# List of the Elements with their Symbols and Atomic Masses*

| Element | Symbol | Atomic Number | Atomic Mass† | Element | Symbol | Atomic Number | Atomic Mass† |
|---|---|---|---|---|---|---|---|
| Actinium | Ac | 89 | (227) | Manganese | Mn | 25 | 54.94 |
| Aluminum | Al | 13 | 26.98 | Meitnerium | Mt | 109 | (266) |
| Americium | Am | 95 | (243) | Mendelevium | Md | 101 | (256) |
| Antimony | Sb | 51 | 121.8 | Mercury | Hg | 80 | 200.6 |
| Argon | Ar | 18 | 39.95 | Molybdenum | Mo | 42 | 95.94 |
| Arsenic | As | 33 | 74.92 | Neodymium | Nd | 60 | 144.2 |
| Astatine | At | 85 | (210) | Neon | Ne | 10 | 20.18 |
| Barium | Ba | 56 | 137.3 | Neptunium | Np | 93 | (237) |
| Berkelium | Bk | 97 | (247) | Nickel | Ni | 28 | 58.69 |
| Beryllium | Be | 4 | 9.012 | Niobium | Nb | 41 | 92.91 |
| Bismuth | Bi | 83 | 209.0 | Nitrogen | N | 7 | 14.01 |
| Bohrium | Bh | 107 | (262) | Nobelium | No | 102 | (253) |
| Boron | B | 5 | 10.81 | Osmium | Os | 76 | 190.2 |
| Bromine | Br | 35 | 79.90 | Oxygen | O | 8 | 16.00 |
| Cadmium | Cd | 48 | 112.4 | Palladium | Pd | 46 | 106.4 |
| Calcium | Ca | 20 | 40.08 | Phosphorus | P | 15 | 30.97 |
| Californium | Cf | 98 | (249) | Platinum | Pt | 78 | 195.1 |
| Carbon | C | 6 | 12.01 | Plutonium | Pu | 94 | (242) |
| Cerium | Ce | 58 | 140.1 | Polonium | Po | 84 | (210) |
| Cesium | Cs | 55 | 132.9 | Potassium | K | 19 | 39.10 |
| Chlorine | Cl | 17 | 35.45 | Praseodymium | Pr | 59 | 140.9 |
| Chromium | Cr | 24 | 52.00 | Promethium | Pm | 61 | (147) |
| Cobalt | Co | 27 | 58.93 | Protactinium | Pa | 91 | (231) |
| Copernicium | Cn | 112 | (227) | Radium | Ra | 88 | (226) |
| Copper | Cu | 29 | 63.55 | Radon | Rn | 86 | (222) |
| Curium | Cm | 96 | (247) | Rhenium | Re | 75 | 186.2 |
| Darmstadtium | Ds | 110 | (281) | Rhodium | Rh | 45 | 102.9 |
| Dubnium | Db | 105 | (262) | Roentgenium | Rg | 111 | (272) |
| Dysprosium | Dy | 66 | 162.5 | Rubidium | Rb | 37 | 85.47 |
| Einsteinium | Es | 99 | (254) | Ruthenium | Ru | 44 | 101.1 |
| Erbium | Er | 68 | 167.3 | Rutherfordium | Rf | 104 | (257) |
| Europium | Eu | 63 | 152.0 | Samarium | Sm | 62 | 150.4 |
| Fermium | Fm | 100 | (253) | Scandium | Sc | 21 | 44.96 |
| Flerovium | Fl | 114 | (285) | Seaborgium | Sg | 106 | (263) |
| Fluorine | F | 9 | 19.00 | Selenium | Se | 34 | 78.96 |
| Francium | Fr | 87 | (223) | Silicon | Si | 14 | 28.09 |
| Gadolinium | Gd | 64 | 157.3 | Silver | Ag | 47 | 107.9 |
| Gallium | Ga | 31 | 69.72 | Sodium | Na | 11 | 22.99 |
| Germanium | Ge | 32 | 72.59 | Strontium | Sr | 38 | 87.62 |
| Gold | Au | 79 | 197.0 | Sulfur | S | 16 | 32.07 |
| Hafnium | Hf | 72 | 178.5 | Tantalum | Ta | 73 | 180.9 |
| Hassium | Hs | 108 | (265) | Technetium | Tc | 43 | (99)† |
| Helium | He | 2 | 4.003 | Tellurium | Te | 52 | 127.6 |
| Holmium | Ho | 67 | 164.9 | Terbium | Tb | 65 | 158.9 |
| Hydrogen | H | 1 | 1.008 | Thallium | Tl | 81 | 204.4 |
| Indium | In | 49 | 114.8 | Thorium | Th | 90 | 232.0 |
| Iodine | I | 53 | 126.9 | Thulium | Tm | 69 | 168.9 |
| Iridium | Ir | 77 | 192.2 | Tin | Sn | 50 | 118.7 |
| Iron | Fe | 26 | 55.85 | Titanium | Ti | 22 | 47.88 |
| Krypton | Kr | 36 | 83.80 | Tungsten | W | 74 | 183.9 |
| Lanthanum | La | 57 | 138.9 | Uranium | U | 92 | 238.0 |
| Lawrencium | Lr | 103 | (257) | Vanadium | V | 23 | 50.94 |
| Lead | Pb | 82 | 207.2 | Xenon | Xe | 54 | 131.3 |
| Lithium | Li | 3 | 6.941 | Ytterbium | Yb | 70 | 173.0 |
| Livermorium | Lv | 116 | (289) | Yttrium | Y | 39 | 88.91 |
| Lutetium | Lu | 71 | 175.0 | Zinc | Zn | 30 | 65.39 |
| Magnesium | Mg | 12 | 24.31 | Zirconium | Zr | 40 | 91.22 |

*All atomic masses have four significant figures. These values are recommended by the Committee on Teaching of Chemistry, International Union of Pure and Applied Chemistry.

†Masses of the longest-lived isotope for radioactive elements are given in parentheses.

# General, Organic, and Biochemistry

## EIGHTH EDITION

### Katherine J. Denniston
Towson University

### Joseph J. Topping
Towson University

### Kim R. Woodrum
University of Kentucky

### Robert L. Caret
University of Massachusetts

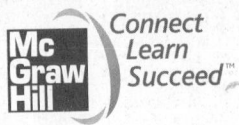

Connect
Learn
Succeed™

GENERAL, ORGANIC, AND BIOCHEMISTRY, EIGHTH EDITION

Published by McGraw-Hill, a business unit of The McGraw-Hill Companies, Inc., 1221 Avenue of the Americas, New York, NY 10020. Copyright © 2014 by The McGraw-Hill Companies, Inc. All rights reserved. Printed in the United States of America. Previous editions © 2011, 2008, and 2007. No part of this publication may be reproduced or distributed in any form or by any means, or stored in a database or retrieval system, without the prior written consent of The McGraw-Hill Companies, Inc., including, but not limited to, in any network or other electronic storage or transmission, or broadcast for distance learning.

Some ancillaries, including electronic and print components, may not be available to customers outside the United States.

This book is printed on acid-free paper.

1 2 3 4 5 6 7 8 9 0 DOW/DOW 1 0 9 8 7 6 5 4 3

ISBN 978-0-07-340276-5
MHID 0-07-340276-1

Senior Vice President, Products & Markets: *Kurt L. Strand*
Vice President, General Manager, Products & Markets: *Marty Lange*
Vice President, Content Production & Technology Services: *Kimberly Meriwether David*
Managing Director: *Thomas Timp*
Brand Manager: *J. Derek Elgin, Ph.D.*
Director of Development: *Rose Koos*
Senior Developmental Editor: *Mary E. Hurley*
Director of Digital Content Development: *Andrea M. Pellerito, Ph.D.*
Marketing Manager: *Heather Chase Wagner*
Senior Project Manager: *Sandy Wille*
Senior Buyer: *Sandy Ludovissy*
Designer: *Tara McDermott*
Cover/Interior Designer: *Greg Nettles/Squarecrow Creative*
Cover Image: *© Seapics.com/Jeff Jaskolski*
Content Licensing Specialist: *Ann Marie Jannette*
Photo Research: *Jerry Marshall*
Compositor: *Laserwords Private Limited*
Typeface: *10/12 Palatino LT Std*
Printer: *R. R. Donnelley*

All credits appearing on page or at the end of the book are considered to be an extension of the copyright page.

### Library of Congress Cataloging-in-Publication Data

Denniston, K. J. (Katherine J.)
  General, organic, and biochemistry.–Eighth edition / Katherine J. Denniston, Joseph J. Topping, Towson University, Kim Woodrum, University of Kentucky.
      pages cm
  Includes index.
  ISBN 978-0-07-340276-5 — ISBN 0-07-340276-1 (hard copy: alk. paper)
  1. Chemistry, Organic—Textbooks. 2. Biochemistry—Textbooks. I. Topping, Joseph J.
  II. Woodrum, Kim, 1963- III. Title.
  QD253.2.D46 2014
  547—dc23
                                                                        2012029427

The Internet addresses listed in the text were accurate at the time of publication. The inclusion of a website does not indicate an endorsement by the authors or McGraw-Hill, and McGraw-Hill does not guarantee the accuracy of the information presented at these sites.

www.mhhe.com

# Brief Contents

# Contents

# ORGANIC CHEMISTRY

viii     Contents

# BIOCHEMISTRY

# Perspectives

## A HUMAN PERSPECTIVE

## A MEDICAL PERSPECTIVE

# GREEN CHEMISTRY

# KITCHEN CHEMISTRY

# CHEMISTRY AT THE CRIME SCENE

# Preface

## To Our Students

Just as some researchers study chemical change, others study learning. The two are related: there are measurable changes in the brain as learning occurs. While the research on brain chemistry and learning continues, the research on learning has taught us some very successful strategies for teaching and learning chemistry. For instance, we now know that building long-term memory requires "repetitions." When you exercise to build muscle strength, you perform some number of "reps" of each exercise for each muscle that you wish to build. That is exactly what you need to do to build your long-term memory and understanding. The Center for Academic Success at the Louisiana State University has devised study tools that have allowed students to improve their performance by a full letter grade, or higher. The following is the Study Cycle with five stages that provide the "reps" needed to perform well in any course:

1. *Preview* the chapter *before* class. Either the evening before or the day of class, skim the material; pay attention to the end-of-chapter summary with boldfaced key terms, chapter map, the learning goals, and headings. Think of questions you would like the instructor to answer. Think of this 10 minutes as your "warm up."

2. *Attend* class! Be an active participant in the class, asking and answering questions and taking thoughtful, meaningful notes. Class time is much more meaningful if you have already familiarized yourself with the organization and key concepts to be discussed.

3. *Review* your notes as soon as possible after class. Fill in any gaps that exist and note any additional questions that arise. This also takes about 10 minutes; think of it as your "cool down" period.

4. *Study.* Since repetition is the key to success, The Center for Academic Success recommends 3–5 short, but intense, study sessions each day. These intense study sessions should have a very structured organization. In the first 2–5 minutes, establish your goal for the session. Spend the next 30–50 minutes studying with focus and action. Organize the material, make flash cards to help you review, draw concept maps to define the relationship among ideas, and practice problem solving. Then reward yourself with a 5–10 minute break. Call a friend, play Angry Birds, or do anything you find enjoyable. Then take 5 minutes to review the material. Finally, about once a week, perhaps on the weekend, review all of the material that you have been studying throughout the week.

5. *Assess* your progress. Are you able to solve the questions and problems at the end of the chapter? Can you explain the concepts to others? The assessment will affirm what you know well and reveal what you need to study further.

The Center for Academic Success has many other suggestions to help students learn how to learn. You can find their online tutorials and workshops at www.cas.lsu.edu.

## To the Instructor

The eighth edition of *General, Organic, and Biochemistry*, like our earlier editions, has been designed to help undergraduate majors in health-related fields understand key concepts and appreciate significant connections among chemistry, health, and the treatment of disease. We have tried to strike a balance between theoretical and practical chemistry, while emphasizing material that is unique to health-related studies. We have written at a level intended for students whose professional goals do not include a mastery of chemistry, but for whom an understanding of the principles and practice of chemistry is a necessity.

Although our emphasis is the importance of chemistry to the health-related professions, we wanted this book to be appropriate for all students who need a one- or two-semester introduction to chemistry. Students learn best when they are engaged. One way to foster that engagement is to help them see clear relationships between the subject and real life. For these reasons, we have included perspectives and essays that focus on medicine and the function of the human body, as well as the environment, forensic science, and even culinary arts.

We begin that engagement with the book cover. Students may wonder why the cover depicts a coral reef featuring a sponge. Then they learn that one of the first drugs used to treat cancer successfully, *cytosine arabinoside,* was synthesized following the discovery of similar compounds from a Caribbean sponge. Because sponges are sessile, they produce a variety of compounds to protect them from predation. Cytosine arabinoside is now used routinely for treatment of acute myeloid leukemia (AAML), acute lymphocytic leukemia (ALL). In fact, a large number of other compounds from sponges are being tested for anticancer and antimicrobial properties.

The cover sets the theme for the book: chemistry is not an abstract study, but one that has an immediate impact on our lives. We try to spark student interest with an art program that uses relevant photography, clear and focused figures, animations that are available on our website and in the e-book, and perspectives and essays that bring life to abstract ideas. We reinforce key concepts by explaining them in a clear and concise way and encouraging students to apply the concept to solve problems. We provide guidance through the inclusion of a large number of in-chapter examples that are solved in a stepwise fashion and that provide students the opportunity to test their understanding through the practice problems that follow and the suggested end-of-chapter questions and problems that apply the same concepts.

## New in This Edition

In the preparation of the eighth edition, we have been guided by the collective wisdom of reviewers who are expert chemists and excellent teachers. They represent experience in community colleges, liberal arts colleges, comprehensive institutions, and research universities. We have followed their recommendations, while remaining true to our overriding goal of writing a readable, student-centered text. The following is a summary of the additions and refinements that we have included in this edition.

Chapter maps are included just before the end-of-chapter summaries to provide students with an overview of the chapter—showing connections among topics, how concepts are related, and outlining the chapter hierarchy.

End-of-chapter summaries have been changed to a bulleted list format of chapter concepts by section, with the bold-faced key terms appearing in context. This more succinct format helps students to quickly identify and review important chapter concepts and to make connections with the incorporated key terms.

Eight new Kitchen Chemistry and two new Green Chemistry applications, and six new Perspectives have been added to the eighth edition to help students see the connections between chemistry and their daily lives and future careers.

Answers to Practice Problems are now supplied at the end of each chapter so that students can quickly check their understanding of important problem-solving skills and chapter concepts.

- **Chapter 1**  The chapter includes a new subsection called Problem Solving Strategies, and was also reorganized to provide a discussion of units prior to the discussion of numbers. Section 1.3 was revised to incorporate information about the English versus the metric system and unit prefixes. The material on significant figures was revised to expand and clarify the discussions of making measurements to the correct number of significant figures, of zeros and significant figures, and of scientific notation and adding numbers in scientific notation. Thirty-seven new end-of-chapter problems were added to correlate to the new and revised material within the text.

- **Chapter 2**  A new subsection and example on writing shorthand electron configurations were added. Also, based on reviewer feedback, the explanations of ions and ion formation, how to use mass number or atomic number to determine the number of neutrons, how to determine the average atomic mass, and of light and the Bohr model were revised to clarify these discussions. Thirty new end-of-chapter problems were added to correlate to the new and revised material within the text.

- **Chapter 3**  New worked examples were added throughout the chapter, including Example 3.3 on how to name ionic compounds using the Stock system and Example 3.16 on exceptions to the octet rule (involving electron pairs on the central atom). The text was revised to expand and clarify the discussion of how to handle molecules with more than

one central atom, and a new Example 3.10, Drawing Lewis Structures for Compounds with Multiple Central Atoms was added. Additionally, based on reviewer feedback, the symbol used for electronegativity was changed. Twenty new end-of-chapter problems were added to correlate to the new and revised material within the text.

- **Chapter 4**  Several of the chapter examples were modified, with color-coding added, and otherwise enhanced for clarity. A new illustration of the conversion between numbers of moles, particles, and grams was added, and other illustrations were revised and improved.

- **Chapter 5**  *A Human Perspective: Gemstones* was added, and *Green Chemistry: The Greenhouse Effect and Global Climate Change* was revised to make the article more current. Six new end-of-chapter problems were added and others revised to correlate to the new and revised material within the text.

- **Chapter 6**  Several of the chapter examples were modified, with reworked solutions, and otherwise enhanced for clarity. A new Example 6.11, Calculating Freezing and Boiling Points of Aqueous Solutions of Ionic, Dissociating Solutes and a new *Kitchen Chemistry: Solubility, Surfactants, and the Dishwasher* were also added. Four new in-text and six new end-of-chapter questions and problems were added, and others revised to correlate to the new and revised material within the text.

- **Chapter 7**  Based on reviewer feedback, *A Human Perspective: An Extraordinary Molecule* was revised and moved to Chapter 7 from Chapter 6 in the previous edition. Several of the chapter examples were modified and otherwise enhanced for clarity. *Green Chemistry: Twenty-First Century Energy* was revised and made more objective. Seven new end-of-chapter questions and problems were added, and others revised to correlate to the new and revised material within the text.

- **Chapter 8**  Based on reviewer feedback, *A Medical Perspective: Control of Blood pH* was made part of the main text in Section 8.4. A new essay *Green Chemistry: Hydrangeas, pH, and Soil Chemistry* was also added. Several of the chapter examples were modified and otherwise enhanced for clarity. Six new in-text and six new end-of-chapter questions and problems were added, and others revised to correlate to the new and revised material within the text.

- **Chapter 9**  Two new worked examples, Example 9.2, Predicting the Product of Beta Decay and Example 9.3, Predicting the Product of Positron Emission, and two new practice problems were added to the chapter. Four new in-text and two new end-of-chapter questions and problems were added, and others revised to correlate to the new and revised material within the text.

- **Chapter 10**  A new *Green Chemistry: Biofuels: A Renewable Resource*, including two For Further Understanding questions, has been added to the revised Chapter 10. More explicit definitions of aliphatic hydrocarbons, alkenes, and alkynes were also added to the text. The subsections

Families of Organic Compounds Structure, Alkyl Groups, *cis-trans* Isomerism in Cycloalkanes, and Cycloalkanes were revised and expanded for clarity. A new subsection Physical Properties adds deeper understanding of properties and the relationship to structure, and includes a discussion of London dispersion forces, which has been woven into all of the organic chapters where appropriate. Several of the chapter examples were modified, with structures added and revised, to further clarify the relationship between structural and condensed formulas. Line formulas were also added throughout to help students understand relationships between line and condensed formulas, and cycloalkane structures were improved to help students visualize three-dimensional structures. Table 10.2 was revised to include a column for names of functional groups, and Table 10.6 was modified with color coding: highlighting the carbon of the alkyl group that bonds to the parent chain to assist students in identifying classification of 1°, 2°, and 3°. Five new questions and problems were added, and nineteen revised to correspond to revisions within the chapter.

- **Chapter 11** Chapter 11 includes a new *Kitchen Chemistry: Amazing Chocolate* and an increased emphasis on line formulas throughout the chapter text.
- **Chapter 12** A new *A Medical Perspective: Resveratrol: Fountain of Youth?* and a new *Kitchen Chemistry: Spicy Phenols* were added. The chapter was reorganized to include alcohol classification within the section on structure. Color-coding was added to the general equations and to the examples of reactions of alcohols to help students visualize the changes occurring in the reactions. An explanation of oxidation and reduction in biochemical/organic reactions was also added to Section 12.5.
- **Chapter 13** Condensed structures were added to the introduction and line formulas to the text to help students better understand the relationships between line and condensed formulas. A new *Kitchen Chemistry: The Allure of Truffles* was added. Numerous figures were revised and color-coding added to help clarify the concepts portrayed. In addition, many areas of the text were revised to improve the clarity of explanations, based on reviewer feedback: added detail to explain polarity of carbonyl groups; improved explanations of oxidation/reduction in organic systems; revised Addition Reactions to update content; and added text art to clarify intramolecular hemiacetal formation. Two new end-of-chapter problems were added and sixteen revised to correlate to the new and revised material within the text.
- **Chapter 14** Line formulas were added where appropriate to help students see relationships with condensed formulas. A new *A Human Perspective: Detergents* and a table of common dicarboxylic acids were also added. In addition, the subsections Nomenclature and Some Important Carboxylic Acids were revised based on reviewer feedback to add detail and further clarity. Section 14.2 was reorganized to clarify the use of nomenclature, and the coverage

of acid chlorides in Section 14.3 was reduced to remove unnecessary material.

- **Chapter 15** A new *Kitchen Chemistry: Browning Reactions and Flavor: The Maillard Reaction* was added. Line formulas were added where appropriate to help students see the relationship with condensed formulas. Many end-of-chapter problems were also revised to use condensed rather than expanded structures.
- **Chapter 16** Chapter 16 includes a new *Kitchen Chemistry: The Chemistry of Caramels* and updated material on intramolecular hemiacetal formation in fructose. Sections 16.2 and 16.3 were also rewritten for clarity and improved comprehension.
- **Chapter 17** Sections 17.2 and 17.3 were reorganized to place Chemical Reactions of Fatty Acids and Glycerides into Section 17.3 for greater clarity. Line formulas were added in Section 17.2 to help students understand the relationship with condensed formulas. Also Examples 17.4 and 17.5 were replaced with clearer examples of the relationship of the reaction (hydrolysis of esters) to monoglycerides. Table 17.1 was revised to add molar mass, and color-coding was added to chemical equations throughout the chapter to better portray chemical changes.
- **Chapter 18** A new *Kitchen Chemistry: Egg Foams: Meringues and Soufflés* was added as well as a new section Proteins in the Blood. Also the sections on stereoisomers, pH, and mechanical stress were revised for greater clarity. One letter codes for the amino acids were added to Table 18.1.
- **Chapter 19** A new *Kitchen Chemistry: Transglutaminase: aka Meat Glue* was added. Also Section 19.12 Uses of Enzymes in Medicine was enhanced to bring greater depth to this topic, which is extremely relevant to health professionals.
- **Chapter 20** New subsections and illustrations of Chemical Composition of DNA and RNA and Nucleosides were added. New material on nucleotide nomenclature was also added.
- **Chapter 21** Chapter 21 includes a new *A Medical Perspective: High Fructose Corn Syrup*. New subsections Biological Effects of Genetic Disorders of Glycolysis and Entry of Fructose into Glycolysis were also added. Section 21.5 The Pentose Phosphate Pathway was revised to focus on key products used in biosynthesis. Four new end-of-chapter problems were added and others revised to correlate to the new and revised material within the text.
- **Chapter 22** A new subsection Biological Effects of Disorders of the Citric Acid Cycle was added to bring medical relevance to the reactions within the chapter. New transition text introduces Summary of the Energy Yield. Five new end-of-chapter problems were added and others revised to correlate to the new and revised material within the text.
- **Chapter 23** A new *A Medical Perspective: Carnitine: The Fat Mover* was added to the revised Chapter 23. Also a new Figure 23.7 illustrates acylation of carnitine and the transport of fatty acids from the cytoplasm into the mitochondria.

## Applications

Each chapter contains applications that present short stories about real-world situations involving one or more topics students will encounter within the chapter. There are over 100 applications throughout the text, so students are sure to find many topics that spark their interest. Global climate change, fingerprinting, the benefits of garlic, and gemstones are just a few examples of application topics.

- **Medical Perspectives** relate chemistry to a health concern or a diagnostic application.
- **Green Chemistry** explores environmental topics, including the impact of chemistry on the ecosystem and how these environmental changes affect human health.
- **Human Perspectives** delve into chemistry and society and include such topics as gender issues in science and historical viewpoints.
- **Chemistry at the Crime Scene** focuses on forensic chemistry, applying the principles of chemistry to help solve crimes.
- **Kitchen Chemistry** discusses the chemistry associated with everyday foods and cooking methods.

## Learning Tools

In designing the original learning system we asked ourselves: "If we were students, what would help us organize and understand the material covered in this chapter?" Based on the feedback of reviewers and users of our text, we include a variety of learning tools:

- **Chapter Overview** pages begin each chapter, listing learning goals and the chapter outline. Both students and professor can see, all in one place, the plan for the chapter.
- **Learning Goal Icons** mark the sections and examples in the chapter that focus on each learning goal.
- **Chapter Cross-References** help students locate pertinent background material. These references to previous chapters, sections, and perspectives are noted in the margins of the text. Marginal cross references also alert students to upcoming topics related to the information currently being studied.
- **End-of-Chapter Questions and Problems** are arranged according to the headings in the chapter outline, with further subdivision into Foundations (basic concepts) and Applications.
- **New Chapter Maps** are included just before the End-of-Chapter Summaries to provide students with an overview of the

### CHEMISTRY AT THE CRIME SCENE

**Adipocere and Mummies of Soap**

One November evening in 1911, widower Patrick Higgins stepped into his local pub in Abercorn, Scotland. To the surprise of his drinking companions, he did not have his two young boys with him. Neighbors knew that the boys had been a great burden on Patrick since the death of his wife; so they believed Patrick's story that he left William, age 6, and John, age 4, with two women in Edinburgh who had offered to adopt the boys.

More than 18 months had passed when an object was seen floating in the Hopetoun Quarry, an unused, flooded quarry near town. When the object was fished out, it was obvious that it was the body of a young boy. To the surprise of the rescuers were stunned to find another small body tied to the first by a rope. How were these bodies preserved after such a long time and why did they float? The answer is that their bodies had almost completely turned into adipocere, or more simply, soap.

Forensic scientists are trying to understand the nature of the reaction that creates adipocere, the technical term for the yellowish-white, greasy, waxlike substance that results from the saponification of fatty tissue. Some researchers hope that this information may allow determination of the postmortem interval (length of time since death). Others simply value the process because it helps preserve the body so well that even after long periods, it can be easily recognized and any wounds or injuries can be observed.

It is known that adipocere is produced when body fat is hydrolyzed (water is needed) to release fatty acids. Because the fatty acids lower the pH in the tissues, they inhibit many of the bacteria that would begin the process of decay. Certain other bacteria, particularly *Clostridium welchii*, an organism that cannot grow in the presence of oxygen, is known to speed up the formation of adipocere in moist, warm, anaerobic (oxygenless) environments. Adipocere forms first in subcutaneous tissues, including the cheeks, breasts, and buttocks. Given appropriate warmth and damp conditions, it may be seen as early as 3 to 4 weeks after death; but more commonly it is not observed until 5 to 6 months after death.

Adipocere formation in John and William Higgins was so extensive that their former neighbors had no trouble recognizing them. At the postmortem, another advantage of adipocere formation became obvious—it had preserved the stomach contents of the boys! From this, the coroner learned that the boys

had eaten Scotch broth about an hour before they died. Investigators were able to find the woman who had given the broth to the boys and, from her testimony, learned that she had fed them on the last day they were seen in the village. Clearly their father had lied about the adoption by two Edinburgh women! In under one and one-half hours, a jury convicted the father of murdering his sons and he was hanged in October 1913.

**For Further Understanding**

▶ Adipocere is the technical term for "soap mummification." It comes from the Latin words *adipis* or fat, as in adipose tissue, and *cera*, which means wax. Draw a triglyceride composed of the fatty acids myristic acid, stearic acid, and oleic acid. Write a balanced equation showing a possible reaction that would lead to the formation of adipocere.

▶ Forensic scientists are studying adipocere formation as a possible source of information to determine postmortem interval (length of time since death) of bodies of murder or accident victims. Among the factors being studied are the type of soil, including pH, moisture, temperature, and presence or absence of lime. How might each of these factors influence the rate of adipocere formation and hence the determination of the postmortem interval?

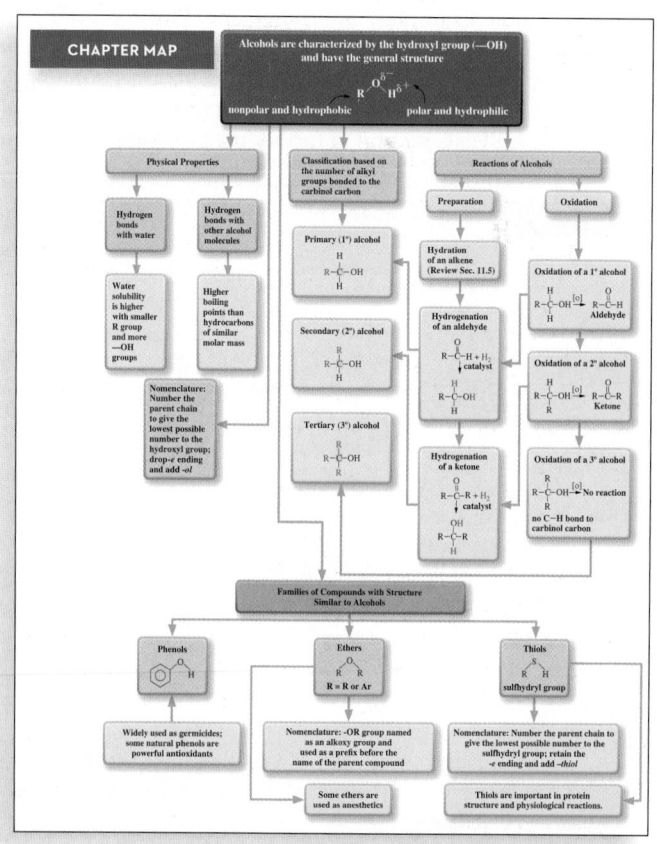

**Question 7.7** Using the conversion factor in Chapter 1, convert the energy released in Example 7.3 to joules (J).

**Question 7.8** Using the conversion factor in Chapter 1, convert the energy absorbed in Example 7.4 to J.

Many chemical reactions that produce heat are combustion reactions. In our bodies many food substances (carbohydrates, proteins, and fats; Chapters 21 and 22) are oxidized to release energy. **Fuel value** is the amount of energy per g of food.

The fuel value of food is an important concept in nutrition science. The fuel value is generally reported in units of *nutritional Calories*. One **nutritional Calorie (Cal)** is equivalent to one kilocalorie (1000 cal). It is also known as the *large Calorie* (uppercase C).

Energy necessary for our daily activity and bodily function comes largely from the reaction of oxygen with carbohydrates. Chemical energy from foods that is not used to maintain normal body temperature or in muscular activity is stored in the bonds of chemical compounds known collectively as fat. Thus consumption of "high-calorie" foods is implicated in the problem of obesity.

A special type of calorimeter, a *bomb calorimeter*, is useful for the measurement of the fuel value (Cal) of foods. Such a device is illustrated in Figure 7.6. Its design is similar, in principle, to that of the "coffee cup" calorimeter discussed earlier.

*Note: Refer to A Human Perspective: Food Calories, Section 1.6.*

**LEARNING GOAL**

**3** Describe experiments that yield thermochemical information and calculate fuel values based on experimental data.

chapter—showing connections among topics, how concepts are related, and outlining the chapter hierarchy.

- **Chapter Summaries** are now a bulleted list format of chapter concepts by major sections, with the integrated bold-faced **Key Terms** appearing in context. This more succinct format helps students to quickly identify and review important chapter concepts and to make connections with the incorporated Key Terms. Each Key Term is defined and listed alphabetically in the **Glossary Terms** at the end of the book.
- **New Answers to Practice Problems** are supplied at the end of each chapter so that students can quickly check their understanding of important problem solving skills and chapter concepts.
- **Summary of Reactions** in the organic chemistry chapters highlight each major reaction type on a tan background. Major chemical reactions are summarized by equations at the end of the chapter, facilitating review.

## Problem Solving and Critical Thinking

Perhaps the best preparation for a successful and productive career is the development of problem-solving and critical thinking skills. To this end, we created a variety of problems that require recall, fundamental calculations, and complex reasoning. In this edition we have used suggestions from our reviewers, as well as from our own experience, to enhance our 2300 problems. This edition includes new problems and hundreds of example problems with step-by-step solutions.

- **In-Chapter Examples, Solutions, and Practice Problems:** Each chapter includes examples that show the student, step-by-step, how to properly reach the correct solution to model problems. Each example contains a practice problem, as well as a referral to further practice questions. These

questions allow students to test their mastery of information and to build self-confidence. The answers to the practice problems can be found at the end of each chapter so students can check their understanding.

- **In-Chapter and End-of-Chapter Questions and Problems:** We have created a wide variety of paired concept problems. The answers to the odd-numbered questions are found in the back of the book as reinforcement for students as they develop problem-solving skills. However, students must then be able to apply the same principles to the related even-numbered problems.
- **Critical Thinking Problems:** Each chapter includes a set of critical thinking problems. These problems are intended to challenge students to integrate concepts to solve more complex problems. They make a perfect complement to the classroom lecture because they provide an opportunity for in-class discussion of complex problems dealing with daily life and the health care sciences.

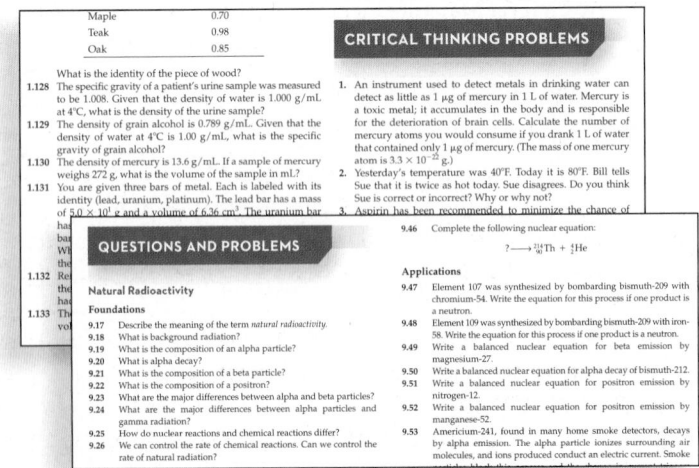

Over the course of the last seven editions, hundreds of reviewers have shared their knowledge and wisdom with us, as well as the reactions of their students to elements of this book. Their contributions, as well as our own continuing experience in the area of teaching and learning science, have resulted in a text that we are confident will provide a strong foundation in chemistry, while enhancing the learning experience of students.

## The Art Program

Today's students are much more visually oriented than previous generations. We have built upon this observation through the use of color, figures, and three-dimensional computer-generated models. This art program enhances the readability of the text and provides alternative pathways to learning.

- **Dynamic Illustrations:** Each chapter is amply illustrated using figures, tables, and chemical formulas. All of these illustrations are carefully annotated for clarity. To help students better understand difficult concepts, there are approximately 350 illustrations and 250 photos in the eighth edition.
- **Color-Coding Scheme:** We have color-coded equations so that chemical groups being added or removed in a reaction can be quickly recognized.

1. **Red print** is used in chemical equations or formulas to draw the reader's eye to key elements or properties in a reaction or structure.
2. **Blue print** is used when additional features must be highlighted.
3. **Green background** screens denote generalized chemical and mathematical equations. In the organic chemistry chapters, the Summary of Reactions at the end of the chapter is also highlighted for ease of recognition.
4. Yellow backgrounds illustrate energy, stored either in electrons or groups of atoms, in the general and biochemistry sections of the text. In the organic chemistry section of the text, yellow background screens also reveal the parent chain of an organic compound.
5. There are situations in which it is necessary to adopt a unique color convention tailored to the material in a particular chapter. For example, in Chapter 18, the structures of amino acids require three colors to draw attention to key features of these molecules. For consistency, blue is used to denote the acid portion of an amino acid and red is used to denote the basic portion of an amino acid. Green print is used to denote the R groups, and a yellow background screen directs the eye to the α-carbon.
- **Computer-Generated Models:** The ability of students to understand the geometry and three-dimensional structure of molecules is essential to the understanding of organic and biochemical reactions. Computer-generated models are used throughout the text because they are both accurate and easily visualized.

The molecule formed by condensing two amino acids is called a *dipeptide*. The amino acid with a free α-N⁺H₃ group is known as the amino terminal, or sim-

Because amines are bases, they react with acids to form alkylammonium salts.

The reaction of methylamine with hydrochloric acid shown is typical of these reactions.

**Figure 18.1** General structure of an

## Learning Resources

This text is supported by a complete package for instructors and students. Several print and media ancillaries have been prepared to accompany the text and make learning as meaningful and up-to-date as possible.

### For the Instructor and Student:

- **McGraw-Hill Connect Chemistry**

Featuring PerkinElmer® ChemDraw

**McGraw-Hill Connect® Chemistry** is a web-based assignment and assessment platform that gives students the means to better connect with their coursework, with their instructors, and with the important concepts that they need to know for success now and in the future.

With Connect Chemistry, instructors can deliver assignments, quizzes, and tests online. Nearly all the questions from the text are presented in an auto-gradable format and tied to the text's learning objectives. Instructors can edit existing questions and write entirely new problems. They can track individual student performance—by question, assignment, or in relation to the class overall—with detailed grade reports. Instructors can also integrate grade reports easily with Learning Management Systems (LMS) such as WebCT and Blackboard, and much more.

By choosing Connect Chemistry, instructors provide their students with a powerful tool for improving academic performance and truly mastering course material. Connect Chemistry allows students to practice important skills at their own pace and on their own schedule. Importantly, students' assessment results and instructors' feedback are all saved online—so students can continually review their progress and plot their course to success.

- **McGraw-Hill ConnectPlus® Chemistry**
  Like Connect Chemistry, ConnectPlus Chemistry provides students with online assignments and assessments, plus 24/7 online access to an eBook—an online edition of the text—to aid them in successfully completing their work, wherever and whenever they choose.

- **McGraw-Hill LearnSmart™**
  **McGraw-Hill LearnSmart** is available as a stand-alone product as well as an integrated feature of McGraw-Hill Connect Chemistry. It is an adaptive learning system designed to help students learn faster, study more efficiently, and retain more knowledge for greater success. LearnSmart assesses a student's knowledge of course content through a series of probes, pinpointing concepts the student does not understand. This innovative study tool also has features that allow instructors to see exactly what students have accomplished and a built-in assessment tool for graded assignments. Visit the following site for a demonstration. www.mhlearnsmart.com

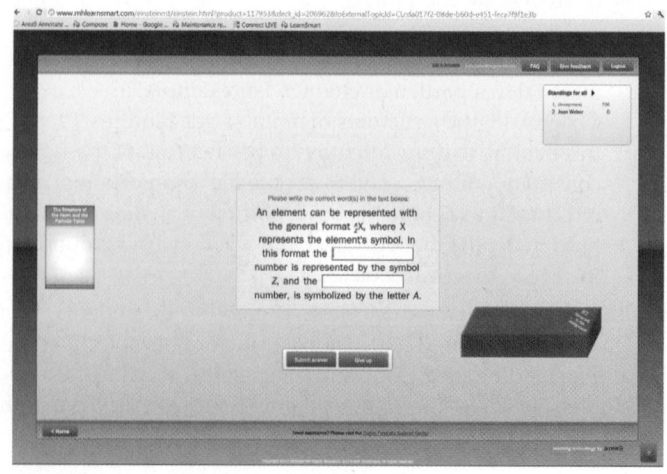

## For the Instructor

- **Instructor's Manual:** Written by the authors and developed for the eighth edition by Cheryl Vaughn and Danae Quirk Dorr, this ancillary contains suggestions for organizing lectures, instructional objectives, perspectives on readings from the text, answers to the even-numbered problems from the text, a list of each chapter's key problems and concepts, and more. The Instructor's Manual is available through the Connect website for this text.

- **Test Bank:** The electronic test bank offers questions that can be used for homework assignments or the preparation of exams. The test bank can be utilized to quickly create customized exams. It allows instructors to sort questions by format or level of difficulty, edit existing questions or add new ones, and scramble questions and answer keys for multiple versions of the same test.

- **Laboratory Manual for General, Organic, and Biochemistry:** The seventh edition, by Charles H. Henrickson, Larry C. Byrd, and Norman W. Hunter of Western Kentucky University, offers clear and concise laboratory experiments to reinforce students' understanding of concepts. Pre-laboratory exercises, questions, and report sheets are coordinated with each experiment to ensure active student involvement and comprehension. An updated student tutorial on graphing with Excel has been added to this edition.

- **Laboratory Instructor's Manual:** Written by Charles H. Henrickson, Larry C. Byrd, and Norman W. Hunter of Western Kentucky University, this helpful guide contains hints that the authors have learned over the years to ensure students' success in the laboratory. This Resource Guide is available through the Connect Chemistry website for this text.

- **McGraw-Hill Presentation Center:** Build instructional material wherever, whenever, and however you want! McGraw-Hill Presentation Center is an online digital library containing assets such as photos, artwork, and other media that can be used to create customized lectures, visually enhanced tests and quizzes, compelling course websites, or attractive printed support materials. The McGraw-Hill Presentation Center Library includes thousands of assets from many McGraw-Hill titles. This ever-growing resource gives instructors the power to use assets specific to an adopted textbook as well as content from all other books in the library. The Presentation Center can be accessed from the instructor side of your textbook's Connect website, and the Presentation Center's dynamic search engine allows you to explore by discipline, course, textbook chapter, asset type, or key word. Simply browse, select, and download the files you need to build engaging course materials. All assets are copyrighted by McGraw-Hill Higher Education but can be used by instructors for classroom purposes.

- **More than 300 animations available through the Connect website:** Many animations are linked to appropriate sections of the textbook using the ▶. They supplement the textbook material in much the same way as instructor demonstrations. However, for students, they are only a few mouse-clicks away, any time, day or night. Because many students are visual learners and quite computer-literate, the animations add another dimension of learning; they bring a greater degree of reality to the written word.

## Customizable Textbooks: Create™

Create what you've only imagined. Introducing **McGraw-Hill Create**—new, self-service website that allows you to create custom course materials—print and eBooks—by drawing upon McGraw-Hill's comprehensive, cross-disciplinary content. Add your own content quickly and easily. Tap into other rights-secured third party sources as well. Then, arrange the content in a way that makes the most sense for your course, and if you wish, personalize your book with your course name and information. Choose the best delivery format for your course: color print, black and white print, or eBook. The eBook is now viewable for the iPad! And when you are finished customizing, you will receive a free PDF review copy in just minutes! Visit McGraw-Hill Create-www.mcgrawhillcreate.com-today and begin building your perfect book.

## Digital Lecture Capture: Tegrity®

**McGraw-Hill Tegrity** records and distributes your lecture with just a click of a button. Students can view anytime/anywhere via computer, iPod, or mobile device. Tegrity indexes as it records your slideshow presentations and anything shown on your computer, so students can use keywords to find exactly what they want to study.

## For the Student

- **Student Study Guide/Solutions Manual:** A separate Student Study Guide/Solutions Manual, prepared by Cheryl Vaughn and Danae Quirk Dorr, is available. It contains the answers and complete solutions for the odd-numbered problems. It also offers students a variety of exercises and keys for testing their comprehension of basic, as well as difficult, concepts.

- **Schaum's Outline of General, Organic, and Biological Chemistry:** Written by George Odian and Ira Blei, this supplement provides students with more than 1400 solved problems with complete solutions. It also teaches effective problem-solving techniques.

## Acknowledgments

We are thankful to our families, whose patience and support made it possible for us to undertake this project. We are also grateful to our many colleagues at McGraw-Hill for their support, guidance, and assistance. In particular, we would like to thank Sandy Wille, Content Project Manager, Mary Hurley, Developmental Editor, Todd Turner, Brand Manager, and Heather Wagner, Marketing Manager. **Connect Chemistry** has been greatly enhanced by the efforts of Danaé Quirk Dorr of Minnesota State University, Mankato, who worked to improve the content, author feedback and hints, and select problems for the eighth edition site, and Shirley Hino of Santa Rosa Junior College, who authored the interactive problem content, also authored feedback and hints, and performed accuracy checking of all Connect Chemistry content.

In addition, the following instructors also did a masterful job of authoring hints and feedback to augment all of the Connect Chemistry homework problems: Eric Elisabeth of Johnson County Community College; Patrick Greco of Sinclair Community College; Paul Root of Henry Ford Community College; Emily Tansey of Otterbein College; John Tansey of Otterbein College; and Dave Tramontozzi of Macomb Community College. The following instructors performed accuracy checks of the Connect Chemistry content to ensure the reliability and correctness: Jennifer Adamski (formally of Old Dominion University); Eric Elisabeth of Johnson County Community College; and Annise Goodman of Eastern Michigan University.

The following individuals helped write and review learning goal-oriented content for **LearnSmart for General, Organic, & Biochemistry:** Susan Bane, Binghamton University; Claire Cohen, University of Toledo; Peter de Lijser, California State University, Fullerton; Anne M. Distler, Cuyahoga Community College; Cynthia Jolly Harwood, Purdue University; David G. Jones, North Carolina Central University; Adam I. Keller, Columbus State Community College; Julia M. Keller, Florida State College at Jacksonville; Jason C. Myers, University of Minnesota; Paul D. Root, Henry Ford Community College; Kathleen Thrush Shaginaw, Particular Solutions, Inc. and the Community College of Philadelphia; and Erin Whitteck.

We are also extremely grateful to the authors of the other ancillaries to accompany *General, Organic, & Biochemistry,* Eighth Edition: Danaé Quirk Dorr of Minnesota State University, Mankato for her authoring of the Instructors' and Students' Solutions Manuals; Cheryl Vaughn of Columbus State Community College for authoring the Student Study Guide and Instructor's Manual; Andrea Leonard of the University of Louisiana at Lafayette for her authoring of the PowerPoint Lecture Outlines; and Jennifer Adamski for her authoring of the Test Bank.

A revision cannot move forward without the feedback of professors teaching the course. The following reviewers have our gratitude and assurance that their comments received serious consideration. The following professors provided reviews, participated in focus groups, or otherwise provided valuable advice for the preparation of the eighth edition:

Augustine Agyeman, *Clayton State University*
Phyllis Arthasery, *Ohio University*
EJ Behrman, *The Ohio State University*
C. Bruce Bradley, *Spartanburg Community College*
Mary Hadley, *Minnesota State University, Mankato*
Thomas Gilbert, *Northern Illinois University*

Emily Halvorson, *Pima Community College*
James Hardy, *The University of Akron*
Amy Hanks, *Brigham Young University-Idaho*
Theresa Hill, *Rochester Community and Technical College*
Shirley Hino, *Santa Rosa Junior College*
Narayan Hosmane, *Northern Illinois University*
Colleen Kelley, *Pima Community College*
Myung-Hoon Kim, *Georgia Perimeter College*
Charlene Kozerow, *University of Maine*
Andrea Leonard, *University of Louisiana at Lafayette*
Lauren E. H. McMills, *Ohio University*
Jonathan McMurry, *Kennesaw State University*
Cynthia Molitor, *Lourdes College*
Matthew Morgan, *Georgia Perimeter College, Covington*
Melekeh Nasiri, *Woodland Community College*
Glenn Nomura, *Georgia Perimeter College*
Kenneth O'Connor, *Marshall University*
Dwight Patterson, *Middle Tennessee State University*
Allan Pinhas, *University of Cincinnati, Cincinnati*
Jerry Poteat, *Georgia Perimeter College*
Danaé R. Quirk Dorr, *Minnesota State University, Mankato*
Michael E. Rennekamp, *Columbus State Community College*
Raymond Sadeghi, *University of Texas at San Antonio*
Paul Sampson, *Kent State University*
Shirish Shah, *Towson University*
Buchang Shi, *Eastern Kentucky University*
Heather Sklenicka, *Rochester Community and Technical College*
Sara Tate, *Northeast Lakeview College*
Kimberley Taylor, *University of Arkansas at Little Rock*
Susan Tansey Thomas, *University of Texas at San Antonio*
Nathan Tice, *Eastern Kentucky University*
Steven Trail, *Elgin Community College*
David A. Tramontozzi, *Macomb Community College*
Pearl Tsang, *University of Cincinnati*
Michael Van Dyke, *Western Carolina University*
Wendy Weeks, *Pima Community College*
Gregg Wilmes, *Eastern Michigan University*
Yakov Woldman, *Valdosta State University*

# 1

# METHODS AND MEASUREMENT
# Chemistry

Chemistry is the study of anything that has mass and occupies space.

## LEARNING GOALS

1 Describe the interrelationship of chemistry with other fields of science and medicine.

2 Discuss the approach to science, the scientific method, and distinguish among the terms *hypothesis, theory,* and *scientific law.*

3 Distinguish between data and results.

4 Describe the properties of the solid, liquid, and gaseous states.

5 Provide specific examples of physical and chemical properties and physical and chemical change.

6 Distinguish between intensive and extensive properties.

7 Classify matter according to its composition as element, compound, or mixture.

8 Learn the major units of measure in the English and metric systems.

9 Report data and results using scientific notation and the proper number of significant figures.

10 Be able to convert between units of the English and metric systems.

11 Know the three common temperature scales and be able to convert from one to another.

12 Use density, mass, and volume in problem solving, and calculate the specific gravity of a substance from its density.

## OUTLINE

# INTRODUCTION

Louis Pasteur, a chemist and microbiologist, said, "Chance favors the prepared mind." In the history of science and medicine there are many examples in which individuals made important discoveries because they recognized the value of an unexpected observation.

One such example is the use of ultraviolet (UV) light to treat infant jaundice. Infant jaundice is a condition in which the skin and the whites of the eyes appear yellow because of high levels of the bile pigment bilirubin in the blood. Bilirubin is a breakdown product of the oxygen-carrying blood protein hemoglobin. If bilirubin accumulates in the body, it can cause brain damage and death. The immature liver of the baby cannot remove the bilirubin.

In 1956, an observant nurse in England noticed that when jaundiced babies were exposed to sunlight, the jaundice faded. Research based on her observation showed that the UV light changes the bilirubin into another substance, which can be excreted. To this day, jaundiced newborns are treated with UV light.

In this first chapter of your study of chemistry, you will learn about the scientific method: the process of developing hypotheses to explain observations and the design of experiments to test those hypotheses.

You will also see that measurement of properties of matter, and careful observation and recording of data, are essential to scientific inquiry. So too is assessment of the precision and accuracy of measurements. Measurements (data) must be reported to allow others to determine their significance. So an understanding of significant figures, and the ability to represent data in the most meaningful units, enables other scientists to interpret data and results.

Helping you develop the skills needed to represent and communicate data and results from scientific inquiry is the goal of this introductory chapter.

## 1.1   The Discovery Process

### Chemistry

Matter and energy are central to our study of chemistry. **Matter** is anything that has mass and occupies space. **Energy** is the ability to do work to accomplish some change. **Chemistry** is the study of matter and the changes it undergoes. As matter undergoes change, it gains or loses energy.

### Major Areas of Chemistry

Chemistry is a broad area of study covering everything from the basic parts of an atom to interactions between huge biological molecules. Because of this, chemistry encompasses the following specialties.

*Biochemistry* is the study of life at the molecular level and the processes associated with life, such as reproduction, growth, and respiration. *Organic chemistry* is the study of matter that is composed principally of carbon and hydrogen. Organic chemists study methods of preparing such diverse substances as plastics, drugs, solvents, and a host of industrial chemicals. *Inorganic chemistry* is the study of matter that consists of all of the elements other than carbon and hydrogen and their combinations. Inorganic chemists have been responsible for the development of unique substances such as semiconductors and high-temperature ceramics for industrial use. *Analytical chemistry* involves the analysis of matter to determine its composition and the quantity of each kind of matter that is present. Analytical chemists detect traces of toxic chemicals in water and air. They also develop methods to analyze human body fluids for drugs, poisons, and levels of medication. *Physical chemistry* is a discipline that attempts to explain the way in which matter behaves. Physical chemists develop theoretical concepts and try to prove them experimentally. This helps us understand how chemical systems behave.

## LEARNING GOAL

**1** Describe the interrelationship of chemistry with other fields of science and medicine.

Over the last 30 years, the boundaries between the traditional sciences of chemistry, physics, and biology, as well as mathematics and computer science, have gradually faded. Medical practitioners, physicians, nurses, and medical technologists use therapies that contain elements of all these disciplines. The rapid expansion of the pharmaceutical industry is based on recognition of the relationship between the function of an organism and its basic chemical makeup. Function is a consequence of changes that chemical substances undergo.

For these reasons, an understanding of basic chemical principles is essential for anyone considering a medically related career; indeed, a worker in any science-related field will benefit from an understanding of the principles and applications of chemistry.

The study of the causes of rapid melting of glaciers is a global application of chemistry. How does this illustrate the interaction of matter and energy?

## The Scientific Method

The **scientific method** is a systematic approach to the discovery of new information. How do we learn about the properties of matter, the way it behaves in nature, and how it can be modified to make useful products? Chemists do this by using the scientific method to study the way in which matter changes under carefully controlled conditions.

The scientific method is not a "cookbook recipe" that, if followed faithfully, will yield new discoveries; rather, it is an organized approach to solving scientific problems. Every scientist brings his or her own curiosity, creativity, and imagination to scientific study. But each field of study has its own set of procedures. Scientists employed by the Food and Drug Administration (FDA) or forensic crime labs, for example, must follow set procedures to the letter. If they do not, their results are deemed invalid. A student's early experience with science laboratories will involve learning set procedures (like recipes). This *cookbook approach* to chemical laboratories is a vital part of learning chemistry.

Characteristics of the scientific process include the following:

**2** Discuss the approach to science, the scientific method, and distinguish among the terms *hypothesis*, *theory*, and *scientific law*.

- *Observation.* The description of, for example, the color, taste, or odor of a substance is a result of observation. The measurement of the temperature of a liquid or the size or mass of a solid results from observation.
- *Formulation of a question.* Humankind's fundamental curiosity motivates questions of why and how things work.
- *Pattern recognition.* If a scientist finds a cause-and-effect relationship, it may be the basis of a generalized explanation of substances and their behavior.
- *Theory development.* When scientists observe a phenomenon, they want to explain it. The process of explaining observed behavior begins with a hypothesis. A **hypothesis** is simply an attempt to explain an observation, or series of observations, in a commonsense way. If many experiments support a hypothesis, it may attain the status of a theory. A **theory** is a hypothesis supported by extensive testing (experimentation) that explains scientific facts and can predict new facts.
- *Experimentation.* Demonstrating the correctness of hypotheses and theories is at the heart of the scientific method. This is done by carrying out carefully designed experiments that will either support or disprove the theory or hypothesis.
- *Information summarization.* A scientific **law** is nothing more than the summary of a large quantity of information. For example, the law of conservation of matter states that matter cannot be created or destroyed, only converted from one form to another. This statement represents a massive body of chemical information gathered from experiments.

The scientific method involves the interactive use of hypotheses, development of theories, and thorough testing of theories using well-designed experiments. It is summarized in Figure 1.1.

**Figure 1.1** The scientific method, an organized way of doing science. A degree of trial and error is apparent here. If experimentation does not support the hypothesis, the cycle must begin again.

## Data and Results

A scientific experiment produces **data.** Each piece of data is the individual result of a single measurement or observation. Examples include the *mass* of a sample and the *time* required for a chemical reaction to occur. Mass, length, volume, time, temperature, and energy are common types of data obtained from chemical experiments.

A **result** is the outcome of an experiment. Data and results may be identical, but more often several related pieces of data are combined, and logic is used to produce a result.

## EXAMPLE 1.1    Distinguishing Between Data and Results

In many cases, a drug is less stable in the presence of moisture, and excess moisture can hasten the breakdown of the active ingredient, leading to loss of potency. Therefore we may wish to know how much water a certain quantity of a drug gains when exposed to air. To do this experiment, we must first weigh the drug sample, then expose it to the air for a period of time and reweigh it. The change in weight,

$$[\text{weight}_{final} - \text{weight}_{initial}] = \text{weight difference}$$

indicates the weight of water taken up by the drug formulation. The initial and final weights are individual bits of *data;* by themselves they do not answer the question, but they do provide the information necessary to calculate the answer: the results. The difference in weight and the conclusions based on the observed change in weight are the *results* of the experiment.

### Practice Problem 1.1

Describe an experiment that demonstrates that the boiling point of water changes when salt (sodium chloride) is added to the water.

▶ For Further Practice: **Questions 1.35 and 1.36.**

The experiment described in Example 1.1 was not a very good experiment because many conditions were not measured. Measurement of the temperature and humidity of the atmosphere and the length of time that the drug was exposed to the air (the creation of a more complete set of data) would make the results less ambiguous.

## Models in Chemistry

Hypotheses, theories, and laws are frequently expressed using mathematical equations. These equations may confuse all but the best of mathematicians. For this reason, a *model* of a chemical unit or system is often used to make ideas more clear. A good model based on everyday experience, although imperfect, gives a great deal of information in a simple fashion. Consider the fundamental unit of methane, the major component of natural gas, which is composed of one carbon atom (symbolized by C) and four hydrogen atoms (symbolized by H).

A geometrically correct model of methane can be constructed from balls and sticks. The balls represent the individual units (atoms) of hydrogen and carbon, and the sticks correspond to the attractive forces that hold the hydrogen and carbon together. The model consists of four balls representing hydrogen symmetrically arranged around a center ball representing carbon. The "carbon" ball is attached to each "hydrogen" ball by sticks, as shown:

## A HUMAN PERSPECTIVE

### The Scientific Method

The discovery of penicillin by Alexander Fleming is an example of the scientific method at work. Fleming was studying the growth of bacteria. One day, his experiment was ruined because colonies of mold were growing on his plates. From this failed experiment, Fleming made an observation that would change the practice of medicine: Bacterial colonies could not grow in the area around the mold colonies. Fleming hypothesized that the mold was making a chemical compound that inhibited the growth of the bacteria. He performed a series of experiments designed to test this hypothesis.

The key to the scientific method is the design of carefully controlled experiments that will either support or disprove the hypothesis. This is exactly what Fleming did.

In one experiment, he used two sets of tubes containing sterile nutrient broth. To one set he added mold cells. The second set (the control tubes) remained sterile. The mold was allowed to grow for several days. Then the broth from each of the tubes (experimental and control) was passed through a filter to remove any mold cells. Next, bacteria were placed in each tube. If Fleming's hypothesis was correct, the tubes in which the mold had grown would contain the chemical that inhibits growth, and the bacteria would not grow. On the other hand, the control tubes (which were never used to grow mold) would allow bacterial growth. This is exactly what Fleming observed.

Within a few years this *antibiotic*, penicillin, was being used to treat bacterial infections in patients.

A nurse administers an injection of penicillin to a young patient.

**For Further Understanding**

▶ What is the purpose of the control tubes used in this experiment?

▶ Match the features of this article with the flowchart items in Figure 1.1.

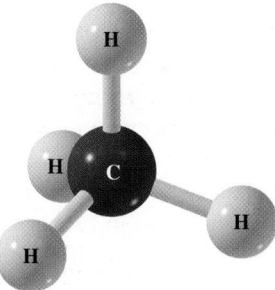

Color-coding the balls distinguishes one type of matter from another; the geometrical form of the model, all of the angles and dimensions of a tetrahedron, are the same for each methane unit found in nature. Methane is certainly not a collection of balls and sticks; but such models are valuable because they help us understand the chemical behavior of methane and other, more complex substances.

Chemists and physicists have used the observed properties of matter to develop models of the individual units of matter. These models collectively make up what we now know as the atomic theory of matter which is discussed in detail in Chapter 2.

The structure-properties concept has advanced so far that compounds are designed and synthesized in the laboratory with the hope that they will perform

**Figure 1.2** Examples of technology originating from scientific inquiry: (a) synthesis of a new drug, (b) solar energy cells, (c) preparation of solid-state electronics, (d) use of a gypsy moth sex attractant for insect control.

(a)    (b)

(c)    (d)

very specific functions, such as curing diseases that have been resistant to other forms of treatment. Figure 1.2 shows some of the variety of modern technology that has its roots in the understanding of the atom.

## 1.2    The Classification of Matter

Matter is a large and seemingly unmanageable concept because it includes everything that has mass and occupies space. Chemistry becomes manageable as we classify matter according to its **properties,** that is, the characteristics of the matter. Chemists look for similarities in properties among various types of materials. Recognizing these likenesses simplifies learning the subject and allows us to predict behavior of new substances based on their relationship to substances already known. Matter will be classified in two ways in this section, by *state* and by *composition*. The properties used to classify matter will also be discussed in this section.

### States of Matter

*We will examine each of the three states in detail in Chapter 5.*

There are three *states of matter:* the **gaseous state,** the **liquid state,** and the **solid state.** A gas is made up of particles that are widely separated. In fact, a gas will expand to fill any container; it has no definite shape or volume. In contrast, particles of a liquid are closer together; a liquid has a definite volume but no definite shape; it takes on the shape of its container. A solid consists of particles that are close together and that often have a regular and predictable pattern of particle arrangement (crystalline). A solid has both fixed volume and fixed shape. Attractive forces, which exist between all particles, are very pronounced in solids and much less so in gases.

(a)                    (b)                    (c)

ANIMATION
• The Three States of Matter

**Figure 1.3** The three states of matter exhibited by water: (a) solid, as ice; (b) liquid, as ocean water; (c) gas, as humidity in the air.

## Physical Properties and Physical Change

Water is the most common example of a substance that can exist in all three states over a reasonable temperature range (Figure 1.3). Conversion of water from one state to another constitutes a *physical change.* A **physical change** produces a recognizable difference in the appearance of a substance without causing any change in its composition or identity. For example, we can warm an ice cube and it will melt, forming liquid water. Clearly its appearance has changed; it has been transformed from the solid to the liquid state. It is, however, still water; its composition and identity remain unchanged. A physical change has occurred. We could in fact demonstrate the constancy of composition and identity by refreezing the liquid water, re-forming the ice cube. This melting and freezing cycle could be repeated over and over. This very process is a hallmark of our global weather changes. The continual interconversion of the three states of water in the environment (snow, rain, and humidity) clearly demonstrates the retention of the identity of water particles or *molecules.*

A **physical property** can be observed or measured without changing the composition or identity of a substance. As we have seen, melting ice is a physical change. We can measure the temperature when melting occurs; this is the *melting point* of water. We can also measure the *boiling point* of water, when liquid water becomes a gas. Both the melting and boiling points of water, and of any other substance, are physical properties.

A practical application of separation of materials based upon their differences in physical properties is shown in Figure 1.4.

## Chemical Properties and Chemical Change

We have noted that physical properties can be exhibited, measured, or observed without any change in identity or composition. In contrast, **chemical properties** do result in a change in composition and can be observed only through chemical reactions. In a **chemical reaction,** a chemical substance is converted to one or more different substances by rearranging, removing, replacing, or adding atoms. For example, the process of photosynthesis can be shown as

$$\text{carbon dioxide} + \text{water} \xrightarrow[\text{Chlorophyll}]{\text{Light}} \text{sugar} + \text{oxygen}$$

This chemical reaction involves the conversion of carbon dioxide and water (the *reactants*) to a sugar and oxygen (the *products*). The products and reactants are clearly different. We know that carbon dioxide and oxygen are gases at room temperature and water is a liquid at this temperature; the sugar is a solid white powder. A chemical property of carbon dioxide is its ability to form sugar under certain conditions. The process of formation of this sugar is the *chemical change.* The term *chemical reaction* is synonymous with **chemical change.**

LEARNING GOAL

**4** Describe the properties of the solid, liquid, and gaseous states.

LEARNING GOAL

**5** Provide specific examples of physical and chemical properties and physical and chemical change.

**Figure 1.4** An example of separation based on differences in physical properties. Magnetic iron is separated from nonmagnetic substances. A large-scale version of this process is important in the recycling industry.

Light is the energy needed to make the reaction happen. Chlorophyll is the energy absorber, converting light energy to chemical energy.

## EXAMPLE 1.2    Identifying Properties

Can the process that takes place when an egg is fried be described as a physical or chemical change?

**5** Provide specific examples of physical and chemical properties and physical and chemical change.

**Solution**

Examine the characteristics of the egg before and after frying. Clearly, some significant change has occurred. Furthermore, the change appears irreversible. More than a simple physical change has taken place. A chemical reaction (actually, several) must be responsible; hence chemical change.

### Practice Problem 1.2

Classify each of the following as either a chemical change or a physical change:
- a. water boiling to become steam
- b. butter becoming rancid
- c. combustion of wood
- d. melting of ice in spring
- e. decay of leaves in winter

▶ For Further Practice: **Questions 1.51 and 1.52.**

**Question 1.1**   Classify each of the following as either a chemical property or a physical property:
- a. color
- b. flammability
- c. hardness

**Question 1.2**   Classify each of the following as either a chemical property or a physical property:
- a. odor
- b. taste
- c. temperature

## Intensive and Extensive Properties

It is important to recognize that properties can also be classified according to whether they depend on the size of the sample. Consequently, there is a fundamental difference between properties such as color and melting point and properties such as mass and volume.

An **intensive property** is a property of matter that is *independent* of the *quantity* of the substance. Boiling and melting points are intensive properties. For example, the boiling point of one single drop of water is exactly the same as the boiling point of a liter (L) of water.

An **extensive property** *depends* on the *quantity* of a substance. Mass and volume are extensive properties. There is an obvious difference between 1 gram (g) of silver and 1 kilogram (kg) of silver; the quantities and, incidentally, the monetary values, differ substantially.

## EXAMPLE 1.3    Differentiating Between Intensive and Extensive Properties

Is temperature an extensive or intensive property?

**Solution**

Imagine two glasses, each containing 100 g of water, and each at 25°C. Now pour the contents of the two glasses into a larger glass. You would predict that the mass of the water in the larger glass would be 200 g (100 g + 100 g) because mass is an *extensive property*, dependent on quantity. However, we would expect the temperature of the water to remain the same (not 25°C + 25°C); hence temperature is an *intensive property* . . . independent of quantity.

**Practice Problem 1.3**

Pure water freezes at 0° Celsius. Is this an intensive or extensive property? Why?

▶ For Further Practice: **Questions 1.45 and 1.46.**

**Question 1.3** Label each property as intensive or extensive:
 a. the length of my pencil   b. the color of my pencil

**Question 1.4** Label each property as intensive or extensive:
 a. the shape of leaves on a tree   b. the number of leaves on a tree

## Composition of Matter

We have seen that matter can be classified by its state as a solid, liquid, or gas. Another way to classify matter is by its composition. This very useful system, described in the following paragraphs and summarized in Figure 1.5, will be utilized throughout the textbook.

All matter is either a *pure substance* or a *mixture*. A **pure substance** has only one component. Pure water is a pure substance. It is made up only of particles containing two hydrogen atoms and one oxygen atom, that is, water molecules ($H_2O$).

There are different types of pure substances. Elements and compounds are both pure substances. An **element** is a pure substance that cannot be changed into a simpler form of matter by any chemical reaction. Hydrogen and oxygen, for example, are elements. Alternatively, a **compound** is a substance resulting from the combination of two or more elements in a definite, reproducible way. The elements hydrogen and oxygen, as noted earlier, may combine to form the compound water, $H_2O$.

A **mixture** is a combination of two or more pure substances in which each substance retains its own identity. Alcohol and water can be combined in a mixture. They coexist as pure substances because they do not undergo a chemical reaction. A mixture has variable composition; there are an infinite number of combinations of quantities of alcohol and water that can be mixed. For example, the mixture may contain a small amount of alcohol and a large amount of water or vice versa. Each is, however, an alcohol-water mixture.

A mixture may be either *homogeneous* or *heterogeneous* (Figure 1.6). A **homogeneous mixture** has uniform composition. Its particles are well mixed, or thoroughly intermingled. A homogeneous mixture, such as alcohol and water, is described as a *solution*. Air, a mixture of gases, is an example of a gaseous solution. A **heterogeneous mixture** has a nonuniform composition. A mixture of salt and pepper is a good example of a heterogeneous mixture. Concrete is also composed of a heterogeneous mixture of materials (various types and sizes of stone and sand with cement in a nonuniform mixture).

**LEARNING GOAL**

7 Classify matter according to its composition as element, compound, or mixture.

At present, more than 100 elements have been characterized. A complete listing of the elements and their symbols is found on the inside front cover of this textbook.

*A detailed discussion of solutions (homogeneous mixtures) and their properties is presented in Chapter 6.*

**Figure 1.5** Classification of matter by composition. All matter is either a pure substance or a mixture of pure substances. Pure substances are either elements or compounds, and mixtures may be either homogeneous (uniform composition) or heterogeneous (nonuniform composition).

**Figure 1.6** Schematic representations of some classes of matter. (a) A pure substance, water, consists of a single component. (b) A homogeneous mixture, blue dye in water, has a uniform distribution of components. The blue spheres represent the blue dye molecules. (c) A heterogeneous mixture, marble, has a nonuniform distribution of components. The lack of homogeneity is readily apparent.

(a)                    (b)                    (c)

| EXAMPLE 1.4 | Classifying Matter by Composition | LEARNING GOAL |
|---|---|---|

**7** Classify matter according to its composition as element, compound, or mixture.

Is seawater a pure substance, a homogeneous mixture, or a heterogeneous mixture?

**Solution**

Imagine yourself at the beach, filling a container with a sample of water from the ocean. Examine it. You would see a variety of solid particles suspended in the water: sand, green vegetation, perhaps even a small fish! Clearly, it is a mixture, and one in which the particles are not uniformly distributed throughout the water; hence a heterogeneous mixture.

**Practice Problem 1.4**

Is each of the following materials a pure substance, a homogeneous mixture, or a heterogeneous mixture?

   a. ethyl alcohol      c. Alka-Seltzer dissolved in water
   b. blood              d. oxygen in a hospital oxygen tank

▶ For Further Practice: **Questions 1.57 and 1.58.**

**Question 1.5**   Provide two examples of homogeneous mixtures that you encounter in everyday life.

**Question 1.6**   Provide two examples of heterogeneous mixtures that you encounter in everyday life.

# 1.3 The Units of Measurement

The study of chemistry requires the collection of data through measurement. The quantities that are most often measured include mass, length, and volume. Measurements require the determination of an amount followed by a **unit,** which defines the basic quantity being measured. A weight of 3 *ounces* (oz) is clearly quite different than 3 *pounds* (lb). A number that is not followed by the correct unit usually conveys no useful information.

The *English system of measurement* is a collection of unrelated units used in the United States in business and industry. However, it is not used in scientific work, primarily because it is difficult to convert one unit to another. In fact, the English "system" is not really a system at all; it is simply a collection of units accumulated throughout English history. Table 1.1 shows relationships among common English units of weight, length, and volume.

The United States has begun efforts, albeit slowly, to convert to the metric system. The *metric system* is truly systematic. It is composed of a set of units that are related to each other decimally, in other words, as powers of ten. Because the metric system is a decimally based system, it is inherently simpler to use and less ambiguous. Table 1.2 shows the meaning of the prefixes used in the metric system.

The metric system was originally developed in France just before the French Revolution in 1789. The more extensive version of this system is the *Systéme Inter-national,* or *S.I. system.* Although the S.I. system has been in existence for over 40 years, it has yet to gain widespread acceptance. Because the S.I. system is truly systematic, it utilizes certain units, especially for pressure, that many find unwieldy.

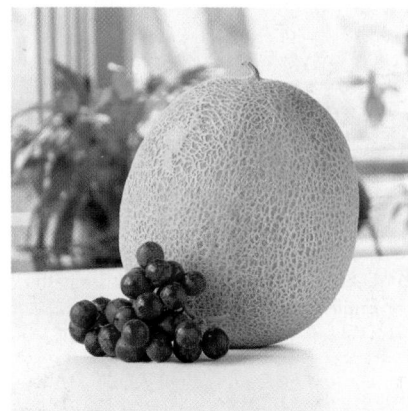

The photo shows 3 oz of grapes versus a 3 lb cantaloupe. Clearly units are important.

**TABLE 1.1 Some Common Relationships Used in the English System**

| | |
|---|---|
| Weight | 1 pound = 16 ounces |
| | 1 ton = 2000 pounds |
| Length | 1 foot = 12 inches |
| | 1 yard = 3 feet |
| | 1 mile = 5280 feet |
| Volume | 1 gallon = 4 quarts |
| | 1 quart = 2 pints |
| | 1 quart = 32 fluid ounces |

**TABLE 1.2 Some Common Prefixes Used in the Metric System**

| Prefix | Abbreviation | Meaning | Decimal Equivalent | Equality with any metric unit g, m, or L (represented with $x$ in each) |
|---|---|---|---|---|
| mega | M | $10^6$ | 1,000,000. | $1\,Mx = 10^6 x$ |
| kilo | k | $10^3$ | 1000. | $1\,kx = 10^3 x$ |
| deka | da | $10^1$ | 10. | $1\,dax = 10^1 x$ |
| deci | d | $10^{-1}$ | 0.1 | $1\,dx = 10^{-1}x$ |
| centi | c | $10^{-2}$ | 0.01 | $1\,cx = 10^{-2}x$ |
| milli | m | $10^{-3}$ | 0.001 | $1\,mx = 10^{-3}x$ |
| micro | μ | $10^{-6}$ | 0.000001 | $1\,mx = 10^{-6}x$ |
| nano | n | $10^{-9}$ | 0.000000001 | $1\,nx = 10^{-9}x$ |

*The mathematical process of converting between units will be covered in detail in Section 1.5.*

**8**  Learn the major units of measure in the English and metric systems.

In this text we will use the metric system, not the S.I. system, and we will use the English system only to the extent of converting from it to the more scientifically useful metric system.

Now let's look at the metric units for mass, length, volume, and time in more detail. In each case, we will compare the unit to a familiar English unit.

## Mass

**Mass** describes the quantity of matter in an object. The terms *weight* and *mass*, in common usage, are often considered synonymous. They are not, in fact. **Weight** is the force of gravity on an object:

$$\text{Weight} = \text{mass} \times \text{acceleration due to gravity}$$

When gravity is constant, mass and weight are directly proportional. But gravity is not constant; it varies as a function of the distance from the center of the earth. Therefore weight cannot be used for scientific measurement because the weight of an object may vary from one place on the earth to the next.

Mass, on the other hand, is independent of gravity; it is a result of a comparison of an unknown mass with a known mass called a *standard mass*. Balances are instruments used to measure the mass of materials.

The metric unit for mass is the gram, g. A common English unit for mass is the pound, lb.

$$1 \text{ lb} = 454 \text{ g}$$

Examples of common balances used for the determination of mass are shown in Figure 1.7.

## Length

The standard metric unit of *length,* the distance between two points, is the meter, m. A meter is close to the English yard, yd.

$$1 \text{ yd} = 0.914 \text{ m}$$

**Figure 1.7** Three common balances that are useful for the measurement of mass. (a) A two-pan comparison balance for approximate mass measurement suitable for routine work requiring accuracy to 0.1 g (or perhaps 0.01 g). (b) A top-loading single-pan electronic balance that is similar in accuracy to (a) but has the advantages of speed and ease of operation. The revolution in electronics over the past 20 years has resulted in electronic balances largely supplant-ing the two-pan comparison balance in routine laboratory usage. (c) An analyti-cal balance of this type is used when the highest level of precision and accuracy is required.

(a)

(b)

(c)

## Volume

The standard metric unit of *volume*, the space occupied by an object, is the liter, L. A L is the volume occupied by 1000 g of water at 4 degrees Celsius (°C).

The English quart, qt, is similar to the liter.

$$1 \text{ qt} = 0.946 \text{ L} \quad \text{or} \quad 1.06 \text{ qt} = 1 \text{ L}$$

Volume can be derived using the formula

$$V = \text{length} \times \text{width} \times \text{height}$$

Therefore, volume is commonly reported with a length cubed unit. A cube with the length of each side equal to 1 m will have a volume of 1 m × 1 m × 1 m, or 1 m³.

$$1 \text{ m}^3 = 1000 \text{ L}$$

The relationships among the L, mL, and cm³ are shown in Figure 1.8.

Typical laboratory devices used for volume measurement are shown in Figure 1.9. These devices are calibrated in units of milliliters (mL) or microliters (μL); 1 mL is, by definition, equal to 1 cm³. The volumetric flask is designed to *contain* a specified volume, and the graduated cylinder, pipet, and buret *dispense* a desired volume of liquid.

## Time

The standard metric unit of time is the second (s). The need for accurate measurement of time by chemists may not be as apparent as that associated with mass, length, and volume. It is necessary, however, in many applications. In fact, matter may be characterized by measuring the time required for a certain process to occur. The rate of a chemical reaction is a measure of change as a function of time.

LEARNING GOAL

**8** Learn the major units of measure in the English and metric systems.

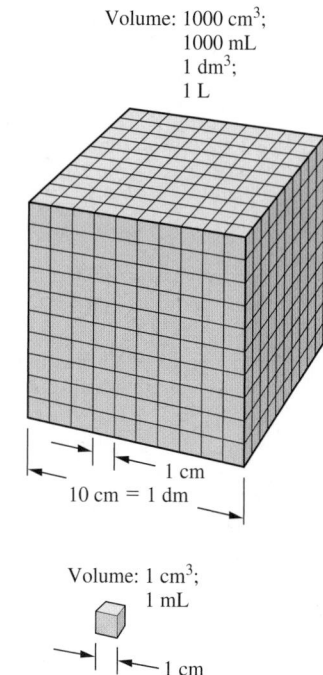

Volume: 1000 cm³;
1000 mL
1 dm³;
1 L

10 cm = 1 dm    1 cm

Volume: 1 cm³;
1 mL

1 cm

**Figure 1.8** The relationships among various volume units.

**Figure 1.9** Common laboratory equipment used for the measurement of volume. Graduated (a) cylinders, (b) pipets, and (c) burets are used for the delivery of liquids. (d) Volumetric flasks are used to contain a specific volume. A graduated cylinder is usually used for measurement of approximate volume; it is less accurate and precise than either pipets or burets.

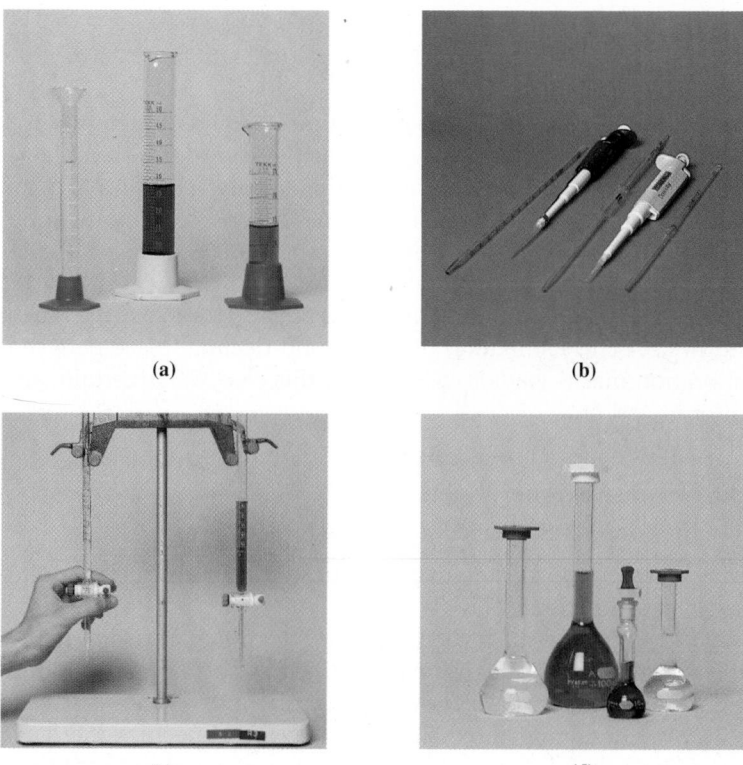

(a)

(b)

(c)

(d)

## 1.4   The Numbers of Measurement

A measurement has two parts: a number and a unit. The English and metric units of mass, length, volume, and time were discussed in the previous section. In this section, we will learn to handle the numbers associated with the measurements.

Information-bearing figures in a number are termed *significant figures*. Data and results arising from a scientific experiment convey information about the way in which the experiment was conducted. The degree of uncertainty or doubt associated with a measurement or series of measurements is indicated by the number of figures used to represent the information.

### Significant Figures

Consider the following situation: A student was asked to obtain the length of a section of wire. In the chemistry laboratory, several different types of measuring devices are usually available. Not knowing which was most appropriate, the student decided to measure the object using each device that was available in the laboratory. To make each measurement, the student determined the mark nearest to the end of the wire. This is depicted in the figure below; the red bar represents the wire being measured. In each case, the student estimated one additional digit by mentally subdividing the marks into ten equal divisions. The following data were obtained:

5.4 cm
(a)

5.36 cm
(b)

In case (a), we are certain that the object is at least 5 centimeters (cm) long and equally certain that it is *not* 6 cm long because the end of the object falls between the calibration lines 5 and 6. We can only estimate between 5 and 6, because there are no calibration indicators between 5 and 6. The end of the wire appears to be approximately four-tenths of the way between 5 and 6, hence 5.4 cm. The 5 is known with certainty, and 4 is estimated.

In case (b), the ruler is calibrated in tenths of cm. The end of the wire is at least 5.3 cm and not 5.4 cm. Estimation of the second decimal place between the two closest calibration marks leads to 5.36 cm. In this case, 5.3 is certain, and the 6 is estimated (or uncertain).

Two questions should immediately come to mind:

Are the two answers equivalent?

If not, which answer is correct?

In fact, the two answers are *not* equivalent, but *both* are correct. How do we explain this apparent contradiction?

The data are not equivalent because each is known to a different degree of certainty. The term **significant figures** is defined to be all digits in a number representing data or results that are known with certainty *plus one uncertain digit*. The answer 5.36 cm, containing three significant figures, specifies the length of the object more exactly than 5.4 cm, which contains only two significant figures.

---

**LEARNING GOAL**

**9** Report data and results using scientific notation and the proper number of significant figures.

---

The uncertain digit results from an estimation.

---

The uncertain digit represents the degree of doubt in a single measurement.

Both answers are correct because each is consistent with the measuring device used to generate the data. An answer of 5.36 cm obtained from a measurement using ruler (a) would be *incorrect* because the measuring device is not capable of that precise specification. On the other hand, a value of 5.4 cm obtained from ruler (b) would be erroneous as well; in that case the measuring device is capable of generating a higher level of certainty (more significant digits) than is actually reported.

In summary, the number of significant figures associated with a measurement is determined by the measuring device. Conversely, the number of significant figures reported is an indication of the precision of the measurement itself.

## Recognition of Significant Figures

Only *significant* digits should be reported as data or results. However, are all digits, as written, significant digits? Let's look at a few examples illustrating the rules that are used to represent data and results with the proper number of significant digits.

- All nonzero digits are significant.
  7.314 has *four* significant digits.
- The number of significant digits is independent of the position of the decimal point.
  73.14 has *four* significant digits, as does 7.314.
- Zeros located between nonzero digits are significant.
  60.052 has *five* significant figures.
- Zeros at the end of a number (often referred to as trailing zeros) are significant or not significant depending upon the existence of a decimal point in the number.
  ○ If there *is* a decimal point, any trailing zeros are significant.
    4.70 has *three* significant figures.
    1000. has *four* significant figures because the decimal point is included.
  ○ If the number *does not* contain a decimal point, trailing zeros are not significant.
    1000 has *one* significant figure.
- Zeros to the left of the first nonzero integer are not significant; they serve only to locate the position of the decimal point.
  0.0032 has *two* significant figures.

**Question 1.7**   How many significant figures are contained in each of the following numbers?
|   |   |   |
|---|---|---|
| a. 7.26 | c. 700.2 | e. 0.0720 |
| b. 726 | d. 7.0 | |

**Question 1.8**   How many significant figures are contained in each of the following numbers?
|   |   |   |
|---|---|---|
| a. 0.042 | c. 24.0 | e. 204 |
| b. 4.20 | d. 240 | |

## Scientific Notation

It is often difficult to express very large numbers to the proper number of significant figures using conventional notation. The solution to this problem lies in the use of **scientific notation,** which involves the representation of a number as a power of ten.

The conversion is illustrated below:

$$6200 = 6.2 \times 1000 = 6.2 \times 10^3$$

LEARNING GOAL

**9** Report data and results using scientific notation and the proper number of significant figures.

Scientific notation is also refered to as exponential notation. When a number is not written in scientific notation it is said to be in standard form.

**A REVIEW OF MATHEMATICS**

If we wish to express 6200 with three significant figures we can write it as:

$$6.20 \times 10^3$$

The trailing zero becomes significant with the existence of the decimal point in the number. Note also that the exponent of 3 has no bearing on the number of significant figures. The value of $6.20 \times 10^{14}$ also contains three significant figures.

When you see this icon in the margin, go to www.mhhe.com/denniston and select the cover for your textbook. On the next screen, select Student Edition from the gray Online Learning Center menu on the left-hand side of your screen. On the following screen, under Course-wide Content (in the menu again in the upper left corner of your screen), select the applicable chapter from the drop down menu and then select the desired topic under More Resources for that chapter. In this example, you may select Chapter 1 from the drop down, then A Review of Mathematics (under More Resources) to view the PDF file for this article. Please be sure to take advantage of all the available resources for each chapter of *General, Organic, and Biochemistry*.

■ RULE:  To convert a number greater than one to scientific notation, the original decimal point is moved $x$ places to the left, and the resulting number is multiplied by $10^x$. The exponent ($x$) is a *positive* number equal to the number of places the original decimal point was moved.

Scientific notation is also useful in representing numbers less than one. The conversion is illustrated below:

$$0.0062 = 6.2 \times \frac{1}{1000} = 6.2 \times \frac{1}{10^3} = 6.2 \times 10^{-3}$$

■ RULE:  To convert a number less than one to scientific notation, the original decimal point is moved $x$ places to the right, and the resulting number is multiplied by $10^{-x}$. The exponent ($-x$) is a *negative* number equal to the number of places the original decimal point was moved.

When a number is exceedingly large or small, scientific notation must be used to enter the number into a calculator. For example, the mass of a single helium atom is

$$0.0000000000000000000006692 \text{ g}$$

This is a very cumbersome number, and most calculators only allow for the input of nine digits. Scientific notation would express this number as $6.692 \times 10^{-24}$ g.

**Question 1.9**  Represent each of the following numbers in scientific notation, showing only significant digits:

a. 0.0024            c. 224
b. 0.0180            d. 673,000

**Question 1.10**  Represent each of the following numbers in scientific notation, showing only significant digits:

a. 48.20             c. 0.126
b. 480.0             d. 9,200

## Error, Accuracy, Precision, and Uncertainty

**Error** is the difference between the true value and our estimation, or measurement, of the value. Some degree of error is associated with any measurement. Two types of error exist: random error and systematic error. *Random error* causes data from multiple measurements of the same quantity to be scattered in a more or less uniform way around some average value. *Systematic error* causes data to be either smaller or larger than the accepted value. Random error is inherent in the experimental approach to the study of matter and its behavior; systematic error can be found and, in many cases, removed or corrected.

Examples of systematic error include such situations as:

- Dust on the balance pan, which causes all objects weighed to appear heavier than they really are.
- Impurities in chemicals used for the analysis of materials, which may interfere with (or block) the desired process.

**Accuracy** is the degree of agreement between the true value and the measured value. **Uncertainty** is the degree of doubt in a single measurement.

When measuring quantities that show continuous variation, for example the weight of this page or the volume of one of your quarters, some doubt or uncertainty is present because the answer cannot be expressed with an infinite number of meaningful digits. The number of meaningful digits is determined by the measuring device. The presence of some error is a natural consequence of any measurement.

The simple process of converting the fraction two-thirds to its decimal equivalent can produce a variety of answers that depend on the device used to perform the calculation: pencil and paper, calculator, computer. The answer might be

$$0.67$$
$$0.667$$
$$0.6667$$

and so forth. All are correct, but each value has a different level of uncertainty. The first number listed, 0.67, has the greatest uncertainty.

It is always best to measure a quantity several times. Modern scientific instruments are designed to perform measurements rapidly; this allows many more measurements to be completed in a reasonable period. Replicate measurements of the same quantity minimize the uncertainty of the result. **Precision** is a measure of the agreement of replicate measurements.

It is important to recognize that accuracy and precision are not the same thing. It is possible to have one without the other. However, when scientific measurements are carefully made, the two most often go hand in hand; high-quality data are characterized by high levels of precision and accuracy.

In Figure 1.10, bull's-eye (a) shows the goal of all experimentation: accuracy *and* precision. Bull's-eye (b) shows the results to be repeatable (good precision); however, some error in the experimental procedure has caused the results to center on an incorrect value. This error is systematic, occurring in each replicate measurement. Occasionally, an experiment may show "accidental" accuracy. The precision is poor, but the average of replicate measurements leads to a correct value. We don't want to rely on accidental success; the experiment should be repeated until the precision inspires faith in the accuracy of the method. Modern measuring devices in chemistry, equipped with powerful computers with immense storage capacity, are capable of making literally thousands of individual replicate measurements to enhance the quality of the result. In bull's-eye (c) we see a representation of poor precision and poor accuracy. Often, poor precision is accompanied by poor accuracy.

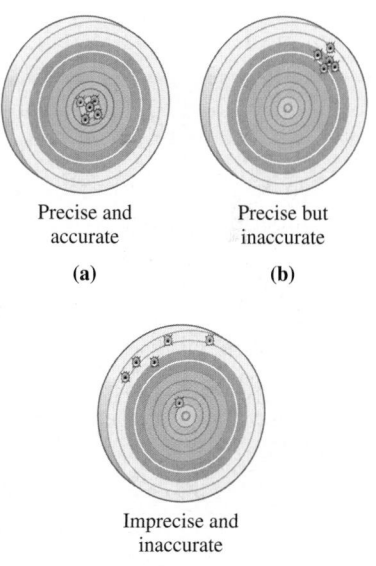

Precise and accurate
(a)

Precise but inaccurate
(b)

Imprecise and inaccurate
(c)

**Figure 1.10** An illustration of precision and accuracy in replicate experiments.

## Significant Figures in Calculation of Results

### Addition and Subtraction

If we combine the following numbers:

$$37.68$$
$$108.428$$
$$6.71864$$

our calculator will show a final result of

$$152.82664$$

Clearly the answer, with eight digits, defines the total much more accurately than *any* of the individual quantities being combined. This cannot be correct; *the answer cannot have greater significance than any of the quantities that produced the answer.* We rewrite the problem:

$$
\begin{aligned}
37.68&xxx \\
108.428&xx \\
+\quad 6.71&864 \\
\hline
152.82&664 \quad \text{(should be 152.83)}
\end{aligned}
$$

*See rules for rounding off discussed later in this section.*

where $x$ = no information; $x$ may be any integer from 0 to 9. Adding 4 to two unknown numbers (in the rightmost column) produces no information. Similar logic prevails for the previous two columns. Thus, five digits remain, all of which are significant. Conventional rules for rounding off would dictate a final answer of 152.83.

**Question 1.11**   Report the result of each of the following to the proper number of significant figures:
   a. 4.26 + 3.831 =    b. 8.321 − 2.4 =    c. 16.262 + 4.33 − 0.40 =

**Question 1.12**   Report the result of each of the following to the proper number of significant figures:
   a. 7.939 + 6.26 =    b. 2.4 − 8.321 =    c. 2.333 + 1.56 − 0.29 =

Adding numbers that are in scientific notation requires a bit more consideration. The numbers must either be converted to standard form or converted to numbers that have the same exponents. Example 1.5 demonstrates this point.

| EXAMPLE 1.5 | Determining Significant Figures When Adding Numbers in Scientific Notation |
|---|---|

LEARNING GOAL

**9**   Report data and results using scientific notation and the proper number of significant figures.

Give the answer to the following calculation using the correct number of significant figures and scientific notation.

$$9.47 \times 10^{-6} + 9.3 \times 10^{-5}$$

**Solution**

We can use either of two strategies to arrive at the correct answer.

**First solution strategy.**
Convert both numbers to standard form and add. Consider significant figures. Then, convert back to scientific notation.

$$
\begin{aligned}
0.00000947& \\
+\quad 0.000093&xx \\
\hline
0.00010247&
\end{aligned}
$$

This gives the answer 0.000102, which when converted to scientific notation gives $1.02 \times 10^{-4}$.

**Second solution strategy.**
Change one of the two exponents so both numbers have the same power of ten. In this example, both numbers will be converted to $10^{-5}$.

$$9.47 \times 10^{-6} = 0.947 \times 10^{-5}$$

$$
\begin{aligned}
0.947 &\times 10^{-5} \\
+\quad 9.3xx &\times 10^{-5} \\
\hline
10.247 &\times 10^{-5}
\end{aligned}
$$

Note: $10^{-5}$ is ten times greater than $10^{-6}$ and 0.967 is ten times smaller than 9.67 so the two numbers are equivalent.

This gives the answer $10.2 \times 10^{-5}$, which is written in standard scientific notation as $1.02 \times 10^{-4}$. (Note that 1.02 is ten times less than 10.2 and $10^{-4}$ is ten times more than $10^{-5}$ so the two numbers are equivalent.)

### Practice Problem 1.5

Report the result of the addition of $6.72 \times 10^5 + 7.4 \times 10^4$ to the proper number of significant figures and in scientific notation.

▶ For Further Practice: **Questions 1.79 b, d; 1.80 d, e.**

## Multiplication and Division

In the preceding discussion of addition and subtraction, the position of the decimal point in the quantities being combined had a bearing on the number of significant figures in the answer. In multiplication and division, this is not the case. The decimal point position is irrelevant when determining the number of significant figures in the answer. It is the number of significant figures in the data that is important. Consider

$$\frac{4.237 \times 1.21 \times 10^{-3} \times 0.00273}{11.125} = 1.26 \times 10^{-6}$$

The answer is limited to three significant figures; the answer can have *only* three significant figures because two numbers in the calculation, $1.21 \times 10^{-3}$ and 0.00273, have three significant figures and "limit" the answer. *The answer can be no more precise than the least precise number from which the answer is derived.* The *least precise number* is the number with the fewest significant figures.

**Question 1.13** Report the result of each of the following operations using the proper number of significant figures:

a. $63.8 \times 0.80 =$

b. $\dfrac{63.8}{0.80} =$

c. $\dfrac{6.1 \times 10^{-4}}{0.3025} =$

**Question 1.14** Report the result of each of the following operations using the proper number of significant figures:

a. $\dfrac{27.2 \times 15.63}{1.84} =$

b. $\dfrac{13.6}{18.02 \times 1.6} =$

c. $\dfrac{4.79 \times 10^5}{0.7911} =$

## Exponents

Now consider the determination of the proper number of significant digits in the result when a value is raised to some power. In each case the number of significant figures in the answer is identical to the number contained in the original term. Therefore

$$(8.314 \times 10^2)^3 = 574.7 \times 10^6 = 5.747 \times 10^8$$

and

$$(8.314 \times 10^2)^{1/2} = 2.883 \times 10^1$$

Each answer contains four significant figures.

### LEARNING GOAL

**9** Report data and results using scientific notation and the proper number of significant figures.

A REVIEW OF MATHEMATICS

## Exact (Counted) and Inexact Numbers

*Inexact numbers,* by definition, have uncertainty (the degree of doubt in the final significant digit). *Exact numbers,* on the other hand, have no uncertainty. Exact numbers may arise from a definition; there are *exactly* 60 minutes (min) in 1 hour (h) or there are exactly 1000 milliliters (mL) in 1 L.

Exact numbers are a consequence of counting. Counting the number of dimes in your pocket or the number of letters in the alphabet are examples. The fact that exact numbers have no uncertainty means that they do not limit the number of significant figures in the result of a calculation.

For example, we may wish to determine the mass of three bolts purchased from the hardware store. Each bolt has a mass of 12.97 g. The total mass is determined by:

$$3 \times 12.97 \text{ g} = 38.91 \text{ g}$$

The number of significant figures in the result is governed by the data (mass of the bolt) and not by the counted (*exact*) number of bolts.

In the following section, we will learn how to convert between units. A good rule of thumb, as we perform the calculations, is to use the measured quantity being converted and *not* the conversion factor to determine the number of significant figures in the answer.

## Rounding Off Numbers

The use of an electronic calculator generally produces more digits for a result than are justified by the rules of significant figures on the basis of the data input. For example, on your calculator,

$$3.84 \times 6.72 = 25.8048$$

The most correct answer would be 25.8, dropping 048. A convenient way to show this is:

$$3.84 \times 6.72 = 25.8048 \approx 25.8$$

A number of acceptable conventions for rounding exist. Throughout this book we will use the following:

■ **RULE:**  When the number to be dropped is less than five, the preceding number is not changed. When the number to be dropped is five or larger, the preceding number is increased by one unit.

**Question 1.15**  Round off each of the following numbers to three significant figures.
a. 61.40      b. 6.171      c. 0.066494

**Question 1.16**  Round off each of the following numbers to two significant figures.
a. 6.2262      b. 3895      c. 6.885

## 1.5   Unit Conversion

Proper use of units is central to all aspects of science. We must be able to convert between units. For example, if we know the mass of an object to be 3.0 lb, we must be able to convert this mass to grams. This section will begin the journey of problem solving. We will utilize our knowledge of the numbers and units of measurement obtained in Sections 1.3 and 1.4 as we learn strategies for problem solving.

### Problem-Solving Strategies

Problem solving is one of the most challenging skills for students in chemistry to master. Although it is tempting to simply memorize facts and mimic steps a teacher took to reach an answer, this method won't allow you to develop strategies that can be used to approach a variety of new problems. Many students come to college with very well developed memorization skills. However, part of the goal of this course is to develop true problem-solving skills.

Problem solving is comparable to planning a road trip and then following the plan to reach a destination. The starting point of the trip and the destination are the *given* information in the problem. Our job is to learn the route (or alternate routes) well enough to plan and complete the trip successfully. Each new skill developed as we proceed through the textbook is like exploring a new road. You may be familiar with interactive mapping websites, where you enter the starting point and the destination but can select from different routes—the quickest trip, familiar roads, the shortest trip, or fewest tolls. You then use your knowledge and skills to select the best route for your trip. In the same way as you develop problem-solving skills, you can select the best routes and roads for working through problems. In this section we will learn the relationships between units of measure. Each relationship is a different road. In this section and Section 1.6 we will learn the first of many mathematical formulas. Again, each formula is a road. As we proceed into the Organic and Biochemistry sections of this textbook, we will still solve problems. However, they will be much less mathematical and will require a whole new set of roads.

As we learn new roads, we will be shown the routes through examples and encouraged to become familiar with them. We will also learn to connect the roads together to plan a lengthy trip.

However, before we proceed with an example, let us consider another important part of problem solving. It is important to look at your final destination when you arrive and determine if you are where you hoped to be. Does your answer seem reasonable? Is the size of the number appropriate? Are the significant figures correct? In other words, do not just try to get an answer; try to get an answer that makes sense. In order to do this, you must understand the concepts behind problems. It is easy to mistakenly transpose numbers, divide instead of multiply, or drop negative signs. If you don't understand the concepts behind the problems, you cannot judge whether your answers are correct. So, *do not* attempt to separate the work in this course into two separate skill sets: "I'm performing a mathematical problem" and "I'm learning a concept." Rather, to judge if answers make sense, you must combine these two skills.

The speed of an automobile is indicated in both English (mi/h) and metric (km/h) units.

## Converting Between Units

Tables 1.1 and 1.2 show the relationships of units within a system, both English and metric, and can be used to convert between units *within* these corresponding systems. It will also be important to convert *between* the English and metric systems. Table 1.3 gives some commonly used units that will assist in conversions between the two systems.

*Tables 1.1 and 1.2 are located in Section 1.3*

## The Factor-Label Method

The *factor-label method*, also called *dimensional analysis*, is a systematic approach to the conversion between units. To convert from one unit to another, whether within the same system or between systems, the equalities found in

**TABLE 1.3 Relationships Between Common English and Metric Units**

| Quantity | English | | Metric |
|----------|---------|---|--------|
| Mass | 1 pound | = | 454 grams |
| | 2.2 pounds | = | 1 kilogram |
| Length | 1 inch | = | 2.54 centimeters |
| | 1 yard | = | 0.914 meter |
| Volume | 1 quart | = | 0.946 liter |
| | 1 gallon | = | 3.78 liters |

Tables 1.1, 1.2, and 1.3 can be set up as a fraction, called a *conversion factor*. For example, from Table 1.1 the relationship between the gallon and the quart is given by:

$$1 \text{ gal} = 4 \text{ qt}$$

The conversion factor is written:

$$\frac{1 \text{ gal}}{4 \text{ qt}} \quad \text{or} \quad \frac{4 \text{ qt}}{1 \text{ gal}}$$

Since the numerator and the denominator both represent the same volume, those ratios are equivalent to one, that is, *unity*. Since multiplying by the number 1 produces the original value, we can take one of these conversion factors and multiply it by a volume and obtain the same magnitude of volume, but with a new unit. Example 1.6 shows the use of this conversion factor to convert from gallons to quarts.

---

## EXAMPLE 1.6    Using Conversion Factors

**LEARNING GOAL**

**10**  Be able to convert between units of the English and metric system.

Convert 12 gallons to quarts.

### Solution

The starting point is 12 gal. The destination is quarts. The information from Table 1.1 that 4 qt = 1 gal is the only road traveled.

12 gal | 1 gal = 4 qt → qt

Write the given quantity or 12 gal. Next, set up the conversion factor so that the unit gal is in the denominator of the conversion factor. This will enable us to cancel the unit of gal and retain the unit of qt.

$$12 \text{ gal} \times \frac{4 \text{ qt}}{1 \text{ gal}} = 48 \text{ qt}$$

*Helpful Hints:*
The unit gal can cancel because anything divided by itself is 1. That is, $\frac{\text{gal}}{\text{gal}} = 1$

If the conversion factor had been set up incorrectly as:

$$12 \text{ gal} \times \frac{1 \text{ gal}}{4 \text{ qt}}$$

the units of gallon would not cancel. Instead, the answer would be

$$3 \frac{\text{gal}^2}{\text{qt}}$$

As a good check of the logic you used to set up the problem, take the time to cancel the units that can be canceled and verify that you are left only with the correct units.

Does the answer make sense? For example, we know that a qt of milk is much smaller than a gal of milk. It makes sense that there will be more qt than there are gal.

---

### Practice Problem 1.6

Convert 360 feet (ft) to miles (mi).

▶ For Further Practice: **Questions 1.91 a, b; 1.92 a, b.**

Sometimes it will be necessary to use more than one conversion factor to convert from the given unit to the desired unit. Keep in mind the equalities we know from Tables 1.1, 1.2, and 1.3 and plan the path accordingly. Example 1.7 demonstrates this process.

## EXAMPLE 1.7    Multi-step Conversions

Convert 4.00 oz to kilograms (kg).

### Solution

The starting point is 4.00 oz. This is an English unit. Our destination is kg, a metric unit. Table 1.3 gives common relationships between English and metric units. For mass, 1 lb = 454 g. We cannot use this relationship until we convert oz to lb. That relationship is given in Table 1.1, 1 lb = 16 oz. Finally the trip ends with the conversion of g to kg using a relationship given in Table 1.2, 1 kg = 1000 g.

4.00 oz → 16 oz = 1 lb → lb → 1 lb = 454 g → g → 1000 g = 1 kg → kg

**First solution strategy.**
This problem can be calculated one step at a time, as follows:

$$4.00 \text{ oz} \times \frac{1 \text{ lb}}{16 \text{ oz}} = 0.250 \text{ lb}$$

$$0.250 \text{ lb} \times \frac{454 \text{ g}}{1 \text{ lb}} = 114 \text{ g}$$

$$114 \text{ g} \times \frac{1 \text{ kg}}{1000 \text{ g}} = 0.114 \text{ kg}$$

**Second solution strategy.**
The calculation can be performed in a single step by arranging the factors in a chain, as demonstrated below:

$$4.00 \text{ oz} \times \frac{1 \text{ lb}}{16 \text{ oz}} \times \frac{454 \text{ g}}{1 \text{ lb}} \times \frac{1 \text{ kg}}{10^3 \text{ g}} = 0.114 \text{ kg}$$

Does the answer make sense?

It is essential to be familiar with the magnitude of these units. An oz is quite small, only one-sixteenth of a lb. It makes sense that this is equal to only a fraction of a kg.

### Practice Problem 1.7

Convert:

|   |   |
|---|---|
| a. 0.50 inch (in) to m | d. 0.50 in to centimeters (cm) |
| b. 0.75 qt to liters (L) | e. 0.75 qt to mL |
| c. 56.8 g to oz | f. 56.8 milligrams (mg) to oz |

▶ For Further Practice: **Questions 1.93 a, b; 1.94 a, b**

The following examples address common issues that arise when using the factor-label method. Example 1.8 demonstrates a conversion between metric units in which both units have a prefix.

**EXAMPLE 1.8**    **Multi-step Conversions Within the Metric System**

Convert 0.0047 kg to mg.

**Solution**

The starting point is 0.0047 kg. The prefixes in Table 1.2 give the relationship between the prefix and the base unit of g, m, and L. Use the meaning of *kilo* to convert to g. Use the meaning of *milli* to convert to mg. There is no information in the table that will take you from kilo to milli in one step.

$$0.0047 \text{ kg} \quad \boxed{1 \text{ kg} = 10^3 \text{ g}} \Rightarrow \text{g} \quad \boxed{10^{-3} \text{ g} = 1 \text{ mg}} \Rightarrow \text{mg}$$

**First solution strategy.**
One step at at time:

$$0.0047 \text{ kg} \times \frac{10^3 \text{ g}}{1 \text{ kg}} = 4.7 \text{ g}$$

$$4.7 \text{ g} \times \frac{1 \text{ mg}}{10^{-3} \text{ g}} = 4.7 \times 10^3 \text{ mg}$$

**Second solution strategy.**
As a single step.

$$0.0047 \text{ kg} \times \frac{10^3 \text{ g}}{1 \text{ kg}} \times \frac{1 \text{ mg}}{10^{-3} \text{ g}} = 4.7 \times 10^3 \text{ mg}$$

Does the answer make sense? Again, it is important to have a feel for the magnitude of these units. A g is 1000 times smaller than a kg and a mg is 1000 times smaller than a g. Therefore it will take many more mg to equal the given quantity of kg.

**Practice Problem 1.8**

Convert the following:

  a. 750 cm to millimeters (mm)
  b. $1.5 \times 10^8$ microliters ($\mu$L) to centiliters (cL)
  c. 0.00055 megagrams (Mg) to kg

▶ For Further Practice: **Questions 1.95 and 1.96.**

The next example demonstrates how to convert units that are squared or cubed.

**EXAMPLE 1.9**    **Using Conversion Factors Involving Exponents**

Convert 1.5 m² to cm².

**Solution**

In a similar fashion to the other factor-label problems, you plan the strategy according to the relationships between units. Table 1.2 gives the relationship between m and cm. This is a one-step process. The only difference is that you must include the exponent (square) in the units.

$$1.5\ \text{m}^2 \quad \boxed{(10^{-2}\,\text{m})^2 = (1\ \text{cm})^2} \longrightarrow \text{cm}^2$$

$$1.5\ \text{m}^2 \times \frac{(1\ \text{cm})^2}{(10^{-2}\ \text{m})^2}$$

$$= 1.5\ \text{m}^2 \times \frac{1\ \text{cm}^2}{(10^{-2})^2\ \text{m}^2}$$

$$= 1.5\ \text{m}^2 \times \frac{1\ \text{cm}^2}{10^{-4}\ \text{m}^2}$$

$$= 1.5 \times 10^4\ \text{cm}^2$$

*Helpful Hint:* The square operation affects both the number *and* the unit within the parentheses.

Does the answer make sense? When converting a squared or cubed unit, the impact of the conversion factor is much greater than if the unit had no exponent. Without the squared unit, the two numbers would be different only by a factor of 100. The two numbers (as the answer shows) are different by a factor of 10,000. This is expected.

**Practice Problem 1.9**

Convert:

   a. $1.5\ \text{cm}^2$ to $\text{m}^2$       b. $3.6\ \text{m}^2$ to $\text{cm}^2$

▶ For Further Practice: **Question 1.97.**

Sometimes the unit to be converted is in the denominator. Be sure to set up your conversion factor accordingly. Example 1.10 demonstrates this process.

**EXAMPLE 1.10**    **Conversions of Units in the Denominator**

LEARNING GOAL

**10** Be able to convert between units of the English and metric system.

The density of air is 1.29 g/L. What is the value in g/mL? (Note: Density will be discussed in more detail in Section 1.6.).

**Solution**

This is a one-step conversion. The L, in the denominator, needs to be converted to mL. Table 1.2 gives the relationship between L and mL.

$$1.29\ \text{g/L} \quad \boxed{10^{-3}\,\text{L} = 1\ \text{mL}} \longrightarrow \text{g/mL}$$

$$1.29\ \frac{\text{g}}{\text{L}} \times \frac{10^{-3}\ \text{L}}{1\ \text{mL}} = 1.29 \times 10^{-3}\ \frac{\text{g}}{\text{mL}}$$

**Practice Problem 1.10**

Convert 0.791 g/mL to kg/L.

▶ For Further Practice: **Question 1.98.**

# A MEDICAL PERSPECTIVE

## Curiosity and the Technology that Leads to Discovery

Curiosity is the basic human trait that leads to scientific discovery. We begin as young children asking, "Why?" Those who become scientists will repeat this question many times throughout their lives. A Web search of "the role of curiosity in science" yields articles and interviews of many scientists who agree that curiosity is fundamental to science. However, curiosity is not enough. The underpinning of modern discovery is a world of technology that is used to develop the devices needed to observe phenomena. Recent research about the brain and its function illustrates this relationship.

In 450 BC, Alcmaeon, a Greek physician, proposed that the brain was the seat of reason and sensation, based on observations that he made while dissecting animals. From that time to the present, curiosity about the brain and its function has persisted and intensified. The study of the brain evolved from this crude dissection of animals to much more sophisticated techniques, which have led scientists to understand what occurs in the brain, even on the molecular level. As experiments get more and more sophisticated, technology plays an ever-increasing role.

The microscope, whose humble beginnings date back to the sixteenth century, has played an important role in the study of the brain function of live animals. However, using a microscope to study the brain of a live, moving animal is a particularly difficult task. Microscopes tend to be large and bulky and require the head of the animal to be fixed in one spot.

The miniature *fluorescence* microscope, developed in 2011 by Mark Schnitzer and Abbas El Gamal of Stanford University, is just one of many examples of how technology assists the curious mind of the scientist. This microscope is so small that it can be attached to the head of a mouse and used to record images of brain activity as the mouse moves about. The 2.4 cubic centimeter (cm$^3$) device weighs only 1.9 g and can record images down to 2.5 micrometers ($\mu$m).

Scientists and engineers have developed a miniature fluorescence microscope that enables the recording of brain image while atop a freely moving mouse.

Using this new technology, scientists observed changes in calcium ion levels in certain regions of the brain that correlated with the motion of the mice. This discovery increases our understanding of the inner workings of the brain at the atomic level; this progress is directly attributable to the development of more sophisticated technology.

This microscope is not as powerful as a conventional laboratory version of the fluorescence microscope (whose instruments record images down to 0.5 $\mu$m) but lab versions obviously cannot be attached to the head of a mouse. Therefore the development of new technology has unlocked more information about the brain and how it functions.

### For Further Understanding

▶ Why is it important for researchers to continue to design and develop new technology for use in scientific discovery?

▶ What is the size of the images that can be recorded by the device in cm?

It is difficult to overstate the importance of paying careful attention to units and unit conversions. Just one example of the tremendous cost that can result from a "small error," is the loss of a 125 million-dollar Mars-orbiting satellite because of failure to convert from English to metric units during one phase of its construction. As a consequence of this error, the satellite established an orbit too close to Mars and burned up in the Martian atmosphere along with 125 million dollars of the National Aeronautics and Space Administration (NASA) budget.

## 1.6  Additional Experimental Quantities

In Section 1.3, we introduced the experimental quantities of mass, length, volume, and time. We will now introduce other commonly measured and derived quantities.

## Temperature

**Temperature** is the degree of "hotness" of an object. This may not sound like a very "scientific" definition, and, in a sense, it is not. We know intuitively the difference between a "hot" and a "cold" object, but developing a precise definition to explain this is not easy. We may think of the temperature of an object as a measure of the amount of heat in the object. However, this is not strictly true. An object increases in temperature because its heat content has increased and vice versa; however, the relationship between heat content and temperature depends on the quantity and composition of the material.

Many substances, such as mercury, expand as their temperature increases, and this expansion provides us with a way to measure temperature and temperature changes. If the mercury is contained within a sealed tube, as it is in a thermometer, the height of the mercury is proportional to the temperature. A mercury thermometer may be calibrated, or scaled, in different units, just as a ruler can be. Three common temperature scales are *Fahrenheit* (°F), *Celsius* (°C), and *Kelvin* (K). Two convenient reference temperatures that are used to calibrate a thermometer are the freezing and boiling temperatures of water. Figure 1.11 shows the relationship between the scales and these reference temperatures.

Although Fahrenheit temperature is most familiar to us, Celsius and Kelvin temperatures are used exclusively in scientific measurements. It is often necessary to convert a temperature reading from one scale to another. To convert from Fahrenheit to Celsius, we use the following formula:

$$T_{°C} = \frac{T_{°F} - 32}{1.8}$$

To convert from Celsius to Fahrenheit, we solve this formula for °F, resulting in

$$T_{°F} = (1.8 \times T_{°C}) + 32$$

To convert from Celsius to Kelvin, we use the formula

$$T_K = T_{°C} + 273.15$$

**Figure 1.11** The freezing point and boiling point of water, body temperature, and room temperature expressed in the three common units of temperature.

The Kelvin scale is of particular importance because it is directly related to molecular motion. As the Kelvin temperature increases, the molecular speed increases proportionately.

The Kelvin symbol does not have a degree sign. The degree sign implies a value that is *relative* to some standard. Kelvin is an *absolute* scale.

**EXAMPLE 1.11    Converting from Fahrenheit to Celsius and Kelvin**

LEARNING GOAL

11  Know the three common temperature scales and be able to convert from one to another.

Normal body temperature is 98.6°F. Calculate the corresponding temperature in both degrees Celsius and Kelvin units.

**Solution**

Using the expression relating °C and °F,

$$T_{°C} = \frac{T_{°F} - 32}{1.8}$$

substituting the information provided,

$$= \frac{98.6 - 32}{1.8} = \frac{66.6}{1.8}$$

results in:

$$= 37.0°C$$

*Continued…*

To calculate the corresponding temperature in Kelvin unit, use the expression relating K and °C.

$$T_K = T_{°C} + 273.15$$

Substituting the value obtained in the first part,

$$= 37.0 + 273.15$$

results in:

$$= 310.2 \text{ K}$$

Does the answer make sense? Until you become familiar with the three temperature scales, look at Figure 1.11. These three temperatures would be at the same place on each thermometer.

### Practice Problem 1.11

a. The freezing temperature of water is 32°F. Calculate the freezing temperature of water in Celsius units and Kelvin units.
b. When a patient is ill, his or her temperature may increase to 104°F. Calculate the temperature of this patient in Celsius units and Kelvin units.

▶ For Further Practice: **Questions 1.115 and 1.116.**

## Energy

Energy, the ability to do work, may be categorized as either **kinetic energy,** the energy of motion, or **potential energy,** the energy of position. Kinetic energy may be considered as energy in process; potential energy is stored energy. All energy is either kinetic or potential.

Another useful way of classifying energy is by form. The principal forms of energy include light, heat, electrical, mechanical, and chemical energy. All of these forms of energy share the following set of characteristics:

- Energy cannot be created or destroyed.
- Energy may be converted from one form to another.
- Conversion of energy from one form to another always occurs with less than 100% efficiency. Energy is not lost (remember, energy cannot be destroyed) but rather, is not useful. We buy gasoline to move our cars from place to place; however, much of the energy stored in the gasoline is released as heat.
- All chemical reactions involve either a "gain" or a "loss" of energy.

The *kilocalorie* (kcal) is the familiar nutritional calorie. It is also known as the large Calorie (C); note that in this term the C is uppercase to distinguish it from the normal calorie. The large Calorie is 1000 small calories. Refer to A Human Perspective: Food Calories for more information.

Energy absorbed or liberated in chemical reactions is usually in the form of heat energy. Heat energy may be represented in units of *calories* (cal) or *joules* (J), their relationship being

$$1 \text{ cal} = 4.18 \text{ J}$$

One calorie is defined as the amount of heat energy required to increase the temperature of 1 g of water 1°C.

Heat energy measurement is a quantitative measure of heat content. It is an extensive property, dependent upon the quantity of material. Temperature, as we have mentioned, is an intensive property, independent of quantity.

Water in the environment (lakes, oceans, and streams) has a powerful effect on the climate because of its ability to store large quantities of energy. In summer, water stores heat energy, moderating temperatures of the surrounding area. In winter, some of this stored energy is released to the air as the water temperature falls; this prevents the surroundings from experiencing extreme changes in temperature.

Not all substances have the same capacity for holding heat; 1 g of iron and 1 g of water, even if they are at the same temperature, do *not* contain the same amount of heat energy. One gram of iron will absorb and store 0.108 cal of heat energy when the temperature is raised 1°C. In contrast, 1 g of water will absorb almost ten times as much energy, 1.00 cal, when the temperature is increased an equivalent amount.

# A HUMAN PERSPECTIVE

## Food Calories

The body gets its energy through the processes known collectively as metabolism, which will be discussed in detail in the chapters on biochemistry and nutrition. The primary energy sources for the body are carbohydrates, fats, and proteins, which we obtain from the foods we eat. The amount of energy available from a given foodstuff is related to the Calories (C) available in the food. Calories are a measure of the energy and heat content that can be derived from the food. One (food) Calorie (symbolized by C) equals 1000 (metric) calories (symbolized by cal):

$$1 \text{ C} = 1000 \text{ cal} = 1 \text{ kcal}$$

The energy available in food can be measured by totally burning the food; in other words, using the food as fuel. The energy given off in the form of heat is directly related to the amount of chemical energy, energy stored in chemical bonds, that is available in the food. Food provides energy to the body through the various metabolic pathways.

The classes of food molecules are not equally energy rich. When oxidized via metabolic pathways, carbohydrates and proteins provide the cell with 4 C/g, whereas fats generate approximately 9 C/g.

In addition, as with all processes, not all the available energy can be efficiently extracted from the food; a certain percentage is always lost. The average person requires between 2000 and 3000 C/day to maintain normal body functions such as the regulation of body temperature, muscle movement, and so on. If a person takes in more C than the body uses, the C-containing substances will be stored as fat, and the person will gain weight. Conversely, if a person uses more C than are ingested, the individual will lose weight.

Excess C are stored in the form of fat, the form that provides the greatest amount of energy per g. Too many C leads to too much fat. Similarly, a lack of C (in the form of food) forces the body to raid its storehouse, the fat. Weight is lost in this process as the fat is consumed. Unfortunately, it always seems easier to add fat to the storehouse than to remove it.

The "rule of thumb" is that 3500 C are equivalent to approximately 1 lb of body weight. You have to take in 3500 C more than you use to gain 1 lb, and you have to expend 3500 C more than you normally use to lose 1 lb. If you eat as few as 100 C/day beyond your body's needs, you could gain about 10–11 lb per year (yr):

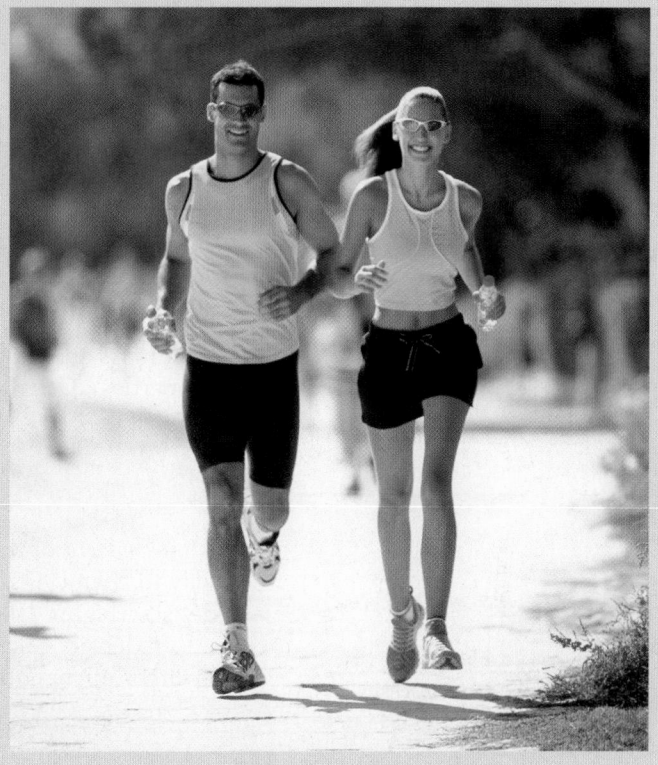

$$\frac{100 \text{ C}}{\text{day}} \times \frac{365 \text{ day}}{1 \text{ yr}} \times \frac{1 \text{ lb}}{3500 \text{ C}} = \frac{10.4 \text{ lb}}{\text{yr}}$$

A frequently recommended procedure for increasing the rate of weight loss involves a combination of dieting (taking in fewer C) and exercise. Running, swimming, jogging, and cycling are particularly efficient forms of exercise. Running burns 0.11 C/min for every lb of body weight, swimming burns approximately 0.05 C/min for every lb of body weight.

### For Further Understanding

► Sarah runs 1 h each day, and Nancy swims 2 h each day. Assuming that Sarah and Nancy are the same weight, which girl burns more calories in 1 week?

► Would you expect a runner to burn more calories in summer or winter? Why?

Units for other forms of energy will be introduced in later chapters.

**Question 1.17**  Convert 595 cal to units of J.

**Question 1.18**  Convert $2.00 \times 10^2$ J to units of cal.

## Concentration

**Concentration** is a measure of the number of particles of a substance, or the mass of those particles, that are contained in a specified volume. Concentration is a widely used way of representing mixtures of different substances. Examples include:

- The concentration of oxygen in the air
- Pollen counts, given during the hay fever seasons, which are simply the number of grains of pollen contained in a measured volume of air
- The amount of an illegal drug in a certain volume of blood, indicating the extent of drug abuse
- The proper dose of an antibiotic, based on a patient's weight

We will describe many situations in which concentration is used to predict useful information about chemical reactions (Sections 6.4 and 8.2, for example). In Chapter 6 we calculate a numerical value for concentration from experimental data.

## Density and Specific Gravity

Both mass and volume are functions of the *amount* of material present (extensive properties). **Density,** the ratio of mass to volume,

$$\text{Density } (d) = \frac{\text{mass}}{\text{volume}} = \frac{m}{V}$$

is *independent* of the amount of material (intensive property). Density is a useful way to characterize or identify a substance because each substance has a unique density (Figure 1.12).

In density calculations, mass is usually represented in g, and volume is given in either mL or cubic centimeters ($cm^3$ or cc):

$$1 \text{ mL} = 1 \text{ cm}^3 = 1 \text{ cc}$$

The unit of density would therefore be g/mL, $g/cm^3$, or g/cc.

A 1 mL sample of air and 1 mL sample of iron have different masses. There is much more mass in 1 mL of iron; its density is greater. Density measurements were used to discriminate between real gold and "fool's gold" during the gold rush era. Today the measurement of the density of a substance is still a valuable analytical technique. The densities of a number of common substances are shown in Table 1.4.

**ANIMATION**
- Solid-Liquid Density

**Figure 1.12** Density (mass/volume) is a unique property of a material. A mixture of wood, water, brass, and mercury is shown, with the cork—the least dense—floating on water. Additionally, brass, with a density greater than water but less than liquid mercury, floats on the interface between these two liquids.

**TABLE 1.4 Densities of Some Common Materials**

| Substance | Density (g/mL) | Substance | Density (g/mL) |
|---|---|---|---|
| Air | 0.00129 (at 0°C) | Methyl alcohol | 0.792 |
| Ammonia | 0.000771 (at 0°C) | Milk | 1.028–1.035 |
| Benzene | 0.879 | Oxygen | 0.00143 (at 0°C) |
| Bone | 1.7–2.0 | Rubber | 0.9–1.1 |
| Carbon dioxide | 0.001963 (at 0°C) | Turpentine | 0.87 |
| Ethyl alcohol | 0.789 | Urine | 1.010–1.030 |
| Gasoline | 0.66–0.69 | Water | 1.000 (at 4°C) |
| Gold | 19.3 | Water | 0.998 (at 20°C) |
| Hydrogen | 0.000090 (at 0°C) | Wood (balsa, least dense; ebony and teak, most dense) | 0.3–0.98 |
| Kerosene | 0.82 | | |
| Lead | 11.3 | | |
| Mercury | 13.6 | | |

**EXAMPLE 1.12**   **Calculating the Density of a Solid**

LEARNING GOAL

A 2.00-cm$^3$ sample of aluminum is found to weigh 5.40 g. Calculate the density of aluminum in units of g/cm$^3$ and g/mL.

**12**   Use density, mass, and volume in problem solving, and calculate the specific gravity of a substance from its density.

**Solution**

To determine density, the formula below is utilized. Initially, this is not a factor-label problem, though it is important to include units.

$$d = \frac{m}{V}$$

To determine the density in units of g/mL, we use the equality 1 mL = 1 cm$^3$ as a conversion factor.

5.40 g, 2.00 cm$^3$  → Density formula →  g/cm$^3$  1 cm$^3$ = 1 mL →  g/mL

Substitute the information given in the problem.

$$d = \frac{5.40 \text{ g}}{2.00 \text{ cm}^3} = 2.70 \text{ g/cm}^3$$

Convert cm$^3$ to mL.

$$2.70\frac{\text{g}}{\text{cm}^3} \times \frac{1 \text{ cm}^3}{1 \text{ mL}} = 2.70 \text{ g/mL}$$

Does the answer make sense? The density of water is 1.0 g/mL. Aluminum is more dense than water (it doesn't float on water); therefore, the value is reasonable.

**Practice Problem 1.12**

A 0.500-mL sample of mercury has a mass of 6.80 g. Calculate the density of mercury in units of g/mL and g/cm$^3$.

▶ For Further Practice: **Questions 1.121 and 1.122.**

**EXAMPLE 1.13**   **Using Density to Calculate the Mass of a Liquid**

LEARNING GOAL

Calculate the mass, in g, of 10.0 mL of mercury (symbolized Hg) if the density of mercury is 13.6 g/mL.

**12**   Use density, mass, and volume in problem solving, and calculate the specific gravity of a substance from its density.

**Solution**

Density has units of g/mL and can be used as a conversion factor from mL to g. This is a one-step conversion.

$$\frac{13.6 \text{ g Hg}}{1 \text{ mL Hg}}$$

10.0 mL → Density → g

$$10.0 \text{ mL Hg} \times \frac{13.6 \text{ g Hg}}{1 \text{ mL Hg}} = 136 \text{ g Hg}$$

Does the answer make sense? If 1.0 mL of mercury has a mass of 13.6 g, it makes sense that the mass of 10 mL is more.

*Continued…*

**Practice Problem 1.13**

The density of ethyl alcohol (200 proof, or pure alcohol) is 0.789 g/mL at 20°C. Calculate the mass of a 30.0-mL sample.

▶ For Further Practice: **Questions 1.125 and 1.126.**

---

**EXAMPLE 1.14      Calculating the Mass of a Gas from Its Density**

LEARNING GOAL

Air has a density of 0.0013 g/mL. What is the mass of a 6.0-L sample of air?

**12**  Use density, mass, and volume in problem solving, and calculate the specific gravity of a substance from its density.

**Solution**

Density has units of g/mL and can be used as a conversion factor from mL to g.

$$\frac{0.0013 \text{ g air}}{1 \text{ mL air}}$$

To use this conversion factor, we must first convert the 6.0 L to mL.

6.0 L → $10^{-3}$ L = 1 mL → mL → density → g

$$6.0 \text{ L air} \times \frac{1 \text{ mL air}}{10^{-3} \text{ L air}} \times \frac{0.0013 \text{ g air}}{1 \text{ mL air}} = 7.8 \text{ g air}$$

Does the answer make sense? Imagine the volume of 6.0 L, a volume equivalent to three 2-L soda bottles. We would expect the mass of air in three "empty" soda bottles to be a small mass. Therefore, 7.8 g is reasonable.

---

**Practice Problem 1.14**

What mass of air, in g, would be found in a 2.0-L party balloon?

▶ For Further Practice: **Questions 1.123 and 1.124.**

---

**EXAMPLE 1.15      Using Density to Calculate the Volume of a Liquid**

LEARNING GOAL

Calculate the volume, in mL, of a liquid that has a density of 1.20 g/mL and a mass of 5.00 g.

**12**  Use density, mass, and volume in problem solving, and calculate the specific gravity of a substance from its density.

**Solution**

In the previous two examples, density was used to convert from volume to mass. Here we will use density as a conversion factor to convert mass to volume.

5.00 g → density → mL

$$5.00 \text{ g liquid} \times \frac{1 \text{ mL liquid}}{1.20 \text{ g liquid}} = 4.17 \text{ mL liquid}$$

*Helpful Hint:*
Notice in the solution that density is inverted with the mass in the denominator. This enables the units to cancel.

Does the answer make sense? If the density were 1 g/mL, 5 g would occupy 5 mL. Since the density is greater than 1, less volume is required; therefore, 4.17 mL is reasonable.

**Practice Problem 1.15**

Calculate the volume, in mL, of 10.0 g of a saline solution that has a density of 1.05 g/mL.

▶ For Further Practice: **Questions 1.130 and 1.133.**

**EXAMPLE 1.16**    **Solving a Problem Requiring Multiple Steps**

LEARNING GOAL

**12**  Use density, mass, and volume in problem solving, and calculate the specific gravity of a substance from its density.

What mass, in kg, is contained in a 3.5-m³ cube of aluminum? The density of aluminum is 2.7 g/cm³.

**Solution**

This requires a multi-step solution. You begin with the given quantity of 3.5 m³. This is a volume. You will need to convert from volume to mass using the density. The density given includes the volume expressed in cm³. Therefore you will need to begin by converting the 3.5 m³ to cm³. Once this is accomplished, the density can be used to convert to g. The last step will be to convert from g to kg.

$$3.5\ m^3\ \boxed{(10^{-2}\ m)^3 = (1\ cm)^3}\ cm^3\ \boxed{density}\ g\ \boxed{10^3\ g = 1\ kg}\ kg$$

Each step is carried out in one calculation as follows:

$$3.5\ m^3 \times \frac{1^3\ cm^3}{(10^{-2})^3\ m^3} \times \frac{2.7\ g}{1\ cm^3} \times \frac{1\ kg}{10^3\ g} = 9.5 \times 10^3\ kg$$

Does the answer make sense? Imagine a cube that is 1 m (approximately 1 yd) on each side, that is, 1 m³. The volume 3.5 m³ is more than three times bigger; 9500 kg is a large mass, quite expected for a large volume.

**Practice Problem 1.16**

What is the volume, in L, of 1.5 kg of rubbing alcohol? The density is 0.786 g/mL.

▶ For Further Practice: **Critical Thinking Problem 3.**

## A MEDICAL PERSPECTIVE

### Assessing Obesity: The Body-Mass Index

Density, the ratio of two extensive properties, mass and volume, is an intensive property that can provide useful information about the identity and properties of a substance. The Body-Mass Index (BMI) is also a ratio of two extensive properties, the weight and height (actually the square of the height) of an individual. As a result, the BMI is also an intensive property. It is widely used by physical trainers, medical professionals, and life insurance companies to quantify obesity, which is a predictor of a variety of potential medical problems.

In metric units, the Body-Mass Index is expressed:

$$BMI = \frac{Weight\ (kg)}{Height\ (m^2)}$$

This can be converted to the English system:

$$BMI = \frac{Weight\ (lb)}{Height\ (in^2)} \times 703$$

The number 703 is the commonly used conversion factor to convert from English units (in and lb) to metric units (m and kg) that are the units in the definition of BMI. The conversion is accomplished in the following way:

$$BMI = \frac{kg}{m^2} = \frac{lb}{in^2} \times \frac{1\ kg}{2.205\ lb} \times \left(\frac{39.37\ in}{1\ m}\right)^2$$

Weight and height (metric)    Weight and height (English)

$$= \frac{lb}{in^2} \times 703\ \frac{kg \cdot in^2}{lb \cdot m^2}$$

The units of the conversion factor are generally not shown, and the BMI in English units is reduced to:

$$BMI = \frac{Weight\ in\ lb}{(Height\ in\ in)^2} \times 703$$

Computer website BMI calculators generally use this form of the equation.

An individual with a BMI of 25 or greater is considered overweight; if the BMI is 30 or greater, the individual is described as obese. The BMI, once known, can be used as a guideline in the design of suitable diet and exercise programs.

BMI values for a variety of weights and heights are shown as a function of individuals' height and weight:

Developed by the National Center for Health Statistics in collaboration with the National Center for Chronic Disease Prevention and Health Promotion

**For Further Understanding**

► Refer to A Human Perspective: Food Calories (p. 29) and describe connections between these two perspectives.
► Calculate your BMI in both metric and English units. Should they agree? Do they?

---

Specific gravity is frequently referenced to water at 4°C, its temperature of maximum density (1.000 g/mL). Other reference temperatures may be used. However, the temperature must be specified.

For convenience, values of density are often related to a standard, well-known reference, the density of pure water at 4°C. This "referenced" density is called the **specific gravity,** the ratio of the density of the object in question to the density of pure water at 4°C.

$$specific\ gravity = \frac{density\ of\ object\ (g/mL)}{density\ of\ water\ (g/mL)}$$

# A HUMAN PERSPECTIVE

## Quick and Useful Analysis

Measurement of the specific gravity of a liquid is fast, easy, and nondestructive of the sample. Changes in specific gravity over time can provide a wealth of information. Two examples follow:

Living cells carry out a wide variety of chemical reactions, which produce molecules and energy essential for proper function of living organisms. Urine, a waste product, contains a wide variety of by-products from these chemical processes. It can be analyzed to indicate abnormalities in cell function or even unacceptable personal behavior (recall the steroid tests in Olympic competition).

Many of these tests must be performed by using sophisticated and sensitive instrumentation. However, a very simple test, the measurement of the specific gravity of urine, can be an indicator of diabetes mellitus or Bright's disease. The normal range for human urine specific gravity is 1.010–1.030.

A hydrometer, a weighted glass bulb inserted in a liquid, may be used to determine specific gravity. The higher it floats in the liquid, the more dense the liquid. A hydrometer that is calibrated to indicate the specific gravity of urine is called a urinometer.

Winemaking is a fermentation process (Chapter 12). The flavor, aroma, and composition of wine depend upon the extent of fermentation. As fermentation proceeds, the specific gravity of the wine gradually changes. Periodic measurement of the specific gravity during fermentation enables the wine-maker to determine when the wine has reached its optimal composition.

### For Further Understanding

▶ Give reasons that may account for such a broad range of "normal" values for urine specific gravity.

▶ Could results for a diabetes test depend on food or medicine consumed prior to the test?

Monitoring the winemaking process.

Normal Urine          Pathological Urine

A hydrometer, used in the measurement of the specific gravity of urine.

Specific gravity is a *unitless* term. Because the density of water at 4.0°C is 1.00 g/mL, the numerical values for the density and specific gravity of a substance are equal. That is, an object with a density of 2.00 g/mL has a specific gravity of 2.00 at 4°C.

Routine hospital tests involving the measurement of the specific gravity of urine and blood samples are frequently used as diagnostic tools. For example, diseases such as kidney disorders and diabetes change the composition of urine. This compositional change results in a corresponding change in the specific gravity. This change is easily measured and provides the basis for a quick preliminary diagnosis. This topic is discussed in greater detail in A Human Perspective: Quick and Useful Analysis.

# CHAPTER MAP

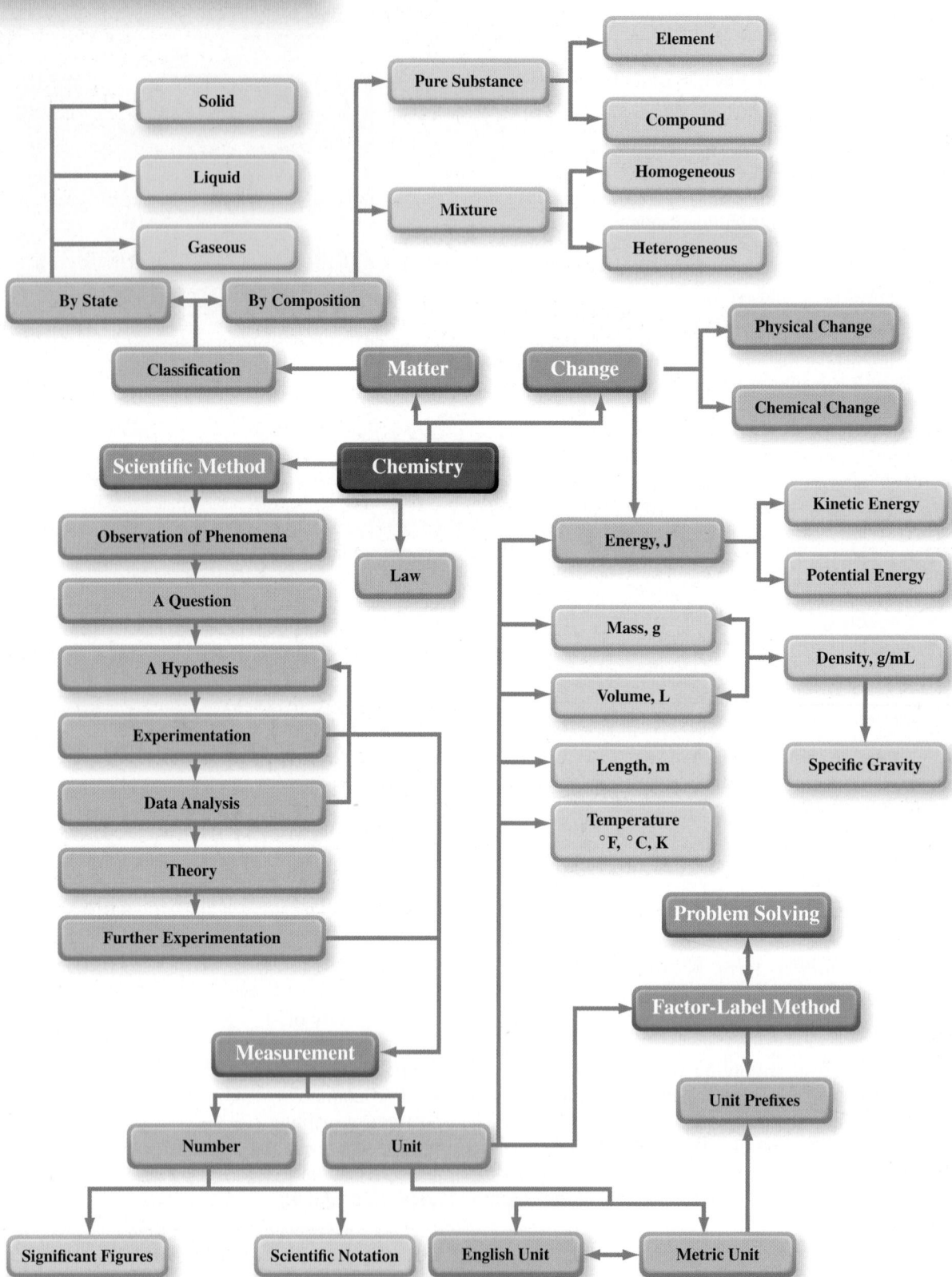

# SUMMARY

## 1.1 The Discovery Process

▶ **Matter** is anything that has mass and occupies space.

▶ **Chemistry** is the study of matter and the changes it undergoes.

▶ Matter gains and loses **energy** at it undergoes change.

▶ The major areas of chemistry include:
  • Inorganic Chemistry
  • Organic Chemistry
  • Biochemistry
  • Analytical Chemistry
  • Physical Chemistry

▶ The **scientific method** is a systematic approach to the discovery of new information. Characteristics of the scientific method include:
  • Observation of a phenomenon.
  • Formulation of a question concerning the observation.
  • Presentation of a **hypothesis,** or answer to the question.
  • Experimentation, with the collection and analysis of **data** and **results** in an attempt to support or disprove the hypothesis.
  • The ultimate goal of the process is to form a **theory,** a hypothesis supported by extensive testing.
  • A **law** is the summary of a large quantity of information.

## 1.2 The Classification of Matter

▶ It is useful to classify matter according to its **properties.**

▶ Matter can be classified by state as a **solid, liquid,** or **gas.**

▶ Properties of matter can be classified as:
  • a **physical property**—observed without changing the composition of the matter or
  • a **chemical property**—observed as the matter is converted to a new substance

▶ Properties can also be classified as:
  • **intensive**—a property that does not depend on the quantity of matter or
  • **extensive**—a property that does depend on the quantity of matter

▶ The changes that matter can undergo can be classified as **physical change** or **chemical change.** Chemical change is synonymous with **chemical reaction.**

▶ Matter can also be classified by composition, which groups matter as a **pure substance** or **mixture.**

▶ Pure substances can be further subdivided into **elements** or **compounds.**

▶ Mixtures can be subdivided into **homogeneous** mixtures or **heterogeneous** mixtures.

## 1.3 The Units of Measurement

▶ The **unit** of a measurement is as vital as the number.

▶ The metric system has an advantage over the English system because metric units are systematically related to each other by powers of ten.

▶ **Mass** is a measure of the quantity of matter. **Weight** is the force of gravity on an object. The metric unit for mass is the gram. A common English mass unit is the pound.

▶ *Length* is the distance between two points. The metric unit is the meter, which is similar to the English yard.

▶ *Volume* is the space occupied by an object. The metric unit of the liter is similar to the English quart.

▶ The metric unit of time is the second.

## 1.4 The Numbers of Measurement

▶ **Significant figures** are all digits in a measurement known with certainty plus one uncertain digit. It is important to be able to:
  • Read a measuring device to the correct number of significant figures.
  • Recognize the number of significant figures in a given written measurement.
  • Report answers to calculations to the correct number of significant figures. The rules for addition and subtraction are different from the rules for multiplication and division.
  • As digits are dropped from the calculation to give the correct number of significant figures, rules for rounding off numbers must be followed.

▶ **Scientific notation** is a way to express a number as a power of ten.

▶ Measurements always have a certain degree of **uncertainty** and **error** associated with them. Care must be taken to obtain a measurement with minimal error and high **accuracy** and **precision.**

## 1.5 Unit Conversion

▶ Problem solving is analogous to planning a road trip. The roads and routes are relationships and concepts presented throughout the textbook. It is not enough to know the roads, a problem solver must be able to connect the relationships to travel from a given piece of information to what is to be determined.

▶ Once a problem is solved, it is important to determine if the answer is reasonable in magnitude and sign.

▶ Conversions between units can be accomplished using the factor-label method.

▶ Conversion factors are fractions in which the numerator and denominator are equivalent in magnitude, and thus, the conversion factor is equivalent to one.

▶ In the factor-label method, undesired units are eliminated by canceling out with units in the conversion factor.

▶ When a unit is squared or cubed, the conversion factor must also be squared or cubed.

## 1.6  Additional Experimental Quantities

▶ **Temperature** is the degree of "hotness" of an object. Common units include Celsius, Kelvin, and the English Fahrenheit. Equations are used to convert between the units.

▶ **Energy,** the ability to do work, is categorized as **kinetic energy** or **potential energy.** Common units of energy are the calorie and the joule.

▶ **Concentration** is a measure of the amount of a substance contained in a specified amount of a mixture.

▶ **Density** is the ratio of mass to volume and is an intensive property.
  • Density is typically reported as g/mL or g/cm³.
  • Density can be used as a conversion factor to convert between the mass and volume of an object.

▶ **Specific gravity** is the ratio of the density of an object to the density of pure water at 4°C. It is numerically equal to density but has no units.

## ANSWERS TO PRACTICE PROBLEMS

**1.1** Fill two beakers with identical volumes of water. Add salt (several grams) to one of the beakers of water. Insert a thermometer into each beaker, and slowly heat the beakers. Record the temperature of each liquid when boiling is observed.

**1.2  a.** Physical change       **d.** Physical change
  **b.** Chemical change      **e.** Chemical change
  **c.** Chemical change

**1.3** Intensive property; the freezing point of a glass of pure water and a gallon of pure water is the same. The freezing point is independent of the quantity of the substance.

**1.4  a.** Pure substance          **c.** Homogeneous mixture
  **b.** Heterogeneous mixture   **d.** Pure substance

**1.5** $7.46 \times 10^5$

**1.6** $6.82 \times 10^{-2}$ mi

**1.7  a.** $1.3 \times 10^{-2}$ m     **d.** 1.3 cm
  **b.** 0.71 L               **e.** $7.1 \times 10^2$ mL
  **c.** 2.00 oz              **f.** $2.00 \times 10^{-3}$ oz

**1.8  a.** $7.5 \times 10^3$ mm
  **b.** $1.5 \times 10^4$ cL
  **c.** 0.55 kg

**1.9  a.** $1.5 \times 10^{-4}$ m²
  **b.** $3.6 \times 10^4$ cm²

**1.10** 0.791 kg/L

**1.11  a.** 0°C
         273 K
   **b.** 40°C
         313 K

**1.12** 13.6 g/mL
         13.6 g/cm³

**1.13** 23.7 g alcohol

**1.14** 2.6 g air

**1.15** 9.52 mL saline

**1.16** 1.9 L rubbing alcohol

## QUESTIONS AND PROBLEMS

### The Discovery Process

#### Foundations

**1.19** Define chemistry and list the major subdivisions of chemistry.

**1.20** Define energy and explain the importance of energy in chemistry.

**1.21** Why is it important for anyone considering a medically related career to have a basic understanding of chemical principles?

**1.22** Why is observation a critical starting point for any scientific study?

**1.23** What data would be required to estimate the total cost of gasoline needed to drive from New York City to Washington, D.C.?

**1.24** What data would be required to estimate the mass of planet earth?

**1.25** What are the characteristics of methane emphasized by the model?

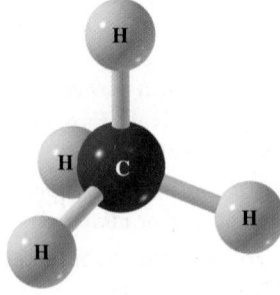

**1.26** The model of methane in Problem 1.25 has limitations, as do all models. What are these limitations?

#### Applications

**1.27** Discuss the difference between *hypothesis* and *theory.*
**1.28** Discuss the difference between *theory* and *law.*

**1.29** We use aspects of the scientific method in our everyday lives. Provide one example of formulating a hypothesis as an aid in solving a practical problem.

**1.30** Provide one example of the utility of pattern recognition in your day-to-day activities.

**1.31** Discuss the meaning of the term *scientific method*.

**1.32** Describe an application of reasoning involving the scientific method that has occurred in your day-to-day life.

**1.33** Stem-cell research has the potential to provide replacement "parts" for the human body. Is this statement a theory, or law? Explain your reasoning.

**1.34** Observed increases in global temperatures are caused by elevated levels of carbon dioxide. Is this statement a theory, or law? Explain your reasoning.

**1.35** Describe an experiment demonstrating that the freezing point of water changes when salt (sodium chloride) is added to water.

**1.36** Describe an experiment that would enable you to determine the amount (g) of solids suspended in a 1-L sample of seawater.

## The Classification of Matter

### Foundations

**1.37** List the three states of matter.

**1.38** Explain the differences among the three states of matter in terms of volume and shape.

**1.39** Describe what is meant by a physical property.

**1.40** Describe what is meant by a physical change.

**1.41** Describe several chemical properties of matter.

**1.42** Describe what is meant by a chemical reaction.

**1.43** Distinguish between a pure substance and a mixture.

**1.44** Give examples of pure substances and mixtures.

**1.45** Describe what is meant by an intensive property and give an example.

**1.46** Describe what is meant by an extensive property and give an example.

**1.47** Distinguish between a homogeneous mixture and a heterogeneous mixture.

**1.48** Distinguish between an intensive property and an extensive property.

### Applications

**1.49** Draw a diagram representing a heterogeneous mixture of two different substances. Use two different colored spheres to represent the two different substances.

**1.50** Draw a diagram representing a homogeneous mixture of two different substances. Use two different colored spheres to represent the two different substances.

**1.51** Label each of the following as either a physical change or a chemical reaction:
**a.** An iron nail rusts.     **c.** A limb falls from a tree.
**b.** An ice cube melts.

**1.52** Label each of the following as either a physical change or a chemical reaction:
**a.** A puddle of water evaporates.
**b.** Food is digested.
**c.** Wood is burned.

**1.53** Label each of the following properties of sodium as either a physical property or a chemical property:
**a.** Sodium is a soft metal (can be cut with a knife).
**b.** Sodium reacts violently with water to produce hydrogen gas and sodium hydroxide.

**1.54** Label each of the following properties of sodium as either a physical property or a chemical property:
**a.** When exposed to air, sodium forms a white oxide.
**b.** Sodium melts at 98°C.
**c.** The density of sodium metal at 25°C is 0.97 g/cm³.

**1.55** Label each of the following as either a pure substance or a mixture:
**a.** water
**b.** table salt (sodium chloride)
**c.** blood

**1.56** Label each of the following as either a pure substance or a mixture:
**a.** sucrose (table sugar)  **c.** urine
**b.** orange juice

**1.57** Label each of the following as either a homogeneous mixture or a heterogeneous mixture:
**a.** a soft drink          **c.** gelatin
**b.** a saline solution

**1.58** Label each of the following as either a homogeneous mixture or a heterogeneous mixture:
**a.** gasoline              **c.** concrete
**b.** vegetable soup

**1.59** Classify the matter represented in the following diagram by state and by composition.

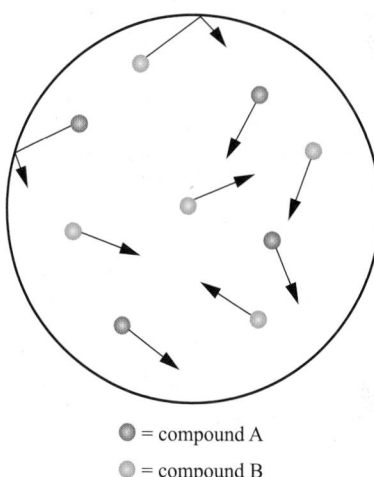

⬤ = compound A
◯ = compound B

**1.60** Classify the matter represented in the following diagram by state and by composition.

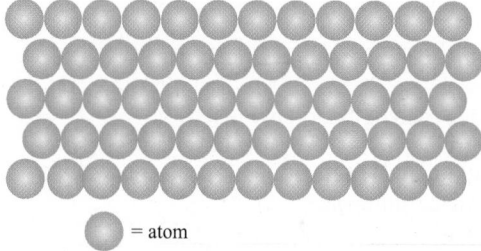

◯ = atom

**1.61** Plant varieties may be distinguished, one from another, by observing properties of their leaves.
**a.** Suggest two extensive properties of leaves that would be useful in the process.
**b.** Suggest two intensive properties of leaves that would be useful in the process.

**1.62** Would you expect that intensive properties or extensive properties would be more useful in distinguishing among plant varieties by inspecting their leaves?

## The Units of Measurement

### Foundations

**1.63** Mass is the measure of what property of matter?
**1.64** Explain the difference between mass and weight.
**1.65** Define length.
**1.66** What metric unit for length is similar to the English yd?
**1.67** How is the metric unit of L defined?
**1.68** What English unit of volume is similar to a L?

### Applications

**1.69** Rank the following from shortest to longest length.

mm, km, m

**1.70** Rank the following from least to greatest mass.

cg, μg, Mg

## The Numbers of Measurement

### Foundations

**1.71** Determine the temperature reading of the following thermometer to the correct number of significant figures.

**1.72** Determine the temperature reading of the following thermometer to the correct number of significant figures.

**1.73** Define each of the following terms:
   a. precision          b. accuracy
**1.74** Define each of the following terms:
   a. error              b. uncertainty
**1.75** How many significant figures are contained in each of the following numbers?
   a. 10.0               d. 2.062
   b. 0.214              e. 10.50
   c. 0.120              f. 1050
**1.76** How many significant figures are contained in each of the following numbers?
   a. $3.8 \times 10^{-3}$     d. 24
   b. $5.20 \times 10^{2}$     e. 240
   c. 0.00261            f. 2.40

**1.77** Round the following numbers to three significant figures:
   a. $3.873 \times 10^{-3}$     d. 24.3387
   b. $5.202 \times 10^{-2}$     e. 240.1
   c. 0.002616           f. 2.407
**1.78** Round the following numbers to three significant figures:
   a. 123700             d. 53.2995
   b. 0.00285792         e. 16.96
   c. $1.421 \times 10^{-3}$     f. 507.5

### Applications

**1.79** Perform each of the following arithmetic operations, reporting the answer with the proper number of significant figures:
   a. (23)(657)          d. $1157.23 - 17.812$
   b. $0.00521 + 0.236$
   c. $\dfrac{18.3}{3.0576}$     e. $\dfrac{(1.987)(298)}{0.0821}$
**1.80** Perform each of the following arithmetic operations, reporting the answer with the proper number of significant figures:
   a. $\dfrac{(16.0)(0.1879)}{45.3}$     d. $18 + 52.1$
   b. $\dfrac{(76.32)(1.53)}{0.052}$     e. $58.17 - 57.79$
   c. $(0.0063)(57.8)$
**1.81** Express the following numbers in scientific notation (use the proper number of significant figures):
   a. 12.3               e. 92,000,000
   b. 0.0569             f. 0.005280
   c. −1527              g. 1.279
   d. 0.000000789        h. −531.77
**1.82** Express each of the following numbers in decimal notation:
   a. $3.24 \times 10^{3}$       e. $-8.21 \times 10^{-2}$
   b. $1.50 \times 10^{4}$       f. $2.9979 \times 10^{8}$
   c. $4.579 \times 10^{-1}$     g. $1.50 \times 10^{0}$
   d. $-6.83 \times 10^{5}$      h. $6.02 \times 10^{23}$
**1.83** The following four measurements were made for an object whose true mass is 4.56 g.

4.55 g, 4.56 g, 4.56 g, 4.57 g

Describe the measurements in terms of their accuracy and their precision.
**1.84** The following four measurements were made for an object whose true volume is 17.55 mL.

18.69 mL, 18.69 mL, 18.70 mL, 18.71 mL

Describe the measurements in terms of their accuracy and their precision.

## Unit Conversion

### Foundations

**1.85** Give a reason why the metric system is a more convenient system than the English system of measurement.
**1.86** Why is it important to *always* include units when recording measurements?
**1.87** Give the abbreviation and meaning of the following metric prefixes:
   a. kilo              c. micro
   b. centi

**1.88** Fill in the blank with the missing abbreviation and name the prefix.
  **a.** $10^6$ m = 1 _____m    **c.** $10^{-9}$ g = 1 _____ g
  **b.** $10^{-3}$ L = 1 _____L

**1.89** Write the two conversion factors that can be written for the relationship between ft and in.

**1.90** Write the two conversion factors that can be written for the relationship between cm and in.

**1.91** Convert 2.0 lb to:
  **a.** oz            **d.** mg
  **b.** tons (t)      **e.** dekagrams (dag)
  **c.** g

**1.92** Convert 5.0 qt to:
  **a.** gal           **d.** mL
  **b.** pints (pt)    **e.** μL
  **c.** L

**1.93** Convert 3.0 g to:
  **a.** lb            **d.** centigrams (cg)
  **b.** oz            **e.** mg
  **c.** kg

**1.94** Convert 3.0 m to:
  **a.** yd            **d.** cm
  **b.** in            **e.** mm
  **c.** ft

**1.95** Convert $1.50 \times 10^4$ μg to mg.

**1.96** Convert $7.5 \times 10^{-3}$ cm to mm.

**1.97** A typical office has 144 ft² of floor space. Calculate the floor space in m².

**1.98** Tire pressure is measured in units of lb/in². Convert 32 lb/in² to g/cm².

**Applications**

**1.99** A 150-lb adult has approximately 9 pt of blood. How many L of blood does the individual have?

**1.100** If a drop of blood has a volume of 0.05 mL, how many drops of blood are in the adult described in Problem 1.99?

**1.101** A patient's temperature is found to be 38.5°C. To what Fahrenheit temperature does this correspond?

**1.102** A newborn is 21 in in length and weighs 6 lb 9 oz. Describe the baby in metric units.

**1.103** Which distance is shorter: 5.0 cm or 5.0 in?

**1.104** Which volume is smaller: 50.0 mL or 0.500 L?

**1.105** Which mass is smaller: 5.0 mg or 5.0 μg?

**1.106** Which volume is smaller: 1.0 L or 1.0 qt?

**1.107** A new homeowner wished to know the perimeter of his property. He found that the front boundary and back boundary were measured in meters: 85 m and 95 m, respectively. The side boundaries were measured in feet: 435 ft and 515 ft.
  **a.** Describe the problem-solving strategy used to determine the perimeter in km.
  **b.** Calculate the perimeter in km.

**1.108** Sally and Gertrude were comparing their weight-loss regimens. Sally started her diet weighing 193 lb. In 1 year she weighed 145 lb. Gertrude started her diet weighing 80 kg. At the end of the year she weighed 65 kg. Who lost the most weight?
  **a.** Describe the problem-solving strategy used to determine who was more successful.
  **b.** Calculate the weight lost in lb and kg by Sally and Gertrude.

## Additional Experimental Quantities

**Foundations**

**1.109** List three major temperature scales.

**1.110** Rank the following temperatures from coldest to hottest:
  zero degrees Celsius, zero degrees Fahrenheit, zero Kelvin

**1.111** List and define the two subgroups of energy.

**1.112** Label each of the following statements as true or false. If false, correct the statement.
  **a.** Energy can be created or destroyed.
  **b.** Energy can be converted from electrical energy to light energy.
  **c.** Conversion of energy from one form to another can occur with 100% efficiency.
  **d.** All chemical reactions involve either a gain or loss of energy.

**1.113** List each of the following as an intensive or extensive property.
  **a.** mass
  **b.** volume
  **c.** density

**1.114** What is the relationship between density and specific gravity?

**Applications**

**1.115** Convert 50.0°F to:
  **a.** °C
  **b.** K

**1.116** Convert −10.0°F to:
  **a.** °C
  **b.** K

**1.117** Convert 20.0°C to:
  **a.** K
  **b.** °F

**1.118** Convert 300.0 K to:
  **a.** °C
  **b.** °F

**1.119** The combustion of a peanut releases 6 kcal of heat. Convert this energy to J.

**1.120** The energy available from the world's total petroleum reserve is estimated at $2.0 \times 10^{22}$ J. Convert this energy to kcal.

**1.121** Calculate the density of a $3.00 \times 10^2$-g object that has a volume of 50.0 mL.

**1.122** Calculate the density of 50.0 g of an isopropyl alcohol–water mixture (commercial rubbing alcohol) that has a volume of 63.6 mL.

**1.123** What volume, in L, will $8.00 \times 10^2$ g of air occupy if the density of air is 1.29 g/L?

**1.124** In Question 1.123, you calculated the volume of $8.00 \times 10^2$ g of air with a density of 1.29 g/L. The temperature of the air sample was lowered and the density increased to 1.50 g/L. Calculate the new volume of the air sample.

**1.125** What is the mass, in g, of a piece of iron that has a volume of $1.50 \times 10^2$ mL and a density of 7.20 g/mL?

**1.126** What is the mass of a femur (leg bone) having a volume of 118 cm³? The density of bone is 1.8 g/cm³.

**1.127** You are given a piece of wood that is maple, teak, or oak. The piece of wood has a volume of $1.00 \times 10^2$ cm$^3$ and a mass of 98 g. The densities of maple, teak, and oak are as follows:

| Wood | Density (g/cm 3) |
|------|------------------|
| Maple | 0.70 |
| Teak | 0.98 |
| Oak | 0.85 |

What is the identity of the piece of wood?

**1.128** The specific gravity of a patient's urine sample was measured to be 1.008. Given that the density of water is 1.000 g/mL at 4°C, what is the density of the urine sample?

**1.129** The density of grain alcohol is 0.789 g/mL. Given that the density of water at 4°C is 1.00 g/mL, what is the specific gravity of grain alcohol?

**1.130** The density of mercury is 13.6 g/mL. If a sample of mercury weighs 272 g, what is the volume of the sample in mL?

**1.131** You are given three bars of metal. Each is labeled with its identity (lead, uranium, platinum). The lead bar has a mass of $5.0 \times 10^1$ g and a volume of 6.36 cm$^3$. The uranium bar has a mass of 75 g and a volume of 3.97 cm$^3$. The platinum bar has a mass of 2140 g and a volume of $1.00 \times 10^2$ cm$^3$. Which of these metals has the lowest density? Which has the greatest density?

**1.132** Refer to Problem 1.131. Suppose that each of the bars had the same mass. How could you determine which bar had the lowest density or highest density?

**1.133** The density of methanol at 20°C is 0.791 g/mL. What is the volume of a 10.0-g sample of methanol?

**1.134** The density of methanol at 20°C is 0.791 g/mL. What is the mass of a 50.0-mL sample of methanol?

## CRITICAL THINKING PROBLEMS

1. An instrument used to detect metals in drinking water can detect as little as 1 µg of mercury in 1 L of water. Mercury is a toxic metal; it accumulates in the body and is responsible for the deterioration of brain cells. Calculate the number of mercury atoms you would consume if you drank 1 L of water that contained only 1 µg of mercury. (The mass of one mercury atom is $3.3 \times 10^{-22}$ g.)

2. Yesterday's temperature was 40°F. Today it is 80°F. Bill tells Sue that it is twice as hot today. Sue disagrees. Do you think Sue is correct or incorrect? Why or why not?

3. Aspirin has been recommended to minimize the chance of heart attacks in persons who have already had one or more occurrences. If a patient takes one aspirin tablet per day for 10 years, how many pounds of aspirin will the patient consume? (Assume that each tablet is approximately 325 mg.)

4. Design an experiment that will allow you to measure the density of your favorite piece of jewelry.

5. The diameter of an aluminum atom is 250 picometers (pm) (1 pm = $10^{-12}$ m). How many aluminum atoms must be placed end to end to make a "chain" of aluminum atoms 1 ft long?

# The Structure of the Atom and the Periodic Table

## LEARNING GOALS

1 Describe the important properties of protons, neutrons, and electrons.

2 Calculate the number of protons, neutrons, and electrons in any atom.

3 Distinguish between the terms *atom* and *isotope* and calculate atomic masses from isotopic abundance.

4 Trace the history of the development of atomic theory, beginning with Dalton.

5 Explain the critical role of spectroscopy in the development of atomic theory and in our everyday lives.

6 State the basic postulates of Bohr's theory, its utility, and its limitations.

7 Recognize the important subdivisions of the periodic table: periods, groups (families), metals, and nonmetals.

8 Use the periodic table to obtain information about an element.

9 Describe the relationship between the electronic structure of an element and its position in the periodic table.

10 Write electron configurations and orbital diagrams for atoms of the most commonly occurring elements.

11 Use the octet rule to predict the charges of common cations and anions.

12 Utilize the periodic table and its predictive power to estimate the relative sizes of atoms and ions, as well as relative magnitudes of ionization energy and electron affinity.

The southern lights, as seen from the space station. The connections between the energy of light and the energy of matter help us understand the structure of atoms.

## OUTLINE

# INTRODUCTION

Why does ice float on water? Why don't oil and water mix? Why does blood transport oxygen to our cells, and why does carbon monoxide inhibit this process? Questions such as these are best answered by understanding the behavior of substances at the atomic level.

In this chapter, we will learn some of the properties of the major particles that make up the atom, and look at early experiments that enabled the development of theories of atomic structure. These theories, in turn, help us to explain the behavior of atoms themselves, as well as the compounds that result from their combination, such as water and carbon dioxide.

The structure of atoms of each element is unique, so it is useful to consider relationships and differences among the elements themselves. The unifying concept is called the periodic law, and it gives rise to an organized "map" of the elements that relates their structure to their chemical and physical properties. This "map" is the periodic table.

As we study the periodic law and periodic table, we shall see that the chemical and physical properties of elements follow directly from the electronic structure of the atoms that make up these elements. A thorough familiarity with the arrangement of the periodic table is vital to the study of chemistry. It not only allows us to predict the structure and properties of the various elements, but it also serves as the basis for developing an understanding of chemical bonding, or the process of forming molecules. Additionally, the properties and behavior of these larger units (bulk properties) are fundamentally related to the properties of the atoms that comprise them.

**Figure 2.1** Sophisticated techniques, such as scanning tunneling electron microscopy, provide visual evidence for the structure of atoms and molecules. Each dot represents the image of a single iron atom. Even more amazing, the iron atoms have been arranged on a copper surface in the form of the Chinese characters representing the word *atom*.

## 2.1   Composition of the Atom

The basic structural unit of an element is the **atom,** which is the smallest unit of an element that retains the chemical properties of that element. A tiny sample of the element copper, too small to be seen by the naked eye, is composed of billions of copper atoms arranged in some orderly fashion. Each atom is incredibly small. Only recently have we been able to "see" atoms using modern instruments such as the scanning tunneling electron microscope (Figure 2.1).

### Electrons, Protons, and Neutrons

We know that the atom is composed of three primary particles: the *electron*, the *proton*, and the *neutron*. Although other subatomic fragments with unusual names (neutrinos, gluons, quarks, and so forth) have also been discovered, we shall concern ourselves only with the primary particles: the protons, neutrons, and electrons.

We can consider the atom to be composed of two distinct regions:

1. The **nucleus** is a small, dense, positively charged region in the center of the atom. The nucleus is composed of positively charged **protons** and uncharged **neutrons.**
2. Surrounding the nucleus is a diffuse region of negative charge populated by **electrons,** the source of the negative charge. Electrons are very low in mass compared to protons and neutrons.

The properties of these particles are summarized in Table 2.1.

**TABLE 2.1 Selected Properties of the Three Basic Subatomic Particles**

| Name | Charge | Mass (amu) | Mass (g) |
|---|---|---|---|
| Electron (e⁻) | −1 | $5.4 \times 10^{-4}$ | $9.1095 \times 10^{-28}$ |
| Proton (p⁺) | +1 | 1.0 | $1.6725 \times 10^{-24}$ |
| Neutron (n) | 0 | 1.0 | $1.6750 \times 10^{-24}$ |

Atoms of various types differ in their number of protons, neutrons, and electrons. The number of protons determines the identity of the atom. As such, the number of protons is *characteristic* of the element. When the number of protons is equal to the number of electrons, the atom is neutral because the charges are balanced and effectively cancel one another. Thus, all atoms have the same number of electrons as protons.

We may represent an element symbolically as follows:

$$\text{Mass number} \longrightarrow {}^{A}_{Z}\mathbf{X} \longleftarrow \text{Element symbol}$$
$$\text{Atomic number} \longrightarrow$$

The **atomic number** (Z) is equal to the number of protons in the atom, and the **mass number** (A) is equal to the *sum* of the number of protons and neutrons (the mass of the electrons is so small as to be insignificant in comparison to that of the nucleus).

The atomic number is the whole number associated with the atom on the periodic table. The mass number is not found on the periodic table.

Since,

mass number = number of protons + number of neutrons

to determine the number of neutrons, we can rearrange the equation to give:

number of neutrons = mass number − number of protons

number of neutrons = mass number − atomic number

number of neutrons = A − Z

**LEARNING GOAL**

**1** Describe the important properties of protons, neutrons, and electrons.

**LEARNING GOAL**

**2** Calculate the number of protons, neutrons, and electrons in any atom.

---

**EXAMPLE 2.1    Determining the Composition of an Atom**

**LEARNING GOAL**

**2** Calculate the number of protons, neutrons, and electrons in any atom.

Calculate the numbers of protons, neutrons, and electrons in an atom of fluorine. The atomic symbol for the fluorine atom is ${}^{19}_{9}$ F.

**Solution**

**Step 1.** The atomic number, Z = 9. There are 9 protons.
**Step 2.** The number of protons = the number of electrons in an atom. There are 9 electrons.
**Step 3.** The mass number, A = 19. The number of neutrons = A − Z.
   Number of neutrons = 19 − 9 = 10. There are 10 neutrons.

**Practice Problem 2.1**

Calculate the numbers of protons, neutrons, and electrons in each of the following atoms:

a. ${}^{32}_{16}$ S

b. ${}^{23}_{11}$ Na

c. ${}^{1}_{1}$ H

d. ${}^{244}_{94}$ Pu

▶ For Further Practice: **Questions 2.35 and 2.36.**

**3** Distinguish between the terms *atom* and *isotope* and calculate atomic masses from isotopic abundance.

## Isotopes

**Isotopes** are atoms of the same element having different masses *because they contain different numbers of neutrons*. In other words, isotopes have different mass numbers. For example, all of the following are isotopes of hydrogen:

| $^1_1 H$ | $^2_1 H$ | $^3_1 H$ |
|---|---|---|
| Hydrogen | Deuterium | Tritium |
| (Hydrogen-1) | (Hydrogen-2) | (Hydrogen-3) |

Isotopes are often written with the name of the element followed by the mass number. For example, the isotopes $^{12}_6 C$ and $^{14}_6 C$ may be written as carbon-12 (or C-12) and carbon-14 (or C-14), respectively.

**Question 2.1** How many protons, neutrons, and electrons are present in a single atom of:

    a. bromine-79        b. bromine-81        c. iron-56

**Question 2.2** How many protons, neutrons, and electrons are present in a single atom of:

    a. phosphorus-30        b. sulfur-32        c. chlorine-35

*A detailed discussion of the use of radioactive isotopes in the diagnosis and treatment of diseases is found in Chapter 9.*

Certain isotopes (radioactive isotopes) of elements emit particles and energy that can be used to trace the behavior of biochemical systems. These isotopes otherwise behave identically to any other isotope of the same element. Their chemical behavior is identical; it is their nuclear behavior that is unique. As a result, a radioactive isotope can be substituted for the "nonradioactive" isotope, and its biochemical activity can be followed by monitoring the particles or energy emitted by the isotope as it passes through the body.

As stated earlier, the atomic number is the whole number associated with every element on the periodic table. The other number associated with each element on the periodic table is its **atomic mass,** the *weighted* average of the masses of each isotope that makes up the element. Atomic mass is measured in *atomic mass units (amu).*

$$1 \text{ amu} = 1.66 \times 10^{-24} \text{ grams (g)}$$

Notice in Table 2.1 that the masses of protons and neutrons are both 1.0 amu.

If we examine the periodic table, we see that the atomic mass of chlorine is 35.45 amu. Two isotopes of chlorine exist, Cl-35 and Cl-37. The atomic mass of chlorine, given as 35.45 amu, is not an average of 35 and 37 (which would be 36), it is a weighted average. There is more Cl-35 in nature than there is Cl-37. The percentage of each isotope, as found in nature, is called its *natural abundance.* A weighted average takes into account the natural abundance of each isotope.

Example 2.2 demonstrates the calculation of the atomic mass of chlorine.

---

**EXAMPLE 2.2**    **Determining Atomic Mass**

**3** Distinguish between the terms *atom* and *isotope* and calculate atomic masses from isotopic abundance.

Calculate the atomic mass of naturally occurring chlorine if 75.77% of chlorine atoms are $^{35}_{17} Cl$ (chlorine-35, atomic mass = 35.0) and 24.23% of chlorine atoms are $^{37}_{17} Cl$ (chlorine-37, atomic mass = 37.0).

## Solution

The weighted average will be between 35 and 37. There is more chlorine-35 than chlorine-37; therefore, we would expect the weighted average to be closer to 35.

**Step 1.** Convert each percentage to a decimal fraction.

$$75.77\% \text{ chlorine-35} \times \frac{1}{100\%} = 0.7577 \text{ chlorine-35}$$

$$24.23\% \text{ chlorine-37} \times \frac{1}{100\%} = 0.2423 \text{ chlorine-37}$$

**Step 2.** Determine the contribution of each isotope to the total atomic mass by multiplying the decimal fraction by the mass of the isotope.

For chlorine-35:  $0.7577 \times 35.0 \text{ amu} = 26.5 \text{ amu}$

For chlorine-37:  $0.2423 \times 37.0 \text{ amu} = 8.97 \text{ amu}$

**Step 3.** Add the mass contributed by each isotope.

Atomic mass $= 26.5 \text{ amu} + 8.97 \text{ amu} = 35.5 \text{ amu}$

Does the answer make sense? The value 35.5 is between 35 and 37 and closer to 35 as expected. This is also close to the value of 35.45 given on the periodic table for the atomic mass of chlorine.

### Practice Problem 2.2

The element nitrogen has two naturally occurring isotopes. One of these has a mass of 14.0 amu and a natural abundance of 99.63%; the other isotope has a mass of 15.0 amu and a natural abundance of 0.37%. Calculate the atomic mass of nitrogen.

▶ For Further Practice: **Question 2.37.**

---

**EXAMPLE 2.3**  **Determining Atomic Mass**

LEARNING GOAL

**3** Distinguish between the terms *atom* and *isotope* and calculate atomic masses from isotopic abundance.

The element neon has three naturally occurring isotopes. The natural abundance and mass of each are given below. Calculate the atomic mass of neon.

|  | Mass | Abundance |
|---|---|---|
| $^{20}$Ne | 20.0 amu | 90.48% |
| $^{21}$Ne | 21.0 amu | 0.27% |
| $^{22}$Ne | 22.0 amu | 9.25% |

## Solution

We can estimate the value by looking at the percent abundances. The isotope of greatest natural abundance is Ne-20. Therefore, the expected value will be close to 20.0 amu. Since the other isotopes are greater in mass than Ne-20, the atomic mass will be slightly greater than 20.0 amu.

*Continued…*

**Step 1.** Convert each percentage to a decimal fraction.

$$90.48\% \text{ Ne-20} \times \frac{1}{100\%} = 0.9048$$

$$0.27\% \text{ Ne-21} \times \frac{1}{100\%} = 0.0027$$

$$9.25\% \text{ Ne-22} \times \frac{1}{100\%} = 0.0925$$

**Step 2.** Determine the contribution of each isotope to the total atomic mass by multiplying the decimal fraction by the mass of the isotope.

For Ne-20:   $0.9048 \times 20.0$ amu = 18.1 amu

For Ne-21:   $0.0027 \times 21.0$ amu = 0.057 amu

For Ne-22:   $0.0925 \times 22.0$ amu = 2.04 amu

**Step 3.** Add the masses contributed by each isotope.

Atomic mass = 18.1 amu + 0.057 amu + 2.04 amu = 20.2 amu.

Does the answer make sense? We estimated that the atomic mass would be slightly greater than 20, and indeed that is what we obtained. As a final check, we can look at the periodic table. Neon has an atomic mass of 20.18 amu.

---

**Practice Problem 2.3**

Calculate the atomic mass of naturally occurring boron if 19.9% of boron atoms are $^{10}B$ (10.0 amu) and 80.1% are $^{11}B$ (11.0 amu).

▶ For Further Practice: **Question 2.38.**

---

LEARNING GOAL

**4** Trace the history of the development of atomic theory, beginning with Dalton.

## 2.2   Development of Atomic Theory

With this overview of our current understanding of the structure of the atom, we now look at a few of the most important scientific discoveries that led to modern atomic theory.

### Dalton's Theory

The first experimentally based theory of atomic structure was proposed by John Dalton, an English schoolteacher, in the early 1800s. Dalton proposed the following description of atoms:

1. All matter consists of tiny particles called atoms.
2. An atom cannot be created, divided, destroyed, or converted to any other type of atom.
3. Atoms of a particular element have identical properties.
4. Atoms of different elements have different properties.
5. Atoms of different elements combine in simple whole-number ratios to produce compounds (stable combinations of atoms).
6. Chemical change involves joining, separating, or rearranging atoms.

# CHEMISTRY AT THE CRIME SCENE

## Microbial Forensics

We have learned that atoms of the same element are not identical; usually elements are a mixture of two or more isotopes, differing in mass because they contain different numbers of neutrons. Furthermore, the atomic mass is the weighted average of the masses of these various isotopes.

It seems to follow from this that the relative amounts of these isotopes would be the same, no matter where in the world we obtain a sample of the element. In reality, this is not true. There exist small, but measurable, differences between elemental isotopic ratios; these differences correlate with their locations.

Water, of course, contains oxygen atoms, and a small fraction of these atoms are oxygen-18. We know that lakes and rivers across the United States contain oxygen-18 in different concentrations. Ocean water is richer in oxygen-18. Consequently, freshwater supplies closest to oceans are similarly enriched, perhaps because water containing oxygen-18 is a bit heavier and falls to earth more rapidly, before the clouds are carried inland, far from the coast. Scientists have been able to map the oxygen-18 distribution throughout the United States, creating contour maps, similar to weather maps, showing regions of varying concentrations of the isotope.

How can we use these facts to our advantage? The Federal Bureau of Investigation (FBI) has an interest in ascertaining the origin of microbes that may be used by terrorists. Anthrax, distributed to several sites shortly after September 11, 2001 through the United States Postal Service (USPS), is but one familiar example. If we could carefully measure the ratio of oxygen-18 to oxygen-16 in weaponized biological materials, it might be possible to match this ratio to that found in water supplies in a specific location. We would then have an indication of the region of the country where the material was cultured, perhaps leading to the arrest and prosecution of the perpetrators of the terrorist activity.

This is certainly not an easy task. However, the FBI has assembled an advisory board of science and forensic experts to study this and other approaches to tracking the origin of biological weapons of mass destruction. Just like the "smoking gun," these strategies, termed *microbial forensics*, could lead to more effective prosecution and a safer society for all of us.

### For Further Understanding

▶ Search the Web for more information on the properties of anthrax.

▶ How might the approach, described above, be applied to determining the origin of an oil spill at sea?

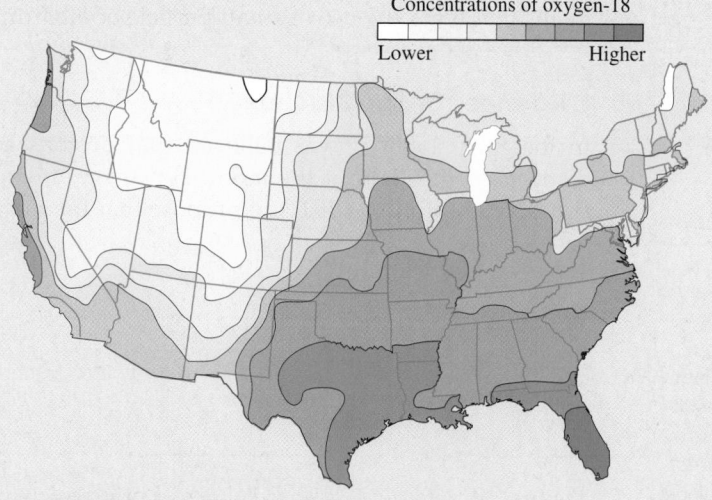

Concentrations of oxygen-18

Lower        Higher

Although Dalton's theory was founded on meager and primitive experimental information, we regard much of it as correct today. Postulates 1, 4, 5, and 6 are currently regarded as true. The discovery of the processes of nuclear fusion, fission ("splitting" of atoms), and radioactivity has disproved the postulate that atoms cannot be created or destroyed. Postulate 3, that all the atoms of a particular element are identical, was disproved by the discovery of isotopes.

Fusion, fission, radioactivity, and isotopes are discussed in some detail in Chapter 9. Figure 2.2 uses a simple model to illustrate Dalton's theory.

Atoms of element X    Atoms of element Y

**(a)**

Compound formed from
elements X and Y

**(b)**

**Figure 2.2** An illustration of John Dalton's atomic theory. (a) Atoms of the same element are identical but different from atoms of any other element. (b) Atoms combine in whole-number ratios to form compounds.

**ANIMATIONS**
• Thomson's Cathode Ray Tube

## Evidence for Subatomic Particles: Electrons, Protons, and Neutrons

The next major discoveries occurred almost a century later (1879–1897). Although Dalton pictured atoms as indivisible, various experiments, particularly those of William Crookes and Eugene Goldstein, indicated that the atom is composed of charged (+ and −) particles.

Crookes connected two metal electrodes (metal disks connected to a source of electricity) at opposite ends of a sealed glass vacuum tube. When the electricity was turned on, rays of light were observed to travel between the two electrodes. They were called *cathode rays* because they traveled from the *cathode* (the negative electrode) to the *anode* (the positive electrode).

Later experiments by J. J. Thomson, an English scientist, demonstrated the electrical and magnetic properties of cathode rays (Figure 2.3). The rays were deflected toward the positive electrode of an external electric field. Because opposite charges attract, this indicates the negative character of the rays. Similar experiments with an external magnetic field showed a deflection as well; hence these cathode rays also have magnetic properties.

A change in the material used to fabricate the electrode disks brought about no change in the experimental results. This suggested that the ability to produce cathode rays is a characteristic of all materials.

In 1897, Thomson announced that cathode rays are streams of negative particles of energy. These particles are *electrons*. Similar experiments, conducted by Goldstein, led to the discovery of particles that are equal in charge to the electron but opposite in sign. These particles, much heavier than electrons (actually 1837 times as heavy), are called *protons*.

As we have seen, the third fundamental atomic particle is the *neutron*. It has a mass virtually identical (it is less than 1% heavier) to that of the proton and has zero charge. The neutron was first postulated in the early 1920s, but it was not until 1932 that James Chadwick demonstrated its existence with a series of experiments involving the use of small-particle bombardment of nuclei.

## Evidence for the Nucleus

In the early 1900s it was believed that protons and electrons were uniformly distributed throughout the atom. However, an experiment by Hans Geiger led Ernest Rutherford (in 1911) to propose that the majority of the mass and positive

**Figure 2.3** Illustration of an experiment demonstrating the charge properties of cathode rays. The cathode rays will strike the fluorescent screen at A. In the presence of an electric field the beam will be deflected to point B.

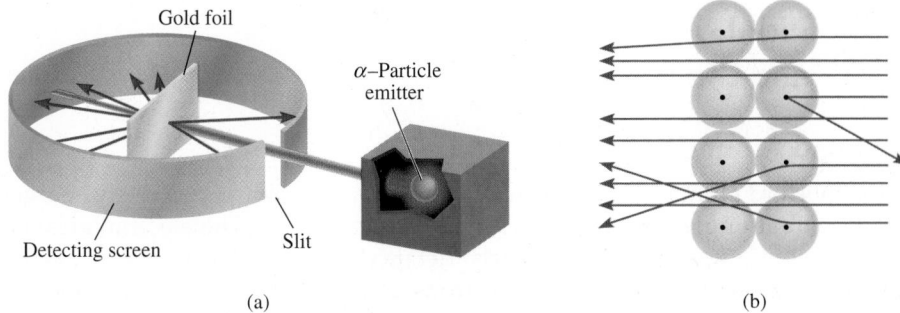

**Figure 2.4** (a) The alpha-particle scattering experiment. Most alpha particles passed through the foil without being deflected; a few were deflected from their path by nuclei in the gold atoms. (b) An enlarged view of the particles passing through the atoms. The nuclei, shown as black dots, deflect some of the alpha particles.

charge of the atom was actually located in a small, dense region, the *nucleus*, with small, negatively charged electrons occupying a much larger volume outside of the nucleus.

To understand how Rutherford's theory resulted from the experimental observations of Geiger, let us examine this experiment in greater detail. Rutherford and others had earlier demonstrated that some atoms spontaneously "decay" to produce three types of radiation: alpha (α), beta (β), and gamma (γ) radiation. This process is known as *natural radioactivity*. Geiger used radioactive materials, such as *radium*, as projectile sources, "firing" alpha particles at a thin metal foil target (gold leaf). He then observed the interaction of the metal and alpha particles with a detection screen (Figure 2.4) and found that:

a. Most alpha particles passed through the foil without being deflected.
b. A small fraction of the particles were deflected, some even *directly back to the source.*

Rutherford interpreted this to mean that most of the atom is empty space, because most alpha particles were not deflected. Further, most of the mass and positive charge must be located in a small, dense region; collision of the heavy and positively charged alpha particle with this small dense and positive region (the nucleus) caused the great deflections. Rutherford summarized his astonishment at observing the deflected particles: "It was almost as incredible as if you fired a 15-inch shell at a piece of tissue and it came back and hit you."

The significance of Rutherford's contribution cannot be overstated. It caused a revolutionary change in the way that scientists pictured the atom (Figure 2.5). His discovery of the nucleus is fundamental to our understanding of chemistry. Chapter 9 will provide much more information about the nucleus and its unique properties.

**ANIMATION**
- The Rutherford Experiment
- Rutherford's Experiment and a New Atomic Model

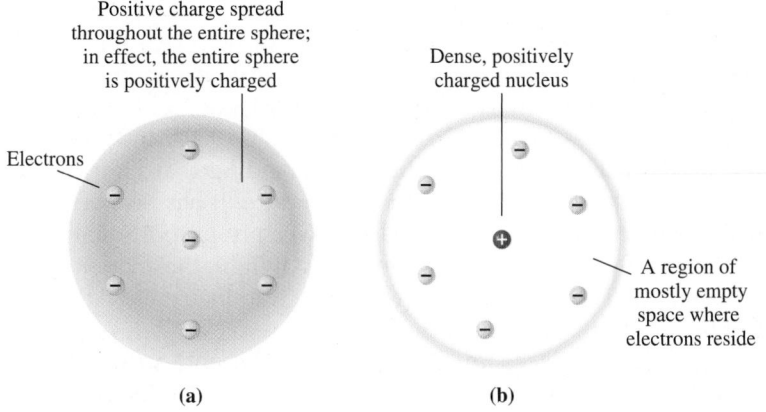

**(a)** Positive charge spread throughout the entire sphere; in effect, the entire sphere is positively charged — Electrons

**(b)** Dense, positively charged nucleus — A region of mostly empty space where electrons reside

**Figure 2.5** (a) A model of the atom (credited to Thomson) prior to the work of Geiger and Rutherford. (b) A model of the atom supported by the alpha-particle scattering experiments of Geiger and Rutherford.

## 2.3   Light, Atomic Structure, and the Bohr Atom

### Light and Atomic Structure

The Rutherford atom leaves us with a picture of a tiny, dense, positively charged nucleus containing protons and surrounded by electrons. The electron arrangement, or configuration, is not clearly detailed. More information is needed regarding the relationship of the electrons to each other and to the nucleus. In dealing with dimensions on the order of $10^{-9}$ meters (m) (the atomic level), conventional methods for measurement of location and distance of separation become impossible. An alternative approach involves the measurement of *energy* rather than the *position* of the atomic particles to determine structure. For example, information obtained from the absorption or emission of *light* by atoms can yield valuable insight into structure. Such studies are referred to as **spectroscopy.**

In a general sense we refer to light as **electromagnetic radiation.** Electromagnetic radiation travels in *waves* from a source. The most recognizable source of this radiation is the sun. We are aware of a rainbow, in which visible white light from the sun is broken up into several characteristic bands of different colors. Similarly, visible white light, when passed through a glass prism, is separated into its various component colors (Figure 2.6). These various colors are simply light of differing *wavelengths*. Light is propagated as a collection of sine waves, and the wavelength is the distance between identical points on successive waves:

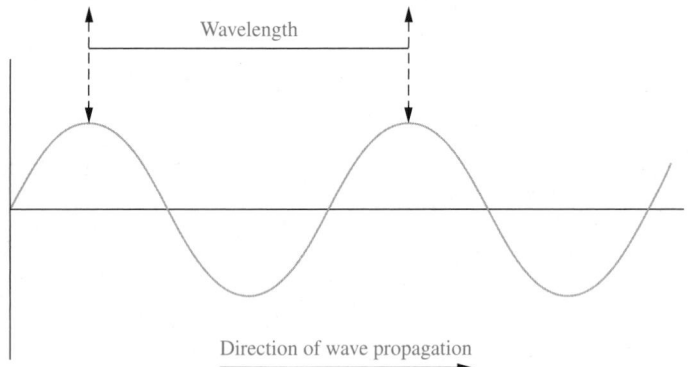

All electromagnetic radiation travels at a speed of $3.0 \times 10^8$ m/s, the **speed of light.** However, each wavelength of light, although traveling with identical velocity, has its own characteristic energy. A collection of all electromagnetic radiation, including each of these wavelengths, is referred to as the *electromagnetic spectrum.* For convenience in discussing this type of radiation, we subdivide electromagnetic radiation into various spectral regions, which are characterized by physical properties of the radiation, such as its *wavelength* or its *energy* (Figure 2.7). Some of these regions are quite familiar to us from our everyday experiences; the visible and microwave regions are two common examples.

Experimental studies by Max Planck in the early 1900s, and interpretation of his results by Albert Einstein, led to the understanding that light is made up of particles called *photons*. Thus, light has a dual nature. It has properties of a wave *and* a particle. The energy of each particle is inversely proportional to the wavelength of the light. By observing the wavelength of light, the energy of the photon can be determined. The understanding of light was instrumental in the understanding of the electron structure of the atom

If hydrogen gas is placed in an evacuated tube and an electric current is passed through the gas, light is emitted. Not all wavelengths (or energies) of

A spectrophotometer, an instrument that utilizes a prism (or similar device) and a light-sensitive detector, is capable of very accurate and precise wavelength measurement.

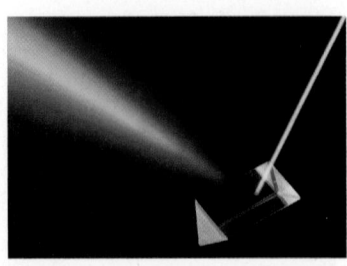

**Figure 2.6** The visible spectrum of light. Light passes through a prism, producing a continuous spectrum. Color results from the way in which our eyes interpret the various wavelengths.

**TABLE 2.2 Summary of the Most Important Elements in Biological Systems**

| Elements Important in Biological Systems | Element Symbols |
| --- | --- |
| Components of major biological molecules | H, C, O, N, P, S |
| Responsible for fluid balance and nerve transmission | K, Na, Cl |
| Necessary for bones and nerve function | Ca, Mg |
| Essential for human metabolism in very small quantities | Zn, Sr, Fe, Cu, Co, Mn |
| "Heavy metals," toxic to living systems | Cd, Hg, Pb |

Group IA (or 1) elements are also known as the **alkali metals;** Group IIA (or 2), the **alkaline earth metals;** Group VIIA (or 17), the **halogens;** and Group VIIIA (or 18), the **noble gases.**

*Representative elements* are also known as *main-group elements*. These terms are synonymous.

## Periods

A **period** is a horizontal row of elements in the periodic table. The periodic table consists of six periods containing two, eight, eight, eighteen, eighteen, and thirty-two elements. The seventh period is still incomplete but potentially holds thirty-two elements. Note that the *lanthanide series*, a collection of fourteen elements that are chemically and physically similar to the element lanthanum, is a part of period six. It is written separately for convenience of presentation and is inserted between lanthanum (La), atomic number 57, and hafnium (Hf), atomic number 72. Similarly, the *actinide series*, consisting of fourteen elements similar to the element actinium, is inserted between actinium, atomic number 89, and rutherfordium, atomic number 104.

**LEARNING GOAL**

**7** Recognize the important subdivisions of the periodic table: periods, groups (families), metals, and nonmetals.

## Metals and Nonmetals

A **metal** is a substance whose atoms tend to lose electrons during chemical change. A **nonmetal,** on the other hand, is a substance whose atoms may gain electrons.

A close inspection of the periodic table reveals a bold zigzag line running from top to bottom, beginning to the left of boron (B) and ending between polonium (Po) and astatine (At). This line acts as the boundary between *metals,* to the left, and *nonmetals,* to the right. Elements straddling the boundary have properties intermediate between those of metals and nonmetals. These elements are referred to as **metalloids.** The metalloids include boron (B), silicon (Si), germanium (Ge), arsenic (As), antimony (Sb), and tellurium (Te).

Note that aluminum (in spite of the fact that it borders the zigzag line) is classified as a metal, not a metalloid.

Metals and nonmetals may be distinguished by differences in their physical properties in addition to their chemical tendency to lose or gain electrons. Metals have a characteristic luster and generally conduct heat and electricity well. Most (except mercury) are solids at room temperature. Nonmetals, on the other hand, are poor conductors, and several are gases at room temperature.

**Question 2.5** Using the periodic table on the inside front cover, write the symbol for each of the following and label as a metal, metalloid, or nonmetal:

a. sodium
b. radium
c. manganese
d. magnesium

**Question 2.6** Using the periodic table on the inside front cover, write the symbol for each of the following and label as a metal, metalloid, a nonmetal.

a. sulfur
b. oxygen
c. phosphorus
d. nitrogen

# A MEDICAL PERSPECTIVE

## Copper Deficiency and Wilson's Disease

An old adage tells us that we should consume all things in moderation. This is very true of many of the trace minerals, such as copper. Too much copper in the diet causes toxicity and too little copper results in a serious deficiency disease.

Copper is extremely important for the proper functioning of the body. It aids in the absorption of iron from the intestine and facilitates iron metabolism. It is critical for the formation of hemoglobin and red blood cells in the bone marrow. Copper is also necessary for the synthesis of collagen, a protein that is a major component of the connective tissue. It is essential to the central nervous system in two important ways. First, copper is needed for the synthesis of norepinephrine and dopamine, two chemicals that are necessary for the transmission of nerve signals. Second, it is required for the formation of the myelin sheath (a layer of insulation) around nerve cells. Release of cholesterol from the liver depends on copper, as does bone development and proper function of the immune and blood clotting systems.

The estimated safe and adequate daily dietary intake (ESADDI) for adults is 1.5–3.0 milligrams (mg). Meats, cocoa, nuts, legumes, and whole grains provide significant amounts of copper.

Although getting enough copper in the diet would appear to be relatively simple, it is estimated that Americans often ingest only marginal levels of copper, and we absorb only 25–40% of that dietary copper. Despite these facts, it appears that copper deficiency is not a serious problem in the United States.

Individuals who are at risk for copper deficiency include people who are recovering from abdominal surgery, which causes decreased absorption of copper from the intestine. Others at risk are premature babies and people who are sustained solely by intravenous feedings that are deficient in copper. In addition, people who ingest high doses of antacids or take excessive supplements of zinc, iron, or vitamin C can develop copper deficiency because of reduced copper absorption. Because copper is involved in so many processes in the body, it is not surprising that the symptoms of copper deficiency are many and diverse. They include anemia; decreased red and white blood cell counts; heart disease; increased levels of serum cholesterol; loss of bone; defects in the nervous system, immune system, and connective tissue; and abnormal hair.

Just as too little copper causes serious problems, so does an excess of copper. At doses greater than about 15 mg, copper causes toxicity that results in vomiting. The effects of extended exposure to excess copper are apparent when we look at Wilson's disease. This is a genetic disorder in which excess copper cannot be removed from the body and accumulates in the cornea of the eye, liver, kidneys, and brain. The symptoms include a greenish ring around the cornea, cirrhosis of the liver, copper in the urine, dementia and paranoia, drooling, and progressive tremors. As a result of the condition, the victim generally dies in early adolescence. Wilson's disease can be treated with medication and diet modification with moderate success, if it is recognized early, before permanent damage has occurred to any tissues.

### For Further Understanding

▶ Why is there an upper limit on the recommended daily amount of copper?

▶ Iron is another essential trace metal in our diet. Go to the Web and find out if upper limits exist for daily iron consumption.

---

## LEARNING GOAL

**8**  Use the periodic table to obtain information about an element.

*See Section 2.1 for an explanation of atomic number and atomic mass.*

## Information Contained in the Periodic Table

Both the atomic number and the average atomic mass of each element are readily available from the periodic table. For example,

```
20      ←——— atomic number
Ca      ←——— symbol
Calcium ←——— name
40.08   ←——— atomic mass
```

More detailed periodic tables may also include such information as the electron arrangement, relative sizes of atoms and ions, and most probable ion charges.

**Question 2.7**   Refer to the periodic table (Figure 2.10) and find the following information:

a. the symbol of the element with an atomic number of 40
b. the atomic mass of the element sodium (Na)
c. the element whose atoms contain 24 protons
d. the known element that should most resemble the as-yet undiscovered element with an atomic number of 117

**Question 2.8**    Refer to the periodic table (Figure 2.10) and find the following information:
    a. the symbol of the noble gas in period 3
    b. the element in Group IVA with the smallest mass
    c. the only metalloid in Group IIIA
    d. the element whose atoms contain 18 protons

**Question 2.9**    For each of the following element symbols, give the name of the element, its atomic number, and its atomic mass.
    a. He            b. F            c. Mn

**Question 2.10**    For each of the following element symbols, give the name of the element, its atomic number, and its atomic mass:
    a. Mg           b. Ne          c. Se

# 2.5  Electron Arrangement and the Periodic Table

A primary objective of studying chemistry is to understand the way in which atoms join together to form chemical compounds. This *bonding process* is a direct consequence of the arrangement of the electrons in the atoms that combine. The **electron configuration** describes the arrangement of electrons in atoms. The organization of the periodic table, originally developed from careful measurement of properties of the elements, also correlates well with similarities in electron configuration. This reveals a very important fact: the properties of collections of atoms are a direct consequence of their electron arrangement.

**LEARNING GOAL**

**9** Describe the relationship between the electronic structure of an element and its position in the periodic table.

## The Quantum Mechanical Atom

As we noted in Section 2.3, the success of Bohr's theory was short-lived. Emission spectra of multi-electron atoms (recall that the hydrogen atom has only one electron) could not be explained by Bohr's theory. Evidence that electrons have wave properties was problematic. Bohr stated that electrons in atoms had very specific locations, now termed *principal energy levels*. The very nature of waves, spread out in space, defies such an exact model of electrons in atoms. Furthermore, the exact model is contradictory to theory and subsequent experiments.

The basic concept of the Bohr theory, that the energy of an electron in an atom is quantized, was refined and expanded by an Austrian physicist, Erwin Schröedinger. He described electrons in atoms in probability terms, developing equations that emphasize the wavelike character of electrons. Although Schröedinger's approach was founded on complex mathematics, we can readily use models of electron probability regions to enable us to gain an insight into atomic structure without the need to understand the underlying mathematics.

Schröedinger's theory, often described as quantum mechanics, incorporates Bohr's principal energy levels ($n = 1, 2$, and so forth); however, it proposes that each of these levels is made up of one or more sublevels. Each sublevel, in turn, contains one or more atomic orbitals. In the following section, we shall look at each of these regions in more detail and learn how to predict the way that electrons are arranged in stable atoms.

## Principal Energy Levels, Sublevels, and Orbitals

### Principal Energy Levels

Bohr concluded that electrons in atoms do not roam freely in space; rather they are confined to certain specific regions of space outside of the nucleus of an atom. **Principal energy levels** (analogous to Bohr's orbits) are regions where electrons may be found, and have integral values designated $n = 1, n = 2, n = 3$, and so forth. The principal energy level is related to the average distance from the nucleus. An $n = 1$ level is closest to the nucleus; the larger the value of $n$, the greater the average distance of an electron in that level from the nucleus.

The maximum number of electrons that a principal energy level can hold is equal to $2(n)^2$. For example:

| | | |
|---|---|---|
| $n = 1$ | $2(1)^2$ | Capacity $= 2e^-$ |
| $n = 2$ | $2(2)^2$ | Capacity $= 8e^-$ |
| $n = 3$ | $2(3)^2$ | Capacity $= 18e^-$ |

### Sublevels

A **sublevel** is a set of equal-energy orbitals within a principal energy level. The sublevels, or subshells, are symbolized as $s$, $p$, $d$, and so forth; they increase in energy in the following order:

$$s < p < d$$

We specify both the principal energy level and type of sublevel when describing the location of an electron—for example, $1s$, $2s$, $2p$. Energy level designations for the first three principal energy levels are as follows:

- The first principal energy level ($n = 1$) has one possible sublevel: $1s$.
- The second principal energy level ($n = 2$) has two possible sublevels: $2s$ and $2p$.
- The third principal energy level ($n = 3$) has three possible sublevels: $3s$, $3p$, and $3d$.

### Orbitals

An **atomic orbital** is a specific region of a sublevel containing a maximum of two electrons.

Figure 2.11 depicts a model of an $s$ orbital. It is spherically symmetrical, much like a Ping-Pong ball. Its volume represents a region where there is a high probability of finding electrons of similar energy. This probability decreases as we approach the outer region of the atom. The nucleus is at the center of the $s$ orbital. At that point the probability of finding the electron is zero; electrons cannot reside in the nucleus. Only one $s$ orbital can be found in any $n$ level. Atoms with many electrons, occupying a number of $n$ levels, have an $s$ orbital in each $n$ level. Consequently $1s$, $2s$, $3s$, and so forth are possible orbitals.

Figure 2.12 illustrates the shapes of the three possible $p$ orbitals within a given level. Each has the same shape, and that shape appears much like a dumbbell; these three orbitals differ only in the direction they extend into space. Imaginary coordinates $x$, $y$, and $z$ are superimposed on these models to emphasize this fact. These three orbitals, termed $p_x$, $p_y$, and $p_z$, may coexist in a single atom.

Figure 2.13 depicts the shapes of the five possible $d$ orbitals within a given $n$ level. These $d$ orbitals are important in determining the properties of the transition metals.

Higher energy orbitals ($f$, $g$, and so forth) also exist, but they are important only in the description of the electron arrangements of the heaviest elements.

It is important to remember that *shape* of the orbital represents regions in the atom (but outside of the nucleus) where electrons *may* be found. Not all orbitals are occupied by electrons; the shaded regions really represent the probability of finding the electrons in specific regions of the atom.

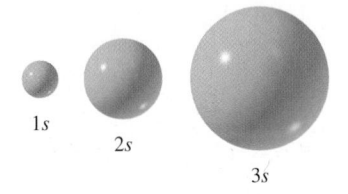

**Figure 2.11** Representation of $s$ orbitals.

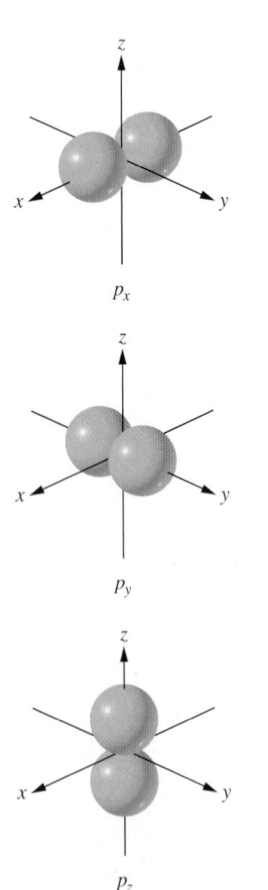

$p_x$

$p_y$

$p_z$

**Figure 2.12** Representation of the three $p$ orbitals, $p_x$, $p_y$, and $p_z$.

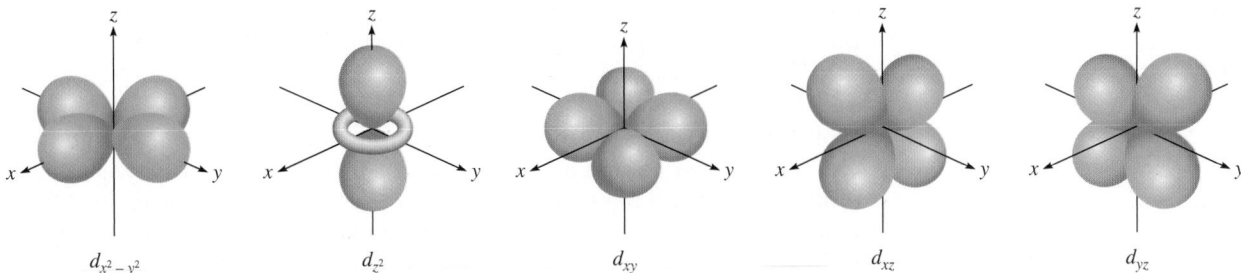

$d_{x^2-y^2}$       $d_{z^2}$       $d_{xy}$       $d_{xz}$       $d_{yz}$

**Figure 2.13** Representation of the five d orbitals.

## Electrons in Sublevels

We can deduce the maximum electron capacity of each sublevel based on the information just given.

For the s sublevel:

$$1 \text{ orbital} \times \frac{2e^- \text{ capacity}}{\text{orbital}} = 2e^- \text{ capacity}$$

For the p sublevel:

$$3 \text{ orbitals} \times \frac{2e^- \text{ capacity}}{\text{orbital}} = 6e^- \text{ capacity}$$

For the d sublevel:

$$5 \text{ orbitals} \times \frac{2e^- \text{ capacity}}{\text{orbital}} = 10e^- \text{ capacity}$$

## Electron Spin

As we have noted, each atomic orbital has a maximum capacity of two electrons. The electrons are perceived to *spin* on an imaginary axis, and the two electrons in the same orbital must have opposite spins: clockwise and counterclockwise. Their behavior is analogous to two ends of a magnet. Remember, electrons have magnetic properties. The electrons exhibit sufficient magnetic attraction to hold themselves together despite the natural repulsion that they "feel" for each other, owing to their similar charge (remember, like charges repel). Electrons must have opposite spins to coexist in an orbital. Two electrons in one orbital that possess opposite spins are referred to as *paired* electrons. The number and arrangement of unpaired electrons in an atom are responsible for the magnetic properties of elements (Figure 2.14.)

## Electron Configurations

We can write the electron arrangement (electron configuration) for an atom of any element if we know a few simple facts. We need to know the number of electrons in the atom, which is readily available from the periodic table. (Remember, the number of electrons in a neutral atom is equal to the atomic number.) We know that each principal energy level has a maximum capacity of $2(n)^2$ electrons. No more than two electrons can be placed in any orbital, and each principal energy level, $n$, can contain only $n$ subshells. Additionally, the aufbau principle, the Pauli exclusion principle, and Hund's rule will complete our strategy.

## Aufbau Principle

The *aufbau*, or building up, *principle* helps us to represent the electron configuration of atoms of various elements. According to this principle, electrons fill the lowest energy orbital that is available. Figure 2.15 is a useful way of depicting the

**Figure 2.14** A compass is a familiar direction-finder that aligns the magnetic field of the compass needle with the earth's natural magnetic field. Unpaired electrons in iron atoms (in the needle and in the earth) are responsible for the magnetic fields.

*Section 2.2 discusses the properties of electrons demonstrated by Thomson.*

LEARNING GOAL

**10** Write electron configurations for atoms of the most commonly occurring elements.

**ANIMATION**
• Electron Configurations

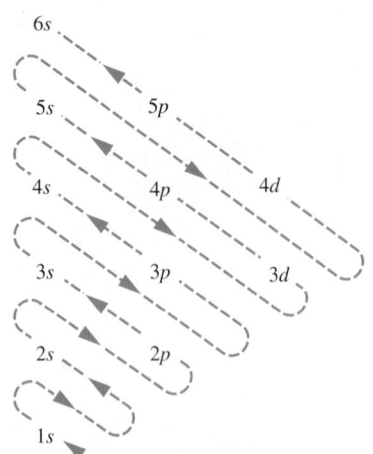

**Figure 2.15** A useful way to remember the filling order for electrons in atoms. Begin adding electrons at the bottom (lowest energy) and follow the arrows. Remember: no more than two electrons in each orbital.

We can also use the periodic table to determine the order in which orbitals are filled. See Figure 2.16.

theoretical order in which orbitals fill with electrons. It is easily memorized and will prove to be a useful guide to constructing electron configurations for the elements.

### Pauli Exclusion Principle

Wolfgang Pauli was a renowned quantum physicist who is credited with providing the most complete explanation of the relationship between electrons in orbitals. Although the theory behind the *Pauli exclusion principle* is rooted in the mathematics of quantum theory, the practical application is straightforward: Each orbital can hold up to two electrons with the electrons spinning in opposite directions (paired).

### Hund's Rule

All electrons in atoms are typically in their lowest energy state, termed the *ground state*, at room temperature. *Hund's rule* is a consequence of this: When there is a set of orbitals of equal energy (for example, three *p* orbitals in the $n = 2$ level) each orbital becomes half-filled (one electron per orbital) before any become completely filled (two electrons).

## Guidelines for Writing Electron Configurations of Atoms

- Obtain the total number of electrons in the atom from the atomic number found on the periodic table. The number of electrons equals the number of protons for an atom.
- Electrons in atoms occupy the lowest energy orbitals that are available, beginning with 1s.
- Fill subshells according to the order depicted in Figure 2.15.
- Remember:
  - The s sublevel has one orbital and can hold two electrons.
  - The p sublevel has three orbitals. The electrons will half-fill before completely filling the orbitals for a maximum of six electrons.
  - The d sublevel has five orbitals. Again, the electrons will half-fill before completely filling the orbitals for a maximum of ten electrons.

Now let us look at several examples:

### Hydrogen

Hydrogen is the simplest atom; it has only one electron. That electron must be in the lowest principal energy level ($n = 1$) and the lowest orbital (s). We indicate the number of electrons in a region with a *superscript*, so we write $1s^1$. The electron configuration for hydrogen is $1s^1$.

An alternate way of depicting electron arrangement in atoms is the *orbital diagram*. Each orbital is represented as a box, and each electron as an arrow, indicating the relative direction of its spin. The orbital diagram for hydrogen is:

1s

### Helium

Helium has two electrons, which will fill the lowest energy level. The ground state (lowest energy) electron configuration for helium is $1s^2$, and the corresponding orbital diagram is:

1s

The arrows show paired (opposite) spins, in accordance with the Pauli exclusion principle.

## Lithium

Lithium has three electrons. The first two are configured the same as helium. The third must go into the orbital of the lowest energy in the second principal energy level; therefore the configuration is $1s^2 2s^1$.
The orbital diagram is:

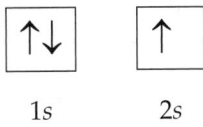

## Beryllium

Beryllium has four electrons. The first three are configured the same as lithium. The fourth electron fills the 2s orbital; therefore the configuration is $1s^2 2s^2$, and the orbital diagram is:

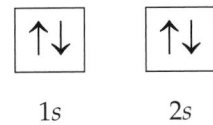

## Boron

Boron has five electrons. The first four are configured the same as beryllium. The fifth electron must go into the 2p level; therefore the configuration is $1s^2 2s^2 2p^1$.
The orbital diagram is:

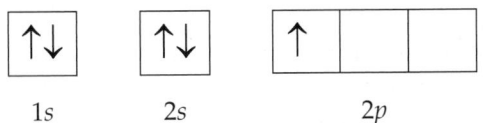

## Carbon

Carbon has six electrons. The first five are configured the same as boron. The sixth electron, according to Hund's rule, enters a second 2p orbital, with the same spin as the fifth electron. The electron configuration for carbon is $1s^2 2s^2 2p^2$, and the orbital diagram is:

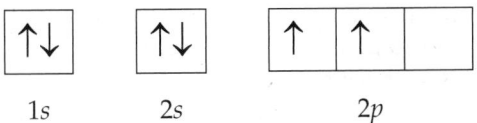

Note that Hund's rule requires the two p electrons to occupy different 2p orbitals.

## Nitrogen

Nitrogen, following the same logic, is $1s^2, 2s^2, 2p^3$, and the orbital diagram is:

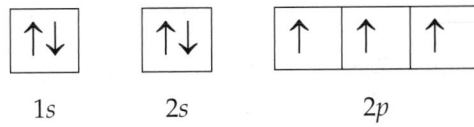

## Oxygen, Fluorine, and Neon

Each of these elements adds one more electron, pairing one of the three unpaired electrons, resulting in:

for oxygen, $1s^2\, 2s^2\, 2p^4$ and

| $\uparrow\downarrow$ | | $\uparrow\downarrow$ | | $\uparrow\downarrow$ | $\uparrow$ | $\uparrow$ |
|---|---|---|---|---|---|---|
| $1s$ | | $2s$ | | | $2p$ | |

for fluorine, $1s^2\, 2s^2\, 2p^5$ and

| $\uparrow\downarrow$ | | $\uparrow\downarrow$ | | $\uparrow\downarrow$ | $\uparrow\downarrow$ | $\uparrow$ |
|---|---|---|---|---|---|---|
| $1s$ | | $2s$ | | | $2p$ | |

for neon, $1s^2\, 2s^2\, 2p^6$ and

| $\uparrow\downarrow$ | | $\uparrow\downarrow$ | | $\uparrow\downarrow$ | $\uparrow\downarrow$ | $\uparrow\downarrow$ |
|---|---|---|---|---|---|---|
| $1s$ | | $2s$ | | | $2p$ | |

### Sodium Through Argon

Electrons in these elements retain the basic $1s^2\, 2s^2\, 2p^6$ arrangement of the preceding element, neon; new electrons enter the third principal energy level:

| | |
|---|---|
| Na | $1s^2\, 2s^2\, 2p^6\, 3s^1$ |
| Mg | $1s^2\, 2s^2\, 2p^6\, 3s^2$ |
| Al | $1s^2\, 2s^2\, 2p^6\, 3s^2\, 3p^1$ |
| Si | $1s^2\, 2s^2\, 2p^6\, 3s^2\, 3p^2$ |
| P | $1s^2\, 2s^2\, 2p^6\, 3s^2\, 3p^3$ |
| S | $1s^2\, 2s^2\, 2p^6\, 3s^2\, 3p^4$ |
| Cl | $1s^2\, 2s^2\, 2p^6\, 3s^2\, 3p^5$ |
| Ar | $1s^2\, 2s^2\, 2p^6\, 3s^2\, 3p^6$ |

Three $3p$ orbitals can hold a maximum of six $e^-$. Argon has a complete $n = 3$ level; that explains its unusual stability.

We have seen that elements in the periodic table are classified as either representative or transition. Representative elements consist of all Group IA–VIIIA elements (1, 2 and 13–18). All others are transition elements. The guidelines that we have developed for writing electron configurations work well for representative elements. Electron configurations for transition elements include several exceptions to the rules, due to more complex interactions among electrons that occur in atoms with large numbers of electrons.

Let us now look at the electron configuration for tin, a representative element with a large number of electrons, hence, a more complex electronic structure.

---

**EXAMPLE 2.4**    **Writing the Electron Configuration of Tin**

LEARNING GOAL

**10** Write electron configurations and orbital diagrams for atoms of the most commonly occurring elements.

Write the electron configuration for tin.

**Solution**

**Step 1.** Tin (Sn) has an atomic number of 50; thus we must place fifty electrons in atomic orbitals.

**Step 2.** Recall the total electron capacities of orbital types: s, two; p, six; and d, ten. The first principal energy level has one sublevel, the second has two sublevels, and so on. The order of filling (Figure 2.15) is $1s$, $2s$, $2p$, $3s$, $3p$, $4s$, $3d$, $4p$.

**Step 3.** The electron configuration is as follows:

$$1s^2\, 2s^2\, 2p^6\, 3s^2\, 3p^6\, 4s^2\, 3d^{10}\, 4p^6\, 5s^2\, 4d^{10}\, 5p^2$$

*Helpful Hint:*
As a check, count electrons in the electron configuration (add all of the superscript numbers) to ensure that we have accounted for all fifty electrons of the Sn atom.

## Practice Problem 2.4

Write the electron configuration for an atom of:

    a. sulfur    b. calcium    c. potassium    d. phosphorus

▶ For Further Practice: **Questions 2.85 and 2.86.**

---

**EXAMPLE 2.5**    **Writing the Electron Configuration and Orbital Diagram for Silicon**

LEARNING GOAL

**10** Write electron configurations and orbital diagrams for atoms of the most commonly occurring elements.

Write the electron configuration and orbital diagram for silicon.

### Solution

**Step 1.** Silicon (Si) has an atomic number of 14; thus we must place fourteen electrons in atomic orbitals.

**Step 2.** Recall the total electron capacities of orbital types (s, two electrons and p, six electrons) and that the first principal energy level has one sublevel, the second two, and so on. The order of filling is $1s, 2s, 2p, 3s, 3p$.

**Step 3.** The electron configuration is as follows:

$$1s^2\ 2s^2\ 2p^6\ 3s^2\ 3p^2$$

**Step 4.** Be sure to count the superscript numbers in the electron configuration to ensure that all fourteen electrons are accounted for.

**Step 5.** Writing the orbital box diagram follows from the electron configuration. Remember that Hund's rule tells us to enter $p$ electrons unpaired until each orbital contains one electron.

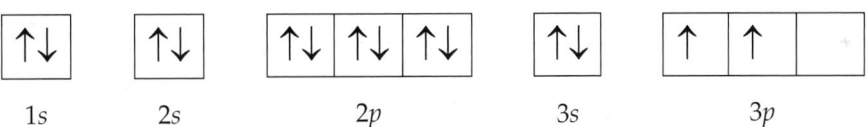

      1s      2s          2p         3s         3p

## Practice Problem 2.5

Write the orbital diagram for each element in Practice Problem 2.4.

▶ For Further Practice: **Questions 2.87 and 2.88.**

---

## Electron Configurations and the Periodic Table

Mendeleev's periodic table was based on extensive observation of physical and chemical properties. Its unusual shape is nicely explained by electron configurations resulting from atomic orbital theory. Elements in the same group (column) have the same outer shell electron configuration. Group IA(1) is $ns^1$, Group IIA(2) is $ns^2$, and so forth. The prefix $n$ corresponds to the period (row) containing the element whose principal energy level (also $n$) is filling. The link between electron configuration and physical properties is, in fact, the periodic table and its unusual shape!

    This relationship is shown in Figure 2.16.

## Shorthand Electron Configurations

Using the periodic table and the layout of sublevels depicted in Figure 2.16, a shorthand version of the electron configuration can be obtained. To use the shorthand

**Figure 2.16** The shape of the periodic table shows four distinct regions, corresponding to the type of subshell that is filling with electrons. Starting with 1s at the top left of the periodic table and proceeding from left to right and down, the same order of sublevels energy can be obtained as is given in Figure 2.15. Take time to examine both figures to see the connection. The application of this figure in writing the shorthand notation for tin is detailed in Example 2.6

method, write the symbol of the nearest noble gas (with atomic number less than the element for which you are determining the shorthand electron configuration) in square brackets. Then finish the electron configuration by writing all additional sublevels that contain electrons.

For example, the full electron configuration of a sodium atom is:

$$1s^2 2s^2 2p^6 3s^1$$

The noble gas that comes before sodium is neon. Putting [Ne] in the configuration accounts for the first ten electrons. The shorthand electron configuration is given as:

$$[Ne]3s^1$$

---

**EXAMPLE 2.6**     **Writing Shorthand Electron Configurations**

Use the periodic table to write the shorthand electron configuration of tin.

**Solution**

**Step 1.** Locate tin (Sn) on the periodic table.

**Step 2.** Find the nearest noble gas that comes before Sn. Write the symbol krypton (element 36) in square brackets:

$$[Kr]$$

**Step 3.** Move to the left side of the periodic table (element 37) and put electrons in the next available sublevels, counting element blocks to determine the number of electrons in the sublevel. Finish at element Sn (Figure 2.16). This gives:

$$[Kr]\ 5s^2 4d^{10} 5p^2$$

**Practice Problem 2.6**

Write the shorthand electron configuration for:

   a. sulfur     b. silicon     c. selenium     d. iron

▶ For Further Practice: **Questions 2.93 and 2.94.**

The advantage to this method is that the electron configurations of atoms with a large number of electrons can be written quickly by examining the periodic table. Example 2.6 demonstrates this method.

## 2.6  Valence Electrons and the Octet Rule

### Valence Electrons

If we picture two spherical objects that we wish to join together, perhaps with glue, the glue can be applied to the surfaces and the two objects can then be brought into contact. We can extend this analogy to two atoms that are modeled as spherical objects. Although this is not a perfect analogy, it is apparent that the surface interaction is of primary importance. Although the positively charged nucleus and "interior" electrons certainly play a role in bonding, we can most easily understand the process by considering only the outermost electrons. We refer to these as *valence electrons*. **Valence electrons** are the outermost electrons in an atom, which are involved, or have the potential to become involved, in the bonding process.

For representative elements the number of valence electrons in an atom corresponds to the number of the *group* (associated with the letter *A*) in which the atom is found. For example, elements such as hydrogen and sodium (in fact, all alkali metals, Group IA or 1) have one valence electron. From left to right in period 2, beryllium, Be (Group IIA or 2), has two valence electrons; boron, B (Group IIIA or 13), has three; carbon, C (Group IVA or 14), has four; and so forth.

> Metals tend to have fewer valence electrons, and nonmetals tend to have more valence electrons.

---

### EXAMPLE 2.7    Determining Electron Arrangement

**LEARNING GOAL**

**10**  Write electron configurations and orbital diagrams for atoms of the most commonly occurring elements.

Provide the total number of electrons, total number of valence electrons, and energy level in which the valence electrons are found for the silicon (Si) atom.

**Solution**

**Step 1.** Determine the position of silicon in the periodic table. Silicon has an atomic number of 14. Silicon is found in Group IVA and period 3 of the table.

**Step 2.** The atomic number provides the number of electrons in an atom. Silicon therefore has fourteen electrons.

**Step 3.** Because silicon is in Group IVA, only four of the fourteen electrons are valence electrons.

**Step 4.** The third period corresponds to the $n = 3$ energy level.

---

**Practice Problem 2.7**

For each of the following elements, provide the *total* number of electrons and *valence* electrons in its atoms as well as the number of the energy level in which the valence electrons are found:

    a. Na      b. Mg     c. S     d. Cl     e. Ar

▶ For Further Practice: **Questions 2.101 and 2.102.**

## The Octet Rule

Elements in the last family, the noble gases, have eight valence electrons, except for helium, which has two. These elements are extremely stable and were often termed *inert gases* because they do not readily bond to other elements, although some of the larger ones (lower on the periodic table) can be made to do so under extreme experimental conditions. A full $n = 1$ energy level (as in helium) or an outer *octet* of electrons (eight valence electrons, two in the $s$ and six in the $p$ sublevel) is responsible for this unique stability.

Atoms of elements in other groups are more reactive than the noble gases because in the process of chemical reaction they try to achieve a more stable "noble gas" configuration by gaining or losing electrons. This is the basis of the **octet rule,** which states that elements usually react in such a way as to attain the electron configuration of the noble gas closest to them in the periodic table (a stable octet of electrons). In chemical reactions they will gain, lose, or share the minimum number of electrons necessary to attain this more stable energy state. The octet rule, although simple in concept, is a remarkably reliable predictor of chemical change, especially for representative elements.

The shorthand electron configuration highlights the valence electrons by placing them after the noble gas core.

## Ions

**Ions** are electrically charged particles that result from a gain of one or more electrons by the parent atom (forming negative ions, or **anions**) or a loss of one or more electrons from the parent atom (forming positive ions, or **cations**).

Formation of an anion may occur as follows:

$$F + 1e^- \longrightarrow F^-$$

The neutral atom     The fluorine anion
gains an electron    is formed

Alternatively, formation of a cation of sodium may proceed as follows:

$$Na \longrightarrow 1e^- + Na^+$$

The neutral atom   The sodium cation
loses an electron   is formed

Note that the electrons gained are written to the left of the reaction arrow (they are reactants), whereas the electrons lost are written as products to the right of the reaction arrow.

**Question 2.11**   Determine the number of protons and electrons in each of the following ions:
  a. $O^{2-}$                 b. $Mg^{2+}$                 c. $Fe^{3+}$

**Question 2.12**   Determine the number of protons and electrons in each of the following ions:
  a. $Ni^{2+}$                 b. $Br^-$                 c. $N^{3-}$

## Ion Formation and the Octet Rule

Metals and nonmetals differ in the way in which they form ions. Metallic elements (located at the left of the periodic table) tend to form positively charged *cations*, by the loss of electrons to obtain a noble gas configuration.

$$\text{Na} \longrightarrow \text{Na}^+ \quad + \text{e}^-$$

Sodium atom     Sodium ion
$[Ne]3s^1$     $[Ne]$

$$\text{Mg} \longrightarrow \text{Mg}^{2+} \quad + 2\text{e}^-$$

Magnesium atom     Magnesium ion
$[Ne]3s^2$     $[Ne]$

$$\text{Al} \longrightarrow \text{Al}^{3+} \quad + 3\text{e}^-$$

Aluminum atom     Aluminum ion
$[Ne]3s^2\,3p^1$     $[Ne]$

These ions are particularly stable. Each ion is **isoelectronic** (that is, it has the same electron configuration) with its nearest noble gas neighbor and has an octet of electrons in its outermost energy level.

The prefix *iso* (Greek *isos*) means equal.

Sodium is typical of each element in its group. Knowing that sodium forms a 1+ ion leads to the prediction that H, Li, K, Rb, Cs, and Fr also will form 1+ ions. Furthermore, magnesium, which forms a 2+ ion, is typical of each element in its group; $Be^{2+}$, $Ca^{2+}$, $Sr^{2+}$, and so forth are the resulting ions.

Nonmetallic elements, located at the right of the periodic table, tend to gain electrons to become isoelectronic with the nearest noble gas element, forming negative *anions*.

*Section 3.2 discusses the naming of ions.*

Consider:

$$\text{F} \quad + 1\text{e}^- \longrightarrow \text{F}^-$$

Fluorine atom     Fluoride ion
$[He]2s^2\,2p^5$     $[He]2s^2\,2p^6$ or $[Ne]$

$$\text{O} \quad + 2\text{e}^- \longrightarrow \text{O}^{2-}$$

Oxygen atom     Oxide ion
$[He]2s^2\,2p^4$     $[He]2s^2\,2p^6$ or $[Ne]$

$$\text{N} \quad + 3\text{e}^- \longrightarrow \text{N}^{3-}$$

Nitrogen atom     Nitride ion
$[He]2s^2\,2p^3$     $[He]2s^2\,2p^6$ or $[Ne]$

As in the case of positive ion formation, each of these negative ions has an octet of electrons in its outermost energy level.

The element fluorine, forming $F^-$, indicates that the other halogens, Cl, Br, and I, behave as a true family and form $Cl^-$, $Br^-$, and $I^-$ ions. Also, oxygen and the other nonmetals in its group form $2^-$ ions; nitrogen and phosphorus form $3^-$ ions. It is important to recognize that ions are formed by gain or loss of *electrons*. No change occurs in the nucleus; the number of protons remains the same.

**Question 2.13**   Give the charge of the most probable ion resulting from each of the following elements. With what element is the ion isoelectronic?

a. Ca      c. S      e. P
b. Sr      d. Mg

**Question 2.14**   Which of the following pairs of atoms and ions are iso-electronic?

a. $Cl^-$, Ar      c. $Mg^{2+}$, $Na^+$      e. $O^{2-}$, $F^-$
b. $Na^+$, Ne      d. $Li^+$, Ne

The transition metals tend to form positive ions by losing electrons, just like the representative metals. Metals, whether representative or transition, share this characteristic. However, the transition elements are characterized as "variable valence"

# A MEDICAL PERSPECTIVE

## Dietary Calcium

"Drink your milk!" "Eat all of your vegetables!" These imperatives are almost universal memories from our childhood. Our parents knew that calcium, present in abundance in these foods, is an essential element for the development of strong bones and healthy teeth.

Recent studies, spanning the fields of biology, chemistry, and nutrition science, indicate that the benefits of calcium go far beyond bones and teeth. This element has been found to play a role in the prevention of disease throughout our bodies.

Calcium is the most abundant mineral (metal) in the body. It is ingested as the calcium ion ($Ca^{2+}$) either in its "free" state or "combined," as a part of a larger compound; calcium dietary supplements often contain ions in the form of calcium carbonate. The acid naturally present in the stomach produces the calcium ion:

$$CaCO_3 + 2H^+ \longrightarrow Ca^{2+} + H_2O + CO_2$$

| calcium carbonate | stomach acid | calcium ion | water | carbon dioxide |
|---|---|---|---|---|

Calcium is responsible for a variety of body functions including:

- transmission of nerve impulses
- release of "messenger compounds" that enable communication among nerves
- blood clotting
- hormone secretion
- growth of living cells throughout the body

The body's storehouse of calcium is bone tissue. When the supply of calcium from external sources, the diet, is insufficient, the body uses a mechanism to compensate for this shortage. With vitamin D in a critical role, this mechanism removes calcium from bone to enable other functions to continue to take place. It is evident then that prolonged dietary calcium deficiency can weaken the bone structure. Unfortunately, current studies show that as much as 75% of the American population may not be consuming sufficient amounts of calcium. Developing an understanding of the role of calcium in premenstrual syndrome, cancer, and blood pressure regulation is the goal of three current research areas.

*Calcium and premenstrual syndrome (PMS).* Dr. Susan Thys-Jacobs, a gynecologist at St. Luke's-Roosevelt Hospital Center in New York City, and colleagues at eleven other medical centers are conducting a study of calcium's ability to relieve the discomfort of PMS. They believe that women with chronic PMS have calcium blood levels that are normal only because calcium is continually being removed from the bone to maintain an adequate supply in the blood. To complicate the situation, vitamin D levels in many young women are very low (as much as 80% of a person's vitamin D is made in the skin, upon exposure to sunlight; many of us now minimize our exposure to the sun because of concerns about ultraviolet radiation and skin cancer). Because vitamin D plays an essential role in calcium metabolism, even if sufficient calcium is consumed, it may not be used efficiently in the body.

*Colon cancer.* The colon is lined with a type of cell (epithelial cell) that is similar to those that form the outer layers of skin. Various studies have indicated that by-products of a high-fat diet are irritants to these epithelial cells and produce abnormal cell growth in the colon. Dr. Martin Lipkin, of Rockefeller University in New York, and his colleagues have shown that calcium ions may bind with these irritants, reducing their undesirable effects. It is believed that a calcium-rich diet, low in fat, and perhaps use of a calcium supplement can prevent or reverse this abnormal colon cell growth, delaying or preventing the onset of colon cancer.

*Blood pressure regulation.* Dr. David McCarron, a blood pressure specialist at the Oregon Health Sciences University, believes that dietary calcium levels may have a significant influence on hypertension (high blood pressure). Preliminary studies show that a diet rich in low-fat dairy products, fruits, and vegetables, all high in calcium, may produce a significant lowering of blood pressure in adults with mild hypertension.

The take-home lesson appears clear: a high-calcium, low-fat diet promotes good health in many ways. Once again, our parents were right!

### For Further Understanding

▶ Distinguish between "free" and "combined" calcium in the diet.

▶ Why might calcium supplements be ineffective in treating all cases of calcium deficiency?

elements; depending on the type of substance with which they react, they may form more than one stable ion. For example, iron has two stable ionic forms:

$$Fe^{2+} \text{ and } Fe^{3+}$$

Copper can exist as

$$Cu^+ \text{ and } Cu^{2+}$$

and elements such as vanadium (V) and manganese (Mn) each can form four different stable ions.

Predicting the charge of an ion or the various possible ions for a given transition metal is not an easy task. Energy differences between valence electrons of transition metals are small and not easily predicted from the position of the element in the periodic table. In fact, in contrast to representative metals, the transition metals show great similarities within a *period* as well as within a *group*.

## 2.7 Trends in the Periodic Table

### Atomic Size

Many atomic properties correlate with electronic structure, hence, with their position in the periodic table. Given that interactions among multiple charged particles are very complex, we would not expect the correlation to be perfect. Nonetheless, the periodic table remains an excellent guide to the prediction of properties.

If our model of the atom is a tiny sphere whose radius is determined by the distance between the center of the nucleus and the boundary of the region where the valence electrons have a probability of being located, the size of the atom will be determined principally by two factors.

1. The energy level (*n* level) in which the outermost electrons are found increases as we go *down* a group. (Recall that the outermost *n* level correlates with period number.) Thus the size of atoms should increase from top to bottom of the periodic table as we fill successive energy levels of the atoms with electrons (Figure 2.17).
2. Across a period, as the magnitude of the positive charge of the nucleus increases, its "pull" on the atom's valence electrons increases. This results in a contraction of the atomic radius from left to right across a period. Hence, atomic size decreases from left to right on the periodic table. Examine Figure 2.17 and notice that there are exceptions.

### Ion Size

Positive ions (cations) are smaller than the parent atom. The cation has more protons than electrons. The decrease in the number of electrons pulls the remaining electrons closer to the nucleus. Also, cation formation often results in the loss of all outer-shell electrons, resulting in a significant decrease in radius.

**LEARNING GOAL**

**12** Utilize the periodic table and its predictive power to estimate the relative sizes of atoms and ions, as well as relative magnitudes of ionization energy and electron affinity.

**ANIMATION**
• Atomic Radius

*The radius of an atom is traditionally defined as one-half of the distance between the nuclei of adjacent bonded atoms.*

**ANIMATION**
• Atomic and Ionic Radii

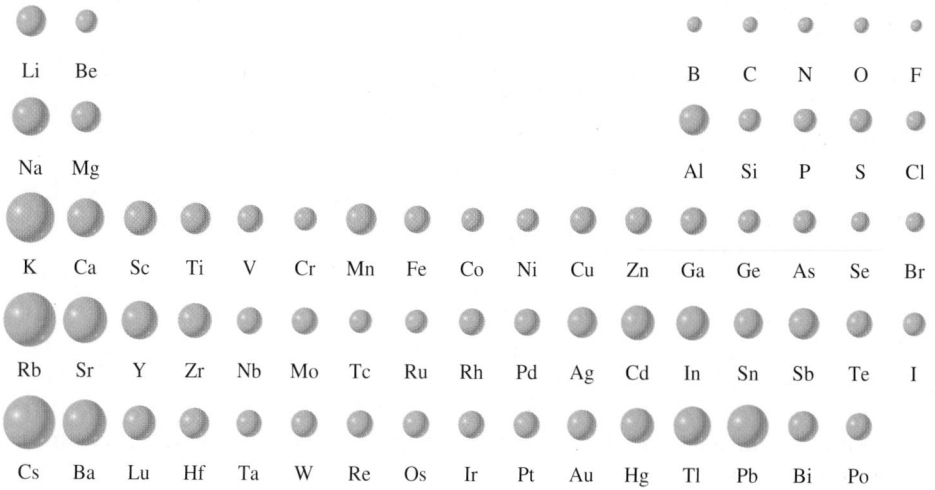

**Figure 2.17** Variation in the size of atoms as a function of their position in the periodic table. Note particularly the decrease in size from left to right in the periodic table and the increase in size as we proceed down the table, although some exceptions do exist. (Lanthanide and actinide elements are not included here.)

**Figure 2.18** Relative size of ions and their parent atoms. Atomic radii are provided in units of picometers (pm).

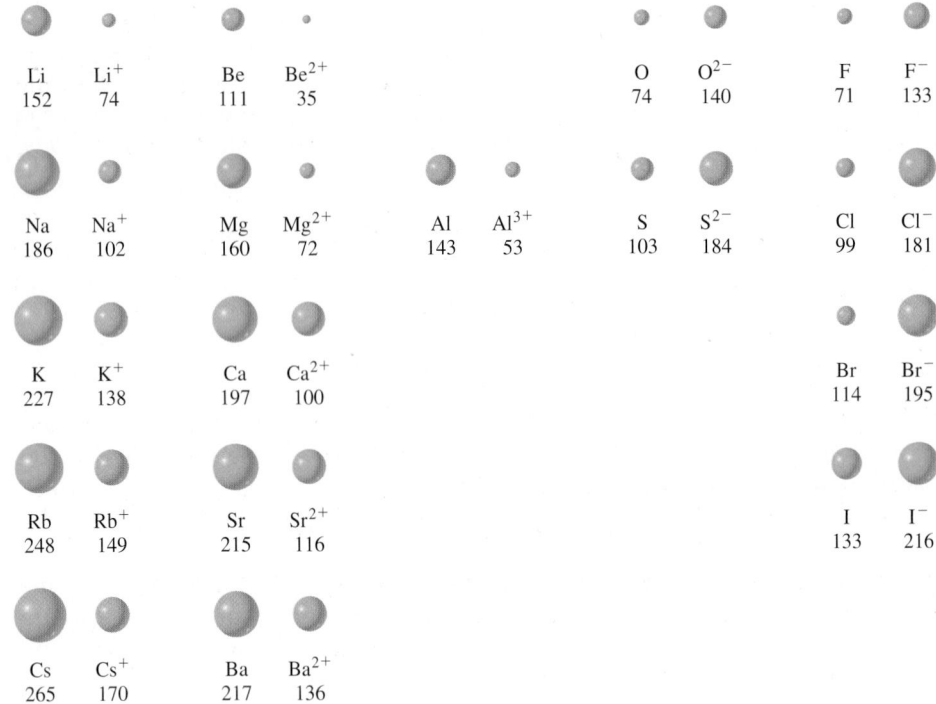

Negative ions (anions) are larger than the parent atom. The anion has more electrons than protons. Owing to the excess negative charge, the nuclear "pull" on each individual electron is reduced. The electrons are held less tightly, resulting in a larger anion radius in contrast to the neutral atom.

Ions with multiple positive charge are even *smaller* than their corresponding monopositive ion. Thus, $Cu^{2+}$ is smaller than $Cu^+$.

Figure 2.18 depicts the relative sizes of several atoms and their corresponding ions.

### Ionization Energy

The energy required to remove an electron from an isolated atom is the **ionization energy**. The process for sodium is represented as follows:

$$\text{ionization energy} + Na \longrightarrow Na^+ + e^-$$

The magnitude of the ionization energy should correlate with the strength of the attractive force between the nucleus and the outermost electron.

- Reading *down* a group, note that the ionization energy decreases, because the atom's size is increasing. The outermost electron is progressively farther from the nuclear charge, hence easier to remove.
- Reading *across* a period, note that atomic size decreases, because the outermost electrons are closer to the nucleus, more tightly held, and more difficult to remove. Therefore the ionization energy generally increases.

A correlation does indeed exist between trends in atomic size and ionization energy. Atomic size generally *decreases* from the bottom to top of a group and from left to right in a period. Ionization energies generally *increase* in the same periodic way. Note also that ionization energies are highest for the noble gases (Figure 2.19a). A high value for ionization energy means that it is difficult to remove electrons from the atom, and this, in part, accounts for the extreme stability and nonreactivity of the noble gases.

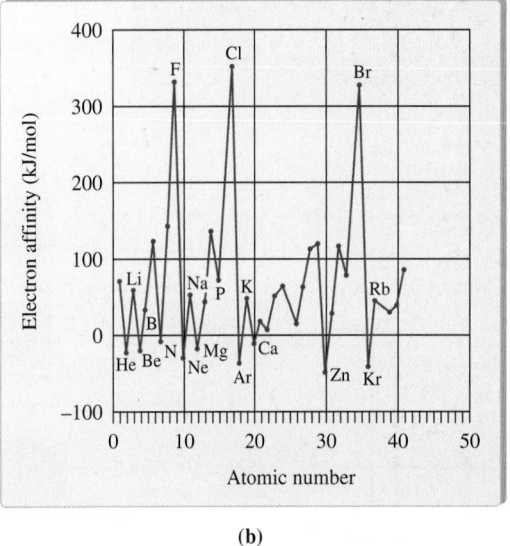

(a)                                                     (b)

**Figure 2.19** (a) The ionization energies of the first forty elements versus their atomic numbers. Note the very high values for elements located on the right in the periodic table, and low values for those on the left. Some exceptions to the trends are evident. (b) The periodic variation of electron affinity. Note the very low values for the noble gases and the elements on the far left of the periodic table. These elements do not form negative ions. In contrast, F, Cl, and Br readily form negative ions.

## Electron Affinity

The energy change when a single electron is added to an isolated atom is the **electron affinity.** If we consider ionization energy in relation to positive ion formation (remember that the magnitude of the ionization energy tells us the ease of *removal* of an electron, hence the ease of forming positive ions), then electron affinity provides a measure of the ease of forming negative ions. A large electron affinity, meaning a large release of energy, indicates that the atom becomes more stable as it becomes a negative ion (through gaining an electron). Consider the gain of an electron by a bromine atom:

$$Br + e^- \longrightarrow Br^- + energy$$
Electron affinity

Periodic trends for electron affinity are as follows:

- Electron affinities generally decrease down a group.
- Electron affinities generally increase across a period.

Remember these trends are not absolute. Exceptions exist, as seen in the many irregularities in Figure 2.19b.

**Question 2.15**   Rank Be, N, and F in order of increasing
   a. atomic size          b. ionization energy       c. electron affinity

**Question 2.16**   Rank Cl, Br, I, and F in order of increasing
   a. atomic size          b. ionization energy       c. electron affinity

**LEARNING GOAL**

**12**   Utilize the periodic table and its predictive power to estimate the relative sizes of atoms and ions, as well as relative magnitudes of ionization energy and electron affinity.

Remember: ionization energy and electron affinity are predictable from *trends* in the periodic table. As with most trends, exceptions occur.

## CHAPTER MAP

# SUMMARY

## 2.1 Composition of the Atom

▶ The basic structural unit of an element is the **atom.**

▶ The **nucleus** is the very small and very dense core at the center of the atom containing:

- Protons—positively charged particles. The number of protons is indicated by the **atomic number,** Z.
- Neutrons—neutral particles. The number of neutrons is calculated from the **mass number** minus the atomic number, A–Z.

▶ **Electrons** are negatively charged particles that are located in a diffuse region. For an atom the number of electrons equals the number of protons.

▶ **Isotopes** are atoms of the same element that have a different number of neutrons. Isotopes of the same element have the same chemical properties.

▶ The **atomic mass** is the weighted average of the masses of the isotopes of an element in atomic mass units; $1$ amu $= 1.66 \times 10^{-24}$ grams (g).

## 2.2 Development of Atomic Theory

▶ Dalton's atomic theory gave the first experimentally based concept of the atom. Many aspects of his theory still hold true.

▶ John Dalton proposed that atoms were indivisible. Experiments by Thomson, Rutherford, and others discovered that the atom contained subatomic particles (electrons, protons, and neutrons) and was divisible.

## 2.3 Light, Atomic Structure, and the Bohr Atom

▶ **Spectroscopy** is the study of the interaction of light and matter and led to the understanding of the electronic structure of the atom.

▶ Features of light (**electromagnetic radiation**) include:

- The **speed of light** equals $3.0 \times 10^{8}$ m/s.
- Light has a wave nature and the wavelength of light determines the energy of the light. The shorter the wavelength, the greater the energy.
- Light has a particle nature. The particles are called photons.

▶ **Niels Bohr** used the emission spectrum of hydrogen to give the first model of the electronic structure of the atom. Some important features of his model include the following:

- Electrons can exist only in certain allowed **energy levels** ($n = 1, 2, 3 \ldots$)., that is, energy is *quantized.* Bohr called these levels orbits.
- Electrons can gain energy and be promoted from the **ground state** to a higher energy level (**excited state**).
- Electrons can lose energy in the form of a photon, and return to a lower energy level.
- The energy difference between the levels can be determined from the wavelength of the emitted light.

- Bohr's model could not explain the emission spectra of systems with more than one electron.

▶ The modern view of the electronic structure of the atom describes **atomic orbitals,** which are regions in space with a high probability of containing electrons, that is, a high **electron density.**

## 2.4 The Periodic Law and the Periodic Table

▶ The **periodic law** relates the structure of elements to their chemical and physical properties. The modern periodic table groups the elements according to these properties.

▶ **Periods** are horizontal rows, numbered 1 thru 7 from top to bottom. The lanthanide series is part of period 6; the actinide series is part of period 7.

▶ Vertical columns are referred to as **groups** or families. Two common numbering systems are used in this textbook:

- Roman numeral system: IA–VIIIA for **representative elements,** IB–VIII B for **transition elements.**
- IUPAC system: 1–18.

▶ Four common names of families are:

- **Alkali metals** (IA, 1)
- **Alkaline earth metals** (IIA, 2)
- **Halogens** (VIIA, 17)
- **Noble gases** (VIIIA, 18)

▶ A bold zigzag line from boron leading to the right and down separates the **metals** from the **nonmetals.**

▶ The elements bordering the line (except aluminum) are **metalloids.**

▶ The blocks on the periodic table commonly give the atomic symbol, name, atomic number, and atomic mass.

## 2.5 Electron Arrangement and the Periodic Table

▶ Electrons are identified by their location in the atom.

▶ **Principal energy levels,** $n$, give the general distance from the nucleus. As $n$ increases, the electron is farther from the nucleus and has more energy.

▶ Each principal energy level, $n$, can have a maximum of $2(n)^2$ electrons located in it.

▶ Each principal energy level contains **sublevels,** named $s$, $p$, and $d$. The number of the principal energy level gives the number of sublevels.

- For $n = 1$, there is one sublevel: $s$
- For $n = 2$, there are two sublevels: $s$, $p$
- For $n = 3$, there are three sublevels: $s$, $p$, $d$

▶ Each sublevel contains atomic orbitals, named the same as the sublevel.

- $s$ sublevels contain one orbital
- $p$ sublevels contain three orbitals
- $d$ sublevels contain five orbitals

▶ The **electron configuration,** shorthand electron configuration, and orbital diagram are three ways to designate where all electrons are located in an atom in its ground state.

## 2.6 Valence Electrons and the Octet Rule

▶ **Valence electrons** are the outermost electrons in the atom (beyond the noble gas core). These are the electrons that are involved in bonding as elements form compounds.

▶ The **octet rule** states that atoms usually react in such a way as to obtain a noble gas configuration.

▶ The octet rule can be used to predict the charge of atoms when they become **ions**.

• Metals tend to lose electrons to become positively charged **cations**.
• Nonmetals tend to gain electrons to become negatively charged **anions**.
• Atoms gain and lose electrons to obtain a noble gas configuration, that is, to be **isoelectronic** with the nearest noble gas.

## 2.7 Trends in the Periodic Table

▶ Atomic size *decreases* from left to right and from bottom to top in the periodic table.

• Cations are smaller than their parent atom.
• Anions are larger than their parent atom.

▶ **Ionization energy** is the energy required to remove an electron from an isolated atom.

• Ionization energy *increases* from left to right and from bottom to top in the periodic table.

▶ **Electron affinity** is the energy change when a single electron is added to a neutral isolated atom.

• Elements with a high electron affinity will *release* a large amount of energy.
• Electron affinity *increases* from left to right and up a group. The halogens have the greatest electron affinity.

## ANSWERS TO PRACTICE PROBLEMS

**2.1  a.**  16 protons, 16 electrons, 16 neutrons
    **b.**  11 protons, 11 electrons, 12 neutrons
    **c.**  1 proton, 1 electron, 0 neutrons
    **d.**  94 protons, 94 electrons, 150 neutrons

**2.2**  14.0 amu

**2.3**  10.8 amu

**2.4  a.**  sulfur: $1s^2\,2s^2\,2p^6\,3s^2\,3p^4$
    **b.**  calcium: $1s^2\,2s^2\,2p^6\,3s^2\,3p^6\,4s^2$
    **c.**  potassium: $1s^2\,2s^2\,2p^6\,3s^2\,3p^6\,4s^1$
    **d.**  phosphorus: $1s^2\,2s^2\,2p^6\,3s^2\,3p^3$

**2.5  a.**

**b.**

**c.**

**d.**

**2.6  a.**  $[\text{Ne}]3s^2\,3p^4$            **c.**  $[\text{Ar}]4s^2 3d^{10}4p^4$
    **b.**  $[\text{Ne}]3s^2\,3p^2$            **d.**  $[\text{Ar}]4s^2 3d^6$

**2.7  a.**  Total electrons = 11, valence electrons = 1, energy level = 3
    **b.**  Total electrons = 12, valence electrons = 2, energy level = 3
    **c.**  Total electrons = 16, valence electrons = 6, energy level = 3
    **d.**  Total electrons = 17, valence electrons = 7, energy level = 3
    **e.**  Total electrons = 18, valence electrons = 8, energy level = 3

## QUESTIONS AND PROBLEMS

### Composition of the Atom

#### Foundations

**2.17**  What information does the atomic number of an atom give?

**2.18**  Why is the number of electrons not part of the mass number of an atom?

**2.19**  Consider the following definitions of isotopes. Are all correct? If not, explain what is wrong with any that have errors.
    **a.** Isotopes are atoms of the same element with different numbers of neutrons.
    **b.** Isotopes are atoms with the same number of protons but different numbers of neutrons.
    **c.** Isotopes are atoms with the same atomic number but different mass numbers.

**2.20**  One of the following isotopic symbols has an error. What is the error?

$$\isotope[12][6]{C} \qquad \isotope[13][7]{C} \qquad \isotope[12]{C}$$

**2.21**  What is the major difference among isotopes of an element?
**2.22**  What is the major similarity among isotopes of an element?
**2.23**  Fill in the blanks:
    **a.** Isotopes of an element differ in mass because the atoms have a different number of _____.
    **b.** The atomic number gives the number of _____ in the nucleus.
    **c.** The mass number of an atom is due to the number of _____ and _____ in the nucleus.
    **d.** Electrons surround the _____ and have a _____ charge.
**2.24**  Label each of the following statements as true or false:
    **a.** An atom with an atomic number of 7 and a mass of 14 is identical to an atom with an atomic number of 6 and a mass of 14.

**b.** Neutral atoms have the same number of electrons as protons.

**c.** The mass of an atom is due to the sum of the number of protons, neutrons, and electrons.

**2.25** Explain the difference between the mass number and the atomic mass of an element.

**2.26** The nuclei of three different atoms are depicted in the diagrams below. Which ones are isotopes, if any?

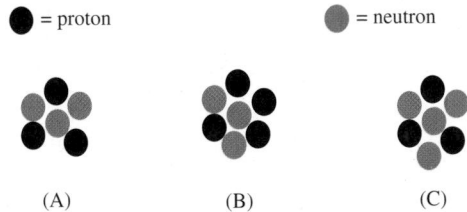

(A)              (B)              (C)

## Applications

**2.27** Calculate the number of protons, neutrons, and electrons in:
**a.** $^{136}_{56}\text{Ba}$        **b.** $^{209}_{84}\text{Po}$

**2.28** Calculate the number of protons, neutrons, and electrons in:
**a.** $^{37}_{17}\text{Cl}$        **b.** $^{23}_{11}\text{Na}$        **c.** $^{84}_{36}\text{Kr}$

**2.29** An atom has nine protons, ten neutrons, and nine electrons. Write the symbol of the atom.

**2.30** An atom has nineteen protons, twenty neutrons, and nineteen electrons. Write the symbol of the atom.

**2.31** How many protons are in the nucleus of the isotope Rn-220?

**2.32** How many neutrons are in the nucleus of the isotope Rn-220?

**2.33** Selenium-80 is a naturally occurring isotope. It is found in over-the-counter supplements.
**a.** How many protons are found in one atom of selenium-80?
**b.** How many neutrons are found in one atom of selenium-80?

**2.34** Iodine-131 is an isotope used in thyroid therapy.
**a.** How many protons are found in one atom of iodine-131?
**b.** How many neutrons are found in one atom of iodine-131?

**2.35** Write symbols for each isotope:
**a.** Each atom contains one proton and zero neutrons.
**b.** Each atom contains six protons and eight neutrons.

**2.36** Write symbols for each isotope:
**a.** Each atom contains one proton and two neutrons.
**b.** Each atom contains 92 protons and 146 neutrons.

**2.37** The element copper has two naturally occurring isotopes. One of these has a mass of 62.93 amu and a natural abundance of 69.09%. A second isotope has a mass of 64.9278 amu and a natural abundance of 30.91%. Calculate the atomic mass of copper.

**2.38** The element lithium has two naturally occurring isotopes. One of these has a mass of 6.0151 amu and a natural abundance of 7.49%. A second isotope has a mass of 7.0160 amu and a natural abundance of 92.51%. Calculate the atomic mass of lithium.

## Development of Atomic Theory

### Foundations

**2.39** What are the major postulates of Dalton's atomic theory?

**2.40** What points of Dalton's theory are no longer current?

**2.41** Note the major accomplishment of each of the following:
**a.** Chadwick        **b.** Goldstein

**2.42** Note the major accomplishment of each of the following:
**a.** Geiger        **b.** Bohr

**2.43** Note the major accomplishment of each of the following:
**a.** Dalton        **b.** Crookes

**2.44** Note the major accomplishment of each of the following:
**a.** Thomson        **b.** Rutherford

## Applications

**2.45** Describe the experiment that provided the basis for our understanding of the nucleus.

**2.46** Describe the series of experiments that characterized the electron.

**2.47** List at least three properties of the electron.

**2.48** What is a cathode ray? Which subatomic particle is detected?

**2.49** Prior to Rutherford's gold foil experiments and the understanding of the existence of a nucleus, how did scientists view the atom?

**2.50** Explain how Rutherford concluded that the atom is principally empty space.

## Light, Atomic Structure, and the Bohr Atom

### Foundations

**2.51** Describe electromagnetic radiation according to its wave nature.

**2.52** Describe electromagnetic radiation according to its particle nature.

**2.53** Is the following statement true or false?
Light of higher energy travels at a faster speed than light of lower energy.

**2.54** What is the relationship between the energy of light and its wavelength?

**2.55** Which form of radiation has greater energy, microwave or infrared?

**2.56** Which form of radiation has the longer wavelength, ultraviolet or infrared?

**2.57** Describe the process that occurs when electrical energy is applied to a sample of hydrogen gas.

**2.58** When electrical energy is applied to an element in its gaseous state, light is produced. How does the light differ among elements?

**2.59** What is meant by the term *spectroscopy*?

**2.60** What is meant by the term *electromagnetic spectrum*?

## Applications

**2.61** Critique this statement: Electrons can exist in any position outside of the nucleus.

**2.62** Critique this statement: Promotion of electrons is accompanied by a release of energy.

**2.63** What are the most important points of the Bohr theory?

**2.64** Give two reasons why the Bohr theory did not stand the test of time.

**2.65** What was the major contribution of Bohr's atomic model?

**2.66** What was the major deficiency of Bohr's atomic model?

## The Periodic Law and the Periodic Table

### Foundations

**2.67** Provide the name of the element represented by each of the following symbols:
**a.** Na        **c.** Mg
**b.** K        **d.** B

**2.68** Provide the name of the element represented by each of the following symbols:
a. Ca          c. Co
b. Cu         d. Si

**2.69** Which group of the periodic table is known as the alkali metals? List them.

**2.70** Which group of the periodic table is known as the alkaline earth metals? List them.

**2.71** Which group of the periodic table is known as the halogens? List them.

**2.72** Which group of the periodic table is known as the noble gases? List them.

### Applications

**2.73** For each of the elements Na, Ni, Al, P, Cl, and Ar, provide the following information:
a. Which are metals?
b. Which are representative metals?
c. Which are inert or noble gases?

**2.74** For each of the elements Ca, K, Cu, Zn, Br, and Kr, provide the following information:
a. Which are metals?
b. Which are representative metals?
c. Which are inert or noble gases?

**2.75** Using the information below, for Group I elements:

| Element | Atomic Number | Melting Point (°C) |
|---------|---------------|--------------------|
| Li | 3 | 180.5 |
| Na | 11 | 97.8 |
| K | 19 | 63.3 |
| Rb | 37 | 38.9 |
| Cs | 55 | 28.4 |

Prepare a graph relating melting point and atomic number. How does this demonstrate the periodic law?

**2.76** Use the graph prepared in Question 2.75 to predict the melting point of francium (Fr).

### Electron Arrangement and the Periodic Table

#### Foundations

**2.77** Distinguish between a principal energy level and a sublevel.

**2.78** Distinguish between a sublevel and an orbital.

**2.79** Sketch a diagram and describe our current model of an $s$ orbital.

**2.80** How is a $2s$ orbital different from a $1s$ orbital?

**2.81** What is the maximum number of electrons in each of the following energy levels?
a. $n = 1$      b. $n = 2$      c. $n = 3$

**2.82** a. What is the maximum number of $s$ electrons that can exist in any one principal energy level?
b. How many $p$ electrons?
c. How many $d$ electrons?

**2.83** State the Pauli exclusion principle. Explain how it is used to determine the number of electrons that can exist in a $d$ subshell.

**2.84** State Hund's rule. Choose the orbital diagram below that violates Hund's rule.

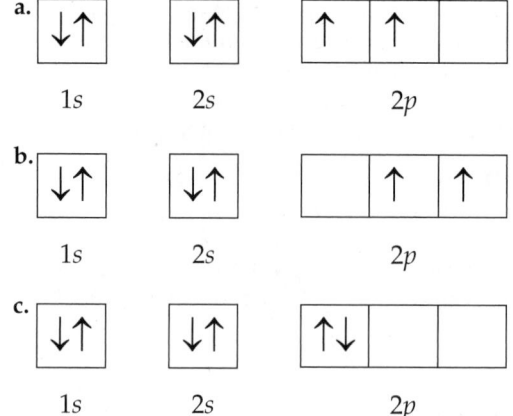

### Applications

**2.85** Using the periodic table, write the electron configuration of each of the following atoms:
a. Al          b. Na          c. Sc

**2.86** Using the periodic table, write the electron configuration of each of the following atoms:
a. Ca          b. Fe          c. Cl

**2.87** Using the periodic table, write the electron configuration and orbital diagram of each of the following atoms:
a. B          b. S          c. Ar

**2.88** Using the periodic table, write the electron configuration and orbital diagram of each of the following atoms:
a. V          b. Cd         c. Te

**2.89** Which of the following electron configurations are not possible? Why?
a. $1s^2 1p^2$        c. $2s^2 2s^2 2p^6 2d^1$
b. $1s^2 2s^2 2p^2$     d. $1s^2 2s^3$

**2.90** For each incorrect electron configuration in Question 2.89, assume that the number of electrons is correct, identify the element, and write the correct electron configuration.

**2.91** Determine whether the following orbital diagrams are correct. If there is an error, fix the diagram.

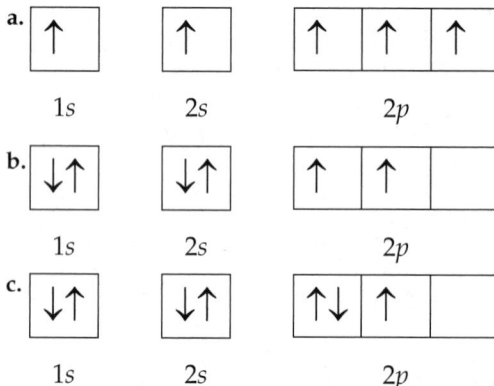

**2.92** Identify the element for each of the orbital diagrams (once corrected) in Question 2.91.

**Figure 3.1** Lewis symbols for representative elements. Each unpaired electron is a potential bond.

## Ionic Bonding

Representative elements form ions that obey the octet rule. Ions of opposite charge attract each other, and this attraction is the essence of the ionic bond. Consider the reaction of a sodium atom and a chlorine atom to produce sodium chloride:

$$Na + Cl \longrightarrow NaCl$$

Recall that the sodium atom has

- a low ionization energy (it readily loses an electron) and
- a low electron affinity (it does not want more electrons).

If sodium loses its valence electron, it will become isoelectronic (same electron configuration) with neon, a very stable noble gas atom. This tells us that the sodium atom would be a good electron donor, forming the sodium ion:

$$Na\cdot \longrightarrow Na^+ + e^-$$

Recall that the chlorine atom has

- a high ionization energy (it will not easily give up an electron) and
- a high electron affinity (it readily accepts another electron).

Chlorine will gain one more electron. By doing so, it will complete an octet (eight outermost electrons) and be isoelectronic with argon, a stable noble gas. Therefore, chlorine behaves as a willing electron acceptor, forming a chloride ion:

$$:\ddot{C}l\cdot + e^- \longrightarrow \left[:\ddot{C}l:\right]^-$$

The electron released by sodium (*electron donor*) is the electron received by chlorine (*electron acceptor*):

$$Na\cdot \longrightarrow Na^+ + e^-$$

$$e^- + \cdot\ddot{C}l: \longrightarrow \left[:\ddot{C}l:\right]^-$$

An **ionic bond** is the *electrostatic force*, the attraction of opposite charges, between the resulting cation and anion (in this case, the $Na^+$ and the $Cl^-$). The electrostatic force is quite strong and holds the ions together as an *ion pair*: $Na^+Cl^-$.

**LEARNING GOAL**

**1** Classify compounds as having ionic, covalent, or polar covalent bonds.

*Refer to Section 2.7 for a discussion of ionization energy and electron affinity.*

Square brackets are placed around Lewis symbols of ions.

The essential features of ionic bonding are the following:

- Metals tend to form cations because they have low ionization energies and low electron affinities.
- Nonmetals tend to form anions because they have high ionization energies and high electron affinities.
- Ions are formed by the transfer of electrons.
- The oppositely charged ions formed are held together by an electrostatic force.
- Reactions between metals and nonmetals tend to form ionic compounds.

---

**EXAMPLE 3.1**    **Predicting the Formula of an Ionic Compound**

**LEARNING GOAL**

Predict the formula of the ionic compound formed from the reaction of sodium and oxygen atoms.

**2**  Write the formula of a compound when provided with the name of the compound.

**Solution**

Determine the charges of the ions from the periodic table. Use subscripts to create a neutral compound.

**Step 1.** Sodium is in Group IA (or 1); it has *one* valence electron. Loss of this electron produces $Na^+$.

**Step 2.** Oxygen is in Group VIA (or 16); it has *six* valence electrons. A gain of two electrons (to create a stable octet) produces $O^{2-}$.

**Step 3.** Two positive charges are necessary to counterbalance two negative charges on the oxygen anion. Because each sodium ion carries a 1+ charge, two sodium ions are needed for each $O^{2-}$.

**Step 4.** The subscript 2 is used to indicate that the formula unit contains two sodium ions. Thus the formula of the compound is $Na_2O$.

Note that the formula for the ionic compound does not show the charges of the ions.

**Practice Problem 3.1**

Predict the formulas of the compounds formed from the combination of ions of the following elements:

   a. lithium and bromine    b. calcium and bromine    c. potassium and chlorine

▶ For Further Practice: **Questions 3.23 and 3.24.**

---

**EXAMPLE 3.2**    **Predicting the Formula of an Ionic Compound**

**LEARNING GOAL**

Predict the formula of the compound formed by the reaction of aluminum and sulfur atoms.

**2**  Write the formula of a compound when provided with the name of the compound.

**Solution**

Determine the charges of the ions from the periodic table. Use subscripts to create a neutral compound.

**Step 1.** Aluminum is in Group IIIA (or 13); it has three valence electrons. Loss of these electrons produces $Al^{3+}$.

**Step 2.** Sulfur is in Group VIA (or 16); it has six valence electrons. A gain of two electrons (to create a stable octet) produces $S^{2-}$.

**Step 3.** How can we combine $Al^{3+}$ and $S^{2-}$ to yield a unit of zero charge? The least common multiple of 2 and 3 is 6. Multiply each charge by a different factor to achieve +6 and −6 charges and a net zero charge for the compound.

$$2 \times (+3) = +6 \text{ and } 3 \times (-2) = -6$$

**Step 4.** The subscript 2 is used to indicate that the formula unit contains two aluminum ions. The subscript 3 is used to indicate that the formula unit contains three sulfide ions. Thus the formula of the compound is $Al_2S_3$.

**Practice Problem 3.2**

Predict the formulas of the compounds formed from the combination of ions of the following elements:

a. calcium and nitrogen      b. magnesium and bromine      c. magnesium and nitrogen

▶ For Further Practice: **Questions 3.25 and 3.26.**

Although ionic compounds are sometimes referred to as ion pairs, in the solid state these ion pairs do not actually exist as individual units. The positive ions exert attractive forces on several negative ions, and the negative ions are attracted to several positive centers. Positive and negative ions arrange themselves in a regular three-dimensional repeating array to produce a stable arrangement known as a **crystal lattice.** The lattice structure for the ionic compound sodium chloride is shown in Figure 3.2.

(a)

(b)

(c)

**Figure 3.2** The arrangement of ions in a crystal of NaCl (sodium chloride, table salt). (a) A sodium atom loses one electron to become a smaller sodium ion, and a chlorine atom gains that electron, becoming a larger chloride ion. (b) Attraction of $Na^+$ and $Cl^-$ forms NaCl ion pairs that aggregate in a three-dimensional crystal lattice structure. (c) An enlarged view of NaCl crystals, magnified 400x, shows their cubic geometry. Each tiny crystal contains billions and billions of sodium and chloride ions.

# A MEDICAL PERSPECTIVE

## Unwanted Crystal Formation

Conventional wisdom says that the painful symptoms associated with the presence of stones in the bladder and kidneys are just one more problem associated with aging. Unfortunately, recent observations by many clinicians and physicians across the country seem to indicate that these problems are not limited to the elderly. Children as young as 5 years old are developing kidney stones while doctors search for reasons to explain this phenomenon.

Kidney stones most often result from the combination of calcium cations ($Ca^{2+}$) with anions such as oxalate ($C_2O_4^{2-}$) and phosphate ($PO_4^{3-}$). Calcium oxalate and calcium phosphate are ionic compounds that are only sparingly soluble in water. They grow in a three-dimensional crystal lattice. When the crystals become large enough to inhibit the flow of urine

in the kidney or bladder, painful symptoms necessitate some strategy to remove the stones.

Conditions that favor stone formation are the same as those that favor the formation of the same material in a beaker: high concentrations of the ions and insufficient water to dissolve the stones.

Many physicians believe that children who tend to form stones share several behavioral characteristics. They do not drink enough water and they consume too much salt. Salt in the diet appears to favor the transport of calcium ions to the kidney. Potato chips, French fries, and other snack foods, as well as processed foods such as frozen dinners, sandwich meats, canned soups, and sport drinks are very high in salt content. Obesity appears associated with stone formation, but this may be linked through the unhealthy diet of many children.

Although limiting calcium ion intake would appear to inhibit stone formation (remember, the stones are calcium compounds), reduction of calcium in the diet is not the answer! Dietary calcium is actually beneficial because it binds with oxalate ions before they reach the kidneys. Dietary calcium is important in preventing osteoporosis and dental caries as well. The take-home lesson? A balanced diet, in moderation, with minimal salt intake, especially in the formative years, is recommended.

**For Further Understanding**

Consult reliable references to answer the following questions:

▶ Describe another disease that is associated with a diet rich in salt.

▶ Describe one useful function of phosphate ion in the diet.

---

## LEARNING GOAL

**1** Classify compounds as having ionic, covalent, or polar covalent bonds.

**ANIMATION**

• Covalent Bonding: Sharing Electrons

## Covalent Bonding

The octet rule is not just for ionic compounds. In covalent bonding, atoms share electrons to complete the octet of electrons for each of the atoms participating in the bond. Consider the bond formed between two hydrogen atoms, producing the diatomic form of hydrogen: $H_2$. Individual hydrogen atoms are not stable, and two hydrogen atoms readily combine to produce diatomic hydrogen:

$$H + H \longrightarrow H_2$$

If a hydrogen atom were to gain a second electron, it would be isoelectronic with the stable electron configuration of helium. However, because two identical hydrogen atoms have an equal tendency to gain or lose electrons, an electron transfer from one atom to the other is unlikely to occur under normal conditions. Each atom may attain a noble gas structure only by *sharing* its electron with the other, as shown with Lewis symbols and a Lewis structure:

$$H^{\cdot} + {\cdot}H \longrightarrow H : H$$

When electrons are shared rather than transferred, the *shared electron pair* is referred to as a *covalent bond* (Figure 3.3). Compounds containing only covalent bonds are called *covalent compounds*. Covalent compounds are typically collections of *molecules*. **Molecules** are neutral (uncharged) species made up of two or more atoms joined by covalent bonds. Molecules are represented by *Lewis structures*. **Lewis structures** depict valence electrons of all atoms in the molecule, arranged to satisfy the octet rule. Covalent bonds tend to form between atoms with similar tendencies to gain or lose electrons. The most obvious examples are the diatomic molecules $H_2$, $N_2$, $O_2$, $F_2$, $Cl_2$, $Br_2$, and $I_2$. Bonding in these molecules is *totally covalent* because there can be no net tendency for electron transfer between identical atoms. The formation of $F_2$, for example, may be represented as

$$:\ddot{F}\cdot \; + \; \cdot\ddot{F}: \; \longrightarrow \; :\ddot{F}:\ddot{F}:$$

As in $H_2$, a single covalent bond is formed. The bonding electron pair is said to be *localized*, or largely confined to the region surrounding the two fluorine nuclei. Paired electrons around an atom that are not shared are termed **lone pairs.** The lone pairs in $F_2$ are shown in red.

Two atoms do not have to be identical to form a covalent bond. Consider compounds such as the following:

$$H:\ddot{F}: \qquad H:\ddot{O}:H \qquad \begin{matrix} H \\ H:\overset{..}{\underset{..}{C}}:H \\ H \end{matrix} \qquad H:\overset{..}{N}:H \; H$$

As you examine each of these structures, notice the number of electrons associated with each atom. The octet rule is satisfied for each atom. The hydrogen atoms have two electrons (shared electrons with the atom to which they are attached), and the other (non-hydrogen) atoms have eight valence electrons, which are counted as follows:

- Fluorine (in HF) has two electrons shared with hydrogen and six lone-pair electrons.
- Oxygen (in $H_2O$) has four electrons shared with the two hydrogen atoms and four lone-pair electrons.
- Carbon (in $CH_4$) has eight electrons shared with the four hydrogen atoms.
- Nitrogen (in $NH_3$) has six electrons shared with the three hydrogen atoms and two lone-pair electrons.

In each of these cases, bond formation satisfies the octet rule. A total of eight electrons surrounds each atom other than hydrogen. Hydrogen has only two electrons (corresponding to the electronic structure of helium).

## Polar Covalent Bonding and Electronegativity

### The Polar Covalent Bond

Covalent bonding is the sharing of an electron pair by two atoms. However, just as we may observe in our day-to-day activities, sharing is not always equal. In a molecule like $H_2$ (or $N_2$, or any other diatomic molecule composed of only one element), the electrons, on average, spend the same amount of time in the vicinity of each atom; the electrons have no preference because both atoms are identical.

Now consider a diatomic molecule composed of two different elements; HF is a common example. It has been experimentally shown that the electrons in the H—F bond between hydrogen and fluorine atoms are not equally shared; the electrons spend more time in the vicinity of the fluorine atom. This unequal sharing results in a **polar covalent bond.** One end of the bond (in this case, the F atom) is more electron rich (higher electron density), hence, more negative. The other end

*There exist large three-dimensional crystals, similar to ionic compounds, which consist of only covalent bonds. The term* molecule *does not apply to these compounds. Covalent solids are discussed in Section 5.3.*

A diatomic molecule is one that is composed of two atoms joined by a covalent bond.

Fourteen valence electrons are arranged in such a way that each fluorine atom is surrounded by eight electrons. The octet rule is satisfied for each fluorine atom.

Hydrogen atoms approach at high velocity.

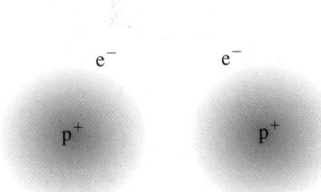

Hydrogen nuclei begin to attract each other's electrons.

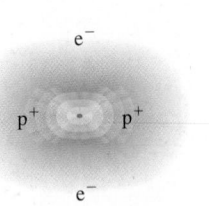

Hydrogen atoms form the hydrogen molecule; atoms are held together by the shared electrons, the covalent bond.

**Figure 3.3** Covalent bonding in hydrogen.

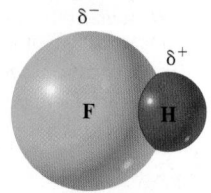

**Figure 3.4** Polar covalent bonding in HF. Fluorine is electron rich ($\delta^-$) and hydrogen is electron deficient ($\delta^+$) due to unequal electron sharing.

**ANIMATION**

• Electronegativity

Linus Pauling is the only person to receive two Nobel Prizes in very unrelated fields; the chemistry award in 1954 and 8 years later, the Nobel Peace Prize. His career is a model of interdisciplinary science, with important contributions ranging from chemical physics to molecular biology.

of the bond (in this case, the H atom) is less electron rich (lower electron density), hence, more positive. These two ends can be described as follows (Figure 3.4):

• Somewhat positive end (partial positive), denoted with a $\delta^+$ symbol.
• Somewhat negative end (partial negative), denoted with a $\delta^-$ symbol.

Once again, we can use the predictive power of the periodic table to help us determine whether a particular bond is polar or nonpolar covalent. We already know that elements that tend to form negative ions (by gaining electrons) are found to the right of the table, whereas positive ion formers (that may lose electrons) are located on the left side of the table. Elements whose atoms strongly attract electrons are described as electronegative elements. Linus Pauling, a chemist noted for his theories on chemical bonding, developed a scale of relative electronegativities that correlates reasonably well with the positions of the elements in the periodic table.

### Electronegativity

**Electronegativity** (EN) is a measure of the ability of an atom to attract electrons in a chemical bond. Elements with high EN have a greater ability to attract electrons than do elements with low EN. Pauling developed a method to assign values of EN to many of the elements in the periodic table. These values range from a low of 0.7 to a high of 4.0, 4.0 being the most electronegative element.

Figure 3.5 shows that the most electronegative elements (excluding the non-reactive noble gas elements) are located in the upper right corner of the periodic table, whereas the least electronegative elements are found in the lower left corner of the table. In general, EN values increase as we proceed left to right and bottom to top of the table. Like other periodic trends, numerous exceptions occur.

If we picture the covalent bond as a competition for electrons between two positive centers, it is the difference in EN, $\Delta$EN, that determines the extent of polarity. Consider: $H_2$ or H—H

$$\Delta EN = \left[\begin{array}{c} EN\ of \\ hydrogen \end{array}\right] - \left[\begin{array}{c} EN\ of \\ hydrogen \end{array}\right]$$

$$\Delta EN = 2.1 - 2.1 = 0$$

**Figure 3.5** Electronegativities of the elements.

The bond in $H_2$ is nonpolar covalent. Bonds between *identical* atoms are *always* nonpolar covalent. Also, $Cl_2$ or Cl—Cl

$$\Delta EN = \begin{bmatrix} EN\ of \\ chlorine \end{bmatrix} - \begin{bmatrix} EN\ of \\ chlorine \end{bmatrix}$$

$$\Delta EN = 3\,0. - 3.0 = 0$$

The bond in $Cl_2$ is nonpolar covalent. Now consider HCl or H—Cl

$$\Delta EN = \begin{bmatrix} EN\ of \\ chlorine \end{bmatrix} - \begin{bmatrix} EN\ of \\ hydrogen \end{bmatrix}$$

$$\Delta EN = 3.0 - 2.1 = 0.9$$

The bond in HCl is polar covalent.

Recall that metals and nonmetals usually react to produce ionic compounds resulting from the transfer of one or more electrons from the metal to the nonmetal.

An EN difference of 2.0 is generally accepted as the boundary between polar covalent and ionic bonds. Although, strictly speaking, any EN difference, no matter how small, produces a polar bond, the degree of polarity for bonds with EN differences less than 0.5 is minimal. Consequently, we shall classify these bonds as nonpolar.

> By convention, the EN difference is calculated by subtracting the less electronegative element's value from the value for the more electronegative element. In this way, negative numbers are avoided.

## 3.2 Naming Compounds and Writing Formulas of Compounds

**Nomenclature** is the assignment of a correct and unambiguous name to each and every chemical compound. Assigning a name to a structure or deducing the structure from a name is a necessary first step in any discussion of these compounds. The system for naming ionic compounds is different from the system for naming covalent compounds.

### Ionic Compounds

The **formula** is the representation of the fundamental compound using chemical symbols and numerical subscripts. It is the "shorthand" symbol for a compound for example,

NaCl    and    $MgBr_2$

> The *formula* of an ionic compound is the smallest whole-number ratio of ions in the substance.

The formula identifies the number and type of the various atoms that make up the compound unit. The number of like atoms in the unit is shown by the use of a subscript. The presence of only one atom is understood when no subscript is present.

The formula NaCl indicates that each ion pair consists of one sodium cation ($Na^+$) and one chloride anion ($Cl^-$). Similarly, the formula $MgBr_2$ indicates that one magnesium ion and two bromide ions combine to form the compound.

### Writing Formulas of Ionic Compounds from the Identities of the Component Ions

It is important to be able to write the formula of an ionic compound when provided with the identities of the ions that make up the compound. The charge of each ion can usually be determined from the group (family) of the periodic table in which the parent element is found. The cations and anions must combine in such a way that the resulting formula unit has a net charge of zero.

> **LEARNING GOAL**
>
> **2** Write the formula of a compound when provided with the name of the compound.

LEARNING GOAL

**3** Name common inorganic compounds using standard naming conventions and recognize the common names of frequently used substances.

## Writing Names of Ionic Compounds from the Formulas of the Compounds

In naming ionic compounds, the name of the cation appears first, followed by the name of the anion. If the ionic compound consists of a metal cation and a non-metal anion, the cation has the name of the metal; the anion is named using the *stem* of the nonmetal name joined to the suffix *-ide*. Some examples follow.

| Formula | cation | and | anion stem | + ide | = | Compound name |
|---------|--------|-----|------------|-------|---|---------------|
| $NaCl$ | sodium | | chlor | + ide | | sodium chloride |
| $Na_2O$ | sodium | | ox | + ide | | sodium oxide |
| $Li_2S$ | lithium | | sulf | + ide | | lithium sulfide |
| $AlBr_3$ | aluminum | | brom | + ide | | aluminum bromide |
| $CaO$ | calcium | | ox | + ide | | calcium oxide |

The metals that exist with only one possible cation charge are the IA and IIA metals, which have +1 and +2 charges, respectively, as well as $Ag^+$, $Cd^{2+}$, $Zn^{2+}$, and $Al^{3+}$.

If the cation and anion exist in only one common charged form, there is no ambiguity between formula and name. Sodium chloride *must be* NaCl, and lithium sulfide *must be* $Li_2S$, so that the sum of positive and negative charges is zero. With many elements, such as the transition metals, several ions of different charge may exist. $Fe^{2+}$, $Fe^{3+}$ and $Cu^+$, $Cu^{2+}$ are two common examples. Clearly, an ambiguity exists if we use the name iron for both $Fe^{2+}$ and $Fe^{3+}$ or copper for both $Cu^+$ and $Cu^{2+}$. Two systems have been developed to avoid this problem: the *Stock system* and the *common nomenclature system*.

In the Stock system (systematic name), a Roman numeral placed immediately after the name of the ion indicates the magnitude of the cation's charge. In the older common nomenclature system, the suffix *-ous* indicates the lower ionic charge, and the suffix *-ic* indicates the higher ionic charge. Consider the examples in Table 3.1.

Systematic names are easier and less ambiguous than common names. Whenever possible, we will use this system of nomenclature. The older, common names (-ous, -ic) are less specific; furthermore, they often use the Latin names of the elements (for example, iron compounds use *ferr-*, from *ferrum*, the Latin word for iron).

---

**EXAMPLE 3.3**    **Naming Ionic Compounds from the Formula Using the Stock System**

LEARNING GOAL

**3** Name common inorganic compounds using standard naming conventions and recognize the common names of frequently used substances.

Name $MnO_2$.

**Solution**

**Step 1.** Decide that the compound is ionic. It contains a metal and a nonmetal.

**Step 2.** Name the cation as the metal name followed by the anion with the *-ide* suffix.

Hence, manganese oxide.

**Step 3.** Determine if a Roman numeral is needed.

Since Mn is not a IA or IIA metal, nor is it Ag, Cd, Zn, or Al, then a Roman numeral *is* needed.

**Step 4.** Determine the charge on the metal. This is determined by using two pieces of information: (1) the charge of the anion, and (2) the overall charge of the compound is zero.

(1)  The charge of oxide is −2, there are two $O^{2-}$ ions.

$$2 \times (-2) = -4$$

(2)  There must be a +4 charge on the metal to balance the −4 of oxide.

**Step 5.** Put a Roman numeral stating this charge (IV) after the metal name.

Giving, manganese(IV) oxide.

### Practice Problem 3.3

Name $CrBr_2$.

▶ For Further Practice: **Questions 3.37, 3.38.**

**Monatomic ions** are ions consisting of a single atom. Common monatomic ions are listed in Table 3.2. The ions that are particularly important in biological systems are highlighted in red.

**Polyatomic ions,** such as the hydroxide ion, $OH^-$, are composed of two or more atoms bonded together. These ions, although bonded to other ions with ionic bonds, are themselves held together by covalent bonds.

**TABLE 3.1** Systematic (Stock) and Common Names for Iron and Copper Ions

| For systematic name: | | | |
|---|---|---|---|
| **Formula** | **+ Ion Charge** | **Cation Name** | **Compound Name** |
| $FeCl_2$ | 2 + | Iron(II) | Iron(II) chloride |
| $FeCl_3$ | 3 + | Iron(III) | Iron(III) chloride |
| $Cu_2O$ | 1 + | Copper(I) | Copper(I) oxide |
| $CuO$ | 2 + | Copper(II) | Copper(II) oxide |
| **For common nomenclature:** | | | |
| **Formula** | **+ Ion Charge** | **Cation Name** | **Common -ous/ic Name** |
| $FeCl_2$ | 2 + | Ferrous | Ferrous chloride |
| $FeCl_3$ | 3 + | Ferric | Ferric chloride |
| $Cu_2O$ | 1 + | Cuprous | Cuprous oxide |
| $CuO$ | 2 + | Cupric | Cupric oxide |

**TABLE 3.2** Common Monatomic Cations and Anions

| Cation | Name | Anion | Name |
|---|---|---|---|
| $H^+$ | Hydrogen ion | $H^-$ | Hydride ion |
| $Li^+$ | Lithium ion | $F^-$ | Fluoride ion |
| $Na^+$ | Sodium ion | $Cl^-$ | Chloride ion |
| $K^+$ | Potassium ion | $Br^-$ | Bromide ion |
| $Cs^+$ | Cesium ion | $I^-$ | Iodide ion |
| $Be^{2+}$ | Beryllium ion | $O^{2-}$ | Oxide ion |
| $Mg^{2+}$ | Magnesium ion | $S^{2-}$ | Sulfide ion |
| $Ca^{2+}$ | Calcium ion | $N^{3-}$ | Nitride ion |
| $Ba^{2+}$ | Barium ion | $P^{3-}$ | Phosphide ion |
| $Al^{3+}$ | Aluminum ion | | |
| $Ag^+$ | Silver ion | | |

*Note:* The ions of principal biological importance are highlighted in red.

**TABLE 3.3 Common Polyatomic Cations and Anions**

| Ion | Name |
|---|---|
| $H_3O^+$ | Hydronium |
| $NH_4^+$ | Ammonium |
| $NO_2^-$ | Nitrite |
| $NO_3^-$ | Nitrate |
| $SO_3^{2-}$ | Sulfite |
| $SO_4^{2-}$ | Sulfate |
| $HSO_4^-$ | Hydrogen sulfate |
| $OH^-$ | Hydroxide |
| $CN^-$ | Cyanide |
| $PO_4^{3-}$ | Phosphate |
| $HPO_4^{2-}$ | Hydrogen phosphate |
| $H_2PO_4^-$ | Dihydrogen phosphate |
| $CO_3^{2-}$ | Carbonate |
| $HCO_3^-$ | Bicarbonate |
| $ClO^-$ | Hypochlorite |
| $ClO_2^-$ | Chlorite |
| $ClO_3^-$ | Chlorate |
| $ClO_4^-$ | Perchlorate |
| $CH_3COO^-$ (or $C_2H_3O_2^-$) | Acetate |
| $MnO_4^-$ | Permanganate |
| $Cr_2O_7^{2-}$ | Dichromate |
| $CrO_4^{2-}$ | Chromate |
| $O_2^{2-}$ | Peroxide |

Note: The most commonly encountered ions are highlighted in red.

The polyatomic ion has an *overall* positive or negative charge. Some common polyatomic ions are listed in Table 3.3. You should memorize the formulas, charges, and names of these polyatomic ions, especially those highlighted in red.

When naming compounds containing polyatomic ions, the same rules apply. That is, name the cation and then the anion. Use Roman numerals where appropriate.

Sodium bicarbonate may also be named sodium hydrogen carbonate, a preferred and less ambiguous name. Likewise, $Na_2HPO_4$ is named sodium hydrogen phosphate, and other ionic compounds are named similarly.

| Formula | Cation | Anion | Name |
|---|---|---|---|
| $NH_4Cl$ | $NH_4^+$ | $Cl^-$ | ammonium chloride |
| $Ca(OH)_2$ | $Ca^{2+}$ | $OH^-$ | calcium hydroxide |
| $Na_2SO_4$ | $Na^+$ | $SO_4^{2-}$ | sodium sulfate |
| $NaHCO_3$ | $Na^+$ | $HCO_3^-$ | sodium bicarbonate |
| $Cu(NO_3)_2$ | $Cu^{2+}$ | $NO_3^-$ | copper(II) nitrate |

**Question 3.1** Name each of the following compounds:

a. KCN     b. MgS     c. $Mg(CH_3COO)_2$

**Question 3.2** Name each of the following compounds:

a. $Li_2CO_3$     b. $FeBr_2$     c. $CuSO_4$

## Writing Formulas of Ionic Compounds from the Names of the Compounds

It is also important to be able to write the correct formula when given the compound name. To do this, we must be able to predict the charge of monatomic ions and remember the charge and formula of polyatomic ions. Equally important, the relative number of positive and negative ions in the unit must result in a net (compound) charge of zero. The compounds are electrically neutral. Two examples follow.

---

**EXAMPLE 3.4**   **Writing a Formula When Given the Name of the Compound**

Write the formula of sodium sulfate.

### Solution

Determine the charges of the ions from the periodic table and by memorization of the polyatomic ions. Use subscripts to create a neutral compound.

**Step 1.**  Determine the charges on the ions:

$$\text{Group IA metal} \longrightarrow \text{Na}^+ \quad \text{SO}_4^{2-} \longleftarrow \text{Polyatomic ion (memorize)}$$

**Step 2.**  Balance the charges. Two positive charges are needed to balance the two negative charges of sulfate.
   Hence the formula is: $Na_2SO_4$

---

**Practice Problem 3.4**

Write the formula for each of the following compounds:

   a. calcium carbonate        b. copper(I) sulfate

▶ For Further Practice: **Questions 3.43 and 3.44.**

---

**EXAMPLE 3.5**   **Writing a Formula When Given the Name of the Compound**

Write the formula of magnesium phosphate.

### Solution

Determine the charges of the ions from the periodic table and by memorization of the polyatomic ions. Use subscripts to create a neutral compound.

**Step 1.**  Determine the charges on the ions:

magnesium phosphate

$$\text{Group II metal} \longrightarrow \text{Mg}^{2+} \quad \text{PO}_4^{3-} \longleftarrow \text{Polyatomic ion (memorize)}$$

*Continued…*

**Step 2.** Balance the charges. The least common multiple for 2 and 3 is 6. Obtain $+6$ and $-6$ charges using subscripts. Three $Mg^{2+}$ and two $PO_4^{3-}$ are needed. Parentheses are needed when more than one polyatomic ion is present.

Hence the formula is: $Mg_3(PO_4)_2$

Note that parentheses must be used whenever a subscript accompanies a polyatomic ion.

---

### Practice Problem 3.5

Write the formula for each of the following compounds:

    a. iron(III) sulfide    b. calcium sulfate    c. aluminum oxide

▶ For Further Practice: **Questions 3.45 and 3.46.**

---

LEARNING GOAL

**3**  Name common inorganic compounds using standard naming conventions and recognize the common names of frequently used substances.

By convention the prefix *mono-* is often omitted from the second element as well (dinitrogen oxide, not dinitrogen monoxide). In other cases, common usage retains the prefix (carbon monoxide, not carbon oxide).

## Covalent Compounds

### Naming Covalent Compounds

Most covalent compounds are formed by the reaction of nonmetals. We saw earlier that ionic compounds are not composed of single units but are a part of a massive three-dimensional crystal structure in the solid state. Covalent compounds typically exist as discrete molecules in the solid, liquid, and gas states. This is a distinctive feature of covalently bonded substances.

The conventions for naming covalent compounds follow:

1. The names of the elements are written in the order in which they appear in the formula.
2. A prefix (Table 3.4) indicating the number of each kind of atom found in the unit is placed before the name of the element.
3. If only one atom of a particular kind is the first element present in the molecule, the prefix *mono-* is usually omitted from that first element.
4. The stem of the name of the last element is used with the suffix *-ide*.
5. The final vowel in a prefix is often dropped before *oxide*.

---

**TABLE 3.4 Prefixes Used to Denote Numbers of Atoms in a Compound**

| Prefix | Number of Atoms |
|---|---|
| Mono- | 1 |
| Di- | 2 |
| Tri- | 3 |
| Tetra- | 4 |
| Penta- | 5 |
| Hexa- | 6 |
| Hepta- | 7 |
| Octa- | 8 |
| Nona- | 9 |
| Deca- | 10 |

| EXAMPLE 3.6 | Naming a Covalent Compound |
|---|---|

Name the covalent compound $N_2O_4$.

LEARNING GOAL

**3** Name common inorganic compounds using standard naming conventions and recognize the common names of frequently used substances.

**Solution**

**Step 1.** two nitrogen atoms     four oxygen atoms

**Step 2.** di-     tetra-

**Step 3.** dinitrogen     tetr(a)oxide

The name is dinitrogen tetroxide.

**Practice Problem 3.6**

Name each of the following compounds:

    a. $B_2O_3$     b. NO     c. ICl     d. $PCl_3$     e. $PCl_5$     f. $P_2O_5$

▶ For Further Practice: **Questions 3.41 and 3.42.**

The following are examples of other covalent compounds.

| Formula | Name |
|---|---|
| $N_2O$ | dinitrogen monoxide |
| $NCl_3$ | nitrogen trichloride |
| $SiO_2$ | silicon dioxide |
| $CF_4$ | carbon tetrafluoride |
| CO | carbon monoxide |

## Writing Formulas of Covalent Compounds

Many compounds are so familiar to us that their *common names* are generally used. For example, $H_2O$ is water, $NH_3$ is ammonia, $C_2H_5OH$ (ethanol) is ethyl alcohol, and $C_6H_{12}O_6$ is glucose. It is useful to be able to correlate both systematic and common names with the corresponding molecular formula and vice versa.

When common names are used, formulas of covalent compounds can be written *only* from memory. You *must* remember that water is $H_2O$, ammonia is $NH_3$, and so forth. This is the major disadvantage of common names. Because of their widespread use, however, they cannot be avoided and must be memorized.

Compounds named by using numeric prefixes are easily converted to formulas. Consider the following examples.

| EXAMPLE 3.7 | Writing the Formula of a Covalent Compound |
|---|---|

Write the formula of dinitrogen tetroxide.

LEARNING GOAL

**2** Write the formula of a compound when provided with the name of the compound.

**Solution**

Use prefix meanings to determine subscripts.

**Step 1.** Nitrogen has the prefix *di*—two nitrogen atoms.

*Continued…*

**Step 2.** Oxygen has the prefix *tetr(a)*—four oxygen atoms.

**Step 3.** Hence the formula is $N_2O_4$.

---

**Practice Problem 3.7**

Write the formula of each of the following compounds:

a. diphosphorus pentoxide
b. silicon dioxide
c. carbon tetrabromide
d. oxygen difluoride

▶ For Further Practice: **Questions 3.51 and 3.52.**

---

## 3.3   Properties of Ionic and Covalent Compounds

LEARNING GOAL

4   Predict differences in physical state, melting and boiling points, solid-state structure, and solution chemistry that result from differences in bonding.

*There exist large three-dimensional crystals, similar to ionic compounds, which consist of only covalent bonds. The term* molecule *does not apply to these compounds. Covalent solids are discussed in Section 5.3.*

The differences in ionic and covalent bonding result in markedly different properties for ionic and covalent compounds. Because covalent compounds are typically made up of molecules, distinct units, they have less tendency to form an extended structure in the solid state. Ionic compounds, with ions joined by electrostatic attraction, do not have definable units but form a crystal lattice composed of enormous numbers of positive and negative ions in an extended three-dimensional network. The effects of this basic structural difference are summarized in this section.

### Physical State

All ionic compounds (for example, NaCl, KCl, and $NaNO_3$) are solids at room temperature; covalent compounds may be solids (sugar), liquids ($H_2O$, ethanol), or gases (carbon monoxide, carbon dioxide). The three-dimensional crystal structure that is characteristic of ionic compounds holds them in a rigid, solid arrangement, whereas molecules of covalent compounds may be fixed, as in a solid, or more mobile, a characteristic of liquids and gases.

### Melting and Boiling Points

The **melting point** is the temperature at which a solid is converted to a liquid, and the **boiling point** is the temperature at which a liquid is converted to a gas at a specified pressure. Considerable energy is required to break apart an ionic crystal lattice with uncountable numbers of ionic interactions and convert the ionic substance to a liquid or a gas. As a result, the melting and boiling temperatures for ionic compounds are generally higher than those of covalent compounds, whose molecules interact less strongly in the solid state. A typical ionic compound, sodium chloride, has a melting point of 801°C; methane, a covalent compound, melts at −182°C. Exceptions to this general rule do exist; quartz, a covalent compound of silicon dioxide with an extremely high melting point, is a familiar example.

### Structure of Compounds in the Solid State

Ionic solids are *crystalline,* characterized by a regular structure, whereas covalent solids may either be crystalline or have no regular structure. In the latter case they are said to be *amorphous.*

### Solutions of Ionic and Covalent Compounds

In Chapter 1 we saw that mixtures are either heterogeneous or homogeneous. A homogeneous mixture is a solution. Many ionic solids dissolve in solvents, such

## A MEDICAL PERSPECTIVE

### Rebuilding our Teeth

Tooth decay (dental caries) is an unpleasant fact of life. Aging, diet, and improper dental hygiene lead to the breakdown of a critical building block of teeth, hydroxyapatite, $Ca_5(PO_4)_3OH$. The hydroxyapatite forms a three-dimensional crystalline structure, and this structural unit is the principal component in the exterior, the enamel part of the tooth. Hydroxyapatite is also a major component in the dentin, which is directly underneath the enamel.

Hydroxyapatite breakdown causes the super-strong enamel to become porous and weak. The pores created are ideal hiding places for bacteria that form acids from foods (especially sugars),

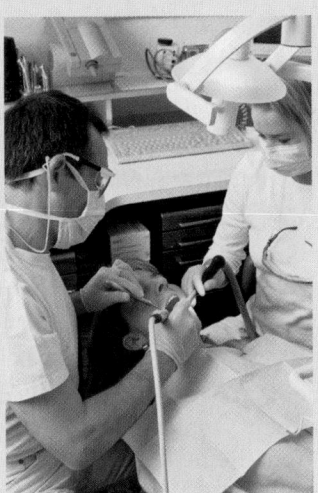

which hasten the decay of the tooth. The traditional remedy is the familiar whine of the drill, removing the decayed material, and unfortunately, some of the unaffected tooth. This step is followed by filling with a carbon-based polymer material or metal amalgam. In extreme cases, removal of the entire tooth is the only suitable remedy.

Researchers at a variety of institutions, such as the University of California, San Francisco, are studying other alternatives, collectively termed *remineralization*. What if teeth, in the early stages of enamel decay, were exposed to solutions containing calcium, phosphate, and fluoride ions? Could the hydroxyapatite be rebuilt through the uptake of its critical components, calcium and phosphate ions? Can the hydroxide ion in the hydroxyapatite be replaced by fluoride ion, producing a more decay-resistant $Ca_5(PO_4)_3F$?

Although conventional drill and fill procedures will be with us for the foreseeable future, early remineralization research is encouraging. Already toothpastes and mouthwashes containing calcium, phosphate, and/or fluoride ions are commercially available. Regular use of these products may at least extend the life of our valuable and irreplaceable natural teeth.

### For Further Understanding

▸ Examine the labels of a variety of toothpastes and mouthwashes on your drugstore's shelves. Do these products contain any of the ions discussed above? Describe their potential benefit.

▸ Many mouthwashes claim to kill bacteria. How can this reduce the incidence of tooth decay?

---

as water. An ionic solid, if soluble, will form positive and negative ions in solution by **dissociation.**

Because ions in water are capable of carrying (conducting) a current of electricity, we refer to these compounds as **electrolytes,** and the solution is termed an *electrolytic solution.* Covalent solids dissolved in solution usually retain their neutral (molecular) character and are **nonelectrolytes.** The solution is not an electrical conductor.

*The role of the solvent in the dissolution of solids is discussed in Section 3.5.*

## 3.4 Drawing Lewis Structures of Molecules and Polyatomic Ions

### Lewis Structures of Molecules

In Section 3.1, we used Lewis symbols of individual atoms to help us understand the bonding process. Lewis symbols for atoms are building blocks that enable construction of *Lewis structures* for compounds and polyatomic ions that depict the role of valence electrons in bonding and structure. To begin to explain the relationship between molecular structure and molecular properties, we will first

### LEARNING GOAL

**5** Draw Lewis structures for covalent compounds and polyatomic ions.

need a set of guidelines to help us write Lewis structures for molecules and poly-atomic ions:

**Step 1.** *Use chemical symbols for the various elements to write the skeletal structure of the compound.* To accomplish this, place the bonded atoms next to one another. This is relatively easy for simple compounds; however, as the number of atoms in the compound increases, the possible number of arrangements increases dramatically. We may be told the pattern of arrangement of the atoms in advance; if not, we can make an intelligent guess and see if a reasonable Lewis structure can be constructed. Three considerations are very important here:

1. *The least electronegative atom will usually be the central atom and often the element written first in the formula.*
2. *Hydrogen and fluorine must occupy terminal (non-central) positions.*
3. *Carbon often forms chains of carbon-carbon covalent bonds.*

**Step 2.** *Determine the number of valence electrons associated with each atom; combine them to determine the total number of valence electrons in the compound.* If we are representing polyatomic cations or anions, we must account for the charge on the ion. Specifically:

1. *For polyatomic cations, subtract one electron for each unit of positive charge. This accounts for the fact that the positive charge arises from electron loss.*
2. *For polyatomic anions, add one electron for each unit of negative charge. This accounts for excess negative charge resulting from electron gain.*

**Step 3.** *Connect the central atom to each of the surrounding atoms with single bonds.* Connection of the atoms uses two electrons per bond. Keep a count of how many valence electrons you placed in the Lewis structure so as not to exceed the previously determined number.

**Step 4.** *Place electrons as lone pairs around the terminal atoms to complete the octet for each.* Remember that hydrogen only needs two electrons. Hydrogen's electron requirement is satisfied simply by a single bond between it and the central atom. Remember to keep a count of electrons used and do not exceed the number of available electrons. Once the terminal atoms have their octet rule satisfied, do the same for the central atom (if you have enough electrons to do so).

**Step 5.** *If the octet rule is not satisfied for all the atoms, move one or more lone pairs on a terminal atom in to make a bond with the central atom.* Double and triple bonds may be formed to ensure that all atoms have an octet.

**Step 6.** *After you are satisfied with the Lewis structure that you have constructed, perform a final electron count.* Count each electron used in the structure; the total must match the number of electrons available.

Now, let us see how these guidelines are applied in the examples that follow.

---

*The central atom is often the element farthest to the left and/or lowest in the periodic table.*

---

*The central atom is often the element in the compound for which there is only one atom.*

---

*Hydrogen is never the central atom.*

---

*Sometimes the octet rule is satisfied for all atoms but electrons are left over from the valence electron count. This problem is addressed under Exceptions to the Octet Rule on page 110.*

---

| EXAMPLE 3.8 | Drawing Lewis Structures of Covalent Compounds | LEARNING GOAL |

Draw the Lewis structure of carbon dioxide, $CO_2$.

**5** Draw Lewis structures for covalent compounds and polyatomic ions.

**Solution**

**Step 1.** Draw a skeletal structure of the molecule, arranging the atoms in their most probable order.

For $CO_2$, two possibilities exist:

C  O  O    and    O  C  O

Our strategy dictates that the least electronegative atom (the one written first in the formula), in this case carbon, is the central atom. Hence the skeletal structure O  C  O may be presumed correct.

**Step 2.** Next, we want to determine the number of valence electrons on each atom and add them to arrive at the total for the compound.

For $CO_2$,

$$1\ C\ atom\ \times 4\ valence\ electrons\ =\ 4\ e^-$$
$$2\ O\ atoms\ \times 6\ valence\ electrons\ =\ 12\ e^-$$
$$\overline{\qquad\qquad\qquad\qquad\qquad\qquad\ 16\ e^-\ total}$$

**Step 3.** Now, use electron pairs to connect the central atom, C, to each oxygen with a single bond.

$$O:C:O$$

**Step 4.** Distribute the electrons around the terminal atoms in pairs, in an attempt to satisfy the octet rule.

$$:\ddot{O}:C:\ddot{O}:$$

**Step 5.** At this point all sixteen electrons have been used. This structure satisfies the octet rule for each oxygen atom, but not the carbon atom (only four electrons surround the carbon). However, when this structure is modified by moving two electrons from each oxygen atom to a position between C and O, each oxygen and carbon atom is surrounded by eight electrons. The octet rule is satisfied, and the structure below is the most probable Lewis structure for $CO_2$.

$$\ddot{O}::C::\ddot{O}$$

In this structure, four electrons (two electron pairs) are located between C and each O, and these electrons are shared in covalent bonds. Because a **single bond** is composed of two electrons (one electron pair) and because four electrons "bond" the carbon atom to each oxygen atom in this structure, there must be two bonds between each oxygen atom and the carbon atom, a **double bond:**

The notation for a single bond : is equivalent to — (one pair of electrons).
The notation for a double bond : : is equivalent to = (two pairs of electrons).

We may write $CO_2$ as shown above or, replacing dots with dashes to indicate bonding electron pairs,

$$\ddot{O}=C=\ddot{O}$$

From this point forward the dash instead of the : will be used to represent the covalent bond.

**Step 6.** Does the answer make sense? As a final step, let us do some "electron accounting." There are eight electron pairs, and they correspond to sixteen valence electrons (8 pair $\times$ 2 e$^-$/pair). Furthermore, there are eight electrons around each atom and the octet rule is satisfied. Therefore

$$\ddot{O}=C=\ddot{O}$$

is a satisfactory way to depict the structure of $CO_2$.

## Practice Problem 3.8

Draw a Lewis structure for each of the following compounds:

a. $H_2O$ (water)   b. $CH_4$ (methane)

▶ For Further Practice: **Question 3.79.**

## A MEDICAL PERSPECTIVE

### Blood Pressure and the Sodium Ion/Potassium Ion Ratio

When you have a physical exam, the physician measures your blood pressure. This indicates the pressure of blood against the walls of the blood vessels each time the heart pumps. A blood pressure reading is always characterized by two numbers. With every heartbeat there is an increase in pressure; this is the systolic blood pressure. When the heart relaxes between contractions, the pressure drops; this is the diastolic pressure. Thus the blood pressure is expressed as two values—for instance, 117/72—measured in millimeters (mm) of mercury. Hypertension is simply defined as high blood pressure. To the body it means that the heart must work too hard to pump blood, and this can lead to heart failure or heart disease.

Heart disease accounts for 50% of all deaths in the United States. Epidemiological studies correlate the following major risk factors with heart disease: heredity, sex, race, age, diabetes, cigarette smoking, high blood cholesterol, and hypertension. Obviously, we can do little about our age, sex, and genetic heritage, but we can stop smoking, limit dietary cholesterol, and maintain a normal blood pressure.

The number of Americans with hypertension is alarmingly high: sixty million adults and children. More than ten million of these individuals take medication to control blood pressure, at a cost of nearly 2.5 billion dollars each year. In many cases, blood pressure can be controlled without medication by increasing physical activity, losing weight, decreasing consumption of alcohol, and limiting intake of sodium.

It has been estimated that the average American ingests 7.5–10 grams (g) of salt (NaCl) each day. Because NaCl is about 40% (by mass) sodium ions, this amounts to 3–4 g of sodium daily. Until 1989 the Food and Nutrition Board of the National Academy of Sciences National Research Council's defined estimated safe and adequate daily dietary intake (ESADDI)

of sodium ion was 1.1–3.3 g. Clearly, Americans exceed this recommendation.

Recently, studies have shown that excess sodium is not the sole consideration in the control of blood pressure. More important is the sodium ion/potassium ion ($Na^+/K^+$) ratio. That ratio should be about 0.6; in other words, our diet should contain about 67% more potassium than sodium. Does the typical American diet fall within this limit? Definitely not! Young American males (25–30 years old) consume a diet with a $Na^+/K^+ = 1.07$, and the diet of females of the same age range has a $Na^+/K^+ = 1.04$. It is little wonder that so many Americans suffer from hypertension.

How can we restrict sodium in the diet, while increasing potassium? A variety of foods are low in sodium and high in potassium. These include fresh fruits and vegetables and fruit juices, a variety of cereals, unsalted nuts, and cooked dried beans (legumes). Unfortunately, some high-sodium, low-potassium foods are very popular. Most of these are processed or prepared foods. This points out how difficult it can be to control sodium in the diet. The majority of the sodium that we ingest comes from commercially prepared foods. The consumer must read the nutritional information printed on cans and packages to determine whether the sodium levels are within acceptable limits.

**For Further Understanding**

▶ Find several processed food products on the shelves of your local grocery store; read the labels and calculate the sodium ion/potassium ion ratio.

▶ Describe each product that you have chosen in terms of its suitability for inclusion in the diet of a person with moderately elevated blood pressure.

---

**EXAMPLE 3.9**    **Drawing Lewis Structures of Covalent Compounds**

LEARNING GOAL

Draw the Lewis structure of ammonia, $NH_3$.

**5** Draw Lewis structures for covalent compounds and polyatomic ions.

**Solution**

**Step 1.** When trying to implement the first step in our strategy, we may be tempted to make H our central atom because it is less electronegative than N. But, remember the margin note in this section:

"Hydrogen is *never* the central atom."

Hence:

H

H  N  H

is our skeletal structure.

**Step 2.** Applying our strategy to determine the total valence electrons for the molecule, we find that there are five valence electrons in nitrogen and one in each of the three hydrogens, for a total of eight valence electrons.

**Step 3.** Applying our strategy for connection of the terminal atoms to the central atom with single bonds results in the following Lewis structure:

$$H-\underset{\displaystyle |}{\overset{\displaystyle H}{N}}-H$$

**Step 4.** The terminal atoms already have the octet rule satisfied since each hydrogen atom requires only two valence electrons. The structure in step 3 only has six valence electrons on the N atom. Place two additional electrons on N, giving the following structure:

$$H-\underset{\displaystyle \underset{..}{|}}{\overset{\displaystyle H}{N}}-H$$

Notice the lines used to represent the sharing of electrons or the bond between the atoms. Each line represents two valence electrons.

Does the answer make sense? This structure uses the eight valence electrons available and satisfies the octet rule for each atom.

**Practice Problem 3.9**

Draw a Lewis structure for each of the following compounds:

a. HCN    b. $N_2$

▶ For Further Practice: **Question 3.80.**

Many compounds have more than one central atom. Example 3.10, illustrates how to draw structures for these compounds.

**EXAMPLE 3.10**   **Drawing Lewis Structures for Compounds with Multiple Central Atoms**

Draw the Lewis structure for ethane, $C_2H_4$.

**LEARNING GOAL**

**5** Draw Lewis structures for covalent compounds and polyatomic ions.

**Solution**

**Step 1.** For the skeletal structure, we know two facts: Hydrogen cannot be the central atom and carbon often forms chains. This gives the structure as follows:

$$\begin{array}{cc} H & H \\ C & C \\ H & H \end{array}$$

**Step 2.** Determine the total number of valence electrons.

$$2\text{ C atoms} \times 4 \text{ valence electrons} = 8\,e^-$$
$$4\text{ H atoms} \times 1 \text{ valence electrons} = 4\,e^-$$
$$12\,e^- \text{ total}$$

**Step 3.** Connect the atoms with single bonds:

*Continued…*

$$
\begin{array}{ccc}
\text{H} & & \text{H} \\
\diagdown & & \diagup \\
& \text{C} - \text{C} & \\
\diagup & & \diagdown \\
\text{H} & & \text{H}
\end{array}
$$

This uses ten valence electrons. We have two more to distribute.

**Step 4.** The hydrogen atoms do not need any more electrons. We can satisfy the octet rule for one of the carbon atoms as follows:

$$
\begin{array}{ccc}
\text{H} & & \text{H} \\
\diagdown & & \diagup \\
& \overset{..}{\text{C}} - \text{C} & \\
\diagup & & \diagdown \\
\text{H} & & \text{H}
\end{array}
$$

**Step 5.** The carbon on the right has only six valence electrons. Shift the lone pair on the left carbon to form a double bond between the carbon atoms.

$$
\begin{array}{ccc}
\text{H} & & \text{H} \\
\diagdown & & \diagup \\
& \text{C} = \text{C} & \\
\diagup & & \diagdown \\
\text{H} & & \text{H}
\end{array}
$$

**Step 6.** Does the answer make sense? Verify that the number of electrons used in the structure matches the number of electrons determined in Step 2, that is 12 e$^-$. There are six bonding pairs, $6 \times 2 = 12$. Therefore the structure above is correct.

*Note:* Compounds that consist of only carbon and hydrogen (hydrocarbons) are often written to convey information concerning connectivity. The compound in this example can be written as $CH_2CH_2$ (a condensed formula). Writing it in this way indicates that the carbons are connected to each other and that each carbon has two hydrogen atoms connected to it.

## Practice Problem 3.10

Draw a Lewis structure for each of the following compounds:

  a. $N_2H_4$     b. $CH_3CH_2CH_3$

▶ For Further Practice: **Questions 3.89 and 3.92.**

## Lewis Structures of Polyatomic Ions

The strategies for writing the Lewis structures of polyatomic ions are similar to those for neutral compounds. There is, however, one major difference: the charge on the ion must be accounted for when computing the total number of valence electrons.

**EXAMPLE 3.11**    **Drawing Lewis Structures of Polyatomic Anions**

Draw the Lewis structure of the carbonate ion, $CO_3^{2-}$.

**Solution**

**Step 1.** Carbon is less electronegative than oxygen. Therefore carbon is the central atom. The carbonate ion has the following skeletal structure and charge:

$$\left[ \begin{array}{c} O \\ O \quad C \quad O \end{array} \right]^{2-}$$

The use of square brackets with the charge outside of the brackets is standard when drawing Lewis structures for polyatomic ions.

**Step 2.** The total number of valence electrons is determined by adding one electron for each unit of negative charge:

$$
\begin{aligned}
1 \text{ C atom} \times 4 \text{ valence electrons} &= 4 \text{ e}^- \\
3 \text{ O atoms} \times 6 \text{ valence electrons} &= 18 \text{ e}^- \\
\text{electrons for } -2 \text{ charge} &= 2 \text{ e}^- \\
\hline
24 \text{ e}^- \text{ total}
\end{aligned}
$$

**Step 3.** Connect the O atoms to the central atom using single bonds. This step uses six of the valence electrons.

$$\left[ \begin{array}{c} O \\ | \\ O - C - O \end{array} \right]^{2-}$$

**Step 4.** Start placing lone-pair electrons around the terminal atoms, giving each an octet. Do not exceed the twenty-four available electrons.

$$\left[ \begin{array}{c} :\ddot{O}: \\ | \\ :\ddot{O} - C - \ddot{O}: \end{array} \right]^{2-}$$

**Step 5.** The central atom only has six valence electrons surrounding it. Move a lone pair from one of the O atoms to form another bond with C. In this example, a lone pair from the top O was moved to make a second bond between it and the C.

$$\left[ \begin{array}{c} :O: \\ \| \\ :\ddot{O} - C - \ddot{O}: \end{array} \right]^{2-}$$

**Step 6.** Does the answer make sense? Each atom has eight valence electrons surrounding it, and the total number of electrons used is twenty-four.

---

**Practice Problem 3.11**

Draw the Lewis structure of $O_2^{2-}$.

▶ For Further Practice: **Questions 3.83 and 3.84.**

---

| EXAMPLE 3.12 | **Drawing Lewis Structures of Polyatomic Anions** |
|---|---|

LEARNING GOAL

Draw the Lewis structure of the acetate ion, $CH_3COO^-$.

**Solution**

**5** Draw Lewis structures for covalent compounds and polyatomic ions.

This species has multiple central atoms and a negative charge.

**Step 1.** A commonly encountered anion, the acetate ion has a skeletal structure that is more complex than any of the examples that we have studied thus far. Which element should we choose as the central atom? We have three choices: H, O, and C. H is eliminated because hydrogen can never be the central atom. Oxygen is more electronegative than carbon, so carbon must be the central atom. There are two carbon atoms; often they are

*Continued…*

joined. Further clues are obtained from the formula itself; $CH_3COO^-$ implies three hydrogen atoms attached to the first carbon atom and two oxygen atoms joined to the second carbon. A plausible skeletal structure is:

$$\left[\begin{array}{ccc} & H & O \\ H & C & C \\ & H & O \end{array}\right]^-$$

**Step 2.** The pool of valence electrons for anions is determined by adding one electron for each unit of negative charge:

$$
\begin{array}{lll}
2\,C\text{ atoms} \times 4\text{ valence electrons} & = & 8\text{ e}^- \\
3\,H\text{ atoms} \times 1\text{ valence electron} & = & 3\text{ e}^- \\
2\,O\text{ atoms} \times 6\text{ valence electrons} & = & 12\text{ e}^- \\
\underline{\text{electron for }-1\text{ charge}} & \underline{=} & \underline{1\text{ e}^-} \\
& & 24\text{ e}^-\text{ total}
\end{array}
$$

**Step 3.** Connect the terminal atoms to the two central carbon atoms.

$$\left[\begin{array}{c} H \quad\quad O \\ | \quad\quad / \\ H-C-C \\ | \quad\quad \backslash \\ H \quad\quad O \end{array}\right]^-$$

This step used twelve valence electrons.

**Step 4.** Place lone-pair electrons around the atoms to give an octet, starting with terminal O atoms. (Remember to keep in mind the twenty-four electrons available, and do not put lone-pair electrons around H.)

$$\left[\begin{array}{c} H \quad\quad :\ddot{O}: \\ | \quad\quad / \\ H-C-C \\ | \quad\quad \backslash \\ H \quad\quad :\ddot{O}: \end{array}\right]^-$$

This structure uses all twenty-four electrons, but one of the C atoms only has six valence electrons.

**Step 5.** Move one of the lone pairs on an O to create an additional bond between C and O.

$$\left[\begin{array}{c} H \quad\quad :O: \\ | \quad\quad // \\ H-C-C \\ | \quad\quad \backslash \\ H \quad\quad :\ddot{O}: \end{array}\right]^-$$

**Step 6.** Does the answer make sense? All twenty-four electrons are used, and the octet rule is satisfied for all atoms in the structure.

## Practice Problem 3.12

Draw a Lewis structure describing the bonding in each of the following polyatomic ions:

    a. the bicarbonate ion, $HCO_3^-$      b. the phosphate ion, $PO_4^{3-}$

▶ For Further Practice: **Question 3.91.**

## Lewis Structure, Stability, Multiple Bonds, and Bond Energies

Hydrogen, oxygen, and nitrogen are present in the atmosphere as diatomic gases, $H_2$, $O_2$, and $N_2$. All are covalent molecules. Their stability and reactivity, however, are quite different. Hydrogen is an explosive material, sometimes used as a fuel. Oxygen, although more stable than hydrogen, reacts with fuels in combustion. The explosion of the space shuttle *Challenger* resulted from the reaction of massive amounts of hydrogen and oxygen. Nitrogen, on the other hand, is extremely non-reactive. Because nitrogen makes up about 80% of the atmosphere, it dilutes the oxygen, which accounts for only about 20% of the atmosphere.

Breathing pure oxygen for long periods, although necessary in some medical situations, causes the breakdown of nasal and lung tissue over time. Oxygen diluted with nonreactive nitrogen is an ideal mixture for humans and animals to breathe.

Why is there such a great difference in reactivity among these three gases? We can explain this, in part, in terms of their bonding characteristics. The Lewis structure for $H_2$ (two valence electrons) is

$$H - H$$

For oxygen (twelve valence electrons, six on each atom), the only Lewis structure that satisfies the octet rule is

$$\overset{..}{O} = \overset{..}{O}$$

The Lewis structure of $N_2$ (ten total valence electrons) must be

$$: N \equiv N :$$

Therefore:

$N_2$ has a *triple bond* (six bonding electrons).
$O_2$ has a *double bond* (four bonding electrons).
$H_2$ has a *single bond* (two bonding electrons).

A **triple bond,** in which three pairs of electrons are shared by two atoms, is very stable. More energy is required to break a triple bond than a double bond, and a double bond is stronger than a single bond. Stability is related to the bond energy. The **bond energy** is the amount of energy, in units of kilocalories (kcal) or kilojoules (kJ), required to break a bond holding two atoms together. Bond energy is therefore a *measure* of stability. The values of bond energies decrease in the order *triple bond > double bond > single bond*. The H—H bond energy is 436 kJ/mol. This amount of energy is necessary to break a H—H bond. In contrast, the O=O bond energy is 499 kJ/mol and the N≡N bond energy is 941 kJ/mol.

The bond length is related to the presence or absence of multiple bonding. The distance of separation of two nuclei is greatest for a single bond, less for a double bond, and still less for a triple bond. The *bond length* decreases in the order *single bond > double bond > triple bond*.

**Question 3.3** Contrast a single and a double bond with regard to:
  a. distance of separation of the bonded nuclei
  b. strength of the bond

How are the distance of separation and bond strength related?

**Question 3.4** Two nitrogen atoms in a nitrogen molecule are held together more strongly than the two chlorine atoms in a chlorine molecule. Explain this fact by comparing their respective Lewis structures.

## Isomers

**Isomers** are compounds that share the same molecular formula but have different structures. Hydrocarbons (compounds that contain only hydrogen and carbon

**6** Describe the relationship between stability and bond energy.

The term *bond order* is sometimes used to distinguish among single, double, and triple bonds. A bond order of one corresponds to a single bond, two corresponds to a double bond, and three corresponds to a triple bond.

The mole (mol) is simply a unit denoting quantity. Just as a *dozen* eggs represents twelve eggs, a mole of bonds is $6.022 \times 10^{23}$ bonds (see Chapter 4).

*n*-pentane

2-methylbutane

2,2-dimethylpropane

---

The compound *n*-pentane, above, is the "straight chain" isomer. Notice that the carbon are attached in a chain; however, they are not actually in a *straight* line.

---

atoms) frequently exhibit this property. For example, butane, C₄H₁₀, has two isomeric forms. One isomer, termed normal butane, *n*-butane, has a structure characterized by the four carbon atoms being linked in a chain; the other, termed isobutane, has a three-carbon chain, with the fourth carbon attached to the middle carbon.

$$\begin{array}{c} \text{H H H H} \\ | \ | \ | \ | \\ \text{H—C—C—C—C—H} \\ | \ | \ | \ | \\ \text{H H H H} \end{array} \qquad \begin{array}{c} \text{H} \\ | \\ \text{H—C—H} \\ \text{H} \ | \ \text{H} \\ | \ | \ | \\ \text{H—C—C—C—H} \\ | \ | \ | \\ \text{H H H} \end{array}$$

*n*-Butane (C₄H₁₀)          Isobutane (C₄H₁₀)

Notice that both structures, although clearly different, contain four carbon atoms and ten hydrogen atoms. Owing to their structural differences, each has a different melting point and boiling point. In fact, all of their physical properties differ at least slightly. These differences in properties clearly show that, in fact, *n*-butane and isobutane are different compounds.

As the size of the hydrocarbon increases, the number of possible isomers increases dramatically. A five-carbon hydrocarbon has three isomers, but a thirty-carbon hydrocarbon has over 400 million possible isomers. Petroleum is largely a complex mixture of hydrocarbons, and the principal reason for this complexity lies in the tremendous variety of possible isomers present.

The three isomers of pentane (a five-carbon hydrocarbon) are depicted in the figure in the margin.

## Lewis Structures and Resonance

In some cases we find that it is possible to write more than one Lewis structure that satisfies the octet rule for a particular compound. Consider sulfur dioxide, SO₂. Its skeletal structure is

O   S   O

Total valence electrons may be calculated as follows:

$$\begin{array}{r} 1 \text{ sulfur atom} \times 6 \text{ valence e}^- / = 6 \text{ e}^- \\ +2 \text{ oxygen atoms} \times 6 \text{ valence e}^- / = 12 \text{ e}^- \\ \hline 18 \text{ e}^- \text{ total} \end{array}$$

The resulting Lewis structures are

Ö=S̈—Ö:    and    :Ö—S̈=Ö

Both satisfy the octet rule. However, experimental evidence shows no double bond in SO₂. The two sulfur-oxygen bonds are equivalent. Apparently, neither structure accurately represents the structure of SO₂, and neither actually exists. The actual structure is said to be an average or *hybrid* of these two Lewis structures. When a compound has two or more Lewis structures that contribute to the real structure, we say that the compound displays the property of **resonance.** The contributing Lewis structures are *resonance forms.* The true structure, a hybrid of the resonance forms, is known as a *resonance hybrid* and may be represented as:

Ö=S̈—Ö:    ↔    :Ö—S̈=Ö

A common analogy might help to clarify this concept. A horse and a donkey may be crossbred to produce a hybrid, the mule. The mule doesn't look or behave exactly like either parent, yet it has attributes of both. The resonance hybrid of a molecule has properties of each resonance form but is not identical to any one form. Unlike the mule, resonance hybrids *do not actually exist*. Rather, they comprise a model that results from the failure of any one Lewis structure to agree with experimentally obtained structural information.

The presence of resonance enhances molecular stability. The more resonance forms that exist, the greater is the stability of the molecule they represent. This concept is important in understanding the chemical reactions of many complex organic molecules and is used extensively in organic chemistry.

> It is a misconception to picture the real molecule as oscillating back and forth among the various resonance structures. Resonance is a modeling strategy designed to help us visualize electron arrangements too complex to be adequately explained by the simple Lewis structure.

---

**EXAMPLE 3.13    Drawing Resonance Hybrids of Covalently Bonded Compounds**

Draw the possible resonance structures of the nitrate ion, $NO_3^-$, and represent them as a resonance hybrid.

LEARNING GOAL

**5** Draw Lewis structures for covalent compounds and polyatomic ions.

**Solution**

**Step 1.** Nitrogen is less electronegative than oxygen; therefore, nitrogen is the central atom and the skeletal structure is:

$$\left[ \begin{array}{ccc} & O & \\ O & N & O \end{array} \right]^-$$

**Step 2.** The pool of valence electrons for anions is determined by adding one electron for each unit of negative charge:

$$
\begin{array}{lcl}
1\ \text{N atom} \times 5\ \text{valence electrons} & = & 5\ e^- \\
3\ \text{O atoms} \times 6\ \text{valence electrons} & = & 18\ e^- \\
\underline{+1\ \text{negative charge} \qquad\qquad\quad = \quad 1\ e^-} \\
& & 24\ e^-\ \text{total}
\end{array}
$$

**Step 3.** First, connect O atoms to the N atom using single bonds.

$$\left[ \begin{array}{c} O \\ | \\ O-N-O \end{array} \right]^-$$

**Step 4.** Place lone-pair electrons around the terminal O atoms until each atom has an octet. Do not exceed twenty-four electrons.

$$\left[ \begin{array}{c} :\ddot{O}: \\ | \\ :\ddot{O}-N-\ddot{O}: \end{array} \right]^-$$

This structure uses twenty-four electrons; however, the central atom only has six valence electrons.

**Step 5.** Shift a lone pair on one of the O atoms to become a bond between the O and N. To draw all possible resonance structures, this shift can be drawn for each of the oxygen atoms.

$$\left[ \begin{array}{c} :\ddot{O}: \\ | \\ \ddot{O}=N-\ddot{O}: \end{array} \right]^- \longleftrightarrow \left[ \begin{array}{c} :O: \\ \| \\ :\ddot{O}-N-\ddot{O}: \end{array} \right]^- \longleftrightarrow \left[ \begin{array}{c} :\ddot{O}: \\ | \\ :\ddot{O}-N=\ddot{O} \end{array} \right]^-$$

**Step 6.** Does the answer make sense? Each resonance structure uses twenty-four valence electrons and the octet rule is obeyed for each atom.

*Continued…*

**Practice Problem 3.13**

a. $SeO_2$, like $SO_2$, has two resonance forms. Draw their Lewis structures.

b. Explain any similarities between the structures for $SeO_2$ and $SO_2$ in light of periodic relationships.

▶ For Further Practice: **Questions 3.87 and 3.88.**

## Lewis Structures and Exceptions to the Octet Rule

The octet rule is remarkable in its ability to realistically model bonding and structure in covalent compounds. But, like any model, it does not adequately describe all systems. Beryllium, boron, and aluminum, in particular, tend to form compounds in which they are surrounded by fewer than eight electrons. This situation is termed an *incomplete octet*. Example 3.14 illustrates how to draw the Lewis structure for such a case.

---

**EXAMPLE 3.14**   **Drawing Lewis Structures of Covalently Bonded Compounds That Are Exceptions to the Octet Rule**

Draw the Lewis structure of beryllium hydride, $BeH_2$.

LEARNING GOAL

**5**  Draw Lewis structures for covalent compounds and polyatomic ions.

**Solution**

**Step 1.** A reasonable skeletal structure of $BeH_2$ is:

$$H \quad Be \quad H$$

**Step 2.** The total number of valence electrons in $BeH_2$ is:

$$1 \text{ beryllium atom} \ \times 2 \text{ valence } e^- = 2\,e^-$$
$$\underline{2 \text{ hydrogen atoms} \times 1 \text{ valence } e^- = 2\,e^-}$$
$$4\,e^- \text{ total}$$

**Step 3.** The resulting Lewis structure must be:

$$H—Be—H$$

**Step 4.** It is apparent that there is no way to satisfy the octet rule for Be in this compound. Consequently, $BeH_2$ is an exception to the octet rule. It contains an incomplete octet.

---

**Practice Problem 3.14**

The $BCl_3$ molecule has an incomplete octet around B. Draw the Lewis structure of $BCl_3$.

▶ For Further Practice: **Questions 3.101 and 102.**

Other molecules, such as nitric oxide:

$$\overset{..}{\underset{.}{N}}=\overset{..}{\underset{..}{O}}$$

are termed *odd-electron* molecules. Note that it is impossible to pair all electrons to achieve an octet simply because the compound contains an odd number of valence electrons.

Elements in the third period and beyond may involve *d* orbitals and form an *expanded octet*, with ten or even twelve electrons surrounding the central atom. Examples 3.15 and 3.16 illustrate the expanded octet.

**EXAMPLE 3.15**   **Drawing Lewis Structures of Covalently Bonded Compounds That Are Exceptions to the Octet Rule**

LEARNING GOAL

**5**  Draw Lewis structures for covalent compounds and polyatomic ions.

Draw the Lewis structure of phosphorus pentafluoride.

**Solution**

**Step 1.**  The formula is $PF_5$. Phosphorus is the central atom, with five terminal fluorine atoms.

$$
\begin{array}{ccc}
 & F & \quad F \\
F & \quad P & \\
 & F & \quad F
\end{array}
$$

**Step 2.**  The total number of valence electrons is:

$$
\begin{array}{rcl}
1 \text{ phosphorus atom} \times 5 \text{ valence } e^- &=& 5\,e^- \\
5 \text{ fluorine atoms} \times 7 \text{ valence } e^- &=& 35\,e^- \\
\hline
 & & 40\,e^- \text{ total}
\end{array}
$$

**Steps 3 and 4.**  Connect five fluorine atoms to the phosphorus atom with single bonds. This gives phosphorus ten valence electrons. Phosphorus is a third period element; it may have an expanded octet. Distribute the electrons around each F in the skeletal structure (completing the fluorine octets), which results in the Lewis structure:

$PF_5$ is an example of a compound with an expanded octet. The central phosphorus atom is surrounded by ten electrons.

**Practice Problem 3.15**

The $SF_6$ molecule has an expanded octet around S. Draw the Lewis structure of $SF_6$.

▶ For Further Practice: **Question 3.103.**

**EXAMPLE 3.16**   **Drawing Lewis Structures of Covalently Bonded Compounds That Are Exceptions to the Octet Rule**

LEARNING GOAL

**5**  Draw Lewis structures for covalent compounds and polyatomic ions.

Draw the Lewis structure of $SF_4$.

**Solution**

**Step 1.**  Sulfur is the central atom with four fluorine atoms surrounding the sulfur.

$$
\begin{array}{ccc}
 & F & \\
F & S & F \\
 & F &
\end{array}
$$

*Continued…*

**Step 2.** The total number of valence electrons is:

$$
\begin{array}{llll}
1 \text{ sulfur atom} & \times\ 6 \text{ valence e}^- & = & 6 \text{ e}^- \\
4 \text{ fluorine atoms} & \times\ 7 \text{ valence e}^- & = & 28 \text{ e}^- \\
\hline
& & = & 34 \text{ e}^- \text{ total}
\end{array}
$$

**Step 3.** Connect the four fluorine atoms with single bonds to the sulfur. This uses eight electrons.

$$
\begin{array}{c}
\text{F} \\
| \\
\text{F} - \text{S} - \text{F} \\
| \\
\text{F}
\end{array}
$$

**Step 4.** Give each terminal atom eight valence electrons.

$$
\begin{array}{c}
:\ddot{\text{F}}: \\
| \\
:\ddot{\text{F}} - \text{S} - \ddot{\text{F}}: \\
| \\
:\ddot{\text{F}}:
\end{array}
$$

**Step 5.** The octet rule *is* satisfied for all atoms. However, we have only used thirty-two electrons and we must use all thirty-four electrons. The two extra electrons will be placed on the central atom.

$$
\begin{array}{c}
:\ddot{\text{F}}: \\
|\cdot \\
:\ddot{\text{F}} - \text{S} - \ddot{\text{F}}: \\
| \\
:\ddot{\text{F}}:
\end{array}
$$

**Step 6.** Now check that the number of electrons used is equal to the number of electrons determined in Step 2.

**Practice Problem 3.16**

Draw the Lewis structure of $SeCl_4$.

▶ For Further Practice: **Question 3.104.**

## Lewis Structures and Molecular Geometry; VSEPR Theory

The shape of a molecule plays a large part in determining its properties and reactivity. We may predict the shapes of various molecules by inspecting their Lewis structures for the orientation of their electron pairs. The covalent bond, for instance, in which bonding electrons are localized between the nuclear centers of the atoms, is *directional;* the bond has a specific orientation in space between the bonded atoms. The specific orientation of electron pairs in covalent molecules imparts a characteristic shape to the molecules. Consider the following series of molecules whose Lewis structures are shown.

$BeH_2$        H—Be—H

$BF_3$

$$:\ddot{F}—\overset{\displaystyle :\ddot{F}:}{\underset{}{B}}—\ddot{F}:$$

$CH_4$

$$H—\overset{\displaystyle H}{\underset{\displaystyle H}{C}}—H$$

$NH_3$

$$H—\overset{\displaystyle ..}{N}—H \atop \displaystyle H$$

$H_2O$        $H—\ddot{O}—H$

**ANIMATIONS**
- Valence-Shell Electron-Pair Repulsion Theory
- VSEPR and Molecular Geometry

The electron pairs around the central atom of the molecule arrange themselves to minimize electronic repulsion. This means that the electron pairs arrange themselves so that they can be as far as possible from each other. We may use this fact to predict molecular shape. This approach is termed the **valence-shell electron-pair repulsion (VSEPR) theory.**

Let's see how the VSEPR theory can be used to describe the bonding and structure of each of the preceding molecules.

### BeH₂

As we saw in Example 3.14, beryllium hydride has two bonded atoms around the beryllium atom. These electron pairs have minimum repulsion if they are located as far apart as possible while still bonding the hydrogen atoms to the central atom. This condition is met if the electron pairs are located on opposite sides of the molecule, resulting in a **linear structure,** 180° apart:

$$H—Be—H$$

The *bond angle,* the angle between H—Be and Be—H bonds, formed by the two bonding pairs is 180° (Figure 3.6).

$BeF_2$, $CS_2$, and HCN are other examples of molecules that exhibit linear geometry. Multiple bonds are treated identically to single bonds in VSEPR theory. For example, the Lewis structure of HCN is H—C≡N:. The bonded atoms on either side of carbon are positioned 180° from each other. Instead of counting bonding electrons to predict molecular shape, it is more appropriate to count bonded atoms. The central atom has two bonded atoms.

### BF₃

Boron trifluoride has three bonded atoms around the central atom. The Lewis structure, as illustrated above shows boron as electron deficient. Placing the electron pairs in a plane, forming a triangle, minimizes the electron-pair repulsion in this molecule, as depicted in Figure 3.7.

Such a structure is **trigonal planar,** and each F—B—F bond angle is 120°. We also find that compounds with central atoms in the same group of the periodic table have similar geometry. Aluminum, in the same group as boron, produces compounds such as $AlH_3$, which is also trigonal planar.

### CH₄

Methane has four bonded atoms around carbon. Here, minimum electron repulsion is achieved by arranging the electrons at the corners of a tetrahedron (Figure 3.8). Each H—C—H bond angle is 109.5°. Methane has a three-dimensional **tetrahedral structure.** Silicon, in the same group as carbon, forms compounds such as $SiCl_4$ and $SiH_4$ that also have tetrahedral structures.

**Figure 3.6** Bonding and geometry in beryllium hydride, $BeH_2$. (a) Linear geometry in $BeH_2$. (b) Computer-generated model of linear $BeH_2$.

**ANIMATIONS**
- The Geometry of $BeF_2$
- The Geometry of $BF_3$

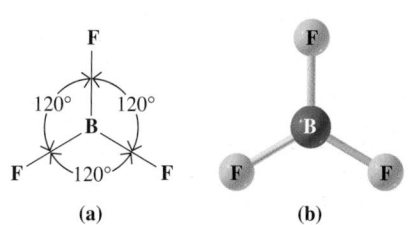

**Figure 3.7** Bonding and geometry in boron trifluoride, $BF_3$. (a) Trigonal planar geometry in $BF_3$. (b) Computer-generated model of trigonal planar $BF_3$.

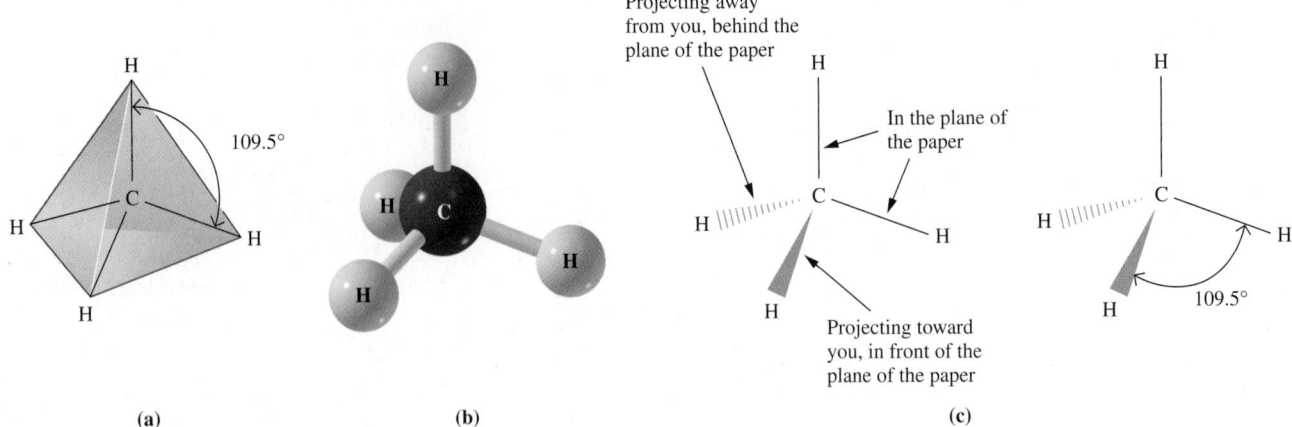

**Figure 3.8** Representations of the three-dimensional structure of methane, $CH_4$. (a) Tetrahedral methane structure. (b) Computer-generated model of tetrahedral methane. (c) Three-dimensional representation of structure (b).

**ANIMATIONS**
- The Geometry of $CH_4$
- The Geometry of $NH_3$
- The Geometry of $H_2O$

## NH₃

Ammonia has three bonded atoms and one lone pair (four groups) about the central atom. In contrast to methane, in which all four electron pairs are bonding, ammonia has three pairs of bonding electrons and one nonbonding lone pair of electrons. We might expect $CH_4$ and $NH_3$ to have electron-pair arrangements that are similar but not identical. The lone pair in ammonia is more negative than the bonding pairs; some of the negative charge on the bonding pairs is offset by the presence of the hydrogen atoms with their positive nuclei. Thus the arrangement of electron pairs in ammonia is distorted.

The hydrogen atoms in ammonia are pushed closer together than in methane (Figure 3.9). The bond angle is 107° because lone pair–bond pair repulsions are greater than bond pair–bond pair repulsions. The structure or shape is termed *trigonal pyramidal*, and the molecule is termed a **trigonal pyramidal molecule.**

## H₂O

Water has two bonded atoms and two lone pairs (four groups) about the central atom. These four electron pairs are approximately tetrahedral to each other; however, because of the difference between bonding and nonbonding electrons, noted earlier, the tetrahedral relationship is only approximate.

The **bent** (or *angular*) **structure** has a bond angle of 104.5°, which is 5° smaller than the tetrahedral angle, because of the repulsive effects of the lone pairs of electrons (Figure 3.10).

**Figure 3.9** The structure of the ammonia molecule. (a) Pyramidal ammonia structure. (b) Computer-generated model of pyramidal ammonia. (c) A three-dimensional sketch showing the H—N—H bond angle.

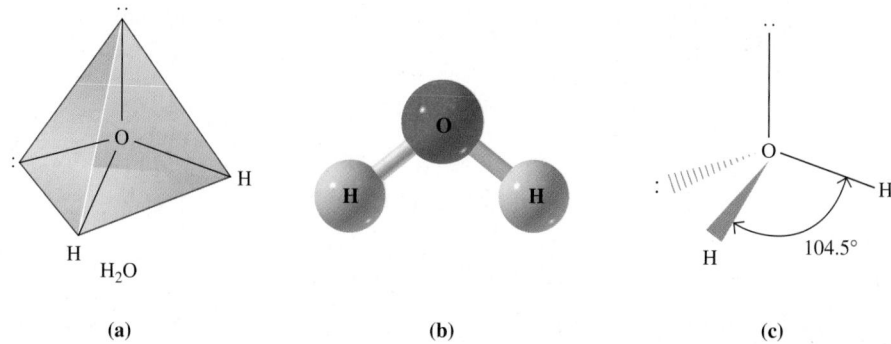

**Figure 3.10** The structure of the water molecule. (a) Bent water structure. (b) Computer-generated model of bent water. (c) A three-dimensional sketch showing the H—O—H bond angle in water.

The characteristics of linear, trigonal planar, trigonal pyramidal, bent, and tetrahedral structures are summarized in Table 3.5.

## Periodic Structural Relationships

The molecules considered previously contain the central atoms Be (Group IIA), B (Group IIIA), C (Group IVA), N (Group VA), and O (Group VIA). We may expect that a number of other compounds containing the same central atom will have structures with similar geometries. This is an approximation, not always true, but still useful in expanding our ability to write reasonable, geometrically accurate structures for a large number of compounds.

The periodic similarity of group members is also useful in predictions involving bonding. Consider Group VIA, oxygen, sulfur, and selenium. Each has six valence electrons. Each needs two more electrons to complete its octet. Each should react with hydrogen, forming $H_2O$, $H_2S$, and $H_2Se$.

If we recall that $H_2O$ is a bent molecule with the following Lewis structure and shape,

$$H-\overset{..}{\underset{..}{O}}-H \qquad \overset{O}{\underset{H \quad H}{\diagup \diagdown}}$$

**TABLE 3.5** Molecular Structure: The Geometry of a Molecule Is Affected by the Number of Nonbonded Electron Pairs Around the Central Atom and the Number of Bonded Atoms

| Bonded Atoms | Nonbonding Electron Pairs | Bond Angle | Molecular Structure | Example | Structure |
|---|---|---|---|---|---|
| 2 | 0 | 180° | Linear | $CO_2$ | |
| 3 | 0 | 120° | Trigonal planar | $SO_3$ | |
| 2 | 1 | <120° | Bent | $SO_2$ | |
| 4 | 0 | 109.5° | Tetrahedral | $CH_4$ | |
| 3 | 1 | ~107° | Trigonal pyramidal | $NH_3$ | |
| 2 | 2 | ~104.5° | Bent | $H_2O$ | |

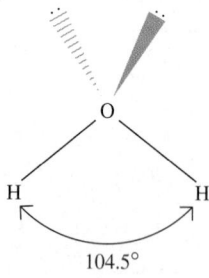

104.5°

Known bond
angle, 104.5°

104°

Predicted bond angle is
approximately 104°

**Figure 3.11** A comparison of the bonding in water and dimethyl ether.

107°

Known bond
angle, 107°

107°

Predicted bond angle is
approximately 107°

**Figure 3.12** A comparison of the bonding in ammonia and trimethylamine.

it follows that $H_2S$ and $H_2Se$ would also be bent molecules with similar Lewis structures and shape.

$$H - \overset{..}{\underset{..}{S}} - H \qquad H \diagdown \overset{S}{\phantom{x}} \diagup H$$

$$H - \overset{..}{\underset{..}{Se}} - H \qquad H \diagdown \overset{Se}{\phantom{x}} \diagup H$$

This logic applies equally well to the other representative elements.

**Question 3.5** Sketch the geometry of each of the following molecules (basing your sketch on the Lewis structure of the molecule):
   a. $PH_3$      b. $SiH_4$

**Question 3.6** Sketch the geometry of each of the following molecules (basing your sketch on the Lewis structure of the molecule):
   a. $C_2H_4$    b. $C_2H_2$

**More Complex Molecules**

For compounds containing more than one central atom, geometry is determined at each central atom. Dimethyl ether, $CH_3—O—CH_3$, has three distinct central atoms. Begin by drawing the Lewis structure

$$H - \overset{\overset{\displaystyle H}{|}}{C} - \overset{..}{\underset{..}{O}} - \overset{\overset{\displaystyle H}{|}}{\underset{\underset{\displaystyle H}{|}}{C}} - H$$

Each carbon atom has four bonded atoms, giving a tetrahedral geometry with bond angles of 109.5°.

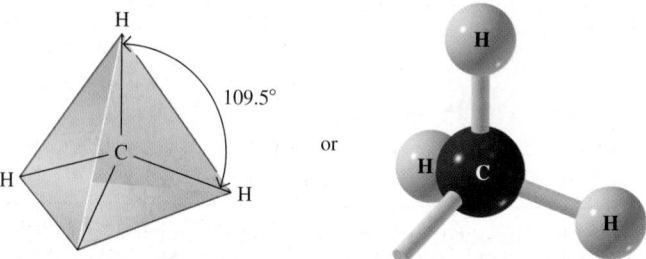

The oxygen has two bonded atoms and two lone pairs, giving a bent geometry with a 104° bond angle, as shown in Figure 3.11.

Trimethylamine, $(CH_3)_3N$, is a member of the amine family. Its Lewis structure is depicted below.

$$H - \overset{\overset{\displaystyle H}{|}}{C} - \overset{..}{N} - \overset{\overset{\displaystyle H}{|}}{C} - H$$

As in the case of dimethyl ether, two different central atoms are present. Carbon and nitrogen determine the geometry of amines. In this case the methyl group should assume the tetrahedral geometry of methane. The nitrogen atom should have the methyl groups in a pyramidal arrangement, similar to the hydrogen atoms in ammonia, as seen in Figure 3.12. This creates a pyramidal geometry around nitrogen. H—N—H bond angles in ammonia are 107°; experimental information shows a very similar C—N—C bond angle in trimethylamine.

It is essential to represent a molecule in its correct geometric form, using the Lewis and VSEPR theories, to understand its physical and chemical behavior. In the rest of this section we use these models to predict molecular behavior.

**ANIMATION**
- Molecular Polarity

## Lewis Structures and Polarity

As discussed in Section 3.1, covalent bonds can be polar or nonpolar. In this section we will examine all the bonds that make up a molecule to determine if the *molecule* is polar or nonpolar. Polar molecules, when placed in an electric field, align themselves with the field (Figure 3.13). These molecules are said to have a *dipole* (having two "poles" or ends, one pole is more negative and the other pole is more positive). Nonpolar molecules do not align with an electric field. It is important to determine if a molecule is polar or nonpolar because this information helps predict properties of solubility as well as melting point and boiling point. These properties will be discussed in Section 3.5.

The hydrogen molecule is the simplest nonpolar molecule. The electrons that make up the bond are shared equally between the two atoms (see Figure 3.3). Any molecule made of only nonpolar bonds is a nonpolar molecule. Therefore, $O_2$, $N_2$, $Cl_2$ and $F_2$ are all nonpolar.

A diatomic molecule that is made of two elements with different electronegativities will contain a polar bond. Since this bond is polar, the molecule is polar. We used the partial positive and partial negative symbols $\delta^+$ and $\delta^-$ in Section 3.1 to represent the polar bond. We can also represent this polar bond using a vector (arrow) pointing in the direction of the most electronegative element in the bond.

**LEARNING GOAL**

**8** Understand the role that molecular geometry plays in determining the polarity of compounds.

**ANIMATIONS**
- The Structure and Dipole Moment of HF
- The Structure and Dipole Moment of $CCl_4$
- The Structure and Dipole Moment of $H_2O$

$$\overset{\delta+}{H} - \overset{\delta-}{F} \qquad \overset{+}{H} \overset{\longrightarrow}{-} F$$

If a molecule contains more than one polar bond, depending on the orientation in space of the polar bonds, the molecule *may* or *may not* be polar. Think of the polarity of a bond as a rope tied around the central atom pulling in the direction of the more electronegative atom. (Or in the case of lone pairs, the pull will always be in the direction of the lone pair.) Each terminal-atom to central-atom connection is a separate tug-of-war. If all the pulls are equal, the molecule is nonpolar; otherwise the molecule is polar. To determine if a molecule with polar bonds is polar or nonpolar, draw the Lewis structure and follow these guidelines:

**Molecules that have no lone pair on the central atom, and all terminal atoms the same are *nonpolar*.** For example, the molecule $CO_2$ has two bonded O atoms and no lone pairs on the central atom. It is linear and nonpolar. The molecule $CCl_4$ has no lone pairs on the central atom and four bonded Cl atoms. Its shape is tetrahedral and it is nonpolar.

**Molecules with one lone pair on the central atom are *polar*.** Ammonia ($NH_3$) is an example. Its nitrogen atom has three bonded H atoms and one lone pair. It is based upon the tetrahedral shape but is a trigonal pyramid. Because the nitrogen atom is more electronegative than the hydrogen atoms, the arrow points toward nitrogen and ammonia is polar. The pull of lone-pair electrons is always away from the atom.

**Figure 3.13** The green ovals represent polar molecule (a) in the absence of an electric field and (b) under the influence of an electric field.

**Molecules that have more than one lone pair on the central atom are *usually* polar, but there are exceptions.** The Lewis structure of water has two lone pairs and two bonded H atoms on the central atom of oxygen. Water is a bent molecule, and it is polar.

The electron density is shifted away from the hydrogens toward oxygen in the water molecule.

**Molecules that are made up of only carbon and hydrogen (hydrocarbons) are nonpolar.** The C—H bond is polar, but the combined effects of the numerous C—H bonds effectively cancel, rendering the molecule nonpolar.

---

**EXAMPLE 3.17    Determining if a Molecule Is Polar Covalent or Nonpolar Covalent**

Is $PCl_3$ a polar or nonpolar covalent compound?

To determine polarity, the geometry must be determined. To determine geometry, draw the Lewis structure.

**LEARNING GOAL**

**7** Predict the geometry of molecules and ions using the octet rule and Lewis structures.

**Solution**

**Step 1.** Follow all steps to correctly draw the Lewis structure.

| Skeletal Structure | Count Valence Electrons | Distribute Valence Electrons |
|---|---|---|
| Cl <br> Cl   P   Cl | $1 P \times 5 e^- = 5 e^-$ <br> $3 Cl \times 7 e^- = 21 e^-$ <br> —————————— <br> $26 e^-$ total | :Cl: <br> &#124; <br> :Cl — P — Cl: |

**LEARNING GOAL**

**8** Understand the role that molecular geometry plays in determining the polarity of compounds.

**Step 2.** Examine the central atom to determine if the molecule is polar. The molecule has three chlorine atoms and one lone pair. The one lone pair makes the molecule polar covalent.

---

**Practice Problem 3.17**

Determine whether the $AsCl_3$ molecule is polar.

▶ For Further Practice: **Questions 3.95 and 3.96.**

---

**Question 3.7** Predict which of the following bonds are polar, and, if polar, use a vector to indicate in which direction the electrons are pulled:
    a. O—S     b. C≡N     c. Cl—Cl     d. I—Cl

**Question 3.8** Predict which of the following bonds are polar, and, if polar, use a vector to indicate in which direction the electrons are pulled:
    a. Si—Cl     b. S—Cl     c. H—C     d. C—C

**Question 3.9** Using Lewis structures and VSEPR, predict whether each of the following molecules is polar:
    a. $BCl_3$     b. $NH_3$     c. HCl     d. $SiCl_4$

**Question 3.10** Using Lewis structures and VSEPR, predict whether each of the following molecules is polar:
    a. $CO_2$     b. $SCl_2$     c. BrCl     d. $CS_2$

## 3.5  Properties Based on Electronic Structure and Molecular Geometry

LEARNING GOAL

**9**  Understand the role of polarity in determining solubility as well as melting and boiling points of compounds.

**Intramolecular forces** are attractive forces *within* molecules. They are the chemical bonds that determine the shape and polarity of individual molecules. **Intermolecular forces,** on the other hand, are forces *between* molecules.

It is important to distinguish between these two kinds of forces. It is the *intermolecular* forces that determine such properties as the solubility of one substance in another and the freezing and boiling points of liquids. But, at the same time, we must realize that these forces are a direct consequence of the *intramolecular* forces in the individual units, the molecules.

In the following section we will see some of the consequences of bonding that are directly attributable to differences in intermolecular forces (solubility, boiling and melting points). In Section 5.2 we will investigate, in some detail, the nature of the intermolecular forces themselves.

### Solubility

**Solubility** is defined as the maximum amount of solute that dissolves in a given amount of solvent at a specified temperature. Polar molecules are most soluble in polar solvents, whereas nonpolar molecules are most soluble in nonpolar solvents. This is the rule of *"like dissolves like."* Substances of similar polarity are mutually soluble, and large differences in polarity lead to insolubility.

*The solute is the substance that is present in lesser quantity, and the solvent is the substance that is present in the greater amount (see Section 6.3).*

#### Case I: Ammonia and Water

Ammonia is soluble in water because both ammonia and water are polar molecules:

*The interaction of water and ammonia is an example of a particularly strong intermolecular force, the hydrogen bond; this phenomenon is discussed in Chapter 5.*

Dissolution of ammonia in water is a consequence of the intermolecular forces present among the ammonia and water molecules. The $\delta^-$ end (a nitrogen) of the ammonia molecule is attracted to the $\delta^+$ end (a hydrogen) of the water molecule; at the same time the $\delta^+$ end (a hydrogen) of the ammonia molecule is attracted to the $\delta^-$ end (an oxygen) of the water molecule. These attractive forces thus "pull" ammonia into water (and water into ammonia), and the ammonia molecules are randomly distributed throughout the solvent, forming a homogeneous solution (Figure 3.14).

#### Case II: Oil and Water

Oil and water do not mix; oil is a nonpolar substance composed primarily of molecules containing carbon and hydrogen. Water molecules, on the other hand, are quite polar. The potential solvent, water molecules, have partially charged ends, whereas the molecules of oil do not. As a result, water molecules exert their attractive forces on other water molecules, not on the molecules of oil; the oil remains insoluble, and because it is less dense than water, the oil simply floats on the surface of the water. This is illustrated in Figure 3.15.

### Boiling Points of Liquids and Melting Points of Solids

Boiling a liquid requires energy. The energy is used to overcome the intermolecular attractive forces in the liquid, driving the molecules into the less-associated gas phase. The amount of energy required to accomplish this is related to the boiling temperature. This, in turn, depends on the strength of the intermolecular attractive

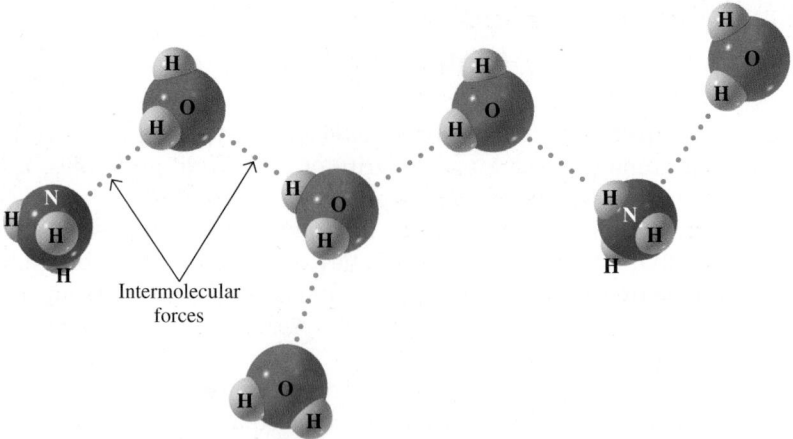

**Figure 3.14** The interaction of polar covalent water molecules (the solvent) with polar covalent solute molecules such as ammonia, resulting in the formation of a solution.

**TABLE 3.6 Melting and Boiling Points of Selected Compounds in Relation to Their Bonding Type**

| Formula (Name) | Bonding Type | M.P. (°C) | B.P. (°C) |
|---|---|---|---|
| $N_2$ (nitrogen) | Nonpolar covalent | −210 | −196 |
| $O_2$ (oxygen) | Nonpolar covalent | −219 | −183 |
| $NH_3$ (ammonia) | Polar covalent | −78 | −33 |
| $H_2O$ (water) | Polar covalent | 0 | 100 |
| NaCl (sodium chloride) | Ionic | 801 | 1413 |
| KBr (potassium bromide) | Ionic | 730 | 1435 |

**Figure 3.15** The interaction of polar water molecules and nonpolar oil molecules. The familiar salad dressing, oil and vinegar, forms two layers. The oil does not dissolve in vinegar, an aqueous solution of acetic acid.

forces in the liquid, which parallels the polarity. This is not the only determinant of boiling point. Molecular mass is also an important consideration. The larger the mass of the molecule, the more difficult it becomes to convert the collection of molecules to the gas phase.

A similar argument can be made for the melting points of solids. The ease of conversion of a solid to a liquid also depends on the magnitude of the attractive forces in the solid. The situation actually becomes very complex for ionic solids because of the complexity of the crystal lattice.

As a general rule, polar compounds have strong attractive (intermolecular) forces, and their boiling and melting points tend to be higher than those of nonpolar substances of similar molecular mass.

Melting and boiling points of a variety of substances are included in Table 3.6.

**Question 3.11** Predict which compound in each of the following pairs should have the higher melting and boiling points (Hint: Write the Lewis structure and determine whether the molecule is polar or nonpolar.):
   a. $H_2O$ and $C_2H_4$    b. CO and $CH_4$    c. $NH_3$ and $N_2$    d. $Cl_2$ and ICl

**Question 3.12** Predict which compound in each of the following pairs should have the higher melting and boiling points (Hint: Write the Lewis structure and determine whether the molecule is polar or nonpolar.):
   a. $C_2H_6$ and $CH_4$    c. $F_2$ and $Br_2$
   b. CO and NO    d. $CHCl_3$ and $CCl_4$

## CHAPTER MAP

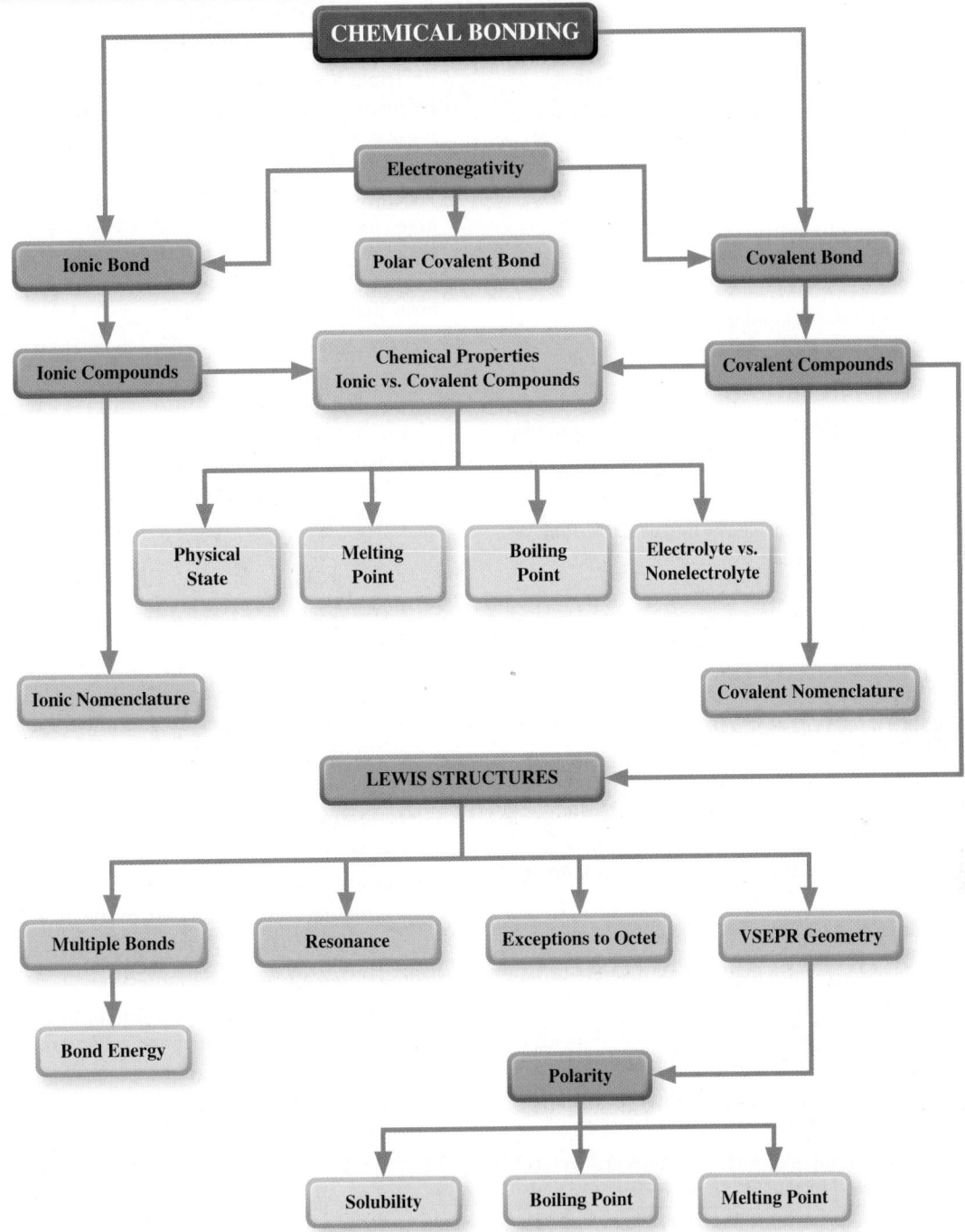

# SUMMARY

## 3.1 Chemical Bonding

► **Lewis symbols** enable the tracking of valence electrons in compounds. They are used to show the types of bonding.

► **Chemical bonding**—the attractive force between atoms in a compound can be classified as

- **Covalent** (or nonpolar covalent)
- **Polar covalent**
- **Ionic**, consisting of cations and anions

► **Electronegativity** is used to help determine the type of chemical bonding.

- Difference of 0.5 and less—nonpolar covalent
- Difference between 0.5 and 2.0—polar covalent
- Difference of 2.0 or larger—ionic

## 3.2 Naming Compounds and Writing Formulas of Compounds

► The system for naming compounds (**nomenclature**) is different for ionic and covalent compounds.

- Ionic compounds: name cation followed by the anion. Use Roman numeral to denote the charge on the metal, when required.
- The charge of a **monatomic ion** can be determined for main-group elements from the periodic table.
- Know the names and charges of the **polyatomic ions.**
- Covalent compounds: name first element first and then second element (with –*ide* ending). Use prefixes of di-, tri-, etc., to denote the number of atoms of each element in the compound.

► When writing **formulas** for ionic compounds be sure the number of positive charges equals the number of negative charges.

► When writing **formulas** for covalent compounds, use the prefix before the element name as the subscript for the element.

## 3.3 Properties of Ionic and Covalent Compounds

► Covalent compounds are typically made up of discrete units called **molecules.**

► Ionic compounds form a **crystal lattice** composed of cations and anions extended out in a three-dimensional network.

► Ionic compounds have higher **melting points** and **boiling points** than covalent compounds.

► When ionic compounds dissolve in water, the ions **dissociate** and the solution conducts electricity. These compounds are **electrolytes.**

► When covalent compounds dissolve in water, the compound does not dissociate. They are **nonelectrolytes.**

## 3.4 Drawing Lewis Structures of Molecules and Polyatomic Ions

► To draw a **Lewis structure**, all valence electrons are placed around the atoms of the compound as bonding electrons or **lone pairs** to satisfy the octet rule.

► If the octet rule cannot be satisfied with **single bonds** connecting the atoms, then **double bonds** and **triple bonds** are used.

► **Bond energy** determines the stability of a bond. Bond energy trend is as follows:

- Single < double < triple

► Bond length trend is the reverse.

- Triple < double < single

► **Isomers** are compounds that have the same molecular formula but have different structures. Hydrocarbons have many possible isomers.

► When two or more Lewis structures contribute to the molecular structure, the compound displays **resonance.** The true structure is a hybrid of the drawn resonance forms. Stability of a compound increases with the number of resonance structures that can be drawn.

► Some molecules have exceptions to the octet rule, these include:

- Odd-electron compounds
- Incomplete octets
- Expanded octets.

► The shapes of molecules can be predicted using **valence-shell electron-pair repulsion theory (VSEPR).** Possible shapes include:

- **Linear**
- **Trigonal planar**
- **Tetrahedral**
- **Bent**
- **Trigonal pyramidal**

► The geometry of a molecule and the knowledge of the polarity of a bond can be used to determine if a molecule is polar (has a dipole) or is nonpolar.

## 3.5 Properties Based on Electronic Structure and Molecular Geometry

► **Intermolecular forces** are attractive forces between molecules. **Intramolecular forces** are chemical bonds.

► Polar molecules are generally attracted to each other more strongly than are nonpolar molecules.

► **Solubility** is the maximum amount of solute that dissolves in a given amount of solvent at a specific temperature.

- Polar molecules are soluble in polar solvents.
- Nonpolar molecules are soluble in nonpolar solvents.

► Polar molecules (of similar mass) have higher melting points and boiling points than nonpolar molecules.

# ANSWERS TO PRACTICE PROBLEMS

3.1  a.  LiBr (one $Li^+$ and one $Br^-$)
     b.  $CaBr_2$ (one $Ca^{2+}$ and two $Br^-$)
     c.  KCl (one $K^+$ and one $Cl^-$)

**3.2 a.** $Ca_3N_2$ (three $Ca^{2+}$ and two $N^{3-}$)
  **b.** $MgBr_2$ (one $Mg^{2+}$ and two $Br^-$)
  **c.** $Mg_3N_2$ (three $Mg^{2+}$ and two $N^{3-}$)

**3.3** Chromium(II) bromide

**3.4 a.** $CaCO_3$      **b.** $Cu_2SO_4$

**3.5 a.** $Fe_2S_3$     **b.** $CaSO_4$     **c.** $Al_2O_3$

**3.6 a.** Nitrogen monoxide
  **b.** Iodine monochloride
  **c.** Iodine chloride
  **d.** Phosphorus trichloride
  **e.** Phosphorus pentachloride
  **f.** Diphosphorus pentoxide

**3.7 a.** $P_2O_5$      **c.** $CBr_4$
  **b.** $SiO_2$      **d.** $OF_2$

**3.8 a.** :Ö—H     **b.** H—C—H (with H above and below, =O type structure)

**3.9 a.** H—C≡N:     **b.** :N≡N:

**3.10 a.** H—N—N—H (with H and lone pairs)

  **b.** H—C—C—C—H (with H substituents)

**3.11** $\left[ \ddot{\text{O}} — \ddot{\text{O}} \right]^{2-}$

**3.12 a.** $\left[ :\ddot{\text{O}} — \overset{\ddot{\text{O}}}{\underset{}{\text{C}}} — \ddot{\text{O}} — H \right]^{-}$

  **b.** $\left[ :\ddot{\text{O}} — \overset{:\ddot{\text{O}}:}{\underset{:\ddot{\text{O}}:}{\text{P}}} — \ddot{\text{O}}: \right]^{3-}$

**3.13 a.** $\ddot{\text{O}} = \ddot{\text{Se}} — \ddot{\text{O}}: \longleftrightarrow :\ddot{\text{O}} — \ddot{\text{Se}} = \ddot{\text{O}}$

**b.** Since both S and Se are in the same family (Group VIA), they have the same number of valence electrons, and therefore, should form the same kinds of bonds.

**3.14**

**3.15** :Ḟ: ·Ḟ: / :Ḟ—S—Ḟ: / ·Ḟ: :Ḟ:

**3.16** :Cl: / :Cl—Se—Cl: / :Cl:

**3.17** $AsCl_3$ is polar.

# QUESTIONS AND PROBLEMS

## Chemical Bonding

### Foundations

**3.13** Describe the differences between covalent bonding and ionic bonding.

**3.14** Describe the difference between nonpolar covalent and polar covalent bonding.

**3.15** What is the periodic trend of electronegativity?

**3.16** What role does electronegativity play in determining the bonding between atoms in a compound?

**3.17** Draw the appropriate Lewis symbol for each of the following atoms:
  **a.** H     **b.** He     **c.** C     **d.** N

**3.18** Draw the appropriate Lewis symbol for each of the following atoms:
  **a.** Be     **b.** B     **c.** F     **d.** S

**3.19** Draw the appropriate Lewis symbol for each of the following ions:
  **a.** $Li^+$     **b.** $Mg^{2+}$     **c.** $Cl^-$     **d.** $P^{3-}$

**3.20** Draw the appropriate Lewis symbol for each of the following ions:
  **a.** $Be^{2+}$     **b.** $Al^{3+}$     **c.** $O^{2-}$     **d.** $S^{2-}$

**3.21** Classify the bonds in each of the following compounds as ionic, polar covalent, or nonpolar covalent.
  **a.** $MgCl_2$    **b.** $CO_2$    **c.** $H_2S$    **d.** $NO_2$

**3.22** Classify the bonds in each of the following compounds as ionic, polar covalent, or nonpolar covalent.
  **a.** NaCl    **b.** CO    **c.** ICl    **d.** $H_2$

## Applications

**3.23** Predict the formula of the ionic compound formed from
  **a.** Li + Br     **b.** Mg + Cl

**3.24** Predict the formula of the ionic compound formed from
  **a.** Na + O     **b.** Na + S

**3.25** Predict the formula of the ionic compound formed from
  **a.** S + H     **b.** P + H

**3.26** Predict the formula of the ionic compound formed from
  **a.** Si + H     **b.** Ca + F

**3.27** Explain, using Lewis symbols and the octet rule, why helium is so nonreactive.

**3.28** Explain, using Lewis symbols and the octet rule, why neon is so nonreactive.

## Naming Compounds and Writing Formulas of Compounds

### Foundations

**3.29** Name each of the following ions:
  **a.** $Na^+$     **b.** $Cu^+$     **c.** $Mg^{2+}$

**3.30** Name each of the following ions:
  **a.** $Cu^{2+}$     **b.** $Fe^{2+}$     **c.** $Fe^{3+}$

**3.31** Name each of the following ions:
  **a.** $S^{2-}$     **b.** $Cl^-$     **c.** $CO_3^{2-}$

**3.32** Name each of the following ions:
  **a.** $ClO^-$     **b.** $NH_4^+$     **c.** $CH_3COO^-$

**3.33** Write the formula for each of the following monatomic ions:
  **a.** the potassium ion     **b.** the bromide ion

**3.34** Write the formula for each of the following monatomic ions:
  **a.** the calcium ion     **b.** the chromium(VI) ion

**3.35** Write the formula for each of the following complex ions:
  **a.** the sulfate ion     **b.** the nitrate ion

**3.36** Write the formula for each of the following complex ions:
  **a.** the phosphate ion     **b.** the bicarbonate ion

### Applications

**3.37** Name each of the following compounds:
  **a.** $MgCl_2$     **b.** $AlCl_3$

**3.38** Name each of the following compounds:
  **a.** $Na_2O$     **b.** $Fe(OH)_3$

**3.39** Name each of the following covalent compounds:
  **a.** $NO_2$     **b.** $SeO_3$

**3.40** Name each of the following covalent compounds:
  **a.** $N_2O_4$     **b.** $CCl_4$

**3.41** Name each covalent compound:
  **a.** $SO_2$     **b.** $SO_3$

**3.42** Name each covalent compound:
  **a.** $N_2O_5$     **b.** $CO$

**3.43** Write the correct formula for each of the following:
  **a.** sodium chloride
  **b.** magnesium bromide

**3.44** Write the correct formula for each of the following:
  **a.** potassium oxide
  **b.** potassium nitride

**3.45** Write the correct formula for each of the following:
  **a.** silver cyanide
  **b.** ammonium chloride

**3.46** Write the correct formula for each of the following:
  **a.** magnesium carbonate
  **b.** magnesium bicarbonate

**3.47** Write the correct formula for each of the following:
  **a.** copper(II) oxide     **b.** iron(III) oxide

**3.48** Write the correct formula for each of the following:
  **a.** manganese(II) oxide
  **b.** manganese(III) oxide

**3.49** Predict the formula of a compound formed from:
  **a.** aluminum and oxygen
  **b.** lithium and sulfur

**3.50** Predict the formula of a compound formed from:
  **a.** boron and hydrogen
  **b.** magnesium and phosphorus

**3.51** Write a suitable formula for:
  **a.** silicon dioxide     **b.** sulfur dioxide

**3.52** Write a suitable formula for:
  **a.** diphosphorus pentoxide
  **b.** dioxygen difluoride

**3.53** Write a suitable formula for:
  **a.** sodium nitrate     **b.** magnesium nitrate

**3.54** Write a suitable formula for:
  **a.** aluminum nitrate     **b.** ammonium nitrate

**3.55** Write a suitable formula for:
  **a.** ammonium iodide     **b.** ammonium sulfate

**3.56** Write a suitable formula for:
  **a.** ammonium acetate     **b.** ammonium cyanide

## Properties of Ionic and Covalent Compounds

### Foundations

**3.57** Contrast ionic and covalent compounds with respect to their solid-state structure.

**3.58** Contrast ionic and covalent compounds with respect to their behavior in solution.

**3.59** Contrast ionic and covalent compounds with respect to their relative boiling points.

**3.60** Contrast ionic and covalent compounds with respect to their relative melting points.

### Applications

**3.61** Would KCl be expected to be a solid at room temperature? Why?

**3.62** Would $CCl_4$ be expected to be a solid at room temperature? Why?

**3.63** Would $H_2O$ or $CCl_4$ be expected to have a higher boiling point? Why?

**3.64** Would $H_2O$ or $CCl_4$ be expected to have a higher melting point? Why?

## Drawing Lewis Structures of Molecules and Polyatomic Ions

### Foundations

**3.65** When drawing a Lewis structure, how is the central atom determined?

**3.66** When drawing a Lewis structure, which elements can never be a central atom?

**3.67** How is the positive charge of a polyatomic *cation* incorporated when determining the number of valence electrons to be used in a Lewis structure?

**3.68** How is the negative charge of a polyatomic *anion* incorporated when determining the number of valence electrons to be used in a Lewis structure?

**3.69** Rank the following in order of increasing bond energy:

single bond, double bond, triple bond

**3.70** Rank the following in order of increasing bond length:

single bond, double bond, triple bond

**3.71** Which will have more isomers: $C_4H_{10}$ or $C_5H_{12}$?

**3.72** Will the number of isomers increase or decrease with the number of carbon atoms in a hydrocarbon?

**3.73** Discuss the concept of resonance, being certain to define the terms *resonance, resonance form,* and *resonance hybrid.*

**3.74** Why is resonance an important concept in bonding?

**3.75** What is the bond angle of a trigonal planar molecule?

**3.76** What is the bond angle of a tetrahedral molecule?

**3.77** True or false? Molecules that have only nonpolar bonds will always be nonpolar.

**3.78** True or false? Molecules that have only polar bonds will always be polar.

**Applications**

**3.79** Give the Lewis structure for each of the following compounds:
a. $NCl_3$    b. $CH_3OH$    c. $CS_2$

**3.80** Give the Lewis structure for each of the following compounds:
a. $HNO_3$    b. $CCl_4$    c. $PBr_3$

**3.81** Using the VSEPR theory, predict the geometry, polarity, and water solubility of each compound in Question 3.79.

**3.82** Using the VSEPR theory, predict the geometry, polarity, and water solubility of each compound in Question 3.80.

**3.83** Draw the Lewis structure of $NO^+$.

**3.84** Draw the Lewis structure of $NO_2^-$.

**3.85** Draw the Lewis structure of $OH^-$.

**3.86** Draw the Lewis structure of $HS^-$.

**3.87** The acetate ion (Example 3.12) exhibits resonance. Draw two resonance forms of the acetate ion.

**3.88** Ozone, $O_3$, has two resonance forms. Draw each form.

**3.89** Ethanol (ethyl alcohol or grain alcohol) has a molecular formula of $C_2H_5OH$. Draw the Lewis structure of ethanol.

**3.90** Formaldehyde, $H_2CO$, in water solution has been used as a preservative for biological specimens. Draw the Lewis structure of formaldehyde.

**3.91** Acetone, $C_3H_6O$, is a common solvent. It is found in such diverse materials as nail polish remover and industrial solvents. Draw its Lewis structure if its skeletal structure is

O

C  C  C

**3.92** Ethylamine is an example of an important class of organic compounds. The molecular formula of ethylamine is $CH_3CH_2NH_2$. Draw its Lewis structure.

**3.93** Draw the Lewis structure of each of the following compounds and predict its geometry using VSEPR.
a. $SO_2$    b. $SO_3$

**3.94** Draw the Lewis structure of each of the following compounds and predict its geometry using VSEPR.
a. $SeO_2$    b. $SeO_3$

**3.95** Predict the polarity of each compound in Question 3.93.

**3.96** Predict the polarity of each compound in Question 3.94.

**3.97** All of the following Lewis structures are incorrect. Find the errors and write the correct structures.

**3.98** All of the following Lewis structures are incorrect. Find the errors and write the correct structures.

a.
$$:\!\ddot{F}\!:$$
$$|$$
$$:\!\ddot{F}\!-\!S\!-\!\ddot{F}\!:$$
$$|$$
$$:\!\ddot{F}\!:$$

c.
H
|
H—C=O=H
|
H

b.
:O:
|
H—C—H

**3.99** Which of the following compounds have polar bonds but are nonpolar covalent compounds?
a. $CO_2$    b. $NF_3$    c. $CF_4$

**3.100** Which of the following compounds have polar bonds but are nonpolar covalent compounds?
a. $SO_2$    b. $CF_4$    c. $NH_3$

**3.101** $BeCl_2$ has an incomplete octet around Be. Draw the Lewis structure of $BeCl_2$.

**3.102** $B(OH)_3$ has an incomplete octet around the B. Draw the Lewis structure of $B(OH)_3$.

**3.103** $SeF_6$ has an expanded octet around Se. Draw the Lewis structure of $SeF_6$.

**3.104** Noble gases in the third period and beyond can undergo covalent bonding. All have an expanded octet. Draw the Lewis structure of $XeF_2$.

## Properties Based on Electronic Structure and Molecular Geometry

**Foundations**

**3.105** What is the relationship between the polarity of a bond and the polarity of the molecule?

**3.106** What effect does polarity have on the solubility of a compound in water?

**3.107** What effect does polarity have on the melting point of a pure compound?

**3.108** What effect does polarity have on the boiling point of a pure compound?

**Applications**

**3.109** Would you expect KCl to dissolve in water?

**3.110** Would you expect ethylamine (Question 3.92) to dissolve in water?

**3.111** In each of the following pairs of compounds, choose the compound with the higher boiling point.
a. $N_2$ and $NH_3$    b. $CS_2$ and $CF_4$    c. NaCl and $Cl_2$

**3.112** In each of the following pairs of compounds, choose the compound with the higher melting point.
a. KF and $F_2$    b. CO and $O_2$    c. $NBr_3$ and $CCl_4$

# CRITICAL THINKING PROBLEMS

1. Predict differences in our global environment that may have arisen if the freezing point and boiling point of water were 20°C higher than they are.
2. Would you expect the compound $C_2S_2H_4$ to exist? Why or why not?
3. Draw the resonance forms of the carbonate ion. What conclusions, based on this exercise, can you draw about the stability of the carbonate ion?

4. Which of the following compounds would be predicted to have the higher boiling point? Explain your reasoning.

$$H-\overset{\overset{\displaystyle H}{|}}{\underset{\underset{\displaystyle H}{|}}{C}}-\overset{\overset{\displaystyle H}{|}}{\underset{\underset{\displaystyle H}{|}}{C}}-O-H$$

Ethanol

$$H-\overset{\overset{\displaystyle H}{|}}{\underset{\underset{\displaystyle H}{|}}{C}}-\overset{\overset{\displaystyle H}{|}}{\underset{\underset{\displaystyle H}{|}}{C}}-H$$

Ethane

5. Why does the octet rule not work well for compounds of lanthanide and actinide elements? Suggest a number other than eight that may be more suitable.

# Calculations and the Chemical Equation

## LEARNING GOALS

1  Know the relationship between the mole and Avogadro's number, and the usefulness of these quantities.

2  Perform calculations using Avogadro's number and the mole.

3  Write chemical formulas for common inorganic substances.

4  Calculate the formula mass and molar mass of a compound.

5  Know the major function served by the chemical equation, the basis for chemical calculations.

6  Classify chemical reactions by type: combination, decomposition, or replacement.

7  Balance chemical equations given the identity of products and reactants.

8  Recognize the various classes of chemical reactions: precipitation, reactions with oxygen, acid-base, and oxidation-reduction.

9  Calculate the number of moles or grams of product resulting from a given number of moles or grams of reactants or the number of moles or grams of reactant needed to produce a certain number of moles or grams of product.

10  Calculate theoretical and percent yield.

Careful measurement is an essential part of the scientific method and its application to real-world problems.

## OUTLINE

# INTRODUCTION

The calculation of chemical quantities based on chemical equations, termed *stoichiometry*, is the application of logic and arithmetic to chemical systems to answer questions such as the following:

A pharmaceutical company wishes to manufacture 1000 kilograms (kg) of a product next year. How much of each of the starting materials must be ordered? If the starting materials cost 20 dollars per gram (g), how much money must be budgeted for the project?

We often need to predict the quantity of a product produced from the reaction of a given amount of material. This calculation is possible. It is equally possible to calculate how much of a material would be necessary to produce a desired amount of product.

What is required is a recipe: a procedure to follow. The basis for our recipe is the chemical equation. A properly written chemical equation provides all of the necessary information for the chemical calculation. That critical information is the combining ratio of elements or compounds that must occur to produce a certain amount of product or products.

In this chapter we define the mole (mol), the fundamental unit of measure of chemical arithmetic; learn to write and balance chemical equations; and use these tools to perform calculations of chemical quantities.

## 4.1   The Mole Concept and Atoms

Atoms are exceedingly small, yet their masses have been experimentally determined for each of the elements. The unit of measurement for these determinations is the **atomic mass unit** (amu):

$$1 \text{ amu} = 1.661 \times 10^{-24} \text{ g}$$

### The Mole and Avogadro's Number

The exact value of the amu is defined in relation to a standard, just as the units of the metric system represent defined quantities. The carbon-12 isotope has been chosen and is assigned a mass of exactly 12 amu. Hence this standard reference point defines an amu as exactly one-twelfth the mass of a carbon-12 atom.

The periodic table provides atomic weights in amu. These atomic weights are average values, based on the contribution of all naturally occurring isotopes of the particular element. For example, the average mass of a carbon atom is 12.01 amu and

$$\frac{12.01 \text{ amu C}}{\text{C atom}} \times \frac{1.661 \times 10^{-24} \text{ g C}}{1 \text{ amu C}} = 1.995 \times 10^{-23} \frac{\text{g C}}{\text{C atom}}$$

The average mass of a helium atom is 4.003 amu and

$$\frac{4.003 \text{ amu He}}{\text{He atom}} \times \frac{1.661 \times 10^{-24} \text{ g He}}{1 \text{ amu He}} = 6.649 \times 10^{-24} \frac{\text{g He}}{\text{He atom}}$$

In everyday work, chemists use much larger quantities of matter (typically g or kg). A more practical unit for defining a "collection" of atoms is the *mole*. The **mole** (mol) is the amount of a substance that contains as many atoms, molecules, or ions as are found in exactly 12 g of the carbon-12 isotope. That number,

## LEARNING GOAL

**1** Know the relationship between the mole and Avogadro's number, and the usefulness of these quantities.

The term *atomic weight* is not correct but is a fixture in common usage. Just remember that atomic weight is really "average atomic mass."

experimentally determined, is **Avogadro's number,** named in honor of the nineteenth-century Italian scientist, Amadeo Avogadro.

Avogadro's number is expressed as:

$$1 \text{ mol of atoms} = 6.022 \times 10^{23} \text{ atoms of an element}$$

The practice of defining a unit for a quantity of small objects is common; a *dozen* eggs, a *ream* of paper, and a *gross* of pencils are well-known examples. Similarly, a mol is $6.022 \times 10^{23}$ individual units of anything. We could, if we desired, speak of a mol of eggs or a mol of pencils. However, in chemistry we use the mol to represent a specific quantity of atoms, ions, or molecules.

The mol and the amu are related. The atomic mass of an element corresponds to the average mass of a single atom in amu and the *molar mass* is the mass of a mole of atoms in grams.

The mass of 1 mol of atoms, in g, is defined as the **molar mass.** Consider this relationship for sodium in Example 4.1.

---

| EXAMPLE 4.1 | Relating Avogadro's Number to Molar Mass |
|---|---|

**LEARNING GOAL**

**2** Perform calculations using Avogadro's number and the mole.

Calculate the mass, in g, of Avogadro's number of sodium atoms.

**Solution**

**Step 1.** The periodic table indicates that the average mass of one sodium atom is 22.99 amu. This may be represented as:

$$\frac{22.99 \text{ amu Na}}{1 \text{ atom Na}}$$

**Step 2.** In order to answer the question, we must calculate the molar mass in units of g/mol. We need two conversion factors; one to convert amu $\longrightarrow$ g and another to convert atoms $\longrightarrow$ mol.

**Step 3.** As previously noted, 1 amu is $1.661 \times 10^{-24}$ g, and $6.022 \times 10^{23}$ atoms of sodium is Avogadro's number. These relationships may be written as:

$$\frac{1.661 \times 10^{-24} \text{ g Na}}{1 \text{ amu Na}} \quad \text{and} \quad \frac{6.022 \times 10^{23} \text{ atoms Na}}{1 \text{ mol Na}}$$

**Step 4.** Representing this information as a series of conversion factors, using the factor-label method, we have

$$\frac{22.99 \text{ amu Na}}{1 \text{ atom Na}} \times \frac{1.661 \times 10^{-24} \text{ g Na}}{1 \text{ amu Na}} \times \frac{6.022 \times 10^{23} \text{ atoms Na}}{1 \text{ mol Na}} = \frac{22.99 \text{ g Na}}{1 \text{ mol Na}}$$

**Step 5.** The average mass of one *atom* of sodium, in units of amu, is *numerically identical* to the mass of *Avogadro's number of atoms*, expressed in units of g. Hence the molar mass of sodium is 22.99 g Na/mol.

*Helpful Hint:* Section 1.5 discusses the use of conversion factors.

---

**Practice Problem 4.1**

Calculate the mass, in g, of Avogadro's number of:

    a. aluminum atoms     b. mercury atoms

▶ For Further Practice: **Questions 4.15 and 4.16.**

**Figure 4.1** The comparison of approximately 1 mol each of silver (as Morgan and Peace dollars), gold (as Canadian Maple Leaf coins), and copper (as pennies) shows the considerable difference in mass (as well as economic value) of equivalent mol of different substances.

The sodium example is not unique. The relationship holds for every element in the periodic table.

Because Avogadro's number of particles (atoms) is 1 mol, it follows that the average mass of one atom of hydrogen is 1.008 amu and the mass of 1 mol of hydrogen atoms is 1.008 g, or the average mass of one atom of carbon is 12.01 amu and the mass of 1 mol of carbon atoms is 12.01 g.

In fact, 1 mol of atoms of *any element* contains the same number, Avogadro's number, of atoms, $6.022 \times 10^{23}$ atoms.

The difference in mass of a mol of two different elements can be quite striking (Figure 4.1). For example, a mol of hydrogen atoms is 1.008 g, and a mol of lead atoms is 207.19 g.

## Calculating Atoms, Moles, and Mass

Performing calculations based on a chemical equation requires a facility for relating the number of atoms of an element to a corresponding number of mol of that element and ultimately to their mass in g. Such calculations involve the use of conversion factors. The use of conversion factors was first described in Chapter 1.

The following examples demonstrate the use of a sequence of conversion factors to proceed from the information *provided* in the problem to the information *requested* by the problem.

---

**EXAMPLE 4.2    Converting Moles to Atoms**

**LEARNING GOAL**

**2** Perform calculations using Avogadro's number and the mole.

How many iron atoms are present in 3.0 mol of iron metal?

**Solution**

**Step 1.** The calculation is based on the choice of the appropriate conversion factor. The relationship

$$\frac{6.022 \times 10^{23} \text{ atoms Fe}}{1 \text{ mol Fe}}$$

follows directly from

$$1 \text{ mol Fe} = 6.022 \times 10^{23} \text{ atoms Fe}$$

**Step 2.** Using this conversion factor, we have

$$\text{number of atoms of Fe} = 3.0 \text{ mol Fe} \times \frac{6.022 \times 10^{23} \text{ atoms Fe}}{1 \text{ mol Fe}}$$
$$= 18 \times 10^{23} \text{ atoms of Fe, or}$$
$$= 1.8 \times 10^{24} \text{ atoms of Fe}$$

---

**Practice Problem 4.2**

How many oxygen atoms are present in 2.50 mol of:

  a. oxygen atoms      b. oxygen molecules

▶ For Further Practice: **Questions 4.17 and 4.18.**

| EXAMPLE 4.3 | Converting Atoms to Moles |

**LEARNING GOAL**

**2** Perform calculations using Avogadro's number and the mole.

Calculate the number of mol of sulfur represented by $1.81 \times 10^{24}$ atoms of sulfur.

**Solution**

**Step 1.** Just as in the previous example, the calculation is based on the choice of the appropriate conversion factor. The relationship

$$\frac{1 \text{ mol S}}{6.022 \times 10^{23} \text{ atoms S}}$$

follows directly from

$$1 \text{ mol S} = 6.022 \times 10^{23} \text{ atoms S}$$

**Step 2.** $1.81 \times 10^{24}$ atoms S $\times \dfrac{1 \text{ mol S}}{6.022 \times 10^{23} \text{ atoms S}} = 3.01$ mol S

Note that this conversion factor is the inverse of that used in Example 4.2. Remember, the conversion factor must cancel units that should not appear in the final answer.

**Practice Problem 4.3**

How many mol of sodium are represented by $9.03 \times 10^{23}$ atoms of sodium?

▶ For Further Practice: **Questions 4.19 and 4.20.**

| EXAMPLE 4.4 | Converting Moles of a Substance to Mass in Grams |

**LEARNING GOAL**

**2** Perform calculations using Avogadro's number and the mole.

What is the mass, in g, of 3.01 mol of sulfur?

**Solution**

**Step 1.** We know from the periodic table that 1 mol of sulfur has a mass of 32.06 g. Setting up a suitable conversion factor between g and mol results in

**Step 2.**
$$\frac{32.06 \text{ g S}}{1 \text{ mol S}}$$

which is based on:

$$1 \text{ mol S} = 32.06 \text{ g S}$$

**Step 3.** Using this conversion factor (ensuring that the units *mol S* cancel):

$$3.01 \text{ mol S} \times \frac{32.06 \text{ g S}}{1 \text{ mol S}} = 96.5 \text{ g S}$$

**Practice Problem 4.4**

What is the mass, in g, of 3.50 mol of the element helium?

▶ For Further Practice: **Questions 4.21 and 4.22.**

## EXAMPLE 4.5    Converting Grams to Number of Atoms

LEARNING GOAL

**2** Perform calculations using Avogadro's number and the mole.

Calculate the number of atoms of sulfur in 1.00 g of sulfur.

### Solution

It is generally useful to map out a pattern for the required conversion. We are given the number of grams and need the number of atoms that correspond to that mass.

Begin by "tracing a path" to the answer:

$$\underset{\text{sulfur}}{\text{grams}} \xrightarrow[\text{ }]{\text{Step 1}} \underset{\text{sulfur}}{\text{moles}} \xrightarrow[\text{ }]{\text{Step 2}} \underset{\text{sulfur}}{\text{atoms}}$$

Two transformations, or conversions, are required:

**Step 1.** Convert g to mol.

**Step 2.** Convert mol to atoms.

To perform step 1, we could consider either

$$\frac{1 \text{ mol S}}{32.06 \text{ g S}} \quad \text{or} \quad \frac{32.06 \text{ g S}}{1 \text{ mol S}}$$

If we want g to cancel, $\dfrac{1 \text{ mol S}}{32.06 \text{ g S}}$ is the correct choice, resulting in

$$\cancel{\text{g S}} \times \frac{1 \text{ mol S}}{32.06 \ \cancel{\text{g S}}} = \text{value in mol S}$$

To perform step 2, the conversion of mol to atoms, the mol of S must cancel; therefore

$$\cancel{\text{mol S}} \times \frac{6.022 \times 10^{23} \text{ atom S}}{1 \ \cancel{\text{mol S}}} = \text{number of atoms S}$$

which are the units necessary for the solution. Combining step 1 and step 2 we have

$$1.00 \ \cancel{\text{g S}} \times \frac{1 \ \cancel{\text{mol S}}}{32.06 \ \cancel{\text{g S}}} \times \frac{6.022 \times 10^{23} \text{ atoms S}}{1 \ \cancel{\text{mol S}}} = 1.88 \times 10^{22} \text{ atoms S}$$

### Practice Problem 4.5

How many oxygen atoms are present in 40.0 g of oxygen molecules?

▶ For Further Practice: **Questions 4.29 and 4.30.**

The conversion between the three principal measures of quantity of matter—the number of g (mass), the number of mol, and the number of individual particles (atoms, ions, or molecules)—is essential to the art of problem solving in chemistry. Their interrelationship is depicted in Figure 4.2.

**Question 4.1**  What is the mass, in g, of $1.00 \times 10^{12}$ mercury (Hg) atoms?

**Question 4.2**  How many mol of lead (Pb) atoms are equivalent to six billion lead atoms?

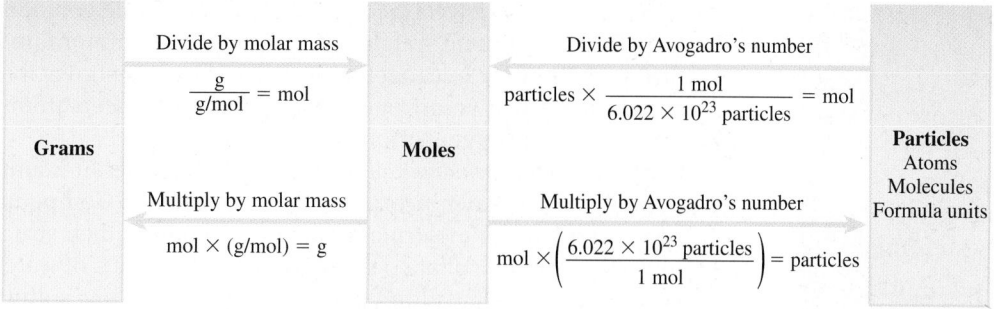

**Figure 4.2** Interconversion between numbers of mol, particles, and g. The mol concept is central to chemical calculations involving measured quantities of matter.

---

**EXAMPLE 4.6**    **Converting Kilograms to Moles**

LEARNING GOAL

Calculate the number of mol of sulfur in 1.00 kg of sulfur.

**2** Perform calculations using Avogadro's number and the mole.

**Solution**

Using the strategy developed in Example 4.5

$$1.00 \ \text{kg S} \times \frac{10^3 \ \text{g S}}{1 \ \text{kg S}} \times \frac{1 \ \text{mol S}}{32.06 \ \text{g S}} = 31.2 \ \text{mol S}$$

**Practice Problem 4.6**

Calculate the number of mol of silver in a silver ring that has a mass of 3.42 g.

▶ For Further Practice: **Questions 4.25 and 4.26.**

---

## **4.2** The Chemical Formula, Formula Mass, and Molar Mass

LEARNING GOAL

### The Chemical Formula

**3** Write chemical formulas for common inorganic substances.

Compounds are pure substances. They are composed of two or more elements that are chemically combined. A **chemical formula** is a combination of symbols of the various elements that make up the compound. It serves as a convenient way to represent a compound. The chemical formula is based on the formula unit. The **formula unit** is the smallest collection of atoms or ions that provides two important pieces of information:

- the identity of the atoms or ions present in the compound and
- the relative numbers of each type of atom or ion.

Let's look at the following formulas:

- *Hydrogen gas*, $H_2$. This indicates that two atoms of hydrogen are chemically bonded forming diatomic hydrogen, hence the subscript two.
- *Water*, $H_2O$. Water is composed of molecules that contain two atoms of hydrogen (subscript two) and one atom of oxygen (lack of a subscript means *one* atom).
- *Sodium chloride*, NaCl. One ion of sodium and one ion of chlorine combine to make sodium chloride.
- *Calcium hydroxide*, $Ca(OH)_2$. Calcium hydroxide contains one ion of calcium and two atoms each of oxygen and hydrogen. One atom of oxygen and one atom of hydrogen are contained in one hydroxide ion (a polyatomic ion). These two hydroxide ions furnish two atoms of both oxygen and hydrogen. Recall that the subscript outside the parentheses applies to *all* atoms inside the parentheses.

**DETERMINATION OF COMPOSITION AND FORMULAS OF COMPOUNDS**

It is possible to determine the correct molecular formula of a compound from experimental data.

**(a)**          **(b)**

**Figure 4.3** The marked difference in color of (a) hydrated, and (b) anhydrous copper sulfate is clear evidence that they are, in fact, different compounds.

**4**  Calculate the formula mass and molar mass of a compound.

- *Ammonium sulfate*, $(NH_4)_2SO_4$. Ammonium sulfate contains two ammonium ions $(NH_4^+)$ and one sulfate ion $(SO_4^{2-})$. Each ammonium ion contains one nitrogen and four hydrogen atoms. The formula shows that ammonium sulfate contains two nitrogen atoms, eight hydrogen atoms, one sulfur atom, and four oxygen atoms.
- *Copper(II) sulfate pentahydrate*, $CuSO_4 \cdot 5H_2O$. This is an example of a compound that has water incorporated in its structure. Compounds containing one or more water molecules as an integral part of their structure are termed **hydrates.** Copper sulfate pentahydrate has five units of water (or ten H atoms and five O atoms) in addition to one copper atom, one sulfur atom, and four oxygen atoms for a total atomic composition of:

1 copper atom

1 sulfur atom

9 oxygen atoms

10 hydrogen atoms

Note that the symbol for water is preceded by a dot, indicating that, although the water is a formula unit capable of standing alone, in this case it is a part of a larger structure. Copper sulfate also exists as a structure free of water, $CuSO_4$. This form is described as anhydrous (no water) copper sulfate. The physical and chemical properties of a hydrate often differ markedly from the anhydrous form (Figure 4.3).

## Formula Mass and Molar Mass

Just as the atomic mass of an element is the average atomic mass for one atom of the naturally occurring element, expressed in amu, the **formula mass** of a compound is the sum of the atomic masses of all atoms in the compound, as represented by its formula. To calculate the formula mass of a compound we *must* know the correct chemical formula. The formula mass is expressed in amu.

When working in the laboratory, we do not deal with individual molecules; instead, we use units of mol or g. Eighteen grams of water (less than 1 ounce) contain approximately Avogadro's number of water molecules ($6.022 \times 10^{23}$ molecules). Defining our working units as mol and g makes good chemical sense.

We earlier concluded that the atomic mass of an element in amu from the periodic table corresponds to the mass of a mol of atoms of that element in units of grams per mole (g/mol). It follows that *molar mass*, the mass of a mol of compound, is numerically equal to the formula mass in amu.

In Example 4.7, $H_2O$ is a covalent compound. In Example 4.8, $Na_2SO_4$ is an ionic compound. As we have seen, it is not technically correct to describe ionic compounds as molecules; similarly, the term *molecular mass* is not appropriate for $Na_2SO_4$. The term *formula mass* may be used to describe the formula unit of a substance, whether it is made up of ions, ion pairs, or molecules. We shall use the term *formula mass* in a general way to represent each of these species.

Figure 4.4 illustrates the difference between molecules and ion pairs.

**Figure 4.4** Formula units of (a) sodium chloride, an ionic compound, and (b) methane, a covalent compound.

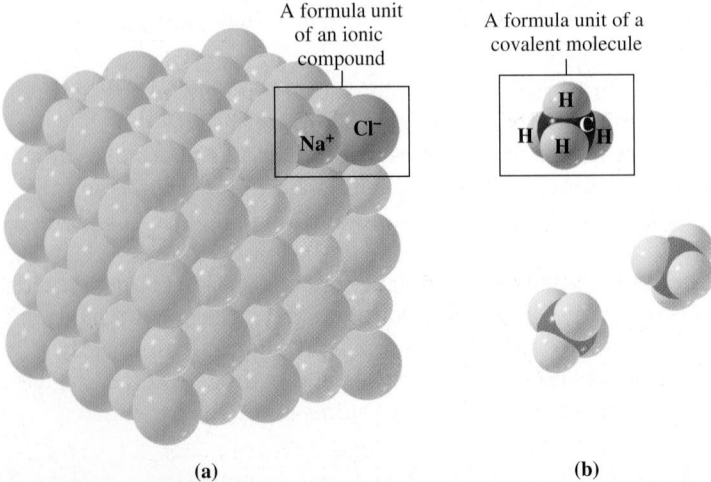

A formula unit of an ionic compound

A formula unit of a covalent molecule

**(a)**          **(b)**

---

**EXAMPLE 4.7**    **Calculating Formula Mass and Molar Mass**

LEARNING GOAL

**4** Calculate the formula mass and molar mass of a compound.

Calculate the formula mass and molar mass of water, $H_2O$.

**Solution**

**Step 1.** Each water molecule contains two hydrogen atoms and one oxygen atom.

**Step 2.** The formula mass is

$$
\begin{array}{ll}
2 \text{ atoms of hydrogen} \times 1.008 \text{ amu/atom} = & 2.016 \text{ amu} \\
1 \text{ atom of oxygen} \quad \times 16.00 \text{ amu/atom} = & 16.00 \text{ amu} \\
\hline
& 18.02 \quad \text{amu}
\end{array}
$$

**Step 3.** The average mass of a single molecule of $H_2O$ is 18.02 amu and is the formula mass. Therefore the mass of a mol of $H_2O$ is 18.02 g or 18.02 g/mol.

*Helpful Hint:* Adding 2.016 and 16.00 shows a result of 18.016 on your calculator. Proper use of significant figures (Chapter 1) dictates rounding that result to 18.02.

**Practice Problem 4.7**

Calculate the formula mass and molar mass of $NH_3$ (ammonia).

▶ For Further Practice: **Questions 4.33 and 4.34.**

---

**EXAMPLE 4.8**    **Calculating Formula Mass and Molar Mass**

LEARNING GOAL

**4** Calculate the formula mass and molar mass of a compound.

Calculate the formula mass and molar mass of sodium sulfate.

**Solution**

**Step 1.** The sodium ion is $Na^+$, and the sulfate ion is $SO_4^{2-}$. Two sodium ions must be present to neutralize the negative charges on the sulfate ion. The formula is $Na_2SO_4$. Sodium sulfate contains two sodium atoms, one sulfur atom, and four oxygen atoms.

**Step 2.** The formula mass is

$$
\begin{array}{ll}
2 \text{ atoms of sodium} \times 22.99 \text{ amu/atom} = & 45.98 \text{ amu} \\
1 \text{ atom of sulfur} \quad \times 32.06 \text{ amu/atom} = & 32.06 \text{ amu} \\
4 \text{ atoms of oxygen} \times 16.00 \text{ amu/atom} = & 64.00 \text{ amu} \\
\hline
& 142.04 \text{ amu}
\end{array}
$$

**Step 3.** The average mass of a single unit of $Na_2SO_4$ is 142.04 amu and is the formula mass. Therefore the mass of a mol of $Na_2SO_4$ is 142.04 g, or 142.04 g/mol.

**Practice Problem 4.8**

Calculate the formula mass and molar mass of $C_6H_{12}O_6$ (a sugar, glucose).

▶ For Further Practice: **Questions 4.35 and 4.36.**

**EXAMPLE 4.9**    **Calculating Formula Mass and Molar Mass**

LEARNING GOAL

**4**    Calculate the formula mass and molar mass of a compound.

Calculate the formula mass and molar mass of calcium phosphate.

**Solution**

**Step 1.** The calcium ion is $Ca^{2+}$, and the phosphate ion is $PO_4^{3-}$. To form a neutral unit, three $Ca^{2+}$ must combine with two $PO_4^{3-}$; $[3 \times (+2)]$ calcium ion charges are balanced by $[2 \times (-3)]$ phosphate ion charges.

**Step 2.** Thus, for calcium phosphate, $Ca_3(PO_4)_2$, the subscript two for phosphate dictates that there are two phosphorus atoms and eight oxygen atoms $(2 \times 4)$ in the formula unit.

**Step 3.** Therefore

$$
\begin{aligned}
&3 \text{ atoms of Ca} \times 40.08 \text{ amu/atom} = 120.24 \text{ amu} \\
&2 \text{ atoms of P} \ \times 30.97 \text{ amu/atom} = \ \ 61.94 \text{ amu} \\
&8 \text{ atoms of O} \ \times 16.00 \text{ amu/atom} = 128.00 \text{ amu} \\
&\hline
&\phantom{3 \text{ atoms of Ca} \times 40.08 \text{ amu/atom}} 310.18 \text{ amu}
\end{aligned}
$$

**Step 4.** The formula mass of calcium phosphate is 310.18 amu, and the molar mass is 310.18 g/mol.

---

**Practice Problem 4.9**

Calculate the formula mass and molar mass of $CoCl_2 \cdot 6H_2O$ (cobalt chloride hexahydrate).

▶ For Further Practice: **Questions 4.37 and 4.38.**

**Question 4.3**    Caffeine occurs naturally in coffee and tea, and is present in many soft drinks. The formula of caffeine is $C_8H_{10}N_4O_2$. Calculate the formula mass and molar mass of caffeine.

**Question 4.4**    The formula of ascorbic acid, commonly known as vitamin C, is $C_6H_8O_6$. Calculate the formula mass and molar mass of vitamin C.

## 4.3    The Chemical Equation and the Information It Conveys

### A Recipe for Chemical Change

LEARNING GOAL

**5**    Know the major function served by the chemical equation, the basis for chemical calculations.

The **chemical equation** is the shorthand notation for a chemical reaction. It describes all of the substances that react and all the products that form. **Reactants,** or starting materials, are all substances that undergo change in a chemical reaction; **products** are substances produced by a chemical reaction.

The chemical equation also describes the physical state of the reactants and products as solid, liquid, or gas. It tells us whether the reaction occurs and identifies the solvent and experimental conditions employed, such as heat, light, or electrical energy added to the system.

Most important, the relative number of mol of reactants and products appears in the equation. According to the **law of conservation of mass,** matter cannot be either gained or lost in the process of a chemical reaction. The total mass of the products must be equal to the total mass of the reactants. In other words, the law of conservation of mass tells us that we must have a balanced chemical equation.

**ANIMATION**

• Conservation of Mass

# Features of a Chemical Equation

Consider the decomposition of calcium carbonate:

$$CaCO_3(s) \xrightarrow{\Delta} CaO(s) + CO_2(g)$$

Calcium carbonate　　　Calcium oxide　Carbon dioxide

This equation reads: One mole of solid calcium carbonate decomposes upon heating to produce one mole of solid calcium oxide and one mole of gaseous carbon dioxide.

The factors involved in writing equations of this type are described as follows:

1. **The identity of products and reactants must be specified using chemical symbols.** In some cases it is possible to predict the products of a reaction. More often, the reactants and products must be verified by chemical analysis. (Generally, you will be given information regarding the identity of the reactants and products.)
2. **Reactants are written to the left of the reaction arrow ($\rightarrow$), and products are written to the right.** The direction in which the arrow points indicates the direction in which the reaction proceeds. In the decomposition of calcium carbonate, the reactant on the left ($CaCO_3$) is converted to products on the right ($CaO + CO_2$) during the course of the reaction.
3. **The physical states of reactants and products may be shown in parentheses.** For example:

   - $Cl_2(g)$ means that chlorine is in the gaseous state.
   - $Mg(s)$ indicates that magnesium is a solid.
   - $Br_2(l)$ indicates that bromine is present as a liquid.
   - $NH_3(aq)$ tells us that ammonia is present as an aqueous solution (ammonia is dissolved in water).

4. **The symbol $\Delta$ over the reaction arrow means that energy is necessary for the reaction to occur.** Often this and other special conditions are noted above or below the reaction arrow. For example, "light" means that a light source provides energy necessary for the reaction. Such reactions are termed photochemical reactions.
5. **The equation must be balanced.** All of the atoms of every reactant must also appear in the products, although in different compounds. We will treat this topic in detail later in this chapter.

According to the factors outlined, the equation for the decomposition of calcium carbonate may now be written as

$$CaCO_3(s) \xrightarrow{\Delta} CaO(s) + CO_2(g)$$

# The Experimental Basis of a Chemical Equation

The chemical equation must represent a chemical change: One or more substances are changed into new substances, with different chemical and physical properties. Evidence for the reaction may be based on observations such as

- the release of carbon dioxide gas when an acid is added to a carbonate,
- the formation of a solid (or precipitate) when solutions of iron ions and hydroxide ions are mixed,
- the production of heat when using hot packs for treatment of injury, and
- the change in color of a solution upon addition of a second substance.

*See discussion of acid-base reactions in Chapter 8.*

*See A Medical Perspective: Hot and Cold Packs in Chapter 7.*

Many reactions are not so obvious. Sophisticated instruments are now available to the chemist. These instruments allow the detection of subtle changes in chemical systems that would otherwise go unnoticed. Such instruments may measure

- heat or light absorbed or emitted as the result of a reaction,
- changes in the way the sample behaves in an electric or magnetic field before and after a reaction, and
- changes in electrical properties before and after a reaction.

Whether we use our senses or a million-dollar computerized instrument, the "bottom line" is the same: We are measuring a change in one or more chemical or physical properties in an effort to understand the changes taking place in a chemical system, the conversion of reactants to new products.

Disease can be described as a chemical system (actually a biochemical system) gone awry. Here, too, the underlying changes may not be obvious. Just as technology has helped chemists see subtle chemical changes in the laboratory, medical diagnosis has been revolutionized in our lifetimes using very similar technology. Some of these techniques are described in A Medical Perspective: Magnetic Resonance Imaging, in Chapter 9.

## Strategies for Writing Chemical Equations

Chemical reactions, whether they involve the formation of precipitate, reaction with oxygen, acids and bases, or oxidation-reduction, generally follow one of a few simple patterns: combination, decomposition, and single- or double-replacement. Recognizing the underlying pattern will improve your ability to write chemical equations and understand chemical reactions.

### Combination Reactions

**Combination reactions** involve the joining of two or more elements or compounds, producing a product of different composition. The general form of a combination reaction is

$$A + B \longrightarrow AB$$

in which $A$ and $B$ represent reactant elements or compounds and $AB$ is the product.

Examples include

1. combination of a metal and a nonmetal to form a salt,

$$Ca(s) + Cl_2(g) \longrightarrow CaCl_2(s)$$

2. combination of hydrogen and chlorine molecules to produce hydrogen chloride,

$$H_2(g) + Cl_2(g) \longrightarrow 2HCl(g)$$

3. formation of water from hydrogen and oxygen molecules,

$$2H_2(g) + O_2(g) \longrightarrow 2H_2O(g)$$

4. reaction of magnesium oxide and carbon dioxide to produce magnesium carbonate,

$$MgO(s) + CO_2(g) \longrightarrow MgCO_3(s)$$

### Decomposition Reactions

**Decomposition reactions** produce two or more products from a single reactant. The general form of these reactions is the reverse of a combination reaction:

$$AB \longrightarrow A + B$$

Some examples are

1. the heating of calcium carbonate to produce calcium oxide and carbon dioxide,

$$CaCO_3(s) \longrightarrow CaO(s) + CO_2(g)$$

2. the removal of water from a hydrated material (a *hydrate* is a substance that has water molecules incorporated in its structure),

$$CuSO_4 \cdot 5H_2O(s) \longrightarrow CuSO_4(s) + 5H_2O(g)$$

*Hydrated compounds are described on page 134.*

## Replacement Reactions

Replacement reactions include both *single-replacement* and *double-replacement*. In a **single-replacement reaction,** one atom replaces another in the compound, producing a new compound:

$$A + BC \longrightarrow AC + B$$

Examples include

1. the replacement of copper by zinc in copper sulfate,

$$Zn(s) + CuSO_4(aq) \longrightarrow ZnSO_4(aq) + Cu(s)$$

*In a single-replacement reaction, an element replaces an ion. In the first example, zinc metal is converted to $Zn^{2+}$ and replaces $Cu^{2+}$ in the $CuSO_4$. $Cu^{2+}$, in turn, is converted to copper metal.*

2. the replacement of aluminum by sodium in aluminum nitrate,

$$3Na(s) + Al(NO_3)_3(aq) \longrightarrow 3NaNO_3(aq) + Al(s)$$

A **double-replacement reaction,** on the other hand, involves *two compounds* undergoing a "change of partners." Two compounds react by exchanging atoms to produce two new compounds:

$$AB + CD \longrightarrow AD + CB$$

Examples include

1. the reaction of an acid (hydrochloric acid) and a base (sodium hydroxide) to produce water and salt, sodium chloride,

$$HCl(aq) + NaOH(aq) \longrightarrow H_2O(l) + NaCl(aq)$$

*Two ions Swap positions.*

2. the formation of solid barium sulfate from barium chloride and potassium sulfate,

$$BaCl_2(aq) + K_2SO_4(aq) \longrightarrow BaSO_4(s) + 2KCl(aq)$$

**Question 4.5**   Classify each of the following reactions as decomposition (D), combination (C), single-replacement (SR), or double-replacement (DR):

a. $HNO_3(aq) + KOH(aq) \longrightarrow KNO_3(aq) + H_2O(aq)$
b. $Al(s) + 3NiNO_3(aq) \longrightarrow Al(NO_3)_3(aq) + 3Ni(s)$
c. $KCN(aq) + HCl(aq) \longrightarrow HCN(aq) + KCl(aq)$
d. $MgCO_3(s) \longrightarrow MgO(s) + CO_2(g)$

**Question 4.6**   Classify each of the following reactions as decomposition (D), combination (C), single-replacement (SR), or double-replacement (DR):

a. $2Al(OH)_3(s) \overset{\Delta}{\longrightarrow} Al_2O_3(s) + 3H_2O(g)$
b. $Fe_2S_3(s) \overset{\Delta}{\longrightarrow} 2Fe(s) + 3S(s)$
c. $Na_2CO_3(aq) + BaCl_2(aq) \longrightarrow BaCO_3(s) + 2NaCl(aq)$
d. $C(s) + O_2(g) \overset{\Delta}{\longrightarrow} CO_2(g)$

## 4.4   Chemical Equations Represent Chemical Change

The chemical equation shows the *molar quantity* of reactants needed to produce a certain *molar quantity* of products.

**LEARNING GOAL**

**7**   Balance chemical equations given the identity of products and reactants.

The coefficients indicate *relative* numbers of mol: 10 mol of $CaCO_3$ produce 10 mol of $CaO$; 0.5 mol of $CaCO_3$ produce 0.5 mol of $CaO$; and so forth.

## Balancing Chemical Equations

The relative number of mol of each product and reactant is indicated by placing a whole-number *coefficient* before the formula of each substance in the chemical equation. A coefficient of two (for example, $2NaCl$) indicates that 2 mol of sodium chloride are involved in the reaction. Also, $3NH_3$ signifies 3 mol of ammonia; it means that 3 mol of nitrogen atoms and $3 \times 3$, or 9, mol of hydrogen atoms are involved in the reaction. The coefficient one is understood, not written. Therefore $H_2SO_4$ would be interpreted as 1 mol of sulfuric acid, or 2 mol of hydrogen atoms, 1 mol of sulfur atoms, and 4 mol of oxygen atoms.

Consider the equation:

$$2Na(s) + Cl_2(g) \longrightarrow 2NaCl(s)$$

The equation is balanced because there are two Na and two Cl on each side of the reaction arrow.

Now consider the equation:

$$CaCO_3(s) \xrightarrow{\Delta} CaO(s) + CO_2(g)$$

It is balanced as written. On the reactant side we have one mol of $CaCO_3$, which is:

1 mol Ca

1 mol C

3 mol O

On the product side there are one mol of CaO and one mol of $CO_2$, which is:

1 mol Ca

1 mol C

3 mol O

**ANIMATION**
• Conservation of Mass

*Therefore the law of conservation of mass is obeyed,* and the equation is balanced as written.

Now consider the reaction of aqueous hydrogen chloride with solid calcium metal in aqueous solution:

$$HCl(aq) + Ca(s) \longrightarrow CaCl_2(aq) + H_2(g)$$

The equation, as written, is not balanced.

| Reactants | Products |
|---|---|
| 1 mol H atoms | 2 mol H atoms |
| 1 mol Cl atoms | 2 mol Cl atoms |
| 1 mol Ca atoms | 1 mol Ca atoms |

Coefficients placed in front of the formula indicate the relative numbers of mol of compound (represented by the formula) that are involved in the reaction. Subscripts placed to the lower right of the atomic symbol indicate the relative number of atoms in the compound.

We need 2 mol of both H and Cl on the left, or reactant, side. An *incorrect* way of balancing the equation is as follows:

$$H_2Cl_2(aq) + Ca(s) \longrightarrow CaCl_2(aq) + H_2(g)$$
NOT a correct equation

Water ($H_2O$) and hydrogen peroxide ($H_2O_2$) illustrate the effect a subscript can have. The two compounds show marked differences in physical and chemical properties.

The equation satisfies the law of conservation of mass; however, we have altered one of the reacting species. Hydrogen chloride is HCl, not $H_2Cl_2$. We must remember that *we cannot alter any chemical substance in the process of balancing the equation.* We can *only* introduce coefficients into the equation. Changing subscripts changes the identity of the substances involved, and that is not permitted. The equation must represent the reaction accurately. The correct equation is

$$2HCl(aq) + Ca(s) \longrightarrow CaCl_2(aq) + H_2(g)$$
Correct equation

This process is illustrated in Figure 4.5.

Many equations are balanced by trial and error. After the identity of the products and reactants, the physical states, and the reaction conditions are known, the following steps provide a method for correctly balancing a chemical equation:

*Step 1.* Count the number of mol of atoms of each element on both product and reactant side.

*Step 2.* Determine which elements are not balanced.

*Step 3.* Balance one element at a time using coefficients.

*Step 4.* When you believe that you have successfully balanced the equation, check, as in step 1, to be certain that mass conservation has been achieved.

Let us apply these steps to the reaction of calcium with aqueous hydrogen chloride:

$$HCl(aq) + Ca(s) \longrightarrow CaCl_2(aq) + H_2(g)$$

*Step 1.* **Reactants**          **Products**

    1 mol H atoms          2 mol H atoms

    1 mol Cl atoms          2 mol Cl atoms

    1 mol Ca atoms          1 mol Ca atoms

*Step 2.* The numbers of mol of H and Cl are not balanced.

Do not dismantle a polyatomic ion. It will retain its identity on both reactant and product sides.

Generally, when using trial and error, save H and O for the very end of the process.

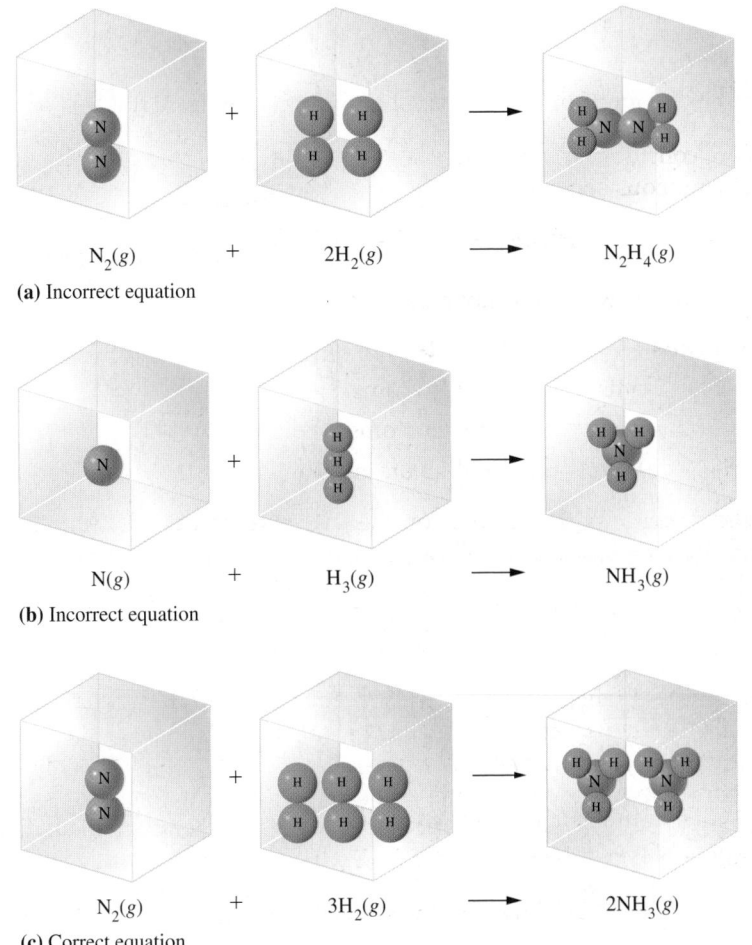

**Figure 4.5** Balancing the equation $N_2(g) + H_2(g) \longrightarrow NH_3(g)$ (a) The product is not the correct chemical species. (b) The reactants, $N_2(g)$ and $H_2(g)$, are incorrectly represented as N and $H_3$. (c) This equation is correct; and species are correct, and the law of conservation of mass is obeyed.

$N_2(g)$ + $2H_2(g)$ $\longrightarrow$ $N_2H_4(g)$

**(a)** Incorrect equation

$N(g)$ + $H_3(g)$ $\longrightarrow$ $NH_3(g)$

**(b)** Incorrect equation

$N_2(g)$ + $3H_2(g)$ $\longrightarrow$ $2NH_3(g)$

**(c)** Correct equation

**Step 3.** Insertion of a 2 before HCl on the reactant side should balance the equation:

$$2HCl(aq) + Ca(s) \longrightarrow CaCl_2(aq) + H_2(g)$$

**Step 4.** Check for mass balance:

| Reactants | Products |
|---|---|
| 2 mol H atoms | 2 mol H atoms |
| 2 mol Cl atoms | 2 mol Cl atoms |
| 1 mol Ca atoms | 1 mol Ca atoms |

Hence the equation is balanced.

---

**EXAMPLE 4.10**    **Balancing Equations**

LEARNING GOAL

**7** Balance chemical equations given the identity of products and reactants.

Balance the following equation: Hydrogen gas and oxygen gas react explosively to produce gaseous water.

**Solution**

Recall that hydrogen and oxygen are diatomic gases; therefore

$$H_2(g) + O_2(g) \longrightarrow H_2O(g)$$

**Step 1.** Count the number of mol of atoms of each element on both product and reactant side.

| Reactants | Products |
|---|---|
| 2 mol H atoms | 2 mol H atoms |
| 2 mol O atoms | 1 mol O atoms |

**Step 2.** Note that the mol of hydrogen atoms are balanced but that the mol of oxygen atoms are not.

**Step 3.** We must first balance the mol of oxygen atoms. Insert 2 before $H_2O$.

$$H_2(g) + O_2(g) \longrightarrow 2H_2O(g)$$

Balancing mol of oxygen atoms creates an imbalance in the number of mol of hydrogen atoms, so

$$2H_2(g) + O_2(g) \longrightarrow 2H_2O(g)$$

**Step 4.** The equation is balanced, with 4 mol of hydrogen atoms and 2 mol of oxygen atoms on each side of the reaction arrow.

**Practice Problem 4.10**

Balance the chemical equation: $Fe(s) + O_2(g) \longrightarrow Fe_2O_3(s)$

▶ For Further Practice: **Questions 4.67 and 4.68.**

---

**EXAMPLE 4.11**    **Balancing Equations**

LEARNING GOAL

**7** Balance chemical equations given the identity of products and reactants.

Balance the following equation: Propane gas, $C_3H_8$, a fuel, reacts with oxygen gas to produce carbon dioxide and water vapor. The reaction is

$$C_3H_8(g) + O_2(g) \longrightarrow CO_2(g) + H_2O(g)$$

## Solution

**Step 1.** Count the number of mol of atoms of each element on both product and reactant side.

| Reactants | Products |
|-----------|----------|
| 3 mol C atoms | 1 mol C atoms |
| 8 mol H atoms | 2 mol H atoms |
| 2 mol O atoms | 3 mol O atoms |

**Step 2.** Note that C, H, and O atoms are not balanced.

**Step 3.** First, balance the carbon atoms; save hydrogen and oxygen for later. There are 3 mol of carbon atoms on the left and only 1 mol of carbon atoms on the right. We need $3CO_2$ on the right side of the equation:

$$C_3H_8(g) + O_2(g) \longrightarrow 3CO_2(g) + H_2O(g)$$

Next, balance the hydrogen atoms; there are 2 mol of hydrogen atoms on the right and 8 mol of hydrogen atoms on the left. We need to place a 4 in front of $H_2O$ on the right side of the equation:

$$C_3H_8(g) + O_2(g) \longrightarrow 3CO_2(g) + 4H_2O(g)$$

There are now 10 mol of oxygen atoms on the right (4 mol O from 4 mol $H_2O$ and 6 mol O from 3 mol $CO_2$) and 2 mol of oxygen atoms (2 mol of O from 1 mol $O_2$) on the left. To balance, we must have $5O_2$ (10 mol oxygen atoms) on the left side of the equation:

$$C_3H_8(g) + 5O_2(g) \longrightarrow 3CO_2(g) + 4H_2O(g)$$

**Step 4.** *Remember:* In every case, be sure to check the final equation for mass balance.

### Practice Problem 4.11

Balance the chemical equation:

$$C_2H_5OH(l) + O_2(g) \longrightarrow CO_2(g) + H_2O(g)$$

▶ For Further Practice: **Questions 4.71, a, b, c, and 4.72, a, b, c.**

---

**EXAMPLE 4.12**   **Balancing Equations**

LEARNING GOAL

Balance the following equation: Butane gas, $C_4H_{10}$, a fuel used in pocket lighters, reacts with oxygen gas to produce carbon dioxide and water vapor. The reaction is

**7** Balance chemical equations given the identity of products and reactants.

$$C_4H_{10}(g) + O_2(g) \longrightarrow CO_2(g) + H_2O(g)$$

## Solution

**Step 1.** Count the number of mol of atoms of each element on both product and reactant side.

| Reactants | Products |
|-----------|----------|
| 4 mol C atoms | 1 mol C atoms |
| 10 mol H atoms | 2 mol H atoms |
| 2 mol O atoms | 3 mol O atoms |

**Step 2.** Note that C, H, and O atoms are not balanced.

**Step 3.** First, balance the carbon atoms; there are 4 mol of carbon atoms on the left and only 1 mol of carbon atoms on the right. Place the coefficient 4 in front of $CO_2$.

$$C_4H_{10}(g) + O_2(g) \longrightarrow 4CO_2(g) + H_2O(g)$$

*Continued...*

Next, balance hydrogen atoms; there are 10 mol of hydrogen atoms on the left and only 2 mol of hydrogen atoms on the right. Place the coefficient 5 in front of $H_2O$.

$$C_4H_{10}(g) + O_2(g) \longrightarrow 4CO_2(g) + 5H_2O(g)$$

There are now 13 mol of oxygen atoms on the right and only 2 mol of oxygen atoms on the left. Therefore a coefficient of 6.5 is necessary (6.5 × 2 mol oxygen atoms equals 13 mol oxygen atoms) for $O_2$.

$$C_4H_{10}(g) + 6.5O_2(g) \longrightarrow 4CO_2(g) + 5H_2O(g)$$

Fractional or decimal coefficients are often needed and used. However, the preferred form requires all integer coefficients. Multiplying each term in the equation by a suitable integer (2, in this case) satisfies this requirement. Hence

$$2C_4H_{10}(g) + 13O_2(g) \longrightarrow 8CO_2(g) + 10H_2O(g)$$

**Step 4.** The equation is balanced, with 8 mol of carbon atoms, 20 mol of hydrogen atoms, and 26 mol of oxygen atoms on each side of the reaction arrow.

*Helpful Hint:* When balancing equations, it is often most efficient to begin by balancing the atoms in the most complicated formulas.

---

**Practice Problem 4.12**

Balance the chemical equation: $C_6H_6(l) + O_2(g) \longrightarrow CO_2(g) + H_2O(g)$

▶ For Further Practice: **Questions 4.71 d, e and 4.72 d, e.**

---

| EXAMPLE 4.13 | **Balancing Equations** |
|---|---|

LEARNING GOAL

Balance the following equation: Aqueous ammonium sulfate reacts with aqueous lead nitrate to produce aqueous ammonium nitrate and solid lead sulfate. The reaction is

**7** Balance chemical equations given the identity of products and reactants.

$$(NH_4)_2SO_4(aq) + Pb(NO_3)_2(aq) \longrightarrow NH_4NO_3(aq) + PbSO_4(s)$$

**Solution**

In this double-replacement reaction the polyatomic ions remain as intact units. Therefore we can balance them as we would balance molecules rather than as atoms.

There are two ammonium ions on the left and only one ammonium ion on the right. Hence

$$(NH_4)_2SO_4(aq) + Pb(NO_3)_2(aq) \longrightarrow 2NH_4NO_3(aq) + PbSO_4(s)$$

No further steps are necessary. The equation is now balanced. There are two ammonium ions, two nitrate ions, one lead ion, and one sulfate ion on each side of the reaction arrow.

---

**Practice Problem 4.13**

Balance the chemical equation:

$$S_2Cl_2(s) + NH_3(g) \longrightarrow N_4S_4(s) + NH_4Cl(s) + S_8(s)$$

▶ For Further Practice: **Questions 4.73 and 4.74.**

## Classifying Chemical Reactions

The most commonly encountered chemical reactions involve:

- the combination of soluble ions to produce an insoluble solid
- the reaction of a substance with oxygen, *oxidation,* to produce a new substance
- the reaction of acids and bases involving the transfer of hydrogen ions
- the transfer of one or more electrons from one reactant to another, *oxidation-reduction*

**ANIMATIONS**
- Types of Reactions
- Predicting Precipitation Reactions

### Precipitation Reactions

Precipitation reactions include any chemical change in solution that results in one or more insoluble product(s). The insoluble product is termed a **precipitate.** For aqueous solution reactions the product is insoluble in water.

An understanding of precipitation reactions is useful in many ways. They may explain natural phenomena, such as the formation of stalagmites and stalactites in caves; these are simply precipitates in rocklike form. Kidney stones may result from the precipitation of calcium oxalate ($CaC_2O_4$). The routine act of preparing a solution requires that none of the solutes will react to form a precipitate.

How do you know whether a precipitate will form? Readily available solubility tables, such as Table 4.1, make prediction rather easy.

The following example illustrates the process.

### Reactions with Oxygen

Many substances react with oxygen. These reactions generally release energy. The combustion of gasoline is used for transportation. Fossil fuel combustion is

---

**LEARNING GOAL**

**8** Recognize the various classes of chemical reactions: precipitation, reactions with oxygen, acid-base, and oxidation-reduction.

---

Precipitation reactions may be written as net ionic equations. See page 147.

---

| EXAMPLE 4.14 | Predicting Whether Precipitation Will Occur |
|---|---|

**LEARNING GOAL**

**8** Recognize the various classes of chemical reactions: precipitation, reactions with oxygen, acid-base, and oxidation-reduction.

Will a precipitate form if two solutions of the soluble salts NaCl and $AgNO_3$ are mixed?

**Solution**

**Step 1.** Two soluble salts, if they react to form a precipitate, will "exchange partners":

$$NaCl(aq) + AgNO_3(aq) \longrightarrow AgCl(?) + NaNO_3(?)$$

**Step 2.** Refer to Table 4.1 to determine the solubility of AgCl and $NaNO_3$. We predict that $NaNO_3$ is soluble and AgCl is not:

$$NaCl(aq) + AgNO_3(aq) \longrightarrow AgCl(s) + NaNO_3(aq)$$

**Step 3.** The fact that solid AgCl is predicted to form classifies this double-replacement reaction as a precipitation reaction.

*Helpful Hints:* (*aq*) indicates a soluble species; (*s*) indicates a solid, an insoluble species.

---

**Practice Problem 4.14**

Predict whether the following reactants, when mixed in aqueous solution, undergo a precipitation reaction. Write a balanced equation for each precipitation reaction.

a. potassium chloride and silver nitrate
b. potassium acetate and silver nitrate
c. sodium hydroxide and ammonium chloride
d. sodium hydroxide and iron(II) chloride

▶ For Further Practice: **Questions 4.77 and 4.78.**

**TABLE 4.1 Solubilities of Some Common Ionic Compounds**

| Soluble Compounds | Exceptions |
|---|---|
| Compounds containing alkali metal ions ($Li^+$, $Na^+$, $K^+$, $Rb^+$, $Cs^+$) and the ammonium ion ($NH_4^+$) | |
| Nitrates ($NO_3^-$), bicarbonates ($HCO_3^-$), and chlorates ($ClO_3^-$) | |
| Halides ($Cl^-$, $Br^-$, $I^-$) | Halides of $Ag^+$, $Hg_2^{2+}$, and $Pb^{2+}$ |
| Sulfates ($SO_4^{2-}$) | Sulfates of $Ag^+$, $Ca^{2+}$, $Sr^{2+}$, $Ba^{2+}$, $Hg_2^{2+}$, and $Pb^{2+}$ |

| Insoluble Compounds | Exceptions |
|---|---|
| Carbonates ($CO_3^{2-}$), phosphates ($PO_4^{3-}$), chromates ($CrO_4^{2-}$), and sulfides ($S^{2-}$) | Compounds containing alkali metal ions and the ammonium ion |
| Hydroxides ($OH^-$) | Compounds containing alkali metal ions and the $Ba^{2+}$ ion |

**ANIMATIONS**
• Precipitation of Barium Sulfate
• Precipitation of Lead Iodide

Formation of a precipitate, BaSO4.

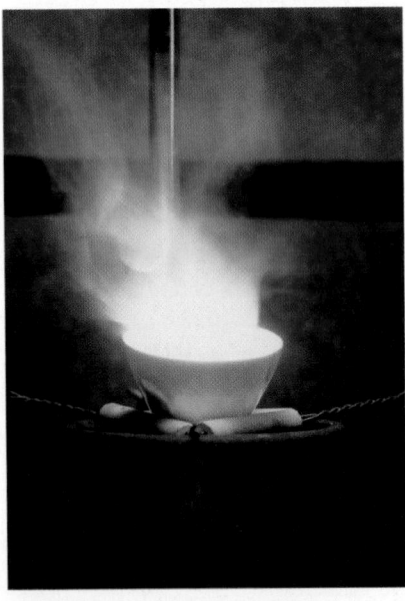

Some reactions of metals with oxygen are very rapid. A dramatic example is the reaction of magnesium with oxygen.

$$2Mg(s) + O_2(g) \longrightarrow 2MgO(s)$$

used to heat homes and provide energy for industry. Reactions involving oxygen provide energy for all sorts of biochemical processes.

When organic (carbon-containing) compounds react with the oxygen in air (burning), carbon dioxide is usually produced. If the compound contains hydrogen, water is the other product.

The reaction between oxygen and methane, $CH_4$, the major component of natural gas, is

$$CH_4(g) + 2O_2(g) \longrightarrow CO_2(g) + 2H_2O(g)$$

$CO_2$ and $H_2O$ are waste products, and $CO_2$ may contribute to the greenhouse effect and global warming. The really important, unseen product is heat energy. That is why we use this reaction in our furnaces!

Inorganic substances also react with oxygen and produce heat, but these reactions usually proceed more slowly. *Corrosion* (rusting iron) is a familiar example:

$$4Fe(s) + 3O_2(g) \longrightarrow 2Fe_2O_3(s)$$
$$\text{Rust}$$

## Acid-Base Reactions

Another approach to the classification of chemical reactions is based on the gain or loss of hydrogen ions. **Acid-base reactions** involve the transfer of a *hydrogen ion*, $H^+$, from one reactant (the acid) to another (the base).

A common example of an acid-base reaction involves hydrochloric acid and sodium hydroxide:

$$HCl(aq) + NaOH(aq) \longrightarrow H_2O(l) + Na^+(aq) + Cl^-(aq)$$
$$\text{Acid} \quad\quad \text{Base} \quad\quad\quad \text{Water} \quad\quad\quad \text{Salt}$$

A hydrogen ion is transferred from the acid to the base, producing water and a salt in solution. Acid and base properties and reactions are important in virtually all aspects of chemistry and biochemistry; for this reason, they are considered in much greater detail in Chapter 8.

## Oxidation-Reduction Reactions

Another important reaction type, **oxidation-reduction,** takes place because of the transfer of negative charge (one or more *electrons*) from one reactant to another.

The reaction of zinc metal with copper(II) ions is one example of oxidation-reduction:

$$Zn(s) \quad + \quad Cu^{2+}(aq) \quad \longrightarrow \quad Zn^{2+}(aq) \quad + \quad Cu(s)$$

| | | | |
|---|---|---|---|
| ↑ | ↑ | ↑ | ↑ |
| Substance to be oxidized | Substance to be reduced | Oxidized product | Reduced product |

Zinc metal atoms each donate two electrons to copper(II) ions; consequently zinc atoms become zinc(II) ions and copper(II) ions become copper atoms. Zinc is oxidized (increased positive charge) and copper is reduced (decreased positive charge) as a result of electron transfer.

Oxidation-reduction processes will be discussed more fully in Section 8.5.

## Writing Precipitation Reactions as Net Ionic Equations

### Writing Net Ionic Equations

The equation that we developed in Example 4.14 is written as a *molecular equation*. Although technically correct and properly balanced, it conveys no information about the way the products and reactants exist in solution, other than the precipitate. In reality, all four species are ionic compounds; both reactants and one product are actually *dissociated* in solution, existing as ions. Only the product, AgCl, is associated. Our solubility rules predicted that AgCl is a solid, crystalline precipitate. A more useful representation would show all of the reactants and products in the form in which they are actually present in solution, solid AgCl surrounded by an aqueous collection of ions. This is an *ionic equation*. Even greater clarity can be achieved by removing the ions that do not change during the course of the reaction (spectator ions), to produce a *net ionic equation*. The net ionic equation only shows the chemical species that actually undergo change. This is the approach that is most faithful to our original concept of a chemical equation: an accurate depiction of chemical *change*. The process we use to write a net ionic equation for a precipitation reaction is as follows:

1. Write a balanced molecular equation for the process being considered. Use the solubility rules to identify any precipitates.
2. Write the ionic equation showing all reactants and products as free ions unless they are precipitates.
3. Ions that appear on both sides of the equation are *spectator ions* (they do not undergo change) and are cancelled out. What remains is the net ionic equation.
4. Ensure that charges and numbers of atoms are balanced, just as they must be in a conventional equation.

Example 4.15 shows how this procedure is applied.

Passing an electrical current through water causes an oxidation-reduction reaction. The products are $H_2$ and $O_2$ in a 2:1 ratio. Is this ratio of products predicted by the equation for the decomposition of water, $2H_2O(l) \longrightarrow 2H_2(g) + O_2(g)$? Explain.

---

All of the reactions with oxygen (discussed earlier) are oxidation-reduction reactions as well.

---

**WRITING NET IONIC EQUATIONS**

---

**EXAMPLE 4.15**    **Writing Net Ionic Equations**

In Example 4.14 we considered the reaction of NaCl and $AgNO_3$. We wrote the chemical equation for this process in the form of a molecular equation. Now, write this process as a net ionic equation.

**LEARNING GOAL**

**8** Recognize the various classes of chemical reactions: precipitation, reactions with oxygen, acid-base, and oxidation-reduction.

**Solution**

**Step 1.** Write the balanced molecular equation. In Example 4.14 we found:

$$NaCl(aq) + AgNO_3(aq) \longrightarrow AgCl(?) + NaNO_3(?)$$

The solubility rules predicted that AgCl is a precipitate; rewriting our equation to show this information results in:

$$NaCl(aq) + AgNO_3(aq) \longrightarrow AgCl(s) + NaNO_3(aq)$$

*Continued…*

**Step 2.** AgCl is a precipitate and should be written in its associated form; all others are not, and should be written in ionic form:

$$\text{Na}^+(aq) + \text{Cl}^-(aq) + \text{Ag}^+(aq) + \text{NO}_3^-(aq) \longrightarrow \text{AgCl}(s) + \text{Na}^+(aq) + \text{NO}_3^-(aq)$$

This is the form of the ionic equation.

**Step 3.** $\text{Na}^+(aq)$ and $\text{NO}_3^-(aq)$ appear on both sides of the equation and are spectator ions that cancel out because they are unchanged during the course of the reaction:

$$\cancel{\text{Na}^+(aq)} + \text{Cl}^-(aq) + \text{Ag}^+(aq) + \cancel{\text{NO}_3^-(aq)} \longrightarrow \text{AgCl}(s) + \cancel{\text{Na}^+(aq)} + \cancel{\text{NO}_3^-(aq)}$$

**Step 4.** We must now ensure that both net charge and number of atoms of each kind are the same on both sides of the reaction arrow.

Counting charges:

**Reactants:** one positive charge, $\text{Ag}^+(aq)$, and one negative charge, $\text{Cl}^-(aq)$, results in a net charge of zero.
**Products:** the only product, AgCl, has a zero charge.

Counting atoms:
**Reactants:** one Ag and one Cl atom.
**Products:** one Ag and one Cl atom.

Charges and numbers of atoms are balanced. The final net ionic equation representing the precipitation of silver chloride is:

$$\text{Ag}^+(aq) + \text{Cl}^-(aq) \longrightarrow \text{AgCl}(s)$$

---

**Practice Problem 4.15**

Write net ionic equations for the following reactions:

    a. $\text{BaCl}_2(aq) + \text{ZnSO}_4(aq) \longrightarrow$      b. $\text{AgNO}_3(aq) + \text{Na}_2\text{SO}_4(aq) \longrightarrow$

▶ For Further Practice: **Questions 4.79 and 4.80.**

---

**WRITING NET IONIC EQUATIONS**

Net ionic equations are useful, not only for precipitation reactions, but for any process involving ionic compounds in aqueous solution. We will see net ionic equations representing acid-base and oxidation-reduction reactions in Chapter 8. Further information about writing these equations may be found on the website under the heading "Writing Net Ionic Equations."

**Question 4.7** Write the net ionic equation representing a solution of $\text{Na}_2\text{S}$ mixed with a solution of $\text{CuCl}_2$.

**Question 4.8** Write the net ionic equation representing a solution of $\text{Na}_2\text{CO}_3$ mixed with a solution of $\text{CaCl}_2$.

---

## 4.5 Calculations Using the Chemical Equation

### General Principles

The calculation of quantities of products and reactants based on a balanced chemical equation is termed *stoichiometry,* and is important in many fields. The synthesis of drugs and other complex molecules on a large scale is conducted on the basis of a balanced equation. This minimizes the waste of expensive chemical compounds used in these reactions. Similarly, the ratio of fuel and air in a home furnace or automobile must be adjusted carefully, according to their combining ratio, to maximize energy conversion, minimize fuel consumption, and minimize pollution.

In carrying out chemical calculations, we apply the following guidelines:

1. The chemical formulas of all reactants and products must be known.
2. The basis for the calculations is a balanced equation because the conservation of mass must be obeyed. If the equation is not properly balanced, the calculation is meaningless.
3. The calculations are performed in terms of mol. The coefficients in the balanced equation represent the relative number of mol of products and reactants.

We have seen that the number of mol of products and reactants often differs in a balanced equation. For example,

$$C(s) + O_2(g) \longrightarrow CO_2(g)$$

is a balanced equation. Two mol of reactants combine to produce 1 mol of product:

$$1 \text{ mol C} + 1 \text{ mol O}_2 \longrightarrow 1 \text{ mol CO}_2$$

However, 1 mol of C *atoms* and 2 mol of O *atoms* produce 1 mol of C *atoms* and 2 mol of O *atoms*. In other words, the number of mol of reactants and products may differ, but the number of mol of atoms cannot. The formation of $CO_2$ from C and $O_2$ may be described as follows:

$$C(s) + O_2(g) \longrightarrow CO_2(g)$$
$$1 \text{ mol C} + 1 \text{ mol O}_2 \longrightarrow 1 \text{ mol CO}_2$$
$$12.0 \text{ g C} + 32.0 \text{ g O}_2 \longrightarrow 44.0 \text{ g CO}_2$$

The mol is the basis of our calculations. However, mol are generally measured in g (or kg). A facility for interconversion of mol and g is fundamental to chemical arithmetic (see Figure 4.2). These calculations, discussed earlier in this chapter, are reviewed in Example 4.16.

## Use of Conversion Factors

### Conversion Between Moles and Grams

Conversion from mol to g, and vice versa, requires only the formula mass of the compound of interest. Consider the following examples.

**ANIMATION**
• Stoichiometry

---

| EXAMPLE 4.16 | Converting Between Moles and Grams |
| --- | --- |

**LEARNING GOAL**

**9** Calculate the number of mol or g of product resulting from a given number of mol or g of reactants or the number of mol or g of reactant needed to produce a certain number of mol or g of product.

a. Convert 1.00 mol of oxygen gas, $O_2$, to g.

**Solution**

**Step 1.** Use the following path:

$$\boxed{\text{mol of oxygen}} \longrightarrow \boxed{\text{g of oxygen}}$$

**Step 2.** The molar mass of oxygen ($O_2$) is 32.00 g $O_2$, and the conversion factor becomes:

$$\frac{32.00 \text{ g O}_2}{1 \text{ mol O}_2}$$

*Continued...*

**Step 3.** Using the conversion factor (ensure that mol cancel):

$$1.00 \ \cancel{mol \ O_2} \times \frac{32.00 \ g \ O_2}{1 \ \cancel{mol \ O_2}} = 32.0 \ g \ O_2$$

b. How many g of carbon dioxide are contained in 10.0 mol of carbon dioxide?

**Solution**

**Step 1.** Use the following path:

$$\boxed{\text{mol of carbon dioxide}} \longrightarrow \boxed{\text{g of carbon dioxide}}$$

**Step 2.** The molar mass of $CO_2$ is 44.01 g $CO_2$, and the conversion factor becomes:

$$\frac{44.01 \ g \ CO_2}{1 \ mol \ CO_2}$$

**Step 3.** Using the conversion factor (ensure that mol cancel):

$$10.0 \ \cancel{mol \ CO_2} \times \frac{44.01 \ g \ CO_2}{1 \ \cancel{mol \ CO_2}} = 44.0 \times 10^1 \ g \ CO_2$$

c. How many mol of sodium are contained in 1 pound (lb) (454 g) of sodium metal?

**Solution**

**Step 1.** Use the following path:

$$\boxed{\text{g of sodium}} \longrightarrow \boxed{\text{mol of sodium}}$$

**Step 2.** The molar mass of Na is 22.99 g Na, and the conversion factor becomes:

$$\frac{1 \ mol \ Na}{22.99 \ g \ Na}$$

**Step 3.** Using the conversion factor (ensure that g Na cancel):

$$454 \ \cancel{g \ Na} \times \frac{1 \ mol \ Na}{22.99 \ \cancel{g \ Na}} = 19.7 \ mol \ Na$$

*Helpful Hint:* Note that each factor can be inverted, producing a second possible factor. Only one will allow the appropriate unit cancellation.

**Practice Problem 4.16**

Perform each of the following conversions:

   a. 5.00 mol of water to g of water
   b. 25.0 g of LiCl to mol of LiCl
   c. $1.00 \times 10^{-5}$ mol of $C_6H_{12}O_6$ to micrograms (μg) of $C_6H_{12}O_6$
   d. 35.0 g of $MgCl_2$ to mol of $MgCl_2$

▶ For Further Practice: **Questions 4.27 and 4.28.**

**Conversion of Moles of Reactants to Moles of Products**

In Example 4.11 we balanced the equation for the reaction of propane and oxygen as follows:

$$C_3H_8(g) + 5O_2(g) \longrightarrow 3CO_2(g) + 4H_2O(g)$$

In this reaction, 1 mol of $C_3H_8$ corresponds to, or results in,

5 mol of $O_2$ being consumed and

3 mol of $CO_2$ being formed and

4 mol of $H_2O$ being formed.

This information may be written in the form of a conversion factor or ratio:

$\dfrac{1 \text{ mol } C_3H_8}{5 \text{ mol } O_2}$  *Translated:* 1 mol of $C_3H_8$ reacts with 5 mol of $O_2$.

$\dfrac{1 \text{ mol } C_3H_8}{3 \text{ mol } CO_2}$  *Translated:* 1 mol of $C_3H_8$ produces 3 mol of $CO_2$.

$\dfrac{1 \text{ mol } C_3H_8}{4 \text{ mol } H_2O}$  *Translated:* 1 mol of $C_3H_8$ produces 4 mol of $H_2O$.

Conversion factors based on the chemical equation permit us to perform a variety of calculations.

Let us look at a few examples, based on the combustion of propane and the equation that we balanced in Example 4.11.

**LEARNING GOAL**

**9** Calculate the number of mol or g of product resulting from a given number of mol or g of reactants or the number of mol or g of reactant needed to produce a certain number of mol or g of product.

---

**EXAMPLE 4.17    Calculating Reacting Quantities**

Calculate the number of g of $O_2$ that will react with 1.00 mol of $C_3H_8$. The balanced equation is: $C_3H_8 (g) + 5O_2(g) \longrightarrow 3CO_2(g) + 4H_2O(g)$.

**Solution**

**Step 1.** Two conversion factors are necessary to solve this problem:

- conversion from mol of $C_3H_8$ to mol of $O_2$ and
- conversion of mol of $O_2$ to g of $O_2$.

**Step 2.** Therefore our path is:

$$\boxed{\text{mol } C_3H_8} \longrightarrow \boxed{\text{mol } O_2} \longrightarrow \boxed{\text{g } O_2}$$

**Step 3.** Set up conversion factors to cancel mol $C_3H_8$ and mol $O_2$:

$$1.00 \text{ mol } C_3H_8 \times \frac{5 \text{ mol } O_2}{1 \text{ mol } C_3H_8} \times \frac{32.00 \text{ g } O_2}{1 \text{ mol } O_2} = 1.60 \times 10^2 \text{ g } O_2$$

**LEARNING GOAL**

**9** Calculate the number of mol or g of product resulting from a given number of mol or g of reactants or the number of mol or g of reactant needed to produce a certain number of mol or g of product.

**Practice Problem 4.17**

When potassium cyanide (KCN) reacts with acids, hydrogen cyanide (HCN), a poisonous gas, is produced. The equation is

$$KCN(aq) + HCl(aq) \longrightarrow KCl(aq) + HCN(g)$$

Calculate the number of g of KCN that will react with 1.00 mol of HCl.

▶ For Further Practice: **Questions 4.85 and 4.86.**

# A HUMAN PERSPECTIVE

## The Chemistry of Automobile Air Bags

Each year, thousands of individuals are killed or seriously injured in automobile accidents. Perhaps most serious is the front-end collision. The car decelerates or stops virtually on impact; the momentum of the passengers, however, does not stop, and the driver and passengers are thrown forward toward the dashboard and the windshield. Suddenly, passive parts of the automobile, such as control knobs, the rearview mirror, the steering wheel, the dashboard, and the windshield, become lethal weapons.

Automobile engineers have been aware of these problems for a long time. They have made a series of design improvements to lessen the potential problems associated with front-end impact. Smooth switches rather than knobs, recessed hardware, and padded dashboards are examples. These changes, coupled with the use of lap and shoulder belts, which help to immobilize occupants of the car, have decreased the frequency and severity of occupant impact and lowered the death rate for this type of accident.

An almost ideal protection would be a soft, fluffy pillow, providing a cushion against impact. Such a device, an air bag inflated only on impact, is now standard equipment for the protection of the driver and front-seat passenger.

How does it work? Ideally, it inflates only when severe front-end impact occurs; it inflates very rapidly (in approximately 40 milliseconds (ms)), then deflates to provide a steady deceleration, cushioning the occupants from impact. A remarkably simple chemical reaction makes this a reality.

When solid sodium azide ($NaN_3$) is detonated by mechanical energy produced by an electrical current, it decomposes to form solid sodium and nitrogen gas:

$$2NaN_3(s) \longrightarrow 2Na(s) + 3N_2(g)$$

The nitrogen gas inflates the air bag, cushioning the driver and front-seat passenger.

The solid sodium azide has a high density (characteristic of solids) and thus occupies a small volume. It can easily be stored in the center of a steering wheel or in the dashboard. The rate of detonation is very rapid. In ms, the reaction produces 3 mol of $N_2$ gas for every 2 mol of $NaN_3$. The $N_2$ gas occupies a relatively large volume because its density is low. This is a general property of gases.

Figuring out how much sodium azide is needed to produce enough nitrogen to properly inflate the bag is an example of a practical application of the chemical arithmetic that we are learning in this chapter.

### For Further Understanding

▶ Why is nitrogen gas preferred for this application?
▶ If this reaction occurs in 5 ms, how many seconds (s) does this represent?

---

**EXAMPLE 4.18** **Calculating Grams of Product from Moles of Reactant**

**LEARNING GOAL**

**9** Calculate the number of mol or g of product resulting from a given number of mol or g of reactants or the number of mol or g of reactant needed to produce a certain number of mol or g of product.

Calculate the number of g of $CO_2$ produced from the combustion of 1.00 mol of $C_3H_8$ using the balanced equation from Example 4.17.

### Solution

**Steps 1. and 2.** Employ logic similar to that used in Example 4.17 and use the following path:

$$\boxed{\text{mol } C_3H_8} \longrightarrow \boxed{\text{mol } CO_2} \longrightarrow \boxed{\text{g } CO_2}$$

**Step 3.** Set up conversion factors to cancel mol $C_3H_8$ and mol $CO_2$:

$$1.00 \ \text{mol } C_3H_8 \times \frac{3 \ \text{mol } CO_2}{1 \ \text{mol } C_3H_8} \times \frac{44.01 \text{g } CO_2}{1 \ \text{mol } CO_2} = 132 \text{ g } CO_2$$

---

### Practice Problem 4.18

Fermentation is a critical step in the process of winemaking. The reaction is

$$\underset{\text{glucose}}{C_6H_{12}O_6(aq)} \longrightarrow \underset{\text{ethanol}}{2CH_3CH_2OH(aq)} + 2CO_2(g)$$

Calculate the number of g of ethanol produced from the fermentation of 5.00 mol of glucose.

▶ For Further Practice: **Questions 4.87 and 4.88.**

---

**EXAMPLE 4.19**    **Relating Masses of Reactants and Products**

Calculate the number of g of $C_3H_8$ required to produce 36.0 g of $H_2O$ using the balanced equation from Example 4.17.

**Solution**

**Steps 1. and 2.**  It is necessary to convert

g of $H_2O$ to mol of $H_2O$,
mol of $H_2O$ to mol of $C_3H_8$, and
mol of $C_3H_8$ to g of $C_3H_8$.
Use the following path:

$$\boxed{\begin{array}{c}g\\H_2O\end{array}} \longrightarrow \boxed{\begin{array}{c}mol\\H_2O\end{array}} \longrightarrow \boxed{\begin{array}{c}mol\\C_3H_8\end{array}} \longrightarrow \boxed{\begin{array}{c}g\\C_3H_8\end{array}}$$

**Step 3.**  Set up conversion factors to cancel g $H_2O$, mol $H_2O$, and mol $C_3H_8$:

$$36.0 \ g\ H_2O \times \frac{1 \ mol\ H_2O}{18.0 \ g\ H_2O} \times \frac{1 \ mol\ C_3H_8}{4 \ mol\ H_2O} \times \frac{44.09g\ C_3H_8}{1 \ mol\ C_3H_8} = 22.0\ g\ C_3H_8$$

---

**LEARNING GOAL**

**9** Calculate the number of mol or g of product resulting from a given number of mol or g of reactants or the number of mol or g of reactant needed to produce a certain number of mol or g of product.

---

**Practice Problem 4.19**

The balanced equation for the combustion of ethanol (ethyl alcohol) is:

$$C_2H_5OH(l) + 3O_2(g) \longrightarrow 2CO_2(g) + 3H_2O(g)$$

a. How many mol of $O_2$ will react with 1 mol of ethanol?
b. How many g of $O_2$ will react with 1 mol of ethanol?
c. How many g of $CO_2$ will be produced by the combustion of 1 mol of ethanol?

▶ For Further Practice: **Questions 4.89 and 4.90.**

Let's consider an example that requires us to write and balance the chemical equation, use conversion factors, and calculate the amount of a reactant consumed in the chemical reaction.

---

**EXAMPLE 4.20**    **Calculating a Quantity of Reactant**

Calcium hydroxide may be used to neutralize (completely react with) aqueous hydrochloric acid. Calculate the number of g of hydrochloric acid that would be neutralized by 0.500 mol of solid calcium hydroxide.

**LEARNING GOAL**

**9** Calculate the number of mol or g of product resulting from a given number of mol or g of reactants or the number of mol or g of reactant needed to produce a certain number of mol or g of product.

*Continued…*

## Solution

**Step 1.** The formula for calcium hydroxide is $Ca(OH)_2$, and that for hydrochloric acid is HCl. The unbalanced equation produces calcium chloride and water as products:

$$Ca(OH)_2(s) + HCl(aq) \longrightarrow CaCl_2(aq) + H_2O(l)$$

**Step 2.** Balance the equation:

$$Ca(OH)_2(s) + 2HCl(aq) \longrightarrow CaCl_2(aq) + 2H_2O(l)$$

**Step 3.** Determine the necessary conversions:
- mol of $Ca(OH)_2$ to mol of HCl and
- mol of HCl to g of HCl

**Step 4.** Use the following path:

$$\boxed{\frac{mol}{Ca(OH)_2}} \longrightarrow \boxed{\frac{mol}{HCl}} \longrightarrow \boxed{\frac{g}{HCl}}$$

**Step 5.** $0.500 \ \text{mol Ca(OH)}_2 \times \dfrac{2 \ \text{mol HCl}}{1 \ \text{mol Ca(OH)}_2} \times \dfrac{36.46 \ \text{g HCl}}{1 \ \text{mol HCl}} = 36.5 \ \text{g HCl}$

This reaction is illustrated in Figure 4.6.

*Helpful Hints:*
1. Recall that the reaction between an acid and a base produces a salt and water (Section 4.4 and further discussed in Chapter 8).
2. Remember to balance the chemical equation; the proper coefficients are essential parts of the subsequent calculations.

### Practice Problem 4.20

Metallic iron reacts with $O_2$ gas to produce iron(III) oxide.

    a. Write and balance the equation.    b. Calculate the number of g of iron needed to produce 5.00 g of product.

▶ For Further Practice: **Questions 4.93 and 4.94.**

| $Ca(OH)_2$ | + | $2HCl$ | ⟶ | $CaCl_2$ | + | $2H_2O$ |
|---|---|---|---|---|---|---|
| 1 mol | | 2 mol | | 1 mol | | 2 mol |
| 74 g/mol | | 36.5 g/mol | | 111 g/mol | | 18.0 g/mol |
| 74 g | | 73 g | | 111 g | | 36 g |

147 g of reactants        147 g of products

**Figure 4.6** An illustration of the law of conservation of mass. In this example, 1 mol of calcium hydroxide and 2 mol of hydrogen chloride react to produce 3 mol of product (2 mol of water and 1 mol of calcium chloride). The total mass, in g, of reactant(s) consumed is equal to the total mass, in g, of product(s) formed. *Note:* In reality, HCl does not exist as discrete molecules in water. The HCl separates to form $H^+$ and $Cl^-$. Ionization in water will be discussed with the chemistry of acids and bases in Chapter 8.

## A MEDICAL PERSPECTIVE

### Carbon Monoxide Poisoning: A Case of Combining Ratios

A fuel, such as methane, $CH_4$, burned in an excess of oxygen produces carbon dioxide and water:

$$CH_4(g) + 2O_2(g) \longrightarrow CO_2(g) + 2H_2O(g)$$

The same combustion in the presence of insufficient oxygen produces carbon monoxide and water:

$$2CH_4(g) + 3O_2(g) \longrightarrow 2CO(g) + 4H_2O(g)$$

The combustion of methane, repeated over and over in millions of gas furnaces, is responsible for heating many of our homes in the winter. The furnace is designed to operate under conditions that favor the first reaction and minimize the second; excess oxygen is available from the surrounding atmosphere. Furthermore, the vast majority of exhaust gases (containing principally CO, $CO_2$, $H_2O$, and unburned fuel) are removed from the home through the chimney. However, if the chimney becomes obstructed, or the burner malfunctions, carbon monoxide levels within the home can rapidly reach hazardous levels.

Why is exposure to carbon monoxide hazardous? Hemoglobin, an iron-containing compound, binds with $O_2$ and transports it throughout the body. Carbon monoxide also combines with hemoglobin, thereby blocking oxygen transport.

The binding affinity of hemoglobin for carbon monoxide is about 200 times as great as for $O_2$. Therefore, to maintain $O_2$ binding and transport capability, our exposure to carbon monoxide must be minimal. Proper ventilation and suitable oxygen-to-fuel ratio are essential for any combustion process in the home, automobile, or workplace. In recent years carbon monoxide sensors have been developed. These sensors sound an alarm when toxic levels of CO are reached. These warning devices have helped to create a safer indoor environment.

The example we have chosen is an illustration of what is termed the *law of multiple proportions*. This law states that identical reactants may produce different products, depending on their combining ratio. The experimental conditions (in this case, the quantity of available oxygen) determine the preferred path of the chemical reaction.

**For Further Understanding**

▶ Why may new, more strict insulation standards for homes and businesses inadvertently increase the risk of carbon monoxide poisoning?

▶ Explain the link between smoking and carbon monoxide that has motivated many states and municipalities to ban smoking in restaurants, offices, and other indoor spaces.

---

**EXAMPLE 4.21**  **Calculating Reactant Quantities**

**LEARNING GOAL**

**9** Calculate the number of mol or g of product resulting from a given number of mol or g of reactants or the number of mol or g of reactant needed to produce a certain number of mol or g of product.

What mass of sodium hydroxide, NaOH, would be required to produce 8.00 g of the antacid milk of magnesia, $Mg(OH)_2$, by the reaction of $MgCl_2$ with NaOH?

**Solution**

**Step 1.** Write and balance the equation:

$$MgCl_2(aq) + 2NaOH(aq) \longrightarrow Mg(OH)_2(s) + 2NaCl(aq)$$

**Step 2.** Determine the strategy:

The equation tells us that 2 mol of NaOH form 1 mol of $Mg(OH)_2$. If we calculate the number of mol of $Mg(OH)_2$ in 8.00 g of $Mg(OH)_2$, we can determine the number of mol of NaOH necessary and then the mass of NaOH required:

$$\text{mass } Mg(OH)_2 \longrightarrow \text{mol } Mg(OH)_2 \longrightarrow \text{mol } NaOH \longrightarrow \text{mass } NaOH$$

**Step 3.** Determine the conversion factor to convert mass to mol $Mg(OH)_2$:

Since 58.3 g $Mg(OH)_2$ = 1 mol $Mg(OH)_2$

The conversion factor is:

$$\frac{1 \text{ mol } Mg(OH)_2}{58.3 \text{ g } Mg(OH)_2}$$

*Continued...*

**Step 4.** $8.00 \text{ g Mg(OH)}_2 \times \dfrac{1 \text{ mol Mg(OH)}_2}{58.3 \text{ g Mg(OH)}_2} = 0.137 \text{ mol Mg(OH)}_2$

**Step 5.** Two moles of NaOH react to give 1 mol of $Mg(OH)_2$. Therefore, using the mol ratio,

$$0.137 \text{ mol Mg(OH)}_2 \times \dfrac{2 \text{ mol NaOH}}{1 \text{ mol Mg(OH)}_2} = 0.274 \text{ mol NaOH}$$

**Step 6.** 40.0 g of NaOH = 1 mol of NaOH. Therefore, using the molar mass of NaOH,

$$0.274 \text{ mol NaOH} \times \dfrac{40.0 \text{ g NaOH}}{1 \text{ mol NaOH}} = 11.0 \text{ g NaOH}$$

However, the calculation may be done in a single step:

$$8.00 \text{ g Mg(OH)}_2 \times \dfrac{1 \text{ mol Mg(OH)}_2}{58.3 \text{ g Mg(OH)}_2} \times \dfrac{2 \text{ mol NaOH}}{1 \text{ mol Mg(OH)}_2} \times \dfrac{40.0 \text{ g NaOH}}{1 \text{ mol NaOH}} = 11.0 \text{ g NaOH}$$

Note once again that we have followed a logical and predictable path to the solution:

$$\begin{array}{ccccccc} \text{g} & & \text{mol} & & \text{mol} & & \text{g} \\ \text{Mg(OH)}_2 & \longrightarrow & \text{Mg(OH)}_2 & \longrightarrow & \text{NaOH} & \longrightarrow & \text{NaOH} \end{array}$$

*Helpful Hint:* Mass is a laboratory unit, whereas mol is a calculation unit. The laboratory balance is calibrated in units of mass (g). Although mol are essential for calculation, often the starting point and objective are in mass units. As a result, our path is often g $\longrightarrow$ mol $\longrightarrow$ g.

---

**Practice Problem 4.21**

Barium carbonate decomposes upon heating to barium oxide and carbon dioxide.

    a. Write and balance the equation.

    b. Calculate the number of g of carbon dioxide produced by heating 50.0 g of barium carbonate.

▶ For Further Practice: **Questions 4.95 and 4.96.**

A general problem-solving strategy is summarized in Figure 4.7. By systematically applying this strategy, you will be able to solve virtually any problem requiring calculations based on the chemical equation.

**For a reaction of the general type:**
$$A + B \longrightarrow C$$

$$\boxed{\text{g } A} \longrightarrow \boxed{\text{mol } A} \longrightarrow \boxed{\text{mol } C}$$
$$\times\left(\dfrac{1 \text{ mol } A}{\text{g } A}\right) \qquad \times\left(\dfrac{\text{mol } C}{\text{mol } A}\right)$$

**(a) Given a specified number of g of A, calculate mol of C.**

$$\boxed{\text{g } A} \longrightarrow \boxed{\text{mol } A} \longrightarrow \boxed{\text{mol } C} \longrightarrow \boxed{\text{g } C}$$
$$\times\left(\dfrac{1 \text{ mol } A}{\text{g } A}\right) \qquad \times\left(\dfrac{\text{mol } C}{\text{mol } A}\right) \qquad \times\left(\dfrac{\text{g } C}{\text{mol } C}\right)$$

**(b) Given a specified number of g of A, calculate g of C.**

$$\boxed{\text{mL } A} \longrightarrow \boxed{\text{g } A} \longrightarrow \boxed{\text{mol } A} \longrightarrow \boxed{\text{mol } C} \longrightarrow \boxed{\text{g } C}$$
$$\times\left(\begin{array}{c}\text{density} \\ \text{of } A\end{array}\right) \qquad \times\left(\dfrac{1 \text{ mol } A}{\text{g } A}\right) \qquad \times\left(\dfrac{\text{mol } C}{\text{mol } A}\right) \qquad \times\left(\dfrac{\text{g } C}{\text{mol } C}\right)$$

**(c) Given a volume of A in milliliters (mL), calculate g of C.**

**Figure 4.7** A general problem-solving strategy, using molar quantities.

## Theoretical and Percent Yield

The **theoretical yield** is the *maximum* amount of product that can be produced (in an ideal world). In the "real" world it is difficult to produce the amount calculated as the theoretical yield. This is true for a variety of reasons. Some experimental error is unavoidable. Moreover, many reactions simply do not go to completion; some amount of reactant remains at the end of the reaction and the *actual* amount of product is less than the *theoretical* (predicted) amount. We will study these processes, termed *equilibrium reactions* in Chapter 7.

A **percent yield**, the ratio of the actual and theoretical yields multiplied by 100%, is often used to show the relationship between predicted and experimental quantities. Thus

$$\% \text{ yield} = \frac{\text{actual yield}}{\text{theoretical yield}} \times 100\%$$

In Example 4.18, the theoretical yield of $CO_2$ is 132 g. For this reaction let's assume that a chemist actually obtained 125 g $CO_2$. This is the actual yield and would normally be provided as a part of the data in the problem.

Calculate the percent yield as follows:

$$\% \text{ yield} = \frac{\text{actual yield}}{\text{theoretical yield}} \times 100\%$$

$$= \frac{125 \text{ g } CO_2 \text{ actual}}{132 \text{ g } CO_2 \text{ theoretical}} \times 100\% = 94.7\%$$

**Question 4.9** It is believed that the reaction responsible for the depletion of ozone in the atmosphere is:

$$O_3(g) + NO(g) \longrightarrow O_2(g) + NO_2(g)$$

a. If 50.0 g of $O_3$ reacts with excess NO, how many g of $NO_2$ will be produced?
b. If the actual yield of $NO_2$ is 25.0 g, what is the % yield?

**Question 4.10** The reaction:

$$2NO(g) + O_2(g) \longrightarrow 2NO_2(g)$$

is one step in the process of forming atmospheric smog.
a. How many g of $NO_2$ can be produced by the reaction of excess $O_2$ with 50.0 g of NO?
b. If the actual yield of $NO_2$ is 50.0 g, what is the % yield?

### A Special Case—The Limiting Reactant

We have learned that reactants combine in molar proportions dictated by the coefficients in the balanced equation. However, we often encounter situations where the reactants are not mixed to match the theoretical proportions. In cases such as this, one reactant will be completely consumed, leaving some of the other reactant unchanged. In effect, the extent of the reaction is *limited* by the amount of the reactant that is completely consumed. This completely consumed reactant is termed the *limiting reactant*. In order to correctly calculate the amount of product formed, the *theoretical yield*, we must base the amount of product formed on the number of mol of the compound "in short supply," the limiting reactant.

Imagine that you are making cheeseburgers. You have twenty buns, eight slices of cheese, and nine hamburger patties. What is the limiting ingredient? How many cheeseburgers can you make? What are the leftover ingredients? If you can answer these questions, you can do limiting reactant problems.

We know that twenty hamburger buns could make twenty cheeseburgers if we had twenty hamburger patties and twenty slices of cheese. But we do not, so it

## A MEDICAL PERSPECTIVE

### Pharmaceutical Chemistry: The Practical Significance of Percent Yield

In recent years, the major pharmaceutical industries have introduced a wide variety of new drugs targeted to cure or alleviate the symptoms of a host of diseases that afflict humanity.

The vast majority of these drugs are synthetic; they are made in a laboratory or by an industrial process. These substances are complex molecules that are patiently designed and constructed from relatively simple molecules in a series of chemical reactions. A series of ten to twenty "steps," or sequential reactions, is not unusual to put together a final product that has the proper structure, geometry, and reactivity for efficacy against a particular disease.

Although a great deal of research occurs to ensure that each of the steps in the overall process is efficient (having a large percent yield), the overall process is still very inefficient (low percent yield). This inefficiency, and the research needed to minimize it, at least in part determines the cost and availability of both prescription and over-the-counter preparations.

Consider a hypothetical five-step sequential synthesis. If each step has a percent yield of 80%, our initial impression might be that this synthesis is quite efficient. However, on closer inspection we find quite the contrary to be true.

The overall yield of the five-step reaction is the product of the decimal fraction of the percent yield of each of the sequential reactions. So, if the decimal fraction corresponding to 80% is 0.80:

$$0.80 \times 0.80 \times 0.80 \times 0.80 \times 0.80 = 0.33$$

Converting the decimal fraction to percentage:

$$0.33 \times 100\% = 33\% \text{ yield}$$

Many reactions are considerably less than 80% efficient, especially those that are used to prepare large molecules with complex arrangements of atoms. Imagine a more realistic scenario in which one step is only 20% efficient (a 20% yield) and the other four steps are 50%, 60%, 70%, and 80% efficient. Repeating the calculation with these numbers (after conversion to a decimal fraction):

$$0.20 \times 0.50 \times 0.60 \times 0.70 \times 0.80 = 0.0336$$

Converting the decimal fraction to a percentage:

$$0.0336 \times 100\% = 3.36\% \text{ yield}$$

a very inefficient process.

If we apply this logic to a fifteen- or twenty-step synthesis we gain some appreciation of the difficulty of producing modern pharmaceutical products. Add to this the challenge of predicting the most appropriate molecular structure that will have the desired biological effect and be relatively free of side effects. All these considerations give new meaning to the term *wonder drug* that has been attached to some of the more successful synthetic products.

We will study some of the elementary steps essential to the synthesis of a wide range of pharmaceutical compounds in later chapters, beginning with Chapter 10.

**For Further Understanding**

▶ Explain the possible connection of this perspective to escalating costs of pharmaceutical products.

▶ Can you describe other situations, not necessarily in the field of chemistry, where multiple-step processes contribute to inefficiency?

---

### EXAMPLE 4.22    Calculation of Percent Yield

Assume that the theoretical yield of iron in the process

$$2Al(s) + Fe_2O_3(s) \longrightarrow Al_2O_3(l) + 2Fe(l)$$

was 30.0 g.

If the actual yield of iron were 25.0 g in the process, calculate the percent yield.

**LEARNING GOAL**

**10**  Calculate theoretical and percent yield.

**Solution**

$$\% \text{ yield} = \frac{\text{actual yield}}{\text{theoretical yield}} \times 100\%$$

$$= \frac{25.0 \text{ g}}{30.0 \text{ g}} \times 100\%$$

$$= 83.3\%$$

**Practice Problem 4.22**

Given the reaction represented by the balanced equation

$$CH_4(g) + 3Cl_2(g) \longrightarrow 3HCl(g) + CHCl_3(g)$$

   a. Calculate the number of g of $CHCl_3$ that could be produced by mixing 105 g $Cl_2$ with excess $CH_4$.

   b. If 10.0 g $CHCl_3$ were actually produced, calculate the % yield.

▶ For Further Practice: **Questions 4.101 and 4.102.**

is obvious that we cannot make twenty cheeseburgers, even though we certainly
have enough buns. It can be reasoned that only eight burgers are possible. We are
limited by the availability of only eight slices of cheese. In our example, cheese is
the limiting reactant. Furthermore, nine minus eight, or one hamburger patty and
twenty minus eight, or twelve buns, would be left over.

    The strategy outlined above is the same as that used in solving problems
involving limiting reactants. You can learn more about this topic on the website,
by referring to "The Limiting Reactant Problem."

**THE LIMITING
REACTANT PROBLEM**

## CHAPTER MAP

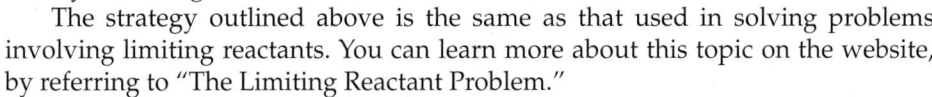

# SUMMARY

## 4.1 The Mole Concept and Atoms

► Atoms are exceedingly small, yet their masses have been experimentally determined for each of the elements. The unit of measurement for these determinations is the **atomic mass unit,** (amu):

$$1\,\text{amu} = 1.661 \times 10^{-24}\,\text{g}$$

► The periodic table provides atomic masses in amu. A more practical unit for defining a "collection" of atoms is the **mole** (mol):

1 mol of atoms = $6.022 \times 10^{23}$ atoms of an element

This number is referred to as **Avogadro's number.**

► The **atomic mass** of a given element is the average mass of a single atom in amu. The mass of 1 mol of atoms, in grams, is termed the **molar mass** of the element. One mole of atoms of any element contains the same number, Avogadro's number, of atoms.

## 4.2 The Chemical Formula, Formula Mass, and Molar Mass

► Compounds are pure substances composed of two or more elements that are chemically combined. They are represented by their **chemical formula,** a combination of symbols of the various elements that make up the compounds. The chemical formula is based on the **formula unit.** This is the smallest collection of atoms that provides the identity of the atoms present in the compound and the relative numbers of each type of atom.

► Just as the mass of a mol of atoms is based on the atomic mass, the mass of a mol of a compound is based on the **formula mass.** The formula mass is calculated by adding the masses of all the atoms or ions of which the unit is composed. To calculate the formula mass, the formula unit must be known. The formula mass of 1 mol of a compound is its **molar mass** in units of g/mol.

## 4.3 The Chemical Equation and the Information It Conveys

► The **chemical equation** is the shorthand notation for a chemical reaction. It describes all of the substances that react to produce the product(s). **Reactants,** or starting materials, are all substances that undergo change in a chemical reaction; **products** are substances produced by a chemical reaction.

► According to the **law of conservation of mass,** matter can neither be gained nor lost in the process of a chemical reaction. The law of conservation of mass states that we must have a balanced chemical equation.

► Features of a correct equation include the following:
  • The identity of products and reactants must be specified.
  • Reactants are written to the left of the reaction arrow ($\rightarrow$) and products to the right.

  • The physical states of reactants and products are shown in parentheses.
  • If heat energy is necessary for the reaction to occur, the symbol $\Delta$ is written over the reaction arrow.
  • The equation must be balanced.

► Chemical reactions involve the **combination** of reactants to produce products, the **decomposition** of reactant(s) into products, or the **replacement** of one or more elements in a compound to yield products. Replacement reactions are subclassified as either **single-** or **double-**replacement.

## 4.4 Chemical Equations Represent Chemical Change

► The chemical equation enables us to determine the quantity of reactants needed to produce a certain molar quantity of products. The chemical equation expresses these quantities in terms of mol.

► The relative number of mol of each product and reactant is indicated by placing a whole-number coefficient before the formula of each substance in the chemical equation.

► Many equations are balanced by trial and error. If the identity of the products and reactants, the physical states, and the reaction conditions are known, the following steps provide a method for correctly balancing a chemical equation:
  • Count the number of atoms of each element on both product and reactant sides.
  • Determine which atoms are not balanced.
  • Balance one element at a time using coefficients.
  • After you believe that you have successfully balanced the equation, check to be certain that mass conservation has been achieved.

► Reactions that produce products with similar characteristics are often classified together. The formation of an insoluble solid, a **precipitate,** is very common. Such reactions are precipitation reactions, and are represented using net ionic equations.

► Chemical reactions that have a common reactant may be grouped together. Reactions involving oxygen are such a class.

► Another approach to the classification of chemical reactions is based on transfer of hydrogen ions (positive charge) or electrons (negative charge). **Acid-base reactions** involve the transfer of a hydrogen ion, $H^+$, from one reactant to another. Another important reaction type, **oxidation-reduction,** takes place because of the transfer of negative charge, one or more electrons, from one reactant to another.

## 4.5 Calculations Using the Chemical Equation

► Calculations involving chemical quantities are based on the following requirements:
  • The basis for the calculations is a balanced equation.
  • The calculations are performed using mole-based conversion factors.
  • The conservation of mass must be obeyed.

► The mol is the basis for calculations. However, masses are generally measured in g (or kg). Therefore you must be able to interconvert mol and g to perform chemical arithmetic.

▶ The calculated amount assumes complete conversion of reactant to product. This amount is the **theoretical yield.** Most reactions are not complete; some reactant(s) remains and the actual amount is less than the theoretical amount. The **percent yield** is the ratio of the actual to theoretical yields multiplied by 100%.

**4.20 a.** $4Fe(s) + 3O_2(g) \longrightarrow 2Fe_2O_3(s)$
**b.** 3.50 g Fe

**4.21 a.** $BaCO_3(s) \xrightarrow{\Delta} BaO(s) + CO_2(g)$
**b.** 11.2 g $CO_2$

**4.22 a.** 58.9 g $CHCl_3$
**b.** 17.0% yield

## ANSWERS TO PRACTICE PROBLEMS

**4.1 a.** $26.98 \dfrac{\text{g Al}}{\text{mol Al}}$

**b.** $200.59 \dfrac{\text{g Hg}}{\text{mol Hg}}$

**4.2 a.** $1.51 \times 10^{24}$ oxygen atoms
**b.** $3.01 \times 10^{24}$ oxygen atoms

**4.3** 1.50 mol Na

**4.4** 14.0 g He

**4.5** $1.51 \times 10^{24}$ O atoms

**4.6** $3.17 \times 10^{-2}$ mol Ag

**4.7** 17.04 g/mol

**4.8** 180.18 g/mol

**4.9** 237.95 g/mol

**4.10** $4Fe(s) + 3O_2(g) \longrightarrow 2Fe_2O_3(s)$

**4.11** $C_2H_5OH(l) + 3O_2(g) \longrightarrow 2CO_2(g) + 3H_2O(g)$

**4.12** $2C_6H_6(l) + 15O_2(g) \longrightarrow 12CO_2(g) + 6H_2O(g)$

**4.13** $6S_2Cl_2(s) + 16NH_3(g) \longrightarrow N_4S_4(s) + 12NH_4Cl(s) + S_8(s)$

**4.14 a.** $KCl(aq) + AgNO_3(aq) \longrightarrow KNO_3(aq) + AgCl(s)$
**b.** $CH_3COOK(aq) + AgNO_3(aq) \longrightarrow$ no reaction
**c.** $NaOH(aq) + NH_4Cl(aq) \longrightarrow$ no reaction
**d.** $2NaOH(aq) + FeCl_2(aq) \longrightarrow 2NaCl(aq) + Fe(OH)_2(s)$

**4.15 a.** $Ba^{2+}(aq) + SO_4^{2-}(aq) \longrightarrow BaSO_4(s)$
**b.** $2Ag^+(aq) + SO_4^{2-}(aq) \longrightarrow Ag_2SO_4(s)$

**4.16 a.** 90.1 g $H_2O$        **c.** $1.80 \times 10^3$ μg $C_6H_{12}O_6$
**b.** 0.590 mol LiCl        **d.** 0.368 mol $MgCl_2$

**4.17** 65.1 g KCN

**4.18** $4.61 \times 10^2$ g ethanol

**4.19 a.** 3 mol $O_2$
**b.** 96.00 g $O_2$
**c.** 88.0 g $CO_2$

## QUESTIONS AND PROBLEMS

### The Mole Concept and Atoms

#### Foundations

**4.11** We purchase eggs by the dozen. Name several other familiar packaging units.
**4.12** One dozen eggs is a convenient consumer unit. Explain why the mol is a convenient chemist's unit.
**4.13** What is the average molar mass of:
   **a.** Si        **b.** Ag
**4.14** What is the average molar mass of:
   **a.** S        **b.** Na
**4.15** What is the mass of Avogadro's number of argon atoms?
**4.16** What is the mass of Avogadro's number of iron atoms?

#### Applications

**4.17** How many carbon atoms are present in $1.0 \times 10^{-4}$ mol of carbon?
**4.18** How many mercury atoms are present in $1.0 \times 10^{-10}$ mol of mercury?
**4.19** How many mol of arsenic correspond to $1.0 \times 10^2$ atoms of arsenic?
**4.20** How many mol of sodium correspond to $1.0 \times 10^{15}$ atoms of sodium?
**4.21** How many g of neon are contained in 2.00 mol of neon atoms?
**4.22** How many g of carbon are contained in 3.00 mol of carbon atoms?
**4.23** What is the mass in g of 1.00 mol of helium atoms?
**4.24** What is the mass in g of 1.00 mol of nitrogen atoms?
**4.25** Calculate the number of mol corresponding to:
   **a.** 20.0 g He        **b.** 0.040 kg Na        **c.** 3.0 g $Cl_2$
**4.26** Calculate the number of mol corresponding to:
   **a.** 0.10 g Ca        **b.** 4.00 g Fe        **c.** 2.00 kg $N_2$
**4.27** What is the mass, in g, of 15.0 mol of silver?
**4.28** What is the mass, in g, of 15.0 mol of carbon?
**4.29** Calculate the number of silver atoms in 15.0 g of silver.
**4.30** Calculate the number of carbon atoms in 15.0 g of carbon.

### The Chemical Formula, Formula Mass, and Molar Mass

#### Foundations

**4.31** Distinguish between the terms *molecule* and *ion pair*.
**4.32** Distinguish between the terms *formula mass* and *molar mass*.
**4.33** Calculate the molar mass, in g/mol, of each of the following formula units:
   **a.** NaCl        **b.** $Na_2SO_4$        **c.** $Fe_3(PO_4)_2$

**4.34** Calculate the molar mass, in g/mol, of each of the following formula units:
   **a.** $S_8$      **b.** $(NH_4)_2SO_4$      **c.** $CO_2$
**4.35** Calculate the molar mass, in g/mol, of oxygen gas, $O_2$.
**4.36** Calculate the molar mass, in g/mol, of ozone, $O_3$.
**4.37** Calculate the molar mass of $CuSO_4 \cdot 5H_2O$.
**4.38** Calculate the molar mass of $CaCl_2 \cdot 2H_2O$.

## Applications

**4.39** Calculate the number of mol corresponding to:
   **a.** 15.0 g NaCl      **b.** 15.0 g $Na_2SO_4$
**4.40** Calculate the number of mol corresponding to:
   **a.** 15.0 g $NH_3$      **b.** 16.0 g $O_2$
**4.41** Calculate the mass in g corresponding to:
   **a.** 1.000 mol $H_2O$      **b.** 2.000 mol NaCl
**4.42** Calculate the mass in g corresponding to:
   **a.** 0.400 mol $NH_3$      **b.** 0.800 mol $BaCO_3$
**4.43** Calculate the mass in g corresponding to:
   **a.** 10.0 mol He      **b.** $1.00 \times 10^2$ mol $H_2$
**4.44** Calculate the mass in g corresponding to:
   **a.** 2.00 mol $CH_4$      **b.** 0.400 mol $Ca(NO_3)_2$
**4.45** How many g are required to have 0.100 mol of each of the following?
   **a.** Mg      **b.** $CaCO_3$
**4.46** How many g are required to have 0.100 mol of each of the following?
   **a.** $C_6H_{12}O_6$ (glucose) **b.** NaCl
**4.47** How many g are required to have 0.100 mol of each of the following compounds?
   **a.** NaOH      **b.** $H_2SO_4$
**4.48** How many g are required to have 0.100 mol of each of the following compounds?
   **a.** $C_2H_5OH$ (ethanol) **b.** $Ca_3(PO_4)_2$
**4.49** How many mol are in 50.0 g of each of the following substances?
   **a.** KBr      **b.** $MgSO_4$
**4.50** How many mol are in 50.0 g of each of the following substances?
   **a.** $Br_2$      **b.** $NH_4Cl$
**4.51** How many mol are in 50.0 g of each of the following substances?
   **a.** $CS_2$      **b.** $Al_2(CO_3)_3$
**4.52** How many mol are in 50.0 g of each of the following substances?
   **a.** $Sr(OH)_2$      **b.** $LiNO_3$

## The Chemical Equation and the Information It Conveys

### Foundations

**4.53** What law is the ultimate basis for a correct chemical equation?
**4.54** List the general types of information that a chemical equation provides.
**4.55** What is the meaning of the subscript in a chemical formula?
**4.56** What is the meaning of the coefficient in a chemical equation?
**4.57** What is the meaning of $\Delta$ over the reaction arrow?
**4.58** What is the meaning of (s), (l), or (g) immediately following the symbol for a chemical substance?

## Applications

**4.59** Will a precipitate form if solutions of the soluble salts $Pb(NO_3)_2$ and KI are mixed?
**4.60** Will a precipitate form if solutions of the soluble salts $AgNO_3$ and NaOH are mixed?

## Chemical Equations Represent Chemical Change

### Foundations

**4.61** When you are balancing an equation, why must the subscripts in the chemical formulas remain unchanged?
**4.62** Describe the process of checking to ensure that an equation is properly balanced.
**4.63** What is a reactant?
**4.64** On which side of the reaction arrow are reactants found?
**4.65** What is a product?
**4.66** On which side of the reaction arrow are products found?

### Applications

**4.67** Balance each of the following equations:
   **a.** $C_2H_6(g) + O_2(g) \longrightarrow CO_2(g) + H_2O(g)$
   **b.** $K_2O(s) + P_4O_{10}(s) \longrightarrow K_3PO_4(s)$
   **c.** $MgBr_2(aq) + H_2SO_4(aq) \longrightarrow HBr(g) + MgSO_4(aq)$
**4.68** Balance each of the following equations:
   **a.** $C_6H_{12}O_6(s) + O_2(g) \longrightarrow CO_2(g) + H_2O(g)$
   **b.** $H_2O(l) + P_4O_{10}(s) \longrightarrow H_3PO_4(aq)$
   **c.** $PCl_5(g) + H_2O(l) \longrightarrow HCl(aq) + H_3PO_4(aq)$
**4.69** Complete, then balance, each of the following equations:
   **a.** $Ca(s) + F_2(g) \longrightarrow$
   **b.** $Mg(s) + O_2(g) \longrightarrow$
   **c.** $H_2(g) + N_2(g) \longrightarrow$
**4.70** Complete, then balance, each of the following equations:
   **a.** $Li(s) + O_2(g) \longrightarrow$
   **b.** $Ca(s) + N_2(g) \longrightarrow$
   **c.** $Al(s) + S(s) \longrightarrow$
**4.71** Balance each of the following equations:
   **a.** $C_4H_{10}(g) + O_2(g) \longrightarrow H_2O(g) + CO_2(g)$
   **b.** $Au_2S_3(s) + H_2(g) \longrightarrow Au(s) + H_2S(g)$
   **c.** $Al(OH)_3(s) + HCl(aq) \longrightarrow AlCl_3(aq) + H_2O(l)$
   **d.** $(NH_4)_2Cr_2O_7(s) \longrightarrow Cr_2O_3(s) + N_2(g) + H_2O(g)$
   **e.** $C_2H_5OH(l) + O_2(g) \longrightarrow CO_2(g) + H_2O(g)$
**4.72** Balance each of the following equations:
   **a.** $Fe_2O_3(s) + CO(g) \longrightarrow Fe_3O_4(s) + CO_2(g)$
   **b.** $C_6H_6(l) + O_2(g) \longrightarrow CO_2(g) + H_2O(g)$
   **c.** $I_4O_9(s) + I_2O_6(s) \longrightarrow I_2(s) + O_2(g)$
   **d.** $KClO_3(s) \longrightarrow KCl(s) + O_2(g)$
   **e.** $C_6H_{12}O_6(s) \longrightarrow C_2H_6O(l) + CO_2(g)$
**4.73** Write a balanced equation for each of the following reactions:
   **a.** Ammonia is formed by the reaction of nitrogen and hydrogen.
   **b.** Hydrochloric acid reacts with sodium hydroxide to produce water and sodium chloride.
**4.74** Write a balanced equation for each of the following reactions:
   **a.** Nitric acid reacts with calcium hydroxide to produce water and calcium nitrate.
   **b.** Butane ($C_4H_{10}$) reacts with oxygen to produce water and carbon dioxide.
**4.75** Write a balanced equation for each of the following reactions:
   **a.** Glucose, a sugar, $C_6H_{12}O_6$, is oxidized in the body to produce water and carbon dioxide.

**b.** Sodium carbonate, upon heating, produces sodium oxide and carbon dioxide.

**4.76** Write a balanced equation for each of the following reactions:

    **a.** Sulfur, present as an impurity in coal, is burned in oxygen to produce sulfur dioxide.

    **b.** Hydrofluoric acid (HF) reacts with glass ($SiO_2$) in the process of etching to produce silicon tetrafluoride and water.

**4.77** Solutions containing $(NH_4)_2CO_3(aq)$ and $CaCl_2(aq)$ are mixed. Will a precipitate form? If so, write its formula.

**4.78** Solutions containing $Mg(NO_3)_2(aq)$ and $NaOH(aq)$ are mixed. Will a precipitate form? If so, write its formula.

**4.79** Write the net ionic equation for the reaction of $NaBr(aq)$ with $AgNO_3(aq)$.

**4.80** Write the net ionic equation for the reaction of $Pb(NO_3)_2(aq)$ with $K_2S(aq)$.

## Calculations Using the Chemical Equation

### Foundations

**4.81** What is the law that forms the basis of chemical calculations?

**4.82** Why is it essential to use balanced equations to solve mol problems?

**4.83** Balancing equations involves changing coefficients, not subscripts. Why?

**4.84** Describe the steps used in the calculation of g of product resulting from the reaction of a specified number of g of reactant.

### Applications

**4.85** How many g of $B_2H_6$ will react with 3.00 mol of $O_2$?

$$B_2H_6(l) + 3O_2(g) \longrightarrow B_2O_3(s) + 3H_2O(l)$$

**4.86** How many g of Al will react with 3.00 mol of $O_2$?

$$4Al(s) + 3O_2(g) \longrightarrow 2Al_2O_3(s)$$

**4.87** Calculate the mass, in grams, of $CrCl_3$ that could be produced from 50.0 g $Cr_2O_3$ according to the equation

$$Cr_2O_3(s) + 3CCl_4(l) \longrightarrow 2CrCl_3(s) + 3COCl_2(aq)$$

**4.88** A 3.5-g sample of water reacts with $PCl_3$ according to the following equation:

$$3H_2O(l) + PCl_3(g) \longrightarrow H_3PO_3(aq) + 3HCl(aq)$$

How many g of $H_3PO_3$ are produced?

**4.89** For the reaction

$$N_2(g) + H_2(g) \longrightarrow NH_3(g)$$

    **a.** Balance the equation.

    **b.** How many mol of $H_2$ would react with 1 mol of $N_2$?

    **c.** How many mol of product would form from 1 mol of $N_2$?

    **d.** If 14.0 g of $N_2$ were initially present, calculate the number of mol of $H_2$ required to react with all of the $N_2$.

    **e.** For conditions outlined in part (d), how many g of product would form?

**4.90** Aspirin (acetylsalicylic acid) may be formed from salicylic acid and acetic acid as follows:

$$C_7H_6O_3(aq) + CH_3COOH(aq) \longrightarrow C_9H_8O_4(s) + H_2O(l)$$

    Salicylic        Acetic              Aspirin
    acid           acid

    **a.** Is this equation balanced? If not, complete the balancing.

    **b.** How many mol of aspirin may be produced from $1.00 \times 10^2$ mol salicylic acid?

    **c.** How many g of aspirin may be produced from $1.00 \times 10^2$ mol salicylic acid?

    **d.** How many g of acetic acid would be required to react completely with the $1.00 \times 10^2$ mol salicylic acid?

**4.91** The proteins in our bodies are composed of molecules called amino acids. One amino acid is methionine; its molecular formula is $C_5H_{11}NO_2S$. Calculate:

    **a.** the formula mass of methionine

    **b.** the number of oxygen atoms in a mol of this compound

    **c.** the mass of oxygen in a mol of the compound

    **d.** the mass of oxygen in 50.0 g of the compound

**4.92** Triglycerides (Chapters 17 and 23) are used in biochemical systems to store energy; they can be formed from glycerol and fatty acids. The molecular formula of glycerol is $C_3H_8O_3$. Calculate:

    **a.** the formula mass of glycerol

    **b.** the number of oxygen atoms in a mol of this compound

    **c.** the mass of oxygen in a mol of the compound

    **d.** the mass of oxygen in 50.0 g of the compound

**4.93** Joseph Priestley discovered oxygen in the eighteenth century by using heat to decompose mercury(II) oxide:

$$2HgO(s) \xrightarrow{\Delta} 2Hg(l) + O_2(g)$$

How much oxygen is produced from $1.00 \times 10^2$ g HgO?

**4.94** Dinitrogen monoxide (also known as nitrous oxide and used as an anesthetic) can be made by heating ammonium nitrate:

$$NH_4NO_3(s) \longrightarrow N_2O(g) + 2H_2O(g)$$

How much dinitrogen monoxide can be made from $1.00 \times 10^2$ g of ammonium nitrate?

**4.95** The burning of acetylene ($C_2H_2$) in oxygen is the reaction in the oxyacetylene torch. How much $CO_2$ is produced by burning 20.0 kg of acetylene in an excess of $O_2$? The unbalanced equation is

$$C_2H_2(g) + O_2(g) \longrightarrow CO_2(g) + H_2O(g)$$

**4.96** The reaction of calcium hydride with water can be used to prepare hydrogen gas:

$$CaH_2(s) + 2H_2O(l) \longrightarrow Ca(OH)_2(aq) + 2H_2(g)$$

How many g of hydrogen gas are produced in the reaction of $1.00 \times 10^2$ g calcium hydride with water?

**4.97** Various members of a class of compounds called alkenes (Chapter 11), react with hydrogen to produce a corresponding alkane (Chapter 10). Termed hydrogenation, this type of reaction is used to produce products such as margarine.

A typical hydrogenation reaction is

$$C_{10}H_{20}(l) + H_2(g) \longrightarrow C_{10}H_{22}(s)$$

Decene                          Decane

How much decane can be produced in a reaction of excess decene with 1.00 g hydrogen?

**4.98**  Chemistry at the Crime Scene: Drinking and Driving (Chapter 12), describes the reaction between the dichromate ion and ethanol to produce acetic acid. How much acetic acid can be produced from a mixture containing excess of dichromate ion and $1.00 \times 10^{-1}$ g of ethanol?

**4.99**  A rocket can be powered by the reaction between dinitrogen tetroxide and hydrazine:

$$N_2O_4(l) + 2N_2H_4(l) \longrightarrow 3N_2(g) + 4H_2O(g)$$

An engineer designed the rocket to hold 1.00 kg $N_2O_4$ and excess $N_2H_4$. How much $N_2$ would be produced according to the engineer's design?

**4.100**  A 4.00-g sample of $Fe_3O_4$ reacts with $O_2$ to produce $Fe_2O_3$:

$$4Fe_3O_4(s) + O_2(g) \longrightarrow 6Fe_2O_3(s)$$

Determine the number of g of $Fe_2O_3$ produced.

**4.101**  If the actual yield of decane in Problem 4.97 is 65.4 g, what is the % yield?

**4.102**  If the actual yield of acetic acid in Problem 4.98 is 0.110 g, what is the % yield?

**4.103**  If the % yield of nitrogen gas in Problem 4.99 is 75.0%, what is the actual yield of nitrogen?

**4.104**  If the % yield of $Fe_2O_3$ in Problem 4.100 is 90.0%, what is the actual yield of $Fe_2O_3$?

## CRITICAL THINKING PROBLEMS

1. Which of the following has fewer mol of carbon: 100 g of $CaCO_3$ or 0.5 mol of $CCl_4$?
2. Which of the following has fewer mol of carbon: $6.02 \times 10^{22}$ molecules of $C_2H_6$ or 88 g of $CO_2$?
3. How many molecules are found in each of the following?
   **a.** 1.0 lb of sucrose, $C_{12}H_{22}O_{11}$ (table sugar)
   **b.** 1.57 kg of $N_2O$ (anesthetic)
4. How many molecules are found in each of the following?
   **a.** $4 \times 10^5$ tons (t) of $SO_2$ (produced by the 1980 eruption of the Mount St. Helens volcano)
   **b.** 25.0 lb of $SiO_2$ (major constituent of sand)
5. Based on the information in Questions 4.9 and 4.10, it appears that we could solve some of our atmospheric problems by reducing the amount of NO that we put into the air. Do some literature (or Internet) research and determine the sources of atmospheric NO. Can we control atmospheric NO? If so, how?

# 5

## GASES, LIQUIDS, AND SOLIDS
# States of Matter

## LEARNING GOALS

1 Describe the major points of the kinetic molecular theory of gases.
2 Explain the relationship between the kinetic molecular theory and the physical properties of measurable quantities of gases.
3 Describe the behavior of gases expressed by the gas laws: Boyle's law, Charles's law, combined gas law, Avogadro's law, the ideal gas law, and Dalton's law.
4 Use gas law equations to calculate conditions and changes in conditions of gases.
5 Describe properties of the liquid state in terms of the properties of the individual molecules that comprise the liquid.
6 Describe the processes of melting, boiling, evaporation, and condensation.
7 Describe the dipolar attractions known collectively as van der Waals forces.
8 Describe hydrogen bonding and its relationship to boiling and melting temperatures.
9 Relate the properties of the various classes of solids (ionic, covalent, molecular, and metallic) to the structure of these solids.

Volcanic activity is a dramatic example of interconversion among the states of matter.

## OUTLINE

# INTRODUCTION

We have learned that the major differences among solids, liquids, and gases are due to the relationships among particles. These relationships include:

- the average distance of separation of particles in each state,
- the kinds of interactions among the particles, and
- the degree of organization of particles.

We have already discovered that the solid state is the most organized, with particles close together, allowing significant interactions among the particles. This results in high melting and boiling points for solid substances. Large amounts of energy are needed to overcome the attractive forces and disrupt the orderly structure.

Substances that are gases, on the other hand, are disordered, with particles widely separated and weak interactions among particles. Their melting and boiling points are relatively low. Gases at room temperature must be cooled a great deal for them to liquefy or solidify. For example, the melting and boiling points of $N_2$ are $-210°C$ and $-196°C$, respectively.

Liquids are intermediate in character. The molecules of a liquid are close together, like those of solids. However, the molecules of a liquid are disordered, like those of a gas.

Can a substance such as $O_2$ gas or $N_2$ gas also exist as a liquid, or even as a solid? We will see that a reduction in temperature or an increase in pressure can force atoms or molecules closer together, allowing them to behave as liquids or solids. Dry ice, for example, is solid carbon dioxide. Changes in state are described as physical changes. When a substance undergoes a change in state, many of its physical properties change. For example, when ice forms from liquid water, changes occur in density and hardness, but it is still water. Table 5.1 summarizes the important differences in physical properties among gases, liquids, and solids.

*Section 1.2 introduces the properties of the three states of matter.*

## 5.1  The Gaseous State

### Ideal Gas Concept

An **ideal gas** is simply a model of the way that gas particles (molecules or atoms) behave at the atomic/molecular level. The behavior of the individual particles can be inferred from the measurable behavior of samples of real gases. We can easily measure temperature, volume, pressure, and quantity (mass) of real gases. Similarly, when we systematically change one of these properties, we can determine the effect on each of the others. For example, putting more molecules in a

**TABLE 5.1 A Comparison of Physical Properties of Gases, Liquids, and Solids**

|  | Gas | Liquid | Solid |
|---|---|---|---|
| **Volume and Shape** | Expands to fill the volume of its container; consequently, it takes the shape of the container | Has a fixed volume at a given mass and temperature; volume principally dependent on its mass and secondarily on temperature; it assumes the shape of its container | Has a fixed volume; volume principally dependent on its mass and secondarily on temperature; it has a definite shape |
| **Density** | Low (typically ~$10^{-3}$ g/mL) | High (typically ~1 g/mL) | High (typically 1–10 g/mL) |
| **Compressibility** | High | Very low | Virtually incompressible |
| **Particle Motion** | Virtually free | Molecules or atoms "slide" past each other | Vibrate about a fixed position |
| **Intermolecular Distance** | Very large | Molecules or atoms are close to each other | Molecules, ions, or atoms are close to each other |

balloon (the act of blowing up a balloon) causes its volume to increase in a predictable way. In fact, careful measurements show a direct proportionality between the number of molecules and the volume of the balloon, an observation made by Amadeo Avogadro more than 200 years ago.

We owe a great deal of credit to the efforts of scientists Boyle, Charles, Avogadro, Dalton, and Gay-Lussac, whose careful work elucidated the relationships among the gas properties. Their efforts are summarized in the ideal gas law and are the subject of the first section of this chapter.

## Measurement of Gases

The gas laws (Boyle's law, Charles's law, Avogadro's law, Dalton's law, and the ideal gas law) involve the relationships among pressure ($P$), volume ($V$), temperature ($T$), and number of moles (mol) ($n$) of gas. We are already familiar with the measurement of temperature, volume, and mass (allowing the calculation of number of mol) from our laboratory experience. Measurement of pressure is perhaps not as obvious.

Gas pressure is a result of the force exerted by the collision of particles with the walls of the container. **Pressure** is force per unit area. The pressure of a gas may be measured with a **barometer,** invented by Evangelista Torricelli in the mid-1600s. The most common type of barometer is the mercury barometer depicted in Figure 5.1. A tube, sealed at one end, is filled with mercury and inverted in a dish of mercury. The pressure of the atmosphere pushing down on the mercury surface in the dish supports the column of mercury. The height of the column is proportional to the atmospheric pressure. The tube can be calibrated to give a numerical reading in millimeters (mm), centimeters (cm), or inches (in) of mercury. A commonly used unit of measurement is the atmosphere (atm). One standard atmosphere (1 atm) of pressure is equivalent to a height of mercury that is equal to

760 mm Hg (millimeters of mercury)

76.0 cm Hg (centimeters of mercury)

1 mm of Hg is also = 1 torr, in honor of Torricelli.

The English system equivalent is a pressure of 14.7 lb/in$^2$ (pounds per square inch, abbreviated psi) or 29.9 in Hg (inches of mercury). A recommended, yet less frequently used, systematic unit is the pascal (or kilopascal), named in honor of Blaise Pascal, a seventeenth-century French mathematician and scientist:

$$1 \text{ atm} = 1.01 \times 10^5 \text{ Pa (pascal)} = 101 \text{ kPa (kilopascal)}$$

Atmospheric pressure is due to the cumulative force of the air molecules ($N_2$ and $O_2$, for the most part) that are attracted to the earth's surface by gravity.

**Question 5.1** Express each of the following in units of atm:
a. 725 mm Hg          b. 29.0 cm Hg          c. 555 torr

**Question 5.2** Express each of the following in units of atm:
a. 10.0 torr          b. 61.0 cm Hg          c. 275 mm Hg

## Kinetic Molecular Theory of Gases

The kinetic molecular theory of gases provides a reasonable explanation of the behavior of gases. The macroscopic properties result from the action of the individual molecules comprising the gas.

The **kinetic molecular theory** can be summarized as follows:

1. Gases are made up of tiny atoms or molecules that are in constant, random motion. The particles are moving linearly.
2. The distance of separation among these atoms or molecules is very large in comparison to the size of the individual atoms or molecules. In other words, a gas is mostly empty space.

**Figure 5.1** A mercury barometer of the type invented by Torricelli. The height of the column of mercury is a function of the magnitude of the surrounding atmospheric pressure. The mercury in the tube is supported by atmospheric pressure.

76 cm

Atmospheric pressure

### LEARNING GOAL

**1** Describe the major points of the kinetic molecular theory of gases.

# A HUMAN PERSPECTIVE

## The Demise of the Hindenburg

One of the largest and most luxurious airships of the 1930s, the Hindenburg completed thirty-six transatlantic flights within a year after its construction. It was the flagship of a new era of air travel. But, on May 6, 1937, while making a landing approach near Lakehurst, New Jersey, the hydrogen-filled airship exploded and burst into flames. In this tragedy, thirty-seven of the ninety-six passengers were killed and many others were injured.

We may never know the exact cause. Many believe that the massive ship (it was more than 800 feet (ft) long) struck an overhead power line. Others speculate that lightning ignited the hydrogen, and some believe that sabotage may have been involved.

In retrospect, such an accident was inevitable. Hydrogen gas is very reactive, it combines with oxygen readily and rapidly, and this reaction liberates a large amount of energy. An explosion is the result of rapid, energy-releasing reactions.

Why was hydrogen chosen? Hydrogen is the lightest element. One mole of hydrogen has a mass of 2 grams (g). Hydrogen can be easily prepared in pure form, an essential requirement; more than seven million cubic feet ($ft^3$) of hydrogen were needed for each airship. Hydrogen has a low density; hence it provides great lift. The lifting power of a gas is based on the difference in density of the gas and the surrounding air (air is composed of gases with much greater molar masses; $N_2$ is 28 g and $O_2$ is 32 g). Engineers believed that the hydrogen would be safe when enclosed by the hull of the airship.

Today, airships are filled with helium (molar mass 4 g), which is far less reactive than hydrogen, and are used principally for advertising and television. A Goodyear blimp can be

Hindenburg

seen hovering over almost every significant outdoor sporting event.

### For Further Understanding

▶ Would a gas such as methane ($CH_4$) provide lifting power for an airship? Why or why not?
▶ What property would immediately rule out methane as a replacement gas for hydrogen in an airship?

---

Kinetic energy (K.E.) is equal to $\frac{1}{2}mv^2$, in which $m$ = mass and $v$ = velocity. Thus increased velocity at higher temperature correlates with an increase in kinetic energy.

---

## LEARNING GOAL

**2** Explain the relationship between the kinetic molecular theory and the physical properties of measurable quantities of gases.

---

3. All of the atoms and molecules behave independently. No attractive or repulsive forces exist between atoms or molecules in a gas.
4. Atoms and molecules collide with each other and with the walls of the container without *losing* energy. The energy is *transferred* from one atom or molecule to another. These collisions cause random changes in direction.
5. The average kinetic energy of the atoms or molecules increases or decreases in proportion to absolute temperature. As the temperature increases, the speed and kinetic energy of the atoms or molecules increase.

## Properties of Gases and the Kinetic Molecular Theory

We know that gases are easily *compressible*. The reason is that a gas is mostly empty space, providing space for the particles to be pushed closer together.

Gases will *expand* to fill any available volume because they move freely with sufficient energy to overcome their attractive forces.

Gases readily *diffuse* through each other simply because they are in continuous motion and paths are readily available owing to the large space between adjacent atoms or molecules. Light molecules diffuse rapidly; heavier molecules diffuse more slowly (Figure 5.2).

Gases have a *low density*. Density is defined as mass per volume. Because gases are mostly empty space, they have a low mass per volume.

Gases exert *pressure* on their containers. Pressure is a force per unit area resulting from collisions of gas particles with the walls of their container.

Gases behave most *ideally at low pressures and high temperatures*. At low pressures, the average distance of separation among atoms or molecules is greatest, minimizing interactive forces. At high temperatures, the atoms and molecules are in rapid motion and are able to overcome interactive forces more easily.

## Boyle's Law

The Irish scientist Robert Boyle found that the volume of a gas varies *inversely* with the pressure exerted by the gas if the number of mol and temperature of gas are held constant. This relationship is known as **Boyle's law.**

Mathematically, the *product* of pressure ($P$) and volume ($V$) is a constant:

$$PV = k_1$$

This relationship is illustrated in Figure 5.3.

Boyle's law is often used to calculate the volume resulting from a pressure change or vice versa. We consider

$$P_i V_i = k_1$$

the *initial* condition and

$$P_f V_f = k_1$$

the *final* condition. Because $PV$, initial or final, is constant and is equal to $k_1$,

$$P_i V_i = P_f V_f$$

Consider a gas occupying a volume of 10.0 liters (L) at 1.00 atm of pressure. The product, $PV = (10.0 \text{ L})(1.00 \text{ atm})$, is a constant, $k_1$. Doubling the pressure, to 2.0 atm, decreases the volume to 5.0 L:

$$(2.0 \text{ atm})(V_x) = (10.0 \text{ L})(1.00 \text{ atm})$$
$$V_x = 5.0 \text{ L}$$

Tripling the pressure decreases the volume by a factor of three:

$$(3.0 \text{ atm})(V_x) = (10.0 \text{ L})(1.00 \text{ atm})$$
$$V_x = 3.3 \text{ L}$$

## LEARNING GOAL

**3** Describe the behavior of gases expressed by the gas laws: Boyle's law, Charles's law, combined gas law, Avogadro's law, the ideal gas law, and Dalton's law.

**A REVIEW OF MATHEMATICS**

(a)

(b)

**Figure 5.2** Gaseous diffusion. (a) Ammonia (17.0 g/mol) and hydrogen chloride (36.5 g/mol) are introduced into the ends of a glass tube containing indicating paper. Red indicates the presence of hydrogen chloride and green indicates ammonia. (b) Note that ammonia has diffused much farther than hydrogen chloride in the same amount of time. This is a verification of the kinetic molecular theory. Light molecules move faster than heavier molecules at a specified temperature.

**Figure 5.3** An illustration of Boyle's law. Note the inverse relationship of pressure and volume.

## EXAMPLE 5.1    Calculating a Final Pressure

A sample of oxygen, at 25°C, occupies a volume of $5.00 \times 10^2$ milliliters (mL) at 1.50 atm pressure. What pressure must be applied to compress the gas to a volume of $1.50 \times 10^2$ mL, with no temperature change?

**4** Use gas law equations to calculate conditions and changes in conditions of gases.

### Solution

**Step 1.** Boyle's law applies directly, because there is no change in temperature or number of mol (no gas enters or leaves the container).

**Step 2.** Begin by identifying each term in the Boyle's law expression:

$$P_i = 1.50 \text{ atm}$$
$$P_f = ?$$
$$V_i = 5.00 \times 10^2 \text{ mL}$$
$$V_f = 1.50 \times 10^2 \text{ mL}$$

**Step 3.** The Boyle's law expression is:

$$P_iV_i = P_fV_f$$

**Step 4.** Solving for $P_f$:

$$P_f = \frac{P_iV_i}{V_f}$$

**Step 5.** Substituting:

$$P_f = \frac{(1.50 \text{ atm})(5.00 \times 10^2 \text{ mL})}{1.50 \times 10^2 \text{ mL}}$$
$$= 5.00 \text{ atm}$$

*Helpful Hint:* The calculation can be done with any volume units. It is important only that the units be the *same* on both sides of the equation.

### Practice Problem 5.1

Complete the following table:

| Sample Number | Initial Pressure (atm) | Final Pressure (atm) | Initial Volume (L) | Final Volume (L) |
|---|---|---|---|---|
| 1 | X | 5.0 | 1.0 | 7.5 |
| 2 | 5.0 | X | 1.0 | 0.20 |
| 3 | 1.0 | 0.50 | X | 0.30 |
| 4 | 1.0 | 2.0 | 0.75 | X |

▶ For Further Practice: **Questions 5.35 and 5.36.**

**3** Describe the behavior of gases expressed by the gas laws: Boyle's law, Charles's law, combined gas law, Avogadro's law, the ideal gas law, and Dalton's law.

## Charles's Law

Jacques Charles, a French scientist, studied the relationship between gas volume and temperature. This relationship, **Charles's law,** states that the volume of a gas varies *directly* with the absolute temperature (K) if pressure and number of mol of gas are constant.

Mathematically, the *ratio* of volume (V) and temperature (T) is a constant:

$$\frac{V}{T} = k_2$$

In a way analogous to Boyle's law, we may establish a set of initial conditions,

$$\frac{V_i}{T_i} = k_2$$

and final conditions,

$$\frac{V_f}{T_f} = k_2$$

Because $k_2$ is a constant, we may equate them, resulting in

$$\frac{V_i}{T_i} = \frac{V_f}{T_f}$$

and we may use this expression to solve some practical problems.

Consider a gas occupying a volume of 10.0 L at 273 K. The ratio V/T is a constant, $k_2$. Doubling the temperature, to 546 K, increases the volume to 20.0 L, as shown here:

$$\frac{10.0\ L}{273\ K} = \frac{V_f}{546\ K}$$
$$V_f = 20.0\ L$$

Tripling the temperature, to 819 K, increases the volume by a factor of three:

$$\frac{10.0\ L}{273\ K} = \frac{V_f}{819\ K}$$
$$V_f = 30.0\ L$$

These relationships are illustrated in Figure 5.4.

Temperature is a measure of the energy of molecular motion. The Kelvin scale is *absolute*, that is, directly proportional to molecular motion. Celsius and Fahrenheit are simply numerical scales based on the melting and boiling points of water. It is for this reason that Kelvin is used for energy-dependent relationships such as the gas laws.

Remember that this equation is only valid at constant n and p.

A REVIEW OF MATHEMATICS

ANIMATION
• Charles's Law

**Figure 5.4** An illustration of Charles's law. Note the direct relationship between volume and temperature.

## EXAMPLE 5.2    Calculating a Final Volume

A balloon filled with helium has a volume of $4.0 \times 10^3$ L at 25°C. What volume will the balloon occupy at 50°C if the pressure surrounding the balloon remains constant?

**Solution**

**Step 1.** Summarize the data, remembering that the temperature must be converted to Kelvin before Charles's law is applied:

$$T_i = 25°C + 273 = 298 \text{ K}$$
$$T_f = 50°C + 273 = 323 \text{ K}$$
$$V_i = 4.0 \times 10^3 \text{ L}$$
$$V_f = ?$$

**Step 2.** Using the Charles's law expression relating initial and final conditions:

$$\frac{V_i}{T_i} = \frac{V_f}{T_f}$$

**Step 3.** Rearrange and solve for $V_f$

$$V_f = \frac{(V_i)(T_f)}{T_i}$$

**Step 4.** Substituting our data, we get

$$V_f = \frac{(V_i)(T_f)}{T_i} = \frac{(4.0 \times 10^3 \text{ L})(323 \text{ K})}{298 \text{ K}} = 4.3 \times 10^3 \text{ L}$$

**Practice Problem 5.2**

A sample of nitrogen gas has a volume of 3.00 L at 25°C. What volume will it occupy at each of the following temperatures if the pressure and number of mol are constant?

a. 100°C   b. 150°F   c. 273 K   d. 546 K   e. 0°C   f. 373 K

▶ For Further Practice: **Questions 5.43 and 5.44.**

**Figure 5.5** Charles's law predicts that the volume of air in the balloon will increase when heated. We assume that the volume of the balloon is fixed; consequently, some air will be pushed out. The air remaining in the balloon is less dense (same volume, less mass) and the balloon will rise. When the heater is turned off the air cools, the density increases, and the balloon returns to earth.

The behavior of a fixed-volume hot-air balloon is a commonplace consequence of Charles's law. The balloon rises because air expands when heated (Figure 5.5). The volume of the balloon is fixed because the balloon is made of an inelastic material; as a result, when the air expands as described by Charles' law, some of it must be forced out. Hence the density of the remaining air is less (less mass contained in the same volume), and the balloon rises. Turning down the heat reverses the process, and the balloon descends.

## Combined Gas Law

Boyle's law describes the inverse proportional relationship between volume and pressure; Charles's law shows the direct proportional relationship between volume and temperature. Often, a sample of gas (a fixed number of mol of gas) undergoes change involving volume, pressure, and temperature simultaneously. It would be useful to have one equation that describes such processes.

The **combined gas law** is such an equation. It can be derived from Boyle's law and Charles's law and takes the form:

$$\frac{P_i V_i}{T_i} = \frac{P_f V_f}{T_f}$$

**ANIMATION**
• Interactive Gas Law

Let's look at two examples that use this expression.

**EXAMPLE 5.3**     Using the Combined Gas Law

**LEARNING GOAL**

Calculate the volume of $N_2$ that results when 0.100 L of the gas is heated from 300.0 K to 350.0 K at 1.00 atm.

**4** Use gas law equations to calculate conditions and changes in conditions of gases.

**Solution**

**Step 1.** Summarize the data:

$$P_i = 1.00 \text{ atm} \qquad P_f = 1.00 \text{ atm}$$
$$V_i = 0.100 \text{ L} \qquad V_f = ? \text{ L}$$
$$T_i = 300.0 \text{ K} \qquad T_f = 350.0 \text{ K}$$

**Step 2.** The combined gas law expression is:

$$\frac{P_i V_i}{T_i} = \frac{P_f V_f}{T_f}$$

**Step 3.** Rearrange:

$$P_f V_f T_i = P_i V_i T_f$$

and

$$V_f = \frac{P_i V_i T_f}{P_f T_i}$$

**Step 4.** Because $P_i = P_f$

$$V_f = \frac{V_i T_f}{T_i}$$

**Step 5.** Substituting gives

$$V_f = \frac{(0.100 \text{ L})(350.0 \text{ K})}{300.0 \text{ K}}$$
$$= 0.117 \text{ L}$$

*Helpful Hint:* In this case, because the pressure is constant, the combined gas law reduces to Charles's law.

**Practice Problem 5.3**

Hydrogen sulfide, $H_2S$, has the characteristic odor of rotten eggs. If a sample of $H_2S$ gas at 760.0 torr and 25.0°C in a 2.00-L container is allowed to expand into a 10.0-L container at 25.0°C, what is the pressure in the 10.0-L container?

▶ For Further Practice: **Questions 5.51 and 5.52.**

**EXAMPLE 5.4**    **Using the Combined Gas Law**

A sample of helium gas has a volume of 1.27 L at 149 K and 5.00 atm. When the gas is compressed to 0.320 L at 50.0 atm, the temperature increases markedly. What is the final temperature?

**4** Use gas law equations to calculate conditions and changes in conditions of gases.

**Solution**

**Step 1.** Summarize the data:

$$P_i = 5.00 \text{ atm} \quad P_f = 50.0 \text{ atm}$$
$$V_i = 1.27 \text{ L} \quad V_f = 0.320 \text{ L}$$
$$T_i = 149 \text{ K} \quad T_f = ? \text{ K}$$

**Step 2.** The combined gas law expression is

$$\frac{P_i V_i}{T_i} = \frac{P_f V_f}{T_f}$$

**Step 3.** Rearrange:

$$P_f V_f T_i = P_i V_i T_f$$

and

$$T_f = \frac{P_f V_f T_i}{P_i V_i}$$

**Step 4.** Substituting yields

$$T_f = \frac{(50.0 \text{ atm})(0.320 \text{ L})(149 \text{ K})}{(5.00 \text{ atm})(1.27 \text{ L})}$$
$$= 375 \text{ K}$$

**Practice Problem 5.4**

Cyclopropane, $C_3H_6$, is used as a general anesthetic. If a sample of cyclopropane stored in a 2.00-L container at 10.0 atm and 25.0°C is transferred to a 5.00-L container at 5.00 atm, what is the resulting temperature?

▶ For Further Practice: **Questions 5.53 and 5.54.**

**3** Describe the behavior of gases expressed by the gas laws: Boyle's law, Charles's law, combined gas law, Avogadro's law, the ideal gas law, and Dalton's law.

▶ **A REVIEW OF MATHEMATICS**

## Avogadro's Law

The relationship between the volume and number of mol of a gas at constant temperature and pressure is known as **Avogadro's law.** It states that equal volumes of any ideal gas contain the same number of mol if measured under the same conditions of temperature and pressure.

Mathematically, the *ratio* of volume ($V$) to number of mol ($n$) is a constant:

$$\frac{V}{n} = k_3$$

Consider 1 mol of gas occupying a volume of 10.0 L; using logic similar to the application of Boyle's and Charles's laws, 2 mol of the gas would occupy 20.0 L, 3 mol would occupy 30.0 L, and so forth. As we have done with the previous laws, we can formulate a useful expression relating initial and final conditions:

$$\frac{V_i}{n_i} = \frac{V_f}{n_f}$$

| EXAMPLE 5.5 | Using Avogadro's Law |
|---|---|

If 5.50 mol of CO occupy 20.6 L, how many L will 16.5 mol of CO occupy at the same temperature and pressure?

**Solution**

**Step 1.** The quantities and volume are related through Avogadro's law. Summarizing the data:

$$V_i = 20.6 \text{ L} \qquad V_f = ? \text{ L}$$
$$n_i = 5.50 \text{ mol} \qquad n_f = 16.5 \text{ mol}$$

**Step 2.** Using the mathematical expression for Avogadro's law:

$$\frac{V_i}{n_i} = \frac{V_f}{n_f}$$

**Step 3.** Rearranging:

$$V_f = \frac{V_i n_f}{n_i}$$

**Step 4.** Substitution yields:

$$V_f = \frac{(20.6 \text{ L})(16.5 \text{ mol})}{(5.50 \text{ mol})}$$
$$= 61.8 \text{ L of CO}$$

**Practice Problem 5.5**

a. A 1.00 mol sample of hydrogen gas occupies 22.4 L. How many mol of hydrogen are needed to fill a 100.0 L container at the same pressure and temperature?

b. How many mol of hydrogen are needed to triple the volume occupied by 0.25 mol of hydrogen, assuming no changes in pressure or temperature?

▶ For Further Practice: **Questions 5.59 and 5.60.**

## Molar Volume of a Gas

The volume occupied by *1 mol* of any gas is referred to as its **molar volume**. At **standard temperature and pressure (STP)**, the molar volume of any gas is 22.4 L. STP conditions are defined as follows:

$$T = 273 \text{ K (or 0°C)}$$
$$P = 1 \text{ atm}$$

Thus, 1 mol of $N_2$, $O_2$, $H_2$, or He all occupy the *same volume, 22.4 L*, at STP.

## Gas Densities

It is also possible to compute the density of various gases at STP. If we recall that density is the mass/unit volume,

Gas densities are most often expressed in units of g/L. Recall that units of g/mL are generally preferred for solids and liquids.

$$d = \frac{m}{V}$$

and that 1 mol of helium weighs 4.00 g,

$$d_{He} = \frac{4.00 \text{ g}}{22.4 \text{ L}} = 0.178 \text{ g/L at STP}$$

or, because 1 mol of nitrogen weighs 28.0 g, then

$$d_{N_2} = \frac{28.0 \text{ g}}{22.4 \text{ L}} = 1.25 \text{ g/L at STP}$$

The large difference in gas densities of helium and nitrogen (which makes up about 80% of the air) accounts for the lifting power of helium. A balloon filled with helium will rise through a predominantly nitrogen atmosphere because its gas density is less than 15% of the density of the surrounding atmosphere:

$$\frac{d_{He}}{d_{N_2}} \times 100\% = \% \text{ density}$$

$$\frac{0.178 \text{ g/L}}{1.25 \text{ g/L}} \times 100\% = 14.2\%$$

Heating a gas, such as air, will decrease its density and have a lifting effect as well.

## The Ideal Gas Law

Boyle's law (relating volume and pressure), Charles's law (relating volume and temperature), and Avogadro's law (relating volume to the number of mol) may be combined into a single expression relating all four terms. This expression is the **ideal gas law:**

$$PV = nRT$$

in which $R$, is a constant based on $k_1$, $k_2$, and $k_3$ (Boyle's, Charles's, and Avogadro's law constants), and is referred to as the *ideal gas constant*:

$$R = 0.0821 \text{ L} \cdot \text{atm} \cdot \text{K}^{-1} \cdot \text{mol}^{-1}$$

which is identical to

$$R = 0.0821 \frac{\text{L} \cdot \text{atm}}{\text{K} \cdot \text{mol}}$$

if the units

    atmospheres, for $P$
    liters, for $V$
    number of moles, for $n$
    and
    Kelvin for $T$

are used.

Consider some examples of the application of the ideal gas equation.

**LEARNING GOAL**

**3** Describe the behavior of gases expressed by the gas laws: Boyle's law, Charles's law, combined gas law, Avogadro's law, the ideal gas law, and Dalton's law.

**ANIMATION**
• Ideal Gas Law

---

**EXAMPLE 5.6**  **Calculating a Molar Volume**

Show by calculation that the molar volume of oxygen gas at STP is 22.4 L.

**Solution**

**Step 1.** At STP,

$$T = 273 \text{ K}$$
$$P = 1.00 \text{ atm}$$

**LEARNING GOAL**

**4** Use gas law equations to calculate conditions and changes in conditions of gases.

and the other terms are

$$n = 1.00 \text{ mol}$$
$$R = 0.0821 \text{ L} \cdot \text{atm} \cdot \text{K}^{-1} \cdot \text{mol}^{-1}$$

**Step 2.** The ideal gas expression is:

$$PV = nRT$$

**Step 3.** Rearrange and solve for $V$:

$$V = \frac{nRT}{P}$$

**Step 4.** Substitute and solve:

$$V = \frac{(1.00 \text{ mol})(0.0821 \text{ L} \cdot \text{atm} \cdot \text{K}^{-1} \cdot \text{mol}^{-1})(273 \text{ K})}{(1.00 \text{ atm})}$$

$$= 22.4 \text{ L}$$

### Practice Problem 5.6

Explain why the molar volume of helium (or any other ideal gas) is also 22.4 L.

▶ For Further Practice: **Questions 5.63 and 5.64.**

---

**EXAMPLE 5.7**    **Calculating the Number of Moles of a Gas**

LEARNING GOAL

Calculate the number of mol of helium in a 1.00-L balloon at 27°C and 1.00 atm of pressure.

**4** Use gas law equations to calculate conditions and changes in conditions of gases.

**Solution**

**Step 1.** The data are:

$$P = 1.00 \text{ atm}$$
$$V = 1.00 \text{ L}$$
$$T = 27°C + 273 = 3.00 \times 10^2 \text{ K}$$
$$R = 0.0821 \text{ L} \cdot \text{atm} \cdot \text{K}^{-1} \cdot \text{mol}^{-1}$$
$$n = ?$$

**Step 2.** The ideal gas expression is:

$$PV = nRT$$

**Step 3.** Rearrange and solve for $n$:

$$n = \frac{PV}{RT}$$

**Step 4.** Substitute and solve:

$$n = \frac{(1.00 \text{ atm})(1.00 \text{ L})}{(0.0821 \text{ L} \cdot \text{atm} \cdot \text{K}^{-1} \cdot \text{mol}^{-1})(3.00 \times 10^2 \text{ K})}$$

$$n = 0.0406 \text{ or } 4.06 \times 10^{-2} \text{ mol}$$

### Practice Problem 5.7

How many mol of $N_2$ gas will occupy a 5.00-L container at STP?

▶ For Further Practice: **Questions 5.65 and 5.71.**

**EXAMPLE 5.8**    **Converting Mass to Volume**

Oxygen used in hospitals and laboratories is often obtained from cylinders containing liquefied oxygen. If a cylinder contains $1.00 \times 10^2$ kilograms (kg) of liquid oxygen, how many L of oxygen can be produced at 1.00 atm of pressure at room temperature (20.0°C)?

**4**  Use gas law equations to calculate conditions and changes in conditions of gases.

**Solution**

**Step 1.** Data include:

mass of oxygen ($O_2$) = $1.00 \times 10^2$ kg
$T = 20.0°C$
$P = 1.00$ atm
$V$ of $O_2$ = ?

**Step 2.** Using conversion factors, we obtain

$$n_{O_2} = 1.00 \times 10^2 \ \text{kg} \, O_2 \times \frac{10^3 \ \text{g} \, O_2}{1 \ \text{kg} \, O_2} \times \frac{1 \ \text{mol} \ O_2}{32.0 \ \text{g} \, O_2}$$

and

$$n_{O_2} = 3.13 \times 10^3 \ \text{mol} \ O_2$$

**Step 3.** Convert °C to K:

$$T = 20.0°C + 273 = 293 \ \text{K}$$

**Step 4.** The ideal gas expression is:

$$PV = nRT$$

**Step 5.** Rearrange and solve for $V$:

$$V = \frac{nRT}{P}$$

**Step 6.** Substitute and solve:

$$V = \frac{(3.13 \times 10^3 \ \text{mol})(0.0821 \ \text{L} \cdot \text{atm} \cdot \text{K}^{-1} \cdot \text{mol}^{-1})(293 \ \text{K})}{1.00 \ \text{atm}}$$

$$= 7.53 \times 10^4 \ \text{L}$$

**Practice Problem 5.8**

What volume is occupied by 10.0 g $N_2$ at 30.0°C and a pressure of 750 torr?

▶ For Further Practice: **Questions 5.67 and 5.68.**

**Question 5.3**   A 20.0-L gas cylinder contains 4.80 g $H_2$ at 25°C. What is the pressure of this gas?

**Question 5.4**   At what temperature will 2.00 mol of He fill a 2.00-L container at standard pressure?

**3**  Describe the behavior of gases expressed by the gas laws: Boyle's law, Charles's law, combined gas law, Avogadro's law, the ideal gas law, and Dalton's law.

## Dalton's Law of Partial Pressures

Our discussion of gases so far has presumed that we are working with a single pure gas. A *mixture* of gases exerts a pressure that is the *sum* of the pressures that each gas would exert if it were present alone under the same conditions. This is known as **Dalton's law** of partial pressures. Dalton's law is based on the

# GREEN CHEMISTRY

## The Greenhouse Effect and Global Climate Change

A greenhouse is a bright, warm, and humid environment for growing plants, vegetables, and flowers even during the cold winter months. It functions as a closed system in which the concentration of water vapor is elevated and visible light streams through the windows; this creates an ideal climate for plant growth.

Some of the visible light is absorbed by plants and soil in the greenhouse and released as infrared radiation. This radiated energy is blocked by the glass or absorbed by water vapor and carbon dioxide ($CO_2$). This trapped energy warms the greenhouse and is a form of solar heating: light energy is converted to heat energy. Hence, water vapor and carbon dioxide are termed *greenhouse gases*.

On a global scale, the same process takes place. Although more than half of the sunlight that strikes the earth's surface is reflected back into space, the fraction of light that is absorbed produces sufficient heat to sustain life. How does this happen? Greenhouse gases, such as $CO_2$, trap energy radiated from the earth's surface and store it in the atmosphere. This moderates our climate. The earth's surface would be much colder and more inhospitable if the atmosphere was not able to capture some reasonable amount of solar energy.

Can we have too much of a good thing? It appears so. Since 1900 the atmospheric concentration of $CO_2$ has increased from 296 parts per million (ppm) to over 350 ppm (approximately 17% increase). The energy demands of technological and population growth have caused massive increases in the combustion of organic matter and carbon-based fuels (coal, oil, and natural gas), adding over 50 billion tons of $CO_2$ to that already present in the atmosphere. Photosynthesis naturally removes $CO_2$ from the atmosphere. However, the removal of forestland to create living space and cropland has decreased the amount of vegetation available to consume atmospheric $CO_2$ through photosynthesis. The rapid destruction of the Amazon rain forest is just the latest of many examples.

Many gases, in addition to $H_2O$ and $CO_2$, behave as greenhouse gases. Any molecule in the gas phase that is capable of absorbing infrared radiation may behave as a greenhouse gas. Many, however, are unimportant in the global climate change discussion simply because they are not present in the atmosphere in significant quantity. Methane ($CH_4$), an infrared absorber, exists at higher levels and is a potent greenhouse gas. It has received little attention principally because we have relatively little control over its atmospheric levels.

If our greenhouse model is correct, an increase in $CO_2$ levels should produce global warming, perhaps changing our climate in unforeseen and undesirable ways.

### For Further Understanding

► What steps might be taken to decrease levels of $CO_2$ in the atmosphere over time?

► In what ways might our climate and our lives change as a consequence of significant global warming?

(a)

(b)

(a) A greenhouse traps solar radiation as heat. (b) Our atmosphere also acts as a solar collector. Carbon dioxide, like the windows of a greenhouse, allows the visible light to enter and traps the heat.

assumption that the behavior of each gas in a mixture of gases is independent of all of the other gases.

Stated another way, the total pressure of a mixture of gases is the sum of the **partial pressures.** That is,

$$P_t = p_1 + p_2 + p_3 + \cdots$$

in which $P_t$ = total pressure and $p_1, p_2, p_3, \ldots$, are the partial pressures of the component gases. For example, the total pressure of our atmosphere is equal to the sum of the pressures of $N_2$ and $O_2$ (the principal components of air):

$$P_{air} = p_{N_2} + p_{O_2}$$

Other gases, such as argon (Ar), carbon dioxide ($CO_2$), carbon monoxide (CO), and methane ($CH_4$) are present in the atmosphere at very low partial pressures.

The ideal gas law applies to mixtures of gases as well as pure gases.

However, their presence may result in dramatic consequences; one such gas is carbon dioxide. Classified as a "greenhouse gas," it exerts a significant effect on our climate. Its role is described in Green Chemistry: The Greenhouse Effect and Global Climate Change.

## Ideal Gases Versus Real Gases

To this point we have assumed, in both theory and calculations, that all gases behave as ideal gases. However, in reality there is no such thing as an ideal gas. As we noted at the beginning of this section, the ideal gas is a model (a very useful one) that describes the behavior of individual atoms and molecules; this behavior translates to the collective properties of measurable quantities of these atoms and molecules. Limitations of the model arise from the fact that interactive forces, even between the widely spaced particles of gas, are not totally absent in any sample of gas.

Attractive forces are present in gases composed of polar molecules. Nonuniform charge distribution on polar molecules creates positive and negative regions, resulting in electrostatic attraction and deviation from ideality.

Calculations involving polar gases such as HF, NO, and $SO_2$ based on ideal gas equations (which presume no such interactions) are approximations. However, at low pressures, such approximations certainly provide useful information. Nonpolar molecules, on the other hand, are only weakly attracted to each other and behave much more ideally in the gas phase.

*See Sections 3.5 and 5.2 for a discussion of interactions of polar molecules.*

Gases behave less ideally as their temperature decreases; they become more like the liquid phase as they approach their condensation temperature.

## 5.2    The Liquid State

LEARNING GOAL

5  Describe properties of the liquid state in terms of the properties of the individual molecules that comprise the liquid.

Molecules in the liquid state are close to one another. Attractive forces are large enough to keep the molecules together, in contrast to gases, whose cohesive forces are so low that a gas expands to fill any volume. However, these attractive forces in a liquid are not large enough to restrict movement, as in solids. Let's look at the various properties of liquids in more detail.

### Compressibility

Liquids are practically incompressible. In fact, the molecules are so close to one another that even the application of very high pressure does not significantly decrease the volume. This makes liquids ideal for the transmission of force, as in the brake lines of an automobile. The force applied by the driver's foot on the brake pedal does not compress the brake fluid in the lines; rather, it transmits the force directly to the brake pads, and the friction between the brake pads and rotors (that are attached to the wheel) stops the car.

### Viscosity

The **viscosity** of a liquid is a measure of its resistance to flow. Viscosity is a function of both the attractive forces between molecules and molecular geometry.

Molecules with complex structures, which do not "slide" smoothly past each other, and polar molecules, tend to have higher viscosity than less structurally complex, less polar liquids. Glycerol, which is used in a variety of skin treatments, has the structural formula:

$$
\begin{array}{c}
\text{H} \\
| \\
\text{H}-\text{C}-\text{O}-\text{H} \\
| \\
\text{H}-\text{C}-\text{O}-\text{H} \\
| \\
\text{H}-\text{C}-\text{O}-\text{H} \\
| \\
\text{H}
\end{array}
$$

# A MEDICAL PERSPECTIVE

## Blood Gases and Respiration

Respiration must deliver oxygen to cells and carbon dioxide, the waste product, to the lungs to be exhaled. Dalton's law of partial pressures helps to explain the way in which this process occurs.

Gases (such as $O_2$ and $CO_2$) move from a region of higher partial pressure to one of lower partial pressure in an effort to establish an equilibrium. At the interface of the lung, the membrane barrier between the blood and the surrounding atmosphere, the following situation exists: Atmospheric $O_2$ partial pressure is high, and atmospheric $CO_2$ partial pressure is low. The reverse is true on the other side of the membrane (blood). Thus $CO_2$ is efficiently removed from the blood, and $O_2$ is efficiently moved into the bloodstream.

At the other end of the line, capillaries are distributed in close proximity to the cells that need to expel $CO_2$ and gain $O_2$. The partial pressure of $CO_2$ is high in these cells, and the partial pressure of $O_2$ is low, having been used up by the energy-harvesting reaction, the oxidation of glucose:

$$C_6H_{12}O_6 + 6O_2 \longrightarrow 6CO_2 + 6H_2O + energy$$

The $O_2$ diffuses into the cells (from a region of high to low partial pressure), and the $CO_2$ diffuses from the cells to the blood (again from a region of high to low partial pressure).

With each breath we take, oxygen is distributed to the cells and used to generate energy, and the waste product, $CO_2$, is expelled by the lungs.

### For Further Understanding

▶ Carbon dioxide and carbon monoxide can be toxic, but for different reasons. Use the Internet to research this topic and:
  ▶ Explain why carbon dioxide is toxic.
  ▶ Explain why carbon monoxide is toxic.

It is quite viscous, owing to its polar nature and its significant intermolecular attractive forces. This is certainly desirable in a skin treatment because its viscosity keeps it on the area being treated. Gasoline, on the other hand, is much less viscous and readily flows through the gas lines of your auto; it is composed of nonpolar molecules.

Viscosity generally decreases with increasing temperature. The increased kinetic energy at higher temperatures overcomes some of the intermolecular attractive forces. The temperature effect is an important consideration in the design of products that must remain fluid at low temperatures, such as motor oils and transmission fluids found in automobiles.

## Surface Tension

The **surface tension** of a liquid is a measure of the attractive forces exerted among molecules at the surface of the liquid. It is only the surface molecules that are not totally surrounded by other liquid molecules (the top of the molecule faces the atmosphere). These surface molecules are surrounded and attracted by fewer liquid molecules than those below and to each side. Hence the net attractive forces on surface molecules pull them downward, into the body of the liquid. As a result, the surface molecules behave as a "skin" that covers the interior.

This increased surface force is responsible for the spherical shape of drops of liquid. Drops of water "beading" on a polished surface, such as a waxed automobile, illustrate this effect.

Because surface tension is related to the attractive forces exerted among molecules, surface tension generally decreases with an increase in temperature or a decrease in the polarity of molecules that make up the liquid.

A **surfactant** is a substance that can be added to a liquid to decrease surface tension. Surfactants have polar and nonpolar regions at opposite ends of their molecules. The polar ends of the molecules interact with polar liquids to decrease attractive forces at the surface (hence, lowering surface tension). Common surfactants include soaps and detergents that reduce water's surface tension; this promotes the interaction of water with grease and dirt, making them easier to remove. For more information on these interesting molecules, see the boxed topic: "Kitchen Chemistry: Solubility, Surfactants, and the Dishwasher" on page 216.

**ANIMATION**
• Surface Tension of Water

Skimming stones is possible due to the surface tension of water. Explain.

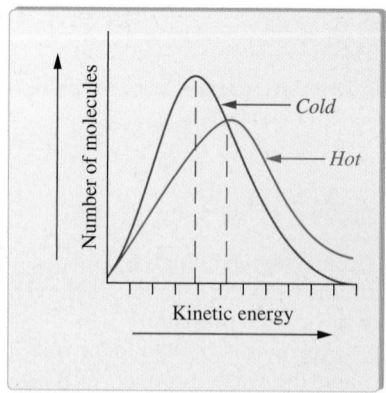

**Figure 5.6** The temperature dependence of liquid vapor pressure is illustrated. The average molecular kinetic energy increases with temperature. Note that the average values are indicated by dashed lines. The small number of high-energy molecules may evaporate.

## LEARNING GOAL

**6** Describe the processes of melting, boiling, evaporation, and condensation.

**ANIMATION**
• Vapor Pressure

The process of evaporation of perspiration from the skin produces a cooling effect, because heat is absorbed by the evaporating molecules.

Symbolizes the rate of evaporation          Symbolizes the rate of condensation

**(a)        (b)        (c)        (d)**

**Figure 5.7** Liquid water in equilibrium with water vapor. (a) Initiation: process of evaporation exclusively. (b, c) After a time, both evaporation and condensation occur, but evaporation predominates. (d) Dynamic equilibrium established. Rates of evaporation and condensation are equal.

**Question 5.5**   What molecular properties favor high viscosity?

**Question 5.6**   What molecular properties favor high surface tension?

## Vapor Pressure of a Liquid

Evaporation, condensation, and the meaning of the term *boiling point* are all related to the concept of liquid vapor pressure. Consider the following example. A liquid, such as water, is placed in a sealed container. After a time the contents of the container are analyzed. Both liquid water and water vapor are found at room temperature, when we might expect water to be found only as a liquid. In this closed system, some of the liquid water was converted to a gas:

$$\text{energy} + H_2O(l) \longrightarrow H_2O(g)$$

How did this happen? The temperature is too low for conversion of a liquid to a gas by boiling. According to the kinetic molecular theory, liquid molecules are in continuous motion, with their *average* kinetic energy directly proportional to the Kelvin temperature. The word *average* is the key. Although the average kinetic energy is too low to allow "average" molecules to escape from the liquid phase to the gas phase, there exists a range of molecules with different energies, some low and some high, that make up the "average" (Figure 5.6). Thus some of these high-energy molecules possess sufficient energy to escape from the bulk liquid.

At the same time, a fraction of these gaseous molecules lose energy (perhaps by collision with the walls of the container) and return to the liquid state:

$$H_2O(g) \longrightarrow H_2O(l) + \text{energy}$$

The process of conversion of liquid to gas, at a temperature too low to boil, is **evaporation**. The reverse process, conversion of the gas to the liquid state, is **condensation**. After some time the rates of evaporation and condensation become *equal*, and this sets up a dynamic equilibrium between liquid and vapor states. The **vapor pressure of a liquid** is defined as the pressure exerted by the vapor *at equilibrium*.

$$H_2O(g) \rightleftarrows H_2O(l)$$

The equilibrium process of evaporation and condensation of water is depicted in Figure 5.7.

The boiling point of a liquid is defined as the temperature at which the vapor pressure of the liquid becomes equal to the atmospheric pressure. The "normal" atmospheric pressure is 760 torr, or 1 atm, and the **normal boiling point** is the temperature at which the vapor pressure of the liquid is equal to 1 atm.

It follows from the definition that the boiling point of a liquid is not constant. It depends on the atmospheric pressure. At high altitudes, where the atmospheric pressure is low, the boiling point of a liquid, such as water, is lower than the normal boiling point (for water, 100°C). High atmospheric pressure increases the boiling point.

Apart from its dependence on the surrounding atmospheric pressure, the boiling point depends on the nature of the attractive forces between the liquid molecules. Polar liquids, such as water, with large intermolecular attractive forces have *higher* boiling points than nonpolar liquids, such as gasoline, which exhibit weak attractive forces.

Compounds may be detected and identified because they have a measurable vapor pressure, as you will see in the discussion Chemistry at the Crime Scene: Explosives at the Airport.

**Question 5.7** Distinguish between the terms *evaporation* and *condensation*.

**Question 5.8** Distinguish between the terms *evaporation* and *boiling*.

## van der Waals Forces

Physical properties of liquids, such as those discussed in the previous section, can be explained in terms of their intermolecular forces. We have seen (see Section 3.5) that attractive forces between polar molecules, **dipole-dipole interactions,** significantly decrease vapor pressure and increase the boiling point. However, nonpolar substances can exist as liquids as well; many are liquids and even solids at room temperature. What is the nature of the attractive forces in these nonpolar compounds?

In 1930, Fritz London demonstrated that he could account for a weak attractive force between any two molecules, whether polar or nonpolar. He postulated that the electron distribution in molecules is not fixed; electrons are in continuous motion, relative to the nucleus. So, for a short time a nonpolar molecule could experience an *instantaneous dipole,* a short-lived polarity caused by a temporary dislocation of the electron cloud. These temporary dipoles could interact with other temporary dipoles, just as permanent dipoles interact in polar molecules. We now call these intermolecular forces **London forces.**

London forces and dipole-dipole interactions are collectively known as **van der Waals forces.** London forces exist among polar and nonpolar molecules because electrons are in constant motion in all molecules. Dipole-dipole attractions occur only among polar molecules. In addition to van der Waals forces, a special type of dipole-dipole force, the *hydrogen bond,* has a very significant effect on molecular properties, particularly in biological systems.

## Hydrogen Bonding

Typical forces in polar liquids, discussed above, are only about 1–2% as strong as ionic and covalent bonds. However, certain liquids have boiling points that are much higher than we would predict from these polar interactions alone. This indicates the presence of some strong intermolecular force. This attractive force is due to **hydrogen bonding.** Molecules in which a hydrogen atom is bonded to a small, highly electronegative atom such as nitrogen, oxygen, or fluorine exhibit this effect. The presence of a highly electronegative atom bonded to a hydrogen atom creates a large dipole:

This arrangement of atoms produces a very polar bond, often resulting in a polar molecule with strong intermolecular attractive forces. Although the hydrogen bond is weaker than bonds formed *within* molecules (covalent and polar covalent *intra*molecular forces), it is the strongest attractive force *between* molecules (intermolecular force).

Consider the boiling points of four small molecules:

| $CH_4$ | $NH_3$ | $H_2O$ | HF |
|---|---|---|---|
| molar mass | molar mass | molar mass | molar mass |
| 16 | 17 | 18 | 20 |
| −161°C | −33°C | +100°C | +19.5°C |

**LEARNING GOAL**

7 Describe the dipolar attractions known collectively as van der Waals forces.

**LEARNING GOAL**

8 Describe hydrogen bonding and its relationship to boiling and melting temperatures.

*Recall that the most electronegative elements are in the upper right corner of the periodic table, and these elements exert strong electron attraction in molecules, as described in Chapter 3.*

# CHEMISTRY AT THE CRIME SCENE

## Explosives at the Airport

The images flash across our television screens: a "bomb sniffing" dog being led through an airport or train station, pausing to sniff packages or passengers, looking for anything of a suspicious nature. Or, perhaps, we see a long line of people waiting to pass through a scanning device surrounded by what appears to be hundreds of thousands of dollars worth of electronic gadgetry.

At one level, we certainly know what is happening. These steps are taken to increase the likelihood that our trip, as well as everyone else's, will be as safe and worry-free as possible. From a scientific standpoint, we may wonder how these steps actually detect explosive materials. What do the dog and some electronic devices have in common? How can a dog sniff a solid or a liquid? Surely everyone knows that the nose can only sense gases, and explosive devices are solids or liquids, or a combination of the two.

One potential strategy is based on the concept of vapor pressure, which you have just studied. We now know that liquids, such as water, have a measurable vapor pressure at room temperature. In fact, most liquids and many solids have vapor pressures large enough to allow detection of the molecules in the gas phase. The challenge is finding devices that are sufficiently sensitive and selective, enabling them to detect low concentrations of molecules characteristic of explosives, without becoming confused by thousands of other compounds routinely present in the air.

Each explosive device has its own "signature," a unique mix of chemicals used in its manufacture and assembly. If only one,

or perhaps a few, of these compounds has a measurable vapor pressure, it may be detected with a sensitive measuring device.

Dogs are renowned for their keen sense of smell, and some breeds are better than others. Dogs can be trained to signal the presence of certain scents by barking or exhibiting unusual agitation. A qualified handler can recognize these cues and alert appropriate authorities.

Scientific instruments are designed to mimic the scenario described here. A device, the mass spectrometer, can detect very low concentrations of molecules in the air. Additionally, it can distinguish certain "target" molecules, because each different compound has its own unique molar mass. Detection of molecules of interest generates an electrical signal, and an alarm is sounded.

Compounds with high vapor pressures are most easily detected. Active areas of forensic research involve designing a new generation of instruments that are even more sensitive and selective than those currently available. Decreased cost and increased portability and reliability will enable many sites not currently being monitored to have the same level of protection as major transit facilities.

### For Further Understanding

▶ Would you expect nonpolar or polar molecules of similar mass to be more easily detected? Why?

▶ Why must an explosives detection device be highly selective?

Hydrogen bond

H  O
H

Water molecule

**Figure 5.8** Hydrogen bonding in water. Note that the central water molecule is hydrogen bonded to four other water molecules. The attractive force between the hydrogen ($\delta^+$) part of one water molecule and the oxygen ($\delta^-$) part of another water molecule constitutes the hydrogen bond.

Clearly, ammonia, water, and hydrogen fluoride boil at significantly higher temperatures than methane. The N—H, O—H, and F—H bonds are far more polar than the C—H bond, owing to the high electronegativity of N, O, and F.

It is interesting to note that the boiling points increase as the electronegativity of the element bonded to hydrogen increases, with one exception: Fluorine, with the highest electronegativity, should cause HF to have the highest boiling point. This is not the case. The order of boiling points is

water > hydrogen fluoride > ammonia > methane

not

hydrogen fluoride > water > ammonia > methane

Why? To answer this question we must look at the *number of potential bonding sites* in each molecule. Water has two partial positive sites (located at each hydrogen atom) and two partial negative sites (two lone pairs of electrons on the oxygen atom); it can form hydrogen bonds at each site. This results in a complex network of attractive forces among water molecules in the liquid state, and the strength of the forces holding this network together accounts for water's unusually high boiling point. This network is depicted in Figure 5.8.

Ammonia and hydrogen fluoride can form only one hydrogen bond per molecule. Ammonia has three partial positive sites (three hydrogen atoms bonded to nitrogen) but only one partial negative site (the lone pair); the single lone pair is the limiting factor. One positive site and one negative site are needed for each hydrogen bond. Hydrogen fluoride has only one partial positive site and three partial negative sites (three lone pairs); the single positive site is the limiting factor. Consequently, hydrogen fluoride, like ammonia, can form only one hydrogen bond per molecule. The network of attractive forces in ammonia and hydrogen fluoride is, therefore, much less extensive than that found in water, and their boiling points are considerably lower than that of water.

Hydrogen bonding has an extremely important influence on the behavior of many biological systems. Molecules such as proteins and DNA require extensive hydrogen bonding to maintain their structures and hence functions. DNA (deoxyribonucleic acid, Section 20.2) is a giant among molecules, with intertwined chains of atoms held together by thousands of hydrogen bonds.

Intramolecular hydrogen bonding between polar regions helps keep proteins folded in their proper three-dimensional structure. See Chapter 18.

**Question 5.9** Arrange the following compounds in order of increasing boiling point:

$$CO_2 \quad CH_3OH \quad CH_3Cl$$

Explain your logic.

**Question 5.10** Explain the large difference in boiling point for the isomers butanol and diethyl ether.

butanol
b.p. = 117°C

diethyl ether
b.p. = 34.5°C

## 5.3 The Solid State

The close packing of the particles of a solid results from attractive forces that are strong enough to restrict motion. This occurs because the kinetic energy of the particles is insufficient to overcome the attractive forces among particles. The particles are "locked" together in a defined and highly organized fashion. This results in fixed shape and volume, although, at the atomic level, vibrational motion is observed.

### Properties of Solids

Solids are virtually incompressible, owing to the small distance between particles. Most will convert to liquids at a higher temperature, when the increased heat energy overcomes some of the attractive forces within the solid. The temperature at which a solid is converted to the liquid phase is its *melting point*. The melting point depends on the strength of the attractive forces in the solid, hence its structure. As we might expect, polar solids have higher melting points than nonpolar solids of the same molecular weight.

A solid may be a **crystalline solid,** having a regular repeating structure, or an **amorphous solid,** having no organized structure. Diamond and sodium chloride (Figure 5.9) are examples of crystalline substances; glass, plastic, and concrete are examples of amorphous solids.

### Types of Crystalline Solids

Crystalline solids may exist in one of four general groups:

1. *Ionic solids.* The units that comprise an **ionic solid** are positive and negative ions. Electrostatic forces hold the crystal together. Ionic solids generally have high melting points, and are hard and brittle. A common example of an ionic solid is sodium chloride.

**LEARNING GOAL**

9 Relate the properties of the various classes of solids (ionic, covalent, molecular, and metallic) to the structure of these solids.

(a) The crystal structure of diamond

Cl⁻     Na⁺

(b) The crystal structure of sodium chloride

(c) The crystal structure of methane, a frozen molecular solid. Only one methane molecule is shown in detail.

**Figure 5.9** Crystalline solids.

(d) The crystal structure of a metallic solid. The gray area represents mobile electrons around fixed metal cations.

*Intermolecular forces are also discussed in Sections 3.5 and 5.2.*

2. *Covalent solids.* The units that comprise a **covalent solid** are atoms held together by covalent bonds. Covalent solids have very high melting points (1200°C to 2000°C or more is not unusual) and are extremely hard. They are insoluble in most solvents. Diamond is a covalent solid composed of covalently bonded carbon atoms. Diamonds are used for industrial cutting because they are so hard and as gemstones because of their crystalline beauty.

3. *Molecular solids.* The units that make up a **molecular solid,** molecules, are held together by intermolecular attractive forces (London forces, dipole-dipole interactions, and hydrogen bonding). Molecular solids are usually soft and have low melting points. They are frequently volatile and are poor electrical conductors. A common example is ice (solid water; Figure 5.10).

4. *Metallic solids.* The units that comprise a **metallic solid** are metal atoms held together by metallic bonds. *Metallic bonds* are formed by the overlap of orbitals of metal atoms, resulting in regions of high electron density surrounding the positive metal nuclei. Electrons in these regions are extremely mobile. They are able to move freely from atom to atom through pathways that are, in reality, overlapping atomic orbitals. This results in the high *conductivity* (ability to carry electrical current) exhibited by many metallic solids. Silver and copper are common examples of metallic solids. Metals are easily shaped and are used for a variety of purposes. Most of these are practical applications such as

= O

= H

**Figure 5.10** The structure of ice, a molecular solid. Hydrogen bonding among water molecules produces a regular open structure that is less dense than liquid water.

# A HUMAN PERSPECTIVE

## Gemstones

When we think of the solid state, we may think of ice, the solid form of water; coal, a major energy source; or, perhaps, concrete and steel, bulwarks of the construction industry. All are commonplace materials with well-defined properties and applications. However, if we turn our thoughts toward beauty and value, diamonds often come to mind. Diamonds are valued for their sparkle, durability, and rarity. Diamonds are the most famous, but certainly not the only gemstones with desirable properties and high price tags.

The diamond market has a value of over twelve billion dollars per year and colored gemstones another six billion dollars. What are these gems made of, and why are they so valuable?

### Diamond

Most of the carbon deposits on earth are amorphous; they have no organized structure. Consequently, they do not share the properties of solids with regular, repeating structure. Much of this carbon is coal. A tiny fraction of the world's solid carbon exists as covalent solids. Recall that covalent solids have strong covalent bonds and a regular, repeating crystal structure. A diamond is a covalent solid comprised of carbon atoms arranged in a 3-dimensional crystalline structure (Figure 5.9(a)).

A one-carat diamond, which is only 0.20 g, has a retail value of thousands of dollars. Just how many thousands is a function of the regularity of the repeating pattern of carbon atoms and freedom from inclusion of impurities. The number of diamonds that meet the highest standards is very small.

### Rubies and Sapphires

These gemstones are variations of the mineral corundum, which is essentially $Al_2O_3$. Rubies and sapphires have similar crystalline structures; however, ruby is red and sapphire is blue. Why? Trace amounts of other elements make all the difference. Chromium replaces some aluminum ions in ruby ($Cr^{3+}$ replaces $Al^{3+}$). This alters the absorption spectrum of the material, favoring transmission of red light (610 nm); hence, the ruby red color. Sapphire appears blue because of the presence of traces of $Fe^{2+}$ and $Ti^{4+}$. Light at the red end of the visible spectrum is absorbed by compounds formed from these trace ions. The blue light is transmitted and the sapphire appears blue.

### Emerald

The $Cr^{3+}$ ion is also responsible for the green color of emerald. It is a trace element incorporated into the base structure of the

A variety of gemstones. Variations in crystal structure are responsible for differences in color and lustre.

mineral beryl (the origin of the name is beryllium, a key element in its structure). Beryl is $Be_3Al_2Si_6O_{18}$ and $Cr^{3+}$ (and vanadium ions as well) replaces $Al^{3+}$ in the crystal structure of the beryl. The resulting color is the familiar emerald green.

### Tanzanite

This blue gem is a product of a mineral with the formula $Ca_2Al_2(SiO_4)(Si_2O_7)O(OH)$. In contrast to other gems we have discussed tanzanite was not discovered and characterized until the 1960s. It was first found in Tanzania, for which it is named. Once again trace elements make all the difference between worthless rock and valuable gemstones. Vanadium ions, substituted for aluminum ions, are responsible for its deep blue color.

We owe the origin of gemstones to the pressure and temperature events associated with earth's formation. We have learned to make synthetic gemstones in the laboratory, but the gem connoisseurs of the world continue to show a preference for the natural product. Not surprisingly, they owe their value to their rarity and intrinsic beauty.

### For Further Understanding

▶ Predict the color of a gemstone that absorbs light mostly in the wavelength range 500–700 nm.

▶ Suggest a reason why a collection of sapphires may appear to be different shades of blue.

hardware, cookware, and surgical and dental tools. Others are purely for enjoyment and decoration, such as silver and gold jewelry.

## Sublimation of Solids

**Sublimation** is the process in which some molecules in the solid state convert directly to the gaseous state.

As we saw in the Chemistry at the Crime Scene discussion of the development of new devices for airport security (p. 184), some molecular solids possess measurable vapor pressures. Recall that vapor pressure of a liquid is the key concept in explaining

Solid-state chemistry is critically important to the semiconductor industry. "Chips," crystalline solids made of silicon and traces of other elements such as arsenic and germanium, are the "brains" behind our computers, cell phones, and a host of other electronic devices.

the conversion of a liquid to a gas by evaporation or by boiling. Certain molecular solids such as dry ice (frozen carbon dioxide) and naphthalene (moth balls) will, at room temperature, convert to a gas without passing through the liquid state because they have a sufficiently high vapor pressure. This process is termed *sublimation*.

If you live in a very cold climate, you may have observed that, over a period of several days, snow and ice "disappear," even though the temperature is continuously below the melting point of water. Snow and ice, molecular solids, have simply sublimed, converting from solid to water vapor.

**Question 5.11**
  a. What properties are associated with ionic solids?
  b. Provide two examples of ionic solids.

**Question 5.12**
  a. What properties are associated with molecular solids?
  b. Provide two examples of molecular solids.

## CHAPTER MAP

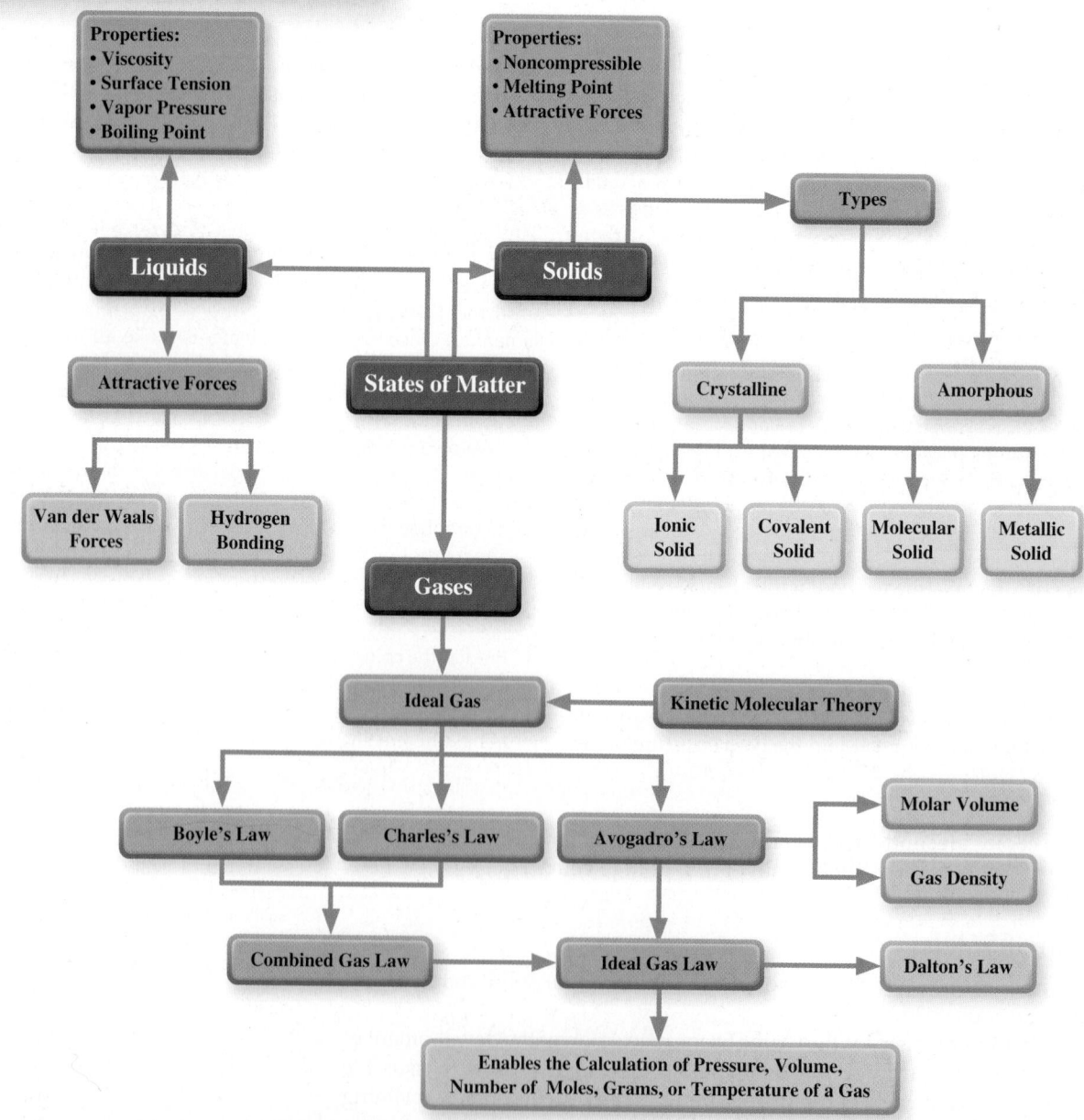

## SUMMARY

### 5.1 The Gaseous State

▶ The **kinetic molecular theory** describes an **ideal gas** in which gas particles exhibit no attractive or repulsive forces and the volumes of the individual gas particles are assumed to be negligible.

▶ Pressure, volume, temperature, and quantity (number of moles) characterize ideal gases. **Pressure** is the force per unit area and is measured using a **barometer.**

▶ **Boyle's law** states that the volume of a gas varies inversely with the pressure exerted by the gas if the number of mol and temperature of the gas are held constant ($PV = k_1$).

▶ **Charles's law** states that the volume of a gas varies directly with the absolute temperature (Kelvin) if pressure and number of mol of gas are constant ($V/T = k_2$).

▶ The **combined gas law** provides a convenient expression for performing gas law calculations involving the most common variables: pressure, volume, and temperature.

▶ **Avogadro's law** states that equal volumes of any gas contain the same number of mol if measured at constant temperature and pressure ($V/n = k_3$).

▶ The volume occupied by 1 mol of any gas is its **molar volume.** At **standard temperature and pressure** (STP), the molar volume of any ideal gas is 22.4 L. STP conditions are defined as 273 K (or 0°C) and 1 atm pressure.

▶ Boyle's law, Charles's law, and Avogadro's law may be combined into a single expression relating all four terms, the **ideal gas law:** $PV = nRT$. $R$ is the ideal gas constant ($0.0821 \; L \cdot atm \cdot K^{-1} \cdot mol^{-1}$) if the units $P$ (atm), $V$(L), $n$ (number of mol), and $T$ (Kelvin) are used.

▶ **Dalton's law of partial pressures** states that a mixture of gases exerts a pressure that is the sum of the pressures that each gas would exert if it were present alone under similar conditions ($P_t = p_1 + p_2 + p_3 + \ldots$).

### 5.2 The Liquid State

▶ Liquids are practically incompressible because of the closeness of their molecules. The **viscosity** of a liquid is a measure of its resistance to flow. Viscosity generally decreases with increasing temperature. The **surface tension** of a liquid is a measure of the attractive forces at the surface of a liquid. **Surfactants** decrease surface tension.

▶ The conversion of liquid to vapor at a temperature below the boiling point of the liquid is **evaporation.** Conversion of the gas to the liquid state is **condensation.** The **vapor pressure** of the liquid is defined as the pressure exerted by the vapor at equilibrium at a specified temperature. The **normal boiling point** of a liquid is the temperature at which the vapor pressure of the liquid is equal to 1 atm.

▶ **Van der Waals forces** include **dipole-dipole interactions,** attractive forces between polar molecules, and **London forces,** attractive forces between molecules exhibiting temporary dipoles.

▶ Molecules in which a hydrogen atom is bonded to a small, highly electronegative atom such as nitrogen, oxygen, or fluorine exhibit **hydrogen bonding.** Hydrogen bonding in liquids is responsible for lower than expected vapor pressures and higher than expected boiling points.

▶ The presence of van der Waals forces and hydrogen bonds significantly affects the *boiling points* of liquids as well as the *melting points* of solids.

### 5.3 The Solid State

▶ Solids have fixed shapes and volumes. They are incompressible, owing to the closeness of their particles. Solids may be **crystalline,** having a regular, repeating structure, or **amorphous,** having no organized structure.

▶ Crystalline solids may exist as **ionic solids, covalent solids, molecular solids,** or **metallic solids.** Electrons in metallic solids are extremely mobile, resulting in the high *conductivity* (ability to carry electrical current) exhibited by many metallic solids. **Sublimation** is a process whereby molecular solids convert directly from solid to gas.

## ANSWERS TO PRACTICE PROBLEMS

**5.1** Sample 1: 38 atm
Sample 2: 25 atm
Sample 3: 0.15 L
Sample 4: 0.38 L

**5.2** 
| | | |
|---|---|---|
| a. 3.76 L | c. 2.75 L | e. 0.15 L |
| b. 3.41 L | d. 5.50 L | f. 3.76 L |

**5.3** 0.200 atm

**5.4** 99.5°C

**5.5** a. 4.46 mol $H_2$   b. 0.75 mol $H_2$

**5.6** The molar volume is based on 1 mol of ANY ideal gas. Hence, for any ideal gas, all quantities substituted in the ideal gas equation are independent of the identity of the ideal gas.

**5.7** 0.223 mol $N_2$

**5.8** 9.00 L

# QUESTIONS AND PROBLEMS

## Kinetic Molecular Theory of Gases

### Foundations

**5.13**  Compare and contrast the gas, liquid, and solid states with regard to the average distance of particle separation.

**5.14**  Compare and contrast the gas, liquid, and solid states with regard to the nature of the interactions among the particles.

**5.15**  Describe the molecular/atomic basis of gas pressure.

**5.16**  Describe the measurement of gas pressure.

### Applications

**5.17**  Why are gases easily compressible?

**5.18**  Why are gas densities much lower than those of liquids or solids?

**5.19**  Why do gases expand to fill any available volume?

**5.20**  Why do gases with lower molar masses diffuse more rapidly than gases with higher molar masses?

**5.21**  Do gases exhibit more ideal behavior at low or high pressures? Why?

**5.22**  Do gases exhibit more ideal behavior at low or high temperatures? Why?

**5.23**  Use the kinetic molecular theory to explain why dissimilar gases mix more rapidly at high temperatures than at low temperatures.

**5.24**  Use the kinetic molecular theory to explain why aerosol cans carry instructions warning against heating or disposing of the container in a fire.

**5.25**  Predict and explain any observed changes taking place when an inflated balloon is cooled (perhaps refrigerated).

**5.26**  Predict and explain any observed changes taking place when an inflated balloon is heated (perhaps microwaved).

## Boyle's Law

### Foundations

**5.27**  State Boyle's law in words.

**5.28**  State Boyle's law in equation form.

**5.29**  The pressure on a fixed mass of a gas is tripled at constant temperature. Will the volume increase, decrease, or remain the same?

**5.30**  By what factor will the volume of the gas in Question 5.29 change?

### Applications

A sample of helium gas was placed in a cylinder and the volume of the gas was measured as the pressure was slowly increased. The results of this experiment are shown graphically.

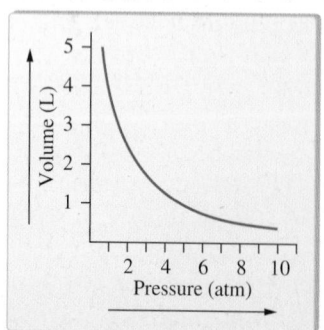

Questions 5.31–5.34 are based on this experiment.

**5.31**  At what pressure does the gas occupy a volume of 5 L?

**5.32**  What is the volume of the gas at a pressure of 5 atm?

**5.33**  Calculate the Boyle's law constant at a volume of 2 L.

**5.34**  Calculate the Boyle's law constant at a pressure of 2 atm.

**5.35**  Calculate the pressure, in atm, required to compress a sample of helium gas from 20.9 L (at 1.00 atm) to 4.00 L.

**5.36**  A balloon filled with helium gas at 1.00 atm occupies 15.6 L. What volume would the balloon occupy in the upper atmosphere, at a pressure of 0.150 atm?

## Charles's Law

### Foundations

**5.37**  State Charles's law in words.

**5.38**  State Charles's law in equation form.

**5.39**  Explain why the Kelvin scale is used for gas law calculations.

**5.40**  The temperature on a summer day may be 90°F. Convert this value to Kelvin units.

### Applications

**5.41**  The temperature of a gas is raised from 25°C to 50°C. Will the volume double if mass and pressure do not change? Why or why not?

**5.42**  Verify your answer to Question 5.41 by calculating the temperature needed to double the volume of the gas.

**5.43**  Determine the change in volume that takes place when a 2.00-L sample of $N_2(g)$ is heated from 250°C to 500°C.

**5.44**  Determine the change in volume that takes place when a 2.00-L sample of $N_2(g)$ is heated from 250 K to 500 K.

**5.45**  A balloon containing a sample of helium gas is warmed in an oven. If the balloon measures 1.25 L at room temperature (20°C), what is its volume at 80°C?

**5.46**  The balloon described in Problem 5.45 was then placed in a refrigerator at 39°F. Calculate its new volume.

**5.47**  A balloon, filled with $N_2$, has a volume of 2.00 L at an indoor temperature of 68°F. When placed outdoors, the volume was observed to increase to 2.20 L. What is the outdoor temperature in °F?

**5.48**  A balloon, filled with an ideal gas, has a volume of 5.00 L at 50°F. At what temperature (°F) would the balloon's volume double?

## Combined Gas Law

### Foundations

**5.49**  Will the volume of gas increase, decrease, or remain the same if the temperature is increased and the pressure is decreased? Explain.

**5.50**  Will the volume of gas increase, decrease, or remain the same if the temperature is decreased and the pressure is increased? Explain.

### Applications

Use the combined gas law,

$$\frac{P_i V_i}{T_i} = \frac{P_f V_f}{T_f}$$

to answer Questions 5.51 and 5.52.

**5.51**  Solve the combined gas law expression for the final volume.

**5.52**  Solve the combined gas law expression for the final temperature.

- Alloys, such as brass and silver and the gold used to make jewelry, are also homogeneous mixtures of two or more kinds of metal atoms in the solid state.

Although solid and gaseous solutions are important in many applications, our emphasis will be on *liquid solutions* because so many important chemical reactions take place in liquid solutions.

## General Properties of Liquid Solutions

Liquid solutions are clear and transparent with no visible particles of solute. They may be colored or colorless, depending on the properties of the solute and solvent. Note that the terms *clear* and *colorless* do not mean the same thing; a clear solution has only one state of matter that can be detected; *colorless* simply means the absence of color.

Recall that solutions of **electrolytes** are formed from solutes that are soluble ionic compounds. These compounds dissociate in solution to produce ions that behave as charge carriers. Solutions of electrolytes are good conductors of electricity. For example, sodium chloride dissolving in water:

$$NaCl(s) \xrightarrow{\text{H}_2\text{O}} Na^+(aq) + Cl^-(aq)$$

Solid sodium          Dissolved sodium
chloride                chloride

In contrast, solutions of **nonelectrolytes** are formed from nondissociating *molecular* solutes (nonelectrolytes), and these solutions are nonconducting. For example, dissolving sugar in water:

$$C_6H_{12}O_6(s) \xrightarrow{\text{H}_2\text{O}} C_6H_{12}O_6(aq)$$

Solid glucose      Dissolved glucose

A *true solution* is a homogeneous mixture with uniform properties throughout. In a true solution the solute cannot be isolated from the solution by filtration. The particle size of the solute is about the same as that of the solvent, and solvent and solute pass directly through the filter paper. Furthermore, solute particles will not "settle out" after a time. All of the molecules of solute and solvent are intimately mixed. The continuous particle motion in solution maintains the homogeneous, random distribution of solute and solvent particles.

Volumes of solute and solvent are not additive; 1 liter (L) of alcohol mixed with 1 L of water does not result in exactly 2 L of solution. The volume of pure liquid is determined by the way in which the individual molecules "fit together." When two or more kinds of molecules are mixed, the interactions become more complex. Solvent interacts with solvent, solute interacts with solvent, and solute may interact with other solute. This will be important to remember when we solve concentration problems later.

## Solutions and Colloids

How can you recognize a solution? A clear liquid in a beaker may be a pure substance, a true solution, or a colloid. Only chemical analysis, determining the identity of all substances in the liquid, can distinguish between a pure substance and a solution. A pure substance has *one* component, pure water being an example. A true solution will contain more than one substance, with the tiny particles homogeneously intermingled.

A **colloidal suspension** also consists of solute particles distributed throughout a solvent. However, the distribution is not completely homogeneous, owing to the size of the colloidal particles. Particles with diameters of $1 \times 10^{-9}$ meter (m) to $2 \times 10^{-7}$ m are colloids. (Recall that $1 \times 10^{-9}$ m = 1 nanometer (nm), therefore $2 \times 10^{-7}$ m = 200 nm.) Particles smaller than 1 nm are solution particles; those larger than 200 nm are precipitates (solid in contact with solvent).

**LEARNING GOAL**

**2** Describe various kinds of solutions and give examples of each.

**ANIMATIONS**
- Dissolution of Compounds
- Salt Dissolving in Water
- Strong, Weak, and Nonelectrolytes

Particles in electrolyte solutions are ions, making the solution an electrical conductor.

Particles in nonelectrolyte solutions are individual molecules. No ions are formed in the dissolution process.

*Section 3.5 relates properties and molecular geometry.*

*See Section 4.4 for more information on precipitates.*

**Figure 6.1** The Tyndall effect. The beaker on the left contains a colloidal suspension, which scatters the light. This scattered light is visible as a haze. The beaker on the right contains a true solution; no scattered light is observed.

To the naked eye, a colloidal suspension and a true solution appear identical; neither solute nor colloid can be seen. However, a simple experiment, using only a bright light source, can readily make the distinction based upon differences in their interaction with light. Colloid particles are large enough to scatter light; solute particles are not. When a beam of light passes through a colloidal suspension, the large particles scatter light, and the liquid appears hazy. We see this effect in sunlight passing through fog. Fog is a colloidal suspension of tiny particles of liquid water dispersed throughout a gas, air. The haze is light scattered by droplets of water. You may have noticed that your automobile headlights are not very helpful in foggy weather. Visibility becomes worse rather than better because light scattering increases.

The light-scattering ability of colloidal suspensions is termed the *Tyndall effect.* True solutions, with very tiny particles, do not scatter light—no haze is observed—and true solutions are easily distinguished from colloidal suspensions by observing their light-scattering properties (Figure 6.1).

A **suspension** is a heterogeneous mixture that contains particles much larger than a colloidal suspension; over time, these particles may settle, forming a second phase. A suspension is not a true solution, nor is it a precipitate.

**Question 6.1**  Describe how you would distinguish experimentally between a pure substance and a true solution.

**Question 6.2**  Describe how you would distinguish experimentally between a true solution and a colloidal suspension.

## Degree of Solubility

*Section 3.5 describes solute-solvent interactions in detail.*

The term *qualitative* implies identity, and the term *quantitative* relates to quantity.

In our discussion of the relationship of polarity and solubility, the rule *"like dissolves like"* was described as the fundamental condition for solubility. Polar solutes are soluble in polar solvents, and nonpolar solutes are soluble in nonpolar solvents. Thus, knowing a little bit about the structure of the molecule enables us to predict qualitatively the solubility of the compound.

The *degree* of **solubility,** *how much* solute can dissolve in a given volume of solvent, is a quantitative measure of solubility. It is difficult to predict the solubility of each and every compound. However, general solubility trends are based on the following considerations:

- *The magnitude of difference between polarity of solute and solvent.* The greater the difference, the less soluble is the solute.
- *Temperature.* An increase in temperature usually, but not always, increases solubility (Figure 6.2). Often, the effect is dramatic. For example, an increase in temperature from 0°C to 100°C increases the water solubility of $KNO_3$ from 10 grams per 100 grams $H_2O$ (10 g/100 g $H_2O$) to 240 g/100 g $H_2O$.
- *Pressure.* Pressure has little effect on the solubility of solids and liquids in liquids. However, the solubility of a gas in liquid is directly proportional to the applied pressure. Carbonated beverages, for example, are made by dissolving carbon dioxide in the beverage under high pressure (hence the term *carbonated*).

When a solution contains all the solute that can be dissolved at a particular temperature, it is a **saturated solution.** When solubility values are given—for example, 13.3 g of potassium nitrate in 100 g of water at 1°C—they refer to the concentration of a saturated solution.

As we have already noted, *increasing* the temperature generally increases the amount of solute a given solution may hold. Conversely, *cooling* a saturated solution often results in a decrease in the

**Figure 6.2** The solubility of a variety of ionic compounds in water as a function of temperature. Note that $Na_2SO_4$ and $Ce_2(SO_4)_3$ become less soluble at higher temperatures.

amount of solute in solution. The excess solute falls to the bottom of the container as a **precipitate** (a solid in contact with the solution). Occasionally, on cooling, the excess solute may remain in solution for a time. Such a solution is described as a **supersaturated solution.** This type of solution is inherently unstable. With time, excess solute will precipitate, and the solution will revert to a saturated solution, which is stable.

## Solubility and Equilibrium

When an excess of solute (beyond the solubility limit) is added to a solvent, it begins to dissolve and continues until it establishes a *dynamic equilibrium* between dissolved and undissolved solute.

Initially, the rate of dissolution is large. After a time the rate of the reverse process, precipitation, increases. The rates of dissolution and precipitation eventually become equal, and there is no further change in the composition of the solution. There is, however, a continual exchange of solute particles between solid and liquid phases because particles are in constant motion. The solution is saturated. The most precise definition of a saturated solution is a solution that is in equilibrium with undissolved solute.

## Solubility of Gases: Henry's Law

When a liquid and a gas are allowed to come to equilibrium, the amount of gas dissolved in the liquid reaches some maximum level. This quantity can be predicted from a very simple relationship. **Henry's law** states that the number of moles (mol) of a gas dissolved in a liquid at a given temperature is proportional to the pressure of the gas. In other words, the gas solubility is directly proportional to the pressure of that gas in the atmosphere that is in contact with the liquid.

Henry's law is expressed mathematically as

$$M = kP$$

Here, $M$ is the molar concentration of the gas in the liquid in units of moles/liter (mol/L). $P$ is the pressure (in atm) of the gas over the solution at equilibrium. For a given gas, $k$ is a constant that depends only on temperature. The constant, $k$, has units of mol/L · atm. In the event that more than one gas is present, $P$ is the partial pressure.

Carbonated beverages are bottled at high pressures of carbon dioxide. When the cap is removed, the fizzing results from the fact that the partial pressure of carbon dioxide in the atmosphere is much less than that used in the bottling process. As a result, the equilibrium quickly shifts to one of lower gas solubility.

Gases are most soluble at low temperatures, and the gas solubility decreases markedly at higher temperatures (Figure 6.3). This explains many common observations. For example, a chilled container of carbonated beverage that is opened quickly goes flat as it warms to room temperature. As the beverage warms up, the solubility of the carbon dioxide decreases.

Henry's law helps to explain the process of respiration. Respiration depends on a rapid and efficient exchange of oxygen and carbon dioxide between the atmosphere and the blood. This transfer occurs through the lungs. The process, oxygen entering the blood and carbon dioxide released to the atmosphere, is accomplished in air sacs called *alveoli*, which are surrounded by an extensive capillary system. Equilibrium is quickly established between alveolar air and the capillary blood. The temperature of the blood is effectively constant. Therefore the equilibrium concentrations of both oxygen and carbon dioxide are determined by the partial pressures of the gases (Henry's law). The oxygen is transported to cells, a variety of reactions take place, and the waste product of respiration, carbon dioxide, is brought back to the lungs to be expelled into the atmosphere.

*The concept of equilibrium was introduced in Section 5.2 and will be discussed in detail in Section 7.4.*

*The concept of partial pressure is a consequence of Dalton's law, discussed in Section 5.1.*

**Figure 6.3** The water solubility of $O_2$ gas decreases markedly as the temperature of the water increases; this may have significant environmental implications.

# A HUMAN PERSPECTIVE

### Scuba Diving: Nitrogen and the Bends

A deep-water diver's worst fear is the interruption of the oxygen supply through equipment malfunction, forcing his or her rapid rise to the surface in search of air. If a diver must ascend too rapidly, he or she may suffer a condition known as "the bends."

Key to understanding this problem is recognition of the tremendous increase in pressure that divers withstand as they descend, because of the weight of the water above them. At the surface the pressure is approximately 1 atmosphere (atm). At a depth of 200 feet (ft) the pressure is approximately six times as great; hence, the blood concentration of $N_2$ increases dramatically. Oxygen solubility increases as well, although its effect is less serious ($O_2$ is 20% of air, $N_2$ is 80%). Recall that Henry's law tells us that the number of mol of gas dissolved in blood is directly proportional to the pressure of the gas.

As the diver quickly rises, the pressure decreases rapidly, and the nitrogen "boils" out of the blood, stopping blood flow and impairing nerve transmission. The joints of the body lock in a bent position, hence the name of the condition: the bends.

To minimize the problem, scuba tanks may be filled with mixtures of helium and oxygen rather than nitrogen and oxygen. Helium has a much lower solubility in blood and, like nitrogen, is inert. To avoid the bends, divers are advised to make several decompression stops while ascending to the water's surface. Such "time-outs" allow a more gradual equilibration of nitrogen concentration in the blood; the ideal is to achieve normal (or close to normal) levels upon reaching the

Scuba diving.

surface. Tables and charts relating pressures and decompression times have been developed to aid divers.

#### For Further Understanding

▶ Why are divers who slowly rise to the surface less likely to be adversely affected?

▶ What design features would be essential in deep-water manned exploration vessels?

*See A Medical Perspective: Blood Gases and Respiration, Chapter 5.*

**Question 6.3**  Explain why, over time, a bottle of soft drink goes "flat" after it is opened.

**Question 6.4**  Would the soft drink in Question 6.3 go "flat" faster if the bottle warmed to room temperature? Why?

The Henry's law constant, $k$, for $CO_2$ in aqueous solution is $3.1 \times 10^{-2}$ mol/(L · atm) at 25°C. Use this information to answer Questions 6.5 and 6.6.

**Question 6.5**  An unopened bottle of soda contains $CO_2$ gas at 6.0 atm. Calculate the equilibrium solubility of $CO_2$ in the unopened soda at 25°C in units of mol/L.

**Question 6.6**  After the soda in Question 6.5 is opened, the "fizz" shows a loss of $CO_2$. If the partial pressure of $CO_2$ in the atmosphere is $5.0 \times 10^{-4}$ atm, calculate the equilibrium $CO_2$ concentration in mol/L in the open bottle of soda.

## 6.2  Concentration Based on Percent by Mass

Solution **concentration** is defined as the amount of solute dissolved in a given amount of solution. The concentration of a solution has a profound effect on the properties of a solution, both *physical* (melting and boiling points) and *chemical* (solution reactivity). Solution concentration may be expressed in many different units. Here we consider concentration units based on percent by mass.

## Mass/Volume Percent

The concentration of a solution is defined as the amount of solute dissolved in a specified amount of solution,

$$\text{concentration} = \frac{\text{amount of solute}}{\text{amount of solution}}$$

LEARNING GOAL

4  Calculate solution concentration in mass/volume percent, mass/mass percent, parts per thousand, and parts per million.

If we define the amount of solute as the *mass* of solute (in g) and the amount of solution in *volume* units (mL), concentration is expressed as the ratio

$$\text{concentration} = \frac{\text{g of solute}}{\text{mL of solution}}$$

This concentration can then be expressed as a percentage by multiplying the ratio by the factor 100%. This results in

$$\% \text{ concentration} = \frac{\text{g of solute}}{\text{mL of solution}} \times 100\%$$

The percent concentration expressed in this way is called **mass/volume percent, or % (m/V)**. Thus

$$\% \left(\frac{m}{V}\right) = \frac{\text{g of solute}}{\text{mL of solution}} \times 100\%$$

Consider the following examples.

---

**EXAMPLE 6.1**    **Calculating Mass/Volume Percent**

LEARNING GOAL

4  Calculate solution concentration in mass/volume percent, mass/mass percent, parts per thousand, and parts per million.

Calculate the mass/volume percent composition, or % (m/V), of $3.00 \times 10^2$ mL of solution containing 15.0 g of glucose.

**Solution**

**Step 1.** The expression for mass/volume percent is:

$$\% \left(\frac{m}{V}\right) = \frac{\text{g of solute}}{\text{mL of solution}} \times 100\%$$

**Step 2.** There are 15.0 g of glucose, the solute, and $3.00 \times 10^2$ mL of total solution. Therefore, substituting in our expression for mass/volume percent:

$$\% \left(\frac{m}{V}\right) = \frac{15.0 \text{ g glucose}}{3.00 \times 10^2 \text{ mL solution}} \times 100\%$$

$$= 5.00\% \left(\frac{m}{V}\right) \text{ glucose}$$

**Practice Problem 6.1**

a. Calculate the % (m/V) of 0.0600 L of solution containing 10.0 g NaCl.
b. Calculate the % (m/V) of 0.200 L of solution containing 15.0 g KCl.
c. 20.0 g of oxygen gas are diluted with 80.0 g of nitrogen gas in a 78.0-L container at standard temperature and pressure. Calculate the % (m/V) of oxygen gas.
d. 50.0 g of argon gas are diluted with 80.0 g of helium gas in a 476-L container at standard temperature and pressure. Calculate the % (m/V) of argon gas.

▶ For Further Practice: **Questions 6.23 and 6.24.**

**EXAMPLE 6.2** **Calculating the Mass or Volume of Solute from a Mass/Volume Percent**

Calculate the number of g of NaCl in $5.00 \times 10^2$ mL of a 10.0% $\left(\dfrac{m}{V}\right)$ solution.

**LEARNING GOAL**

**4** Calculate solution concentration in mass/volume percent, mass/mass percent, parts per thousand, and parts per million.

**Solution**

**Step 1.**  The expression for mass/volume percent is:

$$\% \left(\frac{m}{V}\right) = \frac{\text{g of solute}}{\text{mL of solution}} \times 100\%$$

**Step 2.**  Substitute the data from the problem:

$$10.0\% \left(\frac{m}{V}\right) = \frac{X \text{ g NaCl}}{5.00 \times 10^2 \text{ mL solution}} \times 100\%$$

**Step 3.**  Cross-multiplying to simplify:

$$X \text{ g NaCl} \times 100\% = \left(10.0\% \ \frac{m}{V}\right)(5.00 \times 10^2 \text{ mL solution})$$

**Step 4.**  Dividing both sides by 100% to isolate g NaCl on the left side of the equation:

$$X = 50.0 \text{ g NaCl}$$

Alternatively, the concentration may be used as a conversion factor to arrive at the same result:

$$g \text{ NaCl} = \left(\frac{10\% \text{ g NaCl}}{\text{mL soln}}\right)(5.00 \times 10^2 \text{ mL soln})$$

$$g \text{ NaCl} = 50.0 \text{ g NaCl}$$

---

**Practice Problem 6.2**

  a. Calculate the mass (in g) of sodium hydroxide required to make 2.00 L of a 1.00% (m/V) solution.
  b. Calculate the volume (in mL) of a 25.0% (m/V) solution containing 10.0 g NaCl.

▶ For Further Practice: **Questions 6.33 and 6.34.**

---

*Sections 1.3 and 1.5 discuss units and unit conversion.*

If the units of mass are other than g, or if the solution volume is in units other than mL, the proper conversion factor must be used to arrive at the units used in the equation.

## Mass/Mass Percent

The **mass/mass percent,** or **% (m/m),** is most useful for mixtures of solids, whose masses are easily obtained. The expression used to calculate mass/mass percentage is analogous in form to % (m/V):

$$\% \left(\frac{m}{m}\right) = \frac{\text{g solute}}{\text{g solution}} \times 100\%$$

---

**EXAMPLE 6.3** **Calculating Mass/Mass Percent**

Calculate the % (m/m) of platinum in a gold ring that contains 14.00 g gold and 4.500 g platinum.

**LEARNING GOAL**

**4** Calculate solution concentration in mass/volume percent, mass/mass percent, parts per thousand, and parts per million.

The number of mol of solute *before* and *after* dilution is unchanged, because dilution involves only addition of extra solvent:

$$\underset{\substack{\text{Initial} \\ \text{condition}}}{\text{mol}_1 \text{ solute}} = \underset{\substack{\text{Final} \\ \text{condition}}}{\text{mol}_2 \text{ solute}}$$

or

$$(M_1)(\text{L}_1 \text{ solution}) = (M_2)(\text{L}_2 \text{ solution})$$

$$(M_1)(V_1) = (M_2)(V_2)$$

Knowing any three of these terms enables us to calculate the fourth.

---

**EXAMPLE 6.8**  **Calculating Molarity After Dilution**

LEARNING GOAL

**6** Perform dilution calculations.

Calculate the molarity of a solution made by diluting 0.050 L of 0.10 $M$ HCl solution to a volume of 1.0 L.

**Solution**

**Step 1.** Summarize the information provided in the problem:

$$M_1 = 0.10\ M$$
$$M_2 = X\ M$$
$$V_1 = 0.050\ \text{L}$$
$$V_2 = 1.0\ \text{L}$$

**Step 2.** Use the dilution expression:

$$(M_1)(V_1) = (M_2)(V_2)$$

**Step 3.** Solve for $M_2$, the final solution concentration:

$$M_2 = \frac{(M_1)(V_1)}{V_2}$$

**Step 4.** Substituting,

$$X\ M = \frac{(0.10\ M)(0.050\ \cancel{L})}{(1.0\ \cancel{L})}$$
$$= 0.0050\ M \text{ or } 5.0 \times 10^{-3}\ M \text{ HCl}$$

---

**Practice Problem 6.8**

What volume of 0.200 $M$ sugar solution can be prepared from 50.0 mL of 0.400 $M$ solution?

▶ For Further Practice: **Questions 6.48 and 6.49.**

---

The dilution equation is valid with any concentration units, such as % (m/V) *as well as* molarity, which are used in Examples 6.8 and 6.9. However, you must use the same units for both initial *and* final concentration values. Only in this way can you cancel units properly.

| EXAMPLE 6.9 | Calculating a Dilution Volume |

**LEARNING GOAL**

**6** Perform dilution calculations.

Calculate the volume, in L, of water that must be added to dilute 20.0 mL of 12.0 $M$ HCl to 0.100 $M$ HCl.

**Solution**

**Step 1.** Summarize the information provided in the problem:

$$M_1 = 12.0\ M$$
$$M_2 = 0.100\ M$$
$$V_1 = 20.0\ \text{mL}\ (0.0200\ \text{L})$$
$$V_2 = V_{final}$$

**Step 2.** Then, using the dilution expression:

$$(M_1)(V_1) = (M_2)(V_2)$$

**Step 3.** Solve for $V_2$, the final volume:

$$V_2 = \frac{(M_1)(V_1)}{(M_2)}$$

**Step 4.** Substituting,

$$V_{final} = \frac{(12.0\ M)(0.0200\ \text{L})}{0.100\ M}$$
$$= 2.40\ \text{L solution}$$

Note that this is the *total final volume*. The amount of water added equals this volume *minus* the original solution volume, or

$$2.40\ \text{L} - 0.0200\ \text{L} = 2.38\ \text{L water}$$

**Practice Problem 6.9**

How would you prepare $1.0 \times 10^2$ mL of 2.0 $M$ HCl, starting with concentrated (12.0 $M$) HCl?

▶ For Further Practice: **Questions 6.47 and 6.50.**

## 6.4   Concentration-Dependent Solution Properties

**LEARNING GOAL**

**7** Describe and explain concentration-dependent solution properties.

**Colligative properties** are solution properties that depend on the *concentration of the solute particles*, rather than the *identity of the solute*.

There are four colligative properties of solutions:

• vapor pressure lowering
• freezing point depression
• boiling point elevation
• osmotic pressure

Each of these properties has widespread practical applications. We look at each in some detail in the following sections.

### Vapor Pressure Lowering

**Raoult's law** states that, when a nonvolatile solute is added to a solvent, the vapor pressure of the solvent decreases in proportion to the concentration of the solute.

Perhaps the most important consequence of Raoult's law is the effect of the solute on the boiling point of a solution.

When a nonvolatile solute is added to a solvent, the boiling point of the solution is found to increase because it requires a higher temperature to form the gaseous state.

Raoult's law may be explained in molecular terms by using the following logic: Vapor pressure of a solution results from the escape of solvent molecules from the liquid to the gas phase, thus increasing the partial pressure of the gas-phase solvent molecules until the equilibrium vapor pressure is reached. Presence of solute molecules hinders the escape of solvent molecules, thus lowering the equilibrium vapor pressure (Figure 6.4).

## Freezing Point Depression and Boiling Point Elevation

Freezing point depression may be explained by examining the equilibrium between solid and liquid states. At the freezing point, ice is in equilibrium with liquid water:

$$H_2O(l) \underset{(r)}{\overset{(f)}{\rightleftharpoons}} H_2O(s)$$

Solute molecules interfere with the rate at which liquid water molecules associate to form the solid state, decreasing the rate of the forward reaction. For a true equilibrium, the rate of the forward ($f$) and reverse ($r$) processes must be equal. Lowering the temperature eventually slows the rate of the reverse ($r$) process sufficiently to match the rate of the forward reaction. At the lower temperature, equilibrium is established, and the solution freezes.

Boiling point elevation can be explained by considering the definition of the boiling point, that is, the temperature at which the vapor pressure of the liquid equals the atmospheric pressure. Raoult's law states that the vapor pressure of a solution is decreased by the presence of a solute. Therefore a higher temperature is necessary to raise the vapor pressure to the atmospheric pressure, hence the boiling point elevation.

The extent of the freezing point depression ($\Delta T_f$) is proportional to the solute concentration over a limited range of concentration:

$$\Delta T_f = k_f \times (\text{solute particle concentration})$$

The boiling point elevation ($\Delta T_b$) is also proportional to the solute concentration:

$$\Delta T_b = k_b \times (\text{solute particle concentration})$$

If the value of the proportionality factor ($k_f$ or $k_b$) is known for the solvent of interest, the magnitude of the freezing point depression or boiling point elevation can be calculated for a solution of known concentration.

Solute concentration must be in *mole*-based units. The number of particles (molecules or ions) is critical here, not the mass of solute. One high mass molecule will have exactly the same effect on the freezing or boiling point as one low mass molecule. A mole-based unit, because it is related directly to Avogadro's number, will correctly represent the number of particles in solution.

We have already worked with one mole-based unit, *molarity*, and this concentration unit can be used to calculate either the freezing point depression or the boiling point elevation.

A second mole-based concentration unit, molality, is more commonly used in these types of situations. **Molality** (symbolized $m$) is defined as the number of mol of solute per kilogram (kg) of solvent in a solution:

$$m = \frac{\text{mol solute}}{\text{kg solvent}}$$

Molality does not vary with temperature, whereas molarity is temperature dependent. For this reason, molality is the preferred concentration unit for studies such as freezing point depression and boiling point elevation, in which measurement of *change* in temperature is critical.

Practical applications that take advantage of freezing point depression of solutions by solutes include the following:

- Salt is spread on roads to melt ice in winter. The salt lowers the freezing point of the water, so it exists in the liquid phase below its normal freezing point, 0°C or 32°F.

**Figure 6.4** An illustration of Raoult's law: lowering of vapor pressure by addition of solute molecules. White units represent solvent molecules, and red units are solute molecules. Solute molecules present a barrier to escape of solvent molecules, thus decreasing the vapor pressure.

*Recall that the concept of liquid vapor pressure was discussed in Section 5.2.*

*Section 7.4 discusses equilibrium.*

Molarity is temperature dependent simply because it is expressed as mol/volume. Volume is temperature dependent—most liquids expand measurably when heated and contract when cooled. Molality is mol/mass; both mol and mass are temperature independent.

- Solutes such as ethylene glycol, "antifreeze," are added to car radiators in the winter to prevent freezing by lowering the freezing point of the coolant.

We refer to the concentration of *particles* in our discussion of colligative properties. Why do we stress this term? The reason is that there is a very important difference between electrolytes and nonelectrolytes. That difference is the way that they behave when they dissolve. For example, if we dissolve 1 mol of glucose ($C_6H_{12}O_6$) in 1 kg of water,

$$1\ C_6H_{12}O_6(s) \xrightarrow{H_2O} 1\ C_6H_{12}O_6(aq)$$

1 mol (Avogadro's number, $6.022 \times 10^{23}$ particles) of glucose is present in solution. *Glucose is a covalently bonded nonelectrolyte.* Dissolving 1 mol of sodium chloride in 1 kg of water,

$$1\ NaCl(s) \xrightarrow{H_2O} 1\ Na^+(aq) + 1\ Cl^-(aq)$$

produces 2 mol of particles (1 mol of sodium ions and 1 mol of chloride ions). *Sodium chloride is an ionic electrolyte.*

$$1\text{ mol glucose} \longrightarrow 1\text{ mol of particles in solution}$$
$$1\text{ mol sodium chloride} \longrightarrow 2\text{ mol of particles in solution}$$

It follows that 1 mol of sodium chloride will decrease the vapor pressure, increase the boiling point, or depress the freezing point of 1 kg of water *twice as much* as 1 mol of glucose in the same quantity of water.

**Question 6.9**   Comparing pure water and a 0.10 *m* glucose solution, which has the higher freezing point?

**Question 6.10**   Comparing pure water and a 0.10 *m* glucose solution, which has the higher boiling point?

## Calculating Freezing Points and Boiling Points of Aqueous Solutions

The freezing point depression constant for aqueous solutions is:

$$k_f = \frac{1.86°C}{m}$$

The expression for calculating the change (decrease) in freezing point of an aqueous solution is equal to the product of the freezing point depression constant and the molality of the solution:

$$\Delta T_f = \left(\frac{1.86°C}{m}\right)(m)$$

Correspondingly, for boiling point elevation:

$$k_b = \frac{0.52°C}{m}$$

and

$$\Delta T_b = \left(\frac{0.52°C}{m}\right)(m)$$

If we know the solution molality (*m*),

$$m = \frac{\text{mol solute}}{\text{kg solvent}}$$

we can calculate the decrease (freezing) or increase (boiling) in freezing or boiling temperature. Recalling that pure water freezes at 0°C and boils at 100°C, we can subtract $\Delta T_f$ from 0°C to obtain the solution freezing point and add $\Delta T_b$ to 100°C, resulting in the solution boiling point.

Let's review calculations of this type in Example 6.10.

---

**EXAMPLE 6.10** **Calculating Freezing and Boiling Points of Aqueous Solutions of Covalent, Nondissociating Solutes**

LEARNING GOAL

**8** Perform calculations involving colligative solution properties.

Ethylene glycol, H—O—C—C—O—H, with H H above and H H below the two central C atoms, is a widely used automobile antifreeze.

a. Calculate the freezing point of an 8.38 $m$ aqueous solution of ethylene glycol.
b. Calculate the boiling point of an 8.38 $m$ aqueous solution of ethylene glycol.

**Solution**

We begin by recognizing that ethylene glycol is a nondissociating covalent compound. Consequently, 8.38 $m$ ethylene glycol solute is equivalent to 8.38 $m$ particles of solute.

For part a,

**Step 1.** Using our expression for freezing point depression:

$$\Delta T_f = \left(\frac{1.86°C}{m}\right)(m)$$

and, substituting molality of particles,

$$\Delta T_f = \left(\frac{1.86°C}{m}\right)(8.38\ m) = 15.6°C$$

**Step 2.** The solution freezing point is 15.6°C *below* 0.0°C, the freezing point of pure water. Therefore

$$\text{freezing point} = 0.0°C - 15.6°C = -15.6°C$$

For part b,

**Step 1.** Substituting our value for molality of particles into the boiling point elevation equation:

$$\Delta T_b = \left(\frac{0.52°C}{m}\right)(m)$$

$$= \left(\frac{0.52°C}{m}\right)(8.38\ m) = 4.4°C$$

**Step 2.** This means that the solution boiling point is 4.4°C *above* the boiling point of pure water. Therefore

$$\text{boiling point} = 100.0°C + 4.4°C = 104.4°C$$

---

**Practice Problem 6.10**

Calculate the boiling temperature and freezing temperature of a 1.5 $m$ solution of glucose ($C_6H_{12}O_6$). Remember that glucose is a covalent, nondissociating solute.

▶ For Further Practice: **Questions 6.65a and 6.66a.**

EXAMPLE 6.11 **Calculating Freezing and Boiling Points of Aqueous Solutions of Ionic, Dissociating Solutes**

Calcium chloride is used on roads and sidewalks to prevent ice formation in wintertime.

    a. Calculate the freezing point of a 3.00 $m$ aqueous solution of $CaCl_2$.
    b. Calculate the boiling point of a 3.00 $m$ aqueous solution of $CaCl_2$.

**Solution**

Calcium chloride dissociates in water to form three particles for each $CaCl_2$:

$$\underbrace{CaCl_2(aq)}_{\text{1 particle}} \longrightarrow \underbrace{Ca^{2+}(aq) + 2\,Cl^-(aq)}_{\text{3 particles}}$$

Consequently, a 3.0 $m$ $CaCl_2$ aqueous solution is

$$\frac{3\ m\ \text{particles solute}}{1\ m\ \cancel{CaCl_2}} \times 3.00\ m\ \cancel{CaCl_2} = 9.00\ m\ \text{particles solute}$$

for part a,

**Step 1.** Using our expression for freezing point depression:

$$\Delta T_f = \left(\frac{1.86°C}{m}\right)(m)$$

and substituting molality of particles

$$= \left(\frac{1.86°C}{\cancel{m}}\right)(9.00\ \cancel{m}) = 16.7°C$$

**Step 2.** The solution freezing point is 16.7°C *below* 0.0°C, the freezing point of pure water. Therefore

$$\text{freezing point} = 0.0°C - 16.7°C = -16.7°C$$

for part b,

**Step 1.** Substituting our value for molality of particles into the boiling point elevation equation:

$$\Delta T_b = \left(\frac{0.52°C}{m}\right)(m)$$

$$= \left(\frac{0.52°C}{\cancel{m}}\right)(9.00\ \cancel{m}) = 4.7°C$$

**Step 2.** This means that the solution boiling point is 4.7°C *above* the boiling point of pure water. Therefore

$$\text{boiling point} = 100.0°C + 4.7°C = 104.7°C$$

**Practice Problem 6.11**

Calculate the boiling temperature and freezing temperature of a 1.5 $m$ solution of KCl. (Remember that **1** mol of KCl produces **2** mol of particles.)

▶ For Further Practice: **Questions 6.65b and 6.66b.**

## Osmotic Pressure, Osmosis, and Osmolarity

The cell membrane mediates the interaction of the cell with its environment and is responsible for the controlled passage of material into and out of the cell. One of the principal means of transport is termed *diffusion*. **Diffusion** is the net movement of solute or solvent molecules from an area of high concentration to an area of low concentration. This region where the concentration decreases over a distance is termed the **concentration gradient.** Because of the structure of the cell membrane, only small molecules are able to diffuse freely across this barrier. Large molecules and highly charged ions are restricted by the barrier. In other words, the cell membrane is behaving in a selective fashion. Such membranes are termed **selectively permeable membranes.**

Because a cell membrane is selectively permeable, it is not always possible for solutes to pass through it in response to a concentration gradient. In such cases, the solvent diffuses through the membrane. Such membranes, permeable to solvent but not to solute, are specifically called **semipermeable membranes. Osmosis** is the diffusion of a solvent (water in biological systems) through a semipermeable membrane in response to a (water) concentration gradient.

Suppose that we place a 0.5 *M* glucose solution in a dialysis bag that is composed of a membrane with pores that allow the passage of water molecules but not glucose molecules. Consider what will happen when we place this bag into a beaker of pure water. We have created a gradient in which there is a higher concentration of glucose inside the bag than outside, but the glucose cannot diffuse through the bag to achieve equal concentration on both sides of the membrane.

Now let's think about this situation in another way. We have a higher concentration of water molecules outside the bag (where there is only pure water) than inside the bag (where some of the water molecules are occupied in dipole-dipole interactions with solute particles and are consequently unable to move freely in the system). Because water can diffuse through the membrane, a net diffusion of water will occur through the membrane into the bag. This is the process of osmosis (Figure 6.5).

As you have probably already guessed, this system can never reach equilibrium (equal concentrations inside and outside the bag). Regardless of how much water diffuses into the bag, diluting the glucose solution, the concentration of glucose will always be higher inside the bag (and the accompanying free water concentration will always be lower).

What happens when the bag has taken in as much water as it can, when it has expanded as much as possible? Now the walls of the bag exert a force that will stop the *net* flow of water into the bag. **Osmotic pressure** is the pressure that must be exerted to stop the flow of water across a selectively permeable membrane by osmosis. Stated more precisely, the osmotic pressure of a solution is the net pressure with which water enters it by osmosis from a pure water compartment when the two compartments are separated by a semipermeable membrane.

**ANIMATION**
• Osmosis

The terms *selectively permeable* or *differentially permeable* are used to describe biological membranes because such membranes restrict passage of particles based both on size and charge. Even small ions, such as $H^+$, cannot pass freely across a cell membrane.

● Water
● Solute

**Figure 6.5** Osmosis across a membrane. The solvent, water, diffuses from outside the bag (the membrane) to the region of high solute concentration (inside the bag).

The osmotic pressure, like the pressure exerted by a gas, may be treated quantitatively. Osmotic pressure, symbolized by $\pi$, follows the same form as the ideal gas equation:

| **Ideal Gas** | **Osmotic Pressure** |
|---|---|
| $PV = nRT$ | $\pi V = nRT$ |
| or | or |
| $P = \dfrac{n}{V}RT$ | $\pi = \dfrac{n}{V}RT$ |
| and since | and since |
| $M = \dfrac{n}{V}$ | $M = \dfrac{n}{V}$ |
| then | then |
| $P = MRT$ | $\pi = MRT$ |

The osmotic pressure can be calculated from the solution concentration at any temperature. How do we determine "solution concentration"? Recall that osmosis is a colligative property, dependent on the concentration of solute particles. Again, it becomes necessary to distinguish between solutions of electrolytes and nonelectrolytes. For example, a 1 $M$ glucose solution consists of 1 mol of particles per L; glucose is a nonelectrolyte. A solution of 1 $M$ NaCl produces 2 mol of particles per L (1 mol of $Na^+$ and 1 mol of $Cl^-$). A 1 $M$ $CaCl_2$ solution is 3 $M$ in particles (1 mol of $Ca^{2+}$ and 2 mol of $Cl^-$ per L).

**Osmolarity,** the molarity of particles in solution, and abbreviated osmol, is used for osmotic pressure calculations.

Blood plasma has an osmolarity equivalent to a 0.30 $M$ glucose solution or a 0.15 $M$ NaCl solution. The latter is true because NaCl in solution dissociates into $Na^+$ and $Cl^-$ and thus contributes twice the number of solute particles as a

---

**EXAMPLE 6.12**    **Calculating Solution Osmolarity**

LEARNING GOAL

**8** Perform calculations involving colligative solution properties.

Determine the osmolarity of $5.0 \times 10^{-3}\ M\ Na_3PO_4$.

**Solution**

**Step 1.** $Na_3PO_4$ is an ionic compound and produces an electrolytic solution:

$$Na_3PO_4 \xrightarrow{\ H_2O\ } 3Na^+ + PO_4{}^{3-}$$

**Step 2.** 1 mol of $Na_3PO_4$ yields 4 mol of product ions; consequently

$$5.0 \times 10^{-3}\ \frac{\text{mol } Na_3PO_4}{L} \times \frac{4 \text{ mol particles}}{1 \text{ mol } Na_3PO_4} = 2.0 \times 10^{-2}\ \frac{\text{mol particles}}{L}$$

**Step 3.** Using our definition of osmolarity,

$$2.0 \times 10^{-2}\ \frac{\text{mol particles}}{L} = 2.0 \times 10^{-2}\ \text{osmol}$$

---

**Practice Problem 6.12**

Determine the osmolarity of the following solutions:

    a. $5.0 \times 10^{-3}\ M\ NH_4NO_3$ (electrolyte)    b. $5.0 \times 10^{-3}\ M\ C_6H_{12}O_6$ (nonelectrolyte)

▶ For Further Practice: **Questions 6.81 and 6.82.**

| EXAMPLE 6.13 | Calculating Osmotic Pressure |
|---|---|

Calculate the osmotic pressure of a $5.0 \times 10^{-2}\,M$ solution of NaCl at 25°C (298 K).

**Solution**

**Step 1.** Using our definition of osmotic pressure, $\pi$:

$$\pi = MRT$$

**Step 2.** $M$ should be represented as osmolarity as we have shown in Example 6.12

$$M = 5.0 \times 10^{-2}\,\frac{\text{mol NaCl}}{\text{L}} \times \frac{2\,\text{mol particles}}{1\,\text{mol NaCl}} = 1.0 \times 10^{-1}\,\frac{\text{mol particles}}{\text{L}}$$

**Step 3.** Substituting in our osmotic pressure expression:

$$= 1.0 \times 10^{-1}\,\frac{\text{mol particles}}{\text{L}} \times 0.0821\,\frac{\text{L} \cdot \text{atm}}{\text{K} \cdot \text{mol}} \times 298\,\text{K}$$

$$= 2.4\,\text{atm}$$

**Practice Problem 6.13**

Calculate the osmotic pressure of each solution described in Practice Problem 6.12. Assume that the solutions are at 298 K.

▶ For Further Practice: **Questions 6.71 and 6.72.**

(a)

(b)

(c)

**Figure 6.6** Scanning electron micrographs of red blood cells exposed to (a) hypertonic, (b) isotonic, and (c) hypotonic solutions.

molecule that does not ionize. If red blood cells, which have an osmolarity equal to blood plasma, are placed in a 0.30 $M$ glucose solution, no net osmosis will occur because the osmolarity and water concentration inside the red blood cells are equal to those of the 0.30 $M$ glucose solution. The solutions inside and outside the red blood cells are said to be **isotonic** (*iso* means "same," and *tonic* means "strength") **solutions.** Because the osmolarity is the same inside and outside, the red blood cells will remain the same size (Figure 6.6b).

What happens if we now place the red blood cells into a **hypotonic solution,** in other words, a solution having a lower osmolarity than the cytoplasm of the cells? In this situation there will be a net movement of water into the cells as water diffuses down its concentration gradient. The membranes of the red blood cells do not have the strength to exert a sufficient pressure to stop this flow of water, and the cells will swell and burst (Figure 6.6c). Alternatively, if we place the red blood cells into a **hypertonic solution** (one with a greater osmolarity than the cells), water will pass out of the cells, and they will shrink dramatically (Figure 6.6a).

These principles have important applications in the delivery of intravenous (IV) solutions into an individual (Figure 6.7). Normally, any fluids infused intravenously must have the correct osmolarity; they must be isotonic with the blood cells and the blood plasma. Such infusions are frequently either 5.5% dextrose (glucose) or "normal saline." The first solution is composed of 5.5 g of glucose per 100 mL of solution (0.30 $M$), and the latter of 9.0 g of NaCl per 100 mL of solution (0.15 $M$). In either case, they have the same osmotic pressure and osmolarity as the plasma and blood cells and can therefore be safely

# A MEDICAL PERSPECTIVE

## Oral Rehydration Therapy

Diarrhea kills millions of children before they reach the age of 5 years. This is particularly true in third world countries where sanitation, water supplies, and medical care are poor. In the case of diarrhea, death results from fluid loss, electrolyte imbalance, and hypovolemic shock (multiple organ failure due to insufficient perfusion). Cholera is one of the best-understood bacterial diarrheas. The organism *Vibrio cholera* survives passage through the stomach and reproduces in the intestine, where it produces a toxin called choleragen. The toxin causes the excessive excretion of $Na^+$, $Cl^-$, and $HCO_3^-$ from epithelial cells lining the intestine. The increased ion concentration (hypertonic solution) outside the cell results in movement of massive quantities of water into the intestinal lumen. This causes the severe, abundant, clear vomit and diarrhea that can result in the loss of 10–15 L of fluid per day. Over the 4- to 6-day progress of the disease, a patient may lose from one to two times his or her body mass!

The need for fluid replacement is obvious. Oral rehydration is preferred over intravenous administration of fluids and electrolytes since it is noninvasive. In many third world countries, it is the only therapy available in remote areas. The rehydration formula includes 50–80 g/L rice (or other starch), 3.5 g/L sodium chloride, 2.5 g/L sodium bicarbonate, and 1.5 g/L potassium chloride. Oral rehydration takes advantage of the cotransport of $Na^+$ and glucose across the cells lining the intestine. Thus, the glucose enters the cells, and $Na^+$ is carried along. Movement of these materials into the cells helps alleviate the osmotic imbalance, reduces the diarrhea, and corrects the fluid and electrolyte imbalance.

A woman is shown filtering water through sari cloth.

The disease runs its course in less than a week. In fact, antibiotics are not used to combat cholera. The only effective therapy is oral rehydration, which reduces mortality to less than 1%. A much better option is prevention. In the photo above, a woman is shown filtering water through sari cloth. This simple practice has been shown to reduce the incidence of cholera significantly.

**For Further Understanding**
▶ Explain dehydration in terms of osmosis.
▶ Explain why even severely dehydrated individuals continue to experience further fluid loss.

administered without upsetting the osmotic balance between the blood and the blood cells.

Practical examples of osmosis abound, including the following:

- A sailor, lost at sea in a lifeboat, dies of dehydration while surrounded by water. Seawater, because of its high salt concentration, dehydrates the cells of the body as a result of the large osmotic pressure difference between it and intracellular fluids.
- A cucumber, soaked in brine, shrivels into a pickle. The water in the cucumber is drawn into the brine (salt) solution because of a difference in osmotic pressure (Figure 6.8).
- A Medical Perspective: Oral Rehydration Therapy describes one of the most lethal and pervasive examples of cellular fluid imbalance.

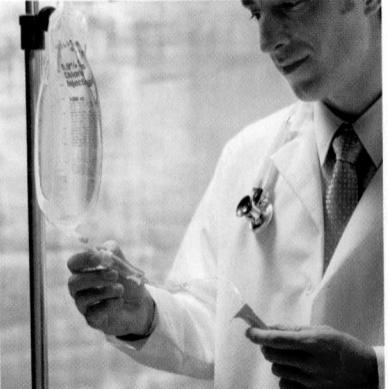

**Figure 6.7** Composition and concentration are critically important in medical intervention. This solution is 0.15% (m/V) KCl and 5% (m/V) glucose.

**Question 6.11**  Refer to the intravenous solution in Figure 6.7 and calculate the osmolarity of its contents.

**Question 6.12**  Is the solution osmolarity that you calculated in Question 6.11 isotonic with blood plasma? Why or why not?

# 6.5 Aqueous Solutions

## Water as a Solvent

Water is by far the most abundant substance on earth. It is an excellent solvent for most inorganic substances, and is the principal biological solvent. Approximately 60% of the adult human body is water, and maintenance of this level is essential for survival. These characteristics are a direct consequence of the molecular structure of water.

As we saw in Chapter 3, water is a bent molecule with a 104.5° bond angle. This angular structure, resulting from the effect of the two lone pairs of electrons around the oxygen atom, is responsible for the polar nature of water. The polarity, in turn, gives water its unique properties.

Because water molecules are polar, water is an excellent solvent for other polar substances ("like dissolves like"). Because much of the matter on earth is polar, hence at least somewhat water soluble, water has been described as the universal solvent. The term *universal solvent* is historical; for centuries, water was known to dissolve many commonly used substances. The solvent in blood is water, and it dissolves and transports compounds as diverse as potassium chloride, glucose, and protein throughout our bodies.

Water is readily accessible and easily purified. It is nontoxic and quite nonreactive. The high boiling point of water, 100°C, compared with molecules of similar size such as $N_2$ (b.p. = −196°C), is also explained by water's polar character. Strong dipole-dipole interactions between a $\delta^+$ hydrogen of one molecule and $\delta^-$ oxygen of a second, referred to as hydrogen bonding, create an interactive molecular network in the liquid phase (see Figure 5.8). The strength of these interactions requires more energy (higher temperature) to cause water to boil. The higher than expected boiling point enhances water's value as a solvent; often, reactions are carried out

## LEARNING GOAL

**9** Describe why the chemical and physical properties of water make it a truly unique solvent.

**ANIMATION**
• The Properties of Water

*See A Human Perspective: An Extraordinary Molecule, in Chapter 7.*

*Refer to Sections 3.4 and 3.5 for a more complete description of the bonding, structure, and polarity of water.*

*Recall the discussion of intermolecular forces in Chapters 3 and 5.*

(a)

(b)

**Figure 6.8** A cucumber (a) in an acidic salt solution undergoes considerable shrinkage on its way to becoming a pickle (b) because of osmosis.

---

| EXAMPLE 6.14 | **Predicting Structure from Observable Properties** |
| --- | --- |

Sucrose is a common sugar and we know that it is used as a sweetener when dissolved in many beverages. What does this allow us to predict about the structure of sucrose?

**LEARNING GOAL**

**9** Describe why the chemical and physical properties of water make it a truly unique solvent.

### Solution

Sucrose is used as a sweetener in teas, coffee, and a host of soft drinks. The solvent in all of these beverages is water, a polar molecule. The rule "like dissolves like" implies that sucrose must also be a polar molecule. Without even knowing the formula or structure of sucrose, we can infer this important information from a simple experiment—dissolving sugar in our morning cup of coffee.

### Practice Problem 6.14

Predict whether ammonia or methane would be more soluble in water. Explain your answer. (Hint: Refer to Section 5.2, the discussion of interactions in the liquid state.)

▶ For Further Practice: **Questions 6.93 and 6.94.**

# KITCHEN CHEMISTRY

## Solubility, Surfactants, and the Dishwasher

Each day we create a new supply of dirty dishes, glasses, pots and pans, and silverware. We may hand wash them, using one of the many commercially available detergents. Or, we may load them in an automatic dishwasher along with a solid or liquid detergent. Close the door, push a few buttons, and, in less than 1 hour, the dishes are clean and reasonably bacteria-free. How does this happen? It is a case of chemistry in action.

The fats, grease, and oils on the dishes are the potential solutes in the solvent water. The dissolution process is unlikely to happen if the solvent is pure water. Remember our rule "like dissolves like." The food residue is composed principally of nonpolar or very slightly polar molecules. Water, on the other hand, is extremely polar. We need some other substance to facilitate the interaction of the polar water and nonpolar food. That substance is a surfactant. Dishwashing detergents are a mixture of many components. Some have nothing to do with the cleaning process itself. Perfumes and dyes may be added to make the product more attractive to the consumer. Some components improve shelf life. The principal *active* ingredient is a surfactant. The role of the surfactant is to form a "bridge" between polar and nonpolar substances. Let us see how this happens.

Many surfactants exist, with a variety of chemical structures. However, all share one structural feature. They are molecules that have both a polar and nonpolar end. The polar end interacts with the solvent water and the nonpolar end dissolves in the less polar (or nonpolar) food residue. Consequently, the surface tension of the water, which serves as a barrier between the water and food particles, is decreased (see p. 181). Agitation of the water removes the water/surfactant/residue aggregate from the surface that is being cleaned. This aggregate remains dissolved in the water until the rinse cycle sends it down the drain.

The structure of the typical surfactant, cocamido DEA,

**(nonpolar region)**        **(polar region)**

is shown above. Note the combination of polar and nonpolar regions in the same molecule:

The −OH groups interact with water; the carbon–hydrogen region (termed *hydrocarbon*) dissolves in the food residue.

The existence of polar and nonpolar sites within the same molecule is certainly the most important feature of a molecule used in a washing formulation. However, it is not the only desirable feature. The molecule should be nontoxic, inexpensive, readily soluble in water, and have a minimal adverse effect on the environment. It should be biodegradable, enabling bacteria, naturally occurring in water, to attack the bonds, destroying the molecules before they can damage aquatic ecosystems. Organic chemists (who study compounds containing mainly carbon and hydrogen atoms) are very adept at synthesizing molecules that optimize desirable properties while minimizing undesirable properties.

Thus, we see that carefully designed surfactants enable us to use clean, attractive, and sanitary utensils to prepare and serve our meals while minimizing the negative impact of our wastewater on the aquatic environment.

(a)                    (b)                    (c)

A surfactant at work. (a) Food residue (nonpolar) is not soluble in water. (b) Nonpolar ends of surfactant molecules dissolve in the food residue. (c) The food residue is removed from the surface and is solubilized in water.

at higher temperatures to increase their rates. Other solvents, with lower boiling points, would simply boil away, and the reaction would stop.

This idea is easily extended to our own chemistry—because 60% of our bodies is water, we should appreciate the polarity of water on a hot day. As a biological solvent in the human body, water is involved in the transport of ions, nutrients, and waste into and out of cells. Water is also the solvent for biochemical reactions in cells and the digestive tract. Water is a reactant or product in some biochemical processes.

## Electrolytes in Solution

Recall (Sections 3.3 and 6.1) that an electrolyte is a material that dissolves in water to produce an *electrolytic solution* that conducts an electrical current. The behavior of many biological systems is critically dependent on the concentration of electrolytic solutions that are a part of these systems.

Molarity (mol/L) is the most commonly used concentration unit; however, another useful concentration unit is based on the *equivalent*. The **equivalent** (eq) is the number of grams of an ion corresponding to Avogadro's number of electrical charges. The resulting concentration unit is eq/L.

When discussing solutions of ionic compounds, molarity emphasizes the number of individual ions. A 1 molar solution of $Na^+$ contains Avogadro's number, $6.022 \times 10^{23}$, of $Na^+$ per L. In contrast, eq/L emphasize charge; 1 eq of $Na^+$ contains Avogadro's number of positive charges.

The concentration of any ion in aqueous solution, in units of eq/L, is equal to the product of the equivalents/mol of the ion and the molar concentration of the ion:

$$eq/L = \left(\frac{eq}{mol\ ion}\right)\left(\frac{mol\ ion}{L}\right)$$

Since

$$\frac{mol\ ion}{L} = M$$

$$eq/L = \left(\frac{eq}{mol\ ion}\right)(M)$$

The eq/mol of the ion is simply the number of charges on the ion, regardless of whether that charge is positive or negative. For example:

For $Na^+$, eq/mol is equal to 1
$\quad$ $Cl^-$, eq/mol is equal to 1
$\quad$ $Mg^{2+}$, eq/mol is equal to 2
$\quad$ $CO_3^{2-}$, eq/mol is equal to 2

and so forth.

The units milliequivalents/liter (meq/L) are often used when describing small amounts or low concentration of ions. These units are routinely used when describing ions in blood, urine, and blood plasma.

We can convert between eq/L and meq/L using conversion factors based on the identity:

$$1\ eq = 10^3\ meq$$

## Biological Effects of Electrolytes in Solution

The concentrations of cations, anions, and other substances in biological fluids are critical to health. Consequently, the osmolarity of body fluids is carefully regulated by the kidney.

The two most important cations in body fluids are $Na^+$ and $K^+$. Sodium ion is the most abundant cation in the blood and intercellular fluids, whereas potassium ion is the most abundant intracellular cation. In blood and intercellular fluid, the $Na^+$ concentration is 135 meq/L and the $K^+$ concentration is 3.5–5.0 meq/L. Inside the cell, the situation is reversed. The $K^+$ concentration is 125 meq/L and the $Na^+$ concentration is 10 meq/L.

**LEARNING GOAL**

**10** Interconvert molar concentrations of ions and milliequivalents/liter.

**LEARNING GOAL**

**11** Explain the role of electrolytes in blood and their relationship to the process of dialysis.

**EXAMPLE 6.15**    **Calculating Ion Concentration**

LEARNING GOAL

**10**  Interconvert molar concentration of ions and milliequivalents/liter.

For a solution that is $5.0 \times 10^{-3}$ M in phosphate ion ($PO_4^{-3}$)
    a. Calculate the concentration of phosphate ion in units of eq/L
    b. Calculate the concentration of phosphate ion in units of meq/L

**Solution**

    a. Substituting in the equation:

$$\text{eq/L} = \left(\frac{\text{eq}}{\text{mol ion}}\right)(M)$$

$$\text{eq/L} = \left(\begin{array}{c} 3 \\ \text{moles of charge} \\ \text{per mol of phosphate ion} \end{array}\right)\left(\begin{array}{c} 5.0 \times 10^{-3}\ M \\ \text{molar concentration} \\ \text{of the phosphate ion} \end{array}\right)$$

$$\text{eq/L} = 1.5 \times 10^{-2}\ \text{eq/L}$$

Note: The mol of charge in this equation is always positive even if the ion is negative. It represents the number of mol of charge, not the sign of the charge.

    b. We need only use the conversion factor

$$\frac{10^3\ \text{meq}}{\text{eq}}$$

$$\text{meq/L} = 1.5 \times 10^{-2}\ \frac{\text{eq}}{\text{L}} \times \frac{10^3\ \text{meq}}{\text{eq}} = 15\ \text{meq/L}$$

**Practice Problem 6.15**

Calculate the number of eq/L of carbonate ion, $CO_3^{2-}$, in a solution that is $6.4 \times 10^{-4}$ M carbonate ion.

▶ For Further Practice: **Questions 6.101 and 6.102.**

**EXAMPLE 6.16**    **Calculating Electrolyte Concentrations**

LEARNING GOAL

**10**  Interconvert molar concentration of ions and milliequivalents/liter.

A typical concentration of calcium ion in blood plasma is 4 meq/L. Represent this concentration in mol/L.

**Solution**

**Step 1.** The calcium ion has a 2+ charge (recall that calcium is in Group IIA of the periodic table; hence, a 2+ charge on the calcium ion).
**Step 2.** We will need two conversion factors:

$$\text{meq} \longrightarrow \text{eq}$$
$$\text{eq} \longrightarrow \text{mol of calcium ion}$$

**Step 3.** Using conversion factors as in Example 6.15,

$$\frac{4\ \text{meq Ca}^{2+}}{1\ \text{L}} \times \frac{1\ \text{eq Ca}^{2+}}{10^3\ \text{meq Ca}^{2+}} = 4 \times 10^{-3}\ \frac{\text{eq Ca}^{2+}}{\text{L}}$$

**Step 4.** Our relationship between meq/L and $M$ is:

$$\text{eq Ca}^{2+}/\text{L} = \left(\frac{\text{eq Ca}^{2+}}{\text{mol Ca}^{2+}}\right)(M)$$

**Step 5.** Rearranging and solving for $M$,

$$M = \left(\frac{\text{eq Ca}^{2+}}{\text{L}}\right)\left(\frac{\text{mol Ca}^{2+}}{\text{eq Ca}^{2+}}\right)$$

**Step 6.** Substituting,

$$M = \left(\frac{4 \times 10^{-3} \text{ eq Ca}^{2+}}{\text{L}}\right)\left(\frac{1 \text{ mol Ca}^{2+}}{2 \text{ eq Ca}^{2+}}\right)$$

and

$$M = \frac{2 \times 10^{-3} \text{ mol Ca}^{2+}}{\text{L}}$$

---

**Practice Problem 6.16**

Sodium chloride [0.9% (m/V)] is a solution administered intravenously to replace fluid loss. It is frequently used to avoid dehydration. The sodium ion concentration is 15.4 meq/L. Calculate the sodium ion concentration in mol/L.

▶ For Further Practice: **Questions 6.105 and 6.106.**

---

**Question 6.13** A typical concentration of chloride ion in blood plasma is 110 meg/L. Represent this concentration in mol/L.

**Question 6.14** A typical concentration of magnesium ion in certain types of intravenous solutions is 3 meg/L. Represent this concentration in mol/L.

If osmosis and simple diffusion were the only mechanisms for transporting water and ions across cell membranes, these concentration differences would not occur. One positive ion would be just as good as any other. However, the situation is more complex than this. Large protein molecules embedded in cell membranes actively pump sodium ions to the outside of the cell and potassium ions into the cell. This is termed *active transport* because cellular energy must be expended to transport those ions. Proper cell function in the regulation of muscles and the nervous system depends on the sodium ion/potassium ion ratio inside and out-side of the cell.

If the $Na^+$ concentration in the blood becomes too low, urine output decreases, the mouth feels dry, the skin becomes flushed, and a fever may develop. The blood level of $Na^+$ may be elevated when large amounts of water are lost. Diabetes, certain high-protein diets, and diarrhea may cause elevated blood $Na^+$ level. In extreme cases, elevated $Na^+$ levels may cause confusion, stupor, or coma.

Concentrations of $K^+$ in the blood may rise to dangerously high levels follow-ing any injury that causes large numbers of cells to rupture, releasing their intra-cellular $K^+$. This may lead to death by heart failure. Similarly, very low levels of $K^+$ in the blood may also cause death from heart failure. This may occur following prolonged exercise that results in excessive sweating. When this happens, both body fluids and electrolytes must be replaced. Salt tablets containing both NaCl and KCl taken with water, and drinks such as Gatorade effectively provide water and electrolytes and prevent serious symptoms.

The cationic charge in blood is neutralized by two major anions, $Cl^-$ and $HCO_3^-$. The chloride ion plays a role in acid-base balance, maintenance of osmotic pressure within an acceptable range, and oxygen transport by hemoglobin. The bicarbonate anion is the form in which most waste $CO_2$ is carried in the blood.

A variety of proteins are also found in the blood. Because of their larger size, they exist in colloidal suspension. These proteins include blood clotting factors,

# A MEDICAL PERSPECTIVE

## Hemodialysis

As we have seen in Section 6.5, blood is the medium for exchange of both nutrients and waste products. The membranes of the kidneys remove waste materials such as urea and uric acid (Chapter 22), excess salts, and large quantities of water. This process of waste removal is termed **dialysis,** a process similar in function to osmosis (Section 6.4). Semipermeable membranes in the kidneys, dialyzing membranes, allow small molecules (principally water and urea) and ions in solution to pass through and ultimately collect in the bladder. From there they can be eliminated from the body.

Unfortunately, a variety of diseases can cause partial or complete kidney failure. Should the kidneys fail to perform their primary function, dialysis of waste products, urea and other waste products rapidly increase in concentration in the blood. This can become a life-threatening situation in a very short time.

The most effective treatment of kidney failure is the use of a machine, an artificial kidney, that mimics the function of the kidney. The artificial kidney removes waste from the blood using the process of hemodialysis (blood dialysis). The blood is pumped through a long semipermeable membrane, the dialysis membrane. The dialysis process is similar to osmosis. However, in addition to water molecules, larger molecules (including the waste products in the blood) and ions can pass across the membrane from the blood into a dialyzing fluid. The dialyzing fluid is isotonic with normal blood; it also is similar in its concentration of all other essential blood components. The waste materials move across the dialysis membrane (from a higher to a lower concentration, as in diffusion). A successful dialysis procedure selectively removes the waste from the body without upsetting the critical electrolyte balance in the blood.

Hemodialysis, although lifesaving, is not by any means a pleasant experience. The patient's water intake must be severely limited to minimize the number of times each week that treatment must be used. Many dialysis patients require

Dialysis patient.

two or three treatments per week and each session may require one-half (or more) day of hospitalization, especially when the patient suffers from complicating conditions such as diabetes.

Improvements in technology, as well as the growth and sophistication of our health care delivery systems over the past several years, have made dialysis treatment much more patient friendly. Dialysis centers, specializing in the treatment of kidney patients, are now found in most major population centers. Smaller, more automated dialysis units are available for home use, under the supervision of a nurse. With the remarkable progress in kidney transplant success, dialysis is becoming, more and more, a temporary solution, sustaining life until a suitable kidney donor match can be found.

### For Further Understanding

▶ In what way is dialysis similar to osmosis?

▶ In what way does dialysis differ from osmosis?

immunoglobulins (antibodies) that help us fight infection, and albumins that act as carriers of nonpolar, hydrophobic substances (fatty acids and steroid hormones) that cannot dissolve in water.

Additionally, blood is the medium for exchange of nutrients and waste products. Nutrients, such as the polar sugar glucose, enter the blood from the intestine or the liver. Because glucose molecules are polar, they dissolve in body fluids and are circulated to tissues throughout the body. As noted above, nonpolar nutrients are transported with the help of carrier proteins. Similarly, nitrogen-containing waste products, such as urea, are passed from cells to the blood. They are continuously and efficiently removed from the blood by the kidneys.

In cases of loss of kidney function, mechanical devices—dialysis machines—mimic the action of the kidney. The process of blood dialysis—hemodialysis—is discussed in A Medical Perspective: Hemodialysis.

# CHAPTER MAP

## SUMMARY

### 6.1 Properties of Solutions

▶ A **solution** is a homogeneous (or uniform) mixture of two or more substances. A solution is composed of one or more **solutes,** dissolved in a **solvent.** When the solvent is water, the solution is called an **aqueous solution.**

▶ Liquid solutions are clear and transparent with no visible particles of solute. They may be colored or colorless, depending on the properties of the solute and solvent.

▶ In solutions of **electrolytes** the solutes are ionic compounds that dissociate in solution to produce ions. They are good conductors of electricity. Solutions of nonelectrolytes are formed from nondissociating molecular solutes (nonelectrolytes), and their solutions do not conduct electricity.

▶ The rule "like dissolves like" is the fundamental condition for **solubility.** Polar solutes are soluble in polar solvents, and nonpolar solutes are soluble in nonpolar solvents.

▶ The degree of solubility depends on the difference between the polarity of solute and solvent, the temperature, and the pressure. Pressure considerations are significant only for solutions of gases.

▶ When a solution contains all the solute that can be dissolved at a particular temperature, it is **saturated.** Excess solute falls to the bottom of the container as a **precipitate.** Occasionally, on cooling, the excess solute may remain in solution for a time before precipitation. Such a solution is a **supersaturated solution.**

▶ When excess solute, the precipitate, contacts solvent, the dissolution process reaches a state of dynamic equilibrium.

▶ **Colloidal suspensions** have particle sizes between those of true solutions and precipitates. A **suspension** is a heterogeneous mixture that contains particles much larger than a colloidal suspension. Over time, these particles may settle, forming a second phase.

▶ **Henry's law** describes the solubility of gases in liquids. At a given temperature the solubility of a gas is proportional to the partial pressure of the gas.

## 6.2 Concentration Based on Percent by Mass

▶ The amount of solute dissolved in a given amount of solution is the solution **concentration**. The more widely used percentage-based concentration units are **mass/volume percent** and **mass/mass percent**. **Parts per thousand** (ppt) and **parts per million** (ppm) are used with very dilute solutions.

## 6.3 Concentration Based on Moles

▶ **Molarity**, symbolized *M*, is defined as the number of moles of solute per liter of solution.

▶ Dilution is often used to prepare less concentrated solutions. The expression for this calculation is $(M_1)(V_1) = (M_2)(V_2)$. Knowing any three of these terms enables us to calculate the fourth. The concentration of solute may be represented as mol/L (molarity) or any other suitable concentration units. However, both concentrations must be in the same units when using the dilution equation.

## 6.4 Concentration-Dependent Solution Properties

▶ Solution properties that depend on the concentration of solute particles, rather than the identity of the solute, are **colligative properties**.

▶ There are four colligative properties of solutions, all of which depend on the concentration of *particles* in solution:

- Vapor pressure lowering. **Raoult's law** states that when a nonvolatile solute is added to a solvent, the vapor pressure of the solvent decreases in proportion to the concentration of the solute.
- Freezing point depression and boiling point elevation. When a nonvolatile solid is added to a solvent, the freezing point of the resulting solution decreases, and the boiling point increases. The magnitudes of both the freezing point depression ($\Delta T_f$) and the boiling point elevation ($\Delta T_b$) are proportional to the solute concentration over a limited range of concentrations. The mole-based concentration unit, molality, is commonly used in calculations involving colligative properties, because molality is temperature independent. **Molality** (symbolized *m)* is defined as the number of mol of solute per kg of solvent in a solution.
- Osmosis and osmotic pressure. The cell membrane mediates the interaction of the cell with its environment and is responsible for the controlled passage of material into and out of the cell. One of the principal means of transport is termed *diffusion*. **Diffusion** is the net movement of

solute or solvent molecules from an area of high concentration to an area of low concentration. This region where the concentration decreases over a distance is termed the **concentration gradient**. Because of the structure of the cell membrane only small molecules are able to diffuse freely across this barrier. Large molecules and highly charged ions are restricted by the barrier. In other words, the cell membrane is behaving in a selective fashion. Such membranes are termed *selectively permeable membranes*. **Osmosis** is the movement of solvent from a dilute solution to a more concentrated solution through a **semipermeable membrane**. The pressure that must be applied to the more concentrated solution to stop this flow is the **osmotic pressure**. The osmotic pressure, like the pressure exerted by a gas, may be treated quantitatively by using an equation similar in form to the ideal gas equation: $\pi = MRT$. By convention the molarity of particles that is used for osmotic pressure calculations is termed *osmolarity (osmol)*.

▶ In biological systems, if the concentration of the fluid surrounding red blood cells is higher than that inside the cell (a **hypertonic solution**), water flows from the cell, causing it to collapse. Too low a concentration of this fluid relative to the solution within the cell (a **hypotonic solution**) will cause cell rupture.

▶ Two solutions are **isotonic** if they have identical osmotic pressures. In that way the osmotic pressure differential across the cell is zero, and no cell disruption occurs.

## 6.5 Aqueous Solutions

▶ The role of water in the solution process deserves special attention. It is often referred to as the "universal solvent" because of the large number of ionic and polar covalent compounds that are at least partially soluble in water. It is the principal biological solvent. These characteristics are a direct consequence of the molecular geometry and structure of water and its ability to undergo hydrogen bonding.

▶ When discussing solutions of ionic compounds, molarity emphasizes the number of individual ions. A 1 *M* solution of $Na^+$ contains Avogadro's number of sodium ions. In contrast, equivalents per liter emphasizes charge; a solution containing 1 eq of $Na^+$ per L contains Avogadro's number of positive charge. One equivalent of an ion is the number of grams of the ion corresponding to Avogadro's number of electrical charges. Changing from mol/L to eq/L (or the reverse) is done using conversion factors.

▶ Concentration of charge in these electrolytic solutions is even more important than the molar concentration of the ions that are responsible for the charge. Consequently, we often use concentration units (eq/L and meq/L) that emphasize charge rather than number of ions in solution.

▶ The concentrations of cations, anions, and other substances in biological fluids are critical to health. As a result, the osmolarity of body fluids is carefully regulated by the kidney using the process of dialysis.

# ANSWERS TO PRACTICE PROBLEMS

**6.1** **a.** 16.7% (m/V) NaCl
  **b.** 7.50% (m/V) KCl
  **c.** $2.56 \times 10^{-2}$% (m/V) oxygen
  **d.** $1.05 \times 10^{-2}$% (m/V)argon

**6.2** **a.** $2.0 \times 10^1$ g NaOH
  **b.** 40.0 mL

**6.3** **a.** 20.0% (m/m) oxygen
  **b.** 38.5% (m/m) argon

**6.4** **a.** $2.00 \times 10^2$ ppt oxygen gas
    and
    $2.00 \times 10^5$ ppm oxygen gas

  **b.** $3.85 \times 10^2$ ppt argon gas
    and
    $3.85 \times 10^5$ ppm argon gas

**6.5** 0.30 $M$

**6.6** $1.25 \times 10^{-2}$ $M$

**6.7** 0.250 L

**6.8** $1.00 \times 10^{-1}$ L (or $1.00 \times 10^2$ mL) of 0.200 $M$ sugar solution

**6.9** To prepare the solution, dilute $1.7 \times 10^{-2}$ L of 12 $M$ HCl with sufficient water to produce $1.0 \times 10^2$ mL of total solution.

**6.10** Boiling point = 100.8° C
   Freezing point = −2.8° C

**6.11** Boiling point = 101.6° C
   Freezing point = −5.6° C

**6.12** **a.** $1.0 \times 10^{-2}$ osmol
   **b.** $5.0 \times 10^{-3}$ osmol

**6.13** **a.** 0.24 atm
   **b.** 0.12 atm

**6.14** Ammonia is a polar substance, as is water. The rule "like dissolves like" predicts that ammonia would be water soluble. Methane, a nonpolar substance, would not be soluble in water.

**6.15**

$$\frac{1.3 \times 10^{-3} \text{ eq } CO_3{}^{2-}}{L}$$

**6.16**

$$1.54 \times 10^{-2} \frac{\text{mol Na}^+}{L}$$

# QUESTIONS AND PROBLEMS

## Properties of Solutions

### Foundations

**6.15** Classify each of the following solutes as an electrolyte or a nonelectrolyte:
  **a.** $NaNO_3$
  **b.** $C_6H_{12}O_6$
  **c.** $FeCl_3$

**6.16** Classify each of the following solutes as an electrolyte or a nonelectrolyte:
  **a.** HCl
  **b.** $Na_2SO_4$
  **c.** Ethanol ($CH_3CH_2OH$)

**6.17** Distinguish among the terms true solution, colloid, and suspension.

**6.18** What is the difference between saturated and supersaturated solutions?

### Applications

**6.19** Fly fishermen in the Northeast have known for a long time that their chances of catching trout are much greater in early spring than in mid-August. Suggest an explanation based on your reading of this chapter.

**6.20** Fish kills (the sudden death of thousands of fish) often occur during periods of prolonged elevated temperatures. Pollution is often, but not always, the cause. Suggest another reason, based on your reading of this chapter.

**6.21** Can a solution be both clear and red? Explain.

**6.22** Two liters of liquid $A$ are mixed with two liters of liquid $B$. The resulting volume is only 3.95 L. Explain what happened on the molecular level.

## Concentration Based on Percent by Mass

### Foundations

**6.23** Calculate the composition of each of the following solutions in mass/volume %:
  **a.** 20.0 g NaCl in 1.00 L solution
  **b.** 33.0 g sugar, $C_6H_{12}O_6$, in $5.00 \times 10^2$ mL solution

**6.24** Calculate the composition of each of the following solutions in mass/volume %:
  **a.** 0.700 g KCl per 1.00 mL
  **b.** 1.00 mol $MgCl_2$ in $2.50 \times 10^2$ mL solution

**6.25** Calculate the composition of each of the following solutions in mass/volume %:
  **a.** 50.0 g ethanol dissolved in 1.00 L solution
  **b.** 50.0 g ethanol dissolved in $5.00 \times 10^2$ mL solution

**6.26** Calculate the composition of each of the following solutions in mass/volume %:
  **a.** 20.0 g acetic acid dissolved in 2.50 L solution
  **b.** 20.0 g benzene dissolved in $1.00 \times 10^2$ mL solution

**6.27** Calculate the composition of each of the following solutions in mass/mass %:
  **a.** 21.0 g NaCl in $1.00 \times 10^2$ g solution
  **b.** 21.0 g NaCl in $5.00 \times 10^2$ mL solution ($d = 1.12$ g/mL)

**6.28**    Calculate the composition of each of the following solutions in mass/mass %:
   **a.** 1.00 g KCl in $1.00 \times 10^2$ g solution
   **b.** 50.0 g KCl in $5.00 \times 10^2$ mL solution ($d = 1.14$ g/mL)

## Applications

**6.29**    How many g of solute are needed to prepare each of the following solutions?
   **a.** $2.50 \times 10^2$ g of 0.900% (m/m) NaCl
   **b.** $2.50 \times 10^2$ g of 1.25% (m/m) $NaC_2H_3O_2$ (sodium acetate)

**6.30**    How many g of solute are needed to prepare each of the following solutions?
   **a.** $2.50 \times 10^2$ g of 5.00% (m/m) $NH_4Cl$ (ammonium chloride)
   **b.** $2.50 \times 10^2$ g of 3.50% (m/m) $Na_2CO_3$

**6.31**    A solution was prepared by dissolving 14.6 g of $KNO_3$ in sufficient water to produce 75.0 mL of solution. What is the mass/volume % of this solution?

**6.32**    A solution was prepared by dissolving 12.4 g of $NaNO_3$ in sufficient water to produce 95.0 mL of solution. What is the mass/volume % of this solution?

**6.33**    How many g of sugar would you use to prepare 100 mL of a 1.00 mass/volume % solution?

**6.34**    How many mL of 4.0 mass/volume % $Mg(NO_3)_2$ solution would contain 1.2 g of magnesium nitrate?

**6.35**    Which solution is more concentrated: a 0.04% (m/m) solution or a 50 ppm solution?

**6.36**    Which solution is more concentrated: a 20 ppt solution or a 200 ppm solution?

**6.37**    A solution contains 1.0 mg of $Cu^{2+}$ per 0.50 kg solution. Calculate the concentration in ppt.

**6.38**    A solution contains 1.0 mg of $Cu^{2+}$ per 0.50 kg solution. Calculate the concentration in ppm.

## Concentration Based on Moles

### Foundations

**6.39**    Why is it often necessary to dilute solutions in the laboratory?

**6.40**    Write the dilution expression and define each term.

**6.41**    Calculate the molarity of 5.0 L of solution containing 2.5 mol $HNO_3$.

**6.42**    Calculate the molarity of 2.75 L of solution containing $1.35 \times 10^{-2}$ mol HCl.

### Applications

**6.43**    Calculate the number of g of solute that would be needed to make each of the following solutions:
   **a.** $2.50 \times 10^2$ mL of 0.100 M NaCl
   **b.** $2.50 \times 10^2$ mL of 0.200 M $C_6H_{12}O_6$ (glucose)

**6.44**    Calculate the number of g of solute that would be needed to make each of the following solutions:
   **a.** $2.50 \times 10^2$ mL of 0.100 M NaBr
   **b.** $2.50 \times 10^2$ mL of 0.200 M KOH

**6.45**    Calculate the volume of a 0.500 M sucrose solution (table sugar, $C_{12}H_{22}O_{11}$) containing 0.133 mol of solute.

**6.46**    Calculate the volume of a $1.00 \times 10^{-2}$ M KOH solution containing $3.00 \times 10^{-1}$ mol of solute.

**6.47**    It is desired to prepare 0.500 L of a 0.100 M solution of NaCl from a 1.00 M stock solution. How many mL of the stock solution must be taken for the dilution?

**6.48**    A 50.0-mL sample of a 0.250 M sucrose solution was diluted to $5.00 \times 10^2$ mL. What is the molar concentration of the resulting solution?

**6.49**    A 50.0-mL portion of a stock solution was diluted to 500.0 mL. If the resulting solution was 2.00 M, what was the molarity of the original stock solution?

**6.50**    A 6.00-mL portion of an 8.00 M stock solution is to be diluted to 0.400 M. What will be the final volume after dilution?

**6.51**    Calculate the molarity of a solution that contains 2.25 mol of $NaNO_3$ dissolved in 2.50 L.

**6.52**    Calculate the molarity of a solution that contains 1.75 mol of $KNO_3$ dissolved in 3.00 L.

**6.53**    How many g of glucose ($C_6H_{12}O_6$) are present in 1.75 L of a 0.500 M solution?

**6.54**    How many g of sodium hydroxide are present in 675 mL of a 0.500 M solution?

**6.55**    A 50.0-mL sample of 0.500 M NaOH was diluted to 500.0 mL. What is the new molarity?

**6.56**    A 300.0-mL portion of $H_2O$ is added to 300.0 mL of 0.250 M $H_2SO_4$. What is the new molarity?

## Concentration-Dependent Solution Properties

### Foundations

**6.57**    What is meant by the term *colligative property*?

**6.58**    Name and describe four colligative solution properties.

**6.59**    Explain, in terms of solution properties, why salt is used to melt ice in the winter.

**6.60**    Explain, in terms of solution properties, why a wilted plant regains its "health" when watered.

**6.61**    State Raoult's law.

**6.62**    What is the major importance of Raoult's law?

**6.63**    Why does 1 mol of $CaCl_2$ lower the freezing point of water more than 1 mol of NaCl?

**6.64**    Using salt to try to melt ice on a day when the temperature is $-20°C$ will be unsuccessful. Why?

**6.65**    **a.** Calculate the freezing temperature of 1.50 *m* Urea, $N_2H_4CO$. Urea is a covalent compound.
   **b.** Calculate the freezing temperature of 1.50 *m* LiBr, an ionic compound.

**6.66**    **a.** Calculate the boiling temperature of 1.50 *m* Urea, $N_2H_4CO$. Urea is a covalent compound.
   **b.** Calculate the boiling temperature of 1.50 *m* LiBr, an ionic compound.

### Applications

Answer Questions 6.67–6.72 by comparing two solutions: 0.50 M sodium chloride (an ionic compound) and 0.50 M sucrose (a covalent compound).

**6.67**    Calculate the freezing temperature of each solution. Assume that the molality of each solution is 0.50 *m*. (The molar and molal concentrations of dilute aqueous solutions are often identical, to two significant figures.)

**6.68**    Calculate the boiling temperature of each solution. Assume that the molality of each solution is 0.50 *m*. (The molar and molal concentrations of dilute aqueous solutions are often identical, to two significant figures.)

**6.69**    Which solution has the higher vapor pressure?

An **endothermic reaction** absorbs energy from the surroundings. The surroundings become colder.

If the energy required to break the $A$—$B$ and $C$—$D$ bonds is *greater* than the energy released when the $A$—$D$ and $C$—$B$ bonds form, the reaction will need an external supply of energy. Insufficient energy is available in the system to initiate the bond-breaking process. Such a reaction is called an endothermic (Greek *endo*, "to take on," and Greek *therm*, "heat") reaction, and energy is a *reactant*.

> Bond breaking is an endothermic process.
> Bond formation is an exothermic process.

The decomposition of ammonia into nitrogen and hydrogen is one example of an endothermic reaction:

$$22 \text{ kcal} + 2NH_3(g) \longrightarrow N_2(g) + 3H_2(g)$$
Endothermic reaction

This thermochemical equation reads: the decomposition of 2 mol of ammonia requires 22 kcal of heat.

The examples used here show the energy absorbed or released as heat energy. Depending on the reaction and the conditions under which the reaction is run, the energy may take the form of light energy or electrical energy. A firefly releases energy as a soft glow of light on a summer evening. An electrical current results from a chemical reaction in a battery, enabling your car to start.

---

**EXAMPLE 7.1**  **Determining Whether a Process Is Exothermic or Endothermic**

LEARNING GOAL

**1** Correlate the terms *endothermic* and *exothermic* with heat flow between a *system* and its *surroundings*.

An ice cube is dropped into a glass of water at room temperature. The ice cube melts. Is the melting of the ice exothermic or endothermic?

**Solution**

**Step 1.** Consider the ice cube to be the system and the water, the surroundings.

**Step 2.** Recognize that the water (the surroundings) will decrease in temperature. The surroundings are transferring heat to the system, the ice cube. The ice cube uses the heat to overcome hydrogen bonding among molecules, and the ice melts.

**Step 3.** The heat flow is from surroundings to system.

**Step 4.** The system gains energy (+energy); hence, the melting process (physical change) is endothermic.

**Practice Problem 7.1**

Are the following processes exothermic or endothermic?

  a. Fuel oil is burned in a furnace.
  b. When solid NaOH is dissolved in water, the solution temperature increases.

▶ For Further Practice: **Questions 7.23 and 7.24.**

---

### Enthalpy of Reactions

A chemical reaction may involve the breaking and forming of many bonds. Our interest is often focused on the total amount of heat released or absorbed by the overall reaction.

**Enthalpy** is the term used to represent heat and is symbolized as H. The *change in enthalpy* is the energy difference between the products and reactants of a chemical reaction and is symbolized as $\Delta H$. By convention, energy released is represented with a negative sign (indicating an exothermic reaction), and energy

LEARNING GOAL

**2** State the meaning of the terms *enthalpy*, *entropy*, and *free energy* and know their implications.

# GREEN CHEMISTRY

## Twenty-First Century Energy

When we purchase gasoline for our automobiles or oil for the furnace we are certainly buying matter. But that matter is only a storage device; we are really purchasing the energy stored in the chemical bonds. Combustion, burning in oxygen, releases the stored energy (potential energy) in a form suited to its function: mechanical energy to power a vehicle or heat energy to warm a home.

Energy release is a consequence of change. In fuel combustion, this change results in the production of waste products that may be detrimental to our environment. This necessitates the expenditure of time, money, and *more* energy to clean up our surroundings.

If we are paying a considerable price for our energy supply, it would be nice to believe that we are at least getting full value for our expenditure. Even that is not the case. Removal of energy from molecules also extracts a price. For example, a properly tuned automobile engine is perhaps 30% efficient. That means that less than one-third of the available energy actually moves the car. The other two-thirds is released into the atmosphere as wasted energy, mostly heat energy. The law of conservation of energy tells us that the energy is not destroyed, but it is certainly no longer available to us in a useful form.

Can we build a 100%-efficient energy transfer system? Is there such a thing as cost-free energy? The answer to these questions is no, on both counts. It is theoretically impossible, and the laws of thermodynamics tell us why this is so.

Although 100% energy conversion is not possible, there is still room for improvement in our current energy usage. Consuming vast quantities of nonrenewable resources (fossil fuels: coal, oil, and natural gas) and expelling the waste products (carbon dioxide and sulfur oxides) into the atmosphere may not be the best energy generation system that human ingenuity can devise.

The process of generating electricity is simply finding ways to move electrons. Converting water to steam, then using the steam pressure to drive a turbine (a mechanical device to "push" electrons) requires massive quantities of heat to boil the water and produce steam. Nuclear reactions produce heat, which is the basis of a nuclear power plant. Combustion of coal, oil, and natural gas (exothermic reactions) also produces heat. So we see that the essential difference among the various types of power plants lies in the identity and technological complexity of the heat source.

Newer approaches to moving electrons involve wind energy and solar energy. It has been estimated that twenty-first century, high-tech windmills erected in unpopulated areas (the shallow waters of the Atlantic Ocean, and the plains of the western portion of the United States), coupled with a modern electrical transmission grid, could satisfy the electrical demands of virtually the entire country. Solar energy, collected by photovoltaic cells arranged in solar panels, is converted to electrical energy.

Despite the tremendous progress in the design and development of new technologies, many problems remain. It will take decades to move away from nonrenewable energy sources. Nuclear energy has serious safety questions raised by the disasters at Three Mile Island, Chernobyl, and Fukushima. Solar energy systems suffer from low efficiencies and cloudy days; they require storage devices that increase the cost of building and maintaining these systems. Wind turbines are perceived by some as unattractive and are most effective in areas with strong prevailing winds. We must remember that electric automobiles replace gasoline with electricity and the electricity (or at least a portion of it) comes from the combustion of fossil fuels.

However, improvement in the design and efficiency of these alternate energy sources holds promise of reducing dependence on polluting, nonrenewable resources.

### For Further Understanding

▶ Solar and wind power have been mentioned as energy alternatives. Suggest a third alternative.

▶ What do you see as potential advantages (and potential shortcomings) of the alternative that you have suggested?

---

absorbed is shown with a positive sign (indicating an endothermic reaction). This is based on the relationship:

$$\Delta H_{\text{reaction}} = H_{\text{products}} - H_{\text{reactants}}$$

If $H_{\text{reactants}} > H_{\text{products}}$, $\Delta H$ must be negative and the reaction is exothermic. On the other hand,

if $H_{\text{reactants}} < H_{\text{products}}$, $\Delta H$ must be positive and the reaction is endothermic.

For the combustion of methane, an exothermic process, energy is a *product* in the thermochemical equation, and

$$\Delta H = -211 \text{ kcal}$$

For the decomposition of ammonia, an endothermic process, energy is a *reactant* in the thermochemical equation, and

$$\Delta H = +22 \text{ kcal}$$

**ANIMATION**
• Heat Flow in Endothermic and Exothermic Reactions

---

In these discussions, we consider the enthalpy change and energy change to be identical. This is true for most common reactions carried out in lab, with minimal volume change.

Diagrams representing changes in enthalpy for exothermic (a) and endothermic (b) reactions are shown in Figure 7.2.

**Question 7.1** Are the following processes exothermic or endothermic?
a. $C_6H_{12}O_6(s) \longrightarrow 2C_2H_5OH(l) + 2CO_2(g)$, $\Delta H = -16$ kcal
b. $N_2O_5(g) + H_2O(l) \longrightarrow 2HNO_3(l) + 18.3$ kcal

**Question 7.2** Are the following processes exothermic or endothermic?
a. $S(s) + O_2(g) \longrightarrow SO_2(g)$, $\Delta H = -71$ kcal
b. $N_2(g) + 2O_2(g) + 16.2$ kcal $\longrightarrow 2NO_2(g)$

## Spontaneous and Nonspontaneous Reactions

It seems that all exothermic reactions should be spontaneous. After all, an external supply of energy does not appear to be necessary; in fact, energy is a product of the reaction. It also seems that all endothermic reactions should be nonspontaneous: energy is a reactant that we must provide. However, these hypotheses are not supported by experimentation.

Experimental measurement has shown that most *but not all* exothermic reactions are spontaneous. Likewise, most *but not all*, endothermic reactions are not spontaneous. There must be some factor in addition to enthalpy that will help us to explain the less obvious cases of nonspontaneous exothermic reactions and spontaneous endothermic reactions. This other factor is entropy.

## The Second Law of Thermodynamics

### Entropy

The first law of thermodynamics considers the enthalpy of chemical reactions. The second law states that the universe spontaneously tends toward increasing disorder or randomness.

A measure of the randomness of a chemical system is its **entropy.** The entropy of a substance is represented by the symbol $S$. A random, or disordered, system is characterized by *high entropy;* a well-organized system has *low entropy.*

What do we mean by disorder in chemical systems? Disorder is simply the absence of a regular repeating pattern. Disorder or randomness increases as we convert from the solid to the liquid to the gaseous state. As we have seen, solids often have an ordered crystalline structure, liquids have, at best, a loose arrangement, and gas particles are virtually random in their distribution. Therefore gases have high entropy, and crystalline solids have very low entropy. Figures 7.3 and 7.4 illustrate properties of entropy in systems.

The second law describes the entire universe or any isolated system within the universe. On a more personal level, we all fall victim to the law of increasing disorder. Chaos in our room or workplace is certainly not our intent! It happens almost effortlessly. However, reversal of this process requires work and energy. The same is true at the molecular level. The gradual deterioration of our cities' infrastructure (roads, bridges, water mains, and so forth) is an all-too-familiar example. Millions of dollars (translated into energy and work) are needed annually just to try to maintain the status quo.

The entropy of a reaction is measured as a difference, $\Delta S$, between the entropies, $S$, of products and reactants.

The drive toward increased entropy, along with a tendency to achieve a lower potential energy, is responsible for spontaneous chemical reactions. Reactions that are exothermic and whose products are more disordered (higher in entropy) will occur spontaneously, whereas endothermic reactions producing products of lower entropy will not be spontaneous. If they are to take place at all, they will need some energy input.

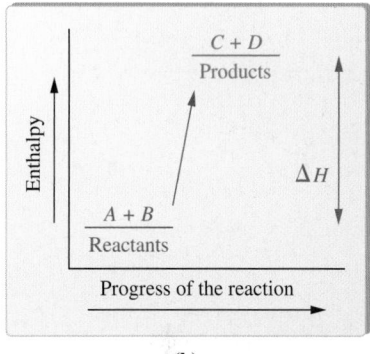

**Figure 7.2** (a) An exothermic reaction. $\Delta H$ represents the energy released during the progress of the exothermic reaction: $A + B \longrightarrow C + D + \Delta H$. (b) An endothermic reaction. $\Delta H$ represents the energy absorbed during the progress of the endothermic reaction: $\Delta H + A + B \longrightarrow C + D$.

**ANIMATION**
• Entropy and Rubber Bands

**Figure 7.3** (a) Gas particles, trapped in the left chamber, spontaneously diffuse into the right chamber, initially under vacuum, when the valve is opened. (b) It is unimaginable that the gas particles will rearrange themselves and reverse the process to create a vacuum. This can only be accomplished using a pump, that is, by doing work on the system.

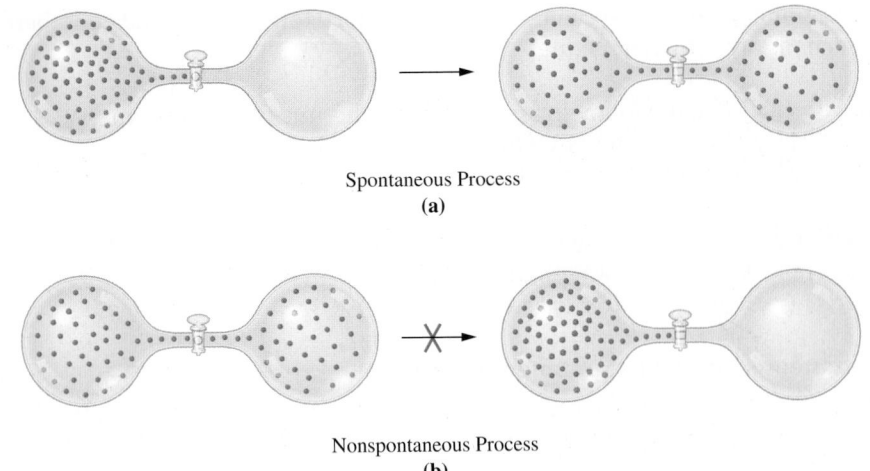

Spontaneous Process
**(a)**

Nonspontaneous Process
**(b)**

**Question 7.3**   Which substance has the greatest entropy, He($g$) or Na($s$)? Explain your reasoning.

**Question 7.4**   Which substance has the greatest entropy, H$_2$O($l$) or H$_2$O($g$)? Explain your reasoning.

**Figure 7.4** Processes such as (a) melting, (b) vaporization, and (c) dissolution increase entropy, or randomness, of the particles.

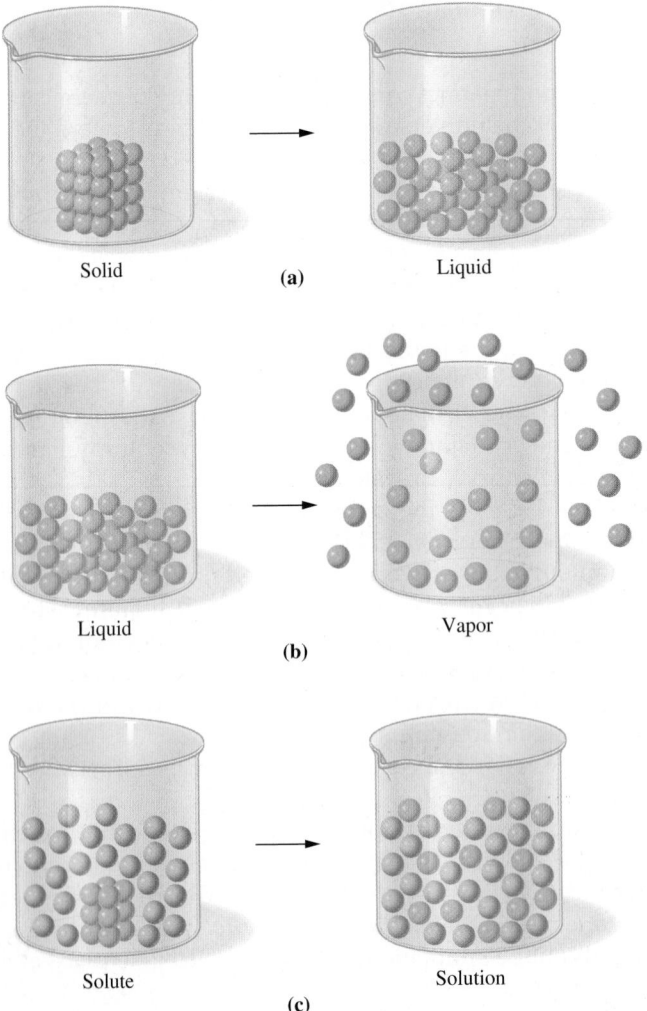

Solid    **(a)**    Liquid

Liquid    **(b)**    Vapor

Solute    **(c)**    Solution

## Free Energy

The two situations just described are clear-cut and unambiguous. In any other situation the reaction may or may not be spontaneous. It depends on the relative size of the enthalpy and entropy values.

**Free energy,** symbolized by $\Delta G$, represents the combined contribution of the enthalpy *and* entropy values for a chemical reaction. Thus free energy is the ultimate predictor of reaction spontaneity and is expressed as

$$\Delta G = \Delta H - T\Delta S$$

$\Delta H$ represents the change in enthalpy between products and reactants, $\Delta S$ represents the change in entropy between products and reactants, and $T$ is the Kelvin temperature of the reaction. A reaction with a negative value of $\Delta G$ will *always* be spontaneous. Reactions with a positive $\Delta G$ will *always* be nonspontaneous.

We need to know both $\Delta H$ and $\Delta S$ in order to predict the sign of $\Delta G$ and make a definitive statement regarding the spontaneity of the reaction. Additionally, the temperature may determine the direction of spontaneity. Consider the four possible situations:

- $\Delta H$ positive and $\Delta S$ negative: $\Delta G$ is always positive, regardless of the temperature. The reaction is always nonspontaneous.
- $\Delta H$ negative and $\Delta S$ positive: $\Delta G$ is always negative, regardless of the temperature. The reaction is always spontaneous.
- Both $\Delta H$ and $\Delta S$ positive: The sign of $\Delta G$ depends on the temperature.
- Both $\Delta H$ and $\Delta S$ negative: The sign of $\Delta G$ depends on the temperature.

**LEARNING GOAL**

**2** State the meaning of the terms *enthalpy*, *entropy*, and *free energy* and know their implications.

---

**EXAMPLE 7.2**    **Determining the Sign of $\Delta G$**

**LEARNING GOAL**

**2** State the meaning of the terms *enthalpy*, *entropy*, and *free energy* and know their implications.

Determine the sign of $\Delta G$ for the following reaction. Is the reaction spontaneous, nonspontaneous, or temperature dependent?

$$42.5 \text{ kcal} + CaCO_3(s) \longrightarrow CaO(s) + CO_2(g)$$

**Solution**

**Step 1.** Determine the sign of $\Delta H$. Because heat is added as a reactant, the reaction is endothermic. This gives a positive sign for $\Delta H$.

**Step 2.** Determine the sign of $\Delta S$. This reaction starts with only solid and produces some gas. Therefore the reaction begins with a small amount of disorder (the solid) and produces products with a high amount of disorder (the gas of $CO_2$). Therefore there is an increase in the disorder and $\Delta S$ is positive.

**Step 3.** Consider the equation $\Delta G = \Delta H - T\Delta S$. Since $\Delta H$ and $\Delta S$ are both positive, $\Delta G$ is temperature dependent. The reaction is only spontaneous if the $T\Delta S$ term becomes so large that when it is subtracted from $\Delta H$ the value for $\Delta G$ will be negative. Therefore this reaction is temperature dependent and is spontaneous at high temperature.

**Practice Problem 7.2**

Determine the sign of $\Delta G$ for the following reaction. Is the reaction spontaneous, nonspontaneous, or temperature dependent?

$$2H_2(g) + O_2(g) \longrightarrow 2H_2O(l) + 137 \text{ kcal}$$

▶ For Further Practice: **Questions 7.41 and 7.42.**

# A MEDICAL PERSPECTIVE

## Hot and Cold Packs

Hot packs provide "instant warmth" for hikers and skiers and are used in treatment of injuries such as pulled muscles. Cold packs are in common use today for the treatment of injuries and the reduction of swelling. These useful items are an excellent example of basic science producing a technologically useful product.

Both hot and cold packs depend on large energy changes taking place during a chemical reaction. Cold packs rely on an endothermic reaction, and hot packs generate heat energy from an exothermic reaction.

A cold pack is fabricated as two separate compartments within a single package. One compartment contains $NH_4NO_3$, and the other contains water. When the package is squeezed, the inner boundary between the two compartments ruptures, allowing the components to mix, and the following reaction occurs:

$$6.7 \text{ kcal/mol} + NH_4NO_3(s) \longrightarrow NH_4^+(aq) + NO_3^-(aq)$$

A cold pack.

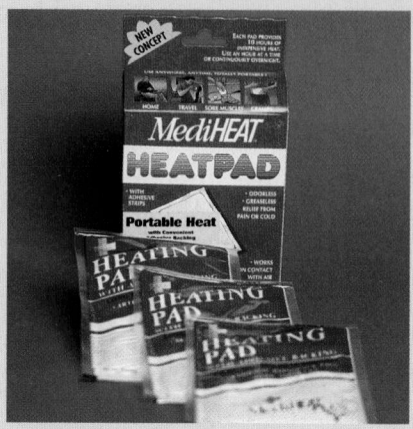

Heating pads.

This reaction is endothermic; heat taken from the surroundings produces the cooling effect.

The design of a hot pack is similar. Here, finely divided iron powder is mixed with oxygen. Production of iron oxide results in the evolution of heat:

$$4Fe(s) + 3O_2(g) \longrightarrow 2Fe_2O_3(s) + 198 \text{ kcal/mol}$$

This reaction occurs via an oxidation-reduction mechanism (see Chapter 8). The iron atoms are oxidized, $O_2$ is reduced. Electrons are transferred from the iron atoms to $O_2$ and $Fe_2O_3$ forms exothermically. The rate of the reaction is slow; therefore the heat is liberated gradually over a period of several hours.

### For Further Understanding

▶ What is the sign of $\Delta H$ for each equation in this story?
▶ Predict whether entropy increases or decreases for each equation in this story.

The introduction to this chapter stated that thermodynamics is used to predict whether or not a reaction will occur. The value of $\Delta G$ determines if a reaction is thermodynamically favorable or unfavorable.

**Question 7.5** Predict whether a reaction with positive $\Delta H$ and negative $\Delta S$ will be spontaneous, nonspontaneous, or temperature dependent. Explain your reasoning.

**Question 7.6** Predict whether a reaction with positive $\Delta H$ and positive $\Delta S$ will be spontaneous, nonspontaneous, or temperature dependent. Explain your reasoning.

# 7.2 Experimental Determination of Energy Change in Reactions

The measurement of heat energy changes in a chemical reaction is **calorimetry.** This technique involves the measurement of the change in the temperature of a quantity of water or solution that is in contact with the reaction of interest and isolated from the surroundings. A device used for these measurements is a *calorimeter,* which measures heat changes in calories.

Think of a calorimeter as a self-contained "universe" where heat can exchange between the system and its surroundings but cannot escape the calorimeter. At the same time, external heat is prevented from entering the calorimeter.

A Styrofoam coffee cup is a simple design for a calorimeter, and it produces surprisingly accurate results. It is a good insulator, and, when filled with solution, it can be used to measure temperature changes taking place as the result of a chemical reaction occurring in that solution (Figure 7.5). The change in the temperature of the solution, caused by the reaction, can be used to calculate the gain or loss of heat energy for the reaction.

For an exothermic reaction, heat released by the reaction is absorbed by the surrounding solution. For an endothermic reaction, the reactants absorb heat from the solution.

The **specific heat** of a substance is defined as the number of calories (cal) of heat needed to raise the temperature of 1 gram (g) of the substance 1 degree Celsius (°C). Knowing the specific heat of the water or the aqueous solution along with the total number of g of solution and the temperature increase (measured as the difference between the final and initial temperatures of the solution), enables the experimenter to calculate the heat released during the reaction.

The solution behaves as a "trap" or "sink" for energy released in an exothermic process. The temperature increase indicates a gain in heat energy. Endothermic reactions, on the other hand, take heat energy away from the solution, lowering its temperature.

The quantity of heat absorbed or released by the reaction ($Q$) is the product of the mass of solution in the calorimeter ($m_s$), the specific heat of the solution ($SH_s$), and the change in temperature ($\Delta T_s$) of the solution as the reaction proceeds from the initial to final state.

The heat is calculated by using the following equation:

$$Q = m_s \times \Delta T_s \times SH_s$$

with units

$$\text{cal} = \cancel{g} \times \cancel{°C} \times \frac{\text{cal}}{\cancel{g} \cdot \cancel{°C}}$$

The details of the experimental approach are illustrated in Example 7.3.

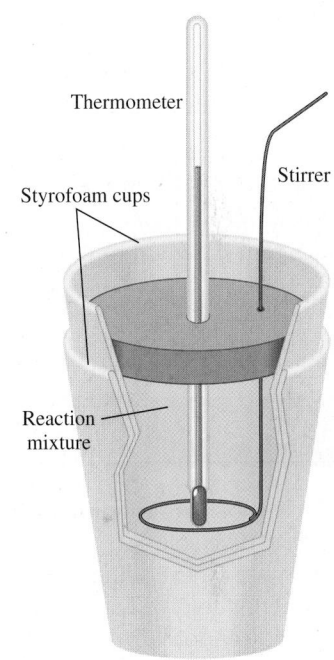

**Figure 7.5** A "coffee cup" calorimeter used for the measurement of heat change in chemical reactions. The concentric Styrofoam cups insulate the solution. Heat released by the chemical reaction (the system) enters the solution (the surroundings), raising its temperature, which is measured by using a thermometer.

Thermometer

Stirrer

Styrofoam cups

Reaction mixture

---

**EXAMPLE 7.3**    **Calculating Energy Involved in Calorimeter Reactions**

If 0.050 mol of hydrochloric acid (HCl) is mixed with 0.050 mol of sodium hydroxide (NaOH) in a "coffee cup" calorimeter, the temperature of $1.00 \times 10^2$ g of the resulting solution increases from 25.0°C to 31.5°C. If the specific heat of the solution is 1.00 cal/g · °C, calculate the quantity of energy involved in the reaction. Also, is the reaction endothermic or exothermic?

*Continued...*

## Solution

**Step 1.** The calorimetry expression is:

$$Q = m_s \times \Delta T_s \times SH_s$$

The reaction is the system; the solution is the surroundings.

**Step 2.** The change in temperature is

$$\Delta T_s = T_{s\,final} - T_{s\,initial}$$
$$= 31.5°C - 25.0°C = 6.5°C$$

The temperature of the solution has increased by 6.5°C; therefore, the reaction is exothermic.

**Step 3.** Substituting:

$$Q = 1.00 \times 10^2 \ \text{g solution} \times 6.5°C \times \frac{1.00 \ \text{cal}}{\text{g solution} \cdot °C}$$

$$= 6.5 \times 10^2 \ \text{cal}$$

$6.5 \times 10^2$ cal (or 0.65 kcal) of heat energy were released by this acid-base reaction to the surroundings, the solution; the reaction is exothermic.

---

### Practice Problem 7.3

Calculate the temperature change that would have been observed if 50.0 g solution were in the calorimeter instead of $1.00 \times 10^2$ g solution.

---

▶ For Further Practice: **Question 7.35.**

---

**EXAMPLE 7.4**    **Calculating Energy Involved in Calorimeter Reactions**

If 0.10 mol of ammonium chloride ($NH_4Cl$) is dissolved in water producing $1.00 \times 10^2$ g solution, the water temperature decreases from 25.0°C to 18.0°C. If the specific heat of the resulting solution is 1.00 cal/g·°C, calculate the quantity of energy involved in the process. Also, is the dissolution of ammonium chloride endothermic or exothermic?

## Solution

**Step 1.** The calorimetry expression is:
$$Q = m_s \times \Delta T_s \times SH_s$$

The reaction is the system; the solution is the surroundings.

**Step 2.** The change in temperature is
$$\Delta T = T_{s\,final} - T_{s\,initial}$$
$$= 18.0°C - 25.0°C = -7.0°C$$

The temperature of the solution has decreased by 7.0°C; therefore, the reaction is endothermic.

**Step 3.** Substituting:
$$Q = 1.00 \times 10^2 \ \text{g solution} \times (-7.0°C) \times \frac{1.00 \ \text{cal}}{\text{g solution} \cdot °C}$$

$$= -7.0 \times 10^2 \ \text{cal}$$

$7.0 \times 10^2$ cal (or 0.70 kcal) of heat energy were absorbed by the dissolution process because the solution lost $7.0 \times 10^2$ cal of heat energy to the system. The reaction is endothermic.

## Practice Problem 7.4

Calculate the temperature change that would have been observed if $1.00 \times 10^2$ g of another liquid, producing a solution with a specific heat capacity of 0.800 cal/g·°C, were substituted for the water in the calorimeter.

▶ For Further Practice: **Question 7.36.**

**Question 7.7** Using the conversion factor in Chapter 1, convert the energy released in Example 7.3 to joules (J).

**Question 7.8** Using the conversion factor in Chapter 1, convert the energy absorbed in Example 7.4 to J.

Many chemical reactions that produce heat are combustion reactions. In our bodies many food substances (carbohydrates, proteins, and fats; Chapters 21 and 22) are oxidized to release energy. **Fuel value** is the amount of energy per g of food.

The fuel value of food is an important concept in nutrition science. The fuel value is generally reported in units of *nutritional Calories*. One **nutritional Calorie (Cal)** is equivalent to one kilocalorie (1000 cal). It is also known as the *large Calorie* (uppercase C).

Energy necessary for our daily activity and bodily function comes largely from the reaction of oxygen with carbohydrates. Chemical energy from foods that is not used to maintain normal body temperature or in muscular activity is stored in the bonds of chemical compounds known collectively as fat. Thus consumption of "high-calorie" foods is implicated in the problem of obesity.

A special type of calorimeter, a *bomb calorimeter,* is useful for the measurement of the fuel value (Cal) of foods. Such a device is illustrated in Figure 7.6. Its design is similar, in principle, to that of the "coffee cup" calorimeter discussed earlier.

*Note: Refer to A Human Perspective: Food Calories, Section 1.6.*

### LEARNING GOAL

**3** Describe experiments that yield thermochemical information and calculate fuel values based on experimental data.

**Figure 7.6** A bomb calorimeter that may be used to measure heat released upon combustion of a sample. This device is commonly used to determine the fuel value of foods. The bomb calorimeter is similar to the "coffee cup" calorimeter. However, note the electrical component necessary to initiate the combustion reaction.

**EXAMPLE 7.5**    **Calculating the Fuel Value of Foods**

A 1-g sample of glucose (a common sugar or carbohydrate) was burned in a bomb calorimeter. The temperature of $1.00 \times 10^3$ g $H_2O$ was raised from 25.0°C to 28.8°C ($\Delta T_w = 3.8$°C). Calculate the fuel value of glucose.

**3**   Describe experiments that yield thermochemical information and calculate fuel values based on experimental data.

**Solution**

**Step 1.** Recall that the fuel value is the number of nutritional Cal liberated by the combustion of 1 g of material, and 1 g of material was burned in the calorimeter.

**Step 2.** Then

$$\text{Fuel value} = Q = m_w \times \Delta T_w \times SH_w$$

**Step 3.** Water is the surroundings in the calorimeter; it has a specific heat capacity equal to 1.00 cal/g $H_2O$·° C. Substituting in our expression for fuel value:

$$\text{Fuel value} = Q = \text{g } H_2O \times °C \times \frac{1.00 \text{ cal}}{\text{g } H_2O \cdot °C}$$

$$= 1.00 \times 10^3 \text{ g } H_2O \times 3.8\,°C \times \frac{1.00 \text{ cal}}{\text{g } H_2O \cdot °C}$$

$$= 3.8 \times 10^3 \text{ cal}$$

**Step 4.** Converting from cal to nutritional Cal:

$$3.8 \times 10^3 \text{ cal} \times \frac{1 \text{ nutritional Cal}}{10^3 \text{ cal}} = 3.8 \text{ Cal (nutritional Calories, or kcal)}$$

Since the quantity of glucose burned in the calorimeter is 1 g, the fuel value of glucose is 3.8 kcal/g.

**Practice Problem 7.5**

A 1.0-g sample of a candy bar (which contains lots of sugar and fats!) was burned in a bomb calorimeter. A 3.0°C temperature increase was observed for $1.00 \times 10^3$ g of water. The entire candy bar weighed 2.5 ounces (oz). Calculate the fuel value (in Cal) of the sample and the total caloric content of the candy bar.

▶ For Further Practice: **Question 7.38.**

It incorporates the insulation from the surroundings, solution pool, reaction chamber, and thermometer. Oxygen gas is added as one of the reactants, and an electrical igniter is inserted to initiate the reaction. However, it is not open to the atmosphere. In the sealed container the reaction continues until the sample is completely oxidized. All of the heat energy released during the reaction is captured in the water.

**4**   Describe the concept of reaction rate and the role of kinetics in chemical and physical change.

**ANIMATIONS**
- Kinetics
- Rates of Chemical Reactions

## 7.3   Kinetics

### Chemical Kinetics

Thermodynamics helps us to decide whether a chemical reaction is spontaneous. Knowing that a reaction can occur spontaneously tells us nothing about the time that it may take.

Chemical **kinetics** is the study of the **rate** (or speed) of chemical reactions. Kinetics also gives an indication of the *mechanism* of a reaction, a step-by-step description of how reactants become products. Kinetic information may be represented as the *disappearance* of reactants or *appearance* of product over time. A typical graph of number of molecules versus time is shown in Figure 7.7.

Information about the rate at which various chemical processes occur is useful. For example, what is the "shelf life" of processed foods? When will slow changes in composition make food unappealing or even unsafe? Many drugs lose their potency with time because the active ingredient decomposes into other substances. The rate of hardening of dental filling material (via a chemical reaction) influences the dentist's technique. Our very lives depend on the efficient transport of oxygen to each of our cells and the rapid use of the oxygen for energy-harvesting reactions.

The diagram in Figure 7.8 is a useful way of depicting the kinetics of a reaction at the molecular level.

Often a color change, over time, can be measured. Such changes are useful in assessing the rate of a chemical reaction (Figure 7.9).

Let's see what actually happens when two chemical compounds react and what experimental conditions affect the rate of a reaction.

## Activation Energy and the Activated Complex

Consider the exothermic reaction that we discussed in Section 7.1:

$$CH_4(g) + 2O_2(g) \longrightarrow CO_2(g) + 2H_2O(g) + 211 \text{ (kcal)}$$

For the reaction to proceed, four C—H and two O=O bonds must be broken, and two C=O and four H—O bonds must be formed. Sufficient energy must be

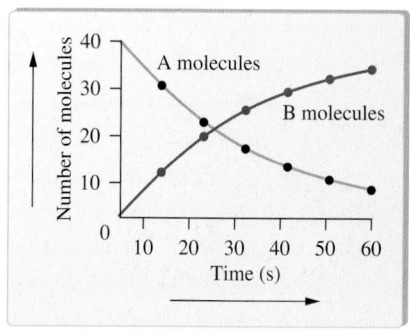

**Figure 7.7** For a hypothetical reaction $A \longrightarrow B$ the number of $A$ molecules (reactant molecules) decreases over time and $B$ molecules (product molecules) increase in number over time.

**LEARNING GOAL**

**5** Describe the importance of *activation energy* and the *activated complex* in determining reaction rate.

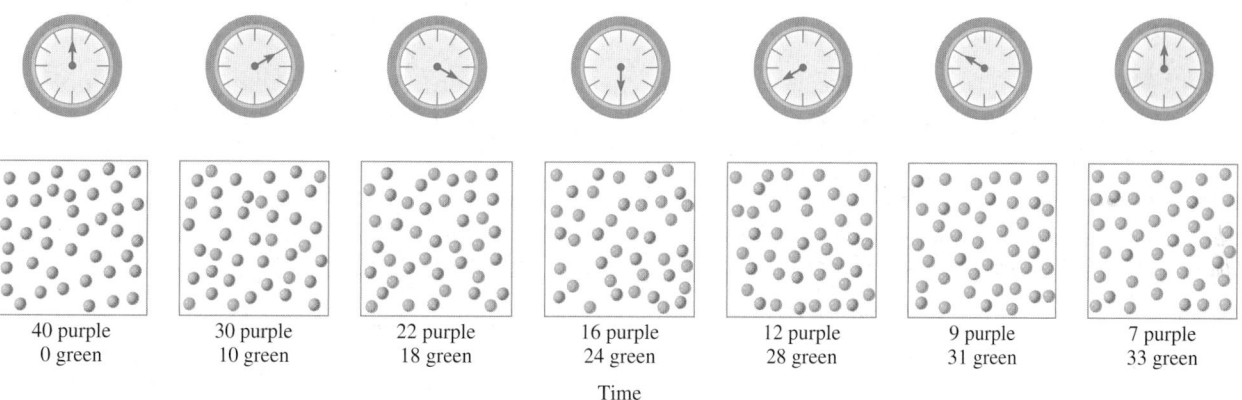

| 40 purple | 30 purple | 22 purple | 16 purple | 12 purple | 9 purple | 7 purple |
| 0 green | 10 green | 18 green | 24 green | 28 green | 31 green | 33 green |

Time

**Figure 7.8** An alternate way of representing the information contained in Figure 7.7.

Time

**Figure 7.9** The conversion of reddish brown $Br_2$ in solution to colorless $Br^-$ over time.

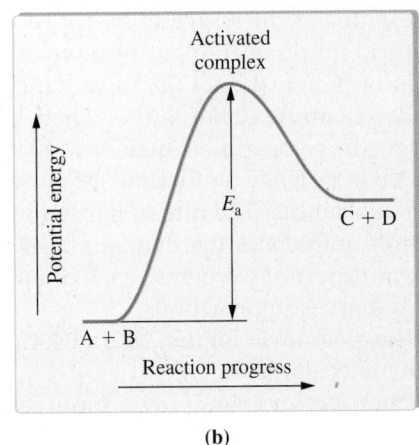

**Figure 7.10** (a) The change in potential energy as a function of reaction time for an exothermic reaction. (b) The change in potential energy as a function of reaction time for an endothermic reaction.

available to cause the bonds to break if the reaction is to take place. This energy is provided by the collision of molecules. If sufficient energy is available at the temperature of the reaction, one or more bonds will break, and the atoms will recombine in a lower energy arrangement, in this case as carbon dioxide and water. A collision producing product molecules is termed an *effective collision*. An effective collision requires sufficient energy and, in the case of complex molecules, the proper orientation of reacting molecules. Only effective collisions lead to chemical reaction.

The minimum amount of energy required to initiate a chemical reaction is called the **activation energy,** $E_a$, for the reaction.

We can picture the chemical reaction in terms of the changes in potential energy that occur during the reaction. Figure 7.10a graphically shows these changes for an exothermic reaction. Important characteristics of this graph include the following:

- The reaction proceeds from reactants to products through an extremely unstable state that we call the **activated complex.** The activated complex cannot be isolated from the reaction mixture but may be thought of as a short-lived group of atoms structured in such a way that it quickly and easily breaks apart into the products of the reaction.
- Formation of the activated complex requires energy. The difference between the energy of reactants and that of the activated complex is the activation energy. This energy must be provided by the collision of the reacting molecules or atoms at the temperature of the reaction.
- Because this is an exothermic reaction, the overall energy change must be a *net* release of energy. The *net* release of energy is the difference in energy between products and reactants.

For an endothermic reaction, such as the decomposition of water,

$$\text{energy} + 2H_2O(l) \longrightarrow 2H_2(g) + O_2(g)$$

the change of potential energy with reaction time is shown in Figure 7.10b.

The reaction takes place slowly because of the large activation energy required for the conversion of water into the elements hydrogen and oxygen.

**Question 7.9**    The act of striking a match illustrates the role of activation energy in a chemical reaction. Explain.

**Question 7.10**    Distinguish between the terms *net energy* and *activation energy*.

## Factors That Affect Reaction Rate

The following six factors influence reaction rate:

### • Structure of the Reacting Species

Reactions among ions in solution are usually very rapid. Ionic compounds in solution are dissociated; consequently, their bonds are already broken, and the activation energy for their reaction should be very low. On the other hand, reactions involving covalently bonded compounds may proceed more slowly. Covalent bonds must be broken and new bonds formed. The activation energy for this process would be significantly higher than that for the reaction of free ions. Bond strengths certainly play a role in determining reaction rates because the magnitude of the activation energy, or energy barrier, is related to bond strength.

### • Molecular Shape and Orientation

The size and shape of reactant molecules influence the rate of the reaction. Large molecules, containing bulky groups of atoms, may block the reactive part of the molecule from interacting with another reactive substance, causing the reaction to proceed slowly. Only molecular collisions that have the correct collision orientation, as well as sufficient energy, lead to product formation. These collisions are termed *effective collisions*.

### • The Concentration of Reactants

The rate of a chemical reaction is often a complex function of the concentration of one or more of the reacting substances. The rate will generally *increase* as concentration *increases* simply because a higher concentration means more reactant molecules in a given volume and therefore a greater number of collisions per unit time. If we assume that other variables are held constant, a larger number of collisions leads to a larger number of effective collisions. For example, the rate at which a fire burns depends on the concentration of oxygen in the atmosphere surrounding the fire, as well as the concentration of the fuel (perhaps methane or propane). A common fire-fighting strategy is the use of fire extinguishers filled with carbon dioxide. The carbon dioxide dilutes the oxygen to a level where the combustion process can no longer be sustained.

### • The Temperature of Reactants

The rate of a reaction increases as the temperature increases, because the average kinetic energy of the reacting particles is directly proportional to the Kelvin temperature. Increasing the speed of particles increases the likelihood of collision, and the higher kinetic energy means that a higher percentage of these collisions will result in product formation (effective collisions). A 10°C rise in temperature has often been found to double the reaction rate.

### • The Physical State of Reactants

The rate of a reaction depends on the physical state of the reactants: solid, liquid, or gas. For a reaction to occur the reactants must collide frequently and have sufficient energy to react. In the solid state, the atoms, ions, or molecules are restricted in their motion. In the gaseous and liquid states, the particles have both free motion and proximity to each other. Hence, reactions tend to be fastest in the gaseous and liquid states and slowest in the solid state.

### • The Presence of a Catalyst

A **catalyst** is a substance that *increases* the reaction rate. If added to a reaction mixture, the catalytic substance undergoes no net change, nor does it alter the outcome of the reaction. However, the catalyst interacts with the reactants to create an alternative pathway for production of products. This alternative path has

## LEARNING GOAL

**6** Predict the way reactant structure, concentration, temperature, and catalysis affect the rate of a chemical reaction.

**ANIMATIONS**
• Activation Energy
• Importance of Molecular Orientation on a Reaction
• Effect of Molecular Orientation on Collision Effectiveness

*Concentration is introduced in section 1.6, and units and calculations are discussed in sections 6.2 and 6.3.*

How does a match illustrate the concept of activation energy?

**Figure 7.12** The synthesis of ammonia, an important industrial product, is facilitated by a solid-phase catalyst (the Haber process). $H_2$ and $N_2$ bind to the surface, their bonds are weakened, dissociation and reformation as ammonia occur, and the newly formed ammonia molecules leave the surface. This process is repeated over and over, with no change in the catalyst.

## LEARNING GOAL

**7**  Write rate laws and use these equations to calculate the effect of concentration on rate.

**(a)** Uncatalyzed reaction

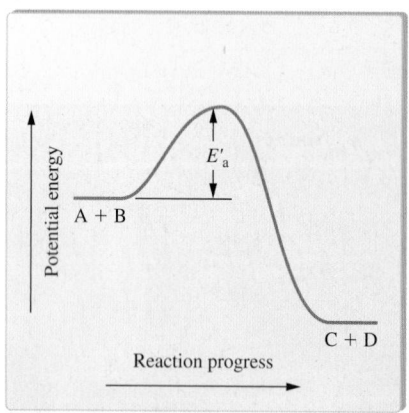

**(b)** Catalyzed reaction

**Figure 7.11** The effect of a catalyst on the magnitude of the activation energy of a chemical reaction: (a) uncatalyzed reaction, (b) catalyzed reaction. Note that the presence of a catalyst decreases the activation energy ($E'_a < E_a$), thus increasing the rate of the reaction.

a lower activation energy. This makes it easier for the reaction to take place and thus increases the rate. This effect is illustrated in Figure 7.11.

Catalysis is important industrially; it may often make the difference between profit and loss in the sale of a product. For example, catalysis is useful in converting double bonds to single bonds. An important application of this principle involves the process of hydrogenation. Hydrogenation converts one or more of the carbon-carbon double bonds of unsaturated fats (e.g., corn oil, olive oil) to single bonds characteristic of saturated fats (such as margarine). The use of a metal catalyst, such as nickel, in contact with the reaction mixture dramatically increases the rate of the reaction.

Thousands of essential biochemical reactions in our bodies are controlled and speeded up by biological catalysts called *enzymes*.

A molecular-level view of the action of a solid catalyst widely used in industrial synthesis of ammonia is presented in Figure 7.12.

**Question 7.11**  Would you imagine that a substance might act as a poison if it interfered with the function of an enzyme? Why?

**Question 7.12**  Bacterial growth decreases markedly in a refrigerator. Why?

## Mathematical Representation of Reaction Rate

Consider the decomposition reaction of $N_2O_5$ (dinitrogen pentoxide) in the gas phase. When heated, $N_2O_5$ decomposes and forms two products: $NO_2$ (nitrogen dioxide) and $O_2$ (diatomic oxygen). The balanced chemical equation for the reaction is

$$2N_2O_5(g) \xrightarrow{\Delta} 4NO_2(g) + O_2(g)$$

# A HUMAN PERSPECTIVE

## Too Fast or Too Slow?

Kinetics plays a vital role in the development of a wide range of commercial products. We will consider a few of these applications that contribute to our health, our enjoyment, and preservation of our environment.

### Refrigeration

Throughout history, few technologies have had a more profound benefit to human health than the development of inexpensive and efficient refrigeration, allowing food to be stored for long periods without spoiling. At room temperature unwanted chemical reactions, with the help of bacteria, rapidly decompose many foods, especially meats and fish, making them unsuitable for human consumption. Storing food at low temperatures slows the rate of decomposition by slowing the rate of bacterial reproduction and the rate of the destructive chemical reactions. Refrigeration is a straightforward application of kinetics: Rates are halved for each 10°C decrease in temperature.

### Dentistry

The most widely used strategy for whitening teeth is bleaching with hydrogen peroxide ($H_2O_2$). Because the reaction is slow, manufacturers of home-use products use devices to trap the $H_2O_2$ and hold it in contact with the teeth. A better strategy involves higher concentrations of $H_2O_2$. (Remember, the rate of a reaction is proportional to the reactant concentration.) However, these treatments must be administered by a dentist; used incorrectly, high concentrations of $H_2O_2$ can damage sensitive tissues, such as the gums and the interior of the mouth.

### Artwork and Photography

Old paintings and photographs are very susceptible to the effects of ultraviolet (UV) light. Chemical reactions that produce discoloration are energized by UV light. More molecules achieve the necessary activation energy, and the quality and value of the artwork degrade more rapidly. Glass that absorbs UV radiation (conservation glass) robs these reactions of needed energy, and the lifetime of these valuable materials is extended.

### The Environment

An essential requirement for herbicides and pesticides is biodegradability. Ideally, these materials enter soil or vegetation, quickly complete their task of killing weeds or bugs and rapidly decompose, often with the help of bacteria. Most people are aware of the problems caused by earlier, nonbiodegradable pesticides, most famously DDT (dichlorodiphenyltrichloroethane). DDT degrades very slowly in the environment. It is fat-soluble, bioaccumulates in animal tissue, and is responsible for many detrimental environmental effects, most notably its interference with bird reproduction. Even though it has been banned in the United States, DDT can still be found in the environment. It has been replaced with compounds that exhibit more favorable decay kinetics.

### Automobiles

The catalytic converter in modern automobiles helps to speed up the rate of conversion of harmful emissions (CO and NO, for example) to less harmful products ($CO_2$ and $N_2$ gas). The converter contains the metals platinum and palladium, which serve as solid catalysts, enabling the almost complete conversion of the auto emissions before they leave the tailpipe.

### Nuclear Waste

Conversion of nuclear waste to harmless products is NOT a chemical process. We wish that chemical kinetics applied to radioactive waste. Perhaps we could heat the waste and it would convert to harmless products. Not so! Radioactive decay (Chapter 9) is a nuclear process and is immune to all of the strategies routinely used to accelerate the rate of chemical reactions. That leaves us with a serious radioactive waste disposal problem. For more details, refer to Green Chemistry: Nuclear Waste Disposal in Chapter 9.

### For Further Understanding

▶ Provide another example of a process that has a less-than-optimal rate. What changes in conditions would improve the rate of this process?

▶ Find the current market values of platinum and palladium in the financial pages of a newspaper. How does this help to explain the high cost of a replacement catalytic converter?

---

When all of the factors that affect the rate of the reaction (except concentration) are held constant (that is, the nature of the reactant, temperature and physical state of the reactant, and the presence or absence of a catalyst), the rate of the reaction is proportional to the concentration of $N_2O_5$, the reactant.

$$\text{rate} \propto \text{concentration } N_2O_5$$

We will represent the concentration of $N_2O_5$ in units of molarity and represent molar concentration using brackets.

$$\text{concentration } N_2O_5 = [N_2O_5]$$

Then,

$$\text{rate} \propto [N_2O_5]$$

Laboratory measurement shows that the rate of the reaction depends on the molar concentration raised to an experimentally determined exponent, which we will symbolize as $n$, the *reaction order*. The **reaction order** represents the number of molecules that are involved in the formation of product.

$$\text{rate} \propto [N_2O_5]^n$$

In expressions such as the one shown, the proportionality symbol, $\propto$, may be replaced by an equality sign and a proportionality constant that we represent as $k$, the **rate constant.**

$$\text{rate} = k[N_2O_5]^n$$

Equations that follow this format, the rate being equal to the rate constant multiplied by the reactant concentration raised to an exponent that is the reaction order, are termed **rate laws.**

For the reaction described here, $n$ has been experimentally determined and is equal to 1; hence the reaction is first order in $N_2O_5$ and the rate law for the reaction is:

$$\text{rate} = k[N_2O_5]$$

In general, the rate of reaction for an equation of the general form:

$$A \longrightarrow product$$

is represented by the rate law

$$rate = k[A]^n$$

in which

$$n = \text{the reaction order}$$
$$k = \text{the rate constant of the reaction}$$
$$[A] = \text{the molar concentration of the reactant}$$

An equation involving two reactants

$$A + B \longrightarrow products$$

has a rate law of the form

$$rate = k[A]^n[B]^{n'}$$

Both the value of the rate constant and the reaction order are deduced from a series of experiments. We cannot predict them by simply looking at the chemical equation.

Knowledge of the form of the rate law, coupled with the experimental determination of the value of the rate constant, $k$, and the order, $n$, are valuable in a number of ways. Industrial chemists use this information to establish optimum conditions for preparing a product in the shortest practical time. The design of an entire manufacturing facility may, in part, depend on the rates of the critical reactions.

Note that the exponent, $n$, in the rate law is not the same as the coefficient of $N_2O_5$ in the balanced equation. However, in some reactions the coefficient in the balanced equation and the exponent $n$ (the order of the reaction) are numerically the same.

*In Section 7.4 we will see how the rate law forms the basis for describing equilibrium reactions.*

EXAMPLE 7.6 **Writing Rate Laws**

Write the rate law for the oxidation of ethanol ($C_2H_5OH$). The reaction has been experimentally determined to be first order in ethanol and third order in oxygen ($O_2$). The chemical reaction for this process is:

$$C_2H_5OH(l) + 3O_2(g) \longrightarrow 2CO_2(g) + 3H_2O(l)$$

**Solution**

**Step 1.** The rate law involves only the reactants, $C_2H_5OH$ and $O_2$. Depict their concentrations as

$$[C_2H_5OH][O_2]$$

**Step 2.** Now raise each to an exponent corresponding to its experimentally determined order

$$[C_2H_5OH][O_2]^3$$

**Step 3.** This is proportional to the rate:

$$\text{rate} \propto [C_2H_5OH][O_2]^3$$

**Step 4.** Proportionality ($\alpha$) is incorporated into an equation using a proportionality constant, $k$.

$$\text{rate} = k[C_2H_5OH][O_2]^3$$

is the rate law. (Remember that 1 is understood as an exponent; $[C_2H_5OH]$ is correct and $[C_2H_5OH]^1$ is not.)

**Practice Problem 7.6**

Write the general form of the rate law for each of the following processes. Represent the order as $n$, $n'$, and so forth.

a. $N_2(g) + O_2(g) \longrightarrow 2NO(g)$     c. $CH_4(g) + 2O_2(g) \longrightarrow CO_2(g) + 2H_2O(g)$

b. $2C_4H_6(g) \longrightarrow C_8H_{12}(g)$     d. $2NO_2(g) \longrightarrow 2NO(g) + O_2(g)$

▶ For Further Practice: **Questions 7.49 and 7.50.**

# 7.4 Equilibrium

## Rate and Reversibility of Reactions

We have assumed that most chemical and physical changes considered thus far proceed to completion. A complete reaction is one in which all reactants have been converted to products. However, many important chemical reactions do not go to completion. As a result, after no further obvious change is taking place, measurable quantities of reactants and products remain. Reactions of this type (incomplete reactions) are called **equilibrium reactions.**

Examples of physical and chemical equilibria abound in nature. Many environmental systems depend on fragile equilibria. The amount of oxygen dissolved in a certain volume of lake water (the oxygen concentration) is governed by the principles of equilibrium because solubility equilibria are temperature dependent (Henry's law, Section 6.1). The lives of plants and animals within this system are critically related to the levels of dissolved oxygen in the water.

The very form and function of the earth is a consequence of a variety of complex equilibria. Stalactite and stalagmite formations in caves are made up of solid calcium carbonate ($CaCO_3$). They owe their existence to an equilibrium process (involving LeChatelier's principle, discussed later in this chapter) described by the following equation:

$$Ca^{2+}(aq) + 2HCO_3^-(aq) \rightleftharpoons CaCO_3(s) + CO_2(aq) + H_2O(l)$$

## Physical Equilibrium

A physical equilibrium, such as sugar dissolving in water, is a reversible reaction. A **reversible reaction** is a process that can occur in both directions. It is indicated by using a double arrow ($\rightleftharpoons$) symbol.

Dissolution of sugar in water, producing a saturated solution, is a convenient illustration of a state of *dynamic equilibrium.*

A **dynamic equilibrium** is a situation in which the rate of the forward process in a reversible reaction is exactly balanced by the rate of the reverse process.

Let's now look at the sugar and water equilibrium in more detail.

### Sugar in Water

Imagine that you mix a small amount of sugar (2 or 3 g) in 100 milliliters (mL) of water. After you stir it for a short time, all of the sugar dissolves; there is no residual solid sugar because the sugar has dissolved *completely.* The reaction clearly has converted all solid sugar to its dissolved state, an aqueous solution of sugar, or

$$sugar(s) \longrightarrow sugar(aq)$$

An excess of sugar in water produces a saturated solution, discussed in Section 6.1.

Now, suppose that you add a very large amount of sugar (100 g), more than can possibly dissolve, to the same volume of water. As you stir the mixture you observe more and more sugar dissolving. After some time the amount of solid sugar remaining in contact with the solution appears constant. Over time, you observe no further decrease in the amount of undissolved sugar. Although nothing further appears to be happening, in reality a great deal of activity is taking place!

An equilibrium situation has been established. Over time the amount of sugar dissolved in the measured volume of water (the concentration of sugar in water) does not change. Hence the amount of undissolved sugar remains the same. However, if you could look at the individual sugar molecules, you would see something quite amazing. Rather than sugar molecules in the solid simply staying in place, you would see them continuing to leave the solid state and go into solution. At the same time, a like number of dissolved sugar molecules would leave the water and form more solid. This active process is described as a *dynamic equilibrium.* The reaction is proceeding in a forward (left to right) and a reverse (right to left) direction at the same time, making it a reversible reaction:

$$sugar(s) \rightleftharpoons sugar(aq)$$

The rates of the forward and reverse reactions are identical and the amount of sugar present as solid and in solution is constant. The system is at equilibrium. The double arrow serves as

- an indicator of a reversible process,
- an indicator of an equilibrium process, and
- a reminder of the dynamic nature of the process.

Dynamic equilibrium may be dangerous for living cells in certain situations because it represents a process in which nothing is getting done. There is no gain. Let's consider an exothermic reaction designed to produce a net gain of energy for the cell. In a dynamic equilibrium, the rate of the forward (energy-releasing) reaction is equal to the rate of the backward (energy-requiring) reaction. Thus there is no net gain of energy to fuel cellular activity, and the cell will die.

**Question 7.13**   Construct an example of a dynamic equilibrium using a subway car at rush hour or a busy restaurant at lunchtime.

**Question 7.14**   A certain change in reaction conditions for an equilibrium process was found to increase the rate of the forward reaction much more than that of the reverse reaction. Did the amount of product increase, decrease, or remain the same? Why?

## Chemical Equilibrium

### The Reaction of $N_2$ and $H_2$

When we mix nitrogen gas ($N_2$) and hydrogen gas ($H_2$) at an elevated temperature (perhaps 500°C), some of the molecules will collide with sufficient energy and proper orientation to break N≡N and H—H bonds. Rearrangement of the atoms will produce the product ($NH_3$):

$$N_2(g) + 3H_2(g) \rightleftharpoons 2NH_3(g)$$

Beginning with a mixture of hydrogen and nitrogen, the rate of the reaction is initially rapid, because the reactant concentration is high; as the reaction proceeds, the concentration of reactants decreases. At the same time the concentration of the product, ammonia, is increasing. At equilibrium the *rate of depletion* of hydrogen and nitrogen *is equal to* the *rate of depletion* of ammonia. In other words, *the rates of the forward and reverse reactions are equal.*

The concentration of the various species is fixed at equilibrium because product is being *consumed and formed at the same rate.* In other words, the reaction continues indefinitely (dynamic), but the concentration of products and reactants is fixed (equilibrium). This is a *dynamic equilibrium.* The rate of this reaction as a function of time is depicted in Figure 7.13.

For systems at equilibrium, an **equilibrium constant** expression can be written; it summarizes the relationship between the concentration of reactants and products in an equilibrium reaction.

### The Generalized Equilibrium Constant Expression for a Chemical Reaction

We write the general form of an equilibrium chemical reaction as

$$aA + bB \rightleftharpoons cC + dD$$

in which $A$ and $B$ represent reactants, $C$ and $D$ represent products, and $a$, $b$, $c$, and $d$ are the coefficients of the balanced equation. The equilibrium constant expression for this general case is

$$K_{eq} = \frac{[C]^c[D]^d}{[A]^a[B]^b}$$

For the ammonia system, it follows that the appropriate equilibrium expression is:

$$K_{eq} = \frac{[NH_3]^2}{[N_2][H_2]^3}$$

It does not matter what initial amounts (concentrations) of reactants or products we choose. When the system reaches equilibrium, the calculated value of $K_{eq}$ will not change. The magnitude of $K_{eq}$ can be altered only by changing the temperature. Thus $K_{eq}$ is temperature dependent. The chemical industry uses this fact to its advantage by choosing a reaction temperature that will maximize the yield of a desired product.

**Question 7.15**   How could we determine when a reaction has reached equilibrium?

**Question 7.16**   Does the attainment of equilibrium imply that no further change is taking place in the system?

**Figure 7.13** The change of the rate of reaction of $H_2$ and $N_2$ as a function of time. The rate of reaction, initially rapid, decreases as the concentration of reactant decreases and product increases. The rate approaches a limiting value at equilibrium.

*Products* of the overall equilibrium reaction
are in the numerator, and *reactants* are in the
denominator.

The exponents correspond to the *coefficients*
of the balanced equation.

## Writing Equilibrium Constant Expressions

An equilibrium constant expression can be written only after a correct, balanced chemical equation that describes the equilibrium system has been developed. A balanced equation is essential because the *coefficients* in the equation become the *exponents* in the equilibrium constant expression.

Each chemical reaction has a unique equilibrium constant value at a specified temperature. Equilibrium constants listed in the chemical literature are often reported at 25°C, to allow comparison of one system with any other. For any equilibrium reaction, the value of the equilibrium constant changes with temperature.

The brackets represent molar concentration or molarity; recall that molarity has units of moles per liter (mol/L). In our discussion of equilibrium, all equilibrium constants are shown as *unitless*.

A properly written equilibrium constant expression may not include all of the terms in the chemical equation upon which it is based. Only the concentrations of gases and substances in solution are shown, because their concentrations can change. Concentration terms for liquids and solids are *not* shown. The concentration of a liquid is constant. Most often, the liquid is the solvent for the reaction under consideration. A solid also has a fixed concentration and, for solution reactions, is not really a part of the solution. When a solid is formed it exists as a solid phase in contact with a liquid phase (the solution).

---

**EXAMPLE 7.7**    **Writing an Equilibrium Constant Expression**

Write an equilibrium constant expression for the reversible reaction:

$$H_2(g) + F_2(g) \rightleftharpoons 2HF(g)$$

### Solution

**Step 1.** Inspection of the chemical equation reveals that no solids or liquids are present. Hence all reactants and products appear in the equilibrium constant expression.

**Step 2.** The numerator term is the product term $[HF]^2$. The exponent for [HF] is identical to the coefficient of HF in the balanced equation.

**Step 3.** The denominator terms are the reactants $[H_2]$ and $[F_2]$. Note that each term contains an exponent identical to the corresponding coefficient in the balanced equation.

**Step 4.** Arranging the numerator and denominator terms as a fraction and setting the fraction equal to $K_{eq}$ yields

$$K_{eq} = \frac{[HF]^2}{[H_2][F_2]}$$

**Practice Problem 7.7**

Write an equilibrium constant expression for each of the following reversible reactions.

   a. $2NO_2(g) \rightleftharpoons N_2(g) + 2O_2(g)$     b. $2H_2O(l) \rightleftharpoons 2H_2(g) + O_2(g)$

▶ For Further Practice: **Questions 7.77 and 7.78.**

**ANIMATION**
• $NO_2/N_2O_4$ Equilibrium

## Interpreting Equilibrium Constants

What utility does the equilibrium constant have? The reversible arrow in the chemical equation alerts us to the fact that an equilibrium exists. Some measurable quantity of the product and reactant remain. However, there is no indication whether products predominate, reactants predominate, or significant concentrations of both products and reactants are present at equilibrium.

| EXAMPLE 7.8 | Writing an Equilibrium Constant Expression |

Write an equilibrium constant expression for the reversible reaction:

$$MnO_2(s) + 4H^+(aq) + 2Cl^-(aq) \rightleftharpoons Mn^{2+}(aq) + Cl_2(g) + 2H_2O(l)$$

**9** Write equilibrium constant expressions and use these expressions to calculate equilibrium constants.

### Solution

**Step 1.** $MnO_2$ is a solid and $H_2O$, although a product, is negligible compared with the water solvent. Thus they are not written in the equilibrium constant expression.

$$MnO_2(s) + 4H^+(aq) + 2Cl^-(aq) \rightleftharpoons Mn^{2+}(aq) + Cl_2(g) + \boxed{2H_2O(l)}$$

Not a part of the $K_{eq}$ expression

**Step 2.** The numerator term includes the remaining products:

$$[Mn^{2+}] \quad \text{and} \quad [Cl_2]$$

**Step 3.** The denominator term includes the remaining reactants:

$$[H^+]^4 \quad \text{and} \quad [Cl^-]^2$$

Note that each exponent is identical to the corresponding coefficient in the chemical equation.

**Step 4.** Arranging the numerator and denominator terms as a ratio and setting the ratio equal to $K_{eq}$ yields

$$K_{eq} = \frac{[Mn^{2+}][Cl_2]}{[H^+]^4[Cl^-]^2}$$

### Practice Problem 7.8

Write an equilibrium constant expression for each of the following reversible reactions.

a. $AgCl(s) \rightleftharpoons Ag^+(aq) + Cl^-(aq)$    b. $PCl_5(s) \rightleftharpoons PCl_3(g) + Cl_2(g)$

▶ For Further Practice: **Questions 7.81 and 7.83.**

The numerical value of the equilibrium constant provides this additional information. It tells us the extent to which reactants have converted to products. This is important information for anyone who wants to manufacture and sell the product. It also is important to anyone who studies the effect of equilibrium reactions on environmental systems and living organisms.

Although an absolute interpretation of the numerical value of the equilibrium constant depends on the form of the equilibrium constant expression, the following generalizations are useful:

- $K_{eq}$ greater than $1 \times 10^3$. A large numerical value of $K_{eq}$ indicates that the numerator (product term) is much larger than the denominator (reactant term) and that at equilibrium mostly product is present.
- $K_{eq}$ less than $1 \times 10^{-3}$. A small numerical value of $K_{eq}$ indicates that the numerator (product term) is much smaller than the denominator (reactant term) and that at equilibrium mostly reactant is present.
- $K_{eq}$ between $1 \times 10^{-3}$ and $1 \times 10^3$. In this case the equilibrium mixture contains significant concentrations of both reactants and products.

**Question 7.17** At a given temperature, the equilibrium constant for a certain reaction is $1 \times 10^{20}$. Does this equilibrium favor products or reactants? Why?

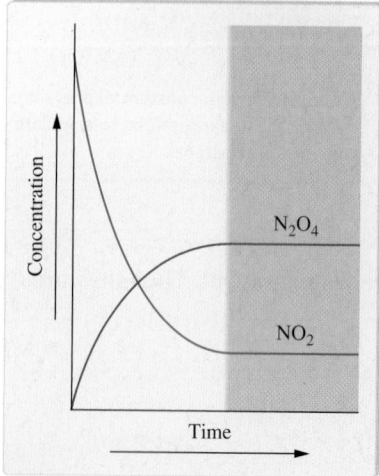

**Figure 7.14** For the reaction $2NO_2(g) \rightleftharpoons N_2O_4(g)$, the concentration of reactant ($NO_2$) diminishes rapidly while the $N_2O_4$ concentration builds. Eventually, the concentrations of both reactant and product become constant over time (blue area). The equilibrium condition has been attained.

**9** Write equilibrium constant expressions and use these expressions to calculate equilibrium constants.

**Question 7.18** At a given temperature, the equilibrium constant for a certain reaction is $1 \times 10^{-18}$. Does this equilibrium favor products or reactants? Why?

### Calculating Equilibrium Constants

The magnitude of the equilibrium constant for a chemical reaction is determined experimentally. The reaction under study is allowed to proceed until the concentration of products and reactants no longer changes (Figure 7.14). This may be a matter of seconds, minutes, hours, or even months or years, depending on the rate of the reaction. The reaction mixture is then analyzed to determine the molar concentration of each of the products and reactants. These concentrations are substituted in the equilibrium constant expression and the equilibrium constant is calculated. The following example illustrates this process.

---

**EXAMPLE 7.9** **Calculating an Equilibrium Constant**

Hydrogen iodide is placed in a sealed container and allowed to come to equilibrium. The equilibrium reaction is:

$$2HI(g) \rightleftharpoons H_2(g) + I_2(g)$$

and the equilibrium concentrations are:

$$[HI] = 0.54 \ M$$
$$[H_2] = 1.72 \ M$$
$$[I_2] = 1.72 \ M$$

Calculate the equilibrium constant.

**Solution**

**Step 1.** Write the equilibrium constant expression:

$$K_{eq} = \frac{[H_2][I_2]}{[HI]^2}$$

**Step 2.** Substitute the equilibrium concentrations of products and reactants to obtain

$$K_{eq} = \frac{[1.72][1.72]}{[0.54]^2} = \frac{2.96}{0.29}$$
$$= 10.1 \text{ or } 1.0 \times 10^1 \text{ (two significant figures)}$$

---

**Practice Problem 7.9**

A container holds the following mixture at equilibrium:

$$[NH_3] = 0.25 \ M$$
$$[N_2] = 0.11 \ M$$
$$[H_2] = 1.91 \ M$$

If the reaction is:

$$N_2(g) + 3H_2(g) \rightleftharpoons 2NH_3(g)$$

calculate the equilibrium constant.

▶ For Further Practice: **Questions 7.82 and 7.84.**

## Using Equilibrium Constants

We have seen that the equilibrium constant for a reaction can be calculated if we know the equilibrium concentrations of all of the reactants and products. Once known, the equilibrium constant can be used to obtain equilibrium concentrations of one or more reactants or products for a variety of different situations. These calculations can be quite complex. Let's look at one straightforward but useful case, one where the equilibrium concentration of reactants is known and we wish to calculate the product concentration.

---

**EXAMPLE 7.10** **Using an Equilibrium Constant**

**LEARNING GOAL**

**9** Write equilibrium constant expressions and use these expressions to calculate equilibrium constants.

Given the equilibrium reaction studied in Example 7.9:

$$2HI(g) \rightleftharpoons H_2(g) + I_2(g)$$

A sample mixture of HI, $H_2$, and $I_2$, at equilibrium, was found to have $[H_2] = 1.0 \times 10^{-2}\ M$ and $[HI] = 4.0 \times 10^{-2}\ M$. Calculate the molar concentration of $I_2$ in the equilibrium mixture.

**Solution**

**Step 1.** From Example 7.9, the equilibrium expression and equilibrium constant are:

$$K_{eq} = \frac{[H_2][I_2]}{[HI]^2}; \quad K_{eq} = 1.0 \times 10^1$$

**Step 2.** To solve the equilibrium expression for $[I_2]$, first multiply both sides of the equation by $[HI]^2$

$$[H_2][I_2] = K_{eq}[HI]^2$$

Then, divide both sides by $[H_2]$

$$[I_2] = \frac{K_{eq}[HI]^2}{[H_2]}$$

**Step 3.** Substitute the values:

$$K_{eq} = 1.0 \times 10^1$$
$$[H_2] = 1.0 \times 10^{-2}\ M$$
$$[HI] = 4.0 \times 10^{-2}\ M$$

**Step 4.** Solve:

$$[I_2] = \frac{[1.0 \times 10^1][4.0 \times 10^{-2}]^2}{[1.0 \times 10^{-2}]}$$
$$[I_2] = 1.6\ M$$

---

**Practice Problem 7.10**

Using the reaction (above), calculate the $[I_2]$ if both $[H_2]$ and $[HI]$ were $1.0 \times 10^{-4}\ M$.

▶ For Further Practice: **Questions 7.85 and 7.86.**

## LEARNING GOAL

**10**  Use LeChatelier's principle to predict changes in equilibrium position.

**ANIMATION**
• LeChatelier's Principle

Addition of products or reactants may have a profound effect on the composition of a reaction mixture but *does not* affect the value of the equilibrium constant.

## LeChatelier's Principle

In the nineteenth century the French chemist LeChatelier discovered that changes in equilibrium depend on the amount of "stress" applied to the system. The stress may take the form of an increase or decrease of the temperature of the system at equilibrium, or perhaps a change in the amount of reactant or product present in a fixed volume (the concentration of reactant or product).

**LeChatelier's principle** states that if a stress is placed on a system at equilibrium, the system will respond by altering the equilibrium composition in such a way as to minimize the stress.

Consider the equilibrium situation discussed earlier:

$$N_2(g) + 3H_2(g) \rightleftharpoons 2NH_3(g)$$

If the reactants and products are present in a fixed volume, such as 1 liter (L), and more $NH_3$ (the *product*) is introduced into the container, the system will be stressed—the equilibrium will be disturbed. The system will try to alleviate the stress (as we all do) by *removing* as much of the added material as possible. How can it accomplish this? By converting some $NH_3$ to $H_2$ and $N_2$. The position of the equilibrium shifts to the left, and a new dynamic equilibrium is soon established.

Adding extra $H_2$ or $N_2$ would apply the stress to the reactant side of the equilibrium. To minimize the stress, the system would "use up" some of the excess $H_2$ or $N_2$ to make product, $NH_3$. The position of the equilibrium would shift to the right.

In summary,

$$N_2(g) + 3H_2(g) \rightleftharpoons 2NH_3(g)$$

Product introduced:  $\leftarrow$ position of the equilibrium shifted

Reactant introduced:  position of the equilibrium shifted $\rightarrow$

What would happen if some of the ammonia molecules were *removed* from the system? The loss of ammonia represents a stress on the system; to relieve that stress, the ammonia would be replenished by the reaction of hydrogen and nitrogen. The position of the equilibrium would shift to the right.

### Effect of Concentration

Addition of extra product or reactant to a fixed reaction volume is just another way of saying that we have increased the concentration of product or reactant. Removal of material from a fixed volume decreases the concentration. Therefore, changing the concentration of one or more components of a reaction mixture is a way to alter the equilibrium composition of an equilibrium mixture (Figure 7.15). Let's look at some additional experimental variables that may change equilibrium composition.

**(a)        (b)        (c)**

**Figure 7.15**  The effect of concentration on equilibrium position of the reaction:

$$FeSCN^{2+}(aq) \rightleftharpoons Fe^{3+}(aq) + SCN^-(aq)$$
(red)      (yellow)   (colorless)

Solution (a) represents this reaction at equilibrium; addition of $SCN^-$ shifts the position of the equilibrium to the left (b) intensifying the red color. Removal of $SCN^-$ shifts the position of the equilibrium to the right (c) shown by the disappearance of the red color.

### Effect of Heat

The change in equilibrium composition caused by the addition or removal of heat from an equilibrium mixture can be explained by treating heat as a product or reactant. The reaction of nitrogen and hydrogen is an exothermic reaction:

$$N_2(g) + 3H_2(g) \rightleftharpoons 2NH_3(g) + 22 \text{ kcal}$$

Adding heat by raising the temperature is similar to increasing the amount of product. The position of the equilibrium will shift to the left, increasing the amounts of $N_2$ and $H_2$ and decreasing the amount of $NH_3$. If the reaction takes place in a fixed volume, the concentrations of $N_2$ and $H_2$ increase and the $NH_3$ concentration decreases.

Removal of heat by lowering the temperature produces the reverse effect. More ammonia is produced from $N_2$ and $H_2$, and the concentrations of these reactants must decrease.

In the case of an endothermic reaction, such as

$$39 \text{ kcal} + 2N_2(g) + O_2(g) \rightleftharpoons 2N_2O(g)$$

addition of heat is analogous to the addition of reactant, and the position of the equilibrium shifts to the right. Removal of heat would shift the reaction to the left, favoring the formation of reactants.

The dramatic effect of heat on the position of equilibrium is shown in Figure 7.16.

## Effect of Pressure

Only gases are affected significantly by changes in pressure because gases are free to expand and compress in accordance with Boyle's law. However, liquids and solids are not compressible, so their volumes are unaffected by pressure.

Therefore pressure changes will alter equilibrium composition only in reactions that involve a gas or variety of gases as products and/or reactants. Again, consider the ammonia example,

$$N_2(g) + 3H_2(g) \rightleftharpoons 2NH_3(g)$$

One mole of $N_2$ and three moles of $H_2$ (total of 4 mol of reactants) react to form two moles of $NH_3$ (2 mol of product). The equilibrium mixture (perhaps at 25°C) contains $N_2$, $H_2$, and $NH_3$. An increase in pressure will cause a stress to the system because the pressure is greater than the equilibrium pressure. To relieve the stress, the system will shift toward the side of the reaction that has fewer mol of gas. As the number of mol decreases, the pressure will decrease. In the example of ammonia, an increase in pressure will shift the position of the equilibrium to the right, producing more $NH_3$ at the expense of $N_2$ and $H_2$.

A decrease in pressure will be countered by the reaction shifting toward the side that contains more mol of gas because the pressure is less than the equilibrium pressure. As the number of mol of gas increases, the pressure will increase. Therefore, in the equilibrium reaction of ammonia, a decrease in pressure will cause the position of the equilibrium to shift to the left, and ammonia decomposes to form more nitrogen and hydrogen.

In contrast, the decomposition of hydrogen iodide,

$$2HI(g) \rightleftharpoons H_2(g) + I_2(g)$$

is unaffected by pressure. The number of mol of gaseous product and reactant are identical. No volume advantage is gained by a shift in equilibrium composition. In summary:

- Pressure affects the equilibrium composition only of reactions that involve at least one gaseous substance.
- Additionally, the relative number of mol of gaseous products and reactants must differ.

**Figure 7.16** The effect of heat on equilibrium position. For the reaction:

$$\begin{aligned} CoCl_4{}^{2-}(aq) + 6H_2O(l) &\rightleftharpoons \\ \text{(blue)} \\ Co(H_2O)_6{}^{2+}(aq) &+ 4Cl^-(aq) \\ \text{(pink)} \end{aligned}$$

heating the solution favors the blue $CoCl_4{}^{2-}$ species; cooling favors the pink $Co(H_2O)_6{}^{2+}$ species.

*Expansion and compression of gases and Boyle's law are discussed in Section 5.1.*

The industrial process for preparing ammonia, the Haber process, uses pressures of several hundred atmospheres (atm) to increase the yield.

• The equilibrium composition will shift to increase the number of mol of gas when the pressure decreases; it will shift to decrease the number of mol of gas when the pressure increases.

### Effect of a Catalyst

A catalyst has no effect on the equilibrium composition. A catalyst increases the rates of both forward and reverse reactions to the same extent. The equilibrium composition *and* equilibrium concentration do not change when a catalyst is used, but the equilibrium composition is achieved in a shorter time. The role of a solid-phase catalyst in the synthesis of ammonia is shown in Figure 7.12 on page 242.

---

**EXAMPLE 7.11    Predicting Changes in Equilibrium Composition**

LEARNING GOAL

Earlier in this section we considered the geologically important reaction that occurs in rock and soil:

**10**  Use LeChatelier's principle to predict changes in equilibrium position.

$$4.67 \text{ kcal} + Ca^{2+}(aq) + 2HCO_3^{-}(aq) \rightleftharpoons CaCO_3(s) + CO_2(aq) + H_2O(l)$$

Predict the effect on the equilibrium composition for each of the following changes.
   a. The concentration of $Ca^{2+}$ is increased by addition of some $CaCl_2$.
   b. Some solid $CaCO_3$ is removed from the mixture.
   c. The concentration of $HCO_3^{-}$ is decreased.
   d. The temperature of the system is increased.
   e. A catalyst is added.

### Solution

   a. The addition of $Ca^{2+}$ ions will cause the position of the equilibrium to shift to the right, and more products will form.
   b. Because $CaCO_3$ is a solid, addition or removal of the substance will have no effect on the equilibrium composition.
   c. If $HCO_3^{-}(aq)$ is removed from the system, the position of the equilibrium will shift to the left to produce more $HCO_3^{-}$ and other reactants.
   d. The reaction is endothermic. The addition of heat by the raising of the temperature will shift the position of the equilibrium to the right, and more products will form.
   e. The addition of a catalyst has no effect on the equilibrium composition.

---

**Practice Problem 7.11**

The reaction

$$382 \text{ cal} + Pb(s) + 2H^{+}(aq) \rightleftharpoons Pb^{2+}(aq) + H_2(g)$$

is carried out at constant pressure. Predict whether the volume of hydrogen gas would increase, decrease, or remain the same for each of the following changes.

   a. Addition of $Pb(s)$.
   b. Addition of $Pb^{2+}$ ions by adding some $Pb(NO_3)_2$ to the solution.
   c. Removal of $H^{+}$ ions.
   d. Lowering of the temperature.
   e. Addition of a catalyst.

▶ For Further Practice: **Questions 7.87 and 7.88.**

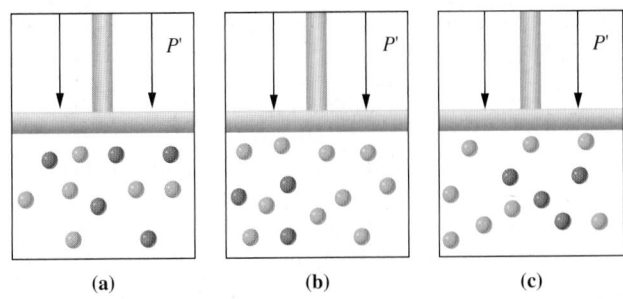

(a)            (b)            (c)

**7.68** The following diagram represents the endothermic reaction at equilibrium at 25°C: heat + $A(g) \rightleftharpoons 2B(g)$

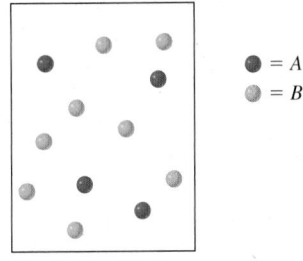

● = A
● = B

**a.** The temperature is increased to 50°C. Which of the following diagrams would represent the system once equilibrium is reestablished?
**b.** The temperature is decreased to 15°C. Which of the following diagrams would represent the system once equilibrium is reestablished?

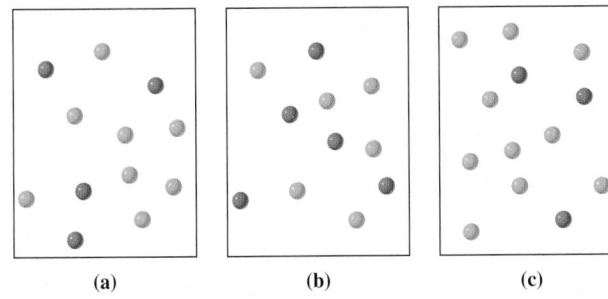

(a)            (b)            (c)

**7.69** Explain LeChatelier's principle.
**7.70** How can LeChatelier's principle help us to increase yields of chemical reactions?
**7.71** Describe the meaning of the term *dynamic equilibrium.*
**7.72** What is the relationship between the forward and reverse rates for a reaction at equilibrium?
**7.73** Describe the meaning of the term *position of the equilibrium.*
**7.74** Can a catalyst alter the position of the equilibrium?
**7.75** Name three factors that can shift the position of an equilibrium.
**7.76** A change in pressure could have the greatest effect on which type of equilibria: gaseous, liquid, or solid?

## Applications

**7.77** Write a valid equilibrium constant expression for the reaction shown in Question 7.61.
**7.78** Write a valid equilibrium constant expression for the reaction shown in Question 7.62.
**7.79** Distinguish between a physical equilibrium and a chemical equilibrium.
**7.80** Distinguish between the rate constant and the equilibrium constant for a reaction.

**7.81** Write the equilibrium constant expression for the reaction:

$$N_2(g) + 3H_2(g) \rightleftharpoons 2NH_3(g)$$

**7.82** Using the equilibrium constant expression in Question 7.81, calculate the equilibrium constant if:

$$[N_2] = 0.071 \, M$$
$$[H_2] = 9.2 \times 10^{-3} \, M$$
$$[NH_3] = 1.8 \times 10^{-4} \, M$$

**7.83** Write the equilibrium constant expression for the reaction:

$$2H_2(g) + S_2(g) \rightleftharpoons 2H_2S(g)$$

**7.84** Using the equilibrium constant expression in Question 7.83, calculate the equilibrium constant if:

$$[H_2] = 2.1 \times 10^{-1} \, M$$
$$[S_2] = 1.1 \times 10^{-6} \, M$$
$$[H_2S] = 7.3 \times 10^{-1} \, M$$

**7.85** Use the equilibrium constant expression you wrote in Question 7.81 and the equilibrium constant you calculated in Question 7.82 to determine the equilibrium concentration of $NH_3$ if:

$$[N_2] = 8.0 \times 10^{-2} \, M$$
$$[H_2] = 5.0 \times 10^{-3} \, M$$

**7.86** Use the equilibrium constant expression you wrote in Question 7.83 and the equilibrium constant you calculated in Question 7.84 to determine the equilibrium concentration of $H_2S$ if:

$$[H_2] = 1.0 \times 10^{-1} \, M$$
$$[S_2] = 1.0 \times 10^{-5} \, M$$

**7.87** For the reaction

$$CH_4(g) + Cl_2(g) \rightleftharpoons CH_3Cl(g) + HCl(g) + 26.4 \, kcal$$

predict the effect on the position of the equilibrium (will it shift to the left or to the right, or will there be no change?) for each of the following changes.
**a.** The temperature is increased.
**b.** The pressure is increased by decreasing the volume of the container.
**c.** A catalyst is added.

**7.88** For the reaction

$$47 \, kcal + 2SO_3(g) \rightleftharpoons 2SO_2(g) + O_2(g)$$

predict the effect on the position of the equilibrium (will it shift to the left or to the right, or will there be no change?) for each of the following changes.
**a.** The temperature is increased.
**b.** The pressure is increased by decreasing the volume of the container.
**c.** A catalyst is added.

**7.89** Label each of the following statements as true or false and explain why.
**a.** A slow reaction is an incomplete reaction.
**b.** The rates of forward and reverse reactions are never the same.

**7.90** Label each of the following statements as true or false and explain why.
   **a.** A reaction is at equilibrium when no reactants remain.
   **b.** A reaction at equilibrium is undergoing continual change.

**7.91** Use LeChatelier's principle to predict whether the amount of $PCl_3$ in a 1.00-L container is increased, is decreased, or remains the same for the equilibrium

$$PCl_3(g) + Cl_2(g) \rightleftharpoons PCl_5(g) + \text{heat}$$

when each of the following changes is made.
   **a.** $PCl_5$ is added.
   **b.** $Cl_2$ is added.
   **c.** $PCl_5$ is removed.
   **d.** The temperature is decreased.
   **e.** A catalyst is added.

**7.92** Use LeChatelier's principle to predict the effects, if any, of each of the following changes on the equilibrium system, described below, in a closed container.

$$C(s) + 2H_2(g) \rightleftharpoons CH_4(g) + 18 \text{ kcal}$$

   **a.** C is added.
   **b.** $H_2$ is added.
   **c.** $CH_4$ is removed.
   **d.** The temperature is increased.
   **e.** A catalyst is added.

**7.93** Will an increase in pressure increase, decrease, or have no effect on the concentration of $H_2(g)$ in the reaction:

$$C(s) + H_2O(g) \rightleftharpoons CO(g) + H_2(g)$$

**7.94** Will an increase in pressure increase, decrease, or have no effect on the concentration of $NO(g)$ in the reaction:

$$N_2(g) + O_2(g) \rightleftharpoons 2NO(g)$$

**7.95** Write the equilibrium constant expression for the reaction described in Question 7.93.

**7.96** Write the equilibrium constant expression for the reaction described in Question 7.94.

**7.97** True or false: The position of the equilibrium will shift to the right when a catalyst is added to the mixture described in Question 7.93. Explain your reasoning.

**7.98** True or false: The position of the equilibrium for an endothermic reaction will shift to the right when the reaction mixture is heated. Explain your reasoning.

**7.99** Why is it dangerous to heat an unopened bottle of cola?

**7.100** Carbonated beverages quickly go flat (lose $CO_2$) when heated. Explain, using LeChatelier's principle.

**7.101** Write the equilibrium constant expression for the reaction:

$$2SO_2(g) + O_2(g) \rightleftharpoons 2 SO_3(g)$$

**7.102** Write the equilibrium constant expression for the reaction:

$$C(s) + H_2O(g) \rightleftharpoons CO(g) + H_2(g)$$

**7.103** Calculate the equilibrium constant for the reaction in Question 7.101 if

$$[SO_2] = 0.10 \ M$$
$$[O_2] = 0.12 \ M$$
$$[SO_3] = 0.60 \ M$$

**7.104** Calculate the equilibrium constant for the reaction in Question 7.102 if

$$[H_2O] = 0.40 \ M$$
$$[CO] = 0.40 \ M$$
$$[H_2] = 0.20 \ M$$

**7.105** Suggest a change in experimental conditions that would increase the yield of $SO_3$ in the reaction in Question 7.101.

**7.106** Suggest a change in experimental conditions that would increase the yield of $H_2$ in the reaction in Question 7.102.

# CRITICAL THINKING PROBLEMS

1. Predict the sign of $\Delta G$ for perspiration evaporating. Would you expect the $\Delta H$ term or the $\Delta S$ term to be more dominant? Explain your reasoning.

2. Can the following statement ever be true? "Heating a reaction mixture increases the rate of a certain reaction but decreases the yield of product from the reaction." Explain why or why not.

3. Molecules must collide for a reaction to take place. Sketch a model of the orientation and interaction of HI and Cl that is most favorable for the reaction:

$$HI(g) + Cl(g) \longrightarrow HCl(g) + I(g)$$

4. Refer to Question 7.88. Choose the statements that are correct.
   **a.** $K_{eq}$ (at 25°C) $> K_{eq}$ (at 50° C)
   **b.** $K_{eq}$ (at 25°C) $< K_{eq}$ (at 50° C)
   **c.** $K_{eq}$ (at 25°C) $= K_{eq}$ (at 50° C)
   **d.** $K_{eq}$ (at 25°C) $> K_{eq}$ (at 15°C)
   **e.** $K_{eq}$ (at 25°C) $< K_{eq}$ (at 15°C)
   **f.** $K_{eq}$ (at 25°C) $= K_{eq}$ (at 15°C)

5. Silver ion reacts with chloride ion to form the precipitate silver chloride:

$$Ag^+(aq) + Cl^-(aq) \rightleftharpoons AgCl(s)$$

   After the reaction reached equilibrium, the chemist filtered 99% of the solid silver chloride from the solution, hoping to shift the equilibrium to the right, to form more product. Critique the chemist's experiment.

6. Human behavior often follows LeChatelier's principle. Provide one example and explain in terms of LeChatelier's principle.

7. A clever device found in some homes is a figurine that is blue on dry, sunny days and pink on damp, rainy days. These figurines are coated with substances containing chemical species that undergo the following equilibrium reaction:

$$Co(H_2O)_6^{2+}(aq) + 4Cl^-(aq) \rightleftharpoons CoCl_4^{2-}(aq) + 6H_2O(l)$$

   **a.** Which substance is blue?
   **b.** Which substance is pink?
   **c.** How is LeChatelier's principle applied here?

8. You have spent the entire morning in a 20°C classroom. As you ride the elevator to the cafeteria, six persons enter the elevator after being outside on a subfreezing day. You suddenly feel chilled. Explain the heat flow situation in the elevator in thermodynamic terms.

# 8

# Acids and Bases and Oxidation-Reduction

## LEARNING GOALS

1 Identify acids and bases and acid-base reactions.

2 Describe the role of the solvent in acid-base reactions.

3 Write equations describing acid-base dissociation and label the conjugate acid-base pairs.

4 Calculate pH from concentration data.

5 Calculate hydronium and/or hydroxide ion concentration from pH data.

6 Provide examples of the importance of pH in chemical and biochemical systems.

7 Describe the meaning and utility of neutralization reactions.

8 Describe the applications of buffers to chemical and biochemical systems, particularly blood chemistry.

9 Explain the meaning of the terms *oxidation* and *reduction*, and describe some practical examples of redox processes.

10 Diagram a voltaic cell and describe its function.

11 Compare and contrast voltaic and electrolytic cells.

Solution properties, including clarity and bacteria levels, are often pH dependent.

## OUTLINE

**Figure 8.1** The yellow solution on the left, containing $CrO_4^{2-}$ (chromate ion), was made acidic, producing the reddish brown solution on the right. The principal component in solution is now $Cr_2O_7^{2-}$. Addition of base to this solution removes $H^+$ ions and regenerates the yellow $CrO_4^{2-}$. This is an example of an acid-base dependent chemical equilibrium.

## LEARNING GOAL

**1**   Identify acids and bases and acid-base reactions.

# INTRODUCTION

In this chapter we will learn about two general classes of chemical change: acid-base reactions and oxidation-reduction reactions. Although superficially quite different, their underlying similarity is that both are essentially processes that involve a transfer of charge from one species to another. An acid-base reaction involves the transfer of one or more positively charged units, protons or hydrogen ions; an oxidation-reduction reaction involves the transfer of one or more negatively charged particles, electrons.

Acids and bases include some of the most important compounds in nature. Historically, it was recognized that certain compounds, acids, had a sour taste, were able to dissolve some metals, and caused vegetable dyes to change color. Bases have long been recognized by their bitter taste, slippery feel, and corrosive nature. Bases react strongly with acids and cause many metal ions in solution to form a solid precipitate.

Digestion of proteins is aided by stomach acid (hydrochloric acid), and many biochemical processes such as enzyme catalysis depend on the proper level of acidity. Indeed, a wide variety of chemical reactions critically depend on the acid-base composition of the solution (Figure 8.1). This is especially true of the biochemical reactions occurring in the cells of our bodies. For this reason the level of acidity must be very carefully regulated. This is done with substances called buffers.

Oxidation-reduction processes are also common in living systems. Respiration is driven by oxidation-reduction reactions. Additionally, oxidation-reduction reactions generate heat that warms our homes and workplaces and fuels our industrial civilization. Moreover, oxidation-reduction is the basis for battery design. Batteries are found in automobiles and electronic devices such as cameras and radios, and are even implanted in the human body to regulate heart rhythm.

## 8.1   Acids and Bases

The properties of acids and bases are related to their chemical structure. All acids have common characteristics that enable them to increase the hydrogen ion concentration in water while all bases lower the hydrogen ion concentration in water.

Two theories, one developed from the other, help us to understand the unique chemistry of acids and bases.

### Arrhenius Theory of Acids and Bases

One of the earliest definitions of acids and bases is the **Arrhenius theory.** According to this theory, an **acid,** dissolved in water, dissociates to form *hydrogen ions or protons* ($H^+$), and a **base,** dissolved in water, dissociates to form *hydroxide ions* ($OH^-$). For example, hydrochloric acid dissociates in solution according to the reaction

$$HCl(aq) \longrightarrow H^+(aq) + Cl^-(aq)$$

Sodium hydroxide, a base, produces hydroxide ions in solution:

$$NaOH(aq) \longrightarrow Na^+(aq) + OH^-(aq)$$

The Arrhenius theory satisfactorily explains the behavior of many acids and bases. However, a substance such as ammonia ($NH_3$) has basic properties but cannot be an Arrhenius base, because it contains no $OH^-$. A new theory was developed to account for the behavior of $NH_3$. The *Brønsted-Lowry theory* gives us a broader view of acid-base theory by considering the central role of the solvent in the dissociation process.

## Brønsted-Lowry Theory of Acids and Bases

The **Brønsted-Lowry theory** defines an **acid** as a proton ($H^+$) donor and a **base** as a proton acceptor.

Hydrochloric acid in solution *donates* a proton to the solvent water, thus behaving as a Brønsted-Lowry acid:

$$HCl(aq) + H_2O(l) \longrightarrow H_3O^+(aq) + Cl^-(aq)$$

$H_3O^+$ is referred to as the hydrated proton or **hydronium ion.**

The basic properties of ammonia are clearly accounted for by the Brønsted-Lowry theory. Ammonia *accepts* a proton from the solvent water, producing $OH^-$, the **hydroxide ion.** An equilibrium mixture of $NH_3$, $H_2O$, $NH_4^+$, and $OH^-$ results.

$$NH_3(aq) + H{-}OH(l) \rightleftharpoons NH_4^+(aq) + OH^-(aq)$$

## Acid-Base Properties of Water

The role that the solvent, water, plays in acid-base reactions is noteworthy. In one example above, the water molecule accepts a proton from the HCl molecule. The water is behaving as a proton acceptor, a Brønsted-Lowry base.

However, when water is a solvent for ammonia ($NH_3$), a base, the water molecule donates a proton to the ammonia molecule. The water, in this situation, is acting as a proton donor, a Brønsted-Lowry acid.

Water, owing to the fact that it possesses *both* acid and base properties, is termed **amphiprotic.** Water is the most commonly used solvent for acids and bases. Solute-solvent interactions between water and acids or bases promote both the solubility and the dissociation of acids and bases.

LEARNING GOAL

2 Describe the role of the solvent in acid-base reactions.

## Acid and Base Strength

The terms *acid (or base) strength* and *acid (or base) concentration* are easily confused. *Strength* is a measure of the *degree of dissociation* of an acid (or base) in solution, independent of its concentration. The degree of dissociation is the fraction of acid or base molecules or ions that produce ions in solution. Concentration, as we have learned, refers to the amount of solute (in this case, the amount of acid or base) per quantity of solution.

The strength of acids and bases in water depends on the extent to which they react with the solvent, water. Acids and bases are classified as *strong* when the reaction with water is virtually 100% complete and as *weak* when the reaction with water is much less than 100% complete.

*Important strong acids include:*

| | |
|---|---|
| Hydrochloric acid | $HCl(aq) + H_2O(l) \longrightarrow H_3O^+(aq) + Cl^-(aq)$ |
| Nitric acid | $HNO_3(aq) + H_2O(l) \longrightarrow H_3O^+(aq) + NO_3^-(aq)$ |
| Sulfuric acid | $H_2SO_4(aq) + H_2O(l) \longrightarrow H_3O^+(aq) + HSO_4^-(aq)$ |

Note that the equation for the dissociation of each of these acids is written with a single arrow. This indicates that the reaction has little or no tendency to proceed in the reverse direction to establish equilibrium. Virtually all of the acid molecules are dissociated to form ions.

All common strong bases are *metal hydroxides.* Strong bases completely dissociate in aqueous solution to produce hydroxide ions and metal cations. Of the

*Concentration of solutions is discussed in Section 6.3.*

The concentration of an acid or base as well as the identity of the solvent do affect the degree of dissociation. However, the major factor in determining the degree of dissociation is the strength of the acid or base.

 **ANIMATIONS**
- The Dissociation of Strong and Weak Acids
- Ionization of a Strong Base and a Weak Base
- Dissociation of Acetic Acid

*Reversibility of reactions is discussed in Section 7.4.*

common metal hydroxides, only NaOH and KOH are soluble in water and are readily usable strong bases:

Sodium hydroxide      $NaOH(aq) \longrightarrow Na^+(aq) + OH^-(aq)$
Potassium hydroxide  $KOH(aq) \longrightarrow K^+(aq) + OH^-(aq)$

Weak acids and weak bases dissolve in water principally in the molecular form. Only a small percentage of the molecules dissociate to form the hydronium or hydroxide ion.

*Two important weak acids are:*

Acetic acid      $CH_3COOH(aq) + H_2O(l) \rightleftharpoons H_3O^+(aq) + CH_3COO^-(aq)$
Carbonic acid  $H_2CO_3(aq) + H_2O(l) \rightleftharpoons H_3O^+(aq) + HCO_3^-(aq)$

> The double arrow implies an equilibrium between dissociated and undissociated species.

We have already mentioned the most common weak base, ammonia. Many organic compounds with a structure derived from ammonia function as weak bases. Several examples of weak bases follow:

Pyridine        $C_5H_5N(aq) + H_2O(l) \rightleftharpoons C_5H_5NH^+(aq) + OH^-(aq)$
Aniline         $C_6H_5NH_2(aq) + H_2O(l) \rightleftharpoons C_6H_5NH_3^+(aq) + OH^-(aq)$
Methylamine  $CH_3NH_2(aq) + H_2O(l) \rightleftharpoons CH_3NH_3^+(aq) + OH^-(aq)$

> *Many organic compounds have acid or base properties. The chemistry of organic acids and bases will be discussed in Chapter 14 (Carboxylic Acids and Carboxylic Acid Derivatives) and 15 (Amines and Amides).*

The fundamental chemical difference between strong and weak acids or bases is their equilibrium ion concentration. A strong acid, such as HCl, does not, in aqueous solution, exist to any measurable degree in equilibrium with its ions, $H_3O^+$ and $Cl^-$. On the other hand, a weak acid, such as acetic acid, establishes a dynamic equilibrium with its ions, $H_3O^+$ and $CH_3COO^-$.

## Conjugate Acids and Bases

The Brønsted-Lowry theory contributed several fundamental ideas that broadened our understanding of solution chemistry. First of all, an acid-base reaction is a process that involves a transfer of charge from one species to another. Second, the transfer process usually involves the solvent. Last, and perhaps most important, the acid-base reaction is seen as a reversible process. This leads to the possibility of a reversible, dynamic equilibrium (see Section 7.4) that can be used to control levels of acidity or basicity.

Consequently, any acid-base reaction can be represented by the general equation

$$\underset{\text{(acid)}}{HA} + \underset{\text{(base)}}{B} \rightleftharpoons BH^+ + A^-$$

In the forward reaction, the acid (HA) donates a proton ($H^+$) to the base (B) leading to the formation of $BH^+$ and $A^-$. However, in the reverse reaction, it is the $BH^+$ that behaves as an acid; it donates its "extra" proton to $A^-$. $A^-$ is therefore a base in its own right because it accepts the proton.

These *product* acids and bases are termed *conjugate acids and bases.*

A **conjugate acid** is the species formed when a base accepts a proton.

A **conjugate base** is the species formed when an acid donates a proton.

The acid and base on the opposite sides of the equation are collectively termed a **conjugate acid-base pair.** In the above equation:

$BH^+$ is the conjugate acid of the base B.

$A^-$ is the conjugate base of the acid HA.

B and $BH^+$ constitute a conjugate acid-base pair.

HA and $A^-$ constitute a conjugate acid-base pair.

Rewriting our model equation:

$$HA + B \rightleftharpoons BH^+ + A^-$$

(acid)  (base)         (acid)   (base)

conjugate acid-base pair

conjugate acid-base pair

Although we show the forward and reverse arrows to indicate the reversibility of the reaction, seldom are the two processes "equal but opposite." One reaction, either forward or reverse, is usually favored. Consider the reaction of hydrochloric acid in water:

↓ Forward reaction: significant

$$HCl(aq) + H_2O(l) \rightleftharpoons H_3O^+(aq) + Cl^-(aq)$$

(acid)       (base)              (acid)       (base)

↑ Reverse reaction: not significant

HCl is a much better proton donor than $H_3O^+$. Consequently the forward reaction predominates, the reverse reaction is inconsequential, and hydrochloric acid is termed a *strong acid*. As we learned in Chapter 7, reactions in which the forward reaction is strongly favored have large equilibrium constants. The dissociation of hydrochloric acid is so favorable that we describe it as 100% dissociated and use only a single forward arrow to represent its behavior in water:

$$HCl(aq) + H_2O(l) \longrightarrow H_3O^+(aq) + Cl^-(aq)$$

**ANIMATIONS**
- Reaction of a Strong Acid with Water
- Reaction of a Weak Acid with Water

The degree of dissociation, or strength, of acids and bases has a profound influence on their aqueous chemistry. For example, vinegar (a 5% m/v aqueous solution of acetic acid) is a consumable product. A 5% m/v aqueous solution of hydrochloric acid is not. Why? Acetic acid is a *weak* acid and, as a result, a dilute solution does no damage to the mouth and esophagus. The following section looks at the strength of acids and bases in solution in more detail.

**Question 8.1**  Write an equation for the reaction of each of the following with water:
   a. HF (a weak acid)
   b. $NH_3$ (a weak base)

**Question 8.2**  Write an equation for the reaction of each of the following with water:
   a. $H_2S$ (a weak acid)
   b. $CH_3NH_2$ (a weak base)

**Question 8.3**  Select the conjugate acid-base pairs for each reaction in Question 8.1.

**Question 8.4**  Select the conjugate acid-base pairs for each reaction in Question 8.2.

The relative strength of an acid or base is determined by the ease with which it donates or accepts a proton. Acids with the greatest proton-donating capability (strongest acids) have the weakest conjugate bases. Good proton acceptors (strong bases) have weak conjugate acids. This relationship is indicated in Figure 8.2. This figure can be used to help us compare and predict relative acid-base strength.

**Figure 8.2** Conjugate acid-base pairs. Strong acids have weak conjugate bases; strong bases have weak conjugate acids. Note the complementary nature of the conjugate acid-base pairs. In every case, the conjugate base has one fewer $H^+$ than the corresponding conjugate acid.

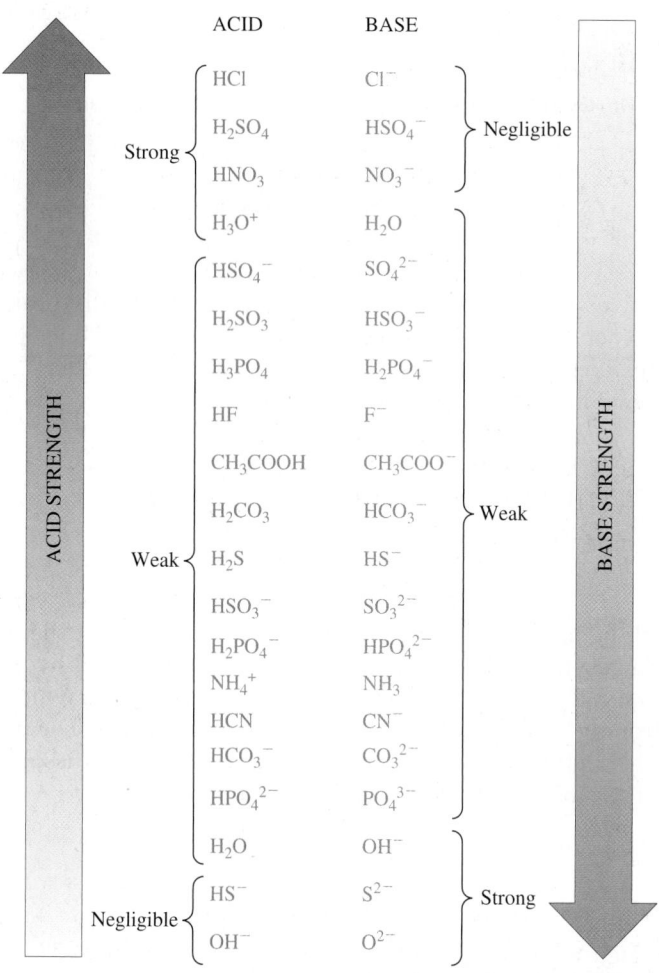

| ACID | BASE |
|---|---|
| HCl | $Cl^-$ |
| $H_2SO_4$ | $HSO_4^-$ |
| $HNO_3$ | $NO_3^-$ |
| $H_3O^+$ | $H_2O$ |
| $HSO_4^-$ | $SO_4^{2-}$ |
| $H_2SO_3$ | $HSO_3^-$ |
| $H_3PO_4$ | $H_2PO_4^-$ |
| HF | $F^-$ |
| $CH_3COOH$ | $CH_3COO^-$ |
| $H_2CO_3$ | $HCO_3^-$ |
| $H_2S$ | $HS^-$ |
| $HSO_3^-$ | $SO_3^{2-}$ |
| $H_2PO_4^-$ | $HPO_4^{2-}$ |
| $NH_4^+$ | $NH_3$ |
| HCN | $CN^-$ |
| $HCO_3^-$ | $CO_3^{2-}$ |
| $HPO_4^{2-}$ | $PO_4^{3-}$ |
| $H_2O$ | $OH^-$ |
| $HS^-$ | $S^{2-}$ |
| $OH^-$ | $O^{2-}$ |

Strong { HCl, $H_2SO_4$, $HNO_3$ } — Negligible

Weak { ... } — Weak

Negligible { HS⁻, OH⁻ } — Strong

ACID STRENGTH          BASE STRENGTH

---

## EXAMPLE 8.1    Predicting Relative Acid-Base Strengths

a. Write the conjugate acid of $HS^-$.
b. Using Figure 8.2, identify the stronger base, $HS^-$ or $F^-$.
c. Using Figure 8.2 identify the stronger acid, $H_2S$ or HF.

**LEARNING GOAL**

**3** Write equations describing acid-base dissociation and label the conjugate acid-base pairs.

### Solution, Part a

The conjugate acid may be constructed by adding a proton ($H^+$) to the base structure, consequently, $H_2S$.

### Solution, Part b

$HS^-$ is the stronger base because it is located farther down the right-hand column.

### Solution, Part c

HF is the stronger acid because its conjugate base is weaker *and* because it is located farther up the left-hand column.

---

### Practice Problem 8.1

a. In each pair, write the conjugate base of each acid and identify the stronger acid.
   $H_2O$ or $NH_4^+$                    $H_2SO_4$ or $H_2SO_3$
b. In each pair, write the conjugate acid of each base and identify the stronger base.
   $CO_3^{2-}$ or $PO_4^{3-}$                    $HCO_3^-$ or $HPO_4^{2-}$

▶ For Further Practice: **Questions 8.29 and 8.30.**

Solutions of acids and bases used in the laboratory must be handled with care. Acids burn because of their exothermic reaction with water present on and in the skin. Bases react with proteins, which are principal components of the skin and eyes.

Solutions of acids or bases are more hazardous if they are strong or concentrated. A strong acid or base produces more $H_3O^+$ or $OH^-$ than does the corresponding weak acid or base. More-concentrated acids or bases contain more $H_3O^+$ or $OH^-$ than do less-concentrated solutions of acids or bases of the same strength.

## The Dissociation of Water

Aqueous solutions of acids and bases are electrolytes. The dissociation of the acid or base produces ions that can conduct an electrical current. As a result of the differences in the degree of dissociation, *strong acids and bases are strong electrolytes while weak acids and bases are weak electrolytes.* The conductivity of these solutions is principally dependent on the solute and not the solvent (water).

*Solutions of electrolytes are discussed in Section 6.5.*

Although pure water is virtually 100% molecular, a small number of water molecules do ionize. This process occurs by the transfer of a proton from one water molecule to another, producing a hydronium ion and a hydroxide ion:

$$H_2O(l) + H_2O(l) \rightleftharpoons H_3O^+(aq) + OH^-(aq)$$

This process is the **autoionization,** or self-ionization, of water. Water is therefore a *very* weak electrolyte and a very poor conductor of electricity. Water has *both* acid and base properties; dissociation produces both the hydronium and hydroxide ion.

It has been determined that pure water at 25°C has a hydronium ion concentration of $1.0 \times 10^{-7}$ M. One hydroxide ion is produced for each hydronium ion. Therefore, the hydroxide ion concentration is also $1.0 \times 10^{-7}$ M. Molar equilibrium concentration is conveniently indicated by brackets around the species whose concentration is represented:

$$[H_3O^+] = 1.0 \times 10^{-7} M$$
$$[OH^-] = 1.0 \times 10^{-7} M$$

The product of hydronium and hydroxide ion concentration in pure water is referred to as the **ion product for water,** symbolized by $K_w$.

$$
\begin{aligned}
K_w = \text{ion product} &= [H_3O^+][OH^-] \\
&= [1.0 \times 10^{-7}][1.0 \times 10^{-7}] \\
&= 1.0 \times 10^{-14}
\end{aligned}
$$

The ion product is constant because its value does not depend on the nature or concentration of the solute, as long as the temperature does not change. The ion product is a temperature-dependent quantity.

The nature and concentration of the solutes added to water alter the relative concentrations of $H_3O^+$ and $OH^-$ present, but the product, $[H_3O^+][OH^-]$, always equals $1.0 \times 10^{-14}$ at 25°C. This relationship is the basis for a scale that is useful in the measurement of the level of acidity or basicity of solutions. This scale, the pH scale, is discussed next.

## 8.2   pH: A Measurement Scale for Acids and Bases

LEARNING GOAL

**4** Calculate pH from concentration data.

### A Definition of pH

The **pH scale** gauges the hydronium ion concentration and reflects the degree of acidity or basicity of a solution. The pH scale is somewhat analogous to the temperature scale used for assignment of relative levels of hot or cold. The temperature scale was developed to allow us to indicate how cold or how hot an object is. The pH scale specifies how acidic or how basic a solution is. The pH scale has

pH values greater than 14 and less than zero are possible, but largely meaningless, due to ion association characteristics of very concentrated solutions.

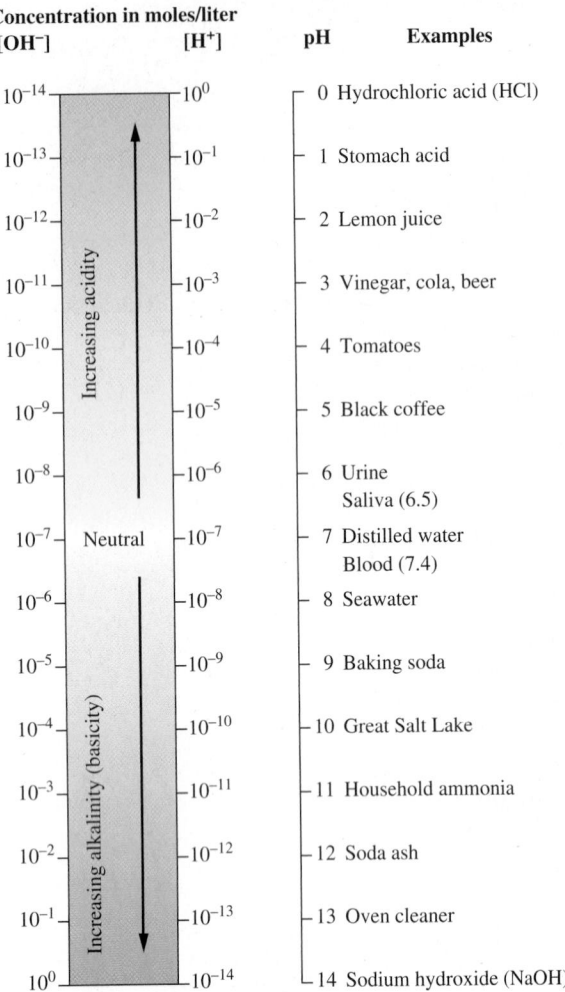

**Figure 8.3** The pH scale. A pH of 7 is neutral ($[H_3O^+] = [OH^-]$). Values less than 7 are acidic ($H_3O^+$ predominates) and values greater than 7 are basic ($OH^-$ predominates).

values that range from 0 (very acidic) to 14 (very basic). A pH of 7, the middle of the scale, is neutral, neither acidic nor basic. Figure 8.3 provides a convenient overview of solution pH.

To help us to develop a concept of pH, let's consider the following:

- Addition of an acid (proton donor) to water *increases* the $[H_3O^+]$ and decreases the $[OH^-]$.
- Addition of a base (proton acceptor) to water *decreases* the $[H_3O^+]$ by increasing the $[OH^-]$.
- $[H_3O^+] = [OH^-]$ when *equal* amounts of acid and base are present.

In all three cases, $[H_3O^+][OH^-] = 1.0 \times 10^{-14}$ = the ion product for water at 25°C.

## Measuring pH

The pH of a solution can be calculated if the concentration of either $H_3O^+$ or $OH^-$ is known. Alternatively, measurement of pH allows the calculation of $H_3O^+$ or $OH^-$ concentration. The pH of aqueous solutions may be approximated by using indicating paper (pH paper) that develops a color related to the solution pH. Alternatively, a pH meter can give us a much more exact pH measurement. A sensor measures an electrical property of a solution that is proportional to pH (Figure 8.4).

## Calculating pH

One of our objectives in this chapter is to calculate the pH of a solution when the hydronium or hydroxide ion concentration is known, and to calculate $[H_3O^+]$ or $[OH^-]$ from the measured pH.

The pH of a solution is defined as the negative logarithm of the molar concentration of the hydronium ion:

$$pH = -\log[H_3O^+]$$

Often, the pH or $[H_3O^+]$ will not be a whole number (pH = 1.5, pH = 5.3, $[H_3O^+] = 1.5 \times 10^{-3}$ and so forth). Consider Examples 8.6 and 8.7.

Examples 8.2–8.7 illustrate the most frequently used pH calculations. It is important to remember that in the case of a base you must convert the $[OH^-]$ to $[H_3O^+]$, using the expression for the ion product for the solvent, water. It is useful to be aware that, because pH is a base 10 logarithmic function, each tenfold change in concentration changes the pH by one unit. A tenfold change in concentration is equivalent to moving the decimal point one place.

**Figure 8.4** The measurement of pH. (a) A strip of test paper impregnated with indicator (a material that changes color as the acidity of the surroundings changes) is put in contact with the solution of interest. The resulting color is matched with a standard color chart (colors shown as a function of pH) to obtain the approximate pH. (b) A pH meter uses a sensor (a pH electrode) that develops an electrical potential that is proportional to the pH of the solution.

(a)

(b)

**EXAMPLE 8.2**    **Calculating pH from Acid Molarity**

**4** Calculate pH from concentration data.

Calculate the pH of a $1.0 \times 10^{-3}$ M solution of HCl.

**Solution**

**Step 1.** Recognize that HCl is a strong acid; consequently, it is 100% dissociated.

**Step 2.** One $H_3O^+$ is produced for each HCl. Therefore a $1.0 \times 10^{-3}$ M HCl solution has $[H_3O^+] = 1.0 \times 10^{-3}$ M, and

**Step 3.** Using our expression for pH:

$$pH = -\log [H_3O^+]$$

**Step 4.** Substituting for $[H_3O^+]$:

$$pH = -\log [1.0 \times 10^{-3}]$$
$$= -[-3.00] = 3.00$$

**Practice Problem 8.2**

Calculate the pH of a $1.0 \times 10^{-4}$ M solution of $HNO_3$.

▶ For Further Practice: **Questions 8.49 and 8.50.**

The proper use of the logarithm function often appears to contradict our understanding of significant figures. This is because the logaithm is an exponent that contains two kinds of information: the information in the measurement and the position of the decimal point.

The operative rule is that the number of decimal places in the logarithm is equal to the number of significant figures in the original number. In both Example 8.2 and 8.3, two significant figures in concentration correspond to two decimal places in pH (the logarithm).

**EXAMPLE 8.3**    **Calculating $[H_3O^+]$ from pH**

**5** Calculate hydronium and/or hydroxide ion concentration from pH data.

Calculate the $[H_3O^+]$ of a solution of hydrochloric acid with pH = 4.00.

**Solution**

**Step 1.** We use the pH expression:

$$pH = -\log [H_3O^+]$$

An alternative mathematical form of this equation is:

$$[H_3O^+] = 10^{-pH}$$

**Step 2.** We can use this expression to solve for $[H_3O^+]$

$$[H_3O^+] = 10^{-4.00}$$

**Step 3.** Performing the calculation on your calculator results in

$$[H_3O^+] = 1.0 \times 10^{-4} M$$

**Practice Problem 8.3**

Calculate the $[H_3O^+]$ of a solution of $HNO_3$ that has a pH = 5.00.

▶ For Further Practice: **Questions 8.51 and 8.52.**

**EXAMPLE 8.4**    **Calculating the pH of a Base**

Calculate the pH of a $1.0 \times 10^{-5}\,M$ solution of NaOH.

**Solution**

**Step 1.** Recognize that NaOH is a strong base; consequently, it is 100% dissociated.

**Step 2.** One [OH$^-$] is produced for each NaOH. Therefore a $1.0 \times 10^{-5}\,M$ NaOH solution has [OH$^-$] = $1.0 \times 10^{-5}\,M$.

**Step 3.** To calculate pH, we need [H$_3$O$^+$]. Recall that

$$[H_3O^+][OH^-] = 1.0 \times 10^{-14}$$

**Step 4.** Solving this equation for [H$_3$O$^+$],

$$[H_3O^+] = \frac{1.0 \times 10^{-14}}{[OH^-]}$$

**Step 5.** Substituting the information provided in the problem,

$$[H_3O^+] = \frac{1.0 \times 10^{-14}}{1.0 \times 10^{-5}}$$
$$= 1.0 \times 10^{-9}\,M$$

**Step 6.** The solution is now similar to that in Example 8.2:

$$pH = -\log[H_3O^+]$$
$$= -\log[1.0 \times 10^{-9}]$$
$$= 9.00$$

**Practice Problem 8.4**

a. Calculate the pH corresponding to a $1.0 \times 10^{-2}\,M$ solution of sodium hydroxide.
b. Calculate the pH corresponding to a $1.0 \times 10^{-6}\,M$ solution of sodium hydroxide.

▶ For Further Practice: **Questions 8.53 and 8.54.**

**EXAMPLE 8.5**    **Calculating Both Hydronium and Hydroxide Ion Concentrations from pH**

Calculate the [H$_3$O$^+$] and [OH$^-$] of a sodium hydroxide solution with a pH = 10.00.

**Solution**

**Step 1.** First, calculate [H$_3$O$^+$] using our expression for pH:

$$pH = -\log[H_3O^+]$$
$$[H_3O^+] = 10^{-pH}$$
$$[H_3O^+] = 10^{-10}\,M$$

**Step 2.** To calculate the [OH$^-$], we need to solve for [OH$^-$] by using the following expression:

$$K_w = [H_3O^+][OH^-] = 1.0 \times 10^{-14}$$
$$[OH^-] = \frac{1.0 \times 10^{-14}}{[H_3O^+]}$$

**Step 3.** Substituting the [H$_3$O$^+$] from the first step, we have

$$[OH^-] = \frac{1.0 \times 10^{-14}}{1.0 \times 10^{-10}}$$
$$= 1.0 \times 10^{-4}\,M$$

**Practice Problem 8.5**

Calculate the $[H_3O^+]$ and $[OH^-]$ of a potassium hydroxide solution with a pH = 8.00.

► For Further Practice: **Questions 8.55 and 8.56.**

---

**EXAMPLE 8.6** | **Calculating pH with Noninteger Numbers**

LEARNING GOAL

**4** Calculate pH from concentration data.

Calculate the pH of a sample of lake water that has a $[H_3O^+] = 6.5 \times 10^{-5}\,M$.

**Solution**

**Step 1.** Use the expression for pH:

$$pH = -\log[H_3O^+]$$

**Step 2.** Substituting

$$pH = -\log[6.5 \times 10^{-5}]$$
$$= 4.19$$

Note: The pH, 4.19, is low enough to suspect acid rain. (See Green Chemistry: Acid Rain in this chapter.)

**Practice Problem 8.6**

Calculate the pH of a sample of blood that has a $[H_3O^+] = 3.3 \times 10^{-8}\,M$.

► For Further Practice: **Questions 8.67 and 8.68.**

---

**EXAMPLE 8.7** | **Calculating $[H_3O^+]$ from pH**

LEARNING GOAL

**5** Calculate hydronium and/or hydroxide ion concentration from pH data.

The measured pH of a sample of lake water is 6.40. Calculate $[H_3O^+]$.

**Solution**

**Step 1.** An alternative mathematical form of

$$pH = -\log[H_3O^+]$$

is the expression

$$[H_3O^+] = 10^{-pH}$$

**Step 2.** We can use this expression to solve for $[H_3O^+]$.

$$[H_3O^+] = 10^{-6.40}$$

**Step 3.** Performing the calculation on your calculator results in $3.98 \times 10^{-7}$ or $4.0 \times 10^{-7}\,M = [H_3O^+]$.

**Practice Problem 8.7**

   a. Calculate the $[H_3O^+]$ corresponding to pH = 8.50.
   b. Calculate the $[H_3O^+]$ corresponding to pH = 4.50.

► For Further Practice: **Questions 8.63 and 8.64.**

# A MEDICAL PERSPECTIVE

## Drug Delivery

When a doctor prescribes medicine to treat a disease or relieve its symptoms, the medication may be administered in a variety of ways. Drugs may be taken orally, injected into a muscle or a vein, or absorbed through the skin. Specific instructions are often provided to regulate the particular combination of drugs that can or cannot be taken. The diet, both before and during the drug therapy, may be of special importance.

To appreciate why drugs are administered in a specific way, it is necessary to understand a few basic facts about medications and how they interact with the body.

Drugs function by undergoing one or more chemical reactions in the body. Few compounds react in only one way, to produce a limited set of products, even in the simple environment of a beaker or flask. Imagine the number of possible reactions that a drug can undergo in a complex chemical factory like the human body. In many cases a drug can react in a variety of ways other than its intended path. These alternative paths are side reactions, sometimes producing *side effects* such as nausea, vomiting, insomnia, or drowsiness. Side effects may be unpleasant and may actually interfere with the primary function of the drug.

The development of safe, effective medication, with minimal side effects, is a slow and painstaking process, and determining the best drug delivery system is a critical step. For example, a drug that undergoes an unwanted side reaction in an acidic solution would not be very effective if administered orally. The acidic digestive fluids in the stomach could prevent the drug from even reaching the intended organ, let alone retaining its potency. The drug could be administered through a vein into the blood; blood is not acidic, in contrast to digestive fluids. In this way the drug may be delivered intact to the intended site in the body, where it is free to undergo its primary reaction.

Drug delivery has become a science in its own right. Pharmacology, the study of drugs and their uses in the treatment of disease, has a goal of creating drugs that are highly selective. In other words, they will undergo only one reaction, the intended reaction. Encapsulation of drugs, enclosing them within larger molecules or collections of molecules, may protect them from unwanted reactions as they are transported to their intended site.

### For Further Understanding

▶ Certain drugs lose potency when consumed with grapefruit juice. Can you propose a possible reason?

▶ Would you expect that the drugs referred to (above) are basic, acidic, or neutral? why?

---

**Question 8.5**   Calculate the $[OH^-]$ of the solution in Example 8.2.

**Question 8.6**   Calculate the $[OH^-]$ of the solution in Example 8.3.

## The Importance of pH and pH Control

Solution pH and pH control play a major role in many facets of our lives. Consider a few examples:

**LEARNING GOAL**

**6**  Provide examples of the importance of pH in chemical and biochemical systems.

*See Green Chemistry: Acid Rain in this chapter.*

- *Agriculture:* Crops grow best in a soil of proper pH. Proper fertilization involves the maintenance of a suitable pH.
- *Physiology:* If the pH of our blood were to shift by one unit, we would die. Many biochemical reactions in living organisms are extremely pH dependent.
- *Industry:* From manufacture of processed foods to the manufacture of automobiles, industrial processes often require rigorous pH control.
- *Municipal services:* Purification of drinking water and treatment of sewage must be carried out at their optimum pH.
- *Acid rain:* Nitric acid and sulfuric acid, resulting largely from the reaction of components of vehicle emissions and electric power generation (nitrogen and sulfur oxides) with water, are carried down by precipitation and enter aquatic systems (lakes and streams), lowering the pH of the water. A less than optimum pH poses serious problems for native fish populations.

In summary, any change that takes place in aqueous solution generally has at least some pH dependence.

## 8.3 Reactions Between Acids and Bases

**7** Describe the meaning and utility of neutralization reactions.

### Neutralization

The reaction of an acid with a base to produce a salt and water is referred to as **neutralization.** In the strictest sense, neutralization requires equal numbers of moles (mol) of $H_3O^+$ and $OH^-$ to produce a neutral solution (no excess acid or base).

Consider the reaction of a solution of hydrochloric acid and sodium hydroxide:

$$\underset{\text{Acid}}{HCl(aq)} + \underset{\text{Base}}{NaOH(aq)} \longrightarrow \underset{\text{Salt}}{NaCl(aq)} + \underset{\text{Water}}{H_2O(l)}$$

Our objective is to make the balanced equation represent the process actually occurring. We recognize that HCl, NaOH, and NaCl are dissociated in solution:

*Equation balancing is discussed in Chapter 4.*

$$H^+(aq) + Cl^-(aq) + Na^+(aq) + OH^-(aq) \longrightarrow Na^+(aq) + Cl^-(aq) + H_2O(l)$$

We also know that $Na^+$ and $Cl^-$ are unchanged in the reaction; they are termed *spectator ions.* If we write only those components that actually change, ignoring the spectator ions, we produce a *net, balanced ionic equation:*

$$H^+(aq) + OH^-(aq) \longrightarrow H_2O(l)$$

If we realize that the $H^+$ occurs in aqueous solution as the hydronium ion, $H_3O^+$, the most correct form of the net, balanced ionic equation is

$$H_3O^+(aq) + OH^-(aq) \longrightarrow 2H_2O(l)$$

**WRITING NET IONIC EQUATIONS**

The equation for any strong acid/strong base neutralization reaction is the same as this equation.

A neutralization reaction may be used to determine the concentration of an unknown acid or base solution. The technique of **titration** involves the addition of measured amounts of a **standard solution** (one whose concentration is known with certainty) to neutralize the second, unknown solution. From the volumes of the two solutions and the concentration of the standard solution, the concentration of the unknown solution may be determined.

**ANIMATIONS**
- The Neutralization Reaction of NaOH and HCl
- Titration of HCl with NaOH

A strategy for carrying out an acid-base titration is summarized in Table 8.1. The calculations involved in an acid-base titration are illustrated in Example 8.8.

---

### TABLE 8.1 Conducting an Acid-Base Titration

1. A known volume, perhaps 25.00 milliliters (mL), of the unknown acid of unknown concentration is measured into a flask using a pipet.

2. An **indicator,** a substance that changes color as the solution reaches a certain pH (Figure 8.5), is added to the unknown solution. We must know, from prior experience, the expected pH at the equivalence point (see step 4). For this titration, phenolphthalein or phenol red would be a logical choice, since the equivalence-point pH is known to be seven.

3. A solution of sodium hydroxide, perhaps 0.1000 M, is carefully added to the unknown solution using a **buret** (Figure 8.6), which is a long glass tube calibrated in mL. A stopcock at the bottom of the buret regulates the amount of liquid dispensed. The standard solution is added until the indicator changes color.

4. At this point, the **equivalence point,** the number of mol of hydroxide ion added is equal to the number of mol of hydronium ion present in the unknown acid. The solution is neutral, with a pH equal to seven.

5. The volume dispensed by the buret, perhaps 35.00 mL, is measured.

6. Using the data from the experiment (volume of the unknown, volume of the titrant, and molarity of the titrant), calculate the molar concentration of the unknown substance.

Phenol red is yellow in acid solution and turns red after all acid is neutralized. Phenolphthalein is colorless in acid solution and turns pink after all acid is neutralized. Phenolphthalein is the indicator of choice because it is easier to discern a change of colorless to a color, rather than one color to another.

**Figure 8.5** The relationship between pH and color of a variety of compounds, some of which are commonly used as acid-base indicators. Many indicators are naturally occurring substances.

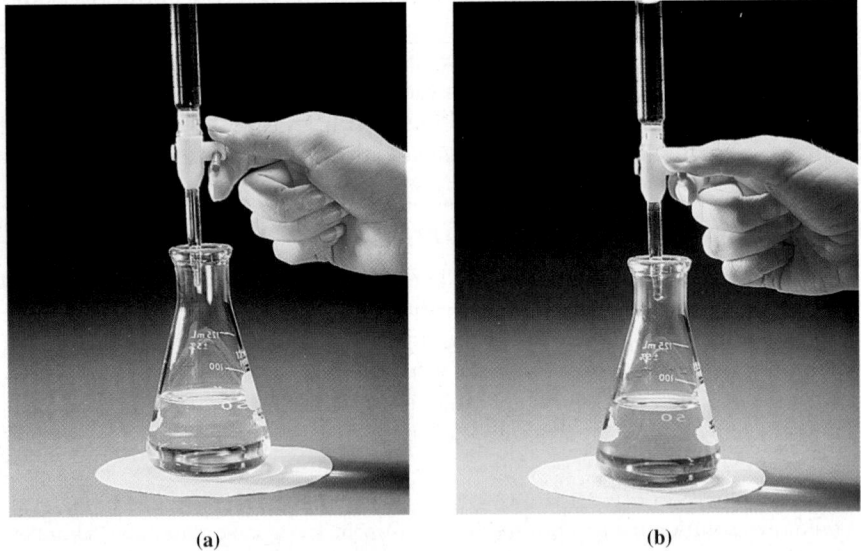

**Figure 8.6** An acid-base titration. (a) An exact volume of a standard solution (in this example, a base) is added to a solution of unknown concentration (in this example, an acid). (b) From the volume (read from the buret) and concentration of the standard solution, coupled with the mass or volume of the unknown, the concentration of the unknown may be calculated.

**Step 4.** Substituting the values given in the problem

$$[H_3O^+] = \frac{[1.0 \times 10^{-1}]1.8 \times 10^{-5}}{[1.0 \times 10^{-1}]}$$

$$[H_3O^+] = 1.8 \times 10^{-5}$$

**Step 5.** Now we can substitute in our expression for pH:

$$pH = -\log[H_3O^+]$$
$$pH = -\log 1.8 \times 10^{-5}$$
$$= 4.74$$

The pH of the buffer solution is 4.74.

### Practice Problem 8.9

A buffer solution is prepared in such a way that the concentrations of propanoic acid and sodium propanoate are each $2.00 \times 10^{-1}$ M. If the buffer equilibrium is described by

$$\underset{\text{Propanoic acid}}{C_2H_5COOH(aq)} + H_2O(l) \rightleftharpoons H_3O^+(aq) + \underset{\text{Propanoate anion}}{C_2H_5COO^-(aq)}$$

with $K_a = 1.34 \times 10^{-5}$, calculate the pH of the solution.

▶ For Further Practice: **Questions 8.87 and 8.88.**

---

**EXAMPLE 8.10**   **Calculating the pH of a Buffer Solution**

LEARNING GOAL

**8** Describe the applications of buffers to chemical and biochemical systems, particularly blood chemistry.

Calculate the pH of a buffer solution similar to that described in Example 8.9 except that the acid concentration is doubled, while the salt concentration remains the same.

**Solution**

**Step 1.** Acetic acid is the acid; [acid] = $2.0 \times 10^{-1}$ M (remember, the acid concentration is twice that of Example 8.9; $2 \times [1.0 \times 10^{-1}] = 2.0 \times 10^{-1}$ M

Sodium acetate is the salt, furnishing the conjugate base; [conjugate base] = $1.0 \times 10^{-1}$ M

**Step 2.** The equilibrium is

$$\underset{\text{acid}}{CH_3COOH(aq)} + H_2O(l) \rightleftharpoons H_3O^+(aq) + \underset{\text{conjugate base}}{CH_3COO^-(aq)}$$

**Step 3.** The hydronium ion concentration is expressed as,

$$[H_3O^+] = \frac{[acid]K_a}{[conjugate\ base]}$$

**Step 4.** Substituting the values given in the problem

$$[H_3O^+] = \frac{[2.0 \times 10^{-1}]1.8 \times 10^{-5}}{[1.00 \times 10^{-1}]}$$

$$[H_3O^+] = 3.60 \times 10^{-5}$$

**Step 5.** Now we can substitute in our expression for pH:

$$pH = -\log [H_3O^+]$$
$$pH = -\log 3.60 \times 10^{-5}$$
$$= 4.44$$

The pH of the buffer solution is **4.44.**

---

### Practice Problem 8.10

Calculate the pH of the buffer solution in Practice Problem 8.9 if the concentration of the sodium propanoate were doubled while the acid concentration remained the same.

▶ For Further Practice: **Questions 8.91 and 8.92.**

---

A comparison of the two solutions described in Examples 8.9 and 8.10 demonstrates a buffer solution's most significant attribute: the ability to stabilize pH. Although the acid concentration of these solutions differs by a factor of two, the difference in their pH is only 0.30 units.

## The Henderson-Hasselbalch Equation

The solution of the equilibrium constant expression and the pH are sometimes combined into one operation. The combined expression is termed the **Henderson-Hasselbalch equation.**

For the acetic acid/sodium acetate buffer system,

$$CH_3COOH(aq) + H_2O(l) \rightleftharpoons H_3O^+(aq) + CH_3COO^-(aq)$$

$$K_a = \frac{[H_3O^+][CH_3COO^-]}{[CH_3COOH]}$$

Taking the $-\log$ of both sides of the equation:

$$-\log K_a = -\log [H_3O^+] - \log \frac{[CH_3COO^-]}{[CH_3COOH]}$$

$$pK_a = pH - \log \frac{[CH_3COO^-]}{[CH_3COOH]}$$

pK_a = −log K_a, analogous to
pH = −log[H_3O^+].

the Henderson-Hasselbalch expression is:

$$pH = pK_a + \log \frac{[CH_3COO^-]}{[CH_3COOH]}$$

The form of this equation is especially amenable to buffer problem calculations. In this expression, $[CH_3COOH]$ represents the molar concentration of the weak acid and $[CH_3COO^-]$ is the molar concentration of the conjugate base of the weak acid. The generalized expression is:

$$pH = pK_a + \log \frac{[\text{conjugate base}]}{[\text{weak acid}]}$$

Substituting concentrations along with the value for the $pK_a$ of the acid allows the calculation of the pH of the buffer solution in problems such as those shown in Examples 8.9 and 8.10.

**Question 8.7** Solve the problem illustrated in Example 8.9 using the Henderson-Hasselbalch equation.

**Question 8.8** Solve the problem illustrated in Example 8.10 using the Henderson-Hasselbalch equation.

**Question 8.9** Solve Practice Problem 8.9 using the Henderson-Hasselbalch equation.

**Question 8.10** Solve Practice Problem 8.10 using the Henderson-Hasselbalch equation.

## Control of Blood pH

A pH of 7.4 is maintained in blood partly by a carbonic acid–bicarbonate buffer system based on the following equilibrium:

$$H_2CO_3(aq) + H_2O(l) \rightleftharpoons H_3O^+(aq) + HCO_3^-(aq)$$

Carbonic acid          Bicarbonate ion
(weak acid)           (salt)

The regulation process based on LeChatelier's principle is similar to the acetic acid–sodium acetate buffer, which we have already discussed.

Red blood cells transport $O_2$, bound to hemoglobin, to the cells of body tissue. The metabolic waste product, $CO_2$, is picked up by the blood and delivered to the lungs.

The $CO_2$ in the blood also participates in the carbonic acid–bicarbonate buffer equilibrium. Carbon dioxide reacts with water in the blood to form carbonic acid:

$$CO_2(aq) + H_2O(l) \rightleftharpoons H_2CO_3(aq)$$

As a result, the buffer equilibrium becomes more complex:

$$CO_2(aq) + 2H_2O(l) \rightleftharpoons H_2CO_3(aq) + H_2O(l) \rightleftharpoons H_3O^+(aq) + HCO_3^-(aq)$$

Through this sequence of relationships the concentration of $CO_2$ in the blood affects the blood pH.

Higher than normal $CO_2$ concentrations shift the above equilibrium to the right (LeChatelier's principle), increasing $[H_3O^+]$ and lowering the pH. The blood becomes too acidic, leading to numerous medical problems. A situation of high blood $CO_2$ levels and low pH is termed *acidosis*. Respiratory acidosis results from various diseases (emphysema, pneumonia) that restrict the breathing process, causing the buildup of waste $CO_2$ in the blood.

Lower than normal $CO_2$ levels, on the other hand, shift the equilibrium to the left, decreasing $[H_3O^+]$ and making the pH more basic. This condition is termed *alkalosis* (from "alkali," implying basic). Hyperventilation, or rapid breathing, is a common cause of respiratory alkalosis.

**Question 8.11** Explain how the molar concentration of $H_2CO_3$ in the blood would change if the partial pressure of $CO_2$ in the lungs were to increase.

**Question 8.12** Explain how the molar concentration of $H_2CO_3$ in the blood would change if the partial pressure of $CO_2$ in the lungs were to decrease.

**Question 8.13** Explain how the molar concentration of hydronium ion in the blood would change under each of the conditions described in Questions 8.11 and 8.12.

**Question 8.14** Explain how the pH of blood would change under each of the conditions described in Questions 8.11 and 8.12.

**Question 8.15** Write the Henderson-Hasselbalch expression for the equilibrium between carbonic acid and the bicarbonate ion.

**Question 8.16** Calculate the $[HCO_3^-]/[H_2CO_3]$ that corresponds to a pH of 7.4. The $K_a$ for carbonic acid is $4.2 \times 10^{-7}$.

**LEARNING GOAL**

**8** Describe the applications of buffers to chemical and biochemical systems, particularly blood chemistry.

**ANIMATION**
• Oxidation-Reduction
  Reactions

**LEARNING GOAL**

**9** Explain the meaning of the terms
*oxidation* and *reduction*, and describe
some practical examples of redox
processes.

Oxidation-reduction reactions are often
termed *redox reactions*.

Oxidation cannot occur without reduction,
and vice versa. The reducing agent becomes
oxidized and the oxidizing agent becomes
reduced.

## 8.5   Oxidation-Reduction Processes

Oxidation-reduction processes are responsible for many types of chemical change. Corrosion, the operation of a battery, and biochemical energy-harvesting reactions are a few examples. In this section we explore the basic concepts underlying this class of chemical reactions.

### Oxidation and Reduction

**Oxidation** is defined as a loss of electrons, loss of hydrogen atoms, or gain of oxygen atoms.

*Magnesium metal,* is, for example, oxidized to a *magnesium ion,* losing two electrons when it reacts with a nonmetal such as chlorine:

$$Mg \longrightarrow Mg^{2+} + 2e^{-}$$

**Reduction** is defined as a gain of electrons, gain of hydrogen atoms, or loss of oxygen atoms.

*Diatomic chlorine* is reduced to *chloride ions* by gaining electrons when it reacts with a metal such as magnesium:

$$Cl_2 + 2e^{-} \longrightarrow 2Cl^{-}$$

Oxidation and reduction are complementary processes. The *oxidation half-reaction* produces electrons that are the reactants for the *reduction half-reaction.* The combination of two half-reactions, one oxidation and one reduction, produces the complete reaction:

Oxidation half-reaction:   $Mg \longrightarrow Mg^{2+} + 2e^{-}$

Reduction half-reaction:   $Cl_2 + 2e^{-} \longrightarrow 2Cl^{-}$

Complete reaction:   $Mg + Cl_2 \longrightarrow Mg^{2+} + 2Cl^{-}$

Half-reactions, one oxidation and one reduction, are exactly that: one-half of a complete reaction. The two half-reactions combine to produce the complete reaction. Note that the electrons cancel: in the electron transfer process, no free electrons remain.

In the preceding reaction, magnesium metal is the **reducing agent.** It releases electrons for the reduction of chlorine. Chlorine is the **oxidizing agent.** It accepts electrons from the magnesium, which is oxidized.

The characteristics of oxidizing and reducing agents may be summarized as follows:

| **Oxidizing Agent** | **Reducing Agent** |
|---|---|
| • Is reduced | • Is oxidized |
| • Gains electrons | • Loses electrons |
| • Causes oxidation | • Causes reduction |

**Question 8.17**   Write the oxidation half-reaction, the reduction half-reaction, and the complete reaction for the formation of calcium sulfide from the elements Ca and S.

**Question 8.18**   Write the oxidation half-reaction, the reduction half-reaction, and the complete reaction for the formation of calcium iodide from calcium metal and $I_2$. Remember, the electron gain *must* equal the electron loss.

**Question 8.19**   Identify the oxidizing agent, reducing agent, substance oxidized, and substance reduced in the reaction described in Question 8.17.

**Question 8.20**   Identify the oxidizing agent, reducing agent, substance oxidized, and substance reduced in the reaction described in Question 8.18.

# A MEDICAL PERSPECTIVE

## Oxidizing Agents for Chemical Control of Microbes

Before the twentieth century, hospitals were not particularly sanitary establishments. Refuse, including human waste, was disposed of on hospital grounds. Because many hospitals had no running water, physicians often cleaned their hands and instruments by wiping them on their lab coats and then proceeded to treat the next patient! As you can imagine, many patients died of infections in hospitals.

By the late nineteenth century a few physicians and microbiologists had begun to realize that infectious diseases are transmitted by microbes, including bacteria and viruses. To decrease the number of hospital-acquired infections, physicians like Joseph Lister and Ignatz Semmelweis experimented with chemicals and procedures that were designed to eliminate pathogens from environmental surfaces and from wounds.

Many common disinfectants and antiseptics are oxidizing agents. A disinfectant is a substance that is used to kill or inhibit the growth of pathogens, disease-causing microorganisms, on environmental surfaces. An antiseptic is a milder chemical that is used to destroy pathogens associated with living tissue.

Hydrogen peroxide is an effective antiseptic that is commonly used to cleanse cuts and abrasions. We are all familiar with the furious bubbling that occurs as the enzyme catalase from our body cells catalyzes the breakdown of $H_2O_2$:

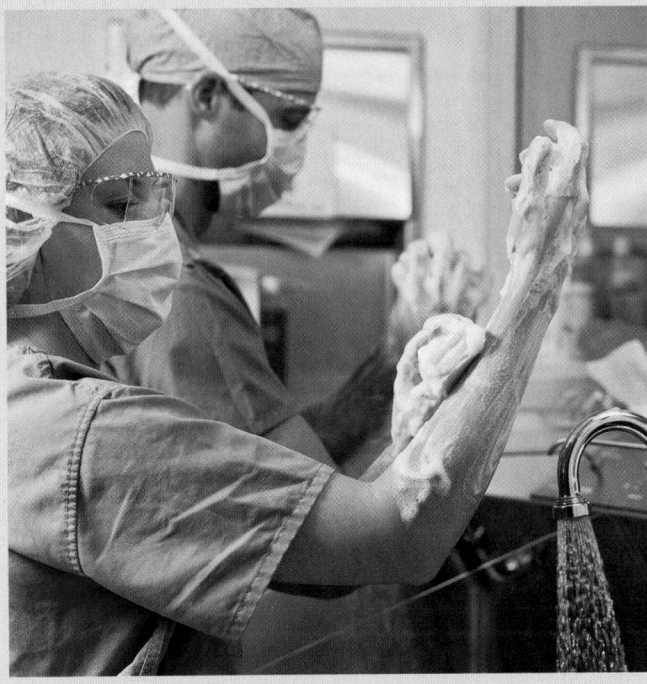

$$2H_2O_2(aq) \longrightarrow 2H_2O(l) + O_2(g)$$

A highly reactive and deadly form of oxygen, the superoxide radical ($O_2^-$), is produced during this reaction. This superoxide inactivates proteins, especially critical enzyme systems.

At higher concentrations (3–6%), $H_2O_2$ is used as a disinfectant. It is particularly useful for disinfection of soft contact lenses, utensils, and surgical implants because there is no residual toxicity. Concentrations of 6–25% are even used for complete sterilization of environmental surfaces.

Benzoyl peroxide is another powerful oxidizing agent. Ointments containing 5–10% benzoyl peroxide have been used as antibacterial agents to treat acne. The compound is currently found in over-the-counter facial scrubs because it is also an exfoliant, causing sloughing of old skin and replacement with smoother-looking skin. A word of caution is in order: in sensitive individuals, benzoyl peroxide can cause swelling and blistering of tender facial skin.

Chlorine is a very widely used disinfectant and antiseptic. Calcium hypochlorite [Ca(OCl)$_2$] was first used in hospital maternity wards in 1847 by the pioneering Hungarian physician Ignatz Semmelweis. Semmelweis insisted that hospital workers cleanse their hands in a Ca(OCl)$_2$ solution and dramatically reduced the incidence of infection. Today, calcium hypochlorite is more commonly used to disinfect bedding, clothing, restaurant eating utensils, slaughterhouses, barns, and dairies.

Sodium hypochlorite (NaOCl), sold as Clorox, is used as a household disinfectant and deodorant but is also used to disinfect swimming pools, dairies, food-processing equipment, and kidney dialysis units. It can be used to treat drinking water of questionable quality. Addition of 1/2 teaspoon (tsp) of household bleach (5.25% NaOCl) to 2 gallons (gal) of clear water renders it drinkable after 1/2 hour (h). The Centers for Disease Control even recommend a 1:10 dilution of bleach as an effective disinfectant against human immunodeficiency virus, the virus that causes acquired immune deficiency syndrome (AIDS).

Chlorine gas (Cl$_2$) is used to disinfect swimming pool water, sewage, and municipal water supplies. This treatment has successfully eliminated epidemics of waterborne diseases. However, chlorine is inactivated in the presence of some organic materials and, in some cases, may form toxic chlorinated organic compounds. For these reasons, many cities are considering the use of ozone (O$_3$) rather than chlorine.

Ozone is produced from O$_2$ by high-voltage electrical discharges. (That fresh smell in the air after an electrical storm is ozone.) Several European cities use ozone to disinfect drinking water. It is a more effective killing agent than chlorine, especially with some viruses: less ozone is required for disinfection; there is no unpleasant residual odor or flavor; and there appear to be fewer toxic by-products. However, ozone is more expensive than chlorine, and maintaining the required concentration in the water is more difficult. Nonetheless, the benefits seem to outweigh the drawbacks, and U.S. cities will continue to follow the example of European cities and convert to the use of ozone for water treatment.

### For Further Understanding

▶ Describe the difference between the terms *disinfectant* and *antiseptic*.

▶ Explain why hydrogen peroxide, at higher concentration, is used as a disinfectant, whereas lower concentrations are used as antiseptics.

Oxidation-reduction processes are more difficult to identify using half-reactions when covalent compounds are involved. For example, consider the reaction of methane with oxygen, discussed in Chapter 4:

$$CH_4(g) + 2O_2(g) \longrightarrow CO_2(g) + 2H_2O(g)$$

Our definitions of oxidation and reduction make it clear that this is an oxidation-reduction reaction. Carbon has lost hydrogen and gained oxygen, becoming $CO_2$ (our definition of oxidation). Oxygen has gained hydrogen, becoming water (the gain of hydrogen indicates reduction).

Consider the reaction of aluminum with atmospheric oxygen:

$$4Al(s) + 3O_2(g) \longrightarrow 2Al_2O_3(s)$$

It is evident that aluminum has been oxidized because it gains oxygen atoms.

## Applications of Oxidation and Reduction

Oxidation-reduction processes are important in many areas as diverse as industrial manufacturing and biochemical processes.

### Corrosion

The deterioration of metals caused by an oxidation-reduction process is termed **corrosion.** Metal atoms are converted to metal ions; the structure, hence the properties, changes dramatically, and usually for the worse.

Millions of dollars are spent annually in an attempt to remedy damage resulting from corrosion. A current area of chemical research is concerned with the development of corrosion-inhibiting processes. In one type of corrosion, elemental iron is oxidized to iron(III) oxide (rust):

$$4Fe(s) + 3O_2(g) \longrightarrow 2Fe_2O_3(s)$$

(a)                                    (b)                                    (c)

The rust (an oxide of iron) that diminishes structural strength and ruins the appearance of (a) automobiles, (b) bridges, and (c) other iron-based objects is a product of a common oxidation-reduction reaction. Can you provide examples of other electron-transfer processes that produce changes in properties?

### Combustion of Fossil Fuels

Burning fossil fuel is an extremely exothermic process. Energy is released to heat our homes, offices, and classrooms. The simplest fossil fuel is methane, $CH_4$, and its oxidation reaction is written:

$$CH_4(g) + 2O_2(g) \longrightarrow CO_2(g) + 2H_2O(g)$$

Methane is a hydrocarbon. The complete oxidation of any hydrocarbon (including those in gasoline, heating oil, liquid propane, and so forth) produces

---

Aluminum is strong and its low density makes it ideal for the wings and cabin exterior of airplanes. Aluminum oxide forms on the metal surface and this oxide coating protects the metal from further reaction.

---

LEARNING GOAL

**9** Explain the meaning of the terms *oxidation* and *reduction*, and describe some practical examples of redox processes.

---

At the same time that iron is oxidized, $O_2$ is being reduced to $O^{2-}$ and is incorporated into the structure of iron(III) oxide. Electrons lost by iron reduce oxygen. This again shows that oxidation and reduction processes go hand in hand.

---

See Green Chemistry: The Greenhouse Effect and Global Climate Change in Chapter 5.

carbon dioxide and water. The energy released by these reactions is of paramount importance. The water and carbon dioxide are viewed as waste products, and the carbon dioxide contributes to the greenhouse effect.

## Bleaching

Bleaching agents are most often oxidizing agents. Sodium hypochlorite (NaOCl) is the active ingredient in a variety of laundry products. It is an effective oxidizing agent. Products containing NaOCl are advertised for their stain-removing capabilities.

Stains are a result of colored compounds adhering to surfaces. Oxidation of these compounds produces products that are not colored or compounds that are subsequently easily removed from the surface, thus removing the stain.

## Biological Processes

### Respiration

There are many examples of biological oxidation-reduction reactions. For example, the electron-transport chain of aerobic respiration involves the reversible oxidation and reduction of iron atoms in cytochrome $c$,

*See Chapters 21 and 22 for the details of these energy-harvesting cellular oxidation-reduction reactions.*

$$\text{cytochrome } c \text{ (Fe}^{3+}) + e^- \longrightarrow \text{cytochrome } c \text{ (Fe}^{2+})$$

The reduced iron ion transfers an electron to an iron ion in another protein, called cytochrome $c$ oxidase, according to the following reaction:

$$\text{cytochrome } c \text{ (Fe}^{2+}) + \text{cytochrome } c \text{ oxidase (Fe}^{3+}) \longrightarrow \text{cytochrome } c \text{ (Fe}^{3+}) + \text{cytochrome } c \text{ oxidase (Fe}^{2+})$$

Cytochrome $c$ oxidase eventually passes four electrons to $O_2$, the final electron acceptor of the chain:

$$O_2 + 4e^- + 4H^+ \longrightarrow 2H_2O$$

### Metabolism

When ethanol is metabolized in the liver, it is oxidized to acetaldehyde (the molecule partially responsible for hangovers). Continued oxidation of acetaldehyde produces acetic acid, which is eventually oxidized to $CO_2$ and $H_2O$. These reactions, summarized as follows, are catalyzed by liver enzymes.

$$\underset{\text{Ethanol}}{CH_3CH_2-OH} \longrightarrow \underset{\text{Acetaldehyde}}{CH_3\overset{\overset{\displaystyle O}{\|}}{C}-H} \longrightarrow \underset{\text{Acetic acid}}{CH_3\overset{\overset{\displaystyle O}{\|}}{C}-OH} \longrightarrow CO_2 + H_2O$$

It is more difficult to recognize these reactions as oxidations because neither the product nor the reactant carries a charge. In previous examples we looked for an increase in positive charge as an indication that an oxidation had occurred. A decrease in positive charge (or increased negative charge) would signify reduction.

Once again our descriptions of oxidation and reduction are useful in identifying these reactions. Recall:

Oxidation is the *gain* of oxygen or *loss* of hydrogen.

Reduction is the *loss* of oxygen or *gain* of hydrogen.

This strategy is most useful for recognizing oxidation and reduction of *organic compounds* and organic compounds of biological interest, *biochemical compounds.*

In our example of the conversion of ethanol to acetaldehyde, ethanol has six hydrogen atoms per molecule; the product acetaldehyde has four hydrogen atoms per molecule. This represents a loss of two hydrogen atoms per molecule. Therefore, ethanol has been oxidized to acetaldehyde. In a subsequent step, the acetaldehyde maybe oxidized to acetic acid.

Acetaldehyde has one oxygen atom per molecule; acetic acid has two. An increase in the number of oxygen atoms per molecule indicates oxidation has occurred. In the process of fermentation of grapes to make wine, the alcohol formed may convert to acetic acid over time, and vinegar, rather than wine, is the result.

Organic compounds and their structures and reactivity are the focus of Chapters 10 through 15, and biochemical compounds are described in Chapters 16 through 23.

## Voltaic Cells

When zinc metal is dipped into a copper(II) sulfate solution, zinc atoms are oxidized to zinc ions and copper(II) ions are reduced to copper metal, which deposits on the surface of the zinc metal (Figure 8.7). This reaction is summarized as follows:

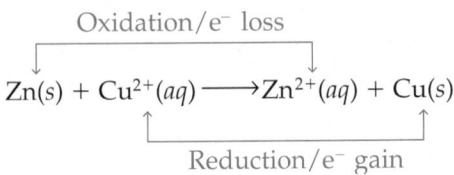

In the reduction of aqueous copper(II) ions by zinc metal, electrons flow from the zinc rod directly to copper(II) ions in the solution. If electron transfer from the zinc rod to the copper ions in solution could be directed through an external electrical circuit, this spontaneous oxidation-reduction reaction could be used to produce an electrical current that could perform some useful function.

However, when zinc metal in one container is connected by a copper wire with a copper(II) sulfate solution in a separate container, no current flows through the wire. A complete, or continuous circuit is necessary for current to flow. To complete the circuit, we connect the two containers with a tube filled with a solution of an electrolyte such as potassium chloride. This tube is described as a *salt bridge*.

Current now flows through the external circuit (Figure 8.8). The device shown in Figure 8.8 is an example of a *voltaic cell*. A **voltaic cell** is an *electrochemical* cell that converts stored *chemical* energy into *electrical* energy.

**LEARNING GOAL**

**10**  Diagram a voltaic cell and describe its function.

**ANIMATIONS**
- The Cu/Zn Voltaic Cell
- Operation of a Voltaic Cell

*Recall that solutions of ionic salts are good conductors of electricity (Chapter 6).*

**Figure 8.7** The spontaneous reaction of zinc metal and $Cu^{2+}$ ions is the basis of the cell depicted in Figure 8.8.

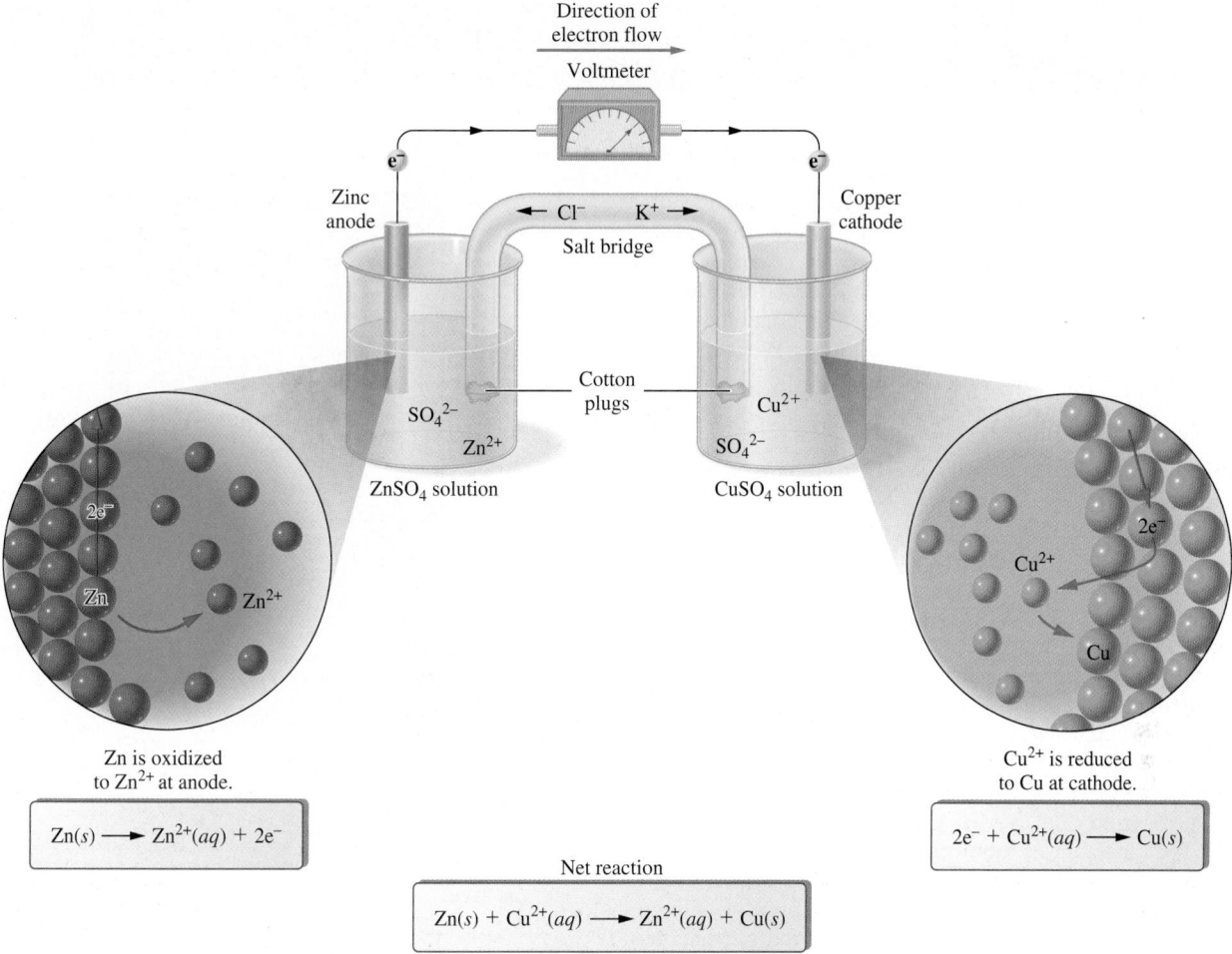

**Figure 8.8**  A voltaic cell generating electrical current by the reaction:

$$Zn(s) + Cu^{2+}(aq) \longrightarrow Zn^{2+}(aq) + Cu(s)$$

Each electrode consists of the pure metal, zinc or copper. Zinc is oxidized, releasing electrons that flow to the copper, reducing $Cu^{2+}$ to Cu. The salt bridge completes the circuit and the voltmeter displays the voltage (or chemical potential) associated with the reaction.

This cell consists of two *half-cells.* The oxidation half-reaction occurs in one half-cell and the reduction half-reaction occurs in the other half-cell. The sum of the two half-cell reactions is the overall oxidation-reduction reaction that describes the cell. The electrode at which oxidation occurs is called the **anode,** and the electrode at which reduction occurs is the **cathode.** In the device shown in Figure 8.8, the zinc metal is the anode. At this electrode the zinc atoms are oxidized to zinc ions:

Anode half-reaction: $Zn(s) \longrightarrow Zn^{2+}(aq) + 2e^-$

Electrons released at the anode travel through the external circuit to the cathode (the copper rod) where they are transferred to copper(II) ions in the solution. Copper(II) ions are reduced to copper atoms that deposit on the copper metal surface, the cathode:

Cathode half-reaction: $Cu^{2+}(aq) + 2e^- \longrightarrow Cu(s)$

The sum of these half-cell reactions is the cell reaction:

$$Zn(s) + Cu^{2+}(aq) \longrightarrow Zn^{2+}(aq) + Cu(s)$$

Voltaic cells are found in many aspects of our lives, as a convenient and reliable source of electrical energy, the battery. Batteries convert stored chemical energy to an

## A MEDICAL PERSPECTIVE

### Electrochemical Reactions in the Statue of Liberty and in Dental Fillings

Throughout history, we have suffered from our ignorance of basic electrochemical principles. For example, during the Middle Ages, our chemistry ancestors (alchemists) placed an iron rod into a blue solution of copper sulfate. They noticed that bright shiny copper plated out onto the iron rod and they thought that they had changed a base metal, iron, into copper. What actually happened was the redox reaction shown in Equation 1.

$$2Fe(s) + 3Cu^{2+}(aq) \longrightarrow 2Fe^{3+}(aq) + 3Cu(s) \qquad (1)$$

This misunderstanding encouraged them to embark on a futile, 1000-year attempt to change base metals into gold.

Over 100 years ago, France presented the United States with the Statue of Liberty. Unfortunately, the French did not anticipate the redox reaction shown in Equation 1 when they mounted the copper skin of the statue on iron support rods. Oxygen in the atmosphere oxidized the copper skin to produce copper ions. Then, because iron is more reactive than copper, the displacement shown in Equation 1 aided the corrosion of the support bars. As a result of this and other reactions, the statue needed refurbishing before we celebrated its one-hundredth anniversary in 1986.

Sometimes dentists also overlook possible redox reactions when placing gold caps over teeth next to teeth with amalgam fillings. The amalgam in tooth fillings is an alloy of mercury, silver, tin, and copper. Because the metals in the amalgam are more reactive than gold, contact between the amalgam fillings and minute numbers of gold ions results in redox reactions such as the following.*

$$3Sn(s) + 2Au^{3+}(aq) \longrightarrow 3Sn^{2+}(aq) + 2Au(s) \qquad (2)$$

As a result, the dental fillings dissolve and the patients are left with a constant metallic taste in their mouths.

These examples show that like our ancestors, we continue to experience unfortunate results because of a lack of understanding of basic electrochemical principles.

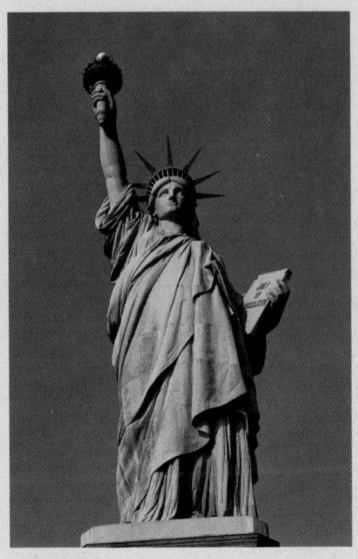

**For Further Understanding**

▶ Label the oxidizing agent, reducing agent, substance oxidized, and substance reduced in each equation in this perspective.

▶ For each equation, state the substance that gains electrons and the substance that loses electrons.

Source: Ronald DeLorenzo, *Journal of Chemical Education*, May 1985, pp. 424–425.

*Equation 2 is oversimplified to illustrate more clearly the basic displacement of gold ions by metallic tin atoms. Actually, only complex ions of gold and tin can exist in aqueous solutions, not the simple cations that are shown.

electrical current to power a wide array of different commercial appliances: radios, cellphones, computers, flashlights, and a host of other useful devices.

Technology has made modern batteries smaller, safer, and more dependable than our crudely constructed copper-zinc voltaic cell. In fact, the silver cell (Figure 8.9) is sufficiently safe and nontoxic that it can be implanted in the human body as a part of a pacemaker circuit that is used to improve heart rhythm.

### Electrolysis

**Electrolysis** reactions use electrical energy to cause nonspontaneous oxidation-reduction reactions to occur. One common application of electrolysis is the rechargeable battery. When it is being used to power a device, such as a laptop computer, it behaves as a voltaic cell. After some time, the chemical reaction approaches completion and the voltaic cell "runs down." The cell reaction is reversible, and the battery is plugged into a battery charger. The charger is really an external source of electrical energy that reverses the chemical reaction in the battery, bringing it back to its original state. The cell has been operated as an

**LEARNING GOAL**

**11** Compare and contrast voltaic and electrolytic cells.

electrolytic cell. Removal of the charging device turns the cell back into a voltaic device, ready to spontaneously react to produce electrical current once again.

Another common example of electrolysis is electroplating. This process is used to cover less expensive and unappealing metal objects with a thin, chemically stable, and (usually) lustrous surface. Chromium (chrome plating) and silver (silver-plated dinnerware) are most common.

The object to be plated (for example, a spoon or fork) is the cathode (negative charge) in an electrolytic cell. The solution surrounding the electrodes contains silver ions ($Ag^+$) that migrate to the negative electrode, undergoing reduction:

$$Ag^+(aq) + e^- \rightarrow Ag(s)$$

The silver metal remains on the surface of the object being plated. The spoon or fork has the appearance of expensive silver at a fraction of the cost.

**Question 8.21**   Chrome plating involves the reduction of $Cr^{3+}(aq)$ at the surface of the electrode to be electroplated.
  a. Must the electrode that is being electroplated have a positive or negative charge? Why?
  b. Is this electrode termed the cathode or the anode?
  c. Write the reduction reaction for $Cr^{3+}(aq)$.

**Question 8.22**   $Cu^{2+}(aq)$ can be reduced in an electrolytic cell to prepare high-purity copper metal.
  a. Does this reduction take place at the positive or negative electrode of the electrolytic cell? Why?
  b. In this electrode termed the cathode or the anode?
  c. Write the reduction reaction for $Cu^{2+}(aq)$.

The relationship between a voltaic cell and an electrolytic cell is illustrated in Figure 8.10.

**Figure 8.9**   A silver battery used in cameras, heart pacemakers, and hearing aids. This battery is small, stable, and nontoxic (hence implantable in the human body).

Electrolytic cells are the reverse of voltaic cells.

(a) Voltaic cell

(b) Electrolytic cell

**Figure 8.10**   (a) A voltaic cell is converted to (b) an electrolytic cell by attaching a battery with a voltage sufficiently large to reverse the reaction. This process underlies commercially available rechargeable batteries.

# CHAPTER MAP

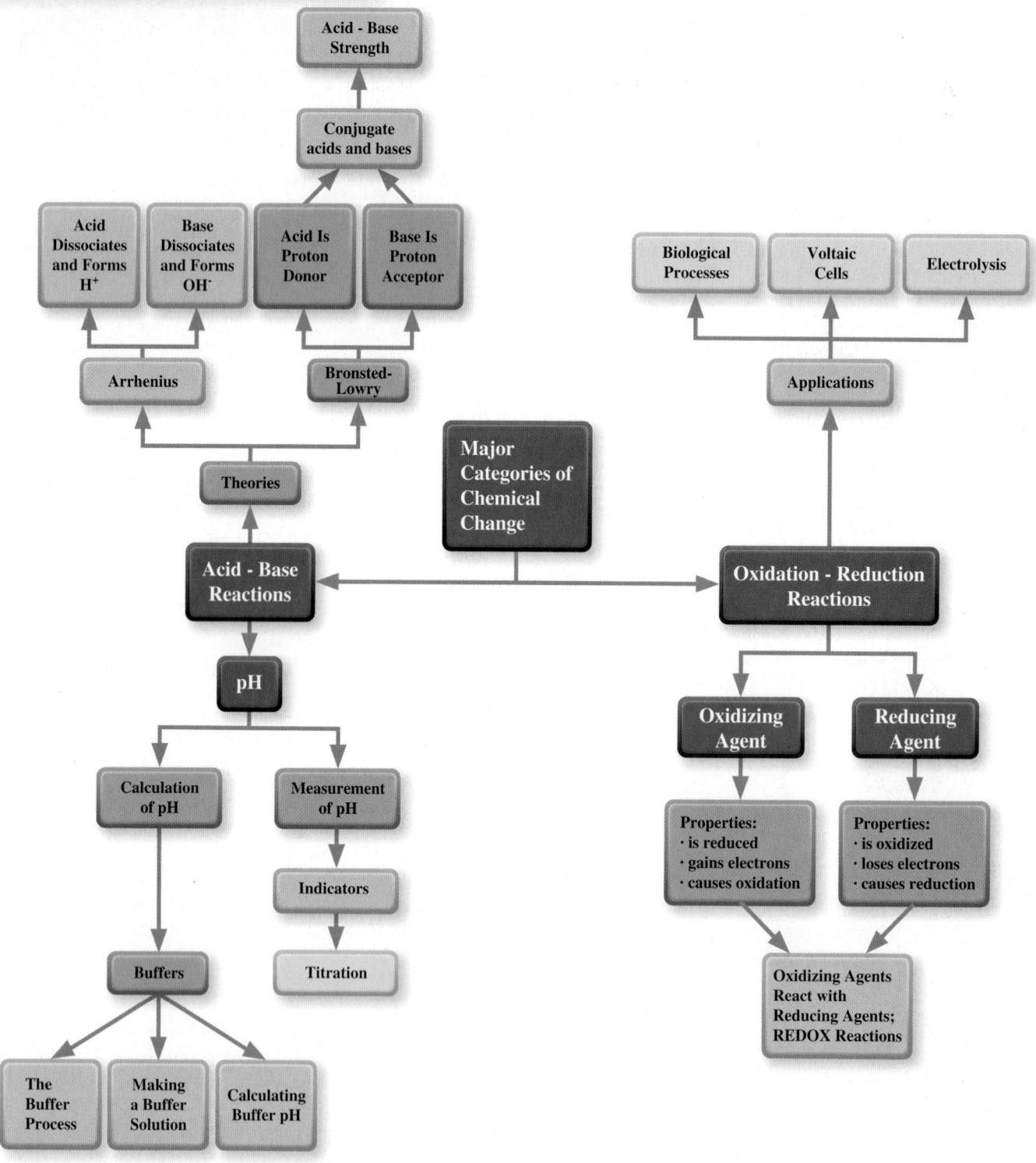

# SUMMARY

## 8.1 Acids and Bases

▶ One of the earliest definitions of acids and bases is the **Arrhenius theory.** According to this theory, an **acid** dissociates to form hydrogen ions, $H^+$, and a **base** dissociates to form hydroxide ions, $OH^-$.

▶ The **Brønsted-Lowry theory** defines an acid as a proton ($H^+$) donor and a base as a proton acceptor.

▶ A **conjugate acid** is the species formed when a base accepts a proton. A **conjugate base** is the species formed when an acid donates a proton. The acid and base on the opposite sides of the equation are collectively termed a **conjugate acid-base pair.**

▶ Water, the solvent in many acid-base reactions, is **amphiprotic.** It has both acid and base properties.

▶ The strength of acids and bases in water depends on their degree of dissociation, the extent to which they react with the solvent, water. Acids and bases are strong when their reaction with water is virtually 100% complete and weak when their reaction with water is much less than 100% complete.

▶ Weak acids and weak bases dissolve in water principally in the molecular form. Only a small percentage of the molecules dissociate to form the **hydronium ion** or **hydroxide ion.**

▶ Aqueous solutions of acids and bases are electrolytes. The dissociation of the acid or base produces ions, which conduct an electrical current. Strong acids and bases are strong electrolytes. Weak acids and bases are weak electrolytes.

▶ Although pure water is virtually 100% molecular, a small number of water molecules do ionize. This process occurs by the transfer of a proton from one water molecule to another, producing a *hydronium ion* and a *hydroxide ion*. This process is the **autoionization,** or self-ionization, of water.

▶ Pure water at room temperature has a hydronium ion concentration of $1.0 \times 10^{-7} M$. One hydroxide ion is produced for each hydronium ion. Therefore, the hydroxide ion concentration is also $1.0 \times 10^{-7} M$. The product of hydronium and hydroxide ion concentration ($1.0 \times 10^{-14}$) is the **ion product for water.**

## 8.2 pH: A Measurement Scale for Acids and Bases

▶ The **pH scale** correlates the hydronium ion concentration with a number, the pH, that serves as a useful indicator of the degree of acidity or basicity of a solution. The pH of a solution is defined as the negative logarithm of the molar concentration of the hydronium ion ($pH = -\log[H_3O^+]$).

## 8.3 Reactions Between Acids and Bases

▶ The reaction of an acid with a base to produce a salt and water is referred to as **neutralization.**

▶ Neutralization requires equal numbers of mol of $H_3O^+$ and $OH^-$ to produce a neutral solution (no excess acid or base).

▶ A neutralization reaction may be used to determine the concentration of an unknown acid or base solution. The technique of **titration** involves the addition of measured amounts of a **standard solution** (one whose concentration is known) from a **buret** to neutralize the second, unknown solution. The **equivalence point** is signaled by an **indicator.** This signal is termed the *end point.*

▶ **Polyprotic substances** donate (as acids) or accept (as bases) more than one proton per formula unit.

## 8.4 Acid-Base Buffers

▶ A **buffer solution** contains components that enable the solution to resist large changes in pH when acids or bases are added.

▶ Buffer action relies on the equilibrium between either a weak acid and its conjugate base or a weak base and its conjugate acid.

▶ A buffer solution follows LeChatelier's principle, which states that an equilibrium system, when stressed, will shift its equilibrium position to alleviate that stress.

▶ Buffering against base is a function of the concentration of the weak acid for an acidic buffer whereas buffering against acid is dependent on the concentration of the anion of the salt.

▶ A buffer solution can be described by an equilibrium constant expression. The equilibrium constant expression for an acidic system can be rearranged and solved for $[H_3O^+]$. In that way, the pH of a buffer solution can be obtained, if the composition of the solution is known. Alternatively, the **Henderson-Hasselbalch equation,** derived from the equilibrium constant expression, may be used to calculate the pH of a buffer solution.

▶ **Buffer capacity** is a measure of the ability of a solution to resist large changes in pH when a strong acid or strong base is added.

## 8.5 Oxidation-Reduction Processes

▶ **Oxidation** is defined as a loss of electrons, loss of hydrogen atoms, or gain of oxygen atoms.

▶ **Reduction** is defined as a gain of electrons, gain of hydrogen atoms, or loss of oxygen atoms.

▶ Oxidation and reduction are complementary processes. The oxidation half-reaction produces an electron that is the reactant for the reduction half-reaction. The combination of two half-reactions, one oxidation and one reduction, produces the complete reaction.

▶ The **reducing agent** releases electrons for the reduction of a second substance to occur. The **oxidizing agent** accepts electrons, causing the oxidation of a second substance to take place.

▶ The deterioration of metals caused by an oxidation-reduction process is termed **corrosion.**

▶ A **voltaic cell** is an electrochemical cell that converts chemical energy into electrical energy. The best-known example of a voltaic cell is the storage battery. **Electrolysis** is the opposite of a battery. It converts electrical energy into chemical potential energy. The electrode at which oxidation occurs is called the **anode,** and the electrode at which reduction occurs is the **cathode.**

## ANSWERS TO PRACTICE PROBLEMS

**8.1  a.** Conjugate base:         $OH^-$    and    $NH_3$
                                     $HSO_4^-$  and    $HSO_3^-$
  Stronger acid of each pair: $NH_4^+$ and $H_2SO_4$

   **b.** Conjugate acid:          $HCO_3^-$   and    $HPO_4^{2-}$
                                    $H_2CO_3$   and    $H_2PO_4^-$
  Stronger base of each pair: $PO_4^{3-}$ and $HPO_4^{2-}$

**8.2  pH = 4.00**

**8.3  $[H_3O^+] = 1.0 \times 10^{-5} M$**

**8.4  a.** pH = 12.00       **b.** pH = 8.00

**8.5  $[H_3O^+] = 1.0 \times 10^{-8} M$**
      $[OH^-] = 1.0 \times 10^{-6} M$

**8.6  pH = 7.48**

**8.7  a.** $[H_3O^+] = 3.2 \times 10^{-9} M$     **b.** $[H_3O^+] = 3.2 \times 10^{-5} M$

**8.8  a.** 0.1000 M NaOH    **b.** 0.1389 M

**8.9  pH = 4.87**

**8.10  pH = 5.17**

## QUESTIONS AND PROBLEMS

### Acids and Bases
#### Foundations

**8.23  a.** Define an acid according to the Arrhenius theory.
     **b.** Define an acid according to the Brønsted-Lowry theory.
**8.24  a.** Define a base according to the Arrhenius theory.
     **b.** Define a base according to the Brønsted-Lowry theory.
**8.25**  What are the essential differences between the Arrhenius and Brønsted-Lowry theories?
**8.26**  Why is ammonia described as a Brønsted-Lowry base and not an Arrhenius base?

#### Applications

**8.27**  Write an equation for the reaction of each of the following with water:
     **a.** $HNO_2$        **b.** HCN
**8.28**  Write an equation for the reaction of each of the following with water:
     **a.** $HNO_3$        **b.** HCOOH
**8.29  a.** Write the conjugate acid of $NO_3^-$.
     **b.** Which is the stronger base, $NO_3^-$ or $CN^-$?
     **c.** Which is the stronger acid, $HNO_3$ or HCN?
**8.30  a.** Write the conjugate acid of $F^-$.
     **b.** Which is the stronger base, $F^-$ or $CH_3COO^-$?
     **c.** Which is the stronger acid, HF or $CH_3COOH$?

**8.31**  Label each of the following as a strong or weak acid (consult Figure 8.2, if necessary):
     **a.** $H_2SO_3$     **b.** $H_2CO_3$     **c.** $H_3PO_4$
**8.32**  Label each of the following as a strong or weak base (consult Figure 8.2, if necessary):
     **a.** KOH        **b.** $CN^-$       **c.** $SO_4^{2-}$
**8.33**  Identify the conjugate acid-base pairs in each of the following chemical equations:
     **a.** $NH_4^+(aq) + CN^-(aq) \rightleftharpoons NH_3(aq) + HCN(aq)$
     **b.** $CO_3^{2-}(aq) + HCl(aq) \rightleftharpoons HCO_3^-(aq) + Cl^-(aq)$
**8.34**  Identify the conjugate acid-base pairs in each of the following chemical equations:
     **a.** $HCOOH(aq) + NH_3(aq) \rightleftharpoons HCOO^-(aq) + NH_4^+(aq)$
     **b.** $HCl(aq) + OH^-(aq) \rightleftharpoons H_2O(l) + Cl^-(aq)$
**8.35**  Distinguish between the terms acid-base *strength* and acid-base *concentration*.
**8.36**  Of the following diagrams, which one represents:
     **a.** a concentrated strong acid   **b.** a dilute strong acid
     **c.** a concentrated weak acid     **d.** a dilute weak acid

I

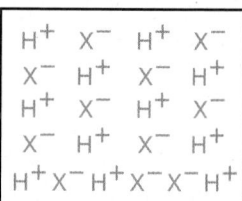

II

III                            IV

**8.37**  Classify each of the following as a Brønsted acid, Brønsted base, or both:
     **a.** $H_3O^+$      **b.** $OH^-$      **c.** $H_2O$
**8.38**  Classify each of the following as a Brønsted acid, Brønsted base, or both:
     **a.** $NH_4^+$      **b.** $NH_3$
**8.39**  Classify each of the following as a Brønsted acid, Brønsted base, or both:
     **a.** $H_2CO_3$     **b.** $HCO_3^-$     **c.** $CO_3^{2-}$
**8.40**  Classify each of the following as a Brønsted acid, Brønsted base, or both:
     **a.** $H_2SO_4$     **b.** $HSO_4^-$     **c.** $SO_4^{2-}$
**8.41**  Write the formula of the conjugate acid of $CN^-$.
**8.42**  Write the formula of the conjugate acid of $Br^-$.
**8.43**  Write the formula of the conjugate base of HI.
**8.44**  Write the formula of the conjugate base of HCOOH.

### pH: A Measurement Scale for Acids and Bases
#### Foundations

**8.45**  Calculate the $[H_3O^+]$ of an aqueous solution that is:
     **a.** $1.0 \times 10^{-7} M$ in $OH^-$     **b.** $1.0 \times 10^{-3} M$ in $OH^-$

Carbon-12 has six protons and six neutrons

Carbon-13 has six protons and seven neutrons

Carbon-14 has six protons and eight neutrons

**Figure 9.1** Three isotopes of carbon. Each nucleus contains the same number of protons. Only the number of neutrons is different; hence, each isotope has a different mass.

to distinguish between the terms *isotope* and *nuclide*. The term *isotope* refers to any atoms that have the same atomic number but different mass numbers. The term **nuclide** refers to any atom characterized by an atomic number and a mass number.

Many elements in the periodic table occur in nature as mixtures of isotopes. Two common examples include carbon (Figure 9.1),

$$^{12}_{6}\text{C} \qquad ^{13}_{6}\text{C} \qquad ^{14}_{6}\text{C}$$

Carbon-12 Carbon-13 Carbon-14

Carbon has three isotopes, three distinct nuclides, C-12, C-13, and C-14.

and hydrogen,

$$^{1}_{1}\text{H} \qquad ^{2}_{1}\text{H} \qquad ^{3}_{1}\text{H}$$

| Hydrogen-1 | Hydrogen-2 | Hydrogen-3 |
| Protium | Deuterium | Tritium |
| | (symbol D) | (symbol T) |

Hydrogen has three isotopes, three distinct nuclides, H-1, H-2, and H-3.

Protium is a stable isotope and makes up more than 99.9% of naturally occurring hydrogen. Deuterium (D) can be isolated from hydrogen; it can form compounds such as "heavy water," $D_2O$. Heavy water is a potential source of deuterium for fusion processes. Tritium (T) is rare and unstable, hence radioactive.

In writing the symbols for a nuclear process, it is essential to indicate the particular isotope involved. This is why the mass number and atomic number are used. These values tell us the number of neutrons in the species, hence the isotope's identity.

Natural radiation emitted by unstable nuclei includes *alpha particles, beta particles, positrons,* and *gamma rays.*

Other radiation particles, such as neutrinos and deuterons, will not be discussed here.

## Alpha Particles

An **alpha particle** (α) contains two protons and two neutrons. An alpha particle is identical to the nucleus of the helium atom (He) or a *helium ion* ($\text{He}^{2+}$), which also contains two protons (atomic number = 2) and two neutrons (mass number − atomic number = 2). Having no electrons to counterbalance the nuclear charge, the alpha particle may be symbolized as

$$^{4}_{2}\text{He}^{2+} \quad \text{or} \quad ^{4}_{2}\text{He} \quad \text{or} \quad \alpha$$

Alpha particles have a relatively large mass compared to other nuclear particles. Consequently, alpha particles emitted by radioisotopes are relatively slow-moving particles (approximately 10% of the speed of light), and they are stopped by barriers as thin as a few pages of this book.

## Beta Particles and Positrons

The **beta particle** (β), in contrast, is a fast-moving electron traveling at approximately 90% of the speed of light as it leaves the nucleus. It is formed in the

**LEARNING GOAL**

**1** Enumerate characteristics of alpha, beta, positron, and gamma radiation.

**ANIMATION**
• The Types of Radioactive Decay

nucleus by the conversion of a neutron into a proton. The beta particle is represented as

$$_{-1}^{0}e \quad \text{or} \quad _{-1}^{0}\beta \quad \text{or} \quad \beta$$

The subscript $-1$ is written in the same position as the atomic number and, like the atomic number (number of protons), indicates the charge of the particle.

Beta particles are smaller and faster than alpha particles. They are more penetrating and are stopped only by more dense materials such as wood, metal, or several layers of clothing.

A *positron* has the same mass as a beta particle but carries a positive charge and is symbolized as $_{+1}^{0}e$ or $_{+1}^{0}\beta$. Positrons are produced by the conversion of a proton to a neutron in the nucleus of the isotope. The proton, in effect, loses its positive charge as well as a tiny bit of mass. This positively charged mass that is released is the positron.

## Gamma Rays

**Gamma rays** ($\gamma$) are the most energetic part of the electromagnetic spectrum (see Section 2.3), and result from nuclear processes; in contrast, alpha radiation and beta radiation are matter. Because electromagnetic radiation has no protons, neutrons, or electrons, the symbol for a gamma ray is simply

$$\gamma$$

Gamma radiation is highly energetic and is the most penetrating form of nuclear radiation. Barriers of lead, concrete, or, more often, a combination of the two are required for protection from this type of radiation.

## Properties of Alpha, Beta, Positron, and Gamma Radiation

Important properties of alpha, beta, positron, and gamma radiation are summarized in Table 9.1.

Alpha, beta, positron, and gamma radiation are collectively termed *ionizing radiation*. **Ionizing radiation** produces a trail of ions throughout the material that it penetrates. The ionization process changes the chemical composition of the material. When the material is living tissue, radiation-induced illness may result (Section 9.6).

The penetrating power of alpha radiation is very low. Damage to internal organs from this form of radiation is negligible except when an alpha particle emitter is actually ingested. Beta particles and positrons have much higher velocities than alpha particles; still, they have limited penetrating power. They cause skin and eye damage and, to a lesser extent, damage to internal organs. Shielding is required when working with beta emitters. Pregnant women must take special precautions. The great penetrating power and high energy of gamma radiation make it particularly difficult to shield. Hence, it can damage internal organs.

Anyone working with any type of radiation must take precautions. Radiation safety is required, monitored, and enforced in the United States by the Occupational Safety and Health Administration (OSHA).

**ANIMATIONS**
- Alpha, Beta, and Gamma Radiation
- Alpha, Beta, and Gamma Rays

**LEARNING GOAL**

**1**  Enumerate characteristics of alpha, beta, positron, and gamma radiation.

**TABLE 9.1 A Summary of the Major Properties of Alpha, Beta, Positron, and Gamma Radiation**

| Name and Symbol | Identity | Charge | Mass (amu) | Velocity | Penetration |
|---|---|---|---|---|---|
| Alpha ($\alpha$) | Helium nucleus | +2 | 4.0026 | 5–10% of the speed of light | Low |
| Beta $_{-1}^{0}\beta$ | Electron | −1 | 0.000549 | Up to 90% of the speed of light | Medium |
| Positron $_{+1}^{0}\beta$ | Electron | +1 | 0.000549 | Up to 90% of the speed of light | Medium |
| Gamma ($\gamma$) | Radiant energy | 0 | 0 | Speed of light | High |

# A HUMAN PERSPECTIVE

## Origin of the Elements

The current, most widely held theory of the origin of the universe is the "big bang" theory. An explosion of very dense matter was followed by expansion into space of the fragments resulting from this explosion. This is one of the scenarios that have been created by scientists fascinated by the origins of matter, the stars and planets, and life as we know it today.

The first fragments, or particles, were protons and neutrons moving with tremendous velocity and possessing large amounts of energy. Collisions involving these high-energy protons and neutrons formed deuterium atoms ($^2H$), which are isotopes of hydrogen. As the universe expanded and cooled, tritium ($^3H$), another hydrogen isotope, formed as a result of collisions of neutrons with deuterium atoms. Subsequent capture of a proton produced helium (He). Scientists theorize that a universe that was principally composed of hydrogen atoms and helium atoms persisted for perhaps 100,000 years until the temperature decreased sufficiently to allow the formation of a simple molecule, hydrogen, two atoms of hydrogen bonded together ($H_2$).

Many millions of years later, the effect of gravity caused these small units to coalesce, first into clouds and eventually into stars, with temperatures of millions of degrees. In this setting, these small collections of protons and neutrons combined to form larger atoms such as carbon (C) and oxygen (O), then sodium (Na), neon (Ne), magnesium (Mg), silicon (Si), and so forth. Subsequent explosions of stars provided the conditions that formed many larger atoms. These fragments, gathered together by the force of gravity, are the most probable origin of the planets in our own solar system.

The reactions that formed the elements as we know them today were a result of a series of *fusion reactions*, the joining of nuclei to produce larger atoms at very high temperatures (millions of degrees Celsius). These fusion reactions are similar to processes that are currently being studied as a possible alternative source of nuclear power.

Nuclear reactions of this type do not naturally occur on the earth today. The temperature is simply too low. As a result we have, for the most part, a collection of stable elements existing as chemical compounds, atoms joined together by chemical bonds while retaining their identity even in the combined state. Silicon exists all around us as sand and soil in a combined form, silicon dioxide; most metals exist as a part of a chemical compound, such as iron ore.

The wonder and complexity of our universe is a legacy of events that happened a long time ago. As our understanding of bonding, molecular structure, and structure-property relationships has developed, our ability to design and synthesize useful new compounds has dramatically increased.

### For Further Understanding

▶ How does tritium differ from "normal" hydrogen?
▶ Would you expect to find similar atoms on other planets?

**Question 9.1** Gamma radiation is a form of *electromagnetic radiation*. Provide examples of other forms of electromagnetic radiation.

**Question 9.2** How does the energy of gamma radiation compare with that of other regions of the electromagnetic spectrum?

# 9.2 Writing a Balanced Nuclear Equation

Nuclear equations represent nuclear change in much the same way as chemical equations represent chemical change.

A **nuclear equation** can be used to represent the process of radioactive decay. In radioactive decay a *nuclide* breaks down, producing a *new nuclide, smaller particles, and/or energy*. The concept of mass balance, required when writing chemical equations, is also essential for nuclear equations. When writing a balanced equation, remember that:

- the total mass on each side of the reaction arrow must be identical, and
- the sum of the atomic numbers on each side of the reaction arrow must be identical.

**LEARNING GOAL**

**2** Write balanced equations for nuclear processes.

## Alpha Decay

Consider the decay of one isotope of uranium, $^{238}_{92}U$, into thorium and an alpha particle. Because an alpha particle is lost in this process, this decay is called *alpha decay*.

Examine the balanced equation for this nuclear reaction:

$$^{238}_{92}U \longrightarrow {}^{234}_{90}Th + {}^{4}_{2}He$$

Uranium-238          Thorium-234      Helium-4

The sum of the mass numbers on the right (234 + 4 = 238) is equal to the mass number on the left. The sum of atomic numbers on the right (90 + 2 = 92) is equal to the atomic number on the left.

## Beta Decay

*Beta decay* is illustrated by the decay of one of the less-abundant nitrogen isotopes, $^{16}_{7}N$. Upon decomposition, nitrogen-16 produces oxygen-16 and a beta particle. Conceptually, a neutron = proton + electron. In beta decay, one neutron in nitrogen-16 is converted to a proton and the electron, the beta particle, is released. The reaction is represented as

$$^{16}_{7}N \longrightarrow {}^{16}_{8}O + {}^{0}_{-1}e$$

or

$$^{16}_{7}N \longrightarrow {}^{16}_{8}O + \beta$$

Note that the mass number of the beta particle is zero, because the electron has no protons or neutrons. Sixteen nuclear particles are accounted for on both sides of the reaction arrow. Note also that the product nuclide has the same mass number as the parent nuclide but the atomic number has *increased* by one unit.

The atomic number on the left (+7) is counterbalanced by [8 + (−1)] or (+7) on the right. Therefore the equation is correctly balanced.

## Positron Emission

The decay of carbon-11 to a stable isotope, boron-11, is one example of positron emission.

$$^{11}_{6}C \longrightarrow {}^{11}_{5}B + {}^{0}_{1}e$$

or

$$^{11}_{6}C \longrightarrow {}^{11}_{5}B + {}^{0}_{+1}\beta$$

A **positron** has the same mass as an electron, or beta particle, but opposite (+) charge. In contrast to beta emission, the product nuclide has the same mass number as the parent nuclide, but the atomic number has *decreased* by one unit.

The atomic number on the left (+6) is counterbalanced by [5 + (+1)] or (+6) on the right. Therefore, the equation is correctly balanced.

## Gamma Production

If *gamma radiation* were the only product of nuclear decay, there would be no measurable change in the mass or identity of the radioactive nuclei. This is so because the gamma emitter has simply gone to a lower energy state. An example of an isotope that decays in this way is technetium-99m. It is described as a *metastable isotope*, meaning that it is unstable and increases its stability through gamma decay without change in the mass or charge of the isotope. The letter *m* is used to denote a metastable isotope. The decay equation for $^{99m}_{43}Tc$ is

$$^{99m}_{43}Tc \longrightarrow {}^{99}_{43}Tc + \gamma$$

More often, gamma radiation is produced along with other products. For example, iodine-131 decays as follows:

$$^{131}_{53}I \longrightarrow {}^{131}_{54}Xe + {}^{0}_{-1}e + \gamma$$

Iodine-131          Xenon-131      Beta          Gamma
                                   particle       ray

This reaction may also be represented as

$$^{131}_{53}\text{I} \longrightarrow ^{131}_{54}\text{Xe} + ^{\phantom{-}0}_{-1}\beta + \gamma$$

An isotope of xenon, a beta particle, and gamma radiation are produced.

## Predicting Products of Nuclear Decay

It is possible to use a nuclear equation to predict one of the products of a nuclear reaction if the others are known. Consider the following example, in which we represent the unknown product as ?:

$$^{40}_{19}\text{K} \longrightarrow ? + ^{\phantom{-}0}_{-1}\text{e}$$

**Step 1.** The mass number of this isotope of potassium is 40. Therefore the sum of the mass number of the products must also be 40, and ? must have a mass number of 40.

**Step 2.** Likewise, the atomic number on the left is 19, and the sum of the unknown atomic number plus the charge of the beta particle ($-1$) must equal 19.

**Step 3.** The unknown atomic number must be 20, because $[20 + (-1) = 19]$. The unknown is

$$^{40}_{20}?$$

**Step 4.** If we consult the periodic table, the element that has atomic number 20 is calcium; therefore $? = ^{40}_{20}\text{Ca}$

---

**EXAMPLE 9.1**    **Predicting the Product of Alpha Decay**

LEARNING GOAL

**2**  Write balanced equations for nuclear processes.

Determine the identity of the unknown product of the alpha decay of curium-245:

$$^{245}_{96}\text{Cm} \longrightarrow ^{4}_{2}\text{He} + ?$$

**Solution**

**Step 1.** The mass number of the curium isotope is 245. Therefore the sum of the mass numbers of the products must also be 245, and ? must have a mass number of 241.

**Step 2.** Likewise, the atomic number on the left is 96, and the sum of the unknown atomic number plus the atomic number of the alpha particle (2) must equal 96.

**Step 3.** The unknown atomic number must be 94, because $[94 + 2 = 96]$. The unknown is

$$^{241}_{94}?$$

**Step 4.** Referring to the periodic table, we find that the element that has atomic number 94 is plutonium; therefore $? = ^{241}_{94}\text{Pu}$.

**Step 5.** Verify the result. The complete equation is:

$$^{245}_{96}\text{Cm} \longrightarrow ^{4}_{2}\text{He} + ^{241}_{94}\text{Pu}$$

Mass number of reactants = 245
Mass number of products = 4 + 241 = 245
and
Atomic number of reactant = 96
Atomic number of products = 2 + 94 = 96

*Continued…*

**Practice Problem 9.1**

Complete each of the following nuclear equations:

a. $? \longrightarrow {}_{2}^{4}He + {}_{86}^{222}Rn$

b. ${}_{5}^{11}B \longrightarrow {}_{3}^{7}Li + ?$

▶ For Further Practice: **Questions 9.44 and 9.50.**

**Question 9.3**   Neodymium-144 is a rare earth isotope that undergoes alpha decay. Write a balanced nuclear equation for this process.

**Question 9.4**   Samarium-147 is one of many rare earth isotopes that undergo alpha decay. Write a balanced nuclear equation for this process.

**EXAMPLE 9.2**    **Predicting the Product of Beta Decay**

LEARNING GOAL

Determine the identity of the unknown product of the beta decay of chromium-55.

$${}_{24}^{55}Cr \longrightarrow {}_{-1}^{0}e + ?$$

**2** Write balanced equations for nuclear processes.

**Solution**

**Step 1.**  The mass number of the chromium isotope is 55. Therefore the sum of the mass numbers of the products must also be 55, and ? must also have a mass number of 55.

**Step 2.**  Likewise, the atomic number on the left is 24, and the sum of the unknown atomic number plus (−1), representing the beta particle, equals the atomic number of the chromium isotope.

**Step 3.**

$$\text{unknown atomic number} + (-1) = 24$$

$$\text{unknown atomic number} = 24 + 1 = 25$$

and the unknown is:

$${}_{25}^{55}?$$

**Step 4.**  Referring to the periodic table, we find that the element having atomic number 25 is manganese; therefore $? = {}_{25}^{55}Mn$.

**Step 5.**  Verify the result. The complete equation is:

$${}_{24}^{55}Cr \longrightarrow {}_{-1}^{0}e + {}_{25}^{55}Mn$$

Mass number of reactants = 55
Mass number of products = 0 + 55 = 55
and
Atomic number of reactants = 24
Atomic number of products = (−1) + 25 = 24

**Practice Problem 9.2**

Complete each of the following nuclear equations:

a. ${}_{36}^{85}Kr \longrightarrow ? + {}_{-1}^{0}e$

b. ${}_{92}^{239}U \longrightarrow ? + {}_{-1}^{0}e$

▶ For Further Practice: **Questions 9.43 and 9.45.**

**Question 9.5** Iodine-131, useful in the treatment of certain kinds of thyroid disease, decays by beta emission. Write a balanced nuclear equation for this process.

**Question 9.6** Phosphorus-31, known to bioaccumulate in the liver, decays by beta emission. Write a balanced nuclear equation for this process.

---

**EXAMPLE 9.3** **Predicting the Product of Positron Emission**

LEARNING GOAL

**2** Write balanced equations for nuclear processes.

Determine the identity of the unknown product of positron emission from xenon-118.

$$^{118}_{54}\text{Xe} \longrightarrow {^0_1}\text{e} + \text{?}$$

**Solution**

**Step 1.** The mass number of the xenon isotope is 118. Therefore the sum of the mass numbers of the products must also be 118 and ? must have a mass number of 118.

**Step 2.** Likewise, the atomic number on the left is 54, and the sum of the unknown atomic number plus (+1), representing the positron, equals the atomic number of the xenon isotope.

**Step 3.**

$$\text{unknown atomic number} + (+1) = 54$$
$$\text{unknown atomic number} = 54 - 1 = 53$$

and the unknown is: $^{118}_{53}$?

**Step 4.** Referring to the periodic table, we find that the element having atomic number 53 is iodine; therefore ? = $^{118}_{53}\text{I}$.

**Step 5.** Verify the result. The complete equation is:

$$^{118}_{54}\text{Xe} \longrightarrow {^0_1}\text{e} + {^{118}_{53}}\text{I}$$

mass number of reactants = 118
mass number of products = 118 + 0 = 118
and
atomic number of reactant = 54
atomic number of products = (+1) + 53 = 54

**Practice Problem 9.3**

Complete each of the following nuclear equations:

a. $^{79}_{37}\text{Rb} \longrightarrow \text{?} + {^0_1}\text{e}$

b. $^{38}_{20}\text{Ca} \longrightarrow \text{?} + {^0_1}\text{e}$

▶ For Further Practice: **Questions 9.51 and 9.52.**

---

**Question 9.7** In what way do beta particles and positrons differ?

**Question 9.8** In what way are beta particles and positrons similar?

## 9.3 Properties of Radioisotopes

Why are some isotopes radioactive but others are not? Do all radioactive isotopes decay at the same rate? Are all radioactive materials equally hazardous? We address these and other questions in this section.

## Nuclear Structure and Stability

A measure of nuclear stability is the **binding energy** of the nucleus. The binding energy of the nucleus is the energy required to break up a nucleus into its component protons and neutrons. This must be very large, because identically charged protons in the nucleus exert extreme repulsive forces on one another. These forces must be overcome if the nucleus is to be stable. When a nuclide decays, some energy is released because the products are more stable than the parent nuclide. This released energy is the source of the high-energy radiation emitted and the basis for all nuclear technology.

Why are some isotopes more stable than others? The answer to this question is not completely clear. Evidence obtained so far points to several important factors that describe stable nuclei:

- Nuclear stability correlates with the ratio of neutrons to protons in the isotope. For example, for light atoms a neutron/proton ratio of 1 characterizes a stable atom.
- Nuclei with large numbers of protons (84 or more) tend to be unstable.
- Naturally occurring isotopes containing 2, 8, 20, 50, 82, or 126 protons or neutrons are stable. These *magic numbers* seem to indicate the presence of energy levels in the nucleus, analogous to electronic energy levels in the atom.
- Isotopes with even numbers of protons or neutrons are generally more stable than those with odd numbers of protons or neutrons.
- All isotopes (except hydrogen-1) with more protons than neutrons are unstable. However, the reverse is not true.

## Half-Life

The **half-life** ($t_{1/2}$) is the time required for one-half of a given quantity of a substance to undergo change. Not all radioactive isotopes decay at the same rate. The rate of nuclear decay is generally represented in terms of the half-life of the isotope. Each isotope has its own characteristic half-life that may be as short as a few millionths of a second or as long as billions of years. Half-lives of some naturally occurring and synthetic isotopes are given in Table 9.2.

The stability of an isotope is indicated by the isotope's half-life. Isotopes with short half-lives decay rapidly; they are very unstable. This is not meant to imply that substances with long half-lives are less hazardous. Often, just the reverse is true.

Imagine that we begin with 100 milligrams (mg) of a radioactive isotope that has a half-life of 24 hours (h). After one half-life, or 24 h, 1/2 of 100 mg will have

**LEARNING GOAL**

**3** Calculate the amount of radioactive substance remaining after a specified time has elapsed.

**ANIMATION**
- Radioactive Half-Life

*Refer to the discussion of radiation exposure and safety in Sections 9.6 and 9.7.*

**TABLE 9.2  Half-Lives of Selected Radioisotopes**

| Name | Symbol | Half-Life |
| --- | --- | --- |
| Carbon-14 | $^{14}_{6}\text{C}$ | 5730 years |
| Cobalt-60 | $^{60}_{27}\text{Co}$ | 5.3 years |
| Hydrogen-3 | $^{3}_{1}\text{H}$ | 12.3 years |
| Iodine-131 | $^{131}_{53}\text{I}$ | 8.1 days |
| Iron-59 | $^{59}_{26}\text{Fe}$ | 45 days |
| Molybdenum-99 | $^{99}_{42}\text{Mo}$ | 67 hours |
| Sodium-24 | $^{24}_{11}\text{Na}$ | 15 hours |
| Strontium-90 | $^{90}_{38}\text{Sr}$ | 28 years |
| Technetium-99m | $^{99m}_{43}\text{Tc}$ | 6 hours |
| Uranium-235 | $^{235}_{92}\text{U}$ | 710 million years |

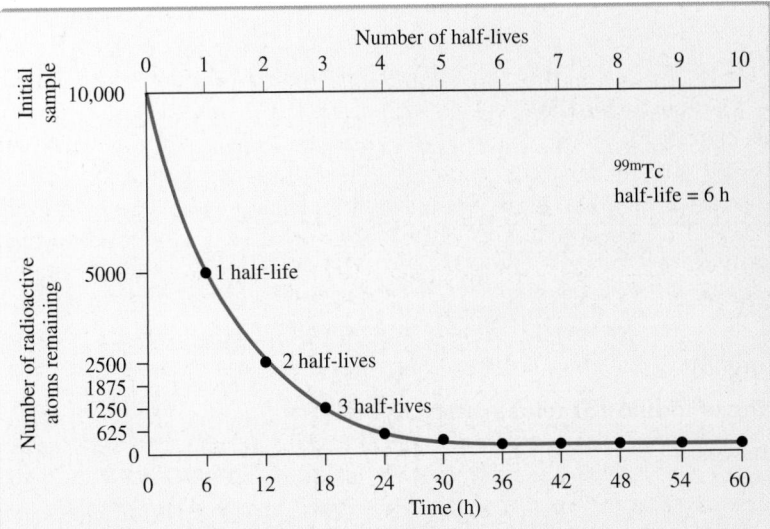

**Figure 9.2** The decay curve for the medically useful radioisotope technetium-99m. Note that the number of radioactive atoms remaining—hence the radioactivity—approaches zero.

decayed to other products, and 50 mg remain. After two half-lives (48 h), 1/2 of the remaining material has decayed, leaving 25 mg, and so forth:

$$100 \text{ mg} \xrightarrow[\substack{\text{Half-life} \\ (24 \text{ h})}]{\text{One}} 50 \text{ mg} \xrightarrow[\substack{\text{Half-life} \\ (48 \text{ h total})}]{\text{A Second}} 25 \text{ mg} \longrightarrow \text{etc.}$$

Decay of a radioisotope that has a reasonably short $t_{1/2}$ is experimentally determined by following its activity as a function of time. Graphing the results produces a radioactive decay curve, as shown in Figure 9.2.

The mass of any radioactive substance remaining after a period may be calculated with a knowledge of the initial mass and the half-life of the isotope, following the scheme just outlined. The general equation for this process is:

$$m_f = m_i (.5)^n$$

where   $m_f$ = final or remaining mass
$m_i$ = initial mass
$n$ = number of half-lives

---

**EXAMPLE 9.4**    **Predicting the Extent of Radioactive Decay**

LEARNING GOAL

**3**  Calculate the amount of radioactive substance remaining after a specified time has elapsed.

A 50.0-mg supply of iodine-131, used in hospitals in the treatment of hyperthyroidism, was stored for 32.4 days (d). If the half-life of iodine-131 is 8.1 d, how many mg remain?

**Solution**

First calculate $n$, the number of half-lives elapsed using the half-life as a conversion factor:

$$n = 32.4 \text{ d} \times \frac{1 \text{ half-life}}{8.1 \text{ d}} = 4.0 \text{ half-lives}$$

Then calculate the amount remaining:

$$\begin{array}{ccccc} & \text{first} & \text{second} & \text{third} & \text{fourth} \\ 50.0 \text{ mg} \longrightarrow & 25.0 \text{ mg} \longrightarrow & 12.5 \text{ mg} \longrightarrow & 6.25 \text{ mg} \longrightarrow & 3.13 \text{ mg} \\ & \text{half-life} & \text{half-life} & \text{half-life} & \text{half-life} \end{array}$$

Hence, 3.13 mg of iodine-131 remain after 32.4 d.

*Continued...*

**An Alternate Strategy**

Use the equation:

$$m_f = m_i (.5)^n$$

Where
$m_i$ is the initial mass
$m_f$ is the final mass
and
$n$ is the number of half-lives
Substituting:

$$m_f = 50.0 \text{ mg}(.5)^4$$
$$m_f = 3.13 \text{ mg of iodine-131 remain after 32.4 d.}$$

Note that both strategies produce the same answer.

**Practice Problem 9.4**

a. A 100.0 nanogram (ng) sample of sodium-24 was stored in a lead-lined cabinet for 2.5 d. How much sodium-24 remained? See Table 9.2 for the half-life of sodium-24.

b. If a patient is administered 10 ng of technetium-99m, how much will remain 1 day later, assuming that no technetium has been eliminated by any other process? See Table 9.2 for the half-life of technetium-99m.

▶ For Further Practice: **Questions 9.63 and 9.64.**

---

**LEARNING GOAL**

**4**  Explain the process of radiocarbon dating.

**Figure 9.3** Radiocarbon dating was used in the authentication study of the Shroud of Turin. It is a minimally destructive technique and is valuable in estimating the age of historical artifacts. It was found that the Shroud is approximately 700 years old, negating the claim that it was used to wrap the body of Jesus.

**Question 9.9**  The half-life of molybdenum-99 is 67 h. A 200 microgram ($\mu$g) quantity decays, over time, to 25 $\mu$g. How much time has elapsed?

**Question 9.10**  The half-life of strontium-87 is 2.8 h. What percentage of this isotope will remain after 8 h and 24 minutes (min)?

## Radiocarbon Dating

Natural radioactivity is useful in establishing the approximate age of objects of archaeological, anthropological, or historical interest. **Radiocarbon dating** is the estimation of the age of objects through measurement of isotopic ratios of carbon.

Radiocarbon dating is based on the measurement of the relative amounts (or ratio) of $^{14}_{6}C$ and $^{12}_{6}C$ present in an object. The $^{14}_{6}C$ is formed in the upper atmosphere by the bombardment of $^{14}_{7}N$ by high-speed neutrons (cosmic radiation):

$$^{14}_{7}N + ^{1}_{0}n \longrightarrow ^{14}_{6}C + ^{1}_{1}H$$

The carbon-14, along with the more abundant carbon-12, is converted into living plant material by the process of photosynthesis. Carbon proceeds up the food chain as the plants are consumed by animals, including humans. When a plant or animal dies, the uptake of both carbon-14 and carbon-12 ceases. However, the amount of carbon-14 slowly decreases because carbon-14 is radioactive ($t_{1/2} = 5730$ years). Carbon-14 decay produces nitrogen:

$$^{14}_{6}C \longrightarrow ^{14}_{7}N + ^{0}_{-1}e$$

When an artifact is found and studied, the relative amounts of carbon-14 and carbon-12 are determined. By using suitable equations involving the $t_{1/2}$ of carbon-14, it is possible to approximate the age of the artifact.

This technique has been widely used to increase our knowledge about the history of the earth, to establish the age of objects (Figure 9.3), and even to detect art forgeries. Early paintings were made with inks fabricated from vegetable dyes (plant material that, while alive, metabolized carbon).

## A HUMAN PERSPECTIVE

### An Extraordinary Woman in Science

The path to a successful career in science, or any other field for that matter, is seldom smooth or straight. That was certainly true for Madame Marie Sklodowska Curie. Her lifelong ambition was to raise a family and do something interesting for a career. This was a lofty goal for a nineteenth-century woman.

The political climate in Poland, coupled with the prevailing attitudes toward women and careers, especially careers in science, certainly did not make it any easier for Mme. Curie. To support herself and her sister, she toiled at menial jobs until moving to Paris to resume her studies.

It was in Paris that she met her future husband and fellow researcher, Pierre Curie. Working with crude equipment in a laboratory that was primitive, even by the standards of the time, she and Pierre made a most revolutionary discovery only 2 years after Henri Becquerel discovered radioactivity. Radioactivity, the emission of energy from certain substances, was released from *inside* the atom and was independent of the molecular form of the substance. The absolute proof of this assertion came only after the Curies processed over 1 *ton* (t) of a material (pitchblende) to isolate less than a gram (g) of pure radium. The difficult conditions under which this feat was accomplished are perhaps best stated by Sharon Bertsch McGrayne in her book *Nobel Prize Women in Science* (Birch Lane Press, New York, 2001):

The only space large enough at the school was an abandoned dissection shed. The shack was stifling hot in summer and freezing cold in winter. It had no ventilation system for removing poisonous fumes, and its roof leaked. A chemist accustomed to Germany's modern laboratories called it "a cross between a stable and a potato cellar and, if I had not seen the work table with the chemical apparatus, I would have thought it a practical joke." This ramshackle shed became the symbol of the Marie Curie legend.

The pale green glow emanating from the radium was beautiful to behold. Mme. Curie would go to the shed in the middle of the night to bask in the light of her accomplishment. She did not realize that this wonderful accomplishment would, in time, be responsible for her death.

Mme. Curie received not one, but two Nobel Prizes, one in physics and one in chemistry. She was the first woman in France to earn the rank of professor.

**For Further Understanding**

▶ Paradoxically, radiation can both cause and cure cancer. Do some Internet research and explain the paradox.

▶ What is the message that you, personally, can take away from this story?

---

The carbon-14 dating technique is limited to objects that are less than fifty thousand years old, or approximately nine half-lives, which is a practical upper limit. Older objects that have geological or archaeological significance may be dated using naturally occurring isotopes having much longer half-lives.

Examples of useful dating isotopes are listed in Table 9.3.

## 9.4 Nuclear Power

### Energy Production

Einstein predicted that a small amount of nuclear mass corresponds to a very large amount of energy that is released when the nucleus breaks apart. Einstein's equation is

$$E = mc^2$$

**TABLE 9.3 Isotopes Useful in Radioactive Dating**

| Isotope | Half-Life (years) | Upper Limit (years) | Dating Applications |
|---------|-------------------|---------------------|---------------------|
| Carbon-14 | 5730 | $5 \times 10^4$ | Charcoal, organic material, artwork |
| Tritium $^3_1H$ | 12.3 | $1 \times 10^2$ | Aged wines, artwork |
| Potassium-40 | $1.3 \times 10^9$ | Age of earth ($4 \times 10^9$) | Rocks, planetary material |
| Rhenium-187 | $4.3 \times 10^{10}$ | Age of earth ($4 \times 10^9$) | Meteorites |
| Uranium-238 | $4.5 \times 10^9$ | Age of earth ($4 \times 10^9$) | Rocks, earth's crust |

in which

$$E = \text{energy}$$
$$m = \text{mass}$$
$$c = \text{speed of light}$$

This kinetic energy, when rapidly released, is the basis for the greatest instruments of destruction developed by humankind, nuclear bombs. However, when heat energy is released in a controlled fashion, as in a nuclear power plant, the heat energy converts liquid water into steam. The steam, in turn, drives an electrical generator, producing electricity. The entire process takes place in a **nuclear reactor.**

## Nuclear Fission

**Fission** (splitting) occurs when a heavy nuclear particle is split into smaller nuclei by a smaller nuclear particle (such as a neutron). This splitting process is accompanied by the release of large amounts of energy.

A nuclear power plant uses a fissionable material (capable of undergoing fission), such as uranium-235, as fuel. The energy released by the fission process in the nuclear core heats water in an adjoining chamber, producing steam. The high pressure of the steam drives a turbine, which converts this heat energy into electricity using an electric power generator. The energy transformation may be summarized as follows:

| nuclear energy $\longrightarrow$ | heat energy $\longrightarrow$ | mechanical energy $\longrightarrow$ | electrical energy |
|---|---|---|---|
| Nuclear reactor | Steam | Turbine | Electricity |

The fission reaction, once initiated, is self-perpetuating. For example, neutrons are used to initiate the reaction:

$$\underset{\text{Fuel}}{{}_{0}^{1}\text{n} + {}_{92}^{235}\text{U}} \longrightarrow \underset{\text{Unstable}}{{}_{92}^{236}\text{U}} \longrightarrow \underset{\text{Products of reaction}}{{}_{36}^{92}\text{Kr} + {}_{56}^{141}\text{Ba} + 3{}_{0}^{1}\text{n} + \text{energy}}$$

Note that three neutrons are released as product for each single reacting neutron. Each of the three neutrons produced is available to initiate another fission process. Nine neutrons are released from this process. These, in turn, react with other nuclei. The fission process continues and intensifies, producing very large amounts of energy (Figure 9.4). This process of intensification is referred to as a **chain reaction.**

To maintain control over the process and to prevent dangerous overheating, rods fabricated from cadmium or boron are inserted into the core. These rods, which are controlled by the reactor's main operating system, absorb free neutrons as needed, thereby moderating the reaction.

A nuclear fission reactor may be represented as a series of energy transfer zones, as depicted in Figure 9.5. A view of the core of a fission reactor is shown in Figure 9.6.

## Nuclear Fusion

**Fusion** (meaning *to join together*) results from the combination of two small nuclei to form a larger nucleus with the concurrent release of large amounts of energy. The best example of a fusion reactor is the sun. Continuous fusion processes furnish our solar system with light and heat.

An example of a fusion reaction is the combination of two isotopes of hydrogen, deuterium (${}_{1}^{2}\text{H}$) and tritium (${}_{1}^{3}\text{H}$), to produce helium, a neutron, and energy:

$$\underset{1}{{}^{2}}\text{H} + {}_{1}^{3}\text{H} \longrightarrow {}_{2}^{4}\text{He} + {}_{0}^{1}\text{n} + \text{energy}$$

LEARNING GOAL

5 Describe how nuclear energy can generate electricity: fission, fusion, and the breeder reactor.

**ANIMATIONS**
• Nuclear Fission
• Nuclear Chain Reaction

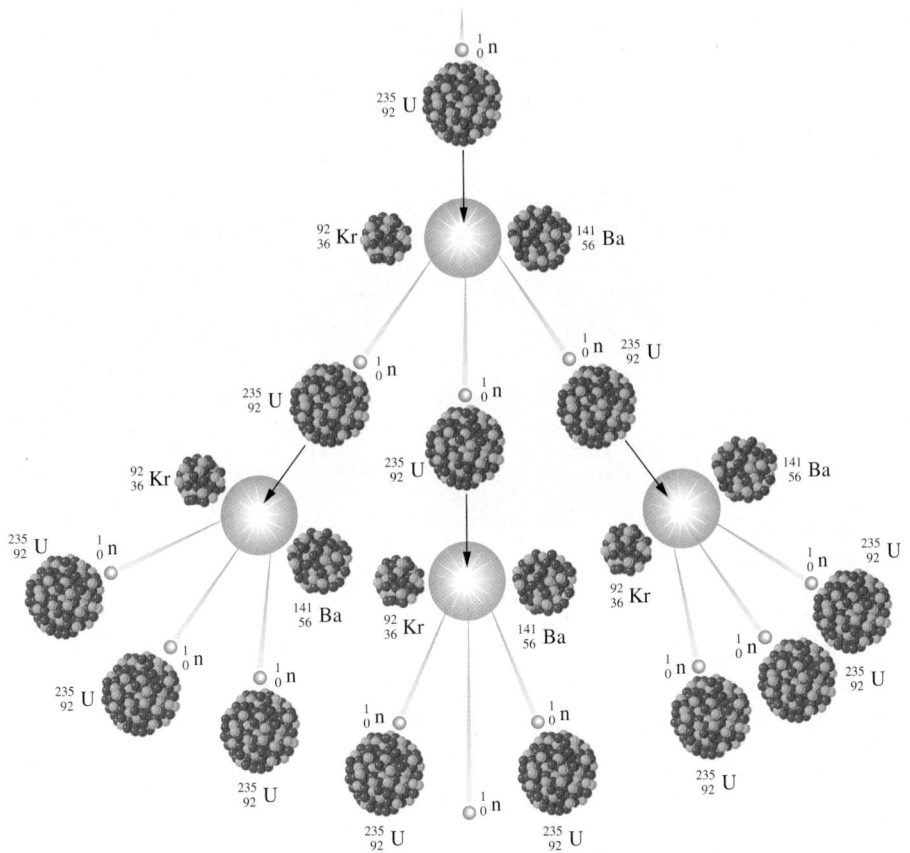

**Figure 9.4** The fission of uranium-235 producing a chain reaction. Note that the number of available neutrons, which "trigger" the decomposition of the fissionable nuclei to release energy, increases at each step in the "chain." In this way the reaction builds in intensity. Control rods stabilize (or limit) the extent of the chain reaction to a safe level.

**Figure 9.5** A representation of the "energy zones" of a nuclear reactor. Heat produced by the reactor core is carried by water in a second zone to a boiler. Water in the boiler (third zone) is converted to steam, which drives a turbine to convert heat energy to electrical energy. The isolation of these zones from each other allows heat energy transfer without actual physical mixing. This minimizes the transport of radioactive material into the environment.

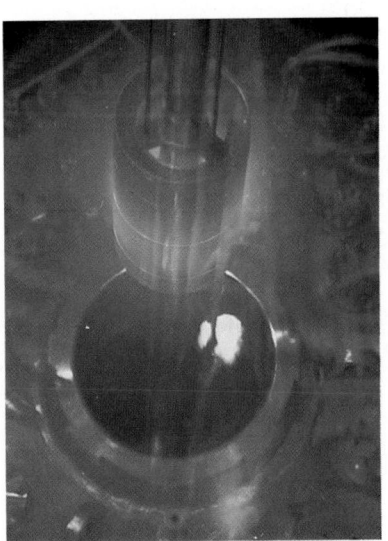

**Figure 9.6** The core of a nuclear reactor located at Oak Ridge National Laboratories in Tennessee.

# GREEN CHEMISTRY

## Nuclear Waste Disposal

Nuclear waste arises from a variety of sources. A major source is the spent fuel from nuclear power plants. Medical laboratories generate significant amounts of low-level waste from tracers and therapy. Even household items with limited lifetimes, such as certain types of smoke detectors, use a tiny amount of radioactive material.

Virtually everyone is aware, through television and newspapers, of the problems of solid waste (nonnuclear) disposal that our society faces. For the most part, this material will degrade in some reasonable amount of time. Still, we are disposing of trash and garbage at a rate that far exceeds nature's ability to recycle it.

Now imagine the problem with nuclear waste. We cannot alter the rate at which it decays. This is defined by the half-life. We can't heat it, stir it, or add a catalyst to speed up the process as we can with chemical reactions. Furthermore, the half-lives of many nuclear waste products are very long: plutonium, for example, has a half-life in excess of 24,000 years. Ten half-lives represents the approximate time required for the radioactivity of a substance to reach background levels. So we are talking about a *very* long storage time, on the order of 250,000 years!

Where on earth can something so very hazardous be contained and stored with reasonable assurance that it will lie undisturbed for a quarter of a million years? Perhaps this is a rhetorical question. Scientists, engineers, and politicians have debated this question for almost 50 years. As yet, no permanent disposal site has been agreed upon. Most agree that the best solution is burial in a stable rock formation, but there is no firm agreement on the location. Fear of earthquakes, which may release large quantities of radioactive materials into the underground water system, is the most serious consideration.

A photograph of the earth, taken from the moon, clearly illustrates the limits of resources and the limits to waste disposal.

Such a disaster could render large sections of the country unfit for habitation.

Many argue for the continuation of temporary storage sites with the hope that the progress of science and technology will, in the years ahead, provide a safer and more satisfactory long-term solution.

The nuclear waste problem, important for its own sake, also affects the development of future societal uses of nuclear chemistry. Before we can fully enjoy its benefits, we must learn to use and dispose of its waste products safely.

### For Further Understanding

► Summarize the major arguments supporting expanded use of nuclear power for electrical energy.
► Enumerate the characteristics of an "ideal" solution to the nuclear waste problem.

---

Although fusion is capable of producing tremendous amounts of energy, no commercially successful fusion plant exists in the United States. Safety concerns relating to problems of containment of the reaction, resulting directly from the technological problems associated with containing high temperatures (millions of degrees) and pressures required to sustain a fusion process, have slowed the development of fusion reactors.

## Breeder Reactors

**ANIMATION**
• Operation of a Nuclear Power Plant

A **breeder reactor** is a variation of a fission reactor that literally manufactures its own fuel. A perceived shortage of fissionable isotopes makes the breeder an attractive alternative to conventional fission reactors. A breeder reactor uses $^{238}_{92}U$, which is abundant but nonfissionable. In a series of steps, the uranium-238 is converted to plutonium-239, which *is* fissionable and undergoes a fission chain reaction, producing energy. The attractiveness of a reactor that makes its own fuel from abundant starting materials is offset by the high cost of the system, potential environmental damage, and fear of plutonium proliferation. Plutonium can be readily used to manufacture nuclear bombs. Currently only France and Japan operate breeder reactors for electrical power generation.

## Nuclear Power

### Foundations

**9.69** Which type of nuclear process splits nuclei to release energy?

**9.70** Which type of nuclear process combines small nuclei to release energy?

**9.71** **a.** Describe the process of fission.
   **b.** How is this reaction useful as the basis for the production of electrical energy?

**9.72** **a.** Describe the process of fusion.
   **b.** How could this process be used for the production of electrical energy?

### Applications

**9.73** Write a balanced nuclear equation for a fusion reaction.

**9.74** What are the major disadvantages of a fission reactor for electrical energy production?

**9.75** What is meant by the term *breeder reactor?*

**9.76** What are the potential advantages and disadvantages of breeder reactors?

**9.77** Describe what is meant by the term *chain reaction.*

**9.78** Why are cadmium rods used in a fission reactor?

**9.79** What is the greatest barrier to development of fusion reactors?

**9.80** What type of nuclear reaction fuels our solar system?

## Medical Applications of Radioactivity

### Foundations

**9.81** Why is radiation therapy an effective treatment for certain types of cancer?

**9.82** Describe how medically useful isotopes may be prepared.

**9.83** What is the source of background radiation?

**9.84** Why do high-altitude jet flights increase a person's exposure to background radiation?

### Applications

**9.85** The isotope indium-111 is used in medical laboratories as a label for blood platelets. To prepare indium-111, silver-108 is bombarded with an alpha particle, forming an intermediate isotope of indium. Write a nuclear equation for the process, and identify the intermediate isotope of indium.

**9.86** Radioactive molybdenum-99 is used to produce the tracer isotope, technetium-99m. Write a nuclear equation for the formation of molybdenum-99 from stable molybdenum-98 bombarded with neutrons.

**9.87** Describe an application of each of the following isotopes:
   **a.** technetium-99m    **b.** xenon-133

**9.88** Describe an application of each of the following isotopes:
   **a.** iodine-131    **b.** thallium-201

## Biological Effects of Radiation

Answer Questions 9.89 through 9.96 based on the assumption that you are employed by a clinical laboratory that prepares radioactive isotopes for medical diagnostic tests. Consider alpha, beta, positron, and gamma emission.

**9.89** What would be the effect on your level of radiation exposure if you increase your average distance from a radioactive source?

**9.90** Would wearing gloves have any significant effect? Why?

**9.91** Would limiting your time of exposure have a positive effect? Why?

**9.92** Would wearing a lab apron lined with thin sheets of lead have a positive effect? Why?

**9.93** Would the use of robotic manipulation of samples have an effect? Why?

**9.94** Would the use of concrete rather than wood paneling help to protect workers in other parts of the clinic? Why?

**9.95** Would the thickness of the concrete in Question 9.94 be an important consideration? Why?

**9.96** Suggest a protocol for radioactive waste disposal.

## Measurement of Radiation

### Foundations

**9.97** What is meant by the term *relative biological effect?*

**9.98** What is meant by the term *lethal dose* of radiation?

**9.99** Define each of the following units:
   **a.** curie    **b.** roentgen

**9.100** Define each of the following radiation units:
   **a.** rad    **b.** rem

### Applications

**9.101** X-ray technicians often wear badges containing photographic film. How is this film used to indicate exposure to X-rays?

**9.102** Why would a Geiger counter be preferred to film for assessing the immediate danger resulting from a spill of some solution containing a radioisotope?

# CRITICAL THINKING PROBLEMS

1. Isotopes used as radioactive tracers have chemical properties that are similar to those of a nonradioactive isotope of the same element. Explain why this is a critical consideration in their use.

2. A chemist proposes a research project to discover a catalyst that will speed up the decay of radioactive isotopes that are waste products of a medical laboratory. Such a discovery would be a potential solution to the problem of nuclear waste disposal. Critique this proposal.

3. A controversial solution to the disposal of nuclear waste involves burial in sealed chambers far below the earth's surface. Describe potential pros and cons of this approach.

4. What type of radioactive decay is favored if the number of protons in the nucleus is much greater than the number of neutrons? Explain.

5. If the proton-to-neutron ratio in Problem 4 (above) were reversed, what radioactive decay process would be favored? Explain.

6. Radioactive isotopes are often used as "tracers" to follow an atom through a chemical reaction, and the following is an example. Acetic acid reacts with methyl alcohol by eliminating a molecule of water to form methyl acetate. Explain how you would use the radioactive isotope oxygen-18 to show whether the oxygen atom in the water product comes from the —OH of the acid or the —OH of the alcohol.

$$\underset{\text{Acetic acid}}{H_3C-\overset{\displaystyle O}{\overset{\|}{C}}-OH} + \underset{\text{Methyl alcohol}}{HOCH_3} \longrightarrow \underset{\text{Methyl acetate}}{H_3C-\overset{\displaystyle O}{\overset{\|}{C}}-O-CH_3} + H_2O$$

7. Chromium-51, used as a tracer to study red blood cells, decays by electron capture. In this process a proton in the chromium nucleus is, in effect, converted to a neutron by combining with (capturing) an electron. Write a balanced equation for this process. What is the identity of the product?

# 10

# THE SATURATED HYDROCARBONS
# An Introduction to Organic Chemistry

The origins of fossil fuels.

## LEARNING GOALS

1 Compare and contrast organic and inorganic compounds.

2 Recognize structures that represent each of the families of organic compounds.

3 Write the names and draw the structures of the common functional groups that characterize the families of organic compounds.

4 Write condensed, structural, and line formulas for saturated hydrocarbons.

5 Describe the relationship between the structure and physical properties of saturated hydrocarbons.

6 Use the basic rules of the IUPAC nomenclature system to name alkanes and substituted alkanes.

7 From the IUPAC name of an alkane or substituted alkane, be able to draw the structure.

8 Draw constitutional (structural) isomers of simple organic compounds.

9 Write the names and draw the structures of simple cycloalkanes.

10 Draw *cis*- and *trans*-isomers of cycloalkanes.

11 Describe conformations of alkanes.

12 Draw the chair and boat conformations of cyclohexane.

13 Write balanced equations for combustion reactions of alkanes.

14 Write balanced equations for halogenation reactions of alkanes.

## OUTLINE

# INTRODUCTION

Organic chemistry is the study of carbon-containing compounds. The term *organic* was coined in 1807 by the Swedish chemist Jöns Jakob Berzelius. At that time it was thought that all organic compounds, such as fats, sugars, coal, and petroleum, were formed by living or once living organisms. All early attempts to synthesize these compounds in the laboratory failed, and it was thought that a vital force, available only in living cells, was needed for their formation.

This idea began to change in 1828 when a 27-year-old German physician, whose first love was chemistry, synthesized the organic molecule urea from inorganic starting materials. This man was Friedrich Wöhler, the "father of organic chemistry."

As a child, Wöhler didn't do particularly well in school because he spent so much time doing chemistry experiments at home. Eventually, he did earn his medical degree, but he decided to study chemistry in the laboratory of Berzelius rather than practice medicine.

After a year he returned to Germany to teach and, as it turned out, to do the experiment that made him famous. The goal of the experiment was to prepare ammonium cyanate from a mixture of potassium cyanate and ammonium sulfate. Wöhler heated a solution of the two salts and crystallized the product. But the product didn't look like ammonium cyanate. It was a white crystalline material that looked exactly like urea! Urea is a waste product of protein breakdown in the body and is excreted in the urine. Wöhler recognized urea crystals because he had previously purified them from the urine of dogs and humans. Excited about his accidental discovery, he wrote to his teacher and friend Berzelius, "I can make urea without the necessity of a kidney, or even an animal, whether man or dog."

$$NH_4^+ \; [N\!=\!C\!=\!O]^-$$

Ammonium cyanate
(inorganic salt)

Urea
(organic compound)

Ironically, Wöhler, the first person to synthesize an organic compound from inorganic substances, devoted the rest of his career to inorganic chemistry. However, other chemists continued this work, and as a result, the "vital force theory" was laid to rest, and modern organic chemistry was born.

In this and later chapters, we will study the amazing array of organic molecules (molecules made up of carbon, hydrogen, and a few other elements), many of which are essential to life. As we will see, all of the structural and functional molecules of the cell, including the phospholipids that make up the cell membrane and the enzymes that speed up biological reactions, are organic molecules. Smaller organic molecules, such as the sugars glucose and fructose, are used as fuel by our cells. Others, such as penicillin and aspirin are useful in the treatment of disease. All these organic compounds, and many more, are the subject of the remaining chapters of this text.

---

## 10.1  The Chemistry of Carbon

The number of possible carbon-containing compounds is almost limitless. The importance of these organic compounds is reflected in the fact that over half of this book is devoted to the study of molecules made with this single element.

Why are there so many organic compounds? There are several reasons. First, carbon can form *stable, covalent* bonds with other carbon atoms. This characteristic can be seen in three inorganic *allotropic forms* of elemental carbon: graphite, diamond, and buckminsterfullerene. Models of these allotropes are shown in Figure 10.1.

Allotropes are forms of an element that have the same physical state but different properties.

**(a)** Graphite                                        **(b)** Diamond                            **(c)** Buckminsterfullerene

**Figure 10.1** Three allotropic forms of elemental carbon.

Coal is a rock composed largely of carbon, with some other impurities. Investigate the conditions required to convert coal into a diamond.

Graphite consists of planar layers in which all carbon-to-carbon bonds extend in two dimensions. Because the planar units can slide over one another, graphite is an excellent lubricant. In contrast, diamond consists of a large, three-dimensional network of carbon-to-carbon bonds. As a result, it is an extremely hard substance used in jewelry and cutting tools.

The third allotropic form of carbon is buckminsterfullerene, affectionately called the *buckey ball*. The buckey ball consists of sixty carbon atoms in the shape of a soccer ball. Discovered in the 1980s, buckminsterfullerene was named for Buckminster Fuller, who used such shapes in the design of geodesic domes.

A second reason for the vast number of organic compounds is that carbon atoms can form stable bonds with other elements. Several families of organic compounds (alcohols, aldehydes, ketones, esters, and ethers) contain oxygen atoms bonded to carbon. Others contain nitrogen, sulfur, or halogens (Group VIIA(17) elements). The presence of these elements confers a wide variety of new chemical and physical properties on an organic compound.

Third, carbon can form double or triple covalent bonds with other carbon atoms to produce a variety of organic molecules with very different properties. Finally, the number of ways in which carbon and other atoms can be arranged is nearly limitless. In addition to linear chains of carbon atoms, ring structures and branched chains are common. Two organic compounds may even have the same number and kinds of atoms but completely different structures and thus different properties. Such organic molecules are called *isomers*.

## Important Differences Between Organic and Inorganic Compounds

The bonds between carbon and another atom are almost always *covalent bonds*, whereas the bonds in many inorganic compounds are *ionic bonds*. Ionic bonds result from the *transfer* of one or more electrons from one atom to another. Thus, ionic bonds are electrostatic, resulting from the attraction between the positive and negative ions formed by the electron transfer. Covalent bonds are formed by sharing one or more pairs of electrons.

Ionic compounds often form three-dimensional crystals made up of many positive and negative ions. Covalent compounds exist as individual units called molecules. Water-soluble ionic compounds often dissociate in water to form ions and are called electrolytes. Most covalent compounds are nonelectrolytes, remaining intact in solution.

As a result of these differences, ionic substances usually have much higher melting and boiling points than covalent compounds. They are more likely to dissolve

LEARNING GOAL

**1** Compare and contrast organic and inorganic compounds.

Polar covalent compounds, such as HCl, dissociate in water and, thus, are electrolytes. Carboxylic acids, the family of organic compounds we will study in Chapter 14, are weak electrolytes when dissolved in water.

**TABLE 10.1 Comparison of the Major Properties of a Typical Organic and an Inorganic Compound: Butane Versus Sodium Chloride**

| Property | Organic Compound (e.g., Butane) | Inorganic Compound (e.g., Sodium Chloride) |
|---|---|---|
| Molar mass | 58 | 58.5 |
| Bonding | Covalent ($C_4H_{10}$) | Ionic ($Na^+$ and $Cl^-$ ions) |
| Physical state at room temperature and atmospheric pressure | Gas | Solid |
| Boiling point | Low ($-0.5°C$) | High ($1413°C$) |
| Melting point | Low ($-139°C$) | High ($801°C$) |
| Solubility in water | Insoluble | High (36 g/100 mL) |
| Solubility in organic solvents (e.g., hexane) | High | Insoluble |
| Flammability | Flammable | Nonflammable |
| Electrical conductivity | Nonconductor | Conducts electricity in solution and in molten liquid |

in water than in a less-polar solvent, whereas organic compounds, which are typically nonpolar or only moderately polar, are less soluble, or insoluble in water. In Table 10.1, the physical properties of the organic compound butane are compared with those of sodium chloride, an inorganic compound of similar molar mass.

**Question 10.1** A student is presented with a sample of an unknown substance and asked to classify the substance as organic or inorganic. What tests should the student carry out?

**Question 10.2** What results would the student expect if the sample in Question 10.1 were an inorganic compound? What results would the student expect if it were an organic compound?

## Families of Organic Compounds

The most general classification of organic compounds divides them into hydrocarbons and substituted hydrocarbons. A **hydrocarbon** molecule contains only carbon and hydrogen. A **substituted hydrocarbon** is one in which one or more hydrogen atoms is replaced by another atom or group of atoms.

The hydrocarbons can be further subdivided into aliphatic and aromatic hydrocarbons (Figure 10.2). **Aliphatic hydrocarbons** are non-aromatic compounds. This means they do not have a benzene ring in the structure. The four families of aliphatic hydrocarbons are the alkanes, cycloalkanes, alkenes, and alkynes.

**Saturated hydrocarbons** contain only carbon and hydrogen and have only carbon-to-hydrogen and carbon-to-carbon single bonds. Alkanes and cycloalkanes are saturated hydrocarbons. **Unsaturated hydrocarbons** contain at least one

**LEARNING GOAL**

**2** Recognize structures that represent each of the families of organic compounds.

**Figure 10.2** The family of hydrocarbons is divided into two major classes: aliphatic and aromatic. The aliphatic hydrocarbons are further subdivided into four major subclasses: alkanes, cycloalkanes, alkenes, and alkynes.

# GREEN CHEMISTRY

## Frozen Methane: Treasure or Threat?

Methane is the simplest hydrocarbon, but it has some unusual behaviors. One of these is the ability to form a clathrate, which is an unusual type of matter in which molecules of one substance form a cage around molecules of another substance. For instance, water molecules can form a latticework around methane molecules to form frozen methane hydrate, possibly one of the biggest reservoirs of fossil fuel on earth.

Typically we wouldn't expect a nonpolar molecule, such as methane, to interact with a polar molecule, such as water. So, then, how is this structure formed? As we have studied earlier, water molecules interact with one another by strong hydrogen bonding. In the frozen state, these hydrogen-bonded water molecules form an open latticework. The nonpolar methane molecule is simply trapped inside one of the spaces within the lattice.

Vast regions of the ocean floor are covered by ice fields of frozen methane. Scientists would like to "mine" this ice to use the methane as a fuel. In fact, the U.S. Geological Survey estimates that the amount of methane hydrate in the United States is worth over 200 times the conventional natural gas resources in this country!

But is it safe to harvest the methane from this ice? Caution will certainly be required. Methane is flammable, and, like carbon dioxide, it is a greenhouse gas. In fact, it is about twenty times more efficient at trapping heat than carbon dioxide. (Greenhouse gases are discussed in greater detail in Green Chemistry: The Greenhouse Effect and Global Climate Change in Chapter 5.) So the U.S. Department of Energy, which is working with industry to develop ways to harvest the methane, must figure out how to do that without releasing much into the atmosphere where it could intensify global warming.

It may be that a huge release of methane from these frozen reserves was responsible for a major global warming that occurred fifty-five million years ago and lasted for one hundred thousand years. NASA scientists using computer simulations hypothesize that a shift of the continental plates may have released vast amounts of methane gas from the ocean floor. This methane raised the temperature of earth by about 13°F. In fact, the persistence of the methane in the atmosphere warmed earth enough to melt the ice in the oceans and at polar caps and completely change the global climate. This theory, if it turns out

Three-dimensional structure of methane hydrate.

A sample of frozen methane hydrate.

to be true, highlights the importance of controlling the amount of methane, as well as carbon dioxide, that we release into the air. Certainly, harvesting the frozen methane of the oceans, if we choose to do it, must be done with great care.

### For Further Understanding

▶ News stories alternatively describe frozen methane as a "New Frontier" and "Armageddon." Explain these opposing views.

▶ What are the ethical considerations involved in mining frozen methane?

---

carbon-to-carbon double or triple bond. An unsaturated hydrocarbon with at least one carbon-to-carbon double bond is an alkene. One with at least one carbon-to-carbon triple bond is an alkyne.

*Recall that each of the lines in these structures represents a shared pair of electrons. See Chapter 3.*

Saturated Hydrocarbon
(Alkane)

Unsaturated Hydrocarbon
(Alkene)

Unsaturated Hydrocarbon
(Alkyne)

Some hydrocarbons are cyclic. Cycloalkanes consist of carbon atoms bonded to one another to produce a ring. **Aromatic hydrocarbons** contain a benzene ring or a derivative of the benzene ring.

A Cycloalkane
(Cyclohexane)

Benzene

A substituted hydrocarbon is produced by replacing one or more hydrogen atoms with a functional group. A **functional group** is an atom or group of atoms arranged in a particular way that is primarily responsible for the chemical and physical properties of the molecule in which it is found. The importance of functional groups becomes more apparent when we consider that hydrocarbons have little biological activity. However, the addition of a functional group confers unique and interesting properties that give the molecule important biological or medical properties.

All compounds that have a particular functional group are members of the same family. We have just seen that the alkenes are characterized by the presence of carbon-to-carbon double bonds. Similarly, all alcohols contain a hydroxyl group (—OH). Since this group is polar and can form hydrogen bonds, an alcohol such as ethanol ($CH_3CH_2OH$) is liquid at room temperature and highly soluble in water, while the alkane of similar molar mass, propane ($CH_3CH_2CH_3$), is nonpolar and is a gas at room temperature and completely insoluble in water. Other common functional groups are shown in Table 10.2, along with an example of a molecule from each family.

The chemistry of organic and biological molecules is usually controlled by the functional group found in the molecule. Just as members of the same family of the periodic table exhibit similar chemistry, organic molecules with the same functional group exhibit similar chemistry. Although it would be impossible to learn the chemistry of each organic molecule, it is relatively easy to learn the chemistry of each functional group. In this way you can learn the chemistry of all members of a family of organic compounds, or biological molecules, just by learning the chemistry of its characteristic functional group or groups.

LEARNING GOAL

**3** Write the names and draw the structures of the common functional groups that characterize the families of organic compounds.

## 10.2 Alkanes

**Alkanes** are saturated hydrocarbons; that is, alkanes contain only carbon and hydrogen bonded together through carbon-hydrogen and carbon-carbon single bonds. $C_nH_{2n+2}$ is the general formula for alkanes. In this formula, $n$ is the number of carbon atoms in the molecule.

### Structure

Four types of formulas, each providing different information, are used in organic chemistry: the molecular formula, the structural formula, the condensed formula, and the line formula.

The **molecular formula** tells the kind and number of each type of atom in a molecule but does not show the bonding pattern. Consider the molecular formulas for simple alkanes:

LEARNING GOAL

**4** Write condensed, structural, and line formulas for saturated hydrocarbons.

$$CH_4 \qquad C_2H_6 \qquad C_3H_8 \qquad C_4H_{10}$$
Methane    Ethane    Propane    Butane

## TABLE 10.2 Common Functional Groups

| Type of Compound | Functional Group | Structural Formula | Condensed Formula | Example Structural Formula | Example IUPAC Name | Common Name |
|---|---|---|---|---|---|---|
| Alcohol | Hydroxyl | *R—O—H | ROH | CH₃CH₂—O—H | Ethanol | Ethyl alcohol |
| Aldehyde | Carbonyl | R—C(=O)—H | RCHO | CH₃C(=O)—H | Ethanal | Acetaldehyde |
| Amide | Carboxamide | R—C(=O)—N(H)—H | RCONH₂ | CH₃C(=O)—N(H)—H | Ethanamide | Acetamide |
| Amine | Amino | R—N(H)—H | RNH₂ | CH₃CH₂N(H)—H | Aminoethane | Ethyl amine |
| Carboxylic acid | Carboxyl | R—C(=O)—O—H | RCOOH | CH₃C(=O)—O—H | Ethanoic acid | Acetic acid |
| Ester | Ester | R—C(=O)—O—R′ | RCOOR′ | CH₃C(=O)—OCH₃ | Methyl ethanoate | Methyl acetate |
| Ether | Ether | R—O—R′ | ROR′ | CH₃OCH₃ | Methoxymethane | Dimethyl ether |
| Halide | Halogen atom | R—Cl (or —Br, —F, —I) | RCl | CH₃CH₂Cl | Chloroethane | Ethyl chloride |
| Ketone | Carbonyl | †R—C(=O)—R′ | RCOR′ | CH₃C(=O)CH₃ | Propanone | Acetone |
| Alkene | Double bond | R₂C=CR₂ | R₂CCR₂ | CH₃CH=CH₂ | Propene | Propylene |
| Alkyne | Triple bond | R—C≡C—R | RCCR | CH₃C≡CH | Propyne | Methyl acetylene |

*R and R′ represent an alkyl group, an aryl group, or H.
†In a ketone, R and R′ must be alkyl or aryl groups.

For the first three compounds, there is only one possible arrangement of the atoms. However, for $C_4H_{10}$ there are two possible arrangements. How do we know which is correct? The problem is solved by using the **structural formula**, which shows each atom and bond in a molecule. The following are the structural formulas for methane, ethane, propane, and the two isomers of butane:

Recall that a covalent bond, representing a pair of shared electrons, can be drawn as a line between two atoms. For the structure to be correct, each carbon atom must show four pairs of shared electrons.

Methane    Ethane    Propane    Butane    Methylpropane (isobutane)

The advantage of a structural formula is that it shows the complete structure, but for large molecules it is time-consuming to draw and requires too much space. The compromise is the **condensed formula**. It shows all the atoms in a molecule and places them in a sequential order that indicates which atoms are bonded to which. The following are the condensed formulas for the preceding five compounds.

| $CH_4$ | $CH_3CH_3$ | $CH_3CH_2CH_3$ | $CH_3(CH_2)_2CH_3$ | $(CH_3)_3CH$ |
|---|---|---|---|---|
| Methane | Ethane | Propane | Butane | Methylpropane (isobutane) |

The names and formulas of the first ten straight-chain alkanes are shown in Table 10.3.

The simplest representation of a molecule is the **line formula.** In the line formula we assume that there is a carbon atom at any location where two or more lines intersect. We also assume that there is a methyl group at the end of any line and that each carbon in the structure is bonded to the correct number of hydrogen atoms. Compare the structural and line formulas for butane and methylpropane, shown here:

Butane
(Straight chain alkane)

Methylpropane
(Branched alkane)

Each carbon atom forms four single covalent bonds, but each hydrogen atom has only a single covalent bond. Although a carbon atom may be involved in single, double, or triple bonds, it always shares four pairs of electrons. The Lewis structure of the simplest alkane, methane, shows the four shared pairs of electrons (Figure 10.3a). When carbon is involved in four single bonds, the *bond angle*, the angle between two atoms or substituents attached to carbon, is 109.5°, as predicted by the valence-shell electron-pair repulsion (VSEPR) theory. Thus, alkanes contain carbon atoms that have tetrahedral geometry.

**ANIMATIONS**
- The Geometry of $CH_4$
- Valence-Shell Electron-Pair Repulsion Theory
- VSEPR and Molecular Geometry

*Molecular geometry is described in Section 3.4.*

**TABLE 10.3  Names and Formulas of the First Ten Straight-Chain Alkanes**

| Name | Molecular Formula | Condensed Formula | Melting Point, °C* | Boiling Point, °C* |
|---|---|---|---|---|
| *Alkanes* | $C_nH_{2n+2}$ | | | |
| Methane | $CH_4$ | $CH_4$ | −182.5 | −162.2 |
| Ethane | $C_2H_6$ | $CH_3CH_3$ | −183.9 | −88.6 |
| Propane | $C_3H_8$ | $CH_3CH_2CH_3$ | −187.6 | −42.1 |
| Butane | $C_4H_{10}$ | $CH_3CH_2CH_2CH_3$ or $CH_3(CH_2)_2CH_3$ | −137.2 | −0.5 |
| Pentane | $C_5H_{12}$ | $CH_3CH_2CH_2CH_2CH_3$ or $CH_3(CH_2)_3CH_3$ | −129.8 | 36.1 |
| Hexane | $C_6H_{14}$ | $CH_3CH_2CH_2CH_2CH_2CH_3$ or $CH_3(CH_2)_4CH_3$ | −95.2 | 68.8 |
| Heptane | $C_7H_{16}$ | $CH_3CH_2CH_2CH_2CH_2CH_2CH_3$ or $CH_3(CH_2)_5CH_3$ | −90.6 | 98.4 |
| Octane | $C_8H_{18}$ | $CH_3CH_2CH_2CH_2CH_2CH_2CH_2CH_3$ or $CH_3(CH_2)_6CH_3$ | −56.9 | 125.6 |
| Nonane | $C_9H_{20}$ | $CH_3CH_2CH_2CH_2CH_2CH_2CH_2CH_2CH_3$ or $CH_3(CH_2)_7CH_3$ | −53.6 | 150.7 |
| Decane | $C_{10}H_{22}$ | $CH_3CH_2CH_2CH_2CH_2CH_2CH_2CH_2CH_2CH_3$ or $CH_3(CH_2)_8CH_3$ | −29.8 | 174.0 |

*Melting and boiling points as reported in the National Institute of Standards and Technology Chemistry Webbook, which can be found at http://webbook.nist.gov/.

**Figure 10.3** The tetrahedral carbon atom: (a) Lewis structure; (b) a tetrahedron; (c) the tetrahedral carbon drawn with dashes and wedges; (d) the stick drawing of the tetrahedral carbon atom; (e) ball-and-stick model of methane.

A tetrahedron is a geometric solid having the structure shown in Figure 10.3b. There are many different ways to draw the tetrahedral carbon (Figures 10.3c–10.3e). In Figure 10.3c, solid lines, dashes, and wedges are used to represent the structure of methane. Dashes go back into the page away from you; wedges come out of the page toward you; and solid lines are in the plane of the page. The structure in Figure 10.3d is the same as that in Figure 10.3c; it just leaves a lot more to the imagination. Figure 10.3e is a ball-and-stick model of the methane molecule. Three-dimensional drawings of two other simple alkanes are shown in Figure 10.4.

**EXAMPLE 10.1**   **Using Different Types of Formulas to Represent Organic Compounds**

LEARNING GOAL

**4** Write condensed, structural, and line formulas for saturated hydrocarbons.

The following line structure represents 2,2,4-trimethylpentane (also called isooctane), which is the standard of excellence used in determining the octane rating of gasoline. See also Green Chemistry: The Petroleum Industry and Gasoline Production later in this chapter.

2,2,4-Trimethylpentane
(isooctane)

Draw the structural and condensed formulas of this molecule.

**Solution**

Remember that each intersection of lines represents a carbon atom and that each line ends in a methyl group. This gives us the following carbon skeleton:

$$
\begin{array}{ccc}
& \text{C} & \text{C} \\
& | & | \\
\text{C}-\text{C}-\text{C}-\text{C}-\text{C} \\
& | \\
& \text{C}
\end{array}
$$

By adding the correct number of hydrogen atoms to the carbon skeleton, we are able to complete the structural formula of this compound.

$$
\begin{array}{ccccc}
& \text{H} & & \text{H} & \\
& | & & | & \\
& \text{H}-\text{C}-\text{H} & & \text{H}-\text{C}-\text{H} & \\
& \text{H} & | & \text{H} & | & \text{H} \\
& | & | & | & | & | \\
\text{H}-\text{C}-\text{C} & & & \text{C}-\text{C}-\text{H} \\
& | & | & | & | \\
& \text{H} & | & \text{H} & \text{H H} \\
& & \text{H}-\text{C}-\text{H} \\
& & | \\
& & \text{H}
\end{array}
$$

From the structural formula, we can write the condensed formula as follows:

$$CH_3C(CH_3)_2\,CH_2CH(CH_3)CH_3$$

**Practice Problem 10.1**

For each of the molecules in Table 10.4, draw the structural and the line formulas.

▶ For Further Practice: **Questions 10.20 and 10.21.**

## Physical Properties

All hydrocarbons are nonpolar molecules. As a result, they are not water soluble but are soluble in nonpolar organic solvents. Furthermore, they have relatively low melting points and boiling points and are generally less dense than water. In general, the longer the hydrocarbon chain (greater the molar mass), the higher the melting and boiling points and the greater the density (see Table 10.3).

At room temperature, alkanes with 1 to 4 carbon atoms are gases, those with 5 to 17 carbon atoms are colorless liquids, and those containing more than 18 carbon atoms are white, waxy solids. These trends in physical properties are the result of London dispersion forces. These attractive forces increase as the mass of the molecule and the number of electrons increase. Knowing this, we can predict that London dispersion forces will be stronger and the attraction greater for molecules having a larger surface area. The longer, higher molar mass alkanes would be expected to exhibit stronger London dispersion forces and therefore higher boiling and melting points.

**LEARNING GOAL**

**5** Describe the relationship between the structure and physical properties of saturated hydrocarbons.

*See Section 5.2 for a discussion of the forces responsible for the physical properties of a substance.*

**Figure 10.4** (a) Drawing and (b) ball-and-stick model of ethane. All the carbon atoms have a tetrahedral arrangement, and all bond angles are approximately 109.5°. (c) Drawing and (d) ball-and-stick model of a more complex alkane, butane.

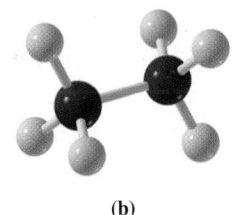

(a)

(b)

(c)

(d)

**TABLE 10.4  Melting and Boiling Points of Five Alkanes of Molecular Formula $C_6H_{14}$**

| Name | Condensed Formula | Boiling Point* °C | Melting Point* °C |
|---|---|---|---|
| Hexane | $CH_3(CH_2)_4CH_3$ | 68.8 | −95.2 |
| 2-Methylpentane | $CH_3CH(CH_3)(CH_2)_2CH_3$ | 60.9 | −153.2 |
| 3-Methylpentane | $CH_3CH_2CH(CH_3)CH_2CH_3$ | 63.3 | −118 |
| 2,3-Dimethylbutane | $CH_3CH(CH_3)CH(CH_3)CH_3$ | 58.1 | −130.2 |
| 2,2-Dimethylbutane | $CH_3C(CH_3)_2CH_2CH_3$ | 49.8 | −100.2 |

*Melting and boiling points as reported in the National Institute of Standards and Technology Chemistry Webbook, which can be found at http://webbook.nist.gov/.

Some alkanes have one or more carbon atoms branching from the main carbon chain. Compare the following two molecules with molecular formula $C_9H_{20}$.

Nonane                    3-Isopropylhexane

The branched-chain form, 3-isopropylhexane, has a much smaller surface area than the straight chain. As a result, the London dispersion forces attracting the molecules to one another are less strong and these molecules have lower melting and boiling points than the straight-chain isomers. The melting and boiling points of the five structural isomers of $C_6H_{14}$ are found in Table 10.4.

## Alkyl Groups

**Alkyl groups** are alkanes with one fewer hydrogen atom. The name of the alkyl group is derived from the name of the alkane containing the same number of carbon atoms. The -*ane* ending of the alkane name is replaced by the -*yl* ending. Thus, —$CH_3$ is a methyl group and —$CH_2CH_3$ is an ethyl group. The dash at the end of these two structures represents the point at which the alkyl group can bond to another atom. The first five continuous-chain alkyl groups are presented in Table 10.5.

Carbon atoms are classified according to the number of other carbon atoms to which they are attached. A **primary (1°) carbon** is directly bonded to one other carbon. A **secondary (2°) carbon** is bonded to two other carbon atoms; a **tertiary (3°) carbon** is bonded to three other carbon atoms, and a **quaternary (4°) carbon** to four.

Alkyl groups are classified according to the number of carbons attached to the carbon atom that joins the alkyl group to a molecule.

**TABLE 10.5  Names and Formulas of the First Five Continuous-Chain Alkyl Groups**

| Alkyl Group Structure | Name |
|---|---|
| —$CH_3$ | Methyl |
| —$CH_2CH_3$ | Ethyl |
| —$CH_2CH_2CH_3$ | Propyl |
| —$CH_2CH_2CH_2CH_3$ | Butyl |
| —$CH_2CH_2CH_2CH_2CH_3$ | Pentyl |

| Primary | Secondary | Tertiary |
| alkyl group | alkyl group | alkyl group |

All of the continuous-chain alkyl groups are primary alkyl groups (see Table 10.5). Several branched-chain alkyl groups are shown in Table 10.6. The carbon atom that attaches the alkyl group to the parent compound is highlighted in red in these structures above and in Table 10.6. Notice that the isopropyl and *sec*-butyl groups are secondary alkyl groups; the isobutyl group is a primary alkyl group; and the *t*-butyl (*tert*-butyl) is a tertiary alkyl group.

**TABLE 10.6  Structures and Names of Some Branched-Chain Alkyl Groups**

| Structure | Classification | Common Name | IUPAC Name |
|---|---|---|---|
| CH₃CH—<br>　\|<br>　CH₃ | 2° | Isopropyl* | 1-Methylethyl |
| 　CH₃<br>　\|<br>CH₃CHCH₂— | 1° | Isobutyl* | 2-Methylpropyl |
| 　　CH₃<br>　　\|<br>CH₃CH₂CH— | 2° | sec-Butyl† | 1-Methylpropyl |
| 　CH₃<br>　\|<br>CH₃C—<br>　\|<br>　CH₃ | 3° | t-Butyl or tert-Butyl‡ | 1,1-Dimethylethyl |

*The prefix *iso*- (isomeric) is used when there are two methyl groups at the end of the alkyl group.
†The prefix *sec*- (secondary) indicates that there are two carbons bonded to the carbon that attaches the alkyl group to the parent molecule.
‡The prefix *t*- or *tert*- (tertiary) means that three carbons are attached to the carbon that attaches the alkyl group to the parent molecule.

**Question 10.3**   Classify each of the carbon atoms in the following structures as primary, secondary, tertiary, or quaternary.

a.　　　　　　　　　b.　　　　　　　　　c.

**Question 10.4**   Classify each of the carbon atoms in the following structures as primary, secondary, tertiary, or quaternary.
　　a.  $CH_3CH_2C(CH_3)_2CH_2CH_3$
　　b.  $CH_3CH_2CH_2CH_2CH(CH_3)CH(CH_3)CH_3$

# CHEMISTRY AT THE CRIME SCENE

## Arson and Alkanes

In September of 2005, Thomas Sweatt was sentenced to life in prison for setting forty-five fires in the Washington, D.C. area. Aside from millions of dollars in property damage, two people died as a result of these fires. Mr. Sweatt confessed to the fires, which terrorized the Washington metropolitan area over a 2-year period, stating that he was "addicted to setting fires."

Authorities estimate that one-third of all fires are arson, and the Federal Bureau of Investigation (FBI) reports that arson is more common in the United States than anywhere else in the world. Although arsonists may set fires as terrorist acts, to defraud insurance companies, to gain revenge, or to cover up another crime, other arsonists are mentally ill pyromaniacs like Mr. Sweatt.

As soon as a fire is extinguished and the scene is secure, investigators gather evidence to determine the cause of the fire. They study the pattern of the fire to determine the point of origin. This is critical, because this is where they must sample for the presence of accelerants, flammable substances that cause fires to burn hotter and spread more quickly. The most common accelerants are mixtures of hydrocarbons, including gasoline, kerosene, or diesel fuel.

Because all of these accelerants contain molecules that evaporate, they may be detected at the point of origin by trained technicians or "sniffer dogs." However, a much more advanced technology is also available; it is called *headspace gas chromatography*. Gas chromatography separates and identifies components of a sample based on differences in their boiling points. Each gas mixture produces its own unique "chemical fingerprint" or chromatogram. Crime scene technicians collect debris from the point of origin and seal it in an airtight vial. In the laboratory, they heat the vial so the hydrocarbons evaporate and are trapped in the headspace of the vial. These gases are then collected with a needle and syringe and injected into the gas chromatograph for analysis and identification.

To be absolutely certain that an accelerant has been used, the crime scene technicians also collect debris from control sites away from the point of origin. The reason for this is that

pyrolysis, the decomposition or transformation of a compound caused by heat, may produce products that simulate accelerants. If an accelerant is found at the point of origin and not among the other pyrolysis products, it can be concluded that arson was the cause of the blaze.

Of course, the next priority is to catch the arsonist. Crime scene technicians collect and analyze physical evidence, including fingerprints, footprints, and other artifacts, found at the crime scene. In the case of Mr. Sweatt, it was DNA fingerprint evidence from articles of clothing left at the crime scenes that led to his capture and conviction and ended his 2-year arson spree.

**For Further Understanding**

▶ Investigate the composition of gasoline, diesel fuel, and kerosene and explain how they can be distinguished from one another using gas chromatography.

▶ Other accelerants that have been used by arsonists include nail polish remover (acetone), grain alcohol (ethanol), and rubbing alcohol (2-propanol or isopropyl alcohol). What properties do these substances share that make them useful as accelerants?

c.

d.

## Nomenclature

Historically, organic compounds were named by the chemist who discovered them. Often the names reflected the source of the compound. For instance, the antibiotic penicillin is named for the mold *Penicillium notatum*, which produces it. The pain reliever aspirin was made by adding an acetate group to a compound first purified from the bark of a willow tree and later from the meadowsweet plant (*Spirea ulmaria*). Thus, the name aspirin comes from *a* (acetate) and *spir* (genus of meadowsweet).

These names are easy for us to remember because we come into contact with these compounds often. However, as the number of compounds increased, organic chemists realized that historical names were not adequate because they revealed nothing about the structure of a compound. Thousands of such compounds and their common names had to be memorized! What was needed was a set of nomenclature (naming) rules that would produce a unique name for every organic compound. Furthermore, the name should be so descriptive that, by knowing the name, a student or scientist could write the structure.

The International Union of Pure and Applied Chemistry (IUPAC) is the organization responsible for establishing and maintaining a standard, universal system for naming organic compounds. The system of nomenclature developed by this group is called the **IUPAC Nomenclature System.** The following rules are used for naming alkanes by the IUPAC system.

1. Determine the name of the **parent compound,** the longest continuous carbon chain in the compound. Refer to Tables 10.3 and 10.7 to determine the parent name. Notice that these names are made up of a prefix related to the number of carbons in the chain and the suffix *-ane,* indicating that the molecule is an alkane (Table 10.7). Write down the name of the parent compound, leaving space before the name to identify the substituents. Parent chains are highlighted in yellow in the following examples, and the names of the parent compounds are shown below each structure.

LEARNING GOAL

**6** Use the basic rules of the IUPAC Nomenclature System to name alkanes and substituted alkanes.

It is important to learn the prefixes for the carbon chain lengths. We will use them in the nomenclature for all organic molecules.

CH₃CHCH₃
     |
    CH₃

Propane

CH₃CH₂CHCH₂CH₃
         |
        CH₃

Pentane

CH₃CH₂CH₂CH₂CH₂CH₂CHCH₃
                      |
                     CH₂CH₃
                      2   1

Nonane

2. Number the parent chain to give the lowest number to the carbon bonded to the first group encountered on the parent chain, regardless of the numbers that result for the other substituents.
3. Name and number each atom or group attached to the parent compound. The number tells you the position of the group on the main chain, and the name tells you what type of substituent is present at that position. For

**TABLE 10.7  Carbon Chain Length and Prefixes Used in the IUPAC Nomenclature System**

| Carbon Chain Length | Prefix | Alkane Name |
|---|---|---|
| 1 | Meth- | Methane |
| 2 | Eth- | Ethane |
| 3 | Prop- | Propane |
| 4 | But- | Butane |
| 5 | Pent- | Pentane |
| 6 | Hex- | Hexane |
| 7 | Hept- | Heptane |
| 8 | Oct- | Octane |
| 9 | Non- | Nonane |
| 10 | Dec- | Decane |

## GREEN CHEMISTRY

### Biofuels: A Renewable Resource

What do a high school science project and a train in the Midwest have in common: biofuels. For their senior project, two young Florida women re-engineered one of the school's maintenance trucks to run on the used oil from a local Chinese restaurant. Aside from the aroma of egg rolls frying, the truck performs very well. There are complications, however. The oil is too viscous to use until the truck engine has warmed up. So the driver needs to start the truck with diesel fuel, warm up the engine, then switch to the cooking oil fuel. Similarly, when preparing to stop the truck, the driver must switch back to diesel fuel so that the biofuel is no longer in the engine when it cools.

In 2010 Amtrak unveiled its first biodiesel-fueled train. The biodiesel fuel is a B20 blend, which means that it is **20%** biodiesel and **80%** regular diesel. The biodiesel is a complex mixture of fatty acids that are a by-product of the beef industry. So it is fitting that this train runs the Oklahoma City to Fort Worth route. This source works well in Texas and Oklahoma, which both produce large numbers of cattle, but what of other locations? Some have suggested corn or soybeans for biodiesel production. The question there is whether it is wise to rely on food crops that, in the event of widespread famine, may be needed for food.

The options are as creative as the minds that have envisioned them. As it turns out, 15 million pounds of alligator fat are dumped into landfills each year as a by-product of processing the meat. Over 60% of that fat can be extracted by microwaving and the resultant fatty acid profile makes it an excellent biodiesel fuel. NASA scientists are developing biodiesel from halophytic (salt-loving) plants. These plants can grow in the desert and can be irrigated with seawater. Thus they take advantage of environments and conditions that traditionally

have not been usefully employed. The scientists even predict that this would create a cooler, wetter land surface that would promote rainfall in areas that are extremely arid.

Boeing Corporation scientists think that biodiesel could cut aircraft emissions by 60–80%, which is a considerable improvement when you consider that 2% of all human emissions are from the aviation industry. Several test flights have shown that aircraft fly very well on fuels that are a mixture of 50% jet fuel and 50% biodiesel produced from a variety of sources including algae, the jatropha plant, and *Camelina* seed.

Biodiesel is much more common in Europe than elsewhere in the world and is produced from palm oil, rapeseed, flax, sunflower, and jatropha. These oils are treated by a transesterification process that produces fatty acid methyl or ethyl esters (FAMES). The resultant fuels are considered safer than traditional diesel because they are biodegradable, are ten times less toxic than table salt, and have high flash points.

We have much to learn about biofuels and their production before we can hope to replace the use of fossil fuels. However, knowing that fossil fuels are a limited resource, it is important to study renewable energy sources so that we can make wise decisions about those processes that provide the greatest benefit with the least negative impact on our environment.

**For Further Understanding**

▶ What are some of the environmental issues that must be studied when considering biodiesel from a variety of sources?

▶ What are some of the economic issues that need to be analyzed when considering biodiesel as a replacement for fossil fuels?

example, it may be one of the halogens [F—fluoro), Cl—(chloro), Br—(bromo), and I—(iodo)] or an alkyl group (Tables 10.5 and 10.6). In the following examples the parent chain is highlighted in yellow:

| Substituent: | 2-Bromo | 3-Methyl | 4-Ethyl |
| --- | --- | --- | --- |
| IUPAC name: | 2-Bromopropane | 3-Methylpentane | 4-Ethyloctane |

4. If the same substituent occurs more than once in the compound, a separate position number is given for each, and the prefixes *di-, tri-, tetra-, penta-,* and so forth are used, as shown in the following examples:

Throughout this book we will primarily use the IUPAC Nomenclature System. When common names are used, they will be shown in parentheses beneath the IUPAC name.

Br
|
CH₃CHCH₂CH₂CHCH₃
|
                Br
1  2   3   4   5  6

2,5-Dibromo
2,5-Dibromohexane

CH₃   CH₃   CH₃
|     |     |
CH₃CH₂CHCH₂CHCH₂CHCH₂CH₂CH₃
1   2   3·  4   5   6   7   8   9   10
10  9   8   7   6   5   4   3   2   1

3,5,7-Trimethyldecane
*NOT* 4,6,8-Trimethyldecane

5. Place the names of the substituents in alphabetical order before the name of the parent compound, which you wrote down in step 1. Numbers are separated by commas, and numbers are separated from names by hyphens. By convention, halogen substituents are placed before alkyl substituents.

CH₃
|
CH₃CHCCH₂CH₃
|   |
Br  CH₃
1  2  3  4  5

2-Bromo-3,3-dimethylpentane
*NOT* 3,3-Dimethyl-2-bromopentane

F
|
CH₃CHCHCHCH₂CH₃
|   |
CH₃  CH₃
1  2  3  4  5  6

3-Fluoro-2,4-dimethylhexane
*NOT* 2,4-Dimethyl-3-fluorohexane

CH₂CH₃
|
CH₃CH₂CHCHCH₂CH₂CH₂CH₃
|
CH₃
1  2  3  4  5  6  7  8

4-Ethyl-3-methyloctane
*NOT* 3-Methyl-4-ethyloctane

| EXAMPLE 10.2 | Naming Substituted Alkanes Using the IUPAC System |
|---|---|

LEARNING GOAL

**6** Use the basic rules of the IUPAC Nomenclature System to name alkanes and substituted alkanes.

a. What is the IUPAC name of the molecule below, which is commonly called Freon-12? This compound is a chlorofluorocarbon (CFC) once used as a refrigerant and aerosol propellant. It has not been manufactured in the United States since 1995 because of the CFC damage to the ozone layer.

$$\text{F—C—Cl}$$ with Cl above and F below

Cl
|
F—C—Cl
|
F

**Solution**

*Helpful Hint:* No numbers are necessary if there is only one carbon or if the numbering is clear cut.

Parent chain: methane
Substituents: dichlorodifluoro (no numbers are necessary)
Name: Dichlorodifluoromethane

b. What is the IUPAC name of the following molecule, which is a component of the tsetse fly pheromone? Molecules such as this are used as attractants in tsetse fly control measures.

CH₃
|
CH₃(CH₂)₁₄CHCH₃

*Continued…*

## Solution

*Helpful Hint:* For alkanes of between eleven and nineteen carbons, a prefix is used before the word decane (see Table 10.8).

> Parent chain: heptadecane
> Substituent: 2-methyl
> Name: 2-Methylheptadecane

c.  What is the IUPAC name of the following molecule, which is the standard of excellence used in determining the octane rating of gasoline?

$$
\underset{\underset{\displaystyle CH_3}{|}}{CH_3}\underset{}{\overset{\overset{\displaystyle CH_3\ \ CH_3}{|\ \ \ \ \ |}}{CH_3CCH_2CHCH_3}} \quad \text{or} \quad
$$

## Solution

> Parent chain: pentane
> Substituents: 2,2,4-trimethyl
> Name: 2,2,4-Trimethylpentane

---

### Practice Problem 10.2

Determine the IUPAC name for each of the following molecules.

a.  $\underset{\underset{}{}}{CH_3}\overset{\overset{CH_3\ \ \ CH_3}{|\ \ \ \ \ \ \ |}}{CH_3CHCH_2CHCH_2CH_2CH_2CH_3}$

b.  $\overset{\overset{Cl}{|}}{\underset{\underset{Cl}{|}}{Cl-C-F}}$

c.  $\overset{\overset{F\ \ Cl\ CH_3}{|\ \ \ |\ \ \ |}}{CH_3CH_2CH_2CHCHCHCH_3}$

▶ For Further Practice: **Questions 10.57, 10.58, and 10.61.**

---

Having learned to name a compound using the IUPAC system, we can easily write the structural formula of a compound, given its name. First, draw and number the parent carbon chain. Add the substituent groups to the correct carbon, and finish the structure by adding the correct number of hydrogen atoms.

### TABLE 10.8  IUPAC Nomenclature for Alkane Parent Chains Longer Than Ten Carbons

| Number of Carbons | IUPAC Name |
|---|---|
| 11 | Undecane |
| 12 | Dodecane |
| 13 | Tridecane |
| 14 | Tetradecane |
| 15 | Pentadecane |
| 16 | Hexadecane |
| 17 | Heptadecane |
| 18 | Octadecane |
| 19 | Nonadecane |

**EXAMPLE 10.3**   **Drawing the Structure of a Compound Using the IUPAC Name**

Draw the structural formula for 1-bromo-4-methylhexane.

LEARNING GOAL

**7** From the IUPAC name of an alkane or substituted alkane, be able to draw the structure.

**Solution**

Begin by drawing the six-carbon parent chain and indicating the four bonds for each carbon atom.

$$-C-C-C-C-C-C-$$

Next, number each carbon atom:

$$-\underset{1}{C}-\underset{2}{C}-\underset{3}{C}-\underset{4}{C}-\underset{5}{C}-\underset{6}{C}-$$

Now add the substituents. In this example a bromine atom is bonded to carbon-1, and a methyl group is bonded to carbon-4:

(structure with Br on C1 and H–C–H on C4, numbered 1 2 3 4 5 6)

Finally, add the correct number of hydrogen atoms so that each carbon has four covalent bonds:

(full structure: Br H H H H H across top, H–C–C–C–C–C–C–H, H H H / H H below, H–C–H with H below C4, numbered 1 2 3 4 5 6)

As a final check of your accuracy, use the IUPAC system to name the compound that you have just drawn, and compare the name with that in the original problem.

The molecular, condensed, and line formulas can be written from the structural formula shown. The molecular formula is $C_7H_{15}Br$, the condensed formula is $BrCH_2(CH_2)_2CH(CH_3)CH_2CH_3$, and the line formula for 1-bromo-4-methylhexane is

(line structure with Br)

**Practice Problem 10.3**

Draw the condensed formula of each of the following compounds:

a. 1-Bromo-2-chlorohexane
b. 2,3-Dimethylpentane
c. 1,3,5-Trichloroheptane
d. 3-Chloro-5-iodo-4-methyloctane
e. 1,2-Dibromo-3-chlorobutane
f. Trifluorochloromethane

▶ For Further Practice: **Questions 10.51, 10.52, and 10.53.**

**ANIMATION**

• Structural Isomers of Hexane

## Constitutional or Structural Isomers

As we saw earlier, there are two arrangements of the atoms represented by the molecular formula $C_4H_{10}$: butane and methylpropane. Molecules having the same molecular formula but a different arrangement of atoms are called **constitutional, or structural, isomers.** These isomers are unique compounds because of their structural differences, and they have different physical and chemical properties. For instance, the data in Table 10.4 show that the branched-chain isomers of $C_6H_{14}$ have lower boiling and melting points than the straight-chain isomer, hexane. These differences reflect the different shapes of the molecules.

---

**EXAMPLE 10.4   Drawing Constitutional or Structural Isomers of Alkanes**

Write all the constitutional isomers having the molecular formula $C_6H_{14}$.

**Solution**

1. Begin with the continuous six-carbon chain structure:

$$\underset{\text{Isomer A}}{\overset{1\quad2\quad3\quad4\quad5\quad6}{CH_3CH_2CH_2CH_2CH_2CH_3}}$$

2. Now try five-carbon chain structures with a methyl group attached to one of the internal carbon atoms of the chain:

$$\overset{1\quad2\quad3\quad4\quad5}{CH_3CHCH_2CH_2CH_3} \quad \text{and} \quad \overset{1\quad2\quad3\quad4\quad5}{CH_3CH_2CHCH_2CH_3}$$
$$\underset{\text{Isomer B}}{\mid \atop CH_3} \qquad\qquad\qquad \underset{\text{Isomer C}}{\mid \atop CH_3}$$

3. Next consider the possibilities for a four-carbon structure to which two methyl groups (—$CH_3$) may be attached:

$$\overset{1\quad2\quad3\quad4}{CH_3CHCHCH_3} \quad \text{and} \quad \overset{1\quad2|3\quad4}{CH_3CCH_2CH_3}$$
$$\underset{CH_3CH_3}{\mid\ \mid} \qquad\qquad \overset{CH_3}{\mid}$$
$$\underset{\text{Isomer D}}{} \qquad\qquad \underset{CH_3}{\mid}$$
$$\qquad\qquad\qquad\qquad \underset{\text{Isomer E}}{}$$

These are the five possible constitutional isomers of $C_6H_{14}$. At first it may seem that other isomers are also possible. But careful comparison will show that they are duplicates of those already constructed. For example, rather than add two methyl groups, a single ethyl group (—$CH_2CH_3$) could be added to the four-carbon chain:

$$CH_3CH_2CHCH_3$$
$$\mid$$
$$CH_2CH_3$$

But close examination will show that this is identical to isomer C. Perhaps we could add one ethyl group and one methyl group to a three-carbon parent chain, with the following result:

$$CH_2CH_3$$
$$\mid$$
$$CH_3CCH_3$$
$$\mid$$
$$CH_3$$

Again we find that this structure is the same as one of the isomers we have already identified, isomer E.

To check whether you have accidentally made duplicate isomers, name them using the IUPAC system. All isomers must have different IUPAC names. So if two names are identical, the structures are also identical. Use the IUPAC system to name the isomers in this example, and prove to yourself that the last two structures are simply duplicates of two of the original five isomers.

### Practice Problem 10.4

Heptane is a very poor fuel and is given a zero on the octane rating scale. Gasoline octane ratings are determined in test engines by comparison with 2,2,4-trimethylpentane (the standard of high quality) and heptane (standard of poor quality). Draw line formula and give the IUPAC name for each of the nine isomers of heptane.

▶ For Further Practice: **Questions 10.62 and 10.63.**

## 10.3 Cycloalkanes

The **cycloalkanes** are a family having C—C single bonds in a ring structure. They have the general molecular formula $C_nH_{2n}$ and thus have two fewer hydrogen atoms than the corresponding alkane ($C_nH_{2n+2}$). The structures and names of some simple cycloalkanes are shown in Figure 10.5.

In the IUPAC system, the cycloalkanes are named by applying the following simple rules.

- Determine the name of the alkane with the same number of carbon atoms as there are within the ring and add the prefix *cyclo*-. For example, cyclopentane is the cycloalkane that has five carbon atoms.
- If the cycloalkane is substituted, place the names of the groups in alphabetical order before the name of the cycloalkane. No number is needed if there is only one substituent.
- If more than one group is present, use numbers that result in the *lowest possible position numbers.*

| EXAMPLE 10.5 | Naming a Substituted Cycloalkane Using the IUPAC Nomenclature System |
| --- | --- |

Name the following cycloalkanes using IUPAC nomenclature.

LEARNING GOAL

**9** Write the names and draw the structures of simple cycloalkanes.

**Solution**

Parent chain: cyclohexane
Substituent: chloro (no number is required because there is only one substituent)
Name: Chlorocyclohexane

Parent chain: cyclopentane
Substituent: methyl (no number is required because there is only one substituent)
Name: Methylcyclopentane

These cycloalkanes could also be shown as line formulas, as shown on the next page. Each line represents a carbon-carbon bond. A carbon atom and the correct number of hydrogen atoms are assumed to be at the point where the lines meet and at the end of a line.

*Continued…*

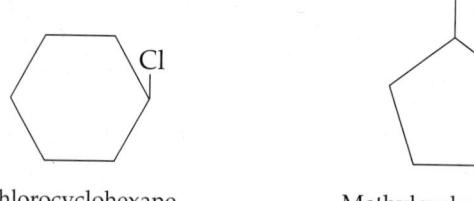

Chlorocyclohexane                    Methylcyclopentane

**Practice Problem 10.5**

Name each of the following cycloalkanes using IUPAC nomenclature:

a.                    b.    CH₃        c.                    d.

Cl                                     CH₂CH₃

▶ For Further Practice: **Questions 10.77 and 10.78.**

**Figure 10.5**  Cycloalkanes: (a) cyclopropane; (b) cyclobutane; (c) cyclohexane.
All of the cycloalkanes are shown using
structural formulas (left column), and line
formulas (right column).

## cis-trans Isomerism in Cycloalkanes

LEARNING GOAL

**10**  Draw cis- and trans-isomers of
cycloalkanes.

Atoms of an alkane can rotate freely around the carbon-carbon single bond, resulting in an unlimited number of arrangements. However, rotation around the bonds
in a cyclic structure is limited by the fact that the carbons of the ring are all bonded
to another carbon within the ring. The formation of **cis-trans isomers**, or **geometric isomers,** is a consequence of the absence of free rotation.

Geometric isomers are a type of *stereoisomer*. **Stereoisomers** are molecules that have the same structural formulas and bonding patterns but different arrangements of atoms in space. The *cis-trans* isomers of cycloalkanes are stereoisomers that differ from one another in the arrangement of substituents in space. Consider the following two views of the *cis-* and *trans*-isomers of 1,2-dichlorocyclohexane:

*Stereoisomers are discussed in detail in Section 16.3.*

Above the ring

Below the ring

*cis*-1,2-Dichlorocyclohexane

*trans*-1,2-Dichlorocyclohexane

*cis*-1,2-Dichlorocyclohexane

*trans*-1,2-Dichlorocyclohexane

In the wedge diagram at the top, it is easy to imagine that you are viewing the ring structures as if an edge were projecting toward you. This will help you understand the more common structural formulas, shown beneath them. In the structure on the left, both Cl atoms are beneath the ring. They are termed *cis* (*Latin*, "on the same side"). The complete name for this compound is *cis*-1,2-dichlorocyclohexane. In the structure on the right, one Cl is above the ring and the other is below it. They are said to be *trans* (*Latin*, "across from") to one another and the complete name of this compound is *trans*-1,2-dichlorocyclohexane. In the line structures, the wedges tell us the same information. The dashed wedges indicate that the bond projects away from you. The solid wedges indicate that the bond is projecting toward you.

Geometric isomers do not readily interconvert. The cyclic structure prevents unrestricted free rotation and, thus, prevents interconversion. Only by breaking carbon-carbon bonds of the ring could interconversion occur. As a result, geometric isomers may be separated from one another in the laboratory.

---

**EXAMPLE 10.6** | **Naming *cis-trans* Isomers of Substituted Cycloalkanes**

Determine whether the following substituted cycloalkanes are *cis-* or *trans*-isomers and write the complete name for each.

**LEARNING GOAL**

**10** Draw *cis-* and *trans*-isomers of cycloalkanes.

**Solution**

Both molecules are cyclopentanes having two methyl group substituents. Thus both would be named 1,2-dimethylcyclopentane. In the structure on the left, one methyl group is above the ring and the other is below the ring; they are in the *trans* configuration, and the structure is named *trans*-1,2-dimethylcyclopentane. In the structure on the right, both methyl groups are on the same side of the ring (above it, in this case); they are *cis* to one another, and the complete name of this compound is *cis*-1,2-dimethylcyclopentane.

*Continued…*

## Practice Problem 10.6

Determine whether each of the following is a *cis*- or a *trans*-isomer.

▶ For Further Practice: **Questions 10.85 and 10.86.**

**EXAMPLE 10.7**   **Naming a Cycloalkane Having Two Substituents Using the IUPAC Nomenclature System**

**LEARNING GOAL**

**9**  Write the names and draw the structures of simple cycloalkanes.

Name the following cycloalkanes using IUPAC nomenclature.

**Solution**

   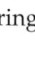

Parent chain: cyclopentane
Substituent: 1,2-dibromo
Isomer: *cis*
Since both bromine atoms are below the ring, the name is: *cis*-1,2-Dibromocyclopentane

Parent chain: cyclohexane
Substituent: 1,3-dimethyl
Isomer: *trans*
Since one of the methyl groups is above the ring and the other is below, the name is: *trans*-1,3-Dimethylcyclohexane

## Practice Problem 10.7

Write the complete IUPAC name for each of the following cycloalkanes.

▶ For Further Practice: **Questions 10.83 and 10.84.**

**LEARNING GOAL**

**11**  Describe conformations of alkanes.

## 10.4  Conformations of Alkanes and Cycloalkanes

Because there is *free rotation* around a carbon-carbon single bond, even a very simple alkane, like ethane, can exist in an unlimited number of forms (Figures 10.6a and 10.6b). These different arrangements are called **conformations,** or **conformers.**

**(a)** Staggered conformation of ethane

**(b)** Eclipsed conformation of ethane

**Figure 10.6** Conformational isomers of ethane and butane. The hydrogen atoms are much more crowded in the eclipsed conformation, depicted in (b) compared with the staggered conformation shown in (a). The staggered form is the most stable. The staggered and eclipsed conformations of butane are shown in (c) and (d).

**(c)** Staggered conformation of butane

**(d)** Eclipsed conformation of butane

## Alkanes

Figures 10.6c and 10.6d show two conformations of a more complex alkane, butane. In addition to these two conformations, an infinite number of intermediate conformers exist. Keep in mind that all these conformations are simply different forms of the same molecule produced by rotation around the carbon-carbon single bonds. Even at room temperature these conformers interconvert rapidly. As a result, they cannot be separated from one another.

Although all conformations can be found in a population of molecules, the *staggered* conformation (see Figures 10.6a and 10.6c) is the most common. One reason for this is that the bonding electrons are farthest from one another in this conformation. Because this minimizes the repulsion between these bonding electrons, the staggered conformation is the most stable of the possible conformations. In the *eclipsed* conformation (Figures 10.6b and 10.6d), the hydrogen atoms are closest to one another. This maximizes the repulsion between electrons. As a result, the eclipsed conformation is the least stable of the conformations.

## Cycloalkanes

Cycloalkanes also exist in different conformations. The only exception to this is cyclopropane. Because it has only three carbon atoms, it is always planar.

The conformations of six-member rings have been the most thoroughly studied. One reason is that many important and abundant biological molecules have six-member ring structures. Among these is the simple sugar glucose, also called *blood sugar*. Glucose is the most important sugar in the human body. It is absorbed by the cells of the body and broken down to provide energy for cellular activities.

The most energetically favorable conformation for a six-member ring is the **chair conformation.** In this conformation the hydrogen atoms are perfectly staggered; that is, they are as far from one another as possible. In addition, the bond angle between carbons is 109.5°, exactly the angle expected for tetrahedral carbon atoms. Because the hydrogen atoms are as far from one another as possible the repulsion between the bonding electrons is minimized. As a result, the chair conformation is the most stable conformation of cyclohexane.

Make a ball-and-stick model of butane and demonstrate these rotational changes for yourself.

**LEARNING GOAL**

**12** Draw the chair and boat conformations of cyclohexane.

*The structure of glucose is found in Section 16.4. The physiological roles of glucose are discussed in Chapters 21 and 22.*

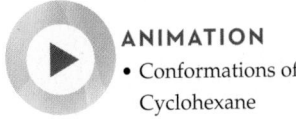

**ANIMATION**
• Conformations of Cyclohexane

# GREEN CHEMISTRY

## The Petroleum Industry and Gasoline Production

Petroleum consists primarily of alkanes and small amounts of alkenes and aromatic hydrocarbons. Substituted hydrocarbons, such as phenol, are also present in very small quantities. Although the composition of petroleum varies with the source (United States, Persian Gulf, etc.), the mixture of hydrocarbons can be separated into its component parts on the basis of differences in the boiling points of various hydrocarbons (distillation). Often several successive distillations of various fractions of the original mixture are required to completely purify the desired component. In the first distillation, the petroleum is separated into several fractions, each of which consists of a mix of hydrocarbons. Each fraction can be further purified by successive distillations. On an industrial scale, these distillations are carried out in columns that may be hundreds of feet (ft) in height.

The gasoline fraction of petroleum, called straight-run gasoline, consists primarily of alkanes and cycloalkanes with six to twelve carbon atoms in the skeleton. This fraction has very poor fuel performance. In fact, branched-chain alkanes are superior to straight-chain alkanes as fuels because they are more volatile, burn less rapidly in the cylinder, and thus reduce "knocking." Alkenes and aromatic hydrocarbons are also good fuels. Methods have been developed to convert hydrocarbons of higher and lower molar masses than gasoline to the appropriate molar mass range and to convert straight-chain hydrocarbons into branched ones. *Catalytic cracking* fragments a large hydrocarbon into smaller ones. *Catalytic re-forming* results in the rearrangement of a hydrocarbon into a more useful form.

The antiknock quality of a fuel is measured as its octane rating. Heptane is a very poor fuel and is given an octane rating of zero. 2,2,4-Trimethylpentane (commonly called isooctane) is an excellent fuel and is given an octane rating of one hundred. Gasoline octane ratings are experimentally determined by comparison with these two compounds in test engines.

Mining the sea for hydrocarbons.

 **ANIMATION**
- Oil Refining Processes

**For Further Understanding**

▶ Explain why the mixture of hydrocarbons in crude oil can be separated by distillation.

▶ Draw the structures of heptane and 2,2,4-trimethylpentane (isooctane).

Compare the structure of this deck chair to the conformation of cyclohexane shown to the right. Explain why this conformation is called the chair conformation.

Chair conformation

Six-member rings can also exist in a **boat conformation,** so-called because it resembles a rowboat. This form is much less stable than the chair conformation because the hydrogen atoms are much more crowded, creating much more repulsion between the electrons.

Boat conformation

Compare the structure of these boats to the conformation of cyclohexane shown to the left. Explain why this conformation is called the boat conformation.

## 10.5   Reactions of Alkanes and Cycloalkanes

### Combustion

Alkanes, cycloalkanes, and other hydrocarbons can be oxidized (by burning) in the presence of excess molecular oxygen. In this reaction, called **combustion,** they burn at high temperatures, producing carbon dioxide and water and releasing large amounts of energy as heat.

**LEARNING GOAL**

**13**  Write balanced equations for combustion reactions of alkanes.

$$C_nH_{2n+2} \quad + \quad O_2 \quad \longrightarrow \quad CO_2 \quad + \quad H_2O \quad + \quad \text{heat energy}$$
Alkane            Oxygen  $\longrightarrow$ Carbon dioxide      Water

The following examples show a combustion reaction for a simple alkane and a simple cycloalkane:

*Combustion reactions are discussed in Section 4.4.*

$$CH_4 + 2O_2 \longrightarrow CO_2 + 2H_2O + \text{heat energy}$$
Methane

(or $C_6H_{12}$) $+ 9O_2 \longrightarrow 6CO_2 + 6H_2O + \text{heat energy}$

Cyclohexane

---

| **EXAMPLE 10.8** | **Balancing Equations for the Combustion of Alkanes** |

Balance the following equation for the combustion of hexane:

$$C_6H_{14} + O_2 \longrightarrow CO_2 + H_2O$$

**LEARNING GOAL**

**13**  Write balanced equations for combustion reactions of alkanes.

**Solution**

First, balance the carbon atoms; there are 6 moles (mol) of carbon atoms on the left and only 1 mol of carbon atoms on the right:

$$C_6H_{14} + O_2 \longrightarrow 6CO_2 + H_2O$$

*Continued…*

Explain why the butane found in the lighter is a liquid only when maintained under pressure. Write an equation representing the complete combustion of butane.

Next, balance hydrogen atoms; there are 14 mol of hydrogen atoms on the left and only 2 mol of hydrogen atoms on the right:

$$C_6H_{14} + O_2 \longrightarrow 6CO_2 + 7H_2O$$

Now there are 19 mol of oxygen atoms on the right and only 2 mol of oxygen atoms on the left. Therefore, a coefficient of 9.5 is needed for $O_2$.

$$C_6H_{14} + 9.5O_2 \longrightarrow 6CO_2 + 7H_2O$$

Although decimal coefficients are sometimes used, it is preferable to have all integer coefficients. Multiplying each term in the equation by 2 will satisfy this requirement, giving us the following balanced equation:

$$2C_6H_{14} + 19O_2 \longrightarrow 12CO_2 + 14H_2O$$

The equation is now balanced with 12 mol of carbon atoms, 28 mol of hydrogen atoms, and 38 mol of oxygen atoms on each side of the equation.

**Practice Problem 10.8**

Write a balanced equation for the complete combustion of each of the following hydrocarbons:

    a. cyclobutane       b. ethane       c. decane

▶ For Further Practice: **Questions 10.93 and 10.94.**

*See Green Chemistry: The Greenhouse Effect and Global Climate Change in Chapter 5.*

The energy released, along with their availability and relatively low cost, makes hydrocarbons very useful as fuels. In fact, combustion is essential to our very existence. It is the process by which we heat our homes, run our cars, and generate electricity. Although combustion of fossil fuels is vital to industry and society, it also represents a threat to the environment. The buildup of $CO_2$ may contribute to global warming and change the face of the earth in future generations.

## Halogenation

Alkanes and cycloalkanes can also react with a halogen (usually chlorine or bromine) in a reaction called **halogenation.** Halogenation is a **substitution reaction,** that is, a reaction that results in the replacement of one group for another. In this reaction a halogen atom is substituted for one of the hydrogen atoms in the alkane. The products of this reaction are an **alkyl halide** or *haloalkane* and a hydrogen halide. Alkanes are not very reactive molecules. However, alkyl halides are very useful reactants for the synthesis of other organic compounds. Thus, the halogenation reaction is of great value because it converts unreactive alkanes into versatile starting materials for the synthesis of desired compounds. This is important in the pharmaceutical industry for the synthesis of some drugs. In addition, alkyl halides having two or more halogen atoms are useful solvents, insecticides, and herbicides.

Halogenation can occur only in the presence of heat and/or light, as indicated by the reaction conditions noted over the reaction arrows. The general equation for the halogenation of an alkane follows. The R in the general structure for the alkane may be either a hydrogen atom or an alkyl group.

**LEARNING GOAL**

**14** Write balanced equations for halogenation reactions of alkanes.

Alkane   Halogen                Alkyl halide   Hydrogen halide

Methane   Bromine              Bromomethane   Hydrogen bromide

$$CH_3CH_3 + Cl_2 \xrightarrow{Light} CH_3CH_2-Cl + H-Cl$$

Ethane      Chlorine         Chloroethane      Hydrogen chloride

Cyclohexane   Chlorine      Chlorocyclohexane   Hydrogen chloride

If the halogenation reaction is allowed to continue, the alkyl halide formed may react with other halogen atoms. When this happens, a mixture of products may be formed. For instance, bromination of methane will produce bromomethane ($CH_3Br$), dibromomethane ($CH_2Br_2$), tribromomethane ($CHBr_3$), and tetrabromomethane ($CBr_4$).

In more complex alkanes, including branched alkanes, halogenation can occur to some extent at all positions to give a mixture of monosubstituted products. For example, bromination of propane produces a mixture of 1-bromopropane and 2-bromopropane. Halogenation of the branched alkane 2-methylpropane results in two alkyl halide products. If the hydrogen atom on carbon-2 is replaced (by chlorine, for example) the product will be 2-chloro-2-methylpropane. If any other hydrogen atom is replaced, the product will be 1-chloro-2-methylpropane.

The alkyl halide may continue to react, forming a mixture of products substituted at multiple sites or substituted multiple times at the same site.

2-Chloro-          1-Chloro-
2-methylpropane   2-methylpropane

**Question 10.5**  Write a balanced equation for each of the following reactions. Show all possible products.
  a. the monobromination of propane
  b. the monochlorination of butane
  c. the monochlorination of cyclobutane
  d. the monobromination of pentane

**Question 10.6**  Provide the IUPAC names for the products of the reactions in Question 10.5.

# A MEDICAL PERSPECTIVE

## Polyhalogenated Hydrocarbons Used as Anesthetics

Polyhalogenated hydrocarbons are hydrocarbons containing two or more halogen atoms. Some polyhalogenated compounds are notorious for the problems they have caused. For instance, some insecticides such as DDT, chlordane, kepone, and lindane do not break down rapidly in the environment. As a result, these toxic compounds accumulate in biological tissue of a variety of animals, including humans, and may cause neurological damage, birth defects, or even death.

Other halogenated hydrocarbons are very useful in medicine. They were among the first anesthetics (pain relievers) used routinely in medical practice. These chemicals played a central role as the studies of medicine and dentistry advanced into modern times.

$$CH_3CH_2Cl \qquad\qquad CH_3Cl$$

Chloroethane      Chloromethane
(ethyl chloride)     (methyl chloride)

Chloroethane and chloromethane are local anesthetics. A local anesthetic deadens the feeling in a portion of the body. Applied topically (on the skin), chloroethane and chloromethane numb the area. Rapid evaporation of these anesthetics lowers the skin temperature, deadening the local nerve endings. They act rapidly, but the effect is brief, and feeling is restored quickly.

$$CHCl_3$$

Trichloromethane
(chloroform)

In the past, chloroform was used as both a general and a local anesthetic. When administered through inhalation, it rapidly causes loss of consciousness. However, the effects of this powerful anesthetic are of short duration. Chloroform is no longer used because it was shown to be carcinogenic.

$$\begin{array}{c} \text{F} \quad \text{H} \\ | \quad\ | \\ \text{F---C---C---Br} \\ | \quad\ | \\ \text{F} \quad \text{Cl} \end{array}$$

2-Bromo-2-chloro-1,1,1-trifluoroethane
(Halothane)

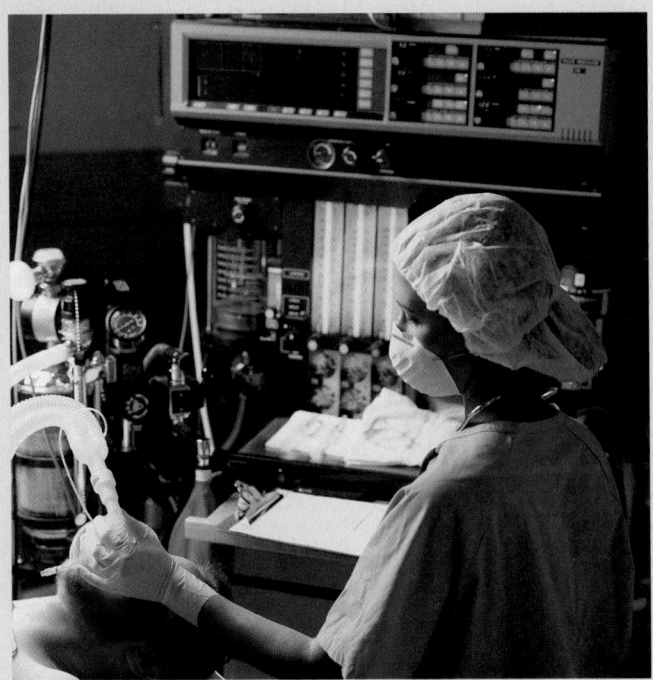

Halothane is administered to a patient.

Halothane is a general anesthetic that is administered by inhalation. It is considered to be a very safe anesthetic and is widely used.

### For Further Understanding

▶ In the first 24 hours (h) following administration, 70% of the halothane is eliminated from the body in exhaled gases. Explain why halothane is so readily eliminated in exhaled gases.

▶ Rapid evaporation of chloroethane from the skin surface causes cooling that causes local deadening of nerve endings. Explain why the skin surface cools dramatically as a result of evaporation of chloroethane.

# CHAPTER MAP

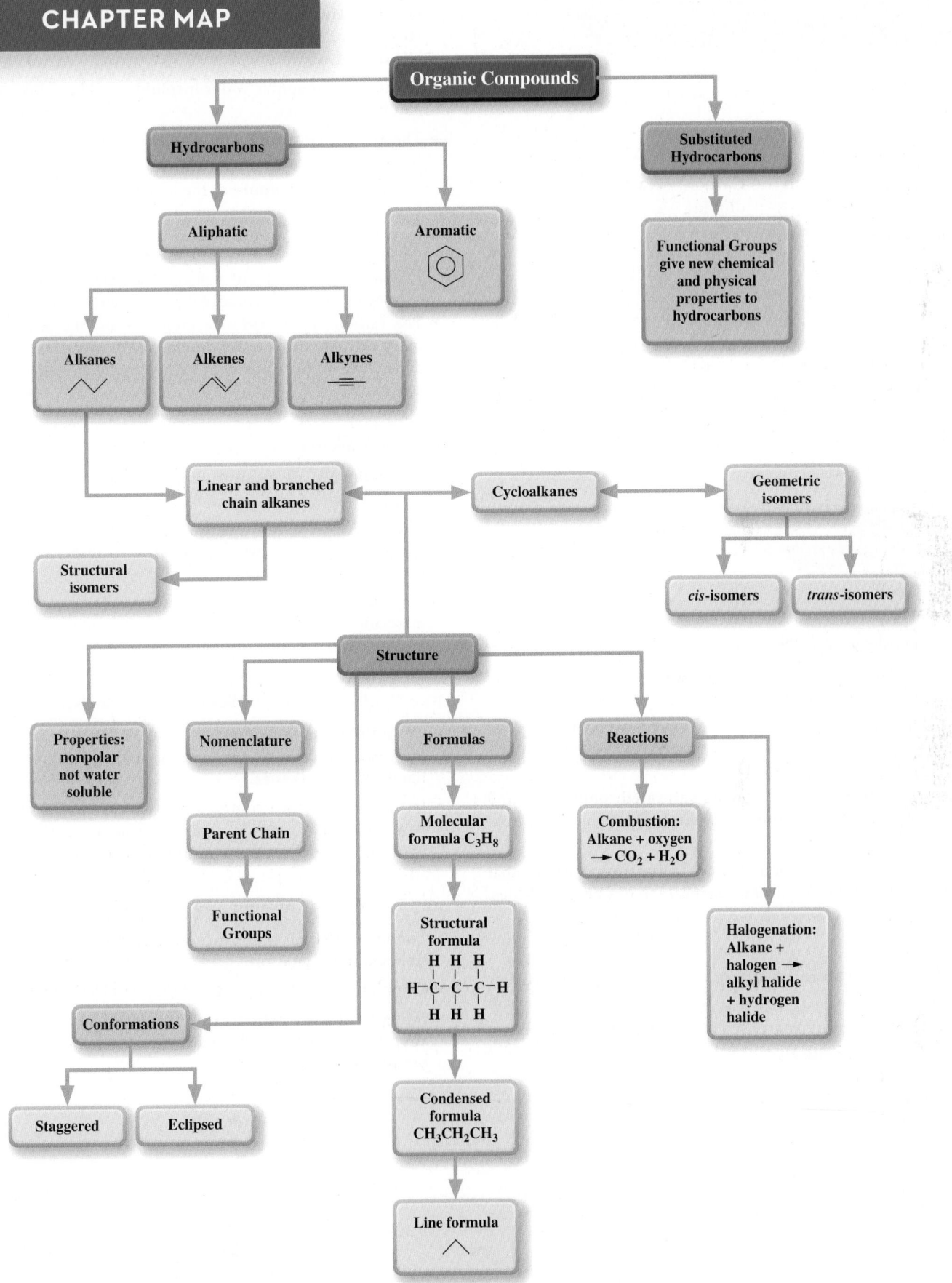

## SUMMARY OF REACTIONS

**Reactions of Alkanes**
**Combustion:**

$$C_nH_{2n+2} + O_2 \longrightarrow CO_2 + H_2O + \text{heat energy}$$

Alkane    Oxygen    Carbon    Water
dioxide

**Halogenation:**

$$\underset{\text{Alkane}}{R-\overset{\overset{\displaystyle H}{|}}{\underset{\underset{\displaystyle H}{|}}{C}}-H} + \underset{\text{Halogen}}{X_2} \xrightarrow{\text{light or heat}} \underset{\substack{\text{Alkyl}\\\text{halide}}}{R-\overset{\overset{\displaystyle H}{|}}{\underset{\underset{\displaystyle H}{|}}{C}}-X} + \underset{\substack{\text{Hydrogen}\\\text{halide}}}{H-X}$$

## SUMMARY

### 10.1 The Chemistry of Carbon

▶ Organic chemistry is the study of carbon-containing compounds.

▶ All organic compounds are classified as **hydrocarbons** or **substituted hydrocarbons.**

▶ Hydrocarbons contain only carbon and hydrogen atoms and may be **aliphatic** (alkanes, alkenes, and alkynes) or **aromatic** (containing a benzene ring.)

▶ Aliphatic hydrocarbons may be **saturated** (only C—C and C—H single bonds) or **unsaturated** (at least one C—C double or triple bond.)

▶ Substituted hydrocarbons include a **functional group** that gives the molecule particular chemical and physical properties.

### 10.2 Alkanes

▶ **Alkanes** are **saturated hydrocarbons** with the general formula $C_nH_{2n+2}$.

▶ Four types of formulas are used to represent organic molecules:
  • **Molecular formulas**
  • **Structural formulas**
  • **Condensed formulas**
  • **Line formulas**

▶ Two organic molecules with the same molecular formula but different bonding patterns have different physical and chemical properties. Such molecules are **structural** or **constitutional isomers.**

▶ Alkanes are nonpolar, water-insoluble, and have low melting and boiling points.

▶ The **IUPAC Nomenclature System** is the universal system for naming organic compounds.
  • The **parent compound,** the longest carbon chain with the characteristic functional group, gives the molecule its primary name.
  • Attached to the parent chain, **alkyl groups** (alkanes with one fewer hydrogen atom), halogens, or other functional groups may replace one or more of the hydrogen atoms in the alkane.

▶ The carbon atoms within a molecule are classified as **primary (1°), secondary (2°), tertiary (3°), or quaternary (4°),** depending on the number of carbon atoms to which they are attached.

### 10.3 Cycloalkanes

▶ **Cycloalkanes** are organic molecules having C—C single bonds in a ring structure.

▶ There is very limited rotation around the C—C bonds in a cycloalkane. As a result, **geometric isomers,** also called *cis-trans* isomers, occur.

▶ Geometric isomers are a type of stereoisomers, which are molecules with the same molecular formulas and bonding patterns, but different arrangements of atoms in space.

### 10.4 Conformations of Alkanes and Cycloalkanes

▶ **Conformations** or **conformers** result from the free rotation of the C—C bonds in alkanes and the limited rotation of C—C bonds in **cycloalkanes.**

▶ In cyclohexane, two common conformers are the **chair** and **boat conformations.** The chair conformation is the most stable and therefore is the more common conformation.

### 10.5 Reactions of Alkanes and Cycloalkanes

▶ Common reactions of alkanes and cycloalkanes are **combustion** and **halogenation.**

▶ Complete combustion produces $CO_2$, $H_2O$, and heat.

▶ Halogenation is a **substitution reaction** in which a halogen atom replaces one of the hydrogen atoms in the molecule, producing an **alkyl halide.**

# ANSWERS TO PRACTICE PROBLEMS

**10.1** Structural Formulas:

Hexane                    2-Methylpentane

3-Methylpentane

2,3-Dimethylbutane        2,2-Dimethylbutane

Line Formulas

Hexane        2-Methylpentane        3-Methylpentane

2,3-Dimethylbutane        2,2-Dimethylbutane

**10.2 a.** 2,4-Dimethyloctane
**b.** Trichlorofluoromethane
**c.** 3-Chloro-4-fluoro-2-methylheptane

**10.3 a.** $CH_2BrCHCl(CH_2)_3CH_3$

**b.** $CH_3CH(CH_3)CH(CH_3)CH_2CH_3$

**c.** $CH_2ClCH_2CHClCH_2CHClCH_2CH_3$

**d.** $CH_3CH_2CHClCH(CH_3)CHI(CH_2)_2CH_3$

**e.** $CH_2BrCHBrCHClCH_3$

**f.** $CF_3Cl$

**10.4** The following are the line structures and IUPAC names of the nine isomers of heptane:

Heptane        2-Methylhexane        3-Methylhexane

2,3-Dimethylpentane  2,4-Dimethylpentane  2,2-Dimethylpentane

3,3-Dimethylpentane    3-Ethylpentane    2,2,3-Trimethylbutane

**10.5 a.** Chlorocycloheptane        **c.** Ethylcyclobutane
**b.** Methylcyclopropane    **d.** 1,1-Difluorocyclohexane
**10.6 a.** *cis*-isomer        **c.** *trans*-isomer
**b.** *cis*-isomer        **d.** *trans*-isomer
**10.7 a.** *cis*-1,2-Dichlorocycloheptane
**b.** *cis*-1,2-Dimethylcyclopropane
**c.** *trans*-1,3-Diethylcyclobutane
**d.** *trans*-1,2-Difluorocyclohexane
**10.8 a.** The complete combustion of cyclobutane:

$\Box$ + $6O_2 \longrightarrow 4CO_2 + 4H_2O$ + heat energy

**b.** The complete combustion of ethane:

$2CH_3CH_3 + 7O_2 \rightarrow 4CO_2 + 6H_2O$ + heat energy

**c.** The complete combustion of decane:

$2C_{10}H_{22} + 31O_2 \rightarrow 20CO_2 + 22H_2O$ + heat energy

# QUESTIONS AND PROBLEMS

## The Chemistry of Carbon

### Foundations

**10.7** Why is the number of organic compounds nearly limitless?
**10.8** Describe the three allotropes of carbon.
**10.9** Why do ionic substances generally have higher melting and boiling points than covalent substances?
**10.10** Why are ionic substances more likely to be water-soluble?

### Applications

**10.11** Based on intermolecular forces or ionic interactions, rank the following compounds from highest to lowest boiling points:
**a.** $H_2O$   $CH_4$   LiCl        **b.** $C_2H_6$   $C_3H_8$   NaCl

**10.12** Based on intermolecular forces or ionic interactions, rank the following compounds from highest to lowest melting points:
a. $H_2O$  $CH_4$  KCl    b. $C_6H_{14}$  $C_{18}H_{38}$  NaCl

**10.13** What would the physical state of each of the compounds in Question 10.11 be at room temperature?

**10.14** Which of the compounds in Question 10.12 would be soluble in water?

**10.15** Consider the differences between organic and inorganic compounds as you answer each of the following questions.
a. Which compounds make good electrolytes?
b. Which compounds exhibit ionic bonding?
c. Which compounds have lower melting points?
d. Which compounds are more likely to be soluble in water?
e. Which compounds are flammable?

**10.16** Describe the major differences between ionic and covalent bonds.

**10.17** For centuries, fishermen have used shark liver oil to treat a variety of ailments, including general weakness, wounds, and inflammation of the respiratory and gastrointestinal tracts. In fact, it is an ingredient in the hemorrhoid cream Preparation H. In addition to chemicals such as vitamins A and D, omega-3 fatty acids, and triglycerides, shark liver oil contains approximately 14% 2,6,10,14-tetramethyl-pentadecane, also known as pristane.
a. Write the molecular formula for pristane.
b. Draw the line and condensed formulas for pristane.
c. Calculate the molar mass of pristane.

**10.18** The tsetse fly *Glossina morsitans* is a large biting fly found in regions of Africa. They carry sleeping sickness, a deadly disease caused by a parasitic protozoan. The pheromone secreted by the tsetse fly contains four straight-chain alkanes: 2-methylheptadecane ($C_{18}H_{38}$), 17,21-dimethylheptatriacontane ($C_{39}H_{80}$), 15,19-dimethylheptatriacontane ($C_{39}H_{80}$), and 15,19,23-trimethylheptatriacontane ($C_{40}H_{82}$). Because this pheromone works by smell over long distances, it has proved useful as an agent to control tsetse fly populations.
a. Draw the line formula for each of these alkanes.
b. Calculate the molar mass of each of these alkanes.

**10.19** Condense each of the following structural formulas:

**10.20** Condense each of the following structural formulas:

**10.21** Convert the following structural formulas into line formulas:

**10.22** Convert the following structural formulas into line formulas:

**10.23** Convert the structural formulas in Question 10.21 into condensed formulas.

**10.24** Convert the structural formulas in Question 10.22 into condensed formulas.

**10.25** Draw a line formula for each of the following alkanes:
a. 4-Ethyl-2-methylhexane    c. 3,3-Dimethylhexane
b. 2,3-Dimethylhexane    d. 3-Ethylpentane

**10.26** Convert the following line formulas into condensed formulas:

**10.27** Certain spider orchids can only be pollinated by a particular sand bee. To ensure pollination, the spider orchid emits a mixture of straight-chain alkanes that is identical to the sex pheromone produced by the female sand bee. The pheromone, a mixture of tricosane ($C_{23}H_{48}$), pentacosane ($C_{25}H_{52}$), and heptacosane ($C_{27}H_{56}$) in the ratio 3:3:1 lures the male sand bee to the spider orchid blooms.
a. Draw the line formula for each of these alkanes.
b. Calculate the molar mass of each of these alkanes.

**10.28** Using the octet rule, explain why carbon forms four bonds in a stable compound.

**10.29** Convert the following condensed formulas into structural formulas:
a. $CH_3CH(CH_3)CH(CH_3)CH_2CH_3$
b. $CH_3CH_2CH_2CH_2CH_3$

**10.30** Convert the following condensed formulas into structural formulas:
a. $CH_3CH_2CH(CH_2CH_3)CH_2CH_2CH_3$
b. $CH_3CH(CH_3)CH(CH_3)CH_2CH_2CH_2CH_3$

**10.31** Convert the following condensed formulas into structural formulas:
a. $CH_3CH_2CH(CH_3)(CH_2)_3CH(CH_3)CH_2CH_3$
b. $CH_3C(CH_3)_2CH_2CH_3$

**10.32** Convert the following condensed formulas into structural formulas:
a. $CH_3CH(CH_3)CH(CH_3)CH(CH_3)CH_2CH_3$
b. $CH_3C(CH_3)_2CH(CH_2CH_3)CH_2CH_2CH_3$

**10.33** Name the functional group in each of the following molecules:
a. $CH_3CH_2CH_2OH$
b. $CH_3CH_2CH_2NH_2$
c. $CH_3CH_2CH_2C{=}O$
    |
    H
d. $CH_3CH_2CH_2C{=}O$
    |
    OH
e. $CH_3CH_2CH_2C{=}O$
    |
    $OCH_2CH_3$
f. $CH_3CH_2OCH_2CH_3$
g. $CH_3CH_2CH_2I$

**10.34** Convert the condensed structures in Question 10.33 into line formulas.

**10.35** Give the general formula for each of the following:
a. An alkane    d. A cycloalkane
b. An alkyne    e. A cycloalkene
c. An alkene

**10.36** Of the classes of compounds listed in Question 10.35, which are saturated? Which are unsaturated?

**10.37** What major structural feature distinguishes the alkanes, alkenes, and alkynes? Give examples.

**10.38** What is the major structural feature that distinguishes between saturated and unsaturated hydrocarbons?

**10.39** Give an example, using condensed formulas, of each of the following families of organic compounds. Each of your examples should contain a minimum of three carbons. (*Hint:* Refer to Table 10.2.)
a. A carboxylic acid    c. An alcohol
b. An amine    d. An ether

**10.40** Folic acid is a vitamin required by the body for nucleic acid synthesis. The structure of folic acid is given below. Circle and identify as many functional groups as possible.

Folic acid

**10.41** The following structure is the artificial sweetener aspartame, found in Equal. Circle and name the functional groups found in this molecule.

**10.42** The following is the structure of the pain reliever ibuprofen, found in Advil. Circle and label the functional groups of the ibuprofen molecule.

Ibuprofen

## Alkanes

### Foundations

**10.43** Why are hydrocarbons not water-soluble?

**10.44** Describe the relationship between the length of hydrocarbon chains and the melting points of the compounds.

### Applications

**10.45** Based on intermolecular forces, rank the following compounds from highest to lowest boiling points:
a. heptane    butane    hexane    ethane
b. $CH_3CH_2CH_2CH_2CH_3$        $CH_3CH_2CH_3$
   $CH_3CH_2CH_2CH_2CH_2CH_2CH_2CH_2CH_3$

**10.46** Based on intermolecular forces, rank the following compounds from highest to lowest melting points:
a. decane    propane    methane    ethane
b. $CH_3CH_2CH_2CH_2CH_3$    $CH_3(CH_2)_8CH_3$    $CH_3(CH_2)_6CH_3$

**10.47** What would the physical state of each of the compounds in Question 10.45 be at room temperature?

**10.48** What would the physical state of each of the compounds in Question 10.46 be at room temperature?

**10.49** Name each of the compounds in Question 10.45b.

**10.50** Name each of the compounds in Question 10.46b.

**10.51** Draw each of the following using line formulas:
a. 2-Bromobutane    c. 2,2-Dimethylhexane
b. 2-Chloro-2-methylpropane

**10.52** Draw each of the following using line formulas:
  **a.** Dichlorodiiodomethane
  **b.** 1,4-Diethylcyclohexane
  **c.** 2-Iodo-2,4,4-trimethylpentane

**10.53** Draw each of the following compounds using structural formulas:
  **a.** 2,2-Dibromobutane    **c.** 1,2-Dichloropentane
  **b.** 2-Iododecane    **d.** 1-Bromo-2-methylpentane

**10.54** Draw each of the following compounds using structural formulas:
  **a.** 1,1,1-Trichlorodecane
  **b.** 1,2-Dibromo-1,1,2-trifluoroethane
  **c.** 3,3,5-Trimethylheptane
  **d.** 1,3,5-Trifluoropentane

**10.55** Name each of the following using the IUPAC Nomenclature System:

  **a.** $CH_3CH_2CHCH_2CH_3$
            |
            $CH_3$

  **c.** $CH_2CH_2CH_2CH_2\,Br$
            |
            $CH_2CH_2CH_3$

  **b.** $CH_3CHCH_2CH_2CHCH_3$
            |              |
            $CH_3$      $CH_3$

  **d.** $CH_2ClCH_2CHCH_3$
                        |
                        $CH_3$

**10.56** Provide the IUPAC name for each of the following compounds:

  **a.** $CH_3CH_2CHCH_2CHCH_2CH_3$
            |           |
            $CH_3$   $CH_2CH_3$

  **c.** $CH_3$
              |
          $CH_3\,C\,Br$
              |
              $CH_3$

  **b.** $CH_3CHClCH_2CH_2CH_2Cl$

**10.57** Give the IUPAC name for each of the following:

  **a.** $CH_3$
            |
          $CH_3CHCl$

  **d.** $CH_3$
            |
          $CH_3CHCH_2Cl$

  **b.** $CH_3CHICH_2CH_3$

  **e.** $CH_3$
            |
          $CH_3CCH_3$
            |
            $I$

  **c.** $CH_3CBr_2CH_3$

**10.58** Name the following using the IUPAC Nomenclature System:

  **a.** $Cl$
            |
          $CH_3CHCHCH_2CH_3$
                  |
                  $Cl$

  **c.** $CH_3$  $CH_3$
              |        |
          $CH_3CH_2CHCHCHCH_3$
                                |
                                $CH_3$

  **b.** $CH_3$
            |
          $CH_3CH_2CCH_2CHCH_3$
            |              |
          $CH_3$       $CH_3$

  **d.** $Br$
            |
          $CHCH_2CH_2CH_3$
            |
            $Br$

**10.59** Draw a complete structural formula for each of the straight-chain isomers of the following alkanes:
  **a.** $C_4H_9Br$    **b.** $C_4H_8Br_2$

**10.60** Name all of the isomers that you obtained in Question 10.59.

**10.61** Name the following using the IUPAC Nomenclature System:
  **a.** $CH_3(CH_2)_3CHClCH_3$    **c.** $CH_3CH_2CHClCH_2CH_3$
  **b.** $CH_2Br(CH_2)_2CH_2Br$    **d.** $CH_3CH(CH_3)(CH_2)_4CH_3$

**10.62** Which of the following pairs of compounds are identical? Which are constitutional isomers? Which are completely unrelated?

**a.**
      $Br$                    $Br$
        |                        |
    $CH_3CH_2CHCH_3$ and $CH_3CHCH_2CH_3$

**b.**
      $Br$    $CH_3$          $CH_3$
        |         |                |
    $CH_3CH_2CHCH_2CHCH_3$ and $CH_3CHCH_2CHCH_2CH_3$
                                              |
                                            $Br$

**c.**
      $Br$                    $Br$
        |                        |
    $CH_3CCH_2CH_3$ and $BrCCH_2CH_3$
        |                        |
      $Br$                    $CH_3$

**d.**
          $CH_3$          $Br$    $CH_2Br$
            |                 |         |
    $BrCH_2CH_2CCH_2CH_3$ and $CH_2CH_2CHCH_2CH_3$
            |
          $Br$

**10.63** Which of the following pairs of molecules are identical compounds? Which are constitutional isomers?
  **a.** $CH_3CH_2CH_2$      $CH_3CHCH_2CH_2CH_3$
          $CH_3CH_2CH_2$          $CH_3$
  **b.** $CH_3CH_2CH_2CH_2CH_2CH_2CH_3$    $CH_3CH_2CH_2CH_2CH_2$
                                                              $CH_3CH_2$

**10.64.** Which of the following pairs of molecules are identical compounds? Which are constitutional isomers?
  **a.** $CH_3CH_2CH(CH_3)CH_2CH_3$    $CH_3C(CH_3)_2CH_2CH_2CH_3$
  **b.** $CH_3CH_2CH_2CH_2C(CH_3)_2CH_2CH(CH_3)CH_3$
        $CH_3CH(CH_3)CH_2CH_2C(CH_3)_2CH_2CH_2CH_3$

**10.65** Which of the following structures are incorrect?
  **a.** $CH_3$  $Br$
              |       |
          $CH_3\,CCH_2CH_2$

  **c.** $CH_3$
              |
          $CH_3CH_2CH_2CH_3$
                        |
                        $Br$

  **b.** $H$
            |
          $CH_3CH_2CCH_3$
            |
          $Br$

  **d.** $Br$
            |
          $CH_3CHCH_2CHCH_3$
                        |
                        $Br$

**10.66.** Which of the following structures are incorrect? Describe the problem in those that are incorrect.
  **a.** $CH_3CH(CH_3)_2CH_2CH_3$  **c.** $CH_2CH_2C(CH_3)CH_2CH_2CH_3$
  **b.** $CH_3(CH_2)_5CH_3$    **d.** $CH_3CH_2CH(CH_3)_3CH_3$

**10.67** Are the following names correct or incorrect? If they are incorrect, give the correct name.
  **a.** 1,3-Dimethylpentane    **c.** 3-Butylbutane
  **b.** 2-Ethylpropane    **d.** 3-Ethyl-4-methyloctane

**10.68** In your own words, describe the steps used to name a compound, using IUPAC nomenclature.

**10.69** Draw the structures of the following compounds. Are the names provided correct or incorrect? If they are incorrect, give the correct name.
  **a.** 2,4-Dimethylpentane  **d.** 1,4-Diethylheptane
  **b.** 1,3-Dimethylhexane  **e.** 1,6-Dibromo-6-methyloctane
  **c.** 1,5-Diiodopentane

**10.70** Draw the structures of the following compounds. Are the names provided correct or incorrect? If they are incorrect, give the correct name.
  **a.** 1,4-Dimethylbutane    **c.** 2,3-Dimethylbutane
  **b.** 1,2-Dichlorohexane    **d.** 1,2-Diethylethane

## Cycloalkanes

### Foundations

**10.71** Describe the structure of a cycloalkane.
**10.72** Describe the IUPAC rules for naming cycloalkanes.

**10.73** What is the general formula for a cycloalkane?

**10.74** How does the general formula of a cycloalkane compare with that of an alkane?

## Applications

**10.75** Name each of the following cycloalkanes, using the IUPAC system:

a.

c.

b.

d.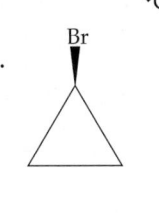

**10.76** Name each of the following cycloalkanes, using the IUPAC system:

a.

c.

b.

d.

**10.77** Draw the structure of each of the following cycloalkanes:
a. 1-Bromo-2-methylcyclobutane
b. Iodocyclopropane
c. 1-Bromo-3-chlorocyclopentane
d. 1,2-Dibromo-3-methylcyclohexane

**10.78** Draw each of the following cycloalkanes:
a. 1,2,3-Trichlorocyclopropane
b. 1,1-Dibromo-3-chlorocyclobutane
c. 1,2,4-Trimethylcycloheptane
d. 1,2-Dichloro-3,3-dimethylcyclohexane

**10.79** How many geometric and structural isomers of dichlorocyclopropane can you construct? Use a set of molecular models to construct the isomers and to contrast their differences. Draw all these isomers.

**10.80** How many isomers of dibromocyclobutane can you construct? As in Question 10.79, use a set of molecular models to construct the isomers and then draw them.

**10.81** Which of the following names are correct and which are incorrect? If incorrect, write the correct name.
a. 2,3-Dibromocyclobutane   c. 1,2-Dimethylcyclopropane
b. 1,4-Diethylcyclobutane   d. 4,5,6-Trichlorocyclohexane

**10.82** Which of the following names are correct and which are incorrect? If incorrect, write the correct name.
a. 1,4,5-Tetrabromocyclohexane c. 1,2-Dichlorocyclopentane
b. 1,3-Dimethylcyclobutane   d. 3-Bromocyclopentane

**10.83** Draw the structures of each of the following compounds:
a. *cis*-1,3-Dibromocyclopentane
b. *trans*-1,2-Dimethylcyclobutane
c. *cis*-1,2-Dichlorocyclopropane
d. *trans*-1,4-Diethylcyclohexane

**10.84** Draw the structures of each of the following compounds:
a. *trans*-1,4-Dimethylcyclooctane
b. *cis*-1,3-Dichlorocyclohexane
c. *cis*-1,3-Dibromocyclobutane

**10.85** Name each of the following compounds:

a.

c.

b.

d.

**10.86** Name each of the following compounds:

a.

c.

b. 

d. 

## Conformations of Alkanes and Cycloalkanes

### Foundations

**10.87** What are conformational isomers?

**10.88** Why is the staggered conformation of ethane more stable than the eclipsed conformation?

### Applications

**10.89** Make a model of cyclohexane and compare the boat and chair conformations. Use your model to explain why the chair conformation is more stable.

**10.90** What is meant by free rotation around a carbon-carbon single bond? Why can't conformations be separated from one another?

## Reactions of Alkanes and Cycloalkanes

### Foundations

**10.91** Define the term *combustion*.

**10.92** Explain why halogenation of an alkane is a substitution reaction.

### Applications

**10.93** Write a balanced equation for the complete combustion of each of the following:
a. propane              c. nonane
b. heptane              d. decane

**10.94** Write a balanced equation for the complete combustion of each of the following:

    **a.** pentane             **c.** octane

    **b.** hexane             **d.** ethane

**10.95** Just as an octane rating is applied to gasoline, a cetane number is used as the measure of the combustion quality of diesel fuel. Cetane, or hexadecane, is an unbranched alkane that ignites easily in a combustion engine. Write a balanced equation for the complete combustion of cetane.

**10.96** For gasoline, isooctane, 2,2,4-trimethylpentane, is the standard of excellence. Write a balanced equation for the complete combustion of isooctane.

**10.97** Complete each of the following equations by supplying the missing reactant or product as indicated by a question mark:

    **a.** $2CH_3CH_2CH_2CH_3 + 13O_2 \xrightarrow{\text{Heat}}$ ? (Complete combustion)

    **b.** $CH_3CH(CH_3)_2 + Br_2 \xrightarrow{\text{Light}}$ ? (Give all possible monobrominated products)

    **c.** ⬡ + ? $\xrightarrow{?}$ Cl—⬡ + HCl

**10.98** Give all the possible monochlorinated products for the following reaction:

$$CH_3CH(CH_3)CH_2CH_3 + Cl_2 \xrightarrow{\text{Light}} ?$$

    Name the products, using IUPAC nomenclature.

**10.99** Draw the constitutional isomers of molecular formula $C_6H_{14}$ and name each using the IUPAC system.

    **a.** Which one gives two and only two monobromo derivatives when it reacts with $Br_2$ and light? Name the products, using the IUPAC system.

    **b.** Which give three and only three monobromo products? Name the products, using the IUPAC system.

    **c.** Which give four and only four monobromo products? Name the products, using the IUPAC system.

**10.100** **a.** Draw and name all of the isomeric products obtained from the monobromination of propane with $Br_2$/light. If halogenation were a completely random reaction and had an equal probability of occurring at any of the C—H bonds in a molecule, what percentage of each of these monobromo products would be expected?

    **b.** Answer part (a) using 2-methylpropane as the starting material.

**10.101** A mol of hydrocarbon formed 8 mol of $CO_2$ and 8 mol of $H_2O$ upon combustion. Determine the molecular formula of the hydrocarbon and write the balanced equation for the combustion reaction. Use line formulas.

**10.102** Highly substituted alkyl fluorides, called perfluoroalkanes, are often used as artificial blood substitutes. These perfluoroalkanes have the ability to transport $O_2$ through the bloodstream as blood does. Some even have twice the $O_2$ transport capability and are used to treat gangrenous tissue. The structure of perfluorodecalin is shown below. How many mol of fluorine must be reacted with 1 mol of decalin to produce perfluorodecalin?

Decalin          Perfluorodecalin

## CRITICAL THINKING PROBLEMS

1. You are given two unlabeled bottles, each of which contains a colorless liquid. One contains hexane and the other contains water. What physical properties could you use to identify the two liquids? What chemical property could you use to identify them?

2. You are given two beakers, each of which contains a white crystalline solid. Both are soluble in water. How would you determine which of the two solids is an ionic compound and which is a covalent compound?

3. Chlorofluorocarbons (CFCs) are man-made compounds made up of carbon and the halogens fluorine and chlorine. One of the most widely used is Freon-12 ($CCl_2F_2$). It was introduced as a refrigerant in the 1930s. This was an important advance because Freon-12 replaced ammonia and sulfur dioxide, two toxic chemicals that were previously used in refrigeration systems. Freon-12 was hailed as a perfect replacement because it has a boiling point of $-30°C$ and is almost completely inert. To what family of organic molecules do CFCs belong? Design a strategy for the synthesis of Freon-12.

4. Over time, CFC production increased dramatically as their uses increased. They were used as propellants in spray cans, as gases to expand plastic foam, and in many other applications. By 1985 production of CFCs reached 850,000 tons (t). Much of this leaked into the atmosphere and in that year the concentration of CFCs reached 0.6 parts per billion (ppb). Another observation was made by groups of concerned scientists: as the level of CFCs rose, the ozone level in the upper atmosphere declined. Does this correlation between CFC levels and ozone levels prove a relationship between these two phenomena? Explain your reasoning.

5. Although manufacture of CFCs was banned on December 31, 1995, the C—F and C—Cl bonds of CFCs are so strong that the molecules may remain in the atmosphere for 120 years. Within 5 years they diffuse into the upper stratosphere where ultraviolet photons can break the C—Cl bonds. This process releases chlorine atoms, as shown here for Freon-12:

$$CCl_2F_2 + photon \longrightarrow CClF_2 + Cl$$

The chlorine atoms are extremely reactive because of their strong tendency to acquire a stable octet of electrons. The following reactions occur when a chlorine atom reacts with an ozone molecule ($O_3$). First, chlorine pulls an oxygen atom away from ozone:

$$Cl + O_3 \longrightarrow ClO + O_2$$

Then ClO, a highly reactive molecule, reacts with an oxygen atom:

$$ClO + O \longrightarrow Cl + O_2$$

Write an equation representing the overall reaction (sum of the two reactions). How would you describe the role of Cl in these reactions?

# ALKENES, ALKYNES, AND AROMATICS
# The Unsaturated Hydrocarbons

## LEARNING GOALS

1 Describe the physical properties of alkenes and alkynes.

2 Draw the structures and write the IUPAC names for simple alkenes and alkynes.

3 Write the names and draw the structures of simple geometric isomers of alkenes.

4 Write equations predicting the products of addition reactions of alkenes and alkynes: hydrogenation, halogenation, hydration, and hydrohalogenation.

5 Apply Markovnikov's rule to predict the major and minor products of the hydration and hydrohalogenation reactions of unsymmetrical alkenes.

6 Write equations representing the formation of addition polymers of alkenes.

7 Draw the structures and write the names of common aromatic hydrocarbons.

8 Write equations for substitution reactions involving benzene.

9 Describe heterocyclic aromatic compounds and list several biological molecules in which they are found.

Ethene gas causes fruit ripening.

## OUTLINE

Oleic acid, the major fatty acid in olive oil, is a monounsaturated fatty acid. What does the term "monounsaturated" mean?

# INTRODUCTION

For many years it was suspected that there existed a gas that stimulated fruit ripening and had other effects on plants. The ancient Chinese observed that their fruit ripened more quickly if incense was burned in the same room. Early in the last century, shippers realized that they could not store oranges and bananas on the same ships because some "emanation" given off by the oranges caused the bananas to ripen too early.

Puerto Rican pineapple growers and Philippine mango growers independently developed a traditional practice of building bonfires near their crops. They believed that the smoke caused the plants to bloom synchronously.

In the mid-nineteenth century, streetlights were fueled with natural gas. Occasionally the pipes leaked, releasing gas into the atmosphere. On some of these occasions, the leaves fell from all the shade trees in the region surrounding the gas leak.

What is the gas responsible for these diverse effects on plants? In 1934, R. Gane demonstrated that the simple alkene ethene (ethylene) was the "emanation" responsible for fruit ripening. More recently, it has been shown that ethene induces and synchronizes flowering in pineapples and mango, induces senescence (aging) and loss of leaves in trees, and effects a wide variety of other responses in various plants.

We can be grateful to ethene for the fresh, unbruised fruits that we purchase at the grocery store. These fruits are picked when they are not yet ripe, while they are still firm. They then can be shipped great distances and gassed with ethene when they reach their destination. Under the influence of ethene, the fruit ripens for display in the store.

In this chapter, we will study the **unsaturated hydrocarbons.** This group of organic compounds includes the alkenes, such as ethene, which all contain at least one carbon-carbon double bond; the alkynes, which all contain at least one carbon-carbon triple bond; and aromatic compounds, particularly stable compounds that contain a benzene ring. The benzene ring is often depicted as having alternating double and single bonds. This arrangement is called a *conjugated system* of double bonds.

## 11.1    Alkenes and Alkynes: Structure and Physical Properties

**LEARNING GOAL**

1    Describe the physical properties of alkenes and alkynes.

*Fatty acids are long hydrocarbon chains having a carboxyl group at the end. Thus by definition they are carboxylic acids. See Chapters 14 and 17.*

**LIPID-SOLUBLE VITAMINS**

Many important biological molecules are characterized by the presence of double bonds or a linear or cyclic conjugated system of double bonds (Figure 11.1). For instance, we classify fatty acids as either monounsaturated (having one double bond), polyunsaturated (having two or more double bonds), or saturated (having single bonds only). Vitamin A (retinol), a vitamin required for vision, contains a nine-carbon conjugated hydrocarbon chain. Vitamin K, a vitamin required for blood clotting, contains an aromatic ring.

**Alkenes** and **alkynes** are unsaturated hydrocarbons. The characteristic functional group of an alkene is the carbon-carbon double bond. The functional group that characterizes the alkynes is the carbon-carbon triple bond. The general formulas shown below compare the structures of alkanes, alkenes, and alkynes.

| | Alkane | Alkene | Alkyne |
|---|---|---|---|
| **General formulas:** | $C_nH_{2n+2}$ | $C_nH_{2n}$ | $C_nH_{2n-2}$ |
| **Structural formulas:** | $H-\overset{\displaystyle H}{\underset{\displaystyle H}{\overset{\displaystyle |}{\underset{\displaystyle |}{C}}}}-\overset{\displaystyle H}{\underset{\displaystyle H}{\overset{\displaystyle |}{\underset{\displaystyle |}{C}}}}-H$ | $\begin{matrix} H \\ \diagdown \\ C \end{matrix} = \begin{matrix} H \\ \diagup \\ C \\ \diagdown \\ H \end{matrix}$ | $H-C\equiv C-H$ |
| | Ethane (ethane) | Ethene (ethylene) | Ethyne (acetylene) |
| **Molecular formulas:** | $C_2H_6$ | $C_2H_4$ | $C_2H_2$ |
| **Condensed formulas:** | $CH_3CH_3$ | $H_2C=CH_2$ | $HC\equiv CH$ |

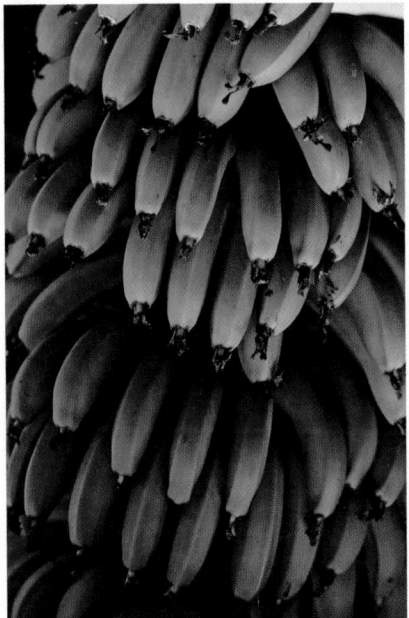

Oleic acid

**(a)**

$CH_2OH$

Vitamin A

**(b)**

Vitamin K

**(c)**

**Figure 11.1** (a) Line formula of the eighteen-carbon monounsaturated fatty acid oleic acid. (b) Line formula of vitamin A, which is required for vision. Notice that the carbon chain of vitamin A is a conjugated system of double bonds. (c) Line formula of vitamin K, a lipid-soluble vitamin required for blood clotting. The six-member ring with the circle represents a benzene ring. See Figure 11.6 for other representations of the benzene ring.

Alkanes, alkenes, and alkynes have the same number of carbon atoms but differ in the number of hydrogen atoms. Alkenes contain two fewer hydrogens than the corresponding alkanes, and alkynes contain two fewer hydrogens than the corresponding alkanes.

In alkanes, the central carbon has four bonds, giving it a tetrahedral molecular geometry. When carbon is bonded by one double bond and two single bonds, as in ethene (an alkene), the molecule is *trigonal planar,* because all atoms lie in a single plane. Each bond angle is approximately 120°. When two carbon atoms are bonded by a triple bond, as in ethyne (an alkyne), each bond angle is 180°. Thus, the molecule is linear, and all atoms are positioned in a straight line. For comparison, examples of a five-carbon alkane, alkene, and alkyne are shown in Figure 11.2.

Alkenes, alkynes, and aromatic compounds are nonpolar and have properties similar to alkanes of the same carbon chain length. They have relatively low melting points and boiling points and are generally less dense than water. In general, the longer the hydrocarbon chain (greater the molar mass), the higher the melting and boiling points and the greater the density. For comparison, the melting points and boiling points of several alkenes and alkynes are presented in Table 11.1. As we saw for the alkanes, these trends in physical properties are the result of London dispersion forces. These attractive forces increase as the mass of the molecule and the

Bananas are picked and shipped while still green. They are treated with the fruit-ripening agent, ethene, once they reach the grocery store. Describe the geometry and bonding of ethene. What is the common name of ethene?

**TABLE 11.1 Physical Properties of Selected Alkenes and Alkynes**

| Name | Molecular Formula | Structural Formula | Melting Point (°C) | Boiling Point (°C) |
|------|-------------------|--------------------|--------------------|--------------------|
| Ethene | $C_2H_4$ | $CH_2{=}CH_2$ | −169.1 | −103.7 |
| Propene | $C_3H_6$ | $CH_2{=}CHCH_3$ | −185.0 | −47.6 |
| 1-Butene | $C_4H_8$ | $CH_2{=}CHCH_2CH_3$ | −185.0 | −6.1 |
| Methylpropene | $C_4H_8$ | $CH_2{=}C(CH_3)_2$ | −140.0 | −6.6 |
| Ethyne | $C_2H_2$ | $HC{\equiv}CH$ | −81.8 | −84.0 |
| Propyne | $C_3H_4$ | $HC{\equiv}CCH_3$ | −101.5 | −23.2 |
| 1-Butyne | $C_4H_6$ | $HC{\equiv}CCH_2CH_3$ | −125.9 | 8.1 |
| 2-Butyne | $C_4H_6$ | $CH_3C{\equiv}CCH_3$ | −32.3 | 27.0 |

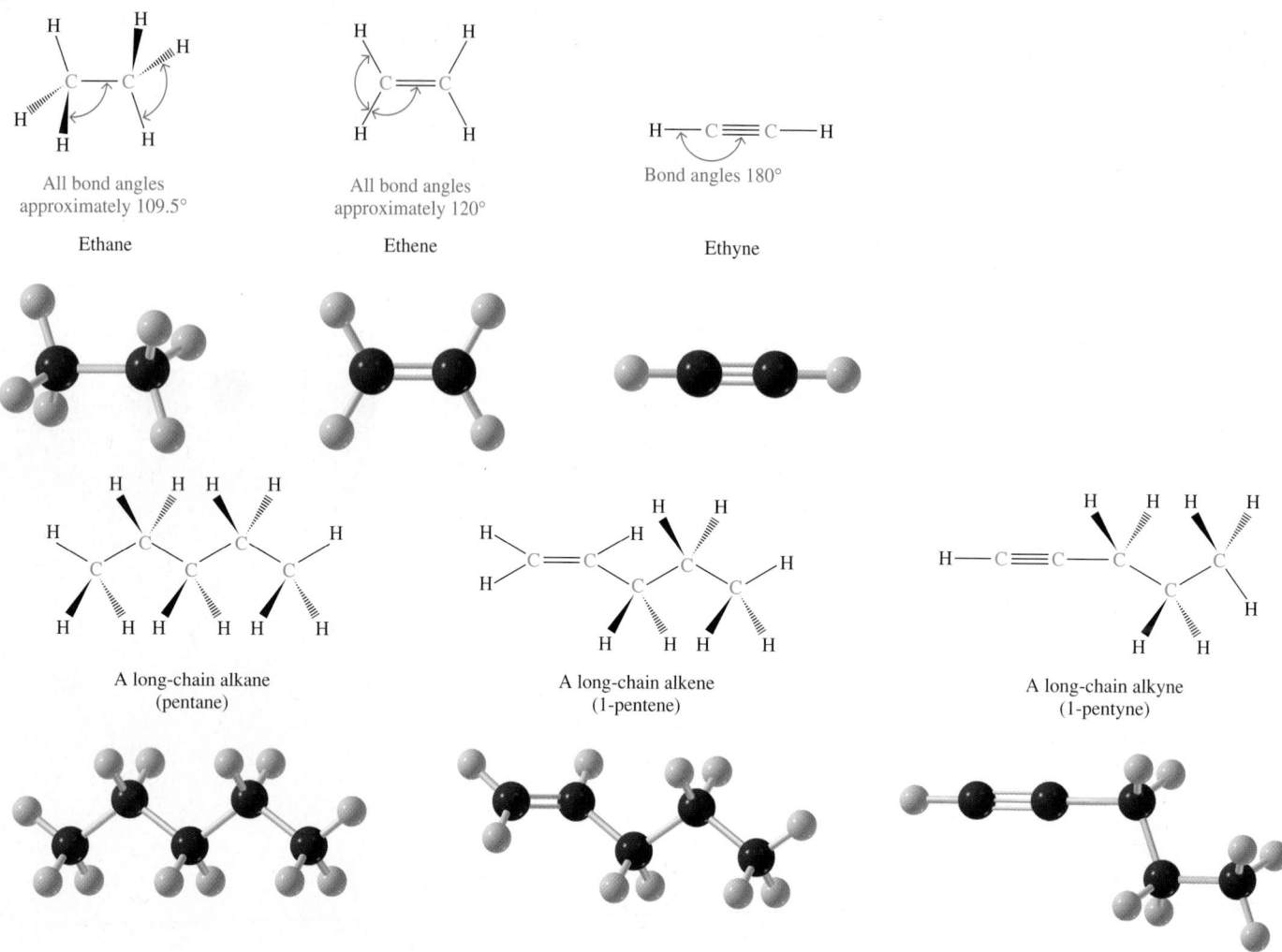

**Figure 11.2** Three-dimensional drawings and ball-and-stick models of typical alkanes, alkenes, and alkynes.

number of electrons increase. Thus, the London dispersion forces are stronger and the attraction greater for molecules having a larger surface area. The longer, higher molar mass alkenes and alkynes would be expected to exhibit stronger London dispersion forces and therefore higher boiling and melting points.

Since they are nonpolar, the "like dissolves like" rule tells us that they are not soluble in water. Like the alkanes, they are very soluble in nonpolar solvents such as other hydrocarbons.

## 11.2    Alkenes and Alkynes: Nomenclature

To determine the name of an alkene or alkyne using the IUPAC. Nomenclature System, use the following simple rules:

- Name the parent compound using the longest continuous carbon chain containing the double bond (alkenes) or triple bond (alkynes).
- Replace the -*ane* ending of the alkane with the -*ene* ending for an alkene or the -*yne* ending for an alkyne. For example:

$CH_3-CH_3$    $CH_2{=}CH_2$    $CH{\equiv}CH$
Ethane        Ethene       Ethyne

$CH_3-CH_2-CH_3$    $CH_2{=}CH-CH_3$    $CH{\equiv}C-CH_3$
Propane          Propene         Propyne

**LEARNING GOAL**

**2**   Draw the structures and write the IUPAC names for simple alkenes and alkynes.

- Number the parent chain to give the double or triple bond the lowest number. For example:

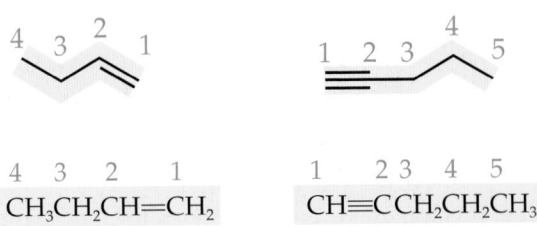

$$CH_3CH_2CH{=}CH_2$$

1-Butene

$$CH{\equiv}CCH_2CH_2CH_3$$

1-Pentyne

- Determine the name and carbon number of each group bonded to the parent alkene or alkyne, and place the name and number in front of the name of the parent compound. Remember that with alkenes and alkynes the double or triple bond takes precedence over a halogen or alkyl group, as shown in the following examples:

Remember, it is the position of the double bond, not the substituent, that determines the numbering of the carbon chain.

$$CH_3CH{=}CClCH_3$$

2-Chloro-2-butene

$$CH_3CHBr\,C{\equiv}CCH_2CH_3$$

2-Bromo-3-hexyne

$$CH_3CHCH{=}CHCH_2CHCH_2CH_3$$

$$\quad\;\;|\qquad\qquad\quad|$$

$$\quad\;\;CH_3\qquad\qquad CH_3$$

2,6-Dimethyl-3-octene

$$CH_3CH_2C{=}CCH_2CH_3$$

$$\qquad\qquad|\quad|$$

$$\qquad\;\;Cl\;\;CH_3$$

3-Chloro-4-methyl-3-hexene

- Alkenes having more than one double bond are called alkadienes (two double bonds) or alkatrienes (three double bonds), as seen in these examples:

Alkenes with many double bonds are often referred to as polyenes (poly—many enes—double bonds).

$$CH_3CH{=}CHCH{=}CHCH_3$$

2,4-Hexadiene

$$CH_2{=}CHCH_2CH{=}CH_2$$

1,4-Pentadiene

3-Methyl-
1, 4-cyclohexadiene

$$CH_3CH{=}CHCH_2CH{=}CHCH_2CH_2CH_3$$

2,5-Nonadiene

$$CH_3CH{=}CHCH{=}CHCH_2CH_3$$

2,4-Heptadiene

**EXAMPLE 11.1**    Naming Alkenes and Alkynes
                    Using IUPAC Nomenclature

LEARNING GOAL

Name the following alkenes and alkyne using IUPAC nomenclature.

**2** Draw the structures and write the IUPAC names for simple alkenes and alkynes.

**Solution**

To determine the IUPAC name, identify the parent chain, number it to give the lowest possible positions for the carbon or carbons with the double bonds, and finally, identify and number each functional group.

The common name of the first molecule below is isoprene. It is the major building block for many important biological molecules, including cholesterol and other steroids, β-carotene, and vitamins A, D, E, and K.

$$CH_2\!=\!CCH\!=\!CH_2$$
        |
       $CH_3$

Isoprene

Longest chain containing the double bond: butene

Positions of the double bonds: 1,3-butadiene

Substituents: 2-methyl

Name: 2-Methyl-1,3-butadiene

$$CH_3CH_2CH_2CH_2C\!=\!CCH_2CH_3$$
                 |           |
               $CH_2CH_3$   $CH_3$

Longest chain containing the double bond: octene

Position of double bond: 3-octene (*not* 5-octene)

Substituents: 3-methyl and 4-ethyl

Name: 4-Ethyl-3-methyl-3-octene

$$CH_3CH_2C\!\equiv\!CCCH_3$$
                 |
               $CH_3$
               $CH_3$

Longest chain containing the triple bond: hexyne

Position of triple bond: 3-hexyne

Substituents: 2,2-dimethyl

Name: 2,2-Dimethyl-3-hexyne

**Practice Problem 11.1**

Name each of the following alkenes and alkynes using IUPAC nomenclature.

a. $CH_3CH\!=\!CHCHCH_2CHCH_3$ (with $CH_3$ and $Cl$ substituents)

b. $CH\!\equiv\!CCH_2C\!\equiv\!CH$

c. $CH_3CH_2C\!\equiv\!CCHCH_2CH_3$ (with $Br$ substituent)

d. $CH_3CH\!=\!CHCH_2CH_2CH\!=\!CH_2$

▶ For Further Practice: **Questions 11.43a–c and 11.44a–c.**

**EXAMPLE 11.2** **Naming Cycloalkenes Using IUPAC Nomenclature**

LEARNING GOAL

**2** Draw the structures and write the IUPAC names for simple alkenes and alkynes.

Name the following cycloalkenes using IUPAC nomenclature.

**Solution**

Parent chain: cyclohexene

Position of double bond: carbon-1 (carbons of the double bond are numbered 1 and 2)

Substituents: 4-chloro

Name: 4-Chlorocyclohexene

Parent chain: cyclopentene

Position of double bond: carbon-1

Substituent: 3-methyl

Name: 3-Methylcyclopentene

**Practice Problem 11.2**

Name each of the following cycloalkenes using IUPAC nomenclature.

a.     b.     c.     d.

► For Further Practice: **Questions 11.43d and 11.44d.**

**Question 11.1** Draw a condensed formula and line formula for each of the following compounds:

a. 1-Bromo-3-hexyne    c. Dichloroethyne
b. 2-Butyne             d. 9-Iodo-1-nonyne

**Question 11.2** Name the following compounds using the IUPAC Nomenclature System:

a. $CH_3C \equiv CCH_2CH_3$

b. $CH_3CH_2CHBrCHBrCH_2C \equiv CH$

c. $CH_3CH(CH_3)CCl = C(CH_3)CH(CH_3)_2$

d. $CH_3CH(CH_2CH_3)C \equiv CCHClCH_3$

# 11.3 Geometric Isomers: A Consequence of Unsaturation

LEARNING GOAL

**3** Write the names and draw the structures of simple geometric isomers of alkenes.

The carbon-carbon double bond is rigid because of the shapes of the orbitals involved in its formation. As a result, rotation around the carbon-carbon double bond is restricted. In Section 10.3, we saw that the rotation around the carbon-carbon bonds of cycloalkanes is also restricted. As a consequence, these molecules

# A MEDICAL PERSPECTIVE

## Killer Alkynes in Nature

There are many examples of alkynes that are beneficial to humans. Among these are *parsalmide*, a pain reliever, *pargyline*, an antihypertensive, and *17-ethynylestradiol*, a synthetic estrogen that is used as an oral contraceptive.

But in addition to these medically useful alkynes, there are in nature a number that are toxic. Some are extremely toxic to mammals, including humans; others are toxic to fungi, fish, or insects. All of these compounds are plant products that may help protect the plant from destruction by predators.

*Capillin* is produced by the oriental wormwood plant. Research has shown that a dilute solution of capillin inhibits the growth of certain fungi. Since fungal growth can damage or destroy a plant, the ability to make capillin may provide a survival advantage to the plants. Perhaps it may one day be developed to combat fungal infections in humans.

*Ichthyothereol* is a fast-acting poison commonly found in plants referred to as fish-poison plants. Ichthyothereol is a very toxic polyacetylenic alcohol that inhibits energy production in the mitochondria. Latin American native tribes use these plants to coat the tips of the arrows used to catch fish. Although ichthyothereol is poisonous to the fish, fish caught by this method pose no risk to the people who eat them!

An extract of the leaves of English ivy has been reported to have antibacterial, analgesic, and sedative effects. The

Falcarinol is extracted from English ivy, like that covering this stone house.

compound thought to be responsible for these characteristics, as well as antifungal activity, is *falcarinol*. Falcarinol, isolated from a tree in Panama, also has been reported by the Molecular Targets Drug Discovery Program to have antitumor activity.

Parsalmide

Pargyline

17-Ethynylestradiol

Alkynes used for medicinal purposes.

form geometric or *cis-trans* isomers. The *cis*-isomers of cycloalkanes have substituent groups on the same side of the ring (*Latin, cis,* "on the same side"). The *trans*-isomers of cycloalkanes have substituent groups located on opposite sides of the ring (*Latin, trans,* "across from").

$$\text{Capillin}$$

$$\text{Ichthyothereol}$$

$$CH_2=CH-CH-C\equiv C-C\equiv C-CH_2-CH=CH-(CH_2)_7CH_3$$
$$\qquad\qquad |$$
$$\qquad\qquad OH$$

Falcarinol

Cicutoxin

Alkynes that exhibit toxic activity.

*Cicuta maculata*, or water hemlock, produces the most deadly toxin indigenous to North America.

Perhaps one day this compound, or a derivative of it, will be useful in treating cancer in humans.

*Cicutoxin* has been described as the most lethal toxin native to North America. It is a neurotoxin that is produced by the water hemlock (*Cicuta maculata*), which is in the same family of plants as parsley, celery, and carrots. Cicutoxin is present in all parts of the plants, but is most concentrated in the root. Eating a portion as small as 2–3 square centimeters (cm$^2$) can be fatal to adults. Cicutoxin acts directly on the nervous system. Signs and symptoms of cicutoxin poisoning include dilation of pupils, muscle twitching, rapid pulse and breathing, violent convulsions, coma, and death. Onset of symptoms is rapid and death may occur within 2 to 3 hours (h). No antidote exists for cicutoxin poisoning. The only treatment involves controlling convulsions and seizures in order to preserve normal heart and lung function. Fortunately, cicutoxin poisoning is a very rare occurrence. Occasionally animals may graze on the plants in the spring, resulting in death within 15 minutes (min). Humans seldom come into contact with the water hemlock. The most recent cases have involved individuals foraging for wild ginseng, or other wild roots, and mistaking the water hemlock root for an edible plant.

**For Further Understanding**

▶ Circle and name the functional groups in parsalmide and pargyline.

▶ The fungus *Tinea pedis* causes athlete's foot. Describe an experiment you might carry out to determine whether capillin might be effective against athlete's foot.

In alkenes, **geometric isomers** occur when there are two different groups or atoms on each of the carbon atoms attached by the double bond. If both groups or atoms are on the same side of the double bond, the molecule is a *cis*-isomer. If the groups or atoms are on opposite sides of the double bond, the molecule is a *trans*-isomer.

Restricted rotation around double bonds is partially responsible for the conformation and hence the activity of many biological molecules that we will study later.

Consider the two isomers of 1,2-dichloroethene:

cis-1,2-Dichloroethene          trans-1,2-Dichloroethene

In these molecules, each carbon atom of the double bond is also bonded to two different atoms: a hydrogen atom and a chlorine atom. In the molecule on the left, both chlorine atoms are on the same side of the double bond; this is the *cis*-isomer and the complete name for this molecule is *cis*-1,2-dichloroethene. In the molecule on the right, the chlorine atoms are on opposite sides of the double bond; this is the *trans*-isomer and the complete name of this molecule is *trans*-1,2-dichloroethene.

If one of the two carbon atoms of the double bond has two identical substituents, there are no *cis-trans* isomers for that molecule. Consider the example of 1,1-dichloroethene:

1,1-Dichloroethene

---

**EXAMPLE 11.3**   **Identifying *cis*- and *trans*-Isomers of Alkenes**

**LEARNING GOAL**

Two isomers of 2-butene are shown below. Which is the *cis*-isomer and which is the *trans*-isomer?

**3**  Write the names and draw the structures of simple geometric isomers of alkenes.

 cis

 trans

**Solution**

As we saw with cycloalkanes, the prefixes *cis* and *trans* refer to the placement of the substituents attached to a bond that cannot undergo free rotation. In the case of alkenes, it is the groups attached to the carbon-carbon double bond (in this example, the H and CH₃ groups). When the groups are on the same side of the double bond, as in the structure on the left, the prefix *cis* is used. When the groups are on the opposite sides of the double bond, as in the structure on the right, *trans* is the appropriate prefix.

cis-2-Butene          trans-2-Butene

**Practice Problem 11.3**

Which of the following alkenes are *cis*-isomers and which are *trans*-isomers?

a. H₃C, H, H, CHBrCHBrCH₃   (cis)

b. CH₃CH₂, Br, Br, CH₂CH₃   (trans)

c. Cl, Cl, H₃C, CH₂CH₂CH₃   (cis)

▶ For Further Practice: **Questions 11.47 and 11.48.**

In alkenes, the orientation of the carbon atoms of the parent chain relative to the double bond determines the *cis-* or *trans-* configuration of the alkene. If the carbon atoms of the parent chain are on opposite sides of the double bond, the alkene is in the *trans-* configuration. If the carbon atoms of the parent chain are on the same side of the double bond, the alkene is in the *cis-* configuration. This can be seen in the *cis-* and *trans-* configurations of 4-nonene shown here:

*trans*-4-Nonene

*cis*-4-Nonene

---

**EXAMPLE 11.4**  **Naming *cis*- and *trans*-Isomers of Alkenes**

**LEARNING GOAL**

**3** Write the names and draw the structures of simple geometric isomers of alkenes.

Name the following geometric isomers.

**Solution**

The longest chain of carbon atoms in each of the following molecules is highlighted in yellow. *The chain must also contain the carbon-carbon double bond.* The orientation of the carbon atoms of the parent chain relative to the double bond is used in determining the appropriate prefix, *cis* or *trans*, to be used in naming each of the molecules.

**Parent chain:** heptene

**Position of double bond:** 3-

**Substituents:** 3,4-dichloro

**Configuration:** *trans* (the carbon atoms of the parent chain are on opposite sides of the double bond)

**Name:** *trans*-3,4-Dichloro-3-heptene

**Parent chain:** octene

**Position of double bond:** 3-

**Substituents:** 3-methyl

**Configuration:** *cis* (the carbon atoms of the parent chain are on the same side of the double bond)

**Name:** *cis*-3-Methyl-3-octene

---

**Practice Problem 11.4**

Name each of the following geometric isomers:

▶ For Further Practice: **Questions 11.51 and 11.52.**

**EXAMPLE 11.5**    **Identifying Geometric Isomers**

LEARNING GOAL

**3** Write the names and draw the structures of simple geometric isomers of alkenes.

Determine whether each of the following molecules can exist as *cis-trans* isomers: (a) 1-pentene and (b) 3-methyl-2-pentene.

**Solution**

a. Examine the structure of 1-pentene,

We see that carbon-1 is bonded to two hydrogen atoms, rather than to two different substituents. In this case there can be no *cis-trans* isomers.

b. Examination of the structure of 3-methyl-2-pentene reveals that both a *cis-* and *trans*-isomer can be drawn.

trans-3-Methyl-2-pentene          cis-3-Methyl-2-pentene

Each of the carbon atoms involved in the double bond is attached to two different groups. In *trans*-3-methyl-2-pentene the carbons of the parent chain are on opposite sides of the double bond. In the *cis*-configuration, the carbons of the parent chain are on the same side of the double bond.

**Practice Problem 11.5**

Which of the following molecules can exist as *cis-* and *trans*-isomers? Draw the *cis-* and *trans*-isomers, where possible. For those molecules that cannot exist as *cis-* and *trans*-isomers, explain why.

a. $CH_3CH=CHCH_2CH_3$

b. $CBr_2=CBrCH_2CH_2CH_3$

c. $CH_2=CHCH_3$

d. $CH_3CBr=CBrCH_2CH_2CH_2CH_3$

▶ For Further Practice: **Questions 11.49 and 11.50.**

The recent debate over the presence of *cis-* and *trans*-isomers of fatty acids in our diet points out the relevance of geometric isomers to our lives. Fatty acids are long-chain carboxylic acids found in vegetable oils (unsaturated fats) and animal fats (saturated fats). Oleic acid,

$$CH_3(CH_2)_7CH=CH(CH_2)_7\overset{\overset{\displaystyle O}{\|}}{C}-OH$$

is the naturally occurring fatty acid in olive oil. Its IUPAC name, *cis*-9-octadecenoic acid, reveals that this is a *cis*-fatty acid.

cis-9-Octadecenoic acid
(oleic acid)

cis-configuration

The *cis*-isomer of oleic acid is V-shaped as a result of the configuration of the double bond and the molecule is more flexible. Its geometric isomer, *trans*-9-octadecenoic acid is a rigid linear molecule.

*trans*-9-Octadecenoic acid
(elaidic acid)

*trans*-configuration

The majority of *trans*-fatty acids found in the diet result from hydrogenation, which is a reaction used to convert oils into solid fats, such as margarine. It has recently been reported that *trans*-fatty acids in the diet elevate levels of "bad" or LDL cholesterol and lower the levels of "good" or HDL cholesterol, thereby increasing the risk of heart disease. Other studies suggest that *trans*-fatty acids may also increase the risk of type 2 diabetes.

cis- *and* trans-*Fatty acids will be discussed in greater detail in Chapter 17. Hydrogenation is described in Section 11.5.*

**Question 11.3**    In each of the following pairs of molecules, identify the *cis*-isomer and the *trans*-isomer.

a.

$$\begin{array}{ccc} H & & H \\ & C=C & \\ CH_3CH_2 & & CH_2CH_3 \end{array}$$
*cis*

$$\begin{array}{ccc} H & & CH_2CH_3 \\ & C=C & \\ CH_3CH_2 & & H \end{array}$$
*trans*

b.

$$\begin{array}{ccc} Br & & CH_3 \\ & C=C & \\ H_3C & & Br \end{array}$$
*trans*

$$\begin{array}{ccc} Br & & Br \\ & C=C & \\ H_3C & & CH_3 \end{array}$$
*cis*

**Question 11.4**   Provide the complete IUPAC name for each of the compounds in Question 11.3.

**Question 11.5**   Which of the following molecules can exist as both *cis-* and *trans-* isomers? Explain your reasoning.

  a. $CH_3CH_2CCl{=}C(CH_2CH_3)_2$     b. $CH_3CH_2CBr{=}CBr_2$     c. $CH_3CCl{=}CClCH_3$

**Question 11.6**   Draw each of the *cis-trans* isomers in Question 11.5 and provide the complete names using the IUPAC Nomenclature System.

**Question 11.7**   Draw condensed formulas for each of the following compounds:

  a. *cis*-3-Octene
  b. *trans*-5-Chloro-2-hexene
  c. *trans*-2,3-Dichloro-2-butene

**Question 11.8**   Name each of the following compounds, using the IUPAC system. Be sure to indicate *cis* or *trans* where applicable.

a. $CH_3$, $CH_3$ C=C H, $CH_3$

c. $CH_3$, H C=C H, $CH_2C(CH_3)_3$

b. $CH_3CH_2$, $CH_2CH_3$ C=C $CH_3$, H

## 11.4   Alkenes in Nature

Folklore tells us that placing a ripe banana among green tomatoes will speed up the ripening process. In fact, this phenomenon has been demonstrated experimentally. The key to the reaction is *ethene*, the simplest alkene. Ethene, produced by ripening fruit, is a plant growth substance. It is produced in the greatest abundance in areas of the plant where cell division is occurring. It is produced during fruit ripening, during leaf fall and flower senescence, as well as under conditions of stress, including wounding, heat, cold, or water stress, and disease.

There are surprising numbers of polyenes, alkenes with several double bonds, found in nature. These molecules, which have wildly different properties and functions, are built from one or more five-carbon units called *isoprene*.

$$CH_2{=}CCH{=}CH_2$$ with $CH_3$

Isoprene

The molecules that are produced are called *isoprenoids*, or *terpenes*. Terpenes include the steroids; chlorophyll and carotenoid pigments that function in photosynthesis; and the lipid-soluble vitamins A, D, E, and K (see Figure 11.1).

Many other terpenes are plant products familiar to us because of their distinctive aromas. *Geraniol*, the familiar scent of geraniums, is a molecule made up of two isoprene units. Purified from plant sources, geraniol is the active ingredient in several natural insect repellants. These can be applied directly to the skin to provide 4 h of protection against a variety of insects, including mosquitoes, ticks, and fire ants.

Geraniol
(Roses and geraniums)

D-*Limonene* is the most abundant component of the oil extracted from the rind of citrus fruits. Because of its pleasing orange aroma, D-limonene is used as a flavor and fragrance additive in foods. However, the most rapidly expanding use of the compound is as a solvent. In this role, D-limonene can be used in place of more toxic solvents, such as mineral spirits, methyl ethyl ketone, acetone, toluene, and fluorinated and chlorinated organic solvents. It can also be formulated as a water-based cleaning product, such as Orange Glo, that can be used in place of more caustic cleaning solutions. There is a form of limonene that is a molecular mirror image of D-limonene. It is called L-limonene and has a pine or turpentine aroma.

D-Limonene
(Oil of lemon and orange)

The terpene *myrcene* is found in bayberry. It is used in perfumes and scented candles because it adds a refreshing, spicy aroma to them. Trace amounts of myrcene may be used as a flavor component in root beer.

Myrcene
(Oil of bayberry)

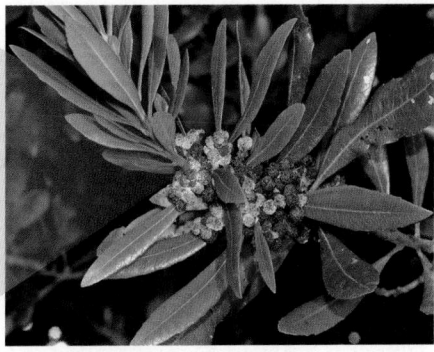

*Farnesol* is a terpene found in roses, orange blossom, wild cyclamen, and lily of the valley. Cosmetics companies began to use farnesol in skin care products in the early 1990s. It is claimed that farnesol smoothes wrinkles and increases skin elasticity. It is also thought to reduce skin aging by promoting regeneration of cells and activation of the synthesis of molecules, such as collagen, that are required for healthy skin.

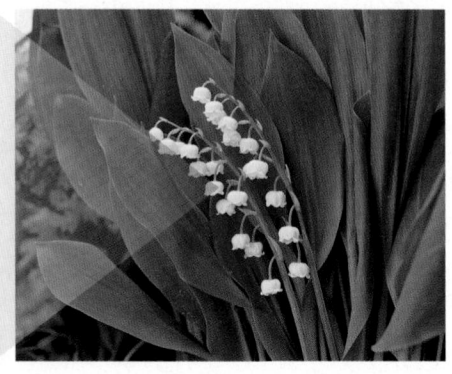

Farnesol
(Lily of the valley)

Another terpene, *retinol,* is a form of vitamin A (see Figure 11.1). It is able to penetrate the outer layers of skin and stimulate the formation of collagen and elastin. This reduces wrinkles by creating skin that is firmer and smoother.

## 11.5 Reactions Involving Alkenes and Alkynes

Reactions of alkenes involve the carbon-carbon double bond. The key reaction of the double bond is the **addition reaction.** This involves the addition of two atoms or groups of atoms to a double bond. The major alkene addition reactions include addition of hydrogen ($H_2$), halogens ($Cl_2$ or $Br_2$), water (HOH), or hydrogen halides (HBr or HCl). A generalized addition reaction is shown here. The R in these structures represents a hydrogen atom or any alkyl or aryl group.

LEARNING GOAL

**4** Write equations predicting the products of addition reactions of alkenes and alkynes: hydrogenation, halogenation, hydration, and hydrohalogenation.

Note that the double bond is replaced by a single bond. The former double bond carbons receive a new single bond to a new atom, producing either an alkane or a substituted alkane.

### Hydrogenation: Addition of $H_2$

**Hydrogenation** is the addition of a molecule of hydrogen ($H_2$) to a carbon-carbon double bond to give an alkane. In this reaction the double bond is broken, and two new C—H single bonds result. One hydrogen molecule is required for each double bond in the alkene. Platinum, palladium, or nickel is needed as a catalyst to speed up the reaction. Heat and/or pressure may also be required.

*Recall that a catalyst itself undergoes no net change in the course of a chemical reaction (see Section 7.3).*

*Note that the alkene is gaining two hydrogens. Thus, hydrogenation is a reduction reaction (see Sections 8.5 and 12.6).*

| EXAMPLE 11.6 | Writing Equations for the Hydrogenation of Alkenes |
|---|---|

Linoleic acid (*cis, cis*-9,12-octadecadienoic acid) is an essential fatty acid. This means that we must obtain it in the diet, because we cannot make it. Fortunately, it is found in abundance in sunflower, safflower, and corn oil. These oils are often hydrogenated to produce margarine. Write a balanced equation showing the hydrogenation of linoleic acid.

**4** Write equations predicting the products of addition reactions of alkenes and alkynes: hydrogenation, halogenation, hydration, and hydrohalogenation.

### Solution

First, notice that there are two double bonds. This means that we will need two molecules of $H_2$ for every molecule of linoleic acid that is hydrogenated.

Linoleic acid

$+ 2H_2$

Ni

Stearic acid

The liquid linoleic acid is converted to stearic acid, which is a rather hard solid. In margarine production today, partial hydrogenation is generally used because it produces a fat that can be more easily spread and has a better "mouth feel." Producers may then add butter flavoring, milk solids, salt, an emulsifying agent, preservatives, vitamin A for nutritional value, and a bit of β-carotene for color.

### Practice Problem 11.6

Write a balanced equation for the hydrogenation of each of the following alkenes.

a. *cis*-2-Heptene      c. 3-Hexene
b. *trans*-2-Pentene      d. Propene

▶ For Further Practice: **Questions 11.55, 11.67a, and 11.83.**

The conditions for the hydrogenation of alkynes are very similar to those for the hydrogenation of alkenes. Two molecules of hydrogen add to the triple bond of the alkyne to produce an alkane, as seen in the following general reaction:

$$R-C\equiv C-R + 2H_2 \xrightarrow[\text{Heat}]{\text{Pt, Pd, or Ni}} \underset{\text{Alkane}}{H-\overset{\displaystyle R}{\underset{\displaystyle H}{C}}-\overset{\displaystyle H}{\underset{\displaystyle R}{C}}-H}$$

Alkyne   Hydrogen

**Question 11.9**   The *trans*-isomer of 2-pentene was used in Practice Problem 11.6b. Would the result be any different if the *cis*-isomer had been used?

**Question 11.10**   Write balanced equations for the hydrogenation of 1-butene and *cis*-2-butene.

Margarine and solid shortening are made by partial hydrogenation of vegetable oils. While natural oils contain only *cis*-fatty acids, the hydrogenation reaction produces *trans*-fatty acids. What are the health risks associated with *trans*-fats?

CH₃—(CH₂)₇—CH=CH—(CH₂)₇—C(=O)—O—CH₂

CH₃—(CH₂)₇—CH=CH—(CH₂)₇—C(=O)—O—CH   →[3H₂, 200°C, 25 psi, metal catalyst]→   CH₃—(CH₂)₇—CH₂—CH₂—(CH₂)₇—C(=O)—O—CH₂

CH₃—(CH₂)₇—CH=CH—(CH₂)₇—C(=O)—O—CH₂

CH₃—(CH₂)₇—CH₂—CH₂—(CH₂)₇—C(=O)—O—CH

CH₃—(CH₂)₇—CH₂—CH₂—(CH₂)₇—C(=O)—O—CH₂

*An oil*                                           *A fat*

**Figure 11.3**   Conversion of a typical oil to a fat involves hydrogenation. In this example, triolein (an oil) is converted to tristearin (a fat).

**Question 11.11**   Write balanced equations for the complete hydrogenation of each of the following alkynes:

a. $H_3CC\equiv CCH_3$          b. $H_3CC\equiv CCH_2CH_3$

**Question 11.12**   Using the IUPAC Nomenclature System, name each of the products and reactants in the reactions described in Question 11.11.

*Saturated and unsaturated dietary fats are discussed in Section 17.2.*

Hydrogenation is used in the food industry to produce margarine, which is a mixture of hydrogenated vegetable oils (Figure 11.3). Vegetable oils are polyunsaturated, that is, they contain many double bonds and as a result have low melting points and are liquid at room temperature. The hydrogenation of these double bonds to single bonds increases the melting point of these oils and results in a fat, such as Crisco, that remains solid at room temperature. Because saturated fats are extended, rigid chains, they tend to stack. This increases the intermolecular attractions (London dispersion forces) and results in higher melting points, producing a fat that is solid at room temperature. A similar process with highly refined corn oil and added milk solids produces corn oil margarine. As we saw in Section 11.3, such margarine may contain *trans*-fatty acids as a result of hydrogenation.

## Halogenation: Addition of X₂

Chlorine (Cl₂) or bromine (Br₂) can be added to a double bond. This reaction, called **halogenation,** proceeds readily and does not require a catalyst:

Alkene        Halogen              Alkyl dihalide

**EXAMPLE 11.7    Writing Equations for the Halogenation of Alkenes**

LEARNING GOAL

Write a balanced equation showing (a) the chlorination of 1-pentene and (b) the bromination of *trans*-2-butene.

**4** Write equations predicting the products of addition reactions of alkenes and alkynes: hydrogenation, halogenation, hydration, and hydrohalogenation.

**Solution**

a. Begin by drawing the structure of 1-pentene and of diatomic chlorine (Cl₂).

1-Pentene        Chlorine

Knowing that one chlorine atom will form a covalent bond with each of the carbon atoms of the carbon-carbon double bond, we can write the product and complete the equation.

1-Pentene        Chlorine        1,2-Dichloropentane

b. Begin by drawing the structure of *trans*-2-butene and of diatomic bromine ($Br_2$).

*trans*-2-Butene        Bromine

Knowing that one bromine atom will form a covalent bond with each of the carbon atoms of the carbon-carbon double bond, we can write the product and complete the equation.

*trans*-2-Butene        Bromine        2,3-Dibromobutane

## Practice Problem 11.7

Write a balanced equation for the chlorination of each of the following alkenes.

a. 2,4-Hexadiene
b. 1,5-Dibromo-2-pentene
c. 2,3-Dimethyl-1-butene
d. 4,6-Dimethyl-2-heptene

▶ For Further Practice: **Questions 11.57, 11.67b, and 11.84.**

Alkynes also react with the halogens bromine or chlorine. Two molecules of halogen add to the triple bond to produce a tetrahaloalkane:

Alkyne    Halogen        Tetrahaloalkane

**Question 11.13** Write a balanced equation for the addition of bromine to each of the following alkenes. Draw the products and reactants for each reaction.
a. $CH_3CH=CH_2$    b. $CH_3CH=CHCH_3$

**Question 11.14** Using the IUPAC Nomenclature System, name each of the products and reactants in the reactions described in Question 11.13.

**Question 11.15** Write balanced equations for the complete chlorination of each of the following alkynes:
a. $H_3CC\equiv CCH_3$    b. $H_3CC\equiv CCH_2CH_3$

**Figure 11.4** Bromination of an alkene. The solution on the left is red because of the presence of bromine and absence of an alkene or alkyne. In the presence of an unsaturated hydrocarbon, the bromine is used in the reaction and the solution becomes colorless.

**Question 11.16**  Using the IUPAC Nomenclature System, name each of the products and reactants in the reactions described in Question 11.15.

The following equation represents the bromination of 1-pentene:

$$CH_3CH_2CH_2CH{=}CH_2 \ + \quad Br_2 \quad \longrightarrow \quad CH_3CH_2CH_2CHCH_2$$
$$\underset{\textstyle Br \ \ Br}{\textstyle | \quad |}$$

| 1-Pentene | Bromine | 1,2-Dibromopentane |
|-----------|---------|--------------------|
| (colorless) | (red) | (colorless) |

This reaction is represented in Figure 11.4. Notice that the solution of reactants is red because of the presence of bromine. However, the product is colorless.

This bromination reaction can be used to show the presence of double or triple bonds in an organic compound. The reaction mixture is red because of the presence of dissolved bromine. If the red color is lost, the bromine has been consumed. Thus bromination has occurred, and the compound must have had a carbon-carbon double or triple bond. The greater the amount of bromine that must be added to the reaction, the more unsaturated the compound is. For instance, a diene or an alkyne would consume twice as much bromine as an alkene with a single double bond.

## Hydration: Addition of $H_2O$

A water molecule can be added to an alkene. This reaction, termed **hydration,** requires a trace of strong acid ($H^+$) as a catalyst. The product is an alcohol, as shown in the following equation:

$$
\begin{array}{ccccc}
\underset{R}{\overset{R}{\diagdown}}C & & H & & R \\
\| & + & | & \xrightarrow{\ H^+\ } & R{-}\overset{\textstyle R}{\underset{\textstyle R}{\overset{|}{C}}}{-}H \\
\underset{R}{\overset{R}{\diagup}}C & & OH & & R{-}C{-}OH \\
& & & & R
\end{array}
$$

| Alkene | Water | Alcohol |
|--------|-------|---------|

The following equation shows the hydration of ethene to produce ethanol.

$$
\begin{array}{ccccc}
\underset{H}{\overset{H}{\diagdown}}C & & H & & H \\
\| & + & | & \xrightarrow{\ H^+\ } & H{-}\overset{\textstyle H}{\underset{\textstyle H}{\overset{|}{C}}}{-}H \\
\underset{H}{\overset{H}{\diagup}}C & & OH & & H{-}C{-}OH \\
& & & & H
\end{array}
$$

| Ethene | Water | Ethanol |
|--------|-------|---------|
| | | (ethyl alcohol) |

With alkenes in which the groups attached to the two carbons of the double bond are different (unsymmetrical alkenes), two products are possible. For example:

LEARNING GOAL

5 Apply Markovnikov's rule to predict the major and minor products of the hydration and hydrohalogenation reactions of unsymmetrical alkenes.

Propene
(propylene)

Major product
2-Propanol
(isopropyl alcohol)

Minor product
1-Propanol
(propyl alcohol)

When hydration of an unsymmetrical alkene, such as propene, is carried out in the laboratory, one product is favored over the other. In this example, 2-propanol is the major product. The Russian chemist Vladimir Markovnikov studied many such reactions and came up with a rule that can be used to predict the major product of such a reaction. **Markovnikov's rule** tells us that the carbon of the carbon-carbon double bond that originally has more hydrogen atoms receives the hydrogen atom being added to the double bond. The remaining carbon forms a bond with the —OH. Simply stated, "the rich get richer"—the carbon with the greater number of hydrogens gets the new one as well. In the preceding example, carbon-1 has two C—H bonds originally, and carbon-2 has only one. The major product, 2-propanol, results from the new C—H bond forming on carbon-1 and the new C—OH bond on carbon-2.

Addition of water to a double bond is a reaction that we find in several biochemical pathways. For instance, the citric acid cycle is a key metabolic pathway in the complete oxidation of the sugar glucose and the release of the majority of the energy used by the body. The citric acid cycle is also the source of starting materials for the synthesis of the biological molecules needed for life. The next-to-last reaction in the citric acid cycle is the hydration of a molecule of fumarate to produce a molecule called malate.

We have seen that hydration of a double bond requires a trace of acid as a catalyst. In the cell, this reaction is catalyzed by an enzyme, or biological catalyst, called fumarase.

Fumarate

Malate

EXAMPLE 11.8

## Writing Equations for the Hydration of Symmetrical and Unsymmetrical Alkenes

LEARNING GOAL

4 Write equations predicting the products of addition reactions of alkenes and alkynes: hydrogenation, halogenation, hydration, and hydrohalogenation.

a. More and more frequently we see ethanol used as an additive in the gasoline we buy. A mixture of 10% ethanol and 90% gasoline significantly raises the octane rating of the fuel. In fact, some cities where auto emissions may reach harmful levels require the use of 10% ethanol gasoline. Bioethanol is produced by fermentation of crops such as corn. However, it can also be manufactured by the hydration of ethene. Write a balanced equation showing the hydration of ethene.

**Solution**

Ethene

Ethanol

*Continued...*

b.  Write an equation showing all the products of the hydration of the
    unsymmetrical alkene 1-pentene.

**Solution**

Begin by drawing the structure of 1-pentene and of water and indicating the
catalyst.

$$\underset{\substack{\\ \\ \underset{\text{CH}_3\text{CH}_2\text{CH}_2}{5\ \ 4\ \ 3}}}{\overset{\text{H}}{\phantom{x}}} \overset{\text{H}}{\underset{2}{\text{C}}}{=}\overset{\text{1}}{\underset{\text{H}}{\text{C}}}\overset{\text{H}}{\phantom{x}} + \text{H—OH} \xrightarrow{\text{H}^+}$$

1-Pentene            Water

Markovnikov's rule tells us that the carbon atom that is already bonded to the greater number of hydrogen atoms is
more likely to receive the hydrogen atom from the water molecule. The other carbon atom is more likely to become
bonded to the hydroxyl group. Thus we can predict that the major product of this reaction will be 2-pentanol and that
the minor product will be 1-pentanol. Now we can complete the equation by showing the products:

$$\underset{\substack{\text{OH H}}}{\underset{\substack{5\ \ 4\ \ 3}}{\text{CH}_3\text{CH}_2\text{CH}_2}}{-}\overset{\overset{2}{\text{H}}}{\underset{}{\text{C}}}{-}\overset{\overset{1}{\text{H}}}{\underset{}{\text{C}}}{-}\text{H} \quad \text{or} \quad \underset{\substack{\text{H  OH}}}{\underset{\substack{5\ \ 4\ \ 3}}{\text{CH}_3\text{CH}_2\text{CH}_2}}{-}\overset{\overset{2}{\text{H}}}{\underset{}{\text{C}}}{-}\overset{\overset{1}{\text{H}}}{\underset{}{\text{C}}}{-}\text{H}$$

2-Pentanol                     1-Pentanol
(major product)                (minor product)

**Practice Problem 11.8**

Write a balanced equation for the hydration of each of the following alkenes.

    a. 1-Butene           c. Propene
    b. 2-Methyl-3-hexene    d. 1,4-Dichloro-2-butene

▶ For Further Practice: **Questions 11.59, 11.68, and 11.79.**

*The chemistry of enols, aldehydes, and
ketones is found in Chapter 13.*

      Hydration of an alkyne is a more complex process because the initial product
is not stable and is rapidly isomerized. As you would expect, the product is an
alcohol but, in this case, one in which the hydroxyl group is bonded to one of the
carbons of a carbon-carbon double bond. This type of molecule is called an *enol*
because it is both an alkene (*ene*) and an alcohol (*ol*). The enol cannot be isolated
from the reaction mixture because it is so quickly isomerized into either an aldehyde or ketone, as shown in the following general reaction:

$$\text{R—C}{\equiv}\text{C—R}' + \text{H}_2\text{O} \longrightarrow \text{R}{-}\overset{\overset{\text{H}}{|}}{\text{C}}{=}\underset{\underset{\text{OH}}{|}}{\text{C}}{-}\text{R}' \longrightarrow \text{R}{-}\overset{\overset{\text{H}}{|}}{\underset{\underset{\text{H}}{|}}{\text{C}}}{-}\overset{}{\underset{\underset{\text{O}}{||}}{\text{C}}}{-}\text{R}'$$

Alkyne        Water                  Enol              Aldehyde if R' = H
                                                        Ketone if R' = alkyl group

**Question 11.17**  Write an equation for the hydration of each of the following
alkenes. Predict the major product of each of the reactions.
    a. $\text{CH}_3\text{CH}{=}\text{CHCH}_3$            c. $\text{CH}_3\text{CH}_2\text{CH}_2\text{CH}{=}\text{CHCH}_2\text{CH}_3$
    b. $\text{CH}_2{=}\text{CHCH}_2\text{CH}_2\text{CH}(\text{CH}_3)_2$    d. $\text{CH}_3\text{CHClCH}{=}\text{CHCHClCH}_3$

**Question 11.18**   Write an equation for the hydration of each of the following alkenes. Predict the major product of each of the reactions.
   a. $CH_2=CHCH_2CH_2CH_3$
   b. $CH_3CH_2CH_2CH=CHCH_3$
   c. $CH_3CHBrCH_2CH=CHCH_2Cl$
   d. $CH_3CH_2CH_2CH_2CH_2CH=CHCH_3$

**Question 11.19**   Write equations for the complete hydration of each of the following alkynes:
   a. $H_3CC\equiv CH$
   b. $H_3CC\equiv CCH_2CH_3$

**Question 11.20**   Is the final product in each of the reactions in Question 11.19 an aldehyde or a ketone?

## Hydrohalogenation: Addition of HX

A hydrogen halide (HBr, HCl, or HI) also can be added to an alkene. The product of this reaction, called **hydrohalogenation,** is an alkyl halide:

Alkene       Hydrogen halide       Alkyl halide

Ethene       Hydrogen bromide       Bromoethane

This reaction also follows Markovnikov's rule. That is, if HX is added to an unsymmetrical alkene, the hydrogen atom will be added preferentially to the carbon atom that originally had the most hydrogen atoms. Consider the following example:

Propene                Major product            Minor product
                     2-Bromopropane          1-Bromopropane

| EXAMPLE 11.9 | **Writing Equations for the Hydrohalogenation of Alkenes** |

Write an equation showing all the products of the hydrohalogenation of 1-pentene with HCl.

**Solution**

Begin by drawing the structure of 1-pentene and of hydrochloric acid.

1-Pentene          Hydrochloric
                     acid

**LEARNING GOAL**

**4** Write equations predicting the products of addition reactions of alkenes and alkynes: hydrogenation, halogenation, hydration, and hydrohalogenation.

**LEARNING GOAL**

**5** Apply Markovnikov's rule to predict the major and minor products of the hydration and hydrohalogenation reactions of unsymmetrical alkenes.

*Continued…*

Markovnikov's rule tells us that the carbon atom that is already bonded to the greater number of hydrogen atoms is more likely to receive the hydrogen atom of the hydrochloric acid molecule. The other carbon atom is more likely to become bonded to the chlorine atom. Thus, we can complete the equation by writing the major and minor products.

$$
\underset{5}{CH_3}\underset{4}{CH_2}\underset{3}{CH_2}-\underset{\underset{Cl}{|}}{\overset{2}{\underset{|}{C}}}-\underset{\underset{H}{|}}{\overset{1}{\underset{|}{\overset{H}{C}}}}-H \ \text{or} \ \underset{5}{CH_3}\underset{4}{CH_2}\underset{3}{CH_2}-\underset{\underset{H}{|}}{\overset{2}{\underset{|}{\overset{H}{C}}}}-\underset{\underset{Cl}{|}}{\overset{1}{\underset{|}{\overset{H}{C}}}}-H
$$

2-Chloropentane            1-Chloropentane
(major product)            (minor product)

As predicted by Markovnikov's rule, the major product is 2-chloropentane and the minor product is 1-chloropentane.

### Practice Problem 11.9

Write a balanced equation for the hydrobromination of each of the following alkenes.

a. 2-Pentene
b. Propene

c. 3-Heptene
d. Ethene

▶ For Further Practice: **Questions 11.69d, 11.70d, and 11.73.**

## Addition Polymers of Alkenes

### LEARNING GOAL

**6** Write equations representing the formation of addition polymers of alkenes.

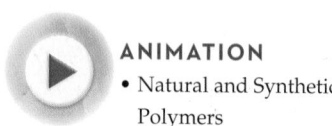

**ANIMATION**

• Natural and Synthetic Polymers

**Polymers** are macromolecules composed of repeating structural units called **monomers**. A polymer may be made up of several thousand monomers. Many commercially important plastics and fibers are addition polymers made from alkenes or substituted alkenes. They are called **addition polymers** because they are made by the sequential addition of the alkene monomer. The general formula for this addition reaction follows:

$$
n \ \underset{\underset{R}{/}}{\overset{\overset{R}{\diagdown}}{C}}=\underset{\underset{R}{\diagdown}}{\overset{\overset{R}{/}}{C}} \ \xrightarrow[\text{Pressure}]{\substack{\text{Catalyst} \\ \text{Heat}}} \ \text{etc.}-\overset{R}{\underset{R}{\overset{|}{\underset{|}{C}}}}-\overset{R}{\underset{R}{\overset{|}{\underset{|}{C}}}}-\overset{R}{\underset{R}{\overset{|}{\underset{|}{C}}}}-\overset{R}{\underset{R}{\overset{|}{\underset{|}{C}}}}-\overset{R}{\underset{R}{\overset{|}{\underset{|}{C}}}}-\overset{R}{\underset{R}{\overset{|}{\underset{|}{C}}}}-\text{etc.}
$$

Alkene monomer                    Addition polymer
R = H, X, or an alkyl group

The product of the reaction is generally represented in a simplified manner:

$$
\left[\begin{matrix} R & R \\ | & | \\ C-C \\ | & | \\ R & R \end{matrix}\right]_n
$$

*Polyethylene* is a polymer made from the monomer ethylene (ethene):

$$
n CH_2=CH_2 \longrightarrow \left[CH_2-CH_2\right]_n
$$

Ethene                    Polyethylene
(ethylene)

It is used to make bottles, injection-molded toys and housewares, and wire coverings.

*Polypropylene* is a plastic made from propylene (propene). It is used to make indoor-outdoor carpeting, packaging materials, toys, and housewares. When propylene polymerizes, a methyl group is located on every other carbon of the main chain:

## A HUMAN PERSPECTIVE

### Life Without Polymers?

What do Nike Air-Sole shoes, disposable diapers, tires, shampoo, and artificial joints and skin share in common? These products and a great many other items we use every day are composed of synthetic or natural polymers. Indeed, the field of polymer chemistry has come a long way since the 1920s and 1930s when DuPont chemists invented nylon and Teflon.

Consider the disposable diaper. The outer, waterproof layer is composed of polyethylene. The polymerization reaction that produces polyethylene is shown in Section 11.5. The diapers have elastic to prevent leaking. The elastic is made of a natural polymer, rubber. The monomer from which natural rubber is formed is 2-methyl-1,3-butadiene. The common name of this monomer is *isoprene*. As we will see in coming chapters, isoprene is an important monomer in the synthesis of many natural polymers.

$$n\text{CH}_2\text{=}\underset{\underset{\text{CH}_3}{|}}{\text{C}}\text{—CH=CH}_2 \longrightarrow \left[\text{CH}_2\text{—}\underset{\underset{\text{CH}_3}{|}}{\text{C}}\text{=CH—CH}_2\right]_n$$

2-Methyl-1,3-butadiene        Rubber polymer
(isoprene)

The diaper is filled with a synthetic polymer called poly(acrylic acid). This polymer has the remarkable ability to absorb many times its own weight in liquid. Polymers that have this ability are called superabsorbers, but polymer chemists have no idea why they have this property! The acrylic acid monomer and resulting poly(acrylic acid) polymer are shown here:

$$n\ \underset{\underset{H}{|}}{\overset{\overset{H}{|}}{C}}\text{=}\underset{\underset{\underset{\underset{\underset{H}{|}}{O}}{|}}{\overset{\overset{H}{|}}{C}}\text{=O}}{C} \longrightarrow \left[\text{CH}_2\text{—}\underset{\underset{\underset{\underset{H}{|}}{O}}{\underset{\underset{C\text{=O}}{|}}{CH}}}{CH}\right]_n$$

Acrylic acid monomer        Poly(acrylic acid)

Another example of a useful polymer is Gore-Tex. This amazing polymer is made by stretching Teflon. Teflon is produced from the monomer tetrafluoroethene, as seen in the following equation:

$$n\ \underset{\underset{F}{|}}{\overset{\overset{F}{|}}{C}}\text{=}\underset{\underset{F}{|}}{\overset{\overset{F}{|}}{C}} \longrightarrow \left[\underset{\underset{F}{|}}{\overset{\overset{F}{|}}{C}}\text{—}\underset{\underset{F}{|}}{\overset{\overset{F}{|}}{C}}\right]_n$$

Tetrafluoroethene        Teflon

Clothing made from this fabric is used to protect firefighters because of its fire resistance. Because it also insulates, Gore-Tex clothing is used by military forces and by many amateur athletes, for protection during strenuous activity in the cold. In addition to its use in protective clothing, Gore-Tex has been used in millions of medical procedures for sutures, synthetic blood vessels, and tissue reconstruction.

**For Further Understanding**

▶ Visit The Macrogalleria, www.pslc.ws/macrog/index.htm, an Internet site maintained by the Department of Polymer Science of the University of Southern Mississippi, to help you answer these questions:
▶ Why does shrink wrap shrink?
▶ What are optical fibers made of and how do they transmit light?

$$n\text{CH}_2\text{=}\underset{\underset{\text{CH}_3}{|}}{\text{CH}} \longrightarrow \left[\text{CH}_2\text{—}\underset{\underset{\text{CH}_3}{|}}{\text{CH}}\right]_n$$

or

$$\text{CH}_2\text{—}\underset{\underset{\text{CH}_3}{|}}{\text{CH}}\text{—CH}_2\text{—}\underset{\underset{\text{CH}_3}{|}}{\text{CH}}\text{—CH}_2\text{—}\underset{\underset{\text{CH}_3}{|}}{\text{CH}}$$

Polymers made from alkenes or substituted alkenes are simply very large alkanes or substituted alkanes. Like the alkanes, they are typically inert. This chemical inertness makes these polymers ideal for making containers to hold juices, chemicals, and fluids used medically. They are also used to make sutures, catheters, and other indwelling devices. A variety of polymers made from substituted alkenes are listed in Table 11.2.

# GREEN CHEMISTRY

## Plastic Recycling

Plastics, first developed by British inventor Alexander Parkes in 1862, are amazing substances. Some serve as containers for many of our foods and drinks, keeping them fresh for long periods. Other plastics serve as containers for detergents and cleansers or are formed into pipes for our plumbing systems. We have learned to make strong, clear sheets of plastic that can be used as windows, and feather-light plastics that can be used as packaging materials. In the United States alone, seventy-five billion pounds (lb) of plastics are produced each year.

But plastics, amazing in their versatility, are a mixed blessing. One characteristic that makes them so useful, their stability, has created an environmental problem. It may take 40 to 50 years for plastics discarded into landfill sites to degrade. Concern that we could soon be knee-deep in plastic worldwide has resulted in a creative new industry: plastic recycling.

Since there are so many types of plastics, it is necessary to identify, sort, and recycle them separately. To help with this sorting process, manufacturers place recycling symbols on their plastic wares. As you can see in the accompanying table, each symbol corresponds to a different type of plastic.

Polyethylene terephthalate, also known as PETE or simply #1, is a form of polyester often used to make bottles and jars to contain food. When collected, it is ground up into flakes and formed into pellets. The most common use for recycled PETE is the manufacture of polyester carpets. But it may also be spun into a cotton candy–like form that can be used as a fiber filling for pillows or sleeping bags. Reuse to produce bottles and jars is also common.

HDPE, or #2, is high-density polyethylene. Originally used for milk and detergent bottles, recycled HDPE is used to produce pipes, plastic lumber, trash cans, or bottles for storage of

materials other than food. Low-density polyethylene (LDPE), or #4, is very similar to HDPE chemically. Because it is a more highly branched polymer, it is less dense and more flexible. Originally used to produce plastic bags, recycled LDPE is also used to make trash bags, grocery bags, and plastic tubing and lumber.

PVC, or #3, is one of the less commonly recycled plastics in the United States, although it is actively recycled in Europe. The recycled material is used to make non-food-bearing containers, shoe soles, flooring, sweaters, and pipes. Polypropylene, PP or #5, is found in margarine tubs, fabrics, and carpets. Recycled polypropylene has many uses, including fabrication of gardening implements.

You probably come into contact with polystyrene, PS or #6, almost every day. It is used to make foam egg cartons and meat

## TABLE 11.2  Some Important Addition Polymers of Alkenes

| Monomer Name | Formula | Polymer | Uses |
|---|---|---|---|
| Styrene | $CH_2{=}CH{-}\bigcirc$ | Polystyrene | Styrofoam containers |
| Acrylonitrile | $CH_2{=}CHCN$ | Polyacrylonitrile (Orlon) | Clothing |
| Methyl methacrylate | $CH_2{=}C(CH_3){-}\overset{\overset{\textstyle O}{\|}}{C}OCH_3$ | Polymethyl methacrylate (Plexiglas, Lucite) | Basketball backboards |
| Vinyl chloride | $CH_2{=}CHCl$ | Polyvinyl chloride (PVC) | Plastic pipe, credit cards |
| Tetrafluoroethene | $CF_2{=}CF_2$ | Polytetrafluoroethylene (Teflon) | Nonstick surfaces |

## 11.6  Aromatic Hydrocarbons

In the early part of the nineteenth century, chemists began to discover organic compounds with chemical properties quite distinct from the alkanes, alkenes, and alkynes. They called these substances *aromatic compounds* because many of the first

| Code | Type | Name | Formula | Description | Examples |
|------|------|------|---------|-------------|----------|
| PETE | 1 | Polyethylene terephthalate | $-CH_2-CH_2-O-\overset{\displaystyle O}{\underset{\displaystyle O}{C}}$—⟨ ⟩—$C-O-$ | Usually clear or green, rigid | Soda bottles, peanut butter jars, vegetable oil bottles |
| HDPE | 2 | High-density polyethylene | $-CH_2-CH_2-$ | Semirigid | Milk and water jugs, juice and bleach bottles |
| PVC | 3 | Polyvinyl chloride | $-\underset{\displaystyle Cl}{CH}-CH_2-$ | Semirigid | Detergent and cleanser bottles, pipes |
| LDPE | 4 | Low-density polyethylene | $-CH_2-CH_2-$ | Flexible, not crinkly | Six-pack rings, bread bags, sandwich bags |
| PP | 5 | Polypropylene | $-\underset{\displaystyle CH_3}{CH}-CH_2-$ | Semirigid | Margarine tubs, straws, screw-on lids |
| PS | 6 | Polystyrene | $-CH-CH_2-$ ⟨ ⟩ | Often brittle | Styrofoam, packing peanuts, egg cartons, foam cups |
| Other | 7 | Multilayer plastics | N/A | Squeezable | Ketchup and syrup bottles |

trays, serving containers for fast food chains, CD "jewel boxes," and "peanuts" used as packing material. At the current time, polystyrene food containers are not recycled. PS from nonfood products can be melted down and converted into pellets that are used to manufacture office desktop accessories, hangers, and plastic trays used to hold plants.

**For Further Understanding**

► Use the Internet or other resources to investigate recycling efforts in your area.

► In some areas, efforts to recycle plastics and paper have been abandoned. What factors contributed to this?

examples were isolated from the pleasant-smelling resins of tropical trees. The carbon/hydrogen ratio of these compounds suggested a very high degree of unsaturation, similar to the alkenes and alkynes. Imagine, then, how puzzled these early organic chemists must have been when they discovered that these compounds do not undergo the kinds of addition reactions common for the alkenes and alkynes.

$$CH_2{=}CH_2 + Br_2 \longrightarrow \underset{\displaystyle Br \quad Br}{CH_2-CH_2}$$

+ Br₂ ⟶ No reaction

We no longer define aromatic compounds as those having a pleasant aroma; in fact, many do not. We now recognize **aromatic hydrocarbons** as those that exhibit a much higher degree of chemical stability than their chemical composition

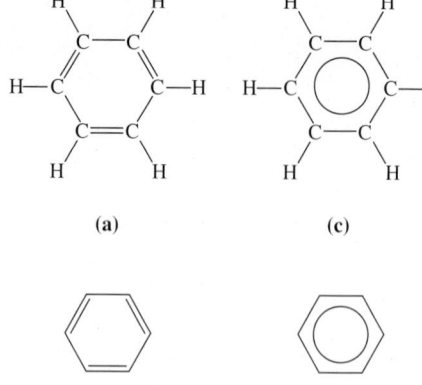

**Figure 11.5** Four ways to represent the benzene molecule. Structure (b) is a simplified diagram of structure (a). Structure (d), a simplified diagram of structure (c), is the most commonly used representation.

*Resonance models are described in Section 3.4.*

LEARNING GOAL

**7**  Draw the structures and write the names of common aromatic hydrocarbons.

would predict. The most common group of aromatic compounds is based on the six-member aromatic ring, the benzene ring. The structure of the benzene ring is represented in various ways in Figure 11.5.

## Structure and Properties

The benzene ring consists of six carbon atoms joined in a planar hexagonal arrangement. Each carbon atom is bonded to one hydrogen atom. Friedrich Kekulé proposed a model for the structure of benzene in 1865. He proposed that single and double bonds alternated around the ring (a conjugated system of double bonds). To explain why benzene did not decolorize bromine—in other words, didn't react like an unsaturated compound—he suggested that the double and single bonds shift positions rapidly.

Actually, the most accurate way to represent the benzene molecules is as a resonance hybrid of two Kekulé structures:

Benzene as a resonance hybrid

The current model of the structure of benzene is based on the idea of overlapping orbitals. Each carbon is bonded to two others by sharing a pair of electrons. Each carbon atom also shares a pair of electrons with a hydrogen atom. The remaining six electrons are located in $p$ orbitals that are perpendicular to the plane of the ring. These $p$ orbitals overlap laterally to form a cloud of electrons above and below the ring (Figure 11.6).

Two symbols are commonly used to represent the benzene ring. The representation in Figure 11.5b is the structure proposed by Kekulé. The structure in Figure 11.5d uses a circle to represent the electron cloud.

## Nomenclature

Most simple aromatic compounds are named as derivatives of benzene. Thus benzene is the parent ring, and the name of any atom or group bonded to benzene is used as a prefix, as in these examples:

Nitrobenzene     Ethylbenzene     Bromobenzene     Benzoic acid     Benzaldehyde

Other members of this family have unique names based on history rather than logic:

Toluene          Phenol           Aniline          Anisole

Other common names include xylene, a benzene ring with two methyl substituents, and cresol, a benzene ring bonded to a methyl group and a hydroxyl group.

When two groups are present on the ring, three possible orientations exist, and they may be named by either the IUPAC Nomenclature System or the common system of nomenclature. If the groups or atoms are located on two adjacent carbons, they are referred to as *ortho* (*o*) in the common system or with the prefix 1,2- in the IUPAC system. If they are on carbons separated by one carbon atom, they are termed *meta* (*m*) in the common system or 1,3- in the IUPAC system. Finally, if the substituents are on carbons separated by two carbon atoms, they are said to be *para* (*p*) in the common system or 1,4- in the IUPAC system. The following examples demonstrate both of these systems:

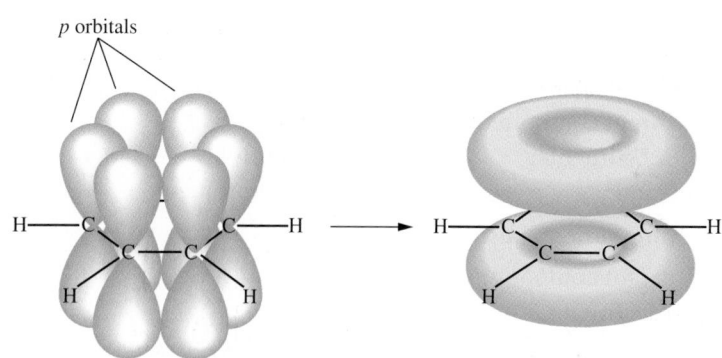

**Figure 11.6** The current model of the bonding in benzene. The overlapping *p* orbitals form a cloud of electrons above and below the ring.

Two groups 1,2 or *ortho*    Two groups 1,3 or *meta*    Two groups 1,4 or *para*

G = Any group

The three orientations of xylene and cresol are shown here:

*ortho*-Xylene    *meta*-Xylene    *para*-Xylene    *ortho*-Cresol    *meta*-Cresol    *para*-Cresol

If three or more groups are attached to the benzene ring, numbers must be used to describe their location. The names of the substituents are given in alphabetical order.

---

**EXAMPLE 11.10**    **Naming Derivatives of Benzene**

Name the following compounds using the IUPAC and common systems of nomenclature.

a.    CH₃
      Cl

b.    NO₂
      OH

c.    CH₂CH₃
      NH₂

**LEARNING GOAL**

**7**  Draw the structures and write the names of common aromatic hydrocarbons.

*Continued…*

## Solution

**IUPAC names:**

| | | | |
|---|---|---|---|
| Parent compound: | toluene | phenol | aniline |
| Substituents: | 2-chloro | 4-nitro | 3-ethyl |
| Name: | 2-Chlorotoluene | 4-Nitrophenol | 3-Ethylaniline |

**Common names:**

| | | | |
|---|---|---|---|
| Parent compound: | toluene | phenol | aniline |
| Substituents: | *ortho*-chloro | *para*-nitro | *meta*-ethyl |
| Name: | *ortho*-Chlorotoluene | *para*-Nitrophenol | *meta*-Ethylaniline |
| Abbreviated name: | *o*-Chlorotoluene | *p*-Nitrophenol | *m*-Ethylaniline |

### Practice Problem 11.10

Name the following compounds using the IUPAC and common nomenclature systems.

a.     b.     c.     d.

▶ For Further Practice: **Questions 11.90, 11.91, and 11.92.**

In IUPAC nomenclature, the group derived by removing one hydrogen from benzene (—C₆H₅), is called the **phenyl group.** An aromatic hydrocarbon attached to a long aliphatic group is named as a phenyl substituted hydrocarbon. For example:

2-Phenylbutane        3-Phenyl-1-butene

One final special name that occurs frequently in aromatic compounds is the benzyl group:

C₆H₅CH₂—     or     ⬡—CH₂—

The use of this group name is illustrated by:

⬡—CH₂Cl        ⬡—CH₂OH

Benzyl chloride        Benzyl alcohol

**Question 11.21**   Draw each of the following compounds:

a. 1,3,5-Trichlorobenzene
b. *ortho*-Cresol
c. 2,5-Dibromophenol
d. *para*-Dinitrobenzene
e. 2-Nitroaniline
f. *meta*-Nitrotoluene

**Question 11.22**  Draw each of the following compounds:

a. 2,3-Dichlorotoluene
b. 3-Bromoaniline
c. 1-Bromo-3-ethylbenzene
d. *o*-Nitrotoluene
e. *p*-Xylene
f. *o*-Dibromobenzene

## Polynuclear Aromatic Hydrocarbons

The polynuclear aromatic hydrocarbons (PAH) are composed of two or more aromatic rings joined together. Many of them have been shown to be carcinogenic, that is, they cause cancer.

   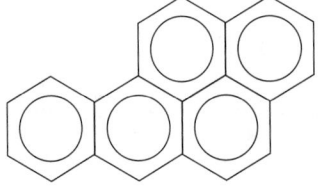

Naphthalene          Anthracene          Phenanthrene          Benzopyrene

Naphthalene has a distinctive aroma. It has been frequently used as mothballs and may cause hemolytic anemia (a condition causing breakdown of red blood cells) in humans, but has not been associated with human or animal cancers. Anthracene, derived from coal tar, is the parent compound of many dyes and pigments. Phenanthrene is common in the environment, although there is no industrial use of the compound. It is a product of incomplete combustion of fossil fuels and wood. Although anthracene is a suspected carcinogen, phenanthrene has not been shown to be one. Benzopyrene is found in tobacco smoke, smokestack effluents, charcoal-grilled meat, and automobile exhaust. It is one of the most potent carcinogens known.

## Reactions Involving Benzene

As we have noted, benzene does not readily undergo addition reactions. The typical reactions of benzene are **substitution reactions,** in which a hydrogen atom is replaced by another atom or group of atoms. Unlike addition reactions of alkenes, no carbon-carbon bonds are broken. In substitution reactions of benzene, the carbon-hydrogen bond is broken and the hydrogen is replaced (substituted) with another atom or group of atoms.

Benzene can react (by substitution) with $Cl_2$ or $Br_2$. These reactions require either iron or an iron halide as a catalyst. For example:

$$\text{Benzene} + Br_2 \xrightarrow{FeBr_3} \text{Benzene}-Br + HBr$$

Benzene          Bromine          Bromobenzene

When a second equivalent of the halogen is added, three isomers—*para, ortho,* and *meta*—are formed.

Benzene also reacts with sulfur trioxide by substitution. Concentrated sulfuric acid is required as the catalyst. Benzenesulfonic acid, a strong acid, is the product:

$$\text{Benzene} + SO_3 \xrightarrow{\text{Concentrated } H_2SO_4} \text{Benzene}-\overset{\overset{O}{\|}}{\underset{\underset{O}{\|}}{S}}-OH + H_2O$$

Benzene     Sulfur trioxide          Benzenesulfonic acid

Benzene can also undergo nitration with concentrated nitric acid dissolved in concentrated sulfuric acid. This reaction requires temperatures in the range of 50–55°C.

$$\text{Benzene} + \text{HNO}_3 \xrightarrow[\text{50--55°C}]{\text{Concentrated H}_2\text{SO}_4} \text{Nitrobenzene} -\text{NO}_2 + \text{H}_2\text{O}$$

Benzene    Nitric acid                                    Nitrobenzene

## 11.7   Heterocyclic Aromatic Compounds

**Heterocyclic aromatic compounds** are those having at least one atom other than carbon as part of the structure of the aromatic ring. The structures and common names of several heterocyclic aromatic compounds are shown:

Pyridine          Pyrimidine          Purine

Imidazole          Furan          Pyrrole

All these compounds are more similar to benzene in stability and chemical behavior than they are to the alkenes. Many of these compounds are components of molecules that have significant effects on biological systems. For instance, the purines and pyrimidines are components of DNA (deoxyribonucleic acid) and RNA (ribonucleic acid). DNA and RNA are the molecules responsible for storing and expressing the genetic information of an organism. The pyridine ring is found in nicotine, the addictive compound in tobacco. The pyrrole ring is a component of the porphyrin ring found in hemoglobin and chlorophyll.

Porphyrin

The imidazole ring is a component of cimetidine, a drug used in the treatment of stomach ulcers. The structure of cimetidine is shown below:

Cimetidine

We will discuss a subset of the heterocyclic aromatic compounds, the heterocyclic amines, in Chapter 15.

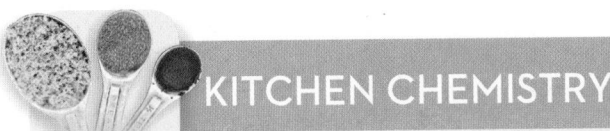

# KITCHEN CHEMISTRY

## Amazing Chocolate

Chocolate has been consumed for over 3000 years. The Mayans and Aztecs enjoyed a frothy drink made from ground up cacao beans. The Mayans preferred it hot and the Aztecs drank it cold. Although the Mayans could grow the cacao tree, the Aztecs couldn't. As a result, the beans became very valuable and were even used as money. The drink that the Aztecs and Mayans enjoyed was very bitter and was sometimes enhanced by adding ground chili peppers or vanilla. They thought that the drink would fight fatigue. Both the bitter taste and the mood enhancement that lifted fatigue are caused by theobromine.

Theobromine

Theobromine is an alkaloid that, in pure form, is a crystalline, bitter powder. Medically it can be used as a vasodilator, a diuretic, and a heart stimulant. One study concluded that theobromine was a better cough suppressant than codeine, and it has been found helpful in the treatment of asthma. As with any pharmacologically active substance, an excess of theobromine can cause theobromine poisoning, which has been observed in some, particularly the elderly, who eat chocolate to excess!

The chocolate that we enjoy is produced by first allowing the cacao seeds to ferment to reduce the bitter taste. The shells are then removed and the inner nib is dried and ground into a powder that is pure chocolate. The powder is generally liquefied, placed in molds to harden, and then processed into cocoa solids and cocoa butter. We can purchase chocolate in many forms. Baking chocolate is generally bitter. No sugar has been added and it primarily consists of the cocoa solids and cocoa butter. Milk chocolate, dark chocolate, and white chocolate are produced by combining the cocoa butter and solids in varying amounts and adding other ingredients, particularly sugar and milk or condensed milk. Dark chocolate has the greatest amount of cocoa solids and, at the extreme, white chocolate has no cocoa solids and is enjoyed by those who have allergies to cocoa solids.

A Mexican sauce made with chili peppers and chocolate brings to mind the drink of the Aztecs. It is a mole sauce (pronounced mole lay). One legend tells us that this sauce was invented by the nuns in Santa Rosa Convent in Puebla, Mexico. The nuns were expecting a visit from the Archbishop. Being poor, they were concerned about the meal that they would prepare for him.

After praying about it, they simply took what they had, some chili peppers, nuts, fruit, bread, tomatillos, spices, and chocolate. They mixed these ingredients into a sauce and served it over turkey. The Archbishop was impressed with the meal and mole sauce over poultry has been a favorite in Mexican cuisine for centuries. It has been said that the secret to the mole sauce is that it combines so many different flavors and sensations; some recipes have 20–30 ingredients! The chili peppers provide "heat;" the tomatillos add a sour note; the dried fruits and sugar contribute sweetness; the spices including cumin, cloves, and anise, add a variety of nuanced flavors; and the nuts and tortillas thicken the sauce. The chocolate, added at the end of the preparation, helps to mellow the heat of the peppers.

Recently scientists have published data to suggest that dark chocolate can reduce blood pressure. Other articles claim that dark chocolate can prevent cancer and heart disease. The molecules responsible for these observed effects are a variety of catechins and derivatives of phenol (see structures below.) Found also in tea, these compounds are antioxidants. It is thought that they prevent the oxidation of lipids in the blood which, in turn, is thought to prevent them from sticking to the surfaces of blood vessels. This reduces the risk of atherosclerosis or hardening of the arteries.

Catechin                    Phenol

We enjoy chocolate in dark, bittersweet form, as creamy milk chocolate, in hot cocoa, and in mole sauces. Whether it is the wide variety of tastes, the melt-in-your mouth sensation, the mild enhancement of mood and energy, or the reported health benefits, chocolate has been enjoyed over the ages and will continue to be a treat in years to come.

### For Further Understanding

► Theobromine has a structure very similar to caffeine. It has one fewer methyl group than caffeine. What are some of the similarities in the biological properties of these two substances that can be traced to the similarity in their structures?

► Why is dark chocolate a richer source of antioxidants than milk chocolate or white chocolate?

**CHAPTER MAP**

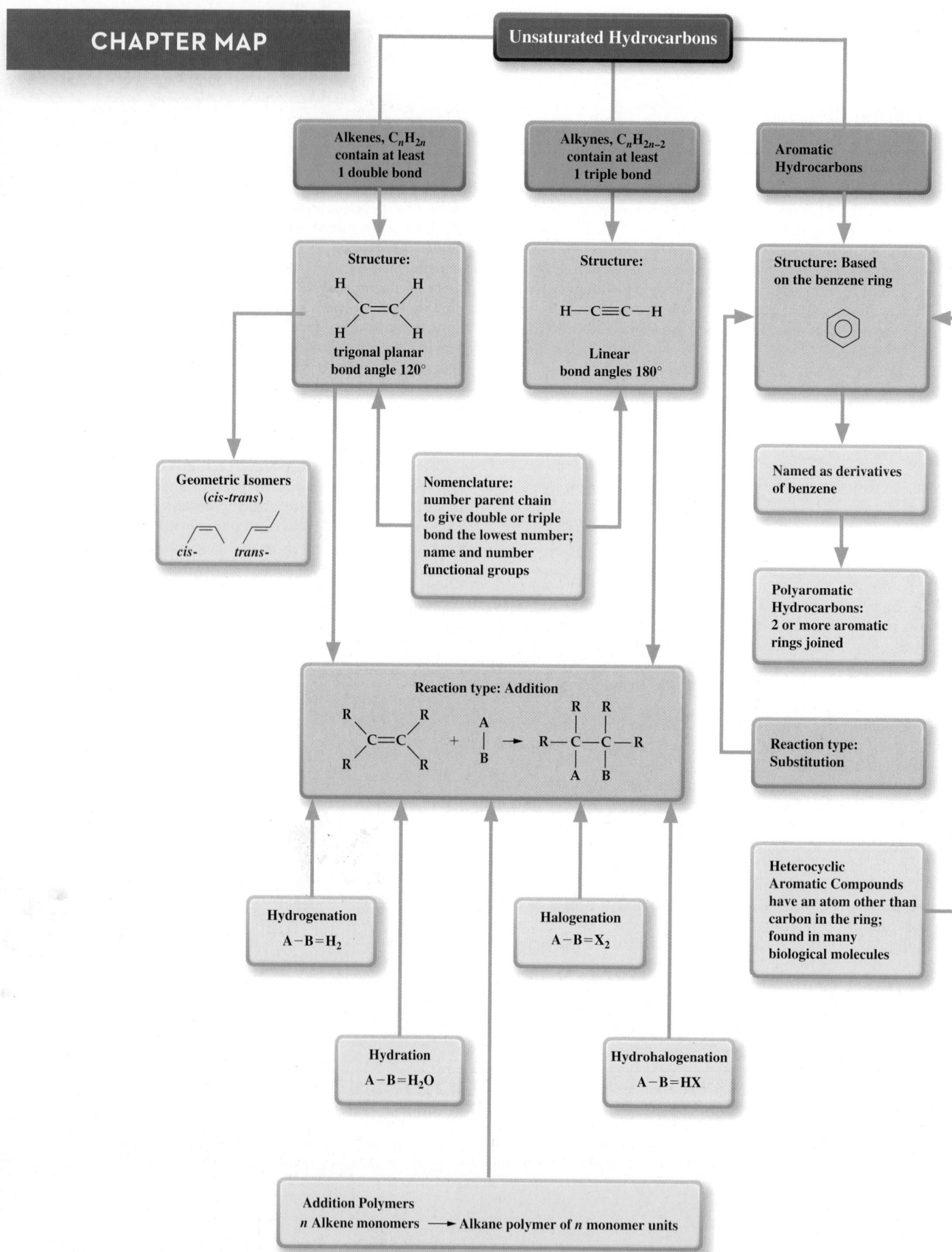

# SUMMARY OF REACTIONS

## Addition Reactions of Alkenes

**Hydrogenation:**

Alkene    Hydrogen      Alkane

**Hydration:**

Alkene    Water     Alcohol

**Halogenation:**

Alkene    Halogen    Alkyl dihalide

**Hydrohalogenation:**

Alkene    Hydrogen halide    Alkyl halide

## Reactions of Benzene

**Halogenation:**

Benzene    Halogen      Halobenzene

**Sulfonation:**

Benzene    Sulfur trioxide

Benzenesulfonic acid

**Nitration:**

Benzene    Nitric acid

Nitrobenzene

## Addition Polymers of Alkenes

Alkene monomer     Addition polymer

# SUMMARY

## 11.1 Alkenes and Alkynes: Structure and Physical Properties

▶ **Alkenes** and **alkynes** are **unsaturated** hydrocarbons because they have at least one C—C double bond (alkenes) or C—C triple bond (alkynes.)

▶ Alkenes have the general formula $C_nH_{2n}$ and alkynes have the general formula $C_nH_{2n-2}$.

▶ Alkenes and alkynes have physical properties like alkanes, but very different chemical properties.

## 11.2 Alkenes and Alkynes: Nomenclature

▶ Identify the parent compound and replace the -*ane* ending with -*ene* for alkenes and -*yne* for alkynes.

▶ Number the parent chain to give the lowest number to the double or triple bond.

▶ Name and number the other groups and place them alphabetically in front of the parent alkene or alkyne name.

## 11.3 Geometric isomers: A Consequence of Unsaturation

▶ Because the carbon-carbon double bond is rigid, **geometric isomers** occur when two different groups are bonded to each of the carbons of the double bond.

▶ When identical groups are on the same side of the double bond, the prefix *cis*- is used. When identical groups are on opposite sides of the double bond, the prefix *trans*- is used.

## 11.4 Alkenes in Nature

▶ Alkenes and polyenes (alkenes with several carbon-carbon double bonds) are common in nature.

▶ Isoprenoids, or terpenes, include steroids, chlorophyll and other photosynthetic pigments, and vitamins A, D, E, and K.

## 11.5 Reactions Involving Alkenes and Alkynes

▶ Alkenes and alkynes undergo **addition reactions** in which two atoms or groups of atoms add to the C—C double or triple bond.

▶ Addition reactions include: **halogenation, hydrohalogenation, hydration,** and **hydrogenation.**

▶ **Markovnikov's rule** predicts the most abundant products in addition reactions involving unsymmetrical alkenes.

▶ **Polymers** are formed by the sequential addition of alkene **monomers.** These are called **addition polymers.**

## 11.6 Aromatic Hydrocarbons

▶ **Aromatic hydrocarbons** contain benzene rings.

▶ Simple aromatic compounds are named as derivatives of benzene. Others have historical common names.

▶ A **phenyl group** is a benzene ring with one hydrogen atom removed. The term may be used in the nomenclature of molecules that include the benzene as a substituent group.

▶ Benzene participates in substitution reactions in which a hydrogen atom is replaced by another atom or group.

▶ Polynuclear aromatic hydrocarbons consist of two or more benzene rings joined.

## 11.7 Heterocyclic Aromatic Compounds

▶ **Heterocyclic aromatic compounds** have at least one atom other than carbon in the structure of the aromatic ring.

▶ Many of these compounds are important components of biological molecules, including DNA, RNA, and hemoglobin.

# ANSWERS TO PRACTICE PROBLEMS

**11.1** a. 6-Chloro-4-methyl-2-heptene    c. 5-Bromo-3-heptyne
b. 1,4-Pentadiyne    d. 1,5-Heptadiene

**11.2** a. l-Chlorocyclopropene    c. 3,4-Dibromocyclopentene
b. 4,5-Dimethylcyclohexene    d. 3-Fluorocyclobutene

**11.3** a. *cis*-isomer    b. *trans*-isomer    c. *cis*-isomer

**11.4** a. *cis*-4,5-Dibromo-2-hexene
b. *trans*-3,4-Dibromo-3-hexene
c. *cis*-2,3-Dichloro-2-hexene

**11.5** a. 2-Pentene can exist as both *cis*- and *trans*-isomers.

*cis*-2-Pentene          *trans*-2-Pentene

b. 1,1,2-Tribromo-1-pentene cannot exist as *cis*- and *trans*-isomers because one of the carbons involved in the double bond is also bonded to two identical atoms (Br).
c. Propene cannot exist as *cis*- and *trans*-isomers because one of the carbons involved in the double bond is also bonded to two identical atoms (H).
d. 2,3-Dibromo-2-heptene can exist as both *cis*- and *trans*-isomers.

*trans*-2,3-Dibromo-2-heptene          *cis*-2,3-Dibromo-2-heptene

**11.6 a.**

$\quad$ + H$_2$ $\xrightarrow{\text{Ni}}$ CH$_3$(CH$_2$)$_5$CH$_3$

cis-2-Heptene $\qquad\qquad$ Heptene

**b.**

$\quad$ + H$_2$ $\xrightarrow{\text{Ni}}$ CH$_3$CH$_2$CH$_2$CH$_2$CH$_3$

trans-2-Pentene $\qquad\qquad$ Pentane

**c.** CH$_3$CH$_2$CH=CHCH$_2$CH$_3$ + H$_2$ $\xrightarrow{\text{Pt}}$ CH$_3$CH$_2$CH$_2$CH$_2$CH$_2$CH$_3$

$\quad$ 3-Hexene $\qquad\qquad\qquad$ Hexane

The product, hexane, would be the same regardless of whether this were cis- or trans-3-hexene.

**d.** CH$_2$=CHCH$_3$ + H$_2$ $\xrightarrow{\text{Pd}}$ CH$_3$CH$_2$CH$_3$

$\quad$ Propene $\qquad\qquad$ Propane

**11.7 a.**

$\quad$ + 2Cl$_2$ $\longrightarrow$

CH$_3$CHClCHClCHClCHClCH$_3$

2,4-Hexadiene $\qquad$ 2,3,4,5-Tetrachlorohexane

**b.** Both cis- and trans-1,5-dibromo-2-pentene would produce 1,5-dibromo-2,3-dichloropentane when chlorinated. The trans-isomer is shown here:

$\quad$ + Cl$_2$ $\longrightarrow$

CH$_2$BrCHClCHClCH$_2$CH$_2$Br

trans-1,5-Dibromo-2-pentene  1,5-Dibromo-2,3-dichloropentane

**c.**

$\quad$ + Cl$_2$ $\longrightarrow$ CH$_2$ClC—CHCH$_3$

2,3-Dimethyl-1-butene $\qquad$ 1,2-Dichloro-2,3 dimethylbutane

**d.** Both cis- and trans-4,6-dimethyl-2-heptene would produce 2,3-dichloro-4,6-dimethylheptane when chlorinated. The cis-isomer is shown here:

$\quad$ + Cl$_2$ $\longrightarrow$

CH$_3$CHClCHClCH(CH$_3$)CH$_2$CH(CH$_3$)CH$_3$

cis-4,6-Dimethyl-2-heptene  2,3-Dichloro-4,6-dimethylheptane

**11.8 a.**

$\quad$ + H$_2$O $\xrightarrow{\text{H}^+}$ CH$_3$CHOHCH$_2$CH$_3$

$\qquad\qquad\qquad\qquad\qquad$ 2-Butanol
$\qquad\qquad\qquad\qquad\qquad$ (major product)

1-Butene

$\qquad\qquad$ + $\;$ CH$_2$OHCH$_2$CH$_2$CH$_3$

$\qquad\qquad\qquad$ 1-Butanol
$\qquad\qquad\qquad$ (minor product)

**b.** 2-Methyl-3-hexanol and 5-methyl-3-hexanol would be produced in equal amounts.

CH$_3$CH(CH$_3$)CH=CHCH$_2$CH$_3$ + H$_2$O $\xrightarrow{\text{H}^+}$

$\qquad\qquad\qquad$ CH$_3$CH(CH$_3$)CHOHCH$_2$CH$_2$CH$_3$

$\quad$ 2-Methyl-3-hexene $\qquad\qquad$ 2-Methyl-3-hexanol

CH$_3$CH(CH$_3$)CH=CHCH$_2$CH$_3$ + H$_2$O $\xrightarrow{\text{H}^+}$

$\qquad\qquad\qquad$ CH$_3$CH(CH$_3$)CH$_2$CHOHCH$_2$CH$_3$

$\quad$ 2-Methyl-3-hexene $\qquad\qquad$ 5-Methyl-3-hexanol

**c.** CH$_2$=CHCH$_3$ + H$_2$O $\xrightarrow{\text{H}^+}$ CH$_3$CHOHCH$_3$

$\quad$ Propene $\qquad\qquad$ 2-Propanol
$\qquad\qquad\qquad$ (major product)

$\qquad\qquad$ + $\;$ CH$_2$OHCH$_2$CH$_3$

$\qquad\qquad\qquad$ 1-Propanol
$\qquad\qquad\qquad$ (minor product)

**d.** CH$_2$ClCH=CHCH$_2$Cl + H$_2$O $\xrightarrow{\text{H}^+}$ CH$_2$ClCHOHCH$_2$CH$_2$Cl

$\quad$ 1,4-Dichloro-2-butene $\qquad\qquad$ 1,4-Dichloro-2-butanol
$\qquad\qquad\qquad\qquad\qquad$ (only product)

**11.9 a.** 2-Bromopentane and 3-bromopentane would be produced in equal amounts.

CH$_2$CH=CHCH$_2$CH$_3$ + HBr $\longrightarrow$ CH$_2$CHBrCH$_2$CH$_2$CH$_3$

$\quad$ 2-Pentene $\qquad\qquad\qquad$ 2-Bromopentane

$\qquad\qquad$ + CH$_3$CH$_2$CHBrCH$_2$CH$_3$

$\qquad\qquad\qquad$ 3-Bromopentane

**b.**
CH$_2$=CHCH$_3$ + HBr $\longrightarrow$ CH$_3$CHBrCH$_3$ + CH$_2$BrCH$_2$CH$_3$

$\quad$ Propene $\qquad\qquad$ 2-Bromopropane  3-Bromopropane
$\qquad\qquad\qquad$ (major product)    (minor product)

**c.** 3-Bromoheptane and 4-bromoheptane would be produced in equal amounts.

CH$_3$CH$_2$CH=CHCH$_2$CH$_2$CH$_3$ + HBr $\longrightarrow$

$\quad$ 3-Heptene $\qquad\qquad$ CH$_3$CH$_2$CHBr(CH$_2$)$_3$CH$_3$

$\qquad\qquad\qquad$ 3-Bromoheptane

$\qquad\qquad\qquad$ CH$_3$(CH$_2$)$_2$CHBr(CH$_2$)$_2$CH$_3$

$\qquad\qquad$ + 4-Bromoheptane

**11.10 a.** IUPAC Name: 2-Bromotoluene
Common name: *ortho*-Bromotoluene or *o*-bromotoluene

**b.** IUPAC Name: 4-Methylphenol
Common name: *para*-Cresol or *p*-cresol

**c.** IUPAC Name: 2, 3-Diethylaniline
Common name: 2, 3-Diethylaniline (Numbers must be used since there are three substituents.)

**d.** IUPAC Name: 1,3-Dibromobenzene
Common name: *meta*-Dibromobenzene or *m*-dibromobenzene

## QUESTIONS AND PROBLEMS

## Alkenes and Alkynes: Structure and Physical Properties

### Foundations

**11.23** Explain why the boiling points of alkynes increase as the length of the hydrocarbon chains increases.

**11.24** Saturated fatty acids have higher melting points than monounsaturated fatty acids. Polyunsaturated fatty acids have even lower melting points. Develop a hypothesis to explain this observation.

**11.25** Write the general formulas for alkanes, alkenes, and alkynes.

**11.26** What are the characteristic functional groups of alkenes and alkynes?

### Applications

**11.27** Describe the geometry of ethene.
**11.28** What are the bond angles in ethene?
**11.29** Compare the bond angles in ethene with those in ethane.
**11.30** Explain the bond angles of ethene in terms of the valence-shell electron-pair repulsion (VSEPR) theory.
**11.31** Describe the geometry of ethyne.
**11.32** What are the bond angles in ethyne?
**11.33** Compare the bond angles in ethane, ethene, and ethyne.
**11.34** Explain the bond angles of ethyne in terms of the valence-shell electron-pair repulsion (VSEPR) theory.
**11.35** Arrange the following groups of molecules from the highest to lowest boiling points:
  **a.** ethyne       propyne       2-pentyne
  **b.** 2-butene    3-decene      ethene
**11.36** Arrange the following groups of molecules from the highest to the lowest melting points.

**a.**

**b.**

## Alkenes and Alkynes: Nomenclature

### Foundations

**11.37** Briefly describe the rules for naming alkenes and alkynes.
**11.38** What is meant by a geometric isomer?
**11.39** Describe what is meant by a *cis*-isomer of an alkene.
**11.40** Describe what is meant by a *trans*-isomer of an alkene.

### Applications

**11.41** Draw a condensed formula for each of the following compounds:
  **a.** 2-Methyl-2-hexene
  **b.** *trans*-3-Heptene
  **c.** *cis*-1-Chloro-2-pentene
  **d.** *cis*-2-Chloro-2-methyl-3-heptene
  **e.** *trans*-5-Bromo-2,6-dimethyl-3-octene

**11.42** Draw a condensed formula for each of the following compounds:
  **a.** 2-Hexyne
  **b.** 4-Methyl-1-pentyne
  **c.** 1-Chloro-4,4,5-trimethyl-2-heptyne
  **d.** 2-Bromo-3-chloro-7,8-dimethyl-4-decyne

**11.43** Name each of the following using the IUPAC Nomenclature System:

  **a.** $CH_3CH_2CH(CH_3)CH{=}CH_2$

  **b.** $CH_2CH_2CH_2CH_2Br$
         $|$
         $CH_2CH{=}CH_2$

  **c.** $CH_3CH_2CH{=}CHCHBrCH_2CH_3$

  **d.**

**11.44** Name each of the following using the IUPAC Nomenclature System:

  **a.** $CH_3CH(CH_3)CH_2CH{=}C(CH_3)_2$

  **b.** $CH_2ClCH(CH_3)C{\equiv}CH$

  **c.** $CH_3CHClCH_2CH_2CH_2C{\equiv}CH$

  **d.**

**11.45** Draw each of the following compounds using condensed formulas:
  **a.** 1,3,5-Trifluoropentane
  **b.** *cis*-2-Octene
  **c.** Dipropylacetylene

**11.46** Draw each of the following compounds using condensed formulas:
  **a.** 3,3,5-Trimethyl-1-hexene
  **b.** 1-Bromo-3-chloro-1-heptyne
  **c.** 3-Heptyne

**11.47** Which of the following alkenes can exist as *cis-trans* isomers? Explain your reasoning.
  **a.** 1-Heptene
  **b.** 2-Heptene
  **c.** 3-Heptene
  **d.** 2-Methyl-2-hexene
  **e.** 3-Methyl-2-hexene
**11.48** Draw the line formula for each of the alkenes in Question 11.47.
**11.49** Which of the following alkenes would not exhibit *cis-trans* geometric isomerism?

**a.**

**b.**

**c.** CH₃CH₂

**d.**

**11.50** Which of the following structures have incorrect IUPAC names? If incorrect, give the correct IUPAC name.
  **a.** CH₃C≡CCH₂CH(CH₃)₂

  2-Methyl-4-hexyne

  **b.**

  3-Ethyl-3-hexene

  **c.** CH₃CH(CH₃)CH₂C≡CCH₂CH(CH₃)CH₂CH₃

  2-Ethyl-7-methyl-4-octyne

  **d.**

  *trans*-6-Chloro-3-heptene

  **e.**

  1-Chloro-5-methyl-2-hexene

**11.51** Which of the following can exist as *cis-* and *trans*-isomers?
  **a.** H₂C=CH₂
  **b.** CH₃CH=CHCH₃
  **c.** Cl₂C=CBr₂
  **d.** ClBrC=CClBr
  **e.** (CH₃)₂C=C(CH₃)₂
**11.52** Draw and name all the *cis-* and *trans*-isomers in Question 11.51.
**11.53** Provide the IUPAC name for each of the following molecules:
  **a.** CH₂=CHCH₂CH₂CH=CHCH₂CH₂CH₃
  **b.** CH₂=CHCH₂CH=CHCH₂CH=CHCH₃
  **c.** CH₃CH=CHCH₂CH=CHCH₂CH₃
  **d.** CH₃CH=CHCH(CH₃)CH=CHCH₃
**11.54** Provide the IUPAC name for each of the following molecules:
  **a.** CH₃CBr=CHCH(CH₃)CH=CBrCH₃
  **b.** CH₂=CHCH(CH₃)CH=CHCH(CH₂CH₃)CH₂CH₃
  **c.** CH₂=CHC(CH₃)₂CH=CHCH₂CH=CHCH(CH₃)₂
  **d.** CH₃CH(CH₃)CH(CH₂CH₃)CH=CHCH₂CH=CHCH(CH₃)CH₂CH₃

## Reactions Involving Alkenes and Alkynes

### Foundations

**11.55** Write a general equation representing the hydrogenation of an alkene.
**11.56** Write a general equation representing the hydrogenation of an alkyne.
**11.57** Write a general equation representing the halogenation of an alkene.
**11.58** Write a general equation representing the halogenation of an alkyne.
**11.59** Write a general equation representing the hydration of an alkene.
**11.60** Write a general equation representing the hydration of an alkyne.
**11.61** What is the principal difference between the hydrogenation of an alkene and hydrogenation of an alkyne?
**11.62** What is the major difference between the hydration of an alkene and hydration of an alkyne?

### Applications

**11.63** Write an equation representing each of the following reactions:
  **a.** 1-Heptene + H₂O (H⁺)
  **b.** 2-Heptene + HBr
  **c.** 3-Heptene + H₂
  **d.** 2-Methyl-2-hexene + HCl
**11.64** Write a balanced equation for each of the following reactions:
  **a.** 1,4-Pentadiene + H₂
  **b.** 3-Methyl-1,4-cyclohexadiene + Cl₂
  **c.** 2,4-Heptadiene + Br₂
  **d.** 3-Methylcyclopentene + H₂O (H⁺)

**11.65** Complete each of the following reactions by supplying the missing reactant or product(s) as indicated by question marks:

a. $CH_3CH_2CH=CHCH_2CH_3 + ? \longrightarrow CH_3(CH_2)_4CH_3$

b.
$$CH_3-\overset{\overset{\displaystyle CH_2}{\|}}{C}-CH_3 + ? \longrightarrow CH_3\overset{\overset{\displaystyle CH_3}{|}}{\underset{\underset{\displaystyle CH_3}{|}}{C}}-OH$$

c. ? + $\longrightarrow$

d. $2CH_3CH_2CH_2CH_2CH_2CH_3 + ?O_2 \xrightarrow{\text{Heat}} ? + ?$
(complete combustion)

e. ? + $\longrightarrow$ + HCl

f. ? $\xrightarrow{\text{H}_2\text{O, H}^+}$

**11.66** Draw and name the product in each of the following reactions:
a. Cyclopentene + $H_2O$ ($H^+$)
b. Cyclopentene + HCl
c. Cyclopentene + $H_2$
d. Cyclopentene + HI

**11.67** Write a balanced equation for each of the following reactions:
a. Hydrogenation of 2-butyne
b. Halogenation of 2-pentyne

**11.68** Write a balanced equation for each of the following reactions:
a. Hydration of 1-butyne
b. Hydration of 2-butyne

**11.69** Predict the major product in each of the following reactions. Name the alkene reactant and the product, using IUPAC nomenclature.
a.
$$\overset{CH_3}{\underset{H}{}}C=C\overset{CH_3}{\underset{H}{}} + H_2 \xrightarrow{\text{Pd}} ?$$
b. $CH_3CH_2CH=CH_2 + H_2O \xrightarrow{H^+} ?$
c. $CH_3CH=CHCH_3 + Cl_2 \longrightarrow ?$
d. $CH_3CH_2CH_2CH=CH_2 + HBr \longrightarrow ?$

**11.70** Predict the major product in each of the following reactions. Name the alkene reactant and the product, using IUPAC nomenclature.
a.
$$\overset{CH_3}{\underset{H}{}}C=C\overset{H}{\underset{CH_3}{}} + H_2 \xrightarrow{\text{Ni}} ?$$
b. $(CH_3)_2C=CHCH_2CH_2CH_3 + H_2O \xrightarrow{H^+} ?$
c. $(CH_3)_2C=CHCH_3 + Br_2 \longrightarrow ?$
d. $CH_3C(CH_3)_2CH=CH_2 + HCl \longrightarrow ?$

**11.71** A hydrocarbon with the formula $C_5H_{10}$ decolorized $Br_2$ and consumed 1 mol of hydrogen upon hydrogenation. Draw all the isomers of $C_5H_{10}$ that are possible based on the above information.

**11.72** Triple bonds react in a manner analogous to that of double bonds. The extra pair of electrons in the triple bond, however, generally allows 2 mol of a given reactant to *add* to the triple bond in contrast to 1 mol with the double bond. The "rich get richer" rule holds. Predict the major product in each of the following reactions:
a. Acetylene with 2 mol HCl
b. Propyne with 2 mol HBr
c. 2-Butyne with 2 mol HI

**11.73** Complete each of the following by supplying the missing product indicated by the question mark:

a. 2-Butene $\xrightarrow{\text{HBr}}$ ?

b. 3-Methyl-2-hexene $\xrightarrow{\text{HI}}$ ?

c. $\xrightarrow{\text{HCl}}$ ?

**11.74** Bromine is often used as a laboratory spot test for unsaturation in an aliphatic hydrocarbon. Bromine in $CCl_4$ is red. When bromine reacts with an alkene or alkyne, the alkyl halide formed is colorless; hence, a disappearance of the red color is a positive test for unsaturation. A student tested the contents of two vials, A and B, both containing compounds with a molecular formula, $C_6H_{12}$. Vial A decolorized bromine, but vial B did not. How may the results for vial B be explained? What class of compound would account for this?

**11.75** What is meant by the term *polymer?*

**11.76** What is meant by the term *monomer?*

**11.77** Write an equation representing the synthesis of polyvinyl chloride from vinyl chloride. (*Hint:* Refer to Table 11.2.) What are some of the uses for polyvinyl chloride?

**11.78** Write an equation representing the synthesis of polypropylene from propene. What are some uses for polypropylene?

**11.79** Provide the IUPAC name for each of the following molecules. Write a balanced equation for the hydration of each.
a. $CH_3CH=CHCH_2CH_3$
b. $CH_2BrCH=CH_2$

c.

**11.80** Provide the IUPAC name for each of the following molecules. Write equations for the hydration of each.
a.
b. $CH_3CH=CHCH_2CH=CHCH_2CH=CHCH_3$
c. $CH_3CH=CHC(CH_3)_2CH_2CH_3$

**11.81** Write an equation for the addition reaction that produced each of the following molecules:

a. $CH_2OHCH_2CH_2CH(CH_3)_2$

b. $CH_3CH_2CHBr(CH_2)_2CH_3$

c.

d.

**11.82** Write an equation for the addition reaction that produced each of the following molecules:

a. $CH_3CH_2CHOHCH(CH_3)CH_2CH_3$

b. $CH_3CHOHCH_2CH_3$

c.

**11.83** Draw the structure of each of the following compounds and write a balanced equation for the complete hydrogenation of each:

a. 1,4-Hexadiene          c. 1,3-Cyclohexadiene
b. 2,4,6-Octatriene        d. 1,3,5-Cyclooctatriene

**11.84** Draw the structure of each of the following compounds and write a balanced equation for the bromination of each:
a. 3-Methyl-1,4-hexadiene
b. 4-Bromo-1,3-pentadiene
c. 3-Chloro-2,4-hexadiene
d. 3-Bromo-1,3-cyclohexadiene

## Aromatic Hydrocarbons

### Foundations

**11.85** Where did the term *aromatic hydrocarbon* first originate?
**11.86** What chemical characteristic of the aromatic hydrocarbons is most distinctive?
**11.87** What is meant by the term *resonance hybrid*?
**11.88** Draw a pair of structures to represent the benzene resonance hybrid.

### Applications

**11.89** Draw the structure for each of the following compounds:
a. 2,4-Dibromotoluene
b. 1,2,4-Triethylbenzene
c. Isopropylbenzene
d. 2-Bromo-5-chlorotoluene
**11.90** Name each of the following compounds, using the IUPAC system.

a.

b.

c.

d.

e.

**11.91** Draw each of the following compounds, using condensed formulas:
a. *meta*-Cresol
b. Propylbenzene
c. 1,3,5-Trinitrobenzene
d. *m*-Chlorotoluene
**11.92** Draw each of the following compounds, using condensed formulas:
a. *p*-Xylene
b. Isopropylbenzene
c. *m*-Nitroanisole
d. *p*-Methylbenzaldehyde
**11.93** Describe the Kekulé model for the structure of benzene.
**11.94** Describe the current model for the structure of benzene.
**11.95** How does a substitution reaction differ from an addition reaction?
**11.96** Give an example of a substitution reaction and of an addition reaction.
**11.97** Write equations for the reactions that would produce each of the following products:

a.          b.          c.

**11.98** Draw all of the products that could be formed in a reaction of benzene with each of the following:
a. $2Cl_2$ in the presence of $FeCl_3$
b. $2SO_3$ in the presence of concentrated sulfuric acid
c. $2HNO_3$ in the presence of concentrated sulfuric acid

## Heterocyclic Aromatic Compounds

**11.99** Draw the general structure of a pyrimidine.
**11.100** What biological molecules contain pyrimidine rings?
**11.101** Draw the general structure of a purine.
**11.102** What biological molecules contain purine rings?

## CRITICAL THINKING PROBLEMS

1. There is a plastic polymer called polyvinylidene difluoride (PVDF) that can be used to sense a baby's breath and thus be used to prevent sudden infant death syndrome (SIDS). The secret is that this polymer can be specially processed so that it becomes piezoelectric (produces an electrical current when it is physically deformed) and pyroelectric (develops

an electrical potential when its temperature changes). When a PVDF film is placed beside a sleeping baby, it will set off an alarm if the baby stops breathing. The structure of this polymer is shown here:

$$\left[ \begin{array}{cccc} F & H & F & H \\ | & | & | & | \\ -C & -C & -C & -C- \\ | & | & | & | \\ F & H & F & H \end{array} \right]$$

Go to the library and investigate some of the other amazing uses of PVDF. Draw the structure of the alkene from which this compound is produced.

2. Isoprene is the repeating unit of the natural polymer rubber. It is also the starting material for the synthesis of cholesterol and several of the lipid-soluble vitamins, including vitamin A and vitamin K. The structure of isoprene is seen below.

$$CH_2{=}CCH{=}CH_2$$
$$\overset{\displaystyle CH_3}{\underset{\displaystyle |}{\phantom{CH_2{=}C}}}$$

What is the IUPAC name for isoprene?

3. When polyacrylonitrile is burned, toxic gases are released. In fact, in airplane fires, more passengers die from inhalation of toxic fumes than from burns. Refer to Table 11.2 for the structure of acrylonitrile. What toxic gas would you predict to be the product of the combustion of these polymers?

4. If a molecule of polystyrene consists of 25,000 monomers, what is the molar mass of the molecule?

5. A factory produces one million tons (t) of polypropylene. How many moles (mol) of propene would be required to produce this amount? What is the volume of this amount of propene at 25°C and 1 atmosphere (atm)?

# 12

# Alcohols, Phenols, Thiols, and Ethers

## LEARNING GOALS

1 Classify alcohols as primary, secondary, or tertiary.

2 Rank selected alcohols by relative water solubility, boiling points, or melting points.

3 Write the names and draw the structures for common alcohols.

4 Discuss the biological, medical, or environmental significance of several alcohols.

5 Write equations representing the preparation of alcohols by the hydration of an alkene.

6 Write equations representing the preparation of alcohols by hydrogenation (reduction) of aldehydes or ketones.

7 Write equations showing the dehydration of an alcohol.

8 Write equations representing the oxidation of alcohols.

9 Discuss the role of oxidation and reduction reactions in the chemistry of living systems.

10 Discuss the use of phenols as germicides.

11 Write names and draw structures for common ethers and discuss their use in medicine.

12 Write equations representing the condensation reaction between two alcohol molecules to form an ether.

13 Write names and draw structures for simple thiols and discuss their biological significance.

Sugar-free chocolates are not calorie free!

## OUTLINE

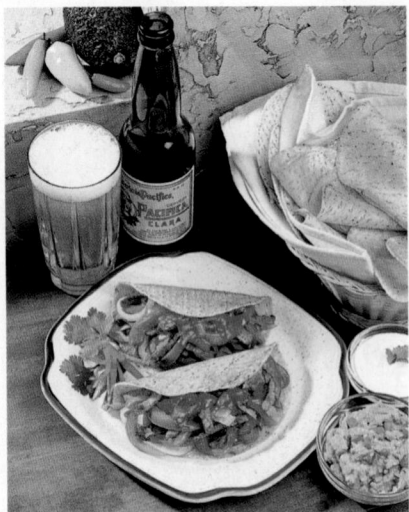

List the types of molecules containing the hydroxyl group that are important elements in the meal shown in this photograph.

# INTRODUCTION

Research tells us that even as babies, we prefer sweet tastes over all others, and the sugar molecules in our diet that satisfy this sweet tooth are all alcohols and are characterized by the presence of a hydroxyl group (—OH). Glucose (blood sugar) and fructose (fruit sugar), sweet individually, can be chemically combined to produce sucrose, or table sugar. The U.S. Department of Agriculture reports that the average American consumes about 152 pounds (lb) of sucrose each year! It is little wonder that physicians, nutritionists, and dentists are concerned about the obesity and tooth decay caused by so much sugar in our diets.

As a result of these concerns, the food chemistry industry has invested billions of dollars in the synthesis of non-nutritive sugar substitutes, such as aspartame (Equal) and Splenda. You can also find a variety of candies, soft drinks, and gums that are labeled "sugar-free." A quick check of the nutritional label reveals that, although they are sugar-free, they are not calorie-free. These sweets contain sugar alcohols, such as sorbitol or mannitol, instead of sucrose. Sorbitol and mannitol molecules look very much like glucose and fructose, except that they are missing the carbonyl (C=O) group.

Carbonyl Group     Hydroxyl Group

D-Glucose          D-Fructose          D-Sorbitol          D-Mannitol

Compared to sucrose, they range in sweetness from about half to nearly the same. They also have fewer calories than table sugar (about one-third to one-half the calories). Sugar alcohols actually absorb heat from the surroundings when they dissolve. As a result, they cause a cooling sensation in the mouth. You may have noticed this when eating certain breath-freshening mints and gums.

In biological systems, the hydroxyl group (—OH) is important to the structures of sugars, fats, and proteins. It allows these biological molecules to undergo a variety of reactions such as oxidation, reduction, hydration, and dehydration, that are essential for life.

In this chapter we will study alcohols and phenols, both of which are characterized by the presence of the hydroxyl group. The difference is that alcohols contain an alkyl group bonded to the hydroxyl group, while phenols have the hydroxyl group bonded to a benzene molecule (aryl group).

An aryl group is an aromatic ring with one hydrogen removed.

General formulas:          Example:

Alcohol     Phenol          Methanol
(methyl alcohol)

We will also be studying ethers, which have two alkyl or aryl groups bonded to oxygen, and thiols, which are similar to alcohols except that the oxygen atom has been replaced by a sulfur atom.

R and R' = alkyl or aryl groups

Ether     Methoxymethane     Thiol     Methanethiol
(dimethyl ether)

# 12.1   Alcohols: Structure and Physical Properties

An **alcohol** is an organic compound that contains a **hydroxyl group** (—OH) attached to an alkyl group (Figure 12.1). The R—O—H portion of an alcohol is similar to the structure of water. The oxygen and the two atoms bonded to it lie in the same plane, and the R—O—H bond angle is approximately 104°, which is very similar to the H—O—H bond angle of water.

Alcohols are classified as **primary (1°)**, **secondary (2°)**, or **tertiary (3°)**, depending on the number of alkyl groups attached to the **carbinol carbon,** the carbon bearing the hydroxyl (—OH) group. If no alkyl groups are attached, the alcohol is methyl alcohol; if there is a single alkyl group, the alcohol is a primary alcohol; an alcohol with two alkyl groups bonded to the carbon bearing the hydroxyl group is a secondary alcohol, and if three alkyl groups are attached, the alcohol is a tertiary alcohol.

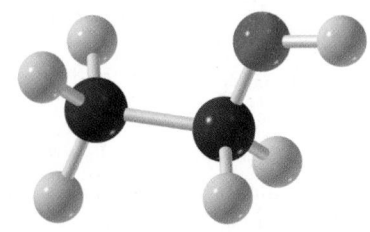

**Figure 12.1** Ball-and-stick model of the simple alcohol ethanol.

Methyl alcohol   1° Alcohol   2° Alcohol   3° Alcohol

Methanol        Ethanol        2-Propanol       2-Methyl-2-propanol
(methyl alcohol)  (1° alcohol)   (2° alcohol)      (3° alcohol)

---

**EXAMPLE 12.1    Classifying Alcohols**

Classify each of the following alcohols as primary, secondary, or tertiary.

**Solution**

a.  Two alcohols contribute to the distinctive flavor of mushrooms. These are 1-octanol and 3-octanol. In each of the structures shown below, the carbinol carbon is shown in red:

$$CH_3(CH_2)_6CH_2OH$$

$$CH_3CH_2CH(CH_2)_4CH_3$$
$$\overset{|}{OH}$$

This alcohol, 1-octanol, is a primary alcohol because there is one alkyl group attached to the carbinol carbon.

This alcohol, 3-octanol, is a secondary alcohol because there are two alkyl groups attached to the carbinol carbon.

*Continued…*

b.

$$CH_3CCH_3$$

with $CH_3$ above and $OH$ below the central carbon

This alcohol, 2-methyl-2-propanol, is a tertiary alcohol because there are three alkyl groups attached to the carbinol carbon.

---

**Practice Problem 12.1**

Classify each of the following alcohols as 1°, 2°, 3°, or aromatic (phenol).

a. $CH_3CH_2CH_2CH_2OH$

b. $CH_3CH_2CHCH_2CH_3$ with $OH$ below

c. cyclopentane ring with $CH_3$ and $OH$

d. benzene ring with $-OH$

e. cyclopentane ring with $HO$

---

▶ For Further Practice: **Questions 12.17 and 12.19.**

---

*Electronegativity is discussed in Section 3.1. Hydrogen bonding is described in detail in Section 5.2.*

**LEARNING GOAL**

**2** Rank selected alcohols by relative water solubility, boiling points, or melting points.

The hydroxyl groups of alcohols are very polar because the oxygen and hydrogen atoms have significantly different electronegativities. Because the two atoms involved in this polar bond are oxygen and hydrogen, hydrogen bonds can form between alcohol molecules (Figure 12.2).

As a result of this intermolecular hydrogen bonding, alcohols boil at much higher temperatures than hydrocarbons of similar molar mass. These higher boiling points are caused by the large amount of heat needed to break the hydrogen bonds that attract the alcohol molecules to one another. Compare the boiling points of butane and propanol, which have similar molar masses:

| | |
|---|---|
| $CH_3CH_2CH_2CH_3$ | $CH_3CH_2CH_2OH$ |
| Butane | 1-Propanol |
| M.M. = 58 | M.M. = 60 |
| b.p. = $-0.5\,°C$ | b.p. = 97.2°C |

Alcohols of one to four carbon atoms are very soluble in water, and those with five or six carbons are moderately soluble in water. This is due to the ability of the alcohol to form intermolecular hydrogen bonds with water molecules (see Figure 12.2b). As the nonpolar, or hydrophobic, portion of an alcohol (the carbon chain) becomes larger relative to the polar, hydrophilic, region (the hydroxyl group), the water solubility of the alcohol decreases. As a result, alcohols of seven carbon atoms or more are nearly insoluble in water. The term *hydrophobic*, which literally means "water fearing," is used to describe a molecule or a region of a molecule that is nonpolar and, thus, more soluble in nonpolar solvents than in water. Similarly, the term *hydrophilic*, meaning "water loving," is used to describe a polar molecule or region of a molecule that is more soluble in the polar solvent water than in a nonpolar solvent.

An increase in the number of hydroxyl groups along a carbon chain will increase the influence of the polar hydroxyl group. It follows, then, that diols and triols are more water-soluble than alcohols with only a single hydroxyl group.

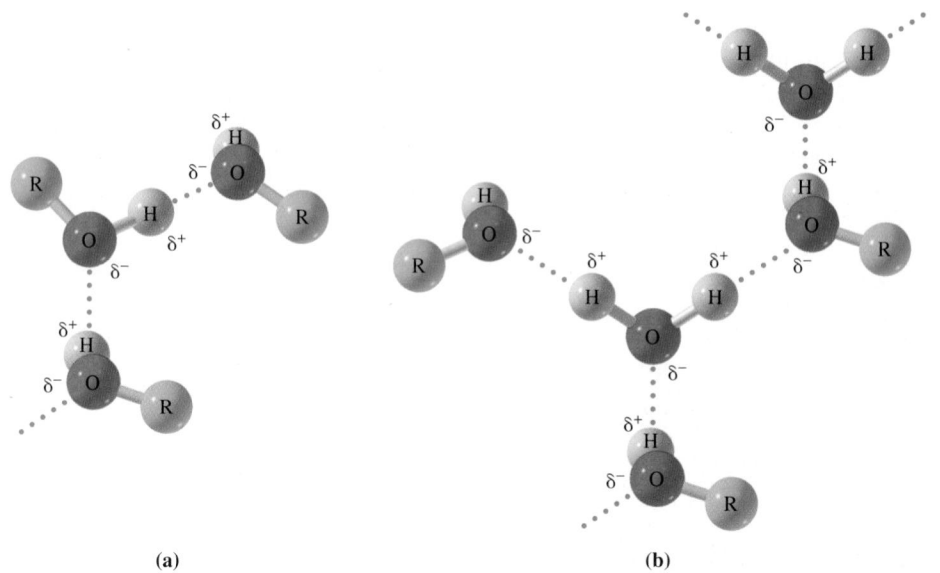

**Figure 12.2** (a) Hydrogen bonding between alcohol molecules. (b) Hydrogen bonding between alcohol molecules and water molecules.

(a)                                    (b)

The presence of polar hydroxyl groups in large biological molecules—for instance, proteins and nucleic acids—allows *intramolecular* hydrogen bonding that keeps these molecules in the shapes needed for biological function.

*Intermolecular* hydrogen bonds are attractive forces between two separate molecules. *Intramolecular* hydrogen bonds are attractive forces between polar groups within the same molecule.

# 12.2   Alcohols: Nomenclature

## IUPAC Names

In the IUPAC Nomenclature System, alcohols are named according to the following steps:

- Determine the name of the *parent compound*, the longest continuous carbon chain or the ring containing the —OH group.
- Replace the *-e* ending of the alkane chain with the *-ol* ending of the alcohol. Following this pattern, an alkane becomes an alkanol. For instance, ethan*e* becomes ethan*ol*, and propan*e* becomes propan*ol*.
- Number the parent chain to give the carbon bearing the hydroxyl group the lowest possible number.
- Name and number all substituents, and add them as prefixes to the "alkanol" name.
- Alcohols containing two hydroxyl groups are named *-diols*. Those bearing three hydroxyl groups are called *-triols*. A number giving the position of each of the hydroxyl groups is needed in these cases and the final *-e* of the parent compound is retained.

**LEARNING GOAL**

**3**   Write the names and draw the structures for common alcohols.

*The way to determine the parent compound was described in Section 10.2.*

| EXAMPLE 12.2 | **Using IUPAC Nomenclature to Name Alcohols** |

**LEARNING GOAL**

**3**   Write the names and draw the structures for common alcohols.

a. The molecule shown here is an alarm-defense pheromone in certain populations of leaf-cutter ants. Provide the IUPAC name for this molecule.

$$\underset{1\quad2\quad3\quad4\quad5\quad6\quad7}{\overset{\overset{\text{CH}_3}{|}}{\text{CH}_3\text{CH}_2\text{CHCHCH}_2\text{CH}_2\text{CH}_3}}$$
OH

*Continued…*

**Solution**

Parent compound: heptane (becomes heptanol)
Position of —OH: carbon-3 (*Not* carbon 5 because the parent chain must be numbered to give the lowest possible number for the carbinol carbon.)
Substituents: 4-methyl
Name: 4-Methyl-3-heptanol

b.  Name the following cyclic alcohol using IUPAC nomenclature.

**Solution**

Parent compound: cyclohexane (becomes cyclohexanol)
Position of —OH: carbon-1 (*Not* carbon-3 because the carbinol carbon is defined as carbon-1.)
Substituents: 3-bromo (*Not* 5-bromo because the lowest possible numbering should be used.)
Name: 3-Bromocyclohexanol (it is assumed that the —OH is on carbon-1 in cyclic structures)

---

**Practice Problem 12.2**

Use the IUPAC Nomenclature System to name each of the following compounds.

a.  $CH_3CHCH_2CH_2CH_2OH$
    |
    $CH_3$

b.  $CH_3CHCH_2CHCH_3$
    |        |
    $OH$    $CH_2CH_3$

c.  $CH_2CHCH_2$
    |   |   |
    $OH$  $OH$  $OH$
    (Common name: Glycerol)

d.  $CH_3CH_2CHCHCH_2CH_2OH$
    |    |
    $Cl$  $CH_3$

▶ For Further Practice: **Questions 12.29 and 12.30.**

---

*See Section 10.2 for the names of the common alkyl groups.*

## Common Names

The common names for alcohols are derived from the alkyl group corresponding to the parent compound. The name of the alkyl group is followed by the word *alcohol*. For some alcohols, such as ethylene glycol and glycerol, historical names are used. The following examples provide the IUPAC and common names of several alcohols:

$CH_3CHCH_3$
|
$OH$

2-Propanol
(isopropyl
alcohol)

$HOCH_2CH_2OH$

1,2-Ethanediol
(ethylene glycol)

$CH_3CH_2OH$

Ethanol
(ethyl alcohol)
(grain alcohol)

**Question 12.1**   Draw structures for each of the following alcohols.
a. 2-Methyl-1-propanol
b. 2-Chlorocyclopentanol
c. 2,4-Dimethylcyclohexanol
d. 2,3-Dichloro-3-hexanol

**Question 12.2**   Give the common name and the IUPAC name for each of the following compounds.

a. $CH_3CH_2CH_2CH_2CH_2CH_2CH_2OH$

b. $CH_3\underset{\underset{OH}{|}}{C}HCH_3$

c.

d.

## 12.3  Medically Important Alcohols

### Methanol

Methanol (methyl alcohol), $CH_3OH$, is a colorless and odorless liquid that is used as a solvent and as the starting material for the synthesis of methanal (formaldehyde). Methanol is often called *wood alcohol* because it can be made by heating wood in the absence of air. In fact, ancient Egyptians produced methanol by this process and, mixed with other substances, used it for embalming. It was not until 1661 that Robert Boyle first isolated pure methanol, which he called *spirit of box,* because he purified it by distillation from boxwood. Methanol is toxic and can cause blindness and perhaps death if ingested. Methanol may also be used as fuel, especially for "formula" racing cars.

### Ethanol

Ethanol (ethyl alcohol), $CH_3CH_2OH$, is a colorless and odorless liquid and is the alcohol in alcoholic beverages. It is also widely used as a solvent and as a raw material for the preparation of other organic chemicals.

The ethanol used in alcoholic beverages comes from the **fermentation** of carbohydrates (sugars and starches). The beverage produced depends on the starting material and the fermentation process: scotch (grain), bourbon (corn), burgundy wine (grapes and grape skins), and chablis wine (grapes without red skins) (Figure 12.3). The following equation summarizes the fermentation process:

$$C_6H_{12}O_6 \xrightarrow[\text{enzyme action}]{\substack{\text{Several steps}\\\text{involving}}} 2CH_3CH_2OH + 2CO_2$$

Sugar
(glucose)

Ethanol
(ethyl alcohol)

The alcoholic beverages listed have quite different alcohol concentrations. Wines are generally 12–13% alcohol because the yeasts that produce the ethanol are killed by ethanol concentrations of 12–13%. To produce bourbon or scotch with an alcohol concentration of 40–45% ethanol (80 or 90 proof), the original fermentation products must be distilled.

The sale and use of pure ethanol (100% ethanol) are regulated by the federal government. To prevent illegal use of pure ethanol, it is *denatured* by the addition of a denaturing agent, which makes it unfit to drink but suitable for many laboratory applications.

**LEARNING GOAL**

**4** Discuss the biological, medical, or environmental significance of several alcohols.

**Figure 12.3** Champagne, a sparkling wine, results when fermentation is carried out in a sealed bottle. Under these conditions, the $CO_2$ produced during fermentation is trapped in the wine.

*Fermentation reactions are described in detail in Section 21.4 and in A Human Perspective: Fermentations: The Good, the Bad, and the Ugly.*

Distillation is the separation of compounds in a mixture based on differences in boiling points.

## A MEDICAL PERSPECTIVE

### Fetal Alcohol Syndrome

The first months of pregnancy are a time of great joy and anticipation but are not without moments of anxiety. On her first visit to the obstetrician, the mother-to-be is tested for previous exposure to a number of infectious diseases that could damage the fetus. She is provided with information about diet, weight gain, and drugs that could harm the baby. Among the drugs that should be avoided are alcoholic beverages.

The use of alcoholic beverages by a pregnant woman can cause *fetal alcohol syndrome (FAS)*. A *syndrome* is a set of symptoms that occur together and are characteristic of a particular disease. In this case, physicians have observed that infants born to women with chronic alcoholism showed a reproducible set of abnormalities including mental retardation, poor growth before and after birth, and facial malformations.

Mothers who report only social drinking may have children with *fetal alcohol effects*, a less severe form of fetal alcohol syndrome. This milder form is characterized by a reduced birth weight, some learning disabilities, and behavioral problems.

How does alcohol consumption cause these varied symptoms? No one is exactly sure, but it is well known that the alcohol consumed by the mother crosses the placenta and enters the bloodstream of the fetus. Within about 15 minutes (min), the concentration of alcohol in the blood of the fetus is as high as that of the mother! However, the mother has enzymes to detoxify the alcohol in her blood; the fetus does not. Now consider that alcohol can cause cell division to stop or be radically altered. It is thought that even a single night on the town could be enough to cause FAS by blocking cell division during a critical developmental period.

This raises the question "How much alcohol can a pregnant woman safely drink?" As we have seen, the severity of the symptoms seems to increase with the amount of alcohol consumed by the mother. However, it is virtually impossible to do the scientific studies that would conclusively determine the risk to the fetus caused by different amounts of alcohol. There is some evidence that suggests that there is a risk associated with

The American Medical Association recommends abstaining from alcohol during pregnancy.

drinking even 1 ounce (oz) of absolute (100%) alcohol each day. Because of these facts and uncertainties, the American Medical Association and the U.S. Surgeon General recommend that pregnant women completely abstain from alcohol.

#### For Further Understanding

▶ In October 2005, the U.S. Centers for Disease Control issued a document entitled *Guidelines for Identifying and Referring Persons with Fetal Alcohol Syndrome*, which can be found at the following Web address: http://www.cdc.gov/ncbddd/fasd/index.html. Refer to this document when answering the following questions.

▶ What is the estimate of the number of babies born each year with fetal alcohol syndrome and why is a more accurate number so difficult to determine?

▶ What are some of the issues, practical and ethical, involved in intervention efforts to prevent fetal alcohol syndrome?

### 2-Propanol

2-Propanol (isopropyl alcohol),

$$\begin{array}{c} CH_3CHCH_3 \\ | \\ OH \end{array}$$

was commonly called *rubbing alcohol* because patients with high fevers were often given alcohol baths to reduce body temperature. Rapid evaporation of the alcohol results in skin cooling. This practice is no longer commonly used.

It is also used as an antiseptic (Figure 12.4), an astringent (skin-drying agent), an industrial solvent, and a raw material in the synthesis of organic chemicals. It is colorless, has a very slight odor, and is toxic when ingested.

### 1,2-Ethanediol

1,2-Ethanediol (ethylene glycol),

$$CH_2{-}CH_2$$
$$\ \ |\quad\ \ |$$
$$OH\ \ \ OH$$

is used as automobile antifreeze. When added to water in the radiator, the ethylene glycol solute lowers the freezing point and raises the boiling point of the water. Ethylene glycol has a sweet taste but is extremely poisonous. For this reason, color additives are used in antifreeze to ensure that it is properly identified.

## 1,2,3-Propanetriol

1,2,3-Propanetriol (glycerol),

$$CH_2{-}CH{-}CH_2$$
$$\ |\qquad |\qquad |$$
$$OH\ \ \ OH\ \ \ OH$$

is a viscous, sweet-tasting, nontoxic liquid. It is very soluble in water and is used in cosmetics, pharmaceuticals, and lubricants. Glycerol is obtained as a by-product of the hydrolysis of fats.

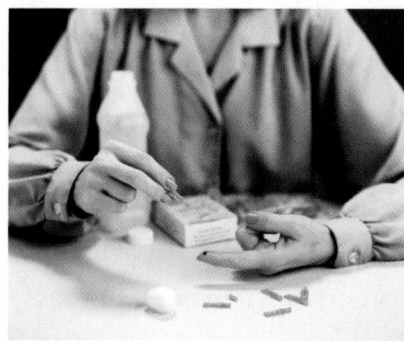

**Figure 12.4** Isopropyl alcohol, or rubbing alcohol, is used as an antiseptic before and after an injection or blood test.

## 12.4   Reactions Involving Alcohols

### Preparation of Alcohols

As we saw in the last chapter, the most important reactions of alkenes are *addition reactions*. Addition of a water molecule to the carbon-carbon double bond of an alkene produces an alcohol. This reaction, called **hydration**, requires a trace of acid ($H^+$) as a catalyst, as shown in the following equation:

**LEARNING GOAL**

**5** Write equations representing the preparation of alcohols by the hydration of an alkene.

*Hydration of alkenes is described in Section 11.5.*

[equation: Alkene + Water → Alcohol]

Alcohols may also be prepared via the hydrogenation (reduction) of aldehydes and ketones. In organic and biochemical reactions, reduction is recognized as the loss of oxygen or the gain of hydrogen. In the reduction of aldehydes and ketones, it is the gain of hydrogen atoms that allows us to recognize that reduction has occurred. The general equations for these reactions can be summarized as follows:

Hydrogenation of aldehydes and ketones will also be discussed in section 13.4.

[equation: Aldehyde + Hydrogen → Primary Alcohol] [equation: Ketone + Hydrogen → Secondary Alcohol]

**EXAMPLE 12.3**   **Writing an Equation Representing the Preparation of an Alcohol by the Hydrogenation (Reduction) of an Aldehyde**

Write an equation representing the preparation of 1-propanol from propanal.

**LEARNING GOAL**

**6** Write equations representing the preparation of alcohols by hydrogenation (reduction) of aldehydes or ketones.

*Continued…*

## Solution

Begin by writing the structure of propanal. Propanal is a three-carbon aldehyde. Aldehydes are characterized by the presence of a carbonyl group (—C=O) attached to the end of the carbon chain of the molecule. After you have drawn the structure of propanal, add diatomic hydrogen to the equation.

Propanal          Hydrogen

Notice that the general equation reveals this reaction to be an example of a hydrogenation reaction. As the hydrogens are added to the carbon-oxygen double bond, it is converted to a carbon-oxygen single bond, and the carbonyl oxygen becomes a hydroxyl group.

Propanal          Hydrogen          1-Propanol

### Practice Problem 12.3

Write an equation representing the reduction of butanal. Provide the structures and names for the reactants and products. *Hint:* Butanal is a four-carbon aldehyde with the structure $CH_3CH_2CH_2C$

▶ For Further Practice: **Questions 12.65a and c and 12.66a and c.**

---

**EXAMPLE 12.4**  **Writing an Equation Representing the Preparation of an Alcohol by the Hydrogenation (Reduction) of a Ketone**

Write an equation representing the preparation of 2-propanol from propanone.

**LEARNING GOAL**

**6** Write equations representing the preparation of alcohols by hydrogenation (reduction) of aldehydes or ketones.

## Solution

Begin by writing the structure of propanone. Propanone is a three-carbon ketone. Ketones are characterized by the presence of a carbonyl group (—C=O) located anywhere within the carbon chain of the molecule. In the structure of propanone, the carbonyl group must be associated with the center carbon. After you have drawn the structure of propanone, add diatomic hydrogen to the equation.

Propanone          Hydrogen

Notice that this reaction is an example of a hydrogenation reaction. As the hydrogens are added to the carbon-oxygen double bond, it is converted to a carbon-oxygen single bond, and the carbonyl oxygen becomes a hydroxyl group.

Propanone          Hydrogen          2-Propanol

## Practice Problem 12.4

Write an equation representing the reduction of butanone. *Hint:* Butanone is a four-carbon ketone with the structure

$$CH_3\overset{\displaystyle O}{\overset{\|}{C}}CH_2CH_3.$$

► For Further Practice: **Questions 12.65b and d and 12.66b and d.**

## Dehydration of Alcohols

Alcohols undergo **dehydration** (lose water) when heated with concentrated sulfuric acid ($H_2SO_4$) or phosphoric acid ($H_3PO_4$). Dehydration is an example of an **elimination reaction,** that is, a reaction in which a molecule loses atoms or ions from its structure. In this case, the —OH and —H are "eliminated" from adjacent carbons in the alcohol to produce an alkene and water. We have just seen that alkenes can be hydrated to give alcohols. Dehydration is simply the reverse process: the conversion of an alcohol back to an alkene. This is seen in the following general reaction and the examples that follow:

**LEARNING GOAL**

**7**  Write equations showing the dehydration of an alcohol.

$$R-\underset{\underset{H}{|}}{\overset{\overset{H}{|}}{C}}-\underset{\underset{OH}{|}}{\overset{\overset{H}{|}}{C}}-H \xrightarrow{H^+, \text{ heat}} R-CH=CH_2 + H-OH$$

Alcohol                          Alkene        Water

$$H-\underset{\underset{H}{|}}{\overset{\overset{H}{|}}{C}}-\underset{\underset{OH}{|}}{\overset{\overset{H}{|}}{C}}-H \xrightarrow{H^+, \text{ heat}} CH_2{=}CH_2 + H-OH$$

Ethanol                          Ethene
(ethyl alcohol)                  (ethylene)

$$CH_3CH_2CH_2OH \xrightarrow{H^+, \text{ heat}} CH_3CH=CH_2 + H_2O$$

1-Propanol                       Propene
(propyl alcohol)                 (propylene)

In some cases, dehydration of alcohols produces a mixture of products, as seen in the following example:

$$CH_3-\underset{\underset{H}{|}}{\overset{\overset{H}{|}}{C}}-\underset{\underset{OH}{|}}{\overset{\overset{H}{|}}{C}}-CH_3 \xrightarrow[\text{heat}]{H^+} CH_3CH=CHCH_3 + H-OH$$

2-Butanol                        2-Butene
                                 (major product)

$$CH_3-\underset{\underset{H}{|}}{\overset{\overset{H}{|}}{C}}-\underset{\underset{OH}{|}}{\overset{\overset{H}{|}}{C}}-CH_3 \xrightarrow[\text{heat}]{H^+} CH_3CH_2CH=CH_2 + H-OH$$

2-Butanol                        1-Butene
                                 (minor product)

Notice in these equations and in Example 12.5, the major product is the more highly substituted alkene. In 1875 the Russian chemist Alexander Zaitsev developed a rule to describe such reactions. **Zaitsev's rule** states that in an elimination reaction, the alkene with the greatest number of alkyl groups on the double bonded carbons (the more highly substituted alkene) is the major product of the reaction.

---

| EXAMPLE 12.5 | **Predicting the Products of Alcohol Dehydration** |
|---|---|

LEARNING GOAL

Predict the products of the dehydration of 3-methyl-2-butanol.

**7** Write equations showing the dehydration of an alcohol.

### Solution

The product(s) of dehydration of an alcohol will contain a double bond in which one of the carbons was the original carbinol carbon—the carbon to which the hydroxyl group is attached. Consider the following reaction:

$$
\begin{array}{c}
CH_3 \\
| \\
CH_3-C{=}CH-CH_3 + H_2O
\end{array}
$$

2-Methyl-2-butene
*(major product)*

$$
\begin{array}{c}
CH_3 \\
| \\
2CH_3-CH-CH-CH_3 \\
| \\
OH
\end{array}
\xrightarrow{\;H^+,\ heat\;}
$$

3-Methyl-2-butanol

$$
\begin{array}{c}
CH_3 \\
| \\
CH_3-CH-CH{=}CH_2 + H_2O
\end{array}
$$

3-Methyl-1-butene
*(minor product)*

It is clear that both the major and minor products have a double bond to carbon number 2, the carbinol carbon in the original alcohol (shown in red). Zaitsev's rule tells us that in dehydration reactions with more than one product possible, the more highly branched alkene predominates. In the reaction shown, 2-methyl-2-butene has three alkyl groups at the double bond, whereas 3-methyl-1-butene has only one alkyl group at the double bond. The more highly branched alkene is more stable and thus is the major product.

### Practice Problem 12.5

Write an equation showing the dehydration of each of the following alcohols. If there are two possible alkene products, indicate which is the major product and which is the minor product.

a. $CH_3CH_2OH$

$$
\begin{array}{c}
CH_3 \\
| \\
c.\ CH_3CH_2CHCHCH_2CH_3 \\
| \\
OH
\end{array}
$$

$$
\begin{array}{c}
OH \\
| \\
b.\ CH_3CHCH_3
\end{array}
$$

$$
\begin{array}{c}
OH \\
| \\
d.\ CH_3CCH_3 \\
| \\
CH_3
\end{array}
$$

▶ For Further Practice: **Questions 12.52 and 12.54.**

---

## Oxidation Reactions

LEARNING GOAL

**8** Write equations representing the oxidation of alcohols.

Alcohols may be oxidized with a variety of oxidizing agents to aldehydes, ketones, and carboxylic acids. The most commonly used oxidizing agents are solutions of basic potassium permanganate ($KMnO_4/OH^-$) and chromic acid ($H_2CrO_4$). The — symbol [O] over the reaction arrow is used throughout this book to designate any general oxidizing agent.

Oxidation of methanol produces the aldehyde methanal:

| Methanol (methyl alcohol) An alcohol | Methanal (formaldehyde) An aldehyde |

Note that the symbol [O] is used throughout this book to designate any oxidizing agent.

In organic and biochemical systems, oxidation is recognized by the loss of hydrogen or the gain of oxygen. In the oxidation of alcohols, two hydrogens are removed from the alcohol. One is removed from the hydroxyl group and a second is removed to form the carbinol carbon.

*As we will see in Section 13.4, aldehydes can undergo further oxidation to produce carboxylic acids.*

Oxidation of a primary alcohol produces an aldehyde, as seen in the following general equation and Example 12.6:

1° Alcohol                An aldehyde

## EXAMPLE 12.6  Writing an Equation Representing the Oxidation of a Primary Alcohol

LEARNING GOAL

Write an equation showing the oxidation of 2,2-dimethylpropanol to produce 2,2-dimethylpropanal.

**8** Write equations representing the oxidation of alcohols.

### Solution

Begin by writing the structure of the reactant, 2,2-dimethylpropanol and indicate the need for an oxidizing agent by placing the designation [O] over the reaction arrow:

2,2-Dimethylpropanol

Now show the oxidation of the hydroxyl group to the aldehyde carbonyl group.

| 2,2-Dimethylpropanol | 2,2-Dimethylpropanal |

### Practice Problem 12.6

Write an equation showing the oxidation of the following primary alcohols:

a. $CH_3C(CH_3)_2CH_2CH_2OH$          b. $CH_3CH_2OH$

▶ For Further Practice: **Questions 12.48 and 12.56.**

Oxidation of a secondary alcohol produces a ketone:

$$R^1-\underset{\underset{H}{|}}{\overset{\overset{OH}{|}}{C}}-R^2 \xrightarrow{[O]} \underset{R^1\quad R^2}{\overset{\overset{O}{\parallel}}{C}} + H_2O$$

2° Alcohol                              A ketone

---

**EXAMPLE 12.7**   **Writing an Equation Representing the Oxidation of a Secondary Alcohol**

LEARNING GOAL

Write an equation showing the oxidation of 2-propanol to produce propanone.

**8** Write equations representing the oxidation of alcohols.

**Solution**

Begin by writing the structure of the reactant, 2-propanol, and indicate the need for an oxidizing agent by placing the designation [O] over the reaction arrow:

$$CH_3-\underset{\underset{H}{|}}{\overset{\overset{OH}{|}}{C}}-CH_3 \xrightarrow{[O]}$$

2-Propanol

Now show the oxidation of the hydroxyl group to the ketone carbonyl group.

Carbonyl Group

$$CH_3-\underset{\underset{H}{|}}{\overset{\overset{OH}{|}}{C}}-CH_3 \xrightarrow{[O]} CH_3-\overset{\overset{O}{\parallel}}{C}-CH_3 + H_2O$$

2-Propanol                              Propanone

**Practice Problem 12.7**

Write an equation showing the oxidation of the following secondary alcohols:

a.   $\overset{\overset{OH}{|}}{CH_3CHCH_2CH_3}$

b.   $\overset{\overset{OH}{|}}{CH_3CHCH_2CH_2CH_3}$

▶ For Further Practice: **Questions 12.49 and 12.55a, b, and c.**

---

Tertiary alcohols cannot be oxidized:

$$R^1-\underset{\underset{R^3}{|}}{\overset{\overset{OH}{|}}{C}}-R^2 \xrightarrow{[O]} \text{No reaction}$$

3° Alcohol

For the oxidation reaction to occur, the carbinol carbon must contain at least one C—H bond. Because tertiary alcohols contain three C—C bonds to the carbinol carbon, they cannot undergo oxidation.

**Question 12.3** Classify the alcohol product in Practice Problem 12.3 at the end of example 12.3 as primary (1°), secondary (2°), or tertiary (3°) and provide the IUPAC and common names.

**Question 12.4** Classify the alcohol product in Practice Problem 12.4, at the end of Example 12.4, as a primary (1°), secondary (2°), or tertiary (3°) alcohol, and provide the IUPAC name.

**Question 12.5** Name the alcohol reactants and alkene products in each of the reactions in Practice Problem 12.5, at the end of Example 12.5, using the IUPAC Nomenclature System, and classify each of these alcohols as primary (1°), secondary (2°), or tertiary (3°).

**Question 12.6** Name each of the reactant alcohols and product aldehydes in Practice Problem 12.6, at the end of Example 12.6, using the IUPAC Nomenclature System. *Hint:* Refer to Example 12.6, as well as to Section 13.2, to name the aldehyde products.

**Question 12.7** Name each of the reactant alcohols and product ketones in Practice Problem 12.7, at the end of Example 12.7, using the IUPAC Nomenclature System. *Hint:* Refer to Example 12.7, as well as to Section 13.2, to name the ketone products.

**Question 12.8** Explain why a tertiary alcohol cannot undergo oxidation.

When ethanol is metabolized in the liver, it is oxidized to ethanal (acetaldehyde). If too much ethanol is present in the body, an overabundance of ethanal is formed, which causes many of the adverse effects of the "morning-after hangover." Continued oxidation of ethanal produces ethanoic acid (acetic acid), which is used as an energy source by the cell and eventually oxidized to $CO_2$ and $H_2O$. These reactions, summarized as follows, are catalyzed by liver enzymes.

$$CH_3CH_2-OH \longrightarrow \underset{\text{Ethanal}}{CH_3\overset{\overset{\displaystyle O}{\|}}{C}-H} \longrightarrow \underset{\text{Ethanoic acid}}{CH_3\overset{\overset{\displaystyle O}{\|}}{C}-OH} \longrightarrow CO_2 + H_2O$$

Ethanol               Ethanal               Ethanoic acid
(ethyl alcohol)     (acetaldehyde)      (acetic acid)

## 12.5 Oxidation and Reduction in Living Systems

Before beginning a discussion of oxidation and reduction in living systems, we must understand how to recognize **oxidation** (loss of electrons) and **reduction** (gain of electrons) in organic compounds. It is easy to determine when an oxidation or a reduction occurs in inorganic compounds because the process is accompanied by a change in charge. For example,

$$Ag^0 \longrightarrow Ag^+ + 1e^-$$

With the loss of an electron, the neutral atom is converted to a positive ion, which is oxidation. In contrast,

$$:\overset{..}{\underset{..}{Br}}\cdot + e^- \longrightarrow :\overset{..}{\underset{..}{Br}}:^-$$

With the gain of one electron, the bromine atom is converted to a negative ion, which is reduction.

When organic compounds are involved, however, there may be no change in charge, and it is often difficult to determine whether oxidation or reduction has occurred. The following simplified view may help.

**LEARNING GOAL**

**9** Discuss the role of oxidation and reduction reactions in the chemistry of living systems.

In organic systems, *oxidation* may be recognized as a gain of oxygen or a loss of hydrogen. A *reduction* reaction may involve a loss of oxygen or gain of hydrogen.

Consider the following compounds. A primary or secondary alcohol may be oxidized to an aldehyde or ketone, respectively, by the loss of hydrogen. An aldehyde may be oxidized to a carboxylic acid by gaining an oxygen.

More oxidized form →

| Alcohol | Aldehyde | Carboxylic acid |

← More reduced form

Thus, the conversion of an alcohol to a carbonyl compound, and a carbonyl compound (aldehyde) to a carboxylic acid are both examples of oxidations. Conversions in the opposite direction are reductions.

Oxidation and reduction reactions also play an important role in the chemistry of living systems. In living systems these reactions are catalyzed by the action of various enzymes called *oxidoreductases*. These enzymes require compounds called *coenzymes* to accept or donate hydrogen in the reactions that they catalyze.

Nicotinamide adenine dinucleotide, $NAD^+$, is a coenzyme commonly involved in biological oxidation-reduction reactions (Figure 12.5). We see $NAD^+$ in action in the final reaction of the citric acid cycle, an energy-harvesting pathway essential to life. In this reaction, catalyzed by the enzyme malate dehydrogenase, malate is oxidized to produce oxaloacetate:

Malate dehydrogenase

Malate                          Oxaloacetate

$NAD^+$ actually accepts a hydride anion, $H^-$, hydrogen with two electrons.

$NAD^+$ participates by accepting hydrogen from the malate. As malate is oxidized, $NAD^+$ is reduced to NADH.

| $NAD^+$ Oxidized form | | NADH Reduced form |

We will study many other biologically important oxidation-reduction reactions in upcoming chapters.

| EXAMPLE 12.8 | Using IUPAC Nomenclature to Name an Ether |
|---|---|

LEARNING GOAL

11 Write names and draw structures for common ethers and discuss their use in medicine.

Name the following ether using IUPAC nomenclature.

**Solution**

$$O—CH_3$$
$$|$$
$$CH_3CH_2CHCH_2CH_2CH_2CH_2CH_2CH_3$$
$$1 \quad 2 \quad 3 \quad 4 \quad 5 \quad 6 \quad 7 \quad 8 \quad 9$$

Parent compound: nonane
Position of alkoxy group: carbon-3 (*Not* carbon-7 because the chain must be numbered to give the lowest number to the carbon bonded to the alkoxy group.)
Substituents: 3-methoxy
Name: 3-Methoxynonane

Figure 12.7 Ball-and-stick model of the ether methoxymethane (dimethyl ether).

**Practice Problem 12.8**

Name the following ethers using IUPAC nomenclature:

a. $CH_3CH_2—O—CH_2CH_2CH_3$
b. $CH_3—O—CH_2CH_2CH_3$
c. $CH_3CH_2—O—CH_2CH_2CH_2CH_2CH_3$
d. $CH_3CH_2CH_2CH_2—O—CH_2CH_2CH_3$

▶ For Further Practice: **Questions 12.85 and 12.88.**

In the common system of nomenclature, ethers are named by placing the names of the two alkyl groups attached to the ether oxygen as prefixes in front of the word *ether*. The names of the two groups can be placed either alphabetically or by size (smaller to larger), as seen in the following examples:

$CH_3—O—CH_3$

Dimethyl ether
or methyl ether

$CH_3—O—CH_2CH_3$

Ethyl methyl ether
or methyl ethyl ether

$CH_3CH_2—O—CH(CH_3)_2$

Ethyl isopropyl ether

| EXAMPLE 12.9 | Naming Ethers Using the Common Nomenclature System |
|---|---|

LEARNING GOAL

11 Write names and draw structures for common ethers and discuss their use in medicine.

Write the common name for each of the following ethers.

**Solution**

|  | $CH_3CH_2—O—CH_2CH_3$ | $CH_3—O—CH_2CH_2CH_3$ |
|---|---|---|
| Alkyl groups: | two ethyl groups | methyl and propyl |
| Name: | Diethyl ether | Methyl propyl ether |

Notice that there is only one correct name for methyl propyl ether because the methyl group is smaller than the propyl group and it would be first in an alphabetical listing also.

**Practice Problem 12.9**

Write the common name for each of the following ethers:

a. $CH_3CH_2—O—CH_2CH_2CH_3$
b. $CH_3—O—CH_2CH_2CH_3$
c. $CH_3CH_2—O—CH_2CH_2CH_2CH_2CH_3$
d. $CH_3CH_2CH_2CH_2—O—CH_2CH_2CH_3$

▶ For Further Practice: **Questions 12.86 and 12.88.**

Chemically, ethers are moderately inert. They do not react with reducing agents or bases under normal conditions. However, they are extremely volatile and highly flammable (easily oxidized in air) and hence must always be treated with great care.

Ethers may be prepared by a condensation reaction (removal of water) between two alcohol molecules, as shown in the following general reaction. The reaction requires heat and acid.

$$\underset{\text{Alcohol}}{R^1-OH} + \underset{\text{Alcohol}}{R^2-OH} \xrightarrow[\text{heat}]{H^+} \underset{\text{Ether}}{R^1-O-R^2} + \underset{\text{Water}}{H_2O}$$

---

**EXAMPLE 12.10    Writing an Equation Representing the Synthesis of an Ether via a Condensation Reaction**

Write an equation showing the synthesis of dimethyl ether.

**LEARNING GOAL**

**12**  Write equations representing the condensation reaction between two alcohol molecules to form an ether.

**Solution**

The alkyl substituents of this ether are two methyl groups. Thus, the alcohol that must undergo condensation to produce dimethyl ether is methanol.

$$\underset{\text{Methanol}}{CH_3OH} + \underset{\text{Methanol}}{CH_3OH} \xrightarrow[\text{heat}]{H^+} \underset{\text{Dimethyl ether}}{CH_3-O-CH_3} + \underset{\text{Water}}{H_2O}$$

**Practice Problem 12.10**

a. Write an equation showing the condensation reaction that would produce diethyl ether. Provide structures and names for all reactants and products.

b. Write an equation showing the condensation reaction between two molecules of 2-propanol. Provide structures and names for all reactants and products.

▶ For Further Practice: **Questions 12.83 and 12.84.**

---

*Diethyl ether* was the first general anesthetic used. The dentist Dr. William Morton is credited with its introduction in the 1800s. Diethyl ether functions as an anesthetic by interacting with the central nervous system. It appears that diethyl ether (and many other general anesthetics) functions by accumulating in the lipid material of the nerve cells, thereby interfering with nerve impulse transmission. This results in analgesia, a lessened perception of pain.

Halogenated ethers are also routinely used as general anesthetics (Figure 12.8). They are less flammable than diethyl ether and are therefore safer to store and work with. *Penthrane* and *Enthrane* (trade names) are two of the more commonly used members of this family:

**Figure 12.8** An anesthesiologist administers Penthrane to a surgical patient.

Penthrane

Enthrane

**Figure 12.9** This skunk on a bed of roses is surrounded by scent molecules. The two most common compounds in the defense spray of the striped skunk are the thiols *trans*-2-butene-1-thiol and 3-methyl-1-butanethiol. Two alcohols, 2-phenylethanol and geraniol, are the major components of the scent of roses.

**Question 12.11** Why do ethers have much lower boiling points than alcohols?

**Question 12.12** Describe the structure of ether molecules.

# 12.8 Thiols

Compounds that contain the sulfhydryl group (—SH) are called **thiols.** They are similar to alcohols in structure, but the sulfur atom replaces the oxygen atom.

Thiols and many other sulfur compounds have nauseating aromas. They are found in substances as different as the defense spray of the North American striped skunk, onions, and garlic. The structures of the two most common compounds in the defense spray of the striped skunk, *trans*-2-butene-1-thiol and 3-methyl-1-butanethiol, are seen in Figure 12.9. These structures are contrasted with the structures of the two molecules that make up the far more pleasant scent of roses: geraniol, an unsaturated alcohol, and 2-phenylethanol, an aromatic alcohol.

The IUPAC rules for naming thiols are similar to those for naming alcohols, except that the full name of the alkane is retained. The suffix *-thiol* follows the name of the parent compound.

**LEARNING GOAL**

**13** Write names and draw structures for simple thiols and discuss their biological significance.

---

| **EXAMPLE 12.11** | **Naming Thiols Using the IUPAC Nomenclature System** |
|---|---|

Write the IUPAC names for the thiols shown below.

**LEARNING GOAL**

**13** Write names and draw structures for simple thiols and discuss their biological significance.

### Solution

Retain the full name of the parent compound and add the suffix *-thiol.*

|  | $CH_3CH_2$—SH | HS—$CH_2CH_2$—SH |
|---|---|---|
| Parent compound: | ethane | ethane |
| Position of —SH: | carbon-1 | carbon-1 and carbon-2 |
| Name: | Ethanethiol | 1,2-Ethanedithiol |

*Continued…*

$$\underset{\underset{SH}{|}}{\overset{\overset{CH_3}{|}}{CH_3CHCH_2CH_2}} \qquad \underset{\underset{SH}{|}}{\overset{\overset{SH}{|}}{CH_3CHCH_2CH_2CH_2}}$$

| | | |
|---|---|---|
| Parent compound: | butane | pentane |
| Position of —SH: | carbon-1 | carbon-1 and carbon-4 |
| Substituent: | 3-methyl | |
| Name: | 3-Methyl-1-butanethiol | 1,4-Pentanedithiol |

## Practice Problem 12.11

Draw the structures of each of the following thiols.

a. 1,3-Butanedithiol
b. 2-Methyl-2-pentanethiol

c. 2-Chloro-2-propanethiol
d. Cyclopentanethiol

▶ For Further Practice: **Questions 12.93 and 12.94.**

---

Amino acids are the subunits from which proteins are made. A protein is a long polymer, or chain, of many amino acids bonded to one another.

The amino acid cysteine is a thiol that plays an important role in the structure and shape of many proteins. Two cysteine molecules can undergo oxidation to form cystine. The new bond formed is called a **disulfide** (—S—S—) bond.

2 Cysteine                                      Cystine

If the two cysteines are in different protein chains, the disulfide bond between them forms a bridge joining them together (Figure 12.10). If the two cysteines are in the same protein chain, a loop is formed. An example of the importance of disulfide bonds is seen in the production and structure of the protein hormone insulin, which controls blood sugar levels in the body. Insulin is initially produced as a protein called preproinsulin. Enzymatic removal of twenty-four amino acids and formation of disulfide bonds between cysteine amino acids produce proinsulin (Figure 12.10). Regions of the protein are identified as the A, B, and C chains. Notice that the A and B chains are covalently bonded to one another by two disulfide bonds. A third disulfide bond produces a hairpin loop in the A chain of the molecule. The molecule is now ready for the final stage of insulin synthesis in which the C chain is removed by the action of protein degrading enzymes (proteases). The active hormone, shown at the bottom of Figure 12.10, consists of the twenty-one amino acid A chain bonded to

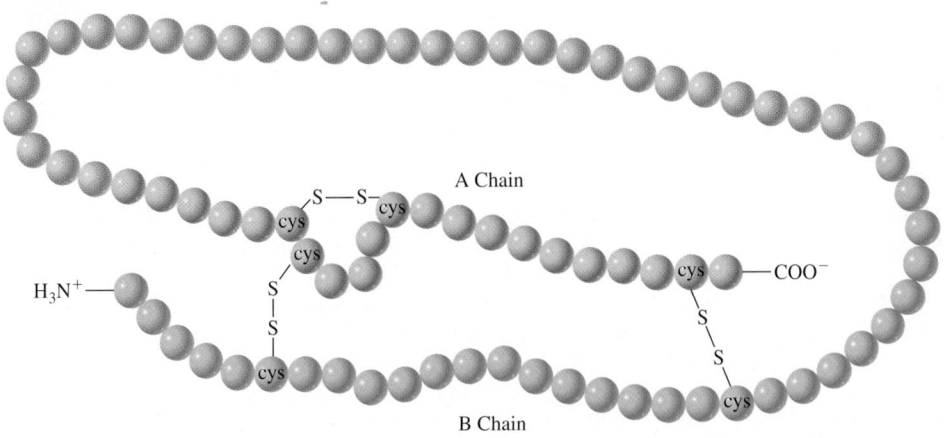

**Figure 12.10** Two steps in the synthesis of insulin. Disulfide bonds hold the A and B chains together and form a hairpin loop in the A chain.

Preproinsulin

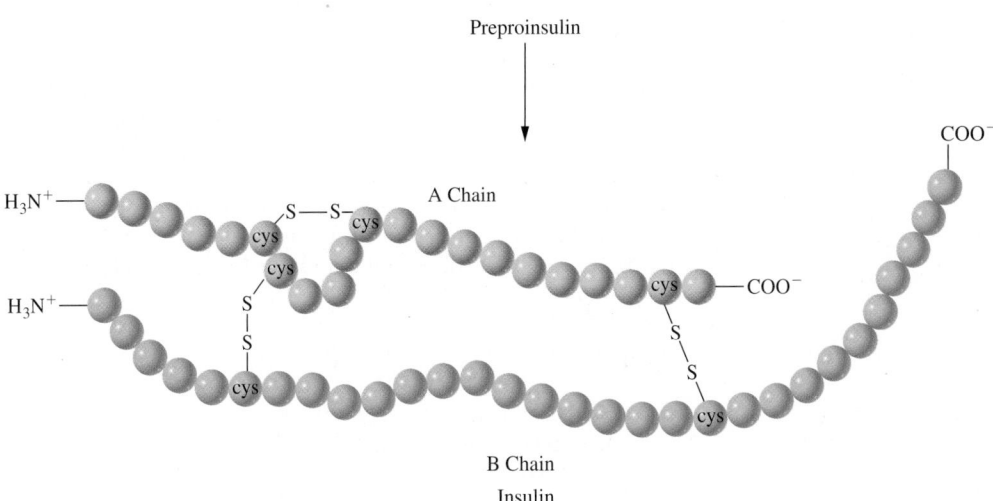

the thirty amino acid B chain by two disulfide bonds. Without these disulfide bonds, functional insulin molecules could not exist because there would be no way to keep the two chains together in the proper shape.

British Anti-Lewisite (BAL) is a dithiol used as an antidote in mercury poisoning. It was originally developed as an antidote to a mustard gas–like chemical warfare agent called Lewisite, which was developed near the end of World War I and never used. By the onset of World War II, Lewisite was considered to be obsolete because of the discovery of BAL, an effective, inexpensive antidote. The two thiol groups of BAL form a water-soluble complex with mercury (or with the arsenic in Lewisite) that is excreted from the body in the urine.

$$CH_2-CH-CH_2$$
$$\ \ |\ \ \ \ \ \ |\ \ \ \ \ \ |$$
$$OH\ \ \ SH\ \ \ SH$$

BAL

*Coenzyme A* is a thiol that serves as a "carrier" of acetyl groups ($CH_3CO-$) in biochemical reactions. It plays a central role in metabolism by shuttling acetyl groups from one reaction to another. When the two-carbon acetate group is attached to coenzyme A, the product is acetyl coenzyme A (acetyl CoA). The bond between coenzyme A and the acetyl group is a high-energy *thioester bond*. In effect, formation of the high-energy thioester bond "energizes" the acetyl group so that it can participate in other biochemical reactions.

*The reactions involving coenzyme A are discussed in detail in Chapters 21, 22, and 23.*

A high-energy bond is one that releases a great deal of energy when it is broken.

# KITCHEN CHEMISTRY

## The Magic of Garlic

Chefs have known for centuries that whole roasted garlic cloves impart a sweet flavor to foods and can even be used to make ice cream! But if you chop or crush the clove of garlic before cooking, the flavors are entirely different, much stronger. The chemistry behind this difference was not understood until the 1940s, when two researchers from the Sandoz Company investigated the chemistry of garlic.

They found that the difference between whole cooked garlic cloves and crushed garlic lies in the presence of the com-pound alliin in certain cells of the garlic clove and the presence of the enzyme allinase in other cells. When the cells are crushed, the enzyme and its substrate are brought together, initiating a chain of chemical reactions that begins with the production of allicin and increases in complexity with time and further cooking. The chemistry becomes even more complex depending on the other ingredients used in the recipe. One set of compounds will form if the garlic is heated in water. Using butter or olive oil or milk will produce quite different products and, thus, quite different flavors in the food.

Some of the compounds produced in these reactions have strong biological activity. For instance, allicin is an antibiotic, having one-fiftieth the power of penicillin and one-tenth the activity of tetracycline. However, allicin is quickly broken down during cooking to produce a complex mixture of compounds that includes propenyl disulfide, which gives onions their aroma, and propenyl sulfenic acid, which causes tears when you cut into an onion. Also among these breakdown products is diallyl disulfide, which has been suggested to have anticancer properties and to be of benefit in reducing cholesterol levels.

### For Further Understanding

► Design an experiment to test the suspected anticancer activity of diallyl disulfide.

► Explain why using a variety of ingredients, such as butter or olive oil, will result in different flavors and aromas in the food that is prepared.

Alliin

Allinase

Allicin

Further breakdown into complex products

Acetyl coenzyme A
(acetyl CoA)

Acetyl CoA is made and used in the energy-producing reactions that provide most of the energy for life processes. It is also required for the biosynthesis of many biological molecules.

# CHAPTER MAP

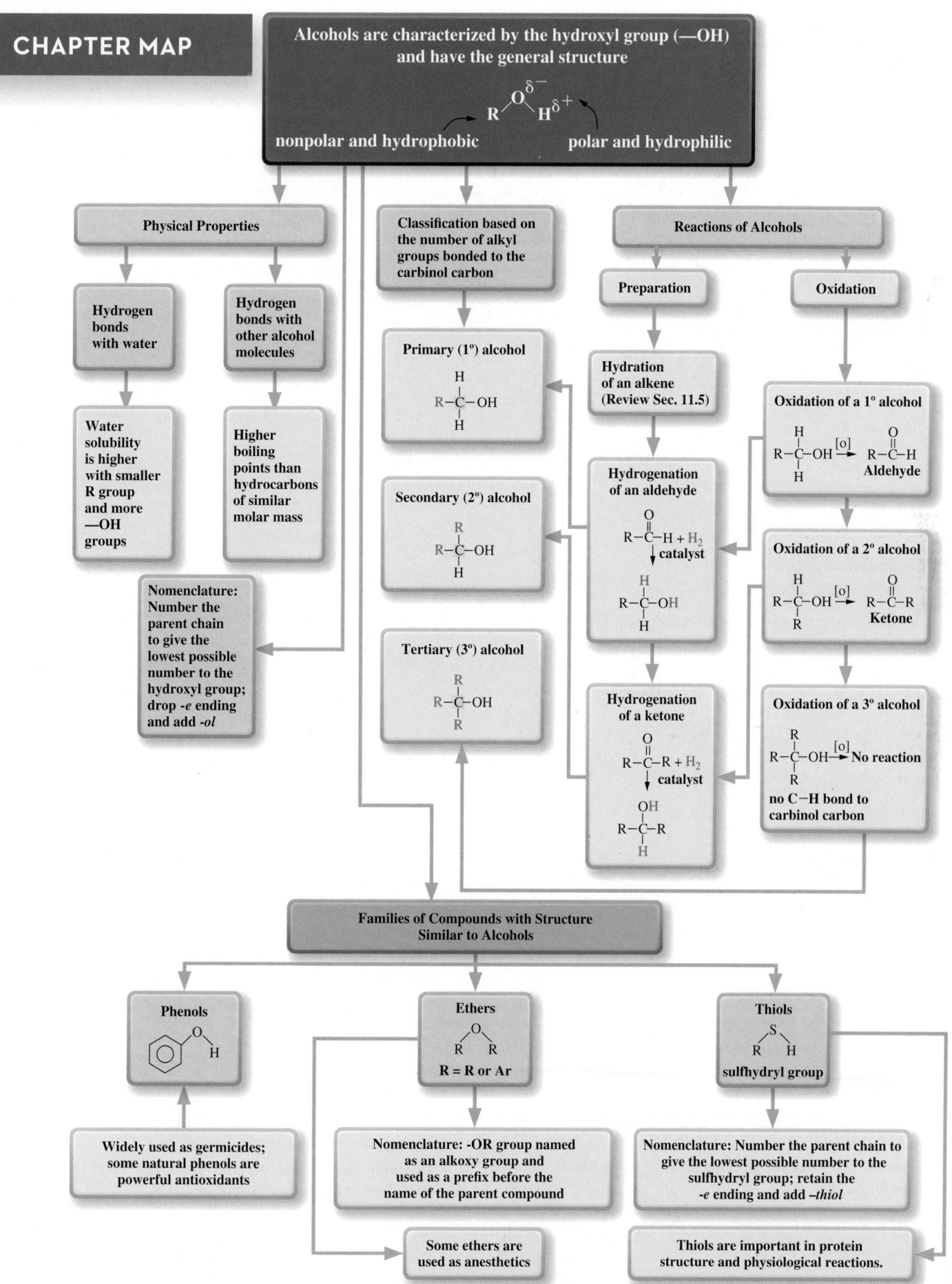

Alcohols are characterized by the hydroxyl group (—OH) and have the general structure

nonpolar and hydrophobic          polar and hydrophilic

**Physical Properties**

Hydrogen bonds with water

Hydrogen bonds with other alcohol molecules

Water solubility is higher with smaller R group and more —OH groups

Higher boiling points than hydrocarbons of similar molar mass

Nomenclature: Number the parent chain to give the lowest possible number to the hydroxyl group; drop -e ending and add -ol

**Classification based on the number of alkyl groups bonded to the carbinol carbon**

Primary (1°) alcohol

Secondary (2°) alcohol

Tertiary (3°) alcohol

**Reactions of Alcohols**

**Preparation**

Hydration of an alkene (Review Sec. 11.5)

Hydrogenation of an aldehyde

Hydrogenation of a ketone

**Oxidation**

Oxidation of a 1° alcohol
Aldehyde

Oxidation of a 2° alcohol
Ketone

Oxidation of a 3° alcohol
No reaction
no C—H bond to carbinol carbon

**Families of Compounds with Structure Similar to Alcohols**

**Phenols**

Widely used as germicides; some natural phenols are powerful antioxidants

**Ethers**

R = R or Ar

Nomenclature: -OR group named as an alkoxy group and used as a prefix before the name of the parent compound

Some ethers are used as anesthetics

**Thiols**

sulfhydryl group

Nomenclature: Number the parent chain to give the lowest possible number to the sulfhydryl group; retain the -e ending and add –thiol

Thiols are important in protein structure and physiological reactions.

# SUMMARY OF REACTIONS

## Preparation of Alcohols

Hydration of alkenes:

Alkene        Water              Alcohol

Reduction of an aldehyde or ketone:

Aldehyde   Hydrogen            Alcohol
or
ketone

## Dehydration of Alcohols

Alcohol                      Alkene      Water

## Oxidation Reactions

Oxidation of a primary alcohol:

1° Alcohol               An aldehyde

Oxidation of a secondary alcohol:

2° Alcohol                A ketone

Oxidation of a tertiary alcohol:

3° Alcohol

## Condensation Synthesis of an Ether

$$R^1-OH + R^2-OH \xrightarrow[\text{heat}]{H^+} R^1-O-R^2 + H_2O$$

Alcohol      Alcohol              Ether      Water

# SUMMARY

## 12.1 Alcohols: Structure and Physical Properties

▶ **Alcohols** are characterized by the **hydroxyl group (—OH).**
▶ Alcohols have the general structure R—OH.
▶ Alcohols are classified as primary, secondary, or tertiary depending on the number of alkyl groups attached to the **carbinol carbon.**
▶ A **primary alcohol** has one alkyl group attached to the carbinol carbon.
▶ A **secondary alcohol** has two alkyl groups attached to the carbinol carbon.

▶ A **tertiary alcohol** has three alkyl groups attached to the carbinol carbon.
▶ They are very polar because the hydroxyl group is polar.
▶ Alcohols form intermolecular hydrogen bonds and as a result have higher boiling points than hydrocarbons of comparable molar mass.
▶ Smaller alcohols are very water-soluble.

## 12.2 Alcohols: Nomenclature

▶ In the IUPAC system, alcohols are named by determining the **parent compound** and replacing the -e ending with -ol.
▶ The parent chain is numbered to give the hydroxyl group the lowest possible number.
▶ Common names are derived from the alkyl group corresponding to the parent compound.

## 12.3 Medically Important Alcohols

▶ Methanol is a toxic alcohol that is used as a solvent.

▶ Ethanol is the alcohol consumed in beer, wine, and distilled liquors. It is produced by the alcohol **fermentation** of sugars.

▶ Isopropanol is used as a an antiseptic.

▶ Ethylene glycol (1,2-ethanediol) is used as antifreeze.

▶ Glycerol (1,2,3-propanetriol) is used in cosmetics and pharmaceuticals.

## 12.4 Reactions Involving Alcohols

▶ Alcohols can be prepared by the **hydration** of alkenes or the **reduction** of aldehydes and ketones.

▶ Alcohols can undergo **dehydration** to produce alkenes.

▶ Dehydration is an example of an **elimination reaction**, that is, one in which a molecule loses atoms or ions from its structure.

▶ **Zaitsev's rule** states that in an elimination reaction, such as the dehydration of an alcohol, the alkene with the greatest number of alkyl groups on the double-bonded carbons (the more highly substituted alkene) will be the major product in the reaction.

▶ Primary and secondary alcohols can undergo **oxidation** reactions to yield aldehydes and ketones, respectively.

▶ Tertiary alcohols do not undergo oxidation.

## 12.5 Oxidation and Reduction in Living Systems

▶ In organic and biological systems, **oxidation** involves the gain of oxygen or the loss of hydrogen and **reduction** involves the loss of oxygen or the gain of hydrogen.

▶ Nicotinamide adenine dinucleotide, $NAD^+$, is a coenzyme involved in many biological oxidation and reduction reactions.

## 12.6 Phenols

▶ **Phenols** are compounds in which the hydroxyl group is attached to a benzene ring.

▶ Phenols have the general structure Ar—OH.

▶ Many phenols are important as antiseptics and disinfectants.

## 12.7 Ethers

▶ **Ethers** are characterized by the R—O—R functional group.

▶ Ethers are generally nonreactive but are extremely flammable.

▶ Diethyl ether was the first general anesthetic used in medical practice.

▶ Penthrane and enthrane, which are much less flammable, have replaced the use of diethyl ether.

## 12.8 Thiols

▶ **Thiols** are characterized by the sulfhydryl group (—SH).

▶ The amino acid cysteine is a thiol that is extremely important for maintaining the correct shapes of proteins by forming **disulfide bonds** with other cysteine molecules within the same or another protein.

▶ Coenzyme A is a thiol that serves as a "carrier" of acetyl groups in important biological reactions.

## ANSWERS TO PRACTICE PROBLEMS

**12.1** a. Primary alcohol    d. Aromatic alcohol (phenol)
     b. Secondary alcohol    e. Secondary alcohol
     c. Tertiary alcohol

**12.2** a. 4-Methyl-1-pentanol    c. 1,2,3-Propanetriol
     b. 4-Methyl-2-hexanol    d. 4-Chloro-3-methyl-1-hexanol

**12.3** $$CH_3CH_2CH_2\overset{\overset{\displaystyle O}{\|}}{C}-H + H_2 \longrightarrow CH_3CH_2CH_2CH_2OH$$

**12.4** $$CH_3CH_2\overset{\overset{\displaystyle O}{\|}}{C}CH_3 + H_2 \longrightarrow CH_3CH_2CH(OH)CH_3$$

**12.5** a. $CH_3CH_2OH \xrightarrow{H^+, heat} CH_2{=}CH_2 + H_2O$

     b. $CH_3CHOHCH_3 \xrightarrow{H^+, heat} CH_3CH{=}CH_2 + H_2O$

     c. There are two possible products

$$CH_3CH_2\underset{\underset{\displaystyle OH}{|}}{C}HCHCH_2CH_3 \xrightarrow{H^+, heat} CH_3CH_2\overset{\overset{\displaystyle CH_3}{|}}{C}{=}CHCH_2CH_3 + H_2O$$

$$CH_3CH_2\underset{\underset{\displaystyle OH}{|}}{C}HCHCH_2CH_3 \xrightarrow{H^+, heat} CH_3CH_2\overset{\overset{\displaystyle CH_3}{|}}{C}HCH{=}CHCH_3$$

     d. $CH_3\underset{\underset{\displaystyle CH_3}{|}}{\overset{\overset{\displaystyle OH}{|}}{C}}CH_3 \xrightarrow{H^+ heat} CH_2{=}\underset{\underset{\displaystyle CH_3}{|}}{C}CH_3 + H_2O$

**12.6** a. $$CH_3\underset{\underset{\displaystyle CH_3}{|}}{\overset{\overset{\displaystyle CH_3}{|}}{C}}CH_2CH_2OH \xrightarrow{[O]} CH_3\overset{\overset{\displaystyle CH_3}{|}}{C}CH_2\overset{\overset{\displaystyle O}{\|}}{C}-H$$

     b. $$CH_3CH_2OH \xrightarrow{[O]} CH_3\overset{\overset{\displaystyle O}{\|}}{C}-H$$

**12.7**  a.
$$\underset{\overset{|}{CH_3\overset{OH}{\underset{}{C}}HCH_2CH_3}}{} \rightarrow \underset{\overset{O}{\overset{\parallel}{CH_3CCH_2CH_3}}}{}$$

b.
$$\underset{CH_3\overset{OH}{\underset{|}{C}}HCH_2CH_2CH_3}{} \rightarrow \underset{CH_3\overset{O}{\overset{\parallel}{C}}CH_2CH_2CH_3}{}$$

**12.8**  a. 1-Ethoxypropane      c. 1-Ethoxypentane
b. 1-Methoxypropane     d. 1-Propoxybutane

**12.9**  a. Ethyl propyl ether      c. Ethyl pentyl ether
b. Methyl propyl ether    d. Propyl butyl ether

**12.10**

a.
$$CH_3CH_2OH + CH_3CH_2OH \xrightarrow[\text{heat}]{H^+} CH_3CH_2-O-CH_2CH_3 + H_2O$$

Ethanol                    Diethyl ether    Water

b.
$$2CH_3\overset{OH}{\underset{|}{C}}HCH_3 \xrightarrow[\text{heat}]{H^+} CH_3CH-O-CHCH_3 + H_2O$$
$$\qquad\qquad\qquad\qquad\underset{CH_3}{|}\quad\underset{CH_3}{|}$$

2-Propanol            Diisopropyl ether

**12.11**  a. 1,3-Butanedithiol
$$\underset{\overset{|}{SH}\quad\overset{|}{SH}}{CH_2CH_2CHCH_3}$$

b. 2-Methyl-2-pentanethiol
$$\underset{\overset{|}{CH_3}}{CH_3\overset{SH}{\overset{|}{C}}CH_2CH_2CH_3}$$

c. 2-Chloro-2-propanethiol
$$\underset{\overset{|}{Cl}}{CH_3\overset{SH}{\overset{|}{C}}CH_3}$$

d. Cyclopentanethiol

**QUESTIONS AND PROBLEMS**

## Alcohols: Structure and Physical Properties

### Foundations

**12.13**  Describe the relationship between the water solubility of alcohols and their hydrocarbon chain length.

**12.14**  Explain the relationship between the water solubility of alcohols and the number of hydroxyl groups in the molecule.

**12.15**  Define the term *carbinol carbon*.

**12.16**  Define the terms *primary, secondary,* and *tertiary alcohol,* and draw a general structure for each.

### Applications

**12.17**  Classify each of the following as a 1°, 2°, or 3° alcohol:
a. 3-Methyl-1-butanol        d. 1-Methylcyclopentanol
b. 2-Methylcyclopentanol     e. 2-Methyl-2-pentanol
c. *t*-Butyl alcohol

**12.18**  1-Heptanol has a pleasant aroma and is sometimes used in cosmetics to enhance the fragrance. Draw the condensed formula for 1-heptanol. Is this a primary, secondary, or tertiary alcohol?

**12.19**  Classify each of the following as a 1°, 2°, or 3° alcohol:
a. $CH_3CH_2CH_2CH_2CH_2CH_2CH_2OH$

b. $CH_3CHCH_3$
$\qquad\underset{}{|}$
$\qquad OH$

c. $CH_3\overset{CH_3}{\underset{CH_2OH}{\overset{|}{\underset{|}{C}}}}CH_3$

d. $CH_3CH_2\overset{Br}{\overset{|}{C}}HCH_2CH_2CH_2OH$

e. $CH_3CH-\overset{CH_3}{\overset{|}{C}}CH_2CH_2CH_3$
$\qquad\underset{OH}{|}\quad\underset{CH_3}{|}$

**12.20**  Classify each of the following as a primary, secondary, or tertiary alcohol:

a. $CH_3CH_2\overset{CH_2CH_3}{\overset{|}{C}}OH$

b. $CH_3CHCH_2CHCH_3$
$\qquad\underset{OH}{|}\qquad\underset{Br}{|}$

c. $CH_3CH_2CH_2OH$

d. $CH_3\overset{CH_3}{\overset{|}{C}}CH_2CH_2CH_3$
$\qquad\underset{OH}{|}$

**12.21**  Stingless bees use complex systems to communicate. One aspect of this communication is chemical: the bees produce 2-nonanol, 2-heptanol, and 2-undecanol in their mouthparts (mandibles) to direct other bees to pollen sources. Draw the condensed structure of each of these alcohols. Classify each as a primary, secondary, or tertiary alcohol.

**12.22**  Classify each of the following as a primary, secondary, or tertiary alcohol:
a. 2-Methyl-2-butanol
b. 1,2-Dimethylcyclohexanol
c. 2,3,4-Trimethylcyclopentanol
d. 3,3-Dimethyl-2-pentanol

**12.23** Arrange the following compounds in order of increasing boiling point, beginning with the lowest:
a. $CH_3CH_2CH_2CH_2CH_3$  c. $CH_3CHCH_2CH_2CH_3$
                                                 |
                                                OH

b. $CH_3CHCH_2CHCH_3$  d. $CH_3CH_2CH_2—O—CH_2CH_3$
        |      |
       OH    OH

**12.24** Why do alcohols have higher boiling points than alkanes?

**12.25** Which member of each of the following pairs is more soluble in water?
a. $CH_3CH_2OH$  or  $CH_3CH_2CH_2CH_2OH$
b. $CH_3CH_2CH_2CH_2CH_3$  or  $CH_3CH_2CH_2CH_2OH$
c.   OH         or      $CH_3CHCH_3$
                                      |
                                     OH

**12.26** Arrange the three alcohols in each of the following sets in order of increasing solubility in water:
a. $CH_3CH_2CH_2CH_2CH_2OH$    $CH_3CHCH_2CHCH_2CH_3$
                                                          |      |
                                                         OH    OH

$CH_3CHCH_2CHCH_2CH_2OH$
        |      |
       OH    OH

b. Pentyl alcohol   1-Hexanol   Ethylene glycol

## Alcohols: Nomenclature

### Foundations

**12.27** Briefly describe the IUPAC rules for naming alcohols.

**12.28** Briefly describe the rules for determining the common names for alcohols.

### Applications

**12.29** Give the IUPAC name for each of the following compounds:
a. $CH_3CH_2CH(OH)CH_2CH_2CH_2OH$
b. $CH_3CH(OH)CH(OH)CH_2CH_3$
c. $CH_3CH(CH_3)CH(OH)CH_2CH_3$

**12.30** Give the IUPAC name for each of the following compounds:
a. $CH_3C(CH_2CH_3)_2CH(CH_3)CH_2CH_2CH_2OH$
b. $CH_3CH_2CH(OH)CH_2CH_2CH_3$
c. $CH_3CH_2CHClCHBrCH_2CH_2OH$

**12.31** Draw each of the following, using complete structural formulas and line formulas:
a. 2-Pentanol
b. 1,2,4-Heptanetriol
c. 2-Methylcyclopentanol

**12.32** Draw each of the following, using condensed formulas and line formulas:
a. 3-Methyl-4-ethyl-3-hexanol
b. 1-Bromo-2-methyl-3-pentanol
c. 2,4-Dimethylcyclohexanol

**12.33** Give the IUPAC name for each of the following compounds:

**12.34** Draw each of the following alcohols:
a. 1-Iodo-2-butanol        c. Cyclobutanol
b. 1,2-Butanediol

**12.35** Give the common name for each of the following compounds:
a. $CH_3OH$                c. $CH_2—CH_2$
                                          |      |
                                        OH    OH
b. $CH_3CH_2OH$            d. $CH_3CH_2CH_2OH$

**12.36** Draw the structure of each of the following compounds:
a. Pentyl alcohol          c. Octyl alcohol
b. Isopropyl alcohol       d. Propyl alcohol

**12.37** Draw a condensed formula for each of the following compounds:
a. 4-Methyl-2-hexanol      d. 2-Nonanol
b. Isobutyl alcohol        e. 1,3,5-Cyclohexanetriol
c. 1,5-Pentanediol

**12.38** Name each of the following alcohols using the IUPAC Nomenclature System:

## Medically Important Alcohols

**12.39** What is denatured alcohol? Why is alcohol denatured?

**12.40** What are the principal uses of methanol, ethanol, and isopropyl alcohol?

**12.41** What is fermentation?

**12.42** Why do wines typically have an alcohol concentration of 12–13%?

**12.43** Why must fermentation products be distilled to produce liquors such as scotch?

**12.44** If a bottle of distilled alcoholic spirits—for example, scotch whiskey—is labeled as 80 proof, what is the percentage of alcohol in the scotch?

## Reactions Involving Alcohols

### Foundations

**12.45** Write a general equation representing the preparation of an alcohol by hydration of an alkene.

**12.46** Write a general equation representing the preparation of an alcohol by hydrogenation of an aldehyde or a ketone.

**12.47** Write a general equation representing the dehydration of an alcohol.

**12.48** Write a general equation representing the oxidation of a 1° alcohol.

**12.49** Write a general equation representing the oxidation of a 2° alcohol.

**12.50** Write a general equation representing the oxidation of a 3° alcohol.

## Applications

**12.51** Predict the products formed by the hydration of the following alkenes:

a. 1-Hexene
b. 2-Hexene
c. 2-Methyl-3-hexene
d. 2,2-Dimethyl-3-heptene

**12.52** Draw the alkene products of the dehydration of the following alcohols:

a. 2-Butanol
b. 1-Butanol
c. 2-Propanol
d. 4-Bromo-2-hexanol

**12.53** Write an equation showing the hydration of each of the following alkenes. Name each of the products using the IUPAC Nomenclature System.

a. 2-Hexene
b. Cyclopentene
c. 1-Octene
d. 1-Methylcyclohexene

**12.54** Write an equation showing the dehydration of each of the following alcohols. Name each of the reactants and products using the IUPAC Nomenclature System.

a. $CH_3CHCH_2CH_3$
    |
    OH

b.

**12.55** What product(s) would result from the oxidation of each of the following alcohols with, for example, potassium permanganate? If no reaction occurs, write N.R.

a. 2-Butanol
b. 2-Methyl-2-hexanol
c. Cyclohexanol
d. 1-Methyl-1-cyclopentanol

**12.56** We have seen that ethanol is metabolized to ethanal (acetaldehyde) in the liver. What would be the product formed, under the same conditions, from each of the following alcohols?

a. $CH_3OH$
b. $CH_3CH_2CH_2OH$
c. $CH_3CH_2CH_2CH_2OH$

**12.57** Using the IUPAC system, name each of the following alcohols and the product formed when it is oxidized. If no reaction occurs, write N.R.

a. $CH_3CH_2CHCH_2CH_3$
                 |
                 OH
b. $CH_3CH_2CH_2OH$

c. $CH_3CHCH_2CHCH_3$
        |       |
        OH     CH_3

d. $CH_3CCH_2CH_3$
        |
        OH  (with CH_3 below)

e.
$-CH_2CH_2CH_2OH$

**12.58** Write an equation demonstrating each of the following chemical transformations:

a. Oxidation of an alcohol to an aldehyde
b. Oxidation of an alcohol to a ketone
c. Dehydration of a cyclic alcohol to a cycloalkene
d. Hydrogenation of an alkene to an alkane

**12.59** Write the reaction, occurring in the liver, that causes the oxidation of ethanol. What is the product of this reaction and what symptoms are caused by the product?

**12.60** Write the reaction, occurring in the liver, that causes the oxidation of methanol. What is the product of this reaction

and what is the possible result of the accumulation of the product in the body?

**12.61** Write an equation for the preparation of 2-butanol from 1-butene. What type of reaction is involved?

**12.62** Write a general equation for the preparation of an alcohol from an aldehyde or ketone. What type of reaction is involved?

**12.63** Show how acetone can be prepared from propene.

$$\underset{\text{Acetone}}{CH_3\overset{\overset{\displaystyle O}{\|}}{C}CH_3}$$

**12.64** Give the oxidation product for cholesterol.

Cholesterol

**12.65** Write a balanced equation for the hydrogenation of each of the following:

a. Hexanal (a six-carbon aldehyde)
b. 2-Hexanone (a six-carbon ketone)
c. 2-Methylbutanal (an aldehyde with a four-carbon parent chain)
d. 6-Ethyl-2-octanone (a ketone with an eight-carbon parent chain)

**12.66** Write a balanced equation for the hydrogenation of each of the following:

a. Propanal (a three-carbon aldehyde)
b. Propanone (a three-carbon ketone)
c. 2,3-Dimethylheptanal (an aldehyde with a seven-carbon parent chain)
d. 3-Methyl-4-heptanone (a ketone with a seven-carbon parent chain)

## Oxidation and Reduction in Living Systems

### Foundations

**12.67** Define the terms *oxidation* and *reduction*.

**12.68** How do we recognize oxidation and reduction in organic compounds?

### Applications

**12.69** Arrange the following compounds from the most reduced to the most oxidized:

$$CH_3CH_2\overset{\overset{\displaystyle O}{\|}}{C}-OH \qquad CH_3CH_2CH_3$$

$$CH_3CH_2\overset{\overset{\displaystyle O}{\|}}{C}-H \qquad CH_3CH_2CH_2OH$$

O
‖
C
R   H
Aldehyde

O
‖
C
R   R'
Ketone

O
‖
C
R   OH
Carboxylic Acid

O
‖
C
R   NR₂
Amide

# 13.1 Structure and Physical Properties

**Aldehydes** and **ketones** are carbonyl group–containing compounds distinguished by the location of the carbonyl group within the carbon chain. In aldehydes the carbonyl group is always located at the end of the carbon chain (carbon-1). In ketones the carbonyl group is located within the carbon chain of the molecule. Thus, in ketones the carbonyl carbon is attached to two other carbon atoms. However, in aldehydes the carbonyl carbon is attached to at least one hydrogen atom; the second atom attached to the carbonyl carbon of an aldehyde may be another hydrogen or a carbon atom (Figure 13.1). Aldehydes and ketones are polar compounds because of the polar carbonyl group.

$$O^{\delta-}$$
$$\|$$
$$C^{\delta+}$$

The carbonyl group is polar because oxygen is more electronegative than carbon (3.5 versus 2.5). This produces a dipole in which the oxygen carries a partial negative charge and the carbon carries a partial positive charge.

Because of the dipole-dipole attractions between molecules, aldehydes and ketones boil at higher temperatures than hydrocarbons or ethers that have the same number of carbon atoms or are of equivalent molar mass. Because they cannot form intermolecular hydrogen bonds, their boiling points are lower than those of alcohols of comparable molar mass. These trends are clearly demonstrated in the following examples:

**LEARNING GOAL**

1 Draw the structures and discuss the physical properties of aldehydes and ketones.

$$\underset{\delta+}{>}C=\underset{\delta-}{O}\cdots\underset{\delta+}{>}C=\underset{\delta-}{O}\cdots\underset{\delta+}{>}C=\underset{\delta-}{O}$$

*Dipole-dipole attraction*

CH₃CH₂CH₂CH₃

Butane
(butane)
M.M. = 58
b.p. −0.5°C

CH₃—O—CH₂CH₃

Methoxyethane
(ethyl methyl ether)
M.M. = 60
b.p. 7.0°C

CH₃CH₂CH₂—OH

1-Propanol
(propyl alcohol)
M.M. = 60
b.p. 97.2°C

O
‖
CH₃CH₂—C—H

Propanal
(propionaldehyde)
M.M. = 58
b.p. 49°C

O
‖
CH₃—C—CH₃

Propanone
(acetone)
M.M. = 58
b.p. 56°C

O
‖
C
R   H
Aldehyde
R = H, R, or Ar

An aldehyde
Propanal

**(a)**

O
‖
C
R   R
Ketone
R = R or Ar

A ketone
Propanone

**(b)**

**Figure 13.1** The structures of aldehydes and ketones. (a) The general structure of an aldehyde and a ball-and-stick model of the aldehyde propanal. (b) The general structure of a ketone and a ball-and-stick model of the ketone propanone.

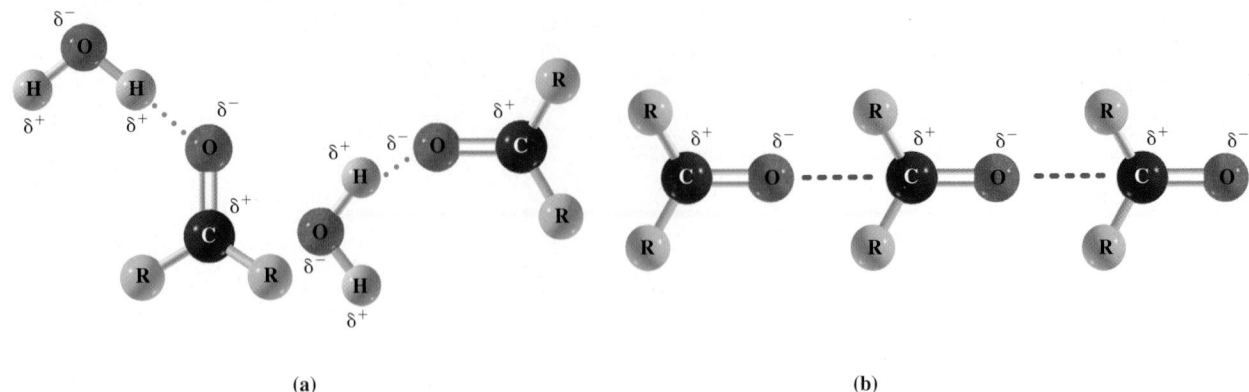

(a)    (b)

**Figure 13.2** (a) Hydrogen bonding between the carbonyl group of an aldehyde or ketone and water. (b) Polar interactions between carbonyl groups of aldehydes or ketones.

Aldehydes and ketones can form intermolecular hydrogen bonds with water (Figure 13.2). As a result, the smaller members of the two families (five or fewer carbon atoms) are reasonably soluble in water. However, as the carbon chain length increases, the compounds become less polar and more hydrocarbonlike. These larger compounds are soluble in nonpolar organic solvents.

**Question 13.1**  Which member in each of the following pairs will be more water-soluble?

a. $CH_3(CH_2)_2CH_3$   or   $CH_3\overset{\displaystyle O}{\overset{\displaystyle \|}{C}}CH_3$

b. $CH_3\overset{\displaystyle O}{\overset{\displaystyle \|}{C}}CH_2CH_2CH_3$   or   $CH_3CHOHCH_2CH_2CH_3$

**Question 13.2**  Which member in each of the following pairs will be more water-soluble?

a.   CH₃   or   H—C=O

b. $HOCH_2CH_2OH$   or   $H\overset{\displaystyle O}{\overset{\displaystyle \|}{C}}\overset{\displaystyle O}{\overset{\displaystyle \|}{C}}H$

**Question 13.3**  Which member in each of the following pairs would have a higher boiling point?

a. $CH_3CH_2\overset{\displaystyle O}{\overset{\displaystyle \|}{C}}OH$   or   $CH_3CH_2\overset{\displaystyle O}{\overset{\displaystyle \|}{C}}H$

b. $CH_3\overset{\displaystyle O}{\overset{\displaystyle \|}{C}}OH$   or   $CH_3\overset{\displaystyle O}{\overset{\displaystyle \|}{C}}CH_3$

**Question 13.4**  Which member in each of the following pairs would have a higher boiling point?

a. $CH_3CH_2OH$   or   $CH_3\overset{\displaystyle O}{\overset{\displaystyle \|}{C}}H$

b. $CH_3(CH_2)_6CH_3$   or   $CH_3(CH_2)_5\overset{\displaystyle O}{\overset{\displaystyle \|}{C}}H$

## 13.2  IUPAC Nomenclature and Common Names

### Naming Aldehydes

In the IUPAC system, aldehydes are named according to the following set of rules:

- Determine the parent compound, that is, the longest continuous carbon chain containing the carbonyl group.
- Replace the final -*e* of the parent alkane with -*al*.
- Number the chain beginning with the carbonyl carbon (or aldehyde group) as carbon-1.

- Number and name all substituents as usual. No number is used for the position of the carbonyl group because it is always at the end of the parent chain. Therefore, it must be carbon-1.

Several examples are provided here with common names given in parentheses:

$$\underset{\substack{\text{Methanal} \\ \text{(formaldehyde)}}}{H-\overset{\overset{\displaystyle O}{\|}}{\underset{1}{C}}-H} \qquad \underset{\substack{\text{Ethanal} \\ \text{(acetaldehyde)}}}{CH_3-\overset{\overset{\displaystyle O}{\|}}{\underset{1}{C}}-H} \qquad \underset{\substack{\text{Propanal} \\ \text{(propionaldehyde)}}}{\underset{3\ \ 2}{CH_3CH_2}-\overset{\overset{\displaystyle O}{\|}}{\underset{1}{C}}-H}$$

$$\underset{\substack{\text{2-Methylpentanal}}}{\underset{5\ \ \ \ 4\ \ \ \ 3\ \ \ \ 2}{CH_3CH_2CH_2}\underset{\underset{\displaystyle CH_3}{|}}{CH}-\overset{\overset{\displaystyle O}{\|}}{\underset{1}{C}}-H}$$

---

**EXAMPLE 13.1**  **Using the IUPAC Nomenclature System to Name Aldehydes**

For many years, scientists were puzzled about what compounds give the nutty flavor to expensive, aged cheddar cheeses. In 2004, Dr. Mary Anne Drake of North Carolina State University solved this puzzle. She identified a group of aldehydes that impart this desirable flavor. Use the IUPAC Nomenclature System to name two of these aldehydes shown below.

LEARNING GOAL

2 From the structures, write the common and IUPAC names of aldehydes and ketones.

**Solution**

$$\underset{3\quad 2\ \underset{\underset{\displaystyle CH_3}{|}}{}\ 1}{CH_3CH\overset{\overset{\displaystyle O}{\|}}{C}-H} \qquad\qquad \underset{4\quad 3\ \underset{\underset{\displaystyle CH_3}{|}}{}\ 2\quad 1}{CH_3CHCH_2\overset{\overset{\displaystyle O}{\|}}{C}-H}$$

| | | |
|---|---|---|
| Parent compound: | propane (becomes propanal) | butane (becomes butanal) |
| Position of carbonyl group: | carbon-1 | carbon-1 |
| Substituents: | 2-methyl | 3-methyl |
| Name: | 2-Methylpropanal | 3-Methylbutanal |

Notice that the position of the carbonyl group is not indicated by a number. By definition, the carbonyl group is located at the end of the carbon chain of an aldehyde. The carbonyl carbon is defined to be carbon-1; thus, it is not necessary to include the position of the carbonyl group in the name of the compound.

**Practice Problem 13.1**

Many molecules contribute to the complex flavors of olive oils. Among these are hexanal and *trans*-2-hexenal, which have flavors described as "green, grassy" and "green, bitter," respectively. Draw the structures of these two compounds.

▶ For Further Practice: **Questions 13.5, 13.29, and 13.36a, b, and c.**

Another aldehyde associated with the nutty flavor of cheddar cheese is 2-methylbutanal. Draw the condensed formula of this molecule.

*Carboxylic acid nomenclature is described in Section 14.1.*

The common names of the aldehydes are derived from the same Latin roots as the corresponding carboxylic acids. The common names of the first five aldehydes are presented in Table 13.1.

In the common system of nomenclature, substituted aldehydes are named as derivatives of the straight-chain parent compound (see Table 13.1). Greek letters are used to indicate the position of the substituents. The carbon atom bonded to the carbonyl group is the α-carbon, the next is the β-carbon, and so on.

$$\overset{\delta}{-}C\overset{\gamma}{-}C\overset{\beta}{-}C\overset{\alpha}{-}C\overset{O}{-}C-H$$

Consider the following examples:

$$\underset{CH_3}{CH_3CH_2CH_2\overset{\delta}{C}H\overset{\gamma}{-}\overset{\beta}{C}\overset{\alpha}{-}\overset{O}{\underset{\|}{C}}-H}$$

2-Methylpentanal
(α-methylvaleraldehyde)

$$\underset{CH_3}{CH_3CH_2\overset{\delta}{C}H\overset{\gamma}{C}H_2\overset{\beta}{-}\overset{\alpha}{\underset{\|}{C}}\overset{O}{-}H}$$

3-Methylpentanal
(β-methylvaleraldehyde)

## Naming Ketones

LEARNING GOAL

**2** From the structures, write the common and IUPAC names of aldehydes and ketones.

The rules for naming ketones in the IUPAC Nomenclature System are directly analogous to those for naming aldehydes. In ketones, however, the -*e* ending of the parent alkane is replaced with the -*one* suffix of the ketone family, and the location of the carbonyl carbon is indicated with a number. The longest carbon chain is numbered to give the carbonyl carbon the lowest possible number. For example,

$$\underset{1 \quad 2 \quad 3}{CH_3\overset{O}{\overset{\|}{-}}C-CH_3}$$

Propanone
(no number necessary)
(acetone)

$$\underset{4 \quad 3 \quad 2 \quad 1}{CH_3CH_2\overset{O}{\overset{\|}{-}}C-CH_3}$$

Butanone
(no number necessary)
(ethyl methyl ketone)

$$\underset{8 \quad 7 \quad 6 \quad 5 \quad 4 \quad 3 \quad 2 \quad 1}{CH_3CH_2CH_2CH_2\overset{O}{\overset{\|}{-}}C-CH_2CH_2CH_3}$$

4-Octanone
(*not* 5-octanone)
(butyl propyl ketone)

**TABLE 13.1 IUPAC and Common Names and Formulas for Several Aldehydes**

| IUPAC Name | Common Name | Formula |
|---|---|---|
| Methanal | Formaldehyde | $\underset{}{H-\overset{O}{\overset{\|}{C}}-H}$ |
| Ethanal | Acetaldehyde | $CH_3\overset{O}{\overset{\|}{C}}-H$ |
| Propanal | Propionaldehyde | $CH_3CH_2\overset{O}{\overset{\|}{C}}-H$ |
| Butanal | Butyraldehyde | $CH_3CH_2CH_2\overset{O}{\overset{\|}{C}}-H$ |
| Pentanal | Valeraldehyde | $CH_3CH_2CH_2CH_2\overset{O}{\overset{\|}{C}}-H$ |

**EXAMPLE 13.2** Comparing the Common and IUPAC Nomenclature Systems to Name Aldehydes

LEARNING GOAL

**2** From the structures, write the common and IUPAC names of aldehydes and ketones.

Name the two aldehydes represented by the following condensed formulas.

**Solution**

$$
\overset{\delta}{C}H_3\overset{\gamma}{C}H\overset{\beta}{C}H_2\overset{\alpha}{C}H_2\overset{O}{\overset{\|}{C}}-H
$$
$$
\underset{Br}{\mid}
$$

$$
\overset{\gamma}{C}H_3\overset{\beta}{C}H\overset{\alpha}{C}H_2\overset{CH_3}{\overset{\mid}{C}}\overset{O}{\overset{\|}{C}}-H
$$
$$
\underset{CH_3}{\mid}
$$

| | | |
|---|---|---|
| Parent compound: | pentane (becomes valeraldehyde) | butane (becomes butyraldehyde) |
| Position of carbonyl group: | carbon-1 | carbon-1 |
| Substituents: | γ-bromo | α, β-dimethyl |
| Common Name: | γ-Bromovaleraldehyde | α, β-Dimethylbutyraldehyde |

In the common system, the carbon atom bonded to the carbonyl group is called the α-carbon, the next is the β-carbon, etc. Greek letters are used to indicate the position of the substituents.

| | | |
|---|---|---|
| Parent compound: | pentane (becomes pentanal) | butane (becomes butanal) |
| Position of carbonyl group: | carbon-1 | carbon-1 |
| Substituents: | 4-bromo | 2,3-dimethyl |
| IUPAC name: | 4-Bromopentanal | 2,3 Dimethylbutanal |

In the IUPAC system, the carbonyl carbon is defined as carbon-1. Any substituents are numbered from that point in the chain to identify their locations.

Also remember that by definition, the carbonyl group is located at the beginning of the carbon chain of an aldehyde. Thus, it is not necessary to include the position of the carbonyl group in the name of the compound.

**Practice Problem 13.2**

Use the common nomenclature system to name each of the following compounds.

a. $CH_3\underset{CH_3}{\overset{CH_3}{\underset{\mid}{C}}}CHCHCH_2\overset{O}{\overset{\|}{C}}H$

b. $CH_3CH_2CH_2\underset{CH_2CH_3}{\overset{\mid}{C}}CH\overset{O}{\overset{\|}{C}}H$

c. $CH_3\underset{Cl}{\overset{\mid}{C}}CH\overset{O}{\overset{\|}{C}}H$

d. $CH_3\underset{OH}{\overset{\mid}{C}}CHCH_2\overset{O}{\overset{\|}{C}}H$

▶ For Further Practice: **Questions 13.6b and d, 13.41c and d, 13.42b.**

The common names of ketones are derived by naming the alkyl groups that are bonded to the carbonyl carbon. These are used as prefixes followed by the word *ketone*. The alkyl groups may be arranged alphabetically or by size (smaller to larger).

**EXAMPLE 13.3** Using the IUPAC Nomenclature System to Name Ketones

LEARNING GOAL

**2** From the structures, write the common and IUPAC names of aldehydes and ketones.

Name the following ketones using the IUPAC Nomenclature System.

*Continued…*

**Solution**

| | |
|---|---|
| Parent compound: | heptane (becomes heptanone) |
| Position of carbonyl group: | carbon-2 |
| Substituents: | 4-methyl |
| IUPAC Name: | 4-Methyl 2-heptanone |

nonane (becomes nonanone)

carbon-2

6, 8-dimethyl

6, 8-Dimethyl-2-nonanone

CH₃CH₂CH₂CHCH₂CCH₃ (positions 7 6 5 4 3 2 1), CH₃ at carbon; O double bond

CH₃CCH₂CH₂CH₂CHCH₂CHCH₃ (positions 1 2 3 4 5 6 7 8 9), CH₃ CH₃; O double bond

**Practice Problem 13.3**

Provide the IUPAC name for each of the following ketones.

a. CH₃CH₂CHCH₂CH₂CH₂CCH₃ with CH₂CH₃ branch, O double bond

b. CH₃CH₂CH₂CCHCH₃ with CH₃ branch, O double bond

c. CH₃CHCCHCH₃ with CH₃ CH₃ branches, O double bond

▶ For Further Practice: **Questions 13.7, 13.33a, 13.34a, 13.35b, 13.38, and 13.39.**

---

**EXAMPLE 13.4    Using the Common Nomenclature System to Name Ketones**

Name the ketones represented by the following condensed and line formulas.

**Solution**

Identify the alkyl groups that are bonded to the carbonyl carbon.

CH₃CH₂CH₂—C(=O)—CH₃     CH₃CH₂—C(=O)—CH₂CH₂CH₂CH₂CH₃

| | | |
|---|---|---|
| Alkyl groups: | propyl and methyl | ethyl and pentyl |
| Common Name: | Methyl propyl ketone | Ethyl pentyl ketone |

**Practice Problem 13.4**

Provide the common names for each of the following ketones:

a. CH₃CH₂CCH₂CH₃, O double bond

b. CH₃CH₂CH₂CH₂CCH₂CH₃, O double bond

c. CH₃CH₂CH₂CH₂CH₂CH₂CCH₃, O double bond

d. CH₃CHCCHCH₃ with CH₃ CH₃ branches, O double bond

▶ For Further Practice: **Questions 13.41a, b, and e and 13.42a and c.**

**LEARNING GOAL**

2  From the structures, write the common and IUPAC names of aldehydes and ketones.

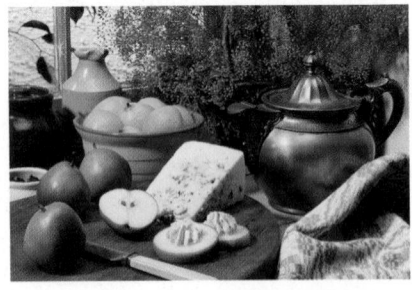

Two molecules that contribute to the aroma of blue cheese are 2-heptanone and 2-nonanone. Draw the condensed formula for each of these molecules.

**Question 13.5**  From the IUPAC names, draw the condensed formula for each of the following aldehydes.

a. 2,3-Dichloropentanal
b. 2-Bromobutanal
c. 4-Methylhexanal
d. Butanal
e. 2,4-Dimethylpentanal

**Question 13.6**  Write the condensed formula for each of the following compounds.

a. 3-Methylnonanal
b. β-Bromovaleraldehyde
c. 4-Fluorohexanal
d. α,β-Dimethylbutyraldehyde

**Question 13.7**  Use the IUPAC Nomenclature System to name each of the following compounds.

a.  $\underset{\underset{I}{|}}{CH_3CHCCH_3}$  (C=O)

c.  $\underset{\underset{CH_3}{|}}{CH_3CHCCH_3}$  (C=O)

e.  $\underset{\underset{F}{|}}{CH_3CHCCH_2CH_3}$  (C=O)

b.  $\underset{\underset{CH_2CH_2CH_2CH_3}{|}}{CH_3CHCH_2CCH_3}$  (C=O)

d.  $\underset{\underset{CH_3}{|}}{CH_3CHCCH_2CH_3}$  (C=O)

**Question 13.8**  Write the condensed formula for each of the following compounds.

a. Methyl isopropyl ketone (What is the IUPAC name for this compound?)
b. 4-Heptanone
c. 2-Fluorocyclohexanone
d. Hexachloroacetone (What is the IUPAC name of this compound?)

## 13.3  Important Aldehydes and Ketones

*Methanal* (formaldehyde) is a gas (b.p. −21°C). It is available commercially as an aqueous solution called *formalin*. Formalin has been used as a preservative for tissues and as an embalming fluid. See A Medical Perspective: Formaldehyde and Methanol Poisoning for more information on methanal.

    *Ethanal* (acetaldehyde) is produced from ethanol in the liver. Ethanol is oxidized in this reaction, which is catalyzed by the liver enzyme alcohol dehydrogenase. The ethanal that is produced in this reaction is responsible for the symptoms of a hangover.

    *Propanone* (acetone), the simplest ketone, is an important and versatile solvent for organic compounds. It has the ability to dissolve organic compounds and is also soluble in water. As a result, it has a number of industrial applications and is used as a solvent in adhesives, paints, cleaning solvents, nail polish, and nail polish remover. Propanone is flammable and should therefore be treated with appropriate care. *Butanone,* a four-carbon ketone, is also an important industrial solvent in the manufacture of plastics, paint remover, varnish, and glue.

    Many aldehydes and ketones are produced industrially as food and fragrance chemicals, medicinals, and agricultural chemicals. They are particularly important to the food industry, in which they are used as artificial and/or natural additives to food. Vanillin, a principal component of natural vanilla, is shown in Figure 13.3. Artificial vanilla flavoring is a dilute solution of synthetic vanillin dissolved in ethanol. Figure 13.3 also shows other examples of important aldehydes and ketones.

**Question 13.9**  Draw the structure of the aldehyde synthesized from ethanol in the liver.

**Question 13.10**  Draw the structure of a ketone that is an important, versatile solvent for organic compounds.

**LEARNING GOAL**

**3**  List several aldehydes and ketones that are of natural, commercial, health, and environmental interest and describe their significance.

Methanal

Ethanal

Propanone

Butanone

Benzaldehyde—almonds

Vanillin—vanilla beans

Cinnamaldehyde—cinnamon

Citral—lemongrass

α-Demascone—berry flavoring

2-Octanone—mushroom flavoring

**Figure 13.3** Important aldehydes and ketones.

## 13.4 Reactions Involving Aldehydes and Ketones

### Preparation of Aldehydes and Ketones

Aldehydes and ketones are prepared primarily by the **oxidation** of the corresponding alcohol. In organic systems, oxidation is recognized as a loss of hydrogen atoms or the gain of oxygen atoms. As we saw in Chapter 12, the oxidation of methyl alcohol gives methanal (formaldehyde). The oxidation of a primary alcohol produces an aldehyde, and the oxidation of a secondary alcohol yields a ketone. Tertiary alcohols do not undergo oxidation under the conditions normally used.

**LEARNING GOAL**

4 Write equations for the preparation of aldehydes and ketones by the oxidation of alcohols.

**EXAMPLE 13.5** Differentiating the Oxidation of Primary, Secondary, and Tertiary Alcohols

**LEARNING GOAL**

4 Write equations for the preparation of aldehydes and ketones by the oxidation of alcohols.

Use specific examples to show the oxidation of a primary, a secondary, and a tertiary alcohol.

**Solution**

The oxidation of a primary alcohol to an aldehyde:

1-Butanol
(butyl alcohol)

Butanal
(butyraldehyde)

The oxidation of a secondary alcohol to a ketone:

2-Hexanol

2-Hexanone

Tertiary alcohols cannot undergo oxidation:

2-Methyl-2-pentanol

In all these examples the symbol [O] is used to represent the oxidizing agent.

**Practice Problem 13.5**

Write equations showing the oxidation of (a) 1-propanol and (b) 2-butanol.

▶ For Further Practice: **Questions 13.57 and 13.58.**

# A MEDICAL PERSPECTIVE

## Formaldehyde and Methanol Poisoning

Most aldehydes have irritating, unpleasant odors, and formaldehyde is no exception. Formaldehyde is also an extremely toxic substance. As an aqueous solution, called formalin, it has been used to preserve biological tissues and for embalming. It has also been used to disinfect environmental surfaces, body fluids, and feces. Under no circumstances is it used as an antiseptic on human tissue because of its toxic fumes and the skin irritations that it causes.

Formaldehyde is used in the production of some killed-virus vaccines. When a potentially deadly virus, such as polio virus, is treated with heat and formaldehyde, the genetic information (RNA) is damaged beyond repair. The proteins of the virus also react with formaldehyde. However, the shape of the proteins, which is critical for a protective immune response against the virus, is not changed. Thus, when a child is injected with the Salk killed-virus polio vaccine, the immune system recognizes viral proteins and produces antibodies that protect against polio virus infection.

Formaldehyde can also be produced in the body! As we saw in Chapter 12, methanol can be oxidized to produce formaldehyde. In the body, the liver enzyme alcohol dehydrogenase, whose function it is to detoxify alcohols by oxidizing them, catalyzes the conversion of methanol to formaldehyde (methanal). The formaldehyde then reacts with cellular macromolecules, including proteins, causing severe damage (remember, it is used as an embalming agent!). As a result, methanol poisoning can cause blindness, respiratory failure, convulsions, and death.

Clever physicians have devised a treatment for methanol poisoning that is effective if administered soon enough after ingestion. Since the same enzyme that oxidizes methanol to formaldehyde (methanal) also oxidizes ethanol to acetaldehyde (ethanal), doctors reasoned that administering an intravenous solution of ethanol to the patient could protect against the methanol poisoning. If the ethanol concentration in the body is higher than the methanol concentration, most of the alcohol dehydrogenase enzymes of the liver will be carrying out the oxidation of the ethanol. This is called *competitive inhibition* because the methanol and ethanol molecules are competing for binding to the enzymes. The molecule that is in the higher concentration will more frequently bind to the enzyme and undergo reaction. In this case, the result is that the alcohol dehydrogenase enzymes are kept busy oxidizing ethanol and producing the less-toxic (not nontoxic) product, acetaldehyde. This gives the body time to excrete the methanol before it is oxidized to the potentially deadly formaldehyde.

### For Further Understanding

▶ Acetaldehyde is described as less toxic than formaldehyde. Do some background research on the effects of these two aldehydes on biological systems.

▶ You have studied enzymes in previous biology courses. Using what you learned in those classes with information from Sections 19.4 and 19.10 in this text, put together an explanation of the way in which competitive inhibition works. Can you think of other types of poisoning for which competitive inhibition might be used to develop an effective treatment?

## Oxidation Reactions

Aldehydes are oxidized to carboxylic acids, whereas ketones do not generally undergo further oxidation. The reason is that a carbon-hydrogen bond, present in the aldehyde but not in the ketone, is needed for the reaction to occur. In fact, aldehydes that are liquids are difficult to store because they can be oxidized by oxygen in the air. In some cases they must be stored under nitrogen gas. The following example shows a general equation for the oxidation of an aldehyde to a carboxylic acid:

$$\underset{\text{Aldehyde}}{R-\overset{\overset{\displaystyle O}{\|}}{C}-H} \quad \xrightarrow{\text{[O]}} \quad \underset{\text{Carboxylic acid}}{R-\overset{\overset{\displaystyle O}{\|}}{C}-OH}$$

In basic solution, the product is the carboxylic acid anion:

$$CH_3-\overset{\overset{\displaystyle O}{\|}}{C}-O^-$$

*The rules for naming carboxylic acid anions are described in Section 14.1.*

Many oxidizing agents can be used. Both basic potassium permanganate and potassium chromate are good oxidizing agents, as the following specific example shows:

$$\underset{\substack{\text{Ethanal}\\\text{(acetaldehyde)}}}{CH_3-\overset{\overset{\displaystyle O}{\|}}{C}-H} \quad \xrightarrow[\text{OH}^-]{\text{KMnO}_4} \quad \underset{\substack{\text{Ethanoate anion}\\\text{(acetate anion)}}}{CH_3-\overset{\overset{\displaystyle O}{\|}}{C}-O^-}$$

The oxidation of benzaldehyde to benzoic acid is an example of the conversion of an aromatic aldehyde to the corresponding aromatic carboxylic acid:

Benzaldehyde                Benzoic acid

Aldehydes and ketones can be distinguished on the basis of the fact that aldehydes are readily oxidized and ketones are not. The most common laboratory test for aldehydes is the **Tollens' test.** When exposed to the Tollens' reagent, a basic solution of $Ag(NH_3)_2^+$, an aldehyde undergoes oxidation. The silver ion ($Ag^+$) is reduced to silver metal ($Ag^0$) as the aldehyde is oxidized to a carboxylic acid anion.

Aldehyde  Silver ammonia complex— Tollens' reagent   Carboxylate anion   Silver metal mirror

Silver metal precipitates from solution and coats the flask, producing a smooth silver mirror, as seen in Figure 13.4. The test is therefore often called the Tollens' silver mirror test. The commercial manufacture of silver mirrors uses a similar process. Ketones cannot be oxidized to carboxylic acids and do not react with the Tollens' reagent.

**EXAMPLE 13.6  Writing Equations for the Reaction of an Aldehyde and of a Ketone with Tollens' Reagent**

Write equations for the reaction of propanal and 2-pentanone with Tollens' reagent.

LEARNING GOAL

5 Write equations representing the oxidation of carbonyl compounds.

**Solution**

Propanal                Propanoate anion

2-Pentanone

**Practice Problem 13.6**

Write equations for the reaction of (a) ethanal and (b) propanone with Tollens' reagent.

▶ For Further Practice: **Questions 13.62 and 13.67.**

Another test that is used to distinguish between aldehydes and ketones is **Benedict's test.** Here, a buffered aqueous solution of copper(II) hydroxide and sodium citrate reacts to oxidize aldehydes but does not generally react with ketones. $Cu^{2+}$ is reduced to $Cu^+$ in the process. $Cu^{2+}$ is soluble and gives a blue solution, whereas the $Cu^+$ precipitates as the red solid copper(I) oxide, $Cu_2O$.

All simple sugars (monosaccharides) are either aldehydes or ketones. Glucose is an aldehyde sugar that is commonly called *blood sugar* because it is the sugar

(a)

(b)

(c)

**Figure 13.4** The silver precipitate produced by the Tollens' reaction is deposited on glass. The progress of the reaction is visualized in panels (a) through (c). Silver mirrors are made in a similar process.

**Figure 13.5** The amount of precipitate formed and thus the color change observed in the Benedict's test are directly proportional to the amount of reducing sugar in the sample.

found transported in the blood and used for energy by many cells. In uncontrolled diabetes, glucose may be found in the urine. One early method used to determine the amount of glucose in the urine was to observe the color change of the Benedict's test. The amount of precipitate formed is directly proportional to the amount of glucose in the urine (Figure 13.5). The reaction of glucose with the Benedict's reagent is represented in the following equation:

$$
\begin{array}{c}
\underset{\text{Glucose}}{
\begin{array}{c}
\text{O}\quad\text{H} \\
\diagdown\text{C}\diagup \\
| \\
\text{H}-\text{C}-\text{OH} \\
| \\
\text{HO}-\text{C}-\text{H} \\
| \\
\text{H}-\text{C}-\text{OH} \\
| \\
\text{H}-\text{C}-\text{OH} \\
| \\
\text{CH}_2\text{OH}
\end{array}
}
+ 2\text{Cu}^{2+}
\xrightarrow{\text{OH}^-}
\begin{array}{c}
\text{O}\quad\text{O}^- \\
\diagdown\text{C}\diagup \\
| \\
\text{H}-\text{C}-\text{OH} \\
| \\
\text{HO}-\text{C}-\text{H} \\
| \\
\text{H}-\text{C}-\text{OH} \\
| \\
\text{H}-\text{C}-\text{OH} \\
| \\
\text{CH}_2\text{OH}
\end{array}
+ \text{Cu}_2\text{O}
\end{array}
$$

We should also note that when the carbonyl group of a ketone is bonded to a $-\text{CH}_2\text{OH}$ group, the molecule will give a positive Benedict's test. This occurs because such ketones are converted to aldehydes under basic conditions. In Chapter 16 we will see that this applies to the ketone sugars, as well. They are converted to aldehyde sugars and react with Benedict's reagent.

## Reduction Reactions

*One way to recognize reduction, particularly in organic chemistry, is the gain of hydrogen. Oxidation and reduction are discussed in Section 12.5.*

Aldehydes and ketones are both readily reduced to the corresponding alcohol by a variety of reducing agents. Throughout the text the symbol [H] over the reaction arrow represents a reducing agent.

The classical method of aldehyde or ketone reduction is **hydrogenation.** The carbonyl compound is reacted with hydrogen gas and a catalyst (nickel, platinum, or palladium metal) in a pressurized reaction vessel. Heating may also be necessary. The carbon-oxygen double bond (the carbonyl group) is reduced to a carbon-oxygen single bond. The addition of hydrogen to a carbon-oxygen double bond is shown in the following general equation:

# A HUMAN PERSPECTIVE

## Alcohol Abuse and Antabuse

According to a study carried out by the Centers for Disease Control and Prevention,[1] more than 75,000 Americans die each year as a result of alcohol abuse. Of these, nearly 35,000 people died of cirrhosis of the liver, cancer, or other drinking-related diseases. The remaining nearly 41,000 died in alcohol-related automobile accidents. Of those who died, 72% were men and 6% were under the age of twenty-one. In fact, a separate study has estimated that 1400 college-age students die each year of alcohol-related causes.

These numbers are striking. Alcohol abuse is now the third leading cause of preventable death in the United States, outranked only by tobacco use and poor diet and exercise habits. As the study concluded, "These results emphasize the importance of adopting effective strategies to reduce excessive drinking, including increasing alcohol excise taxes and screening for alcohol misuse in clinical settings."

Tetraethylthiuram disulfide
(disulfiram)
Antabuse

One approach to treatment of alcohol abuse, the drug tetraethylthiuram disulfide or disulfiram, has been used since 1951. The activity of this drug, generally known by the trade name Antabuse, was discovered accidentally by a group of Danish researchers who were testing it for antiparasitic properties. They made the observation that those who had taken disulfiram became violently ill after consuming any alcoholic beverage.

Further research revealed that this compound inhibits one of the liver enzymes in the pathway for the oxidation of alcohols.

In Chapter 12 we saw that ethanol is oxidized to ethanal (acetaldehyde) in the liver. This reaction is catalyzed by the enzyme alcohol dehydrogenase. Acetaldehyde, which is more toxic than ethanol, is responsible for many of the symptoms of a hangover. The enzyme acetaldehyde dehydrogenase oxidizes acetaldehyde into ethanoic acid (acetic acid), which then is used in biochemical pathways that harvest energy for cellular work or that synthesize fats.

Antabuse inhibits acetaldehyde dehydrogenase. This inhibition occurs within 1 to 2 hours (h) of taking the drug and continues up to 14 days. When a person who has taken Antabuse drinks an alcoholic beverage, the level of acetaldehyde quickly reaches levels that are five to ten times higher than would normally occur after a drink. Within just a few minutes, the symptoms of a severe hangover are experienced and may continue for several hours.

Experts in drug and alcohol abuse have learned that drugs such as Antabuse are generally not effective on their own. However, when used in combination with support groups and/or psychotherapy to solve underlying behavioral or psychological problems, Antabuse is an effective deterrent to alcohol abuse.

1. Alcohol-Attributable Deaths and Years of Potential Life Lost—United States, 2001, Morbidity and Mortality Weekly Report, 53 (37): 866–870, September 24, 2004, also available at http://www.cdc.gov/mmwr/preview/mmwrhtml/mm5337a2.htm.

### For Further Understanding

▶ Antabuse alone is not a cure for alcoholism. Consider some of the reasons why this is so.

▶ Write equations showing the oxidation of ethanal to ethanoic acid as a pathway with the product of the first reaction serving as the reactant for the second. Explain the physiological effects of Antabuse in terms of these chemical reactions.

The hydrogenation (reduction) of a ketone produces a secondary alcohol, as seen in the following equation showing the reduction of the ketone, 3-octanone:

*Hydrogenation was first discussed in Section 11.5 for the hydrogenation of alkenes.*

3-Octanone
(A ketone)          Hydrogen          3-Octanol
(A secondary alcohol)

**EXAMPLE 13.7**  **Writing an Equation Representing the Hydrogenation of a Ketone**

Write an equation showing the hydrogenation of 3-pentanone.

**Solution**

The product of the reduction of a ketone is a secondary alcohol, in this case, 3-pentanol.

$$CH_3CH_2\overset{\overset{\displaystyle O}{\|}}{C}CH_2CH_3 + H_2 \xrightarrow{Pt} CH_3CH_2\overset{\overset{\displaystyle OH}{|}}{\underset{\underset{\displaystyle H}{|}}{C}}CH_2CH_3$$

3-Pentanone                           3-Pentanol

**Practice Problem 13.7**

Write an equation for the hydrogenation of (a) propanone and (b) butanone.

▶ For Further Practice: **Question 13.64.**

The hydrogenation of an aldehyde results in the production of a primary alcohol, as seen in the following equation showing the reduction of the aldehyde, butanal:

$$CH_3CH_2CH_2\overset{\overset{\displaystyle O}{\|}}{C}H + H_2 \xrightarrow{Pt} CH_3CH_2CH_2\overset{\overset{\displaystyle OH}{|}}{\underset{\underset{\displaystyle H}{|}}{C}}H$$

Butanal          Hydrogen          1-Butanol
(An aldehyde)                       (A primary alcohol)

**EXAMPLE 13.8**  **Writing an Equation Representing the Hydrogenation of an Aldehyde**

Write an equation showing the hydrogenation of 3-methylbutanal.

**Solution**

Recall that the reduction of an aldehyde results in the production of a primary alcohol, in this case, 3-methyl-1-butanol.

$$CH_3\underset{\underset{\displaystyle CH_3}{|}}{C}HCH_2\overset{\overset{\displaystyle O}{\|}}{C}H + H_2 \xrightarrow{Pt} CH_3\underset{\underset{\displaystyle CH_3}{|}}{C}HCH_2\overset{\overset{\displaystyle OH}{|}}{\underset{\underset{\displaystyle H}{|}}{C}}H$$

3-Methylbutanal                    3-Methyl-1-butanol

**Practice Problem 13.8**

Write equations for the hydrogenation of 3,4-dimethylhexanal and 2-chloropentanal.

▶ For Further Practice: **Questions 13.65 and 13.66.**

A biological example of the reduction of a ketone occurs in the body, particularly during strenuous exercise when the lungs and circulatory system may not be able to provide enough oxygen to the muscles. Under these circumstances, the lactate fermentation begins. In this reaction, the enzyme *lactate dehydrogenase* reduces pyruvate, the product of glycolysis (a pathway for the breakdown of glucose) into lactate. The reducing agent for this reaction is nicotinamide adenine dinucleotide (NADH).

*The role of the lactate fermentation in exercise is discussed in greater detail in Section 21.4.*

NADH is a donor of hydride anions in biological reduction reactions, such as the formation of lactate from pyruvate, and it is oxidized in the reaction. Let's take a closer look at this reaction:

**Question 13.11**   Label each of the following as an oxidation or a reduction reaction.
  a. Ethanal to ethanol
  b. Benzoic acid to benzaldehyde
  c. Cyclohexanone to cyclohexanol
  d. 2-Propanol to propanone
  e. 2,3-Butanedione (found in butter) to 2,3-butanediol

**Question 13.12**   Write an equation for each of the reactions in Question 13.11.

## Addition Reactions

The principal reaction of the carbonyl group is the **addition reaction** across the polar carbon-oxygen double bond. This reaction is very similar to some that we have already studied, addition across the carbon-carbon double bond of alkenes. Such reactions require that a catalytic amount of acid be present in solution, as shown by the $H^+$ over the arrow for the reactions shown in the following examples.

An example of an addition reaction is the reaction of aldehydes and ketones with alcohols in the presence of catalytic amounts of acid. In this reaction, the hydrogen of the alcohol adds to the carbonyl oxygen. The alkoxy group of the alcohol (—OR) adds to the carbonyl carbon. The predicted product is a **hemiacetal**. A hemiacetal is characterized by a carbon that is bonded to one hydroxyl group (—OH) and one alkoxy group (—OR).

LEARNING GOAL

7  Write equations for the preparation of hemiacetals and acetals.

*Addition reactions of alkenes are described in detail in Section 11.5.*

General structure of a hemiacetal

## KITCHEN CHEMISTRY

### The Allure of Truffles

Truffles are the fruiting body of fungi of the genus *Tuber*. They are remarkably ugly, roughly round and warty in appearance, and have an aroma variously described as "nutty," "musky," and "stinky." Nonetheless, truffles are one of the most highly prized ingredients in most of the finest kitchens in the world. In fact, the white truffle has been described as the "diamond of the kitchen."

Truffles grow under a limited variety of trees, including oak, beech, and poplar. They may be as deep as 1 meter (m) underground and only grow in the fall and winter of the year. Traditionally, they were harvested using truffle-sniffing pigs. These pigs were able to detect the smell of the chemicals the truffle produces to attract animals who will eat them and spread their spores to other sites through their feces. Today trained dogs are used to find the truffles because of a tendency of the pigs to eat the truffles before they could be harvested! With prices as high as $500 per pound (lb) for black truffles and $2000 per lb for white truffles, harvesters couldn't afford to have the pigs feasting on them!

The flavor of the truffles is a direct result of their aroma. The compounds that produce that aroma are only produced as the spores mature, which is why it is useful to use animals to locate the scent of the truffles when they are at their peak. Many have studied the compounds in truffles that produce the aroma, and hence the flavor. They have found as many as thirty-six components of that flavor profile, including alcohols, aldehydes, ketones, carboxylic acids, esters, amines, aromatic compounds, and hydrocarbons—virtually an entire organic chemistry laboratory! Two alcohols and two aldehydes are found in the highest concentrations. These are 2-methylbutanol, 3-methylbutanol, 2-methylbutanal, and 3-methylbutanal. The flavor profile is rounded out by several sulfur compounds, including dimethylsulfide, 2,4-pentanedithiol, and 2,4,6-heptanetrithiol. In fact, it is the dimethylsulfide that attracts animals to the fruiting bodies.

As we have learned in this chapter, alcohols and aldehydes such as these in the truffle flavor profile are easily oxidized. When that happens, the truffle loses the molecules that are characteristic of its aroma and flavor. Fresh truffles must be used quickly and stored carefully to retain the flavor. Often, truffles are sold in a preserved form that has a shelf-life as long as 2 years.

The truffle is becoming much more rare. While it was reported in 1890 that 2200 tons (t) of truffles were harvested, now only about 150 are harvested. The truffle can only grow in association with certain trees and those trees only support truffles for about 15–30 years. To renew the harvest, tree saplings that have been inoculated with spores are being planted in areas with the right type of soil. However, it requires about 7 years before these trees begin to produce the precious fruiting bodies.

Truffles will continue to be a much sought-after delicacy, and science is helping us understand the chemical complexity of this unlovely fungus, as well as ways to ensure that we will be able to enjoy its remarkable flavors in the centuries to come.

#### For Further Understanding

▶ Draw the structures of the molecules that are responsible for the flavor profile of truffles.

▶ Write equations for the oxidation reactions that destroy the complex aroma and flavor of truffles.

In the following reactions notice that the alkoxy group (—OR) of the alcohol adds to the carbonyl carbon and the hydrogen of the hydroxyl group adds to the carbonyl oxygen. The following equations show the addition of ethanol to cyclohexylmethanal and propanone:

$$
\begin{array}{c}
\overset{\displaystyle O}{\underset{\displaystyle H}{\|}}\ \overset{\displaystyle H}{\underset{\displaystyle |}{}} \\
\bigcirc\!\!-\!\!\overset{|}{\underset{|}{C}}\ +\ O\!-\!CH_2CH_3 \quad \xrightleftharpoons{H^+} \quad \bigcirc\!\!-\!\!\overset{O-H}{\underset{H}{\overset{|}{C}}}\!\!-\!OCH_2CH_3
\end{array}
$$

Cyclohexylmethanal   Ethanol                                                    A Hemiacetal

$$CH_3\overset{\overset{\displaystyle O}{\|}}{C} + \overset{\overset{\displaystyle H}{|}}{O} - CH_2CH_3 \;\rightleftharpoons\; CH_3\overset{\overset{\displaystyle O-H}{|}}{\underset{\underset{\displaystyle CH_3}{|}}{C}} - OCH_2CH_3$$

$$\underset{\displaystyle CH_3}{|}$$

Propanone    Ethanol                                A Hemiacetal

Hemiacetals are generally unstable. In the presence of acid and excess alcohol, they undergo a substitution reaction in which the —OH group of the hemiacetal is exchanged for another —OR group from the alcohol. The product of this reaction is an **acetal.** Acetal formation is a reversible reaction, as the general equation shows:

Aldehyde   Alcohol          Hemiacetal                    Acetal
or
Ketone

Notice that the acetal is characterized by a carbon bonded to two alkoxy groups (—OR).

$$\overset{\overset{\displaystyle OR^3}{|}}{R^1 - C - OR^4}$$
$$\underset{\displaystyle R^2}{|}$$

Acetal formation is seen in the following equations that represent the acid-catalyzed reactions between propanal and methanol and between propanone and ethanol.

Propanal        Methanol              Hemiacetal                      Acetal

Propanone        Ethanol               Hemiacetal                      Acetal

**Question 13.13**   Identify each of the following structures as a hemiacetal or acetal.

**Question 13.14**    Identify each of the following structures as a hemiacetal or acetal.

a.
$$CH_2CH_3$$
$$H-\underset{\underset{OCH_3}{|}}{\overset{\overset{|}{}}{C}}-OH$$

c.
$$CH_3$$
$$H-\underset{\underset{OCH_3}{|}}{\overset{\overset{|}{}}{C}}-OCH_2CH_3$$

b.
$$CH_3$$
$$CH_3CH_2-\underset{\underset{OCH_3}{|}}{\overset{\overset{|}{}}{C}}-OH$$

d.
$$CH_3$$
$$H_3C-\underset{\underset{OCH_2CH_3}{|}}{\overset{\overset{|}{}}{C}}-OCH_3$$

Earlier we noted that hemiacetals formed in intermolecular reactions are unstable and continue to react, forming acetals. This is not the case with intramolecular hemiacetal formation, reactions in which the hydroxyl group and the carbonyl group are part of the same molecule, that produce five- or six-membered rings. In these cases the cyclic hemiacetals are very stable. Consider the following reaction in which an intramolecular hemiacetal is formed from 4-hydroxyheptanal:

4-Hydroxyheptanal

Bring carbonyl and hydroxyl groups together

Show bond formation

A Cyclic Hemiacetal

This reaction is very important in the chemistry of the carbohydrates, in which hemiacetals are readily formed. Monosaccharides contain several hydroxyl groups and one carbonyl group. The linear form of a monosaccharide quickly undergoes an intramolecular reaction in solution to produce a cyclic hemiacetal. In these reactions the cyclic or ring form of the molecule is more stable than the linear form. This reaction is shown for the sugar glucose (blood sugar) in Figure 13.6 and is discussed in detail in Section 16.2.

When the hemiacetal of one monosaccharide reacts with the hydroxyl group of another monosaccharide, the product is an acetal. A sugar molecule made up of two monosaccharides is called a *disaccharide*. The C—O—C or acetal bond between the two monosaccharides is called a *glycosidic bond*. An example of this is found in Figure 13.7, which depicts the formation of the disaccharide lactose (milk sugar) from the monosaccharides glucose and galactose. Notice that the acetal is formed between the hemiacetal hydroxyl group of galactose (in blue) and an alcohol hydroxyl group of glucose (in red).

**Figure 13.6** Hemiacetal formation in sugars, shown for the intramolecular reaction of D-glucose.

**Figure 13.7** Acetal formation, demonstrated in the formation of the disaccharide lactose, milk sugar. The reaction between the hemiacetal hydroxyl group of the monosaccharide galactose (blue) and an alcohol hydroxyl group of the monosaccharide glucose (red) produces the acetal lactose. The bond between the two sugars is a glycosidic bond.

## Keto-Enol Tautomers

Many aldehydes and ketones may exist in an equilibrium mixture of two constitutional or structural isomers called tautomers. **Tautomers** differ from one another in the placement of a hydrogen atom and a double bond. One tautomer is the *keto form* (on the left in the following equation). The keto form has the structure typical of an aldehyde or ketone. The other form is called the *enol form* (on the right in the following equation). The **enol** form has a structure containing a carbon-carbon double bond (*en*) and a hydroxyl group, the functional group characteristic of alcohols (*ol*).

**LEARNING GOAL**

**8** Draw the keto and enol forms of aldehydes and ketones.

Keto form          Enol form

Because the keto form of most simple aldehydes and ketones is more stable, they exist mainly in that form.

**EXAMPLE 13.9**   **Writing an Equation Representing the Equilibrium Between the Keto and Enol Forms of a Simple Aldehyde**

Draw the keto form of ethanal and write an equation representing the equilibrium between the keto and enol forms of this molecule.

**Solution**

$$H\underset{\underset{H}{|}}{\overset{\overset{H\ \ O}{|\ \ \|}}{-C-C}}-H \;\rightleftharpoons\; H\underset{\underset{H}{|}}{-C=\overset{\overset{O-H}{|}}{C}}-H$$

Ethanal
Keto form
More stable

Enol form
Less stable

**Practice Problem 13.9**

Draw the keto and enol forms of (a) propanal and (b) 3-pentanone.

▶ For Further Practice: **Questions 13.79 and 13.80.**

Phosphoenolpyruvate is a biologically important phosphorylated enol. Note that the molecule has a phosphoryl group ($-PO_4^{-2}$) in place of a hydroxyl group (–OH). The bond between the carbon and the phosphoryl group is represented by a "squiggle" (~) to show that this is a high energy bond. In fact, phosphoenolpyruvate is the highest energy phosphorylated compound in living systems.

$$^-O-\overset{\overset{O}{\|}}{\underset{\underset{O^-}{|}}{P}}-O{\sim}\overset{\overset{\overset{O^-}{|}}{C=O}}{\underset{\underset{CH_2}{\|}}{C}}$$

Phosphoenolpyruvate

*The glycolysis pathway is discussed in detail in Chapter 21.*

Phosphoenolpyruvate is produced in the next-to-last step in the metabolic pathway called *glycolysis,* which is the first stage of carbohydrate breakdown. In the final reaction of glycolysis, the phosphoryl group from phosphoenolpyruvate, along with energy from the high energy bond, are transferred to adenosine diphosphate (ADP). The reaction produces ATP, the major energy currency of the cell.

The following examples illustrate naming carboxylic acids with two carboxyl groups:

$$\overset{O}{\overset{\|}{HO-C}}-\overset{1\ 2\ 3\ 4\ 5}{CH_2CH_2CH_2CH_2}-\overset{6\ O}{\overset{\|}{C}}-OH$$

Hexanedioic acid
(adipic acid)

$$\overset{O}{\overset{\|}{HO-C}}-\overset{1\ 2}{CH_2}-\overset{3\ O}{\overset{\|}{C}}-OH$$

Propanedioic acid
(malonic acid)

LEARNING GOAL

**2** Determine the common and IUPAC names of carboxylic acids.

---

**EXAMPLE 14.1**  **Use the IUPAC Nomenclature System to Name a Carboxylic Acid**

a. The following compound is one of the monomers from which a biodegradable plastic called Biopol is made (see Green Chemistry: Garbage Bags from Potato Peels? later in this chapter). Name this carboxylic acid using the IUPAC nomenclature system.

$$\overset{5}{\phantom{a}}\overset{4}{\phantom{a}}\overset{3}{\phantom{a}}\overset{2}{\phantom{a}}\overset{1}{COOH}\ \ \ OH$$

$$\overset{5\ 4\ 3\ 2\ 1}{CH_3CH_2CHCH_2C}\overset{O}{\overset{\|}{}}-OH$$
$$\overset{\ \ \ \ \ \ \ \ }{OH}$$

**Solution**

Parent compound: pentane (becomes pentanoic acid)
Position of —COOH: carbon-1 (must be!)
Substituent: 3-hydroxy
Name: 3-Hydroxypentanoic acid

b. Name the following carboxylic acid:

$$\overset{8}{\phantom{a}}\overset{7}{\phantom{a}}\overset{6}{\phantom{a}}\overset{5}{\phantom{a}}\overset{4}{\phantom{a}}\overset{3}{\phantom{a}}\overset{2}{\phantom{a}}\overset{1}{COOH}$$
$$Br\ \ \ Br\ \ \ Br$$

$$\overset{8\ \ \ 7\ \ 6\ \ \ 5\ \ 4\ \ \ 3\ \ 2\ \ \ 1}{CH_3CHCH_2CHCH_2CHCH_2-C}\overset{O}{\overset{\|}{}}-OH$$
$$\ \ \ \ \ \ Br\ \ \ \ \ Br\ \ \ \ \ Br$$

**Solution**

Parent compound: octane (becomes octanoic acid)
Position of —COOH: carbon-1 (must be!)
Substituents: 3,5,7-bromo
Name: 3,5,7-Tribromooctanoic acid

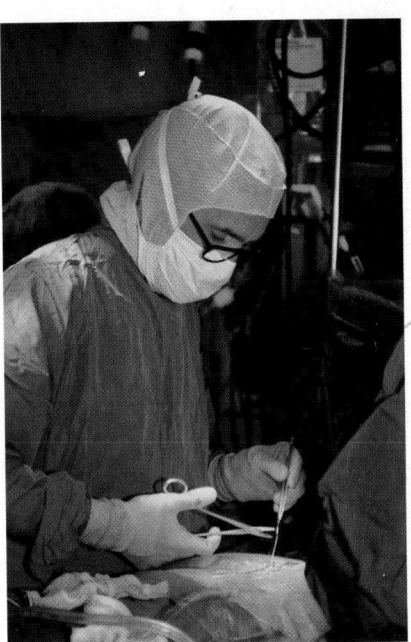

Polymers of lactic acid are used as biodegradable sutures. What is the IUPAC name of lactic acid, shown below?

$$CH_3CHCOOH$$
$$\ \ \ \ \ \ OH$$

---

**Practice Problem 14.1**

Determine the IUPAC name for each of the following structures. Remember that —COOH is an alternative way to represent the carboxyl group.

a. $\overset{CH_3}{\underset{}{CH_3CHCH_2}}\overset{CH_3}{\underset{}{CHCOOH}}$

b. $\underset{Cl\ \ \ \ Cl}{CH_2CH_2CHCOOH}$

c. $\underset{\phantom{a}}{CH_3}\overset{OH}{\underset{OH}{CHCHCOOH}}$

d. $\overset{\ \ \ \ \ \ \ \ \ \ \ \ \ Cl}{CH_3CH_2CHCHCHCOOH}$
$\ \ \ \ \ \ \ \ \ \ \ \ \ CH_3\ \ Br$

▶ For Further Practice: **Questions 14.32, 14.35, and 14.36.**

The carboxylic acid derivatives of cycloalkanes are named by adding the suffix *carboxylic acid* to the name of the cycloalkane or substituted cycloalkane. The carboxyl group is always on carbon-1 and other substituents are named and numbered as usual.

Cyclohexanecarboxylic acid

**Question 14.5** Determine the IUPAC name for each of the following structures.

a.     COOH

CH₃

b.     COOH

CH₂CH₃

**Question 14.6** Write the structure for each of the following carboxylic acids.

a. 1,4-Cyclohexanedicarboxylic acid
b. 4-Hydroxycyclohexanecarboxylic acid

As we have seen so often, the use of common names, rather than systematic names, persists. Often these names have evolved from the source of a given compound. This is certainly true of the carboxylic acids. Table 14.1 shows the IUPAC and common names of several carboxylic acids, as well as their sources and the Latin or Greek words that gave rise to the common names. Not only are the prefixes different than those used in the IUPAC system, the suffix is different as well. Common names end in *-ic acid* rather than *-oic acid*.

In the common system of nomenclature, substituted carboxylic acids are named as derivatives of the parent compound (see Table 14.1). Greek letters are

**LEARNING GOAL**

**2** Determine the common and IUPAC names of carboxylic acids.

**TABLE 14.1 Names and Sources of Some Common Carboxylic Acids**

| Name | Structure | Source | Root |
|---|---|---|---|
| Formic acid (methanoic acid) | HCOOH | Ants | L: *formica*, ant |
| Acetic acid (ethanoic acid) | CH₃COOH | Vinegar | L: *acetum*, vinegar |
| Propionic acid (propanoic acid) | CH₃CH₂COOH | Swiss cheese | Gk: *protos*, first; *pion*, fat |
| Butyric acid (butanoic acid) | CH₃(CH₂)₂COOH | Rancid butter | L: *butyrum*, butter |
| Valeric acid (pentanoic acid) | CH₃(CH₂)₃COOH | Valerian root | |
| Caproic acid (hexanoic acid) | CH₃(CH₂)₄COOH | Goat fat | L: *caper*, goat |
| Caprylic acid (octanoic acid) | CH₃(CH₂)₆COOH | Goat fat | L: *caper*, goat |
| Capric acid (decanoic acid) | CH₃(CH₂)₈COOH | Goat fat | L: *caper*, goat |
| Palmitic acid (hexadecanoic acid) | CH₃(CH₂)₁₄COOH | Palm oil | |
| Stearic acid (octadecanoic acid) | CH₃(CH₂)₁₆COOH | Tallow (beef fat) | Gk: *stear*, tallow |

*Note:* IUPAC names are shown in parentheses.

used to indicate the position of the substituent. The carbon atom bonded to the carboxyl group is the α-carbon, the next is the β-carbon, and so on.

$$\overset{\delta}{-C}-\overset{\gamma}{C}-\overset{\beta}{C}-\overset{\alpha}{C}-\overset{O}{C}-OH$$

Some examples of common names are

$$\overset{\gamma}{CH_3}\overset{\beta}{CH}\overset{\alpha}{CH_2}\overset{O}{C}-OH$$
$$\underset{OH}{|}$$

β-Hydroxybutyric acid

$$\overset{\beta}{CH_3}\overset{\alpha}{CH}\overset{O}{C}-OH$$
$$\underset{OH}{|}$$

α-Hydroxypropionic acid

β-Hydroxybutyric acid is the other monomer used to make the biodegradable plastic Biopol (see Example 14.1).

### EXAMPLE 14.2  Naming Carboxylic Acids Using the Common System of Nomenclature

LEARNING GOAL

2  Determine the common and IUPAC names of carboxylic acids.

Write the common name for each of the following carboxylic acids.

(structure with Br, β α, COOH)   (structure with Cl, γ β α, COOH)

$$\overset{\beta}{CH_3CH_2CH_2}\overset{\alpha}{CH}CH_2\overset{O}{C}-OH$$
$$\underset{Br}{|}$$

$$CH_3\overset{\gamma}{CH}\overset{\beta}{CH_2}\overset{\alpha}{CH_2}\overset{O}{C}-OH$$
$$\underset{Cl}{|}$$

#### Solution

| | | |
|---|---|---|
| Parent compound: | caproic acid | valeric acid |
| Substituents: | β-bromo | γ-chloro |
| Name: | β-Bromocaproic acid | γ-Chlorovaleric acid |

### Practice Problem 14.2

Provide the common name for each of the following molecules. Keep in mind that the carboxyl group can be represented as —COOH.

a. CH₃CHCH₂CHCOOH
    |        |
    CH₃   CH₃

b. CH₂CH₂CHCOOH
   |        |
   Cl      Cl

c. CH₃CHCHCH₂COOH
      |    |
      Br  Br

d. CH₃CH₂CHCH₂CH₂COOH
          |
          OH

▶ For Further Practice: **Questions 14.31, 14.37, and 14.38.**

Benzoic acid is the simplest aromatic carboxylic acid.

(benzene ring with C(=O)—OH)

Benzoic acid

# CHEMISTRY AT THE CRIME SCENE

## Carboxylic Acids and the Body Farm

Dr. Arpad Vass of Oak Ridge National Laboratory explains his unusual vocation in the following way, "Each year there are about 90,000 homicides in this country and for every one, you need to know when the person died. Our research can help answer the where and when, and that should help law enforcement officials solve crimes." Time and location of death are key pieces of information in a criminal investigation. Whether a suspect is convicted or goes free may rest on an accurate estimate of the time since death (TSD). Dr. Vass and graduate student Jennifer Love study decomposing bodies on a research plot in Tennessee. Although its official name is University of Tennessee Anthropological Research Facility, it has been called the "Body Farm" since Patricia Cornwell published a novel of that name in 1994.

Vass and Love are trying to develop an instrument that can sample the air around a corpse to determine the concentrations of certain carboxylic acids, also referred to as volatile fatty acids. What they envision is a "tricorder"-like device that will sample the air for valeric acid, propionic acid, and the straight and branched types of butyric acid. Because the ratio of these carboxylic acids changes in a predictable way following death, measurement of their relative concentrations, from air or from the soil under the corpse, could provide an accurate TSD.

The research is done by taking daily measurements of the air around decomposing bodies at the "Body Farm." At death, the proteins and lipids of the body begin to break down. This decomposition produces, among other substances, the carboxylic acids being studied. The bodies may be placed in various environments so that the researchers can study the effects of different temperature and moisture levels on the process of decomposition. The more that is learned about the amounts and types of organic compounds produced during decomposition under different conditions, the more precise the TSD determinations will be. In fact, Vass considers that these processes are a chemical "clock" and is working to refine the accuracy of that clock so that, eventually, TSD may be measured accurately in hours, rather than days.

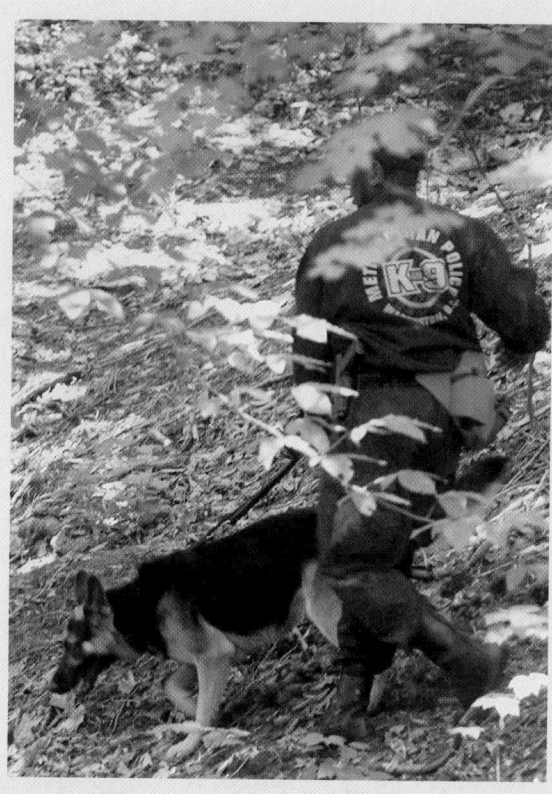

### For Further Understanding

▶ Draw the structures of the carboxylic acids described in this article and write their IUPAC names.

▶ The bones of a murdered 9-year-old boy were found lying on his father's property. Immediately the father was suspected of having killed the child. A sample of the soil under the boy's bones was sent to Dr. Vass for analysis. No volatile fatty acids were found in the soil sample. What can you conclude from these data?

---

*Nomenclature of aromatic compounds is described in Section 11.6.*

In many cases the aromatic carboxylic acids are named, in either system, as derivatives of benzoic acid. Generally, the *-oic acid* suffix is used in the IUPAC system and the *-ic acid* suffix is used in the common system and is attached to the appropriate prefix. However, "common names" of substituted benzoic acids (for example, toluic acid and phthalic acid) are frequently used.

*m*-Toluic acid

*o*-Bromobenzoic acid

*m*-Iodobenzoic acid

Phthalic acid

Often the phenyl group is treated as a substituent, and the name is derived from the appropriate alkanoic acid parent chain. For example:

O
‖
CH₂C—OH

2-Phenylethanoic acid
(α-phenylacetic acid)

O
‖
CH₂CH₂C—OH

3-Phenylpropanoic acid
(β-phenylpropionic acid)

The phenyl group is benzene with one hydrogen removed.

Phenyl group

The benzyl group is toluene with one hydrogen removed from the methyl group:

—CH₂–

Benzyl group

---

**EXAMPLE 14.3**  Naming Aromatic Carboxylic Acids

**LEARNING GOAL**

**2** Determine the common and IUPAC names of carboxylic acids.

a. Name the following aromatic carboxylic acid.

O
‖
C—OH

Cl

**Solution**

It is simplest to name the compound as a derivative of benzoic acid. The substituent, Cl, is attached to carbon-4 of the benzene ring. This compound is 4-chlorobenzoic acid or *p*-chlorobenzoic acid.

b. Name the following aromatic carboxylic acid.

CH₃     O
|       ‖
CHCH₂CH₂C—OH

**Solution**

This compound is most easily named by treating the phenyl group as a substituent. The phenyl group is bonded to carbon-4 (or the γ-carbon, in the common system of nomenclature). The parent compound is pentanoic acid (valeric acid in the common system). Hence the name of this compound is 4-phenylpentanoic acid or γ-phenylvaleric acid.

---

**Practice Problem 14.3**

Draw structures for each of the following compounds.

a. *o*-Toluic acid
b. 2,4,6-Tribromobenzoic acid
c. 2,2,2-Triphenylethanoic acid
d. *p*-Toluic acid
e. 3-Phenylhexanoic acid
f. 3-Phenylcyclohexanecarboxylic acid

▶ For Further Practice: **Questions 14.39 and 14.40.**

# GREEN CHEMISTRY

## Garbage Bags from Potato Peels?

One problem facing society is its enormous accumulation of trash. To try to control the mountains of garbage that we produce, many institutions and towns practice recycling of aluminum, paper, and plastics. One problem that remains, however, is the plastic trash bag. We stuff the trash bag full of biodegradable garbage and bury it in a landfill; but soil bacteria can't break down the plastic to get to the bio-degradable materials inside. Imagine a twenty-fourth century archeologist excavating one of these monuments to our society!

The good news is that laboratory research and products of bacterial metabolism are providing new materials that have the properties of plastics, but are readily biodegradable. For instance, sheets of plastic can be made by making polymers of lactic acid, which is a natural carboxylic acid produced by fermentation of sugars, particularly in milk and working muscle. Because many common soil bacteria can break down polylactic acid (PLA), trash bags made from this polymer would be quickly broken down in landfill soil.

Making plastic from lactic acid requires a huge supply of this carboxylic acid. As it turns out, we can produce an enormous quantity of lactic acid from garbage. When french fries are produced, nearly half of the potato is wasted. That amounts to about ten billion pounds (lb) of potato waste each year. When cheese is made, the curds are separated from the whey, and several billion gallons (gal) of whey are poured down the drain each year. Potato waste and whey can easily be broken down to produce glucose, which, in turn, can be converted into lactic acid used to make biodegradable plastics. PLA plastics have been available since the early 1990s and have been used successfully for sutures, medical implants, and drug delivery systems.

Other researchers have experimented with heteropolymers, polymers composed of two or more different monomers. One such polymer with useful properties is a heteropolymer of β-hydroxybutyric acid and β-hydroxyvaleric acid, which has been given the name Biopol.

$$n\ H_3C-\overset{\overset{\displaystyle H}{|}}{\underset{\underset{\displaystyle OH}{|}}{C}}-\overset{\overset{\displaystyle H}{|}}{\underset{\underset{\displaystyle H}{|}}{C}}-\overset{\displaystyle O}{C}-OH\ +\ n\ H_3C-\overset{\overset{\displaystyle H}{|}}{\underset{\underset{\displaystyle H}{|}}{C}}-\overset{\overset{\displaystyle H}{|}}{\underset{\underset{\displaystyle OH}{|}}{C}}-\overset{\overset{\displaystyle H}{|}}{\underset{\underset{\displaystyle H}{|}}{C}}-\overset{\displaystyle O}{C}-OH$$

β-Hydroxybutyric acid          β-Hydroxyvaleric acid

$$\left[-O-\overset{\overset{\displaystyle CH_3}{|}}{\underset{\underset{\displaystyle H}{|}}{C}}-\overset{\overset{\displaystyle H}{|}}{\underset{\underset{\displaystyle H}{|}}{C}}-\overset{\displaystyle O}{C}-O-\overset{\overset{\displaystyle CH_2CH_3}{|}}{\underset{\underset{\displaystyle H}{|}}{C}}-\overset{\overset{\displaystyle H}{|}}{\underset{\underset{\displaystyle H}{|}}{C}}-\overset{\displaystyle O}{C}-O-\right]_n$$

Biopol—a heteropolymer

Biopol has properties that make it commercially useful, and it is completely broken down into carbon dioxide and water by microorganisms in the soil. Thus, it is completely biodegradable. Because bacteria produced a low yield of Biopol, scientists produced transgenic plants in hopes that they would produce high yields of the polymer. This approach also encountered problems.

For the time being, biodegradable plastics cannot outcompete their nonbiodegradable counterparts. Future research and development will be required to reduce the cost of commercial production and fulfill the promise of an "environmentally friendly" garbage bag.

### For Further Understanding

▶ Why are biodegradable plastics useful as sutures?
▶ Two hydrogen atoms are lost in each reaction that adds a carboxylic acid to the polymers described here. What type of chemical reaction is this?

$$n\ H_3C-\overset{\overset{\displaystyle H}{|}}{\underset{\underset{\displaystyle OH}{|}}{C}}-\overset{\displaystyle O}{C}-OH\ \longrightarrow\ \left[-O-\overset{\overset{\displaystyle CH_3}{|}}{\underset{\underset{\displaystyle H}{|}}{C}}-\overset{\displaystyle O}{C}-O-\overset{\overset{\displaystyle CH_3}{|}}{\underset{\underset{\displaystyle H}{|}}{C}}-\overset{\displaystyle O}{C}-O-\right]_n$$

Lactic acid                   Polylactic acid (PLA)

## Some Important Carboxylic Acids

As Table 14.1 shows, many carboxylic acids occur in nature. The stinging sensation of an ant bite is caused by methanoic (formic) acid, and ethanoic (acetic) acid provides the acidic zip to vinegars. Propanoic (propionic) acid is the product of bacterial fermentation of milk products and is most notable as a tangy component in the characteristic flavor of Swiss cheese.

Several of the larger carboxylic acids have foul odors. For instance, butanoic (butyric) acid is the odor associated with rancid butter and is produced by the bacteria that cause gas gangrene, contributing to the characteristic smell of the necrotic tissue. Pentanoic (valeric) acid is associated with the valerian plant, which has long been known to have an aroma alternately described as over-ripe cheese or a wet dog. Nonetheless, extracts of valerian have been used for thousands of years as a natural sedative. Hexanoic (caproic) acid was first isolated from goats and, fittingly, is described as smelling like a goat. Heptanoic (enanthic) acid is also foul smelling and is associated with the odor of rancid oil.

These foul-smelling carboxylic acids have a far more pleasant potential, however. When carboxylic acids react with alcohols, the products are esters, which contribute to the lovely fragrance and flavor of many fruits.

Octanoic (caprylic) acid has an interesting function in the chemistry of human appetite. The hormone ghrelin, produced in the stomach, is sometimes called the "hunger hormone" because it stimulates the hypothalamus of the brain to signal that the body is hungry. However, the hormone alone does not have this effect. Ghrelin must be covalently bonded to a molecule of octanoic acid in order to have the hunger-stimulating effect on the hypothalamus.

Fatty acids are long-chain monocarboxylic acids and can be isolated from a variety of sources including palm oil, coconut oil, butter, milk, lard, and animal fat, including tallow (beef fat). These fatty acids, in the form of triglycerides, are the major energy storage form in mammals and many plants. When the fatty acids in the triglyceride are saturated, the result is solid fat, as in animal fats. When the fatty acids are unsaturated, the result is a liquid, as in olive oil and canola oil.

Several common dicarboxylic acids are show in Table 14.2. Oxalic acid is a dicarboxylic acid found in spinach and rhubarb. Human kidney stones are often formed from the calcium salt of oxalic acid. In fact, it is toxic in high concentrations and foods with high levels of oxalic acid must be boiled before being eaten. While oxalic acid is used in industry as a bleaching agent and spot remover, the potassium salt is used in clinical laboratories to prevent blood samples from coagulating.

*To learn more about the fragrances and flavors of esters, see A Human Perspective: The Chemistry of Flavor and Fragrance later in this chapter.*

*A triglyceride is a molecule of glycerol (Section 12.3) bonded to three fatty acid molecules by esterification (Sections 14.2 and 17.3).*

**TABLE 14.2 Common Dicarboxylic Acids**

| Common Name | IUPAC Name | Condensed Formula | Line Formula |
|---|---|---|---|
| Oxalic acid | Ethanedioic acid | HOOCCOOH | |
| Malonic acid | Propanedioic acid | $HOOCCH_2COOH$ | |
| Succinic acid | Butanedioic acid | $HOOC(CH_2)_2COOH$ | |
| Glutaric acid | Pentanedioic acid | $HOOC(CH_2)_3COOH$ | |
| Adipic acid | Hexanedioic acid | $HOOC(CH_2)_4COOH$ | |

Malonic acid is used in the synthesis of barbiturates. Succinic acid is one of the intermediates in the citric acid cycle, a metabolic pathway involved in the breakdown of carbohydrates, lipids, and proteins to harvest energy for cellular functions. The name comes from the Latin word for amber (L. *succinum*) because it was first isolated from crushed amber. Glutaric acid is used in the production of several types of condensation polymers, including polyester, polyols, and polyamides. It is useful because it has an odd number of carbons in the chain, which reduces the elasticity of the polymer. Adipic acid (hexanedioic acid) gives tartness to soft drinks and helps retard food spoilage. However, the greatest demand for adipic acid (2.5 billion kilograms (kg) per year) is for the synthesis of nylon and polyurethane, and of plasticizers that are particularly useful in the manufacture of polyvinyl chloride (PVC).

More complex carboxylic acids are found in a variety of foods. For example, citric acid is found in citrus fruits and is often used to give the sharp taste to sour candies. It is also added to foods as a preservative and antioxidant.

Bacteria in milk produce lactic acid as a product of fermentation of sugars. Lactic acid contributes a tangy flavor to yogurt and buttermilk. It is also used as a food preservative to lower the pH to a level that retards microbial growth that causes food spoilage. Lactic acid is produced in muscle cells when an individual is exercising strenuously. If the level of lactic acid in the muscle and bloodstream becomes high enough, the muscle can't continue to work.

Tartaric acid is used in baking powder because it will undergo a reaction with carbonates in the dough, producing $CO_2$ that will cause the bread or cake to rise. It has also been used as a laxative. Malic acid gives the sour taste to green apples. Since the amount of malic acid decreases as a fruit ripens, the fruit becomes sweeter and less tart as it ripens.

Several aromatic carboxylic acids are also of medical interest. The sodium salt of benzoic acid is used as a preservative in soft drinks, pickles, jellies, and many other foods and some cosmetics. It is of value as a preservative because it is colorless, odorless, and tasteless, and will kill bacteria at a concentration of only 0.1%.

Salicylic acid is used as a disinfectant and, in fact, is superior to phenol. It is also used in ointments to remove corns or warts because it causes the top layer of the skin to flake off, leaving the underlying living skin undamaged.

Acetylsalicylic acid is aspirin. As early as the fifth century BC, the revered physician Hippocrates described a bitter extract from willow bark that could reduce fevers and relieve pain. Ancient texts from the Middle East reveal that Egyptian and Sumerian physicians appreciated the medicinal value of willow bark, and Native Americans used it to treat headache, fever, and chills, as well as sore muscles. In 1828, Henri Leroux isolated crystals of the compound that came to be called salicin. Nearly 70 years later, in 1897, chemists at Bayer and Company chemically added an acetyl group to salicin, synthesizing acetylsalicylic acid, a derivative that did not produce the severe gastrointestinal side effects caused by salicin. Thus, aspirin became the first synthetic drug, launching the pharmaceutical industry. Today, aspirin is recommended in low daily doses by the American Heart Association as a preventive measure against heart attacks and strokes caused by blood clots.

Benzoic acid          Salicylic acid          Acetylsalicylic acid

As we will see in the next section, terephthalic acid is primarily used to synthesize polyethylene terephthalate (PETE). Because this polymer is so useful, in excess of 30 million tons (t) of terephthalic acid is needed each year.

Terephthalic acid

## Reactions Involving Carboxylic Acids

### Preparation of Carboxylic Acids

Many of the small carboxylic acids are prepared on a commercial scale. For example, ethanoic (acetic) acid, found in vinegar, is produced commercially by the **oxidation** of either ethanol or ethanal as shown here:

Ethanol          Ethanal          Ethanoic acid

A variety of oxidizing agents, including oxygen, can be used, and catalysts are often required to provide acceptable yields. Other simple carboxylic acids can be made by oxidation of the appropriate primary alcohol or aldehyde. The general reaction is

R−CH₂OH    Primary alcohol          Aldehyde          Carboxylic acid

**LEARNING GOAL**

4 Write equations that show the synthesis of a carboxylic acid.

*Oxidation reactions involving aldehydes and primary alcohols were discussed in Sections 12.4 and 13.4.*

### EXAMPLE 14.4  Writing Equations for the Oxidation of a Primary Alcohol to a Carboxylic Acid

Write an equation showing the oxidation of 1-propanol to propanoic acid.

**LEARNING GOAL**

4 Write equations that show the synthesis of a carboxylic acid.

**Solution**

1-Propanol (propyl alcohol)     Propanal (propionaldehyde)     Propanoic acid (propionic acid)

### Practice Problem 14.4

Write equations showing the synthesis of (a) ethanoic acid, (b) butanoic acid, and (c) octanoic acid by oxidation of the corresponding primary alcohol.

▶ For Further Practice: **Questions 14.49 and 14.50.**

## Acid-Base Reactions

The carboxylic acids behave as acids because they are proton donors. They are weak acids that dissociate to form a carboxylate ion and a hydrogen ion, as shown in the following equation:

*The properties of weak acids are described in Sections 8.1 and 8.2.*

*LeChatelier's principle is described in Section 7.4.*

Carboxylic acids are weak acids because they dissociate only slightly in solution. The majority of the acid remains in solution in the undissociated form. Typically, less than 5% of the acid is ionized (approximately five carboxylate ions to every ninety-five carboxylic acid molecules).

When strong bases are added to a carboxylic acid, neutralization occurs. The acid protons are removed by the $OH^-$ to form water and the carboxylate ion. The position of the equilibrium shown in the reaction above is shifted to the right, owing to removal of $H^+$. This is an illustration of LeChatelier's principle.

The carboxylate anion and the cation of the base form the carboxylic acid salt.

The following examples show the neutralization of acetic acid and benzoic acid in solutions of the strong base NaOH.

Sodium benzoate is commonly used as a food preservative.

Note that the salt of a carboxylic acid is named by replacing the *-ic acid* suffix with *-ate*. Thus acetic acid becomes acetate, and benzoic acid becomes benzoate. This name is preceded by the name of the appropriate cation, sodium in the examples above.

**EXAMPLE 14.5** Writing an Equation to Show the Neutralization of a Carboxylic Acid by a Strong Base

Write an equation showing the neutralization of propanoic acid by sodium hydroxide.

**5** Write equations representing acid-base reactions of carboxylic acids.

**Solution**

The protons of the acid are removed by the $OH^-$ of the base. This produces water. The cation of the base, in this case sodium ion, forms the salt of the carboxylic acid.

$$CH_3CH_2-\overset{\overset{\textstyle O}{\|}}{C}-OH \ + \ NaOH \longrightarrow CH_3CH_2-\overset{\overset{\textstyle O}{\|}}{C}-O^-Na^+ \ + \ H_2O$$

Propanoic acid        Sodium hydroxide        Sodium salt of propanoic acid        Water

**Practice Problem 14.5**

Write the formula of the organic product obtained through each of the following reactions.

a. $CH_3CH_2COOH + KOH \longrightarrow ?$

b. $CH_3CH_2CH_2COOH + Ba(OH)_2 \longrightarrow ?$

c. $CH_3CH_2CH_2CH_2CH_2COOH + KOH \longrightarrow ?$

d. Benzoic acid + sodium hydroxide $\longrightarrow ?$

▶ For Further Practice: **Questions 14.52a, b, and c, 14.55, and 14.56.**

**EXAMPLE 14.6** Naming the Salt of a Carboxylic Acid

Write the common and IUPAC names of the salt produced in the reaction shown in Example 14.5.

**Solution**

$$CH_3CH_2-\overset{\overset{\textstyle O}{\|}}{C}-O^-Na^+$$

| | |
|---|---|
| IUPAC name of the parent carboxylic acid: | Propanoic acid |
| Replace the -ic acid ending with -ate: | Propanoate |
| Name of the cation of the base: | Sodium |
| Name of the carboxylic acid salt: | Sodium propanoate |
| Common name of the parent carboxylic acid: | Propionic acid |
| Replace the -ic acid ending with -ate: | Propionate |
| Name of the cation of the base: | Sodium |
| Name of the carboxylic acid salt: | Sodium propionate |

**Practice Problem 14.6**

Name the products of the reactions in Practice Problem 14.5.

▶ For Further Practice: **Questions 14.57 and 14.58.**

Carboxylic acid salts are ionic substances. As a result, they are very soluble in water. The long-chain carboxylic acid salts (fatty acid salts) are called *soaps*.

*Soaps are made by a process called saponification, which is the base-catalyzed hydrolysis of an ester. This is described in detail in Section 14.2.*

LEARNING GOAL

**6** Write equations representing the preparation of an ester.

## Esterification

Carboxylic acids react with alcohols to form esters and water according to the general reaction:

$$R^1-\overset{\overset{\displaystyle O}{\|}}{C}-OH + R^2OH \underset{\longleftarrow}{\overset{Acid}{\longrightarrow}} R^1-\overset{\overset{\displaystyle O}{\|}}{C}-OR^2 + H_2O$$

Carboxylic    Alcohol         Ester     Water
acid

The details of these reactions will be examined in Section 14.2.

## 14.2   Esters

LEARNING GOAL

**7** Write structures and describe the physical properties of esters.

### Structure and Physical Properties

**Esters** are slightly polar and have pleasant aromas. Many esters are found in natural foodstuffs; banana oil (3-methylbutyl ethanoate; common name, isoamyl acetate), pineapples (ethyl butanoate; common name, ethyl butyrate), and raspberries (isobutyl methanoate; common name, isobutyl formate) are but a few examples.

    Esters boil at approximately the same temperature as aldehydes or ketones of comparable molar mass. The simpler ones are somewhat soluble in water.

*See A Human Perspective: The Chemistry of Flavor and Fragrance later in this chapter.*

### Nomenclature

Esters are **carboxylic acid derivatives,** organic compounds derived from carboxylic acids. They are formed from the reaction of a carboxylic acid with an alcohol, and both of these reactants are reflected in the naming of the ester. They are named according to the following set of rules:

LEARNING GOAL

**8** Determine the common and IUPAC names of esters.

- Use the *alkyl* or *aryl* portion of the alcohol name as the first name.
- The *-ic acid* ending of the name of the carboxylic acid is replaced with *-ate* and follows the first name.

    For example, in the following reaction, ethanoic acid reacts with methanol to produce methyl ethanoate:

$$CH_3\overset{\overset{\displaystyle O}{\|}}{C}-OH + CH_3OH \underset{\longleftarrow}{\overset{H^+,\ heat}{\longrightarrow}} CH_3\overset{\overset{\displaystyle O}{\|}}{C}-OCH_3 + H_2O$$

Ethan*oic acid*   *Methanol*         *Methyl* ethano*ate*
(acetic acid)   (methyl alcohol)      (methyl acetate)

    Similarly, acet*ic acid* and *ethanol* react to produce *ethyl* acet*ate*, and the product of the reaction between benzo*ic acid* and *isopropyl* alcohol is *isopropyl* benzo*ate*.

    Naming esters is analogous to naming the salts of carboxylic acids. Consider the following comparison:

$$CH_3\overset{\overset{\displaystyle O}{\|}}{C}-O^- \quad Na^+ \qquad\qquad CH_3\overset{\overset{\displaystyle O}{\|}}{C}-O-CH_2CH_3$$

Sodium ethanoate          Ethyl ethanoate
(sodium acetate)          (ethyl acetate)

As shown in this example, the alkyl group of the alcohol, rather than $Na^+$, has displaced the acidic hydrogen of the carboxylic acid.

| **EXAMPLE 14.7** | **Naming Esters Using the IUPAC and Common Nomenclature Systems** | **LEARNING GOAL** |

a. The molecule shown below contributes to the flavor of pineapple. Write the IUPAC and common names for this ester.

**8** Determine the common and IUPAC names of esters.

$$CH_3CH_2CH_2\overset{\overset{\displaystyle O}{\|}}{C}-OCH_2CH_3$$

**Solution**

|  | IUPAC | Common |
|---|---|---|
| IUPAC and common names of parent carboxylic acid: | butanoic acid | butyric acid |
| Replace the *-ic acid* ending of the carboxylic acid with *-ate*: | butanoate | butyrate |
| Name of the alkyl portion of the alcohol: | ethyl | ethyl |
| IUPAC and common names of the ester: | Ethyl butanoate | Ethyl butyrate |

b. The molecule shown below is associated with the characteristic flavor of apricots. Write the common and IUPAC names of this ester.

$$CH_3CH_2CH_2\overset{\overset{\displaystyle O}{\|}}{C}-OCH_2CH_2CH_2CH_2CH_3$$

**Solution**

|  | IUPAC | Common |
|---|---|---|
| IUPAC and common names of parent carboxylic acid: | butanoic acid | butyric acid |
| Replace the *-ic acid* ending of the carboxylic acid with *-ate*: | butanoate | butyrate |
| Name of the alkyl portion of the alcohol: | pentyl | pentyl |
| IUPAC and common names of the ester: | Pentyl butanoate | Pentyl butyrate |

**Practice Problem 14.7**

Name each of the following esters using both the IUPAC and common nomenclature systems.

a.
$$CH_3CH_2CH_2\overset{\overset{\displaystyle O}{\|}}{C}-OCH_2CH_2CH_3$$

c.
$$CH_3\overset{\overset{\displaystyle O}{\|}}{C}-OCH_2CH_2CH_3$$

b.
$$CH_3CH_2CH_2\overset{\overset{\displaystyle O}{\|}}{C}-OCH_2CH_3$$

d.
$$CH_3CH_2\overset{\overset{\displaystyle O}{\|}}{C}-OCH_2CH_2CH_2CH_3$$

▶ For Further Practice: **Questions 14.63, 14.64, and 14.66.**

## Reactions Involving Esters

### Preparation of Esters

The conversion of a carboxylic acid to an ester requires heat and is catalyzed by a trace of acid ($H^+$). When esters are prepared directly from a carboxylic acid and an alcohol, a water molecule is lost, as in the reaction:

**6** Write equations representing the preparation of an ester.

$$\underset{\substack{\text{Carboxylic}\\\text{acid}}}{R^1-\overset{\displaystyle O}{\overset{\|}{C}}-OH} + \underset{\text{Alcohol}}{R^2OH} \underset{\xrightarrow{\hspace{1cm}}}{\overset{H^+,\,\text{heat}}{\rightleftharpoons}} \underset{\text{Ester}}{R^1-\overset{\displaystyle O}{\overset{\|}{C}}-OR^2} + \underset{\text{Water}}{H_2O}$$

$$\underset{\substack{\text{Propanoic acid}\\\text{(propionic acid)}}}{CH_3CH_2\overset{\displaystyle O}{\overset{\|}{C}}-OH} + \underset{\substack{\text{Methanol}\\\text{(methyl alcohol)}}}{CH_3OH} \overset{H^+,\,\text{heat}}{\rightleftharpoons} \underset{\substack{\text{Methyl propanoate}\\\text{(methyl propionate)}}}{CH_3CH_2\overset{\displaystyle O}{\overset{\|}{C}}-OCH_3} + H-O-H$$

Esterification is reversible. The direction of the reaction is determined by the conditions chosen. Excess alcohol favors ester formation. The carboxylic acid is favored when excess water is present.

Esterification is a *condensation* reaction, so called because a water molecule is removed during the reaction.

---

**EXAMPLE 14.8**  **Writing Equations Representing Esterification Reactions**

**LEARNING GOAL**

Write an equation showing the esterification reactions that would produce ethyl butanoate and propyl ethanoate.

**6** Write equations representing the preparation of an ester.

**Solution**

The name, ethyl butanoate, tells us that the alcohol used in the reaction is ethanol and the carboxylic acid is butanoic acid. We must remember that a trace of acid and heat are required for the reaction and that the reaction is reversible. With this information, we can write the following equation representing the reaction:

$$\underset{\substack{\text{Butanoic acid}\\\text{(butyric acid)}}}{CH_3CH_2CH_2\overset{\displaystyle O}{\overset{\|}{C}}-OH} + \underset{\text{Ethanol}}{CH_3CH_2OH} \overset{H^+,\,\text{heat}}{\rightleftharpoons} \underset{\substack{\text{Ethyl butanoate}\\\text{(ethyl butyrate)}}}{CH_3CH_2CH_2\overset{\displaystyle O}{\overset{\|}{C}}-OCH_2CH_3} + H_2O$$

Similarly, the name propyl ethanoate reveals that the alcohol used in this reaction is 1-propanol and the carboxylic acid must be ethanoic acid. Knowing that we must indicate that the reaction is reversible and that heat and a trace of acid are required, we can write the following equation:

$$\underset{\substack{\text{Ethanoic acid}\\\text{(acetic acid)}}}{CH_3\overset{\displaystyle O}{\overset{\|}{C}}-OH} + \underset{\substack{\text{1-Propanol}\\\text{(propyl alcohol)}}}{CH_3CH_2CH_2OH} \overset{H^+,\,\text{heat}}{\rightleftharpoons} \underset{\substack{\text{Propyl ethanoate}\\\text{(propyl acetate)}}}{CH_3\overset{\displaystyle O}{\overset{\|}{C}}-OCH_2CH_2CH_3} + H_2O$$

**Practice Problem 14.8**

Write an equation showing the esterification reactions that would produce (a) butyl ethanoate and (b) ethyl propanoate.

▶ For Further Practice: **Questions 14.73 and 14.74.**

**EXAMPLE 14.9**   Designing the Synthesis of an Ester

LEARNING GOAL

6 Write equations representing the preparation of an ester.

Design the synthesis of ethyl propanoate from organic alcohols.

**Solution**

The ease with which alcohols are oxidized to aldehydes, ketones, or carboxylic acids (depending on the alcohol that you start with and the conditions that you employ), coupled with the ready availability of alcohols, provides the pathway necessary to many successful synthetic transformations. For example, let's develop a method for synthesizing ethyl propanoate, using an oxidizing agent and limiting yourself to organic alcohols that contain three or fewer carbon atoms:

$$CH_3CH_2\overset{\overset{\displaystyle O}{\|}}{C}-O-CH_2CH_3$$

Ethyl propanoate
(ethyl propionate)

Ethyl propanoate can be made from propanoic acid and ethanol:

$$CH_3CH_2\overset{\overset{\displaystyle O}{\|}}{C}-OH + CH_3CH_2OH \underset{}{\overset{H^+, heat}{\rightleftharpoons}} CH_3CH_2\overset{\overset{\displaystyle O}{\|}}{C}-O-CH_2CH_3 + H_2O$$

Propanoic acid    Ethanol    Ethyl propanoate
(propionic acid)   (ethyl alcohol)   (ethyl propionate)

Ethanol is a two-carbon alcohol that is an allowed starting material, but propanoic acid is not. Can we now make propanoic acid from an alcohol of three or fewer carbons? Yes!

$$CH_3CH_2CH_2OH \overset{[O]}{\rightarrow} CH_3CH_2\overset{\overset{\displaystyle O}{\|}}{C}-H \overset{[O]}{\rightarrow} CH_3CH_2\overset{\overset{\displaystyle O}{\|}}{C}-OH$$

1-Propanol    Propanal    Propanoic acid
(propyl alcohol)   (propionaldehyde)   (propionic acid)

1-Propanol is a three-carbon alcohol, an allowed starting material. The synthesis is now complete. By beginning with ethanol and 1-propanol, ethyl propanoate can be synthesized easily by the reaction shown in the equation above.

**Practice Problem 14.9**

Design the synthesis of (a) methyl butanoate and (b) propyl methanoate from organic alcohols.

▶ For Further Practice: **Questions 14.75 and 14.76.**

**Hydrolysis of Esters**

**Hydrolysis** refers to cleavage of any bond by the addition of a water molecule. Esters undergo hydrolysis reactions in water, as shown in the general reaction:

LEARNING GOAL

9 Write equations representing the hydrolysis of an ester.

$$R^1-\overset{\overset{\displaystyle O}{\|}}{C}-OR^2 + H_2O \underset{}{\overset{H^+, heat}{\rightleftharpoons}} R^1-\overset{\overset{\displaystyle O}{\|}}{C}-OH + R^2OH$$

Ester    Water    Carboxylic    Alcohol
acid

# A HUMAN PERSPECTIVE

## The Chemistry of Flavor and Fragrance

Carboxylic acids are often foul smelling. For instance, butyric acid is one of the worst smelling compounds imaginable—the smell of rancid butter.

$$CH_3CH_2CH_2\overset{\displaystyle O}{\overset{\displaystyle \|}{C}}{-}OH$$

Butanoic acid
(butyric acid)

Butyric acid is also a product of fermentation reactions carried out by *Clostridium perfringens*. This organism is the most common cause of gas gangrene. Butyric acid contributes to the notable foul smell accompanying this infection.

By forming esters of butyric acid, a chemist can generate compounds with pleasant smells. Ethyl butyrate is the essence of pineapple oil.

Volatile esters are often pleasant in both aroma and flavor. Natural fruit flavors are complex mixtures of many esters and other organic compounds. Chemists can isolate these mixtures and identify the chemical components. With this information they are able to synthesize artificial fruit flavors, using just a few of the esters found in the natural fruit. As a result, the artificial flavors rarely have the full-bodied flavor of nature's original blend.

Raspberries

$$H{-}\overset{\displaystyle O}{\overset{\displaystyle \|}{C}}{-}OCH_2\underset{\displaystyle \underset{\displaystyle CH_3}{|}}{C}HCH_3$$

Isobutyl methanoate
(isobutyl formate)

Pineapple

$$CH_3CH_2CH_2\overset{\displaystyle O}{\overset{\displaystyle \|}{C}}{-}OCH_2CH_3$$

Ethyl butanoate
(ethyl butyrate)

Bananas

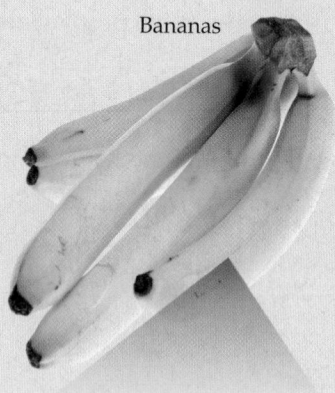

$$CH_3\overset{\displaystyle O}{\overset{\displaystyle \|}{C}}{-}OCH_2CH_2\underset{\displaystyle \underset{\displaystyle CH_3}{|}}{C}HCH_3$$

3-Methylbutyl ethanoate
(isoamyl acetate)

Oranges

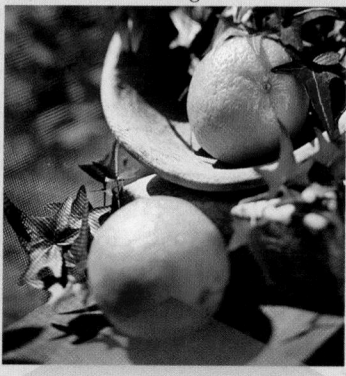

$$CH_3\overset{\displaystyle O}{\overset{\|}{C}}-OCH_2CH_2CH_2CH_2CH_2CH_2CH_2CH_3$$

Octyl ethanoate
(octyl acetate)

Apples

$$CH_3CH_2CH_2\overset{\displaystyle O}{\overset{\|}{C}}-OCH_3$$

Methyl butanoate
(methyl butyrate)

Apricots

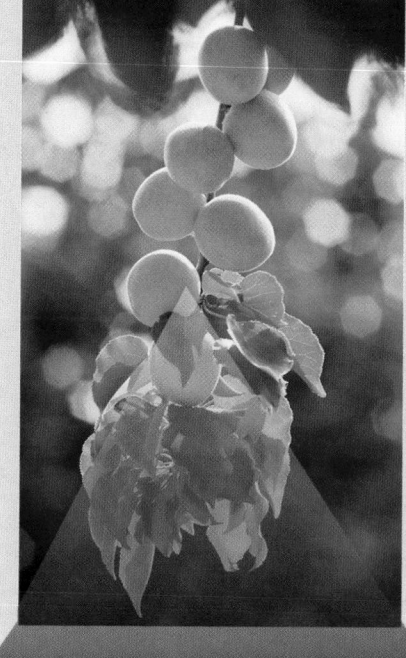

$$CH_3CH_2CH_2\overset{\displaystyle O}{\overset{\|}{C}}-OCH_2CH_2CH_2CH_2CH_3$$

Pentyl butanoate
(pentyl butyrate)

Strawberries

$$CH_3CH_2CH_2\overset{\displaystyle O}{\overset{\|}{C}}-SCH_3$$

Methyl thiobutanoate
(methyl thiobutyrate)
(a thioester in which sulfur replaces oxygen)

**For Further Understanding**

▶ Draw the structure of methyl salicylate, which is found in oil of wintergreen.

▶ Write an equation for the synthesis of each of the esters shown in this Perspective.

This reaction requires heat. A small amount of acid ($H^+$) may be added to catalyze the reaction, as in the following example:

$$CH_3CH_2\overset{\overset{\displaystyle O}{\|}}{C}-OCH_2CH_2CH_3 + H_2O \underset{}{\overset{H^+, heat}{\rightleftharpoons}} CH_3CH_2\overset{\overset{\displaystyle O}{\|}}{C}-OH + CH_3CH_2CH_2OH$$

Propyl propanoate          Propanoic acid     1-Propanol
(propyl propionate)         (propionic acid)    (propyl alcohol)

LEARNING GOAL

**10** Define the term *saponification* and describe how soap works in the emulsification of grease and oil.

The base-catalyzed hydrolysis of an ester is called **saponification.**

$$R^1-\overset{\overset{\displaystyle O}{\|}}{C}-OR^2 + H_2O \overset{OH^-, heat}{\longrightarrow} R^1-\overset{\overset{\displaystyle O}{\|}}{C}-O^- + R^2OH$$

Ester      Water             Carboxylic   Alcohol
                              acid anion

Under basic conditions (NaOH or KOH) the acid cannot exist. Thus, the reaction yields the salt of the carboxylic acid having the cation of the basic catalyst.

$$CH_3\overset{\overset{\displaystyle O}{\|}}{C}-OCH_2CH_2CH_2CH_3 \overset{NaOH, heat}{\longrightarrow} CH_3\overset{\overset{\displaystyle O}{\|}}{C}-O^-Na^+ + CH_3CH_2CH_2CH_2OH$$

Butyl ethanoate            Sodium ethanoate    1-Butanol
(butyl acetate)            (sodium acetate)     (butyl alcohol)

The carboxylic acid is formed when the reaction mixture is neutralized with an acid such as HCl.

$$CH_3\overset{\overset{\displaystyle O}{\|}}{C}-O^-Na^+ + HCl \longrightarrow CH_3\overset{\overset{\displaystyle O}{\|}}{C}-OH + NaCl$$

Sodium ethanoate            Ethanoic acid
(sodium acetate)            (acetic acid)

**Question 14.7**   Complete each of the following reactions by drawing the structure of the missing product(s).

a. $CH_3\overset{\overset{\displaystyle O}{\|}}{C}-OCH_2CH_2CH_3 + H_2O \overset{H^+, heat}{\rightleftharpoons} ?$

b. $CH_3CH_2CH_2CH_2CH_2\overset{\overset{\displaystyle O}{\|}}{C}-OCH_2CH_2CH_3 + H_2O \overset{KOH, heat}{\longrightarrow} ?$

c. $CH_3CH_2CH_2CH_2\overset{\overset{\displaystyle O}{\|}}{C}-OCH_3 + H_2O \overset{NaOH, heat}{\longrightarrow} ?$

d. $CH_3CH_2CH_2CH_2CH_2\overset{\overset{\displaystyle O}{\|}}{C}-O\underset{\underset{\displaystyle CH_3}{|}}{C}HCH_2CH_2CH_3 + H_2O \overset{H^+, heat}{\rightleftharpoons} ?$

**Question 14.8**   Use the IUPAC Nomenclature System to name each of the products in Question 14.7.

*Triesters of glycerol are more commonly referred to as triglycerides. We know them as solid fats, generally from animal sources, and liquid oils, typically from plants. We will study triglycerides in detail in Section 17.3.*

Fats and oils are triesters of the alcohol glycerol. When they are hydrolyzed by saponification, the products are **soaps,** which are the salts of long-chain carboxylic acids (fatty acid salts). According to Roman legend, soap was discovered by washerwomen, following a heavy rain on Mons Sapo ("Mount Soap"). An important

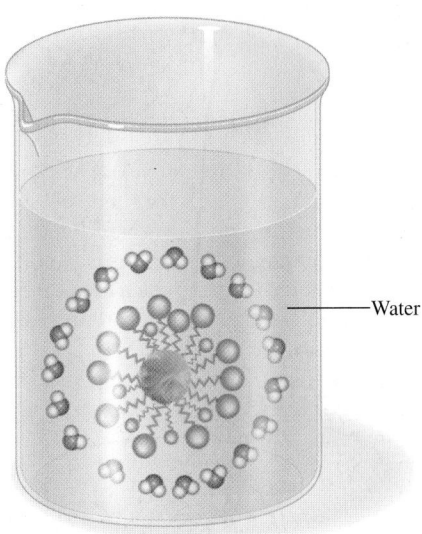

The reaction:

$$CH_2-O-\overset{\overset{\displaystyle O}{\|}}{C}-R^1$$

$$CH-O-\overset{\overset{\displaystyle O}{\|}}{C}-R^2 \quad \xrightarrow[\substack{\text{heat,}\\ H_2O}]{M^+OH^-} \quad \begin{array}{l} CH_2-OH \\ CH-OH \\ CH_2-OH \end{array} \quad + \quad R^1-\overset{\overset{\displaystyle O}{\|}}{C}-O^-M^+ + R^2-\overset{\overset{\displaystyle O}{\|}}{C}-O^-M^+ + R^3-\overset{\overset{\displaystyle O}{\|}}{C}-O^-M^+$$

$$CH_2-O-\overset{\overset{\displaystyle O}{\|}}{C}-R^3$$

Fat or oil                Glycerol            Soap
(triglyceride)                                      (Mixture of carboxylic
                                                    acid salts)

where $M^+ = Na^+$ or $K^+$

**Figure 14.3** Saponification is the base-catalyzed hydrolysis of a glycerol triester.

sacrificial altar was located on the mountain. The rain mixed with the remains of previous animal sacrifices—wood ash and animal fat—at the base of the altar. Thus, the three substances required to make soap accidentally came together—water, fat, and alkali (potassium carbonate and potassium hydroxide, called *potash*, leached from the wood ash). The soap mixture flowed down the mountain and into the Tiber River, where the washerwomen quickly realized its value.

We still use the old Roman recipe to make soap from water, a strong base, and natural fats and oils obtained from animals or plants. The carbon chain length of the fatty acid salts governs the solubility of a soap. The lower-molar-mass carboxylic acid salts (up to twelve carbons) have greater solubility in water and give a lather containing large bubbles. The higher-molar-mass carboxylic acid salts (fourteen to twenty carbons) are much less soluble in water and produce a lather with fine bubbles. The nature of the cation also affects the solubility of the soap. In general, the potassium salts of carboxylic acids are more soluble in water than the sodium salts. The synthesis of a soap is shown in Figure 14.3.

The role of soap in the removal of soil and grease is best understood by considering the functional groups in soap molecules and studying the way in which they interact with oil and water. The long, continuous hydrocarbon side chains of soap molecules resemble alkanes, and they dissolve other nonpolar compounds such as oils and greases ("like dissolves like"). The large nonpolar hydrocarbon part of the molecule is described as *hydrophobic*, which means "water-fearing." This part of the molecule is repelled by water. The highly polar carboxylate end of the molecule is called *hydrophilic*, which means "water-loving."

When soap is dissolved in water, the carboxylate end actually dissolves. When soap solution comes in contact with oil or grease, the hydrocarbon part dissolves in the oil or grease, but the polar carboxylate group remains dissolved in water. When particles of oil or grease are surrounded by soap molecules, the resulting "units" formed are called *micelles*. A simplified view of this phenomenon is shown in Figure 14.4.

Micelles repel one another because they are surrounded on the surface by the negatively charged carboxylate ions. Mechanical action (for example, scrubbing or tumbling in a washing machine) causes oil or grease to be surrounded by soap molecules and broken into small droplets so that relatively small micelles are formed. These small micelles are then washed away. Careful examination of this solution shows that it is an *emulsion* containing suspended micelles.

## Condensation Polymers

As we saw in Chapter 11, *polymers* are macromolecules, very large molecules. They result from the combination of many smaller molecules, usually in a repeating pattern, to give molecules whose molar mass may be 10,000 grams/mole (g/mol) or greater. The small molecules that make up the polymer are called *monomers*.

A polymer may be made from a single type of monomer (A). Such a polymer, called a homopolymer, would have the following general structure:

chain continues~A-A-A-A-A-A-A-A-A-A-A-A-A-A-A-A-A-A-A-A-A-A-A~chain continues

**Figure 14.4** Simplified view of the action of a soap. The wiggly lines represent the long, continuous carbon chains of each soap molecule. Particles of oil and grease are surrounded by soap molecules to form a micelle.

An emulsion is a suspension of very fine droplets of one liquid in another. In this case it is oil in water.

**ANIMATION**
- Natural and Synthetic Polymers

# A HUMAN PERSPECTIVE

## Detergents

Although soaps have served us for centuries as excellent cleansers, they do have some drawbacks. One of these is that they are salts of weak acids and thus may be converted into free fatty acids in the presence of weak acid:

$$CH_3(CH_2)_{16}\overset{O}{\underset{\|}{C}}-O^-Na^+ + HCl \longrightarrow$$

Soap

$$CH_3(CH_2)_{16}\overset{O}{\underset{\|}{C}}-OH + Na^+ + Cl^-$$

Free fatty acid

Free fatty acids are much less water-soluble than the sodium or potassium salts and they tend to precipitate as soap scum. In short, they are no longer effective as soaps because the precipitate cannot emulsify the grease and dirt. Soaps are also ineffective in "hard" water, which is water having relatively high levels of calcium, magnesium, or iron, causing the following reaction:

$$2CH_3(CH_2)_{16}\overset{O}{\underset{\|}{C}}-O^-Na^+ + Ca^{2+} \longrightarrow$$

Soap (sodium salt)
(water-soluble)

$$[CH_3(CH_2)_{16}\overset{O}{\underset{\|}{C}}-O^-]Ca^{2+} + 2Na^+$$

Soap (calcium salt)
(water-insoluble)

The calcium and magnesium salts of the carboxylic acids are much less water-soluble than the sodium salts and as a result precipitate, leaving rings in bathtubs and sinks. The precipitated soaps also leave a film on hair that can make it dull

and may cause laundry to become gray. The solution to these problems with soap has been the detergent.

Detergents were not developed in response to the soap scum problems, but rather in response to a shortage of the natural fats (animal and plant) during World Wars I and II. Without these fats, soaps could not be made and an effective alternative cleaning agent was needed. The answer was detergents.

While soaps clean through emulsifying action, detergents are surfactants. Surfactants lower the surface tension of water so that the molecules are more likely to interact with grease and oil and less likely to interact with other water molecules. The structure of a detergent is very similar to that of a soap: there is a long hydrocarbon chain that is hydrophobic and a highly polar or charged end of the molecule. There are three common types of detergents: anionic, cationic, and nonionic. As the names suggest, these differ in the nature of the polar or charged ends of the molecules.

Anionic detergents have a negatively charged terminus, as you see in the structures of sodium dodecylsulfate (SDS) and sodium dodecylbenzenesulfonate shown here. SDS is primarily used in laundry detergents, but is also found in shampoo, bubble bath, toothpaste, and shaving foams. In higher concentrations it is used in floor cleaners, engine degreasers, and car wash soaps. Like SDS, sodium dodecylbenzenesulfonate is largely used in laundry detergents.

Anionic Detergents

Sodium dodecylbenzensesulfonate

The addition polymers of alkenes that we studied in Chapter 11 are examples of this type of polymer. Alternatively, two different monomers (A and B) may be copolymerized, producing a heteropolymer with the following structure:

chain continues~A-B-A-B-A-B-A-B-A-B-A-B-A-B-A-B~chain continues

Polyesters are heteropolymers. They are also known as condensation polymers. **Condensation polymers** are formed by the polymerization of monomers in a reaction that forms a small molecule such as water or an alcohol. Polyesters are synthesized by reacting a dicarboxylic acid and a dialcohol (diol). Notice that each of the combining molecules has two reactive functional groups, highlighted in red here:

Sodium dodecylsulfate

Cationic detergents have a positively charged head group. In addition to being effective cleansing agents, cationic detergents have also been found to be effective antiseptics. Trimethylhexadecyl ammonium bromide is a cationic detergent found in topical antiseptics because it has been shown to be an effective agent against both bacteria and fungi.

Cationic Detergent

Trimethylhexadecylammonium bromide

Cationic detergents are most often found in shampoos, but are also used as fabric softeners. When added following the wash cycle, the cationic detergent neutralizes the residual charge of the anionic detergent, thereby reducing static cling.

Nonionic detergents have no charge at all on the molecule. As a result, they do not react with hard water ions, making them an excellent choice for toilet bowl cleaners to avoid unsightly buildup and to ensure that the detergent is fully active. Nonionic detergents are also very good at breaking up grease and oils and tend to foam less than ionic detergents. These properties make them very useful as dishwashing detergents. They are also used in a mixture with anionic detergents in formulations of laundry detergents.

Nonionic Detergent

Pentaerythrityl palmitate

Whether brushing our teeth, shampooing our hair, washing the car, or doing the laundry, we find ourselves relying on the action of detergents many times through the course of the day. Our quality of life is much improved by this discovery born of wartime shortages of animal and plant fats!

**For Further Understanding**

▶ Compare and contrast the ways in which soaps and detergents work in the removal of dirt and grease. What is the role of agitation in the process?

▶ Below is one possible structure of an alkyl polyglucoside, the newest generation of environmentally friendly or "green" surfactants. They are synthesized in a reaction between glucose from corn and fatty alcohols from coconut or palm oil. Is this an anionic, cationic, or nonionic detergent? Explain your answer.

$$\left[-OCH_2CH_2O-\overset{\displaystyle O}{\overset{\|}{C}}-\bigcirc-\overset{\displaystyle O}{\overset{\|}{C}}-OCH_2CH_2O-\overset{\displaystyle O}{\overset{\|}{C}}-\bigcirc-\overset{\displaystyle O}{\overset{\|}{C}}-O-\right]_n$$

Polyethylene terephthalate
PETE

Each time a pair of molecules reacts using one functional group from each, a new molecule is formed that still has two reactive groups. The product formed in this reaction is polyethylene terephthalate, or PETE.

When formed as fibers, polyesters are used to make fabric for clothing. These polyesters were trendy in the 1970s, during the "disco" period, but lost their popularity soon thereafter. Polyester fabrics, and a number of other synthetic polymers used in clothing, have become even more fashionable since the introduction of microfiber technology. The synthetic polymers are extruded into fibers that are only half the diameter of fine silk fibers. When these fibers are used to create fabrics, the result is a fabric that drapes freely yet retains its shape. These fabrics are generally lightweight, wrinkle resistant, and remarkably strong.

Polyester can be formed into a film called Mylar. These films, coated with aluminum foil, are used to make balloons that remain inflated for long periods. They are also used as the base for recording tapes and photographic film.

PETE can be used to make shatterproof plastic bottles, such as those used for soft drinks. However, these bottles cannot be recycled and reused directly because they cannot withstand the high temperatures required to sterilize them. PETE can't be used for any foods, such as jellies, that must be packaged at high temperatures. For these uses, a new plastic, PEN, or polyethylene naphthalate, is used.

$$\left[-\overset{\displaystyle O}{\overset{\|}{C}}-\bigcirc\bigcirc-\overset{\displaystyle O}{\overset{\|}{C}}-O-CH_2CH_2-\right]_n$$

Naphthalate group          Ethylene group

*Biodegradable plastics made of both homopolymers and heteropolymers are discussed in Green Chemistry: Garbage Bags from Potato Peels? found on page 478.*

*...found on page 478.*

## LEARNING GOAL

**11**  Determine the common and IUPAC names of acid chlorides.

## 14.3  Acid Chlorides and Acid Anhydrides

### Acid Chlorides

**Acid chlorides** are carboxylic acid derivatives having the general formula

$$R-\overset{\displaystyle O}{\overset{\|}{C}}-Cl$$

They are named by replacing the *-ic acid* ending of the common name with *-yl chloride*, or the *-oic acid* ending of the IUPAC name of the carboxylic acid with *-oyl chloride*. For example,

$$CH_3CH_2CH_2\overset{\displaystyle O}{\overset{\|}{C}}-Cl$$

Butanoyl chloride
(butyryl chloride)

$$CH_3\overset{\displaystyle O}{\overset{\|}{C}}-Cl$$

Ethanoyl chloride
(acetyl chloride)

$$\underset{\displaystyle Br}{CH_2}CH_2\overset{\displaystyle O}{\overset{\|}{C}}-Cl$$

3-Bromopropanoyl chloride
(β-bromopropionyl chloride)

$$Cl-\bigcirc-\overset{\displaystyle O}{\overset{\|}{C}}-Cl$$

4-Chlorobenzoyl chloride
(*p*-chlorobenzoyl chloride)

Acid chlorides are noxious, irritating chemicals and must be handled with great care. They are slightly polar and boil at approximately the same temperature as the corresponding aldehyde or ketone of comparable molar mass. They react violently with water and therefore cannot be dissolved in that solvent. Acid chlorides have little commercial value other than their utility in the synthesis of esters and amides, two of the other carboxylic acid derivatives.

## Acid Anhydrides

**Acid anhydrides** are molecules with the following general formula:

$$R^1-\overset{\overset{\displaystyle O}{\|}}{C}-O-\overset{\overset{\displaystyle O}{\|}}{C}-R^2$$

The name of the family is really quite fitting. The structure above reveals that acid anhydrides are actually two carboxylic acid molecules with a water molecule removed. The word *anhydride* means "without water."

$$R^1-\overset{\overset{\displaystyle O}{\|}}{C}-O-H + HO-\overset{\overset{\displaystyle O}{\|}}{C}-R^2$$

$$\downarrow$$

$$H-OH + R^1-\overset{\overset{\displaystyle O}{\|}}{C}-O-\overset{\overset{\displaystyle O}{\|}}{C}-R^2$$

Acid anhydrides are classified as *symmetrical* if both acyl groups are the same. Symmetrical acid anhydrides are named by replacing the *acid* ending of the carboxylic acid with the word *anhydride*. For example,

$$CH_3\overset{\overset{\displaystyle O}{\|}}{C}-O-\overset{\overset{\displaystyle O}{\|}}{C}CH_3$$

Ethanoic anhydride
(acetic anhydride)

Benzoic anhydride

**LEARNING GOAL**

**12**  Determine the common and IUPAC names of acid anhydrides.

Unsymmetrical anhydrides are those having two different acyl groups. They are named by arranging the names of the two parent carboxylic acids and following them with the word *anhydride*. The names of the carboxylic acids may be arranged by size or alphabetically. For example:

$$CH_3\overset{\overset{\displaystyle O}{\|}}{C}-O-\overset{\overset{\displaystyle O}{\|}}{C}CH_2CH_3$$

Ethanoic propanoic anhydride
(acetic propionic anhydride)

$$CH_3\overset{\overset{\displaystyle O}{\|}}{C}-O-\overset{\overset{\displaystyle O}{\|}}{C}CH_2CH_2CH_2CH_3$$

Ethanoic pentanoic anhydride
(acetic valeric anhydride)

Most acid anhydrides cannot be formed in a reaction between the parent carboxylic acids. One typical pathway for the synthesis of an acid anhydride is the reaction between an acid chloride and a carboxylate anion. This general reaction is seen in the equation below:

**LEARNING GOAL**

**13**  Write equations representing the synthesis of acid anhydrides.

$$R^1-\overset{\overset{\displaystyle O}{\|}}{C}-Cl \quad \underset{\text{Carboxylate ion}}{R^2-\overset{\overset{\displaystyle O}{\|}}{C}-O^-} \quad R^1-\overset{\overset{\displaystyle O}{\|}}{C}-O-\overset{\overset{\displaystyle O}{\|}}{C}-R^2 + Cl^-$$

Acid chloride            Acid anhydride    Chloride ion

The following equation shows the synthesis of ethanoic anhydride from ethanoic acid:

$$CH_3\overset{\overset{\displaystyle O}{\|}}{C}-OH \xrightarrow{SOCl_2} CH_3\overset{\overset{\displaystyle O}{\|}}{C}-Cl \xrightarrow{CH_3\overset{\overset{\displaystyle O}{\|}}{C}-O^-} CH_3\overset{\overset{\displaystyle O}{\|}}{C}-O-\overset{\overset{\displaystyle O}{\|}}{C}CH_3$$

Ethanoic acid
(acetic acid)

Ethanoyl chloride
(acetyl chloride)

Ethanoic anhydride
(acetic anhydride)

Acid anhydrides readily undergo hydrolysis. The rate of the hydrolysis reaction may be increased by the addition of a trace of acid or hydroxide base to the solution.

$$CH_3CH_2\overset{\displaystyle O}{\overset{\|}{C}}-O-\overset{\displaystyle O}{\overset{\|}{C}}CH_2CH_3 + H_2O \xrightarrow{\text{Heat}} 2CH_3CH_2\overset{\displaystyle O}{\overset{\|}{C}}-OH$$

Propanoic anhydride            Propanoic acid
(propionic anhydride)          (propionic acid)

---

**EXAMPLE 14.10**   **Writing Equations Representing the Synthesis of Acid Anhydrides**

Write an equation representing the synthesis of propanoic anhydride.

LEARNING GOAL

**13**  Write equations representing the synthesis of acid anhydrides.

**Solution**

Propanoic anhydride can be synthesized in a reaction between propanoyl chloride and the propanoate anion. This gives us the following equation:

$$CH_3CH_2\overset{\displaystyle O}{\overset{\|}{C}}-Cl \xrightarrow[\text{Propanoate ion}]{CH_3CH_2\overset{\displaystyle O}{\overset{\|}{C}}-O^-} CH_3CH_2\overset{\displaystyle O}{\overset{\|}{C}}-O-\overset{\displaystyle O}{\overset{\|}{C}}CH_2CH_3 + Cl^-$$

Propanoyl                    Propanoic anhydride        Chloride
chloride                                                ion

---

**Practice Problem 14.10**

Write equations representing the synthesis of (a) butanoic anhydride and (b) hexanoic anhydride.

▶ For Further Practice: **Questions 14.93 and 14.94.**

---

**EXAMPLE 14.11**   **Naming Acid Anhydrides**

Write the IUPAC and common names for each of the following acid anhydrides.

LEARNING GOAL

**12**  Determine the common and IUPAC names of acid anhydrides.

$$CH_3CH_2CH_2\overset{\displaystyle O}{\overset{\|}{C}}-O-\overset{\displaystyle O}{\overset{\|}{C}}CH_2CH_2CH_3$$

**Solution**

This is a symmetrical acid anhydride. The IUPAC name of the four-carbon parent carboxylic acid is butanoic acid (common name butyric acid). To name the anhydride, simply replace the word *acid* with the word *anhydride*. The IUPAC name of this compound is butanoic anhydride (common name butyric anhydride).

$$CH_3\overset{\displaystyle O}{\overset{\|}{C}}-O-\overset{\displaystyle O}{\overset{\|}{C}}CH_2CH_2CH_2CH_2CH_3$$

**Solution**

This is an unsymmetrical anhydride. The IUPAC names of the two parent carboxylic acids are ethanoic acid (two-carbon) and hexanoic acid (six-carbon). To name an unsymmetrical anhydride, the term *anhydride* is preceded by the names of the two parent acids. The IUPAC name of this compound is ethanoic hexanoic anhydride. The common names of the two parent carboxylic acids are acetic acid and caproic acid. Thus, the common name of this compound is acetic caproic anhydride.

**Practice Problem 14.11**

Write the common and IUPAC names for each of the following acid anhydrides.

a. $\underset{\quad\quad\quad\;\; \| \quad\quad\quad\quad \|}{CH_3CH_2CH_2C-O-CCH_2CH_2CH_2CH_2CH_3}$

c. $\underset{\quad\quad\quad\quad\quad\quad \| \quad\quad\quad \|}{CH_3CH_2CH_2CH_2C-O-CCH_2CH_3}$

b. $\underset{\quad\; \| \quad\quad\quad \|}{CH_3C-O-CCH_2CH_2CH_2CH_3}$

d. $\underset{\quad\quad\quad\; \| \quad\quad \|}{CH_3CH_2C-O-CCH_3}$

▶ For Further Practice: **Questions 14.89 and 14.90.**

Acid anhydrides can also react with an alcohol. This reaction produces an ester and a carboxylic acid. This is an example of an acyl group transfer reaction. The **acyl group** of a carboxylic acid derivative has the following structure:

$$\underset{R-C-}{\overset{O\;\|}{}}$$

The following general equation represents the acyl group transfer reaction between an alcohol and an acid anhydride.

$$R-OH + R-\overset{O}{\overset{\|}{C}}-O-\overset{O}{\overset{\|}{C}}-R \longrightarrow R-\overset{O}{\overset{\|}{C}}-OR + R-\overset{O}{\overset{\|}{C}}-OH$$

Alcohol     Acid anhydride                    Ester        Carboxylic acid

The acyl group of the acid anhydride is transferred to the oxygen of the alcohol in this reaction. The alcohol and anhydride reactants and ester product are described below. The carboxylic acid product is omitted.

Other acyl group donors include thioesters and esters. As we will see in the final section of this chapter, acyl group transfer reactions are very important in nature, particularly in the pathways responsible for breakdown of food molecules and harvesting cellular energy.

**Question 14.9** Write an equation showing the synthesis of each of the following acid anhydrides. Provide the IUPAC names of the acid chloride and carboxylate anion reactants and the acid anhydride product.

a.  $\underset{\underset{CH_3}{|}}{CH_3CHCH_2}\overset{\overset{O}{\|}}{C}-O-\overset{\overset{O}{\|}}{C}CH_2\underset{\underset{CH_3}{|}}{CHCH_3}$   b.  $H-\overset{\overset{O}{\|}}{C}-O-\overset{\overset{O}{\|}}{C}-CH_3$

**Question 14.10**   Write an equation showing the synthesis of each of the following acid anhydrides. Provide the common names of the acid chloride and carboxylate anion reactants and the acid anhydride products.

a.  $\underset{\underset{CH_2CH_3}{|}}{CH_3CHCH_2}\overset{\overset{O}{\|}}{C}-O-\overset{\overset{O}{\|}}{C}CH_2\underset{\underset{CH_2CH_3}{|}}{CHCH_3}$   b.  $CH_3\overset{\overset{O}{\|}}{C}-O-\overset{\overset{O}{\|}}{C}CH_2CH_2CH_3$

## 14.4   Nature's High-Energy Compounds: Phosphoesters and Thioesters

An alcohol can react with phosphoric acid to produce a phosphate ester, or **phosphoester,** as in

$$ROH + HO-\overset{\overset{O}{\|}}{\underset{\underset{OH}{|}}{P}}-OH \longrightarrow R-O-\overset{\overset{O}{\|}}{\underset{\underset{OH}{|}}{P}}-OH + H_2O$$

| Alcohol | Phosphoric acid | Phosphate ester | Water |

*The many phosphorylated intermediates in the metabolism of sugars will be discussed in Chapter 21.*

Phosphoesters of simple sugars or monosaccharides are very important in the energy-harvesting biochemical pathways that provide energy for all life functions. One such pathway is *glycolysis.* This pathway is the first stage in the breakdown of sugars. The first reaction in this pathway is the formation of a phosphoester of the six-carbon sugar, glucose. The phosphorylation of glucose to produce glucose-6-phosphate is represented in the following equation:

In fact the word *glycolysis* comes from two Greek words that mean "splitting sugars" (*glykos,* "sweet," and *lysis,* "to split"). In this pathway, the six-carbon sugar glucose is split, and then oxidized, to produce two three-carbon molecules, called *pyruvate.*

β-D-Glucose    +    ATP    $\xrightarrow{\text{Hexokinase}}$    β-D-Glucose-6-phosphate    +    ADP

In this reaction the source of the phosphoryl group is **adenosine triphosphate (ATP),** which is the universal energy currency for all living organisms. As such, ATP is used to store energy released in cellular metabolic reactions and to provide the energy required for most of the reactions that occur in the cell. The transfer of a phosphoryl group from ATP to glucose "energizes" the glucose molecule in preparation for other reactions of the pathway.

ATP consists of a nitrogenous base (adenine) and a phosphate ester of the five-carbon sugar ribose (Figure 14.5). The triphosphate group attached to ribose is made up of three phosphate groups bonded to one another by phosphoanhydride bonds. When two phosphate groups react with one another, a water molecule is lost. Because water is lost, the resulting bond is called a **phosphoanhydride** bond.

Phosphate ester  Phosphate group  Phosphoanhydride bond

*Phosphoryl is the term used to describe the functional group derived from phosphoric acid that is part of another molecule.*

The energy of ATP is made available through hydrolysis of either of the two phosphoanhydride bonds, as shown in Figure 14.5. This is an exothermic process; that is, energy is given off. When the phosphoryl group is transferred to another molecule—for instance, glucose—some of that energy resides in the phosphorylated sugar, thereby "energizing" it. The importance of ATP as an energy source becomes apparent when we realize that we synthesize and break down an amount of ATP equivalent to our body weight each day.

*The functions and properties of ATP in energy metabolism are discussed in Section 21.1.*

Cellular enzymes can carry out a reaction between a thiol and a carboxylic acid to produce a **thioester:**

*Thiols are described in Section 12.8.*

$$R^1-S-\overset{\displaystyle O}{\overset{\displaystyle \|}{C}}-R^2$$

Thioester

The reactions that produce thioesters are essential in energy-harvesting pathways as a means of "activating" acyl groups for subsequent breakdown reactions. The complex thiol coenzyme A is the most important acyl group activator in the cell. The detailed structure of coenzyme A appears in Section 12.8, but it is generally abbreviated CoA—SH to emphasize the importance of the sulfhydryl group. The most common thioester is the acetyl ester, called **acetyl coenzyme A** (acetyl CoA).

Acetyl CoA carries the acetyl group from glycolysis or β-oxidation of a fatty acid to an intermediate of the citric acid cycle. This reaction is an example of an acyl group transfer reaction. In this case, the acyl group donor is a thioester—acetyl

*β-Oxidation is the pathway for the breakdown of fatty acids. Like glycolysis, it is an energy-harvesting pathway.*

**Figure 14.5** The hydrolysis of the phosphoanhydride bond of ATP is accompanied by the release of energy that is used for biochemical reactions in the cell.

ATP

Bond cleaved on hydrolysis

$H_2O$

ADP

$+ H_2PO_4^- +$ **energy**

# A HUMAN PERSPECTIVE

## Carboxylic Acid Derivatives of Special Interest

### Analgesics (pain killers) and antipyretics (fever reducers)

Aspirin (*acetylsalicylic acid*), derived from the bark of the willow tree, is the most widely used drug in the world. Hundreds of millions of dollars are spent annually on this compound. It is used primarily as a pain reliever (analgesic) and in the reduction of fever (antipyretic). Aspirin is among the drugs often referred to as NSAIDs, or nonsteroidal anti-inflammatory drugs. These drugs inhibit the inflammatory response by inhibiting an enzyme called cyclooxygenase, which is the first enzyme in the pathway for the synthesis of prostaglandins. Prostaglandins are responsible, in part, for pain and fever. Thus, aspirin and other NSAIDs reduce pain and fever by decreasing prostaglandin synthesis. Aspirin's side effects are a problem for some individuals. Because aspirin inhibits clotting, its use is not recommended during pregnancy, nor should it be used by individuals with ulcers. In those instances, *acetaminophen*, found in the over-the-counter pain-reliever Tylenol, is often prescribed.

The search for NSAIDs that are more effective and yet gentler on the stomach has provided two new analgesics for the over-the-counter market. These are ibuprofen (sold as Motrin, Advil, Nuprin) and naproxen (sold as Naprosyn, Naprelan, Anaprox, and Aleve).

Ibuprofen

Naproxen

Acetylsalicylic acid          Acetaminophen

Some common analgesics.

### Pheromones

*Pheromones*, chemicals secreted by animals, influence the behavior of other members of the same species. They often represent the major means of communication among simpler animals. The term *pheromone* literally means "to carry" and "to

excite" (Greek, *pherein*, to carry; Greek, *horman*, to excite). They are chemicals carried or shed by one member of the species and used to alert other members of the species.

Pheromones may be involved in sexual attraction, trail marking, aggregation or recruitment, territorial marking, or signaling alarm. Others may be involved in defense or in species socialization—for example, designating various classes within the species as a whole. Among all of the pheromones, insect pheromones have been the most intensely studied. Many of the insect pheromones are carboxylic acids or acid derivatives, as seen here:

$$CH_3CH_2CH=CH(CH_2)_9CH_2OCCH_3$$

Tetradecenyl acetate
(European corn borer sex pheromone)

9-Keto-*trans*-2-decenoic acid
(queen bee socializing/royalty pheromone)

*cis*-7-Dodecenyl acetate
(cabbage looper sex pheromone)

### For Further Understanding

▶ A nonsteroidal anti-inflammatory drug can cause side effects if used over a long period. Do some research on the physiological roles of prostaglandins to develop hypotheses concerning these side effects.

▶ How might you make use of pheromones to control pests such as the corn borer?

CoA. The acyl group being transferred is the acetyl group, which is transferred to the carbonyl carbon of oxaloacetate. This reaction follows:

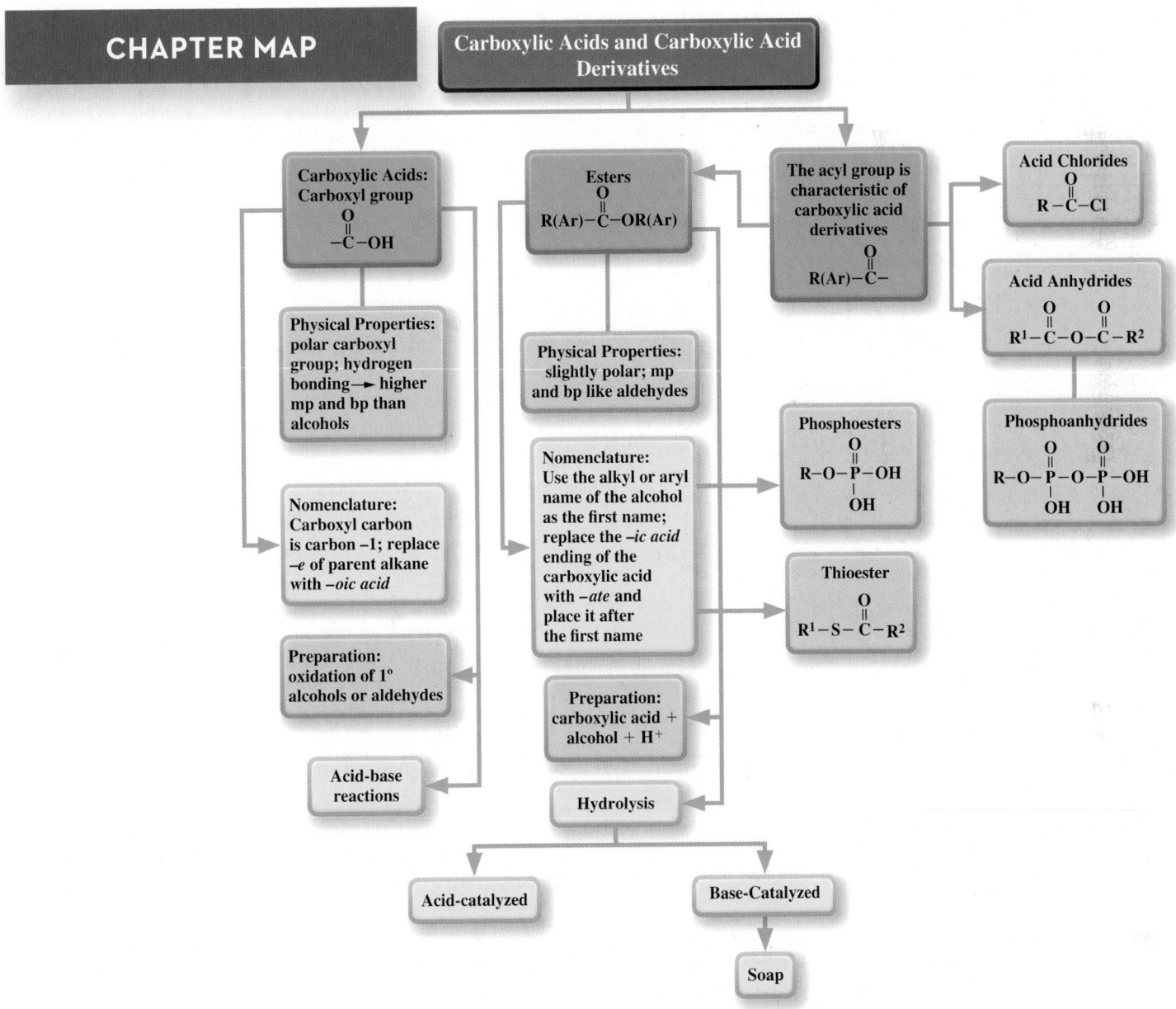

| Acetyl CoA | Oxaloacetate | Citrate | Coenzyme A |

As we will see in Chapter 22, the citric acid cycle is an energy-harvesting pathway that completely oxidizes the acetyl group to two $CO_2$ molecules. The electrons that are harvested in the process are used to produce large amounts of ATP. Coenzyme A also serves to activate the acyl group of fatty acids during β-oxidation, the pathway by which fatty acids are oxidized to produce ATP.

The acyl group of a carboxylic acid is named by replacing the *-oic acid* or *-ic* suffix with *-yl*. For instance, the acyl group of acetic acid is the acetyl group:

$$CoA-S-\overset{\overset{O}{\|}}{C}-CH_3$$

Acetyl coenzyme A
(acetyl CoA)

*Glycolysis, β-oxidation, and the citric acid cycle are cellular energy-harvesting pathways that we will study in Chapters 21, 22, and 23.*

**CHAPTER MAP**

**Carboxylic Acids and Carboxylic Acid Derivatives**

**Carboxylic Acids:**
Carboxyl group
$$-\overset{\overset{O}{\|}}{C}-OH$$

**Esters**
$$R(Ar)-\overset{\overset{O}{\|}}{C}-OR(Ar)$$

**The acyl group is characteristic of carboxylic acid derivatives**
$$R(Ar)-\overset{\overset{O}{\|}}{C}-$$

**Acid Chlorides**
$$R-\overset{\overset{O}{\|}}{C}-Cl$$

**Acid Anhydrides**
$$R^1-\overset{\overset{O}{\|}}{C}-O-\overset{\overset{O}{\|}}{C}-R^2$$

**Physical Properties:** polar carboxyl group; hydrogen bonding→ higher mp and bp than alcohols

**Physical Properties:** slightly polar; mp and bp like aldehydes

**Phosphoesters**
$$R-O-\overset{\overset{O}{\|}}{\underset{\underset{OH}{|}}{P}}-OH$$

**Phosphoanhydrides**
$$R-O-\overset{\overset{O}{\|}}{\underset{\underset{OH}{|}}{P}}-O-\overset{\overset{O}{\|}}{\underset{\underset{OH}{|}}{P}}-OH$$

**Nomenclature:** Carboxyl carbon is carbon –1; replace *-e* of parent alkane with *-oic acid*

**Nomenclature:** Use the alkyl or aryl name of the alcohol as the first name; replace the *-ic acid* ending of the carboxylic acid with *-ate* and place it after the first name

**Thioester**
$$R^1-S-\overset{\overset{O}{\|}}{C}-R^2$$

**Preparation:** oxidation of 1° alcohols or aldehydes

**Preparation:** carboxylic acid + alcohol + $H^+$

**Acid-base reactions**

**Hydrolysis**

**Acid-catalyzed**

**Base-Catalyzed**

**Soap**

## SUMMARY OF REACTIONS

### Preparation of Carboxylic Acids

$$R-CH_2OH \xrightarrow{[O]} R-\overset{\overset{\displaystyle O}{\|}}{C}-H \xrightarrow{[O]} R-\overset{\overset{\displaystyle O}{\|}}{C}-OH$$

Primary alcohol          Aldehyde          Carboxylic acid

### Dissociation of Carboxylic Acids

$$R-\overset{\overset{\displaystyle O}{\|}}{C}-OH \rightleftharpoons R-\overset{\overset{\displaystyle O}{\|}}{C}-O^- \;+\; H^+$$

Carboxylic          Carboxylate          Hydrogen
acid                      anion                    ion

### Neutralization of Carboxylic Acids

$$R-\overset{\overset{\displaystyle O}{\|}}{C}-OH + NaOH \longrightarrow R-\overset{\overset{\displaystyle O}{\|}}{C}-O^-Na^+ \;+\; H_2O$$

Carboxylic      Strong                Carboxylic          Water
acid               base                   acid salt

### Synthesis of Acid Anhydrides

$$R^1-\overset{\overset{\displaystyle O}{\|}}{C}-Cl \xrightarrow[\text{Carboxylate ion}]{R^2-\overset{\overset{\displaystyle O}{\|}}{C}-O^-} R^1-\overset{\overset{\displaystyle O}{\|}}{C}-O-\overset{\overset{\displaystyle O}{\|}}{C}-R^2 + Cl^-$$

Acid                      Acid anhydride          Chloride
chloride                                                ion

### Esterification

$$R^1-\overset{\overset{\displaystyle O}{\|}}{C}-OH + R^2OH \underset{}{\overset{H^+,\,\text{heat}}{\rightleftharpoons}} R^1-\overset{\overset{\displaystyle O}{\|}}{C}-OR^2 + H_2O$$

Carboxylic      Alcohol                Ester          Water
acid

### Acid Hydrolysis of Esters

$$R^1-\overset{\overset{\displaystyle O}{\|}}{C}-OR^2 + H_2O \underset{}{\overset{H^+,\,\text{heat}}{\rightleftharpoons}} R^1-\overset{\overset{\displaystyle O}{\|}}{C}-OH + R^2OH$$

Ester          Water                Carboxylic          Alcohol
                                        acid

### Saponification (Base-catalyzed Hydrolysis of Esters)

$$R^1-\overset{\overset{\displaystyle O}{\|}}{C}-OR^2 + H_2O \xrightarrow{\substack{NaOH,\\ \text{heat}}} R^1-\overset{\overset{\displaystyle O}{\|}}{C}-O^-Na^+ \;+\; R^2OH$$

Ester          Water                Carboxylic          Alcohol
                                        acid salt

### Formation of a Phosphoester

$$ROH + HO-\overset{\overset{\displaystyle O}{\|}}{\underset{\underset{\displaystyle OH}{|}}{P}}-OH \longrightarrow R-O-\overset{\overset{\displaystyle O}{\|}}{\underset{\underset{\displaystyle OH}{|}}{P}}-OH + H_2O$$

Alcohol    Phosphoric                Phosphate      Water
               acid                          ester

## SUMMARY

### 14.1 Carboxylic Acids

▶ The functional group of the **carboxylic acids** is the **carboxyl group** (—COOH).

▶ Because the carboxyl group is extremely polar and carboxylic acids can form intermolecular hydrogen bonds with one another, they have higher boiling points and melting points than alcohols.

▶ The lower-molar-mass carboxylic acids are water-soluble and tend to taste sour and have unpleasant aromas.

▶ The longer-chain carboxylic acids are called **fatty acids**.

▶ In the IUPAC Nomenclature System, carboxylic acids are named by replacing the -e ending of the parent compound with -oic acid. When naming dicarboxylic acids, the -e is retained and the suffix -dioic is added.

▶ Often common names are derived from the source of the carboxylic acid.

▶ Carboxylic acids are synthesized by the **oxidation** of primary alcohols or aldehydes.

▶ Carboxylic acids are weak acids and are neutralized by strong bases to form salts. **Soaps** are salts of long-chain carboxylic acids (fatty acids).

### 14.2 Esters

▶ **Esters** are **carboxylic acid derivatives** that are slightly polar and have pleasant aromas.

- The boiling points and melting points of esters are comparable to those of aldehydes and ketones.
- Esters are formed from the reaction between a carboxylic acid and an alcohol.
- Esters can undergo **hydrolysis** back to the parent carboxylic acid and alcohol.
- The base-catalyzed hydrolysis of an ester is called **saponification**.
- **Condensation polymers** are large molecules formed by combination of many small molecules (monomers) that result from joining of monomers in a reaction that also forms a small molecule, such as water or an alcohol.

## 14.3 Acid Chlorides and Acid Anhydrides

- **Acid chlorides** are noxious chemicals and are useful in the synthesis of a variety of carboxylic acid derivatives.
- **Acid anhydrides** are formed by the combination of an acid chloride and a carboxylate anion.
- Acid anhydrides can react with an alcohol to produce an ester and a carboxylic acid. This is an example of an acyl group transfer.
- The **acyl group** in carboxylic acid derivatives contains the carbonyl group attached to one alkyl or one aryl group.

## 14.4 Nature's High-Energy Compounds: Phosphoesters and Thioesters

- An alcohol can react with phosphoric acid to produce a phosphate ester (**phosphoester**).
- When two phosphate groups are joined, the resulting bond is a **phosphoanhydride** bond.
- The phosphoester and phosphoanhydride bonds are important in the structure of **adenosine triphosphate (ATP)**, the universal energy currency of all cells.
- Cellular enzymes carry out a reaction between a thiol and a carboxylic acid to produce a **thioester**. This reaction is essential for the activation of acyl groups in carbohydrate and fatty acid metabolism.
- Coenzyme A is the important thiol involved in these pathways, forming **acetyl coenzyme A.**

## ANSWERS TO PRACTICE PROBLEMS

**14.1** a. 2,4-Dimethylpentanoic acid
  b. 2,4-Dichlorobutanoic acid
  c. 2,3-Dihydroxybutanoic acid
  d. 2-Bromo-3-chloro-4-methylhexanoic acid
**14.2** a. α,γ-Dimethylvaleric acid
  b. α,γ-Dichlorobutyric acid
  c. β,γ-Dibromovaleric acid
  d. γ-Hydroxycaproic acid

**14.3** a. *o*-Toluic acid:    b. 2,4,6-Tribromobenzoic acid:

  c. 2,2,2-Triphenylethanoic acid:

  d. *p*-Toluic acid:

  e. 3-Phenylhexanoic acid:

  f. 3-Phenylcyclohexanecarboxylic acid:

**14.4** a. The following equation represents the synthesis of ethanoic acid from ethanol.

$$CH_3CH_2OH \xrightarrow{[O]} CH_3\overset{\overset{\displaystyle O}{\|}}{C}-H \xrightarrow{[O]} CH_3\overset{\overset{\displaystyle O}{\|}}{C}-OH$$

Ethanol          Ethanal          Ethanoic acid

  b. The following equation represents the synthesis of butanoic acid from 1-butanol.

$$CH_3CH_2CH_2CH_2OH \xrightarrow{[O]} CH_3CH_2CH_2\overset{\overset{\displaystyle O}{\|}}{C}-H$$

1-Butanol                    Butanal

$$\downarrow {[O]}$$

$$CH_3CH_2CH_2\overset{\overset{\displaystyle O}{\|}}{C}-OH$$

Butanoic acid

c. The following equation represents the synthesis of octanoic acid from 1-octanol.

$$CH_3(CH_2)_6CH_2OH \xrightarrow{[O]} CH_3(CH_2)_6\overset{\overset{\displaystyle O}{\|}}{C}-H$$

1-Octanol                            Octanal

$$\downarrow [O]$$

$$CH_3(CH_2)_6\overset{\overset{\displaystyle O}{\|}}{C}-OH$$

Octanoic acid

**14.5** a. $CH_3CH_2COO^-K^+$
b. $[CH_3CH_2CH_2COO^-]_2Ba^{2+}$
c. $CH_3CH_2CH_2CH_2CH_2COO^-\ K^+$
d.
$$\bigcirc\!-\overset{\overset{\displaystyle O}{\|}}{C}-O^-Na^+$$

**14.6** a. Potassium propanoate    c. Potassium hexanoate
b. Barium butanoate          d. Sodium benzoate
**14.7** a. Propyl butanoate (propyl butyrate)
b. Ethyl butanoate (ethyl butyrate)
c. Propyl ethanoate (propyl acetate)
d. Butyl propanoate (butyl propionate)
**14.8** a. The following reaction between 1-butanol and ethanoic acid produces butyl ethanoate. It requires a trace of acid and heat. It is also reversible.

$$CH_3CH_2CH_2CH_2OH + CH_3COOH$$

$$\updownarrow$$

$$CH_3\overset{\overset{\displaystyle O}{\|}}{C}-OCH_2CH_2CH_2CH_3$$

b. The following reaction between ethanol and propanoic acid produces ethyl propanoate. It requires a trace of acid and heat. It is also reversible.

$$CH_3CH_2OH + CH_3CH_2COOH$$

$$\updownarrow$$

$$CH_3CH_2\overset{\overset{\displaystyle O}{\|}}{C}-OCH_2CH_3$$

**14.9** a. Methyl butanoate is made from methanol and butanoic acid.

$$CH_3OH + CH_3CH_2CH_2COOH \longrightarrow CH_3CH_2CH_2\overset{\overset{\displaystyle O}{\|}}{C}OCH_3$$

Methanol    Butanoic acid        Methyl butanoate

Methanol is an allowed starting material, but butanoic acid is not. However, it can easily be produced by the oxidation of its corresponding alcohol, 1-butanol:

$$CH_3CH_2CH_2CH_2OH \xrightarrow{[O]} CH_3CH_2CH_2CHO$$

1-Butanol                            Butanal

$$\downarrow [O]$$

$$CH_3CH_2CH_2COOH$$

Butanoic acid

b. Propyl methanoate is made from 1-propanol and methanoic acid.

$$CH_3CH_2CH_2OH + HCOOH$$

1-Propanol    Methanoic acid

$$\downarrow$$

$$HCO\overset{\overset{\displaystyle O}{\|}}{}CH_2CH_2CH_3$$

Propyl methanoate

1-Propanol is an allowed starting material, but methanoic acid is not. However, it can easily be produced by the oxidation of its corresponding alcohol, methanol:

$$CH_3OH \xrightarrow{[O]} HCHO \xrightarrow{[O]} HCOOH$$

Methanol    Methanal   Methanoic acid

**14.10** a. The following equation represents the synthesis of butanoic anhydride:

$$CH_3CH_2CH_2\overset{\overset{\displaystyle O}{\|}}{C}O^- + CH_3CH_2CH_2\overset{\overset{\displaystyle O}{\|}}{C}-Cl$$

Butanoate anion    Butanoyl chloride

$$\downarrow$$

$$CH_3CH_2CH_2\overset{\overset{\displaystyle O}{\|}}{C}-O-\overset{\overset{\displaystyle O}{\|}}{C}CH_2CH_2CH_3$$

Butanoic anhydride

b. The following equation represents the synthesis of hexanoic anhydride:

$$CH_3(CH_2)_4\overset{\overset{\displaystyle O}{\|}}{C}O^- + CH_3(CH_2)_4\overset{\overset{\displaystyle O}{\|}}{C}-Cl$$

Hexanoate anion    Hexanoyl chloride

$$\downarrow$$

$$CH_3(CH_2)_4\overset{\overset{\displaystyle O}{\|}}{C}-O-\overset{\overset{\displaystyle O}{\|}}{C}(CH_2)_4CH_3$$

Hexanoic anhydride

**14.11 a.** IUPAC name: Butanoic hexanoic anhydride
Common name: Butyric caproic anhydride
**b.** IUPAC name: Ethanoic pentanoic anhydride
Common name: Acetic valeric anhydride
**c.** IUPAC name: Propanoic pentanoic anhydride
Common name: Propionic valeric anhydride
**d.** IUPAC name: Ethanoic propanoic anhydride
Common name: Acetic propionic anhydride

# QUESTIONS AND PROBLEMS

## Carboxylic Acids: Structure and Properties

### Foundations

**14.11** The functional group is largely responsible for the physical and chemical properties of the various chemical families. Explain why a carboxylic acid is more polar and has a higher boiling point than an alcohol or an aldehyde of comparable molar mass.

**14.12** Explain why carboxylic acids are weak acids.

### Applications

**14.13** Which member of the following pairs has the higher boiling point?
**a.** Pentanoic acid or pentanal
**b.** 3-Pentanone or 2-pentanol
**c.** 2-Pentanol or pentane

**14.14** Which member of the following pairs has the higher boiling point?
**a.** Ethyl propyl ether or pentanal
**b.** 3-Pentanone or pentanoic acid
**c.** Methanol or methanoic acid

**14.15** Arrange the following from highest to lowest melting points:

**14.16** Draw the condensed formula for each of the line formulas in Question 14.15 and provide the IUPAC name for each.

**14.17** Which member in each of the following pairs has the higher boiling point?
**a.** Heptanoic acid or 1-heptanol
**b.** Propanal or 1-propanol
**c.** Methyl pentanoate or pentanoic acid
**d.** 1-Butanol or butanoic acid

**14.18** Which member in each of the following pairs is more soluble in water?

**a.** $CH_3CH_2CH_2CH_2CH_2C{-}OH$   or

$CH_3CH_2CH_2CH_2CH_2C{-}O^-Na^+$
**b.** $CH_3CH_2CH_2CH_2CH_2CH_2CH_2CH_3$   or
$CH_3CH_2CH_2CH_2CH_2CH_2CH_2CH_2OH$
**c.** $CH_3CH_2{-}O{-}CH_2CH_3$   or   $CH_3CH_2C{-}OCH_3$
**d.** $CH_3CH_2{-}O{-}CH_2CH_3$   or   $CH_3CH_2CH_2CH_2CH_2CH_3$
**e.** Decanoic acid or ethanoic acid

**14.19** Describe the properties of low-molar-mass carboxylic acids.

**14.20** What are some of the biological functions of the long-chain carboxylic acids called fatty acids?

**14.21** Why is citric acid added to some food products?

**14.22** What is the function of lactic acid in food products? Of what significance is lactic acid in muscle metabolism?

**14.23** Why is glutaric acid particularly useful in the synthesis of condensation polymers?

**14.24** What is the role of octanoic acid in the control of appetite?

## Carboxylic Acids: Structure and Nomenclature

### Foundations

**14.25** Summarize the IUPAC nomenclature rules for naming carboxylic acids.

**14.26** Describe the rules for determining the common names of carboxylic acids.

### Applications

**14.27** Adipic acid occurs naturally in beets and is used as a food additive. What is the IUPAC name for adipic acid? Why do you think that adipic acid is used as a food additive?

$$HOOCCH_2CH_2CH_2CH_2COOH$$

**14.28** Propionic acid is a liquid fatty acid found in sweat and milk products. It is a bacterial fermentation product that gives the tangy flavor to Swiss cheese. What is the IUPAC name of propionic acid?

$$CH_3CH_2COOH$$

**14.29** Write the condensed formula and the line formula for each of the following carboxylic acids:
**a.** 3-Methylhexanoic acid
**b.** 2-Ethyl-2-methylpentanoic acid
**c.** 3-Methylcyclopentanecarboxylic acid

**14.30** Write the condensed formula and the line formula for each of the following carboxylic acids:
**a.** 2,3-Dibromocycloheptanecarboxylic acid
**b.** 2-Butenoic acid
**c.** 2,4,5-Trimethyloctanoic acid

**14.31** Name each of the following carboxylic acids, using both the common and the IUPAC Nomenclature Systems:

**a.** $H{-}\overset{\displaystyle O}{\overset{\|}{C}}{-}OH$

**c.** $\overset{\displaystyle O}{\overset{\|}{C}}{-}OH$

**b.** $CH_3\overset{\displaystyle CH_3}{\overset{|}{C}}H CH_2\overset{\displaystyle O}{\overset{\|}{C}}{-}OH$

**14.32** Name each of the following carboxylic acids, using both the common and IUPAC Nomenclature Systems:

a. $CH_3CH_2\overset{\overset{\displaystyle Br}{|}}{C}HCHCH_2\overset{\overset{\displaystyle O}{||}}{C}-OH$
      $\underset{\underset{\displaystyle CH_3}{|}}{}$

c. 

b. $CH_3CH_2\overset{\overset{\displaystyle CH_2CH_3}{|}}{C}HCH_2CH_2\overset{\overset{\displaystyle O}{||}}{C}-OH$

**14.33** Write a complete structural formula and determine the IUPAC name for each of the carboxylic acids of molecular formula $C_4H_8O_2$.

**14.34** Write the general structure of an aldehyde, a ketone, a carboxylic acid, and an ester. What similarities exist among these structures?

**14.35** Write the condensed structure of each of the following carboxylic acids:
a. 4,4-Dimethylhexanoic acid
b. 3-Bromo-4-methylpentanoic acid
c. 2,3-Dinitrobenzoic acid
d. 3-Methylcyclohexanecarboxylic acid

**14.36** Use IUPAC nomenclature to write the names for each of the following carboxylic acids:

a.

c.

b.

**14.37** Provide the common and IUPAC names for each of the following compounds:

a. $CH_3\overset{\overset{\displaystyle HO}{|}}{C}H\overset{\overset{\displaystyle O}{||}}{C}-OH$

c. $CH_3\overset{\overset{\displaystyle CH_3}{|}}{C}CH_2CH_2\overset{\overset{\displaystyle O}{||}}{C}-OH$
      $\underset{\underset{\displaystyle CH_3}{|}}{}$

b. $CH_3\overset{\overset{\displaystyle OH}{|}}{C}HCH_2\overset{\overset{\displaystyle O}{||}}{C}-OH$

d. $CH_3CH_2\overset{\overset{\displaystyle Cl}{|}}{C}CH_2\overset{\overset{\displaystyle O}{||}}{C}-OH$
      $\underset{\underset{\displaystyle Cl}{|}}{}$

**14.38** Draw the structure of each of the following carboxylic acids:
a. β-Chlorobutyric acid
b. α,β-Dibromovaleric acid
c. β,γ-Dihydroxybutyric acid
d. δ-Bromo-γ-chloro-β-methylcaproic acid

**14.39** Provide the IUPAC name for each of the following aromatic carboxylic acids.

b.    COOH
             CH₂CH₃

**14.40** Provide the IUPAC name for each of the following aromatic carboxylic acids.

a.    $CH_2CH_2CH_2COOH$

c.  $CH_3CHCOOH$

b.  $CH_3CHCH_2COOH$

## Carboxylic Acids: Reactions

### Foundations

**14.41** Explain what is meant by oxidation in organic molecules and provide an example of an oxidation reaction involving an aldehyde or an alcohol.

**14.42** Write a general equation showing the preparation of a carboxylic acid from an alcohol.

**14.43** Write a general equation showing the dissociation of a carboxylic acid in water.

**14.44** Carboxylic acids are described as weak acids. To what extent do carboxylic acids generally dissociate?

**14.45** What reaction occurs when a strong base is added to a carboxylic acid?

**14.46** Write a general equation showing the reaction of a strong base with a carboxylic acid.

**14.47** How is a soap prepared?

**14.48** How do soaps assist in the removal of oil and grease from clothing?

### Applications

**14.49** Write an equation representing the oxidation of each of the following compounds:
a. 1-Pentanol
b. Butanal
c. Butanone

**14.50** Write an equation representing the oxidation of each of the following compounds:
a. 3-Hexanol
b. 2-Methylpentanal
c. 3-Pentanone

**14.51** Complete each of the following reactions by supplying the missing portion indicated by a question mark:

a. $CH_3\overset{\displaystyle O}{\overset{\|}{C}}-H \xrightarrow{[O]}$ ?

b. $CH_3CH_2CH_2\overset{\displaystyle O}{\overset{\|}{C}}-OH + CH_3OH \xrightarrow{H^+,\text{ heat}}$ ?

c. ⬠$-\overset{\displaystyle O}{\overset{\|}{C}}-OH$ + ? $\longrightarrow$ ⬠$-\overset{\displaystyle O}{\overset{\|}{C}}-OCH_3$

**14.52** Complete each of the following reactions by supplying the missing part(s) indicated by the question mark(s):

a. $CH_3CH_2CH_2OH \xrightarrow{?(1)} CH_3CH_2\overset{\displaystyle O}{\overset{\|}{C}}-OH \underset{?(3)}{\overset{NaOH}{\rightleftarrows}}$ ?(4)

  ↓ ?(2)

  $CH_3CH_2\overset{\displaystyle O}{\overset{\|}{C}}-\underset{\underset{\displaystyle CH_3}{|}}{O}CHCH_3$

b. $CH_3COOH + NaOH \longrightarrow$ ?

c. $CH_3CH_2CH_2CH_2CH_2COOH + NaOH \longrightarrow$ ?

d. ? + $CH_3CH_2\underset{\underset{\displaystyle CH_3}{|}}{C}HOH \xrightarrow{H^+} CH_3\overset{\displaystyle O}{\overset{\|}{C}}-O\underset{\underset{\displaystyle CH_3}{|}}{C}HCH_2CH_3$

**14.53** How might $CH_3CH_2CH_2CH_2CH_2OH$ be converted to each of the following products?

a. $CH_3CH_2CH_2CH_2CHO$
b. $CH_3CH_2CH_2CH_2COOH$

**14.54** Which of the following alcohols can be oxidized to a carboxylic acid? Name the carboxylic acid produced. For those alcohols that cannot be oxidized to a carboxylic acid, name the final product.

a. Ethanol          c. 1-Propanol
b. 2-Propanol       d. 3-Pentanol

**14.55** Write an equation representing the neutralization of pentanoic acid with each of the following bases:

a. NaOH
b. KOH
c. Ca(OH)$_2$

**14.56** Write an equation representing the neutralization of each of the following carboxylic acids with KOH:

a. 3-Chlorohexanoic acid
b. Cyclohexanecarboxylic acid
c. 3,4-Dimethylpentanoic acid

**14.57** The calcium salt of propionic acid is added to breads as a preservative that prevents mold growth. Draw the structure of the calcium salt of propionic acid. What are the common and IUPAC names of this carboxylic acid salt?

**14.58** Oxalic acid is found in the leaves of rhubarb, primarily in the form of the calcium salt. Since high levels of oxalic acid are toxic, only rhubarb stalks are used to make strawberry rhubarb pie. What is the IUPAC name of oxalic acid? Write the structure of the calcium salt of oxalic acid.

## Esters: Structure, Physical Properties, and Nomenclature

### Foundations

**14.59** Explain why esters are described as slightly polar.

**14.60** Compare the boiling points of esters to those of aldehydes or ketones of similar molar mass.

**14.61** Briefly summarize the IUPAC rules for naming esters.

**14.62** How are the common names of esters derived?

### Applications

**14.63** Draw condensed formulas for each of the following compounds:

a. Methyl benzoate
b. Butyl decanoate
c. Methyl propionate
d. Ethyl propionate

**14.64** Draw condensed formulas for each of the following compounds:

a. Ethyl *m*-nitrobenzoate
b. Isopropyl acetate
c. Methyl butyrate

**14.65** Use the IUPAC Nomenclature System to name each of the following esters:

a. $CH_3\overset{\displaystyle O}{\overset{\|}{C}}-OCH_2CH_3$

b. $CH_3CH_2\overset{\displaystyle O}{\overset{\|}{C}}-OCH_3$

c. $CH_3\underset{\underset{\displaystyle CH_3}{|}}{C}HCH_2\overset{\displaystyle O}{\overset{\|}{C}}-OCH_3$

d. ⬡$-\overset{\displaystyle O}{\overset{\|}{C}}-O-$⬠

**14.66** Use the IUPAC Nomenclature System to name each of the following:

a. ⬡$-\overset{\displaystyle O}{\overset{\|}{C}}-OCH_2CH_2CH_3$

b. ⬡$-\overset{\displaystyle O}{\overset{\|}{C}}-OCH_3$

c. $\underset{\underset{\displaystyle Br}{|}}{C}H_2\underset{\underset{\displaystyle Br}{|}}{C}HCH_2CH_2\overset{\displaystyle O}{\overset{\|}{C}}-OCH_2CH_3$

## Esters: Reactions

### Foundations

**14.67** Write a general reaction showing the preparation of an ester.

**14.68** Why is preparation of an ester referred to as a condensation reaction?

**14.69** Write a general reaction showing the hydrolysis of an ester using an acid catalyst.

**14.70** Write a general reaction showing the base-catalyzed hydrolysis of an ester.

**14.71** What is meant by a hydrolysis reaction?

**14.72** Why is the salt of a carboxylic acid produced in a base-catalyzed hydrolysis of an ester?

## Applications

**14.73** Complete each of the following reactions by supplying the missing portion indicated with a question mark:

a. $CH_3CH_2CH_2\overset{\displaystyle O}{\overset{\|}{C}}-OH + CH_3CH_2OH \xrightarrow{\text{H}^+,\ \text{heat}}$ ?

b. $CH_3CH_2\overset{\displaystyle O}{\overset{\|}{C}}-OCH_2CH_3 + H_2O \xrightarrow{\text{H}^+,\ \text{heat}}$ ?

c. $CH_3\overset{\displaystyle CH_3}{\underset{}{\overset{|}{C}H}}CH_2CH_2\overset{\displaystyle O}{\overset{\|}{C}}-OH + ? \xrightarrow{\text{H}^+,\ \text{heat}}$

$CH_3\overset{\displaystyle CH_3}{\underset{}{\overset{|}{C}H}}CH_2CH_2\overset{\displaystyle O}{\overset{\|}{C}}-OCH_2CH_2CH_3$

d. $CH_3CH_2\overset{\displaystyle Br}{\underset{}{\overset{|}{C}H}}CH_2\overset{\displaystyle O}{\overset{\|}{C}}-OCH_2CH_3 + H_2O \xrightarrow{\text{OH}^-,\ \text{heat}}$ ?

**14.74** Complete each of the following reactions by supplying the missing portion indicated with a question mark:

a. $? + CH_3\overset{\displaystyle CH_3}{\underset{\displaystyle CH_3}{\overset{|}{\underset{|}{C}}}}-OH \xrightarrow{\ ?\ } CH_3CH_2\overset{\displaystyle O}{\overset{\|}{C}}-O-\overset{\displaystyle CH_3}{\underset{\displaystyle CH_3}{\overset{|}{\underset{|}{C}}}}-CH_3$

b. $CH_3CH_2CH_2CH_2COOH + CH_3CH_2CH_2CH_2OH \xrightarrow{\text{H}^+,\ \text{heat}}$ ?

c. $CH_3\overset{\displaystyle CH_3}{\underset{\displaystyle CH_3}{\overset{|}{\underset{|}{C}}}}CH_2\overset{\displaystyle O}{\overset{\|}{C}}-OCH_2CH_2\overset{\displaystyle CH_3}{\underset{\displaystyle CH_3}{\overset{|}{\underset{|}{C}}}}CH_3 + H_2O \xrightarrow{\text{H}^+,\ \text{heat}}$ ?

d. $CH_3CH_2\overset{\displaystyle O}{\overset{\|}{C}}-OCH_3 + H_2O \xrightarrow{\text{OH}^-,\ \text{heat}}$ ?

**14.75** Design the synthesis of each of the following esters from organic alcohols.
  **a.** Isobutyl methanoate (raspberries)
  **b.** Pentyl butanoate (apricot)

**14.76** Design the synthesis of each of the following esters from organic alcohols.
  **a.** Methyl butanoate (apples)
  **b.** Octyl ethanoate (oranges)

**14.77** What is saponification? Give an example using specific molecules.

**14.78** When the methyl ester of hexanoic acid is hydrolyzed in aqueous sodium hydroxide in the presence of heat, a homogeneous solution results. When the solution is acidified with dilute aqueous hydrochloric acid, a new product forms. What is the new product? Draw its structure.

**14.79** The structure of salicylic acid is shown. If this acid reacts with methanol, the product is an ester, methyl salicylate.

Methyl salicylate is known as oil of wintergreen and is often used as a flavoring agent. Draw the structure of the product of this reaction.

**14.80** When salicylic acid reacts with acetic anhydride, one of the products is an ester, acetylsalicylic acid. Acetylsalicylic acid is the active ingredient in aspirin. Complete the following equation by drawing the structure of acetylsalicylic acid. (*Hint*: Acid anhydrides are hydrolyzed by water.)

**14.81** Compound A ($C_6H_{12}O_2$) reacts with water, acid, and heat to yield compound B ($C_5H_{10}O_2$) and compound C ($CH_4O$). Compound B is acidic. Deduce possible structures of compounds A, B, and C.

**14.82** What products are formed when methyl *o*-bromobenzoate reacts with each of the following?
  **a.** Aqueous acid and heat
  **b.** Aqueous base and heat

**14.83** Write an equation for the acid-catalyzed hydrolysis of each of the following esters:
  **a.** Propyl propanoate        **c.** Ethyl methanoate
  **b.** Butyl methanoate         **d.** Methyl pentanoate

**14.84** Write an equation for the base-catalyzed hydrolysis of each of the following esters:
  **a.** Pentyl methanoate        **c.** Butyl hexanoate
  **b.** Hexyl propanoate         **d.** Methyl benzoate

## Acid Chlorides and Acid Anhydrides

### Foundations

**14.85** Describe the physical properties of acid chlorides.

**14.86** Describe the chemical properties of acid chlorides.

**14.87** Describe the physical properties of acid anhydrides.

**14.88** Write a general equation for the formation of acid anhydrides.

### Applications

**14.89** Write the condensed formula for each of the following compounds:
  **a.** Decanoic anhydride
  **b.** Acetic anhydride

**14.90** Write the condensed formula for each of the following compounds:
  **a.** Valeric anhydride
  **b.** Benzoyl chloride

**14.91** Write a condensed formula and a line formula for each of the following compounds:
  **a.** Octanoyl chloride
  **b.** Butanoyl chloride
  **c.** Nonanoyl chloride

to one another to produce a protein chain, the amino group of one amino acid reacts with the carboxyl group of another amino acid. The amide bond that results is called a *peptide bond*.

In this chapter we will explore the chemistry of the organic molecules that contain nitrogen. In upcoming chapters we will investigate the structure and properties of the nitrogen-containing biological molecules.

The general structure of an amino acid is

$$H-\overset{\overset{\textstyle H}{|}}{\underset{\underset{\textstyle H}{|}}{N}}-\overset{\overset{\textstyle H}{|}}{\underset{\underset{\textstyle R}{|}}{C}}-\overset{\overset{\textstyle O}{\|}}{C}-OH$$

The amino group is highlighted in red and the carboxyl group in blue. Amino acids are the basic subunits of all proteins.

## 15.1 Amines

### Structure and Physical Properties

**Amines** are organic derivatives of ammonia and, like ammonia, they are basic. In fact, amines are the most important type of organic base found in nature. We can think of them as substituted ammonia molecules in which one, two, or three of the ammonia hydrogens have been replaced by an organic group:

1 Classify amines as primary, secondary, or tertiary.

$$\underset{\text{Ammonia}}{\overset{\cdot\cdot}{N}\underset{H\ H}{\diagup|\diagdown}H} \xrightarrow[\text{for H}]{\text{R substitutes}} \underset{\text{An amine}}{\overset{\cdot\cdot}{N}\underset{H\ H}{\diagup|\diagdown}R}$$

The structures drawn above and in Figure 15.1 reveal that like ammonia, amines are pyramidal. The nitrogen atom has three groups bonded to it and has a non-bonding pair of electrons.

Amines are classified according to the number of alkyl or aryl groups attached to the nitrogen. In a **primary (1°) amine,** one of the hydrogens is replaced by an organic group. In a **secondary (2°) amine,** two hydrogens are replaced. In a **tertiary (3°) amine,** three organic groups replace the hydrogens:

*The geometry of ammonia is described in Section 3.4.*

$$\underset{\text{Ammonia}}{H-\overset{\overset{\textstyle H}{|}}{N}-H} \qquad \underset{\substack{\text{1° amine}\\\text{(primary amine)}}}{R-\overset{\overset{\textstyle H}{|}}{N}-H} \qquad \underset{\substack{\text{2° amine}\\\text{(secondary amine)}}}{R-\overset{\overset{\textstyle H}{|}}{N}-R} \qquad \underset{\substack{\text{3° amine}\\\text{(tertiary amine)}}}{R-\overset{\overset{\textstyle R}{|}}{N}-R}$$

Ammonia     Methanamine (methylamine) (primary amine)     *N*-Methylmethanamine (dimethylamine) (secondary amine)     *N,N*-Dimethylmethanamine (trimethylamine) (tertiary amine)

**Figure 15.1** The trigonal pyramidal structure of amines. Note the similarities in structure between an amine and the ammonia molecule.

The nitrogen atom is more electronegative than the hydrogen atoms in amines. As a result, the N—H bond is polar, and hydrogen bonding between amine molecules or between amine molecules and water can occur (Figure 15.2).

*Hydrogen bonding is described in Section 5.2.*

**Figure 15.2** Hydrogen bonding (a) in methylamine and (b) between methylamine and water. Dotted lines represent hydrogen bonds.

(a)                                    (b)

---

**EXAMPLE 15.1**   **Classifying Amines as Primary, Secondary, or Tertiary**

Classify each of the following compounds as a primary, secondary, or tertiary amine.

**LEARNING GOAL**

**1**  Classify amines as primary, secondary, or tertiary.

**Solution**

Compare the structure of the amine with that of ammonia.

$$\begin{array}{c} CH_3 \\ | \\ H\!-\!N\!-\!H \end{array} \qquad \begin{array}{c} H \\ | \\ H\!-\!N\!-\!H \end{array}$$   1° amine: one hydrogen replaced

$$\begin{array}{c} CH_3 \\ | \\ CH_3\!-\!N\!-\!H \end{array} \qquad \begin{array}{c} H \\ | \\ H\!-\!N\!-\!H \end{array}$$   2° amine: two hydrogens replaced

$$\begin{array}{c} CH_3 \\ | \\ CH_3\!-\!N\!-\!CH_3 \end{array} \qquad \begin{array}{c} H \\ | \\ H\!-\!N\!-\!H \end{array}$$   3° amine: three hydrogens replaced

**Practice Problem 15.1**

Determine whether each of the following amines is primary, secondary, or tertiary.

$$\begin{array}{c} CH_2CH_3 \\ | \\ a.\ CH_3CH_2NCH_3 \end{array} \qquad b.\ CH_3CH_2CH_2NH_2 \qquad \begin{array}{c} H \\ | \\ c.\ CH_3NCH_3 \end{array}$$

▶ For Further Practice: **Questions 15.29 and 15.30.**

**Question 15.1**  Refer to Figure 15.2 and draw a similar figure showing the hydrogen bonding that occurs between water and a 2° amine.

**Question 15.2**  Refer to Figure 15.2 and draw hydrogen bonding between two primary amines.

**TABLE 15.1 Boiling Points of Amines**

| Systematic Name | Common Name | Structure | Boiling Point (°C) |
|---|---|---|---|
| | Ammonia | $NH_3$ | −33.4 |
| Methanamine | Methylamine | $CH_3NH_2$ | −6.3 |
| N-Methylmethanamine | Dimethylamine | $(CH_3)_2NH$ | 7.4 |
| N,N-Dimethylmethanamine | Trimethylamine | $(CH_3)_3N$ | 2.9 |
| Ethanamine | Ethylamine | $CH_3CH_2NH_2$ | 16.6 |
| Propanamine | Propylamine | $CH_3CH_2CH_2NH_2$ | 48.7 |
| Butanamine | Butylamine | $CH_3CH_2CH_2CH_2NH_2$ | 77.8 |

The ability of primary and secondary amines to form N—H···N hydrogen bonds is reflected in their boiling points (Table 15.1). Primary amines have boiling points well above those of alkanes of similar molar mass but considerably lower than those of comparable alcohols. Consider the following examples:

**LEARNING GOAL**

**2** Describe the physical properties of amines.

$CH_3CH_2CH_3$

Propane
M.M. = 44 g/mol
b.p. = −42.2°C

$CH_3CH_2NH_2$

Ethanamine
M.M. = 45 g/mol
b.p. = 16.6°C

$CH_3CH_2OH$

Ethanol
M.M. = 46 g/mol
b.p. = 78.5°C

Tertiary amines do not have an N—H bond. As a result they cannot form intermolecular hydrogen bonds with other tertiary amines. Consequently, their boiling points are lower than those of primary or secondary amines of comparable molar mass. This is seen in a comparison of the boiling points of propanamine (propylamine; M.M. = 59) and N,N-dimethylmethanamine (trimethylamine; M.M. = 59). Trimethylamine, the tertiary amine, has a boiling point of 2.9°C, whereas propylamine, the primary amine, has a boiling point of 48.7°C. Clearly the inability of trimethylamine molecules to form intermolecular hydrogen bonds results in a much lower boiling point.

$CH_3CH_2CH_2—NH_2$

Propanamine
(propylamine)
M.M. = 59 g/mol
b.p. = 48.7°C

$CH_3CH_2—N—CH_3$
         |
         H

N-Methylethanamine
(ethylmethylamine)
M.M. = 59 g/mol
b.p. = 36.7°C

$CH_3—N—CH_3$
       |
       $CH_3$

N,N-Dimethylmethanamine
(trimethylamine)
M.M. = 59 g/mol
b.p. = 2.9°C

The intermolecular hydrogen bonds formed by primary and secondary amines are not as strong as the hydrogen bonds formed by alcohols because nitrogen is not as electronegative as oxygen. For this reason primary and secondary amines have lower boiling points than alcohols (Table 15.2).

All amines can form intermolecular hydrogen bonds with water (O—H···N). As a result, small amines (six or fewer carbons) are soluble in water. As we have noted for other families of organic molecules, water solubility decreases as the length of the hydrocarbon (hydrophobic) portion of the molecule increases.

TABLE 15.2 Comparison of the Boiling Points of Selected Alcohols and Amines

| Name | Molar Mass (g/mol) | Boiling Point (°C) |
|---|---|---|
| Methanol | 32 | 64.5 |
| Methanamine | 31 | −6.3 |
| Ethanol | 46 | 78.5 |
| Ethanamine | 45 | 16.6 |
| Propanol | 60 | 97.2 |
| Propanamine | 59 | 48.7 |

## EXAMPLE 15.2    Predicting the Physical Properties of Amines

Which member of each of the following pairs of molecules has the higher boiling point?

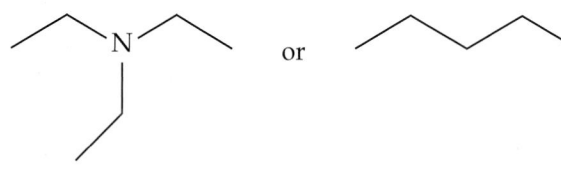
or

### LEARNING GOAL

**2**  Describe the physical properties of amines.

### Solution

The molecule on the right, hexanamine, has a higher boiling point than the molecule on the left, N,N-diethylethanamine (triethylamine). Triethylamine is a tertiary amine; therefore, it has no N—H bond and cannot form intermolecular hydrogen bonds with other triethylamine molecules.

### Solution

The molecule on the left, 1-butanol, has a higher boiling point than the molecule on the right, 1-butanamine. Nitrogen is not as electronegative as oxygen, thus the hydroxyl group is more polar than the amino group and forms stronger hydrogen bonds.

### Practice Problem 15.2

Which compound in each of the following pairs would you predict to have a higher boiling point? Explain your reasoning.

  a. Methanol or methylamine
  b. Dimethylamine or water

  c. Methylamine or ethylamine
  d. Propylamine or butane

▶ For Further Practice: **Questions 15.17 and 15.18.**

## Nomenclature

In systematic nomenclature, primary amines are named according to the following rules:

### LEARNING GOAL

**3**  Draw and name simple amines using systematic and common nomenclature systems.

• Determine the name of the *parent compound,* the longest continuous carbon chain containing the amine group.
• Replace the *-e* ending of the alkane chain with *-amine.* Following this pattern, the alkane becomes an alkan*amine;* for instance, ethan*e* becomes ethan*amine.*

- Number the parent chain to give the carbon bearing the amine group the lowest possible number.
- Name and number all substituents, and add them as prefixes to the "alkanamine" name.

For instance,

$$CH_3—NH_2 \qquad\qquad CH_3CH_2CH_2—NH_2 \qquad\qquad CH_3CH_2CH_2\underset{\underset{NH_2}{|}}{C}HCH_3$$

Methanamine  1-Propanamine  2-Pentanamine

For secondary or tertiary amines the prefix *N*-alkyl is added to the name of the parent compound. For example,

$$CH_3—NH—CH_2CH_3 \qquad\qquad CH_3—\underset{\underset{CH_3}{|}}{\overset{\overset{CH_3}{|}}{N}}—CH_3$$

*N*-Methylethanamine  *N,N*-Dimethylmethanamine

Several aromatic amines have special names that have also been approved for use by IUPAC. For example, the amine of benzene is given the name *aniline*. The systematic name for aniline is *benzenamine*.

Aniline or benzenamine | *m*-Toluidine or *meta*-toluidine | *o*-Toluidine or *ortho*-toluidine | *p*-Toluidine or *para*-toluidine

If additional groups are attached to the nitrogen of an aromatic amine, they are indicated with the letter *N*- followed by the name of the group.

Aniline was first isolated from the blue dye indigo, a product of the indigo plant. It is the starting material in the synthesis of hundreds of dyes. Is aniline a primary, secondary, or tertiary amine?

**LEARNING GOAL**

**3** Draw and name simple amines using systematic and common nomenclature systems.

---

**EXAMPLE 15.3**  **Writing the Systematic Name for an Amine**

a. Determine the systematic name for the following amine, which is used by the German cockroach as a pheromone.

$$CH_3—NH—CH_3$$

**Solution**

Parent compound: methane (becomes methanamine)
Additional group on N: methyl (becomes *N*-methyl)
Name: *N*-Methylmethanamine

b. Name the following amine.

$$CH_3CH_2CH_2—NH—CH_3$$

*Continued...*

*N*-methylmethanamine is used by the German cockroach as a communication pheromone. What is the common name of this amine?

**Solution**

Parent compound: propane (becomes propanamine)
Additional group on N: methyl (becomes *N*-methyl)
Name: *N*-Methyl-1-propanamine

---

**Practice Problem 15.3**

What is the systematic name for each of the following amines?

a. CH$_3$CH$_2$—N—CH$_3$
         |
         CH$_2$CH$_2$CH$_3$

c. CH$_3$CH$_2$CH$_2$—N—CH$_2$CH$_3$
              |
              CH$_2$CH$_3$

b. CH$_3$CH$_2$CHCH$_2$CH$_2$CH$_3$
         |
         NH$_2$

► For Further Practice: **Questions 15.21, 15.27, and 15.28.**

---

Common names are often used for the simple amines. The common names of the alkyl groups bonded to the amine nitrogen are followed by the ending -*amine*. Each group is listed alphabetically in one continuous word followed by the suffix -*amine*:

CH$_3$—NH$_2$           CH$_3$—NH—CH$_3$          
CH$_3$
|
CH$_3$—N—CH$_3$

Methylamine          Dimethylamine          Trimethylamine

CH$_3$CH$_2$—NH$_2$        CH$_3$CH$_2$—NH—CH$_3$

Ethylamine          Ethylmethylamine

Table 15.3 compares these systems of nomenclature for a number of simple amines.

**Question 15.3**   Use the structure of aniline provided and draw the condensed formula for each of the following amines.

a. *N*-Methylaniline
b. *N,N*-Dimethylaniline
c. *N*-Ethylaniline
d. *N*-Isopropylaniline

---

**TABLE 15.3 Systematic and Common Names of Amines**

| Compound | Systematic Name | Common Name |
|---|---|---|
| R—NH$_2$ | Alkan*amine* | Alkyl*amine* |
| CH$_3$—NH$_2$ | Methanamine | Methylamine |
| CH$_3$CH$_2$—NH$_2$ | Ethanamine | Ethylamine |
| CH$_3$CH$_2$CH$_2$—NH$_2$ | 1-Propanamine | Propylamine |
| CH$_3$—NH—CH$_3$ | *N*-Methylmethanamine | Dimethylamine |
| CH$_3$—NH—CH$_2$CH$_3$ | *N*-Methylethanamine | Ethylmethylamine |
| CH$_3$—N—CH$_3$ (with CH$_3$ on N) | *N,N*-Dimethylmethanamine | Trimethylamine |

**Question 15.4** Name each of the following amines using the systematic and common nomenclature systems.

a.

$$NH_2$$
$$CH_3CHCH_2CH_3$$

b.

$$NH_2$$
$$CH_3-C-CH_3$$
$$\quad\quad CH_3$$

c.

$$CH_3$$
$$NH$$
$$CH_3CHCH_2CH_3$$

d.

$$CH_3$$
$$N-CH_2CH_3$$
$$CH_3CHCH_3$$

**Question 15.5** Draw the condensed formula for each of the following compounds.
   a. 2-Propanamine
   b. 3-Octanamine
   c. N-Ethyl-2-heptanamine
   d. 2-Methyl-2-pentanamine
   e. 4-Chloro-5-iodo-1-nonanamine
   f. N,N-Diethyl-1-pentanamine

**Question 15.6** Draw the condensed formula for each of the following compounds.
   a. Diethylmethylamine
   b. 4-Methylpentylamine
   c. N-Methylaniline
   d. Triisopropylamine
   e. Methyl-t-butylamine
   f. Ethylhexylamine

## Medically Important Amines

Although amines play many different roles in our day-to-day lives, one important use is in medicine. A host of drugs derived from amines is responsible for improving the quality of life, whereas others, such as cocaine and heroin, are highly addictive.

*Amphetamines,* such as benzedrine and methedrine, stimulate the central nervous system. They elevate blood pressure and pulse rate and are often used to decrease fatigue. Medically, they have been used to treat depression and epilepsy. Amphetamines have also been prescribed as diet pills because they decrease the appetite. Their use is controlled by federal law because excess use of amphetamines can cause paranoia and mental illness.

1-Phenyl-2-propanamine
(Amphetamine)

Benzedrine

N-Methyl-1-phenyl-2-propanamine
(Methamphetamine)

Methedrine

Many of the medicinal amines are *analgesics* (pain relievers) or *anesthetics* (pain blockers). Novocaine and related compounds, for example, are used as local anesthetics. Demerol is a very strong pain reliever.

Novocaine

Demerol

Ephedrine, its stereoisomer pseudoephedrine, and phenylephrine (also called neosynephrine) are used as decongestants in cough syrups and nasal sprays.

L-*Dopa, dopamine, and other key neurotransmitters are described in detail in Section 15.5.*

By shrinking the membranes that line the nasal passages, they relieve the symptoms of congestion and stuffy nose. These compounds are very closely related to L-dopa and dopamine, which are key compounds in the function of the central nervous system.

Ephedrine

Pseudoephedrine

Phenylephrine
(neosynephrine)

*Methamphetamine use and abuse are discussed in Chemistry at the Crime Scene: Methamphetamine, found on page 523.*

Recently, many states have restricted the sales of products containing ephedrine and pseudoephedrine, and many drugstore chains have moved these products behind the counter. The reason for these precautions is that either ephedrine or pseudoephedrine can be used as the starting material in the synthesis of methamphetamines. In response to this problem, pharmaceutical companies are replacing ephedrine and pseudoephedrine in these decongestants with phenylephrine, which cannot be used as a reactant in the synthesis of methamphetamine.

Ephedrine and pseudoephedrine are also the primary active ingredients in ephedra, a plant found in the deserts of central Asia. Ephedra is used as a stimulant in a variety of products that are sold over-the-counter as aids to boost energy, promote weight loss, and enhance athletic performance. In 2004, the Food and Drug Administration (FDA) banned the use of ephedra in these over-the-counter formulations after reviewing 16,000 reports of adverse side effects including nervousness, heart irregularities, seizures, heart attacks, and 80 deaths, including that of Baltimore Orioles pitcher Steve Bechler, age 23. However, in April 2005, a Federal judge in Texas ruled that the FDA had failed to prove that ephedra is dangerous at doses of 10 milligrams (mg) or lower, opening the way for the sale of ephedra-containing herbal remedies.

The *sulfa drugs*, the first chemicals used to fight bacterial infections, are synthesized from amines.

Sulfanilamide—a sulfa drug

## Reactions Involving Amines

### Preparation of Amines

**4** Write equations representing the synthesis of amines.

In the laboratory, amines are prepared by the reduction of amides and nitro compounds.

Examples of amides

A nitro compound

As we will see in Section 15.3, amides are neutral nitrogen compounds that produce an amine and a carboxylic acid when hydrolyzed. Nitro compounds are prepared by the nitration of an aromatic compound.

Primary amines are readily produced by reduction of a nitro compound, as in the following reaction:

We are using the general symbol [H] to represent any reducing agent just as we used [O] to represent an oxidizing agent in previous chapters. Several different reducing agents may be used to effect the changes shown here; for example, metallic iron and acid may be used to reduce aromatic nitro compounds and LiAlH$_4$ in ether reduces amides.

$$ \underset{\text{A nitro compound}}{\text{NO}_2 \text{ (benzene ring)}} \xrightarrow{\text{[H]}} \underset{\substack{\text{An aromatic} \\ \text{primary} \\ \text{amine}}}{\text{NH}_2 \text{ (benzene ring)}} $$

In this reaction the nitro compound is nitrobenzene and the product is aniline.

Amides may also be reduced to produce primary, secondary, or tertiary amines.

$$ \underset{\text{Amide}}{R^1 - \overset{\overset{\text{O}}{\|}}{C} - N\overset{R^2}{\underset{R^3}{\big\backslash}}} \xrightarrow{\text{[H]}} \underset{\text{Amine}}{R^1CH_2N\overset{R^2}{\underset{R^3}{\big\backslash}}} $$

($R^2$ and $R^3$ may be a hydrogen atom or an organic group.)

If $R^2$ and $R^3$ are hydrogen atoms, the product will be a primary amine:

$$ \underset{\text{Ethanamide}}{CH_3\overset{\overset{\text{O}}{\|}}{C}NH_2} \xrightarrow{\text{[H]}} \underset{\substack{\text{Ethanamine} \\ \text{(ethylamine)}}}{CH_3CH_2NH_2} $$

If either $R^2$ or $R^3$ is an organic group, the product will be a secondary amine:

$$ \underset{\text{N-Methylpropanamide}}{CH_3CH_2\overset{\overset{\text{O}}{\|}}{C}NHCH_3} \xrightarrow{\text{[H]}} \underset{\substack{\text{N-Methyl-1-propanamine} \\ \text{(methylpropylamine)}}}{CH_3CH_2CH_2NHCH_3} $$

If both $R^2$ and $R^3$ are organic groups, the product will be a tertiary amine:

$$ \underset{\text{N,N-Dimethylethanamide}}{CH_3\overset{\overset{\text{O}}{\|}}{C} - N\overset{CH_3}{\underset{}{|}}CH_3} \xrightarrow{\text{[H]}} \underset{\text{N,N-Dimethylethanamine}}{CH_3CH_2\overset{\overset{CH_3}{|}}{N}CH_3} $$

## Basicity

Amines behave as weak bases, accepting H$^+$ when dissolved in water. The nonbonding pair (lone pair) of electrons of the nitrogen atom can be shared with a proton (H$^+$) from a water molecule, producing an **alkylammonium ion.** Hydroxide ions are also formed, so the resulting solution is basic.

LEARNING GOAL

5  Write equations showing the basicity and neutralization of amines.

$$ \underset{\text{Amine}}{R - \overset{\overset{\text{H}}{|}}{\underset{\underset{\text{H}}{|}}{N}}:} + \underset{\text{Water}}{H - OH} \rightleftharpoons \underset{\text{Alkylammonium ion}}{R - \overset{\overset{\text{H}}{|}}{\underset{\underset{\text{H}}{|}}{N^+}} - H} + \underset{\text{Hydroxide ion}}{OH^-} $$

$$\underset{\underset{\text{Methylamine}}{}}{CH_3-\overset{\displaystyle H}{\underset{\displaystyle H}{N}}:} + \underset{\text{Water}}{H-OH} \rightleftharpoons \underset{\underset{\text{Methylammonium ion}}{}}{CH_3-\overset{\displaystyle H}{\underset{\displaystyle H}{N^+}}-H} + \underset{\text{Hydroxide ion}}{OH^-}$$

## Neutralization

Because amines are bases, they react with acids to form alkylammonium salts.

$$\underset{\underset{\text{Amine}}{}}{R-\overset{\displaystyle H}{\underset{\displaystyle H}{N}}:} + \underset{\text{Acid}}{HCl} \longrightarrow \underset{\text{Alkylammonium salt}}{R-\overset{\displaystyle H}{\underset{\displaystyle H}{N^+}}-H\ Cl^-}$$

*Recall that the reaction of an acid and a base gives a salt (Section 8.3).*

The reaction of methylamine with hydrochloric acid shown is typical of these reactions.

$$\underset{\text{Methylamine}}{CH_3-\overset{\displaystyle H}{\underset{\displaystyle H}{N}}:} + \underset{\underset{\text{acid}}{\text{Hydrochloric}}}{HCl} \longrightarrow \underset{\underset{\text{chloride}}{\text{Methylammonium}}}{CH_3-\overset{\displaystyle H}{\underset{\displaystyle H}{N^+}}-H\ Cl^-}$$

Alkylammonium salts are named by replacing the suffix *-amine* with *ammonium*. This is then followed by the name of the anion. The salts are ionic and hence are quite soluble in water.

A variety of important drugs are amines. They are usually administered as alkylammonium salts because the salts are much more soluble in aqueous solutions and in body fluids.

**Question 15.7** Complete each of the following reactions by supplying the missing product(s).

a. NH$_2$⬡ + HBr ⟶ ?

b. $CH_3CH_2NHCH_3 + H_2O \longrightarrow$ ?
c. $CH_3NH_2 + H_2O \longrightarrow$ ?

**Question 15.8** Complete each of the following reactions by supplying the missing product(s).
a. $CH_3NH_2 + HI \longrightarrow$ ?
b. $CH_3CH_2NH_2 + HBr \longrightarrow$ ?
c. $(CH_3CH_2)_2NH + HCl \longrightarrow$ ?

Alkylammonium salts can neutralize hydroxide ions. In this reaction, water is formed and the protonated amine cation is converted into an amine.

$$\underset{\underset{\text{salt}}{\text{Alkylammonium}}}{R-\overset{\displaystyle H}{\underset{\displaystyle H}{N^+}}-H} + \underset{\underset{\text{ion}}{\text{Hydroxide}}}{OH^-} \longrightarrow \underset{\text{Amine}}{R-\overset{\displaystyle H}{\underset{\displaystyle H}{N}}:} + \underset{\text{Water}}{H-OH}$$

# CHEMISTRY AT THE CRIME SCENE

## Methamphetamine

Methamphetamine is an addictive drug known by many names, including "speed," "crystal," "crank," "ice," and "glass." A bitter-tasting, odorless, crystalline powder, it is easily dissolved in either water or alcohol. Methamphetamine was developed early in the twentieth century and used as a decongestant in nasal and bronchial inhalers. Now it is rarely used for medical purposes.

A 2002 Health and Human Services survey revealed that twelve million Americans age twelve and older had used methamphetamine. Use of methamphetamine was once associated with white, male, blue-collar workers; but a much more diverse group now uses the drug. Although it is still used by people in jobs such as long-distance trucking that require long hours and mental and physical alertness, it is disturbing that use of methamphetamine is becoming increasingly associated with sexual activity, teenagers attending "raves," homeless people, and runaway youths.

Methamphetamine can be smoked, taken orally, snorted, or injected, depending on the form of the drug; and it alters the user's mood differently depending on how it is taken. Smoking or injecting intravenously results in a "flash" or intense rush that lasts only a few minutes (min). This may be followed by a high that lasts several hours (h). Snorting and oral ingestion result in a euphoria lasting 3 to 5 min in the case of snorting and up to 20 min in the case of oral ingestion. Because the pleasurable effects are so short-lived, methamphetamine users tend to binge to try to sustain the high.

Both the intense rush and the longer-lasting euphoria are thought to result from a release of dopamine and norepinephrine into regions of the brain that control feelings of pleasure. Once inside nerve cells (neurons), methamphetamine causes the release of dopamine and norepinephrine. At the same time, it inhibits enzymes that would normally destroy these two neurotransmitters and the excess is transported out of neurons, causing the sensations of pleasure and euphoria. The excess norepinephrine may be responsible for the increased attention and decreased fatigue associated with methamphetamine use.

Symptoms of long-term use include addiction, anxiety, violent behavior, confusion, as well as psychotic symptoms of paranoia, hallucinations, and delusions. In severe cases, paranoia causes homicidal and/or suicidal feelings. Methamphetamine also increases heart rate and blood pressure. It can cause strokes, which result from irreversible damage to blood vessels in the brain, as well as respiratory problems, irregular heartbeat, and extreme anorexia. In extreme situations, it can cause cardiovascular collapse and death.

No physical symptoms accompany withdrawal from the drug, but psychological symptoms such as depression, anxiety, aggression, and intense craving are common. Of greatest concern is the brain damage that occurs in long-term users.

Dopamine release may be the cause of the drug's long-term toxic effects. Compare the structure of the neurotransmitter dopamine (Figure 15.7) with that of methamphetamine shown below. Research in humans has shown that even 3 years after chronic methamphetamine use, the former user continues to have a reduced ability to transport dopamine back into nerve cells. Parkinson's disease is characterized by a decrease in the dopamine-producing neurons in the brain; so it was logical to look for similarities between methamphetamine users and those suffering from Parkinson's. In fact, the brains of methamphetamine users showed damage similar to, but not as severe as, that in Parkinson's disease. Research in animals demonstrated that up to 50% of the dopamine-producing cells in parts of the brain may be destroyed by prolonged exposure, and that serotonin-containing neurons may sustain even worse damage.

Methamphetamine use continues to rise, in part, because it is easily synthesized, or "cooked," using "recipes" that are available from many sources, including the Internet. Ephedrine, an over-the-counter decongestant drug, is the starting material. (Pseudoephedrine, a stereoisomer of ephedrine, can also be used.) As shown in the equation below, ephedrine is simply reduced to produce methamphetamine.

$$\text{Ephedrine} \xrightarrow{[H]} \text{Methamphetamine}$$

Ephedrine                    Methamphetamine

While the synthesis involves a variety of dangerous chemicals, including anhydrous ammonia, anhydrous hydrochloric acid, sodium, and sodium hydroxide, most "meth cooks" do not have formal laboratory training. "Meth lab" fires are common, and the synthesis produces toxic wastes. The cleanup that followed the seizure of a major "meth lab" in 2003 took 8 days and required fifty people. Over four million pounds (lb) of toxic soil and 133 drums of hazardous waste were removed from the site, at a cost of $226,000.

### For Further Understanding

► Compare the structures of methamphetamine and dopamine. Develop a hypothesis to explain why dopamine receptors also bind to and transport methamphetamine into neurons. (*Hint:* Receptors are proteins in cell membranes that have a pocket into which a specific molecule can fit.)

► Explain why methamphetamine is soluble in alcohols and in water.

(a)

(b)

**Figure 15.3** (a) Crack cocaine is a non-water-soluble base with a low melting point and a crystalline structure.
(b) Powdered cocaine is a water-soluble salt of cocaine base.
(c) Cocaine is extracted from the leaves of the coca plant.

(c)

---

The local anesthetic novocaine, which is often used in dentistry and for minor surgery, is injected as an amine salt. See Medically Important Amines earlier in this section.

---

Thus, by adding a strong acid to a water-insoluble amine, a water-soluble alkylammonium salt can be formed. The salt can just as easily be converted back to an amine by the addition of a strong base. The ability to manipulate the solubility of physiologically active amines through interconversion of the amine and its corresponding salt is extremely important in the development, manufacture, and administration of many important drugs.

"Crack" cocaine is an amine and a base (see Figure 15.4 and structure below) and is generally found in the form of relatively large crystals (Figure 15.3a) that may vary in color from white to dark brown or black. As we have just seen, when an amine reacts with an acid, an alkylammonium salt is formed. When cocaine reacts with HCl, the product is cocaine hydrochloride:

"Crack" cocaine
(a base)

$+HCl \longrightarrow$

Cocaine hydrochloride
(a salt)

The salt of cocaine is a powder (Figure 15.3b) and is soluble in water. Since it is a powder, it can be snorted, and because it is water-soluble, it dissolves in the fluids of the nasal mucous membranes and is absorbed into the bloodstream. This is a common form of cocaine because it is the direct product of the preparation from coca leaves (Figure 15.3c). A coca paste is made from the leaves and is mixed with HCl and water. After additional processing, the product is the salt of cocaine.

Cocaine hydrochloride salt can be converted into its base form by a process called "free basing." Although the chemistry is simple, the process is dangerous because it requires highly flammable solvents. This pure cocaine is not soluble in water. It has a relatively low melting point, however, and can be smoked. Crack, so called because of the crackling noise it makes when smoked, is absorbed into the body more quickly than the snorted powder and results in a more immediate high.

## Quaternary Ammonium Salts

**Quaternary ammonium salts** are ammonium salts that have four organic groups bonded to the nitrogen. They have the following general structure:

$$R_4N^+X^-$$  (R = any alkyl or aryl group;

X⁻ = a halide anion, most commonly Cl⁻)

Quaternary ammonium salts that have a very long carbon chain, sometimes called "quats," are used as disinfectants and antiseptics because they have detergent activity. Two popular quats are benzalkonium chloride (Zephiran) and cetylpyridinium chloride, found in the mouthwash Scope.

Benzalkonium chloride

Cetylpyridinium chloride

Choline is an important quaternary ammonium salt in the body. It is part of the hydrophilic "head" of the membrane phospholipid lecithin. Choline is also a precursor for the synthesis of the neurotransmitter acetylcholine.

Choline

## 15.2 Heterocyclic Amines

**Heterocyclic amines** are cyclic compounds that have at least one nitrogen atom in the ring structure. The structures and common names of several heterocyclic amines important in nature are shown here. They are represented by their structural formulas and by abbreviated line formulas.

Imidazole

Pyridine

Pyrrole

Pyrimidine

**LEARNING GOAL**

**6** Describe the structure of quaternary ammonium salts and discuss their use as antiseptics and disinfectants.

*Phospholipids and biological membranes are discussed in Sections 17.3 and 17.6.*

*The function of acetylcholine is described in greater detail in Section 15.5.*

**LEARNING GOAL**

**7** Discuss the biological significance of heterocyclic amines.

Coniine is produced by the poison hemlock plant. It is a neurotoxin that causes respiratory paralysis. It is the poison that was used to kill the Greek philosopher Socrates in 399 BC. To what class of molecules does coniine belong?

The heterocyclic amines shown below are examples of fused ring structures. Each ring pair shares two carbon atoms in common. Thus, two fused rings share one or more common bonds as part of their ring backbones. The fused ring structures of purine, indole, and porphyrin, are shown as structural formulas and as line diagrams:

Purine

Indole

M⁺ = metal ion

Porphyrin

*The structures of purines and pyrimidines are presented in Section 20.1.*

*The structure of the heme group found in hemoglobin and myoglobin is presented in Section 18.8.*

The pyrimidine and purine rings are found in DNA and RNA. The porphyrin ring structure is found in hemoglobin (an oxygen-carrying blood protein), myoglobin (an oxygen-carrying protein found in muscle tissue), and chlorophyll (a photosynthetic plant pigment). The indole and pyridine rings are found in many **alkaloids,** which are naturally occurring compounds with one or more nitrogen-containing heterocyclic rings. Alkaloids include cocaine, nicotine, quinine, morphine, heroin, and LSD (Figure 15.4).

Lysergic acid diethylamide (LSD) is a hallucinogenic compound that may cause severe mental disorders. Cocaine is produced by the coca plant. In small doses it is used as an anesthetic for the sinuses and eyes. An **anesthetic** is a drug that causes a lack of sensation in any part of the body (local anesthetic) or causes unconsciousness (general anesthetic). In higher doses, cocaine causes an intense feeling of euphoria followed by a deep depression. Cocaine is addictive because the user needs larger and larger amounts to overcome the depression. Nicotine is one of the simplest heterocyclic amines and appears to be the addictive component of cigarette smoke.

Morphine was the first alkaloid to be isolated from the sap of the opium poppy. Morphine is a strong **analgesic,** a drug that acts as a pain killer. However, it is a powerful and addictive narcotic. Codeine, also produced by the opium poppy, is

Cocaine
(tropane ring skeleton)

Nicotine
(pyridine and pyrrolidine
ring skeleton)

| R=H | R'=H | Morphine |
| R=H | R'=CH₃ | Codeine |
| R=Ac | R'=Ac | Heroin |

(piperidine ring skeleton)

Lysergic acid diethylamide
(LSD)
(indole ring skeleton)

Vitamin B₆
(pyridine ring skeleton)

Strychnine
(indole and piperidine skeleton)

Quinine
(quinoline ring skeleton)

**Figure 15.4** Structures of several heterocyclic amines with biological activity.

a less powerful analgesic than morphine, but it is one of the most effective cough suppressants known. Heroin is produced in the laboratory by adding two acetyl groups to morphine. It was initially made in the hopes of producing a compound with the benefits of morphine but lacking the addictive qualities. However, heroin is even more addictive than morphine.

Strychnine is found in the seeds of an Asiatic tree. It is extremely toxic and was commonly used as a rat poison at one time. Quinine, isolated from the bark of South American trees, was the first effective treatment for malaria. Vitamin B₆ is one of the water-soluble vitamins required by the body.

## 15.3 Amides

**Amides** are the products formed in a reaction between a carboxylic acid derivative and ammonia or an amine. The general structure of an amide is shown here.

From a carboxylic acid                    From an amine

$$(Ar) \ R-\overset{\overset{\displaystyle O}{\|}}{C}-NH_2$$

Ethanamide

# KITCHEN CHEMISTRY

## Browning Reactions and Flavor: The Maillard Reaction

Since earliest times humans have enjoyed the delightful flavors and aromas of meat roasted over a hot fire or seared in a hot pan. The same chemical reaction that produces the aroma of roasted meat is also the reason that bread crust is brown and more flavorful than the inside of the bread, and is responsible for the wonderful smell of roasted coffee and chocolate. The reaction is called the Maillard reaction in honor of Louis Camille Maillard, a French physician who first described it in 1910.

The reaction begins with a carbohydrate molecule, generally glucose or fructose, which binds to an amino acid in a protein chain. This reaction involves a carbonyl group of the sugar and the amino group of the amino acid. The initial product is unstable and is converted into an intermediate that further reacts with other compounds in the food to create a wide variety of aromatic heterocyclic compounds, including heterocyclic amines. Several of the simpler products of the reactions are shown here:

The savory flavors are attributed to the peptides and amino acids in the food. Oxazoles lend a floral note to the flavor. Thiophenes and thiazoles are distinctive meaty and onion flavors. Pyrazines are in part responsible for the aroma of chocolate and pyridines and pyrazines are associated with the flavors of green vegetables.

The Maillard reaction only occurs at approximately 250°F, which is the reason that meats cooked by boiling or steaming are typically pale and don't have the flavor profile of meats that are seared on a hot surface like a sauté pan or on a grill. Meats that are cooked in oil or in a hot oven also undergo the browning reactions because the surface of the meat quickly dehydrates and rises to the temperature of the oven.

Because foods are chemically complex, we may never fully understand the products of the Maillard reaction, but that will not keep us from enjoying the flavors and aromas that they produce.

### For Further Understanding

▶ Many stew recipes begin by browning the meat, vegetables, and flour before adding any water. How will this influence the characteristics of the stew?

▶ Microwave ovens are very useful for heating leftovers or steaming vegetables, but are generally not used to prepare hamburgers or roasts. Explain the reason for this in terms of what you have just learned of the Maillard reaction.

A thiophene    A thiazole    An oxazole

A pyrrole    A pyridine    A pyrazine

The amide group is composed of two portions: the carbonyl group from a carboxylic acid and the amino group from ammonia or an amine. The bond between the carbonyl carbon and the nitrogen of the amine or ammonia is called the **amide bond.**

## Structure and Physical Properties

Most amides are solids at room temperature. They have very high boiling points, and the simpler ones are quite soluble in water. Both of these properties are a result of strong intermolecular hydrogen bonding between the N—H bond of one amide and the C=O group of a second amide, as shown in Figure 15.5.

Unlike amines, amides are not bases (proton acceptors). The reason is that the highly electronegative oxygen atom of the carbonyl group causes a very strong attraction between the lone pair of nitrogen electrons and the carbonyl group. As a result, the unshared pair of electrons cannot "hold" a proton.

Because of the attraction of the carbonyl group for the lone pair of nitrogen electrons, the structure of the C—N bond of an amide is a *resonance hybrid*. In the structures below lines are used to represent pairs of electrons.

### LEARNING GOAL

**8** Describe the physical properties of amides.

*Resonance hybrids are discussed in Section 3.4.*

## Nomenclature

The common and IUPAC names of the amides are derived from the common and IUPAC names of the carboxylic acids from which they were made. Remove the *-ic acid* ending of the common name or the *-oic acid* ending of the IUPAC name of the carboxylic acid, and replace it with the ending *-amide*. Several examples of the common and IUPAC nomenclature are provided in Table 15.4 and in the following structures:

$$CH_3\overset{\displaystyle O}{\overset{\displaystyle \|}{C}}-NH_2 \qquad\qquad CH_3CH_2\overset{\displaystyle O}{\overset{\displaystyle \|}{C}}-NH_2$$

Ethan*oic acid* → Ethan*amide*
or
Acet*ic acid* → Acet*amide*

Propan*oic acid* → Propan*amide*
or
Propion*ic acid* → Propion*amide*

Substituents on the nitrogen are placed as prefixes and are indicated by *N-* followed by the name of the substituent. There are no spaces between the prefix and the amide name. For example:

$$CH_3CH_2\overset{\displaystyle O}{\overset{\displaystyle \|}{C}}-NH-CH_3 \qquad\qquad CH_3CH_2CH_2CH_2CH_2\overset{\displaystyle O}{\overset{\displaystyle \|}{C}}-NH-CH_2CH_2CH_3$$

*N*-Methylpropanamide

*N*-Propylhexanamide

## Medically Important Amides

*Barbiturates*, often called "downers," are derived from amides and are used as sedatives. They are also used as anticonvulsants for epileptics and for people suffering from a variety of brain disorders that manifest themselves in neurosis, anxiety, and tension.

*Nomenclature of carboxylic acids is described in Section 14.1.*

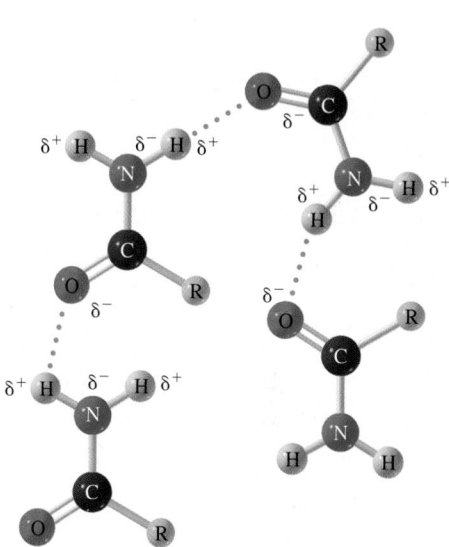

**Figure 15.5** Hydrogen bonding in amides.

## TABLE 15.4 IUPAC and Common Names of Simple Amides

| Compound | IUPAC Name | Common Name |
|---|---|---|
| $R-\overset{O}{\overset{\|}{C}}-NH_2$ | Alkan*amide* (*-amide* replaces the *-oic acid* ending of the IUPAC name of carboxylic acid) | Alkan*amide* (*-amide* replaces the *-ic acid* ending of the common name of carboxylic acid) |
| $H-\overset{O}{\overset{\|}{C}}-NH_2$ | Methanamide | Formamide |
| $CH_3-\overset{O}{\overset{\|}{C}}-NH_2$ | Ethanamide | Acetamide |
| $CH_3CH_2-\overset{O}{\overset{\|}{C}}-NH_2$ | Propanamide | Propionamide |
| $H-\overset{O}{\overset{\|}{C}}-NHCH_3$ | *N*-Methylmethanamide | *N*-Methylformamide |
| $CH_3-\overset{O}{\overset{\|}{C}}-NHCH_3$ | *N*-Methylethanamide | *N*-Methylacetamide |

**EXAMPLE 15.4**   Naming Amides Using Common and IUPAC Nomenclature Systems

a.  Name the following amide using both the IUPAC and common systems.

$$CH_3CH_2CH_2\overset{\displaystyle O}{\overset{\|}{C}}-NH-CH_2CH_2CH_3$$

**Solution**

The names of amides are derived from the common and IUPAC names of the carboxylic acids from which they were made.

|  | IUPAC | Common |
|---|---|---|
| Parent carboxylic acid: | Butanoic acid (becomes butanamide) | Butyric acid (becomes butyramide) |
| Group on N: | propyl | propyl |
| Name: | N-Propylbutanamide | N-Propylbutyramide |

b.  Name the following amide using the IUPAC and common systems.

$$CH_3CH_2\overset{\displaystyle O}{\overset{\|}{C}}-NH-CH_2CH_2CH_2CH_2CH_3$$

**Solution**

| Parent carboxylic acid: | Propanoic acid (becomes propanamide) | Propionic acid (becomes propionamide) |
|---|---|---|
| Group on N: | pentyl | pentyl |
| Name: | N-Pentylpropanamide | N-Pentylpropionamide |

**Practice Problem 15.4**

Provide the common and IUPAC names for each of the following amides.

a.  $CH_3CH_2CH_2CH_2\overset{\displaystyle O}{\overset{\|}{C}}-NH-CH_2CH_2CH_2CH_2CH_3$

b.  $CH_3CH_2CH_2CH_2CH_2\overset{\displaystyle O}{\overset{\|}{C}}-NH-CH_2CH_2CH_2CH_3$

▶ For Further Practice: **Questions 15.53, 15.54, and 15.57.**

Barbital—a barbiturate

Phenacetin and acetaminophen are also amides. Acetaminophen is an aromatic amide that is commonly used in place of aspirin, particularly by people who are allergic to aspirin or who suffer stomach bleeding from the use of aspirin. It was first synthesized in 1893 and is the active ingredient in Tylenol and Datril. Like aspirin, acetaminophen relieves pain and reduces fever. However, unlike aspirin, it is not an anti-inflammatory drug.

Phenacetin was synthesized in 1887 and used as an analgesic for almost a century. Its structure and properties are similar to those of acetaminophen. However, it was banned by the U.S. Food and Drug Administration (FDA) in 1983 because of the kidney damage and blood disorders that it causes.

Phenacetin          Acetaminophen

## Reactions Involving Amides

### Preparation of Amides

Amides are prepared from carboxylic acid derivatives, either acid chlorides or acid anhydrides. Acid chlorides rapidly react with either ammonia or amines, as in:

$$R-\overset{\overset{\displaystyle O}{\|}}{C}-Cl + 2NH_3 \longrightarrow R-\overset{\overset{\displaystyle O}{\|}}{C}-NH_2 + \overset{+}{N}H_4Cl^-$$

| Acid chloride | Ammonia or amine | | Amide | Ammonium chloride or alkylammonium chloride |

Note that two molar equivalents of ammonia or amine are required in this reaction and that this is an acyl group transfer reaction. The **acyl group**

$$R-\overset{\overset{\displaystyle O}{\|}}{C}-$$

of the acid chloride is transferred from the Cl atom to the N atom of one of the ammonia or amine molecules. The second ammonia (or amine) reacts with the HCl formed in the transfer reaction to produce ammonium chloride or alkylammonium chloride.

The reaction between butanoyl chloride and methanamine to produce N-methylbutanamide is an example of an acyl group transfer reaction.

$$CH_3CH_2CH_2\overset{\overset{\displaystyle O}{\|}}{C}-Cl + 2CH_3NH_2 \longrightarrow CH_3CH_2CH_2\overset{\overset{\displaystyle O}{\|}}{C}-NH-CH_3 + CH_3\overset{+}{N}H_3Cl^-$$

Butanoyl chloride     Methanamine     N-Methylbutanamide     Methylammonium chloride

# A MEDICAL PERSPECTIVE

## Semisynthetic Penicillins

The antibacterial properties of penicillin were discovered by Alexander Fleming in 1929. These natural penicillins produced by several species of the mold *Penicillium* had a number of drawbacks. They were effective only against a type of bacteria referred to as Gram positive because of a staining reaction based on their cell wall structure. They were also very susceptible to destruction by bacterial enzymes called β-lactamases, and some were destroyed by stomach acid and had to be administered by injection.

To overcome these problems, chemists have produced semisynthetic penicillins by modifying the core structure. The core of penicillins is 6-aminopenicillanic acid, which consists of a thiazolidine ring fused to a β-lactam ring. In addition, there is an R group bonded via an amide bond to the core structure.

6-Aminopenicillanic acid

The β-lactam ring confers the antimicrobial properties. However, the R group determines the degree of antibacterial activity, the pharmacological properties, including the types of bacteria against which it is active, and the degree of resistance to the β-lactamases exhibited by any particular penicillin antibiotic. These are the properties that must be modified to produce penicillins that are acid resistant, effective with a broad spectrum of bacteria, and β-lactamase resistant.

Chemists simply remove the natural R group by cleaving the amide bond with an enzyme called an amidase. They then replace the R group and test the properties of the "new"

antibiotic. Among the resulting semisynthetic penicillins are ampicillin, methicillin, and oxacillin.

Ampicillin

Methicillin

Oxacillin

### For Further Understanding

▸ Using the Internet and other resources, investigate and describe the properties of some new penicillins and the bacteria against which they are effective.

▸ Why does changing the R group of a penicillin result in altered chemical and physiological properties?

---

The reaction between an amine and an acid anhydride is also an acyl group transfer. The general equation for the synthesis of an amide in the reaction between an acid anhydride and ammonia or an amine is

$$\underset{\text{Acid anhydride}}{R-\overset{O}{\overset{\|}{C}}-O-\overset{O}{\overset{\|}{C}}-R} + \underset{\substack{\text{Ammonia}\\\text{or}\\\text{amine}}}{2NH_3} \longrightarrow \underset{\text{Amide}}{R-\overset{O}{\overset{\|}{C}}-NH_2} + \underset{\substack{\text{Carboxylic acid}\\\text{salt}}}{R-\overset{O}{\overset{\|}{C}}-O^- \overset{+}{N}H_4}$$

When subjected to heat, the carboxylic acid salt loses a water molecule to produce a second amide molecule.

A well-known commercial amide is the artificial sweetener aspartame or NutraSweet. Although the name suggests that it is a sugar, it is not a sugar at all.

Figure 15.6 The amide bond. (a) NutraSweet, the dipeptide aspartame, is a molecule composed of two amino acids joined by an amide (peptide) bond. (b) The sweetener Neotame, is also a dipeptide. One of the amino acids has been modified so that neotame is safe for use by phenylketonurics.

In fact, it is the methyl ester of a molecule composed of two amino acids, aspartic acid and phenylalanine, joined by an amide bond (Figure 15.6a).

Packages of aspartame carry the warning: "Phenylketonurics: Contains Phenylalanine." Digestion of aspartame and heating to high temperatures during cooking break both the ester bond and the amide bond, which releases the amino acid phenylalanine. People with the genetic disorder phenylketonuria (PKU) cannot metabolize this amino acid. As a result, it builds up to toxic levels that can cause mental retardation in an infant born with the condition. This no longer occurs because every child is tested for PKU at the time of birth and each child with the disorder is treated with a diet that limits the amount of phenylalanine to only the amount required for normal growth.

In July 2002 the FDA approved a new artificial sweetener that is related to aspartame. Called neotame, it has the same core structure as aspartame, but a 3,3-dimethylbutyl group has been added to the aspartic acid (Figure 15.6b). Digestion and heating still cause breakage of the ester bond, but the bulky 3,3-dimethylbutyl group blocks the breakage of the amide bond. Neotame can be used without risk by people with PKU and also retains its sweetness during cooking.

Amino acids have both a carboxyl group and an amino group and are discussed in detail in Sections 15.4 and 18.1.

**Question 15.9** What is the structure of the amine that, on reaction with the acid chlorides shown, will give each of the following products?

a. ? + CH₃C(=O)—Cl ⟶ CH₃C(=O)NHCH₃ + CH₃N⁺H₃ Cl⁻

b. ? + CH₃CH₂CH₂CH₂CHC(=O)—Cl (with CH₂CH₃ branch) ⟶ (CH₃)₂NC(=O)CHCH₂CH₂CH₂CH₃ (with CH₂CH₃ branch) + (CH₃)₂N⁺H₂ Cl⁻

**Question 15.10** What are the structures of the acid chlorides and the amines that will react to give each of the following products?

a. N-Ethylhexanamide

b. N-Propylbutanamide

## Hydrolysis of Amides

Hydrolysis of an amide results in breaking the amide bond to produce a carboxylic acid and ammonia or an amine. It is very difficult to hydrolyze the amide bond. In fact, the reaction requires heating the amide in the presence of a strong acid or base.

$$
\underset{\text{Amide}}{R-\overset{\overset{\displaystyle O}{\|}}{C}-NH-R^1} + \underset{\substack{\text{Strong}\\\text{acid}}}{H_3O^+} \longrightarrow \underset{\substack{\text{Carboxylic}\\\text{acid}}}{R-\overset{\overset{\displaystyle O}{\|}}{C}-OH} + \underset{\substack{\text{Alkylammonium}\\\text{ion or ammonium}\\\text{ion}}}{R^1-\overset{+}{N}H_3}
$$

$$
\underset{\substack{\text{Butanamide}\\\text{(butyramide)}}}{CH_3CH_2CH_2\overset{\overset{\displaystyle O}{\|}}{C}-NH_2} + H_3O^+ \longrightarrow \underset{\substack{\text{Butanoic acid}\\\text{(butyric acid)}}}{CH_3CH_2CH_2\overset{\overset{\displaystyle O}{\|}}{C}-OH} + \overset{+}{N}H_4
$$

If a strong base is used, the products are the amine and the salt of the carboxylic acid:

$$
\underset{\text{Amide}}{R-\overset{\overset{\displaystyle O}{\|}}{C}-NH-R^1} + \underset{\substack{\text{Strong}\\\text{base}}}{NaOH} \longrightarrow \underset{\substack{\text{Carboxylic}\\\text{acid salt}}}{R-\overset{\overset{\displaystyle O}{\|}}{C}-O^-Na^+} + \underset{\substack{\text{Amine}\\\text{or}\\\text{ammonia}}}{R^1-NH_2}
$$

$$
\underset{\substack{N\text{-Methylpropanamide}\\(N\text{-methylpropionamide})}}{CH_3CH_2\overset{\overset{\displaystyle O}{\|}}{C}-NHCH_3} + NaOH \longrightarrow \underset{\substack{\text{Sodium propanoate}\\\text{(sodium propionate)}}}{CH_3CH_2\overset{\overset{\displaystyle O}{\|}}{C}-O^-Na^+} + \underset{\substack{\text{Methanamine}\\\text{(methylamine)}}}{CH_3NH_2}
$$

## 15.4  A Preview of Amino Acids, Proteins, and Protein Synthesis

In Chapter 18 we will describe the structure of proteins, the molecules that carry out the majority of the biological processes essential to life. Proteins are polymers of **amino acids.** As the name suggests, amino acids have two essential functional groups, an amino group ($—NH_2$) and a carboxyl group ($—COOH$). Typically amino acids have the following general structure:

$$
H_2N-\overset{\overset{\displaystyle H}{|}}{\underset{\underset{\displaystyle R}{|}}{C}}-COOH \qquad \text{(R may be a hydrogen atom or an organic group.)}
$$

The amide bond that forms between the carboxyl group of one amino acid and the amino group of another is called the **peptide bond.**

In the cell the amino group is usually protonated and the carboxyl group is usually ionized to the carboxylate anion. In the future we will represent an amino acid in the following way:

$$
H_3\overset{+}{N}-\overset{\overset{\displaystyle H}{|}}{\underset{\underset{\displaystyle R}{|}}{C}}-COO^-
$$

The peptide bond is an amide bond.

$$
H_3\overset{+}{N}-\overset{\overset{\displaystyle H}{|}}{\underset{\underset{\displaystyle R}{|}}{C}}-\overset{\overset{\displaystyle O}{\|}}{C}-N-\overset{\overset{\displaystyle H}{|}}{\underset{\underset{\displaystyle R}{|}}{C}}-\overset{\overset{\displaystyle O}{\|}}{C}-O^-
$$

The joining of amino acids by amide bonds produces small *peptides* and larger *proteins*. Because protein structure and function are essential for life processes, it is fortunate indeed that the amide bonds that hold them together are not easily hydrolyzed at physiological pH and temperature.

The process of protein synthesis in the cell mimics amide formation in the laboratory; it involves acyl group transfer. There are several important differences between the chemistry in the laboratory and the chemistry in the cell. During protein synthesis, the **aminoacyl group** of the amino acid is transferred, rather than the acyl group of a carboxylic acid. In addition, the aminoacyl group is not transferred from a carboxylic acid derivative; it is transferred from a special carrier molecule called a **transfer RNA (tRNA)**. When the aminoacyl group is covalently bonded to a tRNA, the resulting structure is called an *aminoacyl tRNA*:

$$\text{Aminoacyl group} \searrow \underset{R}{\overset{H \quad O}{\underset{|}{H_2N-\overset{|}{C}-\overset{\parallel}{C}}}}- \text{transfer RNA}$$

The aminoacyl group of the aminoacyl tRNA is transferred to the amino group nitrogen to form a peptide bond. The transfer RNA is recycled by binding to another of the same kind of aminoacyl group.

More than 100 kinds of proteins, nucleotides, and RNA molecules participate in the incredibly intricate process of protein synthesis. In Chapter 18 we will study protein structure and learn about the many functions of proteins in the life of the cell. In Chapter 20 we will study the details of protein synthesis to see how these aminoacyl transfer reactions make us the individuals that we are.

## 15.5 Neurotransmitters

**Neurotransmitters** are chemicals that carry messages, or signals, from a nerve cell to a target cell, which may be another nerve cell or a muscle cell. Neurotransmitters are classified as being *excitatory*, stimulating their target cell, or *inhibitory*, decreasing activity of the target cell. One feature shared by the neurotransmitters is that they are all nitrogen-containing compounds. Some of them have rather complex structures and one, nitric oxide (NO), consists of only two atoms. Several important neurotransmitters are discussed in the following sections.

### Catecholamines

All of the catecholamine neurotransmitters, including dopamine, epinephrine, and norepinephrine, are synthesized from the amino acid tyrosine (Figure 15.7). *Dopamine* is critical to good health. A deficiency in this neurotransmitter, for example, results in Parkinson's disease, a disorder characterized by tremors, monotonous speech, loss of memory and problem-solving ability, and loss of motor function. It would seem logical to treat Parkinson's disease with dopamine. Unfortunately, dopamine cannot cross the blood-brain barrier to enter brain cells. As a result, L-dopa, which is converted to dopamine in brain cells, is used to treat this disorder.

Just as too little dopamine causes Parkinson's disease, an excess is associated with schizophrenia. Dopamine also appears to play a role in addictive behavior. In proper amounts, it causes a pleasant, satisfied feeling. The greater the amount of dopamine, the more intense the sensation, the "high." Several drugs have been shown to increase the levels of dopamine. Among these are cocaine, heroin, amphetamines, alcohol, and nicotine. Marijuana also causes an increase in brain dopamine, raising the possibility that it, too, has the potential to produce addiction.

**Figure 15.7** The pathway for synthesis of dopamine, epinephrine, and norepinephrine.

# A MEDICAL PERSPECTIVE

## Opiate Biosynthesis and the Mutant Poppy

Hippocrates, the "father of medicine," left us the first record of the therapeutic use of opium (460 BC). Although not recorded, it is probably true that the addictive properties of opium were recognized soon thereafter!

The opium poppy (*Papaver somniferum*) is cultivated, legally and illegally, in many parts of the world. The flowers vary in color from white to deep red, but it is the seed pod that is sought after. In the seed pod is a milky fluid that contains morphine and codeine, and a small amount of an opioid called thebaine. The juice is extracted from the unripe seed pods and dried, and the opium alkaloids are extracted and purified.

In the legal pharmaceutical world, morphine and codeine are used to ease pain and spasmodic coughing. Thebaine is used as a reactant in pharmaceutical synthesis to produce a number of synthetic opioid compounds with a variety of biological effects. These include the analgesics oxycodone (brand name OxyContin), oxymorphone, and nalbuphine; naloxone, which is used to treat opioid overdosage; naltrexone, which is useful in helping people with narcotic or alcohol addictions to remain drug free; and buprenorphine, which is useful in the treatment of opiate addiction because it prevents withdrawal symptoms.

Approximately 40% of the world's legal opium poppies are grown on the Australian island state of Tasmania. This is big business, and the industry has developed an active research program to study the biochemical pathway for the synthesis of morphine and codeine. That pathway begins with the amino acid tyrosine, the same amino acid that is the initial reactant for the synthesis of dopamine and epinephrine (Section 15.5).

|  7 steps | 6 steps | 3 steps | 1 step |
| Tyrosine → | Reticuline → | Thebaine → | Codeine → Morphine |

Through seven chemical reactions, tyrosine is converted to reticuline. Another six reactions convert reticuline to thebaine. Three chemical modifications convert thebaine to codeine, which undergoes an ester hydrolysis to produce morphine.

(a)                                             (b)

(a) Opium poppies are the source of morphine and codeine.
(b) The sap of an opium poppy is white. The sap of the no-morphine mutant poppy is red.

In the course of their studies, researchers produced a mutant strain of poppy that cannot make morphine or codeine, but does produce high levels of thebaine. "Norman," for "No Morphine," has been the most common strain of poppy grown in Tasmania since 1997. The mutation that causes Norman to produce high levels of thebaine is an alteration in one of the enzymes that catalyzes the conversion of thebaine to codeine. Since it can't be converted into codeine, large amounts of thebaine accumulate in the seed pods.

Synthetic opioids, such as naloxone and buprenorphine and the others mentioned above, have become much more important commercially than codeine and morphine. The economic value of Norman is that it produces large amounts of the starting material for the synthesis of these synthetic opioids, as well as the experimental synthesis of new drugs with unknown potential.

Consider the drug formulation Suboxone, a combination of buprenorphine and naloxone, approved for use in the United States in 2003 and produced by the British company Reckitt Benckiser. This combination of synthetic opiates calms the addict's craving for opiates and yet poses little risk of being abused.

Buprenorphine or "bupe" works by binding to the same receptors in the brain to which heroin binds; but the drug is only a partial heroin agonist, so there is no high. As a result,

Both *epinephrine* (adrenaline) and *norepinephrine* are involved in the "fight or flight" response. Epinephrine stimulates the breakdown of glycogen to produce glucose, which is then metabolized to provide energy for the body. Norepinephrine is involved with the central nervous system in the stimulation of other glands and the constriction of blood vessels. All of these responses prepare the body to meet the stressful situation.

## Serotonin

*Serotonin* is synthesized from the amino acid tryptophan (Figure 15.8). A deficiency of serotonin has been associated with depression. It is also thought to be involved in bulimia and anorexia nervosa, as well as the carbohydrate-cravings that characterize seasonal affective disorder (SAD), a depression caused by a decrease in daylight during autumn and winter.

Naloxone

many steps

Thebaine

many steps

Buprenorphine

buprenorphine is much less addictive than drugs such as methadone, leaves patients much more clearheaded, and makes it easier for them to withdraw from the drug after a few months.

Because addicts don't get high from Suboxone, it is much less likely than methadone to be stolen and sold illegally. It has the added advantage that its effects are longer lasting than those of methadone; so addicts need only one pill every 2 or 3 days. In addition, because naloxone is an opioid antagonist, it causes instant withdrawal symptoms if an addict tries to inject Suboxone for a high. As a result, Suboxone can be given to addicts to be taken at home, rather than being dispensed only at clinics, as methadone is. With all of these features, Suboxone begins to sound like a miracle drug; but as with any addiction treatment, it will only help those who want to quit and are willing to work with counselors and support groups to resolve the underlying problems that caused the addiction in the first place.

**For Further Understanding**

▶ In 1998 researchers in England reported that some individuals who had eaten poppy seed rolls or cake tested positive in an opiate drug screen. Using Internet or other resources, investigate the "poppy seed defense" and suggest guidelines for opiate testing that would protect the innocent.

▶ OxyContin is the brand name for a formulation of oxycodone in a timed-release tablet. It is prescribed to provide up to 12 h of relief from chronic pain. Recently, OxyContin has become a commonly abused drug and is thought to be responsible for a number of deaths. Abusers crush the timed-release tablets and ingest or snort the drug, which results in a rapid and powerful high often compared to the euphoria experienced from taking heroin. Use the Internet or other resources to explain why abuse of this prescription medication has overshadowed heroin use in some areas. Consider ways to prevent such abuse.

Tryptophan

Serotonin

$+ CO_2$

**Figure 15.8** Synthesis of serotonin from the amino acid tryptophan.

Serotonin also affects the perception of pain, thermoregulation, and sleep. There are those who believe that a glass of warm milk will help you fall asleep. We have all noticed how sleepy we become after that big Thanksgiving turkey dinner.

**Figure 15.9** Synthesis of histamine from the amino acid histidine.

Both milk protein and turkey are exceptionally high in tryptophan, the precursor of serotonin!

Prozac (fluoxetine), one of the antidepressant drugs, is one of the most widely prescribed drugs in the United States.

Prozac (fluoxetine)

It is a member of a class of drugs called selective serotonin reuptake inhibitors (SSRI). By inhibiting the reuptake, Prozac effectively increases the level of serotonin, relieving the symptoms of depression.

## Histamine

*Histamine* is a neurotransmitter that is synthesized in many tissues by removing the carboxyl group from the amino acid histidine (Figure 15.9). It has many, often annoying, physiological roles. Histamine is released during the allergic response. It causes the itchy skin rash associated with poison ivy or insect bites. It also promotes the red, watery eyes and respiratory symptoms of hay fever.

Many antihistamines are available to counteract the symptoms of histamine release. These act by competing with histamine for binding to target cells. If histamine cannot bind to these target cells, the allergic response stops.

Benadryl is an antihistamine that is available as an ointment to inhibit the itchy rash response to allergens. It is also available as an oral medication to block the symptoms of systemic allergies. You need only visit the "colds and allergies" aisle of your grocery store to find dozens of medications containing antihistamines.

Histamine also stimulates secretion of stomach acid. When this response occurs frequently, the result can be chronic heartburn. The reflux of stomach acid into the esophagus can result in erosion of tissue and ulceration. The excess stomach acid may also contribute to development of stomach ulcers. The drug marketed as Tagamet (cimetidine) has proven to be an effective inhibitor of this histamine response, providing relief from chronic heartburn.

Tagamet (cimetidine)

## γ-Aminobutyric Acid and Glycine

*γ-Aminobutyric acid* (GABA) is produced by removal of a carboxyl group from the amino acid glutamate (Figure 15.10). Both GABA and the amino acid *glycine*

**Figure 15.10** Synthesis of GABA from the amino acid glutamate.

Glycine

are inhibitory neurotransmitters acting in the central nervous system. One class of tranquilizers, the benzodiazopines, relieves aggressive behavior and anxiety. These drugs have been shown to enhance the inhibitory activity of GABA, suggesting one of the roles played by this neurotransmitter.

## Acetylcholine

*Acetylcholine* is a neurotransmitter that functions at the neuromuscular junction, carrying signals from the nerve to the muscle. It is synthesized in a reaction between the quaternary ammonium ion choline and acetyl coenzyme A (Figure 15.11). When it is released from the nerve cell, acetylcholine binds to receptors on the surface of muscle cells. This binding stimulates the muscle cell to contract. Acetylcholine is then broken down to choline and acetate ion.

$$CH_3-\overset{O}{\overset{||}{C}}-O-CH_2CH_2-\overset{+}{N}(CH_3)_3 \longrightarrow HO-CH_2CH_2-\overset{+}{N}(CH_3)_3 + CH_3COO^-$$

Acetylcholine                    Choline                Acetate

These molecules are essentially recycled. They are taken up by the nerve cell where they are used to resynthesize acetylcholine, which is stored in the nerve cell until it is needed.

Nicotine is an agonist of acetylcholine. An agonist is a compound that binds to the receptor for another compound and causes or enhances the biological response. By binding to acetylcholine receptors, nicotine causes the sense of alertness and calm many smokers experience. Nerve cells that respond to nicotine may also signal nerve cells that produce dopamine. As noted above, the dopamine may be responsible for the addictive property of nicotine.

Inhibitors of acetylcholinesterase, the enzyme that catalyzes the breakdown of acetylcholine, are used both as poisons and as drugs. Among the most important poisons of acetylcholinesterase are a class of compounds known as organophosphates. One of these is *diisopropyl fluorophosphate* (DIFP). This molecule forms a covalently bonded intermediate with the enzyme, irreversibly inhibiting its activity.

$$(CH_3)_2CH-O-\overset{O}{\underset{F}{\overset{||}{P}}}-O-CH(CH_3)_2$$

Diisopropyl fluorophosphate (DIFP)

Thus, it is unable to break down the acetylcholine, and nerve transmission continues, resulting in muscle spasm. Death may occur as a result of laryngeal spasm. Antidotes for poisoning by organophosphates, which include many insecticides and nerve gases, have been developed. The antidotes work by reversing the effects of the inhibitor. One of these antidotes is *pyridine aldoxime methiodide* (PAM). This molecule displaces the organophosphate group from the active site of the enzyme, alleviating the effects of the poison.

*Succinylcholine* is a competitive inhibitor of acetylcholine that is used as a muscle relaxant in surgical procedures. Competitive inhibition occurs because the two molecules have structures so similar that both can bind to the acetylcholine receptor (compare the structures on the next page). When administered to a patient, there is more succinylcholine than acetylcholine in the synapse, and thus more succinylcholine binding to the receptor. Because it cannot stimulate muscle contraction, succinylcholine causes muscles to relax. Normal muscle contraction resumes when the drug is no longer administered.

$$HO-CH_2CH_2-\overset{+}{N}(CH_3)_3$$

Choline

+

$$CH_3-\overset{O}{\overset{||}{C}}-S-Coenzyme\ A$$

Acetyl Coenzyme A

$$CH_3-\overset{O}{\overset{||}{C}}-O-CH_2CH_2-\overset{+}{N}(CH_3)_3$$

Acetylcholine

+

Coenzyme A

**Figure 15.11** Synthesis of acetylcholine.

Pyridine aldoxime methiodide

$$CH_3C-O-CH_2CH_2-\overset{+}{N}(CH_3)_3$$

Acetylcholine

$$(CH_3)_3\overset{+}{N}-CH_2CH_2-O-CCH_2CH_2C-O-CH_2CH_2-\overset{+}{N}(CH_3)_3$$

Succinylcholine

Acetylcholine nerve transmission is discussed in further detail in Chemistry at the Crime Scene: Enzymes, Nerve Agents, and Poisoning in Chapter 19.

## Nitric Oxide and Glutamate

*Nitric oxide* (NO) is an amazing little molecule that has been shown to have many physiological functions. Among these is its ability to act as a neurotransmitter. NO is synthesized in many areas of the brain from the amino acid arginine. Research has suggested that NO works in conjunction with another neurotransmitter, the amino acid glutamate (see the structure of glutamate in Figure 15.10). Glutamate released from one nerve cell binds to receptors on its target cell. This triggers the target cell to produce NO, which then diffuses back to the original nerve cell. The NO signals the cell to release more glutamate, thus stimulating this neural pathway even further. This is a kind of positive feedback loop. It is thought that this NO-glutamate mechanism is involved in learning and the formation of memories.

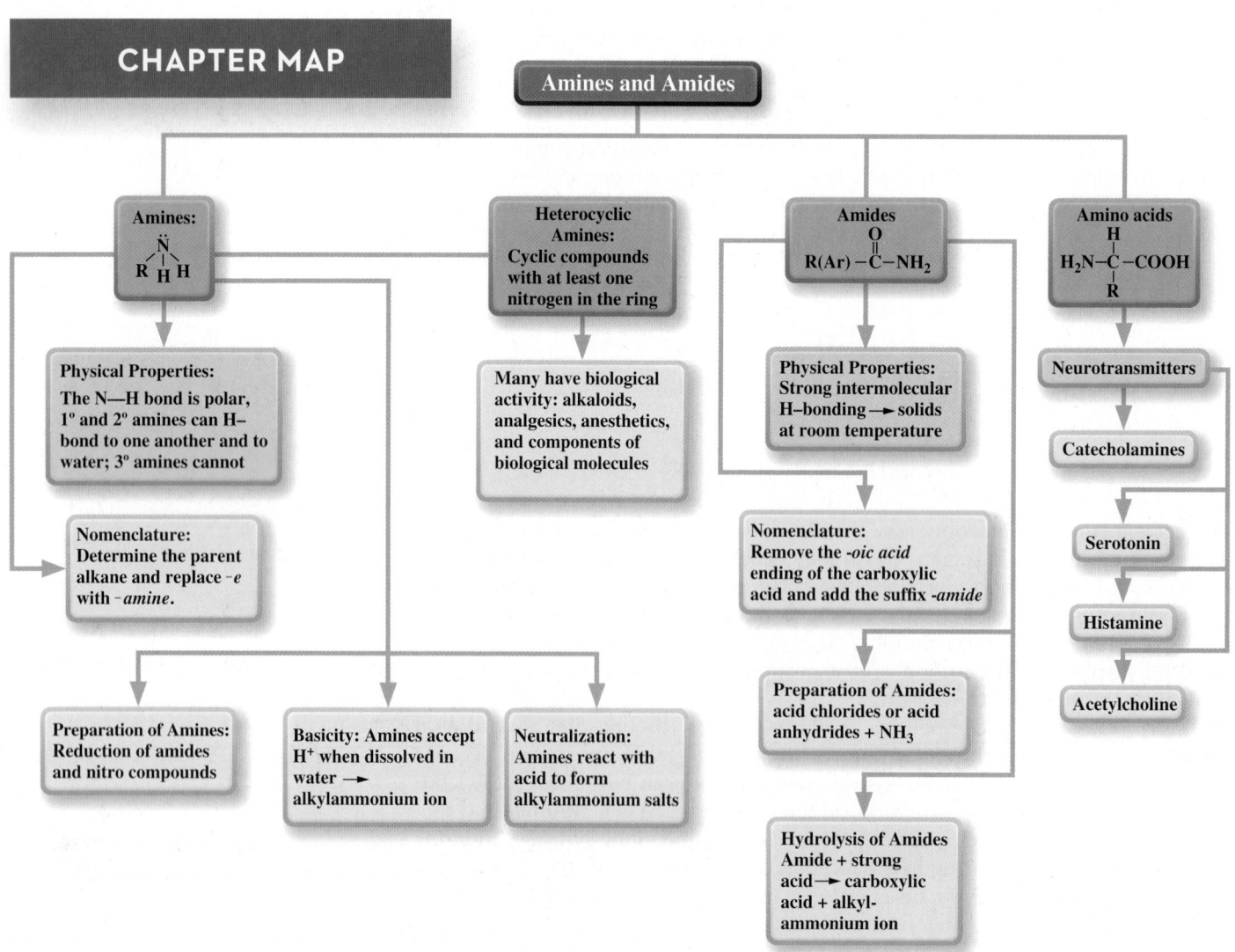

# SUMMARY OF REACTIONS

## Preparation of Amines

A nitro compound → An aromatic primary amine (via [H])

Amide → Amine (via [H])

## Basicity of Amines

$$R-NH_2 + H-OH \rightleftharpoons R-\overset{H}{\underset{H}{N^+}}-H + OH^-$$

Amine    Water    Alkylammonium ion    Hydroxide ion

## Neutralization of Amines

$$R-NH_2 + HCl \longrightarrow R-\overset{H}{\underset{H}{N^+}}-H\ Cl^-$$

Amine    Acid    Alkylammonium salt

## Preparation of Amides

$$R-\overset{O}{\overset{\|}{C}}-Cl + 2NH_3 \longrightarrow$$

Acid chloride    Ammonia or amine

$$R-\overset{O}{\overset{\|}{C}}-NH_2 + \overset{+}{N}H_4Cl^-$$

Amide    Ammonium chloride or alkylammonium chloride

$$R-\overset{O}{\overset{\|}{C}}-O-\overset{O}{\overset{\|}{C}}-R + 2NH_3 \longrightarrow$$

Acid anhydride    Ammonia or amine

$$R-\overset{O}{\overset{\|}{C}}-NH_2 + R-\overset{O}{\overset{\|}{C}}-O^-\overset{+}{N}H_4$$

Amide    Carboxylic acid salt

## Hydrolysis of Amides

$$R-\overset{O}{\overset{\|}{C}}-NH-R^1 + H_3O^+ \longrightarrow R-\overset{O}{\overset{\|}{C}}-OH + R^1-\overset{+}{N}H_3$$

Amide    Strong acid    Carboxylic acid    Alkyl-ammonium ion

$$R-\overset{O}{\overset{\|}{C}}-NH-R^1 + NaOH \longrightarrow R-\overset{O}{\overset{\|}{C}}-O^-Na^+ + R^1-NH_2$$

Amide    Strong base    Carboxylic acid salt    Amine or ammonia

# SUMMARY

## 15.1 Amines

▶ **Amines** are a family of organic compounds that contain an amino group or substituted amino group.

▶ A **primary amine** has the general formula $RNH_2$; a **secondary amine** has the general formula $R_2NH$; and a **tertiary amine** has the general formula $R_3N$.

▶ In the systematic nomenclature system, amines are named as *alkanamines*.

▶ In the common system, they are named as *alkylamines*.

▶ Amines behave as weak bases, forming **alkylammonium ions** in water and alkylammonium salts when they react with acids.

▶ **Quaternary ammonium salts** are ammonium salts that have four organic groups bonded to the nitrogen atom.

## 15.2 Heterocyclic Amines

▶ **Heterocyclic amines** are cyclic compounds having at least one nitrogen atom in the ring structure.

▶ **Alkaloids** are natural plant products that contain at least one heterocyclic ring.

▶ Many alkaloids have powerful biological effects.

▶ Cocaine is an example of an **anesthetic,** which is a drug that causes a lack of sensation in any part of the body or which causes unconsciousness.

▶ Morphine is a strong **analgesic,** a drug that acts as a painkiller.

## 15.3 Amides

▶ **Amides** are formed in a reaction between a carboxylic acid derivative and an amine (or ammonia).

▶ The **amide bond** is the bond between the carbonyl carbon of the **acyl group** and the nitrogen of the amine.

▶ In the IUPAC Nomenclature System, amides are named by replacing the -*oic acid* ending of the carboxylic acid with the -*amide* ending.

▶ In the common system of nomenclature, the -*ic acid* ending of the carboxylic acid is replaced by the -*amide* ending.

▶ Hydrolysis of an amide produces a carboxylic acid and an amine (or ammonia).

## 15.4 A Preview of Amino Acids, Proteins, and Protein Synthesis

▶ Proteins are polymers of **amino acids** joined to one another by amide bonds called **peptide bonds.**

▶ During protein synthesis, the **aminoacyl group** of one amino acid is transferred from a carrier molecule called **transfer RNA (tRNA)** to the amino group nitrogen of another amino acid.

## 15.5 Neurotransmitters

▶ **Neurotransmitters** are chemicals that carry messages, or signals, from a nerve cell to a target cell, which may be another nerve cell or a muscle cell.

▶ Neurotransmitters may be inhibitory or excitatory and all are nitrogen-containing compounds.

▶ The catecholamines include dopamine, norepinephrine, and epinephrine.

- Too little dopamine results in Parkinson's disease. Too much is associated with schizophrenia.
- Dopamine is also associated with addictive behavior.

▶ A deficiency of serotonin is associated with depression and eating disorders. Serotonin is involved in pain perception, regulation of body temperature, and sleep.

▶ Histamine contributes to allergy symptoms.

- Antihistamines block histamine and provide relief from allergies.

▶ γ-Aminobutyric acid (GABA) and glycine are inhibitory neurotransmitters.

- It is believed that GABA is involved in control of aggressive behavior.

▶ Acetylcholine is a neurotransmitter that functions at the neuromuscular junction, carrying signals from the nerve to the muscle.

▶ Nitric oxide and glutamate function in a positive feedback loop that is thought to be involved in learning and the formation of memories.

# ANSWERS TO PRACTICE PROBLEMS

15.1  a. Tertiary amine
   b. Primary amine
   c. Secondary amine
15.2  a. Methanol would have a higher boiling point than methylamine. The intermolecular hydrogen bonds between alcohol molecules will be stronger than those between two amines because oxygen is more electronegative than nitrogen.
   b. Water would have a higher boiling point than dimethylamine. The intermolecular hydrogen bonds between water molecules will be stronger than those between two amines because oxygen is more electronegative than nitrogen.
   c. Ethylamine will have a higher boiling point than methylamine because it has a higher molar mass.
   d. Propylamine will have a higher boiling point than butane because propylamine molecules can form intermolecular hydrogen bonds, and the nonpolar butane cannot do so.
15.3  a. *N*-Ethyl-*N*-methyl-1-propanamine
   b. 3-Hexanamine
   c. *N,N*-Diethyl-1-propanamine
15.4  a. IUPAC name: *N*-Pentylpentanamide
      Common name: *N*-Pentylvaleramide
   b. IUPAC name: *N*-Butylhexanamide
      Common name: *N*-Butylcaproamide

# QUESTIONS AND PROBLEMS

**Amines**

**Foundations**

15.11  Compare the boiling points of amines, alkanes, and alcohols of the same molar mass. Explain these differences in boiling points.

15.12  Describe the water solubility of amines in relation to their carbon chain length.

15.13  Describe the systematic rules for naming amines.

15.14  How are the common names of amines derived?

15.15  Describe the physiological effects of amphetamines.

15.16  Define the terms *analgesic* and *anesthetic* and list some amines that have these activities.

**Applications**

**15.17** For each pair of compounds predict which would have greater solubility in water. Explain your reasoning.
  **a.** Hexane or 1-pentanamine
  **b.** Cyclopentane or 2-butanamine

**15.18** For each pair of compounds predict which would have the higher boiling point. Explain your reasoning.
  **a.** Propanamine or propanol
  **b.** Propane or ethanamine
  **c.** Methanamine or water
  **d.** Propylmethylamine or pentane

**15.19** Explain why a tertiary amine such as triethylamine has a significantly lower boiling point than its primary amine isomer, 1-hexanamine.

**15.20** Draw a diagram to illustrate your answer to Question 15.19.

**15.21** Use systematic nomenclature to name each of the following amines:

  **a.** CH₃CH₂CHNH₂
                |
               CH₃
  **b.** CH₃CH₂CH₂CHCH₂CH₃
                     |
                    NH₂
  **c.**

  ⬠—NH₂

  **d.** (CH₃)₃C—NH₂

**15.22** Use systematic and common nomenclature to name each of the following amines:

  **a.** CH₃CH₂CH₂CH₂CH₂CH₂CH₂CH₂NH₂
  **b.** Cl—⬡—NH₂
  **c.** CH₃CHCH₂CH₃
              |
             NH₂
           CH₃
            |
  **d.** CH₃NCH₂CH₃

**15.23** Draw the condensed formula and line formula of each of the following compounds:
  **a.** Diethylamine        **d.** 3-Bromo-2-pentanamine
  **b.** Butylamine          **e.** Triphenylamine
  **c.** 3-Decanamine

**15.24** Draw the condensed formula and line formula of each of the following compounds:
  **a.** N,N-Dipropylaniline
  **b.** Cyclohexanamine
  **c.** 2-Bromocyclopentanamine
  **d.** Tetraethylammonium iodide
  **e.** 3-Bromobenzenamine

**15.25** Draw the condensed formula for each of the following compounds:
  **a.** 3-Hexanamine        **d.** 2-Methylcyclopentanamine
  **b.** Hexylpentylamine    **e.** Triethylammonium chloride
  **c.** Cyclobutanamine

**15.26** Draw the condensed formula for each of the following compounds:
  **a.** 2,3-Dibromoaniline
  **b.** 2-Octanamine
  **c.** 2-Chloro-2-pentanamine
  **d.** N,N-Diethylpentanamine
  **e.** Diisopropylamine

**15.27** Draw condensed formulas for the eight isomeric amines that have the molecular formula C₄H₁₁N. Name each of the isomers using the systematic names and determine whether each isomer is a 1°, 2°, or 3° amine.

**15.28** Draw all of the isomeric amines of molecular formula C₃H₉N. Name each of the isomers using the systematic names and determine whether each isomer is a primary, secondary, or tertiary amine.

**15.29** Classify each of the following amines as 1°, 2°, or 3°:
  **a.** Cyclohexanamine
  **b.** Dibutylamine
  **c.** 2-Methyl-2-heptanamine
  **d.** Tripentylamine

**15.30** Classify each of the following amines as primary, secondary, or tertiary:
  **a.** Benzenamine            **d.** Tripropylamine
  **b.** N-Ethyl-2-pentanamine  **e.** m-Chloroaniline
  **c.** Ethylmethylamine

**15.31** Write an equation to show a reaction that would produce each of the following products:

  **a.**     **c.**

  **b.**     **d.** NH₂ on cyclohexane (NH₂/CH₂)

**15.32** Write an equation to show a reaction that would produce each of the following amines:
  **a.** 1-Pentanamine
  **b.** N,N-Dimethylethanamine
  **c.** N-Ethylpropanamine

**15.33** Complete each of the following equations by supplying the missing reactant or product indicated by a question mark:
                CH₃                        CH₃
                 |                          |
  **a.** CH₃NH + ?  ⟶  CH₃N⁺H + OH⁻
                                            |
                                            H

                CH₃                        CH₃
                 |                          |
  **b.** CH₃CH₂N    + ? ⟶ CH₃CH₂N⁺H Br⁻
                 |                          |
               CH₂CH₃                     CH₂CH₃

  **c.** CH₃CH₂CH₂NH₂ + H₂O ⟶ ? + OH⁻

               CH₂CH₃
                |
  **d.** CH₃CH₂NH + HCl ⟶ ?

**15.34** Complete each of the following equations by supplying the missing reactant or product indicated by a question mark:

a. $CH_3CH_2NH_2 + H_2O \longrightarrow ? + OH^-$

b. $? + HCl \longrightarrow CH_3CH_2CH_2\overset{\underset{\displaystyle |}{CH_2CH_2CH_3}}{\underset{\underset{\displaystyle H}{|}}{N^+}}H\ Cl^-$

c. $CH_3\overset{\underset{\displaystyle |}{CH_3}}{\underset{\underset{\displaystyle CH_3}{|}}{CH}}NH + H_2O \longrightarrow ? + ?$

d. $NH_3 + HBr \longrightarrow ?$

**15.35** Using condensed formulas, write an equation for the reaction that would produce each of the following amines:
a. Hexanamine
b. N-Methylbutanamine
c. N,N-Dimethylpropanamine

**15.36** Write an equation for the reaction that would produce each of the following amines:
a. Octanamine
b. N-Methylpropanamine
c. N,N-Diethylpentanamine

**15.37** Briefly explain why the lower-molar-mass amines (fewer than five carbons) exhibit appreciable solubility in water.

**15.38** Why is the salt of an amine appreciably more soluble in water than the amine from which it was formed?

**15.39** Most drugs containing amine groups are not administered as the amine but rather as the ammonium salt. Can you suggest a reason why?

**15.40** Why does aspirin upset the stomach, whereas acetaminophen (Tylenol) does not?

**15.41** Putrescine and cadaverine are two odoriferous amines that are produced by decaying flesh. Putrescine is 1,4-butanediamine, and cadaverine is 1,5-pentanediamine. Draw the structures of these two compounds.

**15.42** How would you quickly convert an alkylammonium salt into a water-insoluble amine? Explain the rationale for your answer.

## Heterocyclic Amines

**15.43** Indole and pyridine rings are found in alkaloids.
a. Sketch each ring.
b. Name one compound containing each of the ring structures and indicate its use.

**15.44** What is an alkaloid?

**15.45** List some heterocyclic amines that are used in medicine.

**15.46** Distinguish between the terms *analgesic* and *anesthetic*.

## Amides

### Foundations

**15.47** Why do amides have very high boiling points?

**15.48** Describe the water solubility of amides in relation to their carbon chain length.

**15.49** Explain the IUPAC nomenclature rules for naming amides.

**15.50** How are the common names of amides derived?

**15.51** Describe the physiological effects of barbiturates.

**15.52** Why is acetaminophen often recommended in place of aspirin?

## Applications

**15.53** Use the IUPAC and common systems of nomenclature to name the following amides:

a. $CH_3CH_2\overset{\underset{\displaystyle \|}{O}}{C}NH_2$

b. $CH_3CH_2CH_2CH_2\overset{\underset{\displaystyle \|}{O}}{C}NH_2$

c. $CH_3\overset{\underset{\displaystyle \|}{O}}{C}N(CH_3)_2$

**15.54** Use the IUPAC Nomenclature System to name each of the following amides:

a. $CH_3CH_2\overset{\underset{\displaystyle |}{CH}}{\underset{\underset{\displaystyle Br}{}}{}}CH_2\overset{\underset{\displaystyle \|}{O}}{C}NH_2$

c. $CH_3\overset{\underset{\displaystyle |}{CH}}{\underset{\underset{\displaystyle CH_3}{}}{}}\overset{\underset{\displaystyle \|}{O}}{C}NH_2$

b. benzene ring with $-\overset{\underset{\displaystyle \|}{O}}{C}NH_2$ and Br substituent

**15.55** Draw the condensed formula for each of the following amides:
a. Propanamide
c. 2,3-Diethylpentanamide
b. N,N-Diethylbutanamide
d. N-Methylhexanamide

**15.56** Draw the condensed formula for each of the following amides:
a. N-Propylbutanamide
c. N-Methylpropanamide
b. N-Butyloctanamide
d. N-Isopropylhexanamide

**15.57** Draw the condensed formula and line formula of each of the following amides:
a. Ethanamide
b. N-Methylpropanamide
c. N,N-Diethylbenzenamide
d. 3-Bromo-4-methylhexanamide
e. N,N-Dimethylacetamide

**15.58** Draw the condensed formula and line formula of each of the following amides:
a. Acetamide
b. 4-Methylpentanamide
c. N,N-Dimethylpropanamide
d. Formamide
e. N-Ethylpropionamide

**15.59** The active ingredient in many insect repellents is N,N-diethyl-m-toluamide (DEET). Draw the structure of this compound. Which carboxylic acid and amine would be released by hydrolysis of this compound?

**15.60** When an acid anhydride and an amine are combined, an amide is formed. This approach may be used to synthesize acetaminophen, the active ingredient in Tylenol. Complete the following equation to determine the structure of acetaminophen:

$$CH_3\overset{\underset{\displaystyle \|}{O}}{C}-O-\overset{\underset{\displaystyle \|}{O}}{C}CH_3 + H_2N-\underset{\text{(benzene ring)}}{\bigcirc}-OH \longrightarrow ? + CH_3COOH$$

**15.61** Explain why amides are neutral in the acid-base sense.

A healthy diet contains both complex carbohydrates, such as starches and cellulose, and simple sugars, such as fructose and sucrose (Figure 16.2). However, the quantity of simple sugars, especially sucrose, should be minimized because large quantities of sucrose in the diet promote obesity and tooth decay.

Complex carbohydrates are better for us than the simple sugars. Starch, found in rice, potatoes, breads, and cereals, is an excellent energy source. In addition, the complex carbohydrates, such as cellulose, provide us with an important supply of dietary fiber.

It is hard to determine exactly what percentage of the daily diet *should* consist of carbohydrates. The *actual* percentage varies widely throughout the world, from 80% in the Far East, where rice is the main component of the diet, to 40–50% in the United States. Currently, it is recommended that 45–65% of the calories in the diet should come from carbohydrates and that no more than 10% of the daily caloric intake should be sucrose.

*See A Medical Perspective: Tooth Decay and Simple Sugars on page 551.*

**Question 16.1** What is the current recommendation for the amount of carbohydrates that should be included in the diet? Of the daily intake of carbohydrates, what percentage should be simple sugar?

**Question 16.2** Distinguish between simple and complex carbohydrates. What are some sources of complex carbohydrates?

**Monosaccharides** such as glucose and fructose are the simplest carbohydrates because they contain a single (*mono-*) sugar (*saccharide*) unit. **Disaccharides,** including sucrose and lactose, consist of two monosaccharide units joined through bridging oxygen atoms. Such a bond is called a **glycosidic bond. Oligosaccharides** consist of three to ten monosaccharide units joined by glycosidic bonds. The largest and most complex carbohydrates are the **polysaccharides,** which are long, often highly branched, chains of monosaccharides. Starch, glycogen, and cellulose are all examples of polysaccharides.

**Figure 16.1** Carbohydrates are produced by plants such as this potato in the process of photosynthesis, which uses the energy of sunlight to produce hexoses from $CO_2$ and $H_2O$.

**Figure 16.2** Carbohydrates from a variety of foods are an essential component of the diet.

## 16.2   Monosaccharides

*The importance of phosphorylated sugars in metabolic reactions is discussed in Sections 14.4 and 21.3.*

Monosaccharides are composed of carbon, hydrogen, and oxygen. They can be classified on the basis of the functional groups they contain. A monosaccharide with a ketone (carbonyl) group is a **ketose.** If an aldehyde (carbonyl) group is present, it is called an **aldose.** Sometimes monosaccharides are called *polyhydroxyaldehydes* or *polyhydroxyketones* because they also contain many hydroxyl groups.

**LEARNING GOAL**

2   Apply the systems of classifying and naming monosaccharides according to the functional group and number of carbons in the chain.

Aldehyde functional group

$$
\begin{array}{c}
H \\
| \\
C=O \\
| \\
H-C-OH \\
| \\
H-C-OH \\
| \\
CH_2OH
\end{array}
$$

An aldose

$$
\begin{array}{c}
CH_2OH \\
| \\
C=O \\
| \\
H-C-OH \\
| \\
HO-C-H \\
| \\
CH_2OH
\end{array}
$$

A ketose

Ketone functional group

Another system of classification tells us the number of carbon atoms in the main skeleton. A three-carbon monosaccharide is a *triose,* a four-carbon sugar is a *tetrose,* a five-carbon sugar is a *pentose,* a six-carbon sugar is a *hexose,* and so on. Combining the two classification systems gives even more information about the structure and composition of a sugar. For example, an aldotetrose is a four-carbon sugar that is also an aldehyde.

In addition to these general classification schemes, each monosaccharide has a unique name. These names are shown in blue for the following structures. Because the monosaccharides can exist in several different stereoisomers, it is important to provide the complete name. Thus the complete names of the following structures are D-glyceraldehyde, D-glucose, and D-fructose. These names tell us that the structure represents one particular sugar and also identifies the sugar as one of two possible stereoisomers (D- or L-).

The simplest aldose is D-glyceraldehyde:

$$
\begin{array}{c}
H \\
| \\
C=O \\
| \\
H-C-OH \\
| \\
CH_2OH
\end{array}
$$

The simplest ketose is dihydroxyacetone:

$$
\begin{array}{c}
CH_2OH \\
| \\
C=O \\
| \\
CH_2OH
\end{array}
$$

Stereoisomers are described in detail in the next section.

$$
\begin{array}{c}
H \\
| \\
C=O \\
| \\
H-C-OH \\
| \\
CH_2OH
\end{array}
$$

Aldose
Triose
Aldotriose
D-Glyceraldehyde

$$
\begin{array}{c}
H \\
| \\
C=O \\
| \\
H-C-OH \\
| \\
HO-C-H \\
| \\
H-C-OH \\
| \\
H-C-OH \\
| \\
CH_2OH
\end{array}
$$

Aldose
Hexose
Aldohexose
D-Glucose

$$
\begin{array}{c}
CH_2OH \\
| \\
C=O \\
| \\
HO-C-H \\
| \\
H-C-OH \\
| \\
H-C-OH \\
| \\
CH_2OH
\end{array}
$$

Ketose
Hexose
Ketohexose
D-Fructose

**Question 16.3**   What is the structural difference between an aldose and a ketose?

**Question 16.4**   Explain the difference between:
a. A ketohexose and an aldohexose
b. A triose and a pentose

## A MEDICAL PERSPECTIVE

### Tooth Decay and Simple Sugars

How many times have you heard the lecture from parents or your dentist about brushing your teeth after a sugary snack? Annoying as this lecture might be, it is based on sound scientific data that demonstrate that the cause of tooth decay is plaque and acid formed by the bacterium *Streptococcus mutans* using sucrose as its substrate.

Saliva is teeming with bacteria in concentrations up to 100 million ($10^8$) per milliliter (mL) of saliva! Within minutes after you brush your teeth, sticky glycoproteins in the saliva adhere to tooth surfaces. Then millions of oral bacteria immediately bind to this surface.

Although many oral bacteria stick to the tooth surface, as the diagram shows, only *S. mutans* causes cavities. The reason for this is that this organism alone can make the enzyme *glucosyl transferase*. This enzyme acts only on the disaccharide sucrose, breaking it down into glucose and fructose. The glucose is immediately added to a growing polysaccharide called *dextran*, the glue that allows the bacteria to adhere to the tooth surface, contributing to the formation of plaque.

Now the bacteria embedded in the dextran take in the fructose and use it in the lactic acid fermentation. The lactic acid that is produced lowers the pH on the tooth surface and begins to dissolve calcium from the tooth enamel. Even though we produce about 1 liter (L) of saliva each day, the acid cannot be washed away from the tooth surface because the dextran plaque is not permeable to saliva.

So what can we do to prevent tooth decay? Of course, brushing after each meal and flossing regularly reduce plaque buildup. Eating a diet rich in calcium also helps build strong tooth enamel. Foods rich in complex carbohydrates, such as fruits and vegetables, help prevent cavities in two ways. Glucosyl transferase can't use complex carbohydrates in its cavity-causing chemistry, and eating fruits and vegetables helps to mechanically remove plaque.

Perhaps the most effective way to prevent tooth decay is to avoid sucrose-containing snacks between meals. Studies have shown that eating sucrose-rich foods doesn't cause much tooth decay if followed immediately by brushing. However, even small amounts of sugar eaten between meals actively promote cavity formation.

#### For Further Understanding

▶ It has been suggested that tooth decay could be prevented by a vaccine that would rid the mouth of *Streptococcus mutans*. Explain this from the point of view of the chemical reactions that are described above.

▶ What steps could you take following a sugary snack to help prevent tooth decay, even when it is not possible to brush your teeth?

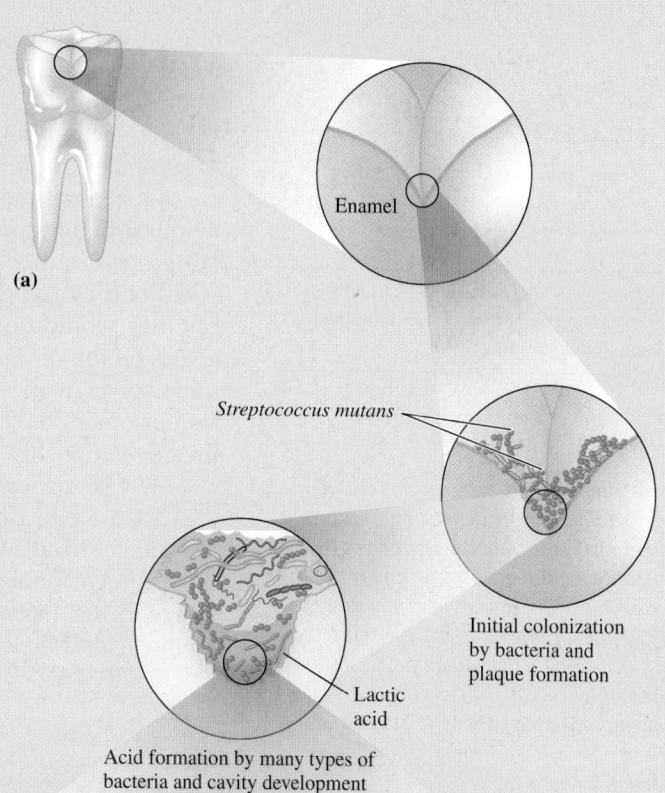

(a)

Enamel

*Streptococcus mutans*

Initial colonization by bacteria and plaque formation

Lactic acid

Acid formation by many types of bacteria and cavity development

(b)

(a) The complex process of tooth decay. (b) Electron micrograph of dental plaque.

## 16.3  Stereoisomers and Stereochemistry

### Stereoisomers

The prefixes D- and L- found in the complete name of a monosaccharide are used to identify one of two possible isomeric forms called **stereoisomers.** By definition, each member of a pair of stereoisomers must have the same molecular formula and the same bonding pattern. How then do stereoisomers of the D-family differ from those of the L-family? D- and L-isomers differ in the spatial arrangements of atoms in the molecule.

**Stereochemistry** is the study of the different spatial arrangements of atoms. A general example of a pair of stereoisomers is shown in Figure 16.3. In this example, the general molecule C-abcd is formed from the bonding of a central carbon to four different groups: a, b, c, and d. This results in two possible ways to arrange the groups, rather than one. Each isomer is bonded together through the exact *same* bonding pattern, yet the two molecules are *not* identical. If they were identical, they would be superimposable. This means that you can place the two molecules on top of one another and every atom and every bond of the two lie in the same space. If they cannot be superimposed, they are stereoisomers. These two stereoisomers have a mirror-image relationship that is analogous to the mirror-image relationship of the left and right hands (see Figure 16.3b).

Two stereoisomers that are nonsuperimposable mirror images of one another are called a pair of **enantiomers.** Molecules that can exist in enantiomeric forms are called **chiral molecules.** The term simply means that as a result of different three-dimensional arrangements of atoms, the molecule can exist in two mirror-image forms. For any pair of nonsuperimposable mirror-image carbohydrates or amino acids, one is always designated D- and the other L-.

*The structures and designations of D- and L-glyceraldehyde are defined by convention. In fact, the D- and L-terminology is generally applied only to carbohydrates and amino acids. For organic molecules, the D- and L-convention has been replaced by a new system that provides the absolute configuration of a chiral carbon. This system, called the (R) and (S) system, is described in Stereochemistry and Stereoisomers Revisited.*

**STEREOCHEMISTRY AND STEREOISOMERS REVISITED**

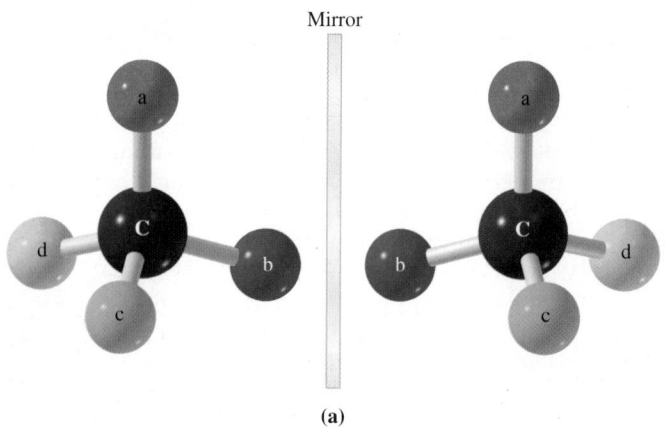

(a)

Nonsuperimposable mirror images:
enantiomers

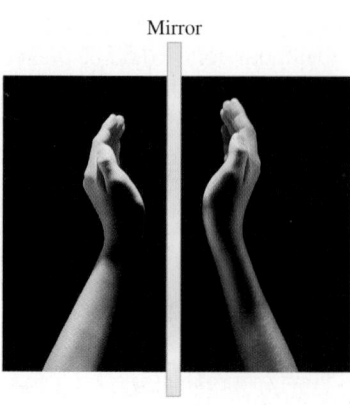

(b)

**Figure 16.3** (a) A pair of enantiomers for the general molecule C-abcd. (b) Mirror-image right and left hands.

Most oxidized end

D-Glyceraldehyde

L-Glyceraldehyde

Chiral center farthest from the most oxidized end

**(a)**

D-Glyceraldehyde

L-Glyceraldehyde

**(b)**

**Figure 16.4** (a) Structural formulas of D- and L-glyceraldehyde. The end of the molecule with the carbonyl group is the most oxidized end. The D- or L-configuration of a monosaccharide is determined by the orientation of the functional groups attached to the chiral carbon farthest from the oxidized end. In the D-enantiomer, the —OH is to the right. In the L-enantiomer, the —OH is to the left. (b) A three-dimensional representation of D- and L-glyceraldehyde.

A carbon atom that has four different groups bonded to it is called a **chiral carbon** atom. Any molecule containing a chiral carbon is a chiral molecule and will exist as a pair of enantiomers. Consider the simplest chiral carbohydrate, **glyceraldehyde**, which is shown in Figure 16.4. Note that the second carbon is bonded to four different groups. It is therefore a chiral carbon. As a result, we can draw two enantiomers of glyceraldehyde that are nonsuperimposable mirror images of one another. Larger biological molecules typically have more than one chiral carbon.

**ANIMATIONS**
- Chiral Molecules
- Chiral Molecules (B)

## Rotation of Plane-Polarized Light

Stereoisomers can be distinguished from one another by their different optical properties. Each member of a pair of stereoisomers will rotate plane-polarized light in a different direction.

As we learned in Chapter 2, white light is a form of electromagnetic radiation that consists of many different wavelengths (colors) vibrating in *planes* that are all perpendicular to the direction of the light beam. To measure optical properties of enantiomers, scientists use special light sources to produce *monochromatic light*, that is, light of a single wavelength. The monochromatic light is passed through a polarizing material, like a Polaroid lens, so that only waves in one plane can pass through. The light that emerges from the lens is *plane-polarized light* (Figure 16.5).

*The polarimeter, measurement of the rotation of plane-polarized light, and the calculation of specific rotation are discussed in detail online in Stereochemistry and Stereoisomers Revisited.*

**STEREOCHEMISTRY AND STEREOISOMERS REVISITED**

Polarized filter mounted on circular dial rotated to give maximum amount of transmitted light

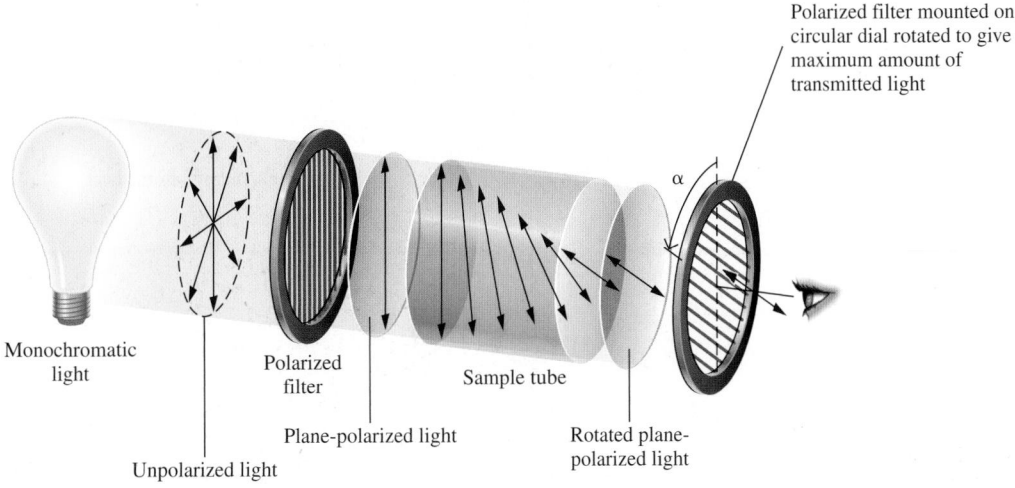

Monochromatic light

Polarized filter

Sample tube

Rotated plane-polarized light

Plane-polarized light

Unpolarized light

**Figure 16.5** Schematic drawing of a polarimeter.

Applying these principles, scientists have developed the *polarimeter* to measure the ability of a compound to change the angle of the plane of plane-polarized light (see Figure 16.5). The polarimeter allows the determination of the specific rotation of a compound, that is, the measure of its ability to rotate plane-polarized light.

Some compounds rotate light in a clockwise direction. These are said to be *dextrorotatory* and are designated by a plus sign (+) before the specific rotation value. Other substances rotate light in a counterclockwise direction. These are called *levorotatory* and are indicated by a minus sign (−) before the specific rotation value.

**STEREOCHEMISTRY AND STEREOISOMERS REVISITED**

## The Relationship Between Molecular Structure and Optical Activity

In 1848, Louis Pasteur was the first to see a relationship between the structure of a compound and the effect of that compound on plane-polarized light. In his studies of winemaking, Pasteur noticed that salts of tartaric acid were formed as a by-product. It is a tribute to his extraordinary powers of observation that he noticed that two types of crystals were formed and that they were mirror images of one another. Using a magnifying glass and forceps, Pasteur separated the left-handed and right-handed crystals into separate piles. When he measured the optical activity of each of the mirror-image forms and of the original mixed sample, he obtained the following results:

- A solution of the original mixture of crystals was optically inactive.
- But both of the mirror-image crystals were optically active. In fact, the specific rotation produced by each was identical in magnitude but was of opposite sign.

Although Pasteur's work opened the door to understanding the relationship between structure and optical activity, it was not until 1874 that the Dutch chemist van't Hoff and the French chemist LeBel independently came up with a basis for the observed optical activity: tetrahedral carbon atoms bonded to four different atoms or groups of atoms. Thus, two enantiomers, which are identical to one another in all other chemical and physical properties, will rotate plane-polarized light to the same degree, but in opposite directions.

## Fischer Projection Formulas

Emil Fischer devised a simple way to represent the structure of stereoisomers. The **Fischer Projection** is a two-dimensional drawing of a molecule that shows a chiral carbon at the intersection of two lines. The horizontal lines represent bonds projecting out of the page, and the vertical lines represent bonds that project into the page. Figure 16.6 demonstrates how to draw the Fischer Projections for the

**Figure 16.6** Drawing a Fischer Projection. (a) The ball-and-stick models for the stereoisomers of bromochlorofluoromethane. (b) The wedge-and-dash and (c) Fischer Projections of these molecules.

stereoisomers of bromochlorofluoromethane. In Figure 16.6a, the two isomers are represented using ball-and-stick models. The molecules are reinterpreted using the wedge-and-dash representations in Figure 16.6b. In the Fischer Projections shown in Figure 16.6c, the point at which two lines cross represents the chiral carbon. Horizontal lines replace the solid wedges indicating that the bonds are projecting toward the reader. Vertical lines replace the dashed wedges, indicating that the bonds are projecting away from the reader. For sugars, the aldehyde or ketone group, the most oxidized carbon, is always represented at the "top."

---

**EXAMPLE 16.1**   **Drawing Fischer Projections for a Sugar**

LEARNING GOAL

Draw the Fischer Projections for the stereoisomers of glyceraldehyde.

**5** Identify monosaccharides as either D- or L-.

### Solution

Review the structures of the two stereoisomers of glyceraldehyde (Figure 16.4b). The ball-and-stick models can be represented using three-dimensional wedge drawings. Remember that for sugars the most oxidized carbon (the aldehyde or ketone group) is always drawn at the top of the structure. Here we show the aldehyde in a condensed form, —CHO.

D-Glyceraldehyde          L-Glyceraldehyde

Remember that in the wedge diagram, the solid wedges represent bonds directed toward the reader. The dashed wedges represent bonds directed away from the reader and into the page. In these molecules, the center carbon is the only chiral carbon in the structure. To convert these wedge representations to a Fischer Projection, simply use a horizontal line in place of each solid wedge and use a vertical line to represent each dashed wedge. The chiral carbon is represented by the point at which the vertical and horizontal lines cross, as shown below.

D-Glyceraldehyde                    L-Glyceraldehyde

---

### Practice Problem 16.1

Draw Fischer Projections for each of the following molecules and for their mirror images.

a.
```
    CH₃
     |
    C=O
     |
 H—C—OH
     |
    CH₂OH
```

b.
```
     H
     |
    C=O
     |
 H—C—OH
     |
 H—C—OH
     |
HO—C—H
     |
    CH₂OH
```

c.
```
   CH₂OH
     |
    C=O
     |
HO—C—H
     |
 H—C—OH
     |
 H—C—OH
     |
    CH₂OH
```

▶ For Further Practice: **Questions 16.45 and 16.46.**

## Racemic Mixtures

When Louis Pasteur measured the specific rotation of the mixture of tartaric acid salt crystals, he observed that it was optically inactive. The reason was that the mixture contained equal amounts of the (+) enantiomer and the (−) enantiomer. A mixture of equal amounts of a pair of enantiomers is called a *racemic mixture*, or simply a *racemate*. The prefix (±) is used to designate a racemic mixture. In this situation the specific rotation is zero because the rotation caused by one enantiomer is canceled by the opposite rotation caused by the mirror-image enantiomer.

## Diastereomers

So far, we have looked only at molecules containing a single chiral carbon. In this case only two enantiomers are possible. However, it is quite common to find molecules with two or more chiral carbons. For a molecule of $n$ chiral carbons the maximum possible number of different configurations is $2^n$. Note that this formula predicts the *maximum* number of configurations. As we will see, there may actually be fewer.

---

**EXAMPLE 16.2**   **Drawing Stereoisomers for Compounds with More Than One Chiral Carbon**

**LEARNING GOALS**

Draw all the possible stereoisomers of 2,3,4-trichlorobutanal.

**3** Determine whether a molecule has a chiral center.

**Solution**

**4** Explain stereoisomerism.

1. There are two chiral carbons in this molecule, C-2 and C-3. Thus there are $2^2$ or 4 possible stereoisomers.
2. There are two possible configurations for each of the chiral carbons (Cl on the left or on the right). Begin by drawing an isomer with both Cl atoms on the right (a). Now draw the mirror image (b). You have now generated the first pair of enantiomers, (a) and (b).

Enantiomers

3. Next, change the location of one of the two Cl atoms bonded to a chiral carbon to produce another possible isomer (c). Finally, draw the mirror image of (c) to produce the second set of enantiomers, (c) and (d).

Enantiomers

4. By this systematic procedure we have drawn the four possible isomers of 2,3,4-trichlorobutanal.

---

**Practice Problem 16.2**

Draw all of the possible stereoisomers of each of the compounds listed below. Indicate which are enantiomers.

　a. 2-Bromo-3-chlorobutane　　　b. 2-Chloro-3-fluoropentane　　　c. 2,3,4-Tribromopentanal

▶ For Further Practice: **Questions 16.47 and 16.48.**

In Example 16.2, structures (a) and (b) are clearly enantiomers, as are (c) and (d). But how do we describe the relationship between structures (a) and (c) or any of the pairs of stereoisomers that are *not* enantiomers? The term **diastereomers** is used to describe a pair of stereoisomers having two or more chiral centers and that are not enantiomers.

Although enantiomers differ from one another only in the direction of rotation of plane-polarized light, diastereomers are different in their chemical and physical properties.

## Meso Compounds

As mentioned previously, the maximum number of configurations for a molecule with two chiral carbons is $2^2$, or 4. However, if each of the two chiral carbons is bonded to the same four nonidentical groups, fewer than four stereoisomers exist. Such compounds are called **meso compounds.** The example of tartaric acid, studied by Pasteur, helps to explain this phenomenon.

| EXAMPLE 16.3 | **Drawing Stereoisomers of Compounds with More Than One Chiral Carbon** |
|---|---|

**LEARNING GOALS**

**3** Determine whether a molecule has a chiral center.

**4** Explain stereoisomerism.

Draw all the possible stereoisomers of tartaric acid,:

### Solution

1. Proceeding as in Example 16.2, you will generate the following four structures:

2. Careful examination of pair (c) and (d) reveals that these molecules are nonsuperimposable mirror images. Thus they are enantiomers.
3. Similar inspection of structures (a) and (b) reveals that, although they are mirror images, they are identical. Structure (b) can simply be rotated 180° to produce structure (a); therefore they are identical.

### Practice Problem 16.3

Draw all of the possible stereoisomers of each of the compounds listed below. Indicate which are enantiomers and which will have a meso compound.

   a. 2,3-Dichlorobutane     b. 1,2-Dibromocyclopentane     c. 3,4-Difluorohexane

▶ For Further Practice: **Questions 16.49 and 16.50.**

Note that if you draw a line between chiral carbon-2 and chiral carbon-3 of the meso compound represented in (a) and (b) in Example 16.3, the top half of the molecule is the mirror image of the bottom half. There is a plane of symmetry within the molecule:

$$
\begin{array}{c}
\text{COOH} \\
\text{H} \!-\! \text{OH} \\
\text{H} \!-\! \text{OH} \\
\text{COOH}
\end{array}
$$

As a result, structure (a) is optically inactive. Even though there are two chiral carbons, the rotation of plane-polarized light by chiral carbon-2 is canceled by the opposite rotation of plane-polarized light caused by chiral carbon-3. This molecule is *achiral* and is termed meso-tartaric acid. Any compound with an internal plane of symmetry (that is, that can be superimposed on its mirror image) is optically inactive and is termed a meso compound.

## The D- and L- System of Nomenclature

In 1891 Emil Fischer devised a nomenclature system that would allow scientists to distinguish between enantiomers. Fischer knew that the two enantiomers of glyceraldehyde rotated plane-polarized light in opposite directions, but he did not have the sophisticated tools needed to make an absolute connection between the structure and the direction of rotation of plane-polarized light. He simply decided that the (+) enantiomer would be the one with the hydroxyl group of the chiral carbon on the right. He called this D-glyceraldehyde. The enantiomer that rotated plane-polarized light in the (−) or levorotatory direction, he called L-glyceraldehyde (see Figure 16.4).

While specific rotation is an experimental value that must be measured, the D- and L-designations of all other monosaccharides are determined by comparison of their structures with D- and L-glyceraldehyde. Sugars with more than three carbons will have more than one chiral carbon. *By convention*, it is the position of the hydroxyl group on the chiral carbon farthest from the carbonyl group (the most oxidized end of the molecule) that determines whether a monosaccharide is in the D- or L-configuration. One way to be sure you are considering the correct chiral carbon is to number the carbon chain, giving the carbonyl group the lowest possible number. It is the chiral carbon with the highest number that is used to determine the D- or L-configuration. If the —OH group is on the right, the molecule is in the D-configuration. If the —OH group is on the left, the molecule is in the L-configuration. Almost all carbohydrates in living systems are members of the D-family.

It was not until 1952 that researchers were able to demonstrate that Fischer had guessed correctly when he proposed the structures of the (+) and (−) enantiomers of glyceraldehyde.

 **STEREOCHEMISTRY AND STEREOISOMERS REVISITED**

D-Glyceraldehyde     D-Glucose     D-Fructose

**Question 16.5** Place an asterisk beside each chiral carbon in the Fischer Projections you drew for Practice Problem 16.1 at the end of Example 16.1.

**Question 16.6** In the Fischer Projections you drew for Practice Problem 16.1 at the end of Example 16.1, indicate which bonds project toward you and which project into the page.

**Question 16.7** Determine the configuration (D- or L-) for each of the molecules in Practice Problem 16.1 at the end of Example 16.1.

**Question 16.8** Explain the difference between the D- and L-designation and the (+) and (−) designation.

## 16.4 Biologically Important Monosaccharides

Monosaccharides, the simplest carbohydrates, have backbones of from three to seven carbons. There are many monosaccharides, but we will focus on those that are most common in biological systems. These include the five- and six-carbon sugars: glucose, fructose, galactose, ribose, and deoxyribose.

### Glucose

**Glucose** is the most important sugar in the human body. It is found in numerous foods and has several common names, including dextrose, grape sugar, and blood sugar. Glucose is broken down in glycolysis and other pathways to release energy for body functions.

The concentration of glucose in the blood is critical to normal body function. As a result, it is carefully controlled by the hormones insulin and glucagon. Normal blood glucose levels are 100–120 mg glucose/100 mL blood, with the highest concentrations appearing after a meal. Insulin stimulates the uptake of the excess glucose by most cells of the body, and after 1 to 2 hours (h), levels return to normal. If blood glucose concentrations drop too low, the individual feels lightheaded and shaky. When this happens, glucagon stimulates the liver to release glucose into the blood, reestablishing normal levels. We will take a closer look at this delicate balancing act in Section 23.6.

The molecular formula of glucose, an aldohexose, is $C_6H_{12}O_6$. The structure of glucose is shown in Figure 16.7, and the method used to draw this structure is described in Example 16.4.

**LEARNING GOAL**

**6** Draw and name the common monosaccharides using structural formulas.

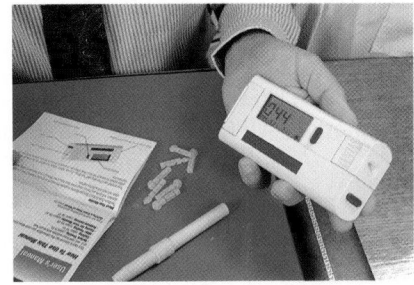

Why do diabetics need to use a blood glucose monitor like the one shown here?

| EXAMPLE 16.4 | Drawing the Structure of a Monosaccharide |
|---|---|

**LEARNING GOAL**

**6** Draw and name the common monosaccharides using structural formulas.

Draw the structure and Fischer Projection for D-glucose.

**Solution**

Glucose is an aldohexose.

**Step 1.** Draw six carbons in a straight vertical line; each carbon is separated from the ones above and below it by a bond:

*Continued...*

**Step 2.** The most highly oxidized carbon is, by convention, drawn as the uppermost carbon (carbon-1). In this case, carbon-1 is an aldehyde carbon:

Most oxidized end of
carbon chain; aldehyde

**Step 3.** The atoms are added to the next to the last carbon atom, at the bottom of the chain, to give either the D- or L-configuration as desired. Remember, when the —OH group is to the right, you have D-glucose. When in doubt, compare your structure to D-glyceraldehyde!

Compare chiral
carbons farthest
from the carbonyl
group

D-Isomer          D-Glyceraldehyde

**Step 4.** All the remaining atoms are then added to give the desired carbohydrate. For example, you would draw the following structure for D-glucose.

D-Glucose

D-Glucose
(Fischer Projection)

The positions for the hydrogen atoms and the hydroxyl groups on the remaining carbons must be learned for each sugar.

## Practice Problem 16.4

Draw the structures of D-ribose and L-ribose. (Information on the structure of D-ribose is found later in this chapter.)

▶ For Further Practice: **Questions 16.9 and 16.10.**

**Figure 16.7** Cyclization of glucose to give α- and β-D-glucose. Note that the carbonyl carbon (C-1) becomes chiral in this process, yielding the α- and β-forms of glucose. The hemiacetal is highlighted in yellow.

In actuality the open-chain form of glucose is present in very small concentrations in cells. It exists in cyclic form under physiological conditions because the carbonyl group at C-1 of glucose reacts with the hydroxyl group at C-5 to give a six-member ring. In the discussion of aldehydes, we noted that the reaction between an aldehyde and an alcohol yields a **hemiacetal.** When the aldehyde portion of the glucose molecule reacts with the C-5 hydroxyl group, the product is a cyclic *intramolecular hemiacetal.* For D-glucose, two isomers can be formed in this reaction (see Figure 16.7). These isomers are called α- and β-D-glucose. The two isomers formed differ from one another in the location of the —OH attached to the hemiacetal carbon, C-1. Such isomers, differing in the arrangement of bonds around the hemiacetal carbon, are called **anomers.** In the α-anomers, the C-1 (*anomeric carbon*) hydroxyl group is below the ring, and in the β-anomers, the C-1 hydroxyl group is above the ring. Like the stereoisomers discussed previously, the α and β forms can be distinguished from one another because they rotate plane-polarized light differently.

*Hemiacetal structure,*

$$R^1 - \underset{\underset{H}{|}}{\overset{\overset{OH}{|}}{C}} - OR^2$$

*and formation are described in Section 13.4.*

**Question 16.9** Draw the structure of D-galactose. (Information on the structure of D-galactose is found later in this chapter.)

**Question 16.10** Draw the structure of L-galactose.

In Figure 16.7 a new type of structural formula, called a **Haworth projection,** is presented. Although on first inspection it appears complicated, it is quite simple to derive a Haworth projection from a structural formula, as Example 16.5 shows.

**EXAMPLE 16.5**   **Drawing the Haworth Projection of a Monosaccharide from the Structural Formula**

Draw the Haworth projections of α- and β-D-glucose.

**7** Given the linear structure of a monosaccharide, draw the Haworth projection of its α- and β-cyclic forms and vice versa.

**Solution**

1. Before attempting to draw a Haworth projection, look at the first steps of ring formation shown here:

Glucose
(open chain)

Glucose
(intermediates in ring formation)

Try to imagine that you are seeing the molecules shown above in three dimensions. Some of the substituent groups on the molecule will be above the ring, and some will be beneath it. The question then becomes: How do you determine which groups to place above the ring and which to place beneath the ring?

2. Look at the two-dimensional structural formula. Note the groups (drawn in blue) to the left of the carbon chain. These are placed above the ring in the Haworth projection.

α-D-Glucose

β-D-Glucose

3. Now note the groups (drawn in red) to the right of the carbon chain. These will be located beneath the carbon ring in the Haworth projection.

α-D-Glucose

β-D-Glucose

4. Thus in the Haworth projection of the cyclic form of any D-sugar the —CH$_2$OH group is always "up." When the —OH group at C-1 is also "up," *cis* to the —CH$_2$OH group, the sugar is β-D-glucose. When the —OH group at C-1 is "down," *trans* to the —CH$_2$OH group, the sugar is α-D-glucose.

Haworth projection
α-D-Glucose

Haworth projection
β-D-Glucose

---

**Practice Problem 16.5**

Refer to the linear structures of D-galactose and D-ribose. Draw the Haworth projections of (a) α- and β-D-galactose and of (b) α- and β-D-ribose. Note that D-ribose is a pentose.

▶ For Further Practice: **Questions 16.55 and 16.56.**

---

## Fructose

**Fructose,** also called levulose and fruit sugar, is the sweetest of all sugars. It is found in large amounts in honey, corn syrup, and sweet fruits. The structure of fructose is similar to that of glucose. When there is a —CH$_2$OH group instead of a —CHO group at carbon-1 and a —C=O group instead of CHOH at carbon-2, the sugar is a ketose. In this case it is D-fructose.

Cyclization of fructose produces α- and β-D-fructose:

D-Fructose

α-D-Fructose

β-D-Fructose

In the equation above, the hemiacetal is highlighted. Fructose forms a five-member ring structure.

Fructose is often called fruit sugar because it contributes sweetness to ripe fruits, such as these peaches. Is fructose an aldose or a ketose?

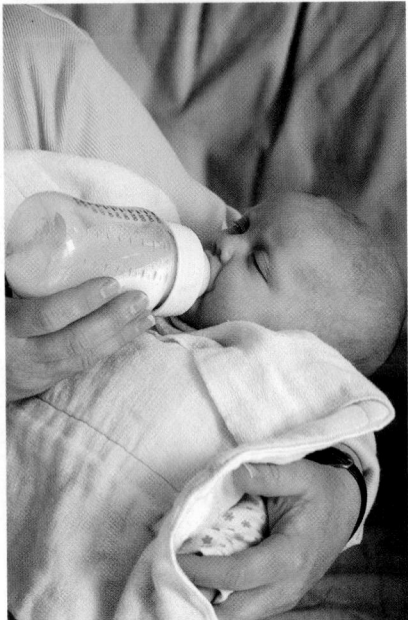

Galactose is one of the components of lactose, or milk sugar. Read about galactosemia in Section 16.5 and describe the symptoms and treatment for this genetic disorder.

## Galactose

Another important hexose is **galactose.** The linear structure of D-galactose and the Haworth projections of α-D-galactose and β-D-galactose are shown here:

D-Galactose

α-D-Galactose

β-D-Galactose

Galactose is found in biological systems as a component of the disaccharide lactose, or milk sugar. This is the principal sugar found in the milk of most mammals. β-D-Galactose and a modified form, β-D-*N*-acetylgalactosamine, are also components of the blood group antigens.

β-D-*N*-Acetylgalactosamine

## Ribose and Deoxyribose, Five-Carbon Sugars

**Ribose** is a component of many biologically important molecules, including RNA and various coenzymes that are required by many of the enzymes that carry out biochemical reactions in the body. The structure of the five-carbon sugar D-ribose is shown in its open-chain form and in the α- and β-cyclic forms.

D-Ribose

α-D-Ribose

β-D-Ribose

β-D-2-Deoxyribose is one of the components of the sugar-phosphate backbone of the DNA molecule. How does this molecule differ from β-D-ribose?

CH$_2$OH  H  H  O  OH  OH  H  H  OH  H  HO  H  OH

β-D-Glucose

CH$_2$OH  HO  H  O  OH  OH  H  H  H  OH  H  H  OH

β-D-Galactose

**Figure 16.9** Comparison of the cyclic forms of glucose and galactose. Note that galactose is identical to glucose except in the position of the C-4 hydroxyl group.

$^6$CH$_2$OH  HO  $^5$H  O  $^4$OH  H  $^1$H  H  $^3$  $^2$  H  OH

β-D-Galactose

+

$^6$CH$_2$OH  $^5$H  $^4$H  O  OH  $^4$OH  H  $^1$  H  $^3$  $^2$  H  OH

β-D-Glucose

→

β(1 → 4) linkage

$^6$CH$_2$OH  HO  $^5$H  O  $^4$OH  H  $^1$  H  OH  H  $^3$  $^2$  H  OH

O

$^6$CH$_2$OH  $^5$H  $^4$H  O  OH  OH  H  $^1$  H  $^3$  $^2$  H  OH

+ H$_2$O

β-Lactose

**Figure 16.10** Glycosidic bond formed between the C-1 hydroxyl group of β-D-galactose and the C-4 hydroxyl group of β-D-glucose. The disaccharide is called β-lactose because the hydroxyl group at the reducing end of the disaccharide has the β-configuration.

through the circulatory system of the plant. It cannot be synthesized by animals. High concentrations of sucrose produce a high osmotic pressure, which inhibits the growth of microorganisms, so it is used as a preservative. Of course, it is also widely used as a sweetener. In fact, it is estimated that the average American consumes 100–125 pounds (lb) of sucrose each year. It has been suggested that sucrose in the diet is undesirable because it represents a source of empty calories; that is, it contains no vitamins or minerals. However, the only negative association that has been scientifically verified is the link between sucrose in the diet and dental caries, or cavities (see A Medical Perspective: Tooth Decay and Simple Sugars on p. 551).

Sucrose is a disaccharide of α-D-glucose joined to β-D-fructose (Figure 16.11). The glycosidic linkage between α-D-glucose and β-D-fructose is quite different from those that we have examined for lactose and maltose. This bond involves the anomeric carbons of *both* sugars! This bond is called an (α1 → β2) glycosidic linkage, since it involves the C-1 anomeric carbon of glucose and the C-2 anomeric carbon of fructose (noted in red in Figure 16.11). Because the (α1 → β2) glycosidic bond joins both anomeric carbons, there is no hemiacetal group. As a result, the ring cannot open to the linear form and sucrose will not react with Benedict's reagent. Thus, sucrose is not a reducing sugar.

Both galactosemia and lactose intolerance are treated by removing milk and milk products from the diet. Explain the difference between these two conditions.

$^6$CH$_2$OH  H  $^5$H  O  H  $^4$OH  H  $^1$  HO  $^3$  $^2$  H  OH

α-Glucose

+

$^6$CH$_2$OH  $^5$H  O  H  HO  $^2$  OH  $^4$  $^3$  OH  H  $^1$CH$_2$OH

β-Fructose

→

$^6$CH$_2$OH  H  $^5$H  O  H  $^4$OH  H  $^1$  HO  $^3$  $^2$  H  OH

O + H$_2$O  (α1 → β2) linkage

$^6$CH$_2$OH  $^5$H  O  H  HO  $^2$  $^4$  $^3$  OH  H  $^1$CH$_2$OH

Sucrose

**Figure 16.11** Glycosidic bond formed between the C-1 hydroxyl of α-D-glucose and the C-2 hydroxyl of β-D-fructose. This bond is called an (α1 → β2) glycosidic linkage. The disaccharide formed in this reaction is sucrose.

# CHEMISTRY AT THE CRIME SCENE

## Blood Group Antigens

Before DNA fingerprinting was available, blood typing was often used to analyze blood from a crime scene. Such evidence could exonerate a suspect or provide further evidence of guilt. But with only four human blood types, you can imagine how inexact conclusions could be drawn from this evidence!

In 1904, Dr. Karl Landsteiner performed a series of experiments on the blood of workers in his laboratory. He separated the blood cells from the serum, the liquid component of the blood, and mixed these samples in test tubes. When he mixed serum from one individual with blood cells of another, Landsteiner observed that, in some instances, the serum samples caused clumping, or *agglutination*, of red blood cells (RBC). (See figure below.) As a result of many such experiments, Landsteiner showed that there are four human blood groups, designated A, B, AB, and O.

We now know that differences among blood groups reflect differences among oligosaccharides attached to the proteins and lipids of the RBC membranes. The oligosaccharides on the RBC surface have a common core, consisting of

ABO blood typing kit. When antibodies bind to antigens on the cell surface, clumping occurs.

$\beta$-D-$N$-acetylgalactosamine, galactose, $N$-acetylneuraminic acid (sialic acid), and L-fucose. It is the terminal monosaccharide of this oligosaccharide that distinguishes the cells and governs the compatibility of the blood types.

The A blood group antigen has $\beta$-D-$N$-acetylgalactosamine at its end, whereas the B blood group antigen has $\alpha$-D-galactose. In type O blood, neither of these sugars is found on the cell surface; only the core oligosaccharide is present. Some oligosaccharides on type AB blood cells have a terminal $\beta$-D-$N$-acetylgalactosamine, whereas others have a terminal $\alpha$-D-galactose.

Why does agglutination occur? The clumping reaction that occurs when incompatible bloods are mixed is an antigen–antibody reaction. Antigens are large molecules, often portions of bacteria or viruses, that stimulate the immune defenses of the body to produce protective antibodies. Antibodies bind to the foreign antigens and help to destroy them.

People with type A blood also have antibodies against type B blood (anti-B antibodies) in the blood serum. If the person with type A blood receives a transfusion of type B blood, the anti-B antibodies bind to the type B blood cells, causing clumping and destruction of those cells that can result in death. Individuals with type B blood also produce anti-A antibodies and therefore cannot receive a transfusion from a type A individual. Those with type AB blood have neither anti-A nor anti-B antibodies in their blood. (If they did, they would destroy their own red blood cells!) Type O blood has no A or B antigens on the RBC but has both anti-A and anti-B antibodies. Because of the presence of both types of antibodies, type O individuals can receive transfusions only from a person who is also type O.

In the forensic laboratory, this same agglutination reaction can be used to determine the blood type of a sample from a crime scene for comparison with the blood of the victim and that of a suspect. The results may clear the suspect or further incriminate him or her. Because there are only four human blood types, significant additional evidence is needed to prove the guilt of a suspect. In fact, DNA fingerprinting is currently being used to reevaluate guilty verdicts obtained with this less reliable evidence.

### For Further Understanding

▶ People with type AB blood are referred to as universal recipients. Explain why these people can receive blood of any of the four ABO types.

▶ Why is blood typing insufficient to prove the guilt of a suspect?

---

## 16.6   Polysaccharides

### LEARNING GOAL

**12**  Discuss the structural, chemical, and biochemical properties of starch, glycogen, and cellulose.

### Starch

Many carbohydrates that are found in nature are large polymers of glucose. Thus a polysaccharide is a large polymer composed of many monosaccharide units (the monomers) joined in one or more chains. **Homopolysaccharides** are those

α (1⟶4) linkage

**(a)**

**Figure 16.12** Structure of amylose. (a) A linear chain of α-D-glucose joined in α(1 → 4) glycosidic linkage makes up the primary structure of amylose. (b) Owing to hydrogen bonding, the amylose chain forms a left-handed helix that contains six glucose units per turn.

**(b)**

composed of a single monosaccharide. **Heteropolysaccharides** are those made up of two or more different monosaccharides. (See A Medical Perspective: Monosaccharide Derivatives and Heteropolysaccharides of Medical Interest on page 573.)

Plants have the ability to use the energy of sunlight to produce monosaccharides, principally glucose, from $CO_2$ and $H_2O$. Although sucrose is the major transport form of sugar in the plant, starch (a homopolysaccharide) is the principal storage form in most plants. These plants store glucose in starch granules. Nearly all plant cells contain some starch granules, but in some seeds, such as corn, as much as 80% of the cell's dry weight is starch.

Starch is a heterogeneous material composed of the glucose polymers **amylose** and **amylopectin**. Amylose, which accounts for about 20% of the starch of a plant cell, is a linear polymer of α-D-glucose molecules connected by glycosidic bonds between C-1 of one glucose molecule and C-4 of a second glucose. Thus the glucose units in amylose are joined by α(1 → 4) glycosidic bonds. A single chain can contain up to 4000 glucose units. Amylose coils up into a helix that repeats every six glucose units. The structure of amylose is shown in Figure 16.12.

Amylose is degraded by two types of enzymes. They are produced in the pancreas, from which they are secreted into the small intestine, and the salivary glands, from which they are secreted into the saliva. α-*Amylase* cleaves the glycosidic bonds of amylose chains at random along the chain, producing shorter polysaccharide chains. The enzyme β-*amylase* sequentially cleaves the disaccharide maltose from the reducing end of the amylose chain. The maltose is hydrolyzed into glucose by the enzyme *maltase*. The glucose is quickly absorbed by intestinal cells and used by the cells of the body as a source of energy.

Amylopectin is a highly branched amylose in which the branches are attached to the C-6 hydroxyl groups by α(1 → 6) glycosidic bonds (Figure 16.13). The main chains consist of α(1 → 4) glycosidic bonds. Each branch contains 20–25 glucose units, and there are so many branches that the main chain can scarcely be distinguished.

## Glycogen

**Glycogen** is the major glucose storage molecule in animals. The structure of glycogen is similar to that of amylopectin. The "main chain" is linked by α(1 → 4) glycosidic bonds, and it has numerous α(1 → 6) glycosidic bonds, which provide many branch points along the chain. Glycogen differs from amylopectin only by having more and shorter branches. Otherwise, the two molecules are virtually identical. The structure of glycogen is shown in Figure 16.13.

Glycogen is stored in the liver and skeletal muscle. Glycogen synthesis and degradation in the liver are carefully regulated. As we will see in Section 21.7, these two processes are intimately involved in keeping blood glucose levels constant.

*A polymer (Section 11.5) is a large molecule made up of many small units, the monomers, held together by chemical bonds.*

**ANIMATION**
• Natural and Synthetic Polymers

Enzymes are proteins that serve as biological catalysts. They speed up biochemical reactions so that life processes can function. α- and β-Amylases are called α(1 → 4) glycosidases because they cleave α(1 → 4) glycosidic bonds.

Potatoes contain large amounts of starch. Describe the composition of this starch.

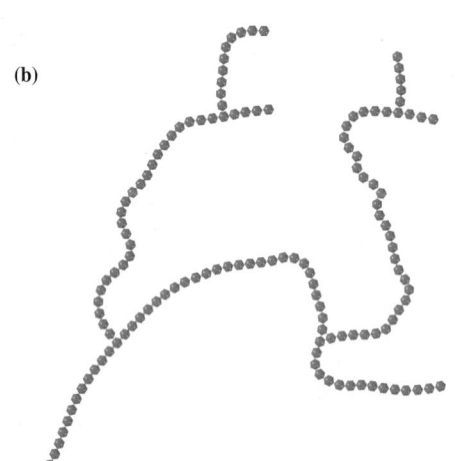

(a)

α(1 → 6) linkage

α(1 → 4) linkage

**Figure 16.13** Structure of amylopectin and glycogen. (a) Both amylopectin and glycogen consist of chains of α-D-glucose molecules joined in α(1 → 4) glycosidic linkages. Branching from these chains are other chains of the same structure. Branching occurs by formation of α(1 → 6) glycosidic bonds between glucose units. (b) A representation of the branched-chain structure of amylopectin. (c) A representation of the branched-chain structure of glycogen. Glycogen differs from amylopectin only in that the branches are shorter and there are more of them.

(b)

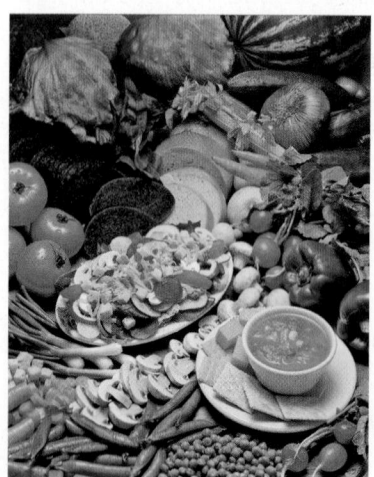

(c)

## Cellulose

The most abundant polysaccharide, indeed the most abundant organic molecule in the world, is **cellulose,** a polymer of β-D-glucose units linked by β(1 → 4) glycosidic bonds (Figure 16.14). A molecule of cellulose typically contains about 3000 glucose units, but the largest known cellulose, produced by the alga *Valonia,* contains 26,000 glucose molecules.

Cellulose is a structural component of the plant cell wall. The unbranched structure of the cellulose polymer and the β(1 → 4) glycosidic linkages allow cellulose molecules to form long, straight chains of parallel cellulose molecules called *fibrils.* These fibrils are quite rigid and are held together tightly by hydrogen bonds; thus it is not surprising that cellulose is a cell wall structural element.

In contrast to glycogen, amylose, and amylopectin, cellulose *cannot* be digested by humans. The reason is that we cannot synthesize the enzyme *cellulase,* which can hydrolyze the β(1 → 4) glycosidic linkages of the cellulose polymer. Indeed, only a few animals, such as termites, cows, and goats, are able to digest cellulose. These animals have, within their digestive tracts, microorganisms that produce the enzyme cellulase. The sugars released by this microbial digestion can then be absorbed and used by these animals. In humans, cellulose from fruits and vegetables serves as fiber in the diet.

Vegetables contribute fiber to our diet. What carbohydrate provides this fiber?

β(1 → 4) glycosidic bond

**Figure 16.14** The structure of cellulose.

nonidentical groups. Therefore, there are only three possible stereoisomers. Compounds A and B are identical and they are meso. Compounds C and D are enantiomers.

**b.**

When 1.2-dibromocyclopentane is drawn as shown in the four structures on the left, it is shown that there are two chiral carbons in this molecule. The set of structures on the right is provided to help you see the stereochemistry around those chiral carbons. Here it should be noted that there is a plane of symmetry within the molecule. Each of the two chiral carbons is bonded to the same four nonidentical groups. Therefore, there are only three possible stereoisomers. Compounds A and B are identical and they are meso. Compounds C and D are enantiomers.

**c.**

There are two chiral carbons in this molecule. But, each of the two chiral carbons is bonded to the same four nonidentical groups. Therefore, there are only three possible stereoisomers. Compounds A and B are identical and they are meso. Compounds C and D are enantiomers.

**16.4**

D-Ribose  L-Ribose

**16.5 a.**

α-D-Galactose  β-D-Galactose

**b.**

α-D-Ribose  β-D-Ribose

# QUESTIONS AND PROBLEMS

## Types of Carbohydrates

### Foundations

**16.13** What is the difference between a monosaccharide and a disaccharide?

**16.14** What is a polysaccharide?

### Applications

**16.15** Read the labels on some of the foods in your kitchen, and see how many products you can find that list one or more carbohydrates among the ingredients in the package. Make a list of these compounds, and attempt to classify them as monosaccharides, disaccharides, or polysaccharides.

**16.16** Some disaccharides are often referred to by their common names. What are the chemical names of (a) milk sugar, (b) beet sugar, and (c) cane sugar?

**16.17** How many kcal of energy are released when 1 g of carbohydrate is "burned" or oxidized?

**16.18** List some natural sources of carbohydrates.

**16.19** Draw and provide the names of an aldohexose and a ketohexose.

**16.20** Draw and provide the name of an aldotriose.

## Monosaccharides

### Foundations

**16.21** Define the term *aldose*.
**16.22** Define the term *ketose*.
**16.23** What is a tetrose?
**16.24** What is a hexose?
**16.25** What is a ketopentose?
**16.26** What is an aldotriose?

### Applications

**16.27** Identify each of the following sugars.

a.

c.

b.

**16.28** Draw the open-chain form of the sugars in Question 16.27.
**16.29** Draw all of the different possible aldotrioses of molecular formula $C_3H_6O_3$.
**16.30** Draw all of the different possible aldotetroses of molecular formula $C_4H_8O_4$.

## Stereoisomers and Stereochemistry

### Foundations

**16.31** Define the term *stereoisomer*.
**16.32** Define the term *enantiomer*.
**16.33** Define the term *chiral carbon*.
**16.34** Draw an aldotetrose. Note each chiral carbon with an asterisk (*).
**16.35** Explain how a polarimeter works.
**16.36** What is plane-polarized light?
**16.37** What is a Fischer Projection?
**16.38** How would you produce a Fischer Projection beginning with a three-dimensional model of a sugar?
**16.39** Define the term *diastereomer*.
**16.40** Define the term *meso compound*.

### Applications

**16.41** Is there any difference between dextrose and D-glucose?
**16.42** The linear structure of D-glucose is shown in Figure 16.7. Draw its mirror image.
**16.43** How are D- and L-glyceraldehyde related?
**16.44** Determine whether each of the following is a D- or L-sugar:

a.

b.

c.

**16.45** Draw a Fischer Projection formula for each of the following compounds. Indicate each of the chiral carbons with an asterisk (*).

a.

b.

c.

**16.46** Draw a Fischer Projection formula for each of the following compounds. Indicate each of the chiral carbons with an asterisk (*).

a.

b.

c.

**16.47** Draw all the possible stereoisomers of each of the following compounds and indicate which are enantiomers, diastereomers, or meso compounds.

a.

b.

**16.48** Draw all the possible stereoisomers of each of the following compounds and indicate which are enantiomers, diastereomers, or meso compounds.

a.

b.

**16.49** Draw all the possible stereoisomers of each of the following compounds and indicate which are enantiomers, diastereomers, or meso compounds.

a.  $CH_3CH_2CHOHCHOHCH_2CH_3$

b.  $CH_2OHCCHFCHClCCH_2OH$ (with two C=O groups shown)

**16.50** Draw all the possible stereoisomers of each of the following compounds and indicate which are enantiomers, diastereomers, or meso compounds.

a. CH₃CCHOHCHOHCCH₃
$$CH_3\overset{O}{\overset{\|}{C}}CHOHCHOH\overset{O}{\overset{\|}{C}}CH_3$$

b. $CH_2OHCHOHCHClCH_2OH$

## Biologically Important Monosaccharides

### Foundations

**16.51** Define the term *anomer*.
**16.52** What is a Haworth projection?
**16.53** What is a hemiacetal?
**16.54** Explain why the cyclization of D-glucose forms a hemiacetal.

### Applications

**16.55** Why does cyclization of D-glucose give two isomers, α- and β-D-glucose?
**16.56** Draw the structure of the open-chain form of D-fructose, and show how it cyclizes to form α- and β-D-fructose.
**16.57** Which of the following would give a positive Benedict's test?
 a. Sucrose         c. β-Maltose
 b. Glycogen        d. α-Lactose
**16.58** Why was the Benedict's reagent useful for determining the amount of glucose in the urine?
**16.59** Describe what is meant by a pair of enantiomers. Draw an example of a pair of enantiomers.
**16.60** What is a chiral carbon atom?
**16.61** When discussing sugars, what do we mean by an intramolecular hemiacetal?
**16.62** Explain why ketoses can be oxidized in the Benedict's test in contrast to ketones, which cannot.

## Biologically Important Disaccharides

### Foundations

**16.63** Define the term *disaccharide*.
**16.64** What is an acetal?
**16.65** What is a glycosidic bond?
**16.66** Why are glycosidic bonds acetals?

### Applications

**16.67** Maltose is a disaccharide isolated from amylose that consists of two glucose units linked by an α(1 → 4) bond. Draw the structure of this molecule.
**16.68** Sucrose is a disaccharide formed by linking α-D-glucose and β-D-fructose by an (α1 → β2) bond. Draw the structure of this disaccharide.
**16.69** What is the major biological source of lactose?
**16.70** What metabolic defect causes galactosemia?
**16.71** What simple treatment prevents most of the ill effects of galactosemia?
**16.72** What are the major physiological effects of galactosemia?
**16.73** What is lactose intolerance?
**16.74** What is the difference between lactose intolerance and galactosemia?

## Polysaccharides

### Foundations

**16.75** What is a polymer?
**16.76** What form of sugar is used as the major transport sugar in a plant?
**16.77** What is the major storage form of sugar in a plant?
**16.78** What is the major structural form of sugar in a plant?
**16.79** What is a homopolysaccharide?
**16.80** What is a heteropolysaccharide?
**16.81** List some examples of homopolysaccharides.
**16.82** List some examples of heteropolysaccharides. (*Hint:* Refer to A Medical Perspective: Monosaccharide Derivatives and Heteropolysaccharides of Medical Interest.)

### Applications

**16.83** What is the difference between the structure of cellulose and the structure of amylose?
**16.84** How does the structure of amylose differ from that of amylopectin and glycogen?
**16.85** What is the major physiological purpose of glycogen?
**16.86** Where in the body do you find glycogen stored?
**16.87** Where are α-amylase and β-amylase produced?
**16.88** Where do α-amylase and β-amylase carry out their enzymatic functions?

# CRITICAL THINKING PROBLEMS

1. The six-member glucose ring structure is not a flat ring. Like cyclohexane, it can exist in the chair conformation. Build models of the chair conformation of α- and β-D-glucose. Draw each of these structures. Which would you predict to be the more stable isomer? Explain your reasoning.
2. The following is the structure of salicin, a bitter-tasting compound found in the bark of willow trees:

Salicin

The aromatic ring portion of this structure is quite insoluble in water. How would forming a glycosidic bond between the aromatic ring and β-D-glucose alter the solubility? Explain your answer.
3. Ancient peoples used salicin to reduce fevers. Write an equation for the acid-catalyzed hydrolysis of the glycosidic bond of salicin. Compare the aromatic product with the structure of acetylsalicylic acid (aspirin). Use this information to develop a hypothesis explaining why ancient peoples used salicin to reduce fevers.

4. Chitin is a modified cellulose in which the C-2 hydroxyl group of each glucose is replaced by

$$\underset{\substack{|| \\ -NHCCH_3}}{O}$$

This nitrogen-containing polysaccharide makes up the shells of lobsters, crabs, and the exoskeletons of insects. Draw a portion of a chitin polymer consisting of four monomers.

5. Pectins are polysaccharides obtained from fruits and berries and used to thicken jellies and jams. Pectins are $\alpha(1 \rightarrow 4)$ linked D-galacturonic acid. D-Galacturonic acid is D-galactose in which the C-6 hydroxyl group has been oxidized to a carboxyl group. Draw a portion of a pectin polymer consisting of four monomers.

6. Peonin is a red pigment found in the petals of peony flowers. Consider the structure of peonin:

Why do you think peonin is bonded to two hexoses? What monosaccharide(s) would be produced by acid-catalyzed hydrolysis of peonin?

# Lipids and Their Functions in Biochemical Systems

## LEARNING GOALS

1 Discuss the physical and chemical properties and biological functions of each of the types of lipids.

2 Write the structures of saturated and unsaturated fatty acids.

3 Compare and contrast the structures and properties of saturated and unsaturated fatty acids.

4 Describe the functions of prostaglandins.

5 Discuss the mechanism by which aspirin reduces pain.

6 Write equations representing the reactions that fatty acids and glycerides undergo.

7 Draw the structure of a phospholipid and discuss its amphipathic nature.

8 Discuss the general classes of sphingolipids and their functions.

9 Draw the structure of the steroid nucleus and discuss the functions of steroid hormones.

10 Describe the function of lipoproteins in triglyceride and cholesterol transport in the body.

11 Draw the structure of the cell membrane and discuss its functions.

The foxglove plant is a source of digitoxin and other cardiotonic steroids. Read A Medical Perspective: Steroids and the Treatment of Heart Disease in this chapter and explain why the ingestion of foxglove can have deadly consequences.

## OUTLINE

# INTRODUCTION

Lipids seem to be the most controversial group of biological molecules, particularly in the fields of medicine and nutrition. We are concerned about the use of anabolic steroids by athletes. Although these hormones increase muscle mass and enhance performance, we are just beginning to understand the damage they cause to the body.

We worry about what types of dietary fat we should consume. We hear frequently about the amounts of saturated fats and cholesterol in our diets because a strong correlation has been found between these lipids and heart disease. Large quantities of dietary saturated fats may also predispose an individual to colon, esophageal, stomach, and breast cancers. As a result, we are advised to reduce our intake of cholesterol and saturated fats.

In this chapter we will study the diverse collection of molecules referred to as lipids. We will see that triglycerides are both a dietary source of energy and a (sometimes unwanted) storage form of energy. Other lipids serve as structural components of the cell; for instance, phospholipids and cholesterol are components of the membranes around each of our cells. Some of the chemical messengers of our bodies are lipids. These include the steroid hormones and the hormonelike prostaglandins. Even some of the vitamins that are required in our diet are lipids and any diet that is completely fat-free will result in deficiencies of these vitamins.

This quick tour through a few of the potential hazards of lipids and their essential roles in our bodies makes it easy to understand why lipids are so controversial and why so much literature has been published about the lipids in our diets. But, in fact, standards of fat intake have not been experimentally determined. The most recent U.S. Dietary Guidelines recommend that our daily fat intake be 20–35% of our daily caloric intake. Fewer than 10% of the calories we consume should be saturated fats, and cholesterol intake should be less than 300 milligrams/day. Overall, the intake of fats and oils that are high in saturated fats or in *trans*-fatty acids should be limited.

## 17.1    Biological Functions of Lipids

The term **lipids** actually refers to a collection of organic molecules of varying chemical composition. They are grouped together on the basis of their solubility in nonpolar solvents. Lipids may be subdivided into four main types:

1. *Fatty acids* (saturated and unsaturated)
2. *Glycerides* (glycerol-containing lipids)
3. *Nonglyceride lipids* (sphingolipids, steroids, waxes)
4. *Complex lipids* (lipoproteins)

In this chapter we examine the structure, properties, chemical reactions, and biological functions of each of the lipid groups shown in Figure 17.1.

As a result of differences in their structures, lipids serve many different functions in the human body. The following brief list will give you an idea of the importance of lipids in biological processes:

- *Energy source.* Like carbohydrates, lipids are an excellent source of energy for the body. When oxidized, each gram of fat releases 9 kilocalories (kcal) of energy, or more than twice the energy released by oxidation of a gram of carbohydrate.
- *Energy storage.* Most of the energy stored in the body is in the form of lipids (triglycerides). Stored in fat cells called *adipocytes,* these fats are a particularly rich source of energy for the body.
- *Cell membrane structural components.* Phosphoglycerides, sphingolipids, and steroids make up the basic structure of all cell membranes. These membranes control the flow of molecules into and out of cells and allow cell-to-cell communication.

# A MEDICAL PERSPECTIVE

## Lifesaving Lipids

In the intensive-care nursery the premature infant struggles for life. Born three and a half months early, the baby weighs only 1.6 pounds (lb), and the lungs labor to provide enough oxygen to keep the tiny body alive. Premature infants often have respiratory difficulties because they have not yet begun to produce *pulmonary surfactant.*

Pulmonary surfactant is a combination of phospholipids and proteins that reduces surface tension in the alveoli of the lungs. (Alveoli are the small, thin-walled air sacs in the lungs.) This allows efficient gas exchange across the membranes of the alveolar cells; oxygen can more easily diffuse from the air into the tissues and carbon dioxide can easily diffuse from the tissues into the air. Without pulmonary surfactant, gas exchange in the lungs is very poor.

Pulmonary surfactant is not produced until early in the sixth month of pregnancy. Premature babies born before they have begun secretion of natural surfactant suffer from *respiratory distress syndrome* (RDS), which is caused by the severe difficulty they have obtaining enough oxygen from the air that they breathe.

Until recently, RDS was a major cause of death among premature infants, but now a lifesaving treatment is available.

A fine aerosol of an artificial surfactant is administered directly into the trachea. The Glaxo-Wellcome Company product EXO-SURF Neonatal contains the phospholipid lecithin to reduce surface tension; 1-hexadecanol, which spreads the lecithin; and a polymer called *tyloxapol,* which disperses both the lecithin and the 1-hexadecanol.

Artificial pulmonary surfactant therapy has dramatically reduced premature infant death caused by RDS and appears to have reduced overall mortality for all babies born weighing less than 700 grams (g) (about 1.5 lb). Advances such as this have come about as a result of research on the makeup of body tissues and secretions in both healthy and diseased individuals. Often, such basic research provides the information needed to develop effective therapies.

**For Further Understanding**

▸ Draw the structure of 1-hexadecanol.
▸ Draw the structure of lecithin. Explain how lecithin reduces surface tension.

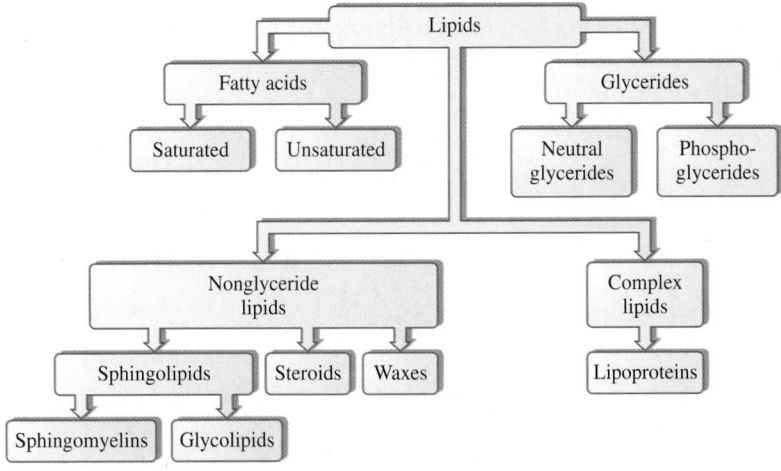

**Figure 17.1** Types of lipids.

- *Hormones.* The steroid hormones are critical chemical messengers that allow tissues of the body to communicate with one another. The hormonelike prostaglandins exert strong biological effects on both the cells that produce them and other cells of the body.
- *Vitamins.* The lipid-soluble vitamins, A, D, E, and K, play a major role in the regulation of several critical biological processes, including blood clotting and vision.
- *Vitamin absorption.* Dietary fat serves as a carrier of the lipid-soluble vitamins. All are transported into cells of the small intestine in association with fat molecules. Therefore a diet that is too low in fat (less than 20% of calories) can result in a deficiency of these four vitamins.

**LIPID-SOLUBLE VITAMINS**

- *Protection.* Fats serve as a shock absorber, or protective layer, for the vital organs. About 4% of the total body fat is reserved for this critical function.
- *Insulation.* Fat stored beneath the skin (subcutaneous fat) serves to insulate the body from extremes of cold temperatures.

## 17.2  Fatty Acids

LEARNING GOAL

**2**  Write the structures of saturated and unsaturated fatty acids.

### Structure and Properties

**Fatty acids** are long-chain monocarboxylic acids. As a consequence of their biosynthesis, fatty acids generally contain an *even number* of carbon atoms. The general formula for a **saturated fatty acid** is $CH_3(CH_2)_nCOOH$, in which $n$ in biological systems is an even integer. Recall that —COOH is a representation of the carboxyl group. If $n = 16$, the result is an 18-carbon saturated fatty acid, stearic acid, having the following structural formula:

*The saturated fatty acids may be thought of as derivatives of alkanes, the saturated hydrocarbons described in Chapter 10.*

Note that each of the carbons in the chain is bonded to the maximum number of hydrogen atoms. To help remember the structure of a saturated fatty acid, you might think of each carbon in the chain being "saturated" with hydrogen atoms. Examples of common saturated fatty acids are given in Table 17.1. An example of an **unsaturated fatty acid** is the eighteen-carbon unsaturated fatty acid oleic acid, which has the following structural formula:

*The unsaturated fatty acids may be thought of as derivatives of the alkenes, the unsaturated hydrocarbons discussed in Chapter 11.*

In the case of unsaturated fatty acids, there is at least one carbon-to-carbon double bond. Because of the double bonds, the carbon atoms involved in these bonds are not "saturated" with hydrogen atoms. The double bonds found in almost all naturally occurring unsaturated fatty acids are in the *cis* configuration. In addition, the double bonds are not randomly located in the hydrocarbon chain. Both the placement and the geometric configuration of the double bonds are dictated by the enzymes that catalyze the biosynthesis of unsaturated fatty acids. Examples of common unsaturated fatty acids are also given in Table 17.1. The similarities and differences between saturated and unsaturated fatty acids are described in Table 17.2.

*A discussion of trans-fatty acids is found in Section 11.3.*

   Examination of Table 17.1 and Figure 17.2 reveals several interesting and important points about the physical properties of fatty acids.

**EXAMPLE 17.1** **Writing the Structural Formula of an Unsaturated Fatty Acid**

Draw the structural formula for palmitoleic acid.

LEARNING GOAL

2 Write the structures of saturated and unsaturated fatty acids.

## Solution

The IUPAC name of palmitoleic acid is *cis*-9-hexadecenoic acid. The name tells us that this is a 16-carbon fatty acid having a carbon-to-carbon double bond between carbons 9 and 10. The name also reveals that this is the *cis* isomer.

16 15 14 13 12 11 10 9 8 7 6 5 4 3 2 1

## Practice Problem 17.1

Draw the line formulas for (a) oleic acid and (b) linoleic acid.

▶ For Further Practice: **Questions 17.27 and 17.28.**

## TABLE 17.1 Common Saturated and Unsaturated Fatty Acids

### Common Saturated Fatty Acids

| Common Name | IUPAC Name | Melting Point (°C) | Molar Mass | Condensed Formula |
|---|---|---|---|---|
| Capric | Decanoic | 32 | 172.26 | $CH_3(CH_2)_8COOH$ |
| Lauric | Dodecanoic | 44 | 200.32 | $CH_3(CH_2)_{10}COOH$ |
| Myristic | Tetradecanoic | 54 | 228.37 | $CH_3(CH_2)_{12}COOH$ |
| Palmitic | Hexadecanoic | 63 | 256.42 | $CH_3(CH_2)_{14}COOH$ |
| Stearic | Octadecanoic | 70 | 284.48 | $CH_3(CH_2)_{16}COOH$ |
| Arachidic | Eicosanoic | 77 | 312.53 | $CH_3(CH_2)_{18}COOH$ |

### Common Unsaturated Fatty Acids

| Common Name | IUPAC Name | Melting Point (°C) | Molar Mass | Number of Double Bonds | Position of Double Bond(s) |
|---|---|---|---|---|---|
| Palmitoleic | *cis*-9-Hexadecenoic | 0 | 254.41 | 1 | 9 |
| Oleic | *cis*-9-Octadecenoic | 16 | 282.46 | 1 | 9 |
| Linoleic | *cis,cis*-9,12-Octadecadienoic | 5 | 280.45 | 2 | 9, 12 |
| Linolenic | All *cis*-9,12,15-Octadecatrienoic | −11 | 278.43 | 3 | 9, 12, 15 |
| Arachidonic | All *cis*-5,8,11,14-Eicosatetraenoic | −50 | 304.47 | 4 | 5, 8, 11, 14 |

### Condensed Formula

| | |
|---|---|
| Palmitoleic | $CH_3(CH_2)_5CH=CH(CH_2)_7COOH$ |
| Oleic | $CH_3(CH_2)_7CH=CH(CH_2)_7COOH$ |
| Linoleic | $CH_3(CH_2)_4CH=CH-CH_2-CH=CH(CH_2)_7COOH$ |
| Linolenic | $CH_3CH_2CH=CH-CH_2-CH=CH-CH_2-CH=CH(CH_2)_7COOH$ |
| Arachidonic | $CH_3(CH_2)_4CH=CH-CH_2-CH=CH-CH_2-CH=CH-CH_2-CH=CH-(CH_2)_3COOH$ |

**Figure 17.2** The melting points of fatty acids. Melting points of both saturated and unsaturated fatty acids increase as the number of carbon atoms in the chain increases. The melting points of unsaturated fatty acids are lower than those of the corresponding saturated fatty acid with the same number of carbon atoms. Also, as the number of double bonds in the chain increases, the melting points decrease.

Explain why the olive oil in the photo above is liquid at room temperature but the beef fat is solid.

**TABLE 17.2 Similarities and Differences Between Saturated and Unsaturated Fatty Acids**

| Property | Saturated Fatty Acid | Unsaturated Fatty Acid |
|---|---|---|
| Chemical composition | Carbon, hydrogen, oxygen | Carbon, hydrogen, oxygen |
| Chemical structure | Hydrocarbon chain with a terminal carboxyl group | Hydrocarbon chain with a terminal carboxyl group |
| Carbon-carbon bonds within the hydrocarbon chain | Only C—C single bonds | At least one C—C double bond |
| Hydrocarbon chains are characteristic of what group of hydrocarbons | Alkanes | Alkenes |
| "Shape" of hydrocarbon chain | Linear, fully extended | Bend in carbon chain at site of C—C double bond |
| Physical state at room temperature | Solid | Liquid |
| Melting point for two fatty acids of the same hydrocarbon chain length | Higher | Lower |
| Relationship between melting point and chain length | Longer chain length, higher melting point | Longer chain length, higher melting point |

**3** Compare and contrast the structures and properties of saturated and unsaturated fatty acids.

*The relationship between alkane chain length and melting point is described in Section 10.2.*

- The melting points of saturated fatty acids increase with increasing carbon number, as is the case with alkanes. Saturated fatty acids containing ten or more carbons are solids at room temperature.
- The melting point of a saturated fatty acid is greater than that of an unsaturated fatty acid of the same chain length. The reason is that saturated fatty acid chains tend to be fully extended and to stack in a regular structure, thereby causing increased intermolecular London dispersion force attraction. Introduction of a *cis* double bond into the hydrocarbon chain produces a rigid 30° bend. Such "kinked" molecules cannot stack in an organized

arrangement and thus have lower intermolecular attractions and lower melting points.
- As in the case for saturated fatty acids, the melting points of unsaturated fatty acids increase with increasing hydrocarbon chain length.

*The relationship between alkene chain length and melting point is described in Section 11.1.*

**Question 17.1** Draw formulas for each of the following fatty acids:

a. Oleic acid  
b. Lauric acid  

c. Linoleic acid  
d. Stearic acid

**Question 17.2** What is the IUPAC name for each of the fatty acids in Question 17.1? (*Hint:* Review the naming of carboxylic acids in Section 14.1, and Table 17.1.)

## Eicosanoids: Prostaglandins, Leukotrienes, and Thromboxanes

Some of the unsaturated fatty acids containing more than one double bond cannot be synthesized by the body. For many years it has been known that linolenic acid, also called α-linolenic acid to distinguish it from isomeric forms, and linoleic acid, called the **essential fatty acids,** are necessary for specific biochemical functions and must be supplied in the diet (see Table 17.1). The function of linoleic acid became clear in the 1960s when it was discovered that linoleic acid is required for the biosynthesis of **arachidonic acid,** the precursor of a class of hormonelike molecules known as **eicosanoids.** The name is derived from the Greek word *eikos,* meaning "twenty," because they are all derivatives of twenty-carbon fatty acids. The eicosanoids include three groups of structurally related compounds: the prostaglandins, the leukotrienes, and the thromboxanes.

**Prostaglandins** are extremely potent biological molecules with hormonelike activity. They got their name because they were originally isolated from seminal fluid produced in the prostate gland. More recently they also have been isolated from most animal tissues. Prostaglandins are unsaturated carboxylic acids consisting of a twenty-carbon skeleton that contains a five-carbon ring.

Several general classes of prostaglandins are grouped under the designations A, B, E, and F, among others. The nomenclature of prostaglandins is based on the arrangement of the carbon skeleton and the number and orientation of double bonds, hydroxyl groups, and ketone groups. For example, in the name PGF₂, PG stands for prostaglandin, F indicates a particular group of prostaglandins with a hydroxyl group bonded to carbon-9, and 2 indicates that there are two carbon-carbon double bonds in the compound. The examples in Figure 17.3 illustrate the general structure of prostaglandins and the current nomenclature system.

Prostaglandins are made in most tissues, and exert their biological effects on the cells that produce them and on other cells in the immediate vicinity. Because the prostaglandins and the closely related leukotrienes and thromboxanes affect so many body processes and because they often cause opposing effects in different tissues, it can be difficult to keep track of their many regulatory functions. The following is a brief summary of some of the biological processes that are thought to be regulated by the prostaglandins, leukotrienes, and thromboxanes.

1. **Blood clotting.** Blood clots form when a blood vessel is damaged, yet such clotting along the walls of undamaged vessels could result in heart attack or stroke. *Thromboxane A₂* (Figure 17.4) is produced by platelets in the blood and stimulates constriction of the blood vessels and aggregation of the platelets. Conversely, PGI₂ (prostacyclin) is produced by the cells lining the blood vessels and has precisely the opposite effect of thromboxane A₂. Prostacyclin inhibits platelet aggregation and causes dilation of blood vessels and thus prevents the untimely production of blood clots.
2. **The inflammatory response.** The inflammatory response is another of the body's protective mechanisms. When tissue is damaged by mechanical injury, burns, or invasion by microorganisms, a variety of white blood cells descend on the

**LEARNING GOAL**

**4** Describe the functions of prostaglandins.

Prostaglandin E₁

Prostaglandin F₁

Prostaglandin E₂

Prostaglandin F₂

**Figure 17.3** The structures of four prostaglandins.

Thromboxane A$_2$

Leukotriene B$_4$

**Figure 17.4** The structures of thromboxane A$_2$ and leukotriene B$_4$.

---

A hormone is a chemical signal that is produced by a specialized tissue and is carried by the bloodstream to send a message to target tissues. Eicosanoids are referred to as hormonelike because they affect the cells that produce them, as well as other target tissues.

---

damaged site to try to minimize the tissue destruction. The result of this response is swelling, redness, fever, and pain. Prostaglandins are thought to promote certain aspects of the inflammatory response, especially pain and fever. Drugs such as aspirin block prostaglandin synthesis and help to relieve the symptoms. We will examine the mechanism of action of these drugs later in this section.

3. **Reproductive system.** PGE$_2$ stimulates smooth muscle contraction, particularly uterine contractions. An increase in the level of prostaglandins has been noted immediately before the onset of labor. PGE$_2$ has also been used to induce second trimester abortions. There is strong evidence that dysmenorrhea (painful menstruation) suffered by many women may be the result of an excess of two prostaglandins. Indeed, drugs such as ibuprofen that inhibit prostaglandin synthesis have been approved by the Food and Drug Administration (FDA) and are found to provide relief from these symptoms.

4. **Gastrointestinal tract.** Prostaglandins have been shown to both inhibit the secretion of acid and increase the secretion of a protective mucus layer into the stomach. In this way, prostaglandins help to protect the stomach lining. Consider for a moment the possible side effect that prolonged use of a drug such as aspirin might have on the stomach—ulceration of the stomach lining. Because aspirin inhibits prostaglandin synthesis, it may actually encourage stomach ulcers by inhibiting the formation of the normal protective mucus layer, while simultaneously allowing increased secretion of stomach acid.

5. **Kidneys.** Prostaglandins produced in the kidneys cause the renal blood vessels to dilate. The greater flow of blood through the kidney results in increased water and electrolyte excretion.

6. **Respiratory tract.** Eicosanoids produced by certain white blood cells, the *leukotrienes* (see Figure 17.4), promote the constriction of the bronchi associated with asthma. Other prostaglandins promote bronchodilation.

As this brief survey suggests, the prostaglandins have numerous, often antagonistic effects. Although they do not fit the formal definition of a hormone (a substance produced in a specialized tissue and transported by the circulatory system to target tissues *elsewhere* in the body), the prostaglandins are clearly strong biological regulators with far-reaching effects.

As mentioned, prostaglandins stimulate the inflammatory response and, as a result, are partially responsible for the cascade of events that cause pain. Aspirin has long been known to alleviate such pain, and we now know that it does so by inhibiting the synthesis of prostaglandins (Figure 17.5).

The first two steps of prostaglandin synthesis (Figure 17.6), the release of arachidonic acid from the membrane and its conversion to PGH$_2$ by the enzyme cyclooxygenase, occur in all tissues that are able to produce prostaglandins. The conversion of PGH$_2$ into the other biologically active forms is tissue-specific and requires the appropriate enzymes, which are found only in certain tissues.

---

**LEARNING GOAL**

**5** Discuss the mechanism by which aspirin reduces pain.

---

**Figure 17.5** Aspirin inhibits the synthesis of prostaglandins by acetylating the enzyme cyclooxygenase. The acetylated enzyme is no longer functional.

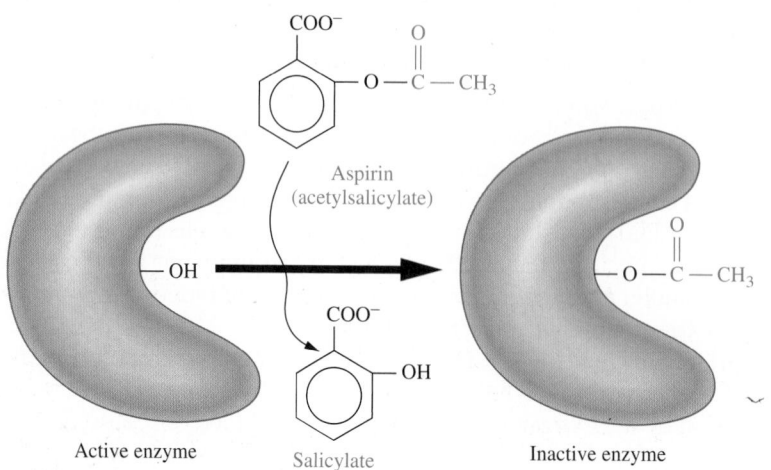

Active enzyme

Aspirin (acetylsalicylate)

Salicylate

Inactive enzyme

**Figure 17.6** A summary of the synthesis of several prostaglandins from arachidonic acid.

Aspirin works by inhibiting the cyclooxygenase, which catalyzes the first step in the pathway leading from arachidonic acid to $PGH_2$. The acetyl group of aspirin becomes covalently bound to the enzyme, thereby inactivating it (Figure 17.5). Because the reaction catalyzed by cyclooxygenase occurs in all cells, aspirin effectively inhibits synthesis of all of the prostaglandins.

## Omega-3 Fatty Acids

In 2002, the American Heart Association (AHA) issued dietary guidelines that recommend that we include at least two servings of "oily" fish in our diet each week. Among the fish recommended are salmon, albacore tuna, sardines, lake trout, and mackerel. The reason for this recommendation is that these fish contain high levels of two omega-3 fatty acids called eicosapentaenoic acid (EPA) and docosahexaenoic acid (DHA). The AHA further recommended a third omega-3 fatty acid, α-linolenic acid, which is found in flax seed, soybeans, and canola, as well as in oil made from these plants.

The name of this group of fatty acids arises from the position of the double bond nearest the terminal *methyl group* of the molecule. In these fatty acids, it is the third carbon from the end, designated omega (ω), which is the location of the double bond.

All *cis*-9,12,15-Octadecatrienoic acid
(α-Linolenic acid or ALA)

All *cis*-5,8,11,14,17-Eicosapentaenoic acid
(EPA)

All *cis*-4,7,10,13,16,19-Docosahexaenoic acid
(DHA)

The reason for this dietary recommendation was research that supported the idea that omega-3 fatty acids reduce the risk of cardiovascular disease by decreasing blood clot formation, blood triglyceride levels, and growth of atherosclerotic plaque. Because of these effects, arterial health improved and blood pressure decreased, as did the risk of sudden death and heart arrhythmias.

In some cases, the reason for the effect can be understood. For instance, EPA is a precursor for the synthesis of prostacyclin, which inhibits clumping of platelets and thus reduces clot formation. DHA is one of the major fatty acids in the phospholipids of sperm and brain cells, as well as in the retina. It has also been shown to reduce triglyceride levels, although the mechanism is not understood.

As we learned earlier, linolenic acid is an essential fatty acid. Although it, too, seems to reduce the incidence of cardiovascular disease, it is not clear whether it acts alone or because it is the precursor of DHA and EPA.

Linoleic acid is also an essential fatty acid, required for the synthesis of arachidonic acid, the precursor for many prostaglandins. These two fatty acids are termed omega-6 fatty acids because the first double bond in the molecule is six carbon atoms from the methyl ($\omega$) end of the molecule.

*cis,cis*-9,12-Octadecadienoic acid
(Linoleic acid)

All *cis*-5,8,11,14-Eicosatetraenoic acid
(Arachidonic acid)

The American Heart Association recommends that we include two meals of fish, such as salmon, in our diets each week. However, there is concern about the amount of heavy metals and other environmental contaminants in wild-caught fish. Go online to investigate the reasons that these contaminants accumulate in these fish.

It is intriguing to note that the omega-3 fatty acids are precursors of prostaglandins that exhibit anti-inflammatory effects, and the omega-6 fatty acids are precursors to prostaglandins that have inflammatory effects. This has led researchers to suggest that the amount of omega-6 fatty acids in our diets should not exceed 4–5 times the amount of omega-3. In fact, in the United States, the diet often contains 10–30 times more omega-6 fatty acids than omega-3 fatty acids. Thus, changing the ratio of the two in the diet could increase the levels of anti-inflammatory prostaglandins and reduce the level of inflammatory prostaglandins. To encourage this dietary change, the National Institutes of Health have issued recommended daily intakes of four of these fatty acids: 650 mg/day of EPA and DHA, 2.22 g/day of α-linolenic acid, and 4.44 g/day of linoleic acid.

## 17.3   Glycerides

### Neutral Glycerides

**Glycerides** are lipid esters that contain the glycerol molecule and fatty acids. They may be subdivided into two classes: neutral glycerides and phosphoglycerides. Neutral glycerides are nonionic and nonpolar. Phosphoglyceride molecules have a polar region, the phosphoryl group, in addition to the nonpolar fatty acid tails. The structures of each of these types of glycerides are critical to their function.

The esterification of glycerol with a fatty acid produces a **neutral glyceride.** Esterification may occur at one, two, or all three positions, producing **monoglycerides, diglycerides,** or **triglycerides.** You will also see these referred to as *mono-, di-,* or *triacylglycerols.*

**EXAMPLE 17.2** **Writing an Equation for the Synthesis of a Monoglyceride**

LEARNING GOAL

**6** Write equations representing the reactions that fatty acids and glycerides undergo.

Write a general equation for the esterification of glycerol and one fatty acid.

**Solution**

Glycerol      Fatty acid      Monoglyceride      Water

**Practice Problem 17.2**

Write equations for the following esterification reactions.

   a. Glycerol with two molecules of stearic acid
   b. Glycerol with one molecule of myristic acid

▶ For Further Practice: **Questions 17.41 and 17.42.**

Although monoglycerides and diglycerides are present in nature, the most important neutral glycerides are the triglycerides, the major component of fat cells. The triglyceride consists of a glycerol backbone (shown in black) joined to three fatty acid units through ester bonds (shown in red). The formation of a triglyceride is shown in the following equation:

Glycerol      Fatty acids      Triglyceride      Water

Because there are no charges (+ or −) on these molecules, they are called *neutral glycerides*. These long molecules readily stack with one another and constitute the majority of the lipids stored in the body's fat cells.

The principal function of triglycerides in biochemical systems is the storage of energy. If more energy-rich nutrients are consumed than are required for metabolic processes, much of the excess is converted to neutral glycerides and stored as triglycerides in fat cells of *adipose tissue*. When energy is needed, the triglycerides are metabolized by the body, and energy is released. For this reason, exercise, along with moderate reduction in caloric intake, is recommended for overweight individuals. Exercise, an energy-demanding process, increases the rate of metabolism of fats and results in weight loss.

*Lipid metabolism is discussed in Chapter 23.*

*See A Human Perspective: Losing Those Unwanted Pounds of Adipose Tissue in Chapter 23.*

## Chemical Reactions of Fatty Acids and Glycerides

*Esterification is described in Sections 14.1 and 14.2.*

The reactions of fatty acids are identical to those of short-chain carboxylic acids. The major reactions that they undergo include esterification, saponification, and addition at the double bond of the carbon chain. Triglycerides can undergo acid hydrolysis and saponification.

### Esterification

In **esterification,** fatty acids react with alcohols to form esters and water according to the following general equation:

$$R^1\!\!-\!\!\overset{\overset{\displaystyle O}{\|}}{C}\!\!-\!\!OH + R^2OH \xrightarrow{\text{H}^+,\,\text{heat}} R^1\!\!-\!\!\overset{\overset{\displaystyle O}{\|}}{C}\!\!-\!\!OR^2 + H\!\!-\!\!OH$$

$$\text{Fatty acid}\qquad\text{Alcohol}\qquad\qquad\text{Ester}\qquad\text{Water}$$

---

**EXAMPLE 17.3**  **Writing Equations Representing the Esterification of Fatty Acids**

Write an equation representing the esterification of capric acid with propyl alcohol and write the IUPAC name of each of the organic reactants and products.

**Solution**

$$CH_3(CH_2)_8\!\!-\!\!\overset{\overset{\displaystyle O}{\|}}{C}\!\!-\!\!OH + CH_3CH_2CH_2OH \xrightarrow{\text{H}^+,\,\text{heat}}$$

$$\quad\text{Decanoic acid}\qquad\qquad\text{1-Propanol}$$

$$CH_3(CH_2)_8\!\!-\!\!\overset{\overset{\displaystyle O}{\|}}{C}\!\!-\!\!O\!\!-\!\!CH_2CH_2CH_3 + H_2O$$

$$\text{Propyl decanoate}$$

### Practice Problem 17.3

Write an equation for the esterification of the following carboxylic acids and alcohols. Write the IUPAC names for all of the organic reactants and products.

a.  Lauric acid and ethyl alcohol
b.  Palmitic acid and 1-pentanol

▶ For Further Practice: **Questions 17.31 and 17.32.**

---

### Acid Hydrolysis

*Acid hydrolysis is discussed in Section 14.2.*

Recall that hydrolysis is the reverse of esterification, producing fatty acids from esters:

$$R^1\!\!-\!\!\overset{\overset{\displaystyle O}{\|}}{C}\!\!-\!\!OR^2 + HO\!\!-\!\!H \xrightarrow{\text{H}^+,\,\text{heat}} R^1\!\!-\!\!\overset{\overset{\displaystyle O}{\|}}{C}\!\!-\!\!OH + R^2OH$$

$$\quad\text{Ester}\qquad\quad\text{Water}\qquad\qquad\text{Fatty acid}\quad\text{Alcohol}$$

## EXAMPLE 17.4 Writing Equations Representing the Acid Hydrolysis of a Monoglyceride

LEARNING GOAL

**6** Write equations representing the reactions that fatty acids and glycerides undergo.

Write an equation representing the acid hydrolysis of a monoglyceride composed of one decanoic acid molecule esterified to glycerol.

### Solution

$$CH_3(CH_2)_8-\overset{\overset{\displaystyle O}{\|}}{C}-O-\overset{H}{\underset{\displaystyle}{C}}-H$$
$$HO-\overset{}{C}-H + H_2O \xrightarrow{H^+, heat} CH_3(CH_2)_8-\overset{\overset{\displaystyle O}{\|}}{C}-OH + $$
$$HO-\overset{}{C}-H$$
$$H$$

Decanoic acid

$$H-\overset{}{C}-OH$$
$$H-\overset{}{C}-OH$$
$$H-\overset{}{C}-OH$$
$$H$$
1,2,3-Propanetriol (glycerol)

### Practice Problem 17.4

Write a complete equation for the acid hydrolysis of the following monoglycerides.

a. Tetradecanoic acid esterified to glycerol
b. Dodecanoic acid esterified to glycerol

▶ For Further Practice: **Questions 17.33 and 17.34.**

## Saponification

**Saponification** is the base-catalyzed hydrolysis of an ester:

*Saponification is described in Section 14.2.*

$$R^1-\overset{\overset{\displaystyle O}{\|}}{C}-OR^2 + NaOH \longrightarrow R^1-\overset{\overset{\displaystyle O}{\|}}{C}-O^-Na^+ + R^2OH$$

Ester    Base      Salt    Alcohol

The product of this reaction, an ionized salt, is a soap. Because soaps have a long uncharged hydrocarbon tail and a negatively charged terminus (the carboxylate group), they form micelles that dissolve oil and dirt particles. Thus the dirt is emulsified and broken into small particles, and can be rinsed away.

*The role of soaps in removal of dirt and grease is described in Section 14.2.*

*Examples of micelles are shown in Figures 14.4 and 23.1.*

## EXAMPLE 17.5 Writing Equations Representing the Base-Catalyzed Hydrolysis of a Monoglyceride

LEARNING GOAL

**6** Write equations representing the reactions that fatty acids and glycerides undergo.

Write an equation representing the base-catalyzed hydrolysis of a monoglyceride composed of dodecanoic acid and glycerol.

### Solution

$$CH_3(CH_2)_{10}-\overset{\overset{\displaystyle O}{\|}}{C}-O-\overset{H}{\underset{}{C}}-H$$
$$HO-\overset{}{C}-H + NaOH \longrightarrow CH_3(CH_2)_{10}-\overset{\overset{\displaystyle O}{\|}}{C}-O^-Na^+ + $$
$$HO-\overset{}{C}-H$$
$$H$$

Sodium dodecanoate

$$H-\overset{}{C}-OH$$
$$H-\overset{}{C}-OH$$
$$H-\overset{}{C}-OH$$
$$H$$
1,2,3-Propanetriol (glycerol)

*Continued…*

**Practice Problem 17.5**

Write a complete equation for the following reactions.

a. A monoglyceride composed of hexadecanoic acid and glycerol with KOH

b. A diglyceride composed of octanoic acid, decanoic acid, and glycerol with NaOH

▶ For Further Practice: **Questions 17.39 and 17.40.**

Problems can arise when "hard" water is used for cleaning because the high concentrations of $Ca^{2+}$ and $Mg^{2+}$ in such water cause fatty acid salts to precipitate. Not only does this interfere with the emulsifying action of the soap, it also leaves a hard scum on the surface of sinks and tubs.

$$2R-\overset{\overset{\displaystyle O}{\|}}{C}-O^- + Ca^{2+} \longrightarrow (R-\overset{\overset{\displaystyle O}{\|}}{C}-O^-)_2Ca^{2+}(s)$$

*Hydrogenation is described in Section 11.5.*

### Reaction at the Double Bond (Unsaturated Fatty Acids)

**Hydrogenation** is an example of an addition reaction. The following is a typical example of the addition of hydrogen to the double bonds of a fatty acid:

$$CH_3(CH_2)_4CH=CHCH_2CH=CH(CH_2)_7COOH \xrightarrow{2H_2,\ Ni} CH_3(CH_2)_{16}COOH$$

Linoleic acid                                     Stearic acid

---

**EXAMPLE 17.6**    **Writing Equations for the Hydrogenation of a Fatty Acid**

Write an equation representing the hydrogenation of oleic acid and write the IUPAC name of each of the organic reactants and products.

**LEARNING GOAL**

**6** Write equations representing the reactions that fatty acids and glycerides undergo.

**Solution**

$$CH_3(CH_2)_7CH=CH(CH_2)_7-\overset{\overset{\displaystyle O}{\|}}{C}-OH \xrightarrow{H_2,\ Ni} CH_3(CH_2)_{16}-\overset{\overset{\displaystyle O}{\|}}{C}-OH$$

*cis*-9-Octadecenoic acid                              Octadecanoic acid

---

**Practice Problem 17.6**

Write balanced equations showing the hydrogenation of (a) *cis*-9-hexadecenoic acid and (b) arachidonic acid.

▶ For Further Practice: **Questions 17.37 and 17.38.**

Hydrogenation is used in the food industry to convert polyunsaturated vegetable oils into saturated solid fats. *Partial hydrogenation* is carried out to add hydrogen to some, but not all, double bonds in polyunsaturated oils. In this way liquid vegetable oils are converted into solid form. Crisco is one example of a hydrogenated vegetable oil.

Margarine is also produced by partial hydrogenation of vegetable oils, such as corn oil or soybean oil. The extent of hydrogenation is carefully controlled so that the solid fat will be spreadable and have the consistency of butter when eaten. If

Hydrogenation of vegetable oils produces a mixture of *cis* and *trans* unsaturated fatty acids. The *trans* unsaturated fatty acids are thought to contribute to atherosclerosis (hardening of the arteries).

too many double bonds were hydrogenated, the resulting product would have the undesirable consistency of animal fat. Artificial color is added to the product, and it may be mixed with milk to produce a butterlike appearance and flavor.

**Question 17.3**  Write the complete equation for the esterification of myristic acid and ethyl alcohol. Write the IUPAC name for each of the organic reactants and products.

**Question 17.4**  Write the complete equation for the esterification of arachidic acid and ethyl alcohol. Write the IUPAC name for each of the organic reactants and products.

**Question 17.5**  Write a complete equation for the acid hydrolysis of pentyl butyrate. Write the IUPAC name for each of the organic reactants and products.

**Question 17.6**  Write a complete equation for the acid hydrolysis of butyl acetate. Write the IUPAC name for each of the organic reactants and products.

**Question 17.7**  Write a complete equation for the reaction of butyl acetate and KOH. Write the IUPAC name for each of the organic reactants and products.

**Question 17.8**  Write a complete equation for the reaction of methyl butyrate and NaOH. Write the IUPAC name for each of the organic reactants and products.

**Question 17.9**  Write a balanced equation for the hydrogenation of linolenic acid.

**Question 17.10**  Write a balanced equation for the hydrogenation of 2-hexenoic acid.

## Phosphoglycerides

**Phospholipids** are a group of lipids that are phosphate esters. The presence of the phosphoryl group results in a molecule with a polar head (the phosphoryl group) and a nonpolar tail (the alkyl chain of the fatty acid). Because the phosphoryl group ionizes in solution, a charged lipid results.

The most abundant membrane lipids are derived from glycerol-3-phosphate and are known as **phosphoglycerides.** Phosphoglycerides contain acyl groups derived from long-chain fatty acids at C-1 and C-2 of glycerol-3-phosphate. At C-3 the phosphoryl group is joined to glycerol by a phosphoester bond. The simplest phosphoglyceride contains a free phosphoryl group and is known as a **phosphatidate** (Figure 17.7). When the phosphoryl group is attached to another hydrophilic molecule, a more complex phosphoglyceride is formed. For example, *phosphatidylcholine (lecithin)* and *phosphatidylethanolamine (cephalin)* are found in the membranes of most cells (Figure 17.7).

Lecithin possesses a polar "head" and a nonpolar "tail." Thus, it is an *amphipathic* molecule. This structure is similar to that of soap and detergent molecules, discussed earlier. The ionic "head" is hydrophilic and interacts with water molecules, whereas the nonpolar "tail" is hydrophobic and interacts with nonpolar molecules. This amphipathic nature is central to the structure and function of cell membranes.

In addition to being a component of cell membranes, lecithin is the major phospholipid in pulmonary surfactant. It is also found in egg yolks and soybeans and is used as an emulsifying agent in ice cream. An **emulsifying agent** aids in the suspension of triglycerides in water. The amphipathic lecithin serves as a bridge, holding together the highly polar water molecules and the nonpolar triglycerides. Emulsification occurs because the hydrophilic head of lecithin dissolves in water and its hydrophobic tail dissolves in the triglycerides.

Cephalin is similar in general structure to lecithin; the amine group bonded to the phosphoryl group is the only difference.

**LEARNING GOAL**

**7** Draw the structure of a phospholipid and discuss its amphipathic nature.

*Phosphoesters are described in Section 14.4.*

*See A Medical Perspective: Lifesaving Lipids, at the beginning of this chapter.*

Phosphatidate

(a)

Phosphatidylcholine (lecithin)

(b)

Phosphatidylethanolamine (cephalin)

(c)

Phosphatidylserine

(d)

Figure 17.7 The structures of (a) phosphatidate and the common membrane phospholipids, (b) phosphatidylcholine (lecithin), (c) phosphatidylethanolamine (cephalin), and (d) phosphatidylserine.

Question 17.11 Using condensed formulas, draw the mono-, di-, and triglycerides that would result from the esterification of glycerol with each of the following fatty acids.

a. Oleic acid

b. Capric acid

Question 17.12 Using condensed formulas, draw the mono-, di-, and triglycerides that would result from the esterification of glycerol with each of the following fatty acids.

a. Palmitic acid

b. Lauric acid

# CHEMISTRY AT THE CRIME SCENE

## Adipocere and Mummies of Soap

One November evening in 1911, widower Patrick Higgins stepped into his local pub in Abercorn, Scotland. To the surprise of his drinking companions, he did not have his two young boys with him. Neighbors knew that the boys had been a great burden on Patrick since the death of his wife; so they believed Patrick's story that he left William, age 6, and John, age 4, with two women in Edinburgh who had offered to adopt the boys.

More than 18 months had passed when an object was seen floating in the Hopetoun Quarry, an unused, flooded quarry near town. When the object was fished out, it was obvious that it was the body of a young boy; the rescuers were stunned to find another small body tied to the first by a rope. How were these bodies preserved after such a long time and why did they float? The answer is that their bodies had almost completely turned into adipocere, or more simply, soap.

Forensic scientists are trying to understand the nature of the reaction that creates *adipocere*, the technical term for the yellowish-white, greasy, waxlike substance that results from the saponification of fatty tissue. Some researchers hope that this information may allow determination of the postmortem interval (length of time since death). Others simply value the process because it helps preserve the body so well that even after long periods, it can be easily recognized and any wounds or injuries can be observed.

It is known that adipocere is produced when body fat is hydrolyzed (water is needed) to release fatty acids. Because the fatty acids lower the pH in the tissues, they inhibit many of the bacteria that would begin the process of decay. Certain other bacteria, particularly *Clostridium welchii*, an organism that cannot grow in the presence of oxygen, is known to speed up the formation of adipocere in moist, warm, anaerobic (oxygenless) environments. Adipocere forms first in subcutaneous tissues, including the cheeks, breasts, and buttocks. Given appropriate warmth and damp conditions, it may be seen as early as 3 to 4 weeks after death; but more commonly it is not observed until 5 to 6 months after death.

Adipocere formation in John and William Higgins was so extensive that their former neighbors had no trouble recognizing them. At the postmortem, another advantage of adipocere formation became obvious—it had preserved the stomach contents of the boys! From this, the coroner learned that the boys

had eaten Scotch broth about an hour before they died. Investigators were able to find the woman who had given the broth to the boys and, from her testimony, learned that she had fed them on the last day they were seen in the village. Clearly their father had lied about the adoption by two Edinburgh women! In under one and one-half hours, a jury convicted the father of murdering his sons and he was hanged in October 1913.

### For Further Understanding

▶ Adipocere is the technical term for "soap mummification." It comes from the Latin words *adipis* or fat, as in adipose tissue, and *cera*, which means wax. Draw a triglyceride composed of the fatty acids myristic acid, stearic acid, and oleic acid. Write a balanced equation showing a possible reaction that would lead to the formation of adipocere.

▶ Forensic scientists are studying adipocere formation as a possible source of information to determine postmortem interval (length of time since death) of bodies of murder or accident victims. Among the factors being studied are the type of soil, including pH, moisture, temperature, and presence or absence of lime. How might each of these factors influence the rate of adipocere formation and hence the determination of the postmortem interval?

## 17.4   Nonglyceride Lipids

### Sphingolipids

**Sphingolipids** are lipids that are not derived from glycerol. Like phospholipids, sphingolipids are amphipathic, having a polar head group and two nonpolar fatty acid tails, and are structural components of cellular membranes. They are derived from sphingosine, a long-chain, nitrogen-containing (amino) alcohol:

$$CH_3(CH_2)_{12}CH{=}CH{-}\overset{\displaystyle OH}{\underset{\displaystyle H_2N-\overset{\displaystyle |}{C}-H}{\overset{\displaystyle |}{C}}}-H$$

CH_2OH

Sphingosine

The sphingolipids include the sphingomyelins and the glycosphingolipids. The **sphingomyelins** are the only class of sphingolipids that are also phospholipids:

Sphingomyelin

Sphingomyelins are located throughout the body, but are particularly important structural lipid components of nerve cell membranes. They are found in abundance in the myelin sheath that surrounds and insulates cells of the central nervous system. In humans, about 25% of the lipids of the myelin sheath are sphingomyelins. Their role is essential to proper cerebral function and nerve transmission.

*Glycosphingolipids,* or *glycolipids,* include the cerebrosides, sulfatides, and gangliosides and are built on a ceramide backbone structure, which is a fatty acid amide derivative of sphingosine:

Ceramide

The *cerebrosides* are characterized by the presence of a single monosaccharide head group. Two common cerebrosides are glucocerebroside, found in the membranes of macrophages (cells that protect the body by ingesting and destroying foreign microorganisms) and galactocerebroside, found almost exclusively in the membranes of brain cells. Glucocerebroside consists of ceramide bonded to the hexose glucose; galactocerebroside consists of ceramide joined to the monosaccharide galactose.

Glucocerebroside

Galactocerebroside

*Sulfatides* are derivatives of galactocerebroside that contain a sulfate group. Notice that they carry a negative charge at physiological pH.

A sulfatide of galactocerebroside

*Gangliosides* are glycolipids that possess oligosaccharide groups, including one or more molecules of *N*-acetylneuraminic acid (sialic acid). First isolated from membranes of nerve tissue, gangliosides are found in most tissues of the body.

A ganglioside associated with Tay-Sachs disease

## Steroids

**Steroids** are a naturally occurring family of organic molecules of biochemical and medical interest. A great deal of controversy has surrounded various steroids. We worry about the amount of cholesterol in the diet and the possible health effects. We are concerned about the use of anabolic steroids by athletes wishing to build muscle mass and improve their performance. However, members of this family of molecules derived from cholesterol have many important functions in the body. The bile salts that aid in the emulsification and digestion of lipids are steroid molecules, as are the sex hormones testosterone and estrone.

The steroids are members of a large, diverse collection of lipids called the *isoprenoids*. All of these compounds are built from one or more five-carbon units called *isoprene*.

**Terpene** is the general term for lipids that are synthesized from isoprene units. Examples of terpenes include the steroids and bile salts, the lipid-soluble vitamins, chlorophyll, and certain plant hormones.

All steroids contain the steroid nucleus (steroid carbon skeleton) as shown here:

Carbon skeleton of the steroid nucleus

Steroid nucleus

The steroid carbon skeleton consists of four fused rings. Each ring pair has two carbons in common. Thus two fused rings share one or more common bonds as part of their ring backbones. For example, rings A and B, B and C, and C and D are all fused in the preceding structure. Many steroids have methyl groups attached to carbons 10 and 13, as well as an alkyl, alcohol, or ketone group attached to carbon-17.

**Cholesterol,** a common steroid, is found in the membranes of most animal cells. It is an amphipathic molecule and is readily soluble in the hydrophobic region of membranes. It is involved in regulation of the fluidity of the membrane as a result of the nonpolar fused ring. However, the hydroxyl group is polar and

LEARNING GOAL

**9** Draw the structure of the steroid nucleus and discuss the functions of steroid hormones.

*Lipid digestion is described in Section 23.1.*

Isoprene

LIPID-SOLUBLE VITAMINS

completely insoluble in water. Waxes are also solid at room temperature, owing to their high molar masses. Two examples of waxes are myricyl palmitate, a major component of beeswax, and whale oil (spermaceti wax), from the head of the sperm whale, which is composed of cetyl palmitate.

Naturally occurring waxes have a variety of uses. Lanolin, which serves as a protective coating for hair and skin, is used in skin creams and ointments. Carnauba wax is used in automobile polish. Whale oil was once used as a fuel, in ointments, and in candles. However, synthetic waxes have replaced whale oil to a large extent, because of efforts to ban the hunting of whales.

$$CH_3(CH_2)_{14}-\overset{O}{\overset{\|}{C}}-O-(CH_2)_{29}CH_3$$

Myricyl palmitate
(beeswax)

$$CH_3(CH_2)_{14}-\overset{O}{\overset{\|}{C}}-O-(CH_2)_{15}CH_3$$

Cetyl palmitate
(whale oil)

## 17.5 Complex Lipids

**Complex lipids** are lipids that are bonded to other types of molecules. The most common and important complex lipids are plasma lipoproteins, which are responsible for the transport of other lipids in the body.

Lipids are only sparingly soluble in water, and the movement of lipids from one organ to another through the bloodstream requires a transport system that uses **plasma lipoproteins.** Lipoprotein particles consist of a core of hydrophobic lipids surrounded by amphipathic proteins, phospholipids, and cholesterol (Figure 17.8).

There are four major classes of human plasma lipoproteins:

- **Chylomicrons,** which have a density of less than 0.95 g/mL, carry dietary triglycerides from the intestine to other tissues. The remaining lipoproteins are classified by their densities.
- **Very low density lipoproteins (VLDL)** have a density of 0.95–1.019 g/mL. They bind triglycerides synthesized in the liver and carry them to adipose and other tissues for storage.
- **Low-density lipoproteins (LDL)** are characterized by a density of 1.019–1.063 g/mL. They carry cholesterol to peripheral tissues and help regulate cholesterol levels in those tissues. These are richest in cholesterol, frequently carrying 40% of the plasma cholesterol.
- **High-density lipoproteins (HDL)** have a density of 1.063–1.210 g/mL. They are bound to plasma cholesterol; however, they transport cholesterol from peripheral tissues to the liver.

A summary of the composition of each of the plasma lipoproteins is presented in Figure 17.9.

Chylomicrons are aggregates of triglycerides and protein that transport dietary triglycerides to cells throughout the body. Not all lipids in the blood are derived directly from the diet. Triglycerides and cholesterol are also synthesized in the liver and also are transported through the blood in lipoprotein packages. Triglycerides are assembled into VLDL particles that carry the energy-rich lipid molecules either to tissues requiring an energy source or to adipose tissue for storage. Similarly, cholesterol is assembled into LDL particles for transport from the liver to peripheral tissues.

Entry of LDL particles into the cell is dependent on a specific recognition event and binding between the LDL particle and a protein receptor embedded within the membrane. Low-density lipoprotein receptors (LDL receptors) are found in the membranes of cells outside the liver and are responsible for the uptake of cholesterol by the cells of various tissues. LDL (lipoprotein bound to cholesterol) binds specifically to the LDL receptor, and the complex is taken into the cell by a process called *receptor-mediated endocytosis* (Figure 17.10). The membrane begins to be pulled into the cell at the site of the LDL receptor complexes. This draws the entire LDL particle into the cell. Eventually, the portion of the membrane

**Figure 17.8** A model for the structure of a plasma lipoprotein. The various lipoproteins are composed of a shell of protein, cholesterol, and phospholipids surrounding more hydrophobic molecules such as triglycerides or cholesterol esters (cholesterol esterified to fatty acids). (a) Cross section, (b) three-dimensional view.

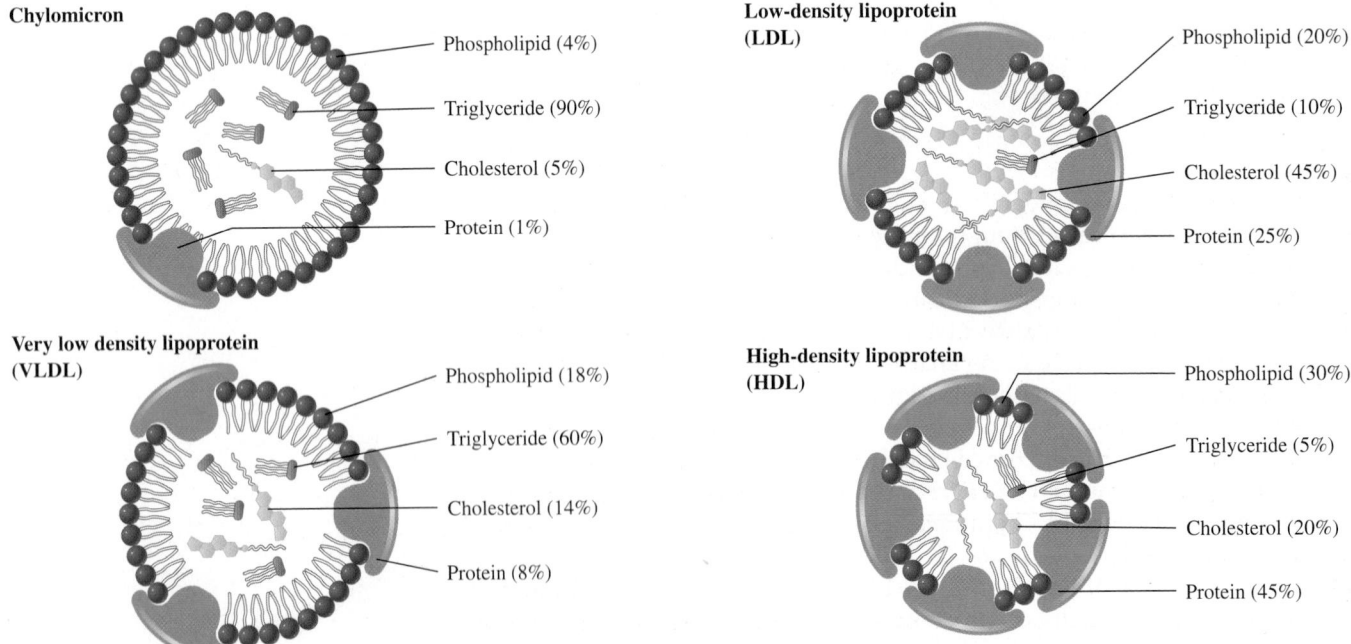

**Chylomicron**

Phospholipid (4%)

Triglyceride (90%)

Cholesterol (5%)

Protein (1%)

**Low-density lipoprotein (LDL)**

Phospholipid (20%)

Triglyceride (10%)

Cholesterol (45%)

Protein (25%)

**Very low density lipoprotein (VLDL)**

Phospholipid (18%)

Triglyceride (60%)

Cholesterol (14%)

Protein (8%)

**High-density lipoprotein (HDL)**

Phospholipid (30%)

Triglyceride (5%)

Cholesterol (20%)

Protein (45%)

**Figure 17.9** A summary of the relative amounts of cholesterol, phospholipid, protein, and triglycerides in the four classes of lipoproteins.

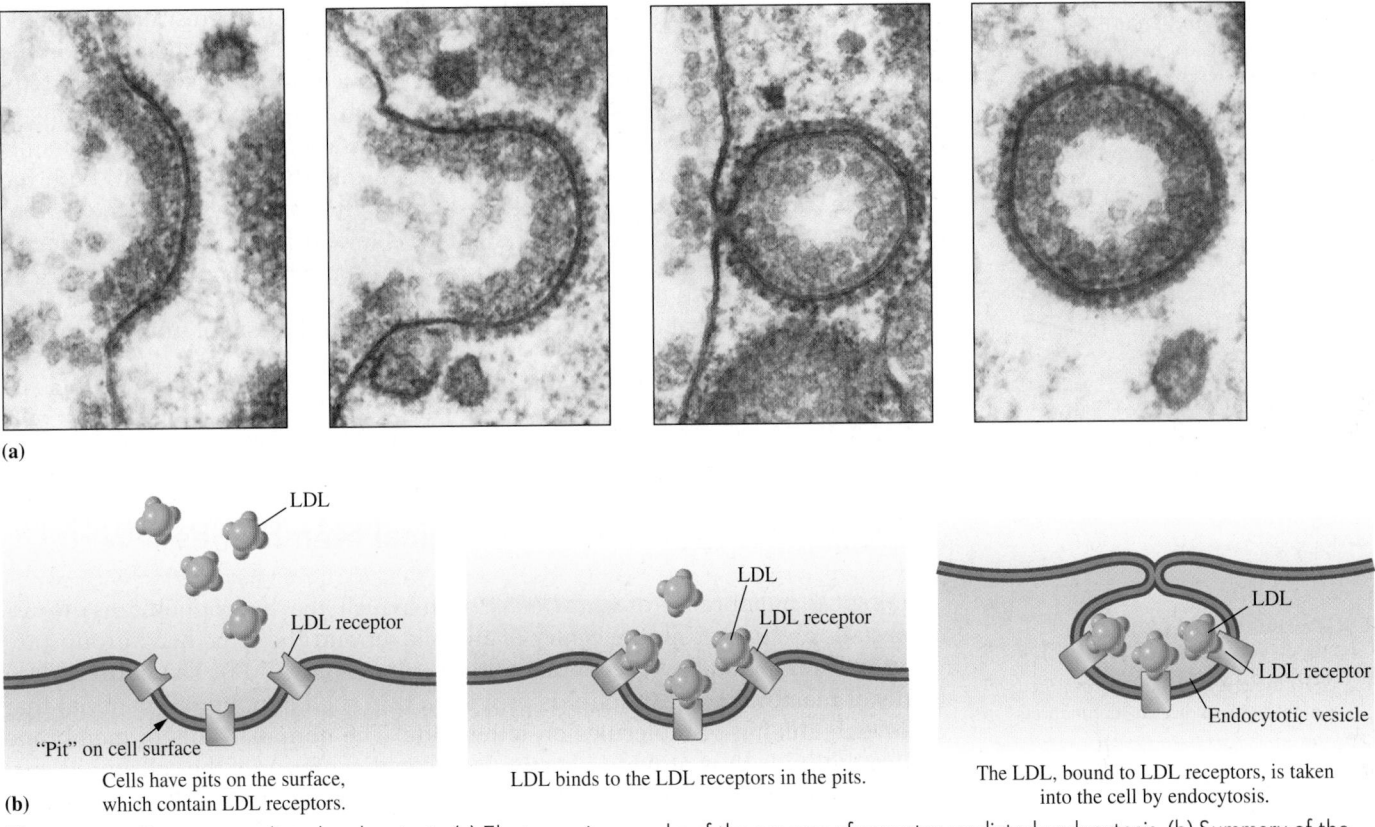

**(a)**

**(b)**

Cells have pits on the surface, which contain LDL receptors.

LDL binds to the LDL receptors in the pits.

The LDL, bound to LDL receptors, is taken into the cell by endocytosis.

**Figure 17.10** Receptor-mediated endocytosis. (a) Electron micrographs of the process of receptor-mediated endocytosis. (b) Summary of the events of receptor-mediated endocytosis of LDL.

surrounding the LDL particles pinches away from the cell membrane and forms a membrane around the LDL particles. As we will see in Section 17.6, membranes are fluid and readily flow. Thus, they can form a vesicle or endosome containing the LDL particles.

Cellular digestive organelles known as *lysosomes* fuse with the endosomes. This fusion is accomplished when the membranes of the endosome and the lysosome flow together to create one larger membrane-bound body or vesicle. Hydrolytic enzymes from the lysosome then digest the entire complex to release cholesterol into the cytoplasm of the cell. There, cholesterol inhibits its own biosynthesis and activates an enzyme that stores cholesterol in cholesterol ester droplets. High concentrations of cholesterol inside the cell also inhibit the synthesis of LDL receptors to ensure that the cell will not take up too much cholesterol. People who have a genetic defect in the gene coding for the LDL receptor do not take up as much cholesterol. As a result they accumulate LDL cholesterol in the plasma. This excess plasma cholesterol is then deposited on the artery walls, causing atherosclerosis. This disease is called *hypercholesterolemia*.

Liver lipoprotein receptors enable large amounts of cholesterol to be removed from the blood, thus ensuring low concentrations of cholesterol in the blood plasma. Other factors being equal, the person with the most lipoprotein receptors will be the least vulnerable to a high-cholesterol diet and have the least likelihood of developing atherosclerosis.

There is also evidence that high levels of HDL in the blood help reduce the incidence of atherosclerosis, perhaps because HDL carries cholesterol from the peripheral tissues back to the liver. In the liver, some of the cholesterol is used for bile synthesis and secreted into the intestines, from which it is excreted.

Recently an inflammatory protein, the C-reactive protein (CRP), has been implicated in atherosclerosis. A test for the level of this protein in the blood is being suggested as a way to predict the risk of heart attack. A high sensitivity CRP test is now widely available.

A final correlation has been made between diet and atherosclerosis. People whose diet is high in saturated fats tend to have high levels of cholesterol in the blood. Although the relationship between saturated fatty acids and cholesterol metabolism is unclear, it is known that a diet rich in unsaturated fats results in decreased cholesterol levels. In fact, the use of unsaturated fat in the diet results in a decrease in the level of LDL and an increase in the level of HDL. With the positive correlation between heart disease and high cholesterol levels, the current dietary recommendations include a diet that is low in fat and the substitution of unsaturated fats (vegetable oils) for saturated fats (animal fats).

**Question 17.15**   What is the mechanism of uptake of cholesterol from plasma?

**Question 17.16**   What is the role of lysosomes in the metabolism of plasma lipoproteins?

## 17.6   The Structure of Biological Membranes

**LEARNING GOAL**

**11**   Draw the structure of the cell membrane and discuss its functions.

Biological membranes are *lipid bilayers* in which the hydrophobic hydrocarbon tails are packed in the center of the bilayer and the ionic head groups are exposed on the surface to interact with water (Figure 17.11). The hydrocarbon tails of membrane phospholipids provide a thin shell of nonpolar material that prevents mixing of molecules on either side. The nonpolar tails of membrane phospholipids thus provide a barrier between the interior of the cell and its surroundings. The polar heads of lipids are exposed to water, and they are highly solvated.

The two layers of the phospholipid bilayer membrane are not identical in composition. For instance, in human red blood cells, approximately 80% of the phospholipids in the outer layer of the membrane are phosphatidylcholine and sphingomyelin; whereas phosphatidylethanolamine and phosphatidylserine make up approximately 80% of the inner layer. In addition, carbohydrate groups are found attached only to those phospholipids found on the outer layer of a membrane. Here they participate in receptor and recognition functions.

### Fluid Mosaic Structure of Biological Membranes

As we have just noted, membranes are not static; they are composed of molecules in motion. The fluidity of biological membranes is determined by the proportions of saturated and unsaturated fatty acid groups in the membrane phospholipids. About half of the fatty acids that are isolated from membrane lipids from all sources are unsaturated.

The unsaturated fatty acid tails of the phospholipids contribute to membrane fluidity because of the bends introduced into the hydrocarbon chain by the double bonds. Because of these "kinks," the fatty acid tails do not pack together tightly.

We also find that the percentage of unsaturated fatty acid groups in membrane lipids is inversely proportional to the temperature of the environment. Bacteria, for example, have different ratios of saturated and unsaturated fatty acids in their membrane lipids, depending on the temperatures of their surroundings. For instance, the membranes of bacteria that grow in the Arctic Ocean have high levels of unsaturated fatty acids so that their membranes remain fluid even at these frigid temperatures. Conversely, the organisms that live in the hot springs of Yellowstone National Park, with temperatures near the boiling point of water, have membranes with high levels of saturated fatty acids. This flexibility in fatty acid content enables the bacteria to maintain the same membrane fluidity over a temperature range of almost 100°C.

The bacteria growing in this hot spring in Yellowstone National Park are called thermophiles because they live at temperatures approaching the boiling point of water. What type of fatty acids do you think will be found in their membrane phospholipids?

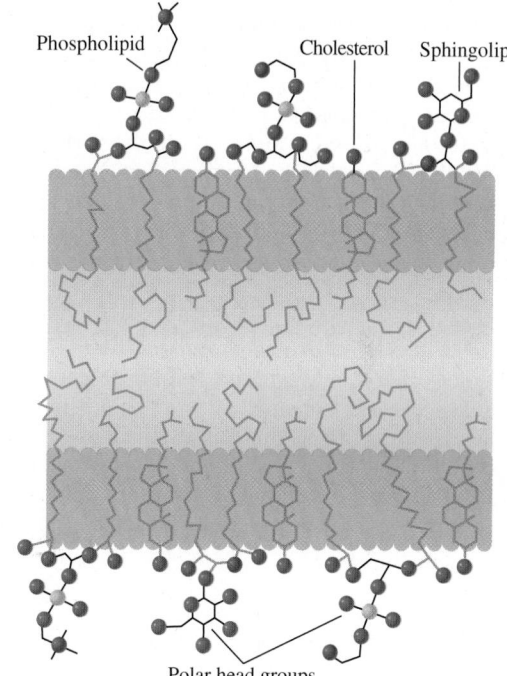

**Figure 17.11** (a) Representation of a phospholipid. (b) Space-filling model of a phospholipid. (c) Representation of a phospholipid bilayer membrane. (d) Line formula structure of a bilayer membrane composed of phospholipids, cholesterol, and sphingolipids.

Generally, the body temperatures of mammals are quite constant, and the fatty acid composition of their membrane lipids is therefore usually very uniform. One interesting exception is the reindeer. Much of the year the reindeer must travel through ice and snow. Thus the hooves and lower legs must function at much colder temperatures than the rest of the body. Because of this, the percentage of unsaturation in the membranes varies along the length of the reindeer leg. We find that the proportion of unsaturated fatty acids increases closer to the hoof, permitting the membranes to function in the low temperatures of ice and snow to which the lower leg is exposed.

Thus, membranes are fluid, regardless of the environmental temperature conditions. In fact, it has been estimated that membranes have the consistency of olive oil.

Although the hydrophobic barrier created by the fluid lipid bilayer is an important feature of membranes, the proteins embedded within the lipid bilayer are equally important and are responsible for critical cellular functions. The presence of these membrane proteins was revealed by an electron microscopic technique called *freeze-fracture.* Cells are frozen to very cold temperatures and then fractured with a very fine diamond knife. Some of the cells are fractured between the two layers of the lipid bilayer. When viewed with the electron microscope, the membrane appeared to be a mosaic, studded with proteins. Because of the fluidity of membranes and the appearance of the proteins seen by electron microscopy, our concept of membrane structure is called the **fluid mosaic model** (Figure 17.12).

Some of the observed proteins, called **peripheral membrane proteins,** are bound only to one of the surfaces of the membrane by interactions between ionic head groups of the membrane lipids and ionic amino acids on the surface of the peripheral protein. Other membrane proteins, called **transmembrane proteins,** are embedded within the membrane and extend completely through it, being exposed both inside and outside the cell.

Just as the phospholipid composition of the membrane is asymmetric, so too is the orientation of transmembrane proteins. Each transmembrane protein has

## A MEDICAL PERSPECTIVE

### Liposome Delivery Systems

Liposomes were discovered by Dr. Alec Bangham in 1961. During his studies on phospholipids and blood clotting, he found that if he mixed phospholipids and water, tiny phospholipid bilayer sacs, called liposomes, would form spontaneously. Since that first observation, liposomes have been developed as efficient delivery systems for everything from antitumor and antiviral drugs, to the hair-loss therapy minoxidil!

If a drug is included in the solution during formation of liposomes, the phospholipids will form a sac around the solution. In this way the drug becomes encapsulated within the phospholipid sphere. These liposomes can be injected intravenously or applied to body surfaces. Sometimes scientists include hydrophilic molecules in the surface of the liposome. This increases the length of time that they will remain in circulation in the bloodstream. These so-called stealth liposomes are being used to carry anticancer drugs, such as doxorubicin and mitoxantrone. Liposomes are also being used as carriers for the antiviral drugs, such as AZT and ddC, that are used to treat human immunodeficiency virus (HIV) infection.

A clever trick to help target the drug-carrying liposome is to include an antibody on the surface of the liposome. These antibodies are proteins designed to bind specifically to the surface of a tumor cell. Upon attaching to the surface of the tumor cell, the liposome "membrane" fuses with the cell membrane. In this way the deadly chemicals are delivered only to those cells targeted for destruction. This helps to avoid many of the unpleasant side effects of chemotherapy treatment that occur when normal healthy cells are killed by the drug.

Another application of liposomes is in the cosmetics industry. Liposomes can be formed that encapsulate a vitamin, herbal agent, or other nutritional element. When applied to the skin, the liposomes pass easily through the outer layer of dead skin, delivering their contents to the living skin cells beneath. As with the pharmaceutical liposomes, these liposomes, sometimes called *cosmeceuticals*, fuse with skin cells. Thus, they directly deliver the beneficial cosmetic agent directly to the cells that can benefit the most.

Since their accidental discovery 50 years ago, much has been learned about the formation of liposomes and ways to engineer them for more efficient delivery of their contents. This is another example of the marriage of serendipity, an accidental discovery, with scientific research and technological application. As the development of new types of liposomes continues, we can expect that even more ways will be found to improve the human condition.

### For Further Understanding

▶ From what you know of the structure of phospholipids, explain the molecular interactions that cause liposomes to form.
▶ Could you use liposome technology to deliver a hydrophobic drug? Explain your answer.

(a) Cross section of a liposome, (b) three-dimensional view of a liposome, and (c) liposome fusing with cell membrane.

hydrophobic regions that associate with the fatty acid tails of membrane phospholipids. Each also has a unique hydrophilic domain that is always found associated with the outer layer of the membrane and is located on the outside of the cell. This region of the protein typically has oligosaccharides covalently attached. Hence these proteins are *glycoproteins*. Similarly, each transmembrane protein has a second hydrophilic domain that is always found associated with the inner layer of the membrane and projects into the cytoplasm of the cell. Typically this region of the transmembrane protein is attached to filaments of the cytoplasmic skeleton.

Membranes are dynamic structures. The mobility of proteins embedded in biological membranes was studied by labeling certain proteins in human and mouse cell membranes with red and green fluorescent dyes. The human and

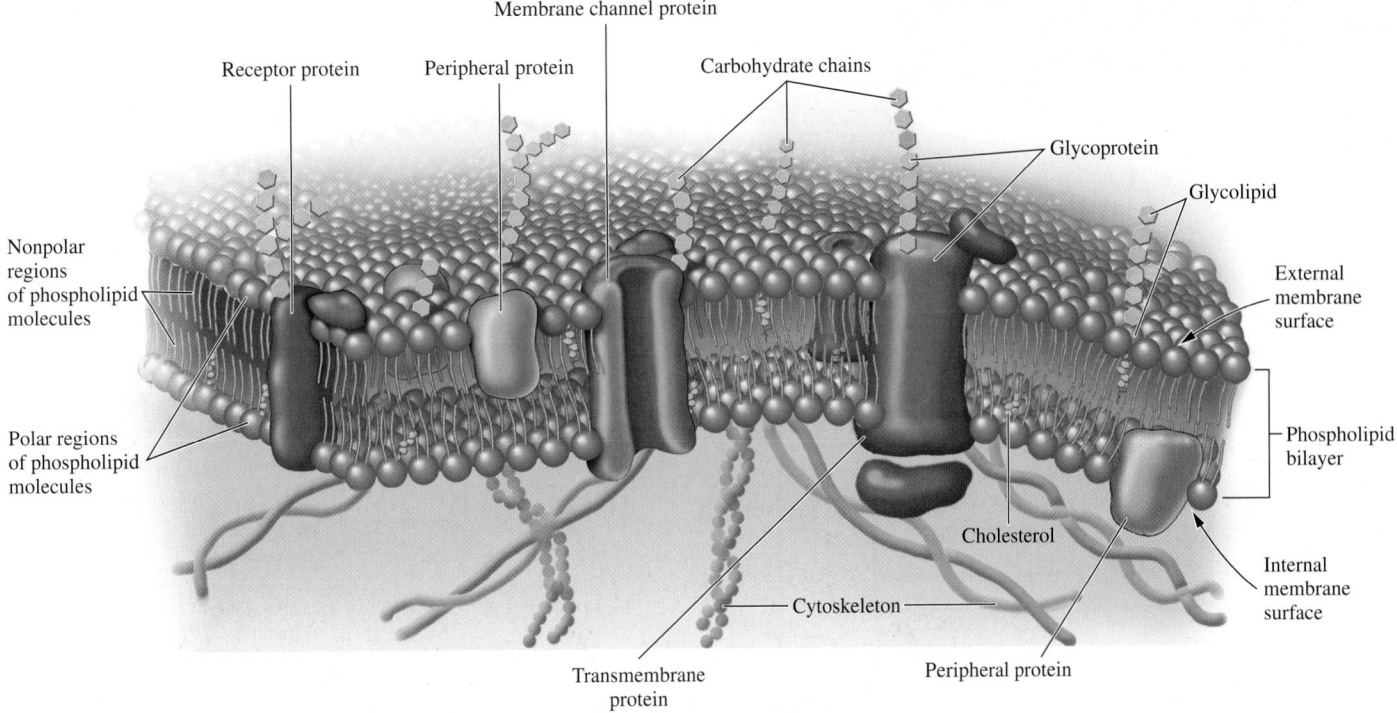

**Figure 17.12**  The fluid mosaic model of membrane structure.

mouse cells were fused; in other words, special techniques were used to cause the membranes of the mouse and human cells to flow together to create a single cell. The new cell was observed through a special ultraviolet or fluorescence microscope. The red and green patches were localized within regions of their original cell membranes when the experiment began. Forty minutes later the color patches were uniformly distributed in the fused cellular membrane (Figure 17.13). This experiment suggests that we can think of the fluid mosaic membrane as an ocean filled with mobile, floating icebergs.

**Figure 17.13**  Demonstration that membranes are fluid and that proteins move freely in the plane of the lipid bilayer.

# CHAPTER MAP

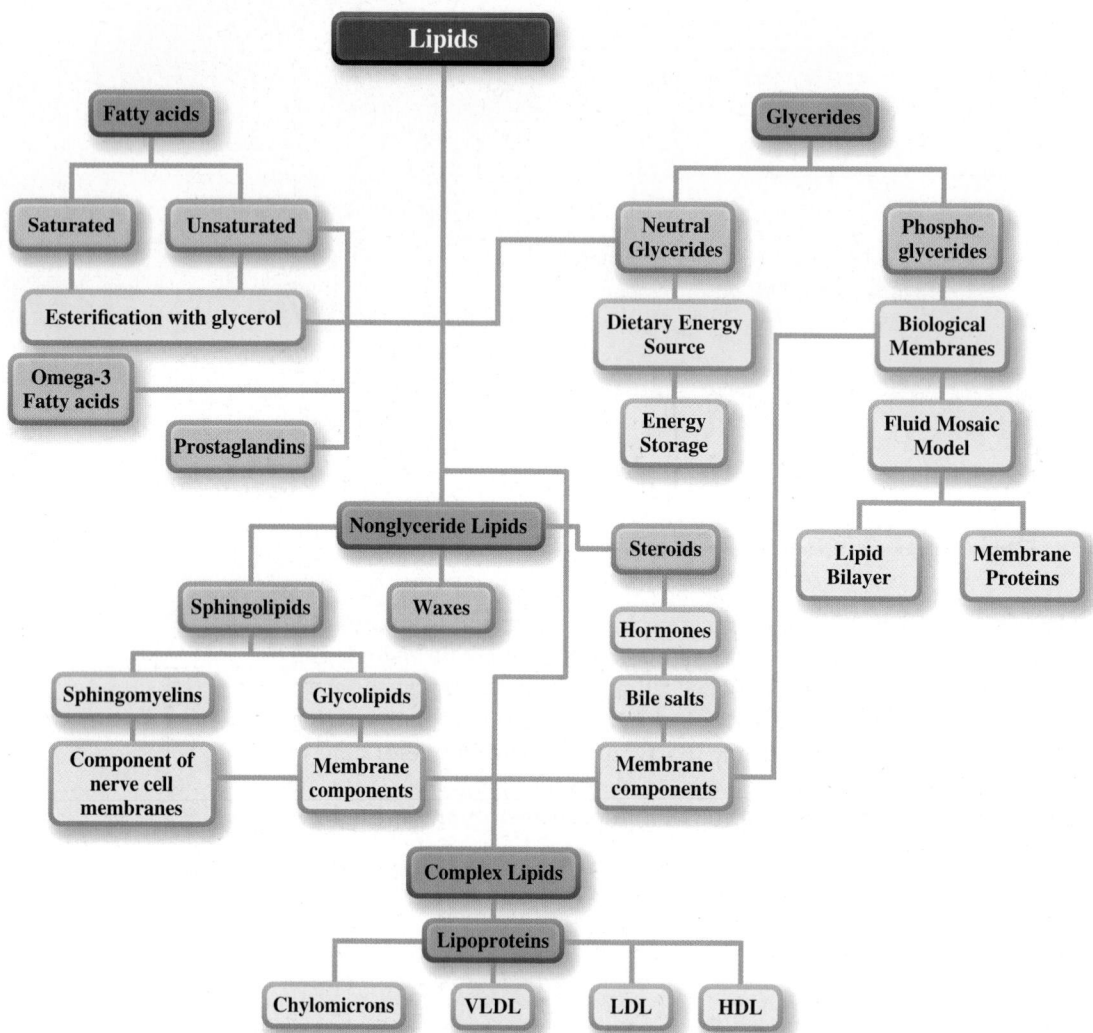

# SUMMARY

## 17.1 Biological Functions of Lipids

▶ **Lipids** are organic molecules characterized by their solubility in nonpolar solvents.

▶ Lipids serve many functions in the body including: energy storage, protection of organs, insulation, absorption of vitamins, energy sources, and hormones.

## 17.2 Fatty Acids

▶ **Fatty acids** may be **saturated** or **unsaturated** carboxylic acids containing 12–24 carbon atoms.

▶ Fatty acids with even numbers of carbon atoms occur most frequently in nature.

▶ **Essential fatty acids** are those that must be provided in the diet. Linoleic and linolenic acids are essential fatty acids.

▶ Linoleic acid is needed for the synthesis of **arachidonic acid,** which is the precursor of the **eicosanoids.**

▶ Among the eicosanoids are the **prostaglandins**, thromboxanes, and leukotrienes, all of which have important physiological effects.

▶ Omega-3 fatty acids are important components of a healthy diet.

## 17.3 Glycerides

▶ **Glycerides** are the most abundant lipids. The **neutral glycerides** are esters of one (**monoglycerides**), two (**diglycerides**), or three (**triglycerides**) fatty acids and glycerol.

▶ The reactions of fatty acids are identical to those of carboxylic acids: **esterification, hydrogenation,** and production by acid hydrolysis of esters. The base-catalyzed hydrolysis of a glyceride is **saponification.**

▶ **Phospholipids** are important components of biological membranes.

▶ **Phosphoglycerides** are esters derived from glycerol-3-phosphate and two fatty acids.

▶ The simplest phosphoglyceride is **phosphatidate.**

▶ Because of their amphipathic nature, phospholipids are excellent **emulsifying agents.**

## 17.4 Nonglyceride Lipids

▶ Nonglyceride lipids include the **sphingolipids, steroids,** and **waxes.**

▶ **Sphingomyelin** is a component of the myelin sheath around cells of the central nervous system.

▶ **Steroids** are important for many biochemical functions. They are **terpenes** because they are synthesized from isoprene units.

- **Cholesterol** is a membrane component. However, high concentrations in the blood can contribute to **atherosclerosis.**

- Testosterone, progesterone, and estrone are sex hormones.
- Cortisone is an anti-inflammatory steroid that is important in the regulation of biological pathways.

## 17.5 Complex Lipids

▶ **Plasma lipoproteins** are **complex lipids** that transport other lipids through the bloodstream.

▶ **Chylomicrons** carry dietary triglycerides from the intestine to other tissues.

▶ **Very low density lipoproteins** carry triglycerides synthesized in the liver to other tissues for storage.

▶ **Low-density lipoproteins** carry cholesterol to peripheral tissues and help regulate cholesterol levels.

▶ **High-density lipoproteins** transport cholesterol from peripheral tissues to the liver.

## 17.6 The Structure of Biological Membranes

▶ The **fluid mosaic model** of membrane structure pictures biological membranes that are composed of lipid bilayers in which proteins are embedded.

▶ Membrane lipids contain polar head groups and nonpolar hydrocarbon tails.

▶ Membrane proteins may be embedded within the membrane (**transmembrane proteins**) or may lie on one surface of the membrane (**peripheral membrane proteins**).

# ANSWERS TO PRACTICE PROBLEMS

17.1  a. Oleic acid:    $CH_3(CH_2)_7CH{=}CH(CH_2)_7COOH$

oleic acid

b. Linoleic acid:   $CH_3(CH_2)_4CH{=}CH{-}CH_2{-}CH{=}CH(CH_2)_7COOH$

linoleic acid

**17.2 a.**

Glycerol    + 2CH₃(CH₂)₁₆COOH ⟶

$+ 2CH_3(CH_2)_{16}COOH$    Stearic acid

**b.**

Glycerol    $+ CH_3(CH_2)_{12}COOH$ ⟶    Myristic acid

**17.3 a.** $CH_3(CH_2)_{10}COOH + CH_3CH_2OH \xrightarrow{H^+, heat}$

Dodecanoic acid        Ethanol
Lauric acid

$CH_3(CH_2)_{10}COCH_2CH_3$

Ethyl dodecanoate

**b.** $CH_3(CH_2)_{14}COOH + CH_3(CH_2)OH \xrightarrow{H^+, heat}$

Hexadecanoic acid    1-Pentanol
Palmitic acid

$CH_3(CH_2)_{14}CO(CH_2)_4CH_3$

Pentyl hexadecanoate

**17.4 a.**

1,2,3-Propanetriol    Tetradecanoic acid

**b.**

$\xrightarrow{H^+, heat}$

1,2,3-Propanetriol    Dodecanoic acid

**17.5 a.**

$+ KOH \longrightarrow$

$+ CH_3(CH_2)_{14}COOH$

1,2,3-Propanetriol    Potassium hexadecanoate

**b.**

$+ 2\,NaOH \longrightarrow$

$+ CH_3(CH_2)_6CO^-Na^+$
Sodium octanoate
$+ CH_3(CH_2)_8CO^-Na^+$

1,2,3-Propanetriol    Sodium decanoate

**17.6 a.** $CH_3(CH_2)_5CH{=}CH(CH_2)_7COOH + H_2$

*cis*-9-Hexadecenoic acid

↓ Ni

$CH_3(CH_2)_{14}COOH$
Hexadecanoic acid

**b.** $CH_3(CH_2)_4CH{=}CH{-}CH_2{-}CH{=}CH{-}CH_2{-}CH{=}$
$CH{-}CH_2{-}CH{=}CH{-}(CH_2)_3COOH + 4H_2$

↓ Ni

$CH_3(CH_2)_{18}COOH$

The α-carbon of each amino acid is also bonded to a hydrogen atom and a side chain, or R group. In a protein, the R groups interact with one another through a variety of weak attractive forces. These interactions participate in folding the protein chain into a precise three-dimensional shape that determines its ultimate function. They also serve to maintain that three-dimensional conformation.

α-Carbon

Figure 18.1  General structure of an α-amino acid. All amino acids isolated from proteins, with the exception of proline, have this general structure.

## Stereoisomers of Amino Acids

The α-carbon is attached to four different groups in all amino acids except glycine. The α-carbon of most α-amino acids is therefore chiral, allowing mirror-image forms, enantiomers, to exist. Glycine has two hydrogen atoms attached to the α-carbon and is the only amino acid commonly found in proteins that is not chiral.

The L-configuration of α-amino acids is isolated from proteins. The D-L notation is very similar to that discussed for carbohydrates, but instead of the —OH group we use the —$N^+H_3$ group to determine which is D- and which is L- (Figure 18.2). In Figure 18.2a we see a comparison of D- and L-glyceraldehyde with D- and L-alanine. Notice that the most oxidized end of the molecule, the carbonyl group of glyceraldehyde or carboxyl group of alanine, is drawn at the top of the molecule. In the D-isomer of glyceraldehyde, the —OH group is on the right. Similarly, in the D-isomer of alanine, the —$N^+H_3$ is on the right. In the L-isomers of the two compounds, the —OH and —$N^+H_3$ groups are on the left. By this comparison with the enantiomers of glyceraldehyde, we can define the D- and L-enantiomers of the amino acids. Figure 18.2b shows ball-and-stick models of the D- and L-isomers of alanine.

**STEREOCHEMISTRY AND STEREOISOMERS REVISITED**

*Stereochemistry is discussed in Section 16.3.*

Figure 18.2  (a) Structures of D- and L-glyceraldehyde and their relationship to D- and L-alanine. (b) Ball-and-stick models of D- and L-alanine.

Mirror plane

L-Isomers          D-Isomers

CHO                CHO

HO—C—H         H—C—OH        Carbohydrate pair

CH₂OH              CH₂OH

L-Glyceraldehyde    D-Glyceraldehyde

COO⁻               COO⁻

H₃N⁺—C—H        H—C—NH₃⁺      Amino acid pair

CH₃                CH₃

L-Alanine          D-Alanine

**(a)**

L-Alanine          D-Alanine

**(b)**

In Chapter 16 we learned that almost all of the monosaccharides found in nature are in the D-family. Just the opposite is true of the α-amino acids. Almost all of the α-amino acids isolated from proteins in nature are members of the L-family. In other words, the orientation of the four groups around the chiral carbon of these α-amino acids resembles the orientation of the four groups around the chiral carbon of L-glyceraldehyde.

## Classes of Amino Acids

Because all amino acids have a carboxyl group and an amino group, all differences between amino acids depend upon their side-chain R groups. The amino acids are grouped in Figure 18.3 according to the polarity of their side chains.

The side chains of some amino acids are nonpolar. They prefer contact with one another over contact with water and are said to be **hydrophobic** ("water-fearing") **amino acids.** They are generally found buried in the interior of proteins, where they can associate with one another and remain isolated from water. Nine amino acids fall into this category: alanine, valine, leucine, isoleucine, proline, glycine, methionine, phenylalanine, and tryptophan. The R group of proline is unique; it is actually bonded to the α-amino group, forming a secondary amine.

The side chains of the remaining amino acids are polar. Because they are attracted to polar water molecules, they are said to be **hydrophilic** ("water-loving") **amino acids.** The hydrophilic side chains are often found on the surfaces of proteins. The polar amino acids can be subdivided into three classes.

- *Polar, neutral amino acids* have R groups that have a high affinity for water but are not ionic at pH 7. Serine, threonine, tyrosine, cysteine, asparagine, and glutamine fall into this category. Most of these amino acids associate with one another by hydrogen bonding; but cysteine molecules form disulfide bonds with one another, as we will discuss in Section 18.5.
- *Negatively charged amino acids* have ionized carboxyl groups in their side chains. At pH 7 these amino acids have a net charge of $-1$. Aspartate and glutamate are the two amino acids in this category. They are acidic amino acids because ionization of the carboxylic acid releases a proton.
- *Positively charged amino acids.* At pH 7, lysine, arginine, and histidine have a net positive charge because their side chains contain positive groups. These amino groups are basic because the side chain reacts with water, picking up a proton and releasing a hydroxide anion.

The names of the amino acids can be abbreviated by a three-letter and by a one-letter code. These abbreviations are shown in Table 18.1.

**Question 18.1**   Write the one-letter and three-letter abbreviations and draw the structure of each of the following amino acids.
  a. Glycine
  b. Proline
  c. Threonine
  d. Aspartate
  e. Lysine

**Question 18.2**   Indicate whether the side chains of each of the amino acids listed in Question 18.1 is polar, nonpolar, basic, or acidic.

---

The hydrophobic interaction between nonpolar R groups is one of the forces that helps maintain the proper three-dimensional shape of a protein.

---

Hydrogen bonding (Section 5.2) is another weak interaction that helps maintain the proper three-dimensional structure of a protein. The positively and negatively charged amino acids within a protein interact with one another to form ionic bridges that also help to keep the protein chain folded in a precise way.

# A HUMAN PERSPECTIVE

## The Opium Poppy and Peptides in the Brain

The seed pods of the oriental poppy contain morphine. *Morphine* is a narcotic that has a variety of effects on the body and the brain, including drowsiness, euphoria, mental confusion, and chronic constipation. Although morphine was first isolated in 1805, not until the 1850s and the advent of the hypodermic was it effectively used as a painkiller. During the American Civil War, morphine was used extensively to relieve the pain of wounds and amputations. It was at this time that the addictive properties were noticed. By the end of the Civil War, over 100,000 soldiers were addicted to morphine.

As a result of the Harrison Act (1914), morphine came under government control and was made available only by prescription.

Why does morphine have such powerful effects on the brain? The drug has been found to bind to *receptors* on the surface of the cells of the brain. The function of these receptors is to bind specific chemical signals and to direct the brain cells to respond. Yet it seemed odd that the cells of our brain should have receptors for a plant chemical. This mystery was solved in 1975, when John Hughes discovered that the brain itself synthesizes small peptide hormones with a morphine-like structure. Two of these opiate peptides are called *methionine enkephalin*, or met-enkephalin, and *leucine enkephalin*, or leu-enkephalin.

These neuropeptide hormones have a variety of effects. They inhibit intestinal motility and blood flow to the gastrointestinal tract. This explains the chronic constipation of morphine users. In addition, it is thought that these *enkephalins* play a role in pain perception, perhaps serving as a pain blockade. This is supported by the observation that they are found in higher concentrations in the bloodstream following painful stimulation. It is further suspected that they may play a role in mood and mental health. The so-called runner's high is thought to be a euphoria brought about by an excessively long or strenuous run!

Morphine
The structure of morphine.

Unlike morphine, the action of enkephalins is short-lived. They bind to the cellular receptor and thereby induce the cells to respond. Then they are quickly destroyed by enzymes in the brain that hydrolyze the peptide bonds of the enkephalin. Once destroyed, they are no longer able to elicit a cellular response.

Morphine binds to these same receptors and induces the cells to respond. However, it is not destroyed and therefore persists in the brain for long periods at concentrations high enough to continue to cause biological effects.

Many researchers are working to understand why drugs like morphine are addictive. Studies with cells in culture have suggested one mechanism for morphine tolerance and addiction. Normally, when the cell receptors bind to enkephalins, this signals the cell to decrease the production of a chemical messenger called *cyclic AMP*, or simply cAMP. (This compound is very closely related to the nucleotide adenosine-5'-monophosphate.) The decrease in cAMP level helps to block pain and elevate mood. When morphine is applied to these cells they initially respond by decreasing cAMP levels. However, with chronic use of morphine the cells become desensitized; that is, they do not decrease cAMP production and thus behave as though no morphine were present. However, a greater amount of morphine will once again cause the decrease in cAMP levels. Thus addiction and the progressive need for more of the drug seem to result from biochemical reactions in the cells.

Tyr-Gly-Gly-Phe-Met
Methionine enkephalin

Tyr-Gly-Gly-Phe-Leu
Leucine enkephalin

Structures of the peptide opiates leucine enkephalin and methionine enkephalin. These are the body's own opiates.

This logic can be extended to understand withdrawal symptoms. When an addict stops using the drug, he or she exhibits withdrawal symptoms that include excessive sweating, anxiety, and tremors. The cause may be that the high levels of morphine were keeping the cAMP levels low, thus reducing pain and causing euphoria. When morphine is removed

*Continued…*

### The Opium Poppy and Peptides in the Brain   (continued)

completely, the cells overreact and produce huge quantities of cAMP. The result is all of the unpleasant symptoms known collectively as the *withdrawal syndrome*.

Clearly, morphine has demonstrated the potential for misuse and is a problem for society in several respects. Nonetheless, morphine remains one of the most effective painkillers known. Certainly, for people suffering from cancer, painful burns, or serious injuries, the risk of addiction is far outweighed by the benefits of relief from excruciating pain.

**For Further Understanding**

▶ Compare the structures of leucine and methionine enkephalin with that of morphine. What similarities do you see that might cause them to bind to the same receptors on the surfaces of nerve cells?

▶ What characteristics might you look for in a nonaddictive drug that could be used both to combat morphine addiction and to treat the symptoms of withdrawal?

---

**Question 18.3**   Write the structure of each of the following peptides at pH 7:
  a. Alanyl-phenylalanine
  b. Lysyl-alanine
  c. Phenylalanyl-tyrosyl-leucine

**Question 18.4**   Write the structure of each of the following peptides at pH 7:
  a. Glycyl-valyl-serine
  b. Threonyl-cysteine
  c. Isoleucyl-methionyl-aspartate

## 18.3   The Primary Structure of Proteins

*The genetic code and the process of protein synthesis are described in Sections 20.5 and 20.6.*

The **primary structure** of a protein is the amino acid sequence of the protein chain. It results from the covalent bonding between the amino acid residues in the chain (peptide bonds). The primary structures of proteins are translations of information contained in genes. Each protein has a different primary structure with different amino acid residues in different places along the chain. This sequence of amino acid residues is dictated by the sequence of the gene.

Ultimately, it is the primary structure of a protein that will determine its biologically active form. The interactions among the R groups of the amino acids in the protein chain depend on the location of those R groups along the chain. These interactions will govern how the protein chain folds, which, in turn, dictates its final three-dimensional structure and its biological function.

## 18.4   The Secondary Structure of Proteins

The primary sequence of a protein, the chain of covalently linked amino acids, folds into regularly repeating structures that resemble designs in a tapestry. These repeating structures define the **secondary structure** of the protein. The secondary structure is the result of hydrogen bonding between the amide hydrogens and carbonyl oxygens of the peptide bonds. Many hydrogen bonds are needed to maintain the secondary structure and thereby the overall structure of the protein. Different regions of a protein chain may have different types of secondary structure. Some regions of a protein chain may have a random or nonregular structure; however, the two most common types of secondary structure are the α-helix and the β-pleated sheet because they maximize hydrogen bonding in the backbone.

## α-Helix

The most common type of secondary structure is a coiled, helical conformation known as the **α-helix** (Figure 18.5). The α-helix has several important features.

- Every amide hydrogen and carbonyl oxygen associated with the peptide backbone is involved in a hydrogen bond when the chain coils into an α-helix. These hydrogen bonds lock the α-helix into place.
- Every carbonyl oxygen is hydrogen-bonded to an amide hydrogen four amino acids away in the chain.
- The hydrogen bonds of the α-helix are parallel to the long axis of the helix (see Figure 18.5).

### LEARNING GOAL

**6**  Discuss the forces that maintain secondary structure.

In the photo above, some of the children have straight hair and some have curly hair. Knowing that the primary structure of a protein is dictated by the sequence of a gene, in this case a keratin gene, develop a hypothesis to explain hair curliness.

(a)          (b)          (c)

**Figure 18.5**  The α-helix. (a) Molecular model showing only the helical backbone. (b) The same molecular model showing that all of the hydrogen bonds between C=O and N—H groups are parallel to the long axis of the helix. (c) Top view of an α-helix. The side chains of the helix point away from the long axis of the helix. The view is into the barrel of the helix.

- The polypeptide chain in an α-helix is right-handed. It is oriented like a normal screw. If you turn a screw clockwise it goes into the wall; turned counterclockwise, it comes out of the wall.
- The repeat distance of the helix, or its pitch, is 5.4 angstroms (Å), and there are 3.6 amino acids per turn of the helix.

**Fibrous proteins** are structural proteins arranged in fibers or sheets that have only one type of secondary structure. The **α-keratins** are fibrous proteins that form the covering (hair, wool, nails, hooves, and fur) of most land animals. Human hair provides a typical example of the structure of the α-keratins. The proteins of hair consist almost exclusively of polypeptide chains coiled up into α-helices. A single α-helix is coiled in a bundle with two other helices to give a three-stranded superstructure called a *protofibril* that is part of an array known as a *microfibril* (Figure 18.6). These structures, which resemble "molecular pigtails," possess great mechanical strength, and they are virtually insoluble in water.

The major structural property of a coiled coil superstructure of α-helices is its great mechanical strength. This property is applied very efficiently in both the fibrous proteins of skin and those of muscle. As you can imagine, these proteins must be very strong to carry out their functions of mechanical support and muscle contraction.

## β-Pleated Sheet

The second common secondary structure in proteins resembles the pleated folds of drapery and is known as the **β-pleated sheet** (Figure 18.7a). All of the carbonyl oxygens and amide hydrogens in a β-pleated sheet are involved in hydrogen bonds, and the polypeptide chain is nearly completely extended. The polypeptide chains in a β-pleated sheet can have two orientations. If the N-termini are head to head, the structure is known as a *parallel* β-pleated sheet. And if the N-terminus of one chain is aligned with the C-terminus of a second chain (head to tail), the structure is known as an *antiparallel* β-pleated sheet.

**Figure 18.6** Structure of the α-keratins. These proteins are assemblies of triple-helical protofibrils that are assembled in an array known as a *microfibril*. These in turn are assembled into macrofibrils. Hair is a collection of macrofibrils and hair cells.

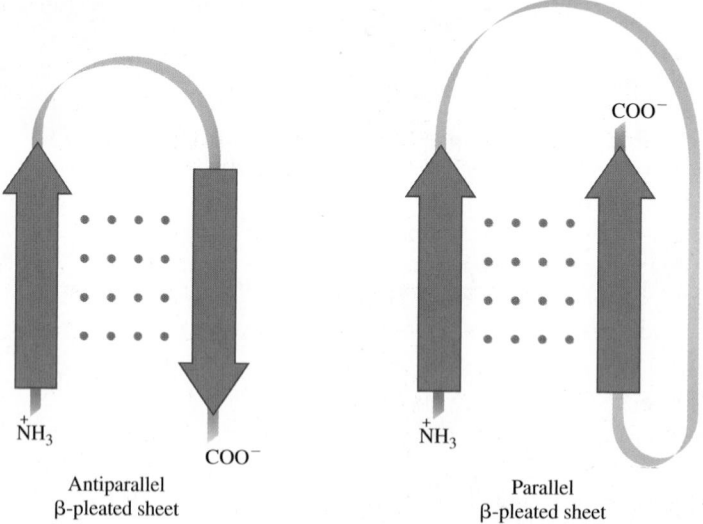

Antiparallel
β-pleated sheet

Parallel
β-pleated sheet

Some fibrous proteins are composed of β-pleated sheets. For example, the silkworm produces *silk fibroin,* a protein whose structure is an antiparallel β-pleated sheet (Figure 18.7). The polypeptide chains of a β-pleated sheet are almost completely extended, and silk does not stretch easily. Glycine accounts for nearly half of the amino acids of silk fibroin. Alanine and serine account for most of the others. The methyl groups of alanines and the hydroxymethyl groups of serines lie on opposite sides of the sheet. Thus the stacked sheets nestle comfortably, like sheets of corrugated cardboard, because the R groups are small enough to allow the stacked-sheet superstructure.

Gly

Ala

**Figure 18.7** The structure of silk fibroin is almost entirely antiparallel β-pleated sheet. (a) The molecular structure of a portion of the silk fibroin protein. (b) A schematic representation of the antiparallel β-pleated sheet with the nestled R groups.

## 18.5 The Tertiary Structure of Proteins

Most fibrous proteins, such as silk, collagen, and the α-keratins, are almost completely insoluble in water. (Our skin would do us very little good if it dissolved in the rain.) The majority of cellular proteins, however, are soluble in the cell cytoplasm. Soluble proteins are usually **globular proteins.** Globular proteins have three-dimensional structures called the **tertiary structure** of the protein, which are distinct from their secondary structure. The polypeptide chain with its regions of secondary structure, α-helix and β-pleated sheet, further folds on itself to achieve the tertiary structure.

We have seen that the forces that maintain the secondary structure of a protein are hydrogen bonds between the amide hydrogen and the carbonyl oxygen of the peptide bond. What are the forces that maintain the tertiary structure of a protein? The globular tertiary structure forms spontaneously and is maintained as a result of interactions among the side chains, the R groups, of the amino acids. The structure is maintained by the following molecular interactions:

- van der Waals forces (London dispersion and dipole-dipole attractions) between the hydrophobic R groups
- Hydrogen bonds between the polar R groups
- Ionic bonds (salt bridges) between the oppositely charged R groups
- Covalent bonds between the thiol-containing amino acid residues. Two of the polar cysteines can be oxidized to a dimeric amino acid called *cystine* (Figure 18.8). The disulfide bond of cystine can be a cross-link between different proteins, or it can tie two segments within a protein together.

The bonds that maintain the tertiary structure of proteins are shown in Figure 18.9. The importance of these bonds becomes clear when we realize that it is the tertiary structure of the protein that defines its biological function. Most of

**LEARNING GOAL**

**8** Describe the tertiary and quaternary structure of a protein.

**LEARNING GOAL**

**9** List the R group interactions that maintain protein conformation.

*Thiols were discussed in Section 12.8.*

*In the next section we will see that some proteins have an additional level of structure, quaternary structure, that also influences function.*

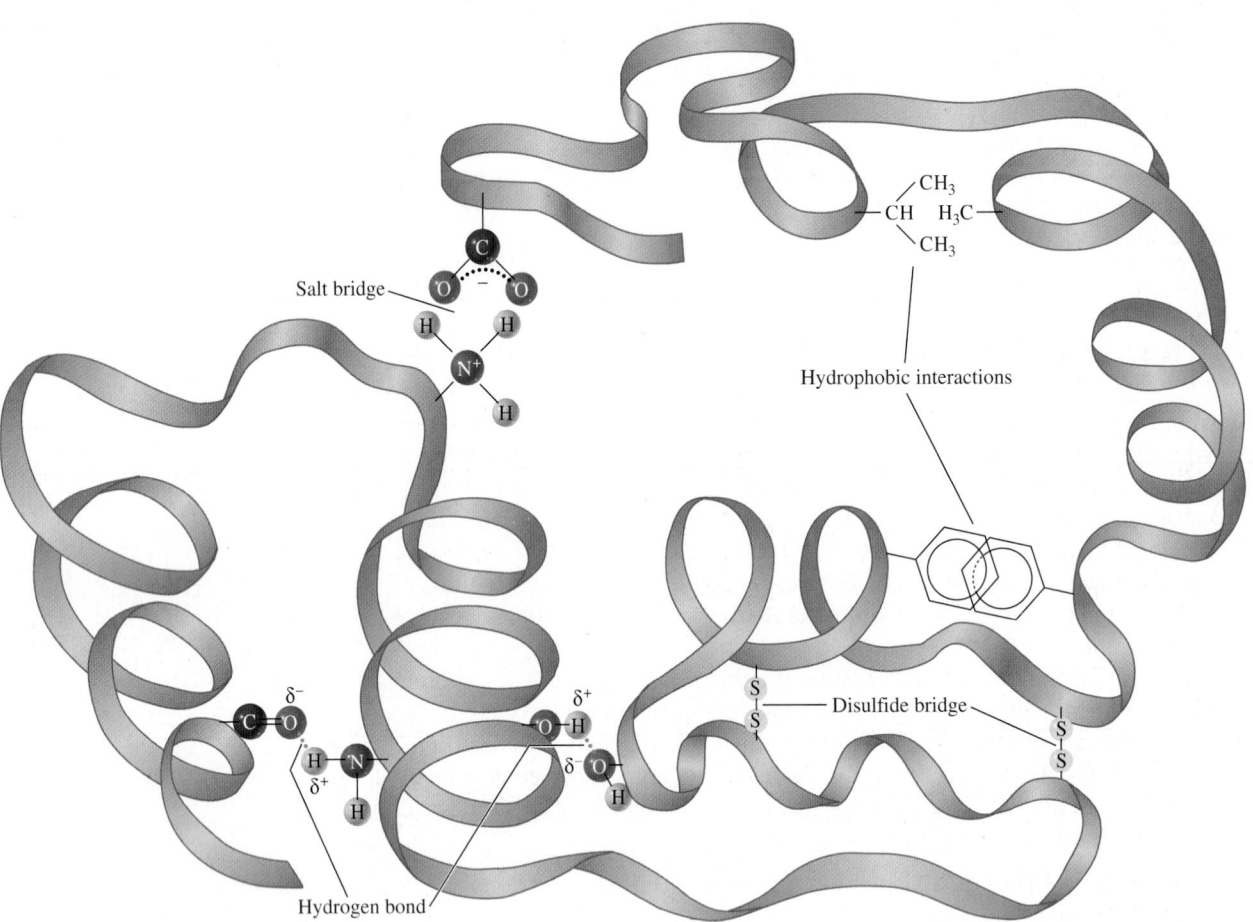

**Figure 18.8** Oxidation of two cysteines to give the dimer cystine. This reaction occurs in cells and is readily reversible.

**Figure 18.9** Summary of the weak interactions that help maintain the tertiary structure of a protein.

the time, nonpolar side chains of amino acid residues are buried, closely packed, in the interior of a globular protein, out of contact with water. Polar and charged side chain amino acid residues lie on the surfaces of globular proteins. Globular proteins are extremely compact. The tertiary structure can contain regions of α-helix and regions of β-pleated sheet. "Hinge" regions of random coil connect regions of α-helix and β-pleated sheet. Because of its cyclic structure, proline disrupts an α-helix. As a result, proline is often found in these hinge regions.

# A MEDICAL PERSPECTIVE

## Collagen, Cosmetic Procedures, and Clinical Applications

*Collagen* is the most abundant protein in the human body, making up about one-third of the total protein content. It provides mechanical strength to bone, tendon, skin, and blood vessels. Collagen fibers in bone provide a scaffolding around which *hydroxyapatite* (a calcium phosphate polymer) crystals are arranged. Skin contains loosely woven collagen fibers that can expand in all directions. The corneas of the eyes are composed of collagen. As we consider these tissues, we realize that they have quite different properties, ranging from tensile strength (tendons) and flexibility (blood vessels) to transparency (cornea).

How could such diverse structures be composed of a single protein? The answer lies in the fact that collagen is actually a family of twenty genetically distinct, but closely related proteins. Although the differences in the amino acid sequence of these different collagen proteins allow them to carry out a variety of functions in the body, they all have a similar three-dimensional structure. Collagen is composed of three left-handed polypeptide helices that are twisted around one another to form a "superhelix" called a *triple helix*. Each of the individual peptide chains of collagen is a left-handed helix, but they are wrapped around one another in the right-handed sense.

Every third amino acid in the collagen chain is glycine. It is important to the structure because the triple-stranded helix forms as a result of interchain hydrogen bonding involving glycine. Thus, every third amino acid on one strand is in very close contact with the other two strands. Glycine has another advantage; it is the only amino acid with an R group small enough for the space allowed by the triple-stranded structure.

Collagen injections have been used in cosmetic procedures to add fullness to lips or minimize the appearance of wrinkled or sunken facial skin. This procedure is no longer very common because of the relatively high frequency of allergic reactions to the bovine collagen used in the injections. Popular alternatives to collagen injections include the patient's own fat and hyaluronic acid (see also A Medical Perspective: Monosaccharide Derivatives and Heteropolysaccharides of Medical Interest in Chapter 16). Another alternative, although an expensive one, is the injection of recombinant human collagen. This reduces the incidence of allergic reactions.

Collagen is also used in the preparation of artificial skin for severe burn patients. The collagen is used in combination with silicones, glycosaminoglycans (such as hyaluronic acid), growth factors, and human fibroblasts, which are the most common type of cell in connective tissue and which promote wound healing.

Collagen even finds its way into our diet. When partially hydrolyzed, the three polypeptide strands separate from one another and then curl up into globular random coils. The product is gelatin, found most notably in gelatin desserts such as

Structure of the
collagen triple helix.

Jello. However, gelatin is found in many other foods, as well as in dietary supplements that claim to improve fingernail and skin condition.

Two unusual, hydroxylated amino acids account for nearly one-fourth of the amino acids in collagen. These amino acids are 4-hydroxyproline and 5-hydroxylysine.

4-Hydroxyproline                    5-Hydroxylysine

Structures of 4-hydroxyproline and 5-hydroxylysine, two amino acids found only in collagen.

These amino acids are an important component of the structure of collagen because they form covalent cross-linkages between adjacent molecules within the triple strand. They can also participate in interstrand hydrogen bonding to further strengthen the structure.

*Continued…*

## Collagen, Cosmetic Procedures, and Clinical Applications    (continued)

When collagen is synthesized, the amino acids proline and lysine are incorporated into the chain of amino acids. These are later modified by two enzymes to form 4-hydroxyproline and 5-hydroxylysine. Both of these enzymes require vitamin C to carry out these reactions. In fact, this is the major known physiological function of vitamin C. Without hydroxylation, hydrogen bonds cannot form and the triple helix is weak, resulting in fragile blood vessels.

Vitamin C
(ascorbic acid)

People who are deprived of vitamin C, as were sailors on long voyages before the eighteenth century, develop *scurvy*, a disease of collagen metabolism. The symptoms of scurvy include skin lesions, fragile blood vessels, and bleeding gums. The British Navy provided the antidote to scurvy by including limes, which are rich in vitamin C, in the diets of its sailors. The epithet *limey*, a slang term for *British*, entered the English language as a result.

**For Further Understanding**

▶ What feature of glycine is responsible for its importance in the hydrogen bonding that maintains the helical structure of collagen?

▶ Collagen may have great tensile strength (as in tendons) and flexibility (as in skin and blood vessels), and may even be transparent (cornea of the eye). Propose a hypothesis to explain the biochemical differences between different forms of collagen that give rise to such different properties.

## 18.6    The Quaternary Structure of Proteins

For many proteins the functional form is not composed of a single peptide but is rather an aggregate of smaller globular peptides. For instance, the protein hemoglobin is composed of four individual globular peptide subunits: two identical α-subunits and two identical β-subunits. Only when the four peptides are bound to one another is the protein molecule functional. The association of several polypeptides to produce a functional protein defines the **quaternary structure** of a protein.

The forces that hold the quaternary structure of a protein are the same as those that hold the tertiary structure. These include, van der Waals forces between hydrophobic R groups, hydrogen bonds between polar R groups, ionic bridges between oppositely charged R groups, and disulfide bridges.

In some cases the quaternary structure of a functional protein involves binding to a nonprotein group. This additional group is called a **prosthetic group.** For example, many of the receptor proteins on cell surfaces are **glycoproteins.** These are proteins with sugar groups covalently attached. Each of the subunits of hemoglobin is bound to an iron-containing heme group. The heme group is a large, unsaturated organic cyclic amine with an iron ion coordinated within it. As in the case of hemoglobin, the prosthetic group often determines the function of a protein. For instance, in hemoglobin it is the iron-containing heme groups that have the ability to bind reversibly to oxygen.

**Question 18.5**    Describe the four levels of protein structure.

**Question 18.6**    What are the weak interactions that maintain the tertiary structure of a protein?

# 18.7 An Overview of Protein Structure and Function

Let's summarize the various types of protein structure and their relationship to one another (Figure 18.10).

- *Primary Structure:* The primary structure of the protein is the amino acid sequence of the protein. The primary structure results from the formation of covalent peptide bonds between amino acids. Peptide bonds are amide bonds formed between the carboxylate group of one amino acid and the amino group of another.
- *Secondary Structure:* As the protein chain grows, numerous opportunities for noncovalent interactions in the backbone of the polypeptide chain become available. These cause the chain to fold and orient itself in a variety of conformational arrangements. The secondary level of structure includes the α-helix and the β-pleated sheet, which are the result of hydrogen bonding between the amide hydrogens and carbonyl oxygens of the peptide bonds. Different portions of the chain may be involved in different types of secondary structure arrangements; some regions might be α-helix and others might be a β-pleated sheet.
- *Tertiary Structure:* When we discuss tertiary structure, we are interested in the overall folding of the entire chain. In other words, we are concerned with the further folding of the secondary structure. Are the two ends of the chain close together or far apart? What general shape is involved? Both noncovalent interactions between the R groups of the amino acids and covalent disulfide bridges play a role in determining the tertiary structure. The noncovalent interactions include hydrogen bonding, ionic bonding, and van der Waals forces (London dispersion forces and dipole-dipole attractions).
- *Quaternary Structure:* Like tertiary structure, quaternary structure is concerned with the topological, spatial arrangements of two or more peptide chains with respect to each other. How is one chain oriented with respect to another? What is the overall shape of the final functional protein?

**Figure 18.10** Summary of the four levels of protein structure, using hemoglobin as an example.

**(a)** Primary structure    **(b)** Secondary structure    **(c)** Tertiary structure    **(d)** Quaternary structure

C    N    R groups

H    O    Heme groups

The quaternary structure is maintained by the same forces that are responsible for the tertiary structure. It is the tertiary and quaternary structures of the protein that ultimately define its function. Some have a fibrous structure with great mechanical strength. These make up the major structural components of the cell and the organism. Often they are also responsible for the movement of the organism. Others fold into globular shapes. Most of the transport proteins, regulatory proteins, and enzymes are globular proteins. The very precise three-dimensional structure of the transport proteins allows them to recognize a particular molecule and facilitate its entry into the cell. Similarly, it is the specific three-dimensional shape of regulatory proteins that allows them to bind to their receptors on the surfaces of the target cell. In this way they can communicate with the cell, instructing it to take some course of action. In Chapter 19 we will see that the three-dimensional structure of enzyme active sites allows them to bind to their specific reactants and speed up biochemical reactions.

As we will see with the example of sickle cell hemoglobin in the next section, an alteration of just a single amino acid within the primary structure of a protein can have far-reaching implications. When an amino acid replaces another in a peptide, there is a change in the R group at that position in the protein chain. This leads to different tertiary and perhaps quaternary structure because the nature of the noncovalent interactions is altered by changing the R group that is available for that bonding. Similarly, replacement of another amino acid with proline can disrupt important regions of secondary structure. Thus changes in the primary amino acid sequence can change the three-dimensional structure of a protein in ways that cause it to be nonfunctional. In the case of sickle cell hemoglobin, this protein malfunction can lead to death.

## 18.8  Myoglobin and Hemoglobin

### Myoglobin and Oxygen Storage

Most of the cells of our bodies are buried in the interior of the body and cannot directly get food molecules or eliminate waste. The circulatory system solves this problem by delivering nutrients and oxygen to body cells and carrying away wastes. Our cells require a steady supply of oxygen, but oxygen is only slightly soluble in aqueous solutions. To overcome this solubility problem, we have an oxygen transport protein, **hemoglobin.** Hemoglobin is found in red blood cells and is the oxygen transport protein of higher animals. **Myoglobin** is the oxygen storage protein of skeletal muscle.

The structure of myoglobin (Mb) is shown in Figure 18.11. The **heme group** (Figure 18.12) is also an essential component of this protein. The $Fe^{2+}$ ion in the heme group is the binding site for oxygen in both myoglobin and hemoglobin. Fortunately, myoglobin has a greater attraction for oxygen than does hemoglobin, which allows efficient transfer of oxygen from the bloodstream to the cells of the body.

### Hemoglobin and Oxygen Transport

Hemoglobin (Hb) is a tetramer composed of four polypeptide subunits: two α-subunits and two β-subunits (Figure 18.13). Because each subunit of hemoglobin contains a heme group, a hemoglobin molecule can bind four molecules of oxygen:

$$Hb \quad + \quad 4O_2 \quad \longrightarrow \quad Hb(O_2)_4$$

Deoxyhemoglobin                 Oxyhemoglobin

The oxygenation of hemoglobin in the lungs and the transfer of oxygen from hemoglobin to myoglobin in the tissues are very complex processes. We begin our investigation of these events with the inhalation of a breath of air.

The oxygenation of hemoglobin in the lungs is greatly favored by differences in the oxygen partial pressure ($pO_2$) in the lungs and in the blood. The $pO_2$ in the

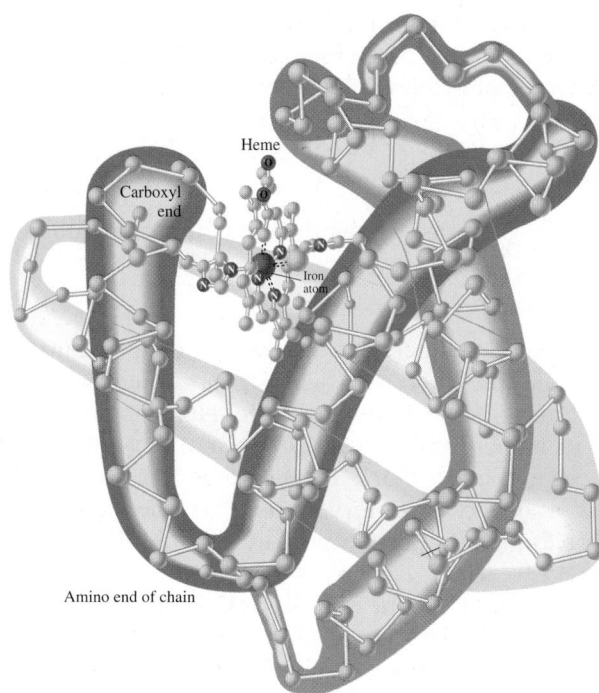

**Figure 18.11** Myoglobin. The heme group has an iron atom to which oxygen binds.

**Figure 18.12** Structure of the heme prosthetic group, which binds to myoglobin and hemoglobin.

air in the lungs is approximately 100 millimeters of mercury (mm Hg); the $pO_2$ in oxygen-depleted blood is only about 40 mm Hg. Oxygen diffuses from the region of high $pO_2$ in the lungs to the region of low $pO_2$ in the blood. There it enters red blood cells and binds to the $Fe^{2+}$ ions of the heme groups of deoxyhemoglobin, forming oxyhemoglobin. This binding actually helps bring more $O_2$ into the blood.

## Oxygen Transport from Mother to Fetus

A fetus receives its oxygen from its mother by simple diffusion across the placenta. If both the fetus and the mother had the same type of hemoglobin, this transfer process would not be efficient, because the hemoglobin of the fetus and the mother would have the same affinity for oxygen. The fetus, however, has a unique type of hemoglobin, called *fetal hemoglobin*. This unique hemoglobin molecule has a greater affinity for oxygen than does the mother's hemoglobin. Oxygen is therefore efficiently transported, via the circulatory system, from the lungs of

**Hemoglobin**
▨ α-chains
▨ β-chains
■ Heme groups

**Figure 18.13** Structure of hemoglobin. The protein contains four subunits, designated α and β. The α- and β-subunits face each other across a central cavity. Each subunit in the tetramer contains a heme group that binds oxygen.

the mother to the fetus. The biosynthesis of fetal hemoglobin stops shortly after birth when the genes encoding fetal hemoglobin are switched "off" and the genes coding for adult hemoglobin are switched "on."

**Question 18.7**   Why is oxygen efficiently transferred from hemoglobin in the blood to myoglobin in the muscles?

**Question 18.8**   How is oxygen efficiently transferred from mother to fetus?

## Sickle Cell Anemia

*The genetic basis of this alteration is discussed in Chapter 20.*

When hemoglobin is carrying $O_2$, it is called oxyhemoglobin. When it is not bound to $O_2$, it is called deoxyhemoglobin.

**Figure 18.14** Scanning electron micrographs of normal and sickled red blood cells.

**Sickle cell anemia** is a human genetic disease that first appeared in tropical west and central Africa. It afflicts about 0.4% of African Americans. These individuals produce a mutant hemoglobin known as sickle cell hemoglobin (Hb S). Sickle cell anemia receives its name from the sickled appearance of the red blood cells that form in this condition (Figure 18.14). The sickled cells are unable to pass through the small capillaries of the circulatory system, and circulation is hindered. This results in damage to many organs, especially bone and kidney, and can lead to death at an early age.

Sickle cell hemoglobin differs from normal hemoglobin by a single amino acid. In the β-chain of sickle cell hemoglobin, a valine (a hydrophobic amino acid) has replaced a glutamic acid (a negatively charged amino acid). This substitution provides a basis for the binding of hemoglobin S molecules to one another. When oxyhemoglobin S unloads its oxygen, individual deoxyhemoglobin S molecules bind to one another as long polymeric fibers. This occurs because the valine fits into a hydrophobic pocket on the surface of a second deoxyhemoglobin S molecule. The fibers generated in this way radically alter the shape of the red blood cell, resulting in the sickling effect.

Sickle cell anemia occurs in individuals who have inherited the gene for sickle cell hemoglobin from both parents. Afflicted individuals produce 90–100% defective β-chains. Individuals who inherit one normal gene and one defective gene produce both normal and altered β-chains. About 10% of African Americans carry a single copy of the defective gene, a condition known as *sickle cell trait*. Although not severely affected, they have a 50% chance of passing the gene to each of their children.

An interesting relationship exists between sickle cell trait and resistance to malaria. In some parts of Africa, up to 20% of the population has sickle cell trait. In those same parts of Africa, one of the leading causes of death is malaria. The presence of sickle cell trait is linked to an increased resistance to malaria because the malarial parasite cannot feed efficiently on sickled red blood cells. People who have sickle cell disease die young; those without sickle cell trait have a high probability of succumbing to malaria. Occupying the middle ground, people who have sickle cell trait do not suffer much from sickle cell anemia and simultaneously resist deadly malaria. Because those with sickle cell trait have a greater chance of survival and reproduction, the sickle cell hemoglobin gene is maintained in the population.

## 18.9   Proteins in the Blood

The blood plasma of a healthy individual typically contains 60–80 grams per liter (g/L) of protein. This protein can be separated into five classes designated α through γ. The separation is based on the overall surface charge on each of the types of protein.

## 18.9 Proteins in the Blood

▶ Blood plasma contains 60–80 g/L of protein.

▶ These proteins can be separated into five classes designated α through γ.

▶ Albumin is the most abundant protein in the blood (55%).

▶ The α-globulins and β-globulins each make up 13% of the blood proteins.

▶ Fibrinogen comprises 7% of the blood proteins.

▶ The remaining proteins in the blood are the γ-globulins.

## 18.10 Denaturation of Proteins

▶ Heat disrupts the hydrogen bonds and hydrophobic interactions that maintain protein structure, causing the protein to unfold and lose its organized structure. This is **denaturation**.

▶ **Coagulation,** or clumping, occurs when the protein chains unfold and become entangled. When this happens, the protein is no longer water-soluble.

▶ Changes in pH interfere with ionic bridges and hydrogen bonds that stabilize and maintain tertiary structure.

## 18.11 Dietary Protein and Protein Digestion

▶ **Essential amino acids** must be acquired in the diet.

▶ **Nonessential amino acids** can be synthesized by the body.

▶ **Complete proteins** contain all the essential and nonessential amino acids.

▶ **Incomplete proteins** are missing one or more essential amino acids.

▶ Protein digestion begins in the stomach, where proteins are degraded by pepsin.

▶ Further digestion occurs in the small intestine by enzymes such as trypsin and chymotrypsin.

## ANSWERS TO PRACTICE PROBLEMS

**18.1 a.** Methionyl-leucyl-cysteine

b. Tyrosyl-seryl-histidine

c. Arginyl-isoleucyl-glutamine

## QUESTIONS AND PROBLEMS

### Introduction to Protein Functions

#### Foundations

**18.13** Define the term *enzyme.*
**18.14** Define the term *antibody.*
**18.15** What is a transport protein?
**18.16** What are the functions of structural proteins?

#### Applications

**18.17** Of what significance are enzymes in the cell?
**18.18** How do antibodies protect us against infection?
**18.19** List two transport proteins and describe their significance to the organism.
**18.20** What is the function of regulatory proteins?
**18.21** Provide two examples of nutrient proteins.
**18.22** Provide two examples of proteins that are required for movement.

### Protein Building Blocks: The α-Amino Acids

#### Foundations

**18.23** Describe the basic general structure of an L-α-amino acid and draw its structure.
**18.24** Draw the D- and L-isomers of valine. Which would you expect to find in nature?

**18.25** What is a zwitterion?

**18.26** Why are amino acids zwitterions at pH 7.0?

### Applications

**18.27** What is a chiral carbon?

**18.28** Why are all of the α-amino acids except glycine chiral?

**18.29** What is the importance of the R groups of the amino acids?

**18.30** Describe the classification of the R groups of the amino acids, and provide an example of each class.

**18.31** Write the structures of the six amino acids that have polar, neutral side chains.

**18.32** Write the structures of the positively charged amino acids. Indicate whether you would expect to find each on the surface or buried in a globular protein.

## The Peptide Bond

### Foundations

**18.33** Define the term *peptide bond.*

**18.34** What type of bond is the peptide bond? Explain why the peptide bond is rigid.

**18.35** What observations led Linus Pauling and his colleagues to hypothesize that the peptide bond exists as a resonance hybrid?

**18.36** Draw the resonance hybrids that represent the peptide bond.

### Applications

**18.37** Write the structure of each of the following peptides:
   **a.** Phe-val-tyr
   **b.** Ala-glu-cys
   **c.** Asn-leu-gly

**18.38** Write the structure of each of the following peptides:
   **a.** Lys-trp-pro
   **b.** Gln-ser-his
   **c.** Arg-met-asp

## The Primary Structure of Proteins

### Foundations

**18.39** Define the *primary structure* of a protein.

**18.40** What type of bond joins the amino acids to one another in the primary structure of a protein?

### Applications

**18.41** How does the primary structure of a protein determine its three-dimensional shape and biological function?

**18.42** Explain the relationship between the primary structure of a protein and the gene for that protein.

**18.43** Write a balanced equation showing peptide bond formation between leucine and arginine.

**18.44** Write a balanced equation showing peptide bond formation between threonine and aspartate.

## The Secondary Structure of Proteins

### Foundations

**18.45** Define the secondary structure of a protein.

**18.46** What are the two most common types of secondary structure?

### Applications

**18.47** What type of secondary structure is characteristic of:
   **a.** The α-keratins?
   **b.** Silk fibroin?

**18.48** Describe the forces that maintain the two types of secondary structure: α-helix and β-pleated sheet.

**18.49** Define fibrous proteins.

**18.50** What is the relationship between the structure of fibrous proteins and their functions?

**18.51** Describe a parallel β-pleated sheet.

**18.52** Compare a parallel β-pleated sheet to an antiparallel β-pleated sheet.

## The Tertiary Structure of Proteins

### Foundations

**18.53** Define the tertiary structure of a protein.

**18.54** Use examples of specific amino acids to show the variety of weak interactions that maintain tertiary protein structure.

### Applications

**18.55** Write the structure of the amino acid produced by the oxidation of cysteine.

**18.56** What is the role of cystine in maintaining protein structure?

**18.57** Explain the relationship between the secondary and tertiary protein structures.

**18.58** Why is the amino acid proline often found in the random coil hinge regions of the tertiary structure?

## The Quaternary Structure of Proteins

### Foundations

**18.59** Describe the quaternary structure of proteins.

**18.60** What weak interactions are responsible for maintaining quaternary protein structure?

### Applications

**18.61** What is a glycoprotein?

**18.62** What is a prosthetic group?

## An Overview of Protein Structure and Function

### Applications

**18.63** Why is hydrogen bonding so important to protein structure?

**18.64** Explain why α-keratins that have many disulfide bonds between adjacent polypeptide chains are much less elastic and much harder than those without disulfide bonds.

**18.65** How does the structure of the peptide bond make the structure of proteins relatively rigid?

**18.66** The primary structure of a protein known as histone H4, which tightly binds DNA, is identical in all mammals and differs by only one amino acid between the calf and pea seedlings. What does this extraordinary conservation of primary structure imply about the importance of that one amino acid?

**18.67** What does it mean to say that the structure of proteins is genetically determined?

**18.68** Explain why genetic mutations that result in the replacement of one amino acid with another can lead to the formation of a protein that cannot carry out its biological function.

## Myoglobin and Hemoglobin

### Foundations

**18.69** What is the function of hemoglobin?
**18.70** What is the function of myoglobin?
**18.71** Describe the structure of hemoglobin.
**18.72** Describe the structure of myoglobin.
**18.73** What is the function of heme in hemoglobin and myoglobin?
**18.74** Write an equation representing the binding to and release of oxygen from hemoglobin.

### Applications

**18.75** Carbon monoxide binds tightly to the heme groups of hemoglobin and myoglobin. How does this affinity reflect the toxicity of carbon monoxide?
**18.76** The blood of the horseshoe crab is blue because of the presence of a protein called *hemocyanin*. What is the function of hemocyanin?
**18.77** Why does replacement of glutamic acid with valine alter hemoglobin and ultimately result in sickle cell anemia?
**18.78** How do sickled red blood cells hinder circulation?
**18.79** What is the difference between sickle cell disease and sickle cell trait?
**18.80** How is it possible for sickle cell trait to confer a survival benefit on the person who possesses it?

## Proteins in the Blood

### Foundations

**18.81** What is the most abundant protein in the blood?
**18.82** List the functions of several α-globulins.

### Applications

**18.83** Develop a hypothesis to explain why albumin in the blood can serve as a nonspecific carrier for such diverse substances as bilirubin, $Ca^{2+}$, and fatty acids. (*Hint:* Consider what you know about the structures of amino acid R groups.)
**18.84** Fibrinogen and prothrombin are both involved in formation of blood clots when they are converted into proteolytic enzymes. However, they are normally found in the blood in an inactive form. Develop an explanation for this observation.

## Denaturation of Proteins

### Foundations

**18.85** Define the term *denaturation*.
**18.86** What is the difference between denaturation and coagulation?

### Applications

**18.87** Why is heat an effective means of sterilization?
**18.88** As you increase the temperature of an enzyme-catalyzed reaction, the rate of the reaction initially increases. It then reaches a maximum rate and finally dramatically declines. Keeping in mind that enzymes are proteins, how do you explain these changes in reaction rate?

**18.89** Yogurt is produced from milk by the action of dairy bacteria. These bacteria produce lactic acid as a by-product of their metabolism. The pH decrease causes the milk proteins to coagulate. Why are food preservatives not required to inhibit the growth of bacteria in yogurt?
**18.90** Wine is made from the juice of grapes by varieties of yeast. The yeast cells produce ethanol as a by-product of their fermentation. However, when the ethanol concentration reaches 12–13%, all the yeast die. Explain this observation.

## Dietary Protein and Protein Digestion

### Foundations

**18.91** Define the term *essential amino acid*.
**18.92** Define the term *nonessential amino acid*.
**18.93** Define the term *complete protein*.
**18.94** Define the term *incomplete protein*.

### Applications

**18.95** Write an equation representing the action of the proteolytic enzyme chymotrypsin. (*Hint:* In order to write the structure of a dipeptide that would be an appropriate reactant, you must consider what is known about where chymotrypsin cleaves a protein chain.)
**18.96** Write an equation representing the action of the proteolytic enzyme trypsin. (*Hint:* In order to write the structure of a dipeptide that would be an appropriate reactant, you must consider what is known about where trypsin cleaves a protein chain.)
**18.97** Why is it necessary to mix vegetable proteins to provide an adequate vegetarian diet?
**18.98** Name some ethnic foods that apply the principle of mixing vegetable proteins to provide all of the essential amino acids.
**18.99** Why must synthesis of digestive enzymes be carefully controlled?
**18.100** What is the relationship between pepsin and pepsinogen?

## CRITICAL THINKING PROBLEMS

1. Calculate the length of an α-helical polypeptide that is twenty amino acids long. Calculate the length of a region of antiparallel β-pleated sheet that is forty amino acids long.
2. Proteins involved in transport of molecules or ions into or out of cells are found in the membranes of all cells. They are classified as transmembrane proteins because some regions are embedded within the lipid bilayer, whereas other regions protrude into the cytoplasm or outside the cell. Review the classification of amino acids based on the properties of their R groups. What type of amino acids would you expect

to find in the regions of the proteins embedded within the membrane? What type of amino acids would you expect to find on the surface of the regions in the cytoplasm or that protrude outside the cell?

3.  A biochemist is trying to purify the enzyme hexokinase from a bacterium that normally grows in the Arctic Ocean at 5° C. In the next lab, a graduate student is trying to purify the same protein from a bacterium that grows in the vent of a volcano at 98° C. To maintain the structure of the protein from the Arctic bacterium, the first biochemist must carry out all her purification procedures at refrigerator temperatures. The second biochemist must perform all his experiments in a warm room incubator. In molecular terms, explain why the same kind of enzyme from organisms with different optimal temperatures for growth can have such different thermal properties.

4.  The α-keratin of hair is rich in the amino acid cysteine. The location of these cysteines in the protein chain is genetically determined; as a result of the location of the cysteines in the protein, a person may have curly, wavy, or straight hair. How can the location of cysteines in α-keratin result in these different styles of hair? Propose a hypothesis to explain how a "perm" causes straight hair to become curly.

5.  Calculate the number of different pentapeptides you can make in which the amino acids phenylalanine, glycine, serine, leucine, and histidine are each found. Imagine how many proteins could be made from the twenty amino acids commonly found in proteins.

# Enzymes

## LEARNING GOALS

1 Classify enzymes according to the type of reaction catalyzed and the type of specificity.

2 Give examples of the correlation between an enzyme's common name and its function.

3 Describe the effect that enzymes have on the activation energy of a reaction.

4 Explain the effect of substrate concentration on enzyme-catalyzed reactions.

5 Discuss the role of the active site and the importance of enzyme specificity.

6 Describe the difference between the lock-and-key model and the induced fit model of enzyme-substrate complex formation.

7 Discuss the roles of cofactors and coenzymes in enzyme activity.

8 Explain how pH and temperature affect the rate of an enzyme-catalyzed reaction.

9 Describe the mechanisms used by cells to regulate enzyme activity.

10 Discuss the mechanisms by which certain chemicals inhibit enzyme activity.

11 Discuss the role of the enzyme chymotrypsin and other serine proteases.

12 Provide examples of medical uses of enzymes.

A hot-spring-fed lake at Yellowstone National Park. Explain how bacteria can thrive at temperatures near the boiling point of water.

## OUTLINE

# INTRODUCTION

Imagine the earth about four billion years ago: it was young then, not even a billion years old. Beginning as a red-hot molten sphere, slowly the earth's surface had cooled and become solid rock. But the interior, still extremely hot, erupted through the crust, spewing hot gases and lava. Eventually these eruptions produced craggy landmasses and an atmosphere composed of gases like hydrogen, carbon dioxide, ammonia, and water vapor. As the water vapor cooled, it condensed into liquid water, forming ponds and shallow seas.

At the dawn of biological life, the surface of the earth was still very hot and covered with rocky peaks and hot shallow oceans. The atmosphere was not very inviting either—filled with noxious gases and containing no molecular oxygen. Yet this is the environment where life on our planet began.

Some scientists think that they have found bacteria—living fossils—that may be very closely related to the first inhabitants of earth. These bacteria thrive at temperatures higher than the boiling point of water. Some need only $H_2$, $CO_2$, and $H_2O$ for their metabolic processes and they quickly die in the presence of molecular oxygen.

But this lifestyle raises some uncomfortable questions. For instance, how do these bacteria survive at these extreme temperatures that would cook the life-forms with which we are more familiar? Researcher Mike Adams of the University of Georgia has found some of the answers. Adams and his students have studied the structure of an enzyme from one of these extraordinary bacteria. He found that the three-dimensional structure of the super-hot enzymes is held together by many more attractive forces than the structure of the low-temperature version of the same enzyme. Thus these proteins are stable and functional even at temperatures above the boiling point of water.

In Chapter 18 we studied the structure and properties of proteins. We are now going to apply that knowledge to the study of a group of proteins that do the majority of the work for the cell. These special proteins, the **enzymes,** catalyze the biochemical reactions that break down food molecules to allow the cell to harvest energy. They also catalyze the biosynthetic reactions that produce the molecules required for cellular life. In this chapter we will study the properties of this extraordinary group of proteins and learn how they dramatically speed up biochemical reactions.

The enzymes discussed in this chapter are proteins; however, several ribonucleic acid (RNA) molecules have been demonstrated to have the ability to catalyze biological reactions. These are called *ribozymes.*

## LEARNING GOAL

**1**  Classify enzymes according to the type of reaction catalyzed and the type of specificity.

*Recall that redox reactions involve electron transfer from one substance to another (Section 8.5).*

## 19.1    Nomenclature and Classification

### Classification of Enzymes

Enzymes may be classified according to the type of reaction that they catalyze. The six classes are as follows.

### Oxidoreductases

**Oxidoreductases** are enzymes that catalyze oxidation–reduction (redox) reactions. *Lactate dehydrogenase* is an oxidoreductase that removes hydrogen from a molecule of lactate. Other subclasses of the oxidoreductases include oxidases and reductases.

$$\underset{\text{Lactate}}{\overset{\displaystyle COO^-}{\underset{\displaystyle CH_3}{HO-\overset{|}{\underset{|}{C}}-H}} + NAD^+} \xrightleftharpoons{\text{Lactate dehydrogenase}} \underset{\text{Pyruvate}}{\overset{\displaystyle COO^-}{\underset{\displaystyle CH_3}{\overset{|}{\underset{|}{C}}=O}} + NADH}$$

## Transferases

**Transferases** are enzymes that catalyze the transfer of functional groups from one molecule to another. For example, a *transaminase* catalyzes the transfer of an amino functional group, and a *kinase* catalyzes the transfer of a phosphate group. Kinases play a major role in energy-harvesting processes involving ATP. In the adrenal glands, norepinephrine is converted to epinephrine by the enzyme *phenylethanolamine-N-methyltransferase* (PNMT), a *transmethylase*.

*The significance of phosphate group transfers in energy metabolism is discussed in Sections 21.1 and 21.3.*

Methyl
group + HO—⬡—CHCH$_2$NH$_2$ $\underset{PNMT}{\rightleftharpoons}$ HO—⬡—CHCH$_2$NH—CH$_3$
donor       OH       OH
     HO           HO

Norepinephrine           Epinephrine

## Hydrolases

**Hydrolases** catalyze hydrolysis reactions, that is, the addition of a water molecule to a bond, resulting in bond breakage. These reactions are important in the digestive process. For example, lipases catalyze the hydrolysis of the ester bonds in triglycerides:

These kittens are adorable, but there is nothing lovely about the aroma of an untended kitty litter box. Urease, a hydrolase, catalyzes the reaction responsible for this smell. Write an equation representing the reaction catalyzed by urease and identify the offending molecule.

$$
\begin{array}{l}
\text{CH}_2\text{—O—}\overset{\text{O}}{\overset{\|}{\text{C}}}\text{(CH}_2)_n\text{CH}_3 \\[4pt]
\text{CH—O—}\overset{\text{O}}{\overset{\|}{\text{C}}}\text{(CH}_2)_n\text{CH}_3 \quad + 3\text{H}_2\text{O} \quad \xrightarrow{\text{Lipase}} \\[4pt]
\text{CH}_2\text{—O—}\overset{\text{O}}{\overset{\|}{\text{C}}}\text{(CH}_2)_n\text{CH}_3
\end{array}
\qquad
\begin{array}{l}
\text{CH}_2\text{OH} \\
\text{CHOH} \quad + \; 3\text{CH}_3\text{(CH}_2)_n\text{COOH} \\
\text{CH}_2\text{OH} \;\cdot
\end{array}
$$

Triglyceride                 Glycerol      Fatty acids

## Lyases

**Lyases** catalyze the addition of a group to a double bond or the removal of a group to form a double bond. *Fumarase* is an example of a lyase. In the citric acid cycle, fumarase catalyzes the addition of a water molecule to the double bond of the substrate fumarate. The product is malate.

*Hydrolysis of esters is described in Section 14.2. The action of lipases in digestion is discussed in Section 23.1.*

$$
\begin{array}{c}
\text{COO}^- \\
\text{C—H} \\
\|\\
\text{H—C} \\
\text{COO}^-
\end{array}
\quad + \text{H}_2\text{O} \quad \xrightarrow{\text{Fumarase}} \quad
\begin{array}{c}
\text{COO}^- \\
\text{HO—C—H} \\
\text{H—C—H} \\
\text{COO}^-
\end{array}
$$

Fumarate                   Malate

*The reactions of the citric acid cycle are described in Section 22.4.*

    *Citrate lyase* catalyzes a far more complicated reaction in which we see the removal of a group and formation of a double bond. Specifically, citrate lyase catalyzes the removal of an acetyl group from a molecule of citrate. The products of this reaction include oxaloacetate, acetyl CoA, ADP, and an inorganic phosphate group ($P_i$):

$$\begin{array}{c}COO^- \\ | \\ CH_2 \\ | \\ ^-OOC-C-OH \\ | \\ CH_2 \\ | \\ COO^-\end{array} + ATP + Coenzyme\ A + H_2O \xrightarrow{\text{Citrate lyase}}$$

Citrate

$$\begin{array}{c}COO^- \\ | \\ CH_2 \\ | \\ C=O \\ | \\ COO^-\end{array} + CH_3-\overset{O}{\underset{\|}{C}}\sim S-CoA + ADP + P_i$$

Oxaloacetate      Acetyl CoA

*This reaction is important in glycolysis, an energy-harvesting pathway described in Chapter 21.*

## Isomerases

**Isomerases** rearrange the functional groups within a molecule and catalyze the conversion of one isomer into another. For example, *phosphoglycerate mutase* converts one structural isomer, 3-phosphoglycerate, into another, 2-phosphoglycerate:

3-Phosphoglycerate                2-Phosphoglycerate

## Ligases

*The use of DNA ligase in recombinant DNA studies is detailed in Section 20.8.*

**Ligases** are enzymes that catalyze a reaction in which a C—C, C—S, C—O, or C—N bond is made or broken. This is accompanied by an ATP-ADP interconversion. For example, *DNA ligase* catalyzes the joining of the hydroxyl group of a nucleotide in a DNA strand with the phosphoryl group of the adjacent nucleotide to form a phosphoester bond:

## Nomenclature of Enzymes

The common names for some enzymes are derived from the name of the **substrate**, the reactant that binds to the enzyme and is converted into product. In many cases, the name of the enzyme is simply derived by adding the suffix -*ase* to the name of the substrate. For instance, *urease* catalyzes the hydrolysis of urea and *lactase* catalyzes the hydrolysis of the disaccharide lactose.

**EXAMPLE 19.1** **Classifying Enzymes According to the Type of Reaction That They Catalyze**

Classify the enzyme that catalyzes each of the following reactions, and explain your reasoning.

Alanyl-glycine    Alanine    Glycine

**Solution**

The reaction occurring here involves breaking a bond, in this case a peptide bond, by adding a water molecule. The enzyme is classified as a *hydrolase*, specifically a *peptidase*.

Glucose    Adenosine triphosphate    Glucose-6-phosphate    Adenosine diphosphate

**Solution**

This is the first reaction in the biochemical pathway called *glycolysis*. A phosphoryl group is transferred from a donor molecule, adenosine triphosphate, to the recipient molecule, glucose. The products are glucose-6-phosphate and adenosine diphosphate. This enzyme, called *hexokinase*, is an example of a *transferase*.

Malate    Oxaloacetate

**Solution**

In this reaction, the reactant malate is oxidized and the coenzyme $NAD^+$ is reduced. The enzyme that catalyzes this reaction, *malate dehydrogenase*, is an *oxidoreductase*.

Dihydroxyacetone phosphate    Glyceraldehyde-3-phosphate

*Continued...*

**Solution**

Careful inspection of the structure of the reactant and the product reveals that they each have the same number of carbon, hydrogen, oxygen, and phosphorus atoms; thus, they must be structural isomers. The enzyme must be an *isomerase*. Its name is *triose phosphate isomerase*.

---

**Practice Problem 19.1**

To which class of enzymes does each of the following belong?

a. Pyruvate kinase    d. Pyruvate dehydrogenase    g. Lipase

b. Alanine transaminase    e. Lactase    h. Acetoacetate decarboxylase

c. Triose phosphate isomerase    f. Phosphofructokinase    i. Succinate dehydrogenase

▶ For Further Practice: **Questions 19.23 and 19.25.**

---

Names of other enzymes reflect the type of reaction that they catalyze. *Dehydrogenases* catalyze the removal of hydrogen atoms from a substrate, while *decarboxylases* catalyze the removal of carboxyl groups. *Hydrogenases* and *carboxylases* carry out the opposite reaction, adding hydrogen atoms or carboxyl groups to their substrates.

Thus, the common name of an enzyme often tells us a great deal about the function of an enzyme. Yet other enzymes have historical names that have no relationship to either the substrates or the reactions that they catalyze. A few examples include catalase, trypsin, pepsin, and chymotrypsin. In these cases, the names of the enzymes and the reactions that they catalyze must simply be memorized.

The systematic names for enzymes tell us the substrate, the type of reaction that is catalyzed, and the name of any coenzyme that is required. For instance, the systematic name of the oxidoreductase lactate dehydrogenase is lactate: NAD oxidoreductase.

*Coenzymes are molecules required by some enzymes to serve as donors or acceptors of electrons, hydrogen atoms, or other functional groups during a chemical reaction. Coenzymes are discussed in Section 19.7.*

**Question 19.1**  Write an equation representing the reaction catalyzed by each of the enzymes listed in Practice Problem 19.1a through d at the end of Example 19.1. (*Hint:* You may need to refer to the index of this book to learn more about the substrates and the reactions that are catalyzed.)

**Question 19.2**  Write an equation representing the reaction catalyzed by each of the enzymes listed in Practice Problem 19.1e through i at the end of Example 19.1. (*Hint:* You may need to refer to the index of this book to learn more about the substrates and the reactions that are catalyzed.)

**Question 19.3**  What is the substrate for each of the following enzymes?
a. Sucrase
b. Pyruvate decarboxylase
c. Succinate dehydrogenase

**Question 19.4**  What chemical reaction is mediated by each of the enzymes in Question 19.3?

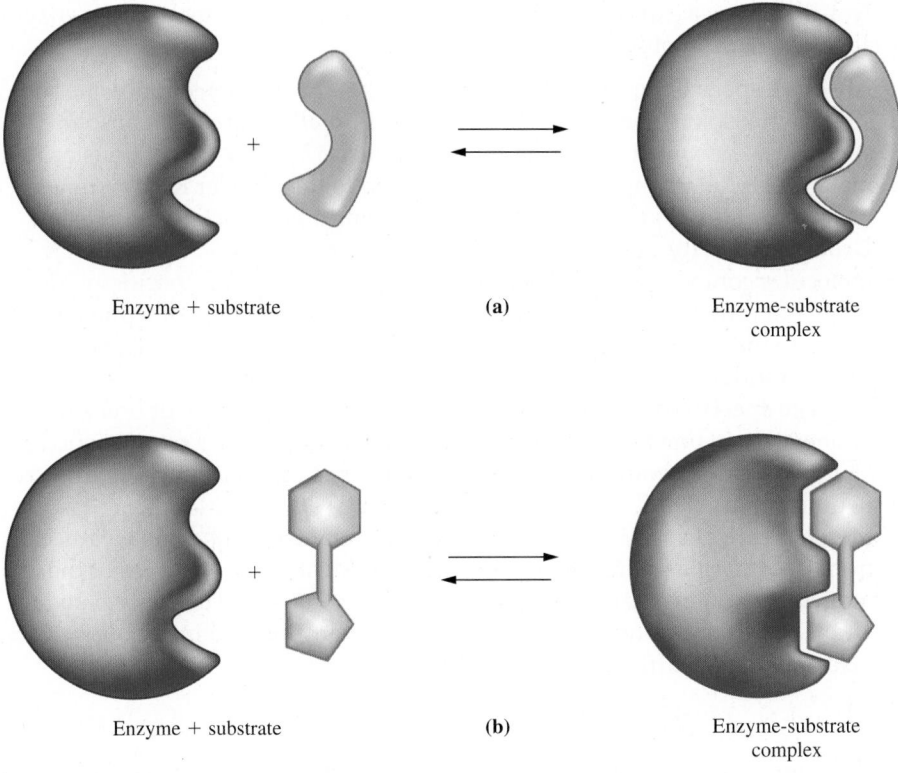

**Figure 19.3** (a) The lock-and-key model of enzyme-substrate binding assumes that the enzyme active site has a rigid structure that is precisely complementary in shape and charge distribution to the substrate. (b) The induced fit model of enzyme-substrate binding. As the enzyme binds to the substrate, the shape of the active site conforms precisely to the shape of the substrate. The shape of the substrate may also change.

**Question 19.5** Compare the lock-and-key and induced fit models of enzyme-substrate binding.

**Question 19.6** What is the relationship between an enzyme active site and its substrate?

## 19.5 Specificity of the Enzyme-Substrate Complex

For an enzyme-substrate interaction to occur, the surfaces of the enzyme and substrate must be complementary. It is this requirement for a specific fit that determines whether an enzyme will bind to a particular substrate and carry out a chemical reaction.

**Enzyme specificity** is the ability of an enzyme to bind only one, or a very few, substrates and thus catalyze only a single reaction. To illustrate the specificity of enzymes, consider the following reactions.

The enzyme urease catalyzes the hydrolysis of urea to carbon dioxide and ammonia as follows:

$$\underset{\text{Urea}}{H_2N-\overset{\overset{\displaystyle O}{\|}}{C}-NH_2} + H_2O \xrightarrow{\text{Urease}} CO_2 + 2NH_3$$

Methylurea, in contrast, though structurally similar to urea, is not affected by urease:

$$\underset{\text{Methylurea}}{H_2N-\overset{\overset{\displaystyle O}{\|}}{C}-NHCH_3} + H_2O \xrightarrow{\text{Urease}} \text{no reaction}$$

**LEARNING GOAL**

**5** Discuss the role of the active site and the importance of enzyme specificity.

*Aminoacyl tRNA synthetases are discussed in Section 20.6. Aminoacyl group transfer reactions were described in Section 15.4.*

*Hexokinase activity is described in Section 21.3.*

*Proteolytic enzymes are discussed in Section 19.11.*

Not all enzymes exhibit the same degree of specificity. Four classes of enzyme specificity have been observed.

- **Absolute specificity:** An enzyme that catalyzes the reaction of only one substrate has absolute specificity. *Aminoacyl tRNA synthetases* exhibit absolute specificity. Each must attach the correct amino acid to the correct transfer RNA molecule. If the wrong amino acid is attached to the transfer RNA, it may be mistakenly added to a peptide chain, producing a nonfunctional protein.
- **Group specificity:** An enzyme that catalyzes processes involving similar molecules containing the same functional group has group specificity. *Hexokinase* is a group-specific enzyme that catalyzes the addition of a phosphoryl group to the hexose sugar glucose in the first step of glycolysis. Hexokinase can also add a phosphoryl group to several other six-carbon sugars.
- **Linkage specificity:** An enzyme that catalyzes the formation or breakage of only certain bonds in a molecule has linkage specificity. *Proteases,* such as trypsin, chymotrypsin, and elastase, are enzymes that selectively hydrolyze peptide bonds. Thus, these enzymes are linkage specific.
- **Stereochemical specificity:** An enzyme that can distinguish one enantiomer from the other has stereochemical specificity. Most of the enzymes of the human body show stereochemical specificity. Because we use only D-sugars and L-amino acids, the enzymes involved in digestion and metabolism recognize only those particular stereoisomers.

## 19.6  The Transition State and Product Formation

How does enzyme-substrate binding result in a faster chemical reaction? To answer this question, we must once again look at the steps of an enzyme-catalyzed reaction, focusing on the steps highlighted in blue:

$$E + S \overset{\text{Step I}}{\rightleftarrows} ES \overset{\text{Step II}}{\rightleftarrows} ES^* \overset{\text{Step III}}{\rightleftarrows} EP \overset{\text{Step IV}}{\rightleftarrows} E + P$$

| Enzyme + substrate | Enzyme– substrate complex | Transition state | Enzyme– product complex | Enzyme + product |

After the formation of the enzyme-substrate complex in Step I, the flexible enzyme and substrate interact, changing the substrate into a configuration that is no longer energetically stable (Step II). This is the **transition state,** a state in which the substrate is in an intermediate form, having features of both the substrate and the product. This state favors conversion of the substrate into product (Step III) and release of the product (Step IV). Notice that the enzyme is completely unchanged by these events.

What kinds of transition state changes might occur in the substrate that would make a reaction proceed more rapidly?

1. The enzyme might put "stress" on a bond and thereby promote bond breakage, as in the example of sucrase. The enzyme catalyzes the hydrolysis of sucrose into glucose and fructose. The formation of the enzyme-substrate complex (Figures 19.4a and 19.4b) results in a change in the shape of the enzyme. This, in turn, may stretch or distort the bond between glucose and fructose, weakening the bond and allowing it to be broken much more easily than in the absence of the enzyme (Figure 19.4c through e).
2. An enzyme may facilitate a reaction by bringing two reactants into close proximity and in the proper orientation for reaction to occur. If we look at the reaction between glucose and fructose to produce sucrose (Figure 19.5a), we see that each of the sugars has five hydroxyl groups that could undergo condensation to produce a disaccharide. By random molecular collision there is a one in twenty-five chance that the two molecules will collide in the

**ANIMATION**
- Enzyme Action and the Hydrolysis of Sucrose

**Figure 19.4** Bond breakage is facilitated by the enzyme as a result of stress on a bond. (a, b) The enzyme-substrate complex is formed. (c) In the transition state, the enzyme changes shape and thereby puts stress on the glycosidic bond holding the two monosaccharides together. This lowers the energy of activation of this reaction. (d, e) The bond is broken, and the products are released.

**Figure 19.5** An enzyme may lower the energy of activation required for a reaction by holding the substrates in close proximity and in the correct orientation. (a) A condensation reaction between glucose and fructose to produce sucrose. (b) The enzyme-substrate complex forms, bringing the two monosaccharides together with the correct hydroxyl groups extended toward one another.

proper orientation to produce sucrose. The probability that the two will react is actually much less than that because at body temperature, most molecular collisions will not have enough energy to overcome the energy of activation, even if the molecules are in the proper orientation. The enzyme can bring the two molecules close together in the correct alignment (Figure 19.5b), forming the transition state and greatly speeding up the reaction.

# A MEDICAL PERSPECTIVE

## HIV Protease Inhibitors and Pharmaceutical Drug Design

In 1981 the Centers for Disease Control in Atlanta, Georgia, recognized a new disease syndrome, acquired immune deficiency syndrome (AIDS). The syndrome is characterized by an impaired immune system, a variety of opportunistic infections and cancer, and brain damage that results in dementia. It soon became apparent that the disease was being transmitted by blood and blood products, as well as by sexual contact.

The earliest drugs that proved effective in the treatment of human immunodeficiency virus (HIV) infections all inhibited replication of the genetic material of the virus. While these treatments were initially effective, prolonging the lives of many, it was not long before viral mutants resistant to these drugs began to appear. Clearly, a new approach was needed.

In 1989 a group of scientists revealed the three-dimensional structure of the HIV protease. This structure is shown in the accompanying figure. This enzyme is necessary for viral replication because the virus has an unusual strategy for making all of its proteins. Rather than make each protein individually, it makes large "polyproteins" that must then be cut by the HIV protease to form the final proteins required for viral replication.

Since scientists realized that this enzyme was essential for HIV replication, they decided to engineer a substance that would inhibit the enzyme by binding irreversibly to the active site, in essence plugging it up. The challenge, then, was to design a molecule that would be the plug. Researchers knew the primary structure (amino acid sequence) of the HIV protease from earlier nucleic acid sequencing studies. By 1989 they also had a very complete picture of the three-dimensional nature of the molecule, which they had obtained by X-ray crystallography.

Putting all of this information into a sophisticated computer modeling program, they could look at the protease from any angle. They could see the location of each of the R groups of each of the amino acids in the active site. This kind of information allowed the scientists to design molecules that would be complementary to the shape and charge distribution of the enzyme active site—in other words, structural analogs of the normal protease substrate. It was not long before the scientists had produced several candidates for the HIV protease inhibitor.

But, there are many tests that a drug candidate must pass before it can be introduced into the market as safe and effective. Scientists had to show that the candidate drugs would bind effectively to the HIV protease and block its function, thereby inhibiting virus replication. Properties such as the solubility, the efficiency of absorption by the body, the period of activity in the body, and the toxicity of the drug candidates all had to be determined.

By 1996 there were three protease inhibitors available to combat HIV infection. There are currently seven of these drugs on the market. In many cases development and testing of a drug candidate can take up to 15 years. In the case of the first HIV protease inhibitors, the first three drugs were on the market in less than 8 years. This is a testament both to the urgent need for HIV treatments and to the technology available to attack the problem.

The human immunodeficiency virus protease.

### For Further Understanding

▶ What particular concerns would you have, as a medical researcher, about administering a drug that is a protease inhibitor?

▶ Often a protease inhibitor is prescribed along with an inhibitor of replication of the viral genetic material. Develop a hypothesis to explain this strategy.

3. The active site of an enzyme may modify the pH of the microenvironment surrounding the substrate. For instance, it may serve as a donor or an acceptor of $H^+$. This would cause a change in the pH in the vicinity of the substrate without disturbing the normal pH elsewhere in the cell.

**Question 19.7** Summarize three ways in which an enzyme might lower the energy of activation of a reaction.

**Question 19.8** What is the transition state in an enzyme-catalyzed reaction?

## 19.7 Cofactors and Coenzymes

In Section 18.6 we saw that some proteins require an additional nonprotein prosthetic group to function. The same is true of some enzymes. In this case, the polypeptide portion is called the **apoenzyme,** and the nonprotein group is called the **cofactor.** Together they form the active enzyme called the **holoenzyme.** Cofactors may be metal ions, organic compounds, or organometallic compounds, and must be bound to the enzyme to maintain the correct shape of the active site (Figure 19.6). Only when the cofactor is bound can the enzyme bind the substrate and catalyze the reaction.

Other enzymes require the temporary binding of a **coenzyme.** Such binding is generally mediated by weak interactions like hydrogen bonds. Coenzymes are organic molecules that serve as carriers of electrons or chemical groups. In chemical reactions, they may either donate groups to the substrate or accept groups that are removed from the substrate. The example in Figure 19.7 shows a coenzyme accepting a functional group from one substrate and donating it to the second substrate in a reaction catalyzed by a transferase.

Often coenzymes contain modified vitamins as part of their structure. A **vitamin** is an organic substance that is required in the diet in only small amounts. Of the water-soluble vitamins, only vitamin C has not been associated with a coenzyme. Table 19.1 is a summary of some coenzymes and the water-soluble vitamins from which they are made.

Nicotinamide adenine dinucleotide ($NAD^+$), shown in Figure 19.8, is an example of a coenzyme that is of critical importance in the oxidation reactions of the cellular energy-harvesting processes. $NAD^+$ can accept a hydride ion, a hydrogen atom with two electrons, from the substrate of these reactions. The substrate is oxidized, and the portion of $NAD^+$ that is derived from the vitamin *niacin* is reduced to produce NADH. The NADH subsequently yields the hydride ion to the first acceptor in an electron transport chain. This regenerates the $NAD^+$ and provides electrons for the production of ATP, the

LEARNING GOAL

**7** Discuss the roles of cofactors and coenzymes in enzyme activity.

**WATER-SOLUBLE VITAMINS**

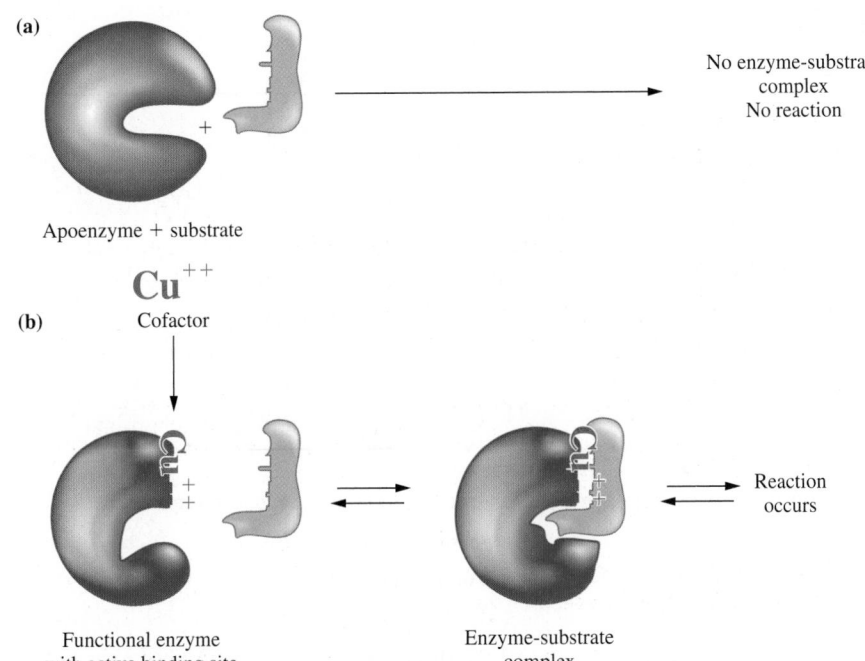

(a) Apoenzyme + substrate

No enzyme-substrate complex
No reaction

$Cu^{++}$

(b) Cofactor

Functional enzyme with active binding site

Enzyme-substrate complex

Reaction occurs

**Figure 19.6** (a) The apoenzyme is unable to bind to its substrate. (b) When the required cofactor, in this case a copper ion, $Cu^{2+}$, is available, it binds to the apoenzyme. Now the active site takes on the correct configuration, the enzyme-substrate complex forms, and the reaction occurs.

**Figure 19.7** Some enzymes require a coenzyme to facilitate the reaction.

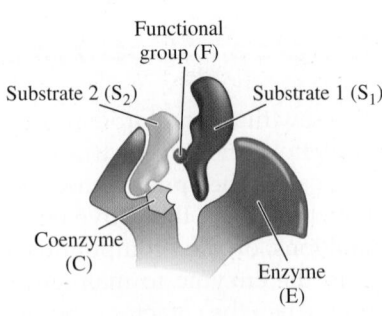

1. An enzyme with a coenzyme positioned to react with two substrates.

2. Coenzyme picks up a functional group from substrate 1.

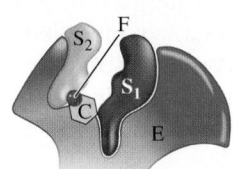

3. Coenzyme transfers the functional group to substrate 2.

4. Products are released from enzyme.

## TABLE 19.1 The Water-Soluble Vitamins and Their Coenzymes

| Vitamin | Coenzyme | Function |
|---|---|---|
| Thiamine ($B_1$) | Thiamine pyrophosphate | Decarboxylation reactions |
| Riboflavin ($B_2$) | Flavin mononucleotide (FMN) | Carrier of H atoms |
| | Flavin adenine dinucleotide (FAD) | |
| Niacin ($B_3$) | Nicotinamide adenine dinucleotide ($NAD^+$) | Carrier of hydride ions |
| | Nicotinamide adenine dinucleotide phosphate ($NADP^+$) | |
| Pyridoxine ($B_6$) | Pyridoxal phosphate | Carriers of amino and carboxyl groups |
| | Pyridoxamine phosphate | |
| Cyanocobalamin ($B_{12}$) | Deoxyadenosyl cobalamin | Coenzyme in amino acid metabolism |
| Folic acid | Tetrahydrofolic acid | Coenzyme for 1-C transfer |
| Pantothenic acid | Coenzyme A | Acyl group carrier |
| Biotin | Biocytin | Coenzyme in $CO_2$ fixation |
| Ascorbic acid | Unknown | Hydroxylation of proline and lysine in collagen |

Sarin

Serine in the acetylcholinesterase active site

HF

Sarin is covalently bonded to the serine in the active site.

Pyridine aldoxime methiodide (PAM)

Sarin is covalently bonded to the serine in the active site.

Complex formed between sarin and PAM

+ HO—| Regenerated enzyme

The covalent intermediate is stable, and acetylcholinesterase is therefore inactive, no longer able to break down acetylcholine. Nerve transmission continues, resulting in muscle spasm. Death may occur as a result of laryngeal spasm. Antidotes for poisoning by organophosphates, which include many insecticides and nerve gases, have been developed. The antidotes work by reversing the effects of the inhibitor. One of these antidotes is known as *PAM*, an acronym for *pyridine aldoxime methiodide*. This molecule displaces the organophosphate group from the active site of the enzyme, alleviating the effects of the poison.

**For Further Understanding**

▶ Botulinum toxin inhibits release of neurotransmitters from the presynaptic membrane. What symptoms do you predict would result from this?

▶ Why must $Na^+$ and $K^+$ enter and exit the cell through a protein channel?

the other hand, if the natural substrate is present in excess, it will more frequently occupy the active site, and there will be little inhibition.

The sulfa drugs, the first antimicrobics to be discovered, are **competitive inhibitors** of a bacterial enzyme needed for the synthesis of the vitamin folic acid. *Folic acid* is a vitamin required for the transfer of methyl groups in the biosynthesis of methionine and the nitrogenous bases required to make DNA and RNA. Humans cannot synthesize folic acid and must obtain it from the diet. Bacteria, on the other hand, must make folic acid because they cannot take it in from the environment.

*para*-Aminobenzoic acid (PABA) is the substrate for an early step in folic acid synthesis. The sulfa drugs, the prototype of which was discovered in the 1930s by

In addition to the folic acid supplied in the diet, we obtain folic acid from our intestinal bacteria.

**Figure 19.12** Competitive inhibition.

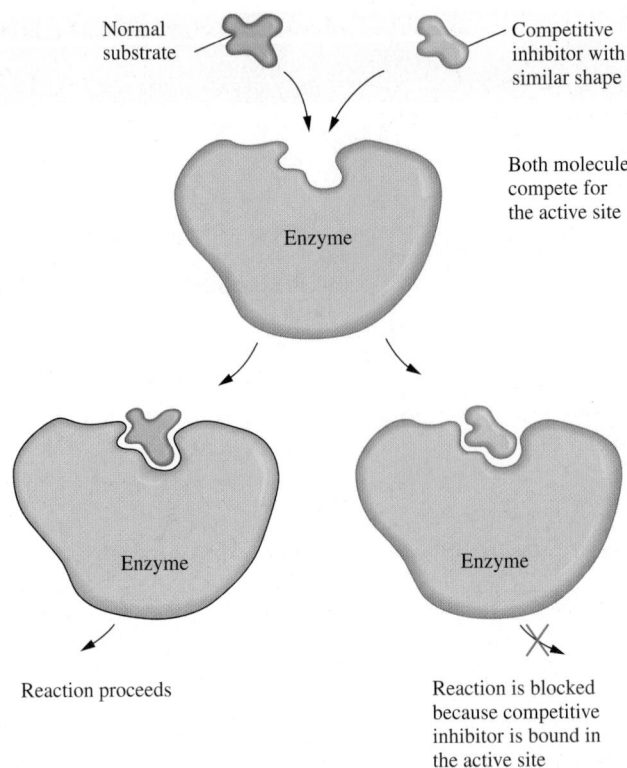

Gerhard Domagk, are structural analogs of PABA and thus competitive inhibitors of the enzyme that uses PABA as its normal substrate.

*p*-Aminobenzoic acid                    Sulfanilamide

If the correct substrate (PABA) is bound by the enzyme, the reaction occurs, and the bacterium lives. However, if the sulfa drug is present in excess over PABA, it binds more frequently to the active site of the enzyme. No folic acid will be produced, and the bacterial cell will die.

Because we obtain our folic acid from our diets, sulfa drugs do not harm us. However, bacteria are selectively killed. Luckily, we can capitalize on this property for the treatment of bacterial infections, and as a result, sulfa drugs have saved countless lives. Although bacterial infection was the major cause of death before the discovery of sulfa drugs and other antibiotics, death caused by bacterial infection is relatively rare at present.

## Reversible, Noncompetitive Inhibitors

**Reversible, noncompetitive enzyme inhibitors** bind to R groups of amino acids or perhaps to the metal ion cofactors. Unlike the situation of irreversible inhibition, however, the binding is weak, and the enzyme activity is restored when the inhibitor dissociates from the enzyme-inhibitor complex. Binding of these inhibitors modifies the shape of the active site in much the same way that the binding of an allosteric effector does. Since this binding is nonspecific, these inhibitors inactivate a broad range of enzymes.

**Question 19.13** Why are irreversible inhibitors considered to be poisons?

**Question 19.14** Explain the difference between an irreversible inhibitor and a reversible, noncompetitive inhibitor.

**Question 19.15** What is a structural analog?

**Question 19.16** How can structural analogs serve as enzyme inhibitors?

# 19.11 Proteolytic Enzymes

**Proteolytic enzymes** break the peptide bonds that maintain the primary protein structure. *Chymotrypsin*, for example, is an enzyme that hydrolyzes dietary proteins in the small intestine. It acts specifically at peptide bonds on the carbonyl side of the peptide bond. The C-terminal amino acids of the peptides released by bond cleavage are methionine, tyrosine, tryptophan, and phenylalanine. The specificity of chymotrypsin depends upon the presence of a *hydrophobic pocket*, a cluster of hydrophobic amino acids brought together by the three-dimensional folding of the protein chain. The flat aromatic side chains of certain amino acids (tyrosine, tryptophan, phenylalanine) slide into this pocket, providing the binding specificity required for catalysis (Figure 19.13).

How can we determine which bond is cleaved by a protease such as chymotrypsin? To know which bond is cleaved, we must write out the sequence of amino acids in the region of the peptide that is being cleaved. This can be determined experimentally by amino acid sequencing techniques. Remember that the N-terminal amino acid is written to the left and the C-terminal amino acid to the right. Consider a protein having within it the sequence —Ala-Phe-Gly—. A reaction is set up in which the enzyme, chymotrypsin, is mixed with the protein substrate. After the reaction has occurred, the products are purified, and their amino acid sequences are determined. Experiments of this sort show that chymotrypsin cleaves the bond between phenylalanine and glycine, which is the peptide bond on the carbonyl side of amino acids having an aromatic side chain.

**Figure 19.13** The specificity of chymotrypsin is determined by a hydrophobic pocket that holds the aromatic side chain of the substrate. This brings the peptide bond to be cleaved into the catalytic domain of the active site.

**LEARNING GOAL**

**11** Discuss the role of the enzyme chymotrypsin and other serine proteases.

The **pancreatic serine proteases** trypsin, chymotrypsin, and elastase all hydrolyze peptide bonds. As the name suggests, they are produced in the pancreas and subsequently transported to the small intestine. These enzymes are the result of *divergent evolution* in which a single ancestral gene was first duplicated. Then each copy evolved individually. They have similar primary structures, similar tertiary structures, and virtually identical mechanisms of action. However, as a result of evolution, these enzymes all have different specificities:

- Chymotrypsin cleaves peptide bonds on the carbonyl side of aromatic amino acids and large, hydrophobic amino acids such as methionine.
- Trypsin cleaves peptide bonds on the carbonyl side of basic amino acids.
- Elastase cleaves peptide bonds on the carbonyl side of glycine and alanine.

These enzymes are called *serine proteases* because they have the amino acid serine in the catalytic region of the active site that is essential for hydrolysis of the peptide bond.

These enzymes have different pockets for the side chains of their substrates; *different keys fit different locks.* This difference manifests itself in the substrate specificity alluded to on the previous page. For example, the binding pocket of trypsin is long, narrow, and negatively charged to accommodate lysine or arginine R groups. Yet although the binding pockets have undergone divergent evolution, the catalytic sites have remained unchanged, and the mechanism of proteolytic action is the same for all the serine proteases. In each case, the mechanism involves a serine R group.

**Question 19.17**  Draw the structural formulas of the following peptides and show which bond would be cleaved by chymotrypsin.
   a. ala-phe-ala        b.  tyr-ala-tyr

**Question 19.18**  Draw the structural formulas of the following peptides and show which bond would be cleaved by chymotrypsin.
   a. trp-val-gly        b.  phe-ala-pro

**Question 19.19**  Draw the structural formula of the peptide val-phe-ala-gly-leu. Which bond would be cleaved if this peptide were reacted with chymotrypsin? With elastase?

**Question 19.20**  Draw the structural formula of the peptide trp-val-lys-ala-ser. Show which bonds would be cleaved by trypsin, chymotrypsin, and elastase.

## 19.12  Uses of Enzymes in Medicine

Analysis of blood serum for levels (concentrations) of certain enzymes can provide a wealth of information about a patient's medical condition. Often, such tests are used to confirm a preliminary diagnosis based on the disease symptoms or clinical picture. These tests, called *enzyme assays,* are very precise and specific because they are based on the specificity of the enzyme-substrate complex.

*Acute myocardial infarction* (AMI) occurs when the blood supply to the heart muscle is blocked for an extended time. If this lack of blood supply, called *ischemia,* is prolonged, the myocardium suffers irreversible cell damage and muscle death, or infarction. When this happens, the concentration of cardiac enzymes in the blood rises dramatically as the dead cells release their contents into the bloodstream.

Three cardiac biomarkers have become the primary tools used to assess myocardial disease and suspected AMI. These are myoglobin, creatine kinase-MB (CK-MB), and cardiac troponin I. Of these three, only troponin is cardiac specific. In fact, it is so reliable that the American College of Cardiology has stated that any elevation of troponin is "abnormal and represents cardiac injury."

Myoglobin is the smallest of these three proteins and diffuses most rapidly through the vascular system. Thus, it is the first cardiac biomarker to appear, becoming elevated as early as 30 min after onset of chest pain. Myoglobin has another benefit in following a myocardial infarction. It is rapidly cleared from the body by the kidneys, returning to normal levels within 16 to 36 h after a heart attack. If the physician sees this decline in myoglobin levels, followed by a subsequent rise, it is an indication that the patient has had a second myocardial infarction.

Creatine kinase-MB is one of the most important cardiac biomarkers, even though it is found primarily in muscle and brain. Levels typically rise 3 to 8 h after chest pains begin. Within another 48 to 72 h, the CK-MB levels return to normal. As a result, like myoglobin, CK-MB can also be used to diagnose a second AMI.

The physician also has enzymes available to treat a heart attack patient. Most AMIs are the result of a *thrombus,* or clot, within a coronary blood vessel. The clot restricts blood flow to the heart muscle. One technique that shows promise for treatment following a coronary thrombosis, a heart attack caused by the formation of a clot, is destruction of the clot by intravenous or intracoronary injection of an enzyme called *streptokinase.* This enzyme, formerly purified from the pathogenic bacterium *Streptococcus pyogenes* but now available through recombinant DNA techniques, catalyzes the production of the proteolytic enzyme plasmin from its proenzyme, plasminogen. Plasmin can degrade a fibrin clot into subunits. This has the effect of dissolving the clot that is responsible for restricted blood flow to the heart, but there is an additional protective function as well. The subunits produced by plasmin degradation of fibrin clots are able to inhibit further clot formation by inhibiting thrombin.

Recombinant DNA technology has provided medical science with yet another, perhaps more promising, clot-dissolving enzyme. *Tissue-type plasminogen activator (TPA)* is a proteolytic enzyme that occurs naturally in the body as a part of the anti-clotting mechanisms. TPA converts the proenzyme, plasminogen, into the active enzyme, plasmin. Injection of TPA within 2 h of the initial chest pain can significantly improve the circulation to the heart and greatly improve the patient's chances of survival.

Elevated blood serum concentrations of the enzymes amylase and lipase are indications of pancreatitis, an inflammation of the pancreas. Liver diseases such as cirrhosis and hepatitis result in elevated levels of alanine aminotransferase/serum glutamate–pyruvate transaminase (ALT/SGPT) and aspartate aminotransferase/serum glutamate–oxaloacetate transaminase (AST/SGOT) in blood serum. In fact, these two enzymes also increase in concentration following heart attack, but the physician can differentiate between these two conditions by considering the relative increase in the two enzymes. If ALT/SGPT is elevated to a greater extent than AST/SGOT, it can be concluded that the problem is liver dysfunction.

Enzymes are also used as analytical reagents in the clinical laboratory owing to their specificity. They often selectively react with one substance of interest, producing a product that is easily measured. An example of this is the clinical analysis of urea in blood. The measurement of urea levels in blood is difficult because of the complexity of blood. However, if urea is converted to ammonia using the enzyme urease, the ammonia becomes an *indicator* of urea, because it is produced from urea, and it is easily measured. This test, called the *blood urea nitrogen (BUN) test,* is useful in the diagnosis of kidney malfunction and serves as one example of the utility of enzymes in clinical chemistry.

Enzyme replacement therapy can also be used in the treatment of certain diseases. One such disease, Gaucher's disease, is a genetic disorder resulting in a deficiency of the enzyme *glucocerebrosidase.* In the normal situation, this enzyme breaks down a glycolipid called *glucocerebroside,* which is an intermediate in the synthesis and degradation of complex glycosphingolipids found in cellular membranes. Glucocerebrosidase is found in the lysosomes, where it hydrolyzes glucocerebroside into glucose and ceramide.

*See A Medical Perspective: Disorders of Sphingolipid Metabolism in Chapter 17.*

Glucocerebroside

Glucocerebrosidase

Glucose                              Ceramide

In Gaucher's disease, the enzyme is not present and glucocerebroside builds up in macrophages found in the liver, spleen, and bone marrow. These cells become engorged with excess lipid that cannot be metabolized and then displace healthy, normal cells in bone marrow. The symptoms of Gaucher's disease include severe anemia, thrombocytopenia (reduction in the number of platelets), and hepatosplenomegaly (enlargement of the spleen and liver). There can also be skeletal problems including bone deterioration and secondary fractures.

Recombinant DNA technology has been used by the Genzyme Corporation to produce the human lysosomal enzyme β-glucocerebrosidase. Given the trade name *Cerezyme,* the enzyme hydrolyzes glucocerebroside into glucose and ceramide so that the products can be metabolized normally. Patients receive Cerezyme intravenously over the course of 1 to 2 h. The dosage and treatment schedule can be tailored to the individual. The results of testing are very encouraging. Patients experience improved red blood cell and platelet counts and reduced hepatosplenomegaly.

## CHAPTER MAP

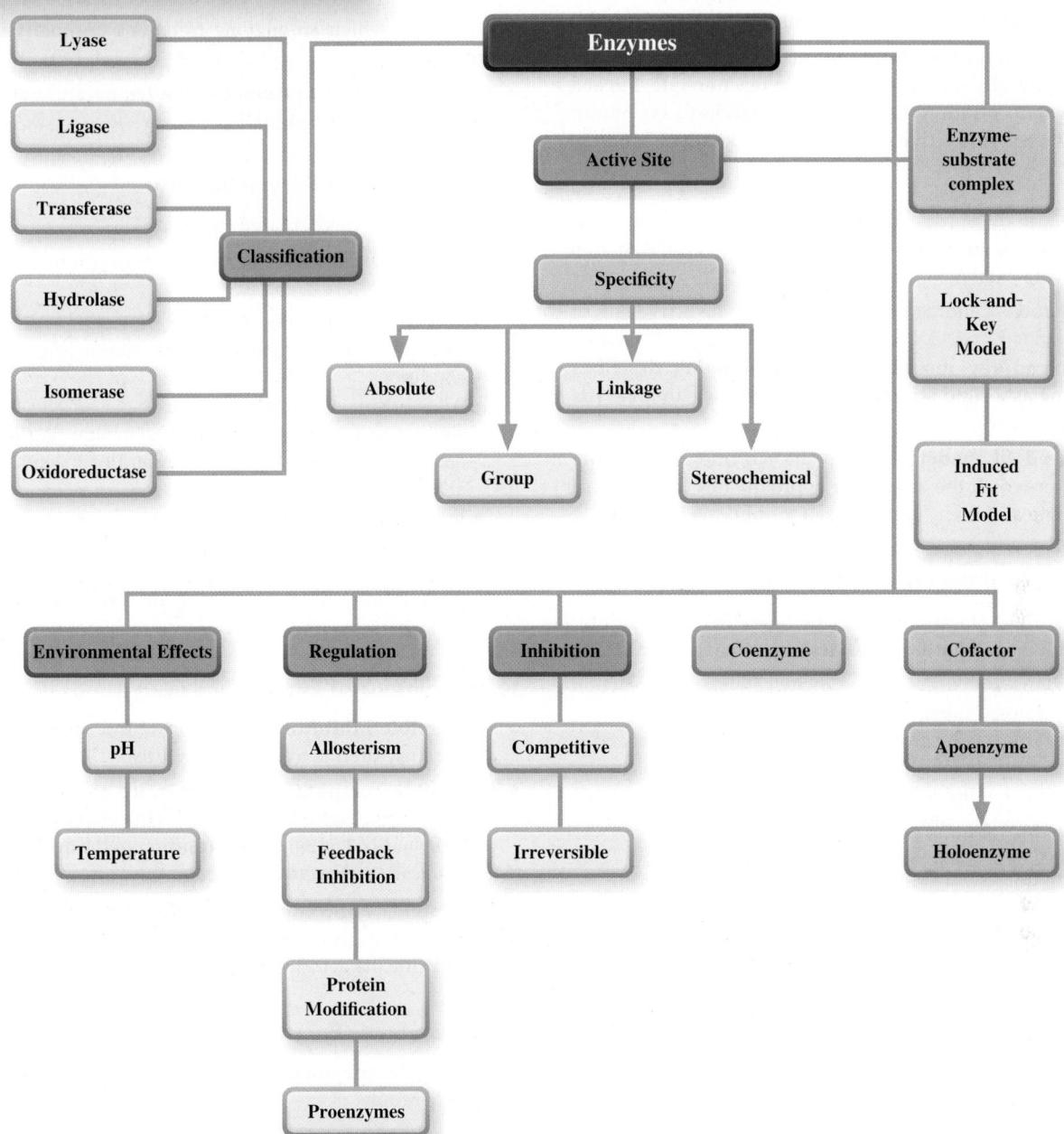

## SUMMARY

### 19.1 Nomenclature and Classification

▶ **Enzymes** are most frequently named by using the common system of nomenclature.

• Common names are useful because they are often derived from the name of the substrate and/or the type of reaction catalyzed by the enzyme.

▶ Enzymes convert one or more **substrates** into one or more **products.**

▶ There are six classes of enzymes on the basis of function: **oxidoreductases, transferases, hydrolases, lyases, isomerases,** and **ligases.**

### 19.2 The Effect of Enzymes on the Activation Energy of a Reaction

▶ Enzymes are biological catalysts that lower the activation energy of a reaction but do not alter the equilibrium constant.

## 19.3  The Effect of Substrate Concentration on Enzyme-Catalyzed Reactions

▶ In uncatalyzed reactions, increases in substrate concentration result in an increase in the reaction rate.

▶ In enzyme-catalyzed reactions, an increase in substrate concentration initially causes an increase in reaction rate, but at a particular concentration the reaction rate reaches a maximum because the enzyme active sites are all filled with substrate.

## 19.4  The Enzyme-Substrate Complex

▶ Formation of an **enzyme-substrate complex** is the first step of an enzyme-catalyzed reaction.
  • This involves binding of the substrate to the **active site** of the enzyme.
▶ The **lock-and-key model** of substrate binding describes the enzyme as a rigid structure into which the substrate fits precisely.
▶ The **induced fit model** describes the enzyme as a flexible molecule in which the active site approximates the shape of the substrate and then "molds" itself around the substrate.

## 19.5  Specificity of the Enzyme-Substrate Complex

▶ There are four classes of **enzyme specificity: absolute, group, linkage,** and **stereochemical specificity.**
  • An enzyme with absolute specificity catalyzes the reaction of only a single substrate.
  • An enzyme with group specificity catalyzes reactions involving similar substrates with the same functional group.
  • An enzyme with linkage specificity catalyzes reactions involving similar substrates with the same kind of bond.
  • An enzyme with stereochemical specificity catalyzes reactions involving only one enantiomer.

## 19.6  The Transition State and Product Formation

▶ An enzyme-catalyzed reaction is mediated through an unstable **transition state.**
▶ Transition states may involve putting "stress" on a bond, bringing reactants into close proximity and in the correct orientation, or altering the local pH.

## 19.7  Cofactors and Coenzymes

▶ **Cofactors** are metal ions, organic compounds, or organometallic compounds that bind to an enzyme and help maintain the correct configuration of the active site.
  • The protein portion is the **apoenzyme;** the protein portion bound to the cofactor is the **holoenzyme.**
▶ **Coenzymes** are organic groups that bind transiently to an enzyme during the reaction and that accept or donate chemical groups.
  • Coenzymes often contain modified **vitamins** as part of their structure.

## 19.8  Environmental Effects

▶ Enzymes are sensitive to pH and temperature and are quickly inactivated by extremes of pH or high temperature.
▶ The pH at which an enzyme functions optimally is the **pH optimum.**
▶ The **temperature optimum** is the temperature at which an enzyme functions optimally.

## 19.9  Regulation of Enzyme Activity

▶ Enzymes may be regulated by the cell.
▶ Some mechanisms of enzyme regulation include the following:
  • Formation of inactive forms or **proenzymes** that are later converted into active enzymes under the appropriate conditions
  • Allosterism: **Allosteric enzymes** have an effector binding site, as well as an active site. Effector binding renders the enzyme active (**positive allosterism**) or inactive (**negative allosterism**).
  • Feedback inhibition: the product of a biosynthetic pathway turns off the entire pathway via negative allosterism.
  • Protein modification: adding or removing a covalently bound group either activates or inactivates the enzyme.

## 19.10  Inhibition of Enzyme Activity

▶ **Irreversible inhibitors,** or poisons, bind tightly to enzymes and destroy their activity permanently.
▶ **Reversible competitive inhibitors** are generally **structural analogs** of the natural substrate for the enzyme that compete with the natural substrate for binding to the active side. They are also called **structural analogs.**
▶ **Reversible noncompetitive inhibitors** bind weakly to amino acid R groups of an enzyme. If they dissociate from the enzyme, its activity is restored.

## 19.11  Proteolytic Enzymes

▶ **Proteolytic enzymes** (proteases) catalyze the hydrolysis of peptide bonds.
▶ The **pancreatic serine proteases** chymotrypsin, trypsin, and elastase have similar structures and mechanisms of action and are thought to have evolved from a common ancestral protease.

## 19.12  Uses of Enzymes in Medicine

▶ Analysis of blood serum for unusually high levels of certain enzymes provides valuable information about the condition of a patient and is used to diagnose heart attack, liver disease, pancreatitis, and other conditions.
▶ Enzymes are used as analytical reagents, as in the blood urea nitrogen (BUN) test, and in the treatment of disease.

## ANSWERS TO PRACTICE PROBLEMS

**19.1** a. Pyruvate kinase is a transferase.
b. Alanine transaminase is a transferase.
c. Triose phosphate isomerase is an isomerase.
d. Pyruvate dehydrogenase is an oxidoreductase.
e. Lactase is a hydrolase.
f. Phosphofructokinase is a transferase.
g. Lipase is a hydrolase.
h. Acetoacetate decarboxylase is a transferase.
i. Succinate dehydrogenase is an oxidoreductase.

## QUESTIONS AND PROBLEMS

### Nomenclature and Classification

**Foundations**

**19.21** How are the common names of enzymes often derived?
**19.22** What is the most common characteristic used to classify enzymes?

**Applications**

**19.23** Match each of the following substrates with its corresponding enzyme:

| 1. Urea | a. Lipase |
| 2. Hydrogen peroxide | b. Glucose-6-phosphatase |
| 3. Lipid | c. Peroxidase |
| 4. Aspartic acid | d. Sucrase |
| 5. Glucose-6-phosphate | e. Urease |
| 6. Sucrose | f. Aspartase |

**19.24** Give a systematic name for the enzyme that would act on each of the following substrates:

| a. Alanine | d. Ribose |
| b. Citrate | e. Methylamine |
| c. Ampicillin | |

**19.25** Describe the function implied by the name of each of the following enzymes:
a. Citrate decarboxylase
b. Adenosine diphosphate phosphorylase
c. Oxalate reductase
d. Nitrite oxidase
e. *cis-trans* Isomerase

**19.26** List the six classes of enzymes based on the type of reaction catalyzed. Briefly describe the function of each class, and provide an example of each.

### The Effect of Enzymes on the Activation Energy of a Reaction

**Foundations**

**19.27** Define the term *substrate*.
**19.28** Define the term *product*.

**Applications**

**19.29** What is the activation energy of a reaction?
**19.30** What is the effect of an enzyme on the activation energy of a reaction?
**19.31** Write and explain the equation for the equilibrium constant of an enzyme-mediated reaction. Does the enzyme alter the $K_{eq}$?
**19.32** If an enzyme does not alter the equilibrium constant of a reaction, how does it speed up the reaction?

### The Effect of Substrate Concentration on Enzyme-Catalyzed Reactions

**Foundations**

**19.33** What is the effect of doubling the substrate concentration on the rate of a chemical reaction?
**19.34** Why doesn't the rate of an enzyme-catalyzed reaction increase indefinitely when the substrate concentration is made very large?

**Applications**

**19.35** What is meant by the term *rate-limiting step*?
**19.36** How does the rate-limiting step influence an enzyme-catalyzed reaction?
**19.37** Draw a graph that describes the effect of increasing the concentration of the substrate on the rate of an enzyme-catalyzed reaction.
**19.38** What does a graph of enzyme activity versus substrate concentration tell us about the nature of enzyme-catalyzed reactions?

### The Enzyme-Substrate Complex

**Foundations**

**19.39** Define the term *enzyme-substrate complex*.
**19.40** Define the term *active site*.
**19.41** What are catalytic groups of an enzyme active site?
**19.42** What is the binding site of an enzyme active site?

**Applications**

**19.43** Name three major properties of enzyme active sites.
**19.44** If enzyme active sites are small, why are enzymes so large?
**19.45** What is the lock-and-key model of enzyme-substrate binding?
**19.46** Why is the induced fit model of enzyme-substrate binding a much more accurate model than the lock-and-key model?

### Specificity of the Enzyme-Substrate Complex

**Foundations**

**19.47** Define the term *enzyme specificity*.
**19.48** What region of an enzyme is responsible for its specificity?
**19.49** What is meant by the term *group specificity*?
**19.50** What is meant by the term *linkage specificity*?
**19.51** What is meant by the term *absolute specificity*?
**19.52** What is meant by the term *stereochemical specificity*?

## Applications

**19.53** Provide an example of an enzyme with group specificity and explain the advantage of group specificity for that particular enzyme.

**19.54** Provide an example of an enzyme with linkage specificity and explain the advantage of linkage specificity for that particular enzyme.

**19.55** Provide an example of an enzyme with absolute specificity and explain the advantage of absolute specificity for that particular enzyme.

**19.56** Provide an example of an enzyme with stereochemical specificity and explain the advantage of stereochemical specificity for that particular enzyme.

## The Transition State and Product Formation

### Foundations

**19.57** Outline the four general stages in an enzyme-catalyzed reaction.

**19.58** Describe the transition state.

### Applications

**19.59** What types of transition states might be envisioned that would decrease the energy of activation of a reaction?

**19.60** If an enzyme catalyzed a reaction by modifying the local pH, what kind of amino acid R groups would you expect to find in the active site?

## Cofactors and Coenzymes

### Foundations

**19.61** What is the role of a cofactor in enzyme activity?

**19.62** How does a coenzyme function in an enzyme-catalyzed reaction?

### Applications

**19.63** List each of the vitamins found in modified form in a coenzyme and list the coenzymes.

**19.64** List the functions of each of the coenzymes. What classes of enzymes would require these coenzymes?

## Environmental Effects

### Foundations

**19.65** Define the temperature optimum for an enzyme.

**19.66** Define the optimum pH for enzyme activity.

**19.67** How will each of the following changes in conditions alter the rate of an enzyme-catalyzed reaction?
a. Decreasing the temperature from 37°C to 10°C
b. Increasing the pH of the solution from 7 to 11
c. Heating the enzyme from 37°C to 100°C

**19.68** Why does an enzyme lose activity when the pH is drastically changed from optimum pH?

### Applications

**19.69** High temperature is an effective mechanism for killing bacteria on surgical instruments. How does high temperature result in cellular death?

**19.70** An increase in temperature will increase the rate of a reaction if a nonenzymatic catalyst is used; however, an increase in temperature will eventually *decrease* the rate of

a reaction when an enzyme catalyst is used. Explain the apparent contradiction of these two statements.

**19.71** What is the function of the lysosome?

**19.72** Of what significance is it that lysosomal enzymes have a pH optimum of 4.8?

**19.73** Why are enzymes that are used for clinical assays in hospitals stored in refrigerators?

**19.74** Why do extremes of pH inactivate enzymes?

## Regulation of Enzyme Activity

### Foundations

**19.75** a. Why is it important for cells to regulate the level of enzyme activity?
b. Why must synthesis of digestive enzymes be carefully controlled?

**19.76** What is an allosteric enzyme?

**19.77** What is the difference between positive and negative allosterism?

**19.78** a. Define feedback inhibition.
b. Describe the role of allosteric enzymes in feedback inhibition.
c. Is this positive or negative allosterism?

**19.79** What is a proenzyme?

**19.80** Three proenzymes that are involved in digestion of proteins in the stomach and intestines are pepsinogen, chymotrypsinogen, and trypsinogen. What is the advantage of producing these enzymes as inactive peptides?

### Applications

**19.81** The blood clotting mechanism consists of a set of proenzymes that act in a cascade that results in formation of a blood clot. Develop a hypothesis to explain the value of this mechanism for blood clotting.

**19.82** What is the benefit for an enzyme such as triacylglycerol lipase to be regulated by covalent modification, in this case phosphorylation?

## Inhibition of Enzyme Activity

### Foundations

**19.83** Define *competitive enzyme inhibition.*

**19.84** How do the sulfa drugs selectively kill bacteria while causing no harm to humans?

**19.85** Describe the structure of a structural analog.

**19.86** How can structural analogs serve as enzyme inhibitors?

**19.87** Define *irreversible enzyme inhibition.*

**19.88** Why are irreversible enzyme inhibitors often called *poisons?*

### Applications

**19.89** Suppose that a certain drug company manufactured a compound that had nearly the same structure as a substrate for a certain enzyme but that could not be acted upon chemically by the enzyme. What type of interaction would the compound have with the enzyme?

**19.90** The addition of phenylthiourea to a preparation of the enzyme polyphenoloxidase completely inhibits the activity of the enzyme.
a. Knowing that phenylthiourea binds all copper ions, what conclusion can you draw about whether polyphenoloxidase requires a cofactor?
b. What kind of inhibitor is phenylthiourea?

called adenosine or guanosine, respectively. If 2'-deoxyribose is the sugar in these nucleosides, they are called 2'-deoxyadenosine and 2'-deoxyguanosine. The ribonucleosides formed from cytosine and uracil are called cytidine and uridine, respectively. The deoxyribonucleosides of cytosine and thymine are called 2'-deoxycytidine and thymidine, respectively. No prefix is needed for thymidine because it is found only in DNA.

## Nucleotide Structure

From the work of Watson and Crick, as well as that of Miescher, Levene, and many others, we now know that deoxyribonucleic acid (DNA) and ribonucleic acid (RNA) are long polymers of **nucleotides.** Every nucleotide is composed of a nitrogenous base, a five-carbon sugar, and at least one phosphoryl group.

Each nucleotide consists of either ribose or deoxyribose, one of the five nitrogenous bases, and one or more phosphoryl groups (Figure 20.3). A nucleotide with the sugar ribose is a **ribonucleotide,** and one having the sugar 2'-deoxyribose is a **deoxyribonucleotide** (Figures 20.1 and 20.3).

The covalent bond between the sugar and the phosphoryl group is a phosphoester bond formed by a condensation reaction between the 5'-OH of the sugar and an —OH of the phosphoryl group. As noted above, the bond between the base and the sugar is a β-N-glycosidic linkage that joins the 1'-carbon of the sugar and a nitrogen atom of the base (N-9 of purines and N-1 of pyrimidines).

To name a nucleotide, simply begin with the name of the nitrogenous base, and apply the following simple rules:

- Remove the -ine ending, and replace it with either -osine for purines or -idine for pyrimidines. Uracil is the one exception to this rule. In this case the -acil ending is replaced with -idine, producing the name uridine.

Figure 20.2  General structures of a purine and a pyrimidine nucleoside. Notice that the N-glycosidic linkage involves the 1' carbon of the sugar and either the N-1 of the pyrimidine or N-9 of the purine.

**Figure 20.3**  (a) The general structures of a deoxyribonucleotide and a ribonucleotide. (b) A specific example of a ribonucleotide, adenosine triphosphate.

**TABLE 20.1 Names and Abbreviations of the Ribonucleotides and Deoxyribonucleotides Containing Adenine**

| Nucleotide | Abbreviation |
| --- | --- |
| Deoxyadenosine monophosphate | dAMP |
| Deoxyadenosine diphosphate | dADP |
| Deoxyadenosine triphosphate | dATP |
| Adenosine monophosphate | AMP |
| Adenosine diphosphate | ADP |
| Adenosine triphosphate | ATP |

- Nucleotides with the sugar ribose are ribonucleotides, and those having the sugar 2'-deoxyribose are deoxyribonucleotides. For a deoxyribonucleotide, the prefix *deoxy-* is placed before the modified nitrogenous base name. No prefix is required for ribonucleotides, or for thymidine, which is found only in DNA.
- Add a prefix to indicate the number of phosphoryl groups that are attached. A *mono*phosphate carries one phosphoryl group; a *di*phosphate carries two phosphoryl groups; and a *tri*phosphate carries three phosphoryl groups.

Because the full names of the nucleotides are so cumbersome, a simple abbreviation is generally used. These abbreviations are summarized in Table 20.1.

**Question 20.1**  Referring to the structures in Figures 20.1 and 20.3, draw the structures for nucleotides consisting of the following units.
    a. Ribose, adenine, two phosphoryl groups
    b. 2'-Deoxyribose, guanine, three phosphoryl groups

**Question 20.2**  Referring to the structures in Figures 20.1 and 20.3, draw the structures for nucleotides consisting of the following units.
    a. 2'-Deoxyribose, thymine, one phosphoryl group
    b. Ribose, cytosine, three phosphoryl groups
    c. Ribose, uracil, one phosphoryl group

## 20.2   The Structure of DNA and RNA

A single strand of DNA is a polymer of nucleotides bonded to one another by 3'–5' phosphodiester bonds. The backbone of the polymer is called the *sugar-phosphate backbone* because it is composed of alternating units of the five-carbon sugar 2'-deoxyribose and phosphoryl groups in phosphodiester linkage. A nitrogenous base is bonded to each sugar by an *N*-glycosidic linkage (Figure 20.4).

### DNA Structure: The Double Helix

James Watson and Francis Crick were the first to describe the three-dimensional structure of DNA, in 1953. They deduced the structure by building models based on the experimental results of others. Irwin Chargaff observed that the amount of adenine in any DNA molecule is equal to the amount of thymine. Similarly, he found that the amounts of cytosine and guanine are also equal. The X-ray diffraction studies of Rosalind Franklin and Maurice Wilkens revealed several repeat distances that characterize the structure of DNA: 0.34 nanometers (nm), 3.4 nm, and 2 nm. (Look at the structure of DNA in Figure 20.5 to see the significance of these measurements.)

With this information, Watson and Crick concluded that DNA is a **double helix** of two strands of DNA wound around one another. The structure of the double helix is often compared to a spiral staircase. The sugar-phosphate backbones

**LEARNING GOAL**

**2**  Describe the structure of DNA and compare it with RNA.

**ANIMATION**
- DNA Structure

**Figure 20.4** The covalent, primary structure of DNA.

of the two strands of DNA spiral around the outside of the helix like the handrails on a spiral staircase. The nitrogenous bases extend into the center at right angles to the axis of the helix. You can imagine the nitrogenous bases forming the steps of the staircase. The structure of this elegant molecule is shown in Figure 20.5.

One noncovalent attraction that helps maintain the double helix structure is hydrogen bonding between the nitrogenous bases in the center of the helix. Adenine forms two hydrogen bonds with thymine, and cytosine forms three hydrogen bonds with guanine (Figure 20.5). These are called **base pairs.** The two strands of DNA are **complementary strands** because the sequence of bases on one automatically determines the sequence of bases on the other. When there is an adenine on one strand, there will always be a thymine in the same location on the opposite strand.

The diameter of the double helix is 2.0 nm. This is dictated by the dimensions of the purine-pyrimidine base pairs. The helix completes one turn every ten base pairs. One complete turn is 3.4 nm. Thus, each base pair advances the helix by 0.34 nm. These dimensions explain the repeat distances observed by X-ray diffraction.

One last important feature of the DNA double helix is that the two strands are **antiparallel strands,** as this example shows:

Base-pairing explains Chargaff's observation that the amount of adenine always equals the amount of thymine and the amount of guanine always equals the amount of cytosine for any DNA sample.

```
5′  P—S—P—S—P—S—P—S—P—S—P—S—OH 3′
    |   |   |   |   |   |
    A   T   G   C   G   A
    :   :   :   :   :   :
    T   A   C   G   C   T
    |   |   |   |   |   |
3′ OH—S—P—S—P—S—P—S—P—S—P—S—P  5′
```

Key Features

- Two strands of DNA form a right-handed double helix.

- The bases in opposite strands hydrogen bond according to the AT/GC rule.

- The two strands are antiparallel with regard to their 5′ to 3′ directionality.

- There are ~10.0 nucleotides in each strand per complete 360° turn of the helix.

**Figure 20.5** Schematic ribbon diagram of the DNA double helix showing the dimensions of the DNA molecule and the antiparallel orientation of the two strands.

In other words, the two strands of the helix run in opposite directions (see Figure 20.5). Only when the two strands are antiparallel can the base pairs form the hydrogen bonds that hold the two strands together.

## Chromosomes

**Chromosomes** are pieces of DNA that carry the genetic instructions, or genes, of an organism. Organisms such as the prokaryotes have only a single chromosome and its structure is relatively simple. Others, the eukaryotes, have many chromosomes, each of which has many different levels of structure. The complete set of genetic information in all the chromosomes of an organism is called the **genome.**

**Prokaryotes** are organisms with a simple cellular structure in which there is no true nucleus surrounded by a nuclear membrane and there are no true membrane-bound organelles. This group includes all of the bacteria. In these organisms the chromosome is a circular DNA molecule that is supercoiled, which means that the helix is coiled on itself. The supercoiled DNA molecule is attached to a complex of proteins at roughly forty sites along its length, forming a series of loops. This structure, called the nucleoid, can be seen in Figure 20.6.

**Eukaryotes** are organisms that have cells containing a true nucleus enclosed by a nuclear membrane. They also have a variety of membrane-bound organelles

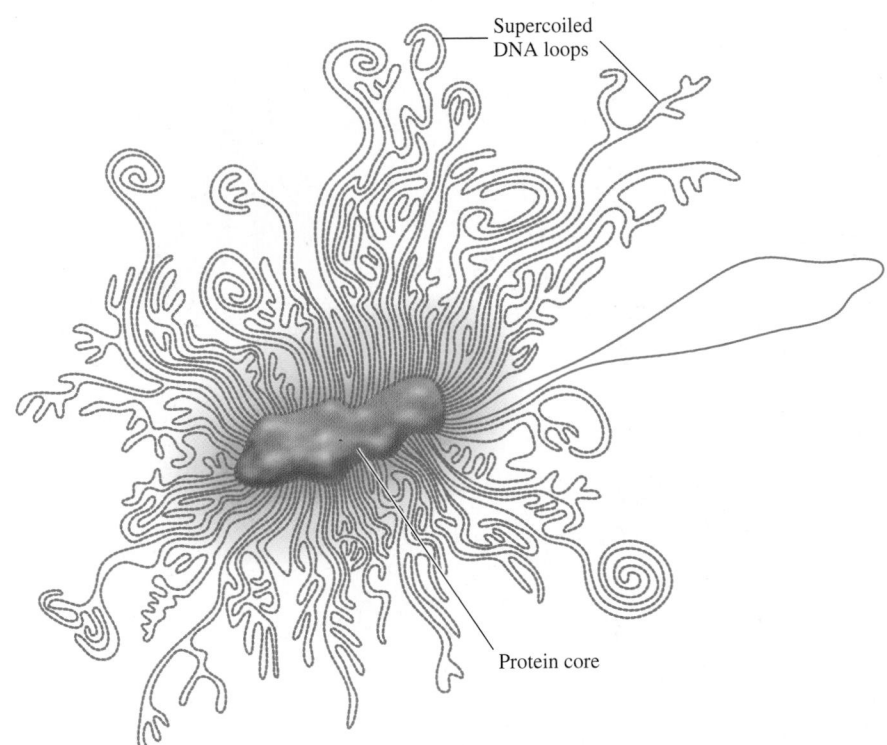

Supercoiled
DNA loops

Protein core

**Figure 20.6** Structure of a bacterial nucleoid. The nucleoid is made up of the supercoiled, circular chromosome attached to a protein core.

that segregate different cellular functions into different compartments. As an example, the reactions of aerobic respiration are located within the mitochondria.

All animals, plants, and fungi are eukaryotes. The number and size of the chromosomes of eukaryotes vary from one species to the next. For instance, humans have twenty-three pairs of chromosomes, while the adder's tongue fern has 631 pairs of chromosomes. But the chromosome structure is the same for all those organisms that have been studied.

Eukaryotic chromosomes are very complex structures (Figure 20.7). The first level of structure is the **nucleosome,** which consists of a strand of DNA wrapped around a small disk made up of histone proteins. At this level the DNA looks like beads along a string. The string of beads then coils into a larger structure called the *30 nm fiber.* These, in turn, are further coiled into a *200 nm fiber.* Other proteins are probably involved in the organization of the 200 nm fiber. The full complexities of the eukaryotic chromosome are not yet understood, but there are probably many such levels of coiled structures.

Some human genetic disorders are characterized by unusual chromosome numbers. For instance, Down syndrome is characterized by an extra copy of chromosome 21. The presence of this additional chromosome causes the traits associated with Down syndrome, including varying degrees of mental challenges, a flattened face, and short stature. The presence of an additional chromosome 18 causes Edward syndrome and an extra chromosome 13 causes Patau syndrome. Both of these are extremely rare and result in extreme mental and physical defects and early death. The presence of extra copies of the sex chromosomes, X or Y, is not lethal. Males with two X chromosomes and one Y suffer from Klinefelter syndrome and show sexual immaturity and breast development. Males with an extra Y chromosome are unusually tall, as are women with three X chromosomes. A woman with only a single X chromosome experiences Turner syndrome, including short stature, a webbed neck, and sexual immaturity. All other abnormalities in chromosome number are thought to be lethal to the fetus. In fact, it is thought that 50% of all miscarriages are the result of abnormal chromosome numbers.

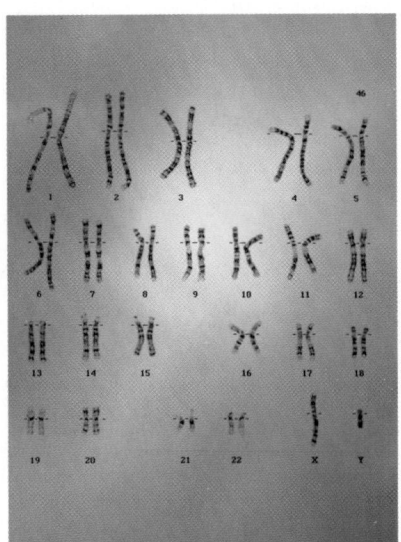

This karyotype shows the twenty-three pairs of chromosomes of humans. What type of genetic disorders could be identified by karyotyping?

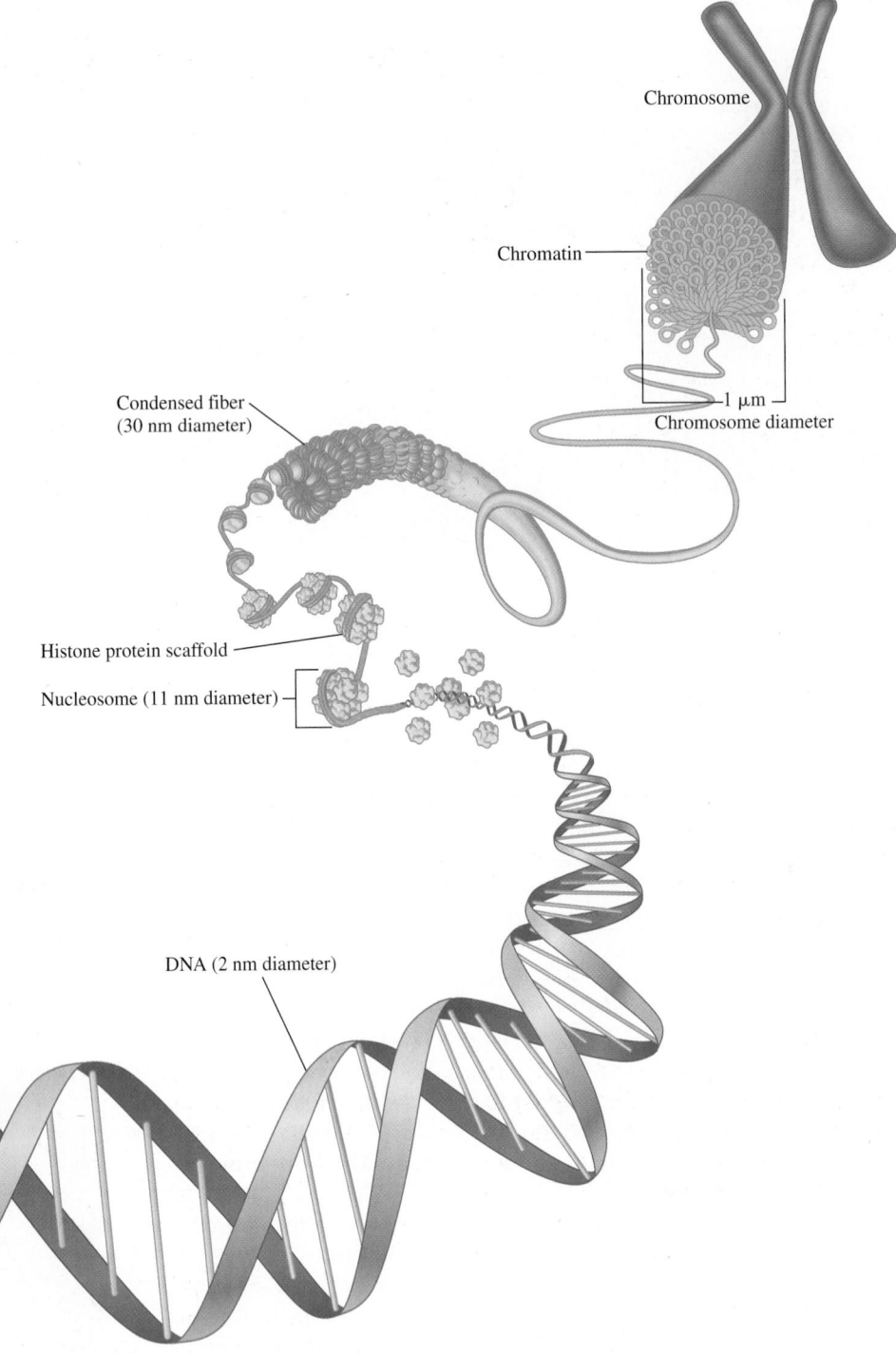

Chromosome

Chromatin

1 μm

Chromosome diameter

Condensed fiber
(30 nm diameter)

Histone protein scaffold

Nucleosome (11 nm diameter)

DNA (2 nm diameter)

**Figure 20.7**  The eukaryotic chromosome has many levels of structure.

## RNA Structure

The sugar-phosphate backbone of RNA consists of ribonucleotides, also linked by 3′–5′ phosphodiester bonds. These phosphodiester bonds are identical to those found in DNA. However, RNA molecules differ from DNA molecules in three basic properties.

- RNA molecules are usually *single-stranded*.
- The sugar-phosphate backbone of RNA consists of *ribonucleotides* linked by 3′–5′ phosphodiester bonds. Thus the sugar *ribose* is found in place of 2′-deoxyribose.
- The nitrogenous base *uracil* (U) replaces thymine (T).

## A MEDICAL PERSPECTIVE

### Molecular Genetics and Detection of Human Genetic Disorders

It is estimated that 3–5% of the human population suffers from a serious genetic defect. That's 350 million people! But what if genetic disease could be detected and "cured"? Two new technologies, *gene therapy* and *preimplantation diagnosis*, may help us realize this dream.

For a couple with a history of genetic disorders in the family, pregnancy is a time of anxiety. Through *genetic counseling* these couples can learn the probability that their child has the defect. For several hundred genetic disorders the uncertainty can be eliminated. *Amniocentesis* (removal of 10–20 milliliters (mL) of fluid from the sac around the fetus) and *chorionic villus sampling* (removal of cells from a fetal membrane) are two procedures that are used to obtain fetal cells for genetic testing. Fetal cells are cultured and tested by enzyme assays and DNA tests to look for genetic disorders. If a genetic defect is diagnosed, the parents must make a difficult decision: to abort the fetus or to carry the child to term and deal with the effects of the genetic disorder.

The power of modern molecular genetics is obvious in our ability to find a "bad" gene from just a few cells. But scientists have developed an even more impressive way to test for genetic defects before the embryo implants into the uterine lining. This technique, called *preimplantation diagnosis*, involves fertilizing a human egg and allowing the resulting zygote to divide in a sterile petri dish. When the zygote consists of eight to sixteen cells, *one* cell is removed for genetic testing. Only genetically

normal embryos are implanted in the mother. Thus, the genetic defects that we can detect could be eliminated from the population by preimplantation diagnosis because only a zygote with "good" genes is used.

Gene therapy is a second way in which genetic disorders may one day be eliminated. Foreign genes, including one for growth hormone, have been introduced into fertilized mouse eggs and the zygotes implanted in female mice. The baby mice born with the foreign growth hormone gene were about three times larger than their normal littermates! One day, this kind of technology may be used to introduce normal genes into human fertilized eggs carrying a defective gene, thereby replacing the defective gene with a normal one.

In this chapter we will examine the molecules that carry and express our genetic information, DNA and RNA. Only by understanding the structure and function of these molecules have we been able to develop the amazing array of genetic tools that currently exists. We hope that as we continue to learn more about human genetics, we will be able to detect and one day correct most of the known genetic disorders.

**For Further Understanding**

▶ Go online to investigate the concerns that limit the use of gene therapy in humans.
▶ What is the advantage of preimplantation diagnosis?

Although RNA molecules are single-stranded, base pairing between uracil and adenine and between guanine and cytosine can still occur. We will show the importance of this property as we examine the way in which RNA molecules are involved in the expression of the genetic information in DNA.

## 20.3 DNA Replication

DNA must be replicated before a cell divides so that each daughter cell inherits a copy of each gene. A cell that is missing a critical gene will die, just as an individual with a genetic disorder, a defect in an important gene, may die early in life. Thus it is essential that the process of DNA replication produces an absolutely accurate copy of the original genetic information. If mistakes are made in critical genes, the result may be lethal mutations.

The structure of the DNA molecule suggested the mechanism for its accurate replication. Since adenine can base pair only with thymine and cytosine with guanine, Watson and Crick first suggested that an enzyme could "read" the nitrogenous bases on one strand of a DNA molecule and add complementary bases to a strand of DNA being synthesized. The product of this mechanism would be a new DNA molecule in which one strand is the original, or parent, strand and the

**LEARNING GOAL**

**3** Explain DNA replication.

Isotopes are atoms of the same element having the same number of protons but different numbers of neutrons and, therefore, different mass numbers.

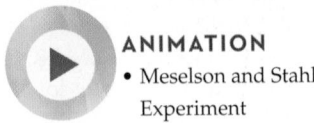

**ANIMATION**
• Meselson and Stahl Experiment

second strand is a newly synthesized, or daughter, strand. This mode of DNA replication is called **semiconservative replication** (Figure 20.8).

Experimental evidence for this mechanism of DNA replication was provided by an experiment designed by Matthew Meselson and Franklin Stahl in 1958. *Escherichia coli* cells were grown in a medium in which $^{15}NH_4^+$ was the sole nitrogen source. $^{15}N$ is a nonradioactive, heavy isotope of nitrogen. Thus, growing the cells in this medium resulted in all of the cellular DNA containing this heavy isotope.

The cells containing only $^{15}NH_4^+$ were then added to a medium containing only the abundant isotope of nitrogen, $^{14}NH_4^+$, and were allowed to grow for one cycle of cell division. When the daughter DNA molecules were isolated and analyzed, it was found that each was made up of one strand of "heavy" DNA, the parental strand, and one strand of "light" DNA, the new daughter strand. After a second round of cell division, half of the isolated DNA contained no $^{15}N$ and half contained a 50/50 mixture of $^{14}N$ and $^{15}N$-labeled DNA (Figure 20.9). This demonstrated conclusively that each parental strand of the DNA molecule serves as the template for the synthesis of a daughter strand and that each newly synthesized DNA molecule is composed of one parental strand and one newly synthesized daughter strand.

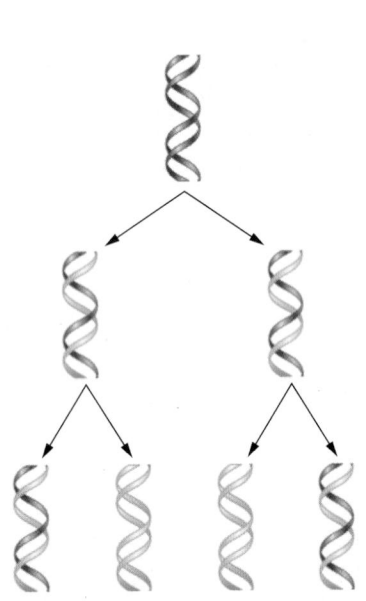

**Figure 20.9** Representation of the Meselson and Stahl experiment. The DNA from cells grown in medium containing $^{15}NH_4^+$ is shown in purple. After a single generation in medium containing $^{14}NH_4^+$, the daughter DNA molecules have one $^{15}N$-labeled parent strand and one $^{14}N$-labeled daughter strand (blue). After a second generation in $^{14}NH_4^+$ containing medium, there are equal numbers of $^{14}N/^{15}N$ DNA molecules and $^{14}N/^{14}N$ DNA molecules.

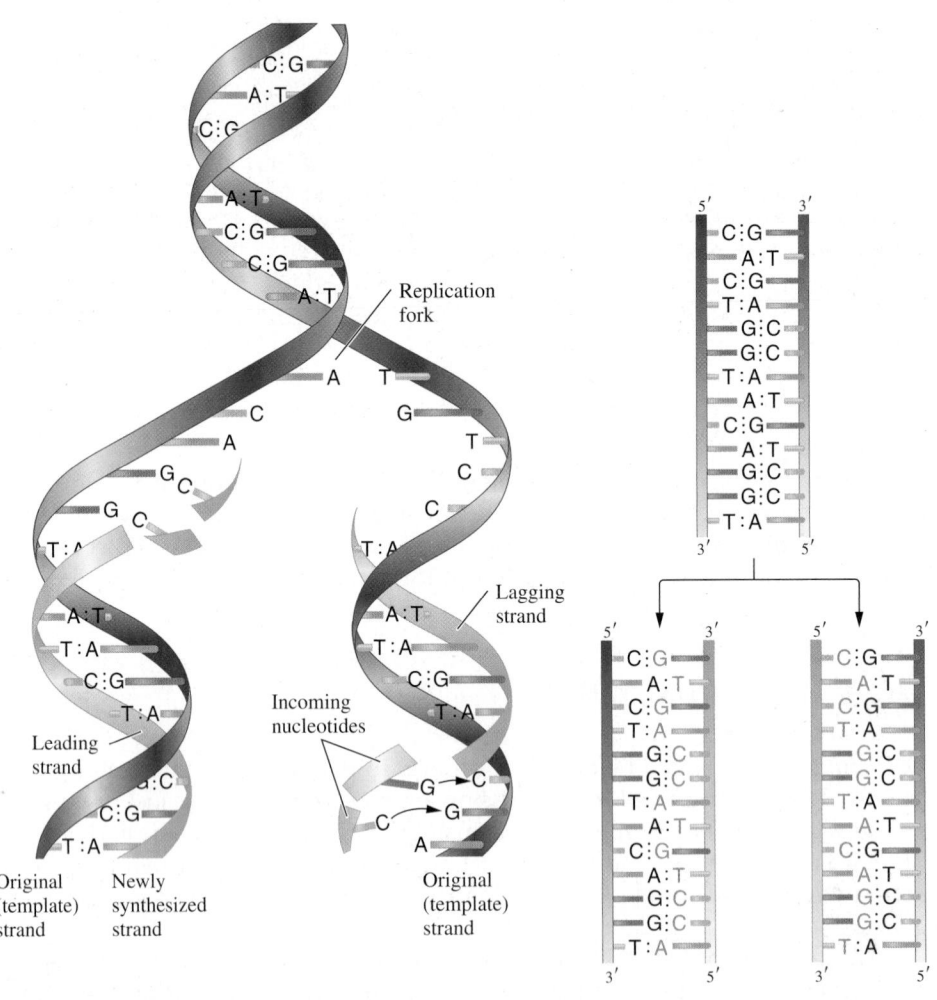

**(a)** The mechanism of DNA replication

**(b)** The products of replication

**Figure 20.8** In semiconservative DNA replication, each parent strand serves as a template for the synthesis of a new daughter strand.

# Bacterial DNA Replication

The bacterial chromosome is a circular molecule of DNA made up of about three million nucleotides. DNA replication begins at a unique sequence on the circular chromosome known as the **replication origin** (Figure 20.10). Replication occurs bidirectionally at the rate of about 500 new nucleotides every second! The point at which the new deoxyribonucleotide is added to the growing daughter strand is called the **replication fork** (Figure 20.10). It is here that the DNA has been opened to allow binding of the various proteins and enzymes responsible for DNA replication. Since DNA synthesis occurs bidirectionally, there are two replication forks moving in opposite directions. Replication is complete when the replication forks collide approximately half way around the circular chromosome.

The first step in DNA replication (Figure 20.11) is the separation of the strands of DNA. The protein *helicase* does this by breaking the hydrogen bonds between the base pairs. This, in turn, causes supercoiling of the molecule. This stress is relieved by the enzyme *topoisomerase*, which travels along the DNA ahead of the replication fork. At this point, *single-strand binding protein* binds to the separated strands, preventing them from coming back together. In the next step, the enzyme *primase* catalyzes the synthesis of a small piece of RNA (ten to twelve nucleotides) called an *RNA primer* that serves to "prime" the process of DNA replication.

Now the enzyme **DNA polymerase III** "reads" each parental strand, also called the *template,* and catalyzes the polymerization of a complementary daughter strand. Deoxyribonucleotide triphosphate molecules are the precursors for DNA replication (Figure 20.12). In this reaction, a pyrophosphate group is released as a phosphoester bond is formed between the 5'-phosphoryl group of the nucleotide being added to the chain and the 3'-OH of the nucleotide on the daughter strand. This is called 5' to 3' synthesis.

One complicating factor in the process of DNA replication is the fact that the two strands of DNA are antiparallel to one another. DNA polymerase III can only catalyze DNA chain elongation in the 5' to 3' direction, yet the replication fork proceeds in one direction, while both strands are replicated simultaneously. Another complication is the need for an RNA primer to serve as the starting point for DNA replication. As a result of these two obstacles, there are different mechanisms for replication of the two strands. One strand, called the **leading strand,** is replicated continuously. The opposite strand, called the **lagging strand,** is replicated discontinuously.

**ANIMATIONS**
- How Nucleotides Are Added in DNA Replication
- DNA Replication Fork
- Bidirectional DNA Replication
- DNA Replication (*E. coli*)

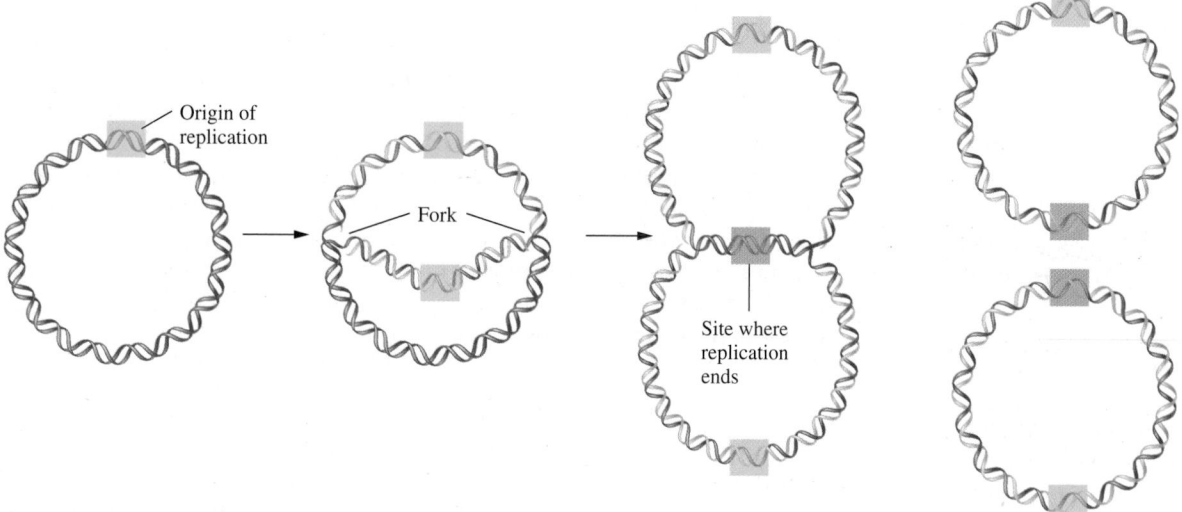

**Figure 20.10** Bacterial chromosome replication.

**Functions of key proteins involved with DNA replication**

- **DNA helicase** breaks the hydrogen bonds between the DNA strands.

- **Topoisomerase** alleviates positive supercoiling.

- **Single-strand binding proteins** keep the parental strands apart.

- **Primase** synthesizes an RNA primer.

- **DNA polymerase III** synthesizes a daughter strand of DNA.

- **DNA polymerase I** excises the RNA primers and fills in with DNA.

- **DNA ligase** covalently links the DNA fragments together.

**Figure 20.11** Because the two strands of DNA are antiparallel and DNA polymerase can only catalyze 5' ⟶ 3' replication, only one of the two DNA strands (top strand) can be read continuously to produce a daughter strand. The other must be synthesized in segments that are extended away from the direction of movement of the replication fork (bottom strand). These discontinuous segments are later covalently joined together by DNA ligase.

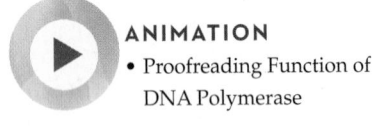

**ANIMATION**
- Proofreading Function of DNA Polymerase

The two mechanisms are shown in Figures 20.11 and 20.12. For the leading strand, a single RNA primer is produced at the replication origin and DNA polymerase III continuously catalyzes the addition of nucleotides in the 5' to 3' direction, beginning with addition of the first nucleotide to the RNA primer.

On the lagging strand, many RNA primers are produced as the replication fork proceeds along the molecule. DNA polymerase III catalyzes DNA chain elongation from each of these primers. When the new strand "bumps" into a previous one, synthesis stops at that site. Meanwhile, at the replication fork, a new primer is being synthesized by primase. The final steps of synthesis on the lagging strand involve removal of the primers, repair of the gaps, and sealing of the fragments into an intact strand of DNA. The enzyme DNA polymerase I catalyzes the removal of the RNA primer and its replacement with DNA nucleotides. In the final step of the process, the enzyme DNA ligase catalyzes the formation of a phosphoester bond between the two adjacent fragments. It is little wonder that this is referred to as lagging strand replication! A more accurate model of the replication fork is shown in Figure 20.13.

Because it is critical to produce an accurate copy of the parental DNA, it is very important to avoid errors in the replication process. In addition to catalyzing the replication of new DNA, DNA polymerase III is able to proofread the newly synthesized strand. If the wrong nucleotide has been added to the growing DNA strand, it is removed and replaced with the correct one. In this way, a faithful copy of the parental DNA is ensured.

## Eukaryotic DNA Replication

DNA replication in eukaryotes is more complex. The human genome consists of approximately three billion nucleotide pairs. Just one chromosome may be nearly 100 times longer than a bacterial chromosome. To accomplish this huge job, DNA replication begins at many replication origins and proceeds bidirectionally along each chromosome.

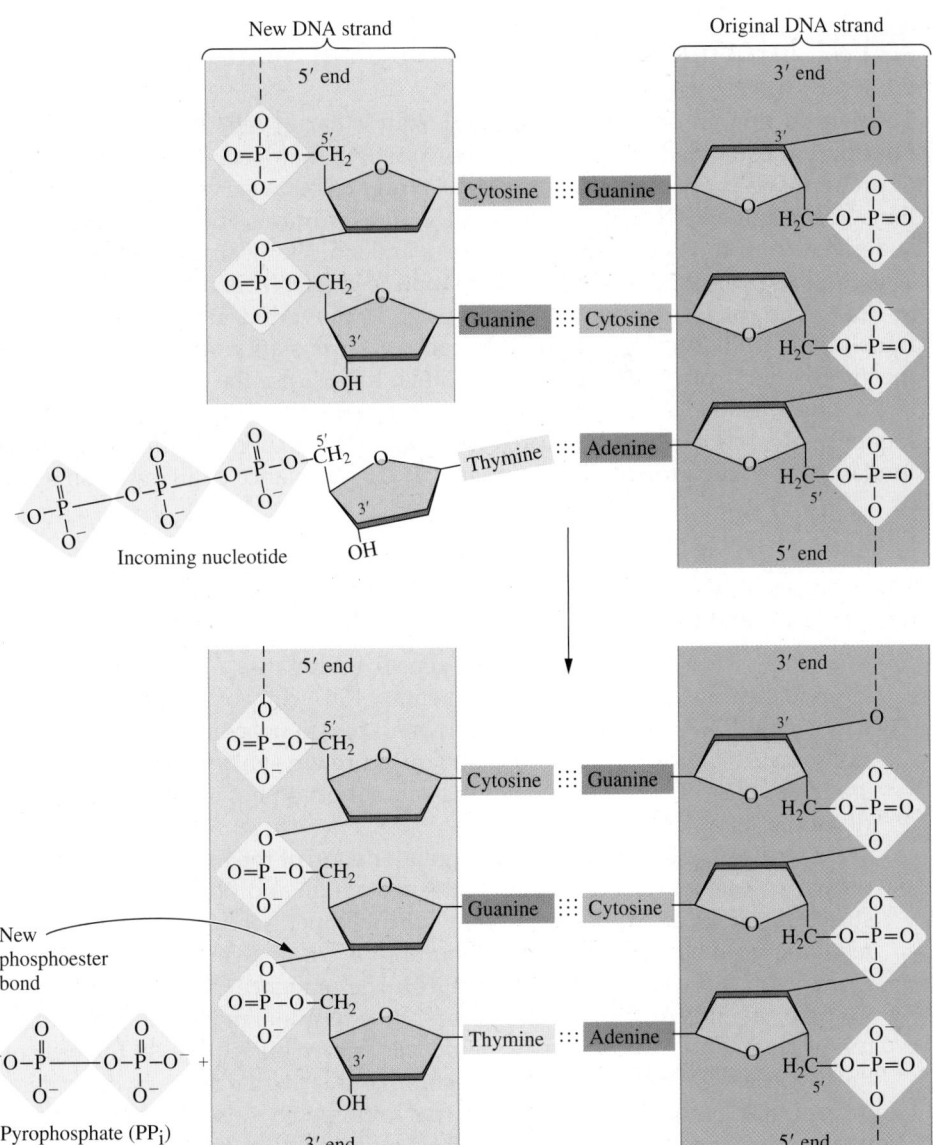

**Figure 20.12** The reaction catalyzed by DNA polymerase.

**Figure 20.13** Model of the complex events occurring at the replication fork. In this representation, the replication fork is moving to the right. On the leading (top) strand, DNA polymerase III synthesizes DNA in the 5' to 3' direction continuously. Thus, replication proceeds in the same direction as the movement of the replication fork. On the lagging strand, DNA polymerase III also synthesizes DNA in the 5' to 3' direction. However, since the DNA strands are antiparallel, DNA polymerase III must read this strand in short segments (discontinuously) and in the opposite direction of the movement of the replication fork.

**ANIMATION**
• Simple Gene Expression

**ANIMATIONS**
• mRNA Synthesis (Transcription)
• Transcription
• Stages of Transcription

## 20.4 Information Flow in Biological Systems

The **central dogma** of molecular biology states that in cells the flow of genetic information contained in DNA is a one-way street that leads from DNA to RNA to protein. The process by which a single strand of DNA serves as a template for the synthesis of an RNA molecule is called **transcription.** The word *transcription* is derived from the Latin word *transcribere* and simply means "to make a copy." Thus, in this process, part of the information in the DNA is copied into a strand of RNA. The process by which the message is converted into protein is called **translation.** Unlike transcription, the process of translation involves converting the information from one language to another. In this case the genetic information in the linear sequence of nucleotides is being translated into a protein, a linear sequence of amino acids. The expression of the information contained in DNA is fundamental to the growth, development, and maintenance of all organisms.

### Classes of RNA Molecules

Three classes of RNA molecules are produced by transcription: messenger RNA, transfer RNA, and ribosomal RNA.

1. **Messenger RNA (mRNA)** carries the genetic information for a protein from DNA to the ribosomes. It is a complementary RNA copy of a gene on the DNA.
2. **Ribosomal RNA (rRNA)** is a structural and functional component of the ribosomes, which are "platforms" on which protein synthesis occurs. There are three types of rRNA molecules in bacterial ribosomes and four in the ribosomes of eukaryotes.
3. **Transfer RNA (tRNA)** translates the genetic code of the mRNA into the primary sequence of amino acids in the protein. In addition to the primary structure, tRNA molecules have a cloverleaf-shaped secondary structure resulting from base pair hydrogen bonding (A—U and G—C) and a roughly L-shaped tertiary structure (Figure 20.14). The sequence CCA is found at the 3' end of the tRNA. The 3'—OH group of the terminal nucleotide, adenosine, can be covalently attached to an amino acid. Three nucleotides at the base of the cloverleaf structure form the **anticodon.** As we will discuss in more detail in Section 20.6, this triplet of bases forms hydrogen bonds to a **codon** (complementary sequence of bases) on a messenger RNA (mRNA) molecule on the surface of a ribosome during protein synthesis. This hydrogen bonding of codon and anticodon brings the correct amino acid to the site of protein synthesis at the appropriate location in the growing peptide chain.

### Transcription

Transcription, shown in Figure 20.15, is catalyzed by the enzyme **RNA polymerase.** The process occurs in three stages. The first, called *initiation,* involves binding of RNA polymerase to a specific nucleotide sequence, the **promoter,** at the beginning of a gene. This interaction of RNA polymerase with specific promoter DNA sequences allows RNA polymerase to recognize the start point for transcription. It also determines which DNA strand will be transcribed. Unlike DNA replication, transcription produces a complementary copy of only one of the two strands of DNA. As it binds to the DNA, RNA polymerase separates the two strands of DNA so that it can "read" the base sequence of the DNA.

The second stage, chain elongation, begins as the RNA polymerase "reads" the DNA template strand and catalyzes the polymerization of a complementary RNA copy. With each step, RNA polymerase transfers a complementary ribonucleotide to the end of the growing RNA chain and catalyzes the formation of a 3'–5' phosphodiester bond between the 5' phosphoryl group of the incoming ribonucleotide and the 3' hydroxyl group of the last ribonucleotide of the growing RNA chain.

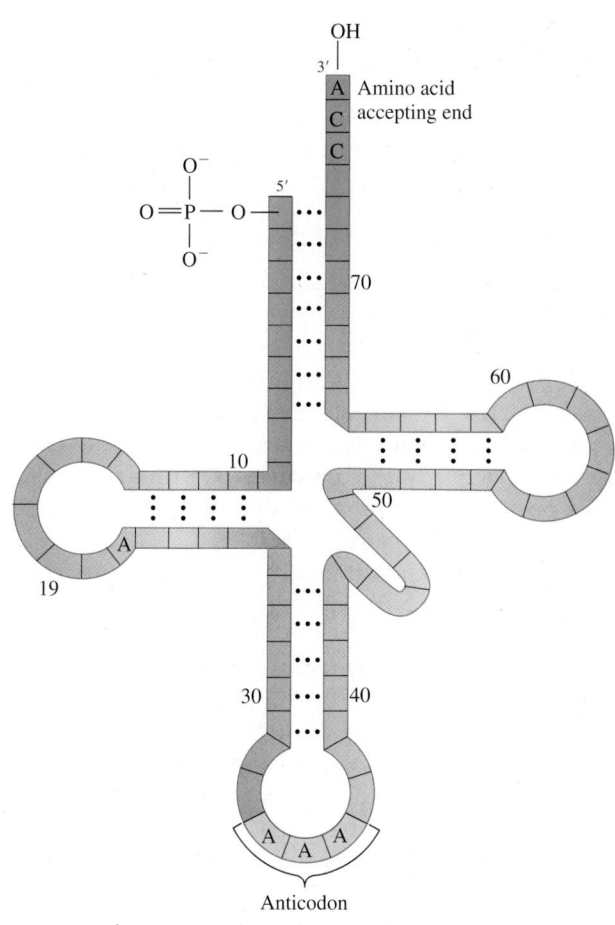

**Figure 20.14** Structure of tRNA. The primary structure of a tRNA is the linear sequence of ribonucleotides. Here we see the hydrogen-bonded secondary structure of a tRNA showing the three loops and the amino acid accepting end.

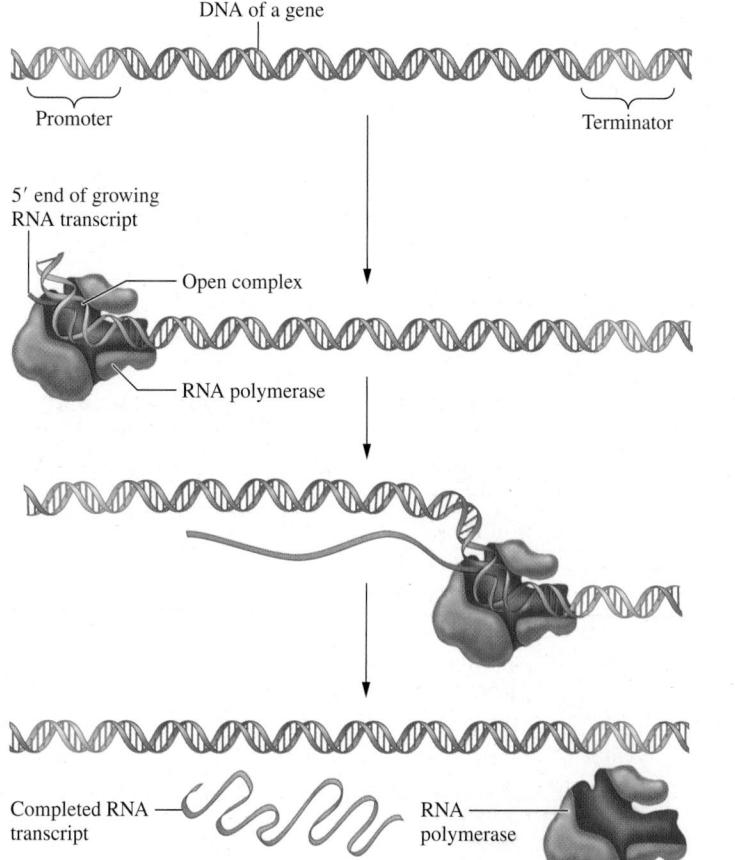

**Figure 20.15** The stages of transcription.

The final stage of transcription is termination. The RNA polymerase finds a termination sequence at the end of the gene and releases the newly formed RNA molecule.

**Question 20.3**  What is the function of RNA polymerase in the process of transcription?

**Question 20.4**  What is the function of the promoter sequence in the process of transcription?

## Post-transcriptional Processing of RNA

In bacteria, which are prokaryotes, termination releases a mature mRNA for translation. In fact, because prokaryotes have no nuclear membrane separating the DNA from the cytoplasm, translation begins long before the mRNA is completed. In eukaryotes, transcription produces a **primary transcript** that must undergo extensive **post-transcriptional modification** before it is exported out of the nucleus for translation in the cytoplasm.

Eukaryotic primary transcripts undergo three post-transcriptional modifications. These are the addition of a 5' cap structure and a 3' poly(A) tail, and RNA splicing.

In the first modification, a **cap structure** is enzymatically added to the 5' end of the primary transcript. The cap structure (Figure 20.16) consists of 7-methyl-guanosine attached to the 5' end of the RNA by a 5'–5' triphosphate bridge. The first two nucleotides of the mRNA are also methylated. The cap structure is required for efficient translation of the final mature mRNA.

The second modification is the enzymatic addition of a **poly(A) tail** to the 3' end of the transcript. *Poly(A) polymerase* uses ATP and catalyzes the stepwise

**Figure 20.16**  The 5'-methylated cap structure of eukaryotic mRNA. $N_1$, $N_2$, and $N_3$ represent any of the four nitrogenous bases adenine, guanine, cytosine, or uracil.

polymerization of 100 to 200 adenosine nucleotides on the 3′ end of the RNA. The poly(A) tail protects the 3′ end of the mRNA from enzymatic degradation and thus prolongs the lifetime of the mRNA.

The third modification, **RNA splicing,** involves the removal of portions of the primary transcript that are not protein coding. Bacterial genes are continuous; all the nucleotide sequences of the gene are found in the mRNA. However, study of the gene structure of eukaryotes revealed a fascinating difference. Eukaryotic genes are discontinuous; there are *extra* DNA sequences within these genes that do not encode any amino acid sequences for the protein. These sequences are called *intervening sequences* or **introns.** The primary transcript contains both the introns and the protein coding sequences, called **exons.** The presence of introns in the mRNA would make it impossible for the process of translation to synthesize the correct protein. Therefore they must be removed, which is done by the process of RNA splicing.

As you can imagine, RNA splicing must be very precise. If too much, or too little, RNA is removed, the mRNA will not carry the correct code for the protein. Thus, there are "signals" in the DNA to mark the boundaries of the introns. The sequence GpU is always found at the intron's 5′ boundary and the sequence ApG is found at the 3′ boundary.

Recognition of the splice boundaries and stabilization of the splicing complex requires the assistance of particles called *spliceosomes.* Spliceosomes are composed of a variety of *small nuclear ribonucleoproteins* (snRNPs, read "snurps"). Each snRNP consists of a small RNA and associated proteins. The RNA components of different snRNPs are complementary to different sequences involved in splicing. By hydrogen bonding to a splice boundary or intron sequences the snRNPs recognize and bring together the sequences involved in the splicing reactions.

One of the first eukaryotic genes shown to contain introns was the gene for the β subunit of adult hemoglobin (Figure 20.17). On the DNA, the gene for β-hemoglobin is 1200 nucleotides long, but only 438 nucleotides carry the genetic information for protein. The remaining sequences are found in two introns of 116 and 646 nucleotides that are removed by splicing before translation. It is interesting that the larger intron is longer than the final β-hemoglobin mRNA! In the genes that have been studied, introns have been found to range in size from 50 to 20,000 nucleotides in length, and there may be many throughout a gene. Thus a typical human gene might be ten to thirty times longer than the final mRNA.

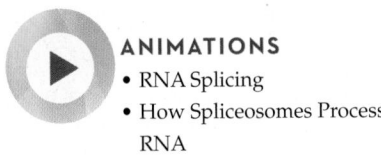

**ANIMATIONS**
• RNA Splicing
• How Spliceosomes Process RNA

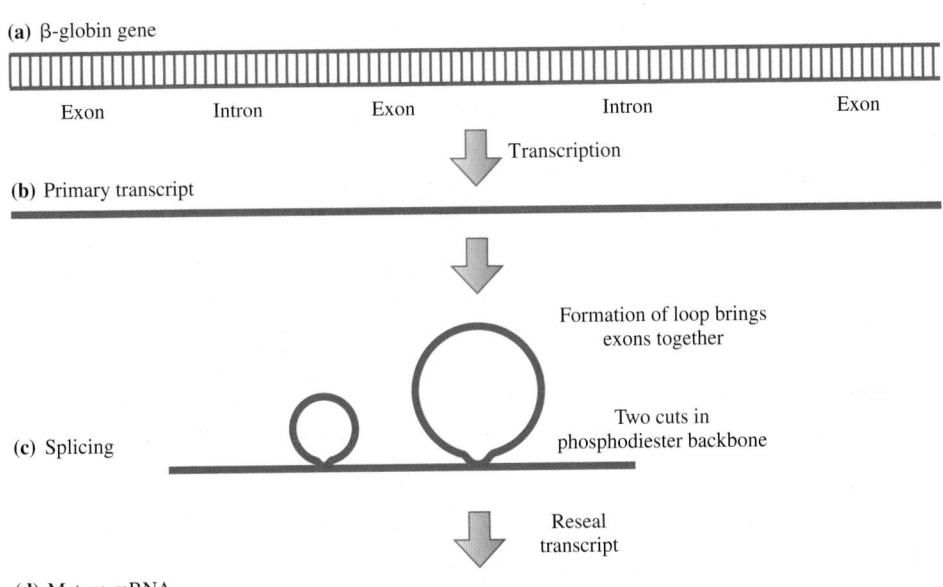

(a) β-globin gene

Exon    Intron    Exon    Intron    Exon

Transcription

(b) Primary transcript

Formation of loop brings exons together

Two cuts in phosphodiester backbone

(c) Splicing

Reseal transcript

(d) Mature mRNA

**Figure 20.17**  Schematic diagram of mRNA splicing. (a) The β-globin gene contains protein coding exons, as well as noncoding sequences called *introns.* (b) The primary transcript of the DNA carries both the introns and the exons. (c) The introns are looped out, the phosphodiester backbone of the mRNA is cut twice, and the pieces are tied together. (d) The final mature mRNA now carries only the coding sequences (exons) of the gene.

## 20.5   The Genetic Code

The mRNA carries the genetic code for a protein. But what is the nature of this code? In 1954, George Gamow proposed that because there are only four "letters" in the DNA alphabet (A, T, G, and C) and because there are twenty amino acids, the genetic code must contain words made of at least three letters taken from the four letters in the DNA alphabet. How did he come to this conclusion? He reasoned that a code of two-letter words constructed from any combination of the four letters has a "vocabulary" of only sixteen words ($4^2$). In other words, there are only sixteen different ways to put A, T, C, and G together two bases at a time (AA, AT, AC, AG, TT, TA, etc.). That is not enough to encode all twenty amino acids. A code of four-letter words gives 256 words ($4^4$), far more than are needed. A code of three-letter words, however, has a possible vocabulary of sixty-four words ($4^3$), sufficient to encode the twenty amino acids but not too excessive.

A series of elegant experiments proved that Gamow was correct by demonstrating that the genetic code is, indeed, a triplet code. Mutations were introduced into the DNA of a bacterial virus. These mutations inserted (or deleted) one, two, or three nucleotides into a gene. The researchers then looked for the protein encoded by that gene. When one or two nucleotides were inserted, no protein was produced. However, when a third base was inserted, the sense of the mRNA was restored, and the protein was made. You can imagine this experiment by using a sentence composed of only three-letter words. For instance,

THE CAT RAN OUT

What happens to the "sense" of the sentence if we insert one letter?

THE FCA TRA NOU T

The reading frame of the sentence has been altered, and the sentence is now nonsense. Can we now restore the sense of the sentence by inserting a second letter?

THE FAC ATR ANO UT

No, we have not restored the sense of the sentence. Once again, we have altered the reading frame, but because our code has only three-letter words, the sentence is still nonsense. If we now insert a third letter, it should restore the correct reading frame:

THE FAT CAT RAN OUT

Indeed, by inserting three new letters we have restored the sense of the message by restoring the reading frame. This is exactly the way in which the message of the mRNA is interpreted. Each group of three nucleotides in the sequence of the mRNA is called a *codon,* and each codes for a single amino acid. If the sequence is interrupted or changed, it can change the amino acid composition of the protein that is produced or even result in the production of no protein at all.

As we noted, a three-letter genetic code contains sixty-four words, called *codons,* but there are only twenty amino acids. Thus, there are forty-four more codons than are required to specify all of the amino acids found in proteins. Three of the codons—UAA, UAG, and UGA—specify termination signals for the process of translation. But this still leaves us with forty-one additional codons. What is the function of the "extra" code words? Francis Crick (recall Watson and Crick and the double helix) proposed that the genetic code is a **degenerate code.** The term *degenerate* is used to indicate that different triplet codons may serve as code words for the same amino acid.

The complete genetic code is shown in Figure 20.18. We can make several observations about the genetic code. First, methionine and tryptophan are the only amino acids that have a single codon. All others have at least two codons, and serine and leucine have six codons each. The genetic code is also somewhat

| FIRST BASE | SECOND BASE | | | | THIRD BASE |
|---|---|---|---|---|---|
| | **U** | **C** | **A** | **G** | |
| **U** | UUU Phenylalanine | UCU Serine | UAU Tyrosine | UGU Cysteine | U |
| | UUC Phenylalanine | UCC Serine | UAC Tyrosine | UGC Cysteine | C |
| | UUA Leucine | UCA Serine | UAA STOP | UGA STOP | A |
| | UUG Leucine | UCG Serine | UAG STOP | UGG Tryptophan | G |
| **C** | CUU Leucine | CCU Proline | CAU Histidine | CGU Arginine | U |
| | CUC Leucine | CCC Proline | CAC Histidine | CGC Arginine | C |
| | CUA Leucine | CCA Proline | CAA Glutamine | CGA Arginine | A |
| | CUG Leucine | CCG Proline | CAG Glutamine | CGG Arginine | G |
| **A** | AUU Isoleucine | ACU Threonine | AAU Asparagine | AGU Serine | U |
| | AUC Isoleucine | ACC Threonine | AAC Asparagine | AGC Serine | C |
| | AUA Isoleucine | ACA Threonine | AAA Lysine | AGA Arginine | A |
| | AUG (START) Methionine | ACG Threonine | AAG Lysine | AGG Arginine | G |
| **G** | GUU Valine | GCU Alanine | GAU Aspartic acid | GGU Glycine | U |
| | GUC Valine | GCC Alanine | GAC Aspartic acid | GGC Glycine | C |
| | GUA Valine | GCA Alanine | GAA Glutamic acid | GGA Glycine | A |
| | GUG Valine | GCG Alanine | GAG Glutamic acid | GGG Glycine | G |

Cys
ACG
tRNA

Asn
UUG
tRNA

**Figure 20.18** The genetic code. The table shows the possible codons found in mRNA. To read the universal biological language from this chart, find the first base in the column on the left, the second base from the row across the top, and the third base from the column to the right. This will direct you to one of the sixty-four squares in the matrix. Within that square you will find the codon and the amino acid that it specifies. In the cell this message is decoded by tRNA molecules like those shown to the right of the table.

mutation-resistant. For those amino acids that have multiple codons, the first two bases are often identical and thus identify the amino acid, and only the third position is variable. Mutations—changes in the nucleotide sequence—in the third position therefore often have no effect on the amino acid that is incorporated into a protein.

**Question 20.5** Why is the genetic code said to be degenerate?

**Question 20.6** Why is the genetic code said to be mutation-resistant?

## 20.6 Protein Synthesis

The process of protein synthesis is called *translation*. It involves translating the genetic information from the sequence of nucleotides into the sequence of amino acids in the primary structure of a protein. Figure 20.19 shows the relationship through which the nucleotide sequence of a DNA molecule is transcribed into a

**LEARNING GOAL**

**8** Describe the process of translation.

**Figure 20.19** Messenger RNA (mRNA) is an RNA copy of one strand of a gene in the DNA. Each codon on the mRNA that specifies a particular amino acid is recognized by the complementary anticodon on a transfer RNA (tRNA).

**ANIMATIONS**
• How Translation Works
• Protein Synthesis

complementary sequence of ribonucleotides, the mRNA molecule. Each mRNA has a short untranslated region followed by the sequences that carry the information for the order of the amino acids in the protein that will be produced in the process of translation. That genetic information is the sequence of codons along the mRNA. The decoding process is carried out by tRNA molecules.

Translation is carried out on **ribosomes,** which are complexes of ribosomal RNA (rRNA) and proteins. Each ribosome is made up of two subunits: a small and a large ribosomal subunit (Figure 20.20a). In eukaryotic cells, the small ribosomal subunit contains one rRNA molecule and thirty-three different ribosomal proteins, and the large subunit contains three rRNA molecules and about forty-nine different proteins.

Protein synthesis involves the simultaneous action of many ribosomes on a single mRNA molecule. These complexes of many ribosomes along a single mRNA are known as *polyribosomes* or **polysomes** (Figure 20.20b). Each ribosome

**Figure 20.20** Structure of the ribosome. (a) The large and small subunits form the functional complex in association with an mRNA molecule. (b) A polyribosome translating the mRNA for a β-globin chain of hemoglobin.

synthesizes one copy of the protein molecule encoded by the mRNA. Thus, many copies of a protein are simultaneously produced.

## The Role of Transfer RNA

The codons of mRNA must be read if the genetic message is to be translated into protein. The molecule that decodes the information in the mRNA molecule into the primary structure of a protein is transfer RNA (tRNA). To decode the genetic message into the primary sequence of a protein, the tRNA must faithfully perform two functions.

*First, the tRNA must covalently bind one, and only one, specific amino acid.* There is at least one transfer RNA for each amino acid. All tRNA molecules have the sequence CCA at their 3' ends. This is the site where the amino acid will be covalently attached to the tRNA molecule. Each tRNA is specifically recognized by the active site of an enzyme called an **aminoacyl tRNA synthetase.** This enzyme also recognizes the correct amino acid and covalently links the amino acid to the 3' end of the tRNA molecule (Figure 20.21). The resulting structure is called an **aminoacyl tRNA.** The covalently bound amino acid will be transferred from the tRNA to a growing polypeptide chain during protein synthesis.

*Second, the tRNA must be able to recognize the appropriate codon on the mRNA that calls for that amino acid.* This is mediated through a sequence of three bases called the *anticodon,* which is located at the bottom of the tRNA cloverleaf (refer to Figure 20.14). The anticodon sequence for each tRNA is complementary to the codon on the mRNA that specifies a particular amino acid. As you can see in Figure 20.19, the anticodon-codon complementary hydrogen bonding will bring the correct amino acid to the site of protein synthesis.

**Question 20.7**   How are codons related to anticodons?

**Question 20.8**   If the sequence of a codon on the mRNA is 5'-AUG-3', what will the sequence of the anticodon be? Remember that the hydrogen bonding rules require antiparallel strands. It is easiest to write the anticodon first 3'⟶5' and then reverse it to the 5'⟶3' order.

## The Process of Translation

### Initiation

The first stage of protein synthesis is *initiation.* Proteins called **initiation factors** assist in the formation of a translation complex composed of an mRNA molecule, the small and large ribosomal subunits, and the initiator tRNA. This initiator tRNA recognizes the codon AUG and carries the amino acid methionine.

The ribosome has two sites for binding tRNA molecules. The first site, called the **peptidyl tRNA binding site (P-site),** holds the peptidyl tRNA, the growing peptide bound to a tRNA molecule. The second site, called the **aminoacyl tRNA binding site (A-site),** holds the aminoacyl tRNA carrying the next amino acid to be added to the peptide chain. Each of the tRNA molecules is hydrogen bonded to the mRNA molecule by codon-anticodon complementarity. The entire complex is further stabilized by the fact that the mRNA is also bound to the ribosome. Figure 20.22a shows the series of events that result in the formation of the initiation complex. The initiator methionyl tRNA occupies the P-site in this complex.

### Chain Elongation

The second stage of translation is *chain elongation.* This occurs in three steps that are repeated until protein synthesis is complete. We enter the action after a

**ANIMATION**
• Aminoacyl tRNA Synthetase

**LEARNING GOAL**

**8**   Describe the process of translation.

**ANIMATION**
• Translation Initiation

**ANIMATION**
• Translation Elongation

**Figure 20.21** Aminoacyl tRNA synthetase binds the amino acid in one region of
the active site and the appropriate tRNA
in another. The acylation reaction occurs
and the aminoacyl tRNA is released.

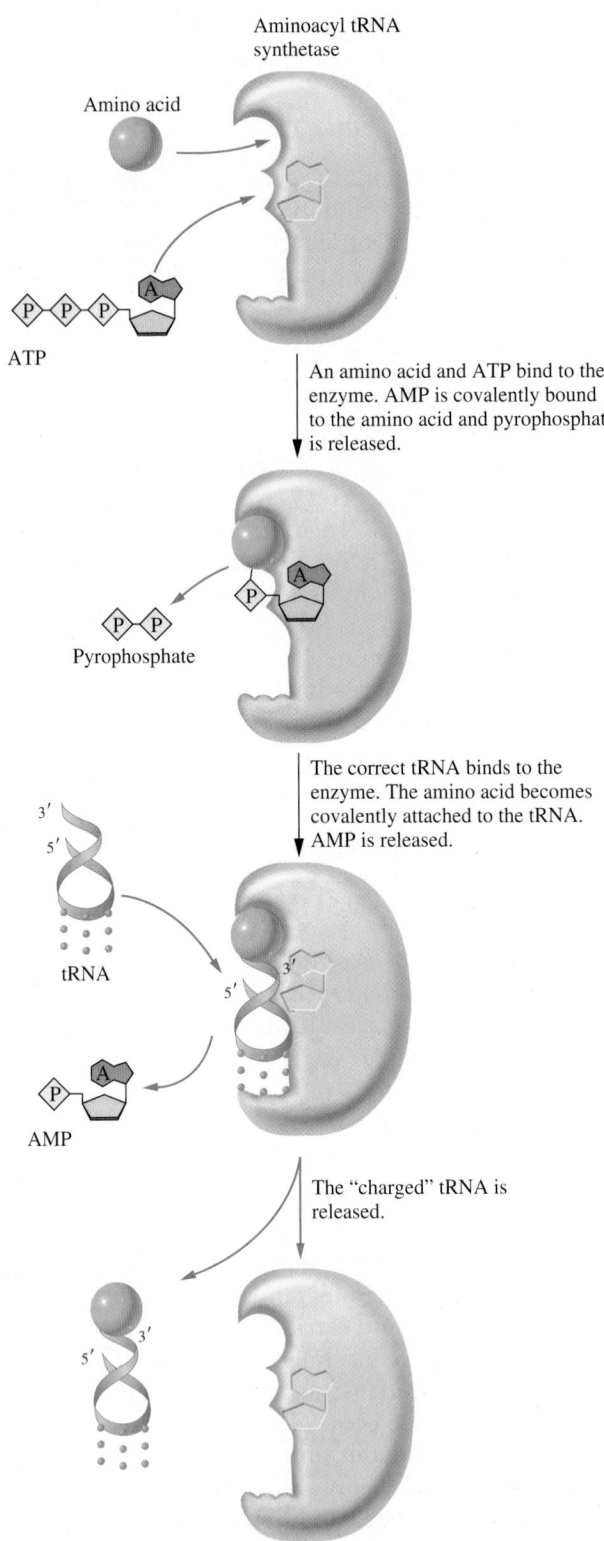

Aminoacyl tRNA
synthetase

Amino acid

ATP

An amino acid and ATP bind to the
enzyme. AMP is covalently bound
to the amino acid and pyrophosphate
is released.

Pyrophosphate

The correct tRNA binds to the
enzyme. The amino acid becomes
covalently attached to the tRNA.
AMP is released.

3′
5′

tRNA

5′    3′

AMP

The "charged" tRNA is
released.

5′    3′

tetrapeptide has already been assembled, and a peptidyl tRNA occupies the P-site
(Figure 20.22b).

The first event is binding of an aminoacyl-tRNA molecule to the empty A-site.
Next, peptide bond formation occurs. This is catalyzed by an enzyme on the ribosome called *peptidyl transferase*. Now the peptide chain is shifted to the tRNA that

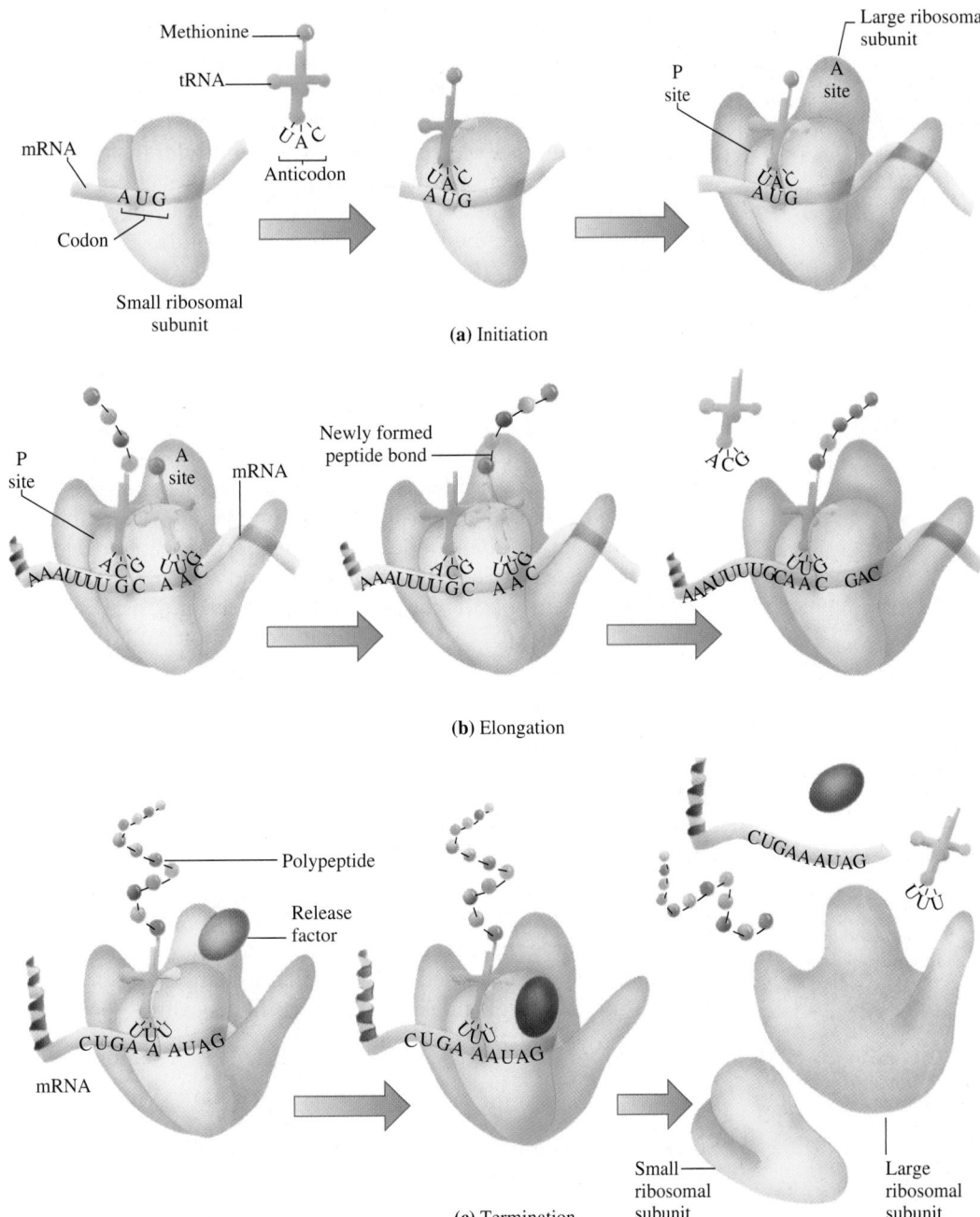

**Figure 20.22** (a) Formation of an initiation complex sets protein synthesis in motion. The mRNA and proteins called *initiation factors* bind to the small ribosomal subunit. Next, a charged methionyl tRNA molecule binds, and finally, the initiation factors are released, and the large subunit binds. (b) The elongation phase of protein synthesis involves addition of new amino acids to the C-terminus of the growing peptide. An aminoacyl tRNA molecule binds at the empty A-site, and the peptide bond is formed. The uncharged tRNA molecule is released, and the peptidyl tRNA is shifted to the P-site as the ribosome moves along the mRNA. (c) Termination of protein synthesis occurs when a release factor binds the stop codon on mRNA. This leads to the hydrolysis of the ester bond linking the peptide to the peptidyl tRNA molecule in the P-site. The ribosome then dissociates into its two subunits, releasing the mRNA and the newly synthesized peptide.

occupies the A-site. Finally, the tRNA in the P-site falls away, and the ribosome changes positions so that the next codon on the mRNA occupies the A-site. This movement of the ribosome is called **translocation.** The process shifts the new peptidyl tRNA from the A-site to the P-site. The chain elongation stage of translation requires the hydrolysis of GTP to GDP and $P_i$. Several **elongation factors** are also involved in this process.

Recent evidence indicates that the peptidyl transferase is a catalytic region of the 28S ribosomal RNA.

ANIMATION
• Translation Termination

*Post-translational proteolytic cleavage of digestive enzymes is discussed in Section 19.11.*

*The quaternary structure of hemoglobin is described in Section 18.8.*

## LEARNING GOAL

**9**  Define mutation and understand how mutations cause cancer and cell death.

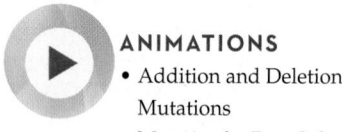

ANIMATIONS
• Addition and Deletion Mutations
• Mutation by Base Substitution

### Termination

The last stage of translation is *termination*. There are three **termination codons**—UAA, UAG, and UGA—for which there are no corresponding tRNA molecules. When one of these "stop" codons is encountered, translation is terminated. A **release factor** binds the empty A-site. The peptidyl transferase that had previously catalyzed peptide bond formation hydrolyzes the ester bond between the peptidyl tRNA and the last amino acid of the newly synthesized protein (Figure 20.22c). At this point the tRNA, the newly synthesized peptide, and the two ribosomal subunits are released.

**Question 20.9**   What is the function of the ribosomal P-site in protein synthesis?

**Question 20.10**   What is the function of the ribosomal A-site in protein synthesis?

The peptide that is released following translation is not necessarily in its final functional form. In some cases the peptide is proteolytically cleaved before it becomes functional. Synthesis of digestive enzymes uses this strategy. Sometimes the protein must associate with other peptides to form a functional protein, as in the case of hemoglobin. Cellular enzymes add carbohydrate or lipid groups to some proteins, especially those that will end up on the cell surface. These final modifications are specific for particular proteins and, like the sequence of the protein itself, are directed by the cellular genetic information.

## 20.7 Mutation, Ultraviolet Light, and DNA Repair

### The Nature of Mutations

Changes can occur in the nucleotide sequence of a DNA molecule. Such a genetic change is called a **mutation.** Mutations can arise from mistakes made by DNA polymerase during DNA replication. They also result from the action of chemicals, called **mutagens,** that damage the DNA.

Mutations are classified by the kind of change that occurs in the DNA. The substitution of a single nucleotide for another is called a **point mutation:**

| ATGGACTTC: | normal DNA sequence |
| ATGCACTTC: | point mutation |

Sometimes a single nucleotide or even large sections of DNA are lost. These are called **deletion mutations:**

| ATGGACTTC: | normal DNA sequence |
| ATGTTC: | deletion mutation |

Occasionally, one or more nucleotides are added to a DNA sequence. These are called **insertion mutations:**

| ATGGACTTC: | normal DNA sequence |
| ATGCTCGACTTC: | insertion mutation |

### The Results of Mutations

Some mutations are **silent mutations;** that is, they cause no change in the protein. Often, however, a mutation has a negative effect on the health of the organism. The effect of a mutation depends on how it alters the genetic code for a protein. Consider the two codons for glutamic acid: GAA and GAG. A point mutation that alters the third nucleotide of GAA to GAG will still result in the incorporation of glutamic acid at the correct position in the protein. Similarly, a GA<u>G</u> to GA<u>A</u> mutation will also be silent.

Many mutations are not silent. There are approximately four thousand human genetic disorders that result from such mutations. These occur because the mutation in the DNA changes the codon and results in incorporation of the wrong amino acid into the protein. This causes the protein to be nonfunctional or to function improperly.

Consider the human genetic disorder sickle cell anemia. In the normal β-chain of hemoglobin, the sixth amino acid is glutamic acid. In the β-chain of sickle cell hemoglobin, the sixth amino acid is valine. How did this amino acid substitution arise? The answer lies in examination of the codons for glutamic acid and valine:

| | |
|---|---|
| Glutamic acid: | GAA or GAG |
| Valine: | GUG, GUC, GUA, or GUU |

A point mutation of A⟶U in the second nucleotide changes some codons for glutamic acid into codons for valine:

$$G\underline{A}A \quad \longrightarrow \quad G\underline{U}A$$
$$G\underline{A}G \quad \longrightarrow \quad G\underline{U}G$$

Glutamic acid codon        Valine codon

This mutation in a single codon leads to the change in amino acid sequence at position 6 in the β-chain of human hemoglobin from glutamic acid to valine. The result of this seemingly minor change is sickle cell anemia in individuals who inherit two copies of the mutant gene.

**Question 20.11**   The sequence of a gene on the mRNA is normally AUGCCC-GACUUU. A point mutation in the gene results in the mRNA sequence AUGC<u>G</u>CGACUUU. What are the amino acid sequences of the normal and mutant proteins? Would you expect this to be a silent mutation?

**Question 20.12**   The sequence of a gene on the mRNA is normally AUGCCC-GACUUU. A point mutation in the gene results in the mRNA sequence AUGCC<u>G</u>GACUUU. What are the amino acid sequences of the normal and mutant proteins? Would you expect this to be a silent mutation?

## Mutagens and Carcinogens

Any chemical that causes a change in the DNA sequence is called a *mutagen*. Often, mutagens are also **carcinogens,** cancer-causing chemicals. Most cancers result from mutations in a single normal cell. These mutations result in the loss of normal growth control, causing the abnormal cell to proliferate. If that growth is not controlled or destroyed, it will result in the death of the individual. We are exposed to many carcinogens in the course of our lives. Sometimes we are exposed to a carcinogen by accident, but in some cases it is by choice. Cigarette smoke has about three thousand chemical components and several are potent mutagens. As a result, people who smoke have a much greater chance of developing lung cancer than those who don't.

## Ultraviolet Light Damage and DNA Repair

Ultraviolet (UV) light is another agent that causes damage to DNA. Absorption of UV light by DNA causes adjacent pyrimidine bases to become covalently linked. The product is called a **pyrimidine dimer.** As a result of pyrimidine dimer formation, there is no hydrogen bonding between these pyrimidine molecules and the complementary bases on the other DNA strand. This stretch of DNA cannot be replicated or transcribed!

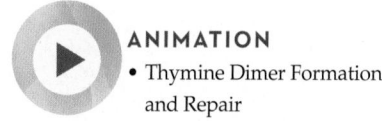

**ANIMATION**
• Thymine Dimer Formation and Repair

# A MEDICAL PERSPECTIVE

## The Ames Test for Carcinogens

Each day we come into contact with a variety of chemicals, including insecticides, food additives, hair dyes, automobile emissions, and cigarette smoke. Some of these chemicals have the potential to cause cancer. How do we determine whether these agents are harmful? More particularly, how do we determine whether they cause cancer?

If we consider the example of cigarette smoke, we see that it can be years, even centuries, before a relationship is seen between a chemical and cancer. Europeans and Americans have been smoking since Sir Walter Raleigh introduced tobacco into England in the seventeenth century. However, it was not until three centuries later that physicians and scientists demonstrated the link between smoking and lung cancer. Obviously, this epidemiological approach takes too long, and too many people die. Alternatively, we can test chemicals by treating laboratory animals, such as mice, and observing them for various kinds of cancer. However, this, too, can take years, is expensive, and requires the sacrifice of many laboratory animals. How, then, can chemicals be tested for carcinogenicity (the ability to cause cancer) quickly and inexpensively? In the 1970s it was recognized that most carcinogens are also mutagens. That is, they cause cancer by causing mutations in the DNA, and the mutations cause the cells of the body to lose growth control. Bruce Ames, a biochemist and bacterial geneticist, developed a test using mutants of the bacterium *Salmonella typhimurium* that can demonstrate in 48–72 hours (h) whether a chemical is a mutagen and thus a suspected carcinogen.

Ames chose several mutants of *S. typhimurium* that cannot grow unless the amino acid histidine is added to the growth medium. The Ames test involves subjecting these bacteria to a chemical and determining whether the chemical causes reversion of the mutation. In other words, the researcher is looking for a mutation that reverses the original mutation. When a reversion occurs, the bacteria will be able to grow in the absence of histidine.

The details of the Ames test are shown in the accompanying figure. Both an experimental and a control test are done. The control test contains no carcinogen and will show the number of spontaneous revertants that occur in the culture. A very small amount of histidine is added to the experimental and control cultures to allow a few rounds of DNA replication. This is needed for the formation of the reverse mutations. If there are many colonies on the surface of the experimental plate and only a few colonies on the negative control plate, it can be concluded that the chemical tested is a mutagen. It is therefore possible that the chemical is also a carcinogen.

The Ames test has greatly accelerated our ability to test new compounds for mutagenic and possibly carcinogenic effects. However, once the Ames test identifies a mutagenic compound, testing in animals must be done to show conclusively that the compound also causes cancer.

### For Further Understanding

▶ A researcher carried out the Ames test in which an experimental sample was exposed to a suspected mutagen and a control sample was not. A sample from each tube was grown on a medium containing no histidine. On the experimental plate, he observed forty-three colonies and on the control plate, he observed thirty-one colonies. He concluded that the substance is a mutagen. When he reported his data and conclusion to his supervisor, she told him that his conclusions were not valid. How can the researcher modify his experimental procedure to obtain better data?

▶ Suppose that the mutation in a strain of *S. typhimurium* produces the codon UUA instead of UUC. What is the amino acid change caused by this mutation? What base substitutions could correct the mutant codon so that it once again calls for the correct amino acid? What base substitutions would not correct the mutant codon?

The Ames test for carcinogenic compounds.

Bacteria such as *Escherichia coli* have four different mechanisms to repair UV light damage. However, even a repair process can make a mistake. Mutations occur when the UV damage repair system makes an error and causes a change in the nucleotide sequence of the DNA.

In medicine, the pyrimidine dimerization reaction is used to advantage in hospitals where germicidal (UV) light is used to kill bacteria in the air and on environmental surfaces, such as in a vacant operating room. This cell death is caused by pyrimidine dimer formation on a massive scale. The repair systems of the bacteria are overwhelmed, and the cells die.

Of course, the same type of pyrimidine dimer formation can occur in human cells as well. Lying out in the sun all day to acquire a fashionable tan exposes the skin to large amounts of UV light. This damages the skin by formation of many pyrimidine dimers. Exposure to high levels of UV from sunlight or tanning booths has been linked to a rising incidence of skin cancer in human populations.

### Consequences of Defects in DNA Repair

The human repair system for pyrimidine dimers is quite complex, requiring at least five enzymes. The first step in repair of the pyrimidine dimer is the cleavage of the sugar-phosphate backbone of the DNA near the site of the damage. The enzyme that performs this is called a *repair endonuclease*. If the gene encoding this enzyme is defective, pyrimidine dimers cannot be repaired. The accumulation of mutations combined with a simultaneous decrease in the efficiency of DNA repair mechanisms leads to an increased incidence of cancer. For example, a mutation in the repair endonuclease gene, or in other genes in the repair pathway, results in the genetic skin disorder called *xeroderma pigmentosum*. People who suffer from xeroderma pigmentosum are extremely sensitive to the ultraviolet rays of sunlight and develop multiple skin cancers, usually before the age of twenty.

Pyrimidine dimers were originally called thymine dimers because thymine is more commonly involved in these reactions than cytosine.

This mother is applying sunscreen to her daughter to shield her from UV radiation. Explain the kind of damage that UV light can cause and what the potential long-term effects may be.

## 20.8  Recombinant DNA

### Tools Used in the Study of DNA

Scientists are often asked why they study such seemingly unimportant subjects as bacterial DNA replication. One very good reason is that such studies often lend insight into the workings of human genetic systems. A second is that such research often produces the tools that allow great leaps into new technologies. Nowhere is this more true than in the development of recombinant DNA technology. Many of the techniques and tools used in recombinant DNA studies were developed or discovered during basic studies on bacterial DNA replication and gene expression. These include many enzymes that catalyze reactions of DNA molecules, gel electrophoresis, cloning vectors, and hybridization techniques.

#### Restriction Enzymes

**Restriction enzymes,** often called *restriction endonucleases*, are bacterial enzymes that "cut" the sugar-phosphate backbone of DNA molecules at specific nucleotide sequences. The first of these enzymes to be purified and studied was called EcoR1. The name is derived from the genus and species name of the bacteria from which it was isolated, in this case *Escherichia coli*, or *E. coli*. The following is the specific nucleotide sequence recognized by EcoR1:

LEARNING GOAL

**10**  Describe the tools used in the study of DNA and in genetic engineering.

**ANIMATION**
• Restriction Endonucleases

```
5' -------------- GAATTC -------------- 3'
3' -------------- CTTAAG -------------- 5'
```

When EcoR1 cuts the DNA at this site, it does so in a staggered fashion. Specifically, it cuts between the G and the first A on both strands. Cutting produces two DNA fragments with the following structure:

```
5' ---------------- G            AATTC -------------- 3'
3' ---------------- CTTAA             G -------------- 5'
```

These staggered termini are called *sticky ends* because they can reassociate with one another by hydrogen bonding. This is a property of the DNA fragments generated by restriction enzymes that is very important to gene cloning.

Examples of other restriction enzymes and their specific recognition sequences are listed in Table 20.2. The sites on the sugar-phosphate backbone that are cut by the enzymes are indicated by slashes.

These enzymes are used to digest large DNA molecules into smaller fragments of specific size. Because a restriction enzyme always cuts at the same site, DNA from a particular individual generates a reproducible set of DNA fragments. This is convenient for the study or cloning of DNA from any source.

### Agarose Gel Electrophoresis

ANIMATION
• Electrophoresis

One means of studying the DNA fragments produced by restriction enzyme digestion is agarose gel electrophoresis. The digested DNA sample is placed in a sample well in the gel, and an electrical current is applied. The negative charge of the phosphoryl groups in the sugar-phosphate backbone causes the DNA fragment to move through the gel away from the negative electrode (cathode) and toward the positive electrode (anode). The smaller DNA fragments move more rapidly than the larger ones, and as a result the DNA fragments end up distributed throughout the gel according to their size. The size of each fragment can be determined by comparison with the migration pattern of DNA fragments of known size.

### Hybridization

Agarose gel electrophoresis allows the determination of the size of a DNA fragment. However, in recombinant DNA research it is also important to identify what gene is carried by a particular DNA fragment.

**Hybridization** is a technique used to identify the presence of a gene on a particular DNA fragment. This technique is based on the fact that complementary DNA sequences will hydrogen bond, or hybridize, to one another. In fact, even RNA can be used in hybridization studies. RNA can hybridize to DNA molecules or to other RNA molecules.

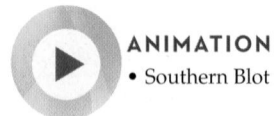
ANIMATION
• Southern Blot

One technique, called Southern blotting, involves hybridization of DNA fragments from an agarose gel (Figure 20.23a). DNA digested by a restriction

**TABLE 20.2  Common Restriction Enzymes and Their Recognition Sequences**

| Restriction Enzyme | Recognition Sequence |
|---|---|
| BamHI | 5'-G/GATCC-3' |
|  | 3'-CCTAG/G-5' |
| HindIII | 5'-A/AGCTT-3' |
|  | 3'-TTCGA/A-5' |
| SalI | 5'-G/TCGAC-3' |
|  | 3'-CAGCT/G-5' |
| BglII | 5'-A/GATCT-3' |
|  | 3'-TCTAG/A-5' |
| PstI | 5'-CTGCA/G-3' |
|  | 3'-G/ACGTC-5' |

A sample of chromosomal DNA is digested into small fragments with a restriction enzyme.

The fragments are separated by gel electrophoresis, and then denatured.

Gel

As shown in part b, the DNA bands are transferred to a nitrocellulose filter.

Nitrocellulose filter (DNA bands would not be visible at this stage.)

The filter is placed in a solution containing a radiolabeled probe. Excess probe is washed away, and the filter is exposed to X-ray film.

Lid

Cathode plate

Blotting paper

Gel

Nitrocellulose filter

Blotting paper

Anode plate

Base

**(a)** The steps in Southern blotting

**(b)** The transfer step in a Southern blotting experiment

**Figure 20.23**  Southern blot hybridization. (a) DNA is digested and the fragments are separated by gel electrophoresis. The DNA is transferred from the gel onto a filter and "melted" into single strands. A radioactive probe is applied and the filter exposed to X-ray film. (b) An electroblotting apparatus for the transfer of DNA from a gel onto a filter.

enzyme is run on an agarose gel. Next the DNA fragments are transferred by blotting onto a special membrane filter. Figure 20.23b shows an apparatus that uses an electric field to transfer DNA from a gel onto a filter. In the next step, the DNA molecules on the filter are "melted" into single DNA strands so that they are ready for hybridization. The filter is then bathed in a solution containing a radioactive DNA or RNA molecule. This probe will hybridize to any DNA fragments on the filter that are complementary to it. X-ray film is used to detect any bands where the radioactive probe hybridized, thus locating the gene of interest.

### DNA Cloning Vectors

DNA cloning experiments combine these technologies with a few additional tricks to isolate single copies of a gene and then produce billions of copies. To produce multiple copies of a gene, it may be joined to a **cloning vector.** A cloning vector is a piece of DNA having its own replication origin so that it can be replicated inside a host cell. Often the bacterium *E. coli* serves as the host cell in which the vector carrying the cloned DNA is replicated in abundance.

There are two major kinds of cloning vectors. The first are bacterial virus or phage vectors. These are bacterial viruses that have been genetically altered to allow the addition of cloned DNA fragments. These viruses have all the genes required to replicate 100 to 200 copies of the virus (and cloned fragment) per infected cell.

The second commonly used vector is a plasmid vector. Plasmids are extra pieces of circular DNA found in most kinds of bacteria. The plasmids that are used as cloning vectors often contain antibiotic resistance genes that are useful in the selection of cells containing a plasmid.

Each plasmid has its own replication origin to allow efficient DNA replication in the bacterial host cell. Most plasmid vectors also have a *selectable marker,* often a gene for resistance to an antibiotic. Finally, plasmid vectors have a gene that has several restriction enzyme sites useful for cloning. The valuable feature of this gene is that it is inactivated when a DNA fragment has been cloned into it. Thus, cells containing a plasmid carrying a cloned DNA fragment can be recognized by their ability to grow in the presence of antibiotic and by loss of function of the gene into which the cloned DNA has been inserted.

### Genetic Engineering

Now that we have assembled most of the tools needed for a cloning experiment, we must decide which gene to clone. The example that we will use is the cloning of the β-globin genes for normal and sickle cell hemoglobin. DNA from an individual with normal hemoglobin is digested with a restriction enzyme. This is the target DNA. The vector DNA must be digested with the same enzyme (Figure 20.24). In our example, the restriction enzyme cuts within the *lacZ* gene, which codes for the enzyme β-galactosidase.

The digested vector and target DNA are mixed together under conditions that encourage the sticky ends of the target and vector DNA to hybridize with one another. The sticky ends are then covalently linked by the enzyme DNA ligase. This enzyme catalyzes the formation of phosphoester bonds between the two pieces of DNA.

Now the recombinant DNA molecules are introduced into bacterial cells by a process called transformation. Next, the cells of the transformation mixture are plated on a solid nutrient agar medium containing the antibiotic ampicillin and the β-galactosidase substrate X-gal (5-bromo-4-chloro-3-indolyl-β-D-galactoside). Only those cells containing the antibiotic resistance gene will survive and grow

Antibiotic resistance causes countless problems in the treatment of bacterial infections.

**ANIMATIONS**
• Construction of a Plasmid Vector
• Steps in Cloning a Gene

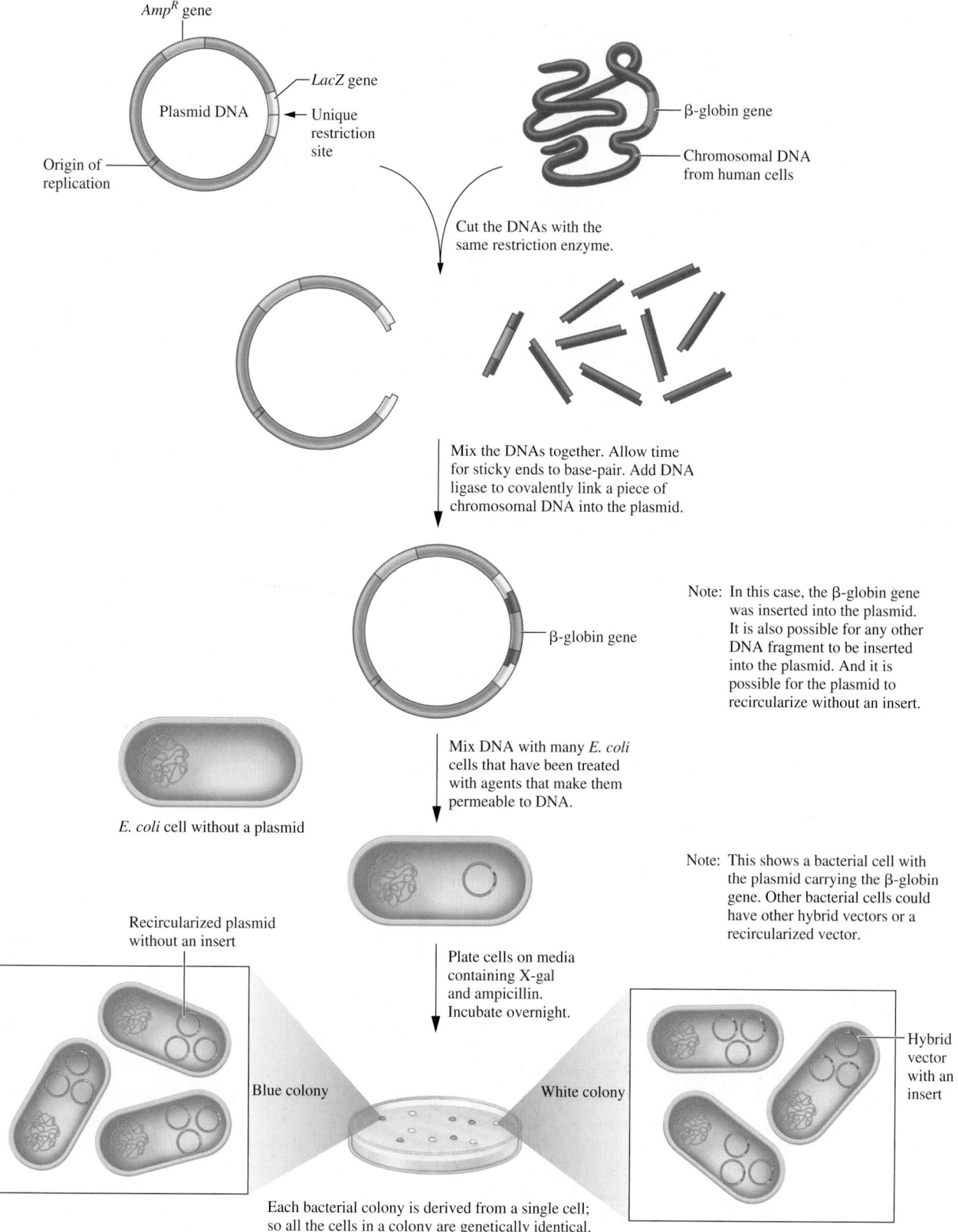

**Figure 20.24** Cloning of eukaryotic DNA into a plasmid cloning vector.

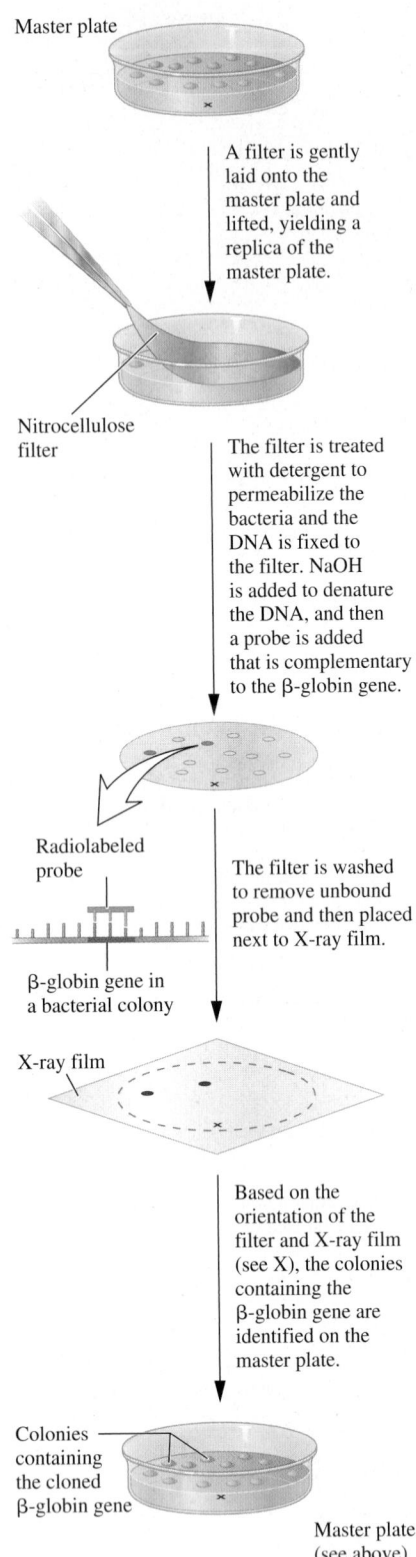

Master plate

A filter is gently laid onto the master plate and lifted, yielding a replica of the master plate.

Nitrocellulose filter

The filter is treated with detergent to permeabilize the bacteria and the DNA is fixed to the filter. NaOH is added to denature the DNA, and then a probe is added that is complementary to the β-globin gene.

Radiolabeled probe

The filter is washed to remove unbound probe and then placed next to X-ray film.

β-globin gene in a bacterial colony

X-ray film

Based on the orientation of the filter and X-ray film (see X), the colonies containing the β-globin gene are identified on the master plate.

Colonies containing the cloned β-globin gene

Master plate (see above)

**Figure 20.25** Colony blot hybridization for detection of cells carrying a plasmid clone of the β-chain gene of hemoglobin.

into bacterial colonies. Cells with an intact *lacZ* gene will produce the enzyme β-galactosidase. The enzyme will hydrolyze X-gal to produce a blue product that will cause the colonies to appear blue. If the *lacZ* gene has been inactivated by insertion of a cloned gene, no β-galactosidase will be produced and the colonies will be white.

Now hybridization can be used to detect the clones that carry the β-globin gene. A replica of the experimental plate is made by transferring some cells from each colony onto a membrane filter. These cells are gently broken open so that the released DNA becomes attached to the membrane. When hybridization is carried out on these filters, the radioactive probe will hybridize only to the complementary sequences of the β-globin gene. When the membrane filter is exposed to X-ray film, a "spot" will appear on the developed film only at the site of a colony carrying the desired clone. By going back to the original plate, we can select cells from that colony and grow them for further study (Figure 20.25).

The same procedure can be used to clone the β-chain gene of sickle cell hemoglobin. Then the two can be studied and compared to determine the nature of the genetic defect.

This simple example makes it appear that all gene cloning is very easy and straightforward. This has proved to be far from the truth. Genetic engineers have had to overcome many obstacles to clone eukaryotic genes of particular medical interest. One of the first obstacles encountered was the presence of introns within eukaryotic genes. Bacteria that are used for cloning lack the enzymatic machinery to splice out introns. Molecular biologists found that a DNA copy of a eukaryotic mRNA could be made by using the enzyme reverse transcriptase from a family of viruses called *retroviruses*. Such a DNA copy of the mRNA carries all the protein-coding sequences of a gene but none of the intron sequences. Thus bacteria are able to transcribe and translate the cloned DNA and produce valuable products for use in medicine and other applications.

This is only one of the many technical problems that have been overcome by the amazing developments in recombinant DNA technology. A brief but impressive list of medically important products of genetic engineering is presented in Table 20.3.

**TABLE 20.3 A Brief List of Medically Important Proteins Produced by Genetic Engineering**

| Protein | Medical Condition Treated |
|---|---|
| Insulin | Insulin-dependent diabetes |
| Human growth hormone | Pituitary dwarfism |
| Factor VIII | Type A hemophilia |
| Factor IX | Type B hemophilia |
| Tissue plasminogen factor | Stroke, myocardial infarction |
| Streptokinase | Myocardial infarction |
| Interferon | Cancer, some virus infections |
| Interleukin-2 | Cancer |
| Tumor necrosis factor | Cancer |
| Atrial natriuretic factor | Hypertension |
| Erythropoietin | Anemia |
| Thymosin α-1 | Stimulate immune system |
| Hepatitis B virus (HBV) vaccine | Prevent HBV viral hepatitis |
| Influenza vaccine | Prevent influenza infection |

## 20.9 Polymerase Chain Reaction

A bacterium originally isolated from a hot spring in Yellowstone National Park provides the key to a powerful molecular tool for the study of DNA. Polymerase chain reaction (PCR) allows scientists to produce unlimited amounts of any gene of interest and the bacterium *Thermus aquaticus* produces a heat-stable DNA polymerase (Taq polymerase) that allows the process to work.

The human genome consists of approximately three billion base pairs of DNA. But suppose you are interested in studying only one gene, perhaps the gene responsible for muscular dystrophy or cystic fibrosis. It's like looking for a needle in a haystack. Using PCR, a scientist can make millions of copies of the gene of interest, while ignoring the thousands of other genes on human chromosomes.

The secret to this specificity is the synthesis of a DNA primer, a short piece of single-stranded DNA that will specifically hybridize to the beginning of a particular gene. DNA polymerases require a primer for initiation of DNA synthesis because they act by adding new nucleotides to the 3'—OH of the last nucleotide of the primer.

To perform PCR, a small amount of DNA is mixed with Taq polymerase, the primer, and the four DNA nucleotide triphosphates. The mixture is then placed in an instrument called a *thermocycler*. The temperature in the thermocycler is raised to 94–96°C for several minutes to separate the two strands of DNA. Because the Taq polymerase is heat-stable, it is not denatured by these temperatures. The temperature is then dropped to 50–56°C to allow the primers to hybridize to the target DNA. Finally, the temperature is raised to 72°C to allow Taq polymerase to act, reading the template DNA strand and polymerizing a daughter strand extended from the primer. At the end of this step, the amount of the gene has doubled (Figure 20.26).

Now the three steps are repeated. With each cycle the amount of the gene is doubled. Theoretically after thirty cycles, you have one billion times more DNA than you started with!

PCR can be used in genetic screening to detect the gene responsible for muscular dystrophy. It can also be used to diagnose disease. For instance, it can be used to amplify small amounts of HIV in the blood. It can also be used by forensic scientists to amplify DNA from a single hair follicle or a tiny drop of blood at a crime scene.

## 20.10 The Human Genome Project

In 1990 the Department of Energy and the National Institutes of Health began the Human Genome Project (HGP), a multinational project that would extend into the next millennium. The goals of the HGP were to identify all of the genes in human DNA and to sequence the entire three billion nucleotide pairs of the genome. In order to accomplish these goals, enormous computer databases had to be developed to store the information and computer software had to be designed to analyze it.

Initially, the HGP planned to complete the work by the year 2005. However, as a result of technological advances made by those in the project, a working draft of the human genome was published in February 2001 and the successful completion of the project was announced on April 14, 2003.

### Genetic Strategies for Genome Analysis

The strategy for the HGP was rather straightforward. In order to determine the DNA sequence of the human genome, genomic libraries had to be produced. A *genomic library* is a set of clones representing the entire genome. The DNA sequences of each of these clones could then be determined. Of course, once the

**Figure 20.26** Polymerase chain reaction.

### LEARNING GOAL

**11** Describe the process of polymerase chain reaction and discuss potential uses of the process.

 **ANIMATIONS**
- PCR Reactions
- Polymerase Chain Reaction
- DNA Fingerprinting

### LEARNING GOAL

**12** Discuss strategies for genome analysis and DNA sequencing.

# CHEMISTRY AT THE CRIME SCENE

### DNA Fingerprinting

Four U.S. Army helicopters swept over the field of illicit coca plants (*Erythroxylum* spp.) growing in a mountainous region of northern Colombia. When the soldiers were certain that the fields were unguarded, a fifth helicopter landed. From it emerged a team of researchers from the Agricultural Research Service of the U.S. Department of Agriculture (ARS-USDA). Quickly the scientists gathered leaves from mature plants, as well as from seedlings growing in a coca nursery, and returned to the helicopter with their valuable samples. With a final sweep over the field, the Army helicopters sprayed herbicides to kill the coca plants.

From 1997 to 2001, this scene was repeated in regions of Colombia known to have the highest coca production. The reason for these collections was to study the genetic diversity of the coca plants being grown for the illegal production of cocaine. The tool selected for this study was DNA fingerprinting.

DNA fingerprinting was developed in the 1980s by Alec Jeffries of the University of Leicester in England. The idea grew out of basic molecular genetic studies of the human genome. Scientists observed that some DNA sequences varied greatly from one person to the next. Such hypervariable regions are made up of variable numbers of repeats of short DNA sequences. They are located at many sites on different chromosomes. Each person has a different number of repeats and when his or her DNA is digested with restriction enzymes, a unique set of DNA fragments is generated. Jeffries invented DNA fingerprinting by developing a set of DNA probes that detect these variable number tandem repeats (VNTRs) when used in hybridization with Southern blots.

Coca nursery next to a mature field in Colombia.

Although several variations of DNA fingerprinting exist, the basic technique is quite simple. DNA is digested with restriction enzymes, producing a set of DNA fragments. These are separated by electrophoresis through an agarose gel. The DNA fragments are then transferred to membrane filters and hybridized with the radioactive probe DNA. The bands that hybridize the radioactive probe are visualized by exposing the membrane to X-ray film and developing a "picture" of the gel. The result is what Jeffries calls a *DNA fingerprint*, a set of twenty-five to sixty DNA bands that are unique to an individual.

sequence of each of these clones is determined, there is no way to know how they are arranged along the chromosomes.

A second technique, called *chromosome walking*, provides both DNA sequence information and a method for identifying the DNA sequences next to it on the chromosome. This method requires clones that are overlapping. To accomplish this, libraries of clones are made using many different restriction enzymes. The DNA sequence of a fragment is determined. Then that information is used to develop a probe for any clones in the library that are overlapping. Each time a DNA fragment is sequenced, the information is used to identify overlapping clones. This process continues, allowing scientists to walk along the chromosome in two directions until the entire sequence is cloned, mapped, and sequenced.

### DNA Sequencing

The method of DNA sequencing that is used is based on a technique developed by Frederick Sanger. A cloned piece of DNA is separated into its two strands. Each of these will serve as a template strand to carry out DNA replication in test tubes.

An example of a DNA fingerprint used in a criminal case. The DNA sample designated *V* is that of the victim and the sample designated *D* is that of the defendant. The samples labeled *jeans* and *shirt* were taken from the clothing of the defendant. The DNA bands from the defendant's clothing clearly match the DNA bands of the victim, providing evidence of the guilt of the defendant.

DNA fingerprinting is now routinely used for paternity testing, testing for certain genetic disorders, and identification of the dead in cases where no other identification is available. DNA fingerprints are used as evidence in criminal cases involving rape and murder. In such cases, the evidence may be little more than a hair with an intact follicle on the clothing of the victim.

Less widely known is the use of DNA fingerprinting to study genetic diversity in natural populations of plants and animals. The greater the genetic diversity, the healthier the population is likely to be. Populations with low genetic diversity face a far higher probability of extinction under adverse conditions. Customs officials have used DNA fingerprinting to determine whether confiscated elephant tusks were taken illegally from an endangered population of elephants or were obtained from a legally harvested population.

In the case of the coca plants, ARS wanted to know whether the drug cartels were developing improved strains that might be hardier or more pest resistant or that have a higher concentration of cocaine. Their conclusions, which you can read in *Phytochemistry* (64: 187–197, 2003), were that the drug cartels have introduced significant genetic modification into coca plants in Colombia in the last two decades. In addition, some of these new variants, those producing the highest levels of cocaine, have been transplanted to other regions of the country. All of this indicates that the cocaine agribusiness is thriving.

**For Further Understanding**

▸ As this sampling of applications suggests, DNA fingerprinting has become an invaluable tool in law enforcement, medicine, and basic research. What other applications of this technology can you think of?

▸ Do some research on the development of DNA fingerprinting as a research and forensics tool. What is the probability that two individuals will have the same DNA fingerprint? How are these probabilities determined?

A primer strand is also needed. This is a short piece of DNA that will hybridize to the template strand. The primer is the starting point for addition of new nucleotides during DNA synthesis.

The DNA is then placed in four test tubes with all of the enzymes and nucleotides required for DNA synthesis. In addition, each tube contains an unusual nucleotide, called a dideoxynucleotide. These nucleotides differ from the standard nucleotides by having a hydrogen atom at the 3′ position of the deoxyribose, rather than a hydroxyl group. When a dideoxynucleotide is incorporated into a growing DNA chain, it acts as a chain terminator. Because it does not have a 3′-hydroxyl group, no phosphoester bond can be formed with another nucleotide and no further polymerization can occur.

Each of the four tubes containing the DNA, enzymes, and an excess of the nucleotides required for replication will also have a small amount of one of the four dideoxynucleotides. In the tube that receives dideoxyadenosine triphosphate (ddA), for example, DNA synthesis will begin. As replication proceeds, either the standard nucleotide or ddA will be incorporated into the growing strand. Since the

**ANIMATION**
• Sanger Sequencing

# A MEDICAL PERSPECTIVE

## A Genetic Approach to Familial Emphysema

Familial emphysema is a human genetic disease resulting from the inability to produce the protein $\alpha_1$-antitrypsin. See also A Medical Perspective: $\alpha_1$-Antitrypsin and Familial Emphysema, in Chapter 19. In individuals who have inherited one or two copies of the $\alpha_1$-antitrypsin gene, this serum protein protects the lungs from the enzyme elastase. Normally, elastase fights bacteria and helps in the destruction and removal of dead lung tissue. However, the enzyme can also cause lung damage. By inhibiting elastase, $\alpha_1$-antitrypsin prevents lung damage. Individuals who have inherited two defective $\alpha_1$-antitrypsin genes do not produce this protein and suffer from familial, or A1AD, emphysema. In the absence of $\alpha_1$-antitrypsin, the elastase and other proteases cause the severe lung damage characteristic of emphysema.

A1AD is the second most common genetic disorder in Caucasians. It is estimated that there are 100,000 sufferers in the United States and that one in five Americans carries the gene. The disorder, discovered in 1963, is often misdiagnosed as asthma or chronic obstructive pulmonary disease. In fact, it is estimated that fewer than 5% of the sufferers are diagnosed with A1AD.

The $\alpha_1$-antitrypsin gene has been cloned. Early experiments with sheep showed that the protein remains stable when administered as an aerosol and remains functional after it has passed through the pulmonary epithelium. This research offers hope of an effective treatment for this disease.

The current treatment involves weekly IV injections of $\alpha_1$-antitrypsin. The supply of the protein, purified from human plasma that has been demonstrated to be virus free, is rather limited. Thus, the injections are expensive. In addition, they are painful. These two factors cause some sufferers to refuse treatment.

Dr. Terry Flotte and his colleagues at the University of Florida have cloned the gene for $\alpha_1$-antitrypsin into the DNA of adeno-associated virus (AAV). This virus is an ideal vector for human gene replacement therapy because it replicates only in cells that are not dividing and it does not stimulate a strong immune or inflammatory response. The researchers injected the virus carrying the cloned $\alpha_1$-antitrypsin gene into the muscle tissue of mice, then tested for the level of $\alpha_1$-antitrypsin in the blood. The results were very promising. Effective levels of $\alpha_1$-antitrypsin were produced in the muscle cells of the mice and secreted into the bloodstream. Furthermore, the level of $\alpha_1$-antitrypsin remained at therapeutic levels for more than four months. In the past 10 years three clinical trials in humans have been completed and a fourth is ongoing. In 2009 Dr. Flotte and his colleagues at the University of Massachusetts Medical School and the University of Florida reported that three patients treated with the recombinant AAV were able to produce $\alpha_1$-antitrypsin for up to 1 year. Although the levels of enzyme produced were not considered to be therapeutic, this clinical trial demonstrated that introduction of a functioning gene can result in production of the protein. Preliminary results of an ongoing Phase 2 clinical trial suggest that therapeutic concentrations of $\alpha_1$-antitrypsin can be achieved. The research team is optimistic that by modifying the design of the recombinant AAV or the method of delivery into the body, they will be able to develop an effective therapy for familial emphysema.

### For Further Understanding

▶ Of the three treatments described in this perspective, which do you think has the highest probability of success in the long term? Defend your answer.

▶ Explain the lung damage that results from A1AD.

standard nucleotide is present in excess, the dideoxynucleotide will be incorporated infrequently and randomly. This produces a family of DNA fragments that terminate at the location of one of the deoxyadenosines in the molecule.

The same reaction is done with each of the dideoxynucleotides. The DNA fragments are then separated by gel electrophoresis on a DNA sequencing gel. The four reactions are placed in four wells, side by side, on the gel. Following electrophoresis, the DNA sequence can be read directly from the gel, as shown in Figure 20.27.

When chain termination DNA sequencing was first done, radioactive isotopes were used to label the DNA strands. However, new technology has

DNA

Labeled primer

DNA polymerase I + 4 dNTPs +

ddATP    ddTTP    ddCTP    ddGTP

Acrylamide gel

T
T
A
G
A
C
C
C
G
A
T
A
A
G
C
C
C
G
C
A

DNA sequence of original strand

**Figure 20.27** DNA sequencing by chain termination requires a template DNA strand and a radioactive primer. These are placed into each of four reaction mixtures that contain DNA polymerase, the four DNA nucleotides (dATP, dCTP, dGTP, and TTP), as well as one of the four dideoxynucleotides. Following the reaction, the products are separated on a DNA sequencing gel. The sequence is read from an autoradiograph of the gel.

resulted in automated systems that employ dideoxynucleotides that are labeled with fluorescent dyes, a different color for each dideoxynucleotide. Because each reaction (A, G, C, and T) will be a different color, all the reactions can be done in a single reaction mixture and the products separated on a single lane of a sequencing gel. A computer then "reads" the gel by distinguishing the color of each DNA band. The sequence information is directly stored into a databank for later analysis.

There is currently a vast amount of DNA information available on the Internet. The complete genomes of many bacteria have been reported, as well as the sequence information generated by the Human Genome Project. Because we know the genetic code, we can predict the amino acid sequence of proteins encoded by the genes. Researchers can also compare the sequences of normal genes with those of people suffering from genetic disorders. The enormity of the DNA information available, as well as the many types of analysis that need to be carried out, have given rise to an entirely new branch of science. The field of **bioinformatics** is a marriage of computer information sciences and DNA technology that is helping to devise methods for understanding, analyzing, and applying the DNA sequence information that we are gathering.

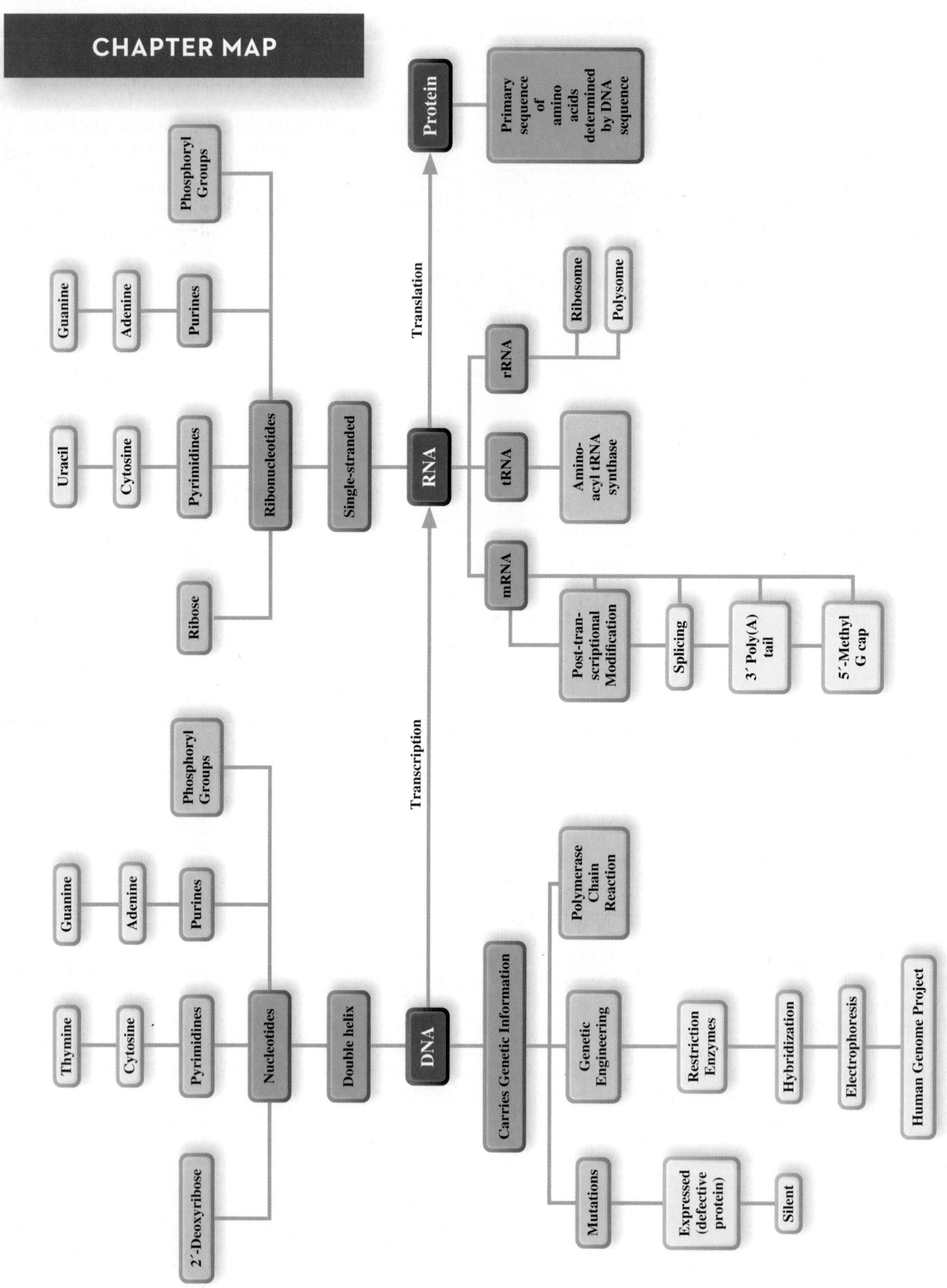

# SUMMARY

## 20.1 The Structure of the Nucleotide

▶ **Deoxyribonucleic acid** (DNA) and **ribonucleic acid** (RNA) are polymers of **nucleotides.**

▶ **Nucleosides** are produced by the combination of a sugar, either ribose in RNA or 2′-deoxyribose in DNA, and a nitrogenous base.

▶ Nucleotides are composed of a nucleoside bonded to one, two, or three phosphoryl groups.

▶ There are two types of nitrogenous bases:
  - Purines: adenine and guanine
  - Pyrimidines: cytosine, thymine, and uracil

▶ **Deoxyribonucleotides** are the subunits of DNA.

▶ **Ribonucleotides** are the subunits of RNA.

## 20.2 The Structure of DNA and RNA

▶ Nucleotides are joined by 3′–5′ phosphodiester bonds in both DNA and RNA.

▶ DNA is a **double helix,** two strands of nucleotide polymers wound around one another with the sugar-phosphate backbone on the outside and complementary pairs of bases extended into the center of the helix.

▶ **Base pairs** are held together by hydrogen bonds.
  - Adenine base pairs with thymine.
  - Cytosine base pairs with guanine.

▶ The two **complementary strands** of DNA are **antiparallel** to one another.

▶ RNA is single-stranded.

▶ **Prokaryotes** are organisms with a simple cellular structure and in which there is no true membrane-bound nucleus and no true membrane-bound organelles.

▶ **Eukaryotes** are organisms that have cells containing a true nucleus with a nuclear membrane and a variety of organelles that segregate a variety of cellular functions from one another.
  - Eukaryotic **chromosomes** are complex structure with a first level structure called the **nucleosome.**

▶ The **genome** is the complete set of genetic information of an organism.

## 20.3 DNA Replication

▶ DNA replication involves synthesis of a faithful copy of the DNA molecule.
  - It begins at a **replication origin** and proceeds at the **replication fork.**

▶ DNA replication is **semiconservative;** each daughter molecule consists of one parental strand and one newly synthesized strand.

▶ **DNA polymerase III** "reads" each parental strand and synthesizes the complementary daughter strand according to the rules of base pairing.

  - The **leading strand** is replicated continuously.
  - The opposite **lagging strand** is replicated discontinuously.

## 20.4 Information Flow in Biological Systems

▶ The **central dogma** states that the flow of biological information in cells is DNA → RNA → protein.

▶ There are three classes of RNA: **messenger RNA** (mRNA), **transfer RNA** (tRNA), and **ribosomal RNA** (rRNA).

▶ **Transcription** is the process by which RNA is synthesized and occurs in three stages: initiation, elongation, and termination.

▶ **RNA polymerase** catalyzes transcription beginning at the **promoter** of the gene.

▶ Eukaryotic genes contain **introns,** sequences that do not encode protein.
  - Introns are removed from the **primary transcript** by RNA **splicing.**
  - The final RNA contains only the protein coding sequences called **exons.**

▶ Eukaryotic mRNA undergoes further **post-transcriptional modification,** including addition of a **5′ cap structure** and a **3′ poly(A) tail.**

## 20.5 The Genetic Code

▶ The genetic code is a triplet code and each code word is called a **codon.**

▶ There are sixty-four codons in the genetic code.
  - There are three termination codons: UAA, UAG, and UGA.
  - The remaining sixty-one specify an amino acid.

▶ Most amino acids have several codons, causing the genetic code to be called **degenerate.**

## 20.6 Protein Synthesis

▶ The process of protein synthesis is called **translation.**

▶ The codons on the mRNA are decoded by tRNA; the **anticodon** on the tRNA is complementary to a codon on the mRNA and the tRNA is covalently linked to the correct amino acid.
  - The tRNA bonded to the correct amino acid is called an **aminoacyl tRNA.**
  - An **aminoacyl tRNA synthetase** catalyzes the bond between the tRNA and the amino acid.

▶ Hydrogen bonding between the codon and anticodon brings the correct amino acid to the site of protein synthesis.

▶ The stages of translation are initiation, chain elongation, and termination.
  - **Initiation factors** and **elongation factors** facilitate initiation and chain elongation.
  - **Translocation** is the movement of the ribosome along the mRNA during chain elongation.
  - A **termination codon** signals the end of the translation process.
  - A **release factor** causes peptidyl transferase to hydrolyze the bond between the peptide and the peptidyl tRNA, releasing the completed peptide.

▶ Protein synthesis occurs on **ribosomes.** The **aminoacyl tRNA binding site** of the ribosome holds the aminoacyl tRNA.

▶ The **peptidyl tRNA binding site** of the ribosome holds the tRNA bonded to the growing peptide chain.

▶ Many ribosomes together translating a single mRNA constitute a **polysome.**

## 20.7  Mutation, Ultraviolet Light, and DNA Repair

▶ Any change in a DNA sequence is a **mutation.**

- Mutations may be **silent mutations** if they do not cause any change in the function of the protein encoded by the gene.
- Mutations that destroy or damage the function of a protein may have effects that range from a mild genetic disorder to death.

▶ Agents that cause mutations are called **mutagens.**

- Mutagens may be **carcinogens,** cancer-causing chemicals.

▶ Mutations are classified by the type of change that occurs in the DNA sequence. They may be **point mutations, deletion mutations,** or **insertion mutations.**

▶ Ultraviolet light causes the formation of **pyrimidine dimers.**

- Errors in the repair of pyrimidine dimers can cause UV-induced mutations.
- Germicidal lamps emit UV light that kills bacteria on environmental surfaces.
- UV light damage to the skin can cause skin cancer.

## 20.8  Recombinant DNA

▶ **Restriction enzymes,** agarose gel electrophoresis, **hybridization,** and **cloning vectors** are all tools required for genetic engineering.

▶ Cloning a DNA fragment involves digestion of the target and the vector DNA with a restriction enzyme.

- DNA ligase joins the target and vector DNA covalently.
- The recombinant DNA molecules are introduced into bacteria by transformation.
- The desired clones are located by using antibiotic selection and hybridization.

▶ Many eukaryotic genes have been cloned for the purpose of producing medically important proteins.

## 20.9  Polymerase Chain Reaction

▶ Using a heat-stable DNA polymerase from the bacterium *Thermus aquaticus* and specific DNA primers, polymerase chain reaction (PCR) allows the amplification of specific DNA fragments that are present in small quantities.

▶ PCR is useful in genetic screening, diagnosis of viral or bacterial disease, and in forensic science.

## 20.10  The Human Genome Project

▶ The Human Genome Project has identified and mapped the genes of the human genome and determined the complete DNA sequence of each of the chromosomes.

▶ DNA libraries were generated and the DNA sequences determined.

▶ Chromosome walking was used to map the sequences along the chromosomes.

▶ DNA sequencing involves reactions in which DNA polymerase copies specific DNA sequences.

- Nucleotide analogs that cause chain termination (dideoxynucleotides) are incorporated randomly into the growing DNA chain.
- This generates a family of DNA fragments that differ in size by one nucleotide.
- DNA sequencing gels separate these fragments and provide DNA sequence data.

▶ **Bioinformatics** is an interdisciplinary field that uses computer information sciences and DNA technology to develop methods to understand, analyze, and apply DNA sequence information.

## QUESTIONS AND PROBLEMS

### The Structure of the Nucleotide

**Foundations**

20.13  What is a heterocyclic amine?

20.14  What components of nucleic acids are heterocyclic amines?

**Applications**

20.15  Draw the structure of the purine ring, and indicate the nitrogen that is bonded to sugars in nucleotides.

20.16  a. Draw the ring structure of the pyrimidines.
      b. In a nucleotide, which nitrogen atom of pyrimidine rings is bonded to the sugar?

20.17  ATP is the universal energy currency of the cell. What components make up the ATP nucleotide?

20.18  One of the energy-harvesting steps of the citric acid cycle results in the production of GTP. What is the structure of the GTP nucleotide?

### The Structure of DNA and RNA

**Foundations**

20.19  The two strands of a DNA molecule are antiparallel. What is meant by this description?

20.20  List three differences between DNA and RNA.

**Applications**

20.21  What is the significance of the following repeat distances in the structure of the DNA molecule: 0.34 nm, 3.4 nm, and 2 nm?

20.22  Except for the functional groups attached to the rings, the nitrogenous bases are largely flat, hydrophobic molecules. Explain why the arrangement of the purines and pyrimidines found in DNA molecules is very stable.

20.23  Draw the adenine-thymine base pair and indicate the hydrogen bonds that link them.

20.24  Draw the guanine-cytosine base pair and indicate the hydrogen bonds that link them.

20.25  Write the structure that results when deoxycytosine-5′-monophosphate is linked by a 3′⟶5′ phosphodiester bond to thymidine-5′-monophosphate.

20.26  Write the structure that results when adenosine-5′-monophosphate is linked by a 3′⟶5′ phosphodiester bond to uridine-5′-monophosphate.

## TABLE 21.1 The Types of Cellular Work That Require Energy

**Biosynthesis: Synthesis of Metabolic Intermediates and Macromolecules**

Synthesis of glucose from $CO_2$ and $H_2O$ in the process of photosynthesis in plants

Synthesis of amino acids

Synthesis of nucleotides

Synthesis of lipids

Protein synthesis from amino acids

Synthesis of nucleic acids

Synthesis of organelles and membranes

**Active Transport: Movement of Ions and Molecules**

Transport of $H^+$ to maintain constant pH

Transport of food molecules into the cell

Transport of $K^+$ and $Na^+$ into and out of nerve cells for transmission of nerve impulses

Secretion of HCl from parietal cells into the stomach

Transport of waste from the blood into the urine in the kidneys

Transport of amino acids and most hexose sugars into the blood from the intestine

Accumulation of calcium ions in the mitochondria

**Motility**

Contraction and flexion of muscle cells

Separation of chromosomes during cell division

Ability of sperm to swim via flagella

Movement of foreign substances out of the respiratory tract by cilia on the epithelial lining of the trachea

Translocation of eggs into the fallopian tubes by cilia in the female reproductive tract

for energy-requiring reactions, we must take a look at the structure of this amazing molecule (Figure 21.1). ATP is a **nucleotide,** which means that it is a molecule composed of a nitrogenous base; a five-carbon sugar; and one, two, or three phosphoryl groups.

In ATP, a phosphoester bond joins the first phosphoryl group to the five-carbon sugar ribose. The next two phosphoryl groups are joined to one another by phosphoanhydride bonds (Figure 21.1). Recall that the phosphoanhydride bond is a *high-energy bond.* When it is broken or hydrolyzed, a large amount of energy is released.

*Nature's high-energy bonds, including phosphoanhydride and phosphoester bonds, are discussed in Section 14.4.*

**Figure 21.1** The structure of the universal energy currency, ATP.

**Figure 21.2** The hydrolysis of the phosphoanhydride bond of ATP releases inorganic phosphate and energy. In this coupled reaction catalyzed by an enzyme, the phosphoryl group and some of the released energy are transferred to β-D-glucose.

*See Sections 14.4 and 20.1 for further information on the structure of ATP and hydrolysis of the phosphoanhydride bonds.*

When the phosphoanhydride bond of ATP is broken, the energy that is released can be used for cellular work. These high-energy bonds are indicated as squiggles (~) in Figure 21.1.

Hydrolysis of ATP yields adenosine diphosphate (ADP), an inorganic phosphate group ($P_i$), and energy (Figure 21.2). The energy released by this hydrolysis of ATP is then used to drive biological processes, for instance, the phosphorylation of glucose or fructose.

An example of the way in which the energy of ATP is used can be seen in the first step of glycolysis, the anaerobic degradation of glucose to harvest chemical energy. The first step involves the transfer of a phosphoryl group, $-PO_3^{2-}$, from ATP to the C-6 hydroxyl group of glucose (Figure 21.2). This reaction is catalyzed by the enzyme hexokinase.

This reaction can be dissected to reveal the role of ATP as a source of energy. Although this is a coupled reaction, we can think of it as a two-step process. The first step is the hydrolysis of ATP to ADP and phosphate, abbreviated $P_i$. This is an exergonic reaction that *releases* about 7 kcal/mol of energy:

$$ATP + H_2O \longrightarrow ADP + P_i + 7 \text{ kcal/mol}$$

The second step, the synthesis of glucose-6-phosphate from glucose and phosphate, is an endergonic reaction that *requires* 3.0 kcal/mol:

$$3.0 \text{ kcal/mol} + \text{glucose} + P_i \longrightarrow \text{glucose-6-phosphate} + H_2O$$

These two chemical reactions can then be added to give the equation showing the way in which ATP hydrolysis is *coupled* to the phosphorylation of glucose:

$$ATP + H_2O \longrightarrow ADP + P_i + 7 \text{ kcal/mol}$$

$$\underline{3.0 \text{ kcal/mol} + \text{glucose} + P_i \longrightarrow \text{glucose-6-phosphate} + H_2O}$$

$$\text{Net: } ATP + \text{glucose} \longrightarrow \text{glucose-6-phosphate} + ADP + 4 \text{ kcal/mol}$$

Because the hydrolysis of ATP releases more energy than is required to synthesize glucose-6-phosphate from glucose and phosphate, there is an overall energy release in this process and the reaction proceeds spontaneously to the right. The product, glucose-6-phosphate, has more energy than the reactant, glucose, because it now carries some of the energy from the original phosphoanhydride bond of ATP.

The primary function of all catabolic pathways is to harvest the chemical energy of fuel molecules and to store that energy by the production of ATP.

This continuous production of ATP is what provides the stored potential energy that is used to power most cellular functions.

**Question 21.1**   Why is ATP called the universal energy currency?

**Question 21.2**   List five biological activities that require ATP.

## 21.2   Overview of Catabolic Processes

Although carbohydrates, fats, and proteins can all be degraded to release energy, carbohydrates are the most readily used energy source. We will begin by examining the oxidation of the hexose glucose. In Chapters 22 and 23 we will see how the pathways of glucose oxidation are also used for the degradation of fats and proteins.

Any catabolic process must begin with a supply of nutrients. When we eat a meal, we are eating quantities of carbohydrates, fats, and proteins. From this point the catabolic processes can be broken down into a series of stages. The three stages of catabolism are summarized in Figure 21.3.

**LEARNING GOAL**

**2**  Describe the three stages of catabolism of dietary proteins, carbohydrates, and lipids.

Food

Proteins → Amino acids
Carbohydrates → Simple sugars
Fats → Fatty acids and glycerol

Stage I: Hydrolysis of macromolecules to subunits

Glycolysis → ATP

Pyruvate

Acetyl CoA

Stage II: Conversion of subunits to a form that can be completely oxidized, usually acetyl CoA

Citric acid cycle

Oxidative phosphorylation

ATP

Stage III: Complete oxidization of acetyl CoA and the production of ATP

**Figure 21.3** The three stages of the conversion of food into cellular energy in the form of ATP.

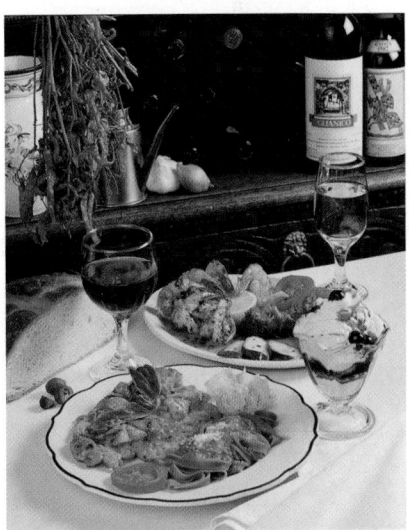

Describe the path of the carbohydrates, lipids, and proteins in this meal from digestion through the biochemical energy-harvesting reactions.

## Stage I: Hydrolysis of Dietary Macromolecules into Small Subunits

The purpose of the first stage of catabolism is to degrade large food molecules into their component subunits. These subunits—simple sugars, amino acids, fatty acids, and glycerol—are then taken into the cells of the body for use as an energy source.

Polysaccharides are hydrolyzed to monosaccharides. This process begins in the mouth, where the enzyme amylase begins the hydrolysis of starch. Digestion continues in the small intestine, where pancreatic amylase further hydrolyzes the starch into maltose (a disaccharide of glucose). Maltase catalyzes the hydrolysis of maltose, producing two glucose molecules. Similarly, sucrose is hydrolyzed to glucose and fructose by the enzyme sucrase, and lactose (milk sugar) is degraded into the monosaccharides glucose and galactose by the enzyme lactase in the small intestine. The monosaccharides are taken up by the epithelial cells of the intestine in an energy-requiring process called *active transport*.

*In the laboratory, a strong acid or base and high temperatures are required for hydrolysis of amide bonds (Section 15.3). However, this reaction proceeds quickly under physiological conditions when catalyzed by enzymes (Section 19.11).*

The digestion of proteins begins in the stomach, where the low pH denatures the proteins so that they are more easily hydrolyzed by the enzyme pepsin. They are further degraded in the small intestine by trypsin, chymotrypsin, elastase, and other proteases. The products of protein digestion—amino acids and short oligopeptides—are taken up by the cells lining the intestine. This uptake also involves an active transport mechanism.

*The digestion and transport of fats are considered in greater detail in Chapter 23.*

Digestion of fats does not begin until the food reaches the small intestine, even though there are lipases in both the saliva and stomach fluid. Fats arrive in the duodenum, the first portion of the small intestine, in the form of large fat globules. Bile salts produced by the liver break these up into an emulsion of tiny fat droplets. Because the small droplets have a greater surface area, the lipids are now more accessible to the action of pancreatic lipase. This enzyme hydrolyzes the fats into fatty acids and glycerol, which are taken up by intestinal cells by a transport process that does not require energy. This process is called *passive transport*. A summary of these hydrolysis reactions is shown in Figure 21.4.

## Stage II: Conversion of Monomers into a Form That Can Be Completely Oxidized

*The citric acid cycle is considered in detail in Section 22.4.*

The monosaccharides, amino acids, fatty acids, and glycerol must now be assimilated into the pathways of energy metabolism. The two major pathways are glycolysis and the citric acid cycle (see Figure 21.3). Sugars usually enter the glycolysis pathway in the form of glucose or fructose. They are eventually converted to acetyl CoA, which is a form that can be completely oxidized in the citric acid cycle. Amino groups are removed from amino acids, and the remaining carbon skeletons enter the catabolic processes at many steps of the citric acid cycle. Fatty acids are converted to acetyl CoA and enter the citric acid cycle in that form. Glycerol, produced by the hydrolysis of fats, is converted to glyceraldehyde-3-phosphate, one of the intermediates of glycolysis, and enters energy metabolism at that level.

## Stage III: The Complete Oxidation of Nutrients and the Production of ATP

*Oxidative phosphorylation is described in Section 22.6.*

Acetyl CoA carries acetyl groups, two-carbon remnants of the nutrients, to the citric acid cycle. Acetyl CoA enters the cycle, and electrons and hydrogen atoms are harvested during the complete oxidation of the acetyl group to $CO_2$. Coenzyme A is released (recycled) to carry additional acetyl groups to the pathway. The electrons and hydrogen atoms that are harvested are used in the process of oxidative phosphorylation to produce ATP.

**Question 21.3**    Briefly describe the three stages of catabolism.

**Question 21.4**    Discuss the digestion of dietary carbohydrates, lipids, and proteins.

Salivary glands secrete amylase, which digests starch.

Disaccharide + Water ⟶ Monosaccharide +

Glycosidase

Stomach secretes HCl, which denatures proteins, and pepsin, which begins the degradation of proteins. Pancreas secretes proteolytic enzymes such as trypsin and chymotrypsin that continue the degradation of proteins. It also secretes lipases that degrade lipids. These act in the duodenum.

Peptidase

Peptide (portion of protein molecule) + Water ⟶ Amino acid + Amino acid

Liver and gallbladder deliver bile salts to the duodenum to emulsify the large fat globules into small fat droplets accessible to the action of pancreatic lipases.

Lipase

Triglyceride + Water ⟶ Fatty acids + Glycerol

**Figure 21.4** A summary of the hydrolysis reactions of carbohydrates, proteins, and fats, and their locations in the digestive tract.

## 21.3 Glycolysis

### An Overview

**Glycolysis,** also known as the Embden-Meyerhof Pathway, is a pathway for carbohydrate catabolism that begins with the substrate D-glucose. The very fact that all organisms can use glucose as an energy source for glycolysis suggests that glycolysis was the first successful energy-harvesting pathway that evolved on the earth. The pathway evolved at a time when the earth's atmosphere was *anaerobic*; no free oxygen was available. As a result, glycolysis requires no oxygen; it is an anaerobic process. Further, it must have evolved in very simple, single-celled organisms, much like bacteria. These organisms did not have complex organelles in the cytoplasm to carry out specific cellular functions. Thus glycolysis was a process carried out by enzymes that were free in the cytoplasm. To this day, glycolysis remains an anaerobic process carried out by cytoplasmic enzymes, even in cells as complex as our own.

The ten steps of glycolysis, catalyzed by ten enzymes, are outlined in Figure 21.5. The first reactions of glycolysis involve an energy investment. ATP molecules are hydrolyzed, energy is released, and phosphoryl groups are added to the hexose sugars. In the remaining steps of glycolysis, energy is harvested to produce a net gain of ATP.

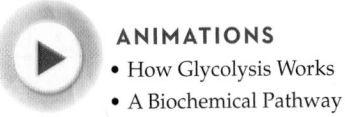

**ANIMATIONS**
- How Glycolysis Works
- A Biochemical Pathway

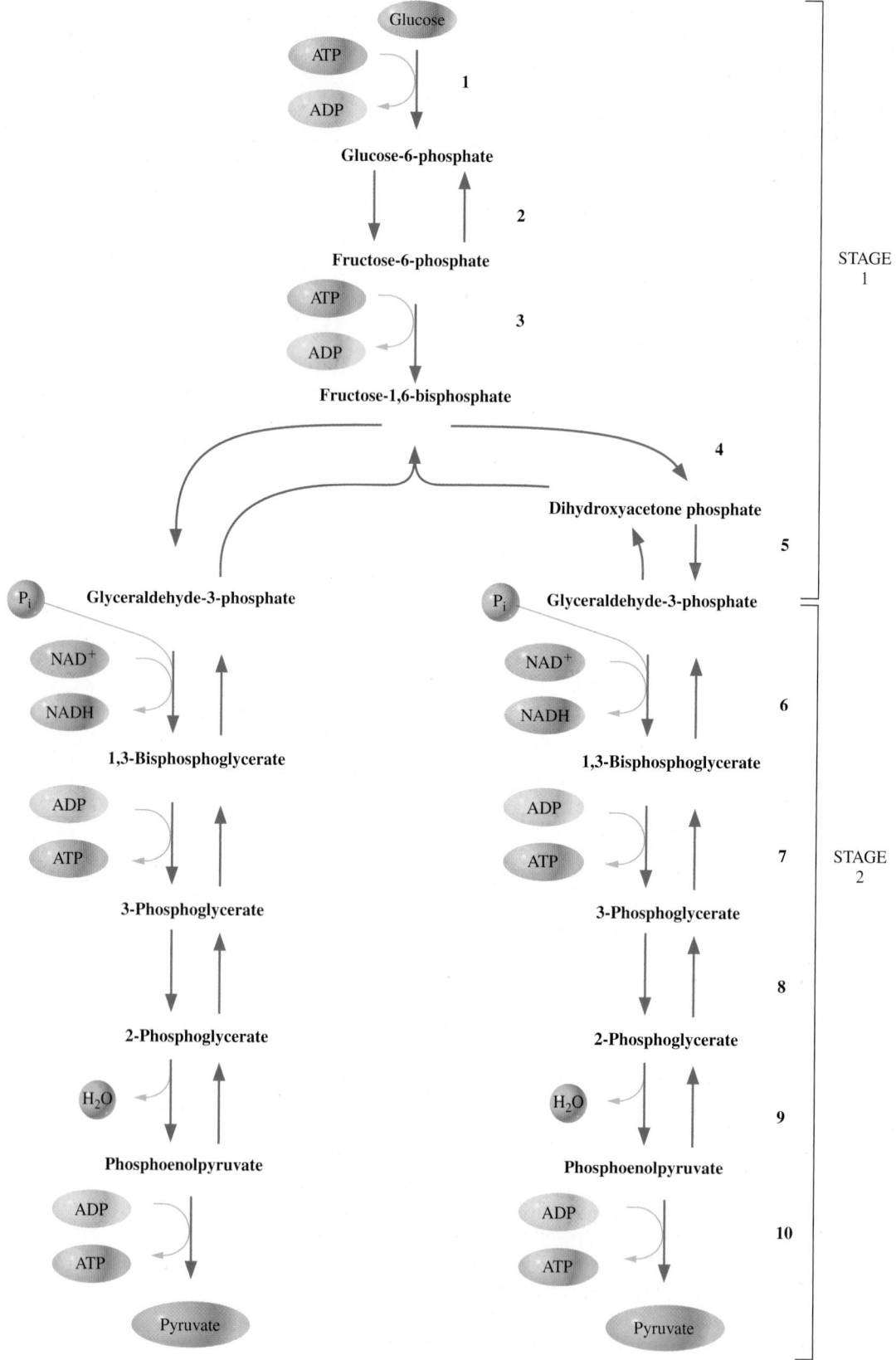

**Figure 21.5** A summary of the reactions of glycolysis. These reactions occur in the cell cytoplasm.

The three major products of glycolysis are seen in Figure 21.5. These are chemical energy in the form of ATP, chemical energy in the form of NADH, and two three-carbon pyruvate molecules. Each of these products is considered below:

- **Chemical energy as ATP.** Four ATP molecules are formed by the process of **substrate-level phosphorylation.** This means that a high-energy phosphoryl group from one of the substrates in glycolysis is transferred to ADP to form ATP. The two substrates involved in these transfer reactions are 1,3-bisphosphoglycerate and phosphoenolpyruvate (see Figure 21.5, steps 7 and 10). Although four ATP molecules are produced during glycolysis, the *net* gain is only two ATP molecules because two ATP molecules are used early in glycolysis (Figure 21.5, steps 1 and 3). The two ATP molecules produced represent only 2.2% of the potential energy of the glucose molecule. Thus glycolysis is not a very efficient energy-harvesting process.
- **Chemical energy in the form of reduced $NAD^+$, NADH. Nicotinamide adenine dinucleotide ($NAD^+$)** is a coenzyme derived from the vitamin niacin. The reduced form of $NAD^+$, NADH, carries hydride anions, hydrogen atoms with two electrons ($H:^-$), removed during the oxidation of glyceraldehyde-3-phosphate (see Figure 21.5, step 6). Under aerobic conditions, the electrons and hydrogen atom are transported from the cytoplasm into the mitochondria. Here they enter an electron transport system for the generation of ATP by **oxidative phosphorylation.** Under anaerobic conditions, NADH is used as a source of electrons in fermentation reactions.
- **Two pyruvate molecules.** At the end of glycolysis the six-carbon glucose molecule has been converted into two three-carbon pyruvate molecules. The fate of the pyruvate also depends on whether the reactions are occurring in the presence or absence of oxygen. Under aerobic conditions it is used to produce acetyl CoA destined for the citric acid cycle and complete oxidation. Under anaerobic conditions it is used as an electron acceptor in fermentation reactions.

*The structure of $NAD^+$ and the way it functions as a hydride anion carrier are shown in Figure 19.8 and described in Section 19.7.*

**ANIMATION**
- How $NAD^+$ Works

In any event these last two products must be used in some way so that glycolysis can continue to function and produce ATP. There are two reasons for this. First, if pyruvate were allowed to build up, it would cause glycolysis to stop, thereby stopping the production of ATP. Thus pyruvate must be used in some kind of follow-up reaction, aerobic or anaerobic. Second, in step 6, glyceraldehyde-3-phosphate is oxidized and $NAD^+$ is reduced (accepts the hydride anion). The cell has only a small supply of $NAD^+$. If all the $NAD^+$ is reduced, none will be available for this reaction, and glycolysis will stop. Therefore NADH must be reoxidized so that glycolysis can continue to produce ATP for the cell.

## Biological Effects of Genetic Disorders of Glycolysis

Before we look at each of the reactions of glycolysis in detail, let's consider the symptoms that arise if a person has a genetic defect in some of the enzymes. Symptoms include muscle myopathy (muscle (*myo*) and disorder (*pathy*)), which involves damage to the muscle as a result of the inability to extract energy from food molecules. In its mildest form, myopathy can cause exercise intolerance, which is the onset of fatigue when exercising. In more severe forms it can cause muscle breakdown (rhabdomyolysis), in which the muscle cells, starved of energy, begin to die. Another symptom of rhabdomyolysis is the release of myoglobin into the blood and eventually into the urine. This condition, called *myoglobinuria,* results in urine that is the color of cola soft drinks, and may even damage the kidneys.

Myopathy may include severe muscle pain. Patients often describe it as a cramp, but it is not a cramp since the muscle is not able to contract because of the lack of energy. Rather, the pain is caused by cell death and tissue damage that result from an inability to produce enough ATP.

Another symptom is hemolytic anemia (anemia that results from the lysis of red blood cells). Red blood cells are completely dependent on glycolysis for their ATP. A defect in one of the enzymes of glycolysis results in insufficient ATP and resultant cell death.

Tarui's disease is caused by a deficiency of phosphofructokinase. Although this is not a sex-linked disorder, the great majority of sufferers are males (nine males to one female). The disorder is most frequently found in U.S. Ashkenazi Jews and Italian families. Onset of symptoms typically occurs between the ages of twenty and forty, although some severe cases have been reported in infants and young children. Patients experiencing the late-onset form of Tarui's disease typically experienced exercise intolerance when they were younger. Vigorous exercise results in myoglobinuria and severe muscle pain. Meals high in carbohydrates worsen the exercise intolerance. Early-onset disease is often associated with respiratory failure, cardiomyopathy (heart muscle disease), seizures, and cortical blindness.

Phosphoglycerate kinase deficiency is a sex-linked genetic disorder (located on the X chromosome). As a result, far more males than females suffer from this disease. There are many clinical features associated with this deficiency, although only rarely are they all found in the same patient. These symptoms range from mental challenge and seizures to a slowly progressive myopathy, and hemolytic anemia.

Phosphoglycerate mutase deficiency has been mapped on chromosome 7. The disorder is found predominantly in U.S African American, Italian, and Japanese families. The clinical features include exercise intolerance, muscle pain, and myoglobinuria following more intense exercise.

These are just three of the disorders associated with deficiencies of the enzymes of glycolysis; but they make it clear that the pathway is critical to our health. The most extreme deficiency of one of these enzymes will cause death of the fetus.

## Reactions of Glycolysis

Glycolysis can be divided into two major segments. The first is the investment of ATP energy. Without this investment, glucose would not have enough energy for glycolysis to continue, and there would be no ATP produced. This segment includes the first five reactions of the pathway. The second major segment involves the remaining reactions of the pathway (steps 6–10), those that result in a net energy yield.

### Reaction 1

The substrate, glucose, is phosphorylated by the enzyme *hexokinase* in a coupled phosphorylation reaction. The source of the phosphoryl group is ATP. At first this reaction seems contrary to the overall purpose of catabolism, the *production* of ATP. The expenditure of ATP in these early reactions must be thought of as an "investment." The cell actually goes into energy "debt" in these early reactions, but this is absolutely necessary to get the pathway started.

**LEARNING GOAL**

3 Discuss glycolysis in terms of its two major segments.

**LEARNING GOAL**

4 Looking at an equation representing any of the chemical reactions that occur in glycolysis, describe the kind of reaction that is occurring and the significance of that reaction to the pathway.

The enzyme name can tell us a lot about the reaction (see Section 19.1). The suffix *-kinase* tells us that the enzyme is a transferase that will transfer a phosphoryl group, in this case from an ATP molecule to the substrate. The prefix *hexo-* gives us a hint that the substrate is a six-carbon sugar. Hexokinase predominantly phosphorylates the six-carbon sugar glucose.

Glucose + ATP $\xrightarrow{\text{Hexokinase}}$ Glucose-6-phosphate + ADP + H$^+$

## Reaction 2

The glucose-6-phosphate formed in the first reaction is rearranged to produce the structural isomer fructose-6-phosphate. The enzyme *phosphoglucose isomerase* catalyzes this isomerization. The result is that the C-1 carbon of the six-carbon sugar is exposed; it is no longer part of the ring structure. Examination of the open-chain structures reveals that this isomerization converts an aldose into a ketose.

The enzyme name, phosphoglucose isomerase, provides clues to the reaction that is being catalyzed (Section 19.1). *Isomerase* tells us that the enzyme will catalyze the interconversion of one isomer into another. *Phosphoglucose* suggests that the substrate is a phosphorylated form of glucose.

Glucose-6-phosphate → (Phosphoglucose isomerase) → Fructose-6-phosphate

Glucose-6-phosphate (an aldose) → (Phosphoglucose isomerase) → Fructose-6-phosphate (a ketose)

## Reaction 3

A second energy "investment" is catalyzed by the enzyme *phosphofructokinase*. The phosphoanhydride bond in ATP is hydrolyzed, and a phosphoester linkage between the phosphoryl group and the C-1 hydroxyl group of fructose-6-phosphate is formed. The product is fructose-1,6-bisphosphate.

The suffix -*kinase* in the name of the enzyme tells us that this is a coupled reaction: ATP is hydrolyzed and a phosphoryl group is transferred to another molecule. The prefix *phosphofructo-* tells us the other molecule is a phosphorylated form of fructose.

Fructose-6-phosphate + ATP → (Phosphofructokinase) → Fructose-1,6-bisphosphate + ADP + H$^+$

## Reaction 4

Fructose-1,6-bisphosphate is split into two three-carbon intermediates in a reaction catalyzed by the enzyme *aldolase*. The products are glyceraldehyde-3-phosphate (G3P) and dihydroxyacetone phosphate.

$$\text{Fructose-1,6-bisphosphate} \xrightleftharpoons{\text{Aldolase}} \text{Dihydroxyacetone phosphate} + \text{Glyceraldehyde-3-phosphate}$$

Fructose-1,6-bisphosphate          Dihydroxyacetone phosphate          Glyceraldehyde-3-phosphate

## Reaction 5

Because G3P is the only substrate that can be used by the next enzyme in the pathway, the dihydroxyacetone phosphate is rearranged to become a second molecule of G3P. The enzyme that mediates this isomerization is *triose phosphate isomerase*.

The enzyme name hints that two isomers of a phosphorylated three-carbon sugar are going to be interconverted (Section 19.1). The ketone dihydroxyacetone phosphate and its isomeric aldehyde, glyceraldehyde-3-phosphate are interconverted through an enediol intermediate.

$$\text{Dihydroxyacetone phosphate} \xrightleftharpoons{\text{Triose phosphate isomerase}} \text{Glyceraldehyde-3-phosphate}$$

Dihydroxyacetone phosphate          Glyceraldehyde-3-phosphate

## Reaction 6

In this reaction the aldehyde glyceraldehyde-3-phosphate is oxidized to a carboxylic acid in a reaction catalyzed by *glyceraldehyde-3-phosphate dehydrogenase*. This is the first step in glycolysis that harvests energy, and it involves the reduction of the coenzyme nicotinamide adenine dinucleotide ($NAD^+$). This reaction occurs in two steps. First, $NAD^+$ is reduced to NADH as the aldehyde group of glyceraldehyde-3-phosphate is oxidized to a carboxyl group. Second, an inorganic phosphate group is transferred to the carboxyl group to give 1,3-bisphosphoglycerate. Notice that the new bond is denoted with a squiggle (~), indicating that this is a high-energy bond. This, and all remaining reactions of glycolysis, occur twice for each glucose because each glucose has been converted into two molecules of glyceraldehyde-3-phosphate.

The name glyceraldehyde-3-phosphate dehydrogenase tells us that the substrate glyceraldehyde-3-phosphate is going to be oxidized. In this reaction, we see that the aldehyde group has been oxidized to a carboxylate group (Section 13.4).

$$\text{Glyceraldehyde-3-phosphate} + NAD^+ + P_i \xrightleftharpoons{\text{Glyceraldehyde-3-phosphate dehydrogenase}} \text{1,3-Bisphosphoglycerate} + NADH$$

Glyceraldehyde-3-phosphate          1,3-Bisphosphoglycerate

## Reaction 7

In this reaction, energy is harvested in the form of *ATP*. The enzyme *phosphoglycerate kinase* catalyzes the transfer of the phosphoryl group of 1,3-bisphosphoglycerate to ADP. This is the first substrate-level phosphorylation of glycolysis, and it produces

ATP and 3-phosphoglycerate. It is a coupled reaction in which the high-energy bond is hydrolyzed and the energy released is used to drive the synthesis of ATP.

1,3-Bisphosphoglycerate      3-Phosphoglycerate

Once again, the enzyme name reveals a great deal about the reaction. The suffix -*kinase* tells us that a phosphoryl group will be transferred. In this case, a phosphoester bond in the substrate 1,3-bisphosphoglycerate is hydrolyzed and ADP is phosphorylated. Note that this is a reversible reaction.

## Reaction 8

3-Phosphoglycerate is isomerized to produce 2-phosphoglycerate in a reaction catalyzed by the enzyme *phosphoglycerate mutase.* The phosphoryl group attached to the third carbon of 3-phosphoglycerate is transferred to the second carbon.

3-Phosphoglycerate      2-Phosphoglycerate

The suffix -*mutase* indicates another type of isomerase. Notice that the chemical formulas of the substrate and reactant are the same. The only difference is in the location of the phosphoryl group.

## Reaction 9

In this step the enzyme *enolase* catalyzes the dehydration (removal of a water molecule) of 2-phosphoglycerate. The energy-rich product is phosphoenolpyruvate, the highest energy phosphorylated compound in metabolism.

2-Phosphoglycerate      Phosphoenolpyruvate

## Reaction 10

Here we see the final substrate-level phosphorylation in the pathway, which is catalyzed by *pyruvate kinase.* Phosphoenolpyruvate serves as a donor of the phosphoryl group that is transferred to ADP to produce ATP. This is another coupled reaction in which hydrolysis of the phosphoester bond in phosphoenolpyruvate provides energy for the formation of the phosphoanhydride bond of ATP. The final product of glycolysis is pyruvate.

The enzyme name indicates that a phosphoryl group will be transferred (kinase) and that the product will be pyruvate.

Phosphoenolpyruvate      Pyruvate

It should be noted that reactions 6 through 10 occur twice per glucose molecule, because the starting six-carbon sugar is split into two three-carbon molecules. Thus in reaction 6, two NADH molecules are generated, and a total of four ATP molecules are made (steps 7 and 10). The net ATP gain from this pathway is, however, only two ATP molecules because there was an energy investment of two ATP molecules in the early steps of the pathway. This investment was paid back by the two ATP molecules produced by substrate-level phosphorylation in step 7. The actual energy yield is produced by substrate-level phosphorylation in reaction 10.

## Entry of Fructose into Glycolysis

Depending on the tissue, fructose enters glycolysis in different ways. In the muscle, where hexokinase is abundant, the enzyme phosphorylates fructose to fructose-6-phosphate, which directly enters glycolysis. There is much less hexokinase in the liver, but fructokinase is present. Fructokinase phosphorylates fructose to produce fructose-1-phosphate. This product is cleaved into dihydroxyacetone phosphate (DHAP) and glyceraldehyde by the enzyme fructose-1-phosphate aldolase. The glyceraldehyde is phosphorylated by triose kinase to produce glyceraldehyde-3-phosphate (G3P). The DHAP and G3P enter glycolysis directly.

**Question 21.5** What is substrate-level phosphorylation?

**Question 21.6** What are the major products of glycolysis?

**Question 21.7** Describe an overview of the reactions of glycolysis.

**Question 21.8** How do the names of the first three enzymes of the glycolytic pathway relate to the reactions they catalyze?

## A MEDICAL PERSPECTIVE

### High Fructose Corn Syrup

A controversy over the health risks of high fructose corn syrup (HFCS) has been raging in recent years. This sweetener was introduced into the food market forty years ago. Some have made the correlation that the increase in the use of HFCS parallels the increase in obesity in the U.S. population. In 1970, approximately 15% of the population was obese. That level currently stands at 33% of the U.S. population.

Until recently, there were no data to suggest that the observed correlation was valid. But in 2010, Dr. Bart Hoebel and his colleagues at Princeton University carried out two experiments in rats that suggest that there is a relationship between HFCS in the diet and obesity.

In the first experiment, one set of rats was given water sweetened with sucrose at a concentration typical of a soft drink. A second set of rats was provided water sweetened with HFCS at a concentration half that found in soft drinks. Both sets of rats were provided their standard diet of rat chow. Dr. Hoebel's group observed that the rats provided water sweetened with HFCS gained much more weight than those given water with sucrose.

In a long-term study of the effects of HFCS, the group monitored weight gain, blood triglycerides, and body fat over a period of 6 months. In this study, rats on rat chow only were compared with rats on a high HFCS diet. Their results were startling. Not only did the HFCS rats gain 48% more weight, they exhibited significant increases in blood triglycerides and deposition of abdominal fat. These are conditions that, in humans, are associated with metabolic syndrome which, in turn, is associated with coronary artery disease, high blood pressure, cancer, and diabetes.

Both HFCS and sucrose contain glucose and fructose; so what differences might cause these results? The primary difference is that HFCS contains a higher concentration of fructose than sucrose (55% compared to 50%). Could this increased amount of fructose be the cause of the symptoms?

The way the body metabolizes HFCS compared to sucrose may provide some clues. First, sucrose is a disaccharide that must be hydrolyzed before it can be absorbed by cells of the body. HFCS is a mixture of the monosaccharides glucose and fructose; these can be immediately absorbed. In addition, unlike glucose, fructose does not stimulate an increase in insulin levels. Since insulin controls the release of leptin, a hormone that signals the satiety center of the brain, thus reducing hunger, a reduced amount of leptin would promote over-eating and weight gain.

The last observation is that fructose enters glycolysis by a different path than glucose. As we saw in the text, fructose is phosphorylated to fructose-1-phosphate in the liver. This is directly cleaved by fructose-1-phosphate aldolase to produce dihydroxyacetone phosphate (DHAP) and glyceraldehye. The DHAP is quickly isomerized and the glyceraldehyde is phosphorylated; both reactions produce glyceraldehyde-3-phosphate. This leads to the production of acetyl CoA via reactions that are unregulated by the normal regulatory steps of glycolysis. The reactions catalyzed by hexokinase and phosphofructokinase, the two earliest regulatory enzymes in glycolysis, are bypassed in fructose metabolism. The final regulatory step, catalyzed by pyruvate kinase, is mediated by fructose-1,6,-bisphosphate, which is reduced when there is an excess of fructose in the cell. The result, some argue, is that high levels of acetyl CoA produced by this unregulated pathway promote the synthesis of fats that are then deposited in adipose tissue.

We must remember that Dr. Hoebel's experiments involved rats and there has been no direct evidence in humans that HFCS causes obesity. Nonetheless, the results do indicate that we need to learn more about the metabolism of fructose and the presence of HFCS in the diet.

**For Further Understanding**

▶ A correlation has been found between the increase of HFCS in the diet and an increase in obesity in the U.S. population. Why is this not proof that a relationship between the two exists?

▶ Discuss the difficulties of proving the effects of foods such as HFCS in humans.

## Regulation of Glycolysis

Energy-harvesting pathways, such as glycolysis, are responsive to the energy needs of the cell. Reactions of the pathway speed up when there is a demand for ATP. They slow down when there is abundant ATP to meet the energy requirements of the cell.

One of the major mechanisms for the control of the rate of glycolysis is the use of *allosteric enzymes*. In addition to the active site, which binds the substrate, allosteric enzymes have an effector binding site, which binds a chemical signal that alters the rate at which the enzyme catalyzes the reaction. Effector binding may increase (positive allosterism) or decrease the rate of reaction (negative allosterism).

The chemical signals, or effectors, that indicate the energy needs of the cell include molecules such as ATP. When the ATP concentration is high, the cell must have sufficient energy. Similarly, ADP and AMP, which are precursors of ATP, are

### LEARNING GOAL

**5** Describe the mechanism of regulation of the rate of glycolysis. Discuss particular examples of that regulation.

*There are additional mechanisms that regulate the rate of glycolysis, but we will focus on those that involve allosteric enzymes (Section 19.9).*

indicators that the cell is in need of ATP. In fact, all of these molecules are allosteric effectors that alter the rate of irreversible reactions catalyzed by enzymes in the glycolytic pathway.

The enzyme hexokinase, which catalyzes the phosphorylation of glucose, is allosterically inhibited by the product of the reaction it catalyzes, glucose-6-phosphate. A buildup of this product indicates that the reactions of glycolysis are not proceeding at a rapid rate, presumably because the cell has enough energy.

Phosphofructokinase, the enzyme that catalyzes the third reaction in glycolysis, is a key regulatory enzyme in the pathway. ATP is an allosteric inhibitor of phosphofructokinase, whereas AMP and ADP are allosteric activators. Another allosteric inhibitor of phosphofructokinase is citrate. As we will see in the next chapter, citrate is the first intermediate in the citric acid cycle, a pathway that results in the complete oxidation of the pyruvate. A high concentration of citrate signals that sufficient substrate is entering the citric acid cycle. The inhibition of phosphofructokinase by citrate is an example of *feedback inhibition:* the product, citrate, allosterically inhibits the activity of an enzyme early in the pathway.

The last enzyme in glycolysis, pyruvate kinase, is also subject to allosteric regulation. In this case, fructose-1,6-bisphosphate, the product of the reaction catalyzed by phosphofructokinase, is the allosteric activator. Thus, activation of phosphofructokinase results in the activation of pyruvate kinase. This is an example of *feedforward activation* because the product of an earlier reaction causes activation of an enzyme later in the pathway.

## 21.4  Fermentations

**LEARNING GOAL**

**6** Discuss the practical and metabolic roles of fermentation reactions.

*Aerobic respiration is discussed in Chapter 22.*

In the overview of glycolysis, we noted that the pyruvate produced must be used up in some way so that the pathway will continue to produce ATP. Similarly, the NADH produced by glycolysis in step 6 (see Figure 21.5) must be reoxidized at a later time, or glycolysis will grind to a halt as the available $NAD^+$ is used up. If the cell is functioning under aerobic conditions, NADH will be reoxidized, and pyruvate will be completely oxidized by aerobic respiration. Under anaerobic conditions, however, different types of fermentation reactions accomplish these purposes. **Fermentations** are catabolic reactions that occur with no net oxidation. Pyruvate or an organic compound produced from pyruvate is reduced as NADH is oxidized. We will examine two types of fermentation pathways in detail: lactate fermentation and alcohol fermentation.

### Lactate Fermentation

Lactate fermentation is familiar to anyone who has performed strenuous exercise. If you exercise so hard that your lungs and circulatory system can't deliver enough oxygen to the working muscles, your aerobic (oxygen-requiring) energy-harvesting pathways are not able to supply enough ATP to your muscles. But the muscles still demand energy. Under these anaerobic conditions, lactate fermentation begins. In this reaction, the enzyme *lactate dehydrogenase* reduces pyruvate to lactate. NADH is the reducing agent for this process (Figure 21.6). As pyruvate is reduced, NADH is oxidized, and $NAD^+$ is again available, permitting glycolysis to continue.

When you exercise beyond the ability of your heart and lungs to provide oxygen to muscle, the lactate fermentation kicks in. Write an equation representing the reaction catalyzed by lactate dehydrogenase and explain how this reaction enables muscle to continue working.

**Figure 21.6** The final reaction of lactate fermentation.

The lactate produced in the working muscle passes into the blood. Eventually, if strenuous exercise is continued, the concentration of lactate becomes so high that this fermentation can no longer continue. Glycolysis, and thus ATP production, stops. The muscle, deprived of energy, can no longer function. This point of exhaustion is called the **anaerobic threshold.**

Of course, most of us do not exercise to this point. When exercise is finished, the body begins the process of reclaiming all of the potential energy that was lost in the form of lactate. The liver takes up the lactate from the blood and converts it back to pyruvate. Now that a sufficient supply of oxygen is available, the pyruvate can be completely oxidized in the much more efficient aerobic energy-harvesting reactions to replenish the store of ATP. Alternatively, the pyruvate may be converted to glucose and used to restore the supply of liver and muscle glycogen. This exchange of metabolites between the muscles and liver is called the *Cori Cycle.*

*The Cori Cycle is described in Section 21.6 and shown in Figure 21.10.*

A variety of bacteria are able to carry out lactate fermentation under anaerobic conditions. This is of great importance in the dairy industry, because these organisms are used to produce yogurt and some cheeses. The tangy flavor of yogurt is contributed by the lactate produced by these bacteria. Unfortunately, similar organisms also cause milk to spoil.

*As we saw in A Medical Perspective: Tooth Decay and Simple Sugars (Chapter 16), the lactate produced by oral bacteria is responsible for the gradual removal of calcium from tooth enamel and the resulting dental cavities.*

## Alcohol Fermentation

Alcohol fermentation has been appreciated, if not understood, since the dawn of civilization. The fermentation process itself was discovered by Louis Pasteur during his studies of the chemistry of wine making and "diseases of wines." Under anaerobic conditions, yeast are able to ferment the sugars produced by fruit and grains. The sugars are broken down to pyruvate by glycolysis. This is followed by the two reactions of alcohol fermentation. First, *pyruvate decarboxylase* removes $CO_2$ from the pyruvate, producing acetaldehyde (Figure 21.7). Second, *alcohol dehydrogenase* catalyzes the reduction of acetaldehyde to ethanol but, more important, reoxidizes NADH in the process. The regeneration of $NAD^+$ allows glycolysis to continue, just as in the case of lactate fermentation.

The two products of alcohol fermentation, then, are ethanol and $CO_2$. We take advantage of this fermentation in the production of wines and other alcoholic beverages and in the process of bread making.

*These applications and other fermentations are described in A Human Perspective: Fermentations: The Good, the Bad, and the Ugly.*

**Question 21.9** How is the alcohol fermentation in yeast similar to lactate production in skeletal muscle?

**Question 21.10** Why must pyruvate be used and NADH be reoxidized so that glycolysis can continue?

**Figure 21.7** The final two reactions of alcohol fermentation.

# A HUMAN PERSPECTIVE

## Fermentations: The Good, the Bad, and the Ugly

In this chapter we have seen that fermentation is an anaerobic, cytoplasmic process that allows continued ATP generation by glycolysis. ATP production can continue because the pyruvate produced by the pathway is utilized in the fermentation and because $NAD^+$ is regenerated.

The stable end products of alcohol fermentation are $CO_2$ and ethanol. These have been used by humankind in a variety of ways, including the production of alcoholic beverages, bread making, and alternative fuel sources.

If alcohol fermentation is carried out by using fruit juices in a vented vat, the $CO_2$ will escape, and the result will be a still wine (not bubbly). But conditions must remain anaerobic; otherwise, fermentation will stop, and aerobic energy-harvesting reactions will ruin the wine. Fortunately for vintners (wine makers), when a vat is fermenting actively, enough $CO_2$ is produced to create a layer that keeps the oxygen-containing air away from the fermenting juice, thus maintaining an anaerobic atmosphere.

Now suppose we want to make a sparkling wine, such as champagne. To do this, we simply have to trap the $CO_2$ produced. In this case the fermentation proceeds in a sealed bottle, a very strong bottle. Both the fermentation products, $CO_2$ and ethanol, accumulate. Under pressure within the sealed bottle the $CO_2$ remains in solution. When the top is "popped," the pressure is released, and the $CO_2$ comes out of solution in the form of bubbles.

In either case the fermentation continues until the alcohol concentration reaches 12–13%. At that point the yeast "stews in its own juices"! That is, 12–13% ethanol kills the yeast cells that produce it. This points out a last generalization about fermentations. The stable fermentation end product, whether it is lactate or ethanol, eventually accumulates to a concentration that is toxic to the organism. Muscle fatigue is the early effect of lactate buildup in the working muscle. In the same way, continued accumulation of the fermentation product can lead to concentrations that are fatal if there is no means of getting rid of the toxic product or of getting away from it. For single-celled organisms the result is generally death. Our bodies have evolved in such a way that lactate buildup contributes to muscle fatigue that causes the exerciser to stop the exercise. Then the lactate is removed from the blood and converted to glucose by the process of gluconeogenesis.

Another application of alcohol fermentation is the use of yeast in bread making. When we mix the water, sugar, and

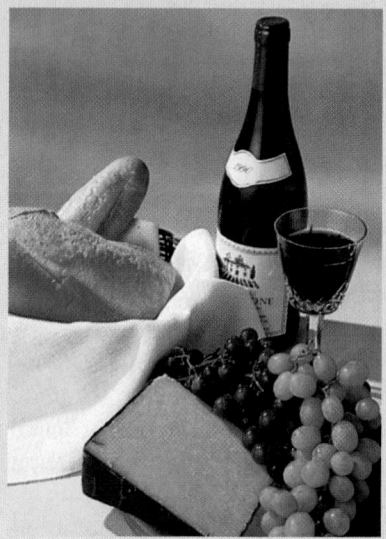

The production of bread, wine, and cheese depends on fermentation processes.

## 21.5  The Pentose Phosphate Pathway

The **pentose phosphate pathway** is an alternative pathway for glucose oxidation. It provides the cell with energy in the form of reducing power for biosynthesis. Specifically, NADPH is produced in the oxidative stage of this pathway. NADPH is the reducing agent required for many biosynthetic pathways.

The details of the pentose phosphate pathway will not be covered in this text. But an overview of the key reactions will allow us to understand the importance of the pathway (Figure 21.8).

$$\text{glucose-6-phosphate} + 2NADP^+ + H_2O \longrightarrow$$

$$\text{ribulose-5-phosphate} + 2NADPH + CO_2$$

The pentose phosphate pathway provides several molecules that are important in biosynthesis. The first is reducing power in the form of NADPH. It also provides sugar phosphates that are required for biosynthesis. For instance, ribose-5-phosphate is used for the synthesis of nucleotides such as ATP. The four-carbon sugar phosphate, *erythrose-4-phosphate,* is produced in the third stage of the pentose phosphate pathway, in a complex set of reactions not shown in the pathway summary in Figure 21.8. It is a precursor of the amino acids phenylalanine, tyrosine, and tryptophan.

dried yeast, the yeast cells begin to grow and carry out the process of fermentation. This mixture is then added to the flour, milk, shortening, and salt, and the dough is placed in a warm place to rise. The yeast continues to grow and ferment the sugar, producing $CO_2$ that causes the bread to rise. Of course, when we bake the bread, the yeast cells are killed, and the ethanol evaporates, but we are left with a light and airy loaf of bread.

Today, alcohol produced by fermentation is being used as an alternative fuel to replace the use of some fossil fuels. Geneticists and bioengineers are trying to develop strains of yeast that can survive higher alcohol concentrations and thus convert more of the sugar of corn and other grains into alcohol.

Bacteria perform a variety of other fermentations. The propionibacteria produce propionic acid and $CO_2$. The acid gives Swiss cheese its characteristic flavor, and the $CO_2$ gas produces the characteristic holes in the cheese. Other bacteria, the clostridia, perform a fermentation that is responsible in part for the horrible symptoms of gas gangrene. When these bacteria are inadvertently introduced into deep tissues by a puncture wound, they find a nice anaerobic environment in which to grow. In fact, these organisms are *obligate anaerobes*; that is, they are killed by even a small amount of oxygen. As they grow, they perform a fermentation called the *butyric acid, butanol, acetone fermentation*. This results in the formation of $CO_2$, the gas associated with gas gangrene. The $CO_2$ infiltrates the local tissues and helps to maintain an anaerobic environment because oxygen from the local blood supply cannot enter the area of the wound. Now able to grow well, these bacteria produce a variety of toxins and enzymes that cause extensive tissue death and necrosis. In addition, the fermentation produces acetic acid, ethanol, acetone, isopropanol, butanol, and butyric acid (which is responsible, along with the necrosis, for

the characteristic foul smell of gas gangrene). Certainly, the presence of these organic chemicals in the wound enhances tissue death.

Gas gangrene is very difficult to treat. Because the bacteria establish an anaerobic region of cell death and cut off the local circulation, systemic antibiotics do not infiltrate the wound and kill the bacteria. Even our immune response is stymied. Treatment usually involves surgical removal of the necrotic tissue accompanied by antibiotic therapy. In some cases a hyperbaric oxygen chamber is employed. The infected extremity is placed in an environment with a very high partial pressure of oxygen. The oxygen forced into the tissues is poisonous to the bacteria, and they die.

These are but a few examples of the fermentations that have an effect on humans. Regardless of the specific chemical reactions, all fermentations share the following traits:

- They use pyruvate produced in glycolysis.
- They reoxidize the NADH produced in glycolysis.
- They are self-limiting because the accumulated stable fermentation end product eventually kills the cell that produces it.

**For Further Understanding**

▶ Write condensed structural formulas for each of the fermentation products made by clostridia in gas gangrene. Identify the functional groups and provide the IUPAC name for each.

▶ Explain the importance of utilizing pyruvate and reoxidizing NADH to the ability of a cell to continue producing ATP.

The pentose phosphate pathway is most active in tissues involved in cholesterol and fatty acid biosynthesis. These two processes require abundant NADPH. Thus the liver, which is the site of cholesterol synthesis and a major site for fatty acid biosynthesis, and adipose (fat) tissue, where active fatty acid synthesis also occurs, have very high levels of pentose phosphate pathway enzymes.

*The pathway for fatty acid biosynthesis is discussed in Section 23.4.*

**Figure 21.8** Summary of the major stages of the pentose phosphate pathway.

## 21.6  Gluconeogenesis: The Synthesis of Glucose

*Under extreme conditions of starvation the brain eventually switches to the use of ketone bodies. Ketone bodies are produced, under certain circumstances, from the breakdown of lipids (Section 23.3).*

Under normal conditions, we have enough glucose to satisfy our needs. However, under some conditions the body must make glucose. This is necessary following strenuous exercise, to replenish the liver and muscle supplies of glycogen. It also occurs during starvation, so that the body can maintain adequate blood glucose levels to supply the brain cells and red blood cells. Under normal conditions these two tissues use only glucose for energy.

Glucose is produced by the process of **gluconeogenesis** (*gleuko*, Greek *sweet*; *neo*, Latin *new*; *genesis*, Latin *produce*), the production of glucose from noncarbohydrate starting materials (Figure 21.9). Gluconeogenesis, an anabolic pathway, occurs primarily in the liver. Lactate, all the amino acids except leucine and lysine, and glycerol from fats can all be used to make glucose. However, the amino acids and glycerol are generally used only under starvation conditions.

**Figure 21.9** Comparison of the reactions of glycolysis and gluconeogenesis.

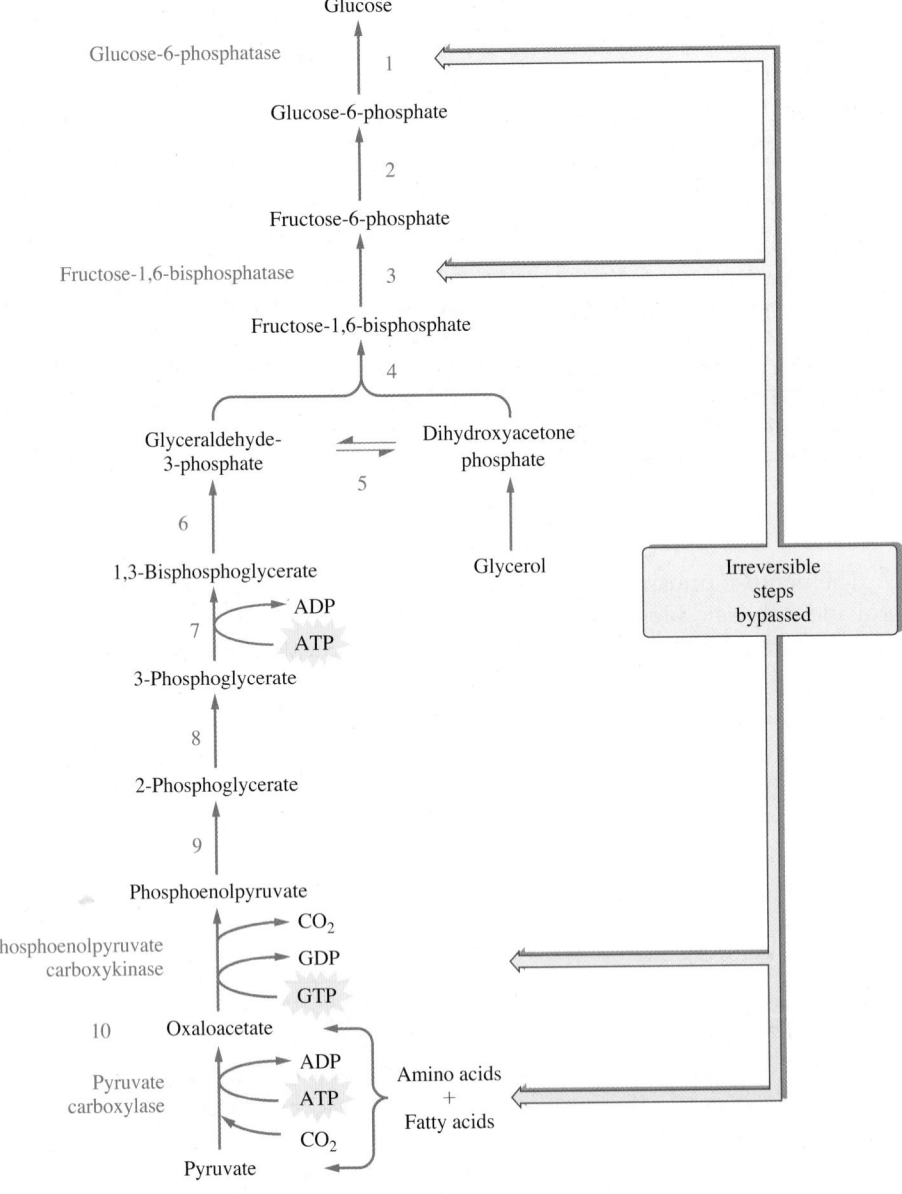

At first glance, gluconeogenesis appears to be simply the reverse of glycolysis (compare Figures 21.9 and 21.5), because the intermediates of the two pathways are identical. But this is not the case, because steps 1, 3, and 10 of glycolysis are irreversible, and therefore the reverse reactions must be carried out by other enzymes. In step 1 of glycolysis, hexokinase catalyzes the phosphorylation of glucose. In gluconeogenesis the dephosphorylation of glucose-6-phosphate is carried out by the enzyme *glucose-6-phosphatase*, which is found in the liver but not in muscle. Similarly, reaction 3, the phosphorylation of fructose-6-phosphate catalyzed by phosphofructokinase, is irreversible. That step is bypassed in gluconeogenesis by using the enzyme *fructose-1,6-bisphosphatase*. Finally, the phosphorylation of ADP catalyzed by pyruvate kinase, step 10 of glycolysis, cannot be reversed. The conversion of pyruvate to phosphoenolpyruvate actually involves two enzymes and some unusual reactions. First, the enzyme *pyruvate carboxylase* adds $CO_2$ to pyruvate. The product is the four-carbon compound oxaloacetate. Then *phosphoenolpyruvate carboxykinase* removes the $CO_2$ and adds a phosphoryl group. The donor of the phosphoryl group in this unusual reaction is **guanosine triphosphate (GTP).** This is a nucleotide like ATP, except that the nitrogenous base is guanine.

This last pair of reactions is complicated by the fact that pyruvate carboxylase is found in the mitochondria, whereas phosphoenolpyruvate carboxykinase is found in the cytoplasm. As we will see in Chapters 22 and 23, mitochondria are organelles in which the final oxidation of food molecules occurs and large amounts of ATP are produced. A complicated shuttle system transports the oxaloacetate produced in the mitochondria through the two mitochondrial membranes and into the cytoplasm. There, phosphoenolpyruvate carboxykinase catalyzes its conversion to phosphoenolpyruvate.

If glycolysis and gluconeogenesis were not regulated in some fashion, the two pathways would occur simultaneously, with the disastrous effect that nothing would get done. Three convenient sites for this regulation are the three bypass reactions. Step 3 of glycolysis is catalyzed by the enzyme phosphofructokinase. This enzyme is stimulated by high concentrations of AMP, ADP, and inorganic phosphate, signals that the cell needs energy. When the enzyme is active, glycolysis proceeds. On the other hand, when ATP is plentiful, phosphofructokinase is inhibited, and fructose-1,6-bisphosphatase is stimulated. The net result is that in times of energy excess (high concentrations of ATP), gluconeogenesis will occur.

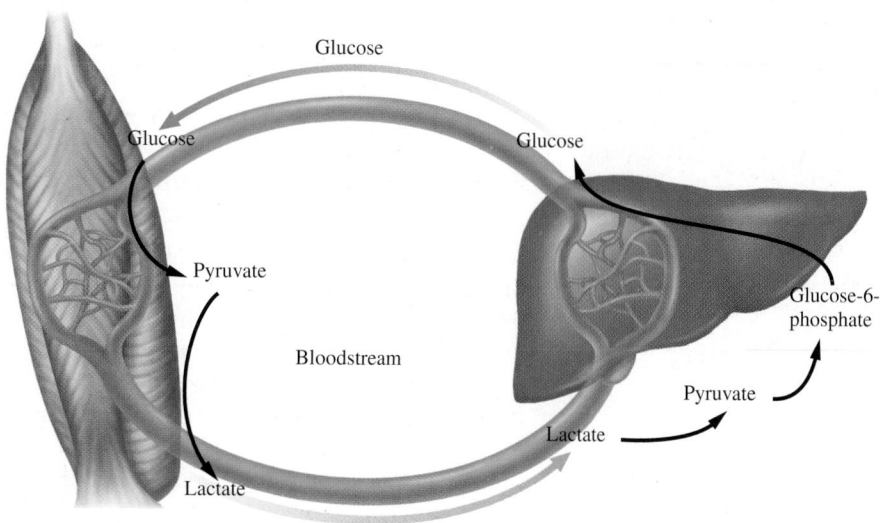

**Figure 21.10** The Cori Cycle.

As we have seen, the conversion of lactate into glucose is important in mammals. As the muscles work, they produce lactate, which is converted back to glucose in the liver. The glucose is transported into the blood and from there back to the muscle. In the muscle it can be catabolized to produce ATP, or it can be used to replenish the muscle stores of glycogen. This cyclic process between the liver and skeletal muscles is called the **Cori Cycle** and is shown in Figure 21.10. Through this cycle, gluconeogenesis produces enough glucose to restore the depleted muscle glycogen reservoir within 48 hours (h).

**Question 21.11**  What are the major differences between gluconeogenesis and glycolysis?

**Question 21.12**  What do the three irreversible reactions of glycolysis have in common?

## 21.7  Glycogen Synthesis and Degradation

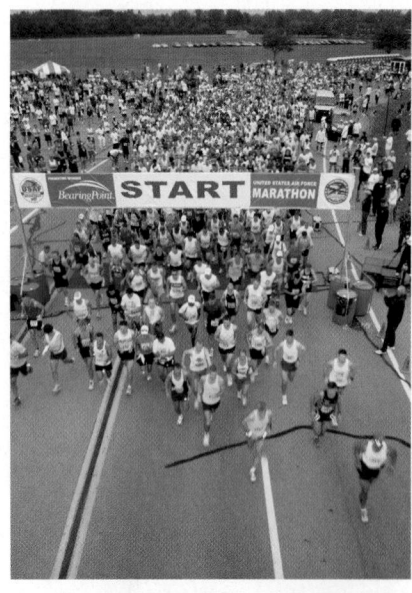

Marathon runners often carbo-load in the days before a race. The goal is to build stores of muscle glycogen. Carbo-loading involves reduced exercise the week before the race, along with a diet that is as high as 70% carbohydrate. Explain how this helps build the runner's endurance.

Glucose is the sole source of energy of mammalian red blood cells and the major source of energy for the brain. Neither red blood cells nor the brain can store glucose; thus a constant supply must be available as blood glucose. This is provided by dietary glucose and by the production of glucose either by gluconeogenesis or by **glycogenolysis,** the degradation of glycogen. Glycogen is a long, branched-chain polymer of glucose. Stored in the liver and skeletal muscles, it is the principal storage form of glucose.

The total amount of glucose in the blood of a 70-kilogram (kg) (approximately 150-pound) adult is about 20 grams (g), but the brain alone consumes 5–6 g of glucose per h. Breakdown of glycogen in the liver mobilizes the glucose when hormonal signals register a need for increased levels of blood glucose. Skeletal muscle also contains substantial stores of glycogen, which provide energy for rapid muscle contraction. However, this glycogen is not able to contribute to blood glucose because muscle cells do not have the enzyme glucose-6-phosphatase. Because glucose cannot be formed from the glucose-6-phosphate, it cannot be released into the bloodstream.

### The Structure of Glycogen

**Glycogen** is a highly branched glucose polymer in which the "main chain" is linked by $\alpha$ (1→4) glycosidic bonds. The polymer also has numerous $\alpha$ (1→6) glycosidic bonds, which provide many branch points along the chain (Figure 21.11). **Glycogen granules** with a diameter of 10–40 nanometers (nm) are found in the cytoplasm of liver and muscle cells. These granules exist in complexes with the enzymes that are responsible for glycogen synthesis and degradation.

### Glycogenolysis: Glycogen Degradation

Two hormones control glycogenolysis, the degradation of glycogen. These are **glucagon,** a peptide hormone synthesized in the pancreas, and *epinephrine*, produced in the adrenal glands. Glucagon is released from the pancreas in response to low blood glucose, and epinephrine is released from the adrenal glands in response to a threat or a stress. Both situations require an increase in blood glucose, and both hormones function by altering the activity of two enzymes, glycogen phosphorylase and glycogen synthase. *Glycogen phosphorylase* is involved in glycogen degradation and is activated; *glycogen synthase* is involved in glycogen synthesis and is inactivated. The steps in glycogen degradation are summarized as follows.

**Step 1.**  The enzyme glycogen phosphorylase catalyzes *phosphorolysis* of a glucose at one end of a glycogen polymer (Figure 21.11). The reaction involves the displacement of a glucose unit of glycogen by a phosphate

**Figure 21.11** The action of glycogen phosphorylase in glycogenolysis.

General reaction:

$$\text{Glycogen (glucose)}_x + n\ HPO_4^{2-} \xrightarrow[\text{phosphorylase}]{\text{Glycogen}} \text{Glycogen (glucose)}_{x-n} + n\ \text{glucose-1-phosphate}$$

group. As a result of phosphorolysis, glucose-1-phosphate is produced without using ATP as the phosphoryl group donor.

**Step 2.** Glycogen contains many branches bound to the α (1→4) backbone by α (1→6) glycosidic bonds. These branches must be removed to allow the complete degradation of glycogen. The extensive action of glycogen phosphorylase produces a smaller polysaccharide with a single glucose bound by an α (1→6) glycosidic bond to the main chain. The enzyme α (1→6) *glycosidase,* also called the *debranching enzyme,* hydrolyzes the α (1→6) glycosidic bond at a branch point and frees one molecule of glucose (Figure 21.12). This molecule of glucose can be phosphorylated and utilized in glycolysis, or it may be released into the bloodstream for use elsewhere. Hydrolysis of the branch bond liberates another stretch of α (1→4)-linked glucose for the action of glycogen phosphorylase.

**Step 3.** Glucose-1-phosphate is converted to glucose-6-phosphate by *phosphoglucomutase* (Figure 21.13). Glucose originally stored in glycogen enters glycolysis through the action of phosphoglucomutase. Alternatively, in the liver and kidneys it may be dephosphorylated for transport into the bloodstream.

**Figure 21.12** The action of α (1→6) glycosidase (debranching enzyme) in glycogen degradation.

**Figure 21.13** The action of phosphoglucomutase in glycogen degradation.

**Question 21.13**   Explain the role of glycogen phosphorylase in glycogenolysis.

**Question 21.14**   How does the action of glycogen phosphorylase and phosphoglucomutase result in an energy savings for the cell if the product, glucose-6-phosphate, is used directly in glycolysis?

## Glycogenesis: Glycogen Synthesis

The hormone **insulin,** produced by the pancreas in response to high blood glucose levels, stimulates the synthesis of glycogen, **glycogenesis.** Insulin is perhaps one of the most influential hormones in the body because it directly alters the metabolism and uptake of glucose in all but a few cells.

When blood glucose rises, as after a meal, the beta cells of the pancreas secrete insulin. It immediately accelerates the uptake of glucose by all the cells of the body except the brain and certain blood cells. In these cells the uptake of glucose is insulin-independent. The increased uptake of glucose is especially marked in the liver, heart, skeletal muscle, and adipose tissue.

In the liver, insulin promotes glycogen synthesis and storage by inhibiting glycogen phosphorylase, thus inhibiting glycogen degradation. It also stimulates glycogen synthase and glucokinase, two enzymes that are involved in glycogen synthesis.

Although glycogenesis and glycogenolysis share some reactions in common, the two pathways are not simply the reverse of one another. Glycogenesis involves some very unusual reactions, which we will now examine in detail.

The first reaction of glycogen synthesis in the liver traps glucose within the cell by phosphorylating it. In this reaction, catalyzed by the enzyme *glucokinase*, ATP serves as a phosphoryl donor, and glucose-6-phosphate is formed:

Glucose                          Glucose-6-phosphate

The second reaction of glycogenesis is the reverse of one of the reactions of glycogenolysis. The glucose-6-phosphate formed in the first step is isomerized to glucose-1-phosphate. The enzyme that catalyzes this step is phosphoglucomutase:

Glucose-6-phosphate                    Glucose-1-phosphate

The glucose-1-phosphate must now be activated before it can be added to the growing glycogen chain. The high-energy compound that accomplishes this is the nucleotide **uridine triphosphate (UTP).** In this reaction, mediated by the enzyme *pyrophosphorylase*, the C-1 phosphoryl group of glucose is linked to the $\alpha$-phosphoryl group of UTP to produce UDP-glucose:

Glucose-1-phosphate     +     UTP          Pyrophosphorylase          UDP-glucose   +   Pyrophosphate

This is accompanied by the release of a pyrophosphate group ($PP_i$). The structure of UDP-glucose is shown in Figure 21.14.

The UDP-glucose can now be used to extend glycogen chains. The enzyme glycogen synthase breaks the phosphoester linkage of UDP-glucose and forms an

# A MEDICAL PERSPECTIVE

## Diagnosing Diabetes

When diagnosing diabetes, doctors take many factors and symptoms into consideration. However, there are two primary tests that are performed to determine whether an individual is properly regulating blood glucose levels. First and foremost is the fasting blood glucose test. A person who has fasted since midnight should have a blood glucose level between 70 and 110 milligrams per deciliter (mg/dL) in the morning. If the level is 140 mg/dL on at least two occasions, a diagnosis of diabetes is generally made.

The second commonly used test is the glucose tolerance test. For this test the subject must fast for at least 10 h. A beginning blood sample is drawn to determine the fasting blood glucose level. This will serve as the background level for the test. The subject ingests 50–100 g of glucose (40 g/m² body surface), and the blood glucose level is measured at 30 minutes (min), and at 1, 2, and 3 h after ingesting the glucose.

A graph is made of the blood glucose levels over time. For a person who does not have diabetes, the curve will show a peak of blood glucose at approximately 1 h. There will be a reduction in the level, and perhaps a slight hypoglycemia (low blood glucose level) over the next hour. Thereafter, the blood glucose level stabilizes at normal levels.

An individual is said to have impaired glucose tolerance if the blood glucose level remains between 140 and 200 mg/dL

2 h after ingestion of the glucose solution. This suggests that there is a risk of the individual developing diabetes and is reason to prescribe periodic testing to allow early intervention.

If the blood glucose level remains at or above 200 mg/dL after 2 h, a tentative diagnosis of diabetes is made. However, this result warrants further testing on subsequent days to rule out transient problems, such as the effect of medications on blood glucose levels.

It was recently suggested that the upper blood glucose level of 200 mg/dL should be lowered to 180 mg/dL as the standard to diagnose impaired glucose tolerance and diabetes. This would allow earlier detection and intervention. Considering the grave nature of long-term diabetic complications, it is thought to be very beneficial to begin treatment at an early stage to maintain constant blood glucose levels. For more information on diabetes, see A Medical Perspective: Diabetes Mellitus and Ketone Bodies, in Chapter 23.

### For Further Understanding

▶ Draw a graph representing blood glucose levels for a normal glucose tolerance test.

▶ Draw a similar graph for an individual who would be diagnosed as diabetic.

α (1→4) glycosidic bond between the glucose and the growing glycogen chain. UDP is released in the process.

UDP-glucose

Glycogen primer
(*n* residues)

Glycogen
synthase

Glycogen
(*n* + 1 residues)

UDP

Figure 21.14 The structure of UDP-glucose.

Figure 21.15 The action of the branching enzyme in glycogen synthesis.

Finally, we must introduce the $\alpha(1\rightarrow6)$ glycosidic linkages to form the branches. The branches are quite important to proper glycogen utilization. As Figure 21.15 shows, the *branching enzyme* removes a section of the linear $\alpha(1\rightarrow4)$ linked glycogen and reattaches it in $\alpha(1\rightarrow6)$ glycosidic linkage elsewhere in the chain.

**Question 21.15**  Describe the way in which glucokinase traps glucose inside liver cells.

**Question 21.16**  Describe the reaction catalyzed by the branching enzyme.

## Compatibility of Glycogenesis and Glycogenolysis

As was the case with glycolysis and gluconeogenesis, it would be futile for the cell to carry out glycogen synthesis and degradation simultaneously. The results achieved by the action of one pathway would be undone by the other. This problem is avoided by a series of hormonal controls that activate the enzymes of one pathway while inactivating the enzymes of the other pathway.

When the blood glucose level is too high, a condition known as **hyperglycemia,** insulin stimulates the uptake of glucose via a transport mechanism. It further stimulates the trapping of the glucose by the elevated activity of glucokinase. Finally, it activates glycogen synthase, the last enzyme in the synthesis of glycogen chains. To further accelerate storage, insulin *inhibits* the first enzyme in glycogen degradation, glycogen phosphorylase. The net effect, seen in Figure 21.16, is that glucose is removed from the bloodstream and converted into glycogen in the liver. When the glycogen stores are filled, excess glucose is converted to fat and stored in adipose tissue.

Glucagon is produced in response to low blood glucose levels, a condition known as **hypoglycemia,** and has an effect opposite to that of insulin. It stimulates glycogen phosphorylase, which catalyzes the first stage of glycogen degradation. This accelerates glycogenolysis and release of glucose into the bloodstream. The effect is further enhanced because glucagon inhibits glycogen synthase. The opposing effects of insulin and glucagon are summarized in Figure 21.16.

**Figure 21.16**  The opposing effects of the hormones insulin and glucagon on glycogen metabolism.

# A HUMAN PERSPECTIVE

## Glycogen Storage Diseases

Glycogen metabolism is important for the proper function of many aspects of cellular metabolism. Many diseases of glycogen metabolism have been discovered. Generally, these are diseases that result in the excessive accumulation of glycogen in the liver, muscle, and tubules of the kidneys. Often they are caused by defects in one of the enzymes involved in the degradation of glycogen.

One example is an inherited defect of glycogen metabolism known as *von Gierke's disease*. This disease results from a defective gene for glucose-6-phosphatase, which catalyzes the final step of gluconeogenesis and glycogenolysis. People who lack glucose-6-phosphatase cannot convert glucose-6-phosphate to glucose. As we have seen, the liver is the primary source of blood glucose, and much of this glucose is produced by gluconeogenesis. Glucose-6-phosphate, unlike glucose, cannot cross the cell membrane, and the liver of a person suffering from von Gierke's disease cannot provide him or her with glucose. The blood sugar level falls precipitously low between meals. In addition, the lack of glucose-6-phosphatase also affects glycogen metabolism. Because glucose-6-phosphatase is absent, the supply of glucose-6-phosphate in the liver is large. This glucose-6-phosphate can also be converted to glycogen. A person suffering from von Gierke's disease has a massively enlarged liver as a result of enormously increased stores of glycogen.

Defects in other enzymes of glycogen metabolism also exist. *Cori's disease* is caused by a genetic defect in the debranching enzyme. As a result, individuals who have this disease cannot completely degrade glycogen and thus use their glycogen stores very inefficiently.

On the other side of the coin, *Andersen's disease* results from a genetic defect in the branching enzyme. Individuals who have this disease produce very long, unbranched glycogen chains. This genetic disorder results in decreased efficiency of glycogen storage.

A final example of a glycogen storage disease is *McArdle's disease*. In this syndrome, the muscle cells lack the enzyme glycogen phosphorylase and cannot degrade glycogen to glucose. Individuals who have this disease have little tolerance for physical exercise because their muscles cannot provide enough glucose for the necessary energy-harvesting processes. It is interesting to note that the liver enzyme glycogen phosphorylase is perfectly normal, and these people respond appropriately with a rise of blood glucose levels under the influence of glucagon or epinephrine.

### For Further Understanding

▶ Write equations showing the reactions catalyzed by the enzymes that are defective in each of the genetic disorders described in this perspective.

▶ There are different forms of glycogen phosphorylase, one found in the liver and the other in skeletal muscle. Discuss the differences you would expect between a defect in the muscle enzyme and a defect in the liver enzyme.

---

This elegant system of hormonal control ensures that the reactions involved in glycogen degradation and synthesis do not compete with one another. In this way they provide glucose when the blood level is too low, and they cause the storage of glucose in times of excess.

**Question 21.17** Explain how glucagon affects the synthesis and degradation of glycogen.

**Question 21.18** How does insulin affect the storage and degradation of glycogen?

## CHAPTER MAP

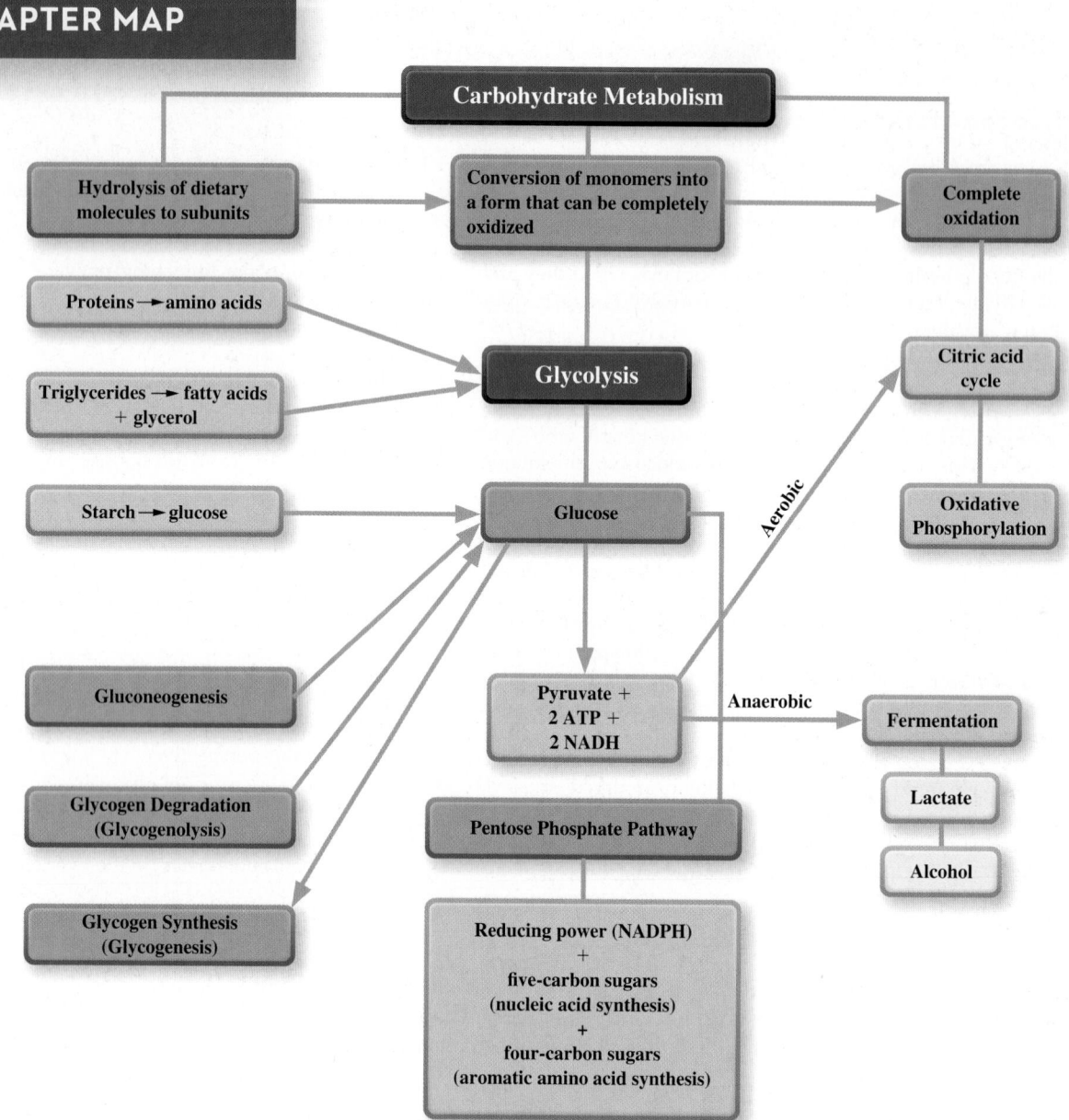

## SUMMARY

### 21.1 ATP: The Cellular Energy Currency

▶ **Adenosine triphosphate (ATP)** is a **nucleotide** composed of adenine, the sugar ribose, and a triphosphate group.

▶ The energy released by the hydrolysis of the phosphoanhydride bond between the second and third phosphoryl groups provides the energy for most cellular work.

▶ The energy harvested during the degradation of fuel molecules, **catabolism,** is stored in ATP.

▶ Biosynthetic reactions, **anabolism,** utilize ATP as an energy source.

### 21.2 Overview of Catabolic Processes

▶ The body needs a supply of ATP to carry out life processes.

▶ To provide this ATP, we consume a variety of energy-rich food molecules: carbohydrates, lipids, and proteins.

▶ In digestion, these food molecules are degraded into smaller molecules that are absorbed by our cells: monosaccharides, fatty acids and glycerol, and amino acids.

▶ Through catabolic reactions, these molecules are used to produce ATP.

### 21.3 Glycolysis

▶ **Glycolysis** is the pathway for glucose catabolism that leads to pyruvate. Glycolysis:
  • is anaerobic
  • occurs in the cytoplasm of the cell

- produces a net harvest of two ATP and two NADH (formed from the coenzyme **nicotinamide adenine dinucleotide (NAD$^+$)**)
▶ The ATP is produced by **substrate-level phosphorylation.**
▶ Under aerobic conditions, the electrons carried by NADH are used to produce ATP by **oxidative phosphorylation.**
▶ The rate of glycolysis responds to the energy demands of the cell.
  - This regulation of the rate of glycolysis occurs through the allosteric enzymes hexokinase, phosphofructokinase, and pyruvate kinase.

## 21.4 Fermentations

▶ **Fermentations** are catabolic reactions that occur with no net oxidation.
▶ Under anaerobic conditions the NADH produced by glycolysis is used to reduce pyruvate.
▶ The lactate fermentation reduces pyruvate to produce lactate.
  - This occurs in working muscles when there is not enough oxygen to provide ATP through aerobic catabolic reactions.
  - If lactate builds up to a high enough concentration, it can inhibit glycolysis and thus ATP production. At this point, the **anaerobic threshold,** there is not enough energy for muscles to continue to function.
▶ The alcohol fermentation reduces pyruvate to ethanol.
  - The alcohol fermentation is used to produce wines and other alcoholic beverages.
  - The alcohol fermentation is also used in bread making.

## 21.5 The Pentose Phosphate Pathway

▶ The **pentose phosphate pathway** is an alternative pathway for glucose degradation and is particularly abundant in the liver and adipose tissue.
▶ Products of the pathway include:
  - NADPH, a reducing agent for biosynthetic reaction.
  - Ribose-5-phosphate for nucleotide synthesis.
  - Erythrose-4-phosphate for biosynthesis of several amino acids (tryptophan, tyrosine, and phenylalanine).

## 21.6 Gluconeogenesis: The Synthesis of Glucose

▶ Gluconeogenesis is the pathway for glucose synthesis from **noncarbohydrate starting materials.**
  - It occurs in the mammalian liver.
  - Starting materials include lactate and all amino acids except lysine and leucine, and glycerol.
▶ Gluconeogenesis is not simply the reverse of glycolysis.
  - Three steps in glycolysis in which ATP is produced or consumed are bypassed by gluconeogenesis by using other enzymes.
  - All the other enzymes in the two pathways are the same.
  - **Guanosine triphosphate (GTP)** is a phosphoryl group donor in a reaction that converts oxaloacetate into phosphoenolpyruvate. The oxaloacetate is produced by the carboxylation of pyruvate.

▶ The **Cori Cycle** is a metabolic pathway in which lactate produced by working muscle is taken up by the liver and converted to glucose by gluconeogenesis.

## 21.7 Glycogen Synthesis and Degradation

▶ **Glycogen** is a long, branched-chain polymer of glucose.
  - It is stored in **glycogen granules** that consist of glycogen and the enzymes required for glycogen synthesis and degradation.
  - It is found in the liver and muscle.
▶ **Glycogenolysis** is the pathway by which the glycogen polymer is broken down into individual monomers (glucose molecules).
▶ **Glycogenesis** is the metabolic pathway by which the polymer glycogen is synthesized from glucose molecules.
  - **Uridine triphosphate (UTP)** is a ribonucleotide involved in glycogenesis.
▶ Glycogen synthesis and degradation are under hormonal control.
  - **Insulin** inhibits glycogen degradation and stimulates glycogen synthesis when blood glucose levels are too high **(hyperglycemia).**
  - **Glucagon** inhibits glycogen synthesis and stimulates glycogen degradation when blood glucose levels are too low **(hypoglycemia).**

# QUESTIONS AND PROBLEMS

## ATP: The Cellular Energy Currency

### Foundations

**21.19** What molecule is primarily responsible for conserving the energy released in catabolism?
**21.20** Describe the structure of ATP.

### Applications

**21.21** Write a reaction showing the hydrolysis of the terminal phosphoanhydride bond of ATP.
**21.22** What is meant by the term *high-energy bond*?
**21.23** What is meant by a coupled reaction?
**21.24** Compare and contrast anabolism and catabolism in terms of their roles in metabolism and their relationship to ATP.

## Overview of Catabolic Processes

### Foundations

**21.25** What is the most readily used energy source in the diet?
**21.26** What is a hydrolysis reaction?

### Applications

**21.27** Write an equation showing the hydrolysis of maltose.
**21.28** Write an equation showing the hydrolysis of sucrose.
**21.29** Write a balanced equation showing the hydrolysis of the following peptide: phe-ala-glu-met-lys.

**21.30** Describe the stages of protein digestion, including the location of each.

**21.31** Write an equation showing the hydrolysis of a triglyceride consisting of glycerol, oleic acid, linoleic acid, and stearic acid.

**21.32** How are fatty acids taken up into the cell?

**21.33** Write an equation showing the hydrolysis of the dipeptide alanyl-leucine.

**21.34** How are amino acids transported into the cell?

## Glycolysis

### Foundations

**21.35** Define glycolysis and describe its role in cellular metabolism.

**21.36** What are the end products of glycolysis?

**21.37** Why does glycolysis require a supply of $NAD^+$ to function?

**21.38** Why must the NADH produced in glycolysis be reoxidized to $NAD^+$?

**21.39** What is the net energy yield of ATP in glycolysis?

**21.40** How many molecules of ATP are produced by substrate-level phosphorylation during glycolysis?

**21.41** Explain how muscle is able to carry out rapid contraction for prolonged periods even though its supply of ATP is sufficient only for a fraction of a second of rapid contraction.

**21.42** Where in the muscle cell does glycolysis occur?

**21.43** Write the balanced chemical equation for glycolysis.

**21.44** Write a chemical equation for the transfer of a phosphoryl group from ATP to fructose-6-phosphate.

**21.45** Match each of the following enzymes with the reaction that it catalyzes.
   **a.** Phosphoglucose isomerase
   **b.** Phosphofructokinase
   **c.** Triose phosphate isomerase
   **d.** Aldolase
   **e.** Hexokinase
   **f.** Enolase
   **g.** Glyceraldehyde-3-phosphate dehydrogenase
   **h.** Phosphoglycerate kinase
   **i.** Pyruvate kinase
   **j.** Phosphoglycerate mutase

   **1.** Phosphorylation of glucose
   **2.** Phosphorylation of fructose-6-phosphate
   **3.** Dephosphorylation of pyruvate
   **4.** Conversion of fructose-1,6-bisphosphate to dihydroxyacetone phosphate and glyceraldehyde-3-phosphate
   **5.** Phosphorylation and oxidation of glyceraldehyde-3-phosphate to produce 1,3-bisphosphoglycerate and NADH
   **6.** Conversion of dihydroxyacetone phosphate into glyceraldehyde-3-phosphate
   **7.** Isomerization of glucose-6-phosphate into fructose-6-phosphate
   **8.** Isomerization of 3-phosphoglycerate into 2-phosphoglycerate
   **9.** Dehydration of 2-phosphoglycerate to produce phosphoenolpyruvate
   **10.** Substrate-level phosphorylation involving transfer of a phosphoryl group from 1,3-bisphosphoglycerate to ADP

**21.46** Match each of the following enzymes with the appropriate class of enzymes that it represents. (*Hint:* An enzyme classification may be used more than once or not at all.)
   **a.** Phosphoglucose isomerase
   **b.** Phosphofructokinase
   **c.** Triose phosphate isomerase
   **d.** Aldolase
   **e.** Hexokinase
   **f.** Enolase
   **g.** Glyceraldehyde-3-phosphate dehydrogenase
   **h.** Phosphoglycerate kinase
   **i.** Pyruvate kinase
   **j.** Phosphoglycerate mutase

   **1.** Transferase
   **2.** Oxidoreductase
   **3.** Kinase
   **4.** Hydrolase
   **5.** Lyase
   **6.** Isomerase

### Applications

**21.47** Describe the symptoms associated with a genetic deficiency of an enzyme in the glycolysis pathway.

**21.48** Why are red blood cells particularly susceptible to a deficiency of an enzyme in the glycolysis pathway?

**21.49** What is the cause of myoglobinuria?

**21.50** Describe exercise intolerance and the cause of the condition.

Examine the following pair of equations and use them to answer Questions 21.51–21.54.

**21.51** What type of enzyme would catalyze each of these reactions?

**21.52** To which family of organic molecules do a and d belong? To which family of organic molecules do b and c belong?

**21.53** What is the name of the type of intermediate formed in each of these reactions?

**21.54** Draw the intermediate that would be formed in each of these reactions.

**21.55** When an enzyme has the term *kinase* in the name, what type of reaction do you expect it to catalyze?

**21.56** What features do the reactions catalyzed by hexokinase and phosphofructokinase share in common?

**21.57** What is the role of NAD$^+$ in a biochemical oxidation reaction?

**21.58** Write the equation for the reaction catalyzed by glyceraldehyde-3-phosphate dehydrogenase. Highlight the chemical changes that show this to be an oxidation reaction.

**21.59** What is the importance of the regulation of glycolysis?

**21.60** Explain the role of allosteric enzymes in control of glycolysis.

**21.61** What molecules serve as allosteric effectors of phosphofructokinase?

**21.62** What molecule serves as an allosteric inhibitor of hexokinase?

**21.63** Explain the role of citrate in the feedback inhibition of glycolysis.

**21.64** Explain the feedforward activation mechanism that results in the activation of pyruvate kinase.

## Fermentations

### Foundations

**21.65** Write a balanced chemical equation for the conversion of acetaldehyde to ethanol.

**21.66** Write a balanced chemical equation for the conversion of pyruvate to lactate.

### Applications

**21.67** After running a 100-meter (m) dash, a sprinter had a high concentration of muscle lactate. What process is responsible for production of lactate?

**21.68** If the muscle of an organism had no lactate dehydrogenase, could anaerobic glycolysis occur in those muscle cells? Explain your answer.

**21.69** What food products are the result of lactate fermentation?

**21.70** Explain the value of alcohol fermentation in bread making.

**21.71** What enzyme catalyzes the reduction of pyruvate to lactate?

**21.72** What enzymes catalyze the conversion of pyruvate to ethanol and carbon dioxide?

**21.73** A child was brought to the doctor's office suffering from a strange set of symptoms. When the child exercised hard, she became giddy and behaved as though drunk. What do you think is the metabolic basis of these symptoms?

**21.74** A family started a batch of wine by adding yeast to grape juice and placing the mixture in a sealed bottle. Two weeks later, the bottle exploded. What metabolic reactions—and specifically, what product of those reactions—caused the bottle to explode?

## The Pentose Phosphate Pathway

**21.75** Of what value are the ribose-5-phosphate and erythrose-4-phosphate that are produced in the pentose phosphate pathway?

**21.76** Of what value is the NADPH that is produced in the pentose phosphate pathway?

## Gluconeogenesis: The Synthesis of Glucose

**21.77** Define gluconeogenesis and describe its role in metabolism.

**21.78** What is the role of guanosine triphosphate in gluconeogenesis?

**21.79** What organ is primarily responsible for gluconeogenesis?

**21.80** What is the physiological function of gluconeogenesis?

**21.81** Lactate can be converted to glucose by gluconeogenesis. To what metabolic intermediate must lactate be converted so that it can be a substrate for the enzymes of gluconeogenesis?

**21.82** L-Alanine can be converted to pyruvate. Can L-alanine also be converted to glucose? Explain your answer.

**21.83** Explain why gluconeogenesis is not simply the reversal of glycolysis.

**21.84** In step 10 of glycolysis, phosphoenolpyruvate is converted to pyruvate, and ATP is produced by substrate-level phosphorylation. How is this reaction bypassed in gluconeogenesis?

**21.85** Which steps in the glycolysis pathway are irreversible?

**21.86** What enzymatic reactions of gluconeogenesis bypass the irreversible steps of glycolysis?

## Glycogen Synthesis and Degradation

### Foundations

**21.87** What organs are primarily responsible for maintaining the proper blood glucose level?

**21.88** Why must the blood glucose level be carefully regulated?

**21.89** What does the term *hypoglycemia* mean?

**21.90** What does the term *hyperglycemia* mean?

### Applications

**21.91** a. What enzymes involved in glycogen metabolism are stimulated by insulin?
  b. What effect does this have on glycogen metabolism?
  c. What effect does this have on blood glucose levels?

**21.92** a. What enzyme is stimulated by glucagon?
  b. What effect does this have on glycogen metabolism?
  c. What effect does this have on blood glucose levels?

**21.93** Explain how a defect in glycogen metabolism can cause hypoglycemia.

**21.94** What defects of glycogen metabolism would lead to a large increase in the concentration of liver glycogen?

**21.95** Write a "word" equation showing the reaction catalyzed by glycogen phosphorylase.

**21.96** Describe the function of the debranching enzyme in glycogen degradation.

**21.97** Write a balanced equation for the reaction catalyzed by phosphoglucomutase. What is the role of this enzyme in glycogen degradation? What is the role of this enzyme in glycogen synthesis?

**21.98** Draw the structure of UDP-glucose and describe its role in glycogen synthesis.

**21.99** Write a balanced equation for the reaction catalyzed by glucokinase. What is the function of this enzyme in glycogen synthesis?

**21.100** Write a "word" equation showing the reaction catalyzed by glycogen synthase.

# CRITICAL THINKING PROBLEMS

1. An enzyme that hydrolyzes ATP (an ATPase) bound to the plasma membrane of certain tumor cells has an abnormally high activity. How will this activity affect the rate of glycolysis?

2. Explain why no net oxidation occurs during anaerobic glycolysis followed by lactate fermentation.

3. A certain person was found to have a defect in glycogen metabolism. The liver of this person could (a) make glucose-6-phosphate from lactate and (b) synthesize glucose-6-phosphate from glycogen but (c) could not synthesize glycogen from glucose-6-phosphate. What enzyme is defective?

4. A scientist added phosphate labeled with radioactive phosphorus ($^{32}$P) to a bacterial culture growing anaerobically (without $O_2$). She then purified all the compounds produced during glycolysis. Look carefully at the steps of the pathway. Predict which of the intermediates of the pathway would be the first one to contain radioactive phosphate. On which carbon of this compound would you expect to find the radioactive phosphate?

5. A 2-month-old baby was brought to the hospital suffering from seizures. He deteriorated progressively over time, showing psychomotor retardation. Blood tests revealed a high concentration of lactate and pyruvate. Although blood levels of alanine were high, they did not stimulate gluconeogenesis. The doctor measured the activity of pyruvate carboxylase in the baby and found it to be only 1% of the normal level. What reaction is catalyzed by pyruvate carboxylase? How could this deficiency cause the baby's symptoms and test results?

# 22

# Aerobic Respiration and Energy Production

## LEARNING GOALS

1 Name the regions of the mitochondria and the function of each region.

2 Describe the reaction that results in the conversion of pyruvate to acetyl CoA, describing the location of the reaction and the components of the pyruvate dehydrogenase complex.

3 Summarize the reactions of aerobic respiration.

4 Looking at an equation representing any of the chemical reactions that occur in the citric acid cycle, describe the kind of reaction that is occurring and the significance of that reaction to the pathway.

5 Explain the mechanisms for the control of the citric acid cycle.

6 Describe the process of oxidative phosphorylation.

7 Describe the conversion of amino acids to molecules that can enter the citric acid cycle.

8 Explain the importance of the urea cycle and describe its essential steps.

9 Discuss the cause and effect of hyperammonemia.

10 Summarize the role of the citric acid cycle in catabolism and anabolism.

Rock climbing demands a great deal of energy.

## OUTLINE

# INTRODUCTION

In this chapter we will be studying the amazing, intricate set of reactions that allow us to completely degrade fuel molecules such as sugars and amino acids. These oxygen-requiring reactions, called *aerobic respiration*, occur in cellular organelles called *mitochondria*.

We are used to thinking of the organelles as a collection of membrane-bound structures that are synthesized under the direction of the genetic information in the nucleus of the cell. Not so with the mitochondria. These organelles have their own genetic information and are able to make some of their own proteins. They grow and multiply in a way very similar to simple bacteria. This, along with other information on the structure and activities of mitochondria, has led researchers to conclude that the mitochondria are actually the descendants of bacteria captured by eukaryotic cells millions of years ago.

We inherit all of our mitochondria from our mothers and, like the mitochondria themselves, some genetic diseases of energy metabolism are maternally inherited. One such disease, Leber's hereditary optic neuropathy (LHON), causes blindness and heart problems. People with LHON have a reduced ability to make ATP. As a result, sensitive tissues that demand a great deal of energy eventually die. LHON sufferers eventually lose their sight because the optic nerve dies from lack of energy.

Researchers have identified and cloned a mutant mitochondrial gene that is responsible for LHON. The defect is a mutant form of *NADH dehydrogenase*, a huge, complex enzyme that accepts electrons from NADH and sends them on through an electron transport system. Passage of electrons through the electron transport system allows the synthesis of ATP. If NADH dehydrogenase is defective, passage of electrons through the electron transport system is less efficient, and less ATP is made. In LHON sufferers, the result is eventual blindness.

In this chapter and the next, we will study some of the important biochemical reactions that occur in the mitochondria. Here, the final oxidations of carbohydrates, lipids, and proteins occur. Here, also, the electrons that are harvested in these oxidation reactions are used to make ATP. In these remarkably efficient reactions, nearly 40% of the potential energy of glucose is stored as ATP.

## LEARNING GOAL

.1  Name the regions of the mitochondria and the function of each region.

An organelle is a compartment within the cytoplasm that has a specialized function.

## 22.1  The Mitochondria

**Mitochondria** are football-shaped organelles that are roughly the size of a bacterial cell. They are surrounded by an **outer mitochondrial membrane** and an **inner mitochondrial membrane** (Figure 22.1). The space between the two membranes is the **intermembrane space,** and the space inside of the inner membrane is the **matrix space.** The enzymes of the citric acid cycle, of the β-oxidation pathway for the breakdown of fatty acids, and for the degradation of amino acids are all found in the mitochondrial matrix space.

### Structure and Function

The outer mitochondrial membrane has many small pores through which small molecules (less than 10,000 g/mol) can pass. Thus, the small molecules to be oxidized for the production of ATP can easily enter the mitochondrial intermembrane space.

The inner membrane is highly folded to create a large surface area. The folded membranes are known as **cristae.** The inner mitochondrial membrane is almost completely impermeable to most substances. For this reason it has many transport proteins to bring particular fuel molecules into the matrix space. Also embedded

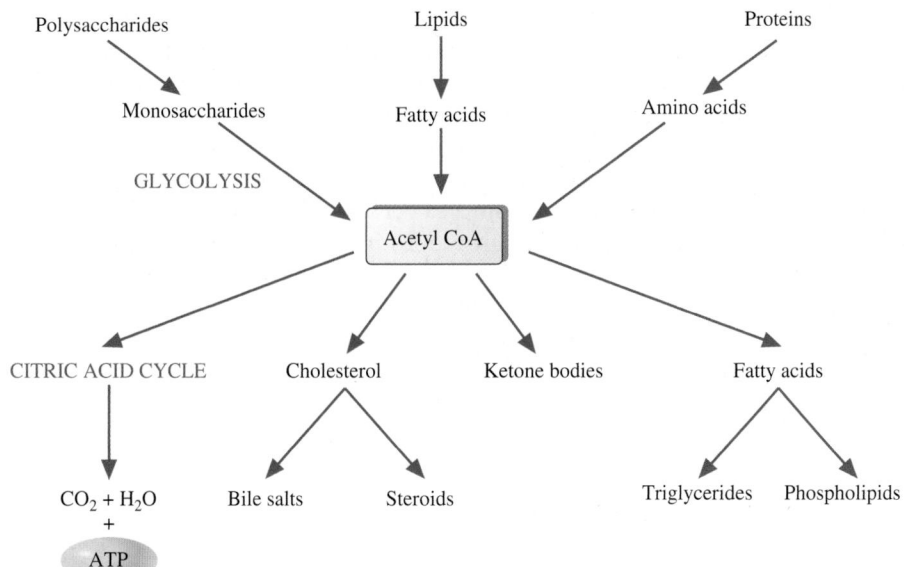

**Figure 22.4** The central role of acetyl CoA in cellular metabolism.

amount of acetyl CoA that our cells could produce. This, in turn, would limit the amount of ATP that the body could make and would contribute to vitamin-deficiency diseases. Fortunately, a well-balanced diet provides an adequate supply of these and other vitamins.

In Figure 22.4, we see that acetyl CoA is a central character in cellular metabolism. It is produced by the degradation of glucose, fatty acids, and some amino acids. The major function of acetyl CoA in energy-harvesting pathways is to carry the acetyl group to the citric acid cycle, in which it will be used to produce large amounts of ATP. In addition to these catabolic duties, the acetyl group of acetyl CoA can also be used for *anabolic* or biosynthetic reactions to produce cholesterol and fatty acids. It is through this intermediate, acetyl CoA, that all the energy sources (fats, proteins, and carbohydrates) are interconvertible.

**Question 22.5** What vitamins are required for acetyl CoA production from pyruvate?

**Question 22.6** What is the major role of coenzyme A in catabolic reactions?

**ANIMATION**
• B Vitamins

## 22.3 An Overview of Aerobic Respiration

**Aerobic respiration** is the oxygen-requiring breakdown of food molecules and production of ATP. The different steps of aerobic respiration occur in different compartments of the mitochondria.

The enzymes for the citric acid cycle are found in the mitochondrial matrix space. The first enzyme catalyzes a reaction that joins the acetyl group of acetyl CoA (two carbons) to a four-carbon molecule (oxaloacetate) to produce citrate (six carbons). The remaining enzymes catalyze a series of rearrangements, decarboxylations (removal of $CO_2$), and oxidation-reduction reactions. The eventual products of this cyclic pathway are two $CO_2$ molecules and oxaloacetate—the molecule we began with.

At several steps in the citric acid cycle, a substrate is oxidized. In three of these steps, a pair of electrons is transferred from the substrate to $NAD^+$, producing NADH (three NADH molecules per turn of the cycle). At another step a pair of electrons is transferred from a substrate to FAD, producing $FADH_2$ (one $FADH_2$ molecule per turn of the cycle).

**LEARNING GOAL**

**3** Summarize the reactions of aerobic respiration.

*Remember (Section 19.7) that it is really the hydride anion with its pair of electrons ($H:^-$) that is transferred to $NAD^+$ to produce NADH. Similarly, a pair of hydrogen atoms (and thus two electrons) are transferred to FAD to produce $FADH_2$.*

**ANIMATIONS**
• How NAD$^+$ Works
• A Biochemical Pathway

The electrons are passed from NADH or FADH$_2$, through an electron transport system located in the inner mitochondrial membrane, and finally to the terminal electron acceptor, molecular oxygen (O$_2$). The transfer of electrons through the electron transport system causes protons (H$^+$) to be pumped from the mitochondrial matrix into the intermembrane compartment. The result is a high-energy H$^+$ reservoir.

In the final step, the energy of the H$^+$ reservoir is used to make ATP. This last step is carried out by the enzyme complex ATP synthase. As protons flow back into the mitochondrial matrix through a pore in the ATP synthase complex, the enzyme catalyzes the synthesis of ATP.

This long, involved process is called *oxidative phosphorylation,* because the energy of electrons from the *oxidation* of substrates in the citric acid cycle is used to *phosphorylate* ADP and produce ATP. The details of each of these steps will be examined in upcoming sections.

**Question 22.7**   What is meant by the term *oxidative phosphorylation?*

**Question 22.8**   What does the term *aerobic respiration* mean?

## 22.4   The Citric Acid Cycle (The Krebs Cycle)

### Biological Effects of Disorders of the Citric Acid Cycle

In Chapter 21 we saw that deficiencies of the enzymes involved in glycolysis cause debilitating conditions and, in severe form, result in death. This is also true of deficiencies of enzymes in the citric acid cycle (Table 22.1). A number of these deficiencies and the mutations that cause them have been studied and, up to this date, no treatment has been found for any of them. As with glycolysis, these genetic deficiencies emphasize the importance of the citric acid cycle to the life of the organism.

Mutations in the fumarase gene cause encephalopathy, which is a syndrome with a variety of symptoms that include neurological symptoms ranging from subtle personality changes to psychosis, lethargy, involuntary muscle spasms, tremors, and seizures. A newborn with a fumarase deficiency may exhibit muscle weakness (hypotonia) and poor feeding. As the child ages, the neurological symptoms become more severe and include severe developmental delay, brain deformation, psychomotor deficits, and seizures. Many children with this deficiency die in infancy or childhood.

A deficiency of α-ketoglutarate dehydrogenase is characterized by chronic lactic acidosis and progressive encephalopathy and hypotonia. The life expectancy of a child born with this deficiency is 2 to 3 years, with death resulting from neurological deterioration.

**TABLE 22.1 Some Citric Acid Cycle Enzyme Deficiencies and the Associated Disorders**

| Enzyme Deficiency | Disorder |
|---|---|
| Fumarase | Early encephalopathy, seizures, and muscular hypotonia |
| α-Ketoglutarate dehydrogenase | Hypotonia, severe encephalopathy, psychotic behavior |
| Succinate dehydrogenase | Leigh disease (subacute necrotizing encephalomyelopathy), paraganglioma |
| Aconitase | Friedreich ataxia |

A variety of mutations in the succinate dehydrogenase gene have been identified. One of these, SdhA, has been associated with Leigh disease, a disorder that generally affects children between 3 months and 2 years of age. It results in loss of motor skills and eventual death. Other mutations lead to tumors called *paragangliomas*. These are typically found in the head and neck regions and, depending on the nature of the mutation, may be malignant or benign.

One manifestation of aconitase deficiency is characterized by myopathy and exercise intolerance. In fact, physical exertion may prove fatal for some patients as a result of circulatory shock. A second manifestation is Friedreich ataxia. Typically symptoms appear in children between the ages of five and fifteen and include muscle weakness, loss of coordination, impaired hearing or speech, and heart disorders.

## Reactions of the Citric Acid Cycle

The **citric acid cycle** is the final stage of the breakdown of carbohydrates, fats, and amino acids released from dietary proteins (Figure 22.5). To understand this important cycle, let's follow the fate of the acetyl group of an acetyl CoA as it passes through the citric acid cycle. The numbered steps listed below correspond to the steps in the citric acid cycle that are summarized in Figure 22.5.

*Reaction 1.* This is a condensation reaction between the acetyl group of acetyl CoA and oxaloacetate. It is catalyzed by the enzyme *citrate synthase.* The product that is formed is citrate:

**LEARNING GOAL**

**4** Looking at an equation representing any of the chemical reactions that occur in the citric acid cycle, describe the kind of reaction that is occurring and the significance of that reaction to the pathway.

$$\underset{\text{Oxaloacetate}}{\begin{array}{c} COO^- \\ | \\ C{=}O \\ | \\ CH_2 \\ | \\ COO^- \end{array}} + \underset{\text{Acetyl CoA}}{H_3C{-}\overset{\displaystyle O}{\overset{\|}{C}}{\sim}S{-}CoA} + H_2O \xrightarrow[\text{synthase}]{\text{Citrate}} \underset{\text{Citrate}}{\begin{array}{c} COO^- \\ | \\ CH_2 \\ | \\ HO{-}C{-}COO^- \\ | \\ H{-}C{-}H \\ | \\ COO^- \end{array}} + \underset{\text{Coenzyme A}}{HS{-}CoA} + H^+$$

**ANIMATION**
• How the Krebs Cycle Works

*Reaction 2.* The enzyme *aconitase* catalyzes the dehydration of citrate, producing *cis*-aconitate. The same enzyme, aconitase, then catalyzes addition of a water molecule to the *cis*-aconitate, converting it to isocitrate. The net effect of these two steps is the isomerization of citrate to isocitrate:

*Notice that the conversion of citrate to cis-aconitate is a biological example of the dehydration of an alcohol to produce an alkene (Section 12.4). The conversion of cis-aconitate to isocitrate is a biochemical example of the hydration of an alkene to produce an alcohol (Sections 11.5 and 12.4).*

$$\underset{\text{Citrate}}{\begin{array}{c} COO^- \\ | \\ CH_2 \\ | \\ HO{-}C{-}COO^- \\ | \\ H{-}C{-}H \\ | \\ COO^- \end{array}} \xrightarrow{\text{Aconitase}} \underset{\text{\textit{cis}-Aconitate}}{\begin{array}{c} COO^- \\ | \\ CH_2 \\ | \\ C{-}COO^- \\ \| \\ C{-}H \\ | \\ COO^- \end{array}} + H_2O \xrightarrow{\text{Aconitase}} \underset{\text{Isocitrate}}{\begin{array}{c} COO^- \\ | \\ CH_2 \\ | \\ H{-}C{-}COO^- \\ | \\ HO{-}C{-}H \\ | \\ COO^- \end{array}}$$

*Reaction 3.* The first oxidative step of the citric acid cycle is catalyzed by *isocitrate dehydrogenase.* It is a complex reaction in which three things happen:

    a. the hydroxyl group of isocitrate is oxidized to a ketone,
    b. carbon dioxide is released, and
    c. $NAD^+$ is reduced to NADH.

*The oxidation of a secondary alcohol produces a ketone (Sections 12.4 and 13.4).*

**Figure 22.5** The reactions of the citric acid cycle.

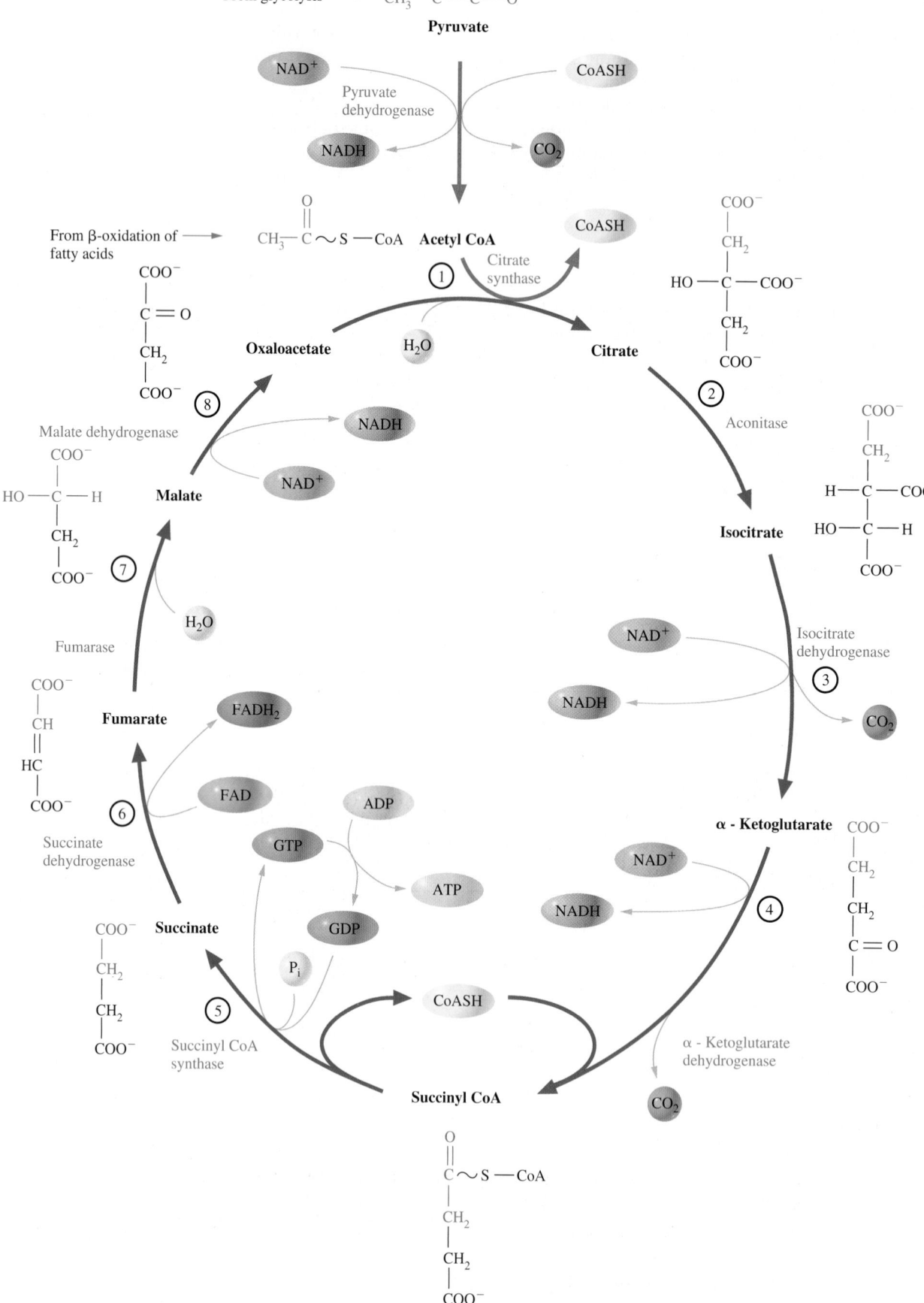

This is an oxidative decarboxylation reaction and the product is α-ketoglutarate:

*The structure of NAD⁺ and its reduction to NADH are shown in Figure 19.8.*

$$
\begin{array}{c}
\text{COO}^- \\
|\\
\text{CH}_2 \\
|\\
\text{H}-\text{C}-\text{COO}^- \\
|\\
\text{HO}-\text{C}-\text{H} \\
|\\
\text{COO}^-
\end{array}
+ \text{NAD}^+
\xrightarrow{\text{Isocitrate dehydrogenase}}
\begin{array}{c}
\text{COO}^- \\
|\\
\text{CH}_2 \\
|\\
\text{CH}_2 \\
|\\
\text{C}=\text{O} \\
|\\
\text{COO}^-
\end{array}
+ \text{CO}_2 + \textbf{NADH}
$$

Isocitrate                                    α-Ketoglutarate

*Remember, in organic (and thus biochemical) reactions, oxidation can be recognized as a gain of oxygen or loss of hydrogen (Section 12.5).*

**Reaction 4.** Coenzyme A enters the picture again as the *α-ketoglutarate dehydrogenase* complex carries out a complex series of reactions similar to those catalyzed by the pyruvate dehydrogenase complex. The same coenzymes are required and, once again, three chemical events occur:

*The pyruvate dehydrogenase complex was described in Section 22.2 and shown in Figure 22.3.*

a. α-ketoglutarate loses a carboxylate group as $CO_2$,
b. it is oxidized and $NAD^+$ is reduced to NADH, and
c. coenzyme A combines with the product, succinate, to form succinyl CoA. The bond formed between succinate and coenzyme A is a high-energy thioester bond.

$$
\begin{array}{c}
\text{COO}^- \\
|\\
\text{CH}_2 \\
|\\
\text{CH}_2 \\
|\\
\text{C}=\text{O} \\
|\\
\text{COO}^-
\end{array}
+ \text{NAD}^+ + \text{Coenzyme A}
\xrightarrow{\begin{array}{c}\text{α-Ketoglutarate}\\\text{dehydrogenase}\\\text{complex}\end{array}}
\begin{array}{c}
\text{COO}^- \\
|\\
\text{CH}_2 \\
|\\
\text{CH}_2 \\
|\\
\text{C}\sim\text{S}-\text{CoA} \\
||\\
\text{O}
\end{array}
+ \text{CO}_2 + \textbf{NADH}
$$

α-Ketoglutarate                                      Succinyl CoA

**Reaction 5.** Succinyl CoA is converted to succinate in this step, which once more is chemically very involved. The enzyme *succinyl CoA synthase* catalyzes a coupled reaction in which the high-energy thioester bond of succinyl CoA is hydrolyzed and an inorganic phosphate group is added to GDP to make GTP:

$$
\begin{array}{c}
\text{COO}^- \\
|\\
\text{CH}_2 \\
|\\
\text{CH}_2 \\
|\\
\text{C}\sim\text{S}-\text{CoA} \\
||\\
\text{O}
\end{array}
+ \text{GDP} + \text{P}_i
\xrightarrow{\begin{array}{c}\text{Succinyl CoA}\\\text{synthase}\end{array}}
\begin{array}{c}
\text{COO}^- \\
|\\
\text{CH}_2 \\
|\\
\text{CH}_2 \\
|\\
\text{COO}^-
\end{array}
+ \textbf{GTP} + \text{Coenzyme A}
$$

Succinyl CoA                                    Succinate

Another enzyme, *dinucleotide diphosphokinase,* then catalyzes the transfer of a phosphoryl group from GTP to ADP to make ATP:

$$
\text{GTP} + \text{ADP} \xrightarrow{\begin{array}{c}\text{Dinucleotide}\\\text{diphosphokinase}\end{array}} \text{GDP} + \text{ATP}
$$

*The structure of FAD was shown in Figure 19.8.*

**Reaction 6.** *Succinate dehydrogenase* then catalyzes the oxidation of succinate to fumarate in the next step. The oxidizing agent, *flavin adenine dinucleotide (FAD)*, is reduced in this step:

*We studied hydrogenation of alkenes to produce alkanes in Section 11.5. This is simply the reverse.*

$$
\begin{array}{c}
\text{COO}^- \\
| \\
\text{CH}_2 \\
| \\
\text{CH}_2 \\
| \\
\text{COO}^-
\end{array}
+ \text{FAD}
\xrightarrow[\text{dehydrogenase}]{\text{Succinate}}
\begin{array}{c}
\text{COO}^- \\
| \\
\text{C—H} \\
\| \\
\text{H—C} \\
| \\
\text{COO}^-
\end{array}
+ \textbf{FADH}_2
$$

Succinate                          Fumarate

**Reaction 7.** Addition of $H_2O$ to the double bond of fumarate gives malate. The enzyme *fumarase* catalyzes this reaction:

*This reaction is a biological example of the hydration of an alkene to produce an alcohol (Sections 11.5 and 12.4).*

$$
\begin{array}{c}
\text{COO}^- \\
| \\
\text{C—H} \\
\| \\
\text{H—C} \\
| \\
\text{COO}^-
\end{array}
+ \text{H}_2\text{O}
\xrightarrow{\text{Fumarase}}
\begin{array}{c}
\text{COO}^- \\
| \\
\text{HO—C—H} \\
| \\
\text{H—C—H} \\
| \\
\text{COO}^-
\end{array}
$$

Fumarate                          Malate

*This reaction is a biochemical example of the oxidation of a secondary alcohol to a ketone, which we studied in Sections 12.4 and 13.4.*

**Reaction 8.** In the final step of the citric acid cycle, *malate dehydrogenase* catalyzes the reduction of $NAD^+$ to NADH and the oxidation of malate to oxaloacetate. Because the citric acid cycle "began" with the addition of an acetyl group to oxaloacetate, we have come full circle.

$$
\begin{array}{c}
\text{COO}^- \\
| \\
\text{HO—C—H} \\
| \\
\text{CH}_2 \\
| \\
\text{COO}^-
\end{array}
+ \text{NAD}^+
\xrightarrow[\text{dehydrogenase}]{\text{Malate}}
\begin{array}{c}
\text{COO}^- \\
| \\
\text{C=O} \\
| \\
\text{CH}_2 \\
| \\
\text{COO}^-
\end{array}
+ \textbf{NADH}
$$

Malate                          Oxaloacetate

## 22.5  Control of the Citric Acid Cycle

LEARNING GOAL

**5** Explain the mechanisms for the control of the citric acid cycle.

Just like glycolysis, the citric acid cycle is responsive to the energy needs of the cell. The pathway speeds up when there is a greater demand for ATP, and it slows down when ATP energy is in excess. In the last chapter we saw that several of the enzymes that catalyze the reactions of glycolysis are *allosteric enzymes*. Similarly, four enzymes or enzyme complexes involved in the complete oxidation of pyruvate are allosteric enzymes. Because the control of the pathway must be precise, there are several enzymatic steps that are regulated. These are summarized in Figure 22.6 and below:

1. *Conversion of pyruvate to acetyl CoA.* The pyruvate dehydrogenase complex is inhibited by high concentrations of ATP, acetyl CoA, and NADH. Of course, the presence of these compounds in abundance signals that the cell has an adequate supply of energy, and thus energy metabolism is slowed.

2. *Synthesis of citrate from oxaloacetate and acetyl CoA.* The enzyme citrate synthase is an allosteric enzyme. In this case, the negative effector is ATP. Again, this is logical because an excess of ATP indicates that the cell has an abundance of energy.

3. *Oxidation and decarboxylation of isocitrate to α-ketoglutarate.* Isocitrate dehydrogenase is also an allosteric enzyme; however, the enzyme is controlled by the positive allosteric effector, ADP. ADP is a signal that the levels of ATP must be low, and therefore the rate of the citric acid cycle should be increased. Interestingly, isocitrate dehydrogenase is also *inhibited* by high levels of NADH and ATP.

4. *Conversion of α-ketoglutarate to succinyl CoA.* The α-ketoglutarate dehydrogenase complex is inhibited by high levels of the products of the reactions that it catalyzes, namely, NADH and succinyl CoA. It is further inhibited by high concentrations of ATP.

*Allosteric enzymes bind to effectors, such as ATP or ADP, that alter the shape of the enzyme active site, either stimulating the rate of the reaction (positive allosterism) or inhibiting the reaction (negative allosterism). For more detail, see Section 19.9.*

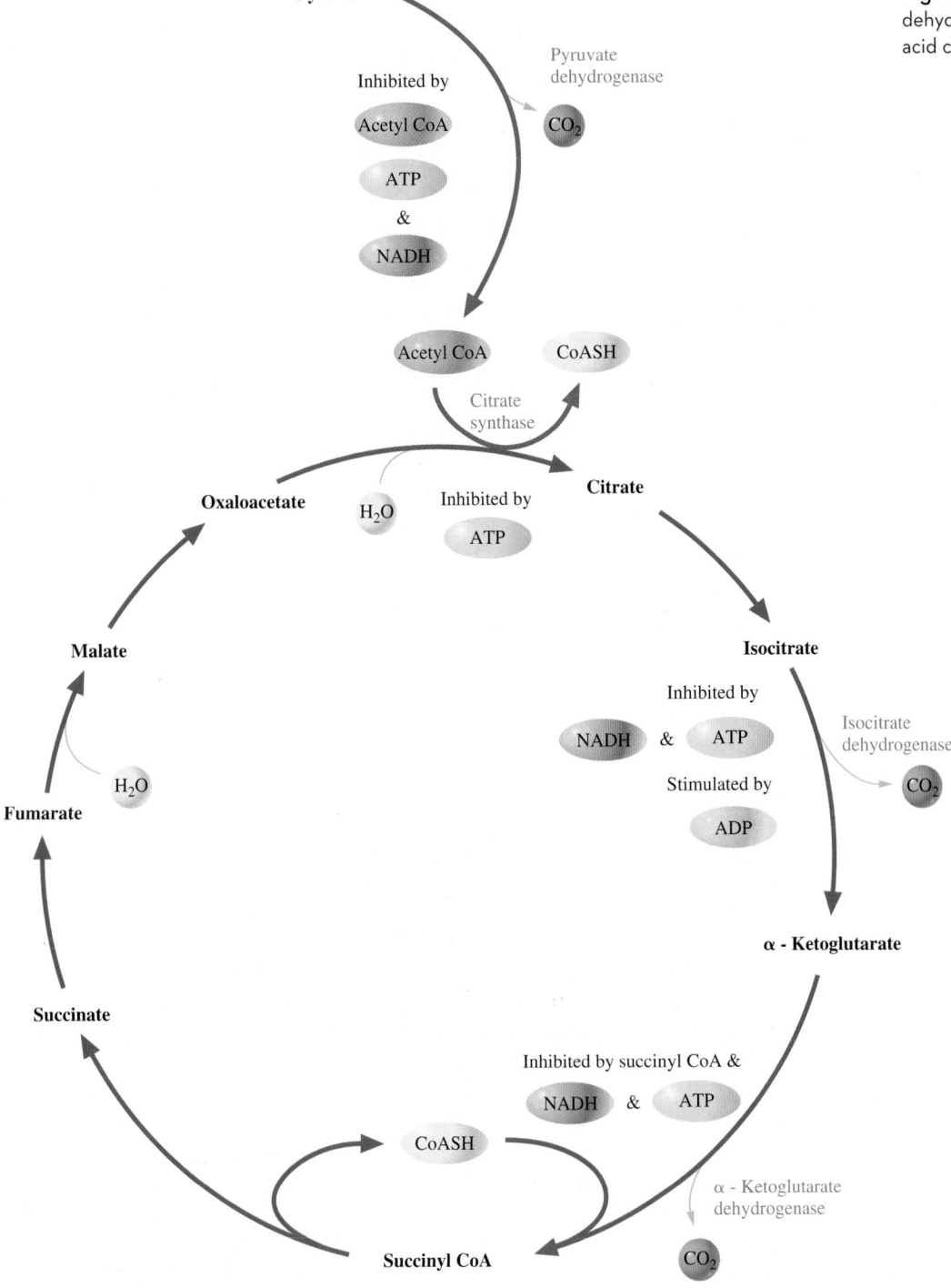

**Figure 22.6** Regulation of the pyruvate dehydrogenase complex and the citric acid cycle.

22.6 Oxidative Phosphorylation

In Section 22.3 we noted that the electrons carried by NADH can be used to produce three ATP molecules, and those carried by FADH$_2$ can be used to produce two ATP molecules. We turn now to the process by which the energy of electrons carried by these coenzymes is converted to ATP energy. It is a series of reactions called **oxidative phosphorylation,** which couples the oxidation of NADH and FADH$_2$ to the phosphorylation of ADP to generate ATP.

### Electron Transport Systems and the Hydrogen Ion Gradient

Before we try to understand the mechanism of oxidative phosphorylation, let's first look at the molecules that carry out this complex process. Embedded within the mitochondrial inner membrane are **electron transport systems.** These are made up of a series of electron carriers, including coenzymes and cytochromes. All these molecules are located within the membrane in an arrangement that allows them to pass electrons from one to the next. This array of electron carriers is called the *respiratory electron transport system* (Figure 22.7). As you would expect in such sequential oxidation-reduction reactions, the electrons lose some energy with each transfer. Some of this energy is used to make ATP.

At three sites in the electron transport system, protons (H$^+$) can be pumped from the mitochondrial matrix to the intermembrane space. These H$^+$ contribute to a high-energy H$^+$ reservoir. At each of the three sites, enough H$^+$ are pumped into the H$^+$ reservoir to produce one ATP molecule. The first site is NADH dehydrogenase. Because electrons from NADH enter the electron transport system by being transferred to NADH dehydrogenase, all three sites actively pump H$^+$, and three ATP molecules are made (see Figure 22.7). FADH$_2$ is a less "powerful" electron donor. It transfers its electrons to an electron carrier that follows NADH

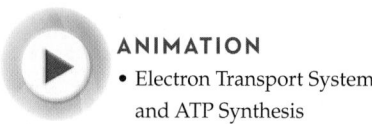

ANIMATION
• Electron Transport System and ATP Synthesis

**Figure 22.7** Electrons flow from NADH to molecular oxygen through a series of electron carriers embedded in the inner mitochondrial membrane. Protons are pumped from the mitochondrial matrix space into the intermembrane space. This results in a hydrogen ion reservoir in the intermembrane space. As protons pass through the channel in ATP synthase, their energy is used to phosphorylate ADP and produce ATP.

dehydrogenase. As a result, when $FADH_2$ is oxidized, only the second and third sites pump $H^+$, and only two ATP molecules are made.

The last component needed for oxidative phosphorylation is a multiprotein complex called **ATP synthase,** also called the **$F_0F_1$ complex** (see Figure 22.7). The $F_0$ portion of the molecule is a channel through which $H^+$ pass. It spans the inner mitochondrial membrane, as shown in Figure 22.7. The $F_1$ part of the molecule is an enzyme that catalyzes the phosphorylation of ADP to produce ATP.

## ATP Synthase and the Production of ATP

How does all this complicated machinery actually function? NADH carries electrons, originally from glucose, to the first carrier of the electron transport system, NADH dehydrogenase (see Figure 22.7). There, NADH is oxidized to $NAD^+$, which returns to the site of the citric acid cycle to be reduced again. As the dashed red line shows, the pair of electrons is passed to the next electron carrier, and $H^+$ are pumped to the intermembrane compartment. The electrons are passed sequentially through the electron transport system, and at two additional sites, $H^+$ from the matrix are pumped into the intermembrane compartment. With each transfer the electrons lose some of their potential energy. It is this energy that is used to transport $H^+$ across the inner mitochondrial membrane and into the $H^+$ reservoir. As mentioned above, $FADH_2$ donates its electrons to a carrier of lower energy and fewer $H^+$ are pumped into the reservoir.

Finally, the electrons arrive at the last carrier. They now have too little energy to accomplish any more work, but they *must* be donated to some final electron acceptor so that the electron transport system can continue to function. In aerobic organisms the **terminal electron acceptor** is molecular oxygen, $O_2$, and the product is water.

As the electron transport system continues to function, a high concentration of protons builds up in the intermembrane space. This creates an $H^+$ gradient across the inner mitochondrial membrane. Such a gradient is an enormous energy source, like water stored behind a dam. The mitochondria make use of the potential energy of the gradient to synthesize ATP energy.

ATP synthase harvests the energy of this gradient by making ATP. $H^+$ pass through the $F_0$ channel back into the matrix. This causes $F_1$ to become an active enzyme that catalyzes the phosphorylation of ADP to produce ATP. In this way the energy of the $H^+$ reservoir is harvested to make ATP.

**Question 22.9** Write a balanced chemical equation for the reduction of $NAD^+$.

**Question 22.10** Write a balanced chemical equation for the reduction of FAD.

## Summary of the Energy Yield

Now that we have studied the reactions of the citric acid cycle and oxidative phosphorylation, we can calculate the total energy yield, in ATP, that is produced from a single glucose molecule.

One turn of the citric acid cycle results in the production of two $CO_2$ molecules, three NADH molecules, one $FADH_2$ molecule, and one ATP molecule. Oxidative phosphorylation yields three ATP molecules per NADH molecule and two ATP molecules per $FADH_2$ molecule. The only exception to these energy yields is the NADH produced in the cytoplasm during glycolysis. Oxidative phosphorylation yields only two ATP molecules per cytoplasmic NADH molecule. The reason for this is that energy must be expended to shuttle electrons from NADH in the cytoplasm to $FADH_2$ in the mitochondrion.

The importance of keeping the electron transport system functioning becomes obvious when we consider what occurs in cyanide poisoning. Cyanide binds to the heme group iron of cytochrome oxidase, one of the electron carriers in the electron transport system, instantly stopping electron transfers and causing death within minutes!

*In some tissues of the body there is a more efficient shuttle system that results in the production of three ATP per cytoplasmic NADH. This system is described online.*

**ENERGY YIELDS FROM AEROBIC RESPIRATION: SOME ALTERNATIVES**

# A HUMAN PERSPECTIVE

## Brown Fat: The Fat That Makes You Thin?

Humans have two types of fat, or adipose, tissue. *White fat* is distributed throughout the body and is composed of aggregations of cells having membranous vacuoles containing stored triglycerides. The size and number of these storage vacuoles determine whether a person is overweight or not. The other type of fat is *brown fat*. Brown fat is a specialized tissue for heat production, called *nonshivering thermogenesis*. As the name suggests, this is a means of generating heat in the absence of the shivering response. The cells of brown fat look nothing like those of white fat. They do contain small fat vacuoles; however, the distinguishing feature of brown fat is the huge number of mitochondria within the cytoplasm. In addition, brown fat tissue contains a great many blood vessels. These provide oxygen for the thermogenic metabolic reactions.

Brown fat is most pronounced in newborns, cold-adapted mammals, and hibernators. One major difficulty faced by a newborn is temperature regulation. The baby leaves an environment in which he or she was bathed in fluid of a constant 37°C, body temperature. Suddenly, the child is thrust into a world that is much colder and in which he or she must generate his or her own warmth internally. By having a good reserve of active brown fat to generate that heat, the newborn is protected against cold shock at the time of birth. However, this thermogenesis literally burns up most of the brown fat tissue, and adults typically have so little brown fat that it can be found only by using a special technique called *thermography*, which detects temperature differences throughout a body. However, in some individuals, brown fat is very highly developed. For instance, the Korean diving women who spend 6–7 h every day diving for pearls in cold water have a massive amount of brown fat to warm them by nonshivering thermogenesis. Thus, development of brown fat is a mechanism of cold adaptation.

When it was noticed that such cold-adapted individuals were seldom overweight, a correlation was made between the amount of brown fat in the body and the tendency to become overweight. Studies done with rats suggest that, to some degree, fatness is genetically determined. In other words, you are as lean as your genes allow you to be. In these studies, cold-adapted and non-cold-adapted rats were fed cafeteria food—as much as they wanted—and their weight gain was monitored. In every case the cold-adapted rats, with their greater quantity of brown fat, gained significantly less weight than their non-cold-adapted counterparts, despite the fact that they ate as much as the non-cold-adapted rats. This and other studies led researchers to conclude that brown fat burns excess fat in a highly caloric diet.

How does brown fat generate heat and burn excess calories? For the answer we must turn to the mitochondrion. In addition to the ATP synthase and the electron transport system proteins that are found in all mitochondria, there is a protein in the inner mitochondrial membrane of brown fat tissue called *thermogenin*. This protein has a channel in the center through which the protons ($H^+$) of the intermembrane space could pass back into the mitochondrial matrix. Under normal conditions, this channel is plugged by a GDP molecule so that it remains closed and the proton gradient can continue to drive ATP synthesis by oxidative phosphorylation.

When brown fat is "turned on," by cold exposure or in response to certain hormones, there is an immediate increase in the rate of glycolysis and β-oxidation of the stored fat (Chapter 23). These reactions produce acetyl CoA, which then fuels the citric acid cycle. The citric acid cycle, of course, produces NADH and $FADH_2$, which carry electrons to the electron transport system. Finally, the electron transport system pumps protons into the intermembrane space. Under usual conditions, the energy of the proton gradient would be used to synthesize ATP. However, when brown fat is stimulated, the GDP that had plugged the pore in thermogenin is lost. Now protons pass freely back into the matrix space, and the proton gradient is dissipated. The energy of the gradient, no longer useful for generating ATP, is released as *heat*, the heat that warms and protects newborns and cold-adapted individuals.

Brown fat is just one of the body's many systems for maintaining a constant internal environment regardless of the conditions in the external environment. Such mechanisms, called *homeostatic mechanisms*, are absolutely essential to allow the body to adapt to and survive in an ever-changing environment.

### For Further Understanding

▶ Hibernators eat a great deal in preparation for their long winter nap. Explain their lifestyle in terms of energy requirements and heat production.

▶ Explain why cold-adapted mammals can eat a high caloric diet and remain thin.

Knowing this information and keeping in mind that two turns of the citric acid cycle are required, we can sum up the total energy yield from the complete oxidation of one glucose molecule.

(a) The inner membrane of brown fat mitochondria contains thermogenin. In the normal state, the pore in the center of thermogenin is plugged by a GDP molecule. (b) When brown fat is activated for thermogenesis, the GDP molecule is removed from the pore, and the protons from the $H^+$ reservoir are free to flow back into the matrix of the mitochondrion. As the gradient dissipates, heat energy is released.

Aerobic metabolism is very much more efficient than anaerobic metabolism. The abundant energy harvested by aerobic metabolism has had enormous consequences for the biological world. Much of the energy released by the oxidation of

**EXAMPLE 22.1    Determining the Yield of ATP from Aerobic Respiration**

Calculate the number of ATP produced by the complete oxidation of one molecule of glucose.

**Solution**

Glycolysis:

| | |
|---|---|
| Substrate-level phosphorylation | 2 ATP |
| 2 NADH × 2 ATP/cytoplasmic NADH | 4 ATP |

Conversion of 2 pyruvate molecules to 2 acetyl CoA molecules:

| | |
|---|---|
| 2 NADH × 3 ATP/NADH | 6 ATP |

Citric acid cycle (two turns):

| | |
|---|---|
| 2 GTP × 1 ATP/GTP | 2 ATP |
| 6 NADH × 3 ATP/NADH | 18 ATP |
| 2 $FADH_2$ × 2 ATP/$FADH_2$ | 4 ATP |
| | 36 ATP |

This represents an energy harvest of about 40% of the potential energy of glucose.

**Practice Problem 22.1**

Calculate the number of ATP produced by the complete oxidation of pyruvate.

▶ For Further Practice: **Questions 22.41, 22.42, and 22.44.**

fuels is not lost as heat but conserved in the form of ATP. Organisms that possess abundant energy have evolved into multicellular organisms and developed specialized functions. As a consequence of their energy requirements, all multicellular organisms are aerobic.

## 22.7  The Degradation of Amino Acids

Carbohydrates are not our only source of energy. As we saw in Chapter 21, dietary protein is digested to amino acids that can also be used as an energy source, although this is not their major metabolic function. Most of the amino acids used for energy come from the diet. In fact, it is only under starvation conditions, when stored glycogen has been depleted, that the body begins to burn its own protein, for instance from muscle, as a fuel.

The fate of the mixture of amino acids provided by digestion of protein depends upon a balance between the need for amino acids for biosynthesis and the need for cellular energy. Only those amino acids that are not needed for protein synthesis are eventually converted into citric acid cycle intermediates and used as fuel.

The degradation of amino acids occurs primarily in the liver and takes place in two stages. The first stage is the removal of the α-amino group, and the second is the degradation of the carbon skeleton. In land mammals the amino group generally ends up in urea, which is excreted in the urine. The carbon skeletons can be converted into a variety of compounds, including citric acid cycle intermediates, pyruvate, acetyl CoA, or acetoacetyl CoA. The degradation of the carbon

**LEARNING GOAL**

**7** Describe the conversion of amino acids to molecules that can enter the citric acid cycle.

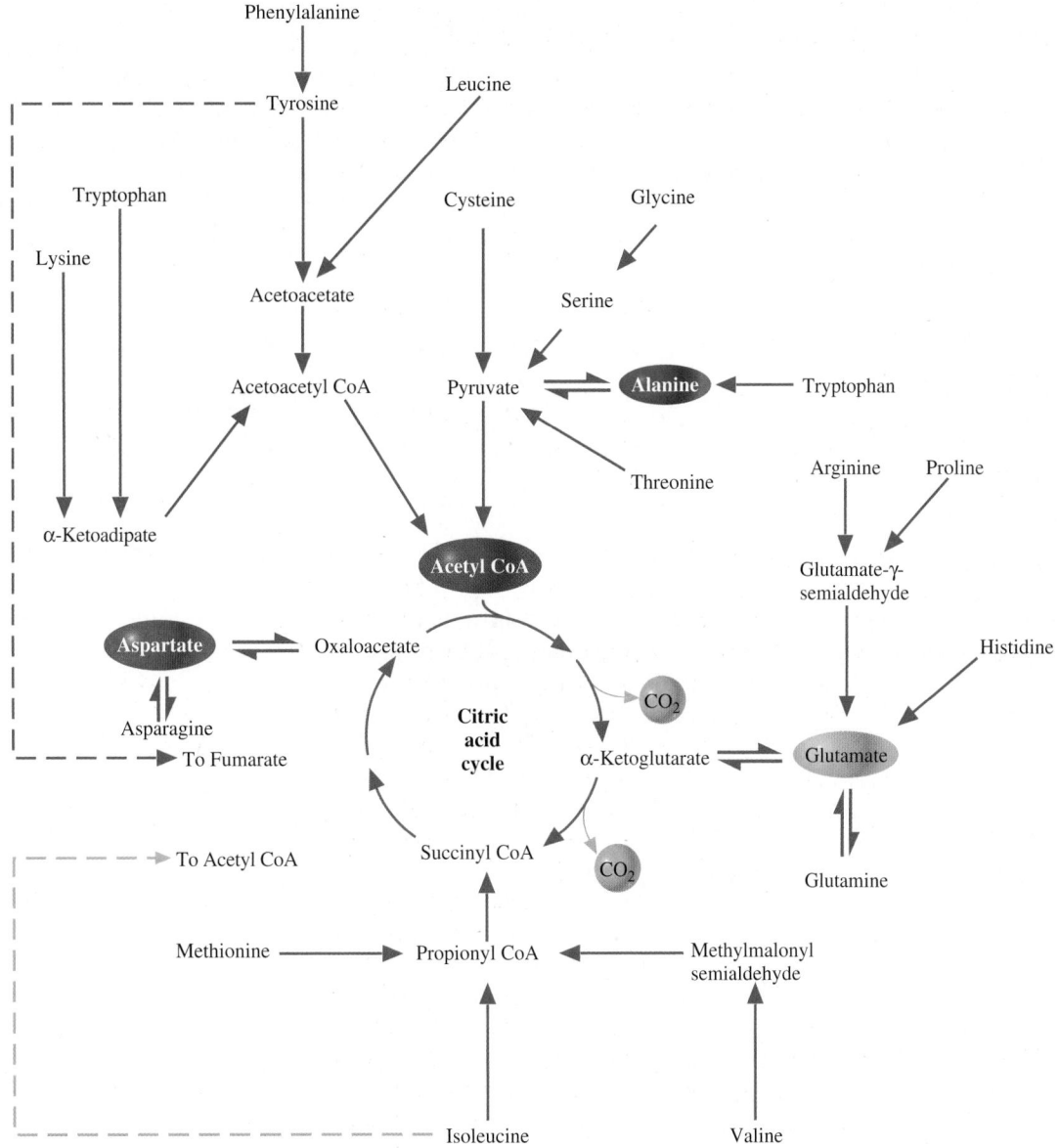

**Figure 22.8** The carbon skeletons of amino acids can be converted to citric acid cycle intermediates and completely oxidized to produce ATP energy.

skeletons is summarized in Figure 22.8. Deamination reactions and the fate of the carbon skeletons of amino acids are the focus of this section.

## Removal of α-Amino Groups: Transamination

The first stage of amino acid degradation, the removal of the α-amino group, is usually accomplished by a **transamination** reaction. **Transaminases** catalyze the transfer of the α-amino group from an α-amino acid to an α-keto acid:

$$
\overset{\overset{+}{NH_3}}{\underset{R^1}{H{-}\overset{|}{\underset{|}{C}}{-}COO^-}} + \overset{O}{\underset{R^2}{\overset{\|}{C}{-}COO^-}} \rightleftharpoons \overset{O}{\underset{R^1}{\overset{\|}{C}{-}COO^-}} + \overset{\overset{+}{NH_3}}{\underset{R^2}{H{-}\overset{|}{\underset{|}{C}}{-}COO^-}}
$$

| Donor amino acid | Acceptor keto acid | α-Keto acid of amino acid | New amino acid |

CH$_2$OH

HOH$_2$C —⟨ring⟩— OH
—CH$_3$
N$^+$
H

Pyridoxine (vitamin B$_6$)

Pyridoxal phosphate

**Figure 22.9** The structure of pyridoxal phosphate, the coenzyme required for all transamination reactions, and pyridoxine, vitamin B$_6$, the vitamin from which it is derived.

The α-amino group of a great many amino acids is transferred to α-ketoglutarate to produce the amino acid glutamate and a new keto acid. This glutamate family of transaminases is especially important because the α-keto acid corresponding to glutamate is α-ketoglutarate, a citric acid cycle intermediate. The glutamate transaminases thus provide a direct link between amino acid degradation and the citric acid cycle.

*Aspartate transaminase* catalyzes the transfer of the α-amino group of aspartate to α-ketoglutarate, producing oxaloacetate and glutamate:

| Aspartate | α-Ketoglutarate | Oxaloacetate | Glutamate |

Another important transaminase in mammalian tissues is *alanine transaminase,* which catalyzes the transfer of the α-amino group of alanine to α-ketoglutarate and produces pyruvate and glutamate:

| Alanine | α-Ketoglutarate | Pyruvate | Glutamate |

All of the more than fifty transaminases that have been discovered require the coenzyme **pyridoxal phosphate.** This coenzyme is derived from vitamin B$_6$ (pyridoxine, Figure 22.9).

The transamination reactions shown above appear to be a simple transfer, but in reality, the reaction is much more complex. The transaminase binds the amino acid (aspartate in Figure 22.10a) in its active site. Then the α-amino group of aspartate is transferred to pyridoxal phosphate, producing pyridoxamine phosphate and oxaloacetate (Figure 22.10b). The amino group is then transferred to an α-keto acid, in this case, α-ketoglutarate (Figure 22.10c), to produce the amino acid glutamate (Figure 22.10d). Next we will examine the fate of the amino group that has been transferred to α-ketoglutarate to produce glutamate.

*For more information on vitamins and the coenzymes that are made from them, look online.*

**WATER-SOLUBLE VITAMINS**

**Question 22.11**  What is the role of pyridoxal phosphate in transamination reactions?

**Question 22.12**  What is the function of a transaminase?

## Removal of α-Amino Groups: Oxidative Deamination

In the next stage of amino acid degradation, ammonium ion is liberated from the glutamate formed by the transaminase. This breakdown of glutamate, catalyzed by the enzyme *glutamate dehydrogenase*, occurs as follows:

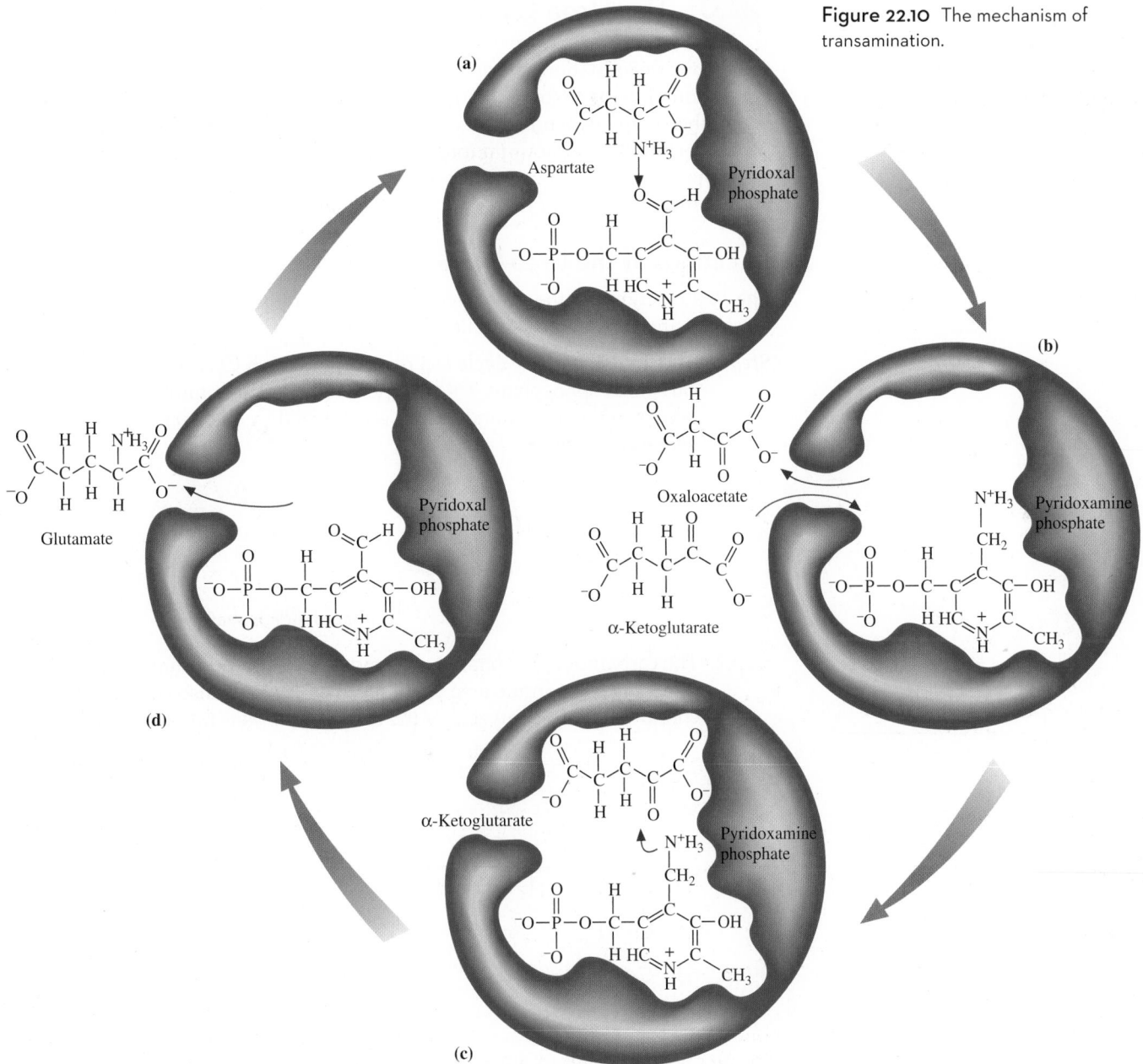

Glutamate

$\alpha$-Ketoglutarate

This is an example of an **oxidative deamination,** an oxidation-reduction process in which NAD$^+$ is reduced to NADH and the amino acid is deaminated (the amino group is removed). A summary of the deamination reactions described is shown in Figure 22.11.

**Figure 22.10** The mechanism of transamination.

(a)

Aspartate

Pyridoxal phosphate

(b)

Oxaloacetate

$\alpha$-Ketoglutarate

Pyridoxamine phosphate

Glutamate

Pyridoxal phosphate

(d)

(c)

$\alpha$-Ketoglutarate

Pyridoxamine phosphate

**Figure 22.11** Summary of the deamination of an α-amino acid and the fate of the ammonium ion ($NH_4^+$).

## The Fate of Amino Acid Carbon Skeletons

The carbon skeletons produced by these and other deamination reactions enter glycolysis or the citric acid cycle at many steps. For instance, we have seen that transamination converts aspartate to oxaloacetate and alanine to pyruvate. The positions at which the carbon skeletons of various amino acids enter the energy-harvesting pathways are summarized in Figure 22.8.

## 22.8  The Urea Cycle

Oxidative deamination produces large amounts of ammonium ion. Because ammonium ions are extremely toxic, they must be removed from the body, regardless of the energy expenditure required. In humans, they are detoxified in the liver by converting the ammonium ions into urea. This pathway, called the **urea cycle,** is the method by which toxic ammonium ions are kept out of the blood. The excess ammonium ions incorporated in urea are excreted in the urine (Figure 22.12).

### Reactions of the Urea Cycle

The five reactions of the urea cycle are shown in Figure 22.12, and details of the reactions are summarized as follows.

*Step 1.* The first step of the cycle is a reaction in which $CO_2$ and $NH_4^+$ form carbamoyl phosphate. This reaction, which also requires ATP and $H_2O$, occurs in the mitochondria and is catalyzed by the enzyme *carbamoyl phosphate synthase.*

Carbamoyl phosphate

The urea cycle involves several unusual amino acids that are not found in polypeptides.

*Step 2.* The carbamoyl phosphate now condenses with the amino acid ornithine to produce the amino acid citrulline. This reaction also occurs in the mitochondria and is catalyzed by the enzyme *ornithine transcarbamoylase.*

Ornithine        Carbamoyl phosphate              Citrulline

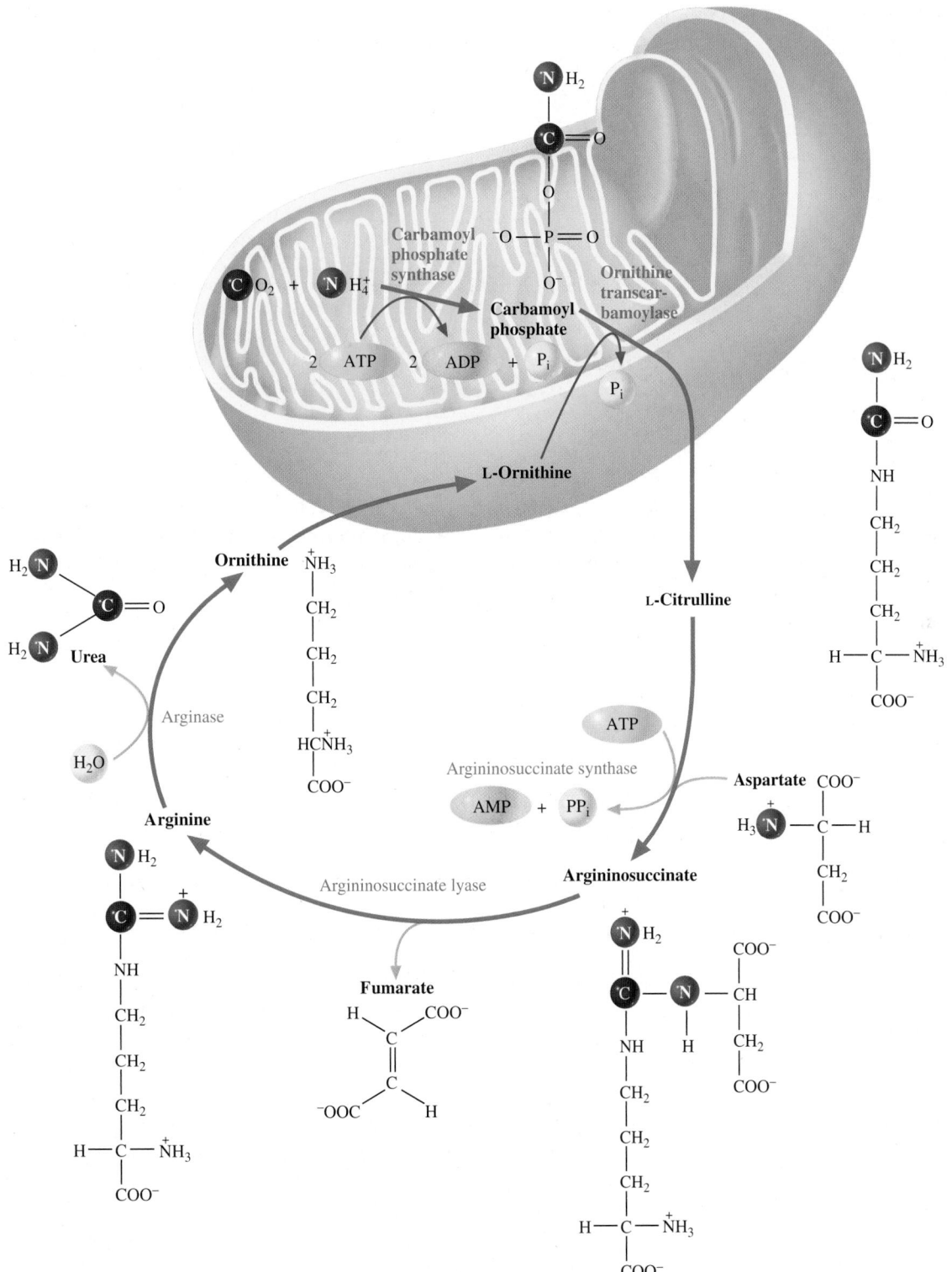

**Figure 22.12** The urea cycle converts ammonium ions into urea, which is less toxic. The intracellular locations of the reactions are indicated. Citrulline, formed in the reaction between ornithine and carbamoyl phosphate, is transported out of the mitochondrion and into the cytoplasm. Ornithine, a substrate for the formation of citrulline, is transported from the cytoplasm into the mitochondrion.

The abbreviation PP$_i$ represents the pyrophosphate group, which consists of two phosphate groups joined by a phosphoanhydride bond:

$$^-O-\overset{\overset{O}{\|}}{P}-O-\overset{\overset{O}{\|}}{P}-O^-$$
$$\quad\quad|\quad\quad\quad|$$
$$\quad\quad O^-\quad\quad O^-$$

*Step 3.* Citrulline is transported into the cytoplasm and now condenses with aspartate to produce argininosuccinate. This reaction, which requires energy released by the hydrolysis of ATP, is catalyzed by the enzyme *argininosuccinate synthase.*

Citrulline + Aspartate $\xrightarrow[\text{ATP} \; \text{AMP + PP}_i]{}$ Argininosuccinate

*Step 4.* Now the argininosuccinate is cleaved to produce the amino acid arginine and the citric acid cycle intermediate fumarate. This reaction is catalyzed by the enzyme *argininosuccinate lyase.*

Argininosuccinate $\longrightarrow$ Arginine + Fumarate

*Step 5.* Finally, arginine is hydrolyzed to generate urea, the product of the reaction to be excreted, and ornithine, the original reactant in the cycle. *Arginase* is the enzyme that catalyzes this reaction.

Arginine + Water $\longrightarrow$ Urea + Ornithine

Note that one of the amino groups in urea is derived from the ammonium ion and the second is derived from the amino acid aspartate.

## A MEDICAL PERSPECTIVE

### Pyruvate Carboxylase Deficiency

Pyruvate carboxylase is the enzyme that converts pyruvate to oxaloacetate.

$$\text{Pyruvate} + CO_2 + ATP + H_2O \longrightarrow$$
$$\text{Oxaloacetate} + ADP + 2H^+$$

This reaction is important because it provides oxaloacetate for the citric acid cycle when the supplies have run low because of the demands of biosynthesis. It is also the enzyme that catalyzes the first step in gluconeogenesis, the pathway that provides the body with needed glucose in times of starvation or periods of exercise that deplete glycogen stores. But somehow these descriptions don't fill us with a sense of the importance of this enzyme and its jobs. It is not until we investigate a case study of a child born with pyruvate carboxylase deficiency that we see the full impact of this enzyme.

Pyruvate carboxylase deficiency is found in about 1 in 250,000 births; however, there is an increased incidence in native North American Indians who speak the Algonquin dialect and in the French. There are two types of genetic disorders that have been described. In the neonatal form of the disease, there is a complete absence of the enzyme. Symptoms are apparent at birth and the child is born with brain abnormalities. In the infantile form, the patient develops symptoms early in infancy. Again, it is neurological symptoms that draw attention to the condition. The infants do not develop mental or psychomotor skills. They may develop seizures and/or respiratory depression. In both cases, it is the brain that suffers the greatest damage. In fact, this is the case in most of the disorders that reduce energy metabolism because the brain has such high energy requirements.

Biochemically, patients exhibit quite a variety of symptoms. They show acidosis (low blood pH) due to accumulations of lactate and extremely high pyruvate concentrations in the blood. Blood levels of alanine are also high and large doses of alanine do not stimulate gluconeogenesis. Furthermore, a patient's cells accumulate lipid.

We can understand each of these symptoms by considering the pathways affected by the absence of this single enzyme.

Lactic acidosis results from the fact that the body must rely on glycolysis and lactate fermentation for most of its energy needs. Alanine levels are high because it isn't being transaminated to pyruvate efficiently, because pyruvate levels are so high. In addition, alanine can't be converted to glucose by gluconeogenesis. Although the excess alanine is taken up by the liver and converted to pyruvate, the pyruvate can't be converted to glucose. Lipids accumulate because a great deal of pyruvate is converted to acetyl CoA. However, the acetyl CoA is not used to produce citrate as a result of the absence of oxaloacetate. So, the acetyl CoA is thus used to synthesize fatty acids, which are stored as triglycerides.

Dietary intervention has been tried. One such regimen is to supplement with aspartic acid and glutamic acid. The theory behind this treatment is as complex as the many symptoms of the disorder. Both amino acids can be aminated (amino groups added) in non-nervous tissue. This produces asparagine and glutamine, both of which are able to cross the blood-brain barrier. Glutamine is deaminated to glutamate, which is then transaminated to $\alpha$-ketoglutarate, indirectly replenishing oxaloacetate. Asparagine can be deaminated to aspartate, which can be converted to oxaloacetate. This serves as a second supply of oxaloacetate. To date, these attempts at dietary intervention have not proved successful. Perhaps in time research will provide the tools for enzyme replacement therapy or gene therapy that could alleviate the symptoms.

#### For Further Understanding

▶ Write an equation showing the reaction catalyzed by pyruvate carboxylase using structural formulas for pyruvate and oxaloacetate.

▶ Supplementing the diet with asparagine and glutamine was tried as a treatment for pyruvate carboxylase deficiency. Write equations showing the reactions that convert these amino acids into citric acid cycle intermediates.

---

There are genetically transmitted diseases that result from a deficiency of one of the enzymes of the urea cycle. The importance of the urea cycle is apparent when we consider the terrible symptoms suffered by afflicted individuals. A deficiency of urea cycle enzymes causes an elevation of the concentration of $NH_4^+$, a condition known as **hyperammonemia.** If there is a complete deficiency of one of the enzymes of the urea cycle, the result is death in early infancy. If there is a partial deficiency of one of the enzymes of the urea cycle, the result may be mental challenge, convulsions, and vomiting. In these milder forms of hyperammonemia, a low-protein diet leads to a lower concentration of $NH_4^+$ in blood and less severe clinical symptoms.

**LEARNING GOAL**

**9** Discuss the cause and effect of hyperammonemia.

**Question 22.13**  What is the purpose of the urea cycle?

**Question 22.14**  Where do the reactions of the urea cycle occur?

## 22.9 Overview of Anabolism: The Citric Acid Cycle as a Source of Biosynthetic Intermediates

LEARNING GOAL

**10** Summarize the role of the citric acid cycle in catabolism and anabolism.

So far, we have talked about the citric acid cycle only as an energy-harvesting mechanism. We have seen that dietary carbohydrates and amino acids enter the pathway at various stages and are oxidized to generate NADH and $FADH_2$, which, by means of oxidative phosphorylation, are used to make ATP.

However, the role of the citric acid cycle in cellular metabolism involves more than just **catabolism.** It plays a key role in **anabolism,** or biosynthesis, as well. Figure 22.13 shows the central role of glycolysis and the citric acid cycle as energy-harvesting reactions, as well as their role as a source of biosynthetic precursors.

As you may already suspect from the fact that amino acids can be converted into citric acid cycle intermediates, these same citric acid cycle intermediates can also be used as starting materials for the synthesis of amino acids. Oxaloacetate provides the carbon skeleton for the one-step synthesis of the amino acid aspartate by the transamination reaction:

$$\text{oxaloacetate} + \text{glutamate} \rightleftharpoons \text{aspartate} + \alpha\text{-ketoglutarate}$$

Aside from providing aspartate for protein synthesis, this reaction provides aspartate for the urea cycle.

Asparagine is made from aspartate by the amination reaction

$$\text{aspartate} + NH_4^+ + \text{ATP} \longrightarrow \text{asparagine} + \text{AMP} + PP_i + H^+$$

The nine amino acids not shown in Figure 22.13 (histidine, isoleucine, leucine, lysine, methionine, phenylalanine, threonine, tryptophan, and valine) are called the essential amino acids (Section 18.11) because they cannot be synthesized by humans. Arginine is an essential amino acid for infants and adults under physical stress.

$\alpha$-Ketoglutarate serves as the starting carbon chain for the family of amino acids including glutamate, glutamine, proline, and arginine. Glutamate is especially important because it serves as the donor of the $\alpha$-amino group of almost all other amino acids. It is synthesized from $NH_4^+$ and $\alpha$-ketoglutarate in a reaction mediated by glutamate dehydrogenase. This is the reverse of the reaction shown in Figure 22.11 and previously described. In this case the coenzyme that serves as the reducing agent is NADPH.

$$NH_4^+ + \alpha\text{-ketoglutarate} + \text{NADPH} \rightleftharpoons \text{L-glutamate} + NADP^+ + H_2O$$

Glutamine, proline, and arginine are synthesized from glutamate.

Actually, in humans tyrosine is made from the essential amino acid phenylalanine.

Examination of Figure 22.13 reveals that serine, glycine, and cysteine are synthesized from 3-phosphoglycerate; alanine is synthesized from pyruvate; and tyrosine is produced from phosphoenolpyruvate and the four-carbon sugar erythrose-4-phosphate, which, in turn, is synthesized from glucose-6-phosphate in the pentose phosphate pathway. In addition to the amino acid precursors, glycolysis and the citric acid cycle also provide precursors for lipids and the nitrogenous bases that are required to make DNA, the molecule that carries the genetic information. They also generate precursors for heme, the prosthetic group that is required for hemoglobin, myoglobin, and the cytochromes.

Clearly, the reactions of glycolysis and the citric acid cycle are central to both anabolic and catabolic cellular activities. Metabolic pathways that function in both anabolism and catabolism are called **amphibolic pathways.** Consider for a moment the difficulties that the dual nature of these pathways could present to the cell. When the cell is actively growing, there is a great demand for biosynthetic precursors to build new cell structures. A close look at Figure 22.13 shows us that periods of active cell growth and biosynthesis may deplete the supply of citric acid cycle intermediates. The problem is, the processes of growth and biosynthesis also require a great deal of ATP!

The solution to this problem is to have an alternative pathway for oxaloacetate synthesis that can produce enough oxaloacetate to supply the anabolic and catabolic requirements of the cell. Although bacteria and plants have several mechanisms, the only way that mammalian cells can produce more oxaloacetate is by the

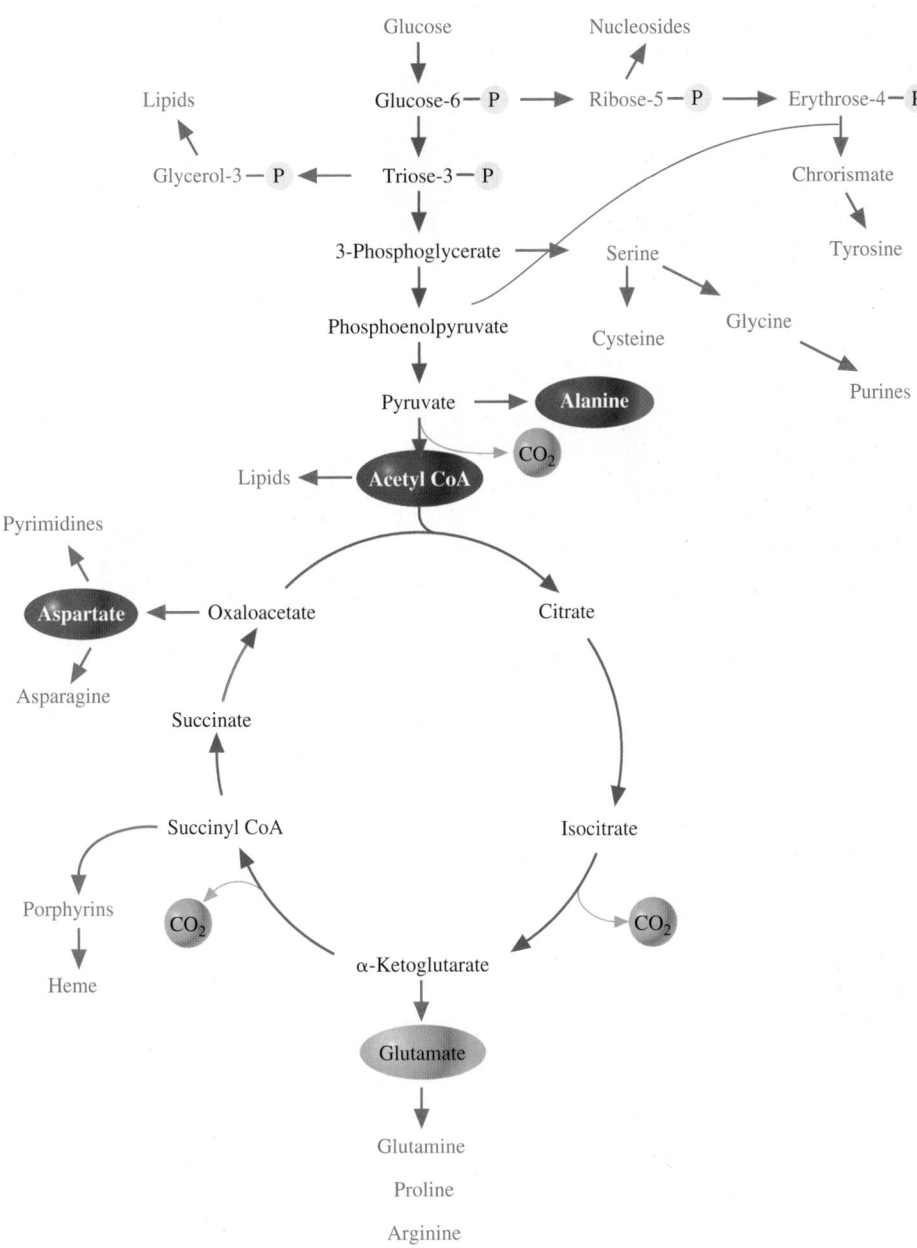

**Figure 22.13** Glycolysis, the pentose phosphate pathway, and the citric acid cycle also provide a variety of precursors for the biosynthesis of amino acids, nitrogenous bases, and porphyrins.

carboxylation of pyruvate, a reaction that is also important in gluconeogenesis. This reaction is

$$\text{pyruvate} + CO_2 + \text{ATP} \longrightarrow \text{oxaloacetate} + \text{ADP} + P_i$$

The enzyme that catalyzes this reaction is *pyruvate carboxylase.* It is a conjugated protein having as its covalently linked prosthetic group the vitamin *biotin.* This enzyme is "turned on" by high levels of acetyl CoA, a signal that the cell requires high levels of the citric acid cycle intermediates, particularly oxaloacetate, the beginning substrate.

The reaction catalyzed by pyruvate carboxylase is called an **anaplerotic reaction.** The term *anaplerotic* means "to fill up." Indeed, this critical enzyme must constantly replenish the oxaloacetate and thus indirectly all the citric acid cycle intermediates that are withdrawn as biosynthetic precursors for the reactions summarized in Figure 22.13.

*Carboxylation of pyruvate during gluconeogenesis is discussed in Section 21.6.*

*See also A Medical Perspective: Pyruvate Carboxylase Deficiency earlier in this chapter.*

**Question 22.15** Explain how the citric acid cycle serves as an amphibolic pathway.

**Question 22.16** What is the function of an anaplerotic reaction?

# CHAPTER MAP

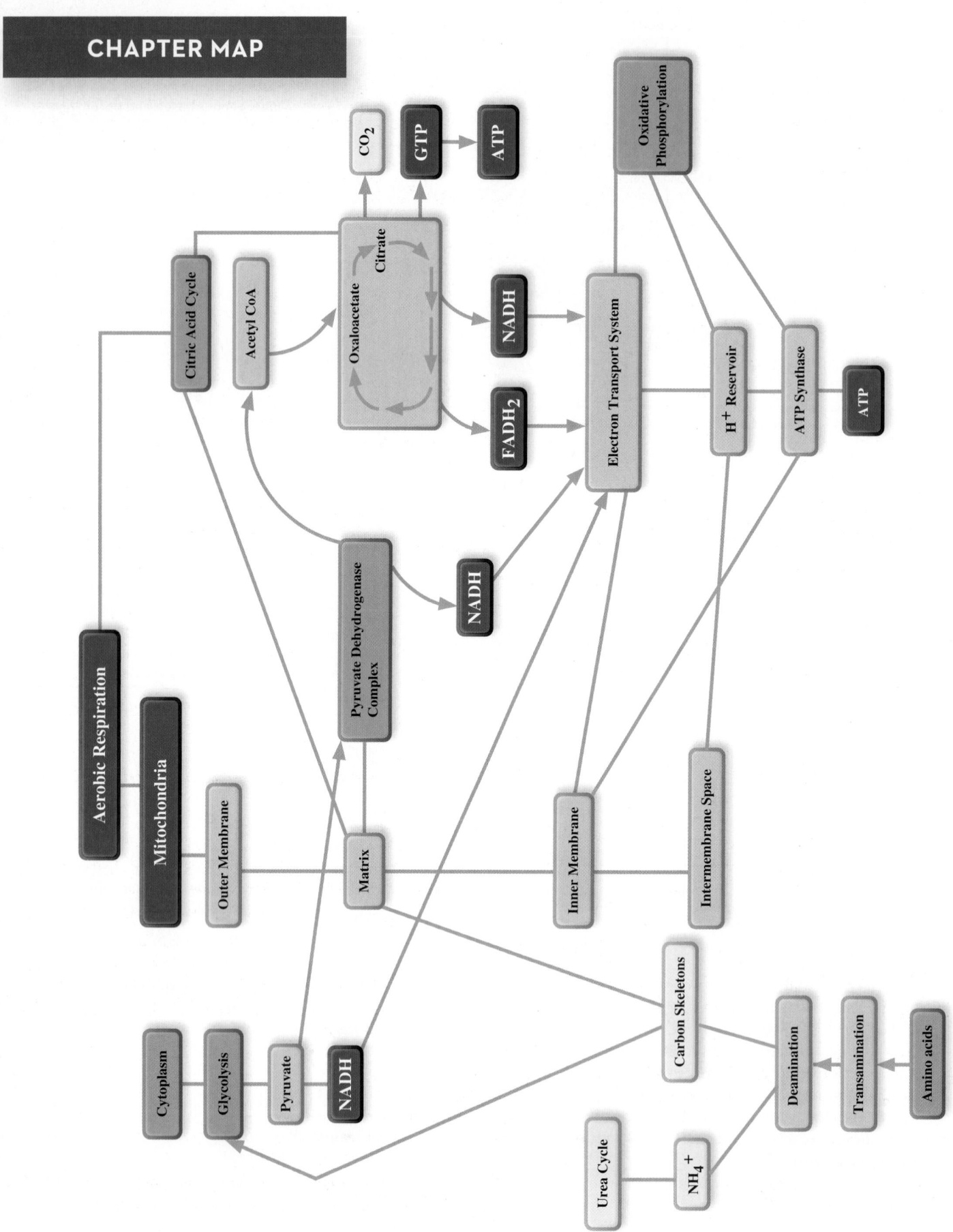

# SUMMARY

## 22.1 The Mitochondria

▶ **Mitochondria** are aerobic cell organelles that are responsible for most of the ATP production in eukaryotic cells.

▶ Mitochondria are enclosed by a double membrane.
  - The **outer mitochondrial membrane** permits low-molar-mass molecules to pass through.
  - The **inner mitochondrial membrane** is almost completely impermeable to most molecules.
    - It is the site of oxidative phosphorylation.
    - It is highly folded into **cristae** to increase the surface area.
  - The **intermembrane space** is the site of the high-energy $H^+$ reservoir.
  - The **matrix space** contains the enzymes of the citric acid cycle.

## 22.2 Conversion of Pyruvate to Acetyl CoA

▶ Under aerobic conditions, pyruvate is oxidized by the **pyruvate dehydrogenase complex.**

▶ In this reaction, **coenzyme A** bonds to an acetyl group through a thioester bond to produce acetyl coenzyme A or **acetyl CoA.**

▶ Acetyl CoA is a central molecule in both anabolism and catabolism.

## 22.3 An Overview of Aerobic Respiration

▶ **Aerobic respiration** is the oxygen-requiring degradation of food molecules and production of ATP.

▶ Oxidative phosphorylation is the process that uses high-energy electrons harvested by oxidation of substrates of the citric acid cycle to produce ATP.

## 22.4 The Citric Acid Cycle (The Krebs Cycle)

▶ The **citric acid cycle** is the final pathway for the degradation of carbohydrates, amino acids, and fatty acids.

▶ This pathway carries out the complete oxidation of carbon skeletons of food molecules.

▶ The enzymes of the citric acid cycle are found in the matrix space of the mitochondria.

## 22.5 Control of the Citric Acid Cycle

▶ Because the rate of ATP production by the cell must vary with the amount of available oxygen and the energy requirements of the body, the citric acid cycle is regulated at several steps. These are:
  - Conversion of pyruvate to acetyl CoA (pyruvate dehydrogenase)
  - Synthesis of citrate from oxaloacetate and acetyl CoA (citrate synthase)
  - Oxidation and decarboxylation of isocitrate to α-ketoglutarate (isocitrate dehydrogenase)
  - Conversion of α-ketoglutarate to succinyl CoA (α-ketoglutarate dehydrogenase)

▶ This regulation allows the cells to produce more ATP when it is needed for activity and less ATP when the body is at rest and the requirement for ATP is lower.

## 22.6 Oxidative Phosphorylation

▶ **Oxidative phosphorylation** is the process by which NADH and $FADH_2$ are oxidized and ATP is produced.
  - Two molecules of ATP are produced when one $FADH_2$ is oxidized.
  - Three molecules of ATP are produced when one NADH is oxidized.

▶ The **electron transport system** is the series of electron transport proteins embedded within the inner mitochondrial membrane that accepts high-energy electrons from NADH and $FADH_2$ and transfers them in stepwise fashion to $O_2$.
  - At three sites in the electron transport system, $H^+$ are pumped into the high-energy $H^+$ reservoir in the intermembrane space.
  - **ATP synthase,** or the $F_0F_1$ **complex,** is a protein complex in the inner mitochondrial membrane.
    - $H^+$ pass through the $F_0$ portion of the complex and return to the matrix space.
    - The $F_1$ portion catalyzes the phosphorylation of ADP to form ATP.
  - The **terminal electron acceptor** is molecular oxygen ($O_2$).

▶ The complete oxidation of a glucose molecule by glycolysis, the citric acid cycle, and oxidative phosphorylation produces thirty-six ATP molecules.

## 22.7 The Degradation of Amino Acids

▶ Amino acid degradation occurs in the liver and has two stages.
  - Removal of the α-amino group
  - Degradation of the carbon skeleton

▶ Removal of the α-amino group occurs in a **transamination** reaction and is catalyzed by a **transaminase.**

▶ All transaminases require the coenzyme **pyridoxal phosphate.**

▶ **Oxidative deamination** is the reaction by which the glutamate produced in transamination is deaminated.

▶ The carbon skeletons of the amino acids enter a number of reactions of glycolysis and the citric acid cycle and are completely oxidized.

## 22.8 The Urea Cycle

▶ In the **urea cycle** the toxic ammonium ions released by deamination of amino acids are incorporated into urea, which is excreted through the urine.

▶ **Hyperammonemia** is a genetic condition that results from a mutation of one of the enzymes of the urea cycle.

## 22.9 Overview of Anabolism: The Citric Acid Cycle as a Source of Biosynthetic Intermediates

▶ The reactions of the citric acid cycle have key roles in both **anabolism** and **catabolism.**

▶ Amino acids, lipids, and nitrogenous bases for nucleic acids all can be synthesized from many intermediates in the citric acid cycle and glycolysis.

▶ Metabolic pathways that function in both anabolism and catabolism are called **amphibolic pathways.**

▶ An **anaplerotic reaction** replenishes a substrate needed for a biochemical reaction.

## ANSWERS TO PRACTICE PROBLEMS

**22.1** The ATP yield from one molecule of pyruvate can be summarized as follows:

Conversion of pyruvate to acetyl CoA

1 NADH × 3 ATP/NADH = 3 ATP

Citric Acid Cycle

| | |
|---|---|
| 1 GTP × 1 ATP/GTP | = 1 ATP |
| 3 NADH × 3 ATP/NADH | = 9 ATP |
| 1 $FADH_2$ × 2 ATP/$FADH_2$ | = 2 ATP |
| Total | = 15 ATP |

## QUESTIONS AND PROBLEMS

### The Mitochondria

#### Foundations

**22.17** Define the term *mitochondrion.*
**22.18** Define the term *cristae.*

#### Applications

**22.19** What is the function of the intermembrane compartment of the mitochondria?
**22.20** What biochemical processes occur in the matrix space of the mitochondria?
**22.21** In what important way do the inner and outer mitochondrial membranes differ?
**22.22** What kinds of proteins are found in the inner mitochondrial membrane?

### Conversion of Pyruvate to Acetyl CoA

#### Foundations

**22.23** What is coenzyme A?
**22.24** What is the role of coenzyme A in the reaction catalyzed by pyruvate dehydrogenase?

**22.25** In the reaction catalyzed by pyruvate dehydrogenase, pyruvate is decarboxylated. What is meant by the term *decarboxylation?*
**22.26** In the reaction catalyzed by pyruvate dehydrogenase, pyruvate is also oxidized. What substance is reduced when pyruvate is oxidized? What is the product of that reduction reaction?

#### Applications

**22.27** Under what metabolic conditions is pyruvate converted to acetyl CoA?
**22.28** Write a chemical equation for the production of acetyl CoA from pyruvate. Under what conditions does this reaction occur?
**22.29** How could a deficiency of riboflavin, thiamine, niacin, or pantothenic acid reduce the amount of ATP the body can produce?
**22.30** In what form are the vitamins riboflavin, thiamine, niacin, and pantothenic acid needed by the pyruvate dehydrogenase complex?

### The Citric Acid Cycle (The Krebs Cycle)

#### Foundations

**22.31** The reaction catalyzed by citrate synthase is a condensation reaction. Define the term *condensation.*
**22.32** The pair of reactions catalyzed by aconitase results in the conversion of isocitrate to its isomer citrate. What are isomers?
**22.33** What general type of reaction is occurring in the conversion of isocitrate to α-ketoglutarate?
**22.34** Write the equation for the conversion of isocitrate to α-ketoglutarate and circle the chemical change that reveals the type of reaction that is occurring.
**22.35** The reaction catalyzed by succinate dehydrogenase is a dehydrogenation reaction. What is meant by the term *dehydrogenation reaction?*
**22.36** The reaction catalyzed by fumarase is an example of the hydration of an alkene to produce an alcohol. Write the equation for this reaction. What is meant by the term *hydration reaction?*
**22.37** Match each of the following enzymes with the class of enzyme to which it belongs. (*Hint:* An enzyme classification may be used more than once or not at all.)

| | |
|---|---|
| a. Citrate synthase | 1. Transferase |
| b. Aconitase | 2. Oxidoreductase |
| c. Isocitrate dehydrogenase | 3. Kinase |
| d. α-Ketoglutarate dehydrogenase | 4. Hydrolase |
| e. Succinyl CoA synthase | 5. Lyase |
| f. Succinate dehydrogenase | 6. Isomerase |
| g. Fumarase | |
| h. Malate dehydrogenase | |

**22.38** Describe the reaction catalyzed by each of the enzymes listed in Question 22.37.
**22.39** Is the following statement true or false? If false, rewrite the statement to make it accurate. Acetyl CoA transfers an acetyl group from pyruvate to citrate.
**22.40** Are the following statements true or false? If false, rewrite the statements to make them accurate. Glycolysis and the citric acid cycle are aerobic processes. These anabolic processes occur in the mitochondria and the cytoplasm, respectively.

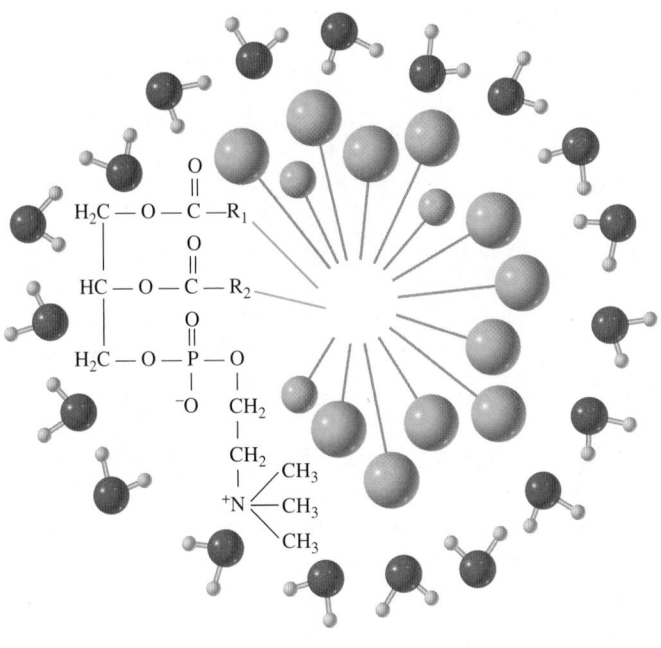

**Figure 23.1** The structure of a micelle formed from the phospholipid lecithin. The straight lines represent the long hydrophobic fatty acid tails, and the spheres represent the hydrophilic heads of the phospholipid.

Cholate

Chenodeoxycholate

**Figure 23.2** Structures of the most common bile salts in human bile: cholate and chenodeoxycholate.

micelles of bile. These micelles are readily absorbed through the membranes of the intestinal epithelial cells (Figure 23.3).

Surprisingly, the monoglycerides and fatty acids are then reassembled into triglycerides that are combined with protein to produce the class of plasma lipoproteins called **chylomicrons** (Figure 23.3). These collections of lipid and protein are secreted into small lymphatic vessels and eventually arrive in the bloodstream. In the bloodstream the triglycerides are once again hydrolyzed to produce glycerol and free fatty acids that are then absorbed by the cells. If the body needs energy, these molecules are degraded to produce ATP. If the body does not need energy, these energy-rich molecules are stored.

*Plasma lipoproteins are described in Section 17.5.*

## Lipid Storage

Fatty acids are stored in the form of triglycerides. Most of the body's triglyceride molecules are stored as fat droplets in the cytoplasm of **adipocytes** (fat cells) that make up **adipose tissue.** Each adipocyte contains a large fat droplet

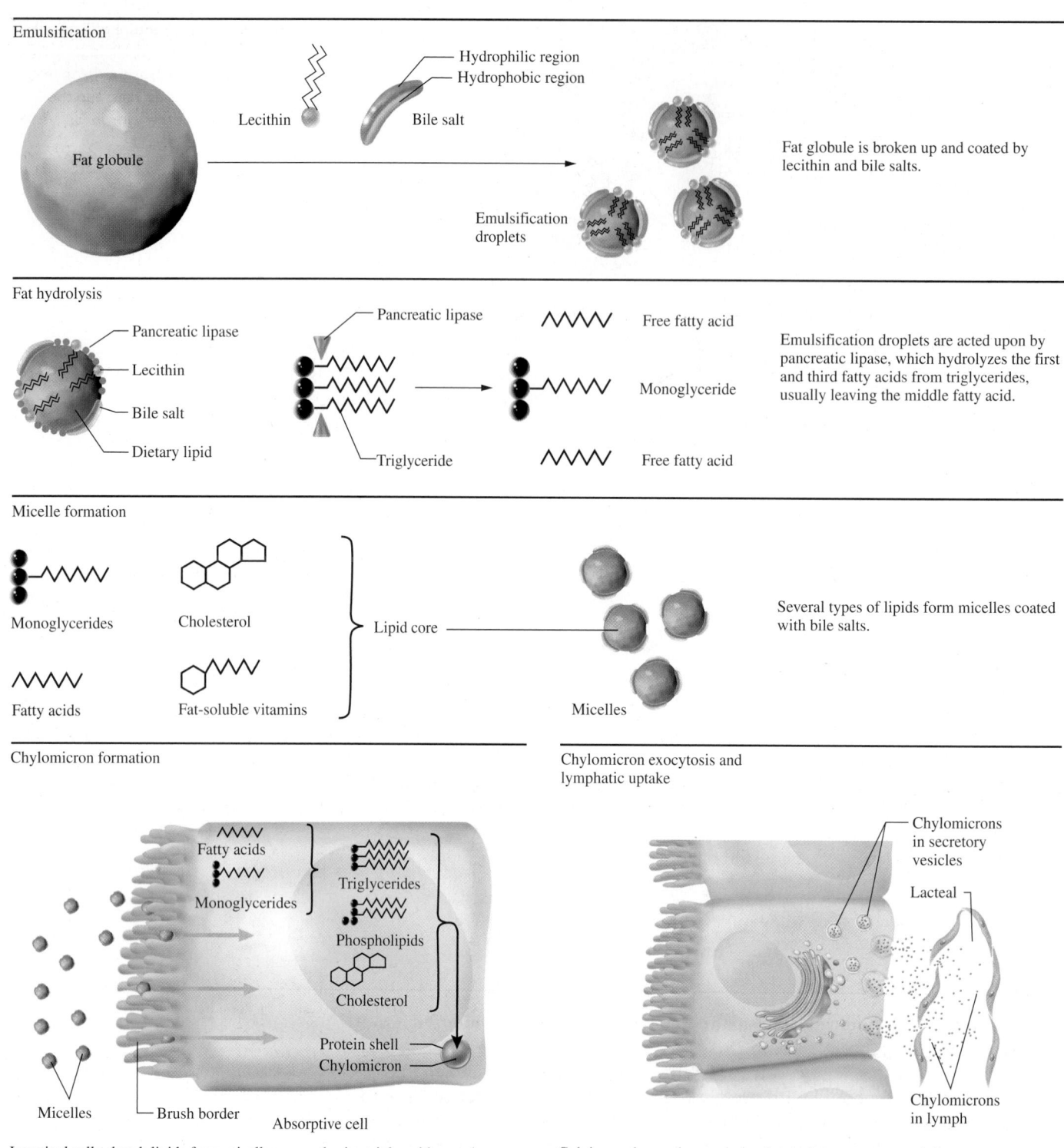

**Emulsification**

Hydrophilic region
Hydrophobic region
Lecithin
Bile salt
Fat globule
Emulsification droplets

Fat globule is broken up and coated by lecithin and bile salts.

**Fat hydrolysis**

Pancreatic lipase
Lecithin
Bile salt
Dietary lipid

Pancreatic lipase
Triglyceride

Free fatty acid
Monoglyceride
Free fatty acid

Emulsification droplets are acted upon by pancreatic lipase, which hydrolyzes the first and third fatty acids from triglycerides, usually leaving the middle fatty acid.

**Micelle formation**

Monoglycerides    Cholesterol
Fatty acids    Fat-soluble vitamins
Lipid core
Micelles

Several types of lipids form micelles coated with bile salts.

**Chylomicron formation**

Fatty acids
Monoglycerides
Triglycerides
Phospholipids
Cholesterol
Protein shell
Chylomicron
Micelles    Brush border
Absorptive cell

Intestinal cells absorb lipids from micelles, resynthesize triglycerides, and package triglycerides, cholesterol, and phospholipids into protein-coated chylomicrons.

**Chylomicron exocytosis and lymphatic uptake**

Chylomicrons in secretory vesicles
Lacteal
Chylomicrons in lymph

Golgi complex packages chylomicrons into secretory vesicles; chylomicrons are released from basal cell membrane by exocytosis and enter the lacteal (lymphatic capillary).

**Figure 23.3** Stages of lipid digestion in the intestinal tract.

that accounts for nearly the entire volume of the cell. Other cells, such as those of cardiac muscle, contain a few small fat droplets. In these cells the fat droplets are surrounded by mitochondria. When the cells need energy, triglycerides are hydrolyzed to release fatty acids that are transported into the matrix space

# A MEDICAL PERSPECTIVE

## Obesity: A Genetic Disorder?

Approximately a third of all Americans are obese; that is, they are more than 20% overweight. One million are morbidly obese; they carry so much extra weight that it threatens their health. Many obese people simply eat too much and exercise too little, but others actually gain weight even though they eat fewer calories than people of normal weight. This observation led many researchers to the hypothesis that obesity in some people is a genetic disorder.

This hypothesis was supported by the 1950 discovery of an obesity mutation in mice. Selective breeding produced a strain of genetically obese mice from the original mutant mouse. The hypothesis was further strengthened by the results of experiments performed in the 1970s by Douglas Coleman. Coleman connected the circulatory systems of a genetically obese mouse and a normal mouse. The obese mouse started eating less and lost weight. Coleman concluded that there was a substance in the blood of normal mice that signals the brain to decrease the appetite. Obese mice, he hypothesized, can't produce this "satiety factor," and thus they continue to eat and gain weight.

In 1987, Jeffrey Friedman assembled a team of researchers to map and then clone the obesity gene that was responsible for appetite control. In 1994, after 7 years of intense effort, the scientists achieved their goal, but they still had to demonstrate that the protein encoded by the cloned obesity gene did, indeed, have a metabolic effect. The gene was modified to be compatible with the genetic system of bacteria so that they could be used to manufacture the protein. When the engineered gene was then introduced into bacteria, they produced an abundance of the protein product. The protein was then purified in preparation for animal testing.

The researchers calculated that a normal mouse has about 12.5 milligrams (mg) of the protein in its blood. They injected that amount into each of ten mice that were so fat they couldn't squeeze into the feeding tunnels used for normal mice. The day after the first injection, graduate student Jeff Halaas observed that the mice had eaten less food. Injections were given daily, and each day the obese mice ate less. After 2 weeks of treatment, each of the ten mice had lost about 30% of its weight. In addition, the mice had become more active and their metabolisms had speeded up.

When normal mice underwent similar treatment, their body fat fell from 12.2% to 0.67%, which meant that these mice had no extra fat tissue. The 0.67% of their body weight represented by fat was accounted for by the membranes that surround each of the cells of their bodies! Because of the dramatic results, Friedman and his colleagues called the protein *leptin*, from the Greek word *leptos*, meaning slender.

The leptin protein is a hormone that functions as a signal in a metabolic thermostat. Fat cells produce leptin and secrete it into the bloodstream. As a result, the leptin concentration in a normal person is proportional to the amount of body fat. The blood concentration of the hormone is monitored by the hypothalamus, a region known to control appetite and set metabolic rates. When the concentration reaches a certain level, it triggers the hypothalamus to suppress the appetite. If no leptin or only small amounts of it are produced, the hypothalamus "thinks" that the individual has too little body fat or is starving. Under these circumstances it does not send a signal to suppress hunger and the individual continues to eat.

The human leptin gene also has been cloned and shown to correct genetic obesity in mice. Unfortunately, the dramatic results achieved with mice were *not* observed with humans. Why? It seems that nearly all of the obese volunteers already produced an abundance of leptin. In fact, fewer than ten people have been found, to date, who do not produce leptin and many obese people have very high levels of leptin in the blood. It appears that, as with type 2 diabetes and insulin, these people are no longer sensitive to the leptin produced by their fat cells.

Ghrelin is another hormone that influences appetite. Produced in the stomach, ghrelin stimulates appetite. As you would predict, the level of ghrelin is high before a meal and decreases following a meal. Many obese people have high levels of ghrelin and therefore experience constant hunger.

Obestatin is another hormone that has been discovered to influence body weight. This hormone decreases appetite. Interestingly, both ghrelin and obestatin are encoded in a single gene. When the protein is produced, it is cleaved into the two peptide hormones.

Clearly lipid metabolism in animals is a complex process and is not yet fully understood. In this chapter we will study other aspects of lipid metabolism: the pathways for fatty acid degradation and biosynthesis and the processes by which dietary lipids are digested and excess lipids are stored.

### For Further Understanding

▶ Go online to learn the cause of type 2 diabetes. Develop a hypothesis to explain the similarities between this condition and leptin insensitivity.

▶ Design an experiment to demonstrate the opposing effects of ghrelin and obestatin.

of the mitochondria. There the fatty acids are completely oxidized, and ATP is produced.

The fatty acids provided by the hydrolysis of triglycerides are a very rich energy source for the body. The complete oxidation of fatty acids releases much more energy than the oxidation of a comparable amount of glycogen.

**Figure 23.4** The action of pancreatic lipase in the hydrolysis of dietary lipids.

Glycerol    Fatty acids

Triglyceride                    Monoglyceride                    Free fatty acids

**Question 23.1**   How do bile salts aid in the digestion of dietary lipids?

**Question 23.2**   Why must dietary lipids be processed before enzymatic digestion can be effective?

## 23.2  Fatty Acid Degradation

### An Overview of Fatty Acid Degradation

Early in the twentieth century, a very clever experiment was done to determine how fatty acids are degraded. Recall from Chapter 9 that radioactive elements can be attached to biological molecules and followed through the body. A German biochemist, Franz Knoop, devised a similar kind of labeling experiment long before radioactive tracers were available. Knoop fed dogs fatty acids in which the usual terminal methyl group had a phenyl group attached to it. Such molecules are called ω-labeled (omega-labeled) fatty acids (Figure 23.5). When he isolated the metabolized fatty acids from the urine of the dogs, he found that phenyl acetate was formed when the fatty acid had an even number of carbon atoms in the chain. But benzoate was formed when the fatty acid had an odd number of carbon atoms. Knoop interpreted these data to mean that the degradation of fatty acids occurs by the removal of two-carbon acetate groups from the carboxyl end of the fatty acid. We now know that the two-carbon fragments produced by the degradation of fatty acids are not acetate, but acetyl CoA. The pathway for the breakdown of fatty acids into acetyl CoA is called β-**oxidation.**

**Figure 23.5** The last carbon of the chain is called the ω-carbon (omega-carbon), so the attached phenyl group is an ω-phenyl group. (a) Oxidation of ω-phenyl-labeled fatty acids occurs two carbons at a time. Fatty acids having an even number of carbon atoms are degraded to phenyl acetate and "acetate." (b) Oxidation of ω-phenyl-labeled fatty acids that contain an odd number of carbon atoms yields benzoate and "acetate."

ω-Phenyl-labeled fatty acid with an even number of carbon atoms                    Phenyl acetate          Acetate

**(a)**

ω-Phenyl-labeled fatty acid having an odd number of carbon atoms                    Benzoate          Acetate

**(b)**

The β-oxidation cycle (steps 2–5, Figure 23.6) consists of a set of four reactions whose overall form is similar to the last four reactions of the citric acid cycle. Each trip through the sequence of reactions releases acetyl CoA and returns a fatty acyl CoA molecule that has two fewer carbons. One molecule of FADH$_2$, equivalent to two ATP molecules, and one molecule of NADH, equivalent to three ATP molecules, are produced for each cycle of β-oxidation.

*Review Section 22.6 for the ATP yields that result from oxidation of FADH$_2$ and NADH.*

---

**EXAMPLE 23.1**  **Predicting the Products of β-Oxidation of a Fatty Acid**

LEARNING GOAL

**2** Describe the degradation of fatty acids by β-oxidation.

What products would be produced by the β-oxidation of 10-phenyldecanoic acid?

**Solution**

This ten-carbon fatty acid would be broken down into four acetyl CoA molecules and one phenyl acetate molecule. Because four cycles through β-oxidation are required to break down a ten-carbon fatty acid, four NADH molecules and four FADH$_2$ molecules would also be produced.

**Practice Problem 23.1**

What products would be formed by β-oxidation of each of the following fatty acids?

   a. 9-Phenylnonanoic acid             c. 7-Phenylheptanoic acid

   b. 8-Phenyloctanoic acid             d. 12-Phenyldodecanoic acid

▶ Further Practice: **Questions 23.41 and 23.42.**

## The Reactions of β-Oxidation

The enzymes that catalyze the β-oxidation of fatty acids are located in the matrix space of the mitochondria. Special transport mechanisms are required to bring fatty acid molecules into the mitochondrial matrix. Once inside, the fatty acids are degraded by the reactions of β-oxidation. As we will see, these reactions interact with oxidative phosphorylation and the citric acid cycle to produce ATP.

LEARNING GOAL

**2** Describe the degradation of fatty acids by β-oxidation.

*Reaction 1.* The first step is an *activation* reaction that results in the production of a fatty acyl CoA molecule. A thioester bond is formed between coenzyme A and the fatty acid:

$$CH_3-(CH_2)_n-CH_2-CH_2-\overset{\overset{\displaystyle O}{\|}}{\underset{\underset{\displaystyle OH}{|}}{C}} \quad \xrightarrow[\text{Coenzyme A}]{\text{ATP}\quad\text{AMP} + \text{PP}_i}$$

Fatty acid

$$CH_3-(CH_2)_n-CH_2-CH_2-\overset{\overset{\displaystyle O}{\|}}{C}\sim S-CoA$$

thioester bond

Fatty acyl CoA

This reaction requires energy in the form of ATP, which is cleaved to AMP and pyrophosphate. This involves hydrolysis of two phosphoanhydride bonds. Here again we see the need to invest a small amount

**Figure 23.6** The reactions in β-oxidation of fatty acids.

Acyl group transfer reactions are described in Section 14.4.

of energy so that a much greater amount of energy can be harvested later in the pathway. Coenzyme A is also required for this step. The product, a fatty acyl CoA, has a *high-energy* thioester bond between the fatty acid and coenzyme A. *Acyl-CoA ligase,* which catalyzes this reaction, is located in the outer membrane of the mitochondria. The mechanism that brings the fatty acyl CoA into the mitochondrial matrix involves a carrier molecule called L-*carnitine.* The first step, catalyzed by the enzyme *carnitine acyltransferase I,* is the transfer of the fatty acyl group to carnitine, producing acylcarnitine and coenzyme A (Figure 23.7a). Next a carrier protein located in the mitochondrial inner membrane transfers the acylcarnitine into the mitochondrial

**(a)**

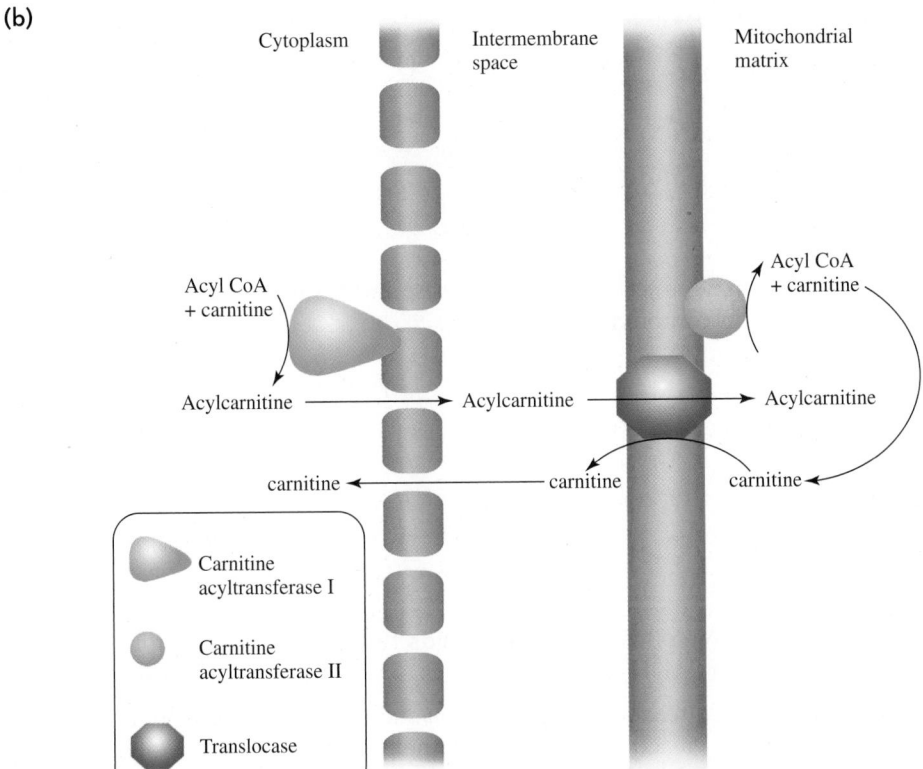

Carnitine

Acyl Coenzyme A

Carnitine acyltransferase I

Acylcarnitine + Coenzyme A

**Figure 23.7** (a) The reaction catalyzed by carnitine acyltransferase I. (b) The transport of fatty acids into the mitochondrial matrix.

**(b)**

Cytoplasm | Intermembrane space | Mitochondrial matrix

Acyl CoA + carnitine

Acylcarnitine → Acylcarnitine → Acylcarnitine

carnitine ← carnitine ← carnitine

Acyl CoA + carnitine

Carnitine acyltransferase I

Carnitine acyltransferase II

Translocase

matrix. There *carnitine acyltransferase II* catalyzes the regeneration of fatty acyl CoA, which now becomes involved in the remaining reactions of β-oxidation (Figure 23.7b).

*Reaction 2.* The next reaction is an *oxidation* reaction that removes a pair of hydrogen atoms from the fatty acid. These are used to reduce FAD to produce FADH₂. This *dehydrogenation* reaction is catalyzed by

# A MEDICAL PERSPECTIVE

## Carnitine: The Fat Mover

Carnitine is a quaternary ammonium compound synthesized in the liver and kidneys from the amino acids lysine and methionine. This synthesis requires vitamin C. Carnitine can also be obtained through the diet. Red meats are an excellent source of carnitine, but it can be found also in nuts, legumes, broccoli, fruits, and cereals.

Carnitine

L-Carnitine, the active enantiomer of carnitine, has been sold as a weight-loss supplement. The idea behind this is that additional carnitine will transport more fatty acids to the site of β-oxidation and in that way promote weight loss. Although the idea is clever, there has never been any scientific evidence to demonstrate that the claim of enhanced weight loss is true. However, a research study in 2007 did find evidence that regular supplements of L-carnitine in the elderly improved energy metabolism and neurotransmitter function in the brain. Further study will be required to fully understand the use of L-carnitine as a nutritional supplement.

Physicians have observed L-carnitine deficiency in children. Systemic primary carnitine deficiency is caused by a mutation in the membrane transport system that brings L-carnitine into the cell. As a result, β-oxidation of fatty acids is defective. The disorder produces a variety of symptoms that present in infancy or childhood. Among these is metabolic decompensation between 3 months and 2 years of age. Decompensation is the inability of the heart to maintain adequate blood circulation, which results in edema and labored breathing. Other symptoms that are more episodic include hypoglycemia, lethargy, irritability, and an enlarged liver. Some children exhibit myopathy of the heart and skeletal muscles between the ages of 2 and 4 years.

If diagnosed before there is irreversible organ damage, the symptoms can be treated with L-carnitine taken orally. A dose of 100–400 mg/kg/day brings about improvement of metabolic decompensation, as well as improved cardiac and skeletal muscle function. Thereafter, the condition can be managed through oral administration of L-carnitine.

**For Further Understanding**

▶ Design an experiment that might demonstrate whether L-carnitine promotes weight loss.
▶ Explain why cardiac and skeletal muscles are particularly susceptible to damage as a result of primary carnitine deficiency.

the enzyme *acyl-CoA dehydrogenase* and results in the formation of a carbon-carbon double bond:

$$CH_3—(CH_2)_n—CH_2—CH_2—\overset{O}{\overset{\|}{C}}{\sim}S—CoA \xrightarrow{\text{FAD} \quad \text{FADH}_2}$$

$$CH_3—(CH_2)_n—\overset{H}{\underset{H}{C}}=C—\overset{O}{\overset{\|}{C}}{\sim}S—CoA$$

Oxidative phosphorylation yields two ATP molecules for each molecule of FADH$_2$ produced by this oxidation-reduction reaction.

*Reaction 3.* The third reaction involves the *hydration* of the double bond produced in reaction 2. As a result, the β-carbon is hydroxylated. This reaction is catalyzed by the enzyme *enoyl-CoA hydrase.*

$$CH_3—(CH_2)_n—\overset{H}{\underset{H}{C}}=C—\overset{O}{\overset{\|}{C}}{\sim}S—CoA \xrightarrow{\text{H}_2\text{O}}$$

$$CH_3—(CH_2)_n—\overset{OH}{\underset{H}{C}}—CH_2—\overset{O}{\overset{\|}{C}}{\sim}S—CoA$$

**Reaction 4.** In this *oxidation* reaction the hydroxyl group of the β-carbon is now dehydrogenated. $NAD^+$ is reduced to form NADH that is subsequently used to produce three ATP molecules by oxidative phosphorylation. L-β-*Hydroxyacyl-CoA dehydrogenase* catalyzes this reaction.

$$CH_3-(CH_2)_n-\overset{\overset{\displaystyle OH}{|}}{\underset{\underset{\displaystyle H}{|}}{C}}-CH_2-\overset{\overset{\displaystyle O}{\|}}{C}\sim S-CoA \xrightarrow{\quad NAD^+ \quad NADH \quad}$$

$$CH_3-(CH_2)_n-\overset{\overset{\displaystyle O}{\|}}{C}-CH_2-\overset{\overset{\displaystyle O}{\|}}{C}\sim S-CoA$$

**Reaction 5.** The final reaction, catalyzed by the enzyme *thiolase*, is the cleavage that releases acetyl CoA. This is accomplished by *thiolysis*, attack of a molecule of coenzyme A on the β-carbon. The result is the release of acetyl CoA and a fatty acyl CoA that is two carbons shorter than the beginning fatty acid:

$$CH_3-(CH_2)_n-\overset{\overset{\displaystyle O}{\|}}{C}-CH_2-\overset{\overset{\displaystyle O}{\|}}{C}\sim S-CoA \xrightarrow{\quad CoA \quad}$$

$$CH_3-(CH_2)_{n-2}-CH_2-CH_2-\overset{\overset{\displaystyle O}{\|}}{C}\sim S-CoA$$
$$+$$
$$\overset{\overset{\displaystyle O}{\|}}{\underset{\underset{\displaystyle S-CoA}{\wr}}{C}}-CH_3$$

The shortened fatty acyl CoA is further oxidized by cycling through reactions 2–5 until the fatty acid carbon chain is completely degraded to acetyl CoA. The acetyl CoA produced by β-oxidation of fatty acids then enters the reactions of the citric acid cycle. Of course, this eventually results in the production of 12 ATP molecules per molecule of acetyl CoA released during β-oxidation.

As an example of the energy yield from β-oxidation, the balance sheet for ATP production when the sixteen-carbon fatty acid palmitic acid is degraded by β-oxidation is summarized in Figure 23.8. Complete oxidation of palmitate results in production of 129 molecules of ATP, *three and one half times more energy than results from the complete oxidation of an equivalent amount of glucose.*

---

| EXAMPLE 23.2 | **Calculating the Amount of ATP Produced in Complete Oxidation of a Fatty Acid** |
|---|---|

How many molecules of ATP are produced in the complete oxidation of stearic acid, an eighteen-carbon saturated fatty acid?

**Solution**

| | |
|---|---|
| Step 1 (activation) | −2 ATP |
| Steps 2–5: | |
| 8 $FADH_2$ × 2 ATP/$FADH_2$ | 16 ATP |
| 8 NADH × 3 ATP/NADH | 24 ATP |

**LEARNING GOAL**

**2** Describe the degradation of fatty acids by β-oxidation.

*Continued…*

9 acetyl CoA (to citric acid cycle):

| | |
|---|---|
| $9 \times 1$ GTP $\times$ 1 ATP/GTP | 9 ATP |
| $9 \times 3$ NADH $\times$ 3 ATP/NADH | 81 ATP |
| $9 \times 1$ FADH$_2$ $\times$ 2 ATP/FADH$_2$ | 18 ATP |
| | 146 ATP |

**Practice Problem 23.2**

Write out the sequence of steps for β-oxidation of butyryl CoA. What is the energy yield from the complete degradation of butyryl CoA via β-oxidation, the citric acid cycle, and oxidative phosphorylation?

▶ For Further Practice: **Questions 23.43 and 23.44.**

**Figure 23.8** Complete oxidation of palmitic acid yields 129 molecules of ATP. Note that the activation step is considered to be an expenditure of two high-energy phosphoanhydride bonds because ATP is hydrolyzed to AMP + PP$_i$.

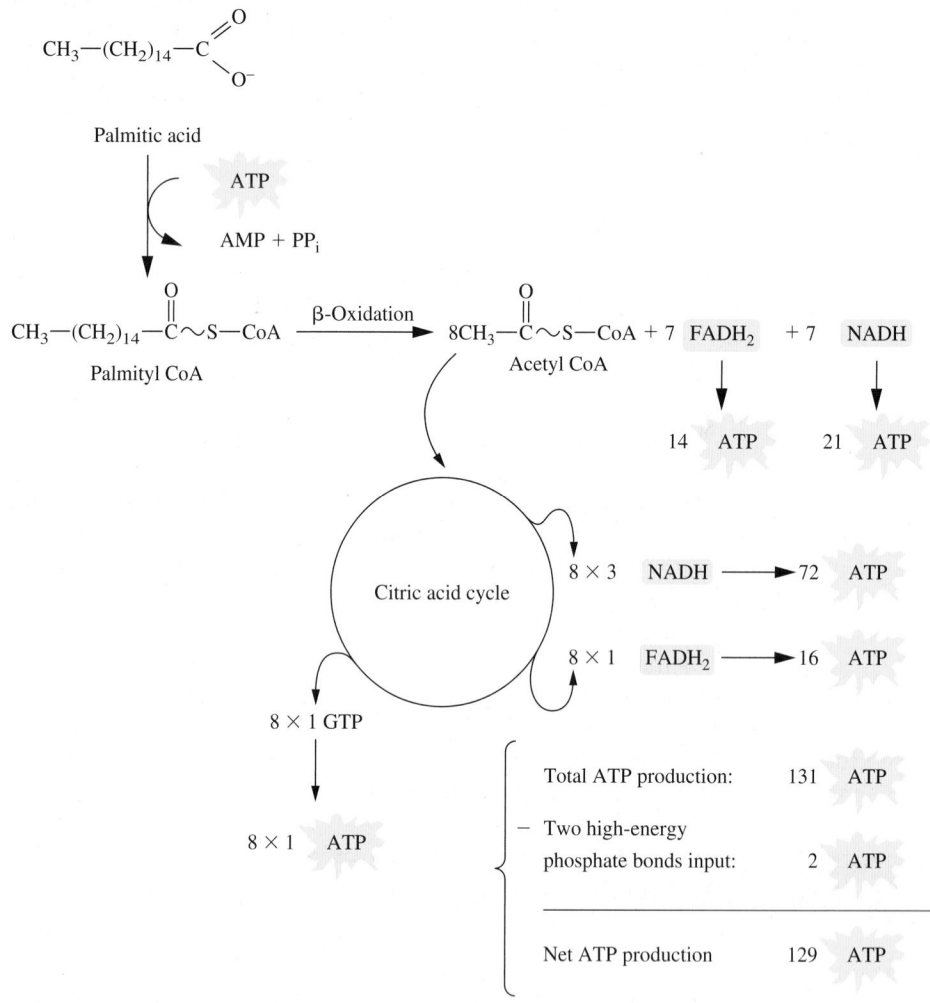

## 23.3 Ketone Bodies

For the acetyl CoA produced by the β-oxidation of fatty acids to efficiently enter the citric acid cycle, there must be an adequate supply of oxaloacetate. If glycolysis and β-oxidation are occurring at the same rate, there will be a steady supply of pyruvate (from glycolysis) that can be converted to oxaloacetate. But what happens

Figure 23.9  Structures of ketone bodies.

β-Hydroxybutyrate          Acetone          Acetoacetate

if the supply of oxaloacetate is too low to allow all of the acetyl CoA to enter the citric acid cycle? Under these conditions, acetyl CoA is converted to the so-called **ketone bodies:** β-hydroxybutyrate, acetone, and acetoacetate (Figure 23.9).

*See Section 22.9 for a review of the reactions that provide oxaloacetate.*

## Ketosis

**Ketosis,** abnormally high levels of blood ketone bodies, is a situation that arises under some pathological conditions, such as starvation, a diet that is extremely low in carbohydrates (as with the high-protein diets), or uncontrolled **diabetes mellitus.** The carbohydrate intake of a diabetic is normal, but the carbohydrates cannot get into the cell to be used as fuel. Thus diabetes amounts to starvation in the midst of plenty. In diabetes the very high concentration of ketone acids in the blood leads to **ketoacidosis.** The ketone acids are relatively strong acids and therefore readily dissociate to release $H^+$. Under these conditions the blood pH becomes acidic, which can lead to death.

Diabetes mellitus is a disease characterized by the appearance of glucose in the urine as a result of high blood glucose levels. The disease is often caused by the inability to produce the hormone insulin.

## Ketogenesis

The pathway for the production of ketone bodies (Figure 23.10) begins with a "reversal" of the last step of β-oxidation. When oxaloacetate levels are low, the enzyme that normally carries out the last reaction of β-oxidation now catalyzes the fusion of two acetyl CoA molecules to produce acetoacetyl CoA:

$$2CH_3-\overset{O}{\overset{||}{C}}\sim S-CoA \rightleftharpoons CH_3-\overset{O}{\overset{||}{C}}-CH_2-\overset{O}{\overset{||}{C}}\sim S-CoA$$

Acetyl CoA          CoA          Acetoacetyl CoA

Acetoacetyl CoA can react with a third acetyl CoA molecule to yield β-hydroxy-β-methylglutaryl CoA (HMG-CoA):

$$CH_3-\overset{O}{\overset{||}{C}}-CH_2-\overset{O}{\overset{||}{C}}\sim S-CoA + CH_3-\overset{O}{\overset{||}{C}}\sim S-CoA + H_2O \rightleftharpoons$$

Acetoacetyl CoA          Acetyl CoA

$$^-OOC-CH_2-\overset{OH}{\underset{CH_3}{\overset{|}{C}}}-CH_2-\overset{O}{\overset{||}{C}}\sim S-CoA + CoA + H^+$$

HMG-CoA

If HMG-CoA were formed in the cytoplasm, it would serve as a precursor for cholesterol biosynthesis. But ketogenesis, like β-oxidation, occurs in the mitochondrial matrix, and here HMG-CoA is cleaved to yield acetoacetate and acetyl CoA:

$$^-OOC-CH_2-\overset{OH}{\underset{CH_3}{\overset{|}{C}}}-CH_2-\overset{O}{\overset{||}{C}}\sim S-CoA \longrightarrow {}^-OOC-CH_2-\overset{O}{\overset{||}{C}}\underset{CH_3}{} + CH_3-\overset{O}{\overset{||}{C}}\sim S-CoA$$

HMG-CoA          Acetoacetate          Acetyl CoA

**Figure 23.10** Summary of the reactions involved in ketogenesis.

$$2CH_3-\overset{O}{\overset{\|}{C}}\sim S-CoA \qquad \text{2 Acetyl CoA}$$

CoA

$$CH_3-\overset{O}{\overset{\|}{C}}-CH_2-\overset{O}{\overset{\|}{C}}\sim S-CoA \qquad \text{Acetoacetyl CoA}$$

Acetyl CoA + H$_2$O

CoA

$$\begin{array}{c} \overset{O}{\overset{\|}{C}}\sim S-CoA \\ | \\ CH_2 \\ | \\ HO-C-CH_3 \\ | \\ CH_2 \\ | \\ COO^- \end{array} \qquad \text{β-Hydroxy-β-methylglutaryl CoA}$$

Acetyl CoA

Acetoacetate
$$\begin{array}{c} O=C-CH_3 \\ | \\ CH_2 \\ | \\ COO^- \end{array}$$
H$^+$
$$O=C\begin{array}{c} CH_3 \\ CH_3 \end{array} \qquad \text{Acetone}$$
CO$_2$

NADH
NAD$^+$

$$\begin{array}{c} H \\ | \\ HO-C-CH_3 \\ | \\ CH_2 \\ | \\ COO^- \end{array} \qquad \text{β-Hydroxybutyrate}$$

In very small amounts, acetoacetate spontaneously loses carbon dioxide to give acetone. This is the reaction that causes the "acetone breath" that is often associated with uncontrolled diabetes mellitus.

$$^-OOC-CH_2-\overset{O}{\overset{\|}{C}}\underset{CH_3}{} + H^+ \longrightarrow CH_3-\overset{O}{\overset{\|}{C}}-CH_3$$
CO$_2$

Acetoacetate                Acetone

More frequently, it undergoes NADH-dependent reduction to produce β-hydroxybutyrate:

$$^-OOC-CH_2-\overset{O}{\overset{\|}{C}}\underset{CH_3}{} \xrightarrow{\text{NADH} \quad \text{NAD}^+} {}^-OOC-CH_2-\overset{OH}{\underset{H}{C}}-CH_3$$

Acetoacetate                β-Hydroxybutyrate

# A HUMAN PERSPECTIVE

## Losing Those Unwanted Pounds of Adipose Tissue

Weight, or overweight, is a topic of great concern to the American populace. A glance through almost any popular magazine quickly informs us that by today's standards, "beautiful" is synonymous with "thin." The models in all these magazines are extremely thin, and there are literally dozens of ads for weight-loss programs. Americans spend millions of dollars each year trying to attain this slim ideal of the fashion models.

Studies have revealed that this slim ideal is often below a desirable, healthy body weight. In fact, the suggested weight for a 6-foot (ft) tall male between 18 and 39 years of age is 179 pounds (lb). For a 5'6" female in the same age range, the desired weight is 142 lb. For a 5'1" female, 126 lb is recommended. Just as being too thin can cause health problems, so too can obesity.

What is obesity, and does it have disadvantages beyond aesthetics? An individual is considered to be obese if his or her body weight is more than 20% above the ideal weight for his or her height. Overweight carries with it a wide range of physical problems, including elevated blood cholesterol levels; high blood pressure; increased incidence of diabetes, cancer, and heart disease; and increased probability of early death. It often causes psychological problems as well, such as guilt and low self-esteem.

Many factors may contribute to obesity. These include genetic factors, a sedentary lifestyle, and a preference for high-calorie, high-fat foods. However, the real concern is how to lose weight. How can we lose weight wisely and safely and keep the weight off for the rest of our lives? Unfortunately, the answer is *not* the answer that most people want to hear. The prevalence and financial success of the quick-weight-loss programs suggest that the majority of people want a program that is rapid and effortless. Unfortunately, most programs that promise dramatic weight reduction with little effort are usually ineffective or, worse, unsafe. The truth is that weight loss and management are best obtained by a program involving three elements.

1. *Reduced caloric intake.* One pound of body fat is equivalent to 3500 Calories (Cal). So if you want to lose 2 lb each week, a reasonable goal, you must reduce your caloric intake by 1000 Cal per day. Remember that diets recommending fewer than 1200 Cal per day are difficult to maintain because they are not very satisfying and may be unsafe because they don't provide all the required vitamins and minerals. The best way to decrease Cal is to reduce fat and increase complex carbohydrates in the diet.
2. *Exercise.* Increase energy expenditures by 200–400 Cal each day. You may choose walking, running, or mowing the lawn; the type of activity doesn't matter, as long as you get moving. Exercise has additional benefits. It increases cardiovascular fitness, provides a psychological lift, and may increase the base rate at which you burn calories after exercise is finished.
3. *Behavior modification.* For some people, overweight is as much a psychological problem as it is a physical problem, and half the battle is learning to recognize the triggers that cause overeating. Several principles of behavior modification have been found to be very helpful.

Reduced caloric intake and exercise are the keys to permanent weight loss.

a. Keep a diary. Record the amount of foods eaten and the circumstances—for instance, a meal at the kitchen table or a bag of chips in the car on the way home.
b. Identify your eating triggers. Do you eat when you feel stress, boredom, fatigue, joy?
c. Develop a plan for avoiding or coping with your trigger situations or emotions. You might exercise when you feel that stress-at-the-end-of-the-day trigger or carry a bag of carrot sticks for the midmorning-boredom trigger.
d. Set realistic goals, and reward yourself when you reach them. The reward should not be food related.

Traditionally, there has been no "quick fix" for safe, effective weight control. A commitment has to be made to modify existing diet and exercise habits. Most important, those habits have to be avoided forever and replaced by new, healthier behaviors and attitudes.

Frustrated by attempts to modify their diet and exercise, growing numbers of people are turning to bariatric surgery, such as the gastric bypass and the reversible laparoscopic stomach banding (lap-band) surgery. One study suggests that the gastric bypass surgery works not only because it reduces the size of the stomach, but because it also reduces the amount of ghrelin produced. Ghrelin is a hormone produced in the stomach that stimulates appetite.

Another interesting approach to the problem of weight loss has been the development of an antiobesity vaccine. A group of researchers at the Scripps Research Institute has developed

*Continued…*

## Losing Those Unwanted Pounds of Adipose Tissue   *(continued)*

a vaccine that slowed weight gain in rats and reduced the amount of stored body fat. The vaccine works by stimulating the body to produce antibodies against ghrelin. These bind the hormone, preventing it from reaching its target in the brain. While this research holds out hope for a safe obesity treatment, it should be noted that the rats in the study were given low-fat, relatively tasteless chow and were rather lean to begin with. It is not clear whether the vaccine would be effective in humans eating a "Western" diet high in calories and fat.

**For Further Understanding**

▶ In terms of the energy-harvesting reactions we have studied in Chapters 22 and 23, explain how reduced caloric intake and increase in activity level contribute to weight loss.

▶ If you increased your energy expenditure by 200 Cal per day and did not change your eating habits, how long would it take you to lose 10 lb?

Acetoacetate and β-hydroxybutyrate are produced primarily in the liver. These metabolites diffuse into the blood and are circulated to other tissues, where they may be reconverted to acetyl CoA and used to produce ATP. In fact, the heart muscle derives most of its metabolic energy from the oxidation of ketone bodies, not from the oxidation of glucose. Other tissues that are best adapted to the use of glucose will increasingly rely on ketone bodies for energy when glucose becomes unavailable or limited. This is particularly true of the brain.

**Question 23.3**  What conditions lead to excess production of ketone bodies?

**Question 23.4**  What is the cause of the characteristic "acetone breath" that is associated with uncontrolled diabetes mellitus?

## 23.4  Fatty Acid Synthesis

All organisms possess the ability to synthesize fatty acids. In humans the excess acetyl CoA produced by carbohydrate degradation is used to make fatty acids that are then stored as triglycerides.

### A Comparison of Fatty Acid Synthesis and Degradation

On first examination, fatty acid synthesis appears to be simply the reverse of β-oxidation. Specifically, the fatty acid chain is constructed by the sequential addition of two-carbon acetyl groups (Figure 23.11). Although the chemistry of fatty acid synthesis and breakdown are similar, there are several major differences between β-oxidation and fatty acid biosynthesis. These are summarized as follows.

- **Intracellular location.** The enzymes responsible for fatty acid biosynthesis are located in the cytoplasm of the cell, whereas those responsible for the degradation of fatty acids are in the mitochondria.
- **Acyl group carriers.** The activated intermediates of fatty acid biosynthesis are bound to a carrier molecule called the **acyl carrier protein (ACP)** (Figure 23.12). In β-oxidation the acyl group carrier was coenzyme A. However, there are important similarities between these two carriers. Both contain the **phosphopantetheine** group, which is made from the vitamin pantothenic acid. In both cases the fatty acyl group is bound by a thioester bond to the phosphopantetheine group.
- **Enzymes involved.** Fatty acid biosynthesis is carried out by a multienzyme complex known as *fatty acid synthase*. The enzymes responsible for fatty acid degradation are not physically associated in such complexes.

**LEARNING GOAL**

**5** Compare β-oxidation of fatty acids and fatty acid biosynthesis.

**Figure 23.11** Summary of fatty acid synthesis. Malonyl ACP is produced in two reactions: carboxylation of acetyl CoA to produce malonyl CoA and transfer of the malonyl acyl group from malonyl CoA to ACP.

Phosphopantetheine prosthetic group of ACP

**Figure 23.12** The structure of the phosphopantetheine group, the reactive group common to coenzyme A and acyl carrier protein, is highlighted in red.

Phosphopantetheine group of coenzyme A

- **Electron carriers.** NADH and $FADH_2$ are produced by fatty acid oxidation, whereas NADPH is the reducing agent for fatty acid biosynthesis. As a general rule, *NADH is produced by catabolic reactions, and NADPH is the reducing agent of biosynthetic reactions.* These two coenzymes differ only by the presence of a phosphate group bound to the ribose ring of NADPH (Figure 23.13). The enzymes that use these coenzymes, however, are easily able to distinguish them on this basis.

Reactive site

**Figure 23.13** Structure of NADPH. The phosphate group shown in red is the structural feature that distinguishes NADPH from NADH.

---

**LEARNING GOAL**

**6** Describe the regulation of lipid and carbohydrate metabolism in relation to the liver, adipose tissue, muscle tissue, and the brain.

---

**Question 23.5** List the four major differences between β-oxidation and fatty acid biosynthesis that reveal that the two processes are not just the reverse of one another.

**Question 23.6** What chemical group is part of coenzyme A and acyl carrier protein and allows both molecules to form thioester bonds to fatty acids?

## 23.5 The Regulation of Lipid and Carbohydrate Metabolism

The metabolism of fatty acids and carbohydrates occurs to a different extent in different organs. As we will see in this section, the regulation of these two related aspects of metabolism is of great physiological importance.

### The Liver

The liver provides a steady supply of glucose for muscle and brain and plays a major role in the regulation of blood glucose concentration. This regulation is under hormonal control. Recall that the hormone insulin causes blood glucose to be taken up by the liver and stored as glycogen (*glycogenesis*). In this way the liver reduces the blood glucose levels when they are too high.

The hormone glucagon, on the other hand, stimulates the breakdown of glycogen and the release of glucose into the bloodstream. Lactate produced by muscles under anaerobic conditions is also taken up by liver cells and is converted to glucose by gluconeogenesis. Both glycogen degradation (*glycogenolysis*) and *gluconeogenesis* are pathways that produce glucose for export to other organs when energy is needed (Figure 23.14).

The liver also plays a central role in lipid metabolism. When excess fuel is available, the liver synthesizes fatty acids. These are used to produce triglycerides that are transported from the liver to adipose tissues by very low density lipoprotein (VLDL) complexes. In fact, VLDL complexes provide adipose tissue with its major source of fatty acids. This transport is particularly active when more calories are eaten than are burned! During fasting or starvation conditions, however, the liver converts fatty acids to acetoacetate and other ketone bodies. The liver cannot use these ketone bodies because it lacks an enzyme for the conversion of acetoacetate to acetyl CoA. Therefore the ketone bodies produced by the liver are exported to other organs where they are oxidized to make ATP.

(a) After a meal

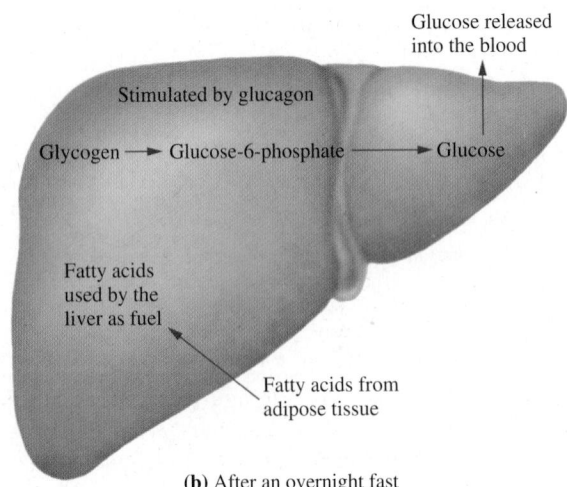

(b) After an overnight fast

**Figure 23.14** The liver controls the concentration of blood glucose.

# A MEDICAL PERSPECTIVE

## Diabetes Mellitus and Ketone Bodies

More than one person, found unconscious on the streets of some metropolis, has been carted to jail only to die of complications arising from uncontrolled diabetes mellitus. Others are fortunate enough to arrive in hospital emergency rooms. A quick test for diabetes mellitus–induced coma is the odor of acetone on the breath of the afflicted person. Acetone is one of several metabolites produced by diabetics that are known collectively as *ketone bodies*.

The term *diabetes* was used by the ancient Greeks to designate diseases in which excess urine is produced. Two thousand years later, in the eighteenth century, the urine of certain individuals was found to contain sugar, and the name *diabetes mellitus* (Latin: *mellitus*, sweetened with honey) was given to this disease. People suffering from diabetes mellitus waste away as they excrete large amounts of sugar-containing urine.

The cause of insulin-dependent diabetes mellitus is inadequate production of insulin by the body. Insulin is secreted

in response to high blood glucose levels. It binds to the membrane receptor protein on its target cells. Binding increases the rate of transport of glucose across the membrane and stimulates glycogen synthesis, lipid biosynthesis, and protein synthesis. As a result, the blood glucose level is reduced. Clearly, the inability to produce sufficient insulin seriously impairs the body's ability to regulate metabolism.

Individuals suffering from diabetes mellitus do not produce enough insulin to properly regulate blood glucose levels. This generally results from the destruction of the β-cells of the islets of Langerhans. One theory to explain the mysterious disappearance of these cells is that a virus infection stimulates the immune system to produce antibodies that cause the destruction of the β-cells.

In the absence of insulin the uptake of glucose into the tissues is not stimulated, and a great deal of glucose is eliminated

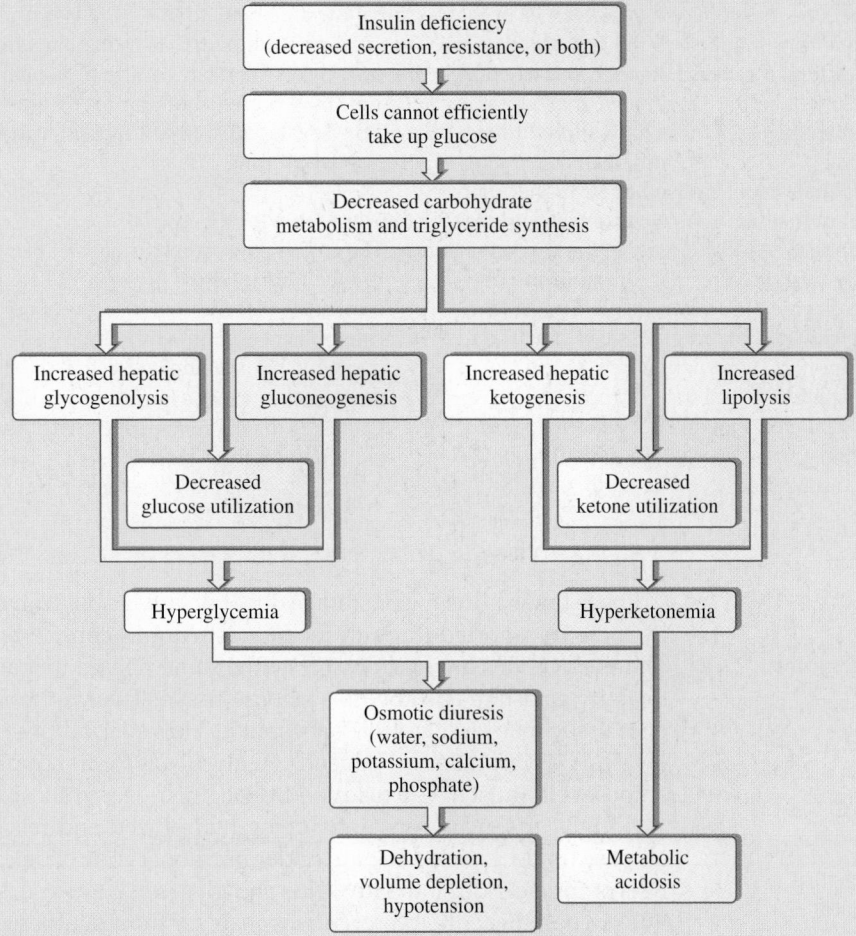

The metabolic events that occur in uncontrolled diabetes and that can lead to coma and death.

*Continued…*

## Diabetes Mellitus and Ketone Bodies   *(continued)*

in the urine. Without insulin, then, adipose cells are unable to take up the glucose required to synthesize triglycerides. As a result, the rate of fat hydrolysis is much greater than the rate of fat resynthesis, and large quantities of free fatty acids are liberated into the bloodstream. Because glucose is not being efficiently taken into cells, carbohydrate metabolism slows, and there is an increase in the rate of lipid catabolism. In the liver this lipid catabolism results in the production of ketone bodies: acetone, acetoacetate, and β-hydroxybutyrate.

A similar situation can develop from improper eating, fasting, or dieting—any situation in which the body is not provided with sufficient energy in the form of carbohydrates. These ketone bodies cannot all be oxidized by the citric acid cycle, which is limited by the supply of oxaloacetate. The acetone concentration in blood rises to levels so high that acetone can be detected in the breath of untreated diabetics. The elevated concentration of ketones in the blood can overwhelm the buffering capacity of the blood, resulting in ketoacidosis. Ketones, too, will be excreted through the kidney. In fact, the presence of excess ketones in the urine can raise the osmotic concentration of the urine so that it behaves as an "osmotic diuretic," causing the excretion of enormous amounts of water. As a result, the patient may become severely dehydrated. In extreme cases the combination of dehydration and ketoacidosis may lead to coma and death.

It has been observed that diabetics also have a higher than normal level of glucagon in the blood. As we have seen, glucagon stimulates lipid catabolism and ketogenesis. It may be that the symptoms previously described result from both the deficiency of insulin and the elevated glucagon levels. The absence of insulin may cause the elevated blood glucose and fatty acid levels, whereas the glucagon, by stimulating ketogenesis, may be responsible for the ketoacidosis and dehydration.

There is no cure for diabetes. However, when the problem is the result of the inability to produce active insulin, blood glucose levels can be controlled moderately well by the injection of human insulin produced from the cloned insulin gene. Unfortunately, one or even a few injections of insulin each day cannot mimic the precise control of blood glucose accomplished by the pancreas.

As a result, diabetics suffer progressive tissue degeneration that leads to early death. One primary cause of this degeneration is atherosclerosis, the deposition of plaque on the walls of blood vessels. This causes a high frequency of strokes, heart attack, and gangrene of the feet and lower extremities, often necessitating amputation. Kidney failure causes the death of about 20% of diabetics under 40 years of age, and diabetic retinopathy (various kinds of damage to the retina of the eye) ranks fourth among the leading causes of blindness in the United States. Nerves are also damaged, resulting in neuropathies that can cause pain or numbness, particularly of the feet.

There is no doubt that insulin injections prolong the life of diabetics, but only the presence of a fully functioning pancreas can allow a diabetic to live a life free of the complications noted here. At present, pancreas transplants do not have a good track record. Only about 50% of the transplants are functioning after 1 year. It is hoped that improved transplantation techniques will be developed so that diabetics can live a normal life span, free of debilitating disease.

### For Further Understanding

▶ The Atkins' low carbohydrate diet recommends that dieters test their urine for the presence of ketone bodies as an indicator that the diet is working. In terms of lipid and carbohydrate metabolism, explain why ketone bodies are being produced and why this is an indication that the diet is working.

▶ An excess of ketone bodies in the blood causes ketoacidosis. Consider the chemical structure of the ketone bodies and explain why they are acids.

Glycerol-3-phosphate

## Adipose Tissue

Adipose tissue is the major storage depot of fatty acids. Triglycerides produced by the liver are transported through the bloodstream as components of VLDL complexes. The triglycerides are hydrolyzed by the same lipases that act on chylomicrons, and the fatty acids are absorbed by adipose tissue. The synthesis of triglycerides in adipose tissue requires glycerol-3-phosphate. However, adipose tissue is unable to make glycerol-3-phosphate and depends on glycolysis for its supply of this molecule. Thus adipose cells must have a ready source of glucose to synthesize and store triglycerides.

Triglycerides are constantly being hydrolyzed and resynthesized in the cells of adipose tissue. Lipases that are under hormonal control determine the rate of hydrolysis of triglycerides into fatty acids and glycerol. If glucose is in limited supply, there will not be sufficient glycerol-3-phosphate for the resynthesis of triglycerides, and the fatty acids and glycerol are exported to the liver for further processing (Figure 23.15).

## Muscle Tissue

The energy demand of resting muscle is generally supplied by the β-oxidation of fatty acids. The heart muscle actually prefers ketone bodies over glucose.

*Working* muscle, however, obtains energy by degradation of its own supply of glycogen. Glycogen degradation produces glucose-6-phosphate, which is directly funneled into glycolysis. If the muscle is working so hard that it doesn't get enough oxygen, it produces large amounts of lactate. This fermentation end product, as well as alanine (from catabolism of proteins and transamination of pyruvate), is exported to the liver. Here they are converted to glucose by gluconeogenesis (Figure 23.16).

## The Brain

Under normal conditions the brain uses glucose as its sole source of metabolic energy. When the body is in the resting state, about 60% of the free glucose of the body is used by the brain. Starvation depletes glycogen stores, and the amount of glucose available to the brain drops sharply. The ketone bodies acetoacetate and β-hydroxybutyrate are then used by the brain as an alternative energy source. Fatty acids are transported in the blood in complexes with proteins and cannot cross the blood-brain barrier to be used by brain cells as an energy source. But ketone bodies, which have a free carboxyl group, are soluble in blood and can enter the brain.

**Question 23.7**  How does the liver regulate blood glucose levels?

**Question 23.8**  Why is regulation of blood glucose levels important to the efficient function of the brain?

**Figure 23.15** Synthesis and degradation of triglycerides in adipose tissue.

## 23.6  The Effects of Insulin and Glucagon on Cellular Metabolism

The hormone **insulin** is produced by the β-cells of the islets of Langerhans in the pancreas. It is secreted from these cells in response to an increase in the blood glucose level. Insulin lowers the concentration of blood glucose by causing a number of changes in metabolism (Table 23.1).

The simplest way to lower blood glucose levels is to stimulate storage of glucose, both as glycogen and as triglycerides. *Insulin therefore activates biosynthetic processes and inhibits catabolic processes.*

Insulin acts only on those cells, known as *target cells*, that possess a specific insulin receptor protein in their plasma membranes. The major target cells for insulin are liver, adipose, and muscle cells.

**LEARNING GOAL**

**7**  Summarize the antagonistic effects of glucagon and insulin.

*The effect of insulin on glycogen metabolism is described in Section 21.7.*

**Figure 23.16** Metabolic relationships between liver and muscle.

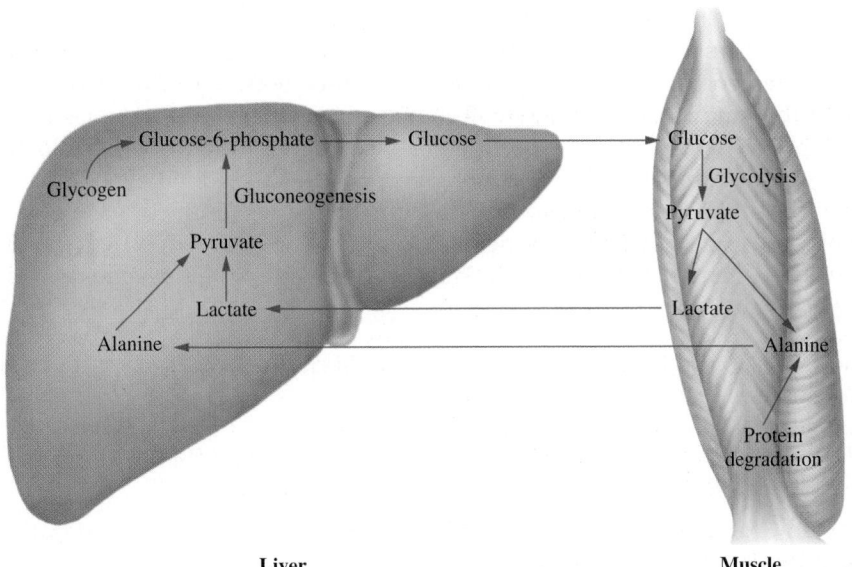

Liver                    Muscle

### TABLE 23.1  Comparison of the Metabolic Effects of Insulin and Glucagon

| Actions | Insulin | Glucagon |
|---|---|---|
| Cellular glucose transport | Increased | No effect |
| Glycogen synthesis | Increased | Decreased |
| Glycogenolysis in liver | Decreased | Increased |
| Gluconeogenesis | Decreased | Increased |
| Amino acid uptake and protein synthesis | Increased | No effect |
| Inhibition of amino acid release and protein degradation | Decreased | No effect |
| Lipogenesis | Increased | No effect |
| Lipolysis | Decreased | Increased |
| Ketogenesis | Decreased | Increased |

The blood glucose level is normally about 10 millimolar (mM). However, a substantial meal increases the concentration of blood glucose considerably and stimulates insulin secretion. Subsequent binding of insulin to the plasma membrane insulin receptor increases the rate of transport of glucose across the membrane and into cells.

Insulin exerts a variety of effects on all aspects of cellular metabolism:

- **Carbohydrate metabolism.** Insulin stimulates glycogen synthesis. At the same time it inhibits glycogenolysis and gluconeogenesis. The overall result of these activities is the storage of excess glucose.
- **Protein metabolism.** Insulin stimulates transport and uptake of amino acids, as well as the incorporation of amino acids into proteins.
- **Lipid metabolism.** Insulin stimulates uptake of glucose by adipose cells, as well as the synthesis and storage of triglycerides. As we have seen, storage of lipids requires a source of glucose, and insulin helps the process by increasing the available glucose. At the same time, insulin inhibits the breakdown of stored triglycerides.

As you may have already guessed, insulin is only part of the overall regulation of cellular metabolism in the body. A second hormone, **glucagon,** is secreted by the α-cells of the islets of Langerhans in response to decreased blood glucose levels. The effects of glucagon, generally the opposite of the effects of insulin, are summarized in Table 23.1. Although it has no direct effect on glucose uptake, glucagon inhibits glycogen synthesis and stimulates glycogenolysis and gluconeogenesis. It also stimulates the breakdown of fats and ketogenesis.

The antagonistic effects of these two hormones, seen in Figure 23.17, are critical for the maintenance of adequate blood glucose levels. During fasting, low blood glucose levels stimulate production of glucagon, which increases blood glucose by stimulating the breakdown of glycogen and the production of glucose by gluconeogenesis. This ensures a ready supply of glucose for the tissues, especially the brain. On the other hand, when blood glucose levels are too high, insulin is secreted. It stimulates the removal of the excess glucose by enhancing uptake and inducing pathways for storage.

**Question 23.9** Summarize the effects of the hormone insulin on carbohydrate, lipid, and amino acid metabolism.

**Question 23.10** Summarize the effects of the hormone glucagon on carbohydrate and lipid metabolism.

**Figure 23.17** A summary of the antagonistic effects of insulin and glucagon.

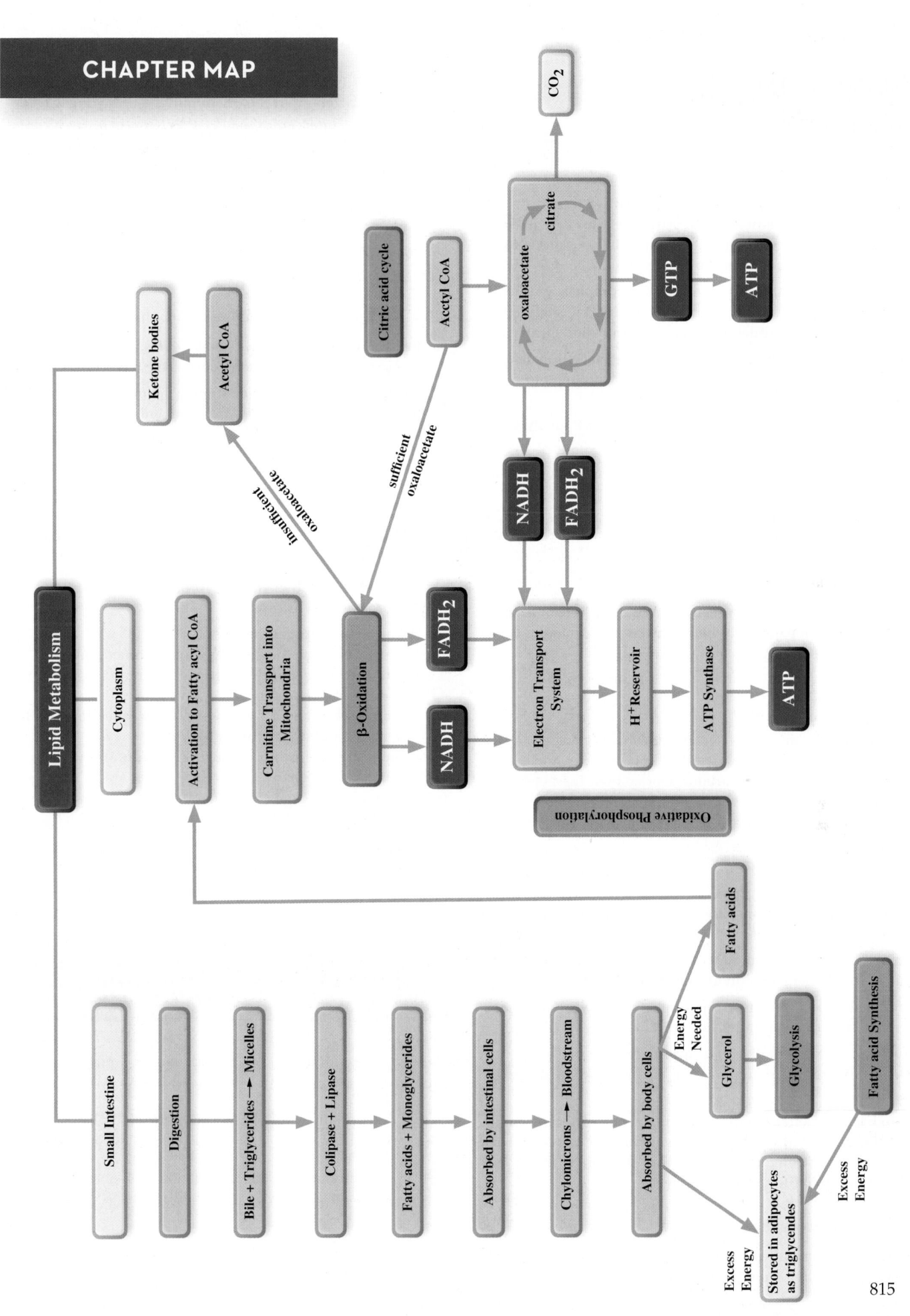

815

# SUMMARY

## 23.1 Lipid Metabolism in Animals

▶ Dietary lipids (triglycerides) are emulsified into tiny fat droplets in the intestine by the action of bile. Bile is composed of micelles consisting of lecithin, cholesterol, protein, bile salts, inorganic ions, and bile pigments.

▶ Colipase binds to the surface of these fat droplets and helps pancreatic lipase stick to the surface so that it can catalyze the hydrolysis of triglycerides into monoglycerides and fatty acids.

▶ These are absorbed by the intestinal epithelial cells, reassembled into triglycerides, and packaged with proteins to form chylomicrons.

▶ Chylomicrons are transported to the cells of the body through the bloodstream.

▶ Fatty acids are stored as triglycerides (triacylglycerols) in fat droplets in the cytoplasm of adipocytes.

▶ Adipose tissue is composed of adipocytes and is a means of energy storage in the body.

## 23.2 Fatty Acid Degradation

▶ Fatty acids are degraded to acetyl CoA in the mitochondria by the β-oxidation pathway, which consists of five steps:
  • Production of a fatty acyl CoA molecule
  • Oxidation of the fatty acid by an FAD-dependent dehydrogenase
  • Hydration
  • Oxidation by an NAD⁺-dependent dehydrogenase
  • Cleavage of the chain with release of acetyl CoA and a fatty acyl CoA that is two carbons shorter than the beginning fatty acid.

▶ The last four reactions are repeated until the fatty acid is completely degraded to acetyl CoA.

## 23.3 Ketone Bodies

▶ Under some conditions, fatty acid degradation occurs more rapidly than glycolysis.

▶ This results in a large amount of acetyl CoA from β-oxidation, but an insufficient amount of oxaloacetate from glycolysis.

▶ In this situation, acetyl CoA is converted to ketone bodies: acetone, acetoacetate, and β-hydroxybutyrate.

▶ Ketosis, an abnormally high level of ketone bodies in the blood, may result from starvation or uncontrolled diabetes mellitus.

▶ A high level of ketone bodies in the blood causes ketoacidosis because the ketone acids β-hydroxybutyrate and acetoacetate are relatively strong acids. When they dissociate, the blood pH may drop to life-threatening levels.

## 23.4 Fatty Acid Synthesis

▶ Fatty acid biosynthesis occurs by sequential addition of acetyl groups, but is not the reverse of β-oxidation.

▶ Although the chemical reactions are similar, fatty acid synthesis differs from β-oxidation in the following ways:
  • It occurs in the cytoplasm.
  • It utilizes acyl carrier protein (ACP) rather than coenzyme A, both of which have the phosphopantetheine group as the functional part of the molecule that binds to the acetyl or acyl group.
  • It utilizes NADPH, rather than NADH.
  • It is carried out by a multienzyme complex called *fatty acid synthase*.

## 23.5 The Regulation of Lipid and Carbohydrate Metabolism

▶ The liver regulates the flow of metabolites to brain, muscle, and adipose tissue, and ultimately controls the blood glucose level.

▶ In adipose tissue, the major storage depot for fatty acids, triglycerides are constantly hydrolyzed and resynthesized.

▶ Muscle can oxidize glucose, fatty acids, and ketone bodies.

▶ The brain uses only glucose as a fuel except in prolonged starvation or fasting, when it will use ketone bodies as fuel.

## 23.6 The Effects of Insulin and Glucagon on Cellular Metabolism

▶ Insulin activates biosynthetic processes and inhibits catabolic processes as follows:
  • Stimulates glycogen synthesis
  • Inhibits glycogen degradation and gluconeogenesis
  • Stimulates transport and uptake of amino acids and their incorporation into proteins
  • Stimulates uptake of glucose by adipose cells, as well as synthesis and storage of triglycerides
  • Inhibits breakdown of stored triglycerides
  • Inhibits ketogenesis

▶ The effects of glucagon are generally the opposite of those of insulin in the following ways:
  • Inhibits glycogen synthesis
  • Stimulates glycogen breakdown and gluconeogenesis
  • Stimulates the breakdown of stored triglycerides
  • Stimulates ketogenesis

# ANSWERS TO PRACTICE PROBLEMS

23.1  a. The products of the β-oxidation of 9-phenylnonanoic acid are 4 acetyl CoA, 1 benzoate, 4 NADH, and 4 FADH₂.

b. The products of the β-oxidation of 8-phenyloctanoic acid are 3 acetyl CoA, 1 phenyl acetate, 3 NADH, and 3 FADH₂.

c. The products of the β-oxidation of 7-phenylheptanoic acid are 3 acetyl CoA, 1 benzoate, 3 NADH, and 3 FADH₂.

d. The products of the β-oxidation of 12-phenyldodecanoic acid are 5 acetyl CoA, 1 phenyl acetate, 5 NADH, and 5 FADH₂.

**23.2** The following equations show the steps for the β-oxidation of butyryl CoA:

$$CH_3CH_2CH_2-\overset{\overset{\displaystyle O}{\|}}{C}\raise2pt{\sim}S-CoA$$

$$\Big\downarrow \curvearrowright FAD$$

$$CH_3CH=CH-\overset{\overset{\displaystyle O}{\|}}{C}\raise2pt{\sim}S-CoA + FADH_2$$

$$\Big\downarrow \curvearrowright H_2O$$

$$CH_3\overset{\overset{\displaystyle OH}{|}}{C}H-CH_2-\overset{\overset{\displaystyle O}{\|}}{C}\raise2pt{\sim}S-CoA$$

$$\Big\downarrow \curvearrowright NAD^+$$

$$CH_3-\overset{\overset{\displaystyle O}{\|}}{C}-CH_2-\overset{\overset{\displaystyle O}{\|}}{C}\raise2pt{\sim}S-CoA + NADH$$

$$\Big\downarrow \curvearrowright Coenzyme\ A$$

$$2\ CH_3-\overset{\overset{\displaystyle O}{\|}}{C}\raise2pt{\sim}S-CoA$$

The energy yield from the complete degradation of butyryl CoA via β-oxidation, the citric acid cycle, and oxidative phosphorylation is summarized below:

Butyryl CoA has already been activated, so no ATP investment is needed.

β-Oxidation:

| | |
|---|---|
| 1 FADH$_2$ × 2 ATP/FADH$_2$ | 2 ATP |
| 1 NADH × 3 ATP/NADH | 3 ATP |

Citric acid cycle (2 acetyl CoA):

| | |
|---|---|
| 6 NADH × 3 ATP/NADH | 18 ATP |
| 2 FADH$_2$ × 2 ATP/FADH$_2$ | 4 ATP |
| 2 GTP × 1 ATP/GTP | 2 ATP |
| | 29 ATP |

## QUESTIONS AND PROBLEMS

### Lipid Metabolism in Animals

#### Foundations

**23.11** Draw the structures of the bile salts cholate and chenodeoxycholate.

**23.12** To what class of lipids do the bile salts belong?

**23.13** Define the term *micelle*.

**23.14** In Figure 23.1, a micelle composed of the phospholipid lecithin is shown. Why is lecithin a good molecule for the formation of micelles?

**23.15** Define the term *triglyceride*.

**23.16** Draw the structure of a triglyceride composed of glycerol, palmitoleic acid, linolenic acid, and oleic acid.

**23.17** Describe the structure of chylomicrons.

**23.18** Why is colipase needed for lipid digestion?

#### Applications

**23.19** What is the major storage form of fatty acids?

**23.20** What tissue is the major storage depot for lipids?

**23.21** What is the outstanding structural feature of an adipocyte?

**23.22** What is the major metabolic function of adipose tissue?

**23.23** What is the general reaction catalyzed by lipases?

**23.24** Why are the lipases that are found in saliva and in the stomach not very effective at digesting triglycerides?

**23.25** List three major biological molecules for which acetyl CoA is a precursor.

**23.26** Why are triglycerides more efficient energy-storage molecules than glycogen?

**23.27** What is the function of chylomicrons?

**23.28** a. What are very low density lipoproteins?
   b. Compare the function of VLDLs with that of chylomicrons.

**23.29** What is the function of the bile salts in the digestion of dietary lipids?

**23.30** What is the function of colipase in the digestion of dietary lipids?

**23.31** Describe the stages of lipid digestion.

**23.32** Describe the transport of lipids digested in the lumen of the intestines to the cells of the body.

### Fatty Acid Degradation

#### Foundations

**23.33** What is the energy source for the activation of a fatty acid in preparation for β-oxidation?

**23.34** Which bond in fatty acyl CoA is a high-energy bond?

**23.35** What is carnitine?

**23.36** Explain the mechanism by which a fatty acyl group is brought into the mitochondrial matrix.

**23.37** Explain why the reaction catalyzed by acyl-CoA dehydrogenase is an example of an oxidation reaction.

**23.38** What is the reactant that is oxidized in the reaction catalyzed by acyl-CoA dehydrogenase? What is the reactant that is reduced in this reaction?

**23.39** What is the product of the hydration of an alkene?

**23.40** Which reaction in β-oxidation is a hydration reaction? What is the name of the enzyme that catalyzes this reaction? Write an equation representing this reaction.

#### Applications

**23.41** What products are formed when the ω-phenyl-labeled carboxylic acid 14-phenyltetradecanoic acid is degraded by β-oxidation?

**23.42** What products are formed when the ω-phenyl-labeled carboxylic acid 5-phenylpentanoic acid is degraded by β-oxidation?

**23.43** Calculate the number of ATP molecules produced by complete β-oxidation of the fourteen-carbon saturated fatty acid tetradecanoic acid (common name: myristic acid).

**23.44** a. Write the sequence of steps that would be followed for one round of β-oxidation of hexanoic acid.
   b. Calculate the number of ATP molecules produced by complete β-oxidation of hexanoic acid.

**23.45** Calculate the number of ATP molecules produced by complete β-oxidation of lauric acid.

**23.46** Calculate the number of ATP molecules produced by the complete β-oxidation of eicosanoic acid.

**23.47**  What is the fate of the acetyl CoA produced by β-oxidation?

**23.48**  How many ATP molecules are produced from each acetyl CoA molecule generated in β-oxidation that enters the citric acid cycle?

## Ketone Bodies

### Foundations

**23.49**  What are ketone bodies?

**23.50**  What are the chemical properties of ketone bodies?

**23.51**  What is ketosis?

**23.52**  Define *ketoacidosis.*

**23.53**  In what part of the cell does ketogenesis occur? Be specific.

**23.54**  What would be the fate of HMG-CoA produced in ketogenesis if it were produced in the cell cytoplasm?

### Applications

**23.55**  Draw the structures of acetoacetate and β-hydroxybutyrate.

**23.56**  Describe the relationship between the formation of ketone bodies and β-oxidation.

**23.57**  Why do uncontrolled diabetics produce large amounts of ketone bodies?

**23.58**  How does the presence of ketone bodies in the blood lead to ketoacidosis?

**23.59**  When does the heart use ketone bodies?

**23.60**  When does the brain use ketone bodies?

## Fatty Acid Synthesis

### Foundations

**23.61**  Where in the cell does fatty acid biosynthesis occur?

**23.62**  What is the acyl group carrier in fatty acid biosynthesis?

**23.63**  Draw the structure of NADPH.

**23.64**  What is the function of NADPH in fatty acid biosynthesis?

### Applications

**23.65**  **a.** What is the role of the phosphopantetheine group in fatty acid biosynthesis?
**b.** From what molecule is phosphopantetheine made?

**23.66**  What molecules involved in fatty acid degradation and fatty acid biosynthesis contain the phosphopantetheine group?

**23.67**  How does the structure of fatty acid synthase differ from that of the enzymes that carry out β-oxidation?

**23.68**  In what cellular compartments do fatty acid biosynthesis and β-oxidation occur?

## The Regulation of Lipid and Carbohydrate Metabolism

### Foundations

**23.69**  Define the term *glycogenesis.*

**23.70**  Define the term *glycogenolysis.*

**23.71**  Define the term *gluconeogenesis.*

**23.72**  How are the fatty acids synthesized in the liver transported to adipose tissue?

### Applications

**23.73**  Which pathway provides the majority of the ATP for *resting* muscle?

**23.74**  Why is the liver unable to utilize ketone bodies as an energy source?

**23.75**  What is the major metabolic function of the liver?

**23.76**  What is the fate of lactate produced in skeletal muscle during rapid contraction?

**23.77**  What are the major fuels of the heart, brain, and liver?

**23.78**  Why can't the brain use fatty acids as fuel?

**23.79**  Briefly describe triglyceride metabolism in an adipocyte.

**23.80**  What is the source of the glycerol molecule that is used in the synthesis of triglycerides?

## The Effects of Insulin and Glucagon on Cellular Metabolism

### Foundations

**23.81**  In general, what is the effect of insulin on catabolic and anabolic or biosynthetic processes?

**23.82**  What is the trigger that causes insulin to be secreted into the bloodstream?

**23.83**  What is meant by the term *target cell?*

**23.84**  What are the primary target cells of insulin?

**23.85**  What is the trigger that causes glucagon to be secreted into the bloodstream?

**23.86**  What are the primary target cells of glucagon?

### Applications

**23.87**  Where is insulin produced?

**23.88**  Where is glucagon produced?

**23.89**  How does insulin affect carbohydrate metabolism?

**23.90**  How does glucagon affect carbohydrate metabolism?

**23.91**  How does insulin affect lipid metabolism?

**23.92**  How does glucagon affect lipid metabolism?

**23.93**  Explain the importance of the antagonistic effects of insulin and glucagon.

**23.94**  How does the presence of the insulin receptor on the surface of a cell identify that cell as a target cell?

# CRITICAL THINKING PROBLEMS

1. Suppose that fatty acids were degraded by sequential oxidation of the α-carbon. What product(s) would Knoop have obtained with fatty acids with even numbers of carbon atoms? What product(s) would he have obtained with fatty acids with odd numbers of carbon atoms?

2. Oil-eating bacteria can oxidize long-chain alkanes. In the first step of the pathway, the enzyme monooxygenase catalyzes a reaction that converts the long-chain alkane into a primary alcohol. Data from research studies indicate that three more reactions are required to allow the primary alcohol to enter the β-oxidation pathway. Propose a pathway that would convert the long-chain alcohol into a product that could enter the β-oxidation pathway.

3. A young woman sought the advice of her physician because she was 30 lb overweight. The excess weight was in the form of triglycerides carried in adipose tissue. Yet when the woman described her diet, it became obvious that she actually ate very moderate amounts of fatty foods. Most of her caloric intake was in the form of carbohydrates. This included candy, cake, beer, and soft drinks. Explain how the excess calories

consumed in the form of carbohydrates ended up being stored as triglycerides in adipose tissue.

4. Olestra is a fat substitute that provides no calories, yet has a creamy, tongue-pleasing consistency. Because it can withstand heating, it can be used to prepare foods such as potato chips and crackers. Olestra is a sucrose polyester produced by esterification of six, seven, or eight fatty acids to molecules of sucrose. Develop a hypothesis to explain why olestra is not a source of dietary calories.

5. Carnitine is a tertiary amine found in mitochondria that is involved in transporting the acyl groups of fatty acids from the cytoplasm into the mitochondria. The fatty acyl group is transferred from a fatty acyl CoA molecule and esterified to carnitine. Inside the mitochondria, the reaction is reversed and the fatty acid enters the β-oxidation pathway.

A 17-year-old male went to a university medical center complaining of fatigue and poor exercise tolerance. Muscle biopsies revealed droplets of triglycerides in his muscle cells. Biochemical analysis showed that he had only one-fifth of the normal amount of carnitine in his muscle cells.

What effect will carnitine deficiency have on β-oxidation? What effect will carnitine deficiency have on glucose metabolism?

6. Acetyl CoA carboxylase catalyzes the formation of malonyl CoA from acetyl CoA and the bicarbonate anion, a reaction that requires the hydrolysis of ATP. Write a balanced equation showing this reaction.

The reaction catalyzed by acetyl CoA carboxylase is the rate-limiting step in fatty acid biosynthesis. The malonyl group is transferred from coenzyme A to acyl carrier protein; similarly, the acetyl group is transferred from coenzyme A to acyl carrier protein. This provides the two beginning substrates of fatty acid biosynthesis shown in Figure 23.11.

Consider the following case study. A baby boy was brought to the emergency room with severe respiratory distress. Examination revealed muscle pathology, poor growth, and severe brain damage. A liver biopsy revealed that the child didn't make acetyl CoA carboxylase. What metabolic pathway is defective in this child? How is this defect related to the respiratory distress suffered by the baby?

# Glossary

## A

**absolute specificity** (19.5) the property of an enzyme that allows it to bind and catalyze the reaction of only one substrate

**accuracy** (1.4) the nearness of an experimental value to the true value

**acetal** (13.4) the family of organic compounds formed via the reaction of two molecules of alcohol with an aldehyde or a ketone in the presence of an acid catalyst

**acetyl coenzyme A (acetyl CoA)** (14.4, 22.2) a molecule composed of coenzyme A and an acetyl group; the intermediate that provides acetyl groups for complete oxidation by aerobic respiration

**acid** (8.1) a substance that behaves as a proton donor

**acid anhydride** (14.3) the product formed by the combination of an acid chloride and a carboxylate ion; structurally they are two carboxylic acids with a water molecule removed:

$$(Ar)R-\overset{\overset{\displaystyle O}{\|}}{C}-O-\overset{\overset{\displaystyle O}{\|}}{C}-R(Ar)$$

**acid-base reaction** (4.4) reaction that involves the transfer of a hydrogen ion ($H^+$) from one reactant to another

**acid chloride** (14.3) member of the family of organic compounds with the general formula

$$(Ar)R-\overset{\overset{\displaystyle O}{\|}}{C}-Cl$$

**activated complex** (7.3) the arrangement of atoms at the top of the potential energy barrier as a reaction proceeds

**activation energy** (7.3) the threshold energy that must be overcome to produce a chemical reaction

**active site** (19.4) the cleft in the surface of an enzyme that is the site of substrate binding

**acyl carrier protein (ACP)** (23.4) the protein that forms a thioester linkage with fatty acids during fatty acid synthesis

**acyl group** (14.3, 15.3) the functional group found in carboxylic acid derivatives that contains the carbonyl group attached to one alkyl or aryl group:

$$(Ar)R-\overset{\overset{\displaystyle O}{\|}}{C}-$$

**addition polymer** (11.5) polymers prepared by the sequential addition of a monomer

**addition reaction** (11.5, 13.4) a reaction in which two molecules add together to form a new molecule; often involves the addition of one molecule to a double or triple bond in an unsaturated molecule; e.g., the addition of alcohol to an aldehyde or ketone to form a hemiacetal

**adenosine triphosphate (ATP)** (14.4, 21.1) a nucleotide composed of the purine adenine, the sugar ribose, and three phosphoryl groups; the primary energy storage and transport molecule used by the cells in cellular metabolism

**adipocyte** (23.1) a fat cell

**adipose tissue** (23.1) fatty tissue that stores most of the body lipids

**aerobic respiration** (22.3) the oxygen-requiring degradation of food molecules and production of ATP

**alcohol** (12.1) an organic compound that contains a hydroxyl group (—OH) attached to an alkyl group

**aldehyde** (13.1) a class of organic molecules characterized by a carbonyl group; the carbonyl carbon is bonded to a hydrogen atom and to another hydrogen or an alkyl or aryl group. Aldehydes have the following general structure:

$$(Ar)-\overset{\overset{\displaystyle O}{\|}}{C}-H \qquad R-\overset{\overset{\displaystyle O}{\|}}{C}-H$$

**aldose** (16.2) a sugar that contains an aldehyde (carbonyl) group

**aliphatic hydrocarbon** (10.1) any member of the alkanes, alkenes, and alkynes or the substituted alkanes, alkenes, and alkynes

**alkali metal** (2.4) an element within Group IA (1) of the periodic table

**alkaline earth metal** (2.4) an element within Group IIA (2) of the periodic table

**alkaloid** (15.2) a class of naturally occurring compounds that contain one or more nitrogen heterocyclic rings; many of the alkaloids have medicinal and other physiological effects

**alkane** (10.2) a hydrocarbon that contains only carbon and hydrogen and is bonded together through carbon-hydrogen and carbon-carbon single bonds; a saturated hydrocarbon with the general molecular formula $C_nH_{2n+2}$

**alkene** (11.1) a hydrocarbon that contains one or more carbon-carbon double bonds; an unsaturated hydrocarbon with the general formula $C_nH_{2n}$

**alkyl group** (10.2) a hydrocarbon group that results from the removal of one hydrogen from the original hydrocarbon (e.g., methyl, —CH$_3$; ethyl, —CH$_2$CH$_3$)

**alkyl halide** (10.5) a substituted hydrocarbon with the general structure R—X, in which R— represents any alkyl group and X = a halogen (F—, Cl—, Br—, or I—)

**alkylammonium ion** (15.1) the ion formed when the lone pair of electrons of the nitrogen atom of an amine is shared with a proton ($H^+$) from a water molecule

**alkyne** (11.1) a hydrocarbon that contains one or more carbon-carbon triple bonds; an unsaturated hydrocarbon with the general formula $C_nH_{2n-2}$

**allosteric enzyme** (19.9) an enzyme that has an effector binding site and an active site; effector binding changes the shape of the active site, rendering it either active or inactive

**alpha particle** (9.1) a particle consisting of two protons and two neutrons; the alpha particle is identical to a helium nucleus

**amide bond** (15.3) the bond between the carbonyl carbon of a carboxylic acid and the amino nitrogen of an amine

**amides** (15.3) the family of organic compounds formed by the reaction between a carboxylic acid derivative and an amine and characterized by the amide group

**amines** (15.1) the family of organic molecules with the general formula RNH$_2$, R$_2$NH, or R$_3$N (R— can represent either an alkyl or aryl group); they may be viewed as substituted ammonia molecules in which one or more of the ammonia hydrogens has been substituted by a more complex organic group

**α-amino acid** (15.4, 18.1) the subunits of proteins composed of an α-carbon bonded to a carboxylate group, a protonated amino group, a hydrogen atom, and a variable R group

**aminoacyl group** (15.4) the functional group that is characteristic of an amino acid; the aminoacyl group has the following general structure:

$$H_3\overset{+}{N}-\overset{\overset{\displaystyle H}{|}}{\underset{\underset{\displaystyle R}{|}}{C}}-\overset{\overset{\displaystyle O}{\|}}{C}-$$

**aminoacyl tRNA** (20.6) the transfer RNA covalently linked to the correct amino acid

**aminoacyl tRNA binding site of ribosome (A-site)** (20.6) a pocket on the surface of a ribosome that holds the aminoacyl tRNA during translation

**aminoacyl tRNA synthetase** (20.6) an enzyme that recognizes one tRNA and covalently links the appropriate amino acid to it

**amorphous solid** (5.3)   a solid with no organized, regular structure

**amphibolic pathway** (22.9)   a metabolic pathway that functions in both anabolism and catabolism

**amphiprotic** (8.1)   a substance that can behave either as a Brønsted acid or a Brønsted base

**amylopectin** (16.6)   a highly branched form of amylose; the branches are attached to the C-6 hydroxyl by $\alpha(1 \rightarrow 6)$ glycosidic linkage; a component of starch

**amylose** (16.6)   a linear polymer of $\alpha$-D-glucose molecules bonded in $\alpha(1 \rightarrow 4)$ glycosidic linkage that is a component of starch; a polysaccharide storage form

**anabolism** (21.1, 22.9)   all of the cellular energy-requiring biosynthetic pathways

**anaerobic threshold** (21.4)   the point at which the level of lactate in the exercising muscle inhibits glycolysis and the muscle, deprived of energy, ceases to function

**analgesic** (15.2)   any drug that acts as a painkiller, e.g., aspirin, acetaminophen

**anaplerotic reaction** (22.9)   a reaction that replenishes a substrate needed for a biochemical pathway

**anesthetic** (15.2)   a drug that causes a lack of sensation in part of the body (local anesthetic) or causes unconsciousness (general anesthetic)

**anion** (2.6)   a negatively charged atom or group of atoms

**anode** (8.5)   the positively charged electrode in an electrical cell

**anomers** (16.4)   isomers of cyclic monosaccharides that differ from one another in the arrangement of bonds around the hemiacetal carbon

**antibodies** (18: Intro)   immunoglobulins; specific glycoproteins produced by cells of the immune system in response to invasion by infectious agents

**anticodon** (20.6)   a sequence of three ribonucleotides on a tRNA that are complementary to a codon on the mRNA; codon-anticodon binding results in delivery of the correct amino acid to the site of protein synthesis

**antigen** (18: Intro)   any substance that is able to stimulate the immune system; generally a protein or large carbohydrate

**antiparallel strands** (20.2)   a term describing the polarities of the two strands of the DNA double helix; on one strand the sugar-phosphate backbone advances in the $5' \rightarrow 3'$ direction; on the opposite, complementary strand, the sugar-phosphate backbone advances in the $3' \rightarrow 5'$ direction

**apoenzyme** (19.7)   the protein portion of an enzyme that requires a cofactor to function in catalysis

**aqueous solution** (6.1)   any solution in which the solvent is water

**arachidonic acid** (17.2)   a fatty acid derived from linoleic acid; the precursor of the prostaglandins

**aromatic hydrocarbon** (10.1, 11.6)   an organic compound that contains the benzene ring or a derivative of the benzene ring

**Arrhenius theory** (8.1)   a theory that describes an acid as a substance that dissociates to produce $H^+$, and a base as a substance that dissociates to produce $OH^-$

**artificial radioactivity** (9.5)   radiation that results from the conversion of a stable nucleus to another, unstable nucleus

**atherosclerosis** (17.4)   deposition of excess plasma cholesterol and other lipids and proteins on the walls of arteries, resulting in decreased artery diameter and increased blood pressure

**atom** (2.1)   the smallest unit of an element that retains the properties of that element

**atomic mass** (2.1, 4.1)   the mass of an atom expressed in atomic mass units

**atomic mass unit** (4.1)   1/12 of the mass of a $^{12}C$ atom, equivalent to $1.661 \times 10^{-24}$ g

**atomic number** (2.1)   the number of protons in the nucleus of an atom; it is a characteristic identifier of an element

**atomic orbital** (2.3, 2.5)   a specific region of space where an electron may be found

**ATP synthase** (22.6)   a multiprotein complex within the inner mitochondrial membrane that uses the energy of the proton ($H^+$) gradient to produce ATP

**autoionization** (8.1)   also known as *self-ionization*, the reaction of a substance, such as water, with itself to produce a positive and a negative ion

**Avogadro's law** (5.1)   a law that states that the volume is directly proportional to the number of moles of gas particles, assuming that the pressure and temperature are constant

**Avogadro's number** (4.1)   $6.022 \times 10^{23}$ particles of matter contained in 1 mol of a substance

## B

**background radiation** (9.6)   the radiation that emanates from natural sources

**barometer** (5.1)   a device for measuring pressure

**base** (8.1)   a substance that behaves as a proton acceptor

**base pair** (20.2)   a hydrogen-bonded pair of bases within the DNA double helix; the standard base pairs always involve a purine and a pyrimidine; in particular, adenine always base pairs with thymine and cytosine with guanine

**Benedict's reagent** (16.4)   a buffered solution of $Cu^{2+}$ ions that can be used to test for reducing sugars or to distinguish between aldehydes and ketones

**Benedict's test** (13.4)   a test used to determine the presence of reducing sugars or to distinguish between aldehydes and ketones; it requires a buffered solution of $Cu^{2+}$ ions that are reduced to $Cu^+$, which precipitates as brick-red $Cu_2O$

**bent structure** (3.4)   a planar molecule with bond angles other than 180°

**beta particle** (9.1)   an electron formed in the nucleus by the conversion of a neutron into a proton

**bile** (23.1)   micelles of lecithin, cholesterol, bile salts, protein, inorganic ions, and bile pigments that aid in lipid digestion by emulsifying fat droplets

**binding energy** (9.3)   the energy required to break down the nucleus into its component parts

**bioinformatics** (20.10)   an interdisciplinary field that uses computer information sciences and DNA technology to devise methods for understanding, analyzing, and applying DNA sequence information

**boat conformation** (10.4)   a form of a six-member cycloalkane that resembles a rowboat. It is less stable than the chair conformation because the hydrogen atoms are not perfectly staggered

**boiling point** (3.3)   the temperature at which the vapor pressure of a liquid is equal to the atmospheric pressure

**bond energy** (3.4)   the amount of energy necessary to break a chemical bond

**Boyle's law** (5.1)   a law stating that the volume of a gas varies inversely with the pressure exerted if the temperature and number of moles of gas are constant

**breeder reactor** (9.4)   a nuclear reactor that produces its own fuel in the process of providing electrical energy

**Brønsted-Lowry theory** (8.1)   a theory that describes an acid as a proton donor and a base as a proton acceptor

**buffer capacity** (8.4)   a measure of the ability of a solution to resist large changes in pH when a strong acid or strong base is added

**buffer solution** (8.4)   a solution containing a weak acid or base and its salt (the conjugate base or acid) that is resistant to large changes in pH upon addition of strong acids or bases

**buret** (8.3)   a device calibrated to deliver accurately known volumes of liquid, as in a titration

## C

**C-terminal amino acid** (18.2)   the amino acid in a peptide that has a free $\alpha$-$CO_2^-$ group; the last amino acid in a peptide

**calorimetry** (7.2)   the measurement of heat energy changes during a chemical reaction

**cap structure** (20.4)   a 7-methylguanosine unit covalently bonded to the 5' end of a mRNA by a 5'-5' triphosphate bridge

**carbinol carbon** (12.1)   that carbon in an alcohol to which the hydroxyl group is attached

**carbohydrate** (16.1)   generally sugars and polymers of sugars; the primary source of energy for the cell

**carbonyl group** (13: Intro)   the functional group that contains a carbon-oxygen double bond: $—C{=}O$; the functional group found in aldehydes and ketones

**carboxyl group** (14.1)  the —COOH functional group; the functional group found in carboxylic acids

**carboxylic acid** (14.1)  a member of the family of organic compounds that contain the —COOH functional group

**carboxylic acid derivative** (14.2)  any of several families of organic compounds, including the esters and amides, that are derived from carboxylic acids and have the general formula

$$\underset{\text{(Ar)}}{\text{(Ar)}}-\overset{\overset{\text{O}}{\|}}{\text{C}}-\text{Z} \qquad \text{R}-\overset{\overset{\text{O}}{\|}}{\text{C}}-\text{Z}$$

Z = —OR or OAr for the esters, and Z = —NH$_2$ for the amides

**carcinogen** (20.7)  any chemical or physical agent that causes mutations in the DNA that lead to uncontrolled cell growth or cancer

**catabolism** (21.1, 22.9)  the degradation of fuel molecules and production of ATP for cellular functions

**catalyst** (7.3)  any substance that increases the rate of a chemical reaction (by lowering the activation energy of the reaction) and that is not destroyed in the course of the reaction

**cathode** (8.5)  the negatively charged electrode in an electrical cell

**cation** (2.6)  a positively charged atom or group of atoms

**cellulose** (16.6)  a polymer of β-D-glucose linked by β(1 → 4) glycosidic bonds

**central dogma** (20.4)  a statement of the directional transfer of the genetic information in cells: DNA → RNA → Protein

**chain reaction** (9.4)  the process in a fission reactor that involves neutron production and causes subsequent reactions accompanied by the production of more neutrons in a continuing process

**chair conformation** (10.4)  the most stable conformation for a six-member cycloalkane; so-called for its resemblance to a lawn chair

**Charles's law** (5.1)  a law stating that the volume of a gas is directly proportional to the temperature of the gas, assuming that the pressure and number of moles of the gas are constant

**chemical bond** (3.1)  the attractive force holding two atomic nuclei together in a chemical compound

**chemical change** (1.2)  a process in which one or more atoms of a substance is rearranged, removed, replaced, or added to produce a new substance

**chemical equation** (4.3)  a record of chemical change, showing the conversion of reactants to products

**chemical equilibrium** (7.4)  the state of a reaction in which the rates of the forward and reverse reactions are equal

**chemical formula** (4.2)  the representation of a compound or ion in which elemental symbols represent types of atoms and subscripts show the relative numbers of atoms

**chemical properties** (1.2)  characteristics of a substance that relate to the substance's participation in a chemical reaction

**chemical reaction** (1.2)  a process in which atoms are rearranged to produce new combinations

**chemistry** (1.1)  the study of matter and the changes that matter undergoes

**chiral carbon** (16.3)  a carbon atom bonded to four different atoms or groups of atoms

**chiral molecule** (16.3)  molecule capable of existing in mirror-image forms

**cholesterol** (17.4)  a twenty-seven-carbon steroid ring structure that serves as the precursor of the steroid hormones

**chromosome** (20.2)  a piece of DNA that carries the genetic instructions, or genes, of an organism

**chylomicron** (17.5, 23.1)  a plasma lipoprotein (aggregate of protein and triglycerides) that carries triglycerides from the intestine to all body tissues via the bloodstream

***cis-trans* isomers** (10.3)  isomers that differ from one another in the placement of substituents on a double bond or ring

**citric acid cycle** (22.4)  a cyclic biochemical pathway that is the final stage of degradation of carbohydrates, fats, and amino acids. It results in the complete oxidation of acetyl groups derived from these dietary fuels

**cloning vector** (20.8)  a DNA molecule that can carry a cloned DNA fragment into a cell and that has a replication origin that allows the DNA to be replicated abundantly within the host cell

**coagulation** (18.10)  the process by which proteins in solution are denatured and aggregate with one another to produce a solid

**codon** (20.5)  a group of three ribonucleotides on the mRNA that specifies the addition of a specific amino acid onto the growing peptide chain

**coenzyme** (19.7)  an organic group required by some enzymes; it generally serves as a donor or acceptor of electrons or a functional group in a reaction

**coenzyme A** (22.2)  a molecule derived from ATP and the vitamin pantothenic acid; coenzyme A functions in the transfer of acetyl groups in lipid and carbohydrate metabolism

**cofactor** (19.7)  an inorganic group, usually a metal ion, that must be bound to an apoenzyme to maintain the correct configuration of the active site

**colipase** (23.1)  a protein that aids in lipid digestion by binding to the surface of lipid droplets and facilitating binding of pancreatic lipase

**colligative property** (6.4)  property of a solution that is dependent only on the concentration of solute particles

**colloidal suspension** (6.1)  a heterogeneous mixture of solute particles in a solvent; distribution of solute particles is not uniform because of the size of the particles

**combination reaction** (4.3)  a reaction in which two substances join to form another substance

**combined gas law** (5.1)  an equation that describes the behavior of a gas when volume, pressure, and temperature may change simultaneously

**combustion** (10.5)  the oxidation of hydrocarbons by burning in the presence of air to produce carbon dioxide and water

**competitive inhibitor** (19.10)  a structural analog; a molecule that has a structure very similar to the natural substrate of an enzyme, competes with the natural substrate for binding to the enzyme active site, and inhibits the reaction

**complementary strands** (20.2)  the opposite strands of the double helix are hydrogen-bonded to one another such that adenine and thymine or guanine and cytosine are always paired

**complete protein** (18.11)  a protein source that contains all the essential and nonessential amino acids

**complex lipid** (17.5)  a lipid bonded to other types of molecules

**compound** (1.2)  a substance that is characterized by constant composition and that can be chemically broken down into elements

**concentration** (1.6, 6.2)  a measure of the quantity of a substance contained in a specified volume of solution

**concentration gradient** (6.4)  region where concentration decreases over distance

**condensation** (5.2)  the conversion of a gas to a liquid

**condensation polymer** (14.2)  a polymer, which is a large molecule formed by combination of many small molecules (monomers) that results from joining of monomers in a reaction that forms a small molecule, such as water or an alcohol

**condensed formula** (10.2)  a structural formula showing all of the atoms in a molecule and placing them in a sequential arrangement that details which atoms are bonded to each other; the bonds themselves are not shown

**conformations, conformers** (10.4)  discrete, distinct isomeric structures that may be converted, one to the other, by rotation about the bonds in the molecule

**conjugate acid** (8.1)  substance that has one more proton than the base from which it is derived

**conjugate acid-base pair** (8.1)  two species related to each other through the gain or loss of a proton

**conjugate base** (8.1)  substance that has one fewer proton than the acid from which it is derived

**constitutional isomers** (10.2)  two molecules having the same molecular formulas, but different chemical structures

**Cori Cycle** (21.6)  a metabolic pathway in which the lactate produced by working muscle is taken up by cells in the liver and converted back to glucose by gluconeogenesis

**corrosion** (8.5)   the unwanted oxidation of a metal

**covalent bonding** (3.1)   a pair of electrons shared between two atoms

**covalent solid** (5.3)   a collection of atoms held together by covalent bonds

**cristae** (22.1)   the folds of the inner membrane of the mitochondria

**crystal lattice** (3.1)   a unit of a solid characterized by a regular arrangement of components

**crystalline solid** (5.3)   a solid having a regular repeating atomic structure

**curie** (9.7)   the quantity of radioactive material that produces $3.7 \times 10^{10}$ nuclear disintegrations per second

**cycloalkane** (10.3)   a cyclic alkane; a saturated hydrocarbon that has the general formula $C_nH_{2n}$

## D

**Dalton's law** (5.1)   also called the law of partial pressures; states that the total pressure exerted by a gas mixture is the sum of the partial pressures of the component gases

**data** (1.1)   facts resulting from an experiment

**decomposition reaction** (4.3)   the breakdown of a substance into two or more substances

**defense proteins** (18: Intro)   proteins that defend the body against infectious diseases; antibodies are defense proteins

**degenerate code** (20.5)   a term used to describe the fact that several triplet codons may be used to specify a single amino acid in the genetic code

**dehydration (of alcohols)** (12.4)   a reaction that involves the loss of a water molecule, in this case the loss of water from an alcohol and the simultaneous formation of an alkene

**deletion mutation** (20.7)   a mutation that results in the loss of one or more nucleotides from a DNA sequence

**denaturation** (18.10)   the process by which the organized structure of a protein is disrupted, resulting in a completely disorganized, nonfunctional form of the protein

**density** (1.6)   mass per unit volume of a substance

**deoxyribonucleic acid (DNA)** (20.1)   the nucleic acid molecule that carries all of the genetic information of an organism; the DNA molecule is a double helix composed of two strands, each of which is composed of phosphate groups, deoxyribose, and the nitrogenous bases thymine, cytosine, adenine, and guanine

**deoxyribonucleotide** (20.1)   a nucleoside phosphate or nucleotide composed of a nitrogenous base in β-N-glycosidic linkage to the 1′ carbon of the sugar 2′-deoxyribose and with one, two, or three phosphoryl groups esterified at the hydroxyl of the 5′ carbon

**diabetes mellitus** (23.3)   a disease caused by the production of insufficient levels of insulin and characterized by the appearance of very high levels of glucose in the blood and urine

**dialysis** (6.5)   the removal of waste material via transport across a membrane

**diastereomers** (16.3)   stereoisomers with at least two chiral carbons that are not mirror images of one another

**diffusion** (6.4)   net movement of solute or solvent molecules from a region of high concentration to a region of low concentration

**diglyceride** (17.3)   the product of esterification of glycerol at two positions

**dipole-dipole interactions** (5.2)   attractive forces between polar molecules

**disaccharide** (16.1)   a sugar composed of two monosaccharides joined through an oxygen atom bridge

**dissociation** (3.3)   production of positive and negative ions when an ionic compound dissolves in water

**disulfide** (12.8)   an organic compound that contains a disulfide group (—S—S—)

**DNA polymerase III** (20.3)   the enzyme that catalyzes the polymerization of daughter DNA strands using the parental strand as a template

**double bond** (3.4)   a bond in which two pairs of electrons are shared by two atoms

**double helix** (20.2)   the spiral staircase–like structure of the DNA molecule characterized by two sugar-phosphate backbones wound around the outside and nitrogenous bases extending into the center

**double-replacement reaction** (4.3)   a chemical change in which cations and anions "exchange partners"

**dynamic equilibrium** (7.4)   the state that exists when the rate of change in the concentration of products and reactants is equal, resulting in no net concentration change

## E

**eicosanoid** (17.2)   any of the derivatives of twenty-carbon fatty acids, including the prostaglandins, leukotrienes, and thromboxanes

**electrolysis** (8.5)   an electrochemical process that uses electrical energy to cause nonspontaneous oxidation-reduction reactions to occur

**electrolyte** (3.3, 6.1)   a material that dissolves in water to produce a solution that conducts an electrical current

**electromagnetic radiation** (2.3)   energy that is propagated as waves at the speed of light

**electron** (2.1)   a negatively charged particle outside of the nucleus of an atom

**electron affinity** (2.7)   the energy released when an electron is added to an isolated atom

**electron configuration** (2.5)   the arrangement of electrons around the nucleus of an atom,

an ion, or a collection of nuclei of a molecule

**electron density** (2.3)   the probability of finding the electron in a particular location

**electron transport system** (22.6)   the series of electron transport proteins embedded in the inner mitochondrial membrane that accept high-energy electrons from NADH and $FADH_2$ and transfer them in stepwise fashion to molecular oxygen $(O_2)$

**electronegativity** (3.1)   a measure of the tendency of an atom in a molecule to attract shared electrons

**element** (1.2)   a substance that cannot be decomposed into simpler substances by chemical or physical means

**elimination reaction** (12.4)   a reaction in which a molecule loses atoms or ions from its structure

**elongation factor** (20.6)   proteins that facilitate the elongation phase of translation

**emulsifying agent** (17.3)   a bipolar molecule that aids in the suspension of fats in water

**enantiomers** (16.3)   stereoisomers that are nonsuperimposable mirror images of one another

**endothermic reaction** (7.1)   a chemical or physical change in which energy is absorbed

**energy** (1.6)   the capacity to do work

**energy level** (2.3)   one of numerous atomic regions where electrons may be found

**enol** (13.4)   a tautomer containing a carbon-carbon double bond and a hydroxyl group

**enthalpy** (7.1)   a term that represents heat energy

**entropy** (7.1)   a measure of randomness or disorder

**enzyme** (18: Intro, 19: Intro)   a protein that serves as a biological catalyst

**enzyme specificity** (19.5)   the ability of an enzyme to bind to only one, or a very few, substrates and thus catalyze only a single reaction

**enzyme-substrate complex** (19.4)   a molecular aggregate formed when the substrate binds to the active site of the enzyme

**equilibrium constant** (7.4)   number equal to the ratio of the equilibrium concentrations of products to the equilibrium concentrations of reactants, each raised to the power corresponding to its coefficient in the balanced equation

**equivalence point** (8.3)   the situation in which reactants have been mixed in the molar ratio corresponding to the balanced equation

**error** (1.4)   the difference between the true value and the experimental value for data or results

**essential amino acid** (18.11)   an amino acid that cannot be synthesized by the body and must therefore be supplied by the diet

**essential fatty acids** (17.2)   the fatty acids linolenic and linoleic acids that must be supplied in the diet because they cannot be synthesized by the body

**ester** (14.2)   a carboxylic acid derivative formed by the reaction of a carboxylic acid and an alcohol. Esters have the following general formula:

$$R-\overset{\overset{\displaystyle O}{\|}}{C}-R \quad R-\overset{\overset{\displaystyle O}{\|}}{C}-(Ar) \quad (Ar)-\overset{\overset{\displaystyle O}{\|}}{C}-(Ar)$$

**esterification** (17.2)   the formation of an ester in the reaction of a carboxylic acid and an alcohol

**ether** (12.7)   an organic compound that contains two alkyl and/or aryl groups attached to an oxygen atom; R—O—R, Ar—O—R, and Ar—O—Ar

**eukaryote** (20.2)   an organism having cells containing a true nucleus enclosed by a nuclear membrane and having a variety of membrane-bound organelles that segregate different cellular functions into different compartments

**evaporation** (5.2)   the conversion of a liquid to a gas below the boiling point of the liquid

**excited state** (2.3)   an electronic state of an atom when energy has been adsorbed by the ground state atom and one or more electrons are promoted into a higher energy level

**exon** (20.4)   protein-coding sequences of a gene found on the final mature mRNA

**exothermic reaction** (7.1)   a chemical or physical change that releases energy

**extensive property** (1.2)   a property of a substance that depends on the quantity of the substance

## F

**$F_0 F_1$ complex** (22.6)   an alternative term for ATP synthase, the multiprotein complex in the inner mitochondrial membrane that uses the energy of the proton gradient to produce ATP

**fatty acid** (14.1, 17.2)   any member of the family of continuous-chain carboxylic acids that generally contain four to twenty carbon atoms; the most concentrated source of energy used by the cell

**feedback inhibition** (19.9)   the process whereby excess product of a biosynthetic pathway turns off the entire pathway for its own synthesis

**fermentation** (12.3, 21.4)   anaerobic (in the absence of oxygen) catabolic reactions that occur with no net oxidation. Pyruvate or an organic compound produced from pyruvate is reduced as NADH is oxidized

**fibrous protein** (18.4)   a protein composed of peptides arranged in long sheets or fibers

**Fischer Projection** (16.3)   a two-dimensional drawing of a molecule, that shows a chiral carbon at the intersection of two lines and horizontal lines representing bonds projecting out of the page and vertical lines representing bonds that project into the page

**fission** (9.4)   the splitting of heavy nuclei into lighter nuclei accompanied by the release of large quantities of energy

**fluid mosaic model** (17.6)   the model of membrane structure that describes the fluid nature of the lipid bilayer and the presence of numerous proteins embedded within the membrane

**formula** (3.2)   the representation of the fundamental compound unit using chemical symbols and numerical subscripts

**formula mass** (4.2)   the mass of a formula unit of a compound relative to a standard (carbon-12)

**formula unit** (4.2)   the smallest collection of atoms from which the formula of a compound can be established

**free energy** (7.1)   the combined contribution of entropy and enthalpy for a chemical reaction

**fructose** (16.4)   a ketohexose that is also called levulose and fruit sugar; the sweetest of all sugars, abundant in honey and fruits

**fuel value** (7.2)   the amount of energy derived from a given mass of material

**functional group** (10.1)   an atom (or group of atoms and their bonds) that imparts specific chemical and physical properties to a molecule

**fusion** (9.4)   the joining of light nuclei to form heavier nuclei, accompanied by the release of large amounts of energy

## G

**galactose** (16.4)   an aldohexose that is a component of lactose (milk sugar)

**galactosemia** (16.5)   a human genetic disease caused by the inability to convert galactose to a phosphorylated form of glucose (glucose-1-phosphate) that can be used in cellular metabolic reactions

**gamma ray** (9.1)   a high-energy emission from nuclear processes, traveling at the speed of light; the high-energy region of the electromagnetic spectrum

**gaseous state** (1.2)   a physical state of matter characterized by a lack of fixed shape or volume and ease of compressibility

**genome** (20.2)   the complete set of genetic information in all the chromosomes of an organism

**geometric isomer** (10.3, 11.3)   an isomer that differs from another isomer in the placement of substituents on a double bond or a ring

**globular protein** (18.5)   a protein composed of polypeptide chains that are tightly folded into a compact spherical shape

**glucagon** (21.7, 23.6)   a peptide hormone synthesized by the α-cells of the islets of Langerhans in the pancreas and secreted in response to low blood glucose levels; glucagon promotes glycogenolysis and gluconeogenesis and thereby increases the concentration of blood glucose

**gluconeogenesis** (21.6)   the synthesis of glucose from noncarbohydrate precursors

**glucose** (16.4)   an aldohexose, the most abundant monosaccharide; it is a component of many disaccharides, such as lactose and sucrose, and of polysaccharides, such as cellulose, starch, and glycogen

**glyceraldehyde** (16.4)   an aldotriose that is the simplest carbohydrate; phosphorylated forms of glyceraldehyde are important intermediates in cellular metabolic reactions

**glyceride** (17.3)   a lipid that contains glycerol

**glycogen** (16.6, 21.7)   a long, branched polymer of glucose stored in liver and muscles of animals; it consists of a linear backbone of α-D-glucose in $\alpha(1 \rightarrow 4)$ linkage, with numerous short branches attached to the C-6 hydroxyl group by $\alpha(1 \rightarrow 6)$ linkage

**glycogenesis** (21.7)   the metabolic pathway that results in the addition of glucose to growing glycogen polymers when blood glucose levels are high

**glycogen granule** (21.7)   a core of glycogen surrounded by enzymes responsible for glycogen synthesis and degradation

**glycogenolysis** (21.7)   the biochemical pathway that results in the removal of glucose molecules from glycogen polymers when blood glucose levels are low

**glycolysis** (21.3)   the enzymatic pathway that converts a glucose molecule into two molecules of pyruvate; this anaerobic process generates a net energy yield of two molecules of ATP and two molecules of NADH

**glycoprotein** (18.6)   a protein bonded to sugar groups

**glycosidic bond** (16.1)   the bond between the hydroxyl group of the C-1 carbon of one sugar and a hydroxyl group of another sugar

**ground state** (2.3)   the electronic state of an atom in which all of the electrons are in the lowest possible energy levels

**group** (2.4)   any one of eighteen vertical columns of elements; often referred to as a *family*

**group specificity** (19.5)   an enzyme that catalyzes reactions involving similar substrate molecules having the same functional groups

**guanosine triphosphate (GTP)** (21.6)   a nucleotide composed of the purine guanosine, the sugar ribose, and three phosphoryl groups

## H

**half-life ( $t_{1/2}$ )** (9.3, 9.6)   the length of time required for one-half of the initial mass of an isotope to decay to products

**halogen** (2.4)   an element found in Group VIIA (17) of the periodic table

**halogenation** (10.5, 11.5)   a reaction in which one of the C—H bonds of a hydrocarbon is replaced with a C—X bond (X = Br or Cl generally)

**Haworth projection** (16.4)   a means of representing the orientation of substituent groups around a cyclic sugar molecule

**heat** (7.1)   energy transferred between a system and its surroundings due to a temperature difference between system and surroundings

**α-helix** (18.4)   a right-handed coiled secondary structure maintained by hydrogen bonds between the amide hydrogen of one amino acid and the carbonyl oxygen of an amino acid four residues away

**heme group** (18.8)   the chemical group found in hemoglobin and myoglobin that is responsible for the ability to carry oxygen

**hemiacetal** (13.4, 16.4)   the family of organic compounds formed via the reaction of one molecule of alcohol with an aldehyde or a ketone in the presence of an acid catalyst; or a ketone

**hemoglobin** (18.8)   the major protein component of red blood cells; the function of this red, iron-containing protein is transport of oxygen

**Henderson-Hasselbalch equation** (8.4)   an equation for calculating the pH of a buffer system:

$$pH = pK_a + \log \frac{[\text{conjugate base}]}{[\text{weak acid}]}$$

**Henry's law** (6.1)   a law stating that the number of moles of a gas dissolved in a liquid at a given temperature is proportional to the partial pressure of the gas

**heterocyclic amine** (15.2)   a heterocyclic compound that contains nitrogen in at least one position in the ring skeleton

**heterocyclic aromatic compound** (11.7)   cyclic aromatic compound having at least one atom other than carbon in the structure of the aromatic ring

**heterogeneous mixture** (1.2)   a mixture of two or more substances characterized by nonuniform composition

**heteropolysaccharide** (16.6)   a polysaccharide composed of two or more different monosaccharides

**hexose** (16.2)   a six-carbon monosaccharide

**high-density lipoprotein (HDL)** (17.5)   a plasma lipoprotein that transports cholesterol from peripheral tissue to the liver

**holoenzyme** (19.7)   an active enzyme consisting of an apoenzyme bound to a cofactor

**homogeneous mixture** (1.2)   a mixture of two or more substances characterized by uniform composition

**homopolysaccharide** (16.6)   a polysaccharide composed of identical monosaccharides

**hybridization** (20.8)   a technique for identifying DNA or RNA sequences that is based on specific hydrogen bonding between a radioactive probe and complementary DNA or RNA sequences

**hydrate** (4.2)   any substance that has water molecules incorporated in its structure

**hydration** (11.5, 12.4)   a reaction in which water is added to a molecule, e.g., the addition of water to an alkene to form an alcohol

**hydrocarbon** (10.1)   a compound composed solely of the elements carbon and hydrogen

**hydrogen bonding** (5.2)   the attractive force between a hydrogen atom covalently bonded to a small, highly electronegative atom and another atom containing an unshared pair of electrons

**hydrogenation** (11.5, 13.4, 17.2)   a reaction in which hydrogen ($H_2$) is added to a double or a triple bond

**hydrohalogenation** (11.5)   the addition of a hydrohalogen (HCl, HBr, or HI) to an unsaturated bond

**hydrolase** (19.1)   an enzyme that catalyzes hydrolysis reactions

**hydrolysis** (14.2)   a chemical change that involves the reaction of a molecule with water; the process by which molecules are broken into their constituents by addition of water

**hydronium ion** (8.1)   a protonated water molecule, $H_3O^+$

**hydrophilic amino acid** (18.1)   "water loving"; a polar or ionic amino acid that has a high affinity for water

**hydrophobic amino acid** (18.1)   "water fearing"; a nonpolar amino acid that prefers contact with other nonpolar molecules over contact with water

**hydroxide ion** (8.1)   the anion consisting of one oxygen atom and one hydrogen atom ($—OH^-$)

**hydroxyl group** (12.1)   the —OH functional group that is characteristic of alcohols

**hyperammonemia** (22.8)   a genetic defect in one of the enzymes of the urea cycle that results in toxic or even fatal elevation of the concentration of ammonium ions in the body

**hyperglycemia** (21.7)   blood glucose levels that are higher than normal

**hypertonic solution** (6.4)   the more concentrated solution of two separated by a semipermeable membrane

**hypoglycemia** (21.7)   blood glucose levels that are lower than normal

**hypothesis** (1.1)   an attempt to explain observations in a commonsense way

**hypotonic solution** (6.4)   the more dilute solution of two separated by a semipermeable membrane

## I

**ideal gas** (5.1)   a gas in which the particles do not interact and the volume of the individual gas particles is assumed to be negligible

**ideal gas law** (5.1)   a law stating that for an ideal gas the product of pressure and volume is proportional to the product of the number of moles of the gas and its temperature; the proportionality constant for an ideal gas is symbolized $R$

**incomplete protein** (18.11)   a protein source that does not contain all the essential and nonessential amino acids

**indicator** (8.3)   a solute that shows some condition of a solution (such as acidity or basicity) by its color

**induced fit model** (19.4)   the theory of enzyme-substrate binding that assumes that the enzyme is a flexible molecule and that both the substrate and the enzyme change their shapes to accommodate one another as the enzyme-substrate complex forms

**initiation factors** (20.6)   proteins that are required for formation of the translation initiation complex, which is composed of the large and small ribosomal subunits, the mRNA, and the initiator tRNA, methionyl tRNA

**inner mitochondrial membrane** (22.1)   the highly folded, impermeable membrane within the mitochondrion that is the location of the electron transport system and ATP synthase

**insertion mutation** (20.7)   a mutation that results in the addition of one or more nucleotides to a DNA sequence

**insulin** (21.7, 23.6)   a hormone released from the pancreas in response to high blood glucose levels; insulin stimulates glycogenesis, fat storage, and cellular uptake and storage of glucose from the blood

**intensive property** (1.2)   a property of a substance that is independent of the quantity of the substance

**intermembrane space** (22.1)   the region between the outer and inner mitochondrial membranes, which is the location of the proton ($H^+$) reservoir that drives ATP synthesis

**intermolecular force** (3.5)   any attractive force that occurs between molecules

**intramolecular force** (3.5)   any attractive force that occurs within molecules

**intron** (20.4)   a noncoding sequence within a eukaryotic gene that must be removed from the primary transcript to produce a functional mRNA

**ion** (2.6)   an electrically charged particle formed by the gain or loss of electrons

**ionic bonding** (3.1)   an electrostatic attractive force between ions resulting from electron transfer

**ionic solid** (5.3)   a solid composed of positive and negative ions in a regular three-dimensional crystalline arrangement

**ionization energy** (2.7)   the energy needed to remove an electron from an atom in the gas phase

**ionizing radiation** (9.1, 9.5)   radiation that is sufficiently high in energy to cause ion formation upon impact with an atom

**ion product for water** (8.1)   the product of the hydronium and hydroxide ion concentrations in pure water at a specified temperature; at 25°C, it has a value of $1.0 \times 10^{-14}$

**irreversible enzyme inhibitor** (19.10)   a chemical that binds strongly to the R groups of an amino acid in the active site and eliminates enzyme activity

**isoelectronic** (2.6)   atoms, ions, and molecules containing the same number of electrons

**isomerase** (19.1)   an enzyme that catalyzes the conversion of one isomer to another

**isomers** (3.4)   molecules having the same molecular formula but different chemical structures

**isotonic solution**  (6.4)   a solution that has the same solute concentration as another solution with which it is being compared; a solution that has the same osmotic pressure as a solution existing within a cell

**isotope**  (2.1)   atom of the same element that differs in mass because it contains different numbers of neutrons

**IUPAC Nomenclature System**  (10.2)   the International Union of Pure and Applied Chemistry (IUPAC) standard, universal system for the nomenclature of organic compounds

## K

**α-keratin**  (18.4)   a member of the family of fibrous proteins that form the covering of most land animals; major components of fur, skin, beaks, and nails

**ketoacidosis**  (23.3)   a drop in the pH of the blood caused by elevated levels of ketone bodies

**ketone**  (13.1)   a family of organic molecules characterized by a carbonyl group; the carbonyl carbon is bonded to two alkyl groups, two aryl groups, or one alkyl and one aryl group; ketones have the following general structures:

$$\text{R} \overset{\overset{\displaystyle O}{\|}}{\text{C}} \text{OR} \quad \text{R} \overset{\overset{\displaystyle O}{\|}}{\text{C}} \text{O(Ar)} \quad \text{(Ar)} \overset{\overset{\displaystyle O}{\|}}{\text{C}} \text{O(Ar)}$$

**ketone bodies**  (23.3)   acetone, acetoacetone, and β-hydroxybutyrate produced from fatty acids in the liver via acetyl CoA

**ketose**  (16.2)   a sugar that contains a ketone (carbonyl) group

**ketosis**  (23.3)   an abnormal rise in the level of ketone bodies in the blood

**kinetic energy**  (1.6)   the energy resulting from motion of an object [kinetic energy = $1/2(\text{mass})(\text{velocity})^2$]

**kinetic molecular theory**  (5.1)   the fundamental model of particle behavior in the gas phase

**kinetics**  (7.3)   the study of rates of chemical reactions

## L

**lactose**  (16.5)   a disaccharide composed of β-D-galactose and either α- or β-D-glucose in β(1 → 4) glycosidic linkage; milk sugar

**lactose intolerance**  (16.5)   the inability to produce the digestive enzyme lactase, which degrades lactose to galactose and glucose

**lagging strand**  (20.3)   in DNA replication, the strand that is synthesized discontinuously from numerous RNA primers

**law**  (1.1)   a summary of a large quantity of information

**law of conservation of mass**  (4.3)   a law stating that, in chemical change, matter cannot be created or destroyed

**leading strand**  (20.3)   in DNA replication, the strand that is synthesized continuously from a single RNA primer

**LeChatelier's principle**  (7.4)   a law stating that when a system at equilibrium is disturbed, the equilibrium shifts in the direction that minimizes the disturbance

**lethal dose (LD$_{50}$)**  (9.7)   the quantity of toxic material (such as radiation) that causes the death of 50% of a population of an organism

**Lewis structure**  (3.1)   representation of a molecule (or polyatomic ion) that shows valence electron arrangement among the atoms in a molecule (or polyatomic ion)

**Lewis symbol**  (3.1)   representation of an atom (or ion) using the atomic symbol (for the nucleus and core electrons) and dots to represent valence electrons

**ligase**  (19.1)   an enzyme that catalyzes the joining of two molecules

**linear structure**  (3.4)   the structure of a molecule in which the bond angle(s) about the central atom(s) is (are) 180°

**line formula**  (10.2)   the simplest representation of a molecule, in which it is assumed that there is a carbon atom at any location where two or more lines intersect, there is a carbon at the end of any line, and each carbon is bonded to the correct number of hydrogen atoms

**linkage specificity**  (19.5)   the property of an enzyme that allows it to catalyze reactions involving only one kind of bond in the substrate molecule

**lipase**  (23.1)   an enzyme that hydrolyzes the ester linkage between glycerol and the fatty acids of triglycerides

**lipid**  (17.1)   a member of the group of biological molecules of varying composition that are classified together on the basis of their solubility in nonpolar solvents

**liquid state**  (1.2)   a physical state of matter characterized by a fixed volume and the absence of a fixed shape

**lock-and-key model**  (19.4)   the theory of enzyme-substrate binding that depicts enzymes as inflexible molecules; the substrate fits into the rigid active site in the same way a key fits into a lock

**London dispersion forces**  (5.2)   weak attractive forces between molecules that result from short-lived dipoles that occur because of the continuous movement of electrons in the molecules

**lone pair**  (3.4)   an electron pair that is not involved in bonding

**low-density lipoprotein (LDL)**  (17.5)   a plasma lipoprotein that carries cholesterol to peripheral tissues and helps to regulate cholesterol levels in those tissues

**lyase**  (19.1)   an enzyme that catalyzes a reaction involving double bonds

## M

**maltose**  (16.5)   a disaccharide composed of α-D-glucose and a second glucose molecule in α(1 → 4) glycosidic linkage

**Markovnikov's rule**  (11.5)   the rule stating that a hydrogen atom, adding to a carbon-carbon double bond, will add to the carbon having the larger number of hydrogens attached to it

**mass**  (1.3)   a quantity of matter

**mass/mass percent [% (m/m)]**  (6.2)   the concentration of a solution expressed as a ratio of mass of solute to mass of solution multiplied by 100%

**mass number**  (2.1)   the sum of the number of protons and neutrons in an atom

**mass/volume percent [% (m/V)]**  (6.2)   the concentration of a solution expressed as a ratio of grams of solute to milliliters of solution multiplied by 100%

**matrix space**  (22.1)   the region of the mitochondrion within the inner membrane; the location of the enzymes that carry out the reactions of the citric acid cycle and β-oxidation of fatty acids

**matter**  (1.1)   anything that has mass and occupies space

**melting point**  (3.3, 5.2)   the temperature at which a solid converts to a liquid

**meso compound**  (16.3)   a special case of stereoisomers that occurs when a molecule has two chiral carbons and each chiral carbon has identical substituents; these molecules are achiral because they have a plane of symmetry within the molecule

**messenger RNA**  (20.4)   an RNA species produced by transcription and that specifies the amino acid sequence for a protein

**metal**  (2.4)   an element located on the left side of the periodic table (left of the "staircase" boundary)

**metallic bond**  (5.3)   a bond that results from the orbital overlap of metal atoms

**metallic solid**  (5.3)   a solid composed of metal atoms held together by metallic bonds

**metalloid**  (2.4)   an element along the "staircase" boundary between metals and nonmetals; metalloids exhibit both metallic and nonmetallic properties

**metastable isotope**  (9.3)   an isotope that will give up some energy to produce a more stable form of the same isotope

**micelle**  (23.1)   an aggregation of molecules having nonpolar and polar regions; the nonpolar regions of the molecules aggregate, leaving the polar regions facing the surrounding water

**mitochondria**  (22.1)   the cellular "power plants" in which the reactions of the citric acid cycle, β-oxidation of fatty acids, the electron transport system, and ATP synthase function to produce ATP

**mixture**  (1.2)   a material composed of two or more substances

**molality**  (6.4)   the number of moles of solute per kilogram of solvent

**molar mass**  (4.1, 4.2)   the mass in grams of 1 mol of a substance

**molar volume**  (5.1)   the volume occupied by 1 mol of a substance

**molarity**  (6.3)   the number of moles of solute per liter of solution

**mole**  (4.1)   the amount of substance containing Avogadro's number of particles

**molecular formula**  (10.2)   a formula that provides the atoms and number of each type of atom in a molecule but gives no information regarding the bonding pattern involved in the structure of the molecule

**molecular solid** (5.3)  a solid in which the molecules are held together by dipole-dipole and London dispersion forces (van der Waals forces)

**molecule** (3.1)  a unit in which the atoms of two or more elements are held together by chemical bonds

**monatomic ion** (3.2)  an ion formed by electron gain or loss from a single atom

**monoglyceride** (17.3)  the product of the esterification of glycerol at one position

**monomer** (11.5)  the individual molecules from which a polymer is formed

**monosaccharide** (16.1)  the simplest type of carbohydrate consisting of a single saccharide unit

**movement protein** (18: Intro)  a protein involved in any aspect of movement in an organism, for instance, actin and myosin in muscle tissue and flagellin that composes bacterial flagella

**mutagen** (20.7)  any chemical or physical agent that causes changes in the nucleotide sequence of a gene

**mutation** (20.7)  any change in the nucleotide sequence of a gene

**myoglobin** (18.8)  the oxygen storage protein found in muscle

# N

**N-terminal amino acid** (18.2)  the amino acid in a peptide that has a free $\alpha$-$N^+H_3$ group; the first amino acid of a peptide

**natural radioactivity** (9.5)  the spontaneous decay of a nucleus to produce high-energy particles or rays

**negative allosterism** (19.9)  effector binding inactivates the active site of an allosteric enzyme

**neurotransmitter** (15.5)  a chemical that carries a message, or signal, from a nerve cell to a target cell

**neutral glyceride** (17.3)  the product of the esterification of glycerol at one, two, or three positions

**neutralization** (8.3)  the reaction between an acid and a base

**neutron** (2.1)  an uncharged particle, with the same mass as the proton, in the nucleus of an atom

**nicotinamide adenine dinucleotide (NAD$^+$)** (21.3)  a molecule synthesized from the vitamin niacin and the nucleotide ATP and that serves as a carrier of hydride anions; a coenzyme that is an oxidizing agent used in a variety of metabolic processes

**noble gas** (2.4)  elements in Group VIIIA (18) of the periodic table

**nomenclature** (3.2)  a system for naming chemical compounds

**nonelectrolyte** (3.3, 6.1)  a substance that, when dissolved in water, produces a solution that does not conduct an electrical current

**nonessential amino acid** (18.11)  any amino acid that can be synthesized by the body

**nonmetal** (2.4)  an element located on the right side of the periodic table (right of the "staircase" boundary)

**nonreducing sugar** (16.5)  a sugar that cannot be oxidized by Benedict's or Tollens' reagent

**normal boiling point** (5.2)  the temperature at which a substance will boil at 1 atm of pressure

**nuclear equation** (9.2)  a balanced equation accounting for the products and reactants in a nuclear reaction

**nuclear imaging** (9.5)  the generation of images of components of the body (organs, tissues) using techniques based on the measurement of radiation

**nuclear medicine** (9.5)  a field of medicine that uses radioisotopes for diagnostic and therapeutic purposes

**nuclear reactor** (9.4)  a device for conversion of nuclear energy into electrical energy

**nucleoside** (20.1)  a molecule composed of a nitrogenous base and a five-carbon sugar

**nucleosome** (20.2)  the first level of chromosome structure consisting of a strand of DNA wrapped around a small disk of histone proteins

**nucleotide** (20.1, 21.1)  a molecule composed of a nitrogenous base, a five-carbon sugar, and one, two, or three phosphoryl groups

**nucleus** (2.1)  the small, dense center of positive charge in the atom

**nuclide** (9.1)  any atom characterized by an atomic number and a mass number

**nutrient protein** (18: Intro)  a protein that serves as a source of amino acids for embryos or infants

**nutritional Calorie** (7.2)  equivalent to 1 kilocalorie (1000 calories); also known as a large Calorie

# O

**octet rule** (2.6)  a rule predicting that atoms form the most stable molecules or ions when they are surrounded by eight electrons in their highest occupied energy level

**oligosaccharide** (16.1)  an intermediate-sized carbohydrate composed of from three to ten monosaccharides

**osmosis** (6.4)  net flow of a solvent across a semipermeable membrane in response to a concentration gradient

**osmotic pressure** (6.4)  the net force with which water enters a solution through a semipermeable membrane; alternatively, the pressure required to stop net transfer of solvent across a semipermeable membrane

**outer mitochondrial membrane** (22.1)  the membrane that surrounds the mitochondrion and separates it from the contents of the cytoplasm; it is highly permeable to small "food" molecules

**$\beta$-oxidation** (23.2)  the biochemical pathway that results in the oxidation of fatty acids and the production of acetyl CoA

**oxidation** (8.5, 12.4, 13.4, 14.1)  a loss of electrons; in organic compounds it may be

recognized as a loss of hydrogen atoms or the gain of oxygen

**oxidation-reduction reaction** (4.4)  also called *redox reaction*, a reaction involving the transfer of one or more electrons from one reactant to another

**oxidative deamination** (22.7)  an oxidation-reduction reaction in which NAD$^+$ is reduced and the amino acid is deaminated

**oxidative phosphorylation** (21.3, 22.6)  production of ATP using the energy of electrons harvested during biological oxidation-reduction reactions

**oxidizing agent** (8.5)  a substance that oxidizes, or removes electrons from, another substance; the oxidizing agent is reduced in the process

**oxidoreductase** (19.1)  an enzyme that catalyzes an oxidation-reduction reaction

# P

**pancreatic serine proteases** (19.11)  a family of proteolytic enzymes, including trypsin, chymotrypsin, and elastase, that arose by divergent evolution

**parent compound or parent chain** (10.2)  in the IUPAC Nomenclature System the parent compound is the longest carbon-carbon chain containing the principal functional group in the molecule that is being named

**partial pressure** (5.1)  the pressure exerted by one component of a gas mixture

**parts per million** (6.2)  number of parts of solute in one million parts of solvent

**parts per thousand** (6.2)  number of parts of solute per thousand parts of solvent

**pentose** (16.2)  a five-carbon monosaccharide

**pentose phosphate pathway** (21.5)  an alternative pathway for glucose degradation that provides the cell with reducing power in the form of NADPH

**peptide bond** (15.4, 18.2)  the amide bond between two amino acids in a peptide chain

**peptidyl tRNA binding site of ribosome (P-site)** (20.6)  a pocket on the surface of the ribosome that holds the tRNA bound to the growing peptide chain

**percent yield** (4.5)  the ratio of the actual and theoretical yields of a chemical reaction multiplied by 100%

**period** (2.4)  any one of seven horizontal rows of elements in the periodic table

**periodic law** (2.4)  a law stating that properties of elements are periodic functions of their atomic numbers (Note that Mendeleev's original statement was based on atomic masses.)

**peripheral membrane protein** (17.6)  a protein bound to either the inner or the outer surface of a membrane

**phenol** (12.6)  an organic compound that contains a hydroxyl group (—OH) attached to a benzene ring

**phenyl group** (11.6)  a benzene ring that has had a hydrogen atom removed, $C_6H_5$—

**pH optimum** (19.8)  the pH at which an enzyme catalyzes the reaction at maximum efficiency

**phosphatidate** (17.3)   a molecule of glycerol with fatty acids esterified to C-1 and C-2 of glycerol and a free phosphoryl group esterified at C-3

**phosphoanhydride** (14.4)   the bond formed when two phosphate groups react with one another and a water molecule is lost

**phosphoester** (14.4)   the product of the reaction between phosphoric acid and an alcohol

**phosphoglyceride** (17.3)   a molecule with fatty acids esterified at the C-1 and C-2 positions of glycerol and a phosphoryl group esterified at the C-3 position

**phospholipid** (17.3)   a lipid containing a phosphoryl group

**phosphopantetheine** (23.4)   the portion of coenzyme A and the acyl carrier protein that is derived from the vitamin pantothenic acid

**pH scale** (8.2)   a numerical representation of acidity or basicity of a solution; $pH = -\log[H_3O^+]$

**physical change** (1.2)   a change in the form of a substance but not in its chemical composition; no chemical bonds are broken in a physical change

**physical property** (1.2)   a characteristic of a substance that can be observed without the substance undergoing change (examples include color, density, melting and boiling points)

**plasma lipoprotein** (17.5)   a complex composed of lipid and protein that is responsible for the transport of lipids throughout the body

**β-pleated sheet** (18.4)   a common secondary structure of a peptide chain that resembles the pleats of an Oriental fan

**point mutation** (20.7)   the substitution of one nucleotide pair for another within a gene

**polar covalent bond** (3.1)   a covalent bond in which the electrons are not equally shared

**poly(A) tail** (20.4)   a tract of 100–200 adenosine monophosphate units covalently attached to the 3′ end of eukaryotic messenger RNA molecules

**polyatomic ion** (3.2)   an ion containing a number of atoms

**polymer** (11.5)   a very large molecule formed by the combination of many small molecules (called *monomers*) (e.g., polyamides, nylons)

**polyprotic substance** (8.3)   a substance that can accept or donate more than one proton per molecule

**polysaccharide** (16.1)   a large, complex carbohydrate composed of long chains of monosaccharides

**polysome** (20.6)   complexes of many ribosomes all simultaneously translating a single mRNA

**positive allosterism** (19.9)   effector binding activates the active site of an allosteric enzyme

**positron** (9.1)   particle that has the same mass as an electron but opposite (+) charge

**post-transcriptional modification** (20.4)   alterations of the primary transcripts produced in eukaryotic cells; these include addition of a poly(A) tail to the 3′ end of the mRNA, addition of the cap structure to the 5′ end of the mRNA, and RNA splicing

**potential energy** (1.6)   stored energy or energy caused by position or composition

**precipitate** (4.4, 6.1)   an insoluble substance formed and separated from a solution

**precision** (1.4)   the degree of agreement among replicate measurements of the same quantity

**pressure** (5.1)   a force per unit area

**primary (1°) alcohol** (12.1)   an alcohol with the general formula $RCH_2OH$

**primary (1°) amine** (15.1)   an amine with the general formula $RNH_2$

**primary (1°) carbon** (10.2)   a carbon atom that is bonded to only one other carbon atom

**primary structure (of a protein)** (18.3)   the linear sequence of amino acids in a protein chain determined by the genetic information of the gene for each protein

**primary transcript** (20.4)   the RNA product of transcription in eukaryotic cells, before post-transcriptional modifications are carried out

**principal energy level** (2.5)   a region where electrons may be found; has integral values $n = 1$, $n = 2$, and so forth

**product** (4.3, 19.1)   the chemical species that results from a chemical reaction and that appears on the right side of a chemical equation

**proenzyme** (19.9)   the inactive form of a proteolytic enzyme

**prokaryote** (20.2)   an organism with simple cellular structure in which there is no true nucleus enclosed by a nuclear membrane and there are no true membrane-bound organelles in the cytoplasm

**promoter** (20.4)   the sequence of nucleotides immediately before a gene that is recognized by the RNA polymerase and signals the start point and direction of transcription

**properties** (1.2)   characteristics of matter

**prostaglandins** (17.2)   a family of hormonelike substances derived from the twenty-carbon fatty acid, arachidonic acid; produced by many cells of the body, they regulate many body functions

**prosthetic group** (18.6)   the nonprotein portion of a protein that is essential to the biological activity of the protein; often a complex organic compound

**protein** (18: Intro)   a macromolecule whose primary structure is a linear sequence of α-amino acids and whose final structure results from folding of the chain into a specific three-dimensional structure; proteins serve as catalysts, structural components, and nutritional elements for the cell

**protein modification** (19.9)   a means of enzyme regulation in which a chemical group is covalently added to or removed from a protein. The chemical modification either turns the enzyme on or turns it off

**proteolytic enzyme** (19.11)   an enzyme that hydrolyzes the peptide bonds between amino acids in a protein chain

**proton** (2.1)   a positively charged particle in the nucleus of an atom

**pure substance** (1.2)   a substance with constant composition

**purine** (20.1)   a family of nitrogenous bases (heterocyclic amines) that are components of DNA and RNA and consist of a six-sided ring fused to a five-sided ring; the common purines in nucleic acids are adenine and guanine

**pyridoxal phosphate** (22.7)   a coenzyme derived from vitamin $B_6$ that is required for all transamination reactions

**pyrimidine** (20.1)   a family of nitrogenous bases (heterocyclic amines) that are components of nucleic acids and consist of a single six-sided ring; the common pyrimidines of DNA are cytosine and thymine; the common pyrimidines of RNA are cytosine and uracil

**pyrimidine dimer** (20.7)   UV light–induced covalent bonding of two adjacent pyrimidine bases in a strand of DNA

**pyruvate dehydrogenase complex** (22.2)   a complex of all the enzymes and coenzymes required for the synthesis of $CO_2$ and acetyl CoA from pyruvate

## Q

**quaternary ammonium salt** (15.1)   an amine salt with the general formula $R_4N^+A^-$ (in which R— can be an alkyl or aryl group or a hydrogen atom and $A^-$ can be any anion)

**quaternary (4°) carbon** (10.2)   a carbon atom that is bonded to four other carbon atoms

**quaternary structure (of a protein)** (18.6)   aggregation of more than one folded peptide chain to yield a functional protein

## R

**rad** (9.7)   abbreviation for *radiation absorbed dose*, the absorption of $2.4 \times 10^{-3}$ calories of energy per kilogram of absorbing tissue

**radioactivity** (9.1)   the process by which atoms emit high-energy particles or rays; the spontaneous decomposition of a nucleus to produce a different nucleus

**radiocarbon dating** (9.3)   the estimation of the age of objects through measurement of isotopic ratios of carbon

**Raoult's law** (6.4)   a law stating that the vapor pressure of a component is equal to its mole fraction times the vapor pressure of the pure component

**rate constant** (7.3)   the proportionality constant that relates the rate of a reaction and the concentration of reactants

**rate law** (7.3)   expresses the rate of a reaction in terms of reactant concentration and a rate constant

**rate of chemical reaction** (7.3)   the change in concentration of a reactant or product per unit time

**reactant** (4.3) starting material for a chemical reaction, appearing on the left side of a chemical equation

**reaction order** (7.3) the exponent of each concentration term in the rate equation

**reducing agent** (8.5) a substance that reduces, or donates electrons to, another substance; the reducing agent is itself oxidized in the process

**reducing sugar** (16.4) a sugar that can be oxidized by Benedict's or Tollens' reagents; includes all monosaccharides and most disaccharides

**reduction** (8.5, 12.4) the gain of electrons; in organic compounds it may be recognized by a gain of hydrogen or loss of oxygen

**regulatory proteins** (18: Intro) proteins that control cell functions such as metabolism and reproduction

**release factor** (20.6) a protein that binds to the termination codon in the empty A-site of the ribosome and causes the peptidyl transferase to hydrolyze the bond between the peptide and the peptidyl tRNA

**rem** (9.7) abbreviation for *roentgen equivalent for man*, the product of rad and RBE

**replication fork** (20.3) the point at which new nucleotides are added to the growing daughter DNA strand

**replication origin** (20.3) the region of a DNA molecule where DNA replication always begins

**representative element** (2.4) member of the groups of the periodic table designated as A

**resonance** (3.4) a condition that occurs when more than one valid Lewis structure can be written for a particular molecule

**restriction enzyme** (20.8) a bacterial enzyme that recognizes specific nucleotide sequences on a DNA molecule and cuts the sugar-phosphate backbone of the DNA at or near that site

**result** (1.1) the outcome of a designed experiment, often determined from individual bits of data

**reversible, competitive enzyme inhibitor** (19.10) a chemical that resembles the structure and charge distribution of the natural substrate and competes with it for the active site of an enzyme

**reversible, noncompetitive enzyme inhibitor** (19.10) a chemical that binds weakly to an amino acid R group of an enzyme and inhibits activity; when the inhibitor dissociates, the enzyme is restored to its active form

**reversible reaction** (7.4) a reaction that will proceed in either direction, reactants to products or products to reactants

**ribonucleic acid (RNA)** (20.1) single-stranded nucleic acid molecules that are composed of phosphoryl groups, ribose, and the nitrogenous bases uracil, cytosine, adenine, and guanine

**ribonucleotide** (20.1) a ribonucleoside phosphate or nucleotide composed of a nitrogenous base in β-$N$-glycosidic linkage

to the 1′ carbon of the sugar ribose and with one, two, or three phosphoryl groups esterified at the hydroxyl of the 5′ carbon of the ribose

**ribose** (16.4) a five-carbon monosaccharide that is a component of RNA and many coenzymes

**ribosomal RNA (rRNA)** (20.4) the RNA species that are structural and functional components of the small and large ribosomal subunits

**ribosome** (20.6) an organelle composed of a large and a small subunit, each of which is made up of ribosomal RNA and proteins; the platform on which translation occurs and that carries the enzymatic activity that forms peptide bonds

**RNA polymerase** (20.4) the enzyme that catalyzes the synthesis of RNA molecules using DNA as the template

**RNA splicing** (20.4) removal of portions of the primary transcript that do not encode protein sequences

**roentgen** (9.7) the dose of radiation producing $2.1 \times 10^9$ ions in 1 cm$^3$ of air at 0°C and 1 atm of pressure

## S

**saccharide** (16.1) a sugar molecule

**saponification** (14.2, 17.3) a reaction in which a soap is produced; more generally, the hydrolysis of an ester by an aqueous base

**saturated fatty acid** (17.2) a long-chain monocarboxylic acid in which each carbon of the chain is bonded to the maximum number of hydrogen atoms

**saturated hydrocarbon** (10.1) an alkane; a hydrocarbon that contains only carbon and hydrogen bonded together through carbon-hydrogen and carbon-carbon single bonds

**saturated solution** (6.1) one in which undissolved solute is in equilibrium with the solution

**scientific method** (1.1) the process of studying our surroundings that is based on experimentation

**scientific notation** (1.4) a system used to represent numbers as powers of ten

**secondary (2°) alcohol** (12.1) an alcohol with the general formula R$_2$CHOH

**secondary (2°) amine** (15.1) an amine with the general formula R$_2$NH

**secondary (2°) carbon** (10.2) a carbon atom that is bonded to two other carbon atoms

**secondary structure (of a protein)** (18.4) folding of the primary structure of a protein into an α-helix or a β-pleated sheet; folding is maintained by hydrogen bonds between the amide hydrogen and the carbonyl oxygen of the peptide bond

**selectively permeable membrane** (6.4) a membrane that restricts diffusion of some ions and molecules (based on size and charge) across the membrane

**semiconservative DNA replication** (20.3) DNA polymerase "reads" each parental strand of DNA and produces a

complementary daughter strand; thus, all newly synthesized DNA molecules consist of one parental and one daughter strand

**semipermeable membrane** (6.4) a membrane permeable to the solvent but not the solute; a material that allows the transport of certain substances from one side of the membrane to the other

**shielding** (9.6) material used to provide protection from radiation

**sickle cell anemia** (18.8) a human genetic disorder resulting from inheriting mutant hemoglobin genes from both parents

**significant figures** (1.4) all digits in a number known with certainty and the first uncertain digit

**silent mutation** (20.7) a mutation that changes the sequence of the DNA but does not alter the amino acid sequence of the protein encoded by the DNA

**single bond** (3.4) a bond in which one pair of electrons is shared by two atoms

**single-replacement reaction** (4.3) also called *substitution reaction,* one in which one atom in a molecule is displaced by another

**soap** (14.1) any of a variety of the alkali metal salts of fatty acids

**solid state** (1.2) a physical state of matter characterized by its rigidity and fixed volume and shape

**solubility** (3.5, 6.1) the amount of a substance that will dissolve in a given volume of solvent at a specified temperature

**solute** (6.1) a component of a solution that is present in lesser quantity than the solvent

**solution** (6.1) a homogeneous (uniform) mixture of two or more substances

**solvent** (6.1) the solution component that is present in the largest quantity

**specific gravity** (1.6) the ratio of the density of a substance to the density of water at 4°C or any specified temperature

**specific heat** (7.2) the quantity of heat (calories) required to raise the temperature of 1 g of a substance 1 degree Celsius

**spectroscopy** (2.3) the measurement of intensity and energy of electromagnetic radiation

**speed of light** (2.3) $2.99 \times 10^8$ m/s in a vacuum

**sphingolipid** (17.4) a phospholipid that is derived from the amino alcohol sphingosine rather than from glycerol

**sphingomyelin** (17.4) a sphingolipid found in abundance in the myelin sheath that surrounds and insulates cells of the central nervous system

**standard solution** (8.3) a solution whose concentration is accurately known

**standard temperature and pressure (STP)** (5.1) defined as 273 K and 1 atm

**stereochemical specificity** (19.5) the property of an enzyme that allows it to catalyze reactions involving only one enantiomer of the substrate

**stereochemistry** (16.3)   the study of the spatial arrangement of atoms in a molecule

**stereoisomers** (10.3, 16.3)   a pair of molecules having the same structural formula and bonding pattern but differing in the arrangement of the atoms in space

**steroid** (17.4)   a lipid derived from cholesterol and composed of one five-sided ring and three six-sided rings; the steroids include sex hormones and anti-inflammatory compounds

**structural analog** (19.10)   a chemical having a structure and charge distribution very similar to those of a natural enzyme substrate

**structural formula** (10.2)   a formula showing all of the atoms in a molecule and exhibiting all bonds as lines

**structural isomers** (10.2)   molecules having the same molecular formula but different chemical structures

**structural protein** (18: Intro)   a protein that provides mechanical support for large plants and animals

**sublevel** (2.5)   a set of equal-energy orbitals within a principal energy level

**sublimation** (5.3)   a process whereby some molecules in the solid state convert directly to the gaseous state

**substituted hydrocarbon** (10.1)   a hydrocarbon in which one or more hydrogen atoms is replaced by another atom or group of atoms

**substitution reaction** (10.5, 11.6)   a reaction that results in the replacement of one group for another

**substrate** (19.1)   the reactant in a chemical reaction that binds to an enzyme active site and is converted to product

**substrate-level phosphorylation** (21.3)   the production of ATP by the transfer of a phosphoryl group from the substrate of a reaction to ADP

**sucrose** (16.5)   a disaccharide composed of α-D-glucose and β-D-fructose in (α1 → β2) glycosidic linkage; table sugar

**supersaturated solution** (6.1)   a solution that is more concentrated than a saturated solution (Note that such a solution is not at equilibrium.)

**surface tension** (5.2)   a measure of the strength of the attractive forces at the surface of a liquid

**surfactant** (5.2)   a substance that decreases the surface tension of a liquid

**surroundings** (7.1)   the universe outside of the system

**suspension** (6.1)   a heterogeneous mixture of particles; the suspended particles are larger than those found in a colloidal suspension

**system** (7.1)   the process under study

**T**

**tautomers** (13.4) structural isomers that differ from one another in the placement of a hydrogen atom and a double bond

**temperature** (1.6)   a measure of the relative "hotness" or "coldness" of an object

**temperature optimum** (19.8)   the temperature at which an enzyme functions optimally and the rate of reaction is maximal

**terminal electron acceptor** (22.6)   the final electron acceptor in an electron transport system that removes the low-energy electrons from the system; in aerobic organisms the terminal electron acceptor is molecular oxygen

**termination codon** (20.6)   a triplet of ribonucleotides with no corresponding anticodon on a tRNA; as a result, translation will end because there is no amino acid to transfer to the peptide chain

**terpene** (17.4)   the general term for lipids that are synthesized from isoprene units; the terpenes include steroids, bile salts, lipid-soluble vitamins, and chlorophyll

**tertiary (3°) alcohol** (12.1)   an alcohol with the general formula $R_3COH$

**tertiary (3°) amine** (15.1)   an amine with the general formula $R_3N$

**tertiary (3°) carbon** (10.2)   a carbon atom that is bonded to three other carbon atoms

**tertiary structure (of a protein)** (18.5)   the globular, three-dimensional structure of a protein that results from folding the regions of secondary structure; this folding occurs spontaneously as a result of interactions of the side chains or R groups of the amino acids

**tetrahedral structure** (3.4)   a molecule consisting of four groups attached to a central atom that occupy the four corners of an imagined regular tetrahedron

**tetrose** (16.2)   a four-carbon monosaccharide

**theoretical yield** (4.5)   the maximum amount of product that can be produced from a given amount of reactant

**theory** (1.1)   a hypothesis supported by extensive testing that explains and predicts facts

**thermodynamics** (7.1)   the branch of science that deals with the relationship between energies of systems, work, and heat

**thioester** (14.4)   the product of a reaction between a thiol and a carboxylic acid

**thiol** (12.8)   an organic compound that contains a thiol group (—SH)

**titration** (8.3)   the process of adding a solution from a buret to a sample until a reaction is complete, at which time the volume is accurately measured and the concentration of the sample is calculated

**Tollens' test** (13.4)   a test reagent (silver nitrate in ammonium hydroxide) used to distinguish aldehydes and ketones; also called the Tollens' silver mirror test

**tracer** (9.5)   a radioisotope that is rapidly and selectively transmitted to the part of the body for which diagnosis is desired

**transaminase** (22.7)   an enzyme that catalyzes the transfer of an amino group from one molecule to another

**transamination** (22.7)   a reaction in which an amino group is transferred from one molecule to another

**transcription** (20.4)   the synthesis of RNA from a DNA template

**transferase** (19.1)   an enzyme that catalyzes the transfer of a functional group from one molecule to another

**transfer RNA (tRNA)** (15.4, 20.4)   small RNAs that bind to a specific amino acid at the 3′ end and mediate its addition at the appropriate site in a growing peptide chain; accomplished by recognition of the correct codon on the mRNA by the complementary anticodon on the tRNA

**transition element** (2.4)   any element located between Groups IIA (2) and IIIA (13) in the long periods of the periodic table

**transition state** (19.6)   the unstable intermediate in catalysis in which the enzyme has altered the form of the substrate so that it now shares properties of both the substrate and the product

**translation** (20.6)   the synthesis of a protein from the genetic code carried on the mRNA

**translocation** (20.6)   movement of the ribosome along the mRNA during translation

**transmembrane protein** (17.6)   a protein that is embedded within a membrane and crosses the lipid bilayer, protruding from the membrane both inside and outside the cell

**transport protein** (18: Intro)   a protein that transports materials across the cell membrane or throughout the body

**triglyceride** (17.3, 23.1)   triacylglycerol; a molecule composed of glycerol esterified to three fatty acids

**trigonal planar** (3.4)   a molecular geometry in which a central atom is bonded to three atoms that lie at the vertices of an equilateral triangle. All atoms lie within one plane and all bond angles are 120°

**trigonal pyramidal molecule** (3.4)   a nonplanar structure involving three groups bonded to a central atom in which each group is equidistant from the central atom

**triose** (16.2)   a three-carbon monosaccharide

**triple bond** (3.4)   a bond in which three pairs of electrons are shared by two atoms

**U**

**uncertainty** (1.4)   the degree of doubt in a single measurement

**unit** (1.3)   a determinate quantity (of length, time, etc.) that has been adopted as a standard of measurement

**unsaturated fatty acid** (17.2)   a long-chain monocarboxylic acid having at least one carbon-to-carbon double bond

**unsaturated hydrocarbon** (10.1, 11: Intro)   a hydrocarbon containing at least one multiple (double or triple) bond

**urea cycle** (22.8)   a cyclic series of reactions that detoxifies ammonium ions by incorporating them into urea, which is excreted from the body

**uridine triphosphate (UTP)** (21.7)   a nucleotide composed of the pyrimidine uracil, the sugar ribose, and three phosphoryl groups and that serves as a carrier of glucose-1-phosphate in glycogenesis

## V

**valence electron** (2.6)   electron in the outermost shell (principal quantum level) of an atom

**valence-shell electron-pair repulsion (VSEPR) theory** (3.4)   a model that predicts molecular geometry using the premise that electron pairs will arrange themselves as far apart as possible, to minimize electron repulsion

**van der Waals forces** (5.2)   a general term for intermolecular forces that include dipole-dipole and London dispersion forces

**vapor pressure lowering** (6.4)   the decrease in the tendency of a liquid to become a gas when a solute is added

**vapor pressure of a liquid** (5.2)   the pressure exerted by the vapor at the surface of a liquid at equilibrium

**very low density lipoprotein (VLDL)** (17.5)   a plasma lipoprotein that binds triglycerides synthesized by the liver and carries them to adipose tissue for storage

**viscosity** (5.2)   a measure of the resistance to flow of a substance at constant temperature

**vitamin** (19.7)   an organic substance that is required in the diet in small amounts; water-soluble vitamins are used in the synthesis of coenzymes required for the function of cellular enzymes; lipid-soluble vitamins are involved in calcium metabolism, vision, and blood clotting

**voltaic cell** (8.5)   an electrochemical cell that converts chemical energy into electrical energy

## W

**wax** (17.4)   a collection of lipids that are generally considered to be esters of long-chain alcohols

**weight** (1.3)   the force exerted on an object by gravity

## Z

**Zaitsev's rule** (12.4)   states that in an elimination reaction, the alkene with the greatest number of alkyl groups on the double-bonded carbon (the more highly substituted alkene) is the major product of the reaction

# Answers to Odd-Numbered Problems

## Chapter 1

**1.1** a. Physical property
b. Chemical property
c. Physical property

**1.3** a. Extensive property
b. Intensive property

**1.5** Many examples exist; two are rubbing alcohol and bottled drinking water.

**1.7** a. Three        d. Two
b. Three        e. Three
c. Four

**1.9** a. $2.4 \times 10^{-3}$        c. $2.24 \times 10^2$
b. $1.80 \times 10^{-2}$        d. $6.73 \times 10^5$

**1.11** a. 8.09
b. 5.9
c. 20.19

**1.13** a. 51
b. $8.0 \times 10^1$
c. $2.0 \times 10^{-3}$ (2 significant figures)

**1.15** a. 61.4
b. 6.17
c. $6.65 \times 10^{-2}$

**1.17** $2.49 \times 10^3$ J

**1.19** Chemistry is the study of matter, its chemical and physical properties, the chemical and physical changes it undergoes, and the energy changes that accompany those processes.
   Major subdivisions include biochemistry, organic chemistry, inorganic chemistry, analytical chemistry and physical chemistry.

**1.21** Medical practitioners, physicians, nurses, and medical technologists use therapies that contain elements of chemistry. There is a relationship between the changes that chemical substances undergo in an organism and its basic chemical makeup.

**1.23** You need the cost per gallon, the average miles per gallon, and the distance between New York City and Washington, D.C.

**1.25** According to the model, methane has one carbon atom and four hydrogen atoms per molecule. The model also provides the spatial relationship of the atoms, and the location and number of bonds that hold the unit together.

**1.27** A hypothesis is essentially an "educated guess." A theory is a hypothesis supported by extensive experimentation; it can explain and predict new facts.

**1.29** Many examples exist; one could involve the time it takes to get to work: hypothesis—taking the "back roads" is faster than choosing the crowded interstate highway. The experiment would involve driving each path several times, starting at the same time, timing each trip, and calculating an average time for each path.

**1.31** The scientific method is an organized way of doing science.

**1.33** A theory.

**1.35** Freeze the contents of two beakers, one containing pure water, and the other containing salt dissolved in water. Slowly warm each container and measure the temperature of each as they convert from the solid to the liquid state. This temperature is the melting point, hence, the freezing point. Note that the melting and freezing point of a solution are the same temperature.

**1.37** The gaseous state, the liquid state, and the solid state are the three states of matter.

**1.39** A physical property is a characteristic of a substance that can be observed without the substance undergoing a change in chemical composition.

**1.41** Chemical properties of matter include flammability and toxicity.

**1.43** A pure substance has constant composition with only a single substance whereas a mixture is composed of two or more substances.

**1.45** An intensive property is a property of matter that is independent of the quantity of the substance. A substance's boiling point is an example of an intensive property.

**1.47** Mixtures are composed of two or more substances. A homogeneous mixture has uniform composition while a heterogeneous mixture has non-uniform composition.

**1.49**
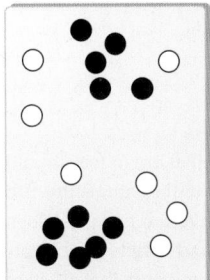

**1.51** a. Chemical reaction
b. Physical change
c. Physical change

**1.53** a. Physical property
b. Chemical property

**1.55** a. Pure substance
b. Pure substance
c. Mixture

**1.57** a. Homogeneous
b. Homogeneous
c. Homogeneous

**1.59** The state of matter represented in the diagram is the gaseous state. The diagram represents a homogeneous mixture.

**1.61** a. Surface area and mass
b. Color and shape

**1.63** Mass describes the quantity of matter in an object.

**1.65** Length is the distance between two points.

**1.67** A liter (L) is the volume occupied by 1000 g of water at 4°C.

**1.69** mm < m < km

**1.71** 23.95

**1.73** a. Precision is a measure of the agreement of replicate results.
b. Accuracy is the degree of agreement between the true value and measured value.

**1.75** a. 3        d. 4
b. 3        e. 4
c. 3        f. 3

**1.77**  a. $3.87 \times 10^{-3}$  d. 24.3
  b. $5.20 \times 10^{-2}$  e. $2.40 \times 10^2$
  c. $2.62 \times 10^{-3}$  f. 2.41
**1.79**  a. $1.5 \times 10^4$  d. 1139.42
  b. $2.41 \times 10^{-1}$  e. $7.21 \times 10^3$
  c. 5.99
**1.81**  a. $1.23 \times 10^1$  e. $9.2 \times 10^7$
  b. $5.69 \times 10^{-2}$  f. $5.280 \times 10^{-3}$
  c. $-1.527 \times 10^3$  g. $1.279 \times 10^0$
  d. $7.89 \times 10^{-7}$  h. $-5.3177 \times 10^2$
**1.83**  These measurements have high levels of precision and accuracy.
**1.85**  Unlike the English system, the metric system is systematic. Since it is composed of a set of units that are related to each other decimally, it is simpler to convert one unit to another.
**1.87**  a. k, $10^3$  c. $\mu$, $10^{-6}$
  b. c, $10^{-2}$
**1.89**  $\dfrac{1\ \text{ft}}{12\ \text{in}}$ and $\dfrac{12\ \text{in}}{1\ \text{ft}}$
**1.91**  a. 32 oz  d. $9.1 \times 10^5$ mg
  b. $1.0 \times 10^{-3}$ t  e. $9.1 \times 10^1$ dag
  c. $9.1 \times 10^2$ g
**1.93**  a. $6.6 \times 10^{-3}$ lb  d. $3.0 \times 10^2$ cg
  b. $1.1 \times 10^{-1}$ oz  e. $3.0 \times 10^3$ mg
  c. $3.0 \times 10^{-3}$ kg
**1.95**  15.0 mg
**1.97**  13.4 m$^2$
**1.99**  4 L
**1.101**  101°F
**1.103**  5 cm is shorter than 5 in.
**1.105**  5.0 µg is smaller that 5.0 mg.
**1.107**  a. First, the boundary measurements that are in feet should be converted to kilometers. Using the unit relationships provided in the textbook, feet can first be converted to yards. Then, yards can be converted to meters, and meters can be converted to kilometers. The boundary measurements that are in meters also need to be converted to kilometers. Finally, after all of the lengths have the same units (km), they can be added together to determine the circumference of the property.
  b. 0.470 km
**1.109**  Celsius, Fahrenheit, and Kelvin
**1.111**  Energy may be categorized as either kinetic energy, the energy of motion, or potential energy, the energy of position.
**1.113**  a. Extensive property  c. Intensive property
  b. Extensive property
**1.115**  a. 10.0°C  b. 283.2 K
**1.117**  a. 293.2 K  b. 68.0°F
**1.119**  $3 \times 10^4$ J
**1.121**  6.00 g/mL
**1.123**  $6.20 \times 10^2$ L
**1.125**  $1.08 \times 10^3$ g
**1.127**  teak
**1.129**  0.789
**1.131**  Lead has the lowest density and platinum has the greatest density.
**1.133**  12.6 mL

## Chapter 2

**2.1**  a. 35 protons, 35 electrons, 44 neutrons
  b. 35 protons, 35 electrons, 46 neutrons
  c. 26 protons, 26 electrons, 30 neutrons
**2.3**  Electron density is the probability that an electron will be found in a particular region of an atomic orbital.

**2.5**  a. Na, metal  c. Mn, metal
  b. Ra, metal  d. Mg, metal
**2.7**  a. Zr (zirconium)  c. Cr (chromium)
  b. 22.99 amu  d. At (astatine)
**2.9**  a. Helium, atomic number = 2, mass = 4.009 amu
  b. Fluorine, atomic number = 9, mass = 19.00 amu
  c. Manganese, atomic number = 25, mass = 54.94 amu
**2.11**  a. 8 protons, 10 electrons
  b. 12 protons, 10 electrons
  c. 26 protons, 23 electrons
**2.13**  a. $Ca^{2+}$ and Ar are isoelectronic
  b. $Sr^{2+}$ and Kr are isoelectronic
  c. $S^{2-}$ and Ar are isoelectronic
  d. $Mg^{2+}$ and Ne are isoelectronic
  e. $P^{3-}$ and Ar are isoelectronic
**2.15**  a. (Smallest) F, N, Be (largest)
  b. (Lowest) Be, N, F (highest)
  c. (Lowest) Be, N, F, (highest)
**2.17**  The number of protons in an atom
**2.19**  All three definitions of isotopes are correct.
**2.21**  Isotopes of an element have different numbers of neutrons.
**2.23**  a. Neutrons  c. Protons, neutrons
  b. Protons  d. Nucleus, negative
**2.25**  The mass number is equal to the sum of the number of protons and neutrons in an atom.
    The atomic mass is the weighted average of the masses of isotopes of an element in amu.
**2.27**  a. 56 protons, 80 neutrons, 56 electrons
  b. 84 protons, 125 neutrons, 84 electrons
**2.29**  $^{19}_{9}$F
**2.31**  All isotopes of Rn have 86 protons.
**2.33**  a. 34  b. 46
**2.35**  a. $^{1}_{1}$H  b. $^{14}_{6}$C
**2.37**  63.55 amu
**2.39**  • All matter consists of tiny particles called atoms.
  • Atoms cannot be created, divided, destroyed, or converted to any other type of atom.
  • All atoms of a particular element have identical properties.
  • Atoms of different elements have different properties.
  • Atoms combine in simple whole-number ratios.
  • Chemical change involves joining, separating, or rearranging atoms.
**2.41**  a. Chadwick demonstrated the existence of the neutron.
  b. Goldstein identified positive charge in the atom.
**2.43**  a. Dalton—developed the Law of Multiple Proportions; determined the relative atomic weights of the elements known at that time; developed the first scientific atomic theory.
  b. Crookes—developed the cathode ray tube and discovered "cathode rays"; characterized electron properties.
**2.45**  Our understanding of the nucleus is based on the gold foil experiment performed by Geiger and interpreted by Rutherford. In this experiment, Geiger bombarded a piece of gold foil with alpha particles, and observed that some alpha particles passed straight through the foil, others were deflected and some simply bounced back. This led Rutherford to propose that the atom consisted of a small, dense nucleus (alpha particles bounced back), surrounded by a cloud of electrons (some alpha particles were deflected). The size of the nucleus is small when compared to the volume of the atom (alpha particles were able to pass through the foil).
**2.47**  Electrons surround the nucleus in a diffuse region. Electrons are negatively charged, and electrons are very low in mass in contrast to protons and neutrons.

**2.49** It was believed that protons and electrons were uniformly distributed throughout the atom.

**2.51** Electromagnetic radiation, or light, travels in waves from its source. Each wavelength of light has its own characteristic energy.

**2.53** False.

**2.55** Infrared radiation has greater energy than microwave radiation.

**2.57** When electrical energy is applied to a sample of hydrogen gas, the electrons in lower orbits are "excited" to higher orbits. As they fall back down into lower orbits, they release an amount of energy equal to the amount of energy they absorbed to jump to the higher orbit. This energy may be released in the form of light and the wavelength is proportional to the energy difference. This produces a line spectrum that is characteristic of hydrogen.

**2.59** Spectroscopy is the measurement of intensity and energy of electromagnetic radiation.

**2.61** According to Bohr, Planck, and others, electrons exist only in certain allowed regions, quantum levels, outside of the nucleus.

**2.63** • Electrons are found in orbits at discrete distances from the nucleus.
• The orbits are quantized—they are of discrete energies.
• Electrons can only be found in these orbits, never in between (they are able to jump instantaneously from orbit to orbit).
• Electrons can undergo transitions—if an electron absorbs energy, it will jump to a higher orbit; when the electron falls back to a lower orbit, it will release energy.

**2.65** Bohr's atomic model was the first to successfully account for electronic properties of atoms, specifically, the interaction of atoms and light (spectroscopy).

**2.67** **a.** Sodium   **c.** Magnesium   **b.** Potassium   **d.** Boron

**2.69** Group IA (or 1) is known collectively as the alkali metals and consists of lithium, sodium, potassium, rubidium, cesium, and francium.

**2.71** Group VIIA (or 17) is known collectively as the halogens and consists of fluorine, chlorine, bromine, iodine, and astatine.

**2.73** **a.** Na, Ni, Al   **c.** Ar   **b.** Na, Al

**2.75**

According to periodic law, the physical and chemical properties of the elements are periodic functions of their atomic numbers. As atomic number increases, the melting point decreases.

**2.77** A principal energy level is designated $n = 1, 2, 3$, and so forth. It is similar to Bohr's orbit in concept. A sublevel is a part of a principal energy level and is designated $s, p, d,$ and $f$.

**2.79** See Figure 2.11 for a sketch of the $s$ atomic orbital. The $s$ orbital represents the probability of finding an electron in a region of space surrounding the nucleus.

**2.81** $2\,e^-$ for $n = 1$
$8\,e^-$ for $n = 2$
$18\,e^-$ for $n = 3$

**2.83** According to the Pauli exclusion principle, each orbital can hold up to two electrons with the electrons spinning in opposite directions (paired). Therefore, since the $d$ sublevel has five orbitals, it can contain a maximum of ten electrons.

**2.85** **a.** $1s^2\,2s^2\,2p^6\,3s^2\,3p^1$
**b.** $1s^2\,2s^2\,2p^6\,3s^1$
**c.** $1s^2\,2s^2\,2p^6\,3s^2\,3p^6\,4s^2\,3d^1$

**2.87** **a.** $1s^2 2s^2 2p^1$

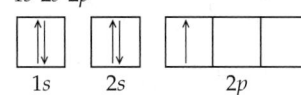

**b.** $1s^2 2s^2 2p^6 3s^2 3p^4$

**c.** $1s^2 2s^2 2p^6 3s^2 3p^6$

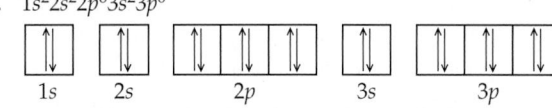

**2.89** **a.** Not possible; $n = 1$ level can have only $s$-level orbitals.
**b.** Possible; the electron configuration that is shown represents the carbon atom.
**c.** Not possible; cannot have two identical orbitals ($2s^2$).
**d.** Not possible; cannot have three electrons in an $s$ orbital ($2s^3$)

**2.91** Diagram A is incorrect.

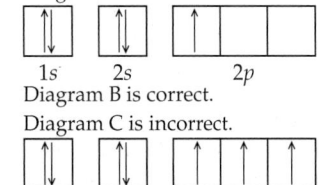

Diagram B is correct.
Diagram C is incorrect.

**2.93** **a.** [Kr] $5s^2\,4d^2$
**b.** [Ar] $4s^2\,3d^{10}\,4p^5$
**c.** [Ar] $4s^1$

**2.95** The total number of electrons in an atom would include all of the electrons in the atom. In a neutral atom, the number of electrons is equal to the number of protons. Valence electrons are the outermost electrons in an atom. For a representative element, the maximum number of valence electrons is eight.

**2.97** The octet rule states that atoms will usually react in such a way as to obtain a noble gas configuration.

**2.99** Metals tend to lose electrons to become positively charged cations.

**2.101**

| Atom | Total electrons | Valence electrons | Principal energy level number |
|---|---|---|---|
| **a.** H | 1 | 1 | 1 |
| **b.** Na | 11 | 1 | 3 |
| **c.** B | 5 | 3 | 2 |
| **d.** F | 9 | 7 | 2 |
| **e.** Ne | 10 | 8 | 2 |
| **f.** He | 2 | 2 | 1 |

**2.103** **a.** 17 protons, 18 electrons
**b.** 20 protons, 18 electrons
**c.** 26 protons, 24 electrons

**2.105** **a.** Two   **c.** One   **b.** One   **d.** Two

**2.107** **a.** $Li^+$   **d.** $Br^-$   **b.** $O^{2-}$   **e.** $S^{2-}$   **c.** $Ca^{2+}$   **f.** $Al^{3+}$

**2.109** **a.** Isoelectronic    **b.** Isoelectronic
**2.111** **a.** $1s^2\,2s^2\,2p^6\,3s^2\,3p^6$    **b.** $1s^2\,2s^2\,2p^6$
**2.113** Atomic size decreases from left to right across a period in the periodic table.
**2.115** Ionization energy is the energy required to remove an electron from an isolated atom.
**2.117** Electron affinity is the energy change when a single electron is added to a neutral isolated atom.
**2.119** **a.** (Smallest) F, O, N (Largest)
   **b.** (Smallest) Li, K, Cs (Largest)
   **c.** (Smallest) Cl, Br, I (Largest)
**2.121** **a.** (Smallest) N, O, F (Largest)
   **b.** (Smallest) Cs, K, Li (Largest)
   **c.** (Smallest) I, Br, Cl (Largest)
**2.123** **a.** A positive ion is always smaller than its parent atom because the positive charge of the nucleus is shared among fewer electrons in the ion. As a result, each electron is pulled closer to the nucleus and the volume of the ion decreases.
   **b.** A negative ion is always larger than its parent atom because the positive charge in the nucleus is shared among a larger number of electrons in the ion. Each electron moves farther from the nucleus and the volume of the ion increases.
**2.125** $Cl^-$ is larger because it has a smaller nuclear (positive) charge.

# Chapter 3

**3.1** **a.** Potassium cyanide    **c.** Magnesium acetate
   **b.** Magnesium sulfide
**3.3** **a.** The bonded nuclei are closer together when a double bond exists, in comparison to a single bond.
   **b.** The bond strength increases as the bond order increases. Therefore, a double bond is stronger than a single bond. The distance of separation and bond strength are inversely related.
**3.5** **a.**
   **b.**
**3.7** **a.** The bond is polar.    **c.** The bond is nonpolar.

   **b.** The bond is polar.    **d.** The bond is polar.

**3.9** **a.** Nonpolar    **c.** Polar
   **b.** Polar    **d.** Nonpolar
**3.11** **a.** $H_2O$    **c.** $NH_3$
   **b.** CO    **d.** ICl
**3.13** Covalent bonding involves a sharing of electrons between atoms to complete the octet of electrons for each atom participating in the bond. Ionic bonding involves a transfer of one or more electrons from one atom to another. An ionic bond is the electrostatic force between the resulting anion and a cation.
**3.15** Electronegativity values increase as we proceed left to right and bottom to top of the table. The most electronegative elements are located in the upper right corner of the periodic table.
**3.17** **a.** H ·    **c.** · Ċ ·
   **b.** He :    **d.** · N̈ ·

**3.19** **a.** $Li^+$    **b.** $Mg^{2+}$    **c.** $\left[:\ddot{C}l:\right]^-$    **d.** $\left[:\ddot{\underset{..}{P}}:\right]^{3-}$
**3.21** **a.** Polar covalent    **c.** Nonpolar covalent
   **b.** Polar covalent    **d.** Polar covalent
**3.23** **a.** $Li\cdot\,+\,:\ddot{Br}\cdot\,\longrightarrow\,Li^+ +\left[:\ddot{Br}:\right]^-$
   **b.** $\cdot Mg\cdot\,+\,2:\ddot{C}l\cdot\,\longrightarrow\,Mg^{2+}+2\left[:\ddot{C}l:\right]^-$
**3.25** **a.** $:\ddot{S}\cdot\,+\,2H\cdot\,\longrightarrow\,$ :S—H with H below
   **b.** $\cdot\ddot{P}\cdot\,+\,3H\cdot\,\longrightarrow\,$ H—P—H with H below
**3.27** He has two valence electrons (electron configuration $1s^2$) and a complete N = 1 level. It has a stable electron configuration, with no tendency to gain or lose electrons, and satisfies the octet rule ($2\,e^-$ for period 1). Hence, it is nonreactive.
   He:
**3.29** **a.** Sodium ion
   **b.** Copper(I) ion (or cuprous ion)
   **c.** Magnesium ion
**3.31** **a.** Sulfide ion    **c.** Carbonate ion
   **b.** Chloride ion
**3.33** **a.** $K^+$    **b.** $Br^-$
**3.35** **a.** $SO_4^{2-}$    **b.** $NO_3^-$
**3.37** **a.** Magnesium chloride    **b.** Aluminum chloride
**3.39** **a.** Nitrogen dioxide    **b.** Selenium trioxide
**3.41** **a.** Sulfur dioxide    **b.** Sulfur trioxide
**3.43** **a.** NaCl    **b.** $MgBr_2$
**3.45** **a.** AgCN    **b.** $NH_4Cl$
**3.47** **a.** CuO    **b.** $Fe_2O_3$
**3.49** **a.** $Al_2O_3$    **b.** $Li_2S$
**3.51** **a.** $SiO_2$    **b.** $SO_2$
**3.53** **a.** $NaNO_3$    **b.** $Mg(NO_3)_2$
**3.55** **a.** $NH_4I$    **b.** $(NH_4)_2SO_4$
**3.57** Ionic solid state compounds exist in regular, repeating, three-dimensional structures; the crystal lattice. The crystal lattice is made up of positive and negative ions. Solid state covalent compounds are made up of molecules which may be arranged in a regular crystalline pattern or in an irregular (amorphous) structure.
**3.59** The boiling points of ionic solids are generally much higher than those of covalent solids.
**3.61** KCl would be expected to exist as a solid at room temperature; it is an ionic compound, and ionic compounds are characterized by high melting points.
**3.63** Water will have a higher boiling point. Water is a polar molecule with strong intermolecular attractive forces, whereas carbon tetrachloride is a nonpolar molecule with weak intermolecular attractive forces. More energy, hence, a higher temperature is required to overcome the attractive forces among the water molecules.
**3.65** The least electronegative atom will usually be the central atom. The central atom is often the element in the compound for which there is only one atom.
**3.67** For polyatomic cations, subtract one electron for each unit of positive charge.
**3.69** Single bond < double bond < triple bond
   (Lowest energy)                (Highest energy)
**3.71** $C_5H_{12}$
**3.73** Resonance can occur when more than one valid Lewis structure can be written for a molecule. Each individual structure which can be drawn is a resonance form. The true nature of the structure

for the molecule is the resonance hybrid, which consists of the "average" of the resonance forms.

**3.75**  120°

**3.77**  True.

**3.79**  **a.** $:\ddot{C}l-\ddot{N}-\ddot{C}l:$  **c.** $:\ddot{S}=C=\ddot{S}:$
$\qquad\qquad\quad |$
$\qquad\qquad\; :\ddot{C}l:$

**b.**  $H-\overset{H}{\underset{H}{\overset{|}{C}}}-\ddot{O}-H$

**3.81**  **a.** $:\ddot{C}l-\ddot{N}-\ddot{C}l:$   **c.** $:\ddot{S}=C=\ddot{S}:$
$\qquad\qquad\quad|$
$\qquad\qquad :\ddot{C}l:$       Linear
$\qquad$ Trigonal       nonpolar
$\qquad$ pyramidal      not water soluble
$\qquad$ polar
$\qquad$ water soluble

**b.**  $H-\overset{H}{\underset{H}{\overset{|}{C}}}-\ddot{O}-H$

Tetrahedral around C
bent around O
polar
water soluble

**3.83**  $[:N\equiv O:]^+$

**3.85**  $[:\ddot{O}-H]^-$

**3.87**

$$\left[\begin{array}{c} H\;\;:\ddot{O}: \\ | \quad\; || \\ H-C-C-\ddot{O}: \\ | \\ H \end{array}\right]^- \longleftrightarrow \left[\begin{array}{c} H\;\;:\ddot{O}: \\ | \quad\; | \\ H-C-C=O \\ | \\ H \end{array}\right]^-$$

**3.89**

$$H-\overset{H}{\underset{H}{\overset{|}{C}}}-\overset{H}{\underset{H}{\overset{|}{C}}}-\ddot{O}-H$$

**3.91**

$$H-\overset{H}{\underset{H}{\overset{|}{C}}}-\overset{\overset{\displaystyle\ddot{O}}{||}}{C}-\overset{H}{\underset{H}{\overset{|}{C}}}-H$$

**3.93**  **a.** Bent

$:\ddot{O}-\ddot{S}=\ddot{O}$

**b.** Trigonal planar

$$\overset{\displaystyle\ddot{O}}{\underset{\ddot{O}\;\;\;\;\ddot{O}}{\overset{||}{S}}}$$

**3.95**  **a.** Polar
$\qquad$ **b.** Nonpolar

**3.97**  **a.** $:C\equiv O:$   **c.** $\ddot{O}=C=\ddot{O}$

**b.**  $\overset{\displaystyle\ddot{O}}{\underset{H\qquad H}{}}$

**3.99**  **a.** $CO_2$
$\qquad$ **c.** $CF_4$

**3.101**  $:\ddot{C}l-Be-\ddot{C}l:$

**3.103**

$$\begin{array}{c} :\ddot{F}: \\ :\ddot{F}\diagdown \;|\; \diagup \ddot{F}: \\ Se \\ :\ddot{F}\diagup \;|\; \diagdown \ddot{F}: \\ :\ddot{F}: \end{array}$$

**3.105**  A molecule containing no polar bonds *must* be nonpolar. A molecule containing polar bonds may or may not itself be polar. It depends upon the number and arrangement of the bonds.

**3.107**  Polar compounds have strong intermolecular attractive forces. Higher temperatures are needed to overcome these forces and convert the solid to a liquid; hence, we predict higher melting points for polar compounds when compared to nonpolar compounds.

**3.109**  Yes

**3.111**  **a.** $NH_3$   **c.** NaCl
$\qquad$ **b.** $CF_4$

## Chapter 4

**4.1**  $3.33 \times 10^{-10}$ g Hg

**4.3**  Formula mass = 194.20 amu
$\qquad$ Molar mass = 194.20 g/mol

**4.5**  **a.** DR   **c.** DR
$\qquad$ **b.** SR   **d.** D

**4.7**  $Cu^{2+}(aq) + S^{2-}(aq) \rightarrow CuS(s)$

**4.9**  **a.** 47.9 g $NO_2$   **b.** 52.2%

**4.11**  Examples of other packaging units include a *ream* of paper (500 sheets of paper), a six-pack of soft drinks, a case of canned goods (24 cans), to name a few.

**4.13**  **a.** 28.09 g   **b.** 107.9 g

**4.15**  39.95 g

**4.17**  $6.0 \times 10^{19}$ carbon atoms

**4.19**  $1.7 \times 10^{-22}$ mol As

**4.21**  40.36 g Ne

**4.23**  4.00 g/mol

**4.25**  **a.** 5.00 mol He   **c.** $4.2 \times 10^{-2}$ mol $Cl_2$
$\qquad$ **b.** 1.7 mol Na

**4.27**  $1.62 \times 10^3$ g Ag

**4.29**  $8.37 \times 10^{22}$ Ag atoms

**4.31**  A molecule is a single unit composed of atoms joined by covalent bonds. An ion pair is composed of positive and negatively charged ions joined by electrostatic attraction, the ionic bond. The ion pairs, unlike the molecule, do not form single units; the electrostatic charge is directed to other ions in a crystal lattice as well.

**4.33**  **a.** 58.44 g/mol   **c.** 357.49 g/mol
$\qquad$ **b.** 142.04 g/mol

**4.35**  32.00 g/mol $O_2$

**4.37**  249.70 g/mol

**4.39**  **a.** 0.257 mol NaCl   **b.** 0.106 mol $Na_2SO_4$

**4.41**  **a.** 18.02 g $H_2O$   **b.** 116.9 g NaCl

**4.43**  **a.** 40.0 g He   **b.** $2.02 \times 10^2$ g $H_2$

**4.45**  **a.** 2.43 g Mg   **b.** 10.0 g $CaCO_3$

**4.47**  **a.** 4.00 g NaOH   **b.** 9.81 g $H_2SO_4$

**4.49**  **a.** 0.420 mol KBr   **b.** 0.415 mol $MgSO_4$

**4.51**  **a.** $6.57 \times 10^{-1}$ mol $CS_2$   **b.** $2.14 \times 10^{-1}$ mol $Al_2(CO_3)_3$

**4.53**  The ultimate basis for a correct chemical equation is the law of conservation of mass. No mass may be gained or lost in a chemical reaction, and the chemical equation must reflect this fact.

**4.55**  The subscript tells us the number of atoms or ions contained in one unit of the compound.

**4.57**  Heat is necessary for the reaction to occur.

**4.59** Yes.

**4.61** If we change the subscript we change the identity of the compound.

**4.63** A reactant is the starting material for a chemical reaction.

**4.65** A product is the chemical species that results from a chemical reaction.

**4.67** **a.** $2C_2H_6(g) + 7O_2(g) \rightarrow 4CO_2(g) + 6H_2O(g)$
**b.** $6K_2O(s) + P_4O_{10}(s) \rightarrow 4K_3PO_4(s)$
**c.** $MgBr_2(aq) + H_2SO_4(aq) \rightarrow 2HBr(g) + MgSO_4(aq)$

**4.69** **a.** $Ca(s) + F_2(g) \rightarrow CaF_2(s)$
**b.** $2Mg(s) + O_2(g) \rightarrow 2MgO(s)$
**c.** $3H_2(g) + N_2(g) \rightarrow 2NH_3(g)$

**4.71** a. $2C_4H_{10}(g) + 13O_2(g) \rightarrow 10H_2O(g) + 8CO_2(g)$
**b.** $Au_2S_3(s) + 3H_2(g) \rightarrow 2Au(s) + 3H_2S(g)$
**c.** $Al(OH)_3(s) + 3HCl(aq) \rightarrow AlCl_3(aq) + 3H_2O(l)$
**d.** $(NH_4)_2Cr_2O_7(s) \rightarrow Cr_2O_3(s) + N_2(g) + 4H_2O(g)$
**e.** $C_2H_5OH(l) + 3O_2(g) \rightarrow 2CO_2(g) + 3H_2O(g)$

**4.73** **a.** $N_2(g) + 3H_2(g) \rightarrow 2NH_3(g)$
**b.** $HCl(aq) + NaOH(aq) \rightarrow NaCl(aq) + H_2O(l)$

**4.75** **a.** $C_6H_{12}O_6(s) + 6O_2(g) \rightarrow 6H_2O(l) + 6CO_2(g)$
**b.** $Na_2CO_3(s) \xrightarrow{\Delta} Na_2O(s) + CO_2(g)$

**4.77** Yes. $CaCO_3$

**4.79** $Ag^+(aq) + Br^-(aq) \rightarrow AgBr(s)$

**4.81** Conservation of mass

**4.83** Changing subscripts changes the identity of the compound. Changing coefficients changes the relative number of moles of compound.

**4.85** 27.7 g $B_2H_6$

**4.87** 104 g $CrCl_3$

**4.89** **a.** $N_2(g) + 3H_2(g) \rightarrow 2NH_3(g)$
**b.** Three moles of $H_2$ will react with one mole of $N_2$
**c.** One mole of $N_2$ will produce two moles of the product $NH_3$
**d.** 1.50 mol $H_2$
**e.** 17.0 g $NH_3$

**4.91** **a.** 149.21 g/mol      **c.** 32.00 g O
**b.** $1.20 \times 10^{24}$ O atoms   **d.** 10.7 g O

**4.93** 7.39 g $O_2$

**4.95** $6.77 \times 10^4$ g $CO_2$

**4.97** 70.6 g $C_{10}H_{22}$

**4.99** $9.13 \times 10^2$ g $N_2$

**4.101** 92.6%

**4.103** $6.85 \times 10^2$ g $N_2$

## Chapter 5

**5.1** **a.** 0.954 atm
**b.** 0.382 atm
**c.** 0.730 atm

**5.3** 2.91 atm

**5.5** Molecules with complex structures, which do not "slide" smoothly past each other, and polar molecules tend to have higher viscosities.

**5.7** Evaporation is the conversion of a liquid to a gas at a temperature lower than the boiling point of the liquid. Condensation is the conversion of a gas to a liquid at a temperature lower than the boiling point of the liquid.

**5.9** $CO_2 < CH_3Cl < CH_3OH$; Only $CH_3OH$ exhibits London dispersion forces, dipole-dipole interactions, and hydrogen bonding. Hence, $CH_3OH$ has the strongest intermolecular forces and therefore, the highest boiling point.

**5.11** **a.** Ionic solids generally have high melting points and a tendency to be hard and brittle.
**b.** Table salt (NaCl) and calcium chloride ($CaCl_2$)

**5.13** In all cases, gas particles are much farther apart than similar particles in the liquid or solid state. In most cases, particles in the liquid state are, on average, farther apart than those in the solid state. Water is the exception; liquid water's molecules are closer together than they are in the solid state.

**5.15** Pressure is a force/unit area. Gas particles are in continuous, random motion. Collisions with the walls of the container result in a force (mass $\times$ acceleration) on the walls of the container. The sum of these collision forces constitutes the pressure exerted by the gas.

**5.17** Gases are easily compressed simply because there is a great deal of space between particles; they can be pushed closer together (compressed) because the space is available.

**5.19** Gas particles are in continuous, random motion. They are free (minimal attractive forces between particles) to roam, up to the boundary of their container.

**5.21** Gases exhibit more ideal behavior at low pressures. At low pressures, gas particles are more widely separated and therefore the attractive forces between particles are less. The ideal gas model assumes negligible attractive forces between gas particles.

**5.23** The kinetic molecular theory states that the average kinetic energy of the gas particles increases as the temperature increases. Kinetic energy is proportional to $(\text{velocity})^2$. Therefore, as the temperature increases the gas particle velocity increases and the rate of mixing increases as well.

**5.25** The volume of the balloon is directly proportional to the pressure the gas exerts on the inside surface of the balloon. As the balloon cools, its pressure drops, and the balloon contracts. (Recall that the speed, hence the force exerted by the molecules, decreases as the temperature decreases.)

**5.27** Boyle's law states that the volume of a gas varies inversely with the gas pressure if the temperature and the number of moles of gas are held constant.

**5.29** Volume will decrease according to Boyle's law. Volume is inversely proportional to the pressure exerted on the gas.

**5.31** 1 atm

**5.33** 5 L-atm

**5.35** 5.23 atm

**5.37** Charles's law states that the volume of a gas varies directly with the absolute temperature if pressure and number of moles of gas are constant.

**5.39** The Kelvin scale is the only scale that is directly proportional to molecular motion, and it is this motion that determines the physical properties of gases.

**5.41** No. The volume is proportional to the temperature in K, not Celsius.

**5.43** 0.96 L

**5.45** 1.51 L

**5.47** 120°F

**5.49** • Volume and temperature are *directly* proportional; increasing T *increases* V.
• Volume and pressure are *inversely* proportional; decreasing P *increases* V.
Therefore, both variables work together to *increase* the volume.

**5.51** $V_f = \dfrac{P_i V_i T_f}{P_f T_i}$

**5.53** $1.82 \times 10^{-2}$ L

**5.55** 1.5 atm

**5.57** Avogadro's law states that equal volumes of any ideal gas contain the same number of moles if measured at constant temperature and pressure.

**5.59** 6.00 L

**5.61** No. One mole of an ideal gas will occupy exactly 22.4 L; however, there is no completely ideal gas and careful measurement will show a different volume.

**5.63** Standard temperature is 273 K.

**5.65** 0.80 mol

**5.67** 22.4 L

**5.69** 1.25 g/L

**5.71** 0.276 mol

**5.73** $5.94 \times 10^{-2}$ L

**5.75** 22.4 L

**5.77** $9.08 \times 10^{3}$ L

**5.79** 172°C

**5.81** Dalton's law states that the total pressure of a mixture of gases is the sum of the partial pressures of the component gases.

**5.83** 0.74 atm

**5.85** 0.29 atm

**5.87** Intermolecular forces in liquids are considerably stronger than intermolecular forces in gases. Particles are, on average, much closer together in liquids and the strength of attraction decreases as the distance of separation increases.

**5.89** The vapor pressure of a liquid increases as the temperature of the liquid increases.

**5.91** Viscosity is the resistance to flow caused by intermolecular attractive forces. Complex molecules may become entangled and not slide smoothly across one another.

**5.93** All molecules exhibit London forces. This is because electrons are in constant motion in all molecules.

**5.95** Only methanol exhibits hydrogen bonding. Methanol has an oxygen atom bonded to a hydrogen atom, a necessary condition for hydrogen bonding.

**5.97** Propylene glycol

**5.99** Solids are essentially incompressible because the average distance of separation among particles in the solid state is small. There is literally no space for the particles to crowd closer together.

**5.101** **a.** High melting temperature, brittle
**b.** High melting temperature, hard

**5.103** Beryllium. Metallic solids are good electrical conductors. Carbon forms covalent solids that are poor electrical conductors.

**5.105** Mercury. Mercury is a liquid at room temperature, whereas chromium is a solid at room temperature. Liquids have higher vapor pressures than solids.

## Chapter 6

**6.1** A chemical analysis must be performed in order to determine the identity of all components, a qualitative analysis. If only one component is found, it is a pure substance; two or more components indicates a true solution.

**6.3** After the container of soft drink is opened, $CO_2$ diffuses into the surrounding atmosphere; consequently the partial pressure of $CO_2$ over the soft drink decreases and the equilibrium

$$CO_2(g) \rightleftharpoons CO_2(aq)$$

shifts to the left, lowering the concentration of $CO_2$ in the soft drink.

**6.5** 0.19 $M$

**6.7** 0.125 mol HCl

**6.9** Pure water

**6.11** $4.0 \times 10^{-2}$ osmol KCl, $3 \times 10^{-1}$ osmol glucose

**6.13** 0.110 mol/L

**6.15** **a.** Electrolyte          **c.** Electrolyte
**b.** Nonelectrolyte

**6.17** A true solution contains more than one substance with the particles having a diameter less than $1 \times 10^{-9}$ m. Particles with

diameters of $1 \times 10^{-9}$ m to $2 \times 10^{-7}$ m are colloids. A suspension contains particles much larger than $2 \times 10^{-7}$ m.

**6.19** Stream temperature is much lower in early spring than mid-August. Henry's law predicts that the concentration of dissolved oxygen in the stream is greater at lower water temperatures. Trout require oxygen and thrive in early spring.

**6.21** A solution is described as clear if it efficiently transmits light, showing no evidence of suspended particles. The solution does not have to be colorless to meet these conditions.

**6.23** **a.** 2.00% NaCl          **b.** 6.60% $C_6H_{12}O_6$

**6.25** **a.** 5.00% ethanol          **b.** 10.0% ethanol

**6.27** **a.** 21.0% NaCl          **b.** 3.75% NaCl

**6.29** **a.** 2.25 g NaCl          **b.** 3.13 g $NaC_2H_3O_2$

**6.31** 19.5% $KNO_3$

**6.33** 1.00 g sugar

**6.35** 0.04% (m/m) solution is more concentrated

**6.37** $2.0 \times 10^{-3}$ ppt

**6.39** Laboratory managers often purchase concentrated solutions for practical reasons such as economy and conservation of storage space.

**6.41** 0.50 $M$

**6.43** **a.** 1.46 g NaCl          **b.** 9.00 g $C_6H_{12}O_6$

**6.45** 0.266 L

**6.47** 50.0 mL

**6.49** 20.0 $M$

**6.51** 0.900 $M$

**6.53** 158 g glucose

**6.55** $5.00 \times 10^{-2}$ $M$

**6.57** A colligative property is a solution property that depends on the concentration of solute particles rather than the identity of the particles.

**6.59** Salt is an ionic substance that dissociates in water to produce positive and negative ions. These ions (or particles) lower the freezing point of water. If the concentration of salt particles is large, the freezing point may be depressed below the surrounding temperature, and the ice would melt.

**6.61** Raoult's law states that when a solute is added to a solvent, the vapor pressure of the solvent decreases in proportion to the concentration of the solute.

**6.63** One mole of $CaCl_2$ produces three moles of particles in solution whereas one mole of NaCl produces two moles of particles in solution. Therefore, a one molar $CaCl_2$ solution contains a greater number of particles than a one molar NaCl solution and will produce a greater freezing-point depression.

**6.65** **a.** −2.79°C          **b.** −5.58°C

**6.67** Freezing Temperature for NaCl Solution = −1.86°C
Freezing Temperature for Sucrose Solution = −0.93°C

**6.69** Sucrose

**6.71** 24 atm

**6.73** A → B

**6.75** No net flow

**6.77** Hypertonic

**6.79** Hypotonic

**6.81** $1.0 \times 10^{-3}$ osmol

**6.83** Water is often termed the "universal solvent" because it is a polar molecule and will dissolve, at least to some extent, most ionic and polar covalent compounds. The majority of our body mass is water and this water is an important part of the nutrient transport system due to its solvent properties. This is true in other animals and plants as well. Because of its ability to hydrogen bond, water has a high boiling point and a low vapor pressure. Also, water is abundant and easily purified.

**6.85**

H—N : δ⁻ δ⁺ H
(with H's around N and O: δ⁻ with H)

**6.87**  The number of particles in solution is dependent on the degree of dissociation.

**6.89**  In dialysis, sodium ions move from a region of high concentration to a region of low concentration. If we wish to remove (transport) sodium ions from the blood, they can move to a region of lower concentration, the dialysis solution.

**6.91**  The shelf life is a function of the stability of the ammonia-water solution. The ammonia can react with the water to convert to the extremely soluble and stable ammonium ion. Also, ammonia and water are polar molecules. Polar interactions, particularly hydrogen bonding, are strong and contribute to the long-term solution stability.

**6.93**

$\delta^+$H, O $\delta^-$ Na$^+$, $\delta^+$H

**6.95**  Polar; like dissolves like ($H_2O$ is polar)

**6.97**  Elevated concentrations of sodium ion in the blood may cause confusion, stupor, or coma.

**6.99**  Elevated concentrations of sodium ion in the blood may occur whenever large amounts of water are lost. Diarrhea, diabetes, and certain high-protein diets are particularly problematic.

**6.101**  0.10 eq/L

**6.103**  **a.** 0.154 mol/L        **b.** 0.154 mol/L

**6.105**  $4.0 \times 10^{-2}$ mol/L

## Chapter 7

**7.1**  **a.** Exothermic        **b.** Exothermic

**7.3**  He(g). Gases have a greater degree of disorder than solids.

**7.5**  $\Delta G = (+) - T(-)$
$\Delta G$ must always be positive. A positive value for $\Delta G$ indicates a nonspontaneous process.

**7.7**  $2.7 \times 10^3$ J

**7.9**  Heat energy produced by the friction of striking the match provides the activation energy necessary for this combustion process.

**7.11**  If the enzyme catalyzed a process needed to sustain life, the substance interfering with that enzyme would be classified as a poison.

**7.13**  At rush hour, approximately the same number of passengers enter and exit the train at any given stop. Throughout the trip, the number of passengers on the train may be essentially unchanged, but the identity of the individual passengers is continually changing.
At a busy restaurant during lunchtime, approximately the same number of people will enter and exit the restaurant at any given moment. Throughout lunchtime, the number of people in the restaurant may be essentially unchanged, but the identity of the individuals in the restaurant is continually changing.

**7.15**  Measure the concentrations of products and reactants at a series of times until no further concentration change is observed.

**7.17**  Product formation

**7.19**  Joule

**7.21**  An exothermic reaction is one in which energy is released during chemical change.

**7.23**  A fuel must release heat in the combustion (oxidation) process.

**7.25**  The temperature of the water (or solution) is measured in a calorimeter. If the reaction being studied is exothermic, released energy heats the water and the temperature increases. In an endothermic reaction, heat flows from the water to the reaction and the water temperature decreases.

**7.27**  Double-walled containers, used in calorimeters, provide a small airspace between the part of the calorimeter (inside wall) containing the sample solution and the outside wall, contacting the surroundings. This gap makes heat transfer more difficult.

**7.29**  Free energy is the combined contribution of entropy and enthalpy for a chemical reaction.

**7.31**  The first law of thermodynamics, the law of conservation of energy, states that the energy of the universe is constant.

**7.33**  Enthalpy is a measure of heat energy.

**7.35**  $1.20 \times 10^3$ cal

**7.37**  $5.02 \times 10^3$ J

**7.39**  **a.** Entropy increases. Conversion of a solid to a liquid results in an increase in disorder of the substance. Solids retain their shape while liquids will flow and their shapes are determined by their container.
**b.** Entropy increases. Conversion of a liquid to a gas results in an increase in disorder of the substance. Gas paricles move randomly with very weak interactions between particles, much weaker than those interactions in the liquid state.

**7.41**  $\Delta G = (-) - T(+)$
$\Delta G$ must always be negative and the process is always spontaneous.

**7.43**  Isopropyl alcohol quickly evaporates (liquid → gas) after being applied to the skin. Conversion of a liquid to a gas requires heat energy. The heat energy is supplied by the skin. When this heat is lost, the skin temperature drops.

**7.45**  Decomposition of leaves and twigs to produce soil.

**7.47**  The activated complex is the arrangement of reactants in an unstable transition state as a chemical reaction proceeds. The activated complex must form in order to convert reactants to products.

**7.49**  The rate of a reaction is the change in concentration of a reactant or product per unit time. The rate constant is the proportionality constant that relates rate and concentration. The order is the exponent of each concentration term in the rate equation.

**7.51**  Increase

**7.53**  A catalyst increases the rate of a reaction without itself undergoing change.

**7.55**

**Non-catalyzed reaction
Higher activation energy**

**Catalyzed reaction
Lower activation energy**

**7.57**  The rate of the reaction increases four-fold.

**7.59**  An increase in concentration of reactants means that there are more molecules in a certain volume. The probability of collision is enhanced because they travel a shorter distance before meeting another molecule. The rate is proportional to the number of collisions per unit time.

**7.61** Rate = $k[N_2O_4]$

**7.63** A catalyst speeds up a chemical reaction by facilitating the formation of the activated complex, thus lowering the activation energy, the energy barrier for the reaction.

**7.65** Products

**7.67** (A)

**7.69** LeChatelier's principle states that when a system at equilibrium is disturbed, the equilibrium shifts in the direction that minimizes the disturbance.

**7.71** A dynamic equilibrium has fixed concentrations of all reactants and products—these concentrations do not change with time. However, the process is dynamic because products and reactants are continuously being formed and consumed. The concentrations do not change because the rates of production and consumption are equal.

**7.73** The position of the equilibrium addresses the question of whether products or reactants are favored. In a hypothetical equilibrium, if the equilibrium position shifts to the left, that means more reactants are formed. If the equilibrium position shifts to the right, that means more products are formed.

**7.75** 1. Concentration      3. Pressure
     2. Heat

**7.77** $K_{eq} = \dfrac{[NO_2]^2}{[N_2O_4]}$

**7.79** A physical equilibrium describes physical change; examples include the equilibrium between ice and water, or the equilibrium vapor pressure of a liquid. A chemical equilibrium describes chemical change; examples include the reactions shown in Questions 7.81 and 7.83.

**7.81** $K_{eq} = \dfrac{[NH_3]^2}{[N_2][H_2]^3}$

**7.83** $K_{eq} = \dfrac{[H_2S]^2}{[H_2]^2[S_2]}$

**7.85** $7.7 \times 10^{-5}\,M$

**7.87** **a.** Equilibrium shifts to the left.
     **b.** No change      **c.** No change

**7.89** **a.** False      **b.** False

**7.91** **a.** $PCl_3$ increases      **d.** $PCl_3$ decreases
     **b.** $PCl_3$ decreases      **e.** $PCl_3$ remains the same
     **c.** $PCl_3$ decreases

**7.93** Decrease

**7.95** $K_{eq} = \dfrac{[CO][H_2]}{[H_2O]}$

**7.97** False. The position of equilibrium is not affected by a catalyst, only the rate at which equilibrium is attained.

**7.99** Carbon dioxide is dissolved in cola. Heating shifts the equilibrium to the right.
$$CO_2(l) \rightleftharpoons CO_2(g)$$
Since gases are less soluble at elevated temperatures, the pressure build-up from the carbon dioxide gas in the sealed bottle can lead to an explosion.

**7.101** $K_{eq} = \dfrac{[SO_3]^2}{[SO_2]^2[O_2]}$

**7.103** $3.0 \times 10^2$

**7.105** Adding $SO_2(g)$ or $O_2(g)$ or increasing the pressure

# Chapter 8

**8.1** **a.** $HF(aq) + H_2O(l) \rightleftharpoons H_3O^+(aq) + F^-(aq)$
     **b.** $NH_3(aq) + H_2O(l) \rightleftharpoons NH_4^+(aq) + OH^-(aq)$

**8.3** **a.** HF and $F^-$; $H_2O$ and $H_3O^+$
     **b.** $NH_3$ and $NH_4^+$; $H_2O$ and $OH^-$

**8.5** $1.0 \times 10^{-11}\,M$

**8.7** 4.74

**8.9** 4.87

**8.11** $CO_2 + H_2O \rightleftharpoons H_2CO_3 \rightleftharpoons H_3O^+ + HCO_3^-$
An increase in the partial pressure of $CO_2$ is a stress on the left side of the equilibrium. The equilibrium will shift to the right in an effort to decrease the concentration of $CO_2$. This will cause the molar concentration of $H_2CO_3$ to increase.

**8.13** In Question 8.11, the equilibrium shifts to the right. Therefore the molar concentration of $H_3O^+$ should increase.
     In Question 8.12, the equilibrium shifts to the left. Therefore the molar concentration of $H_3O^+$ should decrease.

**8.15** $pH = pK_a + \log\dfrac{[HCO_3^-]}{[H_2CO_3]}$

**8.17** $Ca \rightarrow Ca^{2+} + 2\,e^-$ (oxidation ½ reaction)
$S + 2\,e^- \rightarrow S^{2-}$ (reduction ½ reaction)
$Ca + S \rightarrow CaS$ (complete reaction)

**8.19** Oxidizing agent: S
Reducing agent: Ca
Substance oxidized: Ca
Substance reduced: S

**8.21** **a.** In order for $Cr^{3+}(aq)$ to form $Cr(s)$ at the electrode to be electroplated, $Cr^{3+}$ must gain 3 electrons and undergo reduction. Therefore, the electrode must have a negative charge.
     **b.** Cathode
     **c.** $Cr^{3+}(aq) + 3e^- \rightarrow Cr(s)$

**8.23** **a.** An Arrhenius acid is a substance that dissociates, producing hydrogen ions.
     **b.** A Brønsted-Lowry acid is a substance that behaves as a proton donor.

**8.25** The Brønsted-Lowry theory provides a broader view of acid-base theory than does the Arrhenius theory. Brønsted-Lowry emphasizes the role of the solvent in the dissociation process.

**8.27** **a.** $HNO_2(aq) + H_2O(l) \rightleftharpoons H_3O^+(aq) + NO_2^-(aq)$
     **b.** $HCN(aq) + H_2O(l) \rightleftharpoons H_3O^+(aq) + CN^-(aq)$

**8.29** **a.** $HNO_3$      **c.** $HNO_3$
     **b.** $CN^-$

**8.31** **a.** Weak      **c.** Weak
     **b.** Weak

**8.33** **a.** $CN^-$ and HCN; $NH_3$ and $NH_4^+$
     **b.** $CO_3^{2-}$ and $HCO_3^-$; $Cl^-$ and HCl

**8.35** Concentration refers to the quantity of acid or base contained in a specified volume of solvent. Strength refers to the degree of dissociation of the acid or base.

**8.37** **a.** Brønsted acid      **c.** Both
     **b.** Brønsted base

**8.39** **a.** Brønsted acid      **c.** Brønsted base
     **b.** Both

**8.41** HCN

**8.43** $I^-$

**8.45** **a.** $1.0 \times 10^{-7}\,M$      **b.** $1.0 \times 10^{-11}\,M$

**8.47** The beaker containing $0.10\,M$ $CH_3COOH$. $CH_3COOH$ is a weaker acid than HCl, thus, a higher pH than HCl.

**8.49** **a.** 2.00      **b.** 4.00

**8.51** **a.** $[H_3O^+] = 1.0 \times 10^{-1}\,M$
     **b.** $[H_3O^+] = 1.0 \times 10^{-5}\,M$

**8.53** 11.00

**8.55** **a.** $[H_3O^+] = 5.0 \times 10^{-2}\,M$
        $[OH^-] = 2.0 \times 10^{-13}\,M$
     **b.** $[H_3O^+] = 2.0 \times 10^{-10}\,M$
        $[OH^-] = 5.0 \times 10^{-5}\,M$

**8.57** A neutralization reaction is one in which an acid and a base react to produce water and a salt (a "neutral" solution).

**8.59** **a.** $[H_3O^+] = 1.0 \times 10^{-6}\,M$
  $[OH^-] = 1.0 \times 10^{-8}\,M$
 **b.** $[H_3O^+] = 6.3 \times 10^{-6}\,M$
  $[OH^-] = 1.6 \times 10^{-9}\,M$
 **c.** $[H_3O^+] = 1.6 \times 10^{-8}\,M$
  $[OH^-] = 6.3 \times 10^{-7}\,M$

**8.61** The statement is incorrect. The pH = 3 solution is 1000 times as acidic as the pH = 6 solution because pH is a logarithmic function.

**8.63** **a.** $[H_3O^+] = 1.0 \times 10^{-5}\,M$
 **b.** $[H_3O^+] = 1.0 \times 10^{-12}\,M$
 **c.** $[H_3O^+] = 3.2 \times 10^{-6}\,M$

**8.65** **a.** pH = 6.00    **c.** pH = 3.25
 **b.** pH = 8.00

**8.67** pH = 3.12

**8.69** pH = 10.74

**8.71** $HNO_3(aq) + NaOH(aq) \rightarrow H_2O(l) + NaNO_3(aq)$

**8.73** $H^+(aq) + OH^-(aq) \longrightarrow H_2O(l)$ or
  $H_3O^+(aq) + OH^-(aq) \longrightarrow 2H_2O(l)$

**8.75** Color change tells us that the proper volume of titrant has been added.

**8.77** 0.1800 $M$

**8.79** 13.33 mL

**8.81** **a.** $NH_3$ and $NH_4Cl$ can form a buffer solution.
 **b.** $HNO_3$ and $KNO_3$ cannot form a buffer solution.

**8.83** $HCl/NaCl$ is not a buffer solution. It is a strong acid and a salt. The NaOH would produce a significant pH change. On the other hand, $CH_3COOH/CH_3COONa$ is a buffer solution because it is a weak acid and its salt. Therefore, it would resist significant pH change upon addition of a strong base.

**8.85** **a.** Addition of strong acid is equivalent to adding $H_3O^+$. This is a stress on the right side of the equilibrium and the equilibrium will shift to the left. Consequently the $[CH_3COOH]$ increases.
 **b.** Water, in this case, is a solvent and does not appear in the equilibrium expression. Hence, it does not alter the position of the equilibrium.

**8.87** $[H_3O^+] = 2.32 \times 10^{-7}\,M$

**8.89** $CH_3COO^-$, a conjugate base, reacts with added $H_3O^+$ to maintain pH.

**8.91** pH = 4.74

**8.93** $11.2 = \dfrac{[HCO_3^-]}{[H_2CO_3]}$

**8.95** The species oxidized *loses* electrons.

**8.97** During an oxidation-reduction reaction the species *oxidized* is the reducing agent.

**8.99**  $Cl_2$  +  2KI  $\rightarrow$ 2KCl + $I_2$
 substance reduced  substance oxidized
  oxidizing agent  reducing agent

**8.101** $2I^- \rightarrow I_2 + 2e^-$ (oxidation ½ reaction)
  $Cl_2 + 2e^- \rightarrow 2Cl^-$ (reduction ½ reaction)

**8.103** An oxidation-reduction reaction must take place to produce electron flow in a voltaic cell.

**8.105** Storage battery.

## Chapter 9

**9.1** X-ray, ultraviolet, visible, infrared, microwave, and radiowave.

**9.3** $^{144}_{60}Nd \rightarrow {}^{140}_{58}Ce + {}^{4}_{2}He$

**9.5** $^{131}_{53}I \rightarrow {}^{131}_{54}Xe + {}^{0}_{-1}e$

**9.7** A positron has a positive charge and a beta particle has a negative charge.

**9.9** 201 hours

**9.11** 1/4 of the radioisotope remains after two half-lives.

**9.13** Isotopes with short half-lives release their radiation rapidly. There is much more radiation per unit time observed with short half-life substances; hence, the signal is stronger and the sensitivity of the procedure is enhanced.

**9.15** The rem takes into account the relative biological effect of the radiation in addition to the quantity of radiation. This provides a more meaningful estimate of potential radiation damage to human tissue.

**9.17** Natural radioactivity is the spontaneous decay of a nucleus to produce high-energy particles or rays.

**9.19** Two protons and two neutrons

**9.21** An electron with a $-1$ charge.

**9.23** • charge, $\alpha = +2$, $\beta = -1$
  • mass, $\alpha = 4$ amu, $\beta = 0.000549$ amu
  • velocity, $\alpha = 10\%$ of the speed of light, $\beta = 90\%$ of the speed of light

**9.25** Chemical reactions involve joining, separating and rearranging atoms; valence electrons are critically involved. Nuclear reactions involve only changes in nuclear composition.

**9.27** $^{4}_{2}He$

**9.29** $^{235}_{92}U$

**9.31** $^{1}_{1}H = 0$ neutrons and 1 proton
  $^{2}_{1}H = 1$ neutron and 1 proton
  $^{3}_{1}H = 2$ neutrons and 1 proton

**9.33** $^{15}_{7}N$

**9.35** Alpha and beta particles are matter; gamma radiation is pure energy. Alpha particles are large and relatively slow moving. They are the least energetic and least penetrating. Gamma radiation moves at the speed of light, is highly energetic, and is most penetrating.

**9.37** A helium atom has two electrons; an alpha particle has no electrons.

**9.39** $^{60}_{27}Co \rightarrow {}^{60}_{28}Ni + {}^{0}_{-1}\beta + \gamma$

**9.41** $^{23}_{11}Na + {}^{2}_{1}H \rightarrow {}^{24}_{11}Na + {}^{1}_{1}H$

**9.43** $^{24}_{10}Ne \rightarrow \beta + {}^{24}_{11}Na$

**9.45** $^{140}_{55}Cs \rightarrow {}^{140}_{56}Ba + {}^{0}_{-1}e$

**9.47** $^{209}_{83}Bi + {}^{54}_{24}Cr \rightarrow {}^{262}_{107}Bh + {}^{1}_{0}n$

**9.49** $^{27}_{12}Mg \rightarrow {}^{0}_{-1}e + {}^{27}_{13}Al$

**9.51** $^{12}_{7}N \rightarrow {}^{12}_{6}C + {}^{0}_{1}e$

**9.53** $^{241}_{95}Am \rightarrow {}^{4}_{2}\alpha + {}^{237}_{93}Np$

**9.55** Natural radioactivity is a spontaneous process; artificial radioactivity is nonspontaneous and results from a nuclear reaction that produces an unstable nucleus.

**9.57** • Nuclei for light atoms tend to be most stable if their neutron/proton ratio is close to 1.
  • Nuclei with more than 84 protons tend to be unstable.
  • Isotopes with a "magic number" of protons or neutrons (2, 8, 20, 50, 82, or 126 protons or neutrons) tend to be stable.
  • Isotopes with even numbers of protons or neutrons tend to be more stable.

**9.59** $^{20}_{8}O$; Oxygen-20 has $20 - 8 = 12$ neutrons, an n/p of 12/8, or 1.5. The n/p is probably too high for stability even though it does have a "magic number" of protons and an even number of protons and neutrons.

**9.61**  $^{48}_{24}$Cr; Chromium-48 has $48 - 24 = 24$ neutrons, an n/p of 24/24, or 1.0. It also has an even number of protons and neutrons. It would probably be stable.

**9.63**  0.40 mg of iodine-131 remains

**9.65**  13 mg of iron-59 remains

**9.67**  Radiocarbon dating is a process used to determine the age of objects. The ratio of the masses of the stable isotope, carbon-12, and unstable isotope, carbon-14, is measured. Using this value and the half-life of carbon-14, the age of the coffin may be calculated.

**9.69**  Fission

**9.71**  **a.** The fission process involves the breaking down of large, unstable nuclei into smaller, more stable nuclei. This process releases some of the binding energy in the form of heat and/or light.
  **b.** The heat generated during the fission process could be used to generate steam, which is then used to drive a turbine to create electricity.

**9.73**  $^{3}_{1}$H + $^{1}_{1}$H → $^{4}_{2}$He + energy

**9.75**  A "breeder" reactor creates the fuel that can be used by a conventional fission reactor during its fission process.

**9.77**  The reaction in a fission reactor that involves neutron production and causes subsequent reactions accompanied by the production of more neutrons in a continuing process.

**9.79**  High operating temperatures

**9.81**  Radiation therapy provides sufficient energy to destroy molecules critical to the reproduction of cancer cells.

**9.83**  Background radiation, radiation from natural sources, is emitted by the sun as cosmic radiation, and from naturally radioactive isotopes found throughout our environment.

**9.85**  $^{108}_{47}$Ag + $^{4}_{2}$He → $^{112}_{49}$In

**9.87**  **a.** Technetium-99 m is used to study the heart (cardiac output, size, and shape), kidney (follow-up procedure for kidney transplant), and liver and spleen (size, shape, presence of tumors).
  **b.** Xenon-133 is used to locate regions of reduced ventilation and presence of tumors in the lung.

**9.89**  Level decreases

**9.91**  Yes, it would lead to a positive effect. Potential damage is often directly proportional to the time of exposure.

**9.93**  Yes, it would lead to a positive effect. The operator of the robotic device could be located far from the source, no physical contact with the source is necessary, and barriers of lead or other shielding can isolate the control and the robot.

**9.95**  Yes. Concrete has a higher density than wood and thus serves as a better radiation shield.

**9.97**  Relative biological effect is a measure of the damage to biological tissue caused by different forms of radiation.

**9.99**  **a.** The curie is the amount of radioactive material needed to produce $3.7 \times 10^{10}$ atomic disintegrations per second.
  **b.** The roentgen is the amount of radioactive material needed to produce $2 \times 10^{9}$ ion-pairs when passing through 1 cc of air at 0°C.

**9.101**  A film badge detects gamma radiation by darkening photographic film in proportion to the amount of radiation exposure over time. Badges are periodically collected and evaluated for their level of exposure. This mirrors the level of exposure of the personnel wearing the badges.

## Chapter 10

**10.1**  The student could test the solubility of the substance in water and in an organic solvent, such as hexane. Solubility in hexane would suggest an organic substance; whereas solubility in water would indicate an inorganic compound. The student could also determine the melting and boiling points of the substance. If the melting and boiling points are very high, an inorganic substance would be suspected.

**10.3**  **a.**

```
    H  H  H  H
    |  |2°|2°|
 H—C—C—C—C—H
   1°|  |  |  |1°
    H  H  H  H
          1°
```

  **b.**

```
         H
      H  |1°
      |
   H—C—H
   1° H     H
      |  |  |1°
   H—C—C—C—H
      | 4°|
      H  |
       H—C—H
          |
          H
          1°
```

  **c.**

```
          H
          |1°
       H—C—H
    H  H  |  H  H
    | 3°|3°|  | 2°|
 H—C—C—C—C—C—H
   1°|  |  |  |  |1°
    H  H  H  H
       H—C—H
          |1°
          H
```

**10.5**  **a.** The monobromination of propane will produce two products, as shown in the following two equations:
$$CH_3CH_2CH_3 + Br_2 \xrightarrow{\text{Light or heat}} CH_3CH_2CH_2Br + HBr$$
$$CH_3CH_2CH_3 + Br_2 \xrightarrow{\text{Light or heat}} CH_3CHBrCH_3 + HBr$$
  **b.** The monochlorination of butane will produce two products, as shown in the following two equations:
$$CH_3CH_2CH_2CH_3 + Cl_2 \xrightarrow{\text{Light or heat}} CH_3CH_2CH_2CH_2Cl + HCl$$
$$CH_3CH_2CH_2CH_3 + Cl_2 \xrightarrow{\text{Light or heat}} CH_3CH_2CHClCH_3 + HCl$$
  **c.** The monochlorination of cyclobutane:

☐ + $Cl_2$ $\xrightarrow{\text{Light}}$ ☐ + HCl

  **d.** The monobromination of pentane will produce three products as shown in the following equations:
$$CH_3CH_2CH_2CH_2CH_3 + Br_2 \xrightarrow{\text{Light or heat}} CH_3CH_2CH_2CH_2CH_2Br + HBr$$
$$CH_3CH_2CH_2CH_2CH_3 + Br_2 \xrightarrow{\text{Light or heat}} CH_3CH_2CH_2CHBrCH_3 + HBr$$
$$CH_3CH_2CH_2CH_2CH_3 + Br_2 \xrightarrow{\text{Light or heat}} CH_3CH_2CHBrCH_2CH_3 + HBr$$

**10.7**  The number of organic compounds is nearly limitless because carbon forms stable covalent bonds with other carbon atoms in a variety of different patterns. In addition, carbon can form stable bonds with other elements and functional groups. Finally, carbon can form double or triple bonds with other carbon atoms to produce organic molecules with different properties.

**10.9**  Because ionic substances often form three-dimensional crystals made up of many positive and negative ions, they generally have much higher melting and boiling points than covalent compounds.

**10.11**  **a.** LiCl > $H_2O$ > $CH_4$   **b.** NaCl > $C_3H_8$ > $C_2H_6$

**10.13**  **a.** LiCl would be a solid; $H_2O$ would be a liquid; and $CH_4$ would be a gas.
  **b.** NaCl would be a solid; both $C_3H_8$ and $C_2H_6$ would be gases.

**10.15**  **a.** Water-soluble inorganic compounds
  **b.** Inorganic compounds
  **c.** Organic compounds
  **d.** Inorganic compounds
  **e.** Organic compounds

**10.17**  **a.** $C_{19}H_{40}$
  **b.**

$$CH(CH_3)_2(CH_2)_3CH(CH_3)(CH_2)_3CH(CH_3)(CH_2)_3CH(CH_3)_2$$
  **c.** 268.51 g/mol

**10.19**  **a.** $CH_3CH_2CH(CH_3)_2$
 **b.** $CH_3CH_2C(CH_3)_2(CH_2)_2CH(CH_3)_2$
 **c.** $CH_3CH_2C(CH_3)_2(CH_2)_3CH(CH_3)CH(CH_3)_2$

**10.21**  **a.**        **b.**        **c.**

**10.23**  **a.** $(CH_3)_3CCH(CH_2CH_3)_2$
 **b.** $CH_3CHCH_2$
 **c.** $CH_3CH_2CH_3$

**10.25**

 **a.**        **b.**

 **c.**        **d.**

**10.27**  **a.**        Tricosane.

 Pentacosane.

 Heptacosane.

 **b.** Tricosane: 324.61 g/mol
 Pentacosane: 352.67 g/mol
 Heptacosane: 380.72 g/mol

**10.29**  **a.**        **b.**

**10.31**

 **a.**        **b.**

**10.33**  **a.** Hydroxyl group        **e.** Ester group
 **b.** Amino group        **f.** Ether group
 **c.** Carbonyl group        **g.** Halide
 **d.** Carboxyl group

**10.35**  **a.** $C_nH_{2n+2}$        **c.** $C_nH_{2n}$        **e.** $C_nH_{2n-2}$
 **b.** $C_nH_{2n-2}$        **d.** $C_nH_{2n}$

**10.37**  Alkanes have only carbon-to-carbon and carbon-to-hydrogen single bonds, as in the molecule ethane:

Alkenes have at least one carbon-to-carbon double bond, as in the molecule ethene:

Alkynes have at least one carbon-to-carbon triple bond, as in the molecule ethyne:
$$H-C\equiv C-H$$

**10.39**  **a.** A carboxylic acid:

$$CH_3CH_2-\overset{\overset{\displaystyle O}{\|}}{C}-OH$$

 **b.** An amine: $CH_3CH_2CH_2-NH_2$
 **c.** An alcohol: $CH_3CH_2CH_2-OH$
 **d.** An ether: $CH_3CH_2-O-CH_2CH_3$

**10.41**

Amide Group
Carboxyl Group
Aromatic Ring
Ester Group
Amino Group

**10.43**  Hydrocarbons are nonpolar molecules, and hence are not soluble in water.

**10.45**  **a.** Heptane > Hexane > Butane > Ethane
 **b.** $CH_3CH_2CH_2CH_2CH_2CH_2CH_2CH_2CH_3$ > $CH_3CH_2CH_2CH_2CH_3$ > $CH_3CH_2CH_3$

**10.47**  **a.** Heptane and hexane would be liquid at room temperature; butane and ethane would be gases.
 **b.** $CH_3CH_2CH_2CH_2CH_2CH_2CH_2CH_2CH_3$ and $CH_3CH_2CH_2CH_2CH_3$ would be liquids at room temperature; $CH_3CH_2CH_3$ would be a gas.

**10.49**  Nonane: $CH_3CH_2CH_2CH_2CH_2CH_2CH_2CH_2CH_3$
 Pentane: $CH_3CH_2CH_2CH_2CH_3$
 Propane: $CH_3CH_2CH_3$

**10.51**  **a.**        **c.**

 **b.**

**10.53**  **a.** 2,2-Dibromobutane:

 **b.** 2-Iododecane:

 **c.** 1,2-Dichloropentane:

**d.** 1-Bromo-2-methylpentane:

**10.55  a.** 3-Methylpentane          **c.** 1-Bromoheptane
  **b.** 2,5-Dimethylhexane     **d.** 1-Chloro-3-methylbutane

**10.57  a.** 2-Chloropropane          **d.** 1-Chloro-2-methylpropane
  **b.** 2-Iodobutane            **e.** 2-Iodo-2-methylpropane
  **c.** 2,2-Dibromopropane

**10.59  a.** The straight chain isomers of molecular formula $C_4H_9Br$:

H—C—C—C—C—Br     H—C—C—C—C—H

  **b.** The straight chain isomers of molecular formula $C_4H_8Br_2$:

H—C—C—C—C—Br     H—C—C—C—C—Br

H—C—C—C—C—Br     Br—C—C—C—C—Br

H—C—C—C—C—H     H—C—C—C—C—H

**10.61  a.** 2-Chlorohexane         **c.** 3-Chloropentane
  **b.** 1,4-Dibromobutane     **d.** 2-Methylheptane

**10.63  a.** The first pair of molecules are constitutional isomers: hexane and 2-methylpentane.
  **b.** The second pair of molecules are identical. Both are heptane.

**10.65** Structures "a" and "c"

**10.67  a.** Incorrect: 3-Methylhexane     **c.** Incorrect: 3-Methylheptane
  **b.** Incorrect: 2-Methylbutane     **d.** Correct

**10.69  a.**
  $CH_3CHCH_2CHCH_3$          The name given in the problem is correct.
  (CH₃ groups shown)

  **b.**          The correct name is 4-methylheptane.
  $CH_3CH_2CH_2CHCH_2CH_2CH_3$

  **c.** I—$CH_2CH_2CH_2CH_2CH_2$—I     The name given in the problem is correct.

  **d.** $CH_3CH_2CH_2CH_2CH_2CHCH_2CH_2CH_3$     The correct name is 4-ethylnonane.
  $CH_2CH_3$

  **e.** Br                   Br
  $CH_2CH_2CH_2CH_2CH_2CH_2CCH_2CH_3$     The name given in the problem is correct.
  $CH_3$

**10.71** Cycloalkanes are a family of molecules having carbon-to-carbon bonds in a ring structure.

**10.73** The general formula for a cycloalkane is $C_nH_{2n}$.

**10.75  a.** Chlorocyclopropane
  **b.** cis-1,2-Dichlorocyclopropane
  **c.** trans-1,2-Dichlorocyclopropane
  **d.** Bromocyclopropane

**10.77  a.**          **c.**

  **b.**          **d.**

**10.79** There are three structural isomers of dichlorocyclopropane. Two of these isomers are geometric isomers.

**10.81  a.** Incorrect—1,2-Dibromocyclobutane
  **b.** Incorrect—1,2-Diethylcyclobutane
  **c.** Correct
  **d.** Incorrect—1,2,3-Trichlorocyclohexane

**10.83  a.** cis-l,3-Dibromocyclopentane    **c.** cis-1, 2-Dichlorocyclopropane

  **b.** trans-1,2-Dimethylcyclobutane    **d.** trans-1,4-Diethylcyclohexane

**10.85  a.** cis-1,2-Dibromocyclopentane
  **b.** trans-1,3-Dibromocyclopentane
  **c.** cis-1,2-Dimethylcyclohexane
  **d.** cis-1,2-Dimethylcyclopropane

**10.87** Conformational isomers are distinct isomeric structures that may be converted into one another by rotation about the bonds in the molecule.

**10.89** In the chair conformation the hydrogen atoms, and thus the electron pairs of the C—H bonds, are farther from one another. As a result, there is less electron repulsion and the structure is more stable. In the boat conformation, the electron pairs are more crowded. This causes greater electron repulsion, producing a less stable conformation.

**10.91** Combustion is the oxidation of hydrocarbons by burning in the presence of air to produce carbon dioxide and water.

**10.93  a.** $C_3H_8 + 5O_2 \rightarrow 4H_2O + 3CO_2$
  **b.** $C_7H_{16} + 11O_2 \rightarrow 8H_2O + 7CO_2$
  **c.** $C_9H_{20} + 14O_2 \rightarrow 10H_2O + 9CO_2$
  **d.** $2C_{10}H_{22} + 31O_2 \rightarrow 22H_2O + 20CO_2$

**10.95** $2C_{16}H_{34} + 49O_2 \rightarrow 32CO_2 + 34H_2O$

**10.97  a.** $8CO_2 + 10H_2O$
  **b.**     $CH_3$                   $CH_3$
  Br—C—$CH_3$ + $CH_3CHCH_2Br$ + $2HBr$
        $CH_3$
  **c.** $Cl_2$ and light

**10.99** The following molecules are all isomers of $C_6H_{14}$.

$CH_3CH_2CH_2CH_2CH_2CH_3$

Hexane

$$CH_3CHCH_2CH_2CH_3$$
$$\overset{\displaystyle CH_3}{|}$$

2-Methylpentane

$$CH_3CH_2CHCH_2CH_3$$
$$\overset{\displaystyle CH_3}{|}$$

3-Methylpentane

$$CH_3CHCHCH_3$$
$$\overset{\displaystyle CH_3}{|} \quad \overset{\displaystyle CH_3}{|}$$

2,3-Dimethylbutane

$$CH_3CCH_2CH_3$$
$$\overset{\displaystyle CH_3}{|}$$
$$\underset{\displaystyle CH_3}{|}$$

2,2-Dimethylbutane

**a.** 2,3-Dimethylbutane produces only two monobrominated derivatives: 1-bromo-2,3-dimethylbutane and 2-bromo-2, 3-dimethylbutane.

**b.** Hexane produces three monobrominated products: 1-bromohexane, 2-bromohexane, and 3-bromohexane. 2,2-Dimethylbutane also produces three monobrominated products: 1-bromo-2,2-dimethylbutane, 2-bromo-3, 3-dimethylbutane, and 1-bromo-3,3-dimethylbutane.

**c.** 3-Methylpentane produces four monobrominated products: 1-bromo-3-methylpentane, 2-bromo-3-methylpentane, 3-bromo-3-methylpentane, and 1-bromo-2-ethylbutane.

**10.101** The hydrocarbon is cyclooctane, and it has the molecular formula $C_8H_{16}$.

$+ 12\ O_2 \longrightarrow 8\ CO_2 + 8\ HO_2 +$ heat energy

# Chapter 11

**11.1** **a.** $CH_2BrCH_2C\equiv CCH_2CH_3$

**b.** $CH_3C\equiv CCH_3$

**c.** $ClC\equiv CCl$     Cl———≡———Cl

**d.** $HC\equiv C(CH_2)_7I$

**11.3** **a.**

cis-3-Hexene       trans-3-Hexene

**b.**

trans-2,3-Dibromo-2-butene    cis-2,3-Dibromo-2-butene

**11.5** Molecule "c" can exist as cis- and trans-isomers because there are two different groups on each of the carbon atoms attached by the double bond.

**11.7** **a.**

**b.**

**c.**

**11.9** The hydrogenation of the cis and trans isomers of 2-pentene would produce the same product, pentane.

**11.11** **a.**

$$H_3C-C\equiv C-CH_3 + 2\ H_2 \xrightarrow{\text{Ni}}$$

2-Butyne      Butane

**b.**

$$H_3C-C\equiv C-CH_2CH_3 + 2\ H_2 \xrightarrow{\text{Ni}}$$

2-Pentyne      Pentane

**11.13**

**a.** $CH_3CH=CH_2 + Br_2 \longrightarrow$

**b.** $CH_3CH=CHCH_3 + Br_2 \longrightarrow$

**11.15**

**a.** $CH_3C\equiv CCH_3 + 2\ Cl_2 \longrightarrow$

**b.** $CH_3C\equiv CCH_2CH_3 + 2\ Cl_2 \longrightarrow$

**11.17** **a.** $CH_3CH=CHCH_3 + H_2O \xrightarrow{\text{H+}} CH_3CHOHCH_2CH_3$

**b.** $H_2C=CHCH_2CH_2CH(CH_3)_2 + H_2O \xrightarrow{\text{H+}}$
$$CH_3CHOHCH_2CH_2CH(CH_3)_2$$
$$\text{(Major product)}$$

$H_2C=CHCH_2CH_2CH(CH_3)_2 + H_2O \xrightarrow{\text{H+}}$
$$CH_2OHCH_2CH_2CH_2CH(CH_3)_2$$
$$\text{(Major product)}$$

**c.** $CH_3CH_2CH_2CH=CHCH_2CH_3 + H_2O \xrightarrow{\text{H+}}$
$$CH_3CH_2CH_2CHOHCH_2CH_2CH_3$$

$CH_3CH_2CH_2CH=CHCH_2CH_3 + H_2O \xrightarrow{\text{H+}}$
$$CH_3CH_2CH_2CH_2CHOHCH_2CH_3$$

**d.** $CH_3CHClCH=CHCHClCH_3 + H_2O \xrightarrow{\text{H+}}$
$$CH_3CHClCHOHCH_2CHClCH_3$$
$$\text{Only product}$$

**11.19 a.** $H_3CC\equiv CH + H_2O \xrightarrow{H^+}$

Or

$H_3CC\equiv CH + H_2O \xrightarrow{H^+}$

**b.**

$H_3CC\equiv CCH_2CH_3 + H_2O \xrightarrow{H^+}$

Or

$H_3CC\equiv CCH_2CH_3 + H_2O \xrightarrow{H^+}$

**11.21 a.**

**b.**

**c.**

**d.**

**e.**

**f.**

**11.23** As the length of the hydrocarbon chain increases, the London dispersion forces between the molecules increase. The stronger these attractive forces between molecules are, the higher the boiling point will be.

**11.25** The general formula for an alkane is $C_nH_{2n+2}$.
The general formula for an alkene is $C_nH_{2n}$.
The general formula for an alkyne is $C_nH_{2n-2}$.

**11.27** Ethene is a planar molecule. All of the bond angles are 120°.

**11.29** In alkanes, such as ethane, the four bonds around each carbon atom have tetrahedral geometry. The bond angles are 109.5°. In alkenes, such as ethene, each carbon is bonded by two single bonds and one double bond. The molecule is planar and each bond angle is approximately 120°.

**11.31** Ethyne is a linear molecule. All of the bond angles are 180°.

**11.33** In alkanes, such as ethane, the four bonds around each carbon atom have tetrahedral geometry. The bond angles are 109.5°. In alkenes, such as ethene, each carbon is bonded by two single bonds and one double bond. The molecule is planar and each bond angle is approximately 120°. In alkynes, such as ethyne, each carbon is bonded by one single bond and one triple bond. The molecule is linear and the bond angles are 180°.

**11.35 a.** 2-Pentyne > Propyne > Ethyne
**b.** 3-Decene > 2-Butene > Ethene

**11.37** Identify the longest carbon chain containing the carbon-to-carbon double or triple bond. Replace the *–ane* suffix of the alkane name with *–ene* for an alkene or *-yne* for an alkyne. Number the chain to give the lowest number to the first of the two carbons involved in the double or triple bond. Determine the name and carbon number of each substituent group and place that information as a prefix in front of the name of the parent compound.

**11.39** Geometric isomers of alkenes differ from one another in the placement of substituents attached to each of the carbon atoms of the double bond. Of the pair of geometric isomers, the *cis-* isomer is the one in which identical groups are on the same side of the double bond.

**11.41 a.**

**b.**

**c.**

**d.**

**e.**

**11.43 a.** 3-Methyl-1-pentene
**b.** 7-Bromo-1-heptene
**c.** 5-Bromo-3-heptene
**d.** 1-*t*-Butyl-4-methylcyclohexene

**11.45 a.** $CH_2FCH_2CHFCH_2CH_2F$
**b.**

**c.** $CH_3CH_2CH_2C\equiv CCH_2CH_2CH_3$

**11.47 a.** 1-Heptene can only be drawn one way. Therefore, a *cis-trans* isomer does not exist.
**b.** 2-Heptene can be drawn two ways. Therefore, *cis-trans* isomers do exist.

**c.** 3-Heptene can be drawn two ways. Therefore, *cis-trans* isomers do exist.

**d.** 2-Methyl-2-hexene can only be drawn one way. Therefore, *cis-trans* isomers do not exist.

**e.** 3-Methyl-2-hexene can be drawn two ways. Therefore, *cis-trans* isomers do exist.

**11.49** Alkenes b and c would not exhibit *cis-trans* isomerism.

**11.51** Alkenes b and d can exist as both *cis-* and *trans-* isomers.

**11.53** **a.** 1,5-Nonadiene  **c.** 2,5-Octadiene
 **b.** 1,4,7-Nonatriene  **d.** 4-Methyl-2,5-heptadiene

**11.55**

**11.57**

**11.59**

**11.61** The primary difference between complete hydrogenation of an alkene and an alkyne is that 2 moles of $H_2$ are required for the complete hydrogenation of an alkyne.

**11.63** **a.** $CH_2=CH(CH_2)_4CH_3 + H_2O \xrightarrow{H^+}$

$CH_3CHOH(CH_2)_4CH_3$  Major Product
+
$CH_2OH(CH_2)_5CH_3$  Minor Product

**b.** $CH_3CH=CH(CH_2)_3CH_3 + HBr \longrightarrow$

$CH_3CH_2CHBr(CH_2)_3CH_3$
+
$CH_3CHBr(CH_2)_4CH_3$

**c.** $CH_3CH_2CH=CH(CH_2)_2CH_3 + H_2 \xrightarrow[\text{heat or pressure}]{\text{Pt, Pd, or Ni}}$

$CH_3(CH_2)_5CH_3$

**d.**

**11.65** **a.** $H_2$  **d.** $19O_2 \rightarrow 12CO_2 + 14H_2O$
 **b.** $H_2O$  **e.** $Cl_2$
 **c.** HBr  **f.**

**11.67** **a.**

$H_3CC\equiv CCH_3 + 2H_2 \xrightarrow[\text{heat or pressure}]{\text{Pt, Pd, or Ni}}$

2-Butyne

**b.**

$CH_3CH_2C\equiv CCH_3 + 2X_2 \longrightarrow$

2-Pentyne

**11.69** **a.** Reactant—*cis*-2-butene; Only product—butane
 **b.** Reactant—1-butene; Major product—2-butanol
 **c.** Reactant—2-butene; Only product—2,3-dichlorobutane
 **d.** Reactant—1-pentene; Major product— 2-bromopentane

**11.71** $CH_2=CHCH_2CH_2CH_3$, $CH_3CH=CHCH_2CH_3$,

**11.73** **a.**  Br
$CH_3CHCH_2CH_3$

**b.**

(Major product)    (Minor product)

**c.**

**11.75** A polymer is a macromolecule composed of repeating structural units called *monomers.*

**11.77** Polyvinyl chloride (PVC) is used in pipes, detergent bottles, and cleanser bottles.

**11.79** The IUPAC name for (a) is 2-pentene, for (b) is 3-bromo-1-propene, and for (c) is 3,4-dimethylcyclohexene.

**a.** These products will be formed in approximately equal amounts.

$CH_3CH=CHCH_2CH_3 + H_2O \xrightarrow{H^+}$

$CH_3CHOHCH_2CH_2CH_3$

$CH_3CH=CHCH_2CH_3 + H_2O \xrightarrow{H^+}$

$CH_3CH_2CHOHCH_2CH_3$

**b.** $CH_3BrCH=CH_2 + H_2O \xrightarrow{H^+}$

$CH_2BrCH_2CH_2OH + CH_2BrCHOHCH_3$
Minor product    Major product

**c.** These products will be formed in approximately equal amounts.

**11.91  a.**  OH ... CH₃  **b.**  CH₂CH₂CH₃

**c.**  NO₂ ... O₂N ... NO₂  **d.**  CH₃ ... Cl

**11.93** Kekulé proposed that single and double carbon-carbon bonds alternate around the benzene ring. To explain why benzene does not react like other unsaturated compounds, he proposed that the double and single bonds shift positions rapidly.

**11.95** An addition reaction involves addition of a molecule to a double or triple bond in an unsaturated molecule. In a substitution reaction, one chemical group replaces another.

**11.97  a.**

$$\bigcirc + Br_2 \xrightarrow{FeBr_3} \bigcirc^{Br} + HBr$$

**b.**

$$\bigcirc + Cl_2 \xrightarrow{FeCl_3} \bigcirc^{Cl} + HCl$$

**c.**

$$\bigcirc + HNO_3 \xrightarrow[50-55°C]{\text{Concentrated } H_2SO_4} \bigcirc^{NO_2} + H_2O$$

**11.99**

Pyrimidine

**11.101**

Purine

---

The reaction at top left:

$$\text{(ring with CH}_3\text{, CH}_3\text{)} + H_2O \xrightarrow{H^+} \text{(HO-ring with CH}_3\text{, CH}_3\text{)}$$

**11.81  a.** This is the minor product of this reaction.

$$H_2C=CHCH_2CH(CH_3)_2 + H_2O \xrightarrow{H^+}$$
$$CH_2OHCH_2CH_2CH(CH_3)_2$$

**b.**  $CH_3CH=CHCH_2CH_2CH_3 + HBr \xrightarrow{H^+}$
$$CH_3CH_2CHBrCH_2CH_2CH_3$$

and

$$CH_3CH_2CH=CHCH_2CH_3 + HBr \longrightarrow$$
$$CH_3CH_2CHBrCH_2CH_2CH_3$$

**c.**

$$\text{(ring with CH}_3) + HBr \longrightarrow \text{(Br-ring with CH}_3)$$

**d.**

$$\text{(ring)}-CH_2CH_3 + H_2O \xrightarrow{H^+} \text{(ring with OH)}-CH_2CH_3$$

**11.83  a.**

$$CH_2=CHCH_2CH=CHCH_3 + 2H_2 \xrightarrow[\text{heat}]{Pt} CH_3(CH_2)_4CH_3$$

1,4-Hexadiene    Hexane

**b.**

$$CH_3CH=CHCH=CHCH=CHCH_3 + 3H_2$$

2,4,6-Octatriene  $\xrightarrow[\text{heat}]{Ni} CH_3(CH_2)_6CH_3$

Octane

**c.**

$$\text{(ring)} + 2H_2 \xrightarrow[\text{Pressure}]{Pd} \text{(ring)}$$

1,3-Cyclohexadiene    Cyclohexane

**d.**

$$\text{(ring)} + 3H_2 \xrightarrow[\text{heat}]{Ni} \text{(ring)}$$

1,3,5-Cyclooctatriene    Cyclooctane

**11.85** The term aromatic hydrocarbon was first used as a term to describe the pleasant-smelling resins of tropical trees.

**11.87** Resonance hybrids are molecules for which more than one valid Lewis structure can be written.

**11.89  a.**  CH₃ ... Br ... Br  **b.**  CH₂CH₃ ... CH₂CH₃ ... CH₂CH₃

**c.**  CH₃CHCH₃   **d.**  CH₃ ... Br ... Cl

# Chapter 12

**12.1  a.** 2-Methyl-1-propanol
$$CH_3CHCH_2OH$$
$$\quad | $$
$$\quad CH_3$$

**b.** 2-Chlorocyclopentanol
Cl ... HO-(cyclopentane ring)

**c.** 2,4-Dimethylcyclohexanol

**d.** 2,3-Dichloro-3-hexanol

$$CH_3CHCCH_2CH_2CH_3$$

with OH on top and Cl Cl below

**12.3**  IUPAC name: 1-Butanol
Common name: Butyl alcohol
Primary alcohol

**12.5**  **a.** Ethanol is a primary alcohol. The product is ethene.
**b.** 2-Propanol is a secondary alcohol. The product is propene.
**c.** 4-Methyl-3-hexanol is a secondary alcohol. The products are 3-methyl-3-hexene and 4-methyl-2-hexene.
**d.** 2-Methyl-2-propanol is a tertiary alcohol. The product is 2-methyl-1-propene.

**12.7**  **a.** The reactant is 2-butanol and the product is butanone.
**b.** The reactant is 2-pentanol and the product is 2-pentanone.

**12.9**  Simple phenols are somewhat soluble in water because they have the polar hydroxyl group.

**12.11**  Ethers have much lower boiling points than alcohols because ether molecules cannot hydrogen bond to one another.

**12.13**  The longer the hydrocarbon tail of an alcohol becomes, the less water soluble it will be.

**12.15**  The carbinol carbon is the one to which the hydroxyl group is bonded.

**12.17**  **a.** Primary alcohol
**b.** Secondary alcohol
**c.** Tertiary alcohol
**d.** Tertiary alcohol
**e.** Tertiary alcohol

**12.19**  **a.** Primary alcohol
**b.** Secondary alcohol
**c.** Primary alcohol
**d.** Primary alcohol
**e.** Secondary alcohol

**12.21**  **a.** 2-Nonanol is a secondary alcohol:
$CH_3CHOHCH_2CH_2CH_2CH_2CH_2CH_2CH_3$
**b.** 2-Heptanol is a secondary alcohol:
$CH_3CHOHCH_2CH_2CH_2CH_2CH_3$
**c.** 2-Undecanol is a secondary alcohol:
$CH_3CHOHCH_2CH_2CH_2CH_2CH_2CH_2CH_2CH_2CH_3$

**12.23**  a < d < c < b

**12.25**  **a.** $CH_3CH_2OH$
**b.** $CH_3CH_2CH_2CH_2OH$
**c.** $CH_3CHCH_3$
     with OH below

**12.27**  The IUPAC rules for the nomenclature of alcohols require you to name the parent compound, that is the longest continuous carbon chain bonded to the —OH group. Replace the –e ending of the parent alkane with –ol of the alcohol. Number the parent chain so that the carbon bearing the hydroxyl group has the lowest possible number. Name and number all other substituents. If there is more than one hydroxyl group, the –ol ending will be modified to reflect the number. If there are two —OH groups, the suffix –diol is used; if it has three —OH groups, the suffix –triol is used, etc.

**12.29**  **a.** 1,4-Hexanediol          **c.** 2-Methyl-3-pentanol
**b.** 2,3-Pentanediol

**12.31  a.**

**b.**

**c.**

**12.33**  **a.** Cyclopentanol
**b.** Cycloheptanol
**c.** 3-Methylcyclohexanol

**12.35**  **a.** Methyl alcohol          **c.** Ethylene glycol
**b.** Ethyl alcohol          **d.** Propyl alcohol

**12.37**  **a.** $CH_3CHOHCH_2CH(CH_3)CH_2CH_3$
**b.** $CH(CH_3)_2CH_2OH$
**c.** $CH_2OH(CH_2)_3CH_2OH$
**d.** $CH_3CHOH(CH_2)_6CH_3$
**e.**

**12.39**  Denatured alcohol is 100% ethanol to which benzene or methanol is added. The additive makes the ethanol unfit to drink and prevents illegal use of pure ethanol.

**12.41**  Fermentation is the anaerobic degradation of sugar that involves no net oxidation. The alcohol fermentation, carried out by yeast, produces ethanol and carbon dioxide.

**12.43**  When the ethanol concentration in a fermentation reaches 12–13%, the yeast producing the ethanol are killed by it. To produce a liquor of higher alcohol concentration, the product of the original fermentation must be distilled.

**12.45**

**12.47**

**12.49**

$$\underset{\substack{\text{Secondary alcohol}}}{R-\underset{\underset{H}{|}}{\overset{\overset{R}{|}}{C}}-OH} \xrightarrow{[O]} \underset{\substack{\text{Ketone}}}{\underset{R}{}\overset{\overset{O}{\|}}{C}_{R}}$$

**12.51**  **a.** The predicted products are 1-hexanol (minor) and 2-hexanol (major).
**b.** The predicted products are 2-hexanol and 3-hexanol. These products will be formed in approximately equal amounts.
**c.** The predicted products are 5-methyl-3-hexanol and 2-methyl-3-hexanol. These products will be formed in approximately equal amounts.
**d.** The predicted products are 2,2-dimethyl-4-heptanol and 2,2-dimethyl-3-heptanol. These products will be formed in approximately equal amounts.

**12.53**  **a.**

$$\underset{\substack{\text{2-Hexene}}}{CH_3C\underset{\underset{H}{|}}{\overset{\overset{H}{|}}{=}}CCH_2CH_2CH_3} + H_2O \xrightarrow{H^+}$$

$$\underset{\substack{\text{2-Hexanol}}}{CH_3\underset{\underset{OH}{|}}{C}HCH_2CH_2CH_2CH_3}$$

and

$$\underset{\substack{\text{3-Hexanol}}}{CH_3CH_2\underset{\underset{OH}{|}}{C}HCH_2CH_2CH_3}$$

These products will be formed in approximately equal amounts.

**b.**

Cyclopentene + $H_2O$ $\xrightarrow{H^+}$ Cyclopentanol

**c.** $CH_2{=}CHCH_2CH_2CH_2CH_2CH_2CH_3 + H_2O \xrightarrow{H^+}$
1-Octene

$$\underset{\substack{\text{2-Octanol}\\\text{(Major product)}}}{CH_3\underset{\underset{OH}{|}}{C}HCH_2CH_2CH_2CH_2CH_2CH_3}$$

and

$$\underset{\substack{\text{1-Octanol}\\\text{(Minor product)}}}{CH_2CH_2CH_2CH_2CH_2CH_2CH_2CH_3}$$ with OH

**d.**

1-Methylcyclohexene + $H_2O$ $\xrightarrow{H^+}$

1-Methylcyclohexanol (Major product) and 2-Methylcyclohexanol (Minor product)

**12.55**  **a.** Butanone          **c.** Cyclohexanone
**b.** N.R.               **d.** N.R.

**12.57**  **a.** 3-Pentanol; 3-Pentanone
**b.** 1-Propanol; Propanal (Upon further oxidation, propanoic acid would be formed.)
**c.** 4-Methyl-2-pentanol; 4-Methyl-2-pentanone
**d.** 2-Methyl-2-butanol; N.R.
**e.** 3-Phenyl-1-propanol; 3-Phenylpropanal (Upon further oxidation, 3-phenylpropanoic acid will be formed.)

**12.59**

$$\underset{\substack{\text{Ethanol}}}{CH_3CH_2OH} \xrightarrow{\text{liver enzymes}} \underset{\substack{\text{Ethanal}}}{CH_3-\overset{\overset{O}{\|}}{C}-H}$$

The product, ethanal, is responsible for the symptoms of a hangover.

**12.61**  The reaction in which a water molecule is added to 1-butene is a hydration reaction.

$$\underset{\substack{\text{1-Butene}}}{CH_3CH_2CH{=}CH_2} + H_2O \xrightarrow{H^+} \underset{\substack{\text{2-Butanol}}}{CH_3CH_2\underset{\underset{OH}{|}}{C}HCH_3}$$

**12.63**

$$\underset{\substack{\text{Propene}\\\text{(propylene)}}}{CH_3CH{=}CH_2} \xrightarrow{H_2O, H^+} \underset{\substack{\text{2-Propanol}\\\text{(isopropanol)}}}{CH_3\underset{\underset{OH}{|}}{C}HCH_3} \xrightarrow{[O]} \underset{\substack{\text{Propanone}\\\text{(acetone)}}}{CH_3\overset{\overset{O}{\|}}{C}CH_3}$$

**12.65**  **a.**

(aldehyde) + $H_2$ $\xrightarrow{\text{catalyst}}$ (alcohol)

**b.**

(ketone) + $H_2$ $\xrightarrow{\text{catalyst}}$ (alcohol)

**c.**

(aldehyde) + $H_2$ $\xrightarrow{\text{catalyst}}$ (alcohol)

**d.**

(ketone) + $H_2$ $\xrightarrow{\text{catalyst}}$ (alcohol)

**12.67**  Oxidation is a loss of electrons, whereas reduction is a gain of electrons.

**12.69**

$$CH_3CH_2CH_3 < CH_3CH_2CH_2OH < CH_3CH_2\overset{\overset{O}{\|}}{C}-H < CH_3CH_2\overset{\overset{O}{\|}}{C}-OH$$

**12.71**  Phenols are compounds with an —OH attached to a benzene ring.

**12.73**

Picric acid:                    2,4,6,-Trinitrotoluene:

(Picric acid structure: benzene ring with OH, $O_2N$, $NO_2$, $NO_2$)    (Trinitrotoluene structure: benzene ring with $CH_3$, $O_2N$, $NO_2$, $NO_2$)

Picric acid is water-soluble because of the polar hydroxyl group that can form hydrogen bonds with water.

**12.75**  Hexachlorophene, hexylresorcinol, and o-phenylphenol are phenol compounds used as antiseptics or disinfectants.

**12.77** Ethers have much lower boiling points than alcohols of similar molar mass, but higher boiling points than alkanes of similar molar mass. The boiling points are higher than alkanes because the R—O—R bond is polar. However, there is no —OH group, so ether molecules cannot hydrogen bond to one another. This is the reason that the boiling points are lower than alcohols of similar molar mass.

**12.79** Alcohols of molecular formula $C_4H_{10}O$

$CH_3CH_2CH_2CH_2OH$,    $\underset{\underset{}{OH}}{CH_3CHCH_2CH_3}$,

$\underset{\underset{}{CH_3}}{CH_3CHCH_2OH}$,    $\underset{\underset{}{CH_3}}{CH_3\overset{\overset{OH}{|}}{\underset{|}{C}}CH_3}$

Ethers of molecular formula $C_4H_{10}O$
$CH_3—O—CH_2CH_2CH_3$    $CH_3CH_2—O—CH_2CH_3$
$\underset{\underset{}{CH_3}}{CH_3—O—CHCH_3}$

**12.81** Penthrane: 2,2-Dichloro-1,1-difluoro-1-methoxyethane
Enthrane: 2-Chloro-1-(difluoromethoxy)-1,1,2-trifluoroethane

**12.83**  **a.** $CH_3CH_2—O—CH_2CH_3 + H_2O$
  **b.** $CH_3CH_2—O—CH_2CH_3 + CH_3—O—CH_3 +$
  $CH_3—O—CH_2CH_3 + H_2O$
  **c.** $CH_3—O—CH_3 + CH_3—O—CHCH_3 +$
  $\phantom{CH_3—O—CH_3 + CH_3—O—}\underset{}{CH_3}$

$\underset{\underset{}{CH_3}\phantom{xxx}\underset{}{CH_3}}{CH_3CH—O—CHCH_3 + H_2O}$

  **d.**

+ $H_2O$

**12.85**  **a.** 2-Ethoxypentane    **c.** 1-Ethoxybutane
  **b.** 2-Methoxybutane    **d.** Methoxycyclopentane

**12.87**  **a.**

  **b.**

  **c.**

  **d.**

**12.89** Thiols contain the sulfhydryl group (—SH). The sulfhydryl group is similar to the hydroxyl group (—OH) of alcohols, except that a sulfur atom replaces the oxygen atom.

**12.91** Cystine:

**12.93**  **a.** 1-Propanethiol    **c.** 2-Methyl-2-butanethiol
  **b.** 2-Butanethiol    **d.** 1,4-Cyclohexanedithiol

## Chapter 13

**13.1**  **a.**    $\underset{\underset{}{}}{CH_3—\overset{\overset{O}{||}}{C}—CH_3}$    **b.**    $\underset{\underset{}{}}{CH_3CH\overset{\overset{OH}{|}}{}CH_2CH_2CH_3}$

**13.3**  **a.**    $CH_3CH_2\overset{\overset{O}{||}}{C}—OH$    **b.**    $CH_3\overset{\overset{O}{||}}{C}—OH$

**13.5**  **a.** 2,3-Dichloropentanal    **d.** Butanal

$CH_3CH_2CHClCHClCH\overset{\overset{O}{||}}{}$    $CH_3CH_2CH_2CH\overset{\overset{O}{||}}{}$

  **b.** 2-Bromobutanal    **e.** 2,4-Dimethylpentanal

$CH_3CH_2CHBrCH\overset{\overset{O}{||}}{}$    $CH_3CH(CH_3)CH_2CH(CH_3)CH\overset{\overset{O}{||}}{}$

  **c.** 4-Methylhexanal

$CH_3CH_2CH(CH_3)CH_2CH_2CH\overset{\overset{O}{||}}{}$

**13.7**  **a.** 3-Iodobutanone    **d.** 2-Methyl-3-pentanone
  **b.** 4-Methyl-2-octanone    **e.** 2-Fluoro-3-pentanone
  **c.** 3-Methylbutanone

**13.9**

$CH_3—\overset{\overset{O}{||}}{C}—H$

---

**13.11** a. Reduction  d. Oxidation
b. Reduction  e. Reduction
c. Reduction

**13.13** a. Hemiacetal  c. Acetal
b. Acetal  d. Hemiacetal

**13.15** As the carbon chain length increases, the compounds become less polar and more hydrocarbon-like. As a result, their solubility in water decreases.

**13.17** A good solvent should dissolve a wide range of compounds. Simple ketones are considered to be universal solvents because they have both a polar carbonyl group and nonpolar side chains. As a result, they dissolve organic compounds and are also miscible in water.

**13.19**

**13.21** Alcohols have higher boiling points than aldehydes or ketones of comparable molar mass because alcohol molecules can form intermolecular hydrogen bonds with one another. Aldehydes and ketones cannot form intermolecular hydrogen bonds.

**13.23** a.

b.

**13.25** To name an aldehyde using the IUPAC Nomenclature System, identify and name the longest carbon chain containing the carbonyl group. Replace the final -e of the alkane name with -al. Number and name all substituents as usual. Remember that the carbonyl carbon is always carbon-1 and does not need to be numbered in the name of the compound.

**13.27** The common names of aldehydes are derived from the same Latin roots as the corresponding carboxylic acids. For instance, methanal is formaldehyde; ethanal is acetaldehyde; propanal is propionaldehyde, *etc.*

Substituted aldehydes are named as derivatives of the straight-chain parent compound. Greek letters are used to indicate the position of substituents. The carbon nearest the carbonyl group is the α-carbon, the next is the β-carbon, and so on.

**13.29** a.

b.

$(CH_3)_2CHCH(CH_3)CH_2CH$

c.

$CH_3(CH_2)_4CH(CH_2CH_3)CH$

**d.**

$CH_2ClCH_2CHCl(CH_2)_3CH$

**13.31** a. $CH_3CH(CH_3)CCH_2CH_3$

b. $CH_3(CH_2)_2CCH_2CH_3$

c. $CH_3(CH_2)_3C(CH_2)_3CH_3$

d. $CH_3(CH_2)_5C(CH_2)_6CH_3$

**13.33** a. Butanone
b. 2-Ethylhexanal

**13.35** a. 3-Nitrobenzaldehyde
b. 3,4-Dihydroxycyclopentanone

**13.37** 7-Hydroxy-3,7-dimethyloctanal

**13.39** a. 4,6-Dimethyl-3-heptanone
b. 3,3-Dimethylcyclopentanone

**13.41** a. Acetone  d. Propionaldehyde
b. Ethyl methyl ketone  e. Methyl isopropyl ketone
c. Acetaldehyde

**13.43** a. 3-Hydroxybutanal  d. 3-Iodopentanal

$CH_3CHOHCH_2CH$  $CH_3CH_2CHICH_2CH$

b. 2-Methylpentanal  e. 2-Hydroxy-3-methylheptanal

$CH_3(CH_2)_2CH(CH_3)CH$  $CH_3(CH_2)_3CH(CH_3)CHOHCH$

c. 4-Bromohexanal

$CH_3CH_2CHBr(CH_2)_2CH$

**13.45** Acetone is a good solvent because it can dissolve a wide range of compounds. It has both a polar carbonyl group and nonpolar side chains. As a result, it dissolves organic compounds and is also miscible in water.

**13.47** The liver

**13.49** In organic molecules, oxidation may be recognized as a gain of oxygen or a loss of hydrogen. An aldehyde may be oxidized to form a carboxylic acid as in the following example in which ethanal is oxidized to produce ethanoic acid.

Ethanal → Ethanoic acid

**13.51** Addition reactions of aldehydes or ketones are those in which a second molecule is added to the double bond of the carbonyl group.

**13.53** The following equation represents the oxidation of an aldehyde. The product is a carboxylic acid.

Aldehyde → Carboxylic acid

**13.55** The following general equation represents the addition of one alcohol molecule to an aldehyde:

$$\underset{\text{Aldehyde}}{R-\overset{\overset{\displaystyle O}{\|}}{C}-H} + R'OH \underset{\longleftarrow}{\overset{H^+}{\longrightarrow}} \underset{\text{Hemiacetal}}{R-\overset{\overset{\displaystyle OH}{|}}{\underset{\underset{\displaystyle H}{|}}{C}}-OR'}$$

The following general equation represents the addition of one alcohol molecule to a ketone:

$$\underset{\text{Ketone}}{R-\overset{\overset{\displaystyle O}{\|}}{C}-R} + R'OH \underset{\longleftarrow}{\overset{H^+}{\longrightarrow}} \underset{\text{Hemiacetal}}{R-\overset{\overset{\displaystyle OH}{|}}{\underset{\underset{\displaystyle R}{|}}{C}}-OR'}$$

**13.57 a.**

4-Methyl-2-heptanol $\xrightarrow{[O]}$ 4-Methyl-2-heptanone

**b.**

3,4-Dimethyl-1-pentanol $\xrightarrow{[O]}$ 3,4-Dimethylpentanal

**c.**

4-Ethyl-2-heptanol $\xrightarrow{[O]}$ 4-Ethyl-2-heptanone

**d.**

5,7-Dichloro-3-heptanol $\xrightarrow{[O]}$ 5,7-Dichloro-3-heptanone

**13.59** $\underset{\substack{\text{Primary}\\\text{alcohol}}}{R-CH_2OH} \xrightarrow{[O]} \underset{\text{Aldehyde}}{R-\overset{\overset{\displaystyle O}{\|}}{C}-H} \xrightarrow{[O]} \underset{\substack{\text{Carboxylic}\\\text{acid}}}{R-\overset{\overset{\displaystyle O}{\|}}{C}-OH}$

**13.61 a.** Reduction reaction

$$\underset{\text{Ethanal}}{CH_3-\overset{\overset{\displaystyle O}{\|}}{C}-H} + H_2 \xrightarrow{Pt} \underset{\text{Ethanol}}{CH_3CH_2OH}$$

**b.** Reduction reaction

$$\underset{\text{Cyclohexanone}}{\bigcirc\!\!=\!O} + H_2 \xrightarrow{Pt} \underset{\text{Cyclohexanol}}{\bigcirc\!\!-\!OH}$$

**c.** Oxidation reaction

$$\underset{\text{2-Propanol}}{CH_3\overset{\overset{\displaystyle OH}{|}}{C}HCH_3} \xrightarrow{[O]} \underset{\text{Propanone}}{CH_3-\overset{\overset{\displaystyle O}{\|}}{C}-CH_3}$$

**13.63 a.**

$$+ H_2 \xrightarrow{Pt}$$

**b.**

$$+ H_2 \xrightarrow{Pt}$$

**c.**

$$+ H_2 \xrightarrow{Pt}$$

**d.**

$$+ H_2 \xrightarrow{Pt}$$

**13.65 a.**

$$\underset{\text{Butanal}}{CH_3CH_2CH_2\overset{\overset{\displaystyle O}{\|}}{C}H} + H_2 \xrightarrow{Pt} \underset{\text{1-Butanol}}{CH_3CH_2CH_2CH_2OH}$$

**b.**

$$\underset{\text{3-Methylpentanal}}{CH_3CH_2\overset{\overset{\overset{\displaystyle }{|}}{\underset{\displaystyle CH_3}{}}}{C}HCH_2\overset{\overset{\displaystyle O}{\|}}{C}H} + H_2 \xrightarrow{Pt} \underset{\text{3-Methyl-1-pentanol}}{CH_3CH_2\overset{\overset{\displaystyle }{|}}{\underset{\displaystyle CH_3}{C}}HCH_2CH_2OH}$$

**c.**

$$\underset{\text{2-Methylpropanal}}{CH_3\overset{\overset{\displaystyle }{|}}{\underset{\displaystyle CH_3}{C}}H\overset{\overset{\displaystyle O}{\|}}{C}H} + H_2 \xrightarrow{Pt} \underset{\text{2-Methyl-1-propanol}}{CH_3\overset{\overset{\displaystyle }{|}}{\underset{\displaystyle CH_3}{C}}HCH_2OH}$$

**13.67** Only (c) 3-methylbutanal and (f) acetaldehyde would give a positive Tollens' test.

**13.69 a.**

$$CH_3CH_2\overset{\overset{\displaystyle O}{\|}}{C}H + CH_3CH_2OH \xrightarrow{H^+} CH_3CH_2-\overset{\overset{\displaystyle OH}{|}}{\underset{\underset{\displaystyle OCH_2CH_3}{|}}{C}}-H$$

**b.**

$$CH_3\overset{\overset{\displaystyle O}{\|}}{C}H + CH_3CH_2OH \xrightarrow{H^+} CH_3-\overset{\overset{\displaystyle OH}{|}}{\underset{\underset{\displaystyle OCH_2CH_3}{|}}{C}}-H$$

**13.71 a.**

$$CH_3CH_2\overset{\overset{\displaystyle O}{\|}}{C}H + 2\,CH_3OH \xrightarrow{H^+} CH_3CH_2-\overset{\overset{\displaystyle OCH_3}{|}}{\underset{\underset{\displaystyle OCH_3}{|}}{C}}-H + H_2O$$

**b.**

$$CH_3\overset{\overset{\displaystyle O}{\|}}{C}H + 2\,CH_3OH \xrightarrow{H^+} CH_3-\overset{\overset{\displaystyle OCH_3}{|}}{\underset{\underset{\displaystyle OCH_3}{|}}{C}}-H + H_2O$$

**13.73 a.**

**b.**

**c.**

**d.**

**13.75**  **a.** Methanal          **b.** Propanal

**13.77**  **a.** False          **c.** False
          **b.** True           **d.** False

**13.79**

Keto form of          Enol form of
Propanone             Propanone

**13.81**  **a.**

          **c.**

          **b.**

**13.83**  **(1)** $2CH_3CH_2OH$
          **(2)** $KMnO_4/OH^-$
          **(3)** $CH_3CH=CH_2$

# Chapter 14

**14.1**  **a.** Ketone          **c.** Alkane
          **b.** Ketone

**14.3**  The carboxyl group consists of two very polar groups, the carbonyl group and the hydroxyl group. Thus, carboxylic acids are very polar, in addition to which, they can hydrogen bond to one another. Aldehydes are polar, as a result of the carbonyl group, but cannot hydrogen bond to one another. As a result, carboxylic acids have higher boiling points than aldehydes of the same carbon chain length.

**14.5**  **a.** 3-Methylcyclohexanecarboxylic acid
          **b.** 2-Ethylcyclopentanecarboxylic acid

**14.7**  **a.** $CH_3COOH + CH_3CH_2CH_2OH$
              Ethanoic acid    1-Propanol
          **b.** $CH_3CH_2CH_2CH_2CH_2COO^-K^+ + CH_3CH_2CH_2OH$
              Potassium hexanoate                1-Propanol
          **c.** $CH_3CH_2CH_2CH_2COO^-Na^+ + CH_3OH$
              Sodium pentanoate        Methanol
          **d.** $CH_3CH_2CH_2CH_2CH_2COOH + CH_3CHCH_2CH_2CH_3$
                                                        |
                                                       OH
              Hexanoic acid                      2-Pentanol

**14.9**  **a.**

3-Methylbutanoyl
chloride

3-Methylbutanoic
anhydride

          **b.**

Methanoyl          Ethanoic methanoic
chloride           anhydride

**14.11**  Aldehydes are polar, as a result of the carbonyl group, but cannot hydrogen bond to one another. Alcohols are polar and can hydrogen bond as a result of the polar hydroxyl group. The carboxyl group of the carboxylic acids consists of both of these groups: the carbonyl group and the hydroxyl group. Thus, carboxylic acids are more polar than either aldehydes or alcohols, in addition to which, they can hydrogen bond to one another. As a result, carboxylic acids have higher boiling points than aldehydes or alcohols of comparable molar mass.

**14.13**  **a.** Pentanoic acid
          **b.** 2-Pentanol
          **c.** 2-Pentanol

**14.15**

Propanoic acid        2-Butanol

Butanal        2-Methylbutane

**14.17**  **a.** Heptanoic acid        **c.** Pentanoic acid
          **b.** 1-Propanol           **d.** Butanoic acid

**14.19**  The smaller carboxylic acids are water-soluble. They have sharp, sour tastes and unpleasant aromas.

**14.21**  Citric acid is found naturally in citrus fruits. It is added to foods to give them a tart flavor or to act as a food preservative and antioxidant.

**14.23**  Glutaric acid is useful in the synthesis of condensation polymers because it has an odd number of carbons in the chain, which reduces the elasticity of the polymer.

**14.25**  Determine the name of the parent compound, that is, the longest carbon chain containing the carboxyl group. Change the -e ending of the alkane name to -oic acid. Number the chain so that the carboxyl carbon is carbon-1. Name and number substituents in the usual way.

**14.27**  The IUPAC name for adipic acid is hexanedioic acid. Adipic acid is a natural food additive that reduces spoilage by lowering the pH and thereby inhibiting the growth of bacteria and fungi.

**14.29  a.** $CH_3(CH_2)_2CH(CH_3)CH_2COOH$

**b.** $CH_3(CH_2)_2C(CH_3)(CH_2CH_3)COOH$

**c.**

**14.31  a.** IUPAC name: Methanoic acid
Common name: Formic acid
**b.** IUPAC name: 3-Methylbutanoic acid
Common name: β-Methylbutyric acid
**c.** IUPAC name: Cyclopentanecarboxylic acid
Common name: Cyclovalericcarboxylic acid

**14.33**

Butanoic acid          Methylpropanoic acid

**14.35  a.**

$$CH_3CH_2\overset{\overset{\displaystyle CH_3}{|}}{\underset{\underset{\displaystyle CH_3}{|}}{C}}CH_2CH_2COOH$$

**b.**

$$CH_3\overset{\overset{\displaystyle CH_3}{|}}{C}HCH\underset{\underset{\displaystyle Br}{|}}{C}H_2COOH$$

**c.**

**d.**

**14.37  a.** IUPAC name: 2-Hydroxypropanoic acid
Common name: α-Hydroxypropionic acid
**b.** IUPAC name: 3-Hydroxybutanoic acid
Common name: β-Hydroxybutyric acid
**c.** IUPAC name: 4,4-Dimethylpentanoic acid
Common name: γ,γ-Dimethylvaleric acid
**d.** IUPAC name: 3, 3-Dichloropentanoic acid
Common name: β,β-Dichlorovaleric acid

**14.39  a.** 3-Bromobenzoic acid (or *meta*-bromobenzoic acid or *m*-bromobenzoic acid)
**b.** 2-Ethylbenzoic acid (or *ortho*-ethylbenzoic acid or *o*-ethylbenzoic acid)
**c.** 4-Hydroxybenzoic acid (or *para*-hydroxybenzoic acid or *p*-hydroxybenzoic acid)

**14.41** In organic molecules, oxidation may be recognized as a gain of oxygen or a loss of hydrogen. An aldehyde may be oxidized to form a carboxylic acid as in the following example in which ethanal is oxidized to produce ethanoic acid.

Ethanal                    Ethanoic acid

**14.43** The following general equation represents the dissociation of a carboxylic acid.

**14.45** When a strong base is added to a carboxylic acid, neutralization occurs.

**14.47** Soaps are made from water, a strong base, and natural fats or oils.

**14.49**

**a.**

**b.**

**c.**

**14.51  a.** $CH_3COOH$
**b.**

$$CH_3CH_2CH_2{-}\overset{\overset{\displaystyle O}{||}}{C}{-}O{-}CH_3 + H_2O$$

**c.** $CH_3OH$

**14.53  a.** The oxidation of 1-pentanol yields pentanal.
**b.** Continued oxidation of pentanal yields pentanoic acid.

**14.55**

**a.**

**b.**

**c.**

**14.57** The structure of the calcium salt of propionic acid is $[CH_3CH_2COO^-]_2Ca^{2+}$. The common name of this salt is calcium propionate and the IUPAC name is calcium propanoate.

**14.59** Esters are slightly polar as a result of the polar carbonyl group within the structure.

**14.61** Esters are formed in the reaction of a carboxylic acid with an alcohol. The name is derived by using the alkyl or aryl portion of the alcohol IUPAC name as the first name. The *-ic* acid ending of the IUPAC name of the carboxylic acid is replaced with *-ate* and follows the name of the aryl or alkyl group.

**14.63  a.**

**b.**

$$CH_3CH_2CH_2CH_2CH_2CH_2CH_2CH_2CH_2{-}\overset{\overset{\displaystyle O}{||}}{C}{-}O{-}CH_2CH_2CH_2CH_3$$

**c.**

$$CH_3CH_2{-}\overset{\overset{\displaystyle O}{||}}{C}{-}O{-}CH_3$$

**d.**

$$CH_3CH_2{-}\overset{\overset{\displaystyle O}{||}}{C}{-}O{-}CH_2CH_3$$

**14.65 a.** Ethyl ethanoate  **c.** Methyl-3-methylbutanoate
**b.** Methyl propanoate  **d.** Cyclopentyl benzoate

**14.67** The following equation shows the general reaction for the preparation of an ester:

$$R-\overset{\overset{\displaystyle O}{\|}}{C}-OH \;+\; R-OH \underset{}{\overset{H^+,\,heat}{\rightleftharpoons}} R-\overset{\overset{\displaystyle O}{\|}}{C}-OR \;+\; H_2O$$

Carboxylic acid    Alcohol    Ester    Water

**14.69** The following equation shows the general reaction for the acid-catalyzed hydrolysis of an ester:

$$R-\overset{\overset{\displaystyle O}{\|}}{C}-OR \;+\; H_2O \overset{H^+,\,heat}{\rightleftharpoons} R-\overset{\overset{\displaystyle O}{\|}}{C}-OH \;+\; R-OH$$

Ester    Water    Carboxylic acid    Alcohol

**14.71** A hydrolysis reaction is the cleavage of any bond by the addition of a water molecule.

**14.73 a.**
$$CH_3CH_2CH_2-\overset{\overset{\displaystyle O}{\|}}{C}-O-CH_2CH_3$$

**b.**
$$CH_3CH_2-\overset{\overset{\displaystyle O}{\|}}{C}-OH + CH_3CH_2OH$$

**c.** $CH_3CH_2CH_2OH$

**d.**
$$CH_3CH_2\overset{\overset{\displaystyle Br}{|}}{C}HCH_2-\overset{\overset{\displaystyle O}{\|}}{C}-O^- + CH_3CH_2OH$$

**14.75 a.** Isobutyl methanoate is made from isobutyl alcohol (IUPAC name 2-methyl-1-propanol) and methanoic acid.

$$CH_3\overset{\overset{\displaystyle CH_3}{|}}{C}HCH_2OH + HCOOH \rightarrow HCOOCH_2\overset{\overset{\displaystyle CH_3}{|}}{C}HCH_3$$
Isobutyl alcohol  Methanoic acid  Isobutyl methanoate

Isobutyl alcohol is an allowed starting material, but methanoic acid is not. However, it can easily be produced by the oxidation of its corresponding alcohol, methanol:

$$CH_3OH \overset{[O]}{\rightarrow} HCHO \overset{[O]}{\rightarrow} HCOOH$$
Methanol    Methanal    Methanoic acid

**b.** Pentyl butanoate is made from 1-pentanol and butanoic acid.

$$CH_3(CH_2)_3CH_2OH + CH_3CH_2CH_2COOH$$
1-Pentanol    Butanoic acid

$$\rightarrow CH_3CH_2CH_2\overset{\overset{\displaystyle O}{\|}}{C}OCH_2(CH_2)_3CH_3$$
Pentyl butanoate

Pentanol is an allowed starting material but butanoic acid is not. However, it can easily be produced by the oxidation of its corresponding alcohol, 1-butanol:

$$CH_3CH_2CH_2CH_2OH \overset{[O]}{\rightarrow} CH_3CH_2CH_2CHO$$
1-Butanol    Butanal $\overset{[O]}{\rightarrow}$
$$\rightarrow CH_3CH_2CH_2COOH$$
Butanoic acid

**14.77** Saponification is a reaction in which soap is produced. More generally, it is the hydrolysis of an ester in the presence of a base. The following reaction shows the base-catalyzed hydrolysis of an ester:

$$CH_3(CH_2)_{14}-\overset{\overset{\displaystyle O}{\|}}{C}-O-CH_3 + NaOH \longrightarrow$$

$$CH_3(CH_2)_{14}-\overset{\overset{\displaystyle O}{\|}}{C}-O^-\,Na^+ + CH_3OH$$

**14.79**

$$\text{(Salicylic acid)}-\overset{\overset{\displaystyle O}{\|}}{C}-OH + CH_3OH \overset{H^+}{\longrightarrow}$$

Salicylic acid

$$\text{(ring)}-\overset{\overset{\displaystyle O}{\|}}{C}-OCH_3 + H_2O$$

Methyl salicylate

**14.81** Compound A is
$$CH_3CH_2CH_2CH_2-\overset{\overset{\displaystyle O}{\|}}{C}-O-CH_3$$

Compound B is
$$CH_3CH_2CH_2CH_2-\overset{\overset{\displaystyle O}{\|}}{C}-OH$$

Compound C is $CH_3OH$

**14.83 a.**
$$CH_3CH_2-\overset{\overset{\displaystyle O}{\|}}{C}-OCH_2CH_2CH_3 \overset{H^+,\,heat}{\rightleftharpoons} CH_3CH_2-\overset{\overset{\displaystyle O}{\|}}{C}-OH$$
Propyl propanoate    Propanoic acid
$$+ CH_3CH_2CH_2OH$$
1-Propanol

**b.**
$$H-\overset{\overset{\displaystyle O}{\|}}{C}-OCH_2CH_2CH_2CH_3 \overset{H^+,\,heat}{\rightleftharpoons} H-\overset{\overset{\displaystyle O}{\|}}{C}-OH$$
Butyl methanoate    Methanoic acid
$$+ CH_3CH_2CH_2CH_2OH$$
1-Butanol

**c.**
$$H-\overset{\overset{\displaystyle O}{\|}}{C}-OCH_2CH_3 \overset{H^+,\,heat}{\rightleftharpoons} H-\overset{\overset{\displaystyle O}{\|}}{C}-OH$$
Ethyl methanoate    Methanoic acid
$$+ CH_3CH_2OH$$
Ethanol

**d.**
$$CH_3CH_2CH_2CH_2-\overset{\overset{\displaystyle O}{\|}}{C}-OCH_3 \overset{H^+,\,heat}{\rightleftharpoons}$$
Methyl pentanoate

$$CH_3CH_2CH_2CH_2-\overset{\overset{\displaystyle O}{\|}}{C}-OH + CH_3OH$$
Pentanoic acid    Methanol

**14.85** Acid chlorides are noxious, irritating chemicals. They are slightly polar and have boiling points similar to comparable aldehydes or ketones. They cannot be dissolved in water because they react violently with it.

**14.87** Acid anhydrides have much lower boiling points than carboxylic acids of comparable molar mass. They are also less soluble in water, and often react with it.

**14.89 a.**
$$CH_3(CH_2)_8-\overset{\overset{\displaystyle O}{\|}}{C}-O-\overset{\overset{\displaystyle O}{\|}}{C}-(CH_2)_8CH_3$$

**b.**
$$CH_3-\overset{\overset{\displaystyle O}{\|}}{C}-O-\overset{\overset{\displaystyle O}{\|}}{C}-CH_3$$

**14.91**   **a.**  $CH_3(CH_2)_6\overset{\overset{\displaystyle O}{\|}}{C}Cl$

   **b.**  $CH_3(CH_2)_2\overset{\overset{\displaystyle O}{\|}}{C}Cl$

   **c.**  $CH_3(CH_2)_7\overset{\overset{\displaystyle O}{\|}}{C}Cl$

**14.93**   The following equation represents the synthesis of methanoic anhydride:

$$HCO^- + HC\!-\!Cl \rightarrow HC\!-\!O\!-\!CH$$

Methanoate   Methanoic   Methanoic
anion        chloride     anhydride

**14.95**   **a.**

$$CH_3CH_2OH + CH_3CH_2\!-\!\overset{O}{\overset{\|}{C}}\!-\!O\!-\!\overset{O}{\overset{\|}{C}}\!-\!CH_2CH_3 \longrightarrow$$

$$CH_3CH_2\!-\!\overset{O}{\overset{\|}{C}}\!-\!OCH_2CH_3$$
$$+$$
$$CH_3CH_2\!-\!\overset{O}{\overset{\|}{C}}\!-\!OH$$

   **b.**

$$CH_3CH_2OH + CH_3\!-\!\overset{O}{\overset{\|}{C}}\!-\!O\!-\!\overset{O}{\overset{\|}{C}}\!-\!CH_3 \longrightarrow$$

$$CH_3\!-\!\overset{O}{\overset{\|}{C}}\!-\!OCH_2CH_3 + CH_3\!-\!\overset{O}{\overset{\|}{C}}\!-\!OH$$

   **c.**

$$CH_3CH_2OH + H\!-\!\overset{O}{\overset{\|}{C}}\!-\!O\!-\!\overset{O}{\overset{\|}{C}}\!-\!H \longrightarrow$$

$$H\!-\!\overset{O}{\overset{\|}{C}}\!-\!OCH_2CH_3 + H\!-\!\overset{O}{\overset{\|}{C}}\!-\!OH$$

**14.97**   **a.** Monoester:

$$HO\!-\!\overset{\overset{\displaystyle O}{\|}}{\underset{\underset{\displaystyle OH}{|}}{P}}\!-\!OCH_2CH_3$$

   **b.** Diester:

$$HO\!-\!\overset{\overset{\displaystyle O}{\|}}{\underset{\underset{\displaystyle OCH_2CH_3}{|}}{P}}\!-\!OCH_2CH_3$$

   **c.** Triester:

$$CH_3CH_2\!-\!O\!-\!\overset{\overset{\displaystyle O}{\|}}{\underset{\underset{\displaystyle OCH_2CH_3}{|}}{P}}\!-\!OCH_2CH_3$$

**14.99**   ATP is the molecule used to store the energy released in metabolic reactions. The energy is stored in the phosphoanhydride bonds between two phosphoryl groups. The energy is released when the bond is hydrolyzed. A portion of the energy can be transferred to another molecule if the phosphoryl group is transferred from ATP to the other molecule.

**14.101**

$$CH_3\!-\!\overset{\overset{\displaystyle O}{\|}}{C}\!\sim\!S\!-\!COENZYME\ A$$

The squiggle denotes a high energy bond.

**14.103**

# Chapter 15

**15.1**

**15.3**   **a.**

   **b.**

   **c.**

   **d.**

**15.5**   **a.**

$$\underset{CH_3CHCH_3}{\overset{\overset{\displaystyle NH_2}{|}}{}}$$

   **b.**

$$\underset{CH_3CH_2CH(CH_2)_4CH_3}{\overset{\overset{\displaystyle NH_2}{|}}{}}$$

   **c.**

$$\underset{CH_3CH(CH_2)_4CH_3}{\overset{\overset{\displaystyle NHCH_2CH_3}{|}}{}}$$

**d.** $NH_2C(CH_3)_2(CH_2)_2CH_3$

**e.** $NH_2(CH_2)_3CHCH(CH_2)_3CH_3$
$\qquad\qquad\quad\ \ |\quad\ |$
$\qquad\qquad\quad\ Cl\ \ I$

**f.** $(CH_3CH_2)_2N(CH_2)_4CH_3$

**15.7  a.**

$N^+H_3Br^-$

**b.**
$\qquad\qquad\quad H$
$\qquad\qquad\quad |$
$CH_3CH_2—N^+—CH_3 + OH^-$
$\qquad\qquad\quad |$
$\qquad\qquad\quad H$

**c.** $CH_3—N^+H_3 + OH^-$

**15.9  a.** $CH_3—NH_2$
$\qquad\qquad\quad CH_3$
$\qquad\qquad\quad\ |$
**b.** $CH_3—NH$

**15.11** The nitrogen atom is more electronegative than the hydrogen atom in amines; thus, the N—H bond is polar and hydrogen bonding can occur between primary or secondary amine molecules. Thus, amines have a higher boiling point than alkanes, which are nonpolar. Because nitrogen is not as electronegative as oxygen, the N—H bond is not as polar as the O—H. As a result, intermolecular hydrogen bonds between primary and secondary amine molecules are not as strong as the hydrogen bonds between alcohol molecules. Thus, alcohols have a higher boiling point.

**15.13** In systematic nomenclature, primary amines are named by determining the name of the parent compound, the longest continuous carbon chain containing the amine group. The *-e* ending of the alkane chain is replaced with *-amine*. Thus, an alkane becomes an alkanamine. The parent chain is then numbered to give the carbon bearing the amine group the lowest possible number. Finally, all substituents are named and numbered and added as prefixes to the "alkanamine" name.

**15.15** Amphetamines elevate blood pressure and pulse rate. They also decrease the appetite.

**15.17  a.** 1-Pentamine would be more soluble in water because it has a polar amine group that can form hydrogen bonds with water molecules.
**b.** 2-Butamine would be more soluble in water because it has a polar amine group that can form hydrogen bonds with water molecules.

**15.19** Triethylamine molecules cannot form hydrogen bonds with one another, but 1-hexanamine molecules are able to do so.

**15.21  a.** 2-Butanamine
**b.** 3-Hexanamine
**c.** Cyclopentanamine
**d.** 2-Methyl-2-propanamine

**15.23  a.** $CH_3CH_2NHCH_2CH_3$

**b.** $CH_3(CH_2)_3NH_2$

**c.**
$\qquad\qquad\quad NH_2$
$\qquad\qquad\quad\ |$
$CH_3(CH_2)_6CHCH_2CH_3$

**d.**
$\qquad\ NH_2$
$\qquad\ |$
$CH_3CHCHCH_2CH_3$
$\qquad\qquad |$
$\qquad\quad Br$

**e.**

**15.25  a.** $CH_3CH_2CH(NH)(CH_2)_2CH_3$

**b.** $CH_3(CH_2)_5NH(CH_2)_4CH_3$

**c.**
$\qquad\qquad NH_2$
$\qquad\qquad\ |$
$H_2C—CH$
$\ \ |\qquad\ |$
$H_2C—CH_2$

**d.**

**e.**
$\qquad\qquad\qquad Cl^-$
$CH_3CH_2N^+HCH_2CH_3$
$\qquad\qquad |$
$\qquad\quad CH_2CH_3$

**15.27** $CH_3CH_2CH_2CH_2NH_2$      $CH_3CH_2CHCH_3$
$\qquad\qquad\qquad\qquad\qquad\qquad\qquad |$
$\qquad\qquad\qquad\qquad\qquad\qquad\ NH_2$

1-Butanamine          2-Butanamine
(Primary amine)      (Primary amine)

$CH_3CHCH_2NH_2$           $\qquad CH_3$
$\quad |\qquad\qquad\qquad\qquad\qquad\ \ |$
$\ CH_3\qquad\qquad\qquad CH_3—C—CH_3$
$\qquad\qquad\qquad\qquad\qquad\qquad |$
$\qquad\qquad\qquad\qquad\qquad\quad NH_2$

2-Methyl-1-propanamine    2-Methyl-2-propanamine
(Primary amine)          (Primary amine)

$\qquad\qquad CH_3$
$\qquad\qquad |$
$CH_3CH_2—N—CH_3$          $CH_3CH_2—NH—CH_2CH_3$

*N,N*-Dimethylethanamine     *N*-Ethylethanamine
(Tertiary amine)          (Secondary amine)

$CH_3CHCH_3$
$\quad |$
$\ NH—CH_3$              $CH_3CH_2CH_2—NH—CH_3$

*N*-Methyl-2-propanamine     *N*-Methyl-1-propanamine
(Secondary amine)          (Secondary amine)

**15.29  a.** Primary
**b.** Secondary
**c.** Primary
**d.** Tertiary

**15.31** **a.**

**b.** NO₂ → NH₂ (with OH substituent)

NO₂ with OH → [H] → NH₂ with OH

**c.** NO₂ → [H] → NH₂

**d.**

amide structure → [H] → amine structure

**15.33** **a.** H₂O
**b.** HBr
**c.** CH₃CH₂CH₂—N⁺H₃
**d.** CH₃CH₂—N⁺H₂Cl⁻
          |
          CH₂CH₃

**15.35**

**a.** CH₃(CH₂)₄CNH₂  —[H]→  CH₃(CH₂)₅NH₂

**b.** CH₃(CH₂)₂CNHCH₃  —[H]→  CH₃(CH₂)₃NHCH₃

**c.** CH₃CH₂CNCH₃  —[H]→  CH₃(CH₂)₂NCH₃
              |                              |
              CH₃                          CH₃

**15.37** Lower molar mass amines are soluble in water because the N—H bond is polar and can form hydrogen bonds with water molecules.

**15.39** Drugs containing amine groups are generally administered as ammonium salts because the salt is more soluble in water and, hence, in body fluids.

**15.41** Putrescine (1,4-Butanediamine):
CH₂CH₂CH₂CH₂
|              |
NH₂         NH₂

Cadaverine (1,5-Pentanediamine):
CH₂CH₂CH₂CH₂CH₂
|                    |
NH₂               NH₂

**15.43** **a.**

Pyridine                    Indole

**b.** The indole ring is found in lysergic acid diethylamide, which is a hallucinogenic drug. The pyridine ring is found in vitamin B₆, an essential water-soluble vitamin.

**15.45** Morphine, codeine, quinine, and vitamin B₆

**15.47** Amides have very high boiling points because the amide group consists of two very polar functional groups, the carbonyl group and the amino group. Strong intermolecular hydrogen bonding between the N—H bond of one amide and the C=O group of a second amide results in very high boiling points.

**15.49** The IUPAC names of amides are derived from the IUPAC names of the carboxylic acids from which they are derived. The *-oic acid* ending of the carboxylic acid is replaced with the *-amide* ending.

**15.51** Barbiturates are often called "downers" because they act as sedatives. They are sometimes used as anticonvulsants for epileptics and people suffering from other disorders that manifest as neurosis, anxiety, or tension.

**15.53** **a.** IUPAC name: Propanamide
          Common name: Propionamide
**b.** IUPAC name: Pentanamide
          Common name: Valeramide
**c.** IUPAC name: N,N-Dimethylethanamide
          Common name: N,N-Dimethylacetamide

**15.55** **a.** CH₃CH₂CNH₂

**c.** (CH₃CH₂)₂CHCH(CH₂CH₃)CNH₂

**b.** CH₃(CH₂)₂CN(CH₂CH₃)₂

**d.** CH₃(CH₂)₄CNHCH₃

**15.57** **a.** CH₃—C—NH₂,

**b.** CH₃CH₂—C—NHCH₃,

**c.** benzene—C—N—CH₂CH₃
                        |
                        CH₂CH₃

**d.** CH₃
        |
CH₃CH₂CHCHCH₂—C—NH₂,
              |
              Br

**e.** CH₃—C—N—CH₃,
                |
                CH₃

**15.59** N,N-Diethyl-*m*-toluamide:

C—NCH₂CH₃
      |
      CH₂CH₃

H₃C

Hydrolysis of this compound would release the carboxylic acid *m*-toluic acid and the amine N-ethylethanamine (diethylamine).

**15.61** Amides are not proton acceptors (bases) because the highly electronegative carbonyl oxygen has a strong attraction for the nitrogen lone pair of electrons. As a result they cannot "hold" a proton.

**15.63**

Amide group

Lidocaine hydrochloride

**15.65**

Penicillin BT

**15.67 a.**

N-Methylethanamide

$CH_3COOH$ + $CH_3N^+H_3$

Ethanoic acid    Methylammonium ion

**b.**

N-Methylbutanamide

$CH_3CH_2CH_2COOH + CH_3N^+H_3$

Butanoic acid    Methylammonium ion

**c.**

N-Ethyl-3-methylbutanamide

3-Methylbutanoic acid    Ethylammonium ion

**15.69 a.**

**b.**

$CH_3CH_2$—C—$NH_2$ + $NH_4^+Cl^-$

**c.**

$CH_3CH_2CH_2$—C—Cl + 2$CH_3CH_2NH_2$

**15.71**

**15.73** Glycine:                Alanine:

**15.75**

**15.77** In an acyl group transfer reaction, the acyl group of an acid chloride is transferred from the Cl of the acid chloride to the N of an amine or ammonia. The product is an amide.

**15.79** A chemical that carries messages or signals from a nerve to a target cell

**15.81 a.** Tremors, monotonous speech, loss of memory and problem-solving ability, and loss of motor function
**b.** Parkinson's disease
**c.** Schizophrenia, intense satiety sensations

**15.83** In proper amounts, dopamine causes a pleasant, satisfied feeling. This feeling becomes intense as the amount of dopamine increases. Several drugs, including cocaine, heroin, amphetamines, alcohol, and nicotine increase the levels of dopamine. It is thought that the intense satiety response this brings about may contribute to addiction to these substances.

**15.85** Epinephrine is a component of the flight or fight response. It stimulates glycogen breakdown to provide the body with glucose to supply the needed energy for this stress response.

**15.87** The amino acid tryptophan

**15.89** Perception of pain, thermoregulation, and sleep

**15.91** Promotes the itchy skin rash associated with poison ivy and insect bites; the respiratory symptoms characteristic of hay fever; secretion of stomach acid

**15.93** Inhibitory neurotransmitters

**15.95** When acetylcholine is released from a nerve cell, it binds to receptors on the surface of muscle cells. This binding stimulates the muscle cell to contract. To stop the contraction, the acetylcholine is then broken down to choline and acetate ion. This is catalyzed by the enzyme acetylcholinesterase.

**15.97** Organophosphates inactivate acetylcholinesterase by binding covalently to it. Since acetylcholine is not broken down, nerve transmission continues, resulting in muscle spasm. Pyridine aldoxime methiodide (PAM) is an antidote to organophosphate poisoning because it displaces the organophosphate, thereby allowing acetycholinesterase to function.

# Chapter 16

**16.1** It is currently recommended that 45–55% of the calories in the diet should be carbohydrates. Of that amount, no more than 10% should be simple sugars.

**16.3** An aldose is a sugar with an aldehyde functional group. A ketose is a sugar with a ketone functional group.

**16.5 a.**

**16.7**   **a.** D-
    **b.** L-
    **c.** D-

**16.9**

```
        CHO
   H——————OH
  HO——————H
  HO——————H
   H——————OH
       CH₂OH
```

D-Galactose

**16.11**   α-Amylase and β-amylase are digestive enzymes that break down the starch amylose. α-Amylase cleaves glycosidic bonds of the amylose chain at random, producing shorter polysaccharide chains. β-Amylase sequentially cleaves maltose (a disaccharide of glucose) from the reducing end of the polysaccharide chain.

**16.13**   A monosaccharide is the simplest sugar and consists of a single saccharide unit. A disaccharide is made up of two monosaccharides joined covalently by a glycosidic bond.

**16.15**   Mashed potato flakes, rice, and corn starch contain amylose and amylopectin, both of which are polysaccharides. A candy bar contains sucrose, a disaccharide. Orange juice contains fructose, a monosaccharide. It may also contain sucrose if the label indicates that sugar has been added.

**16.17**   Four

**16.19**

```
        O                        CH₂OH
        ‖                          |
        C—H                       C=O
        |                          |
   H—C—OH                    HO—C—H
        |                          |
  HO—C—H                     H—C—OH
        |                          |
  HO—C—H                     H—C—OH
        |                          |
   H—C—OH                        CH₂OH
        |
      CH₂OH
```

D-Galactose              D-Fructose
(An aldohexose)          (A ketohexose)

**16.21**   An aldose is a sugar that contains an aldehyde (carbonyl) group.

**16.23**   A tetrose is a sugar with a four-carbon backbone.

**16.25**   A ketopentose is a sugar with a five-carbon backbone and containing a ketone (carbonyl) group.

**16.27**   **a.** β-D-Glucose
    **b.** β-D-Fructose
    **c.** α-D-Galactose

**16.29**

```
        O                        O
        ‖                        ‖
        C—H                      C—H
        |                         |
   H—C—OH                   HO—C—H
        |                         |
      CH₂OH                     CH₂OH
```

D-Glyceraldehyde          L-Glyceraldehyde

**16.31**   Stereoisomers are a pair of molecules that have the same structural formula and bonding pattern but that differ in the arrangement of the atoms in space.

**16.33**   A chiral carbon is one that is bonded to four different chemical groups.

**16.35**   A polarimeter converts monochromatic light into monochromatic plane-polarized light. This plane-polarized light is passed through a sample and into an analyzer. If the sample is optically active, it will rotate the plane of the light. The degree and angle of rotation are measured by the analyzer.

**16.37**   A Fischer Projection is a two-dimensional drawing of a molecule that shows a chiral carbon at the intersection of two lines. Horizontal lines at the intersection represent bonds projecting out of the page and vertical lines represent bonds that project into the page.

**16.39**   Diastereomers are a pair of stereoisomers that are not enantiomers.

**16.41**   Dextrose is a common name used for D-glucose.

**16.43**   D- and L-Glyceraldehyde are a pair of enantiomers, that is, they are nonsuperimposable mirror images of one another.

**16.45**

**16.47**   **a.**

```
    HC=O          HC=O          HC=O          HC=O
  H——OH        HO——H        HO——H         H——OH
  H——OH        HO——H         H——OH        HO——H
    HC=O          HC=O          CH=O          HC=O
     A             B             C             D
```

The stereoisomers are A, C, and D. Compounds A and B are identical and they are meso compounds because they have an internal plane of symmetry. Compounds C and D are enantiomers. Compound A is a diastereomer to both compounds C and D.

**b.**

```
   CH₂OH         CH₂OH         CH₂OH         CH₂OH
  H——Br        Br——H        Br——H         H——Br
  H——CH₃      H₃C——H        H——CH₃      H₃C——H
   CH₂OH         CH₂OH         CH₂OH         CH₂OH
     A             B             C             D
```

There are four possible stereoisomers. The two pairs of enantiomers are A with B and C with D. Compounds A and B are both diastereomers to compounds C and D.

**16.49**   **a.**

```
   CH₂CH₃        CH₂CH₃        CH₂CH₃        CH₂CH₃
  H——OH        HO——H        HO——H         H——OH
  H——OH        HO——H         H——OH        HO——H
   CH₂CH₃        CH₂CH₃        CH₂CH₃        CH₂CH₃
     A             B             C             D
```

The stereoisomers are A, C, and D. Compounds A and B are identical and they are meso compounds because they have an internal plane of symmetry. Compounds C and D are enantiomers. Compound A is a diastereomer to both compounds C and D.

**b.**

| CH$_2$OH | CH$_2$OH | CH$_2$OH | CH$_2$OH |
|---|---|---|---|
| =O | =O | =O | =O |
| H——F | F——H | F——H | H——F |
| H——Cl | Cl——H | H——Cl | Cl——H |
| =O | =O | =O | =O |
| CH$_2$OH | CH$_2$OH | CH$_2$OH | CH$_2$OH |
| A | B | C | D |

There are four possible stereoisomers. Compounds A and B are enantiomers, and compounds C and D are enantiomers. Compounds A and B are diastereomers to both compounds C and D.

**16.51** Anomers are isomers that differ in the arrangement of bonds around the hemiacetal carbon.

**16.53** A hemiacetal is a member of the family of organic compounds formed in the reaction of one molecule of alcohol with an aldehyde or a ketone.

**16.55** When the carbonyl group at C-1 of d-glucose reacts with the C-5 hydroxyl group, a new chiral carbon is created (C-1). In the α-isomer of the cyclic sugar, the C-1 hydroxyl group is below the ring; and in the β-isomer, the C-1 hydroxyl group is above the ring.

**16.57** β-Maltose and α-lactose would give positive Benedict's tests. Glycogen would give only a weak reaction because there are fewer reducing ends for a given mass of the carbohydrate.

**16.59** Enantiomers are stereoisomers that are nonsuperimposable mirror images of one another. For instance:

| CHO | CHO |
|---|---|
| H——OH | HO——H |
| CH$_2$OH | CH$_2$OH |
| D-Glyceraldehyde | L-Glyceraldehyde |

**16.61** An aldehyde sugar forms an intramolecular hemiacetal when the carbonyl group of the monosaccharide reacts with a hydroxyl group on one of the other carbon atoms.

**16.63** A disaccharide is a simple carbohydrate composed of two monosaccharides.

**16.65** A glycosidic bond is the bond formed between the hydroxyl group of the C-1 carbon of one sugar and a hydroxyl group of another sugar.

**16.67**

β-Maltose

**16.69** Milk

**16.71** Eliminating milk and milk products from the diet

**16.73** Lactose intolerance is the inability to produce the enzyme lactase that hydrolyzes the milk sugar lactose into its component monosaccharides, glucose and galactose.

**16.75** A polymer is a very large molecule formed by the combination of many small molecules, called monomers.

**16.77** Starch

**16.79** Homopolysaccharides are a class of polysaccharides that are composed of a single monosaccharide.

**16.81** Starch, glycogen, and cellulose are examples of homopolysaccharides. These homopolysaccharides are all made up of glucose.

**16.83** The glucose units of amylose are joined by α (1 → 4) glycosidic bonds and those of cellulose are bonded together by β (1 → 4) glycosidic bonds.

**16.85** Glycogen serves as a storage molecule for glucose.

**16.87** The salivary glands and the pancreas

# Chapter 17

**17.1**
  **a.** CH$_3$(CH$_2$)$_7$CH=CH(CH$_2$)$_7$COOH
  **b.** CH$_3$(CH$_2$)$_{10}$COOH
  **c.** CH$_3$(CH$_2$)$_4$CH=CH—CH$_2$—CH=CH(CH$_2$)$_7$COOH
  **d.** CH$_3$(CH$_2$)$_{16}$COOH

**17.3**

$$CH_3(CH_2)_{12}\overset{O}{\overset{\|}{C}}-OH + CH_3CH_2OH \xrightarrow[\text{heat}]{H^+} CH_3(CH_2)_{12}\overset{O}{\overset{\|}{C}}\text{-O-}CH_2CH_3$$

Tetradecanoic acid   Ethanol   Ethyl tetradecanoate

**17.5**

$$CH_3CH_2CH_2\overset{O}{\overset{\|}{C}}-O-CH_2(CH_2)_3CH_3 \xrightarrow[\text{heat}]{H^+}$$

Pentyl butanoate

$$CH_3CH_2CH_2\overset{O}{\overset{\|}{C}}-OH + CH_3(CH_2)_3CH_2OH$$

Butanoic acid    1-Pentanol

**17.7**

$$CH_3\overset{O}{\overset{\|}{C}}-O-CH_2(CH_2)_2CH_3 + KOH \rightarrow$$

Butyl acetate

$$CH_3\overset{O}{\overset{\|}{C}}-O^-K^+ + CH_3(CH_2)_2CH_2OH$$

Potassium    1-Butanol
acetate

**17.9**

CH$_3$CH$_2$CH=CHCH$_2$CH=CHCH$_2$CH=CH(CH$_2$)$_7$COOH + 3H$_2$

All cis-9,12,15-Octadecatrienoic acid

↓ Ni

CH$_3$(CH$_2$)$_{16}$COOH

Octadecanoic acid

**17.11**  **a.**

CH$_3$(CH$_2$)$_7$CH=CH(CH$_2$)$_7$—C—O—CH$_2$
‖
O
|
CH—OH
|
CH$_2$—OH

CH$_3$(CH$_2$)$_7$CH=CH(CH$_2$)$_7$—C—O—CH$_2$
‖
O
|
CH$_3$(CH$_2$)$_7$CH=CH(CH$_2$)$_7$—C—O—CH
‖
O
|
CH$_2$—OH

CH$_3$(CH$_2$)$_7$CH=CH(CH$_2$)$_7$—C—O—CH$_2$
‖
O
|
CH$_3$(CH$_2$)$_7$CH=CH(CH$_2$)$_7$—C—O—CH
‖
O
|
CH$_3$(CH$_2$)$_7$CH=CH(CH$_2$)$_7$—C—O—CH$_2$
‖
O

**b.**

**17.13**

Steroid nucleus

**17.15** Receptor-mediated endocytosis

**17.17** Fatty acids, glycerides, nonglyceride lipids, and complex lipids

**17.19** Lipid-soluble vitamins are transported into cells of the small intestine in association with dietary fat molecules. Thus, a diet low in fat reduces the amount of vitamins A, D, E, and K that enters the body.

**17.21** A saturated fatty acid is one in which the hydrocarbon tail has only carbon-to-carbon single bonds. An unsaturated fatty acid has at least one carbon-to-carbon double bond.

**17.23** The melting points increase.

**17.25** The melting points of fatty acids increase as the length of the hydrocarbon chains increase. This is because the intermolecular attractive forces, including London dispersion forces, increase as the length of the hydrocarbon chain increases.

**17.27** **a.** Decanoic acid $CH_3(CH_2)_8COOH$
**b.** Stearic acid $CH_3(CH_2)_{16}COOH$

**17.29** **a.** IUPAC name: Hexadecanoic acid
Common name: Palmitic acid
**b.** IUPAC name: Dodecanoic acid
Common name: Lauric acid

**17.31** Esterification of glycerol with three molecules of myristic acid:

**17.33**

Glycerol          3 Oleic Acid Molecules

**17.35**

**17.37** This line drawing of EPA shows the bends or "kinks" introduced into the molecule by the double bonds.

All *cis*-5,8,11,14,17-Eicosapentaenoic acid (EPA)

**17.39**

**17.41**

H—C—OH   +   HO—C—$(CH_2)_8CH_3$     Decanoic acid

H—C—OH   +   HO—C—$(CH_2)_{10}CH_3$     Dodecanoic acid

H—C—OH   +   HO—C—$(CH_2)_{14}CH_3$     Hexadecanoic acid

Glycerol

$\downarrow$ $H^+$, heat

H—C—O—C—$(CH_2)_8CH_3$

H—C—O—C—$(CH_2)_{10}CH_3$ + $3H_2O$

H—C—O—C—$(CH_2)_{14}CH_3$

**17.43**  The essential fatty acid linoleic acid is required for the synthesis of arachidonic acid, a precursor for the synthesis of the prostaglandins, a group of hormonelike molecules.

**17.45**  Aspirin effectively decreases the inflammatory response by inhibiting the synthesis of all prostaglandins. Aspirin works by inhibiting cyclooxygenase, the first enzyme in prostaglandin biosynthesis. This inhibition results from the transfer of an acetyl group from aspirin to the enzyme. Because cyclooxygenase is found in all cells, synthesis of all prostaglandins is inhibited.

**17.47**  Smooth muscle contraction, enhancement of fever and swelling associated with the inflammatory response, bronchial dilation, inhibition of secretion of acid into the stomach.

**17.49**  The name of these fatty acids arises from the position of the double bond nearest the terminal *methyl group* of the molecule. The terminal methyl group is designated omega ($\omega$). In $\omega$-3 fatty acids the double bond nearest the $\omega$ methyl group is three carbons along the chain. In $\omega$-6 fatty acids, the nearest double bond is six carbons from the end.

**17.51**  Omega-3 fatty acids reduce the risk of cardiovascular disease by decreasing blood clot formation, blood triglyceride levels, and growth of atherosclerotic plaque.

**17.53**  The decrease in blood clot formation, along with the reduced blood triglyceride levels and decreased atherosclerotic plaque result in improved arterial health. This, in turn, results in lower blood pressure and a decreased risk of sudden death and heart arrhythmias.

**17.55**  Omega-3 fatty acids are precursors of prostaglandins that exhibit anti-inflammatory effects. On the other hand, omega-6 fatty acids are precursors to prostaglandins that have inflammatory effects. To reduce the inflammatory response contribution to cardiovascular disease, it is logical to increase the amount of omega-3 fatty acids in the diet and to decrease the amount of omega-6 fatty acids.

**17.57**  A glyceride is a lipid ester that contains the glycerol molecule and from one to three fatty acids.

**17.59**  An emulsifying agent is a molecule that aids in the suspension of triglycerides in water. They are amphipathic molecules, such as lecithin, that serve as bridges holding together the highly polar water molecules and the nonpolar triglycerides.

**17.61**  A triglyceride with three saturated fatty acid tails would be a solid at room temperature. The long, straight fatty acid tails would stack with one another because of strong intermolecular and intramolecular London dispersion force attractions.

**17.63**

$CH_3(CH_2)_{14}$—C—O—$CH_2$

$CH_3(CH_2)_4CH_2$, H   C=C   $CH_2(CH_2)_6$—C—O—CH

$CH_3(CH_2)_4CH_2$, C=C, H   H   $CH_2(CH_2)_6$—C—O—$CH_2$

**17.65**

$CH_3CH_2CH_2CH_2CH_2CH_2CH_2CH_2CH_2$—C—O—$CH_2$

$CH_3CH_2CH_2CH_2CH_2CH_2CH_2CH_2CH_2CH_2$—C—O—CH

$CH_2$—O—P—$O^-$ / $O^-$

**17.67**  Triglycerides consist of three fatty acids esterified to the three hydroxyl groups of glycerol. In phospholipids there are only two fatty acids esterified to glycerol. A phosphoryl group is esterified (phosphoester linkage) to the third hydroxyl group.

**17.69**  A sphingolipid is a lipid that is not derived from glycerol, but rather from sphingosine, a long-chain, nitrogen-containing (amino) alcohol. Like phospholipids, sphingolipids are amphipathic.

**17.71**  A glycosphingolipid or glycolipid is a lipid that is built on a ceramide backbone structure. Ceramide is a fatty acid derivative of sphingosine.

**17.73**  Sphingomyelins are important structural lipid components of nerve cell membranes. They are found in the myelin sheath that surrounds and insulates cells of the central nervous system.

**17.75**  Cholesterol is readily soluble in the hydrophobic region of biological membranes. It is involved in regulating the fluidity of the membrane.

**17.77**  Progesterone is the most important hormone associated with pregnancy. Testosterone is needed for development of male secondary sexual characteristics. Estrone is required for proper development of female secondary sexual characteristics.

**17.79**  Cortisone is used to treat rheumatoid arthritis, asthma, gastrointestinal disorders, and many skin conditions.

**17.81**  Myricyl palmitate (beeswax) is made up of the fatty acid palmitic acid and the alcohol myricyl alcohol—$CH_3(CH_2)_{28}CH_2OH$.

**17.83**  Isoprenoids are a large, diverse collection of lipids that are synthesized from the isoprene unit:

$CH_2$=C—CH=$CH_2$ / $CH_3$

**17.85**  Steroids and bile salts, lipid-soluble vitamins, certain plant hormones, and chlorophyll

**17.87**  Chylomicrons, high-density lipoproteins, low-density lipoproteins, and very low density lipoproteins

**17.89**  The terms "good" and "bad" cholesterol refer to two classes of lipoprotein complexes. The high-density lipoproteins, or HDL, are considered to be "good" cholesterol because a correlation has been made between elevated levels of HDL and a reduced incidence of atherosclerosis. Low-density lipoproteins, or LDL, are considered to be "bad" cholesterol because evidence suggests that a high level of LDL is associated with increased risk of atherosclerosis.

**17.91** Atherosclerosis results when cholesterol and other substances coat the arteries, causing a narrowing of the passageways. As the passageways become narrower, greater pressure is required to provide adequate blood flow. This results in higher blood pressure (hypertension).

**17.93** If the LDL receptor is defective, it cannot function to remove cholesterol-bearing LDL particles from the blood. The excess cholesterol, along with other substances, will accumulate along the walls of the arteries, causing atherosclerosis.

**17.95** The basic structure of a biological membrane is a bilayer of phospholipid molecules arranged so that the hydrophobic hydrocarbon tails are packed in the center and the hydrophilic head groups are exposed on the inner and outer surfaces.

**17.97** A peripheral membrane protein is bound to only one surface of the membrane, either inside or outside the cell.

**17.99** Cholesterol is freely soluble in the hydrophobic layer of a biological membrane. It moderates the fluidity of the membrane by disrupting the stacking of the fatty acid tails of membrane phospholipids.

**17.101** Specific membrane proteins on human and mouse cells were labeled with red and green fluorescent dyes, respectively. The human and mouse cells were fused into single-celled hybrids and were observed using a microscope with an ultraviolet light source. The ultraviolet light caused the dyes to fluoresce. Initially the dyes were localized in regions of the membrane representing the original human or mouse cell. Within an hour, the proteins were evenly distributed throughout the membrane of the fused cell.

**17.103** If the fatty acid tails of the membrane phospholipids are converted from saturated to unsaturated, the fluidity of the membrane will increase.

## Chapter 18

**18.1**  **a.** Glycine (gly or G):

$$H_3^+N-\underset{\overset{|}{H}}{\overset{COO^-}{\overset{|}{C}}}-H$$

**b.** Proline (pro or P):

**c.** Threonine (thr or T):

$$H_3^+N-\underset{\overset{|}{H-C-OH}}{\overset{COO^-}{\overset{|}{C}}}-H$$
$$\overset{|}{CH_3}$$

**d.** Aspartate (asp or D):

$$H_3^+N-\overset{COO^-}{\overset{|}{C}}-H$$
$$H-\overset{|}{C}-H$$
$$\overset{|}{COO^-}$$

**e.** Lysine (lys or K):

$$H_3^+N-\overset{COO^-}{\overset{|}{C}}-H$$
$$H-\overset{|}{C}-H$$
$$H-\overset{|}{C}-H$$
$$H-\overset{|}{C}-H$$
$$H-\overset{|}{C}-H$$
$$\overset{|}{N^+H_3}$$

**18.3  a.** Alanyl-phenylalanine:

$$H_3^+N-\overset{H}{\overset{|}{C}}-\overset{O}{\overset{\|}{C}}-\overset{H}{\overset{|}{N}}-\overset{H}{\overset{|}{C}}-COO^-$$

**b.** Lysyl-alanine:

$$H_3^+N-\overset{H}{\overset{|}{C}}-\overset{O}{\overset{\|}{C}}-\overset{H}{\overset{|}{N}}-\overset{H}{\overset{|}{C}}-COO^-$$

**c.** Phenylalanyl-tyrosyl-leucine:

$$H_3^+N-\overset{H}{\overset{|}{C}}-\overset{O}{\overset{\|}{C}}-\overset{H}{\overset{|}{N}}-\overset{H}{\overset{|}{C}}-\overset{O}{\overset{\|}{C}}-\overset{H}{\overset{|}{N}}-\overset{H}{\overset{|}{C}}-COO^-$$

**18.5** The primary structure of a protein is the amino acid sequence of the protein chain. Regular, repeating folding of the peptide chain caused by hydrogen bonding between the amide nitrogens and carbonyl oxygens of the peptide bond is the secondary structure of a protein. The two most common types of secondary structure are the α-helix and the β-pleated sheet. Tertiary structure is the further folding of the regions of α-helix and β-pleated sheet into a compact, spherical structure. Formation and maintenance of the tertiary structure results from weak attractions between amino acid R groups. The binding of two or more peptides to produce a functional protein defines the quaternary structure.

**18.7** Oxygen is efficiently transferred from hemoglobin to myoglobin in the muscle because myoglobin has a greater affinity for oxygen.

**18.9** High temperature disrupts the hydrogen bonds and other weak interactions that maintain protein structure.

**18.11** Vegetables vary in amino acid composition. No single vegetable can provide all of the amino acid requirements of the body.

By eating a variety of different vegetables, all the amino acid requirements of the human body can be met.

**18.13** An enzyme is a protein that serves as a biological catalyst, speeding up biological reactions.

**18.15** A transport protein is a protein that transports materials across the cell membrane or throughout the body.

**18.17** Enzymes speed up reactions that might take days or weeks to occur on their own. They also catalyze reactions that might require very high temperatures or harsh conditions if carried out in the laboratory. In the body, these reactions occur quickly under physiological conditions.

**18.19** Transferrin is a transport protein that carries iron from the liver to the bone marrow, where it is used to produce the heme group for hemoglobin and myoglobin. Hemoglobin transports oxygen in the blood.

**18.21** Egg albumin is a nutrient protein that serves as a source of protein for the developing chick. Casein is the nutrient storage protein in milk, providing protein, a source of amino acids, for mammals.

**18.23** The general structure of an L-α-amino acid has a carbon in the center that is referred to as the alpha carbon. Bonded to the alpha carbon are an amino group, a carboxyl group, a hydrogen atom, and a side chain, R.

$$\begin{array}{c} COO^- \\ | \\ H_3{}^+N-C-H \\ | \\ R \end{array}$$

**18.25** A zwitterion is a neutral molecule with equal numbers of positive and negative charges. Under physiological conditions, amino acids are zwitterions.

**18.27** A chiral carbon is one that has four different atoms or groups of atoms attached to it.

**18.29** Interactions between the R groups of the amino acids in a polypeptide chain are important for the formation and maintenance of the tertiary and quaternary structures of proteins.

**18.31**

L-Serine, L-Threonine, L-Cysteine, L-Tyrosine, L-Asparagine, L-Glutamine (amino acid structures shown)

**18.33** A peptide bond is an amide bond between two amino acids in a peptide chain.

**18.35** Linus Pauling and his colleagues carried out X-ray diffraction studies of protein. Interpretation of the pattern formed when X-rays were diffracted by a crystal of pure protein led Pauling to conclude that peptide bonds are both planar (flat) and rigid and that the N—C bonds are shorter than expected. In other words, they deduced that the peptide bond has a partial double bond character because it exhibits resonance. There is no free rotation

about the amide bond because the carbonyl group of the amide bond has a strong attraction for the amide nitrogen lone pair of electrons. This can best be described using a resonance model:

(resonance structure diagram)

The partially double bonded character of the resonance structure restricts free rotation.

**18.37**
a. (tripeptide structure)
b. (tripeptide structure)
c. (tripeptide structure)

**18.39** The primary structure of a protein is the sequence of amino acids bonded to one another by peptide bonds.

**18.41** The primary structure of a protein determines its three-dimensional shape and biological function because the location of R groups along the protein chain is determined by the primary structure. The interactions among the R groups, based on their location in the chain, will govern how the protein folds. This, in turn, dictates its three-dimensional structure and biological function.

**18.43** (reaction scheme of two amino acids forming a dipeptide + H₂O)

**18.45** The secondary structure of a protein is the folding of the primary structure into an α-helix or β-pleated sheet.

**18.47** a. α-Helix
b. β-Pleated sheet

**18.49** A fibrous protein is one that is composed of peptides arranged in long sheets or fibers.

**18.51** A parallel β-pleated sheet is one in which the hydrogen bonded peptide chains have their amino-termini aligned head-to-head.

**18.53**  The tertiary structure of a protein is the globular, three-dimensional structure of a protein that results from folding the regions of secondary structure.

**18.55**

$$
\begin{array}{c}
COO^- \\
|\\
H_3{}^+N-C-H \\
|\\
CH_2 \\
|\\
S \\
|\\
S \\
|\\
CH_2 \\
|\\
H_3{}^+N-C-H \\
|\\
COO^-
\end{array}
$$

**18.57**  The tertiary structure is a level of folding of a protein chain that has already undergone secondary folding. The regions of α-helix and β-pleated sheet are folded into a globular structure.

**18.59**  Quaternary protein structure is the aggregation of two or more folded peptide chains to produce a functional protein.

**18.61**  A glycoprotein is a protein with covalently attached sugars.

**18.63**  Hydrogen bonding maintains the secondary structure of a protein and contributes to the stability of the tertiary and quaternary levels of structure.

**18.65**  The peptide bond exhibits resonance, which results in a partially double bonded character. This causes the rigidity of the peptide bond.

$$
\begin{array}{c}
-C \\
\quad\diagdown \\
\qquad C-N \\
\diagup\quad\quad\diagdown \\
O\qquad\quad C-
\end{array}
\quad\longleftrightarrow\quad
\begin{array}{c}
-C \\
\quad\diagdown \\
\qquad C=N^+ \\
\diagup\quad\quad\diagdown \\
{}^-O\qquad\quad C-
\end{array}
$$

**18.67**  The code for the primary structure of a protein is carried in the genetic information (DNA).

**18.69**  The function of hemoglobin is to carry oxygen from the lungs to oxygen-demanding tissues throughout the body. Hemoglobin is found in red blood cells.

**18.71**  Hemoglobin is a protein composed of four subunits—two α-globin and two β-globin subunits. Each subunit holds a heme group, which in turn carries an $Fe^{2+}$ ion.

**18.73**  The function of the heme group in hemoglobin and myoglobin is to bind to molecular oxygen.

**18.75**  Because carbon monoxide binds tightly to the heme groups of hemoglobin, it is not easily removed or replaced by oxygen. As a result, the effects of oxygen deprivation (suffocation) occur.

**18.77**  When sickle cell hemoglobin (HbS) is deoxygenated, the amino acid valine fits into a hydrophobic pocket on the surface of another HbS molecule. Many such sickle cell hemoglobin molecules polymerize into long rods that cause the red blood cell to sickle. In normal hemoglobin, glutamic acid is found in the place of the valine. This negatively charged amino acid will not "fit" into the hydrophobic pocket.

**18.79**  When individuals have one copy of the sickle cell gene and one copy of the normal gene, they are said to carry the sickle cell trait. These individuals will not suffer serious side effects, but may pass the trait to their offspring. Individuals with two copies of the sickle cell globin gene exhibit all the symptoms of the disease and are said to have sickle cell anemia.

**18.81**  Albumin

**18.83**  Albumin in the blood can serve as a carrier for $Ca^{2+}$ because it contains acidic amino acids. The negative charges in the acidic amino acids can form salt bridges (or ionic bonds) with $Ca^{2+}$. Albumin can also serve as a carrier for fatty acids because it contains basic amino acids. The positive charges in the basic amino acids can form salt bridges with the anionic fatty acids.

**18.85**  Denaturation is the process by which the organized structure of a protein is disrupted, resulting in a completely disorganized, nonfunctional form of the protein.

**18.87**  Heat is an effective means of sterilization because it destroys the proteins of microbial life-forms, including fungi, bacteria, and viruses.

**18.89**  The low pH of the yogurt denatures the proteins of microbial contaminants, inhibiting their growth.

**18.91**  An essential amino acid is one that must be provided in the diet because it cannot be synthesized in the body.

**18.93**  A complete protein is one that contains all of the essential and nonessential amino acids.

**18.95**  Chymotrypsin catalyzes the hydrolysis of peptide bonds on the carbonyl side of aromatic amino acids.

Site of chymotrypsin-catalyzed hydrolysis

Phenylalanyl-alanine     Phenylalanine

+

Alanine

**18.97**  In a vegetarian diet, vegetables are the only source of dietary protein. Because individual vegetable sources do not provide all the needed amino acids, vegetables must be mixed to provide all the essential and nonessential amino acids in the amounts required for biosynthesis.

**18.99**  Synthesis of digestive enzymes must be carefully controlled because the active enzyme would digest, and thus destroy, the cell that produces it.

## Chapter 19

**19.1**  **a.** Pyruvate kinase catalyzes the transfer of a phosphoryl group from phosphoenolpyruvate to adenosine diphosphate.

Phosphoenolpyruvate     Pyruvate kinase     Pyruvate

**b.** Alanine transaminase catalyzes the transfer of an amino group from alanine to α-ketoglutarate, producing pyruvate and glutamate.

Alanine + Alanine transaminase → Pyruvate

α-Ketoglutarate + Glutamate

**c.** Triose phosphate isomerase catalyzes the isomerization of the ketone dihydroxyacetone phosphate to the aldehyde glyceraldehyde-3-phosphate.

Dihydroxyacetone phosphate → Glyceraldehyde-3-phosphate

**d.** Pyruvate dehydrogenase catalyzes the oxidation and decarboxylation of pyruvate, producing acetyl coenzyme A and $CO_2$.

Pyruvate + Coenzyme A → Acetyl coenzyme A + $CO_2$

**19.3** **a.** Sucrose
   **b.** Pyruvate
   **c.** Succinate

**19.5** The induced fit model assumes that the enzyme is flexible. Both the enzyme and the substrate are able to change shape to form the enzyme-substrate complex. The lock-and-key model assumes that the enzyme is inflexible (the lock) and the substrate (the key) fits into a specific rigid site (the active site) on the enzyme to form the enzyme-substrate complex.

**19.7** An enzyme might distort a bond, thereby catalyzing bond breakage. An enzyme could bring two reactants into close proximity and in the proper orientation for the reaction to occur. Finally, an enzyme could alter the pH of the microenvironment of the active site, thereby serving as a transient donor or acceptor of $H^+$.

**19.9** Water-soluble vitamins are required by the body for the synthesis of coenzymes that are required for the function of a variety of enzymes.

**19.11** A decrease in pH will change the degree of ionization of the R groups within a peptide chain. This disturbs the weak interactions that maintain the structure of an enzyme, which may denature the enzyme. Less drastic alterations in the charge of R groups in the active site of the enzyme can inhibit enzyme-substrate binding or destroy the catalytic ability of the active site.

**19.13** Irreversible inhibitors bind very tightly, sometimes even covalently, to an R group in enzyme active sites. They generally inhibit many different enzymes. The loss of enzyme activity impairs normal cellular metabolism, resulting in death of the cell or the individual.

**19.15** A structural analog is a molecule that has a structure and charge distribution very similar to that of the natural substrate of an enzyme. Generally they are able to bind to the enzyme active site. This inhibits enzyme activity because the normal substrate must compete with the structural analog to form an enzyme-substrate complex.

**19.17** **a.**

ala-phe-ala

**b.**

tyr-ala-tyr

**19.19**

**19.21** The common name of an enzyme is often derived from the name of the substrate and/or the type of reaction that it catalyzes.

**19.23** **1.** Urease
   **2.** Peroxidase
   **3.** Lipase
   **4.** Aspartase
   **5.** Glucose-6-phosphatase
   **6.** Sucrase

**19.25** **a.** Citrate decarboxylase catalyzes the cleavage of a carboxyl group from citrate.
   **b.** Adenosine diphosphate phosphorylase catalyzes the addition of a phosphate group to ADP.
   **c.** Oxalate reductase catalyzes the reduction of oxalate.
   **d.** Nitrite oxidase catalyzes the oxidation of nitrite.
   **e.** *cis-trans* Isomerase catalyzes interconversion of *cis* and *trans* isomers.

**19.27** A substrate is the reactant in an enzyme-catalyzed reaction that binds to the active site of the enzyme and is converted into product.

**19.29**  The activation energy of a reaction is the energy required for the reaction to occur.

**19.31**  The equilibrium constant for a chemical reaction is a reflection of the difference in energy of the reactants and products. Consider the following reaction:
$$aA + bB \rightarrow cC + dD$$
The equilibrium constant for this reaction is:
$$K_{eq} = [D]^d[C]^c/[A]^a[B]^b = [products]/[reactants]$$
Because the difference in energy between reactants and products is the same regardless of what path the reaction takes, an enzyme does not alter the equilibrium constant of a reaction.

**19.33**  The rate of an uncatalyzed chemical reaction typically doubles every time the substrate concentration is doubled.

**19.35**  The rate-limiting step is that step in an enzyme-catalyzed reaction that is the slowest, and hence limits the speed with which the substrate can be converted into product.

**19.37**

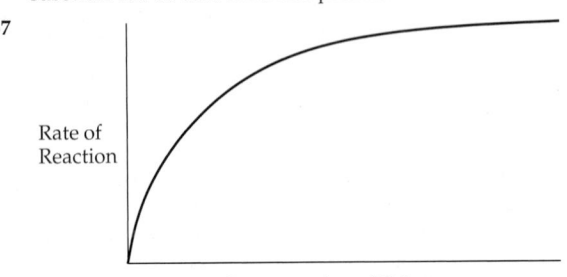

Concentration of Substrate

**19.39**  The enzyme-substrate complex is the molecular aggregate formed when the substrate binds to the active site of an enzyme.

**19.41**  The catalytic groups of an enzyme active site are those functional groups that are involved in carrying out catalysis.

**19.43**  Enzyme active sites are pockets in the surface of an enzyme that include R groups involved in binding and R groups involved in catalysis. The shape of the active site is complementary to the shape of the substrate. Thus, the conformation of the active site determines the specificity of the enzyme. Enzyme-substrate binding involves weak, noncovalent interactions.

**19.45**  The lock-and-key model of enzyme-substrate binding was proposed by Emil Fischer in 1894. He thought that the active site was a rigid region of the enzyme into which the substrate fit perfectly. Thus, the model purports that the substrate simply snaps into place within the active site, like two pieces of a jigsaw puzzle fitting together.

**19.47**  Enzyme specificity is the ability of an enzyme to bind to only one, or a very few, substrates and thus catalyze only a single reaction.

**19.49**  Group specificity means that an enzyme catalyzes reactions involving similar molecules having the same functional group.

**19.51**  Absolute specificity means that an enzyme catalyzes the reaction of only one substrate.

**19.53**  Hexokinase has group specificity. The advantage is that the cell does not need to encode many enzymes to carry out the phosphorylation of six-carbon sugars. Hexokinase can carry out many of these reactions.

**19.55**  Methionyl tRNA synthetase has absolute specificity. This is the enzyme that attaches the amino acid methionine to the transfer RNA (tRNA) that will carry the amino acid to the site of protein synthesis. If the wrong amino acid were attached to the tRNA, it could be incorporated into the protein, destroying its correct three-dimensional structure and biological function.

**19.57**  The first step of an enzyme-catalyzed reaction is the formation of the enzyme-substrate complex. In the second step, the transition state is formed. This is the state in which the substrate assumes a form intermediate between the original substrate and the product. In step 3 the substrate is converted to product and the enzyme-product complex is formed. Step 4 involves the release of the product and regeneration of the enzyme in its original form.

**19.59**  In a reaction involving bond breaking, the enzyme might distort a bond, producing a transition state in which the bond is stressed. An enzyme could bring two reactants into close proximity and in the proper orientation for the reaction to occur, producing a transition state in which the proximity of the reactants facilitates bond formation. Finally, an enzyme could alter the pH of the microenvironment of the active site, thereby serving as a transient donor or acceptor of $H^+$.

**19.61**  A cofactor helps maintain the shape of the active site of an enzyme.

**19.63**  Thiamine ($B_1$) is found in the coenzyme thiamine pyrophosphate. Riboflavin ($B_2$) is found in both flavin mononucleotide and flavin adenine dinucleotide. Niacin ($B_3$) is found in both nicotinamide adenine dinucleotide and nicotinamide adenine dinucleotide phosphate. Pyridoxine ($B_6$) is found in both pyridoxal phosphate and pyridoxamine phosphate. Cyanocobalamin ($B_{12}$) is found in deoxyadenosyl cobalamin. Folic acid is found in tetrahydrofolic acid. Pantothenic acid is found in coenzyme A. Biotin is found in biocytin.

**19.65**  At the temperature optimum, the enzyme is functioning optimally and the rate of the reaction is maximal. Above the temperature optimum, increasing temperature begins to denature the enzyme and stop the reaction.

**19.67**  Each of the following answers assumes that the enzyme was purified from an organism with optimal conditions for life near 37°C, pH 7.
  **a.** Decreasing the temperature from 37°C to 10°C will cause the rate of an enzyme-catalyzed reaction to decrease because the frequency of collisions between enzyme and substrate will decrease as the rate of molecular movement decreases.
  **b.** Increasing the pH from 7 to 11 will generally cause a decrease in the rate of an enzyme-catalyzed reaction. In fact, most enzymes would be denatured by a pH of 11 and enzyme activity would cease.
  **c.** Heating an enzyme from 37°C to 100°C will destroy enzyme activity because the enzyme would be denatured by the extreme heat.

**19.69**  High temperature denatures bacterial enzymes and structural proteins. Because the life of the cell is dependent on the function of these proteins, the cell dies.

**19.71**  A lysosome is a membrane-bound vesicle in the cytoplasm of cells that contains approximately fifty hydrolytic enzymes. Some of the enzymes in the lysosomes can degrade proteins to amino acids, others hydrolyze polysaccharides into monosaccharides, and some degrade lipids and nucleic acids. The lysosome contains these enzymes to prevent degradation of large biological molecules that are important to maintain cell integrity.

**19.73**  Enzymes used for clinical assays in hospitals are typically stored at refrigerator temperatures to ensure that they are not denatured by heat. In this way they retain their activity for long periods.

**19.75**  **a.** Cells regulate the level of enzyme activity to conserve energy. It is a waste of cellular energy to produce an enzyme if its substrate is not present or if its product is in excess.
  **b.** Production of proteolytic digestive enzymes must be carefully controlled because the active enzyme could destroy the cell that produces it. Thus, they are produced in an inactive form in the cell and are only activated at the site where they carry out digestion.

**19.77** In positive allosterism, binding of the effector molecule turns the enzyme on. In negative allosterism, binding of the effector molecule turns the enzyme off.

**19.79** A proenzyme is the inactive form of an enzyme that is converted to the active form at the site of its activity.

**19.81** Blood clotting is a critical protective mechanism in the body, preventing excessive loss of blood following an injury. However, it can be a dangerous mechanism if it is triggered inappropriately. The resulting clot could cause a heart attack or stroke. By having a cascade of proteolytic reactions leading to the final formation of the clot, there are many steps at which the process can be regulated. This ensures that it will only be activated under the appropriate conditions.

**19.83** Competitive enzyme inhibition occurs when a structural analog of the normal substrate occupies the enzyme active site so that the reaction cannot occur. The structural analog and the normal substrate compete for the active site. Thus, the rate of the reaction will depend on the relative concentrations of the two molecules.

**19.85** A structural analog has a shape and charge distribution that are very similar to those of the normal substrate for an enzyme.

**19.87** Irreversible inhibitors bind tightly to and block the active site of an enzyme and eliminate catalysis at the site.

**19.89** The compound would be a competitive inhibitor of the enzyme.

**19.91** A proteolytic enzyme catalyzes the cleavage of the peptide bond that maintains the primary protein structure.

**19.93** The structural similarities among chymotrypsin, trypsin, and elastase suggest that these enzymes evolved from a single ancestral gene that was duplicated. Each copy then evolved independently.

**19.95**

Bond cleaved by chymotrypsin

tyr-lys-ala-phe

**19.97** Elastase will cleave the peptide bonds on the carbonyl side of alanine and glycine. Trypsin will cleave the peptide bonds on the carbonyl side of lysine and arginine. Chymotrypsin will cleave the peptide bonds on the carbonyl side of tryptophan and phenylalanine.

**19.99** Analysis of blood serum for levels of certain enzymes can confirm a preliminary diagnosis that was made based on disease symptoms or a clinical picture. When cells die, they release their enzymes into the bloodstream. Enzyme assays can measure amounts of certain enzymes in the blood.

**19.101** Creatine kinase-MB and aspartate aminotransferase (AST/SGOT)

**19.103** Urease is used in the clinical analysis of urea in blood. In a test called the blood urea nitrogen test (BUN), urea is converted to ammonia using the enzyme urease; the ammonia becomes an indicator of urea. This allows for the levels of urea to be measured. This measurement is useful in the diagnosis of kidney malfunction.

## Chapter 20

**20.1** **a.** Adenosine diphosphate:

**b.** Deoxyguanosine triphosphate:

**20.3** The RNA polymerase recognizes the promoter site for a gene, separates the strands of DNA, and catalyzes the polymerization of an RNA strand complementary to the DNA strand that carries the genetic code for a protein. It recognizes a termination site at the end of the gene and releases the RNA molecule.

**20.5** The genetic code is said to be degenerate because several different triplet codons may serve as code words for a single amino acid.

**20.7** The nitrogenous bases of the codons are complementary to those of the anticodons. As a result they are able to hydrogen bond to one another according to the base pairing rules.

**20.9** The ribosomal P-site holds the peptidyl tRNA during protein synthesis. The peptidyl tRNA is the tRNA carrying the growing peptide chain. The only exception to this is during initiation of translation when the P-site holds the initiator tRNA.

**20.11** The normal mRNA sequence, AUG-CCC-GAC-UUU, would encode the peptide sequence methionine-proline-aspartate-phenylalanine. The mutant mRNA sequence, AUG-CGC-GAC-UUU, would encode the mutant peptide sequence methionine-arginine-aspartate-phenylalanine. This would not be a silent mutation because a hydrophobic amino acid (proline) has been replaced by a positively charged amino acid (arginine).

**20.13** A heterocyclic amine is a compound that contains nitrogen in at least one position of the ring skeleton.

**20.15** It is the N-9 of the purine that forms the *N*-glycosidic bond with C-1 of the five-carbon sugar. The general structure of the purine ring is shown below:

**20.17** The ATP nucleotide is composed of the five-carbon sugar ribose, the purine adenine, and a triphosphate group.

**20.19** The two strands of DNA in the double helix are said to be antiparallel because they run in opposite directions. One strand progresses in the $5' \rightarrow 3'$ direction, and the opposite strand progresses in the $3' \rightarrow 5'$ direction.

**20.21**    The DNA double helix is 2 nm in width. The nitrogenous bases are stacked at a distance of 0.34 nm from one another. One complete turn of the helix is 3.4 nm, or 10 base pairs.

**20.23**

**20.25**

**20.27**    The prokaryotic chromosome is a circular DNA molecule that is supercoiled, that is, the helix is coiled on itself.

**20.29**    The term semiconservative DNA replication refers to the fact that each parental DNA strand serves as the template for the synthesis of a daughter strand. As a result, each of the daughter DNA molecules is made up of one strand of the original parental DNA and one strand of newly synthesized DNA.

**20.31**    The two primary functions of DNA polymerase III are to read a template DNA strand and catalyze the polymerization of a new daughter strand, and to proofread the newly synthesized strand and correct any errors by removing the incorrectly inserted nucleotide and adding the proper one.

**20.33**    3′-TACGGGCTCGACTAACTAGTCT-5′

**20.35**    The replication origin of a DNA molecule is the unique sequence on the DNA molecule where DNA replication begins.

**20.37**    The enzyme helicase separates the strands of DNA at the origin of DNA replication so that the proteins involved in replication can interact with the nitrogenous base pairs.

**20.39**    The RNA primer "primes" DNA replication by providing a 3′—OH which can be used by DNA polymerase III for the addition of the next nucleotide in the growing DNA chain.

**20.41**    DNA → RNA → Protein

**20.43**    Anticodons are found on transfer RNA molecules.

**20.45**    3′-AUGCCCGUAUCCGGAAUUUCGAUCGAA-5′

**20.47**    RNA splicing is the process by which the noncoding sequences (introns) of the primary transcript of a eukaryotic mRNA are removed and the protein coding sequences (exons) are spliced together.

**20.49**    Messenger RNA, transfer RNA, and ribosomal RNA

**20.51**    Spliceosomes are small ribonucleoprotein complexes that carry out RNA splicing.

**20.53**    The poly(A) tail is a stretch of 100–200 adenosine nucleotides polymerized onto the 3′ end of a mRNA by the enzyme poly(A) polymerase.

**20.55**    The cap structure is made up of the nucleotide 7-methylguanosine attached to the 5′ end of a mRNA by a 5′-5′ triphosphate bridge. Generally the first two nucleotides of the mRNA are also methylated.

**20.57**    Sixty-four

**20.59**    The reading frame of a gene is the sequential set of triplet codons that carries the genetic code for the primary structure of a protein.

**20.61**    Methionine and tryptophan

**20.63**    The codon 5′-UUU-3′ encodes the amino acid phenylalanine. The mutant codon 5′-UUA-3′ encodes the amino acid leucine. Both leucine and phenylalanine are hydrophobic amino acids, however, leucine has a smaller R group. It is possible that the smaller R group would disrupt the structure of the protein.

**20.65**    The ribosomes serve as a platform on which protein synthesis can occur. They also carry the enzymatic activity that forms peptide bonds.

**20.67**    5′-AUG GCU GGG CUU UGU AUG UGG UAU UCU AUU GGG UAA-3′

**20.69**    The sequence of DNA nucleotides in a gene is transcribed to produce a complementary sequence of RNA nucleotides in a messenger RNA (mRNA). In the process of translation the sequence of the mRNA is read sequentially in words of three nucleotides (codons) to produce a protein. Each codon calls for the addition of a particular amino acid to the growing peptide chain. If one of those codons has been altered by mutation, it may now call for the addition of the wrong amino acid to the growing peptide chain. This could result in improper folding of the protein and in loss of biological function.

**20.71**    An ester bond

**20.73**    A point mutation is the substitution of one nucleotide pair for another in a gene.

**20.75**    Some mutations are silent because the change in the nucleotide sequence does not alter the amino acid sequence of the protein. This can happen because there are many amino acids encoded by multiple codons.

**20.77**    UV light causes the formation of pyrimidine dimers, the covalent bonding of two adjacent pyrimidine bases. Mutations occur when the UV damage repair system makes an error during the repair process. This causes a change in the nucleotide sequence of the DNA.

**20.79**    **a.** A carcinogen is a compound that causes cancer. Cancers are caused by mutations in the genes responsible for controlling cell division.

   **b.** Carcinogens cause DNA damage that results in changes in the nucleotide sequence of the gene. Thus, carcinogens are also mutagens.

**20.81**  A restriction enzyme is a bacterial enzyme that "cuts" the sugar–phosphate backbone of DNA molecules at a specific nucleotide sequence.

**20.83**  A selectable marker is a genetic trait that can be used to detect the presence of a plasmid in a bacterium. Many plasmids have antibiotic resistance genes as selectable markers. Bacteria containing the plasmid will be able to grow in the presence of the antibiotic; those without the plasmid will be killed.

**20.85**  Human insulin, interferon, human growth hormone, and human blood clotting factor VIII

**20.87**  4096 copies

**20.89**  The goals of the Human Genome Project were to identify and map all of the genes of the human genome and to determine the DNA sequences of the complete three billion nucleotide pairs.

**20.91**  A genome library is a set of clones that represents all of the DNA sequences in the genome of an organism.

**20.93**  A dideoxynucleotide is one that has hydrogen atoms rather than hydroxyl groups bonded to both the 2′ and 3′ carbons of the five-carbon sugar.

**20.95**  Sequences that these DNA sequences have in common are highlighted in bold.

    **a.**  5′-**AGCTCCT**GATTTCATACAGTTTCTACT**ACCTACTA**-3′

    **b.**  5′-AGACATTCTATCTACCTAGACTATG**TTCAGAA**-3′

    **c.**  5′-**TTCAGAA**CTCATTCAGACCTACTACTATACCTTGG**GAGCTCCT**-3′

    **d.**  5′-**ACCTACTA**GACTATACTACTACTAAGGGGACTATT CCAGACTT-3′

    The 5′ end of sequence (a) is identical to the 3′ end of sequence (c). The 3′ end of sequence (a) is identical to the 5′ end of sequence (d). The 3′ end of sequence (b) is identical to the 5′ end of sequence (c). From 5′ to 3′, the sequences would form the following map:

## Chapter 21

**21.1**  ATP is called the universal energy currency because it is the major molecule used by all organisms to store energy.

**21.3**  The first stage of catabolism is the digestion (hydrolysis) of dietary macromolecules in the stomach and intestine.

    In the second stage of catabolism, monosaccharides, amino acids, fatty acids, and glycerol are converted by metabolic reactions into molecules that can be completely oxidized.

    In the third stage of catabolism, the two-carbon acetyl group of acetyl CoA is completely oxidized by the reactions of the citric acid cycle. The energy of the electrons harvested in these oxidation reactions is used to make ATP.

**21.5**  Substrate level phosphorylation is one way the cell can make ATP. In this reaction, a high-energy phosphoryl group of a substrate in the reaction is transferred to ADP to produce ATP.

**21.7**  Glycolysis is a pathway involving ten reactions. In reactions 1–3, energy is invested in the beginning substrate, glucose. This is done by transferring high-energy phosphoryl groups from ATP to the intermediates in the pathway. The product is fructose-1,6-bisphosphate. In the energy-harvesting reactions of glycolysis, fructose-1,6-bisphosphate is split into two three-carbon molecules that begin a series of rearrangement, oxidation-reduction, and substrate-level phosphorylation reactions that produce four ATP, two NADH, and two pyruvate molecules. Because of the investment of two ATP in the early steps of glycolysis, the net yield of ATP is two.

**21.9**  Both the alcohol and lactate fermentations are anaerobic reactions that use the pyruvate and re-oxidize the NADH produced in glycolysis.

**21.11**  Gluconeogenesis (synthesis of glucose from noncarbohydrate sources) appears to be the reverse of glycolysis (the first stage of carbohydrate degradation) because the intermediates in the two pathways are the same. However, reactions 1, 3, and 10 of glycolysis are not reversible reactions. Thus, the reverse reactions must be carried out by different enzymes.

**21.13**  The enzyme glycogen phosphorylase catalyzes the phosphorolysis of a glucose unit at one end of a glycogen molecule. The reaction involves the displacement of the glucose by a phosphate group. The products are glucose-1-phosphate and a glycogen molecule that is one glucose unit shorter.

**21.15**  Glucokinase traps glucose within the liver cell by phosphorylating it. Because the product, glucose-6-phosphate, is charged, it cannot be exported from the cell.

**21.17**  Glucagon indirectly stimulates glycogen phosphorylase, the first enzyme of glycogenolysis. This speeds up glycogen degradation. Glucagon also inhibits glycogen synthase, the first enzyme in glycogenesis. This inhibits glycogen synthesis.

**21.19**  ATP

**21.21**

Adenosine triphosphate

Adenosine diphosphate

Inorganic phosphate group

**21.23**  A coupled reaction is one that can be thought of as a two-step process. In a coupled reaction, two reactions occur simultaneously. Frequently one of the reactions releases the energy that drives the second, energy-requiring, reaction.

**21.25**  Carbohydrates

**21.27** The following equation represents the hydrolysis of maltose:

β-Maltose $+ H_2O$

$\longrightarrow$  2  β-D-Glucose

**21.29**

$H_3^+N-CH-C-HN-CH-C-HN-CH-C-HN-CH-C-HN-CH-C-O^-$

with side chains: $CH_2$ (benzyl/phenyl ring); $CH_3$; $CH_2$ $CH_2$ $C=O$ $O^-$; $CH_2$ $CH_2$ $S$ $CH_3$; $CH_2$ $CH_2$ $CH_2$ $CH_2$ $NH_3^+$

$+ 4H_2O$ $\downarrow$

$H_3^+N-CH-C-O^-$ with $CH_3$   +   $H_3^+N-CH-C-O^-$ with $CH_2$ $CH_2$ $S$ $CH_3$

$H_3^+N-CH-C-O^-$ (benzyl)   +   $H_3^+N-CH-C-O^-$ with $CH_2$ $CH_2$ $C=O$ $O^-$   +   $H_3^+N-CH-C-O^-$ with $CH_2$ $CH_2$ $CH_2$ $CH_2$ $NH_3^+$

**21.31** The hydrolysis of a triglyceride containing oleic acid, stearic acid, and linoleic acid is represented in the following equations:

$H-C-O-C-(CH_2)_7CH=CH(CH_2)_7CH_3$
$H-C-O-C-(CH_2)_{16}CH_3$   $+ 3H_2O$   $\longrightarrow$
$H-C-O-C-(CH_2)_7CH=CHCH_2CH=CH(CH_2)_4CH_3$
$H$

$H-C-OH$
$H-C-OH$   +   $HO-C-(CH_2)_7CH=CH(CH_2)_7CH_3$   Oleic acid
$H-C-OH$
$H$   Glycerol
   +   $HO-C-(CH_2)_{16}CH_3$   Stearic acid
   +   $HO-C-(CH_2)_7CH=CHCH_2CH=CH(CH_2)_4CH_3$   Linoleic acid

**21.33** The hydrolysis of the dipeptide alanyl leucine is represented in the following equation:

$H_3^+N-CH-C-N-CH-C-O^- + H_2O \longrightarrow$
with $CH_3$; $CH_2$ $CH-CH_3$ $CH_3$   Alanyl leucine

$H_3^+N-CH-C-O^-$ with $CH_3$   Alanine   +   $H_3^+N-CH-C-O^-$ with $CH_2$ $CH-CH_3$ $CH_3$   Leucine

**21.35** Glycolysis is the enzymatic pathway that converts a glucose molecule into two molecules of pyruvate. The pathway generates a net energy yield of two ATP and two NADH. Glycolysis is the first stage of carbohydrate catabolism.

**21.37** Glycolysis requires $NAD^+$ for reaction 6 in which glyceraldehyde-3-phosphate dehydrogenase catalyzes the oxidation of glyceraldehyde-3-phosphate. $NAD^+$ is reduced.

**21.39** Two ATP per glucose

**21.41** Although muscle cells have enough ATP stored for only a few seconds of activity, glycolysis speeds up dramatically when there is a demand for more energy. If the cells have a sufficient supply of oxygen, aerobic respiration (the citric acid cycle and oxidative phosphorylation) will contribute large amounts of ATP. If oxygen is limited, the lactate fermentation will speed up. This will use up the pyruvate and re-oxidize the NADH produced by glycolysis and allow continued synthesis of ATP for muscle contraction.

**21.43** $C_6H_{12}O_6 + 2ADP + 2P_i + 2NAD^+ \rightarrow$
Glucose         $2C_3H_3O_3 + 2ATP + 2NADH + 2H_2O$
                Pyruvate

**21.45**  a. 7      f. 9
      b. 2      g. 5
      c. 6      h. 10
      d. 4      i. 3
      e. 1      j. 8

**21.47** Myopathy and hemolytic anemia are symptoms associated with a genetic defect in some of the enzymes of glycolysis. Myopathy can lead to exercise intolerance, muscle breakdown, and blood in the urine. Tarui's disease is also caused by a deficiency in one of the enzymes of glycolysis. Its symptoms include muscle pain, exercise intolerance, respiratory failure, heart muscle disease, seizures, and blindness.

**21.49** If a person is deficient in some of the enzymes of glycolysis, muscle cells may begin to die, which can lead to the release of myoglobin into the blood and the urine. This condition is called myoglobinuria, and it results in urine that is the color of cola soft drinks.

**21.51** Isomerase

**21.53** Enediol

**21.55** A kinase transfers a phosphoryl group from one molecule to another.

**21.57** $NAD^+$ is reduced, accepting a hydride anion.

**21.59** To optimize efficiency and minimize waste, it is important that energy-harvesting pathways, such as glycolysis, respond to the energy demands of the cell. If energy in the form of ATP is abundant, there is no need for the pathway to continue at a rapid rate. When this is the case, allosteric enzymes that catalyze the reactions of the pathway are inhibited by binding to their negative effectors. Similarly, when there is a great demand for ATP, the pathway speeds up as a result of the action of allosteric enzymes binding to positive effectors.

**21.61** ATP and citrate are allosteric inhibitors of phosphofructokinase, whereas AMP and ADP are allosteric activators.

**21.63** Citrate, which is the first intermediate in the citric acid cycle, is an allosteric inhibitor of phosphofructokinase. The citric acid cycle is a pathway that results in the complete oxidation of the pyruvate produced by glycolysis. A high concentration of citrate signals that sufficient substrate is entering the citric acid cycle. The inhibition of phosphofructokinase by citrate is an example of feedback inhibition: the product, citrate, allosterically inhibits the activity of an enzyme early in the pathway.

**21.65**

$$CH_3-\overset{\overset{\displaystyle O}{\|}}{C}-H \xrightarrow[\text{Acetaldehyde}]{\quad NADH \quad NAD^+\quad} CH_3CH_2OH$$
Acetaldehyde                          Ethanol

**21.67** Lactate fermentation

**21.69** Yogurt and some cheeses

**21.71** Lactate dehydrogenase

**21.73** This child must have the enzymes to carry out the alcohol fermentation. When the child exercised hard, there was not enough oxygen in the cells to maintain aerobic respiration. As a result, glycolysis and the alcohol fermentation were responsible for the majority of the ATP production by the child. The accumulation of alcohol (ethanol) in the child caused the symptoms of drunkenness.

**21.75** The ribose-5-phosphate is used for the biosynthesis of nucleotides. The erythrose-4-phosphate is used for the biosynthesis of aromatic amino acids.

**21.77** Gluconeogenesis is production of glucose from noncarbohydrate starting materials. This pathway can provide glucose when starvation or strenuous exercise leads to a depletion of glucose from the body.

**21.79** The liver

**21.81** Lactate is first converted to pyruvate.

**21.83** Because steps 1, 3, and 10 of glycolysis are irreversible, gluconeogenesis is not simply the reverse of glycolysis. The reverse reactions must be carried out by different enzymes.

**21.85** Steps 1, 3, and 10 of glycolysis are irreversible. Step 1 is the transfer of a phosphoryl group from ATP to carbon-6 of glucose and is catalyzed by hexokinase. Step 3 is the transfer of a phosphoryl group from ATP to carbon-1 of fructose-6-phosphate and is catalyzed by phosphofructokinase. Step 10 is the substrate-level phosphorylation in which a phosphoryl group is transferred from phosphoenolpyruvate to ADP and is catalyzed by pyruvate kinase.

**21.87** The liver and pancreas

**21.89** Hypoglycemia is the condition in which blood glucose levels are too low.

**21.91** **a.** Insulin stimulates glycogen synthase, the first enzyme in glycogen synthesis. It also stimulates uptake of glucose from the bloodstream into cells and phosphorylation of glucose by the enzyme glucokinase.

**b.** This traps glucose within liver cells and increases the storage of glucose in the form of glycogen.

**c.** These processes decrease blood glucose levels.

**21.93** Any defect in the enzymes required to degrade glycogen or export glucose from liver cells will result in a reduced ability of the liver to provide glucose at times when blood glucose levels are low. This will cause hypoglycemia.

**21.95** Glycogen phosphorylase catalyzes phosphorylysis of a glucose at one end of a glycogen polymer. The reaction involves the displacement of a glucose unit of glycogen by a phosphate group. As a result, glucose-1-phosphate is produced.

Glycogen(glucose)$_x$ + $n$HPO$_4^{2-}$ → Glycogen(glucose)$_{n-x}$ + $n$glucose-1-phosphate

**21.97** In glycogen degradation, phosphoglucomutase converts glucose-1-phosphate to glucose-6-phosphate. In glycogen synthesis, phosphoglucomutase converts glucose-6-phosphate to glucose-1-phosphate.

**21.99** Glucokinase converts glucose to glucose-6-phosphate as the first reaction of glycogen synthesis.

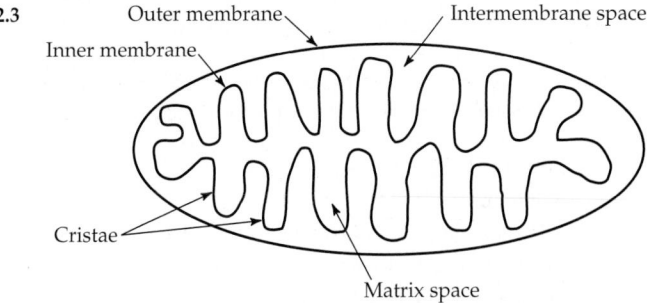

## Chapter 22

**22.1** Mitochondria are the organelles responsible for aerobic respiration.

**22.3**

Outer membrane · Intermembrane space · Inner membrane · Cristae · Matrix space

**22.5** Pyruvate is converted to acetyl CoA by the pyruvate dehydrogenase complex. This huge enzyme complex requires four coenzymes, each of which is made from a different vitamin.

The four coenzymes are thiamine pyrophosphate (made from thiamine), FAD (made from riboflavin), $NAD^+$ (made from niacin), and coenzyme A (made from the vitamin pantothenic acid). The coenzyme lipoamide is also involved in this reaction.

**22.7** Oxidative phosphorylation is the process by which the energy of electrons harvested from oxidation of a fuel molecule is used to phosphorylate ADP to produce ATP.

**22.9** $NAD^+ + H:^- \rightarrow NADH$

**22.11** During transamination reactions, the $\alpha$-amino group is transferred to the coenzyme pyridoxal phosphate. In the last part of the reaction, the $\alpha$-amino group is transferred from pyridoxal phosphate to an $\alpha$-keto acid.

**22.13** The purpose of the urea cycle is to convert toxic ammonium ions to urea, which is excreted in the urine of land animals.

**22.15** An amphibolic pathway is a metabolic pathway that functions both in anabolism and catabolism. The citric acid cycle is amphibolic because it has a catabolic function—it completely oxidizes the acetyl group carried by acetyl CoA to provide electrons for ATP synthesis. Because citric acid cycle intermediates are precursors for the biosynthesis of many other molecules, it also serves a function in anabolism.

**22.17** The mitochondrion is an organelle that serves as the cellular power plant. The reactions of the citric acid cycle, the electron transport system, and ATP synthase function together within the mitochondrion to harvest ATP energy for the cell.

**22.19** The intermembrane compartment is the location of the high-energy proton $(H^+)$ reservoir produced by the electron transport system. The energy of this $H^+$ reservoir is used to make ATP.

**22.21** The outer mitochondrial membrane is freely permeable to substances of molar mass less than 10,000 g/mol. The inner mitochondrial membrane is highly impermeable. Embedded within the inner mitochondrial membrane are the electron carriers of the electron transport system, and ATP synthase, the multisubunit enzyme that makes ATP.

**22.23** Coenzyme A is a molecule derived from ATP and the vitamin pantothenic acid. It functions in the transfer of acetyl groups in lipid and carbohydrate metabolism.

**22.25** Decarboxylation is a chemical reaction in which a carboxyl group is removed from a molecule.

**22.27** Under aerobic conditions pyruvate is converted to acetyl CoA.

**22.29** The coenzymes $NAD^+$, FAD, thiamine pyrophosphate, and coenzyme A are required by the pyruvate dehydrogenase complex for the conversion of pyruvate to acetyl CoA. These coenzymes are synthesized from the vitamins niacin, riboflavin, thiamine, and pantothenic acid, respectively. If the vitamins are not available, the coenzymes will not be available and pyruvate cannot be converted to acetyl CoA. Because the complete oxidation of the acetyl group of acetyl CoA produces the vast majority of the ATP for the body, ATP production would be severely inhibited by a deficiency of any of these vitamins.

**22.31** A condensation is a reaction in which aldehydes or ketones react to form larger molecules.

**22.33** Oxidation reduction

**22.35** A dehydrogenation reaction is an oxidation reaction in which protons and electrons are removed from a molecule.

**22.37**
   **a.** 1            **e.** 4
   **b.** 6            **f.** 2
   **c.** 2            **g.** 5
   **d.** 2            **h.** 2

**22.39** True

**22.41** Three

**22.43** Two ATP per glucose

**22.45** The function of acetyl CoA in the citric acid cycle is to bring the two-carbon remnant (acetyl group) of pyruvate from glycolysis and transfer it to oxaloacetate. In this way the acetyl group enters the citric acid cycle for the final stages of oxidation.

**22.47** The high-energy phosphoryl group of the GTP is transferred to ADP to produce ATP. This reaction is catalyzed by the enzyme dinucleotide diphosphokinase.

**22.49** Fumarate contains an alkene carbon-carbon double bond. Addition of water to the double bond of fumarate gives malate. The enzyme fumarase catalyzes this reaction. When water is added to the alkene double bond, one of the carbons forms a new bond to $-OH$, and the other carbon forms a new bond to $-H$. As a result, the alkene becomes an alcohol.

**22.51** First, pyruvate is converted to acetyl CoA:

Then, citrate is formed from oxaloacetate and the radiolabeled acetyl CoA.

The following structures are the intermediates of the citric acid cycle. An asterisk is on the radiolabeled carbon, and circles are on the $-COO^-$ groups that are released as $CO_2$.

**22.53** This reaction is an example of the oxidation of a secondary alcohol to a ketone. The two functional groups are the hydroxyl group of the alcohol and the carbonyl group of the ketone.

**22.55** It is a kinase because it transfers a phosphoryl group from one molecule to another. Kinases are a specific type of transferase.

**22.57** Mutations of the citric acid cycle enzymes frequently appear first in the central nervous system because of the high energy (ATP) demands of this tissue.

**22.59** Deficiencies of citric acid cycle enzymes cause hypotonia because there is insufficient ATP.

**22.61** An allosteric enzyme is one that has an effector binding site and an active site. Effector binding can change the shape of the active site, causing it to be active or inactive.

**22.63** Allosteric enzymes are an efficient means to regulate a biochemical pathway because they bind to effectors, such as ATP or ADP, that alter the shape of the enzyme active site, either stimulating the rate of the reaction or inhibiting the reaction.

**22.65** The citric acid cycle is regulated by the following four enzymes or enzyme complexes: pyruvate dehydrogenase complex, citrate synthase, isocitrate dehydrogenase, and the $\alpha$-ketoglutarate dehydrogenase complex.

**22.67** Energy-harvesting pathways, such as the citric acid cycle, must be responsive to the energy needs of the cell. If the energy requirements are high, as during exercise, the reactions must speed up. If energy demands are low and ATP is in excess, the reactions of the pathway slow down.

**22.69** ADP

**22.71** The electron transport system is a series of electron transport proteins embedded in the inner mitochondrial membrane that accept high-energy electrons from NADH and $FADH_2$ and transfer them in stepwise fashion to molecular oxygen ($O_2$).

**22.73** Three ATP

**22.75** The oxidation of a variety of fuel molecules, including carbohydrates, the carbon skeletons of amino acids, and fatty acids provides the electrons. The energy of these electrons is used to produce an $H^+$ reservoir. The energy of this proton reservoir is used for ATP synthesis.

**22.77** The electron transport system passes electrons harvested during oxidation of fuel molecules to molecular oxygen. At three sites protons are pumped from the mitochondrial matrix into the intermembrane compartment. Thus, the electron transport system builds the high-energy $H^+$ reservoir that provides energy for ATP synthesis.

**22.79** **a.** Two ATP per glucose (net yield) are produced in glycolysis, whereas the complete oxidation of glucose in aerobic respiration (glycolysis, the citric acid cycle, and oxidative phosphorylation) results in the production of 36 ATP per glucose.

**b.** Thus, aerobic respiration harvests nearly 40% of the potential energy of glucose, and anaerobic glycolysis harvests only about 2% of the potential energy of glucose.

**22.81** Transaminases transfer amino groups from amino acids to ketoacids.

**22.83** The glutamate family of transaminases is very important because the ketoacid corresponding to glutamate is $\alpha$-ketoglutarate, one of the citric acid cycle intermediates. This provides a link between the citric acid cycle and amino acid metabolism. These transaminases provide amino groups for amino acid synthesis and collect amino groups during catabolism of amino acids.

**22.85** **a.** Pyruvate        **d.** Acetyl CoA
        **b.** $\alpha$-Ketoglutarate     **e.** Succinate
        **c.** Oxaloacetate       **f.** $\alpha$-Ketoglutarate

**22.87** Transaminase binds to the amino acid in its active site. Then, the $\alpha$-amino group is transferred to pyridoxal phosphate, producing pyridoxamine phosphate. The amino group is then transferred to an $\alpha$-keto acid.

**22.89** Hyperammonemia

**22.91** **a.** The source of one amino group of urea is the ammonium ion and the source of the other is the $\alpha$-amino group of the amino acid aspartate.

**b.** The carbonyl group of urea is derived from $CO_2$.

**22.93** Anabolism is a term used to describe all of the cellular energy-requiring biosynthetic pathways.

**22.95** $\alpha$-Ketoglutarate

**22.97** Citric acid cycle intermediates are the starting materials for the biosynthesis of many biological molecules.

**22.99** An essential amino acid is one that cannot be synthesized by the body and must be provided in the diet.

**22.101**

$$\underset{\text{Pyruvate}}{\overset{\displaystyle O}{\underset{\displaystyle CH_3}{\overset{\|}{C}-COO^-}}} + CO_2 + ATP \longrightarrow \underset{\text{Oxaloacetate}}{\overset{\displaystyle O}{\underset{\displaystyle \underset{COO^-}{\overset{|}{CH_2}}}{\overset{\|}{C}-COO^-}}} + ADP + P_i$$

## Chapter 23

**23.1** Because dietary lipids are hydrophobic, they arrive in the small intestine as large fat globules. The bile salts emulsify these fat globules into tiny fat droplets. This greatly increases the surface area of the lipids, allowing them to be more accessible to pancreatic lipases and thus more easily digested.

**23.3** Starvation, a diet low in carbohydrates, and diabetes mellitus are conditions that lead to the production of ketone bodies.

**23.5** **(1)** Fatty acid biosynthesis occurs in the cytoplasm whereas $\beta$-oxidation occurs in the mitochondria.

**(2)** The acyl group carrier in fatty acid biosynthesis is acyl carrier protein while the acyl group carrier in $\beta$-oxidation is coenzyme A.

**(3)** The seven enzymes of fatty acid biosynthesis are associated as a multienzyme complex called *fatty acid synthase*. The enzymes involved in $\beta$-oxidation are not physically associated with one another.

**(4)** NADPH is the reducing agent used in fatty acid biosynthesis. NADH and $FADH_2$ are produced by $\beta$-oxidation.

**23.7** The liver regulates blood glucose levels under the control of the hormones insulin and glucagon. When blood glucose levels are too high, insulin stimulates the uptake of glucose by liver cells and the storage of the glucose in glycogen polymers. When blood glucose levels are too low, the hormone glucagon stimulates the breakdown of glycogen and release of glucose into the bloodstream. Glucagon also stimulates the liver to produce glucose for export into the bloodstream by the process of gluconeogenesis.

**23.9** Insulin stimulates uptake of glucose and amino acids by cells, glycogen and protein synthesis, and storage of lipids. It inhibits glycogenolysis, gluconeogenesis, breakdown of stored triglycerides, and ketogenesis.

**23.11**

Cholate

Chenodeoxycholate

**23.13** A micelle is an aggregation of molecules having nonpolar and polar regions; the nonpolar regions of the molecules aggregate, leaving the polar regions facing the surrounding water.

**23.15** A triglyceride is a molecule composed of glycerol esterified to three fatty acids.

**23.17** Triglycerides, cholesterol, and phospholipids are packaged into a protein-coated shell to produce the class of plasma lipoproteins called chylomicrons.

**23.19** Triglycerides

**23.21** The large fat globule that takes up nearly the entire cytoplasm

**23.23** Lipases catalyze the hydrolysis of the ester bonds of triglycerides.

**23.25** Acetyl CoA is the precursor for fatty acids, several amino acids, cholesterol, and other steroids.

**23.27** Chylomicrons carry dietary triglycerides from the intestine to all tissues via the bloodstream.

**23.29** Bile salts are detergents that emulsify the lipids, increasing their surface area and making them more accessible to digestive enzymes (pancreatic lipases).

**23.31** When dietary lipids in the form of fat globules reach the duodenum, they are emulsified by bile salts. The triglycerides in the resulting tiny fat droplets are hydrolyzed into monoglycerides and fatty acids by the action of pancreatic lipases, assisted by colipase. The monoglycerides and fatty acids are absorbed by cells lining the intestine.

**23.33** The hydrolysis of ATP into AMP and $PP_i$

**23.35** Carnitine is a carrier molecule that brings fatty acyl groups into the mitochondrial matrix.

**23.37** The following equation represents the reaction catalyzed by acyl-CoA dehydrogenase. Notice that the reaction involves the loss of two hydrogen atoms. Thus, this is an oxidation reaction.

**23.39** An alcohol is the product of the hydration of an alkene.

**23.41** Six acetyl CoA, one phenyl acetate, six NADH, and six $FADH_2$

**23.43** 112 ATP

**23.45** 95 ATP

**23.47** The acetyl CoA produced by β-oxidation will enter the citric acid cycle.

**23.49** Ketone bodies include the compounds acetone, acetoacetone, and β-hydroxybutyrate, which are produced from fatty acids in the liver via acetyl CoA.

**23.51** Ketosis is an abnormal rise in the level of ketone bodies in the blood.

**23.53** Matrix of the mitochondrion.

**23.55**

Acetoacetate                    β-Hydroxybutyrate

**23.57** In those suffering from uncontrolled diabetes, the glucose in the blood cannot get into the cells of the body. The excess glucose is excreted in the urine. Body cells degrade fatty acids because glucose is not available. β-oxidation of fatty acids yields enormous quantities of acetyl CoA, so much acetyl CoA, in fact, that it cannot all enter the citric acid cycle because there is not enough oxaloacetate available. Excess acetyl CoA is used for ketogenesis.

**23.59** Ketone bodies are the preferred energy source of the heart.

**23.61** Cytoplasm

**23.63**

**23.65** **a.** The phosphopantetheine group allows formation of a high-energy thioester bond with a fatty acid.

**b.** It is derived from the vitamin pantothenic acid.

**23.67** Fatty acid synthase is a huge multienzyme complex consisting of the seven enzymes involved in fatty acid synthesis. It is found in the cell cytoplasm. The enzymes involved in β-oxidation are not physically associated with one another. They are free in the mitochondrial matrix space.

**23.69** Glycogenesis is the synthesis of the polymer glycogen from glucose monomers.

**23.71** Gluconeogenesis is the synthesis of glucose from noncarbohydrate precursors.

**23.73** β-oxidation of fatty acids

**23.75** The major metabolic function of the liver is to regulate blood glucose levels.

**23.77** Ketone bodies are the major fuel for the heart. Glucose is the major energy source of the brain, and the liver obtains most of its energy from the oxidation of amino acid carbon skeletons.

**23.79** Fatty acids are absorbed from the bloodstream by adipocytes. Using glycerol-3-phosphate, produced as a by-product of glycolysis, triglycerides are synthesized. Triglycerides are constantly being hydrolyzed and resynthesized in adipocytes. The rates of hydrolysis and synthesis are determined by lipases that are under hormonal control.

**23.81** In general, insulin stimulates anabolic processes and inhibits catabolic processes.

**23.83** A target cell is one that has a receptor for a particular hormone.

**23.85** Decreased blood glucose levels

**23.87** In the β-cells of the islets of Langerhans in the pancreas.

**23.89** Insulin stimulates the uptake of glucose from the blood into cells. It enhances glucose storage by stimulating glycogenesis and inhibiting glycogen degradation and gluconeogenesis.

**23.91** Insulin stimulates synthesis and storage of triglycerides.

**23.93** Insulin is secreted when blood glucose levels are high. It facilitates the uptake and storage of glucose by target cells to restore normal blood glucose levels. Glucagon is secreted when blood glucose levels are too low. It stimulates release of glucose into the blood to restore normal levels.

# Credits

# Index

China, ancient, 364, 512
chiral molecules, 552, 553, 556, 557, 558
chlorates, 146T
chloride, 219, 284
chlorine
    atomic mass, 46–47
    chemical equations, 137
    as disinfectant and antiseptic, 285B
    halogenation, 380, 381
    oxidation-reduction processes, 284
4-chlorobenzoyl chloride, 494
2-chloro-2-butene, 367
chlorocyclohexane, 345–46, 369
chloroethane, 354B
chlorofluorocarbon (CFC), 341
chloroform, 354B
chloromethane, 354B
3-chloro-4-methyl-3-hexene, 367
2-chloro-2-methylpropane, 353
1-chloropentane and 2-chloropentane, 386
chlorophyll, 7, 394, 526
γ-chlorovaleric acid, 475
chocolate, 395B, 424B
cholate, 603, 794, 795F
cholera, 214B
cholesterol, 375, 600–603, 605, 607, 794
choline, 525
chondroitin sulfate, 573B
chorionic villus sampling, 693B
chromate, 146T, 262F
chromic acid, 416
chromium, 187B, 291, 304
chromosomes, 685, 690–91
chromosome walking, 718
chylomicrons, 605, 606F, 795, 796F
chymotrypsin, 642, 675–76
chymotrypsinogen A, 671T
cicutoxin, 371B
cigarette smoking, 667B, 709, 710B
cimetidine, 394, 538
cinnamaldehyde, 448F
citral, 448F
citrate, 742, 770F, 772
citrate lyase, 651
citric acid, 480
citric acid cycle
    adenosine triphosphate (ATP), 501
    aerobic respiration, 764, 767, 768–69
    biosynthetic intermediates, 786–87
    carbohydrate metabolism, 732
    carboxylic acids, 480
    chemical reactions, 769–72
    control of, 772–73
    exercise and energy metabolism, 764B
    hydration, 383
    regulation of glycolysis, 742
citrulline, 782, 783F, 784
classification. See also nomenclature
    of chemical reactions, 145–47
    of elements on periodic table, 57–61
    of matter, 6–10
clathrate, 330B
clear versus colorless, 195
climate
    acid rain, 272, 276B
    global warming, 179B, 330B, 352
    water in environment, 28, 255B
cloning and cloning vectors, 714, 715F, 716
*Clostridium perfringens*, 488B
*Clostridium welchii*, 597B
coagulation, of proteins, 638
coal, 276B, 328F. See also fossil fuels
cobalt-60, 306T, 313
coca plants (*Erythroxylum* spp.), 718B

cocaine, 524–25, 526, 718B
cocamido DEA, 216B
codeine, 526–27, 536B
codons, 698, 702–703
coefficient, 140
coenzyme(s), 420, 429, 499, 539, 663–66. See also
    acetoacetyl CoA; acetyl coenzyme A; acyl
    CoA; coenzyme A; succinyl CoA
coenzyme A, 664T, 732, 765, 766
cold adaptation, and brown fat, 776B. See also
    freezing point; ice
cold packs, 234B
Coleman, Douglas, 797B
colipase, 794
colitis, 573B, 631–32B
colligative properties, 206
colloid(s), 195–96
colloidal suspension, 195
Colombia, 718B
colon cancer, 72B
color
    Benedict's reagent, 567
    breathalyzer test, 421B
    bromination of alkenes, 382
    fluid mosaic membrane, 611
    pH indicators, 274F
colorless, use of term, 195
combination reactions, 138
combined gas law, 172–74
combustion, of hydrocarbons, 351–52
common names, and nomenclature systems
    alcohols, 410–11
    aldehydes and ketones, 443, 444, 445, 446
    amines, 518
    aromatic compounds, 391
    carboxylic acids, 474, 475
    esters, 485
    ionic compounds, 92
    iron and copper ions, 93T
compass, 63F
competitive inhibition, 450B, 539, 673
complementary strands, of DNA, 689
complete protein, 642
complex carbohydrates, 549
complex lipids, 582, 605–608
composition, of matter, 9–10
compounds. See also covalent compounds; ionic
    compounds; nitro compounds
    definition of, 9
    naming and writing formulas of, 91–98
    organic compared to inorganic, 328–29
compressibility, and physical properties of gases,
    liquids, and solids, 166T, 168, 180
computerized tomography (CT) imaging, 54B, 319
concentration, of solutions
    acid strength, 263
    chemical equilibrium, 248, 252
    measurement of, 30–33
    moles, 202–206
    percent by mass, 198–200
    properties dependent on, 206–14
    rate of chemical reactions, 241
concentration gradient, 211
condensation, 182
condensation polymers, 491–94
condensation reaction, 426, 486
condensed formula, 332–33
conductivity, of metallic solids, 186
conformations, of alkanes and cycloalkanes, 348–50
congestive heart failure, 602B
coniine, 526F
conjugate acids and bases, 264–67
conservation of energy, law of, 230B
conservation of mass, law of, 136, 140, 154F

constitutional isomers. See structural isomers
continental drift, 330B
contour maps, and microbial forensics, 49B
conversion factors, 22–26, 149–56
cookbook approach, to chemical laboratories, 3
copper
    common names for ions, 93T
    cooking pots, 639B
    fireworks, 56B
    ionic forms, 72
    metallic solids, 186
    molar mass, 130F
    oxidation-reduction reactions, 147, 288, 289
    single-replacement reaction, 139
    Wilson's disease and deficiency of, 60B
copper hydroxide, 451
copper sulfate, 134, 139
Cori Cycle, 743, 747F, 748
Cori's disease, 755B
Cornwell, Patricia, 476B
coronary artery, 314T
corrosion, 146, 286
cortisone, 604
corundum, 187B
cosmeceuticals, 610B
cosmetics industry, 610B, 631B
covalent bonds, 84, 88–89, 328, 629
covalent compounds
    definition of, 89
    Lewis structures, 100–103, 111–12
    naming of, 96–98
    properties of, 98–99
    rate of chemical reactions, 241
covalent solids, 186
crack cocaine, 524–25
creatine kinase-MB (CK-MB), 676, 677
creatine phosphate, 764B
C-reactive protein (CRP), 608
cresol, 391
Crick, Francis, 686, 687, 688, 693, 702
crime scenes
    adipocere and mummies of soap, 597B
    arson and alkanes, 338B
    automobile accidents, 421B
    blood group antigens, 570B
    carboxylic acids and forensic anthropology, 476B
    DNA fingerprinting, 718–19B
    enzymes, nerve agents, and poisoning, 672–73B
    explosives at airports, 184B
    methamphetamines, 523B
    microbial forensics, 49B
cristae, 762
Crookes, William, 50
crotonyl ACP, 809F
CRP. See C-reactive protein
crystal lattice, 87, 98
crystalline solids, 98, 185–87
C-terminal amino acid (C-terminus), 622
CT scan. See computerized tomography imaging
cube, 13
Curie, Marie and Pierre, 309B, 320B
curie (unit of measurement), 320–21
curiosity, and scientific discovery, 26B
curium-245, 303
cyanide, 775
cyanocobalamin, 664T
cyclic AMP (cAMP), 625B
cycloalkanes, 329F, 331, 345–53, 474
cyclobutane, 346F
cyclohexanal ethanal, 456
cyclohexane, 331, 346F, 349, 351
cyclohexanecarboxylic acid, 474
cyclooxygenase, 500B, 588, 589
cyclopropane, 174, 346F